MW00345836

Purchased with funds provided by
The Estate of Louis H. Brush
In Memory of his Father
Professor James Alpheus Brush
Librarian of Mount Union College
1869-1873

APA Dictionary *of* Clinical Psychology

Ψ

APA Dictionary *of* Clinical Psychology

Gary R. VandenBos, PhD
Editor in Chief

American Psychological Association
Washington, DC

Published by
American Psychological Association
750 First Street, NE
Washington, DC 20002
www.apa.org

To order
APA Order Department
P.O. Box 92984
Washington, DC 20090-2984
Tel: (800) 374-2721; Direct: (202) 336-5510
Fax: (202) 336-5502; TDD/TTY: (202) 336-6123
Online: www.apa.org/pubs/books/
E-mail: order@apa.org

In the U.K., Europe, Africa, and the Middle East, copies may be ordered from
American Psychological Association
3 Henrietta Street
Covent Garden, London
WC2E 8LU England

AMERICAN PSYCHOLOGICAL ASSOCIATION STAFF
Gary R. VandenBos, PhD, Publisher
Julia Frank-McNeil, Senior Director, APA Books
Theodore J. Baroody, Director, Reference, APA Books
Patricia D. Mathis, Senior Reference Development Editor, APA Books
Marion Osmun, Senior Reference Development Editor

Typeset in Aylesbury, England, by Market House Books, Ltd.
Printer: Maple-Vail Book Manufacturing Group, York, PA
Cover Designer: Naylor Design, Washington, DC

Library of Congress Cataloging-in-Publication Data

APA dictionary of clinical psychology. — 1st ed.
p. cm.
ISBN 978-1-4338-1207-1 -- ISBN 1-4338-1207-X 1. Clinical psychology--Dictionaries. 2. Psychotherapy—Dictionaries. I. American Psychological Association. II. Title: A.P.A. dictionary of clinical psychology. III. Title: Dictionary of clinical psychology.
RC467.A63 2013
616.89'1403--dc23
2012022203

British Library Cataloguing-in-Publication Data
A CIP record is available from the British Library.

The citation for this publication is American Psychological Association. (2013). *APA dictionary of clinical psychology*. Washington, DC: Author.

Printed in the United States of America
First Edition

DOI: 10.1037/13945-000

Contents

Preface

This dictionary is the fourth in a family of lexicographical works published by the American Psychological Association (APA). The parent reference, the 25,000-entries *APA Dictionary of Psychology*—the culmination of some ten years of research and lexicographic activity—was released in 2006, winning wide critical endorsement and recognition from both the publishing and reference library communities. We are pleased to note that a considerably revised and expanded second edition of this work is well under way and will be available in 2014.

An abridgment of the parent dictionary in 10,000 entries, the *APA Concise Dictionary of Psychology,* was released in 2008. Whereas the original dictionary offered a deeply layered approach to the lexicon of the field, *Concise,* through an editorial process of reduction and synthesis, offered an equally informative exploration of the fundamental vocabulary, but with broader general appeal. This version is now available both in print and as an app for iPhone, iPad, and Android.

A collegiate version, the popular *APA College Dictionary of Psychology,* in 5,000 entries, followed in 2009, offering an even more highly concentrated, easily portable, and economical alternative for the student of psychology—whether he or she is at the advanced placement level in high school, a college undergraduate enrolled in Intro Psych, or an undergraduate considering or making psychology his or her major field of study.

Thus, the *APA Dictionary of Clinical Psychology* is the latest offspring in the dictionary branch of the APA Reference family—one that we hope will prove a convenient and highly focused alternative for the women and men at the very heart of the psychological enterprise: the clinicians who interpret the theory, read the research, and who, ultimately, are directly involved in the care and treatment of patients, whether they work in health and mental health clinics; in independent and group practices; or as consultants to professionals in such fields as medicine, law, social work, and consumer relations. Students—especially those in training as clinicians—will likewise find this dictionary a well-focused and economical alternative to the broader coverage of the parent work.

As with *Concise* and *College,* the *APA Dictionary of Clinical Psychology* is primarily a derivative: In order to delimit an appropriately representative universe of terms for inclusion in a clinical dictionary, APA reference staff culled those entries (largely in the 2006 parent work) that either directly or closely relate to clinical psychology—whether they are terms specific to the assessment, evaluation, diagnosis, prevention, and treatment of emotional and behavioral disorders; to clinical training and supervision, or to clinical research and practice; or they are terms more generally relevant to various biological, cognitive, developmental, and personality/social psychological underpinnings of physical and mental health. As with the two previous derivatives, we have retained much of the historical lexicon in this first edition of *Clinical* on the assumption that it remains useful for reading in the older literature of the late 19th and early and mid-20th centuries.

In addition, we have slightly expanded coverage, with some updating of pharmacological entries and of etymological information, as well as a very limited "preview" of some of the new clinical entries that will appear in the second edition of the full *APA Dictionary of Psychology.*

Finally, we take another opportunity to recognize the earlier contributions of the full editorial board of the *APA Dictionary of Psychology,* whose efforts remain the foundation upon which this clinical psychology dictionary rests.

Gary R. VandenBos, PhD
Editor in Chief
APA Publisher

Editorial Staff

Editor in Chief

Gary R. VandenBos, PhD

Senior Editors (American Psychological Association)

Theodore J. Baroody
Julia Frank-McNeil
Patricia D. Mathis
Marion Osmun

Senior Editors (Market House Books, Ltd.)

Jonathan Law
Elizabeth Martin

Editorial Board

Mark Appelbaum, PhD
Elizabeth D. Capaldi, PhD
Debra L. Dunivin, PhD
Alan E. Kazdin, PhD
Joseph D. Matarazzo, PhD
Susan H. McDaniel, PhD
Susan K. Nolen-Hoeksema, PhD
Suparna Rajaram, PhD

Editorial Contributors

John G. Albinson, PhD
Mark Appelbaum, PhD
Bernard J. Baars, PhD
Andrew S. Baum, PhD
Roy F. Baumeister, PhD
Daniel S. Beasley, PhD
Leonard Berkowitz, PhD
David F. Bjorklund, PhD
C. Alan Boneau, PhD
Marc N. Branch, PhD
Laura S. Brown, PhD
Joseph J. Campos, PhD
Daniel Cervone, PhD
Stanley H. Cohen, PhD
Deborah J. Coon, PhD
James C. Coyne, PhD
Robert L. Dipboye, PhD
Maria L. Dittrich, PhD
Gail Donaldson, PhD
Deborah K. Elliott-DeSorbo, PhD
David G. Elmes, PhD
Gary W. Evans, PhD
Leandre R. Fabrigar, PhD
Erica L. Fener, PhD
Donelson R. Forsyth, PhD
Robert G. Frank, PhD
Donald K. Freedheim, PhD
Charles J. Golden, PhD
Maria A. Gomez, DVM, PhD
Kenji Hakuta, PhD
Dennis C. Harper, PhD
Curtis P. Haugtvedt, PhD
Morton A. Heller, PhD
John W. Jacobson, PhD
Robert J. Kastenbaum, PhD
John F. Kihlstrom, PhD
Bruce E. Kline, PsyD
Debra L. Kosch, PhD
Michael J. Lambert, PhD
Joseph LoPiccolo, PhD
George F. Luger, PhD
Raelynn Maloney, PhD
A. David Mangelsdorff, PhD
Colin Martindale, PhD
Kenneth I. Maton, PhD
Randi E. McCabe, PhD, CPsych

Editorial Contributors (continued)

Katharine McGovern, PhD
Barbara G. Melamed, PhD
Theodore Millon, PhD, DSc
Bryan P. Myers, PhD
Peter E. Nathan, PhD
Raymond S. Nickerson, PhD
Andrea Farkas Patenaude, PhD
Christopher Peterson, PhD
Robert W. Proctor, PhD
Stacey M. Rosenfeld, PhD
Robert Rosenthal, PhD
Mark R. Rosenzweig, PhD
Preeti Saigal, PhD
Morgan T. Sammons, PhD
Julie H. Sandell, PhD
Thomas R. Scott, PhD
Anderson D. Smith, PhD
Tonya L. Smith-Jackson, PhD
Charles T. Snowdon, PhD
Michael A. Stadler, PhD
Robert J. Sternberg, PhD
Cheryl V. Tan, PhD
W. Scott Terry, PhD
J. Kevin Thompson, PhD
Mieke H. Verfaellie, PhD
Neal F. Viemeister, PhD
Kathleen D. Vohs, PhD
Kim-Phuong L. Vu, PhD
Leighton C. Whitaker, PhD
Richard N. Williams, PhD
Abraham W. Wolf, PhD
Charles E. Wright, PhD
Josef Zihl, PhD

Quick Guide to Format

Headword — **bariatrics** *n.* a field of medicine that focuses on the study of overweight: its causes, prevention, and treatment. — **Part-of-speech label**

Beck Anxiety Inventory (**BAI**) a self-report, 21-item measure used to assess the severity of anxiety in adults and to discriminate anxiety from depression. [Aaron T. **Beck** (1921–), U.S. Psychiatrist] — **Abbreviation**; **Etymology**

Plural form — **benny** *n.* (*pl.* **bennies**) slang for an amphetamine tablet. See AMPHETAMINES.

behavior hierarchy a ranking of possible responses based on the relative probabilities of their being elicited, with more probable behaviors ranked higher than less probable behaviors. Also called **behavioral hierarchy**. — **Alternative name**

behaviorism *n.* an approach to psychology, formulated in 1913 by U.S. psychologist John B. Watson (1878–1958), based on the study of objective, observable facts rather than subjective, qualitative processes, such as feelings, motives, and consciousness. To make psychology a naturalistic science, Watson proposed to limit it to quantitative events, such as stimulus–response relationships, effects of conditioning, physiological processes, and a study of human and animal behavior, all of which can best be investigated through laboratory experiments that yield objective measures under controlled conditions. Historically, behaviorists held that mind was not a proper topic for scientific study since mental events are subjective and not independently verifiable. With its emphasis on activity as an adaptive function, behaviorism is seen as an outgrowth of FUNCTIONALISM. See DESCRIPTIVE BEHAVIORISM; METHODOLOGICAL BEHAVIORISM; NEOBEHAVIORISM; RADICAL BEHAVIORISM. — **Etymology**; **Cross-references**

biogenesis *n.* the origin of living things from other living things. **Biogenetics** is the scientific study of the principles and processes governing the production of living organisms from other living organisms, including the mechanisms of heredity. **—biogenetic** *adj.* — **Hidden entry**; **Derived word**

body narcissism **1.** an exaggerated preoccupation or fascination with one's own body and its erogenous zones. See also NARCISSISM. **2.** in psychoanalytic theory, the PRIMARY NARCISSISM of the young infant. — **Sense number**; **Sense number**; **Cross-reference**

Aa

AA abbreviation for ALCOHOLICS ANONYMOUS.

AAAP abbreviation for AMERICAN ASSOCIATION OF APPLIED PSYCHOLOGY.

AAAPP abbreviation for AMERICAN ASSOCIATION OF APPLIED AND PREVENTIVE PSYCHOLOGY.

AACP abbreviation for AMERICAN ASSOCIATION OF CLINICAL PSYCHOLOGISTS.

AACS abbreviation for AMERICAN ACADEMY OF CLINICAL SEXOLOGISTS.

AAI abbreviation for ADULT ATTACHMENT INTERVIEW.

AAIDD see AMERICAN ASSOCIATION ON INTELLECTUAL AND DEVELOPMENTAL DISABILITIES.

AAMI abbreviation for AGE-ASSOCIATED MEMORY IMPAIRMENT.

AAMR abbreviation for American Association of Mental Retardation. See AMERICAN ASSOCIATION ON INTELLECTUAL AND DEVELOPMENTAL DISABILITIES.

AAP abbreviation for ASSOCIATION FOR THE ADVANCEMENT OF PSYCHOLOGY.

AASECT abbreviation for AMERICAN ASSOCIATION OF SEX EDUCATORS, COUNSELORS AND THERAPISTS.

ABA abbreviation for APPLIED BEHAVIOR ANALYSIS.

A-B-A-B design a SINGLE-CASE EXPERIMENTAL DESIGN in which a baseline or other initial condition (A) is followed by a different condition (B), which is followed by a return to the initial condition (A), which is then followed by a return to the second condition (B).

A-B-A design a SINGLE-CASE EXPERIMENTAL DESIGN in which a baseline or other initial condition (A) is followed by a different condition (B) and then by a return to the initial condition (A).

abaissement *n.* a mental state in which the threshold of consciousness lowers and unconscious thoughts become conscious, as when slipping into sleep and becoming aware of dream content. [from French, in full: *abaissement du niveau mental,* first recognized and defined by French physician and psychologist Pierre Janet (1859–1947)]

abandonment *n.* desertion of a dependent by a parent or primary caregiver. Dependents are usually children but may be entire families or individuals who are ill. **—abandon** *vb.*

abandonment reaction a feeling of emotional deprivation, loss of support, and loneliness experienced by children who have been deserted or neglected by one or both parents. Abandonment reaction is also experienced by adults who have lost a loved one on whom they have depended.

abasement need a need to surrender oneself to another person, accept blame or punishment, or confess and atone. See also MASOCHISM. [defined by U.S. psychologist Henry A. Murray (1893–1988)]

abasia *n.* severe impairment or complete loss of the ability to walk due to problems in motor coordination. **—abasic** *adj.*

abatement *n.* a reduction or lessening in the severity of pain or other symptoms of illness or disorder.

ABCDE technique a procedure used in RATIONAL EMOTIVE BEHAVIOR THERAPY, on the basis of ABC THEORY, which suggests that *A*ctivating events (i.e., adversities) are mediated by irrational *B*eliefs in determining inappropriate emotional and behavioral *C*onsequences. ABCDE technique involves *D*isputing these beliefs (i.e., under the guidance of a therapist), which results in several types of *E*ffects (e.g., rational beliefs, appropriate feelings, desirable behaviors).

ABC theory the theory underlying RATIONAL EMOTIVE BEHAVIOR THERAPY, which suggests that *A*ctivating events (i.e., adversities) are mediated by irrational *B*eliefs in determining inappropriate behavioral *C*onsequences. See also ABCDE TECHNIQUE. [devised by U.S. psychologist Albert Ellis (1913–2007)]

A-B design the simplest SINGLE-CASE EXPERIMENTAL DESIGN, in which the DEPENDENT VARIABLE is measured throughout the pretreatment or baseline period (the A phase) and then again following the treatment period (the B phase). Numerous variations of this basic design exist, such as the A-B-A design, A-B-A-B design, A-B-B-A design, and A-B-BC-B design. The latter involves two treatment periods (the B phase and the C phase) and is intended to assess the effect of B both in combination with C and apart from C.

abdominal migraine recurrent, severe episodes of abdominal pain that may be accompanied by nausea and vomiting. The episodes last from 1 to 72 hours and occur most frequently in children.

aberrant response an abnormal or atypical behavior, commonly targeted during a behavioral intervention.

aberration *n.* any deviation, particularly a sig-

A

nificant or undesirable one, from the normal or typical. See also MENTAL ABERRATION.

abience *n.* a response or behavior that results in movement away from a stimulus, either by physical withdrawal from the stimulus or by an action designed to avoid the stimulus entirely. Compare ADIENCE. **—abient** *adj.*

Abilify *n.* a trade name for ARIPIPRAZOLE.

ability level an index of achievement or performance that reports the absolute or relative ability of the organism being evaluated.

ability trait a personality trait that involves an individual's capacity to attain his or her goals. It is one of three classes of SOURCE TRAITS in CATTELL'S PERSONALITY TRAIT THEORY, the other two being DYNAMIC TRAITS and TEMPERAMENT TRAITS.

abiotrophy *n.* loss of function or loss of resistance to a disease through degeneration or failure of body tissues, organs, or systems. Abiotrophy is used particularly to refer to premature degeneration caused by a genetic defect, as in Huntington's disease. **—abiotrophic** *adj.*

ablation *n.* the removal or destruction of part of a biological tissue or structure by a surgical procedure or a toxic substance, usually for treatment or to study its function. When the entire tissue or structure is excised, the process is called **extirpation**.

ablution *n.* **1.** a largely obsolete therapeutic technique utilizing water (such as wrapping wet towels around the body or immersing in water) to calm agitated patients. It was abandoned with the advent of psychotropic drugs. **2.** a symbolic cleansing of the body, or of possessions, with the intent of purification.

abnormal *adj.* relating to any deviation from what is considered typical, usual, or healthy, particularly if the deviation is considered harmful or maladaptive. In statistics, for example, abnormal scores are those that are outside the usual or expected range. The term, however, is most often applied to behavior that differs from a culturally accepted norm, especially when indicative of a mental disorder. **—abnormality** *n.* **—abnormally** *adv.*

abnormal behavior behavior that is atypical or statistically uncommon within a particular culture or that is maladaptive or detrimental to an individual. Such behavior is often regarded as evidence of a mental or emotional disturbance, ranging from minor adjustment problems to severe mental disorder.

abnormality *n.* **1.** the state or condition of being ABNORMAL. **2.** a defect or malformation in structure or function.

abnormal psychology the branch of psychology devoted to the study, prevention, assessment, and treatment of maladaptive behavior. See also PSYCHOPATHOLOGY.

aboiement *n.* the involuntary, uncontrollable production of animalistic sounds. Aboiement (French, "barking") is a symptom sometimes occurring in schizophrenia and Tourette's disorder.

abortifacient *n.* any agent that induces abortion. Also called **abortient**.

abortion *n.* the expulsion from the uterus of an embryo or fetus before it is able to survive independently. An abortion may be either spontaneous, in which case it occurs naturally and is also called a **miscarriage**, or induced, in which case it is produced deliberately by artificial means such as drugs or surgery and done for therapeutic reasons or as an elective decision. The practice is controversial and may involve **abortion counseling**, the provision of guidance, advice, information, and support on issues concerning termination of pregnancy and the alternatives of adoption or raising the child.

aboulia *n.* see ABULIA.

ABPP abbreviation for AMERICAN BOARD OF PROFESSIONAL PSYCHOLOGY.

abreaction *n.* the therapeutic process of bringing forgotten or inhibited material (i.e., experiences, memories) from the unconscious into consciousness, with concurrent emotional release and discharge of tension and anxiety. See also CATHARSIS.

ABS abbreviation for the American Association on Intellectual and Developmental Disabilities' (formerly American Association on Mental Retardation's) Adaptive Behavior Scale, in separate editions for school and adult service settings. See ADAPTIVE BEHAVIOR SCALE.

abscess *n.* a contained but often enlarging area of infection that includes pus and dead tissue. A brain abscess raises INTRACRANIAL PRESSURE and can cause substantial neurological deficits, such as poor coordination, decreased sensation, confusion, and other altered mental states.

absence *n.* a brief LOSS OF CONSCIOUSNESS or period of mental inattentiveness, particularly when associated with a seizure (see ABSENCE SEIZURE), with no memory for the event afterward.

absence seizure a type of GENERALIZED SEIZURE, formerly called **petit mal seizure**, in which the individual abruptly ceases activity and cannot afterward remember the event. The absences usually last from 5 to 15 s, during which the individual is unresponsive and motionless, staring blankly. Seizures of this type typically begin between ages 4 and 12 and rarely persist into adulthood.

absent-mindedness *n.* a state of heedlessness or inattention marked by a tendency to be occupied by one's own thoughts and not to be fully aware of concurrent situations or the external reality of the moment.

absolute error the degree to which an observation is inaccurate without specification of whether it errs by being too high or too low. Absolute error is computed as the average absolute difference between the intended or expected value and the actual value. This measure may also describe the overall accuracy of a set of movements with a well-defined goal. Compare CONSTANT ERROR; RANDOM ERROR.

absolute judgment a psychophysical judgment in which a single stimulus is placed in a particular category (e.g., "bright," "loud"), as opposed to one in which several stimuli are compared to one another or to a given standard (e.g., "brighter," "louder").

absorption *n.* **1.** the uptake of fluid and dissolved substances into a cell across the plasma membrane. For example, an administered drug moves through various biological membranes from its site of administration to its target organ. Absorption into the target organ is dependent on a number of factors, including the method of ADMINISTRATION (e.g., oral, intravenous); the properties of the drug (e.g., molecular size, ability to cross lipid membranes); the amount of drug administered; and the characteristics or state of the individual (e.g., body mass, sex, age, presence of disease, presence of other drugs). **2.** an extreme involvement or preoccupation with one object, idea, or pursuit, with inattention to other aspects of the environment. See also TELLEGEN ABSORPTION SCALE.

abstinence *n.* the act of refraining from the use of something, particularly alcohol or drugs, or from participation in sexual or other activity. In most instances, abstinence from drugs or alcohol is the primary goal of substance abuse treatment. See also SUBSTANCE WITHDRAWAL. **—abstinent** *adj.*

abstinence delirium a form of DELIRIUM that occasionally accompanies withdrawal from alcohol or drugs of abuse. See ALCOHOL WITHDRAWAL DELIRIUM; DELIRIUM TREMENS.

abstinence rule see RULE OF ABSTINENCE.

abstinence syndrome the characteristic set of physiological and behavioral events that accompanies withdrawal from dependence-inducing substances.

abstract attitude a COGNITIVE STYLE that involves the ability to grasp essentials and common properties, to keep different aspects of a situation in mind and shift from one to another, to predict and plan ahead, and to think symbolically and draw conclusions. These capacities are often impaired in people with certain neurological or psychological disorders. Also called **categorical attitude**. Compare CONCRETE ATTITUDE. See also ABSTRACT THINKING. [defined by German-born U.S. neurologist Kurt Goldstein (1878–1965)]

abstract conceptualization the process of forming abstract concepts, which may be general and apply to numerous particular instances (e.g., "dog" or "fish") or wholly intangible and have no specific material referent (e.g., "liberty" or "youth"). See ABSTRACTION; CONCEPTUALIZATION.

abstract intelligence the intellectual ability to think in terms of abstract concepts. Also called **abstract ability**. See ABSTRACT THINKING. Compare CONCRETE INTELLIGENCE.

abstraction *n.* **1.** the formation of general ideas or concepts by extracting similarities from particular instances. The precise cognitive processes by which this occurs remain a subject of investigation. **2.** such a concept, especially a wholly intangible one, such as "goodness" or "truth." **—abstract** *vb.*

abstract representation in cognitive theory, a MENTAL REPRESENTATION of a stimulus in an abstract or essential form that is not tied to any one of its variable surface forms. For example, the letter *A* can be thought about at an abstract level with no reference to specific surface forms, such as *a*, *A*, or **a**.

abstract thinking thinking characterized by the use of abstractions and generalizations. Compare CONCRETE THINKING. See also ABSTRACT ATTITUDE; CATEGORICAL THOUGHT.

abulia (aboulia) *n.* extreme loss of initiative and willpower, resulting in an inability to make decisions or initiate voluntary actions. **—abulic** *adj.*

abuse 1. *n.* interactions in which one person behaves in a cruel, violent, demeaning, or invasive manner toward another person or an animal. The term most commonly implies physical mistreatment but also encompasses sexual and psychological (emotional) mistreatment. **2.** *vb.* to subject a person or animal to such treatment. **3.** *n.* see SUBSTANCE ABUSE. **4.** *n.* colloquially, the misuse of a substance to an extent that it causes the individual difficulty, whether or not it meets the *DSM–IV–TR* definition of substance abuse. See also ALCOHOL ABUSE. **—abuser** *n.*

abuse potential the ability of a drug to reinforce drug-taking behavior. Factors that determine abuse potential include route of drug administration (e.g., intravenous, inhalation, oral) and the speed of onset, duration, and nature of the drug effect. These factors are themselves determined by complex interactions between the individual, the substance, and the social environment. Substances with a high abuse potential include intravenous heroin, crack cocaine, morphine, and smoked opium. Substances with a low abuse potential include the hallucinogens and marijuana. Also called **abuse liability**.

academic intervention the active involvement of school officials and teachers in developing and implementing an effective plan for the prevention or remediation of inappropriate and disruptive student behavior. Successful programs of intervention are most often individualized, child focused, and minimally restrictive. Academic intervention is the antithesis of reactive strategies, such as loss of privileges and time out.

academic skills disorder in *DSM–III* and earlier editions, a disorder that in *DSM–IV–TR* is classified as a LEARNING DISORDER.

acalculia *n.* loss of the ability to perform simple arithmetic operations that results from brain injury or disease, usually to the PARIETAL LOBE. It is an acquired condition, whereas DYSCALCULIA is developmental.

acamprosate *n.* an analog of the inhibitory neurotransmitter GAMMA-AMINOBUTYRIC ACID (GABA) used in the management of alcohol dependence. Although exact mechanisms of action are unclear, acamprosate may act by directly binding to the GABA receptor complex (see $GABA_A$ RECEPTOR; $GABA_B$ RECEPTOR); it may also act by inhibiting the actions of the excitatory amino acid GLUTAMATE, for example by inhibiting NMDA RECEPTORS. When administered in combination with behavioral treatments, it has some efficacy in reducing alcohol intake or increasing alcohol-free periods in people recovering from alcohol dependence. U.S. trade name: **Campral**.

acarophobia *n.* a persistent and irrational fear of skin parasites (mites), ants, worms, and, by extension, small objects such as pins and needles. The condition is believed to be related to the sensation of insects crawling on or under the skin, which occurs in alcoholism, cocaine use, narcotic addiction, and delirium resulting from meningitis, encephalitis, rheumatic fever, or diphtheria. See also FORMICATION; LILLIPUTIAN HALLUCINATION. **—acarophobic** *adj.*

acataphasia (**akataphasia**) *n.* the use of inappropriate or grammatically incorrect words and expressions. It is a speech disturbance frequently found in individuals with schizophrenia or APHASIA. See also AGRAMMATISM.

acathisia *n.* see AKATHISIA.

accelerated interaction the intensification of group processes and emotional interaction that occurs in experiential groups when the group sessions are continuous and secluded. See MARATHON GROUP; TIME-EXTENDED THERAPY.

acceleration–deceleration injury a form of HEAD INJURY caused by the head suddenly being placed into motion or abruptly stopped, as, for example, when the individual is in a car accident. The sudden motion or stop causes diffuse stretching and tearing of white matter tracts in addition to bleeding and other neurological effects. The injury may have a variety of consequences, including personality change, attention problems, memory disorders, and EXECUTIVE DYSFUNCTION.

acceptance *n.* **1.** a favorable attitude toward an idea, situation, person, or group. In the context of psychotherapy and counseling, it is the receptive, nonjudgmental attitude of therapists or counselors, which conveys an implicit respect and regard for their clients as individuals. **2.** willing acknowledgment of validity or correctness. In the context of recovery from substance abuse and other addictions, it is essential for a person to accept that he or she has a problem before any interventions can be effective.

acceptance and commitment therapy (**ACT**) a form of COGNITIVE BEHAVIOR THERAPY based on the premise that ineffective strategies to control thoughts and feelings actually lead to problem behaviors. It helps clients to abandon these ineffective control strategies and instead willingly experience difficult thoughts and feelings as a necessary part of a worthy life. Clients then clarify their personal values and life goals, and learn to make life-enhancing behavioral changes accordingly. ACT has been applied to a wide variety of problems, including depression, anxiety, stress, and substance abuse.

access *vb.* to retrieve or recall a memory.

accessible *adj.* **1.** receptive or responsive to personal interaction and other external stimuli. A client in psychotherapy, for example, is thought to be accessible if he or she responds to the therapist in a way that facilitates the development of rapport and, ultimately, fosters the examination of cognitive, emotional, and behavioral issues. **2.** retrievable through memory or other cognitive processes. **3.** a characteristic of a building and its facilities and fixtures, or of any site, that makes it easy to approach, enter, or use, particularly by people with disabilities. **4.** in a tissue, reachable by means of standard surgical or diagnostic procedures. **—accessibility** *n.*

accessory symptoms see SECONDARY SYMPTOMS.

accidental stimulus any stimulus that intrudes into a dream, such as the sound of a telephone ringing or a muscle cramp. Such stimuli may be incorporated into dreams. Compare DREAM STIMULUS.

accident prevention the use of scientifically tested methods to reduce the number and severity of accidents. These include the systematic study of accidents and the circumstances in which they occur; the identification and control of workplace hazards; the evaluation and redesign of systems and processes; and the use of training programs, instruction, and other forms of safety education.

accident proneness a chronic susceptibility to accidents. This concept has been heavily debated since its introduction around 1920, and many question the existence of a fixed accident-prone personality. However, several individual variables and sociological and situational factors have been identified as important predictors of accident involvement, including aggressiveness, impulsiveness, thrill and adventure seeking, workload and cognitive demand, and stress.

acclimatization *n.* adjustment or adaptation to new circumstances or environmental conditions, particularly the physiological changes that improve an individual's ability to tolerate environmental alterations. Also called **acclimation**. **—acclimatize** *vb.*

accommodation *n.* **1.** adjustment or modification. For example, regarding individuals with disabilities, it refers to REASONABLE ACCOMMODATIONS made to meet their needs, whereas in the theory of cognitive development proposed by Jean PIAGET it refers to the adjustment of mental SCHEMAS according to information acquired through experience; and in the context of bargaining and interpersonal negotiations it refers to modification of the various parties' demands or actions in order to achieve agreement or a mutually beneficial outcome. **2.** the process by which the focus of the eye is changed to allow near or distant objects to form sharp images on the retina. **—accommodate** *vb.*

accountability *n.* in health care, the responsibility of individual providers, clinics, or hospitals to document their efforts, their resource utilization, and the outcome of their services and to report this information to insurance companies or state or federal agencies. **—accountable** *adj.*

accreditation *n.* the formal process in which an agency or organization evaluates and approves an institution or program of study as meeting predetermined standards. Accreditation applies to institutions as CERTIFICATION applies to individuals. **—accredited** *adj.*

accuracy standards criteria used to assess the scientific value of the information and conclusions presented in an evaluation report. Such standards include ensuring the completeness of data collection and the reliability and validity of procedures and measures, conducting appropriate qualitative and quantitative analyses, and impartially reporting results to arrive at justified conclusions. See also FEASIBILITY STANDARDS; PROPRIETY STANDARDS; UTILITY STANDARDS.

Accutane *n.* a trade name for ISOTRETINOIN.

acenesthesia *n.* **1.** loss of the sensation of physical existence. **2.** a lack of awareness of one's own body. See DEPERSONALIZATION.

acetaldehyde *n.* a toxic and volatile initial product of alcohol (ethanol) metabolism that is responsible for the variety of unpleasant effects associated with a hangover, including nausea, vomiting, and headache. It is produced when alcohol is broken down by a liver enzyme called alcohol dehydrogenase and is itself further broken down by another liver enzyme (acetaldehyde dehydrogenase) into acetate and, ultimately, into carbon dioxide and water. Acetaldehyde is widely studied to determine its relationship to and influence upon the development and progression of alcoholism. See also DISULFIRAM.

acetaminophen *n.* a common ANALGESIC and ANTIPYRETIC agent with an efficacy similar to aspirin, except that it does not possess antirheumatic or anti-inflammatory properties. It is rapidly distributed in the body and has a short HALF-LIFE (around 2 hours). Acetaminophen is a widely used alternative to aspirin, especially when usage of the latter is inadvisable (e.g., in patients with bleeding disorders). It is also sold in combination with other analgesics, antihistamines, decongestants, or cough suppressants. However, acute overdose or chronic daily dosing of acetaminophen may cause liver damage (hepatotoxicity), and consumption of alcohol increases the risk of liver damage. Rapid intervention, including the administration of *N*-acetylcysteine, is required to prevent fatal hepatotoxicity after acetaminophen poisoning. Also called **APAP**; **paracetamol**. U.S. trade name (among others): **Tylenol**.

acetanilide *n.* see ANILIDES.

acetazolamide *n.* see CARBONIC ANHYDRASE INHIBITOR.

acetylcholine (**ACh**) *n.* a major, predominantly excitatory but also inhibitory, neurotransmitter in the central nervous system, where it plays an important role in memory formation and learning and is implicated in Alzheimer's disease; and in the peripheral nervous system, where it mediates skeletal, cardiac, and smooth muscle contraction and is implicated in MYASTHENIA GRAVIS and other movement disorders.

acetylcholine receptor (**AChR**) any of certain protein molecules in cell membranes in the central and peripheral nervous systems that are stimulated by acetylcholine or acetylcholine-like substances. There are two main types: MUSCARINIC RECEPTORS and NICOTINIC RECEPTORS.

acetylcholinesterase inhibitors drugs that block the ability of the enzyme acetylcholinesterase (see CHOLINESTERASE) to degrade the neurotransmitter acetylcholine in the SYNAPTIC CLEFT of cholinergic neurons. Some acetylcholinesterase inhibitors are used clinically as NOOTROPICS to slow the progression of dementia in Alzheimer's disease. Also called **anticholinesterases**; **cholinesterase inhibitors**. See DONEPEZIL; GALANTAMINE; RIVASTIGMINE; TACRINE. See also CARBAMATE.

acetylsalicylic acid (**ASA**) the chemical name for ASPIRIN.

acetylureas *pl. n.* drugs that are analogs of HYDANTOINS used in the treatment of partial seizures.

ACh abbreviation for ACETYLCHOLINE.

acheiria (**achiria**) *n.* **1.** the condition of being born with only one or no hands. See also APODIA. **2.** a disorder of sensation in which an individual cannot tell which side of the body is being touched. It is considered a **dyscheiria**, a disordered representation of one side of the body.

achievement drive a strong impulse to do one's best to achieve a goal and, often, to be recognized and approved for attaining it. Students with a strong achievement drive have been found to earn better grades than equally gifted students with a weaker achievement drive. Studies of the literature of different societies indicate that achievement themes predominate during periods of rapid economic growth. See also ACHIEVEMENT MOTIVATION.

achievement motivation **1.** the desire to perform well and be successful. In this sense, the term often is used synonymously with NEED FOR ACHIEVEMENT. **2.** the desire to overcome obstacles and master difficult challenges. High scorers in achievement motivation are likely to set higher standards and work with greater perseverance than equally gifted low scorers. David MCCLELLAND found a significant relationship between high achievement motivation and early independence in childhood; in addition, there is a positive correlation between high achievement motivation and actual achievement in later life. See ACHIEVEMENT DRIVE; NEED FOR ACHIEVEMENT. [first described by U.S. psychologist Henry Alexander Murray (1893–1988)]

achiria *n.* see ACHEIRIA.

acid *n.* slang for LSD. See also HALLUCINOGEN.

acid flashback the experience reported by some users of LSD in which some part of the LSD experience recurs later when the individual has not been using the drug.

acid head slang for a user of LSD.

acidosis *n.* an abnormally high level of acidity (hydrogen ion concentration) in the blood and tissues, which upsets the body's acid–base balance. The condition has numerous causes and symptoms vary with each, potentially including such neurological abnormalities as confusion, fatigue or lethargy, and irritability. Rapid breathing is often seen as well. Compare ALKALOSIS. **—acidotic** *adj.*

acid trip slang for an episode of LSD intoxication.

acme *n.* the highest point of sexual pleasure. Also called **summa libido**.

acmesthesia *n.* a form of PARESTHESIA in which a cutaneous stimulus normally sensed as pain is perceived instead as sharp touch or pressure.

ACOA abbreviation for ADULT CHILDREN OF ALCOHOLICS.

aconuresis *n.* involuntary passage of urine. It is a rare synonym of ENURESIS.

acoria (**akoria**) *n.* a form of POLYPHAGIA marked by an excessive appetite and a loss of the sensation of satiety. See also BULIMIA NERVOSA.

acquaintance rape see DATE RAPE.

acquiescence *n.* agreement or acceptance, typically without protest or argument. **—acquiesce** *vb.* **—acquiescent** *adj.*

acquired *adj.* denoting a response, behavior, idea, or information that has been learned or developed on the basis of experience rather than being innate or inborn.

acquired characteristic a structural or functional characteristic or a psychological feature (e.g., a trait or behavior) of a organism that arises from experience or through environmental factors rather than being the result of inheritance. Also called **acquired character**.

acquired dyspraxia DYSPRAXIA that is manifested as the loss of a previously acquired ability to perform coordinated movements. It usually follows or is associated with brain injury or stroke. Compare DEVELOPMENTAL DYSPRAXIA.

acquired immune deficiency syndrome see AIDS.

acquisition *n.* the attainment by an individual of new behavior, information, or skills or the process by which this occurs. Although often used interchangeably with LEARNING, acquisition tends to be defined somewhat more concretely as the period during which progressive, measurable increases in response strength are seen. **—acquire** *vb.*

acquisitiveness *n.* the tendency or desire to acquire and accumulate objects or possessions. Compare HOARDING. **—acquisitive** *adj.*

acroanesthesia *n.* an absence of sensitivity in the extremities.

acrocephalosyndactyly *n.* any of several related inherited disorders (all dominant traits) that cause abnormalities of the skull, face, hands, and feet. APERT'S SYNDROME, Apert–Crouzon syndrome, and PFEIFFER'S SYNDROME (acrocephalosyndactyly Types I, II, and V) are due to different mutations in the *FGFR2* gene (encoding fibroblast growth factor receptor) on chromosome 10. CHOTZEN'S SYNDROME (Type III) is due to a mutation in the *TWIST* gene on chromosome 7 (locus 7p21.3–21.2), which affects the expression of *FGFR2.*

acrocinesis *n.* excessive motion or movement. Also called **acrocinesia**; **acrokinesia**.

acroesthesia *n.* an abnormal sensitivity to stimuli applied to the extremities.

acromegaloid-hypertelorism-pectus carinatum syndrome a congenital condition, believed to be hereditary, marked by short stature, mental retardation, widely set eyes, and skeletal anomalies, including an enlarged head and a deformed sternum. Only males are known to be affected. All show slow psychomotor development and IQs estimated in the 20s.

acromegaloid personality a personality pattern observed in a large proportion of patients with ACROMEGALY. The chief features are frequent changes in mood, impulsiveness, temper outbursts, impatience, and, in advanced cases, loss of initiative, egocentricity, and somnolence.

acromegaly *n.* an abnormal enlargement of the bones in the hands, feet, face, and skull due to excessive secretion of growth hormone by the pituitary gland during adulthood. **—acromegalic** *adj.*

acroparesthesia *n.* a feeling of numbness, tingling, or other abnormal sensation in the extremities. Kinds of acroparesthesia include **Nothnagel's acroparesthesia**, which is accompanied by circulatory disorders, and **Schultze's**

acroparesthesia, marked by peripheral-nerve irritability but without circulatory abnormalities.

acrophobia *n.* an excessive, irrational fear of heights, resulting in the avoidance of elevations or marked distress when unable to avoid high places. **—acrophobic** *adj.*

acrotomophilia *n.* pathological interest in amputations. It may be expressed as a PARAPHILIA in which the person is sexually aroused by people whose body parts, typically arms or legs, have been amputated or by amputation sites in the body. Also called **acrotophilia**; **apotemnophilia**.

ACT 1. abbreviation for ACCEPTANCE AND COMMITMENT THERAPY. **2.** abbreviation for ATROPINE-COMA THERAPY. **3.** abbreviation for ATTENTION-CONTROL TRAINING. **4.** abbreviation for AUDITORY CONSONANT TRIGRAM.

acting in 1. in psychoanalysis, a form of RESISTANCE in which the patient defends against repressed wishes, memories, or both by using actions (e.g., getting up and walking about) to impede the flow of FREE ASSOCIATION. **2.** the patient's reenactment of past relationships in the TRANSFERENCE relationship with the analyst.

acting out 1. the uncontrolled and inappropriate behavioral expression of denied emotions that serves to relieve tension associated with these emotions or to communicate them in a disguised, or indirect, way to others. Such behaviors may include arguing, fighting, stealing, threatening, or throwing tantrums. Acting out is often assumed to underlie antisocial or delinquent behavior in children and adolescents. **2.** in psychoanalytic theory, reenactment of past events as an expression of unconscious emotional conflicts, feelings, or desires—often sexual or aggressive—with no attempt to understand the origin or meaning of these behaviors.

action disorganization syndrome (**ADS**) a cognitive deficit resulting from damage to the FRONTAL LOBES of the brain and causing individuals to make errors on multistepped but familiar or routine tasks. Types of errors include omissions or additions of steps, disordered sequencing of steps, and object substitutions or misuse.

action interpretation the nonverbal reaction of a therapist to a patient's behavior or remarks.

action-oriented therapy any therapy that emphasizes doing and taking action rather than verbal communication or discussion.

action painting a form of painting, often used in ART THERAPY, in which individuals spontaneously create unplanned abstract works using unconventional techniques, for example, splashing, dribbling, trickling, or slapping the paint more or less randomly onto the canvas. When used therapeutically, these productions are reviewed and incorporated into treatment. Also called **tachisme**.

action potential (**AP**) the change in electric potential that propagates along a cell during the transmission of a nerve impulse or the contraction of a muscle. It is marked by a rapid, transient depolarization of the cell's plasma membrane, from a resting potential of about –70 mV (inside negative) to about +30 mV (inside positive), and back again, after a slight hyperpolarization, to the resting potential. Each action potential takes just a few milliseconds. Also called **action current**; **spike potential**.

action readiness a state of preparedness for action that is elicited as part of an emotional response and associated with such physiological indicators as changes in heart rate, respiratory rate, and muscle tension. The term is often used synonymously with ACTION TENDENCY but also refers to a general readiness for action that does not involve an urge to carry out a specific behavior.

action slip any error that involves some kind of cognitive lapse and results in an unintended action, as in putting one's spectacles in the refrigerator. Action slips are commonly referred to as "absent-minded" mistakes. See ABSENT-MINDEDNESS.

action tendency an urge to carry out certain expressive or instrumental behaviors that is linked to a specific emotion. For example, the action tendency of fear involves an urge to escape, and that of anger involves an urge to attack. Some theorists argue that the action tendency of an emotional reaction should be regarded as its essential defining characteristic. Compare ACTION READINESS.

action theory all those theories, collectively, that explain behavior in terms of goal-directed human beings acting intentionally with reference to the environment and present situation. Action theory was known originally as **will psychology**, founded in Germany by Wilhelm WUNDT, who emphasized and distinguished between motivation and volition of human behavior.

Actiq *n.* a trade name for FENTANYL.

activated sleep see REM SLEEP.

activating event in RATIONAL EMOTIVE BEHAVIOR THERAPY, an event—current, past, or anticipated—that triggers irrational beliefs and disruptive emotions.

activation *n.* **1.** in many theories of memory, an attribute of the representational units that varies from weaker to stronger, with more strongly activated representations competing to control processing. **2.** the process of alerting an organ or body system for action, particularly arousal of one organ or system by another. **—activate** *vb.* **—activational** *adj.*

activation–elaboration a dual-process theory of memory holding that concepts stored in memory vary in their levels both of ACTIVATION and ELABORATION.

activation hypothesis 1. the principle that numerical weightings on the links or nodes of cognitive network models can represent their degree of activity or processing. Consciousness is sometimes attributed to the subset of most highly weighted elements in such models. **2.** the hypothesis that high metabolic activity reflects activation of brain areas subserving mental tasks.

activation–synthesis hypothesis a hypothesis that explains dreams as a product of cortical interpretation of random activation rising from the lower brain structures, including the PONS. See PGO SPIKES. [originated by U.S. psychiatrists J. Allan Hobson (1933–) and Robert W. McCarley]

activation theory of emotion the theory that emotion is measurable as change in the individual's level of neural excitation of the RETICULAR FORMATION and associated degree of cortical and thalamic alertness, as revealed via ELECTROENCEPHALOGRAPHY. It was a refinement of an earlier **activation–arousal theory** equating emotion to change in the difficult-to-measure level of an individual's energy expenditure. Also called **arousal theory**.

active algolagnia arousal of sexual excitement by causing pain to another person. See SEXUAL SADISM.

active analytic psychotherapy the therapeutic approach of German psychoanalyst Wilhelm Stekel (1868–1940) in which the analyst takes a much more active role than prescribed in CLASSICAL PSYCHOANALYSIS and gives more attention to the intrapsychic conflicts in the patient's current life than to exploring early childhood experiences. The therapist intervenes in the process of free association to discuss important issues, confronts the patient's resistances directly, offers advice and exhortation, and helps the patient interpret his or her dreams intuitively in the light of current attitudes and problems. Through these methods, and by avoiding many of the Freudian steps such as ANALYSIS OF THE TRANSFERENCE, Stekel sought to shorten the therapeutic process considerably. Also called **active analysis**.

active avoidance a type of OPERANT CONDITIONING in which an explicit act prevents or postpones the delivery of an AVERSIVE STIMULUS, such as when pressing a lever blocks the delivery of an electric shock. That is, avoidance is achieved by an overt action. Compare PASSIVE AVOIDANCE.

active concretization in schizophrenia, the process of transforming abstract concepts into concrete representations or forms. For example, an individual with paranoid schizophrenia who experiences feelings that the whole world is hostile may later become convinced that the neighbors are trying to harm him or her. If this individual should then begin to have specific perceptual experiences that support this conviction, such as auditory hallucinations of threatening remarks made by the neighbors, PERCEPTUALIZATION of the concept has occurred; this is the most advanced level of active concretization. [defined by Italian-born U.S. psychiatrist Silvano Arieti (1914–1982)]

active coping a stress-management strategy in which a person directly works to control a stressor through appropriately targeted behavior, embracing responsibility for resolving the situation using one's available internal resources. This type of COPING STRATEGY may take various forms, including getting answers to questions or changing established habits. Active coping generally is considered adaptive, having been associated with fewer mood disturbances, enhanced SELF-EFFICACY, and other favorable consequences. It is similar to the earlier conceptualization of PROBLEM-FOCUSED COPING but distinguished by its focus upon one's internal resources. Compare PASSIVE COPING. [identified in 1987 by Gregory K. Brown and Perry M. Nicassio (1947–), U.S. clinical psychologists]

active deception the process of intentionally misleading research participants, for example, by giving them false information about the purpose of the research or by having them unwittingly interact with CONFEDERATES. Also called **deception by commission**. Compare PASSIVE DECEPTION.

active euthanasia direct action performed to terminate the life of a person (or animal) who is suffering greatly and is considered to have no chance for recovery. Administering a lethal injection is the most common method of active euthanasia today. This practice is distinguished from PASSIVE EUTHANASIA, in which treatments are withheld but no direct action to terminate the life is taken. See also ASSISTED DEATH.

active learning 1. learning that occurs through the actual performance of behavior or acting out of an idea. Also called **action learning**. **2.** the active seeking out of new information, rather than simply being a passive recipient of a learning experience. Active learners set goals, select strategies, recognize when they understand, and work with others to further learning.

active listening a psychotherapeutic technique in which the therapist listens to a client closely and attentively, asking questions as needed, in order to fully understand the content of the message and the depth of the client's emotion. The therapist typically restates what has been said to ensure accurate understanding. Active listening is particularly associated with CLIENT-CENTERED THERAPY.

active memory a memory that is currently the focus of consciousness or was recently in awareness, as distinct from the vast body of stored memories that are currently inactive. Activation occurs through RETRIEVAL, cuing (see CUE), or prompting. According to one theory, an item in short-term memory is an item from long-term memory that has been activated.

active negativism see NEGATIVISM.

active performance the actual performance of behavior or acting out an idea, in contrast to mentally rehearsing or imagining the action.

active placebo an agent used in double-BLIND controlled trials of pharmacological products that has no therapeutic effect but—unlike a completely inert DUMMY placebo—may produce side effects characteristic of the drug under investigation. Active placebos are therefore considered by some to be more likely to reveal true differences in drug–placebo responding.

active scopophilia pathological interest in viewing other people engaged in sexual activity or in viewing their genitals. It may be expressed as a PARAPHILIA in which the person is sexually aroused by these actions. See also SCOPOPHILIA.

active therapy any form of psychotherapy in which the therapist departs from classic psychoanalytic practice by assuming an active, directive role. An **active therapist** may express opinions, offer interpretations, make suggestions and recommendations, give advice about the client's actions and decisions, issue injunctions and prohibitions, or urge the client to take a particular action, such as facing an anxiety-provoking situation directly.

activities of daily living (**ADLs**) activities essential to an individual's personal care, such as getting into and out of bed and chairs, dressing, eating, toileting and bathing, and grooming. A person's ability to perform ADLs is often used as a measure of functional capabilities during the course of a disease or following an injury. See also INSTRUMENTAL ACTIVITIES OF DAILY LIVING.

activity analysis the objective evaluation of activity engaged in by an individual over a specified period, usually by breaking it down into smaller components, such as eating, working, social activities, resting, and so on.

activity drive an organism's hypothetical innate desire or urge to be physically active, often expressed as a need to move about, even in the absence of any apparent stimuli motivating movement, such that activity deprivation may cause distress.

activity-group therapy a form of GROUP THERAPY for children and young adolescents that emphasizes active participation in games, crafts, and other age-appropriate activities and interplay. Activity-group therapy provides children with opportunities to express their feelings in a permissive, nonthreatening atmosphere. [introduced in the 1930s by 20th-century Russian-born U.S. psychotherapist Samuel Richard Slavson]

activity-interview group psychotherapy a form of ANALYTIC GROUP PSYCHOTHERAPY for children in the latency period (i.e., between infancy and adolescence). Hobbies and recreational activities are used to stimulate communication and the expression of conflicts and fantasies. During the process, the therapist asks questions that encourage the children to understand how their immediate problems (e.g., fears) are affecting their behavior and attitudes. [introduced by 20th-century Russian-born U.S. psychotherapist Samuel Richard Slavson]

activity–passivity in psychoanalytic theory, polarities characterizing instinctual aims (see AIM OF THE INSTINCT). Sigmund FREUD asserted that instincts are always active but that their aims can be either active (e.g., SADISM and VOYEURISM) or passive (e.g., EXHIBITIONISM and MASOCHISM). Freud's equation of activity with masculinity and passivity with femininity was much criticized early on by women analysts, including Melanie KLEIN and German-born U.S. psychoanalyst Karen Horney (1885–1952), and has been rejected by many theorists, researchers, and therapists since.

activity-play therapy a controlled play technique in which a child is given a set of dolls and other play materials and encouraged to express and explore his or her feelings about them—such as sadness, guilt, and hostility—based on the theory that the child will then become less afraid of these emotions and will express them more freely.

activity theory 1. a school of thought, developed primarily by Soviet psychologists, that focuses on activity in general—rather than the distinct concepts of behavior or mental states—as the primary unit of analysis. In this context, an **activity** is a nonadditive unit that orients an organism in the world; it is essentially a system comprising an **operation** (a routine behavior requiring little thought, e.g., typing) that serves to accomplish an **action** (a behavior that involves planning, e.g., creating a bibliography) in the minimum meaningful context that provides understanding of the function of the individual in interacting with the environment (e.g., preparing a paper for a university course as part of a network of students). The theory emphasizes a hierarchical structure of activity, object-orientedness, internalization and externalization, mediation (by tools, language, and other cultural artifacts or instruments), and continuous development. Also called **activity psychology**. **2.** a theory proposing that old age is a lively, creative experience characterized by maintaining existing social roles, activities, and relationships or replacing any lost ones with new ones. Compare DISENGAGEMENT THEORY.

activity therapy any type of therapy centered around various activities, such as arts and crafts, exercise, music, and dramatics groups.

act psychology a philosophical and psychological approach based on the proposition that the act and CONTENT of psychological processes are separate functions; for example, the act of seeing color leads to a perception of the visual content, or image. Historically, proponents of act psychology held that acts (mental representation and transformation, judgment, emotion), rather

A

than contents, are the proper subject of psychology, in contrast to Wilhelm WUNDT's emphasis on introspection and conscious contents. Compare CONTENT PSYCHOLOGY. See also INTENTIONALITY.

actualization *n.* the process of mobilizing one's potentialities and realizing them in concrete form. According to U.S. psychologist Carl ROGERS (1902–1987), all humans have an innate **actualizing tendency** to grow and actualize the self fully. See also SELF-ACTUALIZATION. **—actualize** *vb.*

actualizing tendency in the humanistic personality theory of Carl ROGERS, the innate tendency of humans to develop and actualize the self fully. See ACTUALIZATION; SELF-ACTUALIZATION.

actual neurosis in the classical psychoanalytic theory of Sigmund FREUD, a neurosis that stems from current sexual frustrations (e.g., coitus interruptus, otherwise incomplete sexual experience, or forced abstinence), as contrasted with one that stems from past experiences or psychological conflicts. The term, which was applied primarily to ANXIETY NEUROSIS and NEURASTHENIA, is now rarely used.

actual self in various psychodynamic writings, the REAL SELF or TRUE SELF as it exists at a particular point in time, as opposed to an idealized, grandiose, or otherwise distorted self.

actuarial prediction prediction based on quantified experience and data rather than on more subjective (e.g., clinical) experience. See also ACTUARIAL RISK ASSESSMENT.

actuarial risk assessment a statistically calculated prediction of the likelihood that an individual will pose a threat to others or engage in a certain behavior (e.g., violence) within a given period. Unlike CLINICAL RISK ASSESSMENT, it relies on data from specific, measurable variables (e.g., age, gender, prior criminal activity) that have been validated as predictors and uses mathematical analyses and formulas to calculate the probability of DANGEROUSNESS or violent behavior.

aculalia *n.* nonsensical speech associated with lack of comprehension of written or spoken language, as occurs in WERNICKE'S APHASIA.

acupressure *n.* a form of COMPLEMENTARY AND ALTERNATIVE MEDICINE in which pressure is applied with the fingers or thumbs to specific points on the body to relieve pain, treat symptoms of disease, or improve overall health.

acupuncture *n.* a form of COMPLEMENTARY AND ALTERNATIVE MEDICINE in which fine needles are inserted into the body at specific points to relieve pain, induce anesthesia (ACUPUNCTURE ANESTHESIA), or treat disease. It is based on the concept in traditional Chinese medicine that "meridians," or pathways, conduct life-force energy known as CHI between places on the skin and the body's organ systems. Western scientists are unable to explain specifically how acupuncture produces its effects but theorize that the needling sites may be related to trigger points in the GATE-CONTROL THEORY of pain or may stimulate the release of ENDOGENOUS OPIOIDS. The technique is highly popular in many Western societies and has been deemed appropriate by the World Health Organization for use in treating more than 40 medical conditions. Compare ACUPRESSURE. See also COMPLEMENTARY AND ALTERNATIVE MEDICINE. **—acupuncturist** *n.*

acupuncture anesthesia the loss of sensation, often of pain, that results from the insertion of ACUPUNCTURE needles into the body at specific points. The technique may be used alone or in combination with other PAIN-MANAGEMENT techniques during surgery.

acute *adj.* **1.** denoting conditions or symptoms of sudden onset, short duration, and often great intensity. Compare CHRONIC. **2.** sharp, keen, or very sensitive (e.g., acute hearing).

acute alcoholic hallucinosis the rapid or sudden onset of alcoholic hallucinosis (see ALCOHOL-INDUCED PSYCHOTIC DISORDER), usually either during a heavy drinking episode or during withdrawal. See also ALCOHOL WITHDRAWAL.

acute alcoholic myopathy a condition of severe pain, tenderness, and swelling of the muscles, accompanied by cramps and muscular weakness, that develops after a period of heavy drinking. The effects may be general or focused in one body area. In some cases, muscle fibers may undergo necrosis (death of constituent cells). Recovery may require several weeks to several months.

acute alcoholism the unusually rapid onset of the symptoms of ALCOHOL DEPENDENCE.

acute anxiety a sudden feeling of dread and apprehension accompanied by somatic symptoms of tension, usually precipitated by a threatening situation, such as an examination or court hearing. The feeling typically subsides as soon as the situation is over. See PERFORMANCE ANXIETY.

acute anxiety attack see PANIC ATTACK.

acute brain disorder any pattern of symptoms resulting from temporary, reversible impairment of brain functioning.

acute cerebellar ataxia a disorder that occurs suddenly, most often in children, following a viral infection. It is characterized by slurred speech, muscular incoordination (ATAXIA), rapid, involuntary eye movements (NYSTAGMUS), and body tremors. Also called **acute cerebral tremor**.

acute cerebrovascular accident see CEREBROVASCULAR ACCIDENT.

acute confusional state severe confusion that can include symptoms of agitation, memory disturbance, disorientation, and DELIRIUM. It often occurs as a result of severe mental or physical illness.

acute delirium a disorder of brain function, of

sudden onset and brief duration, characterized by a disturbance in consciousness that ranges from extreme hyperactivity to near coma. Resulting from metabolic disturbance (e.g., high fever) or toxic agents (e.g., excessive amounts of alcohol), it is marked by illusions, hallucinations, delusions, excitement, restlessness, and incoherence.

acute delusional psychosis a diagnostic entity specific to French psychiatry, in which it is known as **bouffée délirante** (French, "delirious outburst"), involving the sudden onset of schizophrenic symptoms in response to a stressful life event. It is temporary (lasting no longer than 3 months), has no strong evidence of a genetic link, and has a favorable prognosis; spontaneous resolution of symptoms is not uncommon. Acute delusional psychosis is essentially equivalent to SCHIZOPHRENIFORM DISORDER. See also ACUTE SCHIZOPHRENIC EPISODE.

acute depression 1. a recent, sudden onset of depression. **2.** a severe episode of depression, characterized by many more symptoms than are necessary to meet the criteria for a MAJOR DEPRESSIVE EPISODE.

acute hallucinosis the sudden onset of hallucinations resulting from alcohol or drug intoxication or withdrawal. The condition usually remits within hours, though it may persist for a few days. See SUBSTANCE-INDUCED PSYCHOTIC DISORDER.

acute mania the manic phase of bipolar I disorder (see BIPOLAR DISORDER), characterized by an extremely unstable euphoric or irritable mood with hyperactivity, excessively rapid thought and speech, uninhibited and reckless behavior, and FLIGHT OF IDEAS. See MANIC EPISODE.

acute onset a sudden, rapid, or unanticipated development of a disease or its symptoms.

acute psychotic episode an appearance of florid (blatant) psychotic symptoms, such as hallucinations, delusions, and disorganized speech, that is of sudden onset and usually short duration.

acute schizophrenic episode an appearance of florid (blatant) schizophrenic symptoms, such as disordered thinking and disturbances in emotional responsiveness and behavior, that is of sudden onset and usually short duration.

acute stress disorder (**ASD**) a disorder representing the immediate psychological aftermath of exposure to a traumatic stressor. Symptoms are the same as those of POSTTRAUMATIC STRESS DISORDER but do not last longer than 4 weeks. This disorder also includes elements of dissociation, such as DEPERSONALIZATION and DEREALIZATION.

acute tolerance a type of TOLERANCE (physical dependence) that develops rapidly, sometimes in response to a single small dose of a particular drug. See also TACHYPHYLAXIS.

ADAMHA abbreviation for ALCOHOL, DRUG ABUSE AND MENTAL HEALTH ADMINISTRATION.

adaptability *n.* **1.** the capacity to make appropriate responses to changed or changing situations. **2.** the ability to modify or adjust one's behavior in meeting different circumstances or different people. **—adaptable** *adj.*

adaptation *n.* **1.** modification to suit different or changing circumstances, as in behavior that enables an individual to adjust to the environment effectively and function optimally in various domains, such as coping with daily stressors. Compare MALADAPTATION. **2.** adjustments to the demands, restrictions, and mores of society, including the ability to live and work harmoniously with others and to engage in satisfying social interactions and relationships. Also called **social adaptation**. **3.** in Jean PIAGET's theory of cognitive development, the process of adjusting one's cognitive structures to meet environmental demands, which involves the complementary processes of assimilation, in which new information is incorporated into already existing cognitive structures, and accommodation in which new information that does not fit into already existing cognitive structures is used to create new cognitive structures. **—adapt** *vb.* **—adaptational** *adj.* **—adaptive** *adj.*

adaptational approach a form of psychoanalytic psychiatry that avoids the orthodox analytic emphasis on childhood experience and focuses instead on the nature and development of the patient's maladaptive behavior and the steps he or she should take to develop new, more effective patterns. Also called **adaptational psychodynamics**. [developed by Hungarian-born U.S. psychoanalyst Sandor Rado (1890–1972)]

adaptation syndrome see GENERAL ADAPTATION SYNDROME.

adapted child one of the child ego states in TRANSACTIONAL ANALYSIS, characterized as compliant, orderly, and manipulative. Compare NATURAL CHILD.

adaptive act the process whereby an organism learns to make the appropriate responses that are needed for an adjustment to the environment.

adaptive behavior 1. the level of everyday performance of tasks that is required for a person to fulfill typical roles in society, including maintaining independence and meeting cultural expectations regarding personal and social responsibility. Specific categories in which adaptive behavior is usually assessed include self-help, mobility, health care, communi- cation, domestic skills, consumer skills, com- munity use, practical academic skills, and vocational skills. Limitations in adaptive be- havior are one of the criteria for diagnosis or classification of MENTAL RETARDATION. See also ADAPTIVE BEHAVIOR SCALE. **2.** any behavior that enables an individual to adjust to the environment appropriately and effectively. It is often discussed in the context of evolution. See also ADAPTIVE ACT; ADJUSTMENT PROCESS.

adaptive behavior scale **1.** any standardized assessment protocol with established psychometric properties used to document and quantify everyday performance of skills necessary for personal independence and social responsibility, consistent with cultural expectations (see ADAPTIVE BEHAVIOR). Examples include the American Association on Intellectual and Developmental Disabilities' (formerly American Association on Mental Retardation's) Adaptive Behavior Scale (ABS), Vineland Adaptive Behavior Scales (VABS), and Scales of Independent Behavior (SIB). **2.** any protocol assessing behavioral and social performance that is based on developmental norms, with domains structured in developmental sequence or degree of ascending task complexity or difficulty. **3.** a component of the BAYLEY SCALES OF INFANT AND TODDLER DEVELOPMENT.

adaptive hypothesis the view that the function of the primary autonomous ego is to cope with an "average expectable environment" through perception, memory, affect regulation, and motility. This is the view taken by Austrian-born U.S. psychoanalyst Heinz Hartmann (1894–1970) in his version of EGO PSYCHOLOGY.

adaptive intelligence the ability to apply knowledge to novel situations, such as solving problems and conversing with others, demonstrating an effective ability to interact with, and learn from, the environment.

adaptive nonresponding theory a theory that sleep evolved as a means of creating species-specific daily periods of inactivity concurrent with periods of greatest threat from predators.

adaptive process see ADJUSTMENT PROCESS.

adaptive response see ADAPTIVE BEHAVIOR.

adaptive skills activities that require self-management, such as controlling impulses, being able to adjust to a new environment, and a willingness to learn new things.

adaptive testing a testing technique designed to adjust to the response characteristics of individual examinees by presenting items of varying difficulty based on the examinee's responses to previous items. The process continues until a stable estimate of the ABILITY LEVEL of the examinee can be determined.

ADC abbreviation for AIDS DEMENTIA COMPLEX.

ADD abbreviation for ATTENTION-DEFICIT DISORDER.

ADDH abbreviation for attention-deficit disorder with hyperactivity. See ATTENTION-DEFICIT/HYPERACTIVITY DISORDER.

addict *n.* a person who has developed a SUBSTANCE DEPENDENCE.

addicted athlete an individual habitually involved in an athletic activity who will experience withdrawal symptoms if deprived of participating in the activity. See also COMPULSIVE EXERCISER.

addiction *n.* a state of psychological or physical dependence (or both) on the use of alcohol or other drugs. The equivalent term SUBSTANCE DEPENDENCE is preferred to describe this state because it refers more explicitly to the criteria by which it is diagnosed, which include tolerance, withdrawal, loss of control, and compulsive use of the substance. Chemical substances with significant potential for producing dependence are called ADDICTIVE DRUGS. **—addictive** *adj.*

addictive alcoholism see GAMMA ALCOHOLISM.

addictive drugs drugs or other substances that cause SUBSTANCE DEPENDENCE. They include alcohol, AMPHETAMINES and amphetamine-like CNS STIMULANTS, caffeine, COCAINE and CRACK, HALLUCINOGENS, INHALANTS, NICOTINE, OPIOIDS, PCP (phencyclidine) and phencyclidine-like substances, and CNS DEPRESSANTS.

addictive personality a hypothetical personality pattern thought to increase the likelihood a person will become dependent on one or more substances. Research has not supported this view, although it has identified personality traits associated with substance abuse, such as impulsivity and neuroticism.

Addison's disease a disorder caused by a malfunction of the adrenal glands resulting in a deficiency of adrenal hormones. A major symptom is muscle fatigue with trembling, due in part to an inability to maintain a stable level of blood sugar for energy. Mental effects include depression, anxiety, and mood changes. [Thomas **Addison** (1793–1860), British physician]

additive effect the joint effect of two or more independent variables on a dependent variable equal to the sum of their individual effects: The value of either independent variable is unconditional upon the value of the other one. Compare INTERACTION EFFECT.

additive scale a scale with all points distributed equally so that a meaningful result can be obtained by addition (e.g., a metric ruler).

adenosine *n.* a compound in living cells consisting of an adenine molecule and a ribose sugar molecule. Adenosine functions as a neuromodulator: By binding to special **adenosine receptors**, it influences the release of several neurotransmitters in the central nervous system. Combined with three phosphate units, adenosine becomes ATP (adenosine triphosphate), which functions as an energy source in metabolic activities.

ADHD abbreviation for ATTENTION-DEFICIT/HYPERACTIVITY DISORDER.

adherence *n.* the ability of an individual to conform to a treatment regimen, especially one involving drug treatment, as outlined by a health care provider. External factors affecting adherence may include appropriate education regarding a drug and its use, the individual's ability to pay for or otherwise obtain the treatment recommended, and familial or cultural value systems influencing the acceptability of the treatment to the individual. Internal factors include the individual's belief in the potency of the treatment, the presence or absence of unpleasant side effects, and the individual's capability to understand or conform to instructions given by the health care provider. See also NONADHERENCE. Also called **compliance**.

adience *n.* a response or behavior that results in movement toward a stimulus, either by physical approach or by an action that increases contact with the stimulus. Compare ABIENCE. **—adient** *adj.*

adinazolam *n.* a BENZODIAZEPINE of the triazolobenzodiazepine class with antidepressant as well as anxiolytic properties. It currently is not available in the United States. Italian trade name: **Deracyn**.

Adipex *n.* a trade name for PHENTERMINE.

adipsia *n.* an absence of thirst, manifest as a lack of drinking. Adipsia is associated with lesions of the thirst center in the anterior hypothalamus, but may also be caused by head injury, stroke, or other conditions. Compare POLYDIPSIA.

adjective checklist a self-inventory, used in personality assessment, consisting of a list of adjectives (e.g., intelligent, lazy, productive) that the respondent checks off as descriptive of or applicable to him- or herself.

adjudicative competence an umbrella term that encompasses all forms of meaningful participation in proceedings of the criminal justice system, including COMPETENCY TO STAND TRIAL, competency to plead guilty, and competency to waive Miranda rights.

adjunct *n.* **1.** a drug that is used concurrently with another drug in treating a condition in order to provide additional therapeutic effects. It may have a mechanism of action that differs from that of the main drug used in treatment. **2.** more generally, a supplementary or nonessential part of something. **—adjunctive** *adj.*

adjunctive therapist **1.** in psychotherapy, a provider of any secondary ADJUNCTIVE THERAPY. **2.** in health care, a member of a multidisciplinary treatment team whose functions are ancillary to the main therapeutic program. Such therapists provide direct clinical services to patients in such areas as improvement of daily living skills, behavior management, coordination of educational activities, and management of leisure time.

adjunctive therapy one or more secondary interventions used concurrently with a primary intervention to enhance treatment effectiveness. For example, medication may be used concurrently with COGNITIVE BEHAVIOR THERAPY, with the latter as the primary form of intervention; GROUP THERAPY may be used secondarily to individual PSYCHODYNAMIC PSYCHOTHERAPY, with each intervention bringing its own characteristic perspectives and methods to bear on the client's mental awareness and healing. Adjunctive therapy is typically conducted by a different practitioner than is the primary intervention, which distinguishes it from COMBINATION THERAPY. The term is sometimes used synonymously with ADJUVANT THERAPY. See also COLLABORATIVE CARE. Compare ADJUVANT THERAPY; COMBINATION THERAPY.

adjusted mean in the ANALYSIS OF COVARIANCE, the numerical average of a batch of scores on a dependent variable that is obtained after the effects of a covariate are removed.

adjustive behavior any response of an organism that effectively incorporates environmental or situational demands.

adjustment *n.* a change in attitude, behavior, or both by an individual on the basis of some recognized need or desire to change, particularly to account for the current environment or changing, atypical, or unexpected conditions. It may be assessed via a type of survey called an **adjustment inventory**, which compares one's emotional and social adjustment with a representative sample of other individuals. A well-adjusted person is one who satisfies his or her needs in a healthy, beneficial manner and demonstrates appropriate social and psychological responses to situations and demands. **—adjust** *vb.*

adjustment disorder in *DSM–IV–TR*, impairment in social or occupational functioning and unexpected severe emotional or behavioral symtoms occurring within three months after an individual experiences a specific identifiable stressful event, such as a divorce, business crisis, or family discord. The event is not as stressful as a traumatic stressor, which can result in POSTTRAUMATIC STRESS DISORDER. Symptoms may include anxiety, depression, and conduct disturbances and tend to remit following elimination of the stressors. In **chronic adjustment disorder**, the symptoms last more than six months due to either the persistence or the severity of the stressor.

adjustment inventory a survey form used to assess a person's emotional and social adjustment as compared with a large and representative sample of individuals from the same population.

adjustment mechanism a habitual behavioral pattern that enables the individual to meet the demands of life.

adjustment process any means through which human beings modify attitudes and behaviors in response to environmental demands. Such attempts to maintain a balance between needs and the circumstances that influence the satisfaction of those needs are influenced by numerous factors that vary widely across situations and individuals and are a frequent subject of research.

adjustment reaction a temporary, maladjustive psychological response to a situation. Such reactions were subsumed under the category TRANSIENT SITUATIONAL PERSONALITY DISORDER in *DSM–I*, comprising adjustment reactions of infancy, childhood, adolescence, and later life, and under TRANSIENT SITUATIONAL DISTURBANCE in *DSM–II*; the corresponding category for these reactions in *DSM–III* and *DSM–IV–TR* is ADJUSTMENT DISORDER.

adjuvant therapy therapy provided after the initial (primary) form of treatment to enhance effectiveness or to increase the chances of a cure. Adjuvant therapy typically refers to medical rather than psychotherapeutic treatment, particularly any drug therapy used in support of nondrug interventions. For example, in the treatment of cancer, chemotherapy and radiation are often used as adjuvant therapies after the primary intervention of surgery. The term is sometimes used in psychotherapy as a synonym for the preferred ADJUNCTIVE THERAPY.

Adler, Alfred (1870–1937) Austrian psychiatrist. Trained at the University of Vienna and receiving his MD in 1895, Adler was the first disciple of Sigmund FREUD to break away and form his own school, known as INDIVIDUAL PSYCHOLOGY. This was based on the theory that human beings are governed by a conscious drive to express and fulfill themselves, as opposed to Freud's theory of dominance by early sexual trauma and blind unconscious instincts. The school revolved around such concepts as the STRIVING FOR SUPERIORITY, the INFERIORITY COMPLEX, COMPENSATION and overcompensation, social interests, and the creative development of an individual style of life that incorporates both personal and social goals. See also GUIDING FICTION; LIFE GOAL; LIFE PLAN; PERSUASION THERAPY; SOCIAL INSTINCT; SOCIAL INTEREST; WILL TO POWER. **—Adlerian** *adj.*

Adlerian psychology see INDIVIDUAL PSYCHOLOGY.

ADLs abbreviation for ACTIVITIES OF DAILY LIVING.

administration *n.* **1.** the application of a drug or other agent in the diagnosis or treatment of a disorder. This may be accomplished **enterally** (via the digestive tract) or **parenterally** (via all other means). The former includes oral and sublingual (under the tongue) routes, whereas the latter includes subcutaneous, intramuscular, and intravenous injection; rectal and vaginal suppositories; inhalation; and absorption through skin or mucous membranes. **2.** the giving of a test for the purpose of obtaining information.

admission *n.* the act of registering an individual for treatment or observation in a health care facility. See FIRST ADMISSION; READMISSION; VOLUNTARY ADMISSION. **—admit** *vb.*

admission certification an aspect of UTILIZATION REVIEW in which the medical necessity of a patient's admission to a health care facility is determined.

admission procedures the administrative and medical procedures of admitting a person as an inpatient to a health care facility.

adolescence *n.* the period of human development that starts with puberty (10–12 years of age) and ends with physiological maturity (approximately 19 years of age), although the exact age span varies across individuals. During this period major changes occur at varying rates in physical characteristics, sexual characteristics, and sexual interest, resulting in significant effects on body image, self-concept, and self-esteem. Major cognitive and social developments take place as well: Most young people acquire enhanced abilities to think abstractly, evaluate reality hypothetically, reconsider prior experiences from altered points of view, assess data from multiple dimensions, reflect inwardly, create complex models of understanding, and project complicated future scenarios. Adolescents also increase their peer focus and involvement in peer-related activities, place greater emphasis on social acceptance, and seek more independence and autonomy from parents. **—adolescent** *adj., n.*

adolescent counseling the provision of professional guidance, advice, and information to adolescents through such means as personal interviews, analysis of case-history data, and the use of psychological tests.

adolescent crisis the emotional turmoil that may occur during adolescence as individuals seek to achieve independence (by casting off old emotional ties and developing new relationships) and adapt to a changed body.

adolescent homosexuality same-sex activity during the pubertal period. It has been estimated that at least 20% of boys and 3% of girls have engaged in such activity, resulting in orgasm, before the end of adolescence, and about twice that number have had casual or relatively uninvolved gay or lesbian experiences during adolescence. Many of these experiences, especially for boys, actually involve mutual masturbation to heterosexual stimuli and thus do not indicate same-sex eroticism or predict adult gay or lesbian sexual orientation.

adolescent psychotherapy psychotherapy for adolescents who are experiencing social, emotional, or behavioral problems.

adolescent rebellion the rejection by adolescents of family values and family control over their behavior, reflecting their desire for increased independence.

adoption *n.* the legal process by which an infant or child is permanently placed with a family other than his or her birth family. An adoption may be private, in which a birth parent voluntarily plans for the placement of the child with adoptive parents through intermediaries, or public, in which a child removed from his or her birth parent(s) because of neglect or abuse is placed with adoptive parents through public child welfare agencies. Adoptions may also be closed, allowing no contact between the birth and adoptive parents, or open, permitting varying degrees of pre- and postplacement contact and making possible a relationship between all three parties.

adoption study a research design that investigates the relationships among genetic and environmental factors in the development of personality, behavior, or disorder by comparing the similarities of biological parent–child pairs with those of adoptive parent–child pairs.

ADR abbreviation for ADVERSE DRUG REACTION.

adrenal androgen any of the androgenic hormones (chiefly dehydroepiandrosterone and androstenedione) secreted by the ADRENAL CORTEX. See ADRENARCHE; ANDROGEN.

adrenal cortex the outer layer of the ADRENAL GLAND. It secretes a number of hormones, including ADRENAL ANDROGENS, GLUCOCORTICOIDS, and MINERALOCORTICOIDS. Adrenal cortical functions are controlled by CORTICOTROPIN, secreted by the anterior PITUITARY GLAND.

adrenal cortical hyperfunction the excessive production of one or more of the hormones of the adrenal cortex. The manifestations vary with the hormone but potentially include (among others) hypertension, sudden weight gain, torso obesity, and low blood levels of potassium. Causes may include a tumor or congenital adrenal hyperplasia, a disorder marked by increased adrenal production of cortisol precursors and androgens.

adrenal gland an endocrine gland adjacent to the kidney. Its outer layer, the **adrenal cortex**, secretes a number of hormones, including ANDROGENS, GLUCOCORTICOIDS, and MINERALOCORTICOIDS. Its inner core, the **adrenal medulla**, secretes the hormones EPINEPHRINE and NOREPINEPHRINE, both of which are CATECHOLAMINES and also serve as neurotransmitters. Also called **suprarenal gland**.

adrenaline *n.* see EPINEPHRINE.

adrenarche *n.* the stage of prepubertal development marked by the start of androgen secretion by the adrenal cortex. Normally, it occurs between 6 to 8 years of age and does not result in ANDROGENIZATION. Premature adrenarche, characterized by pubertal levels of ADRENAL ANDROGENS, is manifested by the early appearance of pubic hair. It may be associated with psychological disturbances. By parent report on the DIAGNOSTIC INTERVIEW SCHEDULE for Children, 44% of the children with premature adrenarche met the diagnostic criteria for psychological disorders, primarily anxiety disorders. The condition is also associated with self-reported depression and parent-reported behavior problems and low scores on various intelligence tests.

adrenergic blocking agent any pharmacological substance that either partially or completely inhibits the binding of the neurotransmitters norepinephrine or epinephrine to ADRENERGIC RECEPTORS and thus blocks or disrupts the action of these neurotransmitters. Such blocking agents are classed according to which of the two types of receptors they inhibit binding to: **alpha blockers**, used primarily to widen blood vessels in the treatment of hypertension, or **beta blockers**, used to treat hypertension as well but by reducing the rate and force of heart contractions, arrhythmia, tremor, and anxiety-related symptoms. Also called **adrenoceptor blocking agent**; **adrenoreceptor blocking agent**.

adrenergic drug see SYMPATHOMIMETIC DRUG.

adrenergic receptor a molecule in a cell membrane that specifically binds and responds to norepinephrine and, to a lesser extent, epinephrine, which act as neurotransmitters in the sympathetic nervous system. There are two types: ALPHA-ADRENERGIC RECEPTORS (or alpha receptors) and BETA-ADRENERGIC RECEPTORS (or beta receptors). Also called **adrenoceptor**; **adrenoreceptor**.

adrenoleukodystrophy *n.* a genetic disease characterized by destruction of the MYELIN SHEATH surrounding the nerves of the brain (i.e., demyelination) and progressive dysfunction of the adrenal gland. Nerve function becomes erratic, resulting in a variety of physiological and behavioral symptoms involving changes in body tone, motor movements, gait, speech, ability to eat, vision, hearing, memory, attention, and cognitive processes. There are several types of adrenoleukodystrophy, of which the childhood X-chromosome-linked form is the most common and the most severe.

adult *n.* **1.** a person who has reached ADULTHOOD. **2.** a person who has reached the legal age of maturity. Although it may vary across jurisdictions, an individual 18 years of age is typically considered an adult.

Adult Attachment Interview (**AAI**) an hour-long interview used for classifying a person's subjective evaluation of his or her own attachment experiences with his or her parents, especially centering on hurtful experiences, separations, and discipline. The categories of adult attachment that emerge are **dismissing** (interviewees idealize their early relationships but cannot provide specific supporting examples); **preoccupied** (interviewees describe their early parental relationships as overly involving and angry); and **secure** or **autonomous** (interviewees provide objective, coherent accounts of relationships). A fourth category, **unresolved** or **disorganized**, is used for individuals who have experienced loss of attachment figures and who show lapses in reasoning when discussing such.

Adult Children of Alcoholics (**ACOA**) a TWELVE-STEP PROGRAM for adults who were raised in a family environment where alcoholism or other family dysfunctions were present. See also SELF-HELP GROUP.

adult day care a group program for the nonresidential care and supervision of adults with functional impairments, designed to meet their health, social, and functional needs in a setting other than their homes. See DAY CARE CENTER.

adult foster care the provision of community-based living arrangements to adults who require supervision, personal care, or other services in daily living on a 24-hour basis. Host families open their own homes to, and act as caregivers for, such adults who are unable safely to live independently, which is what distinguishes **adult foster homes** from other RESIDENTIAL CARE facilities.

adult home an ASSISTED-LIVING residence that provides shared rooms, common meals, personal care services, activities, and protective oversight to adults who are unable to live independently. Intensive medical or nursing services are generally not available.

adulthood *n.* the period of human development in which full physical growth and maturity have been achieved and certain biological, cognitive, social, personality, and other changes associated with the aging process occur. Beginning after adolescence, adulthood is sometimes divided into **young adulthood** (roughly 20 to 35 years of age); **middle adulthood** (about 36 to 64 years); and **later adulthood** (age 65 and beyond). The last is sometimes subdivided into **young-old** (65 to 74), **old-old** (75 to 84), and **oldest old** (85 and beyond). The oldest old group is the fastest growing segment of the population in many developed countries.

adultomorphism *n.* **1.** the attribution of adult traits or motives to children. Also called **enelicomorphism**. Compare PEDOMORPHISM. **2.** more specifically, the tendency to reconstruct developmental phases by extrapolating from adult psychopathology. **—adultomorphic** *adj.*

advance directive a legal mechanism for individuals to specify their wishes and instructions about prospective health care in the event they later become unable to make such decisions. This can be achieved by means of a **durable power of attorney**, a legal document designating someone to make health care decisions on that person's behalf, or a **living will**, a legal document clarifying a person's wishes regarding future medical or, increasingly, mental health treatment.

advantage by illness see SECONDARY GAIN.

adverse drug reaction (**ADR**) any unintended, harmful, and potentially fatal response to a drug. Reactions may be genetically determined (as in the case of HYPERSENSITIVITY), in which case they are highly individual and can be difficult to predict, or they may arise through interactions with other prescribed or nonprescribed drugs or with dietary items (as in the case of MONOAMINE OXIDASE INHIBITORS). This term sometimes is used synonymously with SIDE EFFECT, but an adverse drug reaction more properly denotes an unexpected negative occurrence, whereas side effects may be positive or negative and are usually anticipated. Also called **adverse drug event (ADE)**; **adverse event**; **adverse reaction**.

adverse event **1.** in health care, an injury or harmful effect resulting from medical intervention or research. **2.** in pharmacology, see ADVERSE DRUG REACTION.

advice giving a COUNSELING technique in which the therapist advises the client on alternatives or options for consideration.

advocacy *n.* speaking or acting on behalf of an individual or group to uphold their rights or explain their point of view. For example, health care advocates represent consumers to protect their rights to effective treatment, while therapists may act as advocates for clients in court hearings or other situations involving decisions based on the clients' mental health or related issues.

advocate *n.* an individual who represents and defends the interests of another individual or of a group or cause. In health care, advocates represent consumers to protect their rights to effective treatment. There are two general types of such advocates: A **case advocate** represents a single individual, and a **class advocate** represents a whole group. See OMBUDSMAN. See also CHILD ADVOCACY.

aerobic exercise physical activity, typically prolonged and of moderate intensity (e.g., jogging or cycling), that involves the use of oxygen in the muscles to provide the needed energy. Aerobic exercise strengthens the cardiovascular and respiratory systems and is associated with a variety of health benefits including increased endurance, reduction of body fat, and decreased depression and anxiety. Compare ANAEROBIC EXERCISE.

affect *n.* any feeling or emotion, which may be irreflexive or reflexive. **Irreflexive affect** is the direct experience in consciousness of a particular emotional state (as in a person's feeling of elation upon receiving good news). **Reflexive affect** occurs when a person makes his or her feelings objects of scrutiny (as when a person wonders why he or she does not feel particularly elated upon receiving good news). A distinction may also be made between NEGATIVE AFFECT and POSITIVE AFFECT. Along with cognition and conation, affect is one of the three traditionally identified components of mind.

affect-block *n.* a condition marked by an inability to adequately express or experience emotions, especially strong ones, because of a dissociation of these emotions from ideas or thoughts. It is characteristically seen in individuals with schizophrenia or obsessive-compulsive disorder.

affect display a facial, vocal, or gestural behavior that serves as an indicator of AFFECT. See EMOTIONAL EXPRESSION.

affect hunger a craving for affection and loving care.

affect intensity the tendency to experience emotional states very strongly, irrespective of the nature (e.g., positive versus negative) of those states.

affect inversion see REVERSAL OF AFFECT.

affection *n.* fondness, tenderness, and liking, especially when nonsexual. Feelings of emotional attachment between individuals, particularly human infants and their caregivers, are called **affectional bonds**. They are particularly important to ATTACHMENT THEORY, and their presence is evidenced by proximity-seeking behaviors and distress if loss or involuntary separation occurs. **—affectionate** *adj.*

affective *adj.* demonstrating, capable of producing, or otherwise pertaining to emotion or feelings. **—affectivity** *n.*

affective amnesia see FUNCTIONAL AMNESIA.

affective assessment evaluation of an individual's emotional or psychological state and degree of emotional intensity.

affective–cognitive structure the combination of an emotional experience with a thought or image, such as the linking of the emotions of relief and fear reduction to the idea of a parent as a haven of safety.

affective development see EMOTIONAL DEVELOPMENT.

affective discharge the expression of strong emotions (e.g., sorrow or anger) by clients undergoing therapy in which the therapist uses techniques aimed at facilitating deeper exploration of past experiences. Affective discharge is believed to be a release of psychic energy. Also called **cathectic discharge**.

affective disorder see MOOD DISORDER.

affective education any program in which learning is focused on or derived from emotion rather than reason, for example, a curriculum designed to enhance students' emotional and social growth and encourage positive behavior change. The concept is gaining popularity as a means of reducing conflict and aggression in schools.

affective experience any emotionally charged experience.

affective forecasting predicting one's own future emotional states, especially in connection with some event or outcome that one faces. People often "forecast" more extreme and lasting emotional reactions to events than they actually experience.

affective hallucination a hallucination that occurs in the context of AFFECTIVE PSYCHOSIS and has a manic or depressive content.

affective interaction highly emotional interpersonal interactions, as may occur in GROUP THERAPY or in a family.

affective logic the hypothesis that emotions have their own independent set of mental operations, distinct from those governing other forms of mental life. [proposed by French psychologist Théodule A. Ribot (1839–1916)]

affective meaning the attitude or emotion elicited by a stimulus, such as a musical piece, a drawing, or—especially—a word or phrase.

affective neuroscience a discipline that addresses the brain mechanisms underlying emotions. In seeking to understand the particular roles of major subcortical and cortical structures in the elicitation, experience, and regulation of emotion, affective neuroscience provides an important framework for understanding the neural processes that underlie psychopathology, particularly the mood and substance-related disorders.

affective psychosis originally, a mood alteration so profound as to impair one's capacity to interact with the environment appropriately and effectively. In essence, it was a synonym for affective disorder, which itself is now a synonym for MOOD DISORDER. In contemporary usage the term refers to a mood disorder accompanied by delusions or hallucinations (i.e., PSYCHOTIC FEATURES). The mood disruption precedes the psychotic symptoms, and the psychotic symptoms only occur during a MAJOR DEPRESSIVE EPISODE or a MANIC EPISODE.

affective rigidity a condition in which emotions or feelings remain unchanged through varying situations in which such changes would normally occur. Affective rigidity is common in obsessive-compulsive disorder and schizophrenia.

affective state any type of emotional state. The term is often used in situations where emotions dominate the person's awareness.

affective theory a framework underlying certain approaches to psychotherapy that emphasizes the importance of feelings and emotions in therapeutic change.

affective tone the mood or feeling associated with a particular experience or stimulus. In psychotherapy, when a client fails to recognize his or her affective tone, the therapist may draw the client's attention to it as a primary element of the therapeutic interaction. Also called **feeling tone**.

affectivity *n.* the degree of a person's response or susceptibility to pleasure, pain, and other emotional stimuli. Evaluation of affectivity is an important component of a psychological examination; the therapist or clinician may look for evidence of such reactions as BLUNTED AFFECT, INAPPROPRIATE AFFECT, LOSS OF AFFECT, AMBIVALENCE, DEPERSONALIZATION, ELATION, DEPRESSION, or ANXIETY.

affect regulation the attempt to alter or prolong one's mood or emotional state. Trying to get out of a bad mood is the most common example. Because people cannot usually change their emotions simply by deciding to feel differently, they use many indirect strategies for affect regulation.

affect scale any of several psychometric measures for quantifying the intensity of the subjective aspects of emotion. An example is the BECK DEPRESSION INVENTORY.

affiliation *n.* a social relationship with one or more other individuals, usually based on liking or a personal attachment rather than on perceived material benefits. Affiliation appears to be a basic source of emotional security, given the anxiety, frustration, and loneliness stemming from the absence of such relationships. Some propose that the seeking of cooperative, friendly association with others who resemble or like one or whom one likes is a fundamental human desire, referring to it variously as the **affiliative drive** or **affiliative need**. **—affiliative** *adj.*

affiliative behavior any action that is carried out with the aim of maintaining or enhancing one's personal relationship with one or more other individuals or that is associated more generally with the urge to form, maintain, or enhance personal attachments. See AFFILIATION.

affinity *n.* **1.** an inherent attraction to or liking for a particular person, place, or thing, often based on some commonality. **2.** relationship by marriage or adoption rather than blood. **3.** in pharmacology, the tendency of a particular neurotransmitter or drug to bind to a particular receptor.

affirmative defense a defense in which the defendant admits committing the act with which he or she is charged but provides evidence that undermines the prosecution's or plaintiff's claim of criminal intent. The INSANITY DEFENSE, DIMINISHED RESPONSIBILITY, contributory negligence (the defendant's claim that the plaintiff acted carelessly or with disregard and was partially at fault), and self-defense are examples of affirmative defenses.

affirmative therapy a socioculturally informed intervention that empowers clients and their communities, particularly in situations in which ethnic, gender, or sexual orientation diversity has been resisted or in which normal conditions (e.g., gay identity) have been pathologized. Emphasizing self- and cultural awareness, this therapy may be practiced as a distinct intervention or within the context of other psychotherapies.

African trypanosomiasis see SLEEPING SICKNESS.

aftercare *n.* **1.** a program of outpatient treatment and support services provided for individuals discharged from an institution, such as a hospital or mental health facility, to help maintain improvement, prevent relapse, and aid adjustment of the individual to the community. Aftercare may also refer to inpatient services provided for convalescent patients, such as those who are recovering from surgery. **2.** a form of day care, as in programs designed to care for children after school. See CHILD CARE.

afterplay *n.* affectionate and sensual activity (e.g., hugging, caressing, kissing) that continues after orgasm is achieved in sexual activity.

age-appropriate maturity the ability to deal effectively and resiliently with experience and to perform satisfactorily in developmental tasks (biological, social, cognitive) characteristic of one's age level.

age-associated memory impairment (**AAMI**) the minor memory deficits often associated with normal aging, for example, forgetting the name of a recently read book. These changes are not associated with dementias, such as Alzheimer's disease, and affect the ability to acquire and recall new information rather than the recall of established memories (e.g., the name of one's hometown). Also called **benign senescence**; **benign senescent forgetfulness**.

age-equivalent scale a system of expressing test scores in terms of age norms or averages.

agency *n.* the state of being active, usually in the service of a goal, or of having the power and capability to produce an effect or exert influence.

agenesis *n.* the failure of a body part to develop fully or to develop at all. An example is **callosal agenesis** (or **corpus callosum agenesis**), in which the nerve tract joining the two cerebral hemispheres (see CORPUS CALLOSUM) fails to develop. **—agenetic** *adj.*

age norm the standard score or range of scores that represent the average achievement level of people of a particular chronological age.

agent *n.* **1.** a person or entity that acts or has the capacity to act. **2.** a person who acts on behalf of another or of a group. **3.** in PSYCHOTHERAPY, a therapist who helps a client gain self-understanding. **4.** in GROUP THERAPY, the therapist or any individual client who helps another client. **5.** a means by which something is done or caused. For example, an infectious agent is a bacterium or other microorganism that causes a particular disease. **—agentive** *adj.*

agentic orientation an emphasis on achieving, doing, succeeding, and making one's own mark in the world, which may be expressed through such traits as competitiveness and SELF-FOCUS.

age of consent the age at which an individual is considered legally competent to assent to something, especially sexual intercourse or marriage.

age of onset the chronological age at which symptoms of a disease or disorder first appear in an individual. One of the hallmarks of some genetic syndromes is that the age of onset is earlier in individuals with hereditary susceptibility than in sporadic cases.

age regression a hypnotic technique in which the therapist helps the client recall a crucial experience by inducing amnesia for the present, then suggesting that he or she return, year by year, to the earlier date when a particular experience took place. This technique is also used in forensic contexts to help eyewitnesses and victims recall their experiences. The use of age regression in either context is controversial, given the potential for FALSE MEMORIES and the debatable legitimacy of RECOVERED MEMORIES.

aggravating factor a fact relating to a crime or to the defendant that makes the offense more serious or supports the argument for a harsher sentence. An example of an aggravating factor is the use of a deadly weapon in the commission of a crime. Also called **aggravating circumstance**. Compare MITIGATING FACTOR.

aggregate score a combination of two or more scores on variables that are related to one another conceptually or empirically.

aggregation problems the difficulty of separating individual effects from situational effects when established groups or institutions are used as the unit of analysis in an evaluation. For example, investigators are likely to attribute characteristics of the institution to the individual.

aggression *n.* behavior that harms others physically or psychologically or destroys property. It can be distinguished from anger in that anger is oriented at overcoming the target but not necessarily through harm or destruction. When such behavior is purposively performed with the primary goal of intentional injury or destruction it is termed **hostile aggression.** Other types of aggression are less deliberately damaging and may be instrumentally motivated (proactive) or affectively motivated (reactive). **Instrumental aggression** involves an action carried out principally to achieve another goal, such as acquiring a desired resource. **Affective aggression** involves an emotional response to an aversive state of affairs, which tends to be targeted toward the perceived source of the distress but may be displaced onto other people or objects if the disturbing agent cannot be attacked (see DISPLACED AGGRESSION). In the classical psychoanalytic theory of Sigmund FREUD, the aggressive impulse is innate and derived from the DEATH INSTINCT, but most nonpsychoanalytically oriented psychologists view it as socially learned or as a reaction to frustration (see FRUSTRATION–AGGRESSION HYPOTHESIS). **—aggressive** *adj.*

aggressive character a personality characterized by a hostile or competitive attitude to others and the pursuit of power, prestige, and material possessions. German-born U.S. psychoanalyst Karen D. Horney (1885–1952) defined the development of such a character as one of three basic NEUROTIC TRENDS used as a defense against BASIC ANXIETY. Compare COMPLIANT CHARACTER; DETACHED CHARACTER.

aggressive cue a signal or stimulus in a person's environment that is interpreted as aggressive or that is typically associated with aggression.

aggressive erotic containing both violent and sexual elements. It may describe a type of pornography or behavior (e.g., rape).

aggressive instinct in psychoanalytic theory, a derivative of the DEATH INSTINCT that directs destructive impulses away from the self and toward the outside world.

aggressiveness *n.* a tendency toward social dominance, threatening behavior, and hostility. It may cause a transient change in behavior within an individual or be a characteristic trait of an individual. **—aggressive** *adj.*

aggressive script a SCRIPT based on anger, hostility, and overcompetitiveness that becomes stored in the memory of some individuals and guides their judgments and behavior. It is thought that such scripts are acquired from early family experiences, association with aggressive peers, and exposure to media violence.

aging *n.* the biological and psychological changes associated with chronological age. A distinction is often made between changes that are due to normal biological processes (see PRIMARY AGING) and changes that are caused by age-related pathologies (see SECONDARY AGING).

aging disorder any disruption of the gradual structural and immune changes that occur with the passage of time, leading to increased probability of early death. An example is **progeria** (or **Hutchinson–Gilford syndrome**), a very rare inherited disorder in which children age extremely rapidly and typically die of a heart attack or stroke between the ages of 10 and 15 years. A more common example is Alzheimer's disease.

agitated depression a MAJOR DEPRESSIVE EPISODE in which psychomotor agitation (excessive but purposeless activity), restlessness, and irritability predominate.

agitation *n.* a state of increased but typically purposeless and repetitious activity, as in PSYCHOMOTOR AGITATION.

agitophasia *n.* very rapid and cluttered speech in which sounds, words, or parts of words are omitted or distorted. Also called **agitolalia**.

agnosia *n.* loss or impairment of the ability to recognize or appreciate the nature of sensory stimuli due to brain damage or disorder. Recognition impairment is profound and specific to a particular sensory modality. AUDITORY AGNOSIA, TACTILE AGNOSIA, and VISUAL AGNOSIA are the most common types, and each has a variety of subtypes.

agnus castus an herbal preparation derived from the flowers of the chasteberry tree and approved by Commission E of the German Federal Institute for Drugs and Medical Devices for use in the management of symptoms associated with the late luteal phase of the menstrual cycle (see PREMENSTRUAL DYSPHORIC DISORDER) and in the alleviation of menstrual cycle abnormalities or irregularities. Also called **vitex agnus castus**.

A

agonist *n.* a drug or other chemical agent that binds to a particular receptor and produces a physiological effect, typically one similar to that of the body's own neurotransmitter at that receptor. There are PARTIAL AGONISTS, which stimulate the receptor only somewhat to produce the same physiological effect as the natural neurotransmitter but to a lesser degree, and **inverse agonists**, which act at the receptor to produce a physiological effect opposite to that produced by another agonist at that same receptor. Compare ANTAGONIST. **—agonism** *n.* **—agonistic** *adj.*

agonist–antagonist a substance that simultaneously binds to multiple receptors, mimicking the action of the body's natural neurotransmitter at one type of receptor and inhibiting that action at another, different type of receptor.

agoraphobia *n.* an excessive, irrational fear of being in open or unfamiliar places, resulting in the avoidance of public situations from which escape may be difficult, such as standing in line or being in a crowd. Agoraphobia may accompany PANIC DISORDER (**panic disorder with agoraphobia**), in which an individual experiences unexpected panic attacks, or it may occur in the absence of panic disorder (**agoraphobia without history of panic disorder**), when an individual fears paniclike symptoms or limited symptom attacks but has not experienced full-blown panic attacks. See also ANXIETY DISORDER. **—agoraphobic** *adj.*

agrammatism *n.* a manifestation of APHASIA characterized by loss or impairment of the ability to use speech that conforms to grammatical rules, such as those governing word order, verb tense, and subject–verb agreement. It is distinct from **syntactic aphasia**, which is a more specific manifestation involving loss or impairment only of the ability to adhere to rules governing syntax, that is, to correctly combine or sequence words in sentences. Also called **dysgrammatism**.

agranulocytosis *n.* a decline in the number of certain white blood cells (neutrophils), typically as a result of an immune reaction to a drug or other chemical or the toxic effect of this substance on the bone marrow, causing production of white blood cells to fall. Agranulocytosis is diagnosed when the neutrophil count is below $200/mm^3$ or when the total white-blood-cell count is below $500/mm^3$. The condition results in suppression of the immune response, rendering individuals vulnerable to opportunistic infections. Psychotropic drugs, such as CLOZAPINE and PHENOTHIAZINE antipsychotics, can induce agranulocytosis.

agraphia *n.* loss or impairment of the ability to write as a result of neurological damage or disorder. The specific forms of writing difficulties vary considerably, but may include problems with such things as spelling irregular or ambiguous words, writing numbers or particular letters, or performing the motor movements needed for handwriting. Agraphia generally is seen in APHASIA, although there is considerable variability of writing ability within a given aphasia type. Also called **dysgraphia**. **—agraphic** *adj.*

agreeableness *n.* the tendency to act in a cooperative, unselfish manner, construed as one end of a dimension of individual differences (agreeableness versus disagreeableness) in the BIG FIVE PERSONALITY MODEL. It is also a dimension in the FIVE-FACTOR PERSONALITY MODEL. **—agreeable** *adj.*

agrypnia *n.* see INSOMNIA.

aha experience the emotional reaction that typically occurs at a moment of sudden insight into a problem or other puzzling issue. For example, in psychotherapy it is a client's sudden insight into his or her motives for cognitions, affects, or behaviors. Also called **aha reaction**.

ahedonia *n.* see ANHEDONIA.

ahistoric therapy a therapeutic approach that focuses on here-and-now situations and behaviors. This approach is distinguished from approaches that place a strong emphasis on earlier events and circumstances.

AHP abbreviation for ALLIED HEALTH PROFESSIONAL.

ahypnia *n.* see INSOMNIA.

ahypnosia *n.* see INSOMNIA.

AI abbreviation for ARTIFICIAL INSEMINATION.

aided recall the process of remembering something under circumstances where a prompt is given to assist recall. Aided recall is used, for example, to assist an eyewitness or victim of a crime to retrieve memories relevant to the event.

AIDS *a*cquired *i*mmune *d*eficiency *s*yndrome: a clinical condition in which the immune system is so severely damaged from infection with human immunodeficiency virus (see HIV) as to result in certain serious opportunistic infections and diseases.

AIDS counseling counseling in which guidance, advice, and information are provided to individuals on issues related to HIV infection and AIDS. Such counseling typically covers ways to avoid exposure to HIV infection, provision of HIV antibody testing, and the importance of adhering to medication, as well as dealing with the myriad psychological and social issues associated with AIDS, including stigma, the anxiety in dealing with a life-threatening illness, and the nature of friendships and other support systems. Also called **HIV/AIDS counseling**.

AIDS dementia complex (**ADC**) neuropsychological dysfunction directly attributable to HIV infection, found most commonly in those who have developed AIDS. It is marked by impairment in four areas: (a) cognition (e.g., memory loss, inability to concentrate); (b) behavior (e.g., inability to perform normal activities of daily living); (c) motor coordination (e.g., unsteady gait, loss of balance, incontinence); and (d) mood (e.g., severe depression, psychosis).

Brain scans of affected individuals reveal cortical atrophy. Also called **HIV dementia**.

aim *n.* **1.** the symbolic or internal representation of a goal that may motivate and direct behavior toward achieving that goal: an intention or purpose. **2.** a goal toward which an organism voluntarily directs behavior, effort, or activity: an objective. **3.** in psychoanalytic theory, see AIM OF THE INSTINCT; OBJECT OF INSTINCT.

aim-inhibited *adj.* in psychoanalytic theory, describing a behavior—particularly an interpersonal behavior—in which the underlying drives are deflected from their original object and remain unconscious. According to the theory, aim inhibition characterizes those situations in which an INSTINCT fails to achieve direct satisfaction of its aim but obtains reduced gratification through activities or relationships similar to the original aim. Sigmund FREUD used this idea to explain affectional relationships within families and platonic friendships as deriving from an aim-inhibited sexual instinct.

aim of the instinct in psychoanalytic theory, the activity through which an INSTINCT is gratified, resulting in the release of internal tension. For example, kissing may satisfy the oral instinct. Also called **instinctual aim**. See also REVERSAL OF AFFECT.

akathisia (**acathisia**) *n.* extreme restlessness characterized by an inability to sit or stand still for at least several minutes and by fidgety movements or jitteriness, as well as a subjective report of inner restlessness. It occurs as an EXTRAPYRAMIDAL SYMPTOM resulting from exposure to a neuroleptic (antipsychotic) medication (**neuroleptic-induced acute akathisia**) or in response to SSRI antidepressant medications (**medication-induced movement disorder not otherwise specified**). Akathisia is also a feature of some neurological and general medical conditions (e.g., Parkinson's disease and iron-deficiency anemia).

akinesia algera a condition in which pain is experienced with any body movement, a disorder often associated with psychogenic factors.

akinetic *adj.* characterized by loss of voluntary movement not due to paralysis.

akinetic mutism an absence or gross reduction of voluntary movements and speech, although the individual does follow eye movements. The condition is associated with damage to the anterior CINGULATE GYRUS and supplementary motor area in the mesial part of the FRONTAL LOBES.

Akineton *n.* a trade name for BIPERIDEN.

alalia *n.* partial or total inability to speak. Although mostly historical now, the term is occasionally used as a synonym for MUTISM.

Al-Anon *n.* an international self-help organization for people who have been affected by the compulsive use of alcohol by a family member or friend. Founded in the United States in 1951, it uses the TWELVE-STEP PROGRAM adapted from ALCOHOLICS ANONYMOUS and includes **Alateen** for younger individuals. Al-Anon members share their experiences with and offer support to one another in order to promote personal recovery and growth.

alarm reaction see GENERAL ADAPTATION SYNDROME.

alcohol *n.* **1.** ETHANOL (ethyl alcohol). **2.** any other member of the class of chemical compounds to which ethanol belongs.

Alcohol, Drug Abuse and Mental Health Administration (**ADAMHA**) an agency in the U.S. Department of Health and Human Services that was replaced in 1992 by the SUBSTANCE ABUSE AND MENTAL HEALTH SERVICES ADMINISTRATION (SAMHSA). In this reorganization, the three ADAMHA research institutes, the National Institute on Alcohol Abuse and Alcoholism (NIAAA), the National Institute on Drug Abuse (NIDA), and the NATIONAL INSTITUTE OF MENTAL HEALTH (NIMH), were moved to the National Institutes of Health. The substance abuse and mental health services programs provided by ADAMHA remain the responsibility of SAMHSA.

alcohol abuse a pattern of alcohol consumption that persists despite recurrent significant adverse consequences resulting directly from alcohol use, including neglect of important personal, financial, social, occupational, or recreational activities; absenteeism from work or school; repeated encounters with the police; and the use of alcohol in situations in which drinking is hazardous (e.g., driving while intoxicated). It is distinct from alcohol dependence in that it does not involve tolerance or withdrawal.

alcohol addiction see ADDICTION; ALCOHOL DEPENDENCE.

alcohol-amnestic disorder the *DSM–III* designation for the condition classified in *DSM–IV–TR* as ALCOHOL-INDUCED PERSISTING AMNESTIC DISORDER.

alcohol dependence a pattern of repeated or compulsive use of alcohol despite significant behavioral, physiological, and psychosocial problems, including indications of physical and psychological dependence—tolerance and characteristic withdrawal symptoms if use is suspended—resulting in impaired control. It is further differentiated from alcohol abuse by the preoccupation with obtaining alcohol or recovering from its effects, and the overwhelming desire for experiencing alcohol's intoxicating result (i.e., craving). Alcohol dependence is known popularly as **alcoholism**.

alcohol derivatives drugs that use the sedative and hypnotic effects of alcohols for therapeutic purposes. In the 1890s, it was found that compounds derived from methyl alcohol had CNS DEPRESSANT effects. In the 1950s, a new generation of alcohol-based compounds with greater hypnotic activity was introduced. They included ETHCHLORVYNOL and **ethinamate**; the latter is a

A

more potent sleep inducer than ethchlorvynol, but its abuse potential is similar to that of barbiturates. Due to their toxicity, alcohol derivatives are rarely used in modern clinical practice.

alcohol hallucinosis see ALCOHOL-INDUCED PSYCHOTIC DISORDER.

alcoholic *n.* a person who meets the *DSM–IV–TR* criteria for ALCOHOL DEPENDENCE.

alcoholic blackout see BLACKOUT.

alcoholic brain syndrome any of several syndromes associated with the acute or chronic effects of alcohol on brain function, including ALCOHOL INTOXICATION DELIRIUM, ALCOHOL WITHDRAWAL DELIRIUM, ALCOHOL-INDUCED PERSISTING DEMENTIA, ALCOHOL-INDUCED PERSISTING AMNESTIC DISORDER, and ALCOHOL-INDUCED PSYCHOTIC DISORDER.

alcoholic cerebellar degeneration degeneration of the CEREBELLUM caused by long-term alcohol abuse, commonly producing gait disturbances.

alcoholic dementia see ALCOHOL-INDUCED PERSISTING DEMENTIA.

alcoholic hallucinosis see ALCOHOL-INDUCED PSYCHOTIC DISORDER.

alcoholic Korsakoff's syndrome a form of KORSAKOFF'S SYNDROME caused by long-term alcohol abuse. See ALCOHOL-INDUCED PERSISTING AMNESTIC DISORDER.

alcoholic myopathy see ACUTE ALCOHOLIC MYOPATHY.

alcoholic neuropathy any of various neurological disturbances, including weakness and abnormal skin sensations, such as numbness, tingling, and burning, that are secondary to chronic heavy consumption of alcohol. Specific causative factors are not well understood, but appear to include vitamin deficiencies and a directly toxic effect of alcohol on nerves.

alcoholic psychosis in *DSM–II*, a category of mental disorders associated with the detrimental neurological effects of alcohol abuse. The equivalent *DSM–IV–TR* disorders include the following: ALCOHOL INTOXICATION DELIRIUM, ALCOHOL WITHDRAWAL DELIRIUM, ALCOHOL-INDUCED PSYCHOTIC DISORDER, ALCOHOL-INDUCED PERSISTING DEMENTIA, and ALCOHOL-INDUCED PERSISTING AMNESTIC DISORDER.

Alcoholics Anonymous (**AA**) a worldwide voluntary organization of men and women who, through a TWELVE-STEP PROGRAM, seek to help each other stay sober and learn to live healthy, fulfilling lives. The only requirement for membership is a desire to stop drinking. Two critical components of the AA program are its focus on alcoholics helping alcoholics and its desire to put principles above personalities in conducting its business. Founded in the United States in 1935, AA is the oldest, largest, and best-known self-help organization.

alcohol idiosyncratic intoxication in *DSM–III*, a condition characterized by marked behavioral change associated with consumption of an amount of alcohol usually insufficient to intoxicate most people. The idiosyncratic behavior is atypical of the individual when he or she is not drinking: for example, a quiet, shy person may become belligerent and assaultive. Although this diagnosis was removed from *DSM–IV* because of its rarity, controversy over the decision to remove it remains.

alcohol-induced persisting amnestic disorder a disturbance in memory caused by the persisting effects of alcohol. The ability to learn new information or to recall previously learned information is impaired severely enough to interfere markedly with social or occupational functioning and to represent a significant decline from a previous level of functioning. See also KORSAKOFF'S SYNDROME; WERNICKE–KORSAKOFF SYNDROME.

alcohol-induced persisting dementia a deterioration of mental function resulting from the persisting effects of alcohol abuse. It is characterized by multiple COGNITIVE DEFICITS, especially of memory but also including impairment of speech (see APHASIA), movement (see APRAXIA), and sensory capabilities (see AGNOSIA), and EXECUTIVE DYSFUNCTION. Also called **alcoholic dementia**. See also SUBSTANCE-INDUCED PERSISTING DEMENTIA.

alcohol-induced psychotic disorder hallucinations or delusions due to the direct physiological effects of alcohol. Also called **alcoholic** (or **alcohol**) **hallucinosis**. See also SUBSTANCE-INDUCED PSYCHOTIC DISORDER.

alcohol intoxication a reversible condition that develops after the ingestion of alcohol. It comprises behavioral or psychological changes, such as inappropriate or aggressive behavior, impaired judgment, or impaired social functioning; and physiological changes, such as slurred speech, unsteady gait, and disruption of attention or memory. The effects typically become more marked with increased alcohol intake. See also SUBSTANCE INTOXICATION.

alcohol intoxication delirium a reversible syndrome that develops over a short period of time (usually hours to days) following heavy alcohol consumption. Disturbance of consciousness (e.g., reduced ability to focus, sustain, or shift attention) is accompanied by changes in cognition (e.g., memory deficit, disorientation, or language disturbance) in excess of those usually associated with ALCOHOL INTOXICATION. See also SUBSTANCE INTOXICATION DELIRIUM.

alcoholism *n.* see ALCOHOL DEPENDENCE.

alcoholism treatment interventions designed to enable the alcohol-dependent person either to achieve and maintain abstinence, which is the generally accepted goal of treatment for alcohol dependence, or to reach and maintain a stable pattern of nonproblem drinking, which is a controversial, less common goal of treatment. Also called **alcohol rehabilitation**.

alcohol withdrawal a group of physical symptoms that arise after cessation of repeated and prolonged heavy alcohol consumption. Withdrawal symptoms include autonomic hyperactivity (sweating, pounding heart, dry mouth, etc.), hand tremor, insomnia, nausea or vomiting, PSYCHOMOTOR AGITATION, anxiety, and in some cases hallucinations or illusions, seizures, and DELIRIUM TREMENS.

alcohol withdrawal delirium a reversible syndrome that develops over a short period of time (usually hours to days) following cessation of prolonged, heavy alcohol consumption. The features are disturbed consciousness (e.g., reduced ability to focus, sustain, or shift attention) and changes in cognition (e.g., memory deficit, disorientation, or language disturbance) in excess of those usually associated with ALCOHOL WITHDRAWAL. See also DELIRIUM TREMENS.

Aldomet *n.* a trade name for METHYLDOPA.

alertness *n.* the state of being awake, aware, attentive, and prepared to act or react. Neurologically, alertness corresponds with high-frequency, low-amplitude brain waves resulting from stimulation of the RETICULAR FORMATION. See also AROUSAL.

alexia *n.* loss or impairment of the ability to comprehend written or printed words as a result of lesions, stroke, or other forms of neurological damage or disorder. It is generally seen in APHASIA but may occur in isolation, in which case it is called **pure alexia** (or **alexia without agraphia**) and characterized by reading impairment with preserved language production and auditory comprehension. Individuals with pure alexia can also write but are frequently unable to read what they have written. See also DYSLEXIA.

alexithymia *n.* an inability to express, describe, or distinguish between one's emotions. It may occur in a variety of disorders (e.g., depression), especially psychosomatic and some substance use disorders, or following repeated exposure to a traumatic stressor.

Alfenta *n.* a trade name for alfentanil. See FENTANYL.

alfentanil *n.* see FENTANYL.

algedonic *adj.* relating to pain associated with pleasure, or the pleasantness–unpleasantness dimension of experience. **Algedonics** is the study of the mixture of pleasure and pain.

algesia *n.* the ability to experience the sensation of pain. Compare ANALGESIA. **—algesic** *adj.*

algolagnia *n.* a sexual disorder in which sexual excitement is achieved by experiencing or inflicting pain. See ACTIVE ALGOLAGNIA; PASSIVE ALGOLAGNIA; SEXUAL MASOCHISM; SEXUAL SADISM.

algophilia *n.* liking for the experience or infliction of pain. See also ALGOLAGNIA; MASOCHISM; SADISM.

algopsychalia *n.* physical pain recognized by the patient as being of mental rather than physical origin, which sometimes accompanies mental difficulties (e.g., anxiety, schizophrenia, depression). See also PSYCHIC PAIN.

alien abduction a claim by individuals that they have been kidnapped by extraterrestrial beings. Although this phenomenon is commonly associated with delusional thinking, POSTTRAUMATIC STRESS DISORDER, and acute stress reactions, many of these individuals have no other clear symptoms of mental disorder. Historically, there is no conclusive physical evidence to support the validity of their claims. Also called **extraterrestrial kidnapping**.

alienation *n.* **1.** estrangement from others, resulting in the absence of close or friendly relationships with people in one's social group (e.g., family, workplace, community). **2.** estrangement from oneself. An individual experiences life as a search for his or her true personal identity, which is believed to have been hidden through socialization and nurturing, and as a continuous failure to reach an ideal but unattainable level of personal fulfillment. This creates a deep-seated sense of dissatisfaction with one's personal existence and lack of trust in one's social or physical environment or in oneself. **3.** the experience of being separated from reality or isolated from one's thoughts or feelings, as in DEREALIZATION and DEPERSONALIZATION. **—alienated** *adj.*

alienation test an evaluation of an individual's feelings of estrangement or separation from his or her milieu, work, or self.

alien limb syndrome a motor disorder characterized by involuntary hand, arm, or leg movements in place of or in addition to intended movements (e.g., grabbing objects or throwing things) and the person's feeling that he or she has no control over the limb or that it is "foreign," sometimes to the extent that the person does not recognize the limb as his or her own in the absence of visual clues. The syndrome may be associated with lesions to the SUPPLEMENTARY MOTOR AREA or the motor regions of the CORPUS CALLOSUM. **Alien hand syndrome** is a specific kind of the disorder.

aliphatic phenothiazines PHENOTHIAZINE antipsychotic agents containing an aliphatic (fatty acid) side chain in their molecular structure. Including chlorpromazine, promazine, and triflupromazine, they are the least potent of the phenothiazines and are now rarely used.

alkalosis *n.* an abnormally high level of alkalinity (bicarbonate ion concentration) in the blood and tissues, which upsets the body's acid–base balance. The condition is often marked by slow, shallow breathing. It has a variety of causes and additional symptoms vary with each, potentially including neurological abnormalities such as muscle twitching, confusion, tremors or spasms, and numbness. Compare ACIDOSIS. **—alkalotic** *adj.*

allele *n.* an alternate form of a gene that occupies a given position on each of a pair of HOMOLO-

GOUS chromosomes. Each person typically has two alleles of each gene: One is inherited from the mother and the other from the father. Alleles may be alike (**homozygous**) or different (**heterozygous**), and are responsible for variation in inherited characteristics, such as hair color or blood type. See also DOMINANT ALLELE; RECESSIVE ALLELE. —**allelic** *adj.*

allied health professional (**AHP**) a licensed health care professional with specialized education and training who assists other professional staff in the prevention, treatment, and rehabilitation process.

allocation decision 1. a choice in which an individual must decide how to distribute a limited resource across entities (e.g., hypothetical factories or hospitals). **2.** in group problem solving, the group's allocation of particular roles or jobs to individual members.

allocentric 1. *adj.* denoting externality to the self, particularly an orientation toward or focus on groups and connections to others. **2.** *adj.* in anthropology, respecting the values and customs of other cultures (i.e., not ethnocentric). **3.** *n.* an individual who is dispositionally predisposed to put the goals and needs of the group above his or her own. Just as societies based on COLLECTIVISM stress connections among members and the welfare of the group, allocentrics emphasize their connections to others and are group-centered. They are more likely to join groups and to base their identities on their memberships. Also called **interdependent**. Compare IDIOCENTRIC. See also SOCIOCENTRISM. —**allocentrism** *n.*

allochthonous *adj.* stemming from sources or forces external to a particular system: not indigenous or innate. Compare AUTOCHTHONOUS.

allocortex *n.* those regions of the cerebral cortex that are phylogenetically older and have fewer than six main layers of cells. The allocortex is involved primarily in olfactory functions and limbic functions related to memory and emotion, and comprises the three-layered **archicortex** (or **archipallium**), found mostly in the hippocampus, and the four- or five-layered **paleocortex** (or **paleopallium**), found mostly in the pyriform area and parahippocampal gyrus. Compare NEOCORTEX.

alloeroticism *n.* the extension of erotic feelings toward and the derivation of sexual satisfaction from others, as opposed to AUTOEROTICISM. Also called **alloerotism**. —**alloerotic** *adj.*

allopathy *n.* a system of medicine in which a disease or disorder is treated with agents that produce effects different from or incompatible with those caused by the disease or disorder. Allopathy is often equated with conventional or pharmacological medical practice. Compare HOMEOPATHY. —**allopathic** *adj.*

allophasis *n.* disorganized, incoherent speech.

alloplasty *n.* **1.** a process of adaptive response that aims to alter the environment, as opposed to altering the self. Also called **alloplastic adaptation**. **2.** surgical repair of diseased or damaged tissue through implantation using synthetic or organic material from outside the patient's body. Compare AUTOPLASTY. —**alloplastic** *adj.*

allopsychic delusion see AUTOPSYCHIC DELUSION.

allostasis *n.* stability through change. Allostasis refers particularly to the idea that parameters of most physiological regulatory systems change to accommodate environmental demands. Although allostatic processes are critical for adaptive functioning, chronic or repeated activation of physiological systems in response to life's challenges are hypothesized to exact a toll on such systems.

allosteric modulation the binding of a substance (called an **allosteric modulator**) to a certain site on a RECEPTOR in a way that alters the conformation of other sites on the receptor, thereby increasing or decreasing the affinity of the receptor for other molecules. Allosteric modulation recently has been recognized as an alternative pharmacological approach to gain selectivity in drug action.

allotriophagy *n.* a desire to eat inappropriate foods or nonnutritive substances. Also called **allotriophagia**. See also PICA.

all-payer system a health care system in which prices for health care services and payment methods are the same regardless of who is paying (e.g., the patient or an insurance company). Also called **multipayer system**.

Allport, Gordon Willard (1897–1967) U.S. psychologist. Allport received his PhD from Harvard University in 1922. He is widely recognized as the originator of a theory of personality based on three categories of traits (see ALLPORT'S PERSONALITY TRAIT THEORY) and as coauthor of two personality inventories, the ALLPORT–VERNON–LINDZEY STUDY OF VALUES and the Allport AS Reaction Study. Allport was also a major contributor to the field of social psychology, emphasizing the role of attitudes in motivation and making major theoretical contributions to the study of prejudice. See also DIRECTEDNESS; FUNCTIONAL AUTONOMY; GROUP RELATIONS THEORY; HUMANISTIC PERSPECTIVE; PERSONALISTIC PSYCHOLOGY; PERSONALITY STRUCTURE; PROPRIATE STRIVING; PROPRIUM; SELF-EXTENSION; SELF-OBJECTIFICATION.

Allport's personality trait theory the theory that an individual's PERSONALITY TRAITS are the key to the uniqueness and consistency of his or her behavior. Traits are regarded as dynamic forces that interact with each other and the environment to determine the characteristic actions or reactions that define the self (see PROPRIUM). They develop largely from experience, learning, and imitation and fall into three main categories: (a) cardinal traits or master qualities (e.g., overweening ambition); (b) central traits, or clusters of distinctive attitudes and characteristics; and (c) secondary traits, which are more limited and not essential to personality description. [Gordon W. ALLPORT]

Allport–Vernon–Lindzey Study of Values (**SOV**) a two-part personality test designed to show the relative importance of six basic values in the participant's life: theoretical, economic, aesthetic, social, political, and religious. The categories are presented in the form of 45 items to which participants respond. Part one consists of 30 statements, each describing a situation with two alternative choices; participants must choose which option they prefer and indicate the strength of that preference by distributing three points between the two alternatives. Part two consists of 15 questions, each with four alternative answers; participants must rank the answers in order of preference. The SOV was originally published in 1931 as the **Allport–Vernon Study of Values** but in 1951 was revised and renamed. The most recent version of the test was published in 1960. Also called **Study of Values**. [Gordon W. ALLPORT; Philip E. **Vernon** (1905–1987), British psychologist; Gardner **Lindzey** (1920–2008), U.S. psychologist]

allusive thinking a type of thinking marked by inference and suggestion rather than traditional logic and direct communication of ideas. The concepts employed may seem diffuse and indistinct. See also ANALOGICAL THINKING.

alogia *n.* inability to speak because of dysfunction in the central nervous system. In a less severe form, it is sometimes referred to as **dyslogia**.

alpha (symbol: α) *n.* the probability of a TYPE I ERROR.

alpha-adrenergic receptor a receptor that binds NOREPINEPHRINE and causes stimulation of smooth muscle in responses of the SYMPATHETIC NERVOUS SYSTEM, such as pupil dilation and increased vascular resistance (vasoconstriction). There are two types, α_1-adrenoreceptors and α_2-adrenoreceptors, each of which is divided into subtypes designated by subscript capital letters (α_{1A}-adrenoreceptor, α_{2A}-adrenoreceptor, etc.). Also called **alpha adrenoceptor**; **alpha adrenoreceptor**; **alpha receptor**. Compare BETA-ADRENERGIC RECEPTOR.

L-alpha-acetyl-methadol *n.* see LAAM.

alpha-adrenoreceptor blocking agent see ADRENERGIC BLOCKING AGENT.

alpha alcoholism one of five types of alcoholism defined by U.S. physician Elvin M. Jellinek (1890–1963), the others being BETA ALCOHOLISM, GAMMA ALCOHOLISM, DELTA ALCOHOLISM, and EPSILON ALCOHOLISM. It is characterized by undisciplined drinking that disturbs interpersonal and family relationships and work life and a reliance on the effects of alcohol for the relief of physical or emotional pain, but it does not involve losing control or inability to abstain.

alpha-block conditioning the training of humans or other animals to block ALPHA WAVES by reinforcement or biofeedback. See ALPHA BLOCKING.

alpha blocker see ADRENERGIC BLOCKING AGENT.

alpha blocking the suppression of ALPHA WAVES that occurs upon deviation from a wakeful but relaxed state, as, for example, when focusing the eyes on an unexpected stimulus or performing an active mental task. It is sometimes taken as an indicator of orienting or attention. Typically, blocked alpha waves are replaced by faster, low-amplitude, irregular waveforms on the electroencephalogram, a phenomenon called DESYNCHRONIZATION.

alpha coefficient see CRONBACH'S ALPHA.

alpha error see TYPE I ERROR.

alpha level see SIGNIFICANCE LEVEL.

alpha wave in electroencephalography, a type of low-amplitude BRAIN WAVE (frequency 8–12 Hz) that typically occurs when the eyes are unfocused and no active mental processes are taking place, indicating a wakeful but relaxed state. The occurrence of alpha waves may be increased, for example, through meditation or **alpha-wave training**, a type of BIOFEEDBACK TRAINING that involves providing a feedback stimulus (typically an auditory tone) when alpha waves appear on the electroencephalogram (EEG). Also called **alpha rhythm**; **Berger rhythm**.

Alport's syndrome a familial condition characterized by hematuria (bloody urine), nephropathy (disease of the kidney), and deafness. Hematuria may first appear in infancy, while deafness is likely to develop around the age of puberty. The condition also may be accompanied by cataracts and mental retardation. It is caused by mutation of the genes *COL4A3*, *COL4A4*, *COL4A5*, or *COL4A6*, which specify chains of basement membrane (Type IV) collagen. [described in 1927 by Arthur Cecil **Alport** (1879–1959), British physician]

alprazolam *n.* a BENZODIAZEPINE used for the treatment of generalized anxiety disorder and panic disorder. It is rapidly absorbed and has a relatively brief duration of action. Common side effects include drowsiness, light-headedness, headache, and confusion. U.S. trade name: **Xanax**.

ALS abbreviation for AMYOTROPHIC LATERAL SCLEROSIS.

Alström–Hallgren syndrome a familial disorder that is characterized by obesity, deafness, visual disorders, and diabetes and is occasionally associated with mental disorders. [Carl-Henry **Alström** (1907–1993), Swedish physician; Bertil **Hallgren**, 20th-century Swedish geneticist]

alter *n.* **1.** any of the SECONDARY PERSONALITIES in a person with DISSOCIATIVE IDENTITY DISORDER. **2.** the other person in a social interaction.

alteration hypothesis a theoretical explana-

A

tion of the MISINFORMATION EFFECT stating that misleading information introduced after a witnessed event replaces, transforms, or impairs the original memory of the event, leading to erroneous reporting of that event. Also called **substitution hypothesis**. Compare COEXISTENCE HYPOTHESIS.

altered state of consciousness (**ASC**) a state of psychological functioning that is significantly different from ordinary states of CONSCIOUSNESS, being characterized by altered levels of self-awareness, affect, reality testing, orientation to time and place, wakefulness, responsiveness to external stimuli, or memorability or by a sense of ecstasy, boundlessness, or unity with the universe.

alter ego 1. a second identity or aspect of a person that exists metaphorically as his or her substitute or representative, with different characteristics. **2.** an intimate, supportive friend with whom an individual can share all types of problems and experiences, as if he or she were "another self." **3.** in psychodrama, a group member, other than the therapist, who assumes the role of a significant figure in the PROTAGONIST's life (see AUXILIARY EGO) but who also speaks as part of the protagonist in order to give voice to and portray actions felt but not expressed by the protagonist.

alter-egoism *n.* an altruistic concern or a feeling of empathy for another person in the same situation as oneself.

alternate-forms reliability an estimate of the extent to which a test yields consistent reproducible results that is obtained from the correlation of scores on different versions of that test. These **alternate forms** of the test may be of three types: **comparable forms** have items of similar content and difficulty; **equivalent forms** have items of similar content and difficulty but demonstrate differences in certain statistical characteristics (e.g., standard deviations); and **parallel forms** have items of similar content and difficulty and are similar in all statistical characteristics (e.g., means, standard deviations, correlations with other measures). Comparable forms have the least degree of similarity to one another, while parallel forms have the greatest degree of similarity and are essentially interchangeable.

alternating personality a personality with components that appear alternately. See DISSOCIATIVE IDENTITY DISORDER.

alternative behavior completion a technique in BEHAVIOR THERAPY for extinguishing unwanted habits by substituting an incompatible behavior for the nondesired behavior (e.g., substituting nail care for nail biting). This technique can be practiced in vivo (see IN VIVO DESENSITIZATION) or imaginally in the therapy session or assigned as homework. It is often used as an alternative to mild AVERSION THERAPY. See also COMPETING RESPONSE TRAINING.

alternative dispute resolution the resolving of disputes between parties using neutral third parties, who act as arbitrators or mediators, rather than by engaging in a lawsuit.

alternative hypothesis (symbol: H_1) a statement of the position opposite to that of the NULL HYPOTHESIS. It usually outlines the predicted relationship between variables that a researcher is seeking to demonstrate empirically as true. In HYPOTHESIS TESTING, the alternative hypothesis may be considered plausible only when the null hypothesis is rejected at a predetermined SIGNIFICANCE LEVEL.

alternative medicine see COMPLEMENTARY AND ALTERNATIVE MEDICINE.

alternative psychotherapy any treatment approach not considered to be within the mainstream of psychotherapy. PRIMAL THERAPY and REICHIAN ANALYSIS are considered alternative approaches by most therapists.

altruism *n.* an apparently unselfish concern for others or behavior that provides benefit to others at some cost to the individual. In humans, it covers a wide range of behaviors, including volunteerism and martyrdom, but the degree to which such behaviors are legitimately without egotistic motivation is subject to much debate. **—altruistic** *adj.* **—altruist** *n.*

altruistic behavior behavior performed for the benefit of others. Altruistic behavior covers a wide range of actions, including expressions of interest, support, and sympathy; special favors performed for others; active defense of the rights of the oppressed or deprived; VOLUNTEERISM; and martyrdom (see ALTRUISTIC SUICIDE). The degree to which altruistic behavior is true—that is, without egoistic motivation—is subject to much debate. See also EGOISTIC HELPING; EMPATHY–ALTRUISM HELPING; HELPING; PROSOCIAL BEHAVIOR.

altruistic suicide suicide committed, or suicidal actions undertaken, in the belief that this will benefit the group or serve a greater good, as exemplified by terrorist suicide bombings, the Japanese kamikaze attacks of World War II, or suicides by older adults who believe they are a burden to their families. Altruistic suicide is generally committed by members of highly integrated groups. See also MASS SUICIDE. [defined by French sociologist Emile Durkheim (1858–1917)]

Alzheimer's disease a progressive neurodegenerative disease characterized by cortical atrophy, neuronal death, synapse loss, and accumulation of SENILE PLAQUES and NEUROFIBRILLARY TANGLES, causing DEMENTIA and a significant decline in functioning. Early features include deficits in memory (e.g., rapid forgetting of new information, impaired recall and recognition), executive dysfunction, and subtle personality changes such as decreased energy, social withdrawal, indifference, and impulsivity. As the disease progresses, there is global deterioration of cognitive capacities with intellectual decline, APHASIA, AGNOSIA, and APRAXIA as well as behavioral features including apathy, emotional blunting, mood-dependent delusions, decreased sleep and appetite, and increased motor activity (e.g., restlessness and wandering). Onset of Alzheimer's disease is insidious and typically after age 65, although early-onset cases do occur. Major risk factors for Alzheimer's disease include advanced age, a family history of the disease, and genetic factors, particularly the presence of the ApoE4 allele on chromosome 19. [first described in 1907 by Alois **Alzheimer** (1864–1915), German neurologist]

Alzheimer's Disease and Related Disorders Association, Inc. an organization that provides support groups, assistance, and information for caregivers of patients with Alzheimer's disease.

amae *n.* an indigenous Japanese concept that describes a behavioral pattern roughly translated as indulgent dependency in which people ask others to perform actions for them that they could actually perform for themselves. Typically found in mother–child relationships, amae is distinguished from true dependency by the inappropriateness of the requests and their presumed acceptance. [first described by Japanese psychologist Takeo Doi (1920–2009)]

amantadine *n.* an ANTIVIRAL DRUG that is also a DOPAMINE-RECEPTOR AGONIST and is occasionally used to ameliorate the EXTRAPYRAMIDAL SYMPTOMS of antipsychotic drugs active at dopamine receptors. U.S. trade name: **Symmetrel**.

amative intercourse sexual intercourse that occurs as part of a loving, caring relationship. This is distinguished from sexual activity between people who neither know each other nor have an emotional relationship (e.g., a prostitute and a client).

ambenomium *n.* an anticholinesterase (see CHOLINERGIC DRUG) that can be taken orally to relieve the symptoms of MYASTHENIA GRAVIS. U.S. trade name: **Mytelase**.

Ambien *n.* a trade name for ZOLPIDEM.

ambiguity *n.* **1.** the property of a behavior, behavior pattern, or situation that might lead to interpretation in more than one way. **2.** the property of a word, phrase, or sentence that has more than one possible meaning. In psychoanalytic theory, ambiguous words or phrases are usually interpreted as a symptom of the speaker's hidden feelings or unconscious wishes about the subject. **—ambiguous** *adj.*

ambiguity scale any questionnaire used in evaluating tolerance or intolerance for vagueness, ambiguity, and indefiniteness.

ambiguity tolerance the degree to which one is able to accept, and to function without distress or disorientation in, situations having conflicting or multiple interpretations or outcomes.

ambiguous stimulus a stimulus in any sensory modality that can be interpreted in more than one way.

ambisexual *adj.* **1.** denoting individuals or characteristics that manifest no sex or gender dominance. Compare ASEXUAL. **2.** an older term for bisexual (see BISEXUALITY), now rarely used. **—ambisexuality** *n.*

ambitendency *n.* **1.** the tendency to act in opposite ways, based on conflicting behavioral motivations. **2.** a pattern of incomplete motor responses in anticipation of a voluntary action. It occurs in catatonic states as a type of PSYCHOMOTOR RETARDATION in which the individual appears motorically stuck and exhibits hesitant, indecisive motions in the absence of voluntary movement. **3.** in Jungian psychology, the psychic ambivalence that is caused by the existence of opposing tendencies.

ambivalence *n.* **1.** the simultaneous existence of contradictory feelings and attitudes, such as pleasantness and unpleasantness or friendliness and hostility, toward the same person, object, event, or situation. Conflicting feelings are often strong toward parents, since they are agents of both discipline and affection. Swiss psychiatrist Eugen Bleuler (1857–1939), who first defined ambivalence in a psychological sense and referred to it as **affective ambivalence**, regarded extreme ambivalence, such as an individual expressing great love for his or her mother while also asking how to kill her, as a major symptom of schizophrenia. **2.** uncertainty or indecisiveness about a course of action. **—ambivalent** *adj.*

ambivalent attachment in the STRANGE SITUATION, a form of INSECURE ATTACHMENT in which infants show a combination of positive and negative responses toward a parent. After separation, for example, infants may simultaneously seek and resist close contact with the returning parent. Also called **resistant attachment**.

ambiversion *n.* the tendency to display characteristics of introversion and extraversion in approximately equal degrees. Such a person would be referred to as an **ambivert**.

ambulation *n.* the act of walking from place to place. Ambulation training often is necessary in the rehabilitation of individuals who have had a spinal injury, stroke, or other trauma affecting the neuromuscular system and in the physical therapy of individuals with certain genetic or congenital disorders.

ambulatory care medical or psychological services provided to individuals on an outpatient, nonemergency basis. Such services may include observation, diagnosis, treatment (referred to as **ambulatory treatment**), and rehabilitation and are often provided at such places as a doctor's office, health center, or hospital outpatient department.

ambulatory schizophrenia a condition in which a person who was previously hospitalized from extreme symptoms and then diagnosed as having schizophrenia no longer requires hospitalization but nonetheless behaves eccentrically and cannot function in a manner consistent with social expectations.

ambulatory services mental health, counseling, or medical services provided on an outpatient basis, that is, without the client needing to be in or remain in a hospital, clinic, or other provider facility. See also WALK-IN CLINIC.

amenorrhea *n.* the absence of menstruation. When menstruation fails to begin after puberty, the condition is called **primary amenorrhea.** If menstrual periods stop, in the absence of pregnancy or menopause, after starting, the condition is known as **secondary amenorrhea.** Changes in physical or mental health can be a causal factor.

American Academy of Clinical Sexologists (AACS) an institution founded in 1986 as the educational arm of the American Board of Sexology. Since 1995 it has provided professional training for sex therapists at Maimonides University, Miami Beach, Florida.

American Association of Applied and Preventive Psychology (AAAPP) a professional organization whose purpose is to promote the interests of clinical and preventive psychology. It encourages a research orientation toward clinical and preventive work, emphasizing the consumer and public interest above guild or personal interests. Its main publication is the journal *Applied and Preventive Psychology: Current Scientific Perspectives.*

American Association of Applied Psychology (AAAP) a professional organization founded in 1937 by a group of consulting, clinical, educational, and industrial psychologists who broke from the AMERICAN PSYCHOLOGICAL ASSOCIATION in order to represent the applied interests of U.S. psychologists more effectively. Their main publication was the *Journal of Consulting Psychology.* In 1944 the group rejoined the American Psychological Association.

American Association of Clinical Psychologists (AACP) a professional organization founded in 1917 when clinical psychologists broke from the AMERICAN PSYCHOLOGICAL ASSOCIATION in order to promote training and certification standards for the practice of clinical psychology. The AACP returned to the American Psychological Association in 1919 as its first special-interest group, the Section of Clinical Psychology.

American Association of Mental Retardation (AAMR) see AMERICAN ASSOCIATION ON INTELLECTUAL AND DEVELOPMENTAL DISABILITIES.

American Association of Sex Educators, Counselors and Therapists (AASECT) a nonprofit, interdisciplinary, professional accrediting organization founded in 1967 whose mission is to provide professional education and certification of sex educators, counselors, and therapists and to promote understanding of human sexuality and healthy sexual behavior.

American Association on Intellectual and Developmental Disabilities (AAIDD) a professional organization, founded in 1876, whose mission is to promote progressive policies, sound research, and effective practices in the field of mental retardation, together with universal human rights for people with intellectual and developmental disabilities. It is the oldest and largest interdisciplinary organization in this field. Formerly called **American Association of Mental Retardation (AAMR).**

American Board of Professional Psychology (ABPP) the umbrella organization for 13 psychological specialty boards in the United States. Established in 1947, its purpose is to establish, implement, and maintain standards and set examinations for specialty areas in the practice of psychology. A "specialty" is defined as a focused area in which special competency has been acquired through an organized sequence of education, training, and practical experience.

American Law Institute Model Penal Code Insanity Test a legal standard for establishing CRIMINAL RESPONSIBILITY, adopted in 1962, that combines elements of the MCNAUGHTEN RULE and the IRRESISTIBLE IMPULSE RULE. According to this standard, individuals are not responsible for criminal conduct if at the time of such conduct, as a result of mental illness or defect, they lacked substantial capacity either to appreciate the criminality of their conduct or to conform their conduct to the requirements of the law. Also called **American Law Institute Guidelines (ALI Guidelines); Brawner decision; Brawner rule.**

American Orthopsychiatric Association (AOA) an interdisciplinary professional organization engaged in preventive, treatment, and advocacy approaches to mental health. The prefix *ortho-* (from the Greek *orthos,* "straight") emphasizes the need for preventive approaches. The *American Journal of Orthopsychiatry* is its major publication. [founded in 1924 by U.S. physician Karl Menninger (1893–1990)]

American Parkinson Disease Association, Inc. an organization that provides support groups, information, and referrals for individuals with Parkinson's disease and their families.

American Psychiatric Association (APA) a national medical and professional organization whose physician members specialize in the diagnosis, treatment, and prevention of mental disorders. It was founded in 1844 as the Association of Medical Superintendents of American Institutes for the Insane and renamed the American Medico-Psychological Association in 1892. The current name was adopted in 1922. Its objectives include the improvement of care for people with mental illnesses, the promotion of research and professional education in psychiatry, and the dissemination of psychological knowledge through nationwide public information, education, and awareness programs and materials. Its extensive publications include the *Diagnostic and Statistical Manual of Mental Disorders* (see DSM-IV-TR), the most widely used psychiatric reference in the world.

American Psychoanalytic Association (**APsaA**) a professional organization for psychoanalysts that focuses on education, research, and membership development. Founded in 1911, it is the oldest national psychoanalytic organization, with 29 accredited training institutes and 42 affiliate psychoanalytic societies. It is the U.S. chapter of the International Psychoanalytic Association. Its major publication is the *Journal of the American Psychoanalytic Association.*

American Psychological Association (**APA**) a scientific and professional organization founded in 1892 that represents psychology in the United States and is the largest association of psychologists worldwide. Its mission is to advance psychology as a science, as a profession, and as a means of promoting health and human welfare. Among its specific goals are the promotion of psychological research and improvement of research methods and conditions; the establishment and maintenance of high standards of professional ethics and conduct of its members; and the increase and diffusion of psychological knowledge through a variety of means, including over 50 scholarly journals, the APA *Publication Manual,* 75 books and videotapes per year, and 7 electronic databases.

American Psychological Association code see CODE OF ETHICS.

American Psychological Society (**APS**) a professional organization founded in 1988 to advance the needs and interests of scientific, applied, and academic psychologists as opposed to those engaged in clinical practice. Its mission is to promote, protect, and advance the interests of scientifically oriented psychology in research, application, and the improvement of human welfare. The APS publishes three journals: *Psychological Science, Current Directions in Psychological Science,* and *Psychological Science in the Public Interest.*

American Psychosomatic Society (**APS**) an interdisciplinary professional organization founded in 1942 whose mission is to promote a scientific understanding of the interrelationships among biological, psychological, social, and behavioral factors in human health and disease. Its main publication is *Psychosomatic Medicine.*

amethystic *n.* see ANTI-INTOXICANT.

amino acid an organic compound that contains an amino group ($-NH_2$) and a carboxyl group ($-COOH$), 20 of which are constituents of proteins; 9 of these are **essential amino acids**, that is, they cannot be synthesized by the body and must be obtained from foods. Other amino acids (e.g., GLUTAMIC ACID, GLYCINE) are neurotransmitters or precursors to neurotransmitters.

amino acid imbalance a disorder, genetic or acquired, characterized by a deficiency in the body's ability to transport or utilize certain amino acids. The cause is usually an absence or lack of an enzyme needed to carry an amino acid or its components through a step of a metabolic cycle. More than 80 kinds of amino acid imbalance have been identified, and many (e.g., PHENYLKETONURIA, HOMOCYSTINURIA) affect the central nervous system.

aminoketone *n.* the chemical classification of the antidepressant agent BUPROPION, whose structure and mechanism of action differ from other marketed antidepressants. Although the specific method of action is unknown it is presumed to involve noradrenergic or dopaminergic mechanisms.

aminopterin *n.* a drug similar to methotrexate (also called **amethopterin** and used in treating leukemia) that is sometimes used in nonclinical settings to induce abortions. Surviving infants show teratogenic effects (see TERATOGEN), such as HYDROCEPHALUS, craniosynostosis (premature skull ossification) with skull defects, and mild to moderate mental retardation. Aminopterin is in current use as a rodenticide and is under investigation as a treatment for certain forms of leukemia.

amitriptyline *n.* a TRICYCLIC ANTIDEPRESSANT introduced into clinical use in 1961; with IMIPRAMINE, it was the first widely used antidepressant agent. Its tertiary amine structure makes it a more potent inhibitor of SEROTONIN reuptake than secondary amines (thereby increasing the availability of serotonin for neurotransmission), but also contributes to its significant antihistamine, anticholinergic, and adrenoreceptor-blocking activity (producing adverse side effects). It is an effective antidepressant, but its side effects and toxicity in overdose have led to a decline in its use in favor of the SSRIS and other agents. Although still used as an antidepressant, amitriptyline is no longer considered FIRST-LINE MEDICATION and is more likely to be employed in low doses for chronic pain management or the prevention of migraine. It is also sold in combination with a benzodiazepine ANXIOLYTIC (as **Limbitrol** in the United States) or an antipsychotic (as **Etrafon** or **Triavil** in the United States). U.S. trade name: **Elavil.**

amnesia *n.* partial or complete loss of memory. Either temporary or permanent, it may be due to physiological factors such as injury, disease, or substance use, or to psychological factors such as a traumatic experience. A disturbance in memory marked by inability to learn new information is called **anterograde amnesia** and one marked by inability to recall previously learned

A

information or past events is called **retrograde amnesia**. When severe enough to interfere markedly with social or occupational functioning or to represent a significant decline from a previous level of functioning, the memory loss is known as **amnestic disorder**. **—amnesiac** *adj., n.* **—amnesic** or **amnestic** *adj.*

amnestic apraxia an inability to remember and therefore carry out a command, although there is no loss of ability to perform the task. Also called **amnesic apraxia**.

amnestic disorder in *DSM–IV–TR*, a disturbance in memory marked by inability to learn new information (anterograde amnesia) or to recall previously learned information or past events (retrograde amnesia) that is severe enough to interfere markedly with social or occupational functioning or represents a significant decline from a previous level of functioning. A distinction is made between **amnestic disorder due to a general medical condition**, SUBSTANCE-INDUCED PERSISTING AMNESTIC DISORDER, and **amnestic disorder not otherwise specified**. The first of these can be caused by a variety of conditions, including head injury, ANOXIA, and posterior cerebral artery stroke, resulting in lesions in specific brain regions, including the MEDIAL TEMPORAL LOBE and the DIENCEPHALON, and their connections with various cortical areas. It may be transient, lasting from several hours to no more than a month (see also TRANSIENT GLOBAL AMNESIA), or chronic (lasting more than 1 month). In *DSM–III*, amnestic disorder was called **amnesic** (or **amnestic**) **syndrome**.

amniocentesis *n.* a method of examining fetal chromosomes for any abnormality or for determination of sex. A hollow needle is inserted through the mother's abdominal wall into the uterus, enabling the collection of amniotic fluid, which contains fetal cells. Compare CHORIONIC VILLUS SAMPLING.

amobarbital *n.* an intermediate-acting, rapidly excreted BARBITURATE that was formerly used as a sedative and hypnotic. Like other barbiturates, its toxicity has led to its clinical eclipse by safer agents, such as the BENZODIAZEPINES. Amobarbital abuse can result in addiction, stupor, and death. Amobarbital was occasionally used to conduct interviews (**Amytal interviews**) designed to elicit subconscious material from patients, as well as information that was consciously withheld. Such interviews were also used in attempting to distinguish between patients who were malingering and those who had a bona fide conversion disorder. Due to numerous legal and ethical issues surrounding amobarbital interviews, in addition to the medical risks associated with administration of barbiturates, such techniques are no longer acceptable in modern clinical practice. U.S. trade name: **Amytal**.

amok (**amuck**) *n.* a CULTURE-BOUND SYNDROME observed among males in Malaysia, the Philippines, and other parts of southeast Asia. The individual experiences a period of social withdrawal and apathy, followed by a violent, unprovoked attack on nearby individuals. If not overpowered or killed, the affected male eventually collapses from exhaustion and afterward has no memory of the event. See also MAL DE PELEA.

amotivational syndrome a behavior pattern associated with chronic use of cannabis, characterized by loss of drive and initiative. The concept is mainly conjectural and anecdotal, based on observations of the lifestyles of chronic cannabis users in various cultures around the world. See CANNABIS ABUSE; CANNABIS DEPENDENCE.

amoxapine *n.* an antidepressant, one of the secondary amine TRICYCLIC ANTIDEPRESSANTS (TCAs), that inhibits the reuptake of norepinephrine and serotonin. It may also have ANTIPSYCHOTIC activity due to the strong dopamine-receptor-blocking activity of one of its metabolites. Amoxapine may cause EXTRAPYRAMIDAL SYMPTOMS and TARDIVE DYSKINESIA but is less associated with anticholinergic side effects than other TCAs. U.S. trade name: **Asendin**.

AMPA receptor a type of GLUTAMATE RECEPTOR that binds the agonist AMPA (alpha-amino-3-hydroxy-5-methyl-4-isoxazole-propionic acid) as well as glutamate. AMPA receptors are coupled to ligand-gated ION CHANNELS and are responsible for most of the activity at synapses where glutamate is the neurotransmitter. Compare NMDA RECEPTOR.

amphetamine *n.* a CNS STIMULANT, closely related in structure and activity to ephedrine (see EPHEDRA), that is the prototype of the group of drugs known as the AMPHETAMINES. U.S. trade name: **Benzedrine**.

amphetamine abuse in *DSM–IV–TR*, a pattern of use of amphetamines or amphetamine-like substances manifested by recurrent significant adverse consequences related to the repeated ingestion of these substances. This diagnosis is preempted by the diagnosis of AMPHETAMINE DEPENDENCE: If the criteria for amphetamine abuse and amphetamine dependence are both met, only the latter diagnosis is given. See also SUBSTANCE ABUSE; SUBSTANCE DEPENDENCE.

amphetamine dependence in *DSM–IV–TR*, a cluster of cognitive, behavioral, and physiological symptoms indicating continued use of an amphetamine or amphetamine-like substance despite significant substance-related problems. There is a pattern of repeated substance ingestion resulting in tolerance, characteristic symptoms if use is suspended (see AMPHETAMINE WITHDRAWAL), and an uncontrollable drive to continue use. See also AMPHETAMINE ABUSE.

amphetamine-induced psychotic disorder a condition marked by paranoid delusions due to the direct physiological effects of an amphetamine or amphetamine-like substance. The delusions can continue as long as the use of these substances continues and might persist for weeks or months after withdrawal from the substances has been completed. Also called **amphetamine psychosis**.

amphetamine intoxication a reversible syndrome caused by the recent ingestion of amphetamines or amphetamine-like substances. It is characterized by behavioral or psychological changes (e.g., inappropriate aggressive behavior, impaired judgment, suspiciousness, and paranoia), as well as one or more signs of physiological involvement (e.g., unsteady gait, impairment in attention or memory). See also SUBSTANCE INTOXICATION.

amphetamine intoxication delirium a reversible syndrome that develops over a short period of time (usually hours to days) following the heavy ingestion of amphetamines or amphetamine-like substances. The features include disturbed consciousness (e.g., reduced ability to focus, sustain, or shift attention) and changes in cognition (e.g., memory deficit, disorientation, or language disturbance) in excess of those usually associated with AMPHETAMINE INTOXICATION. See also SUBSTANCE INTOXICATION DELIRIUM.

amphetamine psychosis see AMPHETAMINE-INDUCED PSYCHOTIC DISORDER.

amphetamines *pl. n.* a group of drugs (substituted PHENYLETHYLAMINES) that stimulate the RETICULAR FORMATION in the brain and cause a release of stored norepinephrine. The effect is a prolonged state of arousal and relief from feelings of fatigue (see CNS STIMULANT). Amphetamines were introduced in 1932 for a variety of clinical uses. AMPHETAMINE ABUSE can result in dependence and a well-defined state of psychosis (see AMPHETAMINE DEPENDENCE; AMPHETAMINE-INDUCED PSYCHOTIC DISORDER). Although widely used in the past for weight loss, relief of depression, and other indications, modern use of amphetamines is more circumscribed because of their adverse effects. They are now used mainly in short- and long-acting preparations to manage symptoms of attention deficit/hyperactivity disorder and to treat certain cases of severe depression or narcolepsy. Amphetamines include AMPHETAMINE itself (the prototype), DEXTROAMPHETAMINE, and METHAMPHETAMINE. Related drugs, with a similar mode of action but different molecular structure, include METHYLPHENIDATE. In addition, some forms and derivatives (including DOM, MDA, and MDMA) have been manufactured as recreational hallucinogenic drugs.

amphetamine withdrawal a characteristic withdrawal syndrome that develops after cessation of (or reduction in) prolonged, heavy consumption of an amphetamine or amphetamine-like substance. The essential characteristic is depressed mood, sometimes severe, and there may also be fatigue, disturbed sleep, increased appetite, vivid and unpleasant dreams, or PSYCHOMOTOR RETARDATION or agitation, or all of these features. Marked withdrawal symptoms (see CRASH) often follow an episode of intense, high-dose use. See also SUBSTANCE WITHDRAWAL.

amputation fetish see ACROTOMOPHILIA.

Amsterdam dwarf disease a congenital disorder characterized by delayed growth, small stature, MICROCEPHALY, and such features as cleft lip and palate, upturned nose, and hirsutism. Other manifestations can include malformed or missing limbs, fingers, or hands, seizure disorders, bowel abnormalities, and cardiac defects. Developmental delays are common, as is some degree of mental retardation (usually moderate to severe). Also called **Amsterdam type of retardation**; **Brachmann–de Lange syndrome**. See also DE LANGE'S SYNDROME.

amuck *n.* see AMOK.

amurakh *n.* a CULTURE-BOUND SYNDROME observed among Siberian women and characterized by compulsive mimicking of other people's words or behaviors. See also LATAH.

amygdala *n.* an almond-shaped structure in the TEMPORAL LOBE that is a component of the LIMBIC SYSTEM and considered part of the BASAL GANGLIA. It comprises two main groups of nuclei—the **corticomedial group** and the **basolateral group**—and through widespread connections with other brain areas has numerous viscerosensory and autonomic functions as well as an important role in memory, emotion, perception of threat, and fear learning. Also called **amygdaloid body**; **amygdaloid complex**; **amygdaloid nuclei**. **—amygdaloid** *adj.*

amyl nitrite an organic nitrite, administered by nasal inhalation, that dilates (widens) arteries by relaxing smooth muscles in arterial walls. The main effects are to dilate the coronary arteries supplying the heart and to reduce blood pressure. Amyl nitrite has been used therapeutically in the treatment of angina pectoris and as an antidote in the treatment of cyanide poisoning. It is now best known as a recreational drug that is reputed to enhance orgasm and other aspects of the sexual experience; adverse effects can include anxiety, nausea, dizziness, faintness associated with a drop in blood pressure, and impaired oxygen-carrying capacity of the blood.

amyloid plaque see SENILE PLAQUE.

amyotrophic lateral sclerosis (**ALS**) a rapidly progressive adult-onset disease involving degeneration of both lower MOTOR NEURONS, responsible for muscle contraction, and upper motor neurons, responsible for MUSCLE SPINDLE sensitivity, and leading to death within 5 years of diagnosis. Symptoms include muscular atrophy and weakness, partial and complete paralysis, speech impairment, and difficulties swallowing or breathing. Amyotrophic lateral sclerosis is often used interchangeably with motor neuron disease, especially in the United States. Also called **Lou Gehrig's disease**.

Amytal *n.* a trade name for AMOBARBITAL.

A

Amytal interview see AMOBARBITAL.

anabolic-androgenic steroids steroids that are used to increase muscle bulk and also affect the secondary sex characteristics.

anaclisis *n.* **1.** an extreme dependence on another person for emotional and in some cases physical support, just as an infant is dependent on the parents for the satisfaction of his or her basic needs. See ANACLITIC OBJECT CHOICE. **2.** in the classical psychoanalytic theory of Sigmund FREUD, the attachment of the sex drive to the satisfaction of another instinct, such as hunger or defecation. **—anaclitic** *adj.*

anaclitic depression dependent depression: intense sadness and DYSPHORIA stemming from early disruptions in caring relationships, such as deprivation, inconsistency, or overindulgence, that lead to an indefinite fear of loss of love, abandonment, and impoverishment. The individual expresses a child-like dependency; has little capacity for frustration; and desires to be soothed directly and immediately. Compare INTROJECTIVE DEPRESSION.

anaclitic identification in psychoanalytic theory, the first phase of the IDENTIFICATION process, which is rooted in the child's initial total dependence on the mother (as well as others) for basic biological and emotional needs. The child acquires the mother's characteristics in the service of becoming his or her own source of reinforcement and comfort. The child incorporates the mother into his or her superego (see EGO-IDEAL). A weaker version of this is seen with other significant figures in the child's life (e.g., teachers).

anaclitic object choice in psychoanalytic theory, the selection of a mate or other LOVE OBJECT who will provide the same type of assistance, comfort, and support that the individual received from the parents during infancy and early childhood: A woman chooses a man resembling or modeled on her father and a man chooses a woman like his mother. Sigmund FREUD contrasted this with NARCISSISTIC OBJECT CHOICE, which involves selecting a mate who is similar to oneself. According to Freud, these are the only two possible types of object choice. Also called **anaclitic love**. See also ANACLISIS.

anaclitic personality according to some psychoanalytic theories, a line of personality development that is focused on feelings of loneliness or fear of abandonment with regard to interpersonal relationships and—if the personality fails to develop properly—may result in psychopathological dependency. Compare INTROJECTIVE PERSONALITY.

anaerobic exercise strength-based physical activity, such as weight training and sprinting, that occurs in short, intense bursts with limited oxygen intake. The **anaerobic threshold** is the point at which energy use by the body is so great as to require the muscles to begin producing energy in the absence of adequate oxygen. Compare AEROBIC EXERCISE.

anaesthesia *n.* see ANESTHESIA.

Anafranil *n.* a trade name for CLOMIPRAMINE.

anagogic interpretation the interpretation of dreams and other unconscious material as expressions of ideals or spiritual forces, in contrast to the instinct-based interpretations of psychoanalysis. [introduced by Carl JUNG and developed by Austrian psychoanalyst Herbert Silberer (1882–1923)]

anagram problem solving in studies of problem solving, a common task in which participants are asked to determine the word that corresponds to a series of scrambled letters (e.g., *rlmoebp–problem*).

anal-aggressive personality in psychoanalytic theory, a personality type characterized by obstinacy, obstructionism, defiance, and passive resistance. Such traits are held to stem from the ANAL STAGE, in which the child asserted himself or herself by withholding feces. Also called **anal-aggressive character**. See also ANAL PERSONALITY; ANAL SADISM; ANAL-SADISTIC PHASE.

anal character see ANAL PERSONALITY.

analeptics *pl. n.* stimulants other than amphetamines that produce subjective effects similar to those caused by amphetamine use. These effects may include alertness, elevated mood, increased feeling of energy, decreased appetite, irritability, and insomnia. The group includes DIETHYLPROPION, METHYLPHENIDATE, and PEMOLINE. See also APPETITE SUPPRESSANT.

anal eroticism in psychoanalytic theory, pleasurable sensations associated with expulsion, retention, or observation of the feces or through stimulation of the anus. These sensations first arise in the ANAL STAGE of PSYCHOSEXUAL DEVELOPMENT, between the ages of 1 and 3. Also called **anal erotism**. See also ANAL PERSONALITY; COPROPHILIA.

anal-expulsive phase in psychoanalytic theory, a phase of the ANAL STAGE in which pleasure is obtained by expelling feces and the sadistic instinct is linked to destruction of the OBJECT. According to the theory, fixation at this phase results in an adult ANAL PERSONALITY. See also ANAL-SADISTIC PHASE. Compare ANAL-RETENTIVE PHASE.

analgesia *n.* absence of or reduction in the sensation of pain. Compare ALGESIA. **—analgesic** *adj.*

analgesics *pl. n.* drugs or other agents that alleviate pain. Analgesic drugs usually are classed as opioid (narcotic) or nonopioid (nonnarcotic), depending on their chemical composition and potential for physical dependence. OPIOID ANALGESICS are generally the most effective in relieving pain. The most widely used of the less potent nonopioid analgesics are the NSAIDS (nonsteroidal anti-inflammatory drugs)—most notably ASPIRIN—and ACETAMINOPHEN.

anal intercourse a form of sexual activity in which pleasure is achieved through the insertion of the penis into the anus. Also called **coitus analis**; **coitus in ano**. See also SODOMY.

anal masturbation a form of anal eroticism in which sexual excitement is achieved through manual or mechanical self-stimulation of the anus.

analogical thinking thinking characterized by extrapolations from the familiar to the unfamiliar, rather than the use of formal logic or consecutive reasoning. It is particularly important in problem solving and learning, in which known similarities between aspects of certain entities are used to make assumptions about other aspects or entities. Also called **analogical reasoning**.

analogue experiment an experiment in which a phenomenon is produced in the laboratory in order to obtain greater control over the phenomenon. Examples include the use of hypnosis, drugs, and sensory deprivation to produce brief periods of abnormal behavior that simulate those of psychopathological conditions.

analogue study a research design in which the procedures or participants used are similar but not identical to the situation of interest. For example, if researchers are interested in the effects of therapist gender on client perceptions of therapist trustworthiness, they may use undergraduate students who are not clients and provide simulated counseling dialogues that are typed and identified as offered by a male or female therapist. The results of such studies are assumed to offer a high degree of experimental control and to generalize to actual clinical practice. Also called **analogue model**.

anal personality in psychoanalytic theory, a pattern of personality traits believed to stem from the ANAL STAGE of PSYCHOSEXUAL DEVELOPMENT, when defecation is a primary source of pleasure. Special satisfaction from retention of the feces will result in an adult **anal-retentive personality**, marked by frugality, obstinacy, and orderliness, whereas fixation on expelling feces will produce an aggressive and disorderly **anal-expulsive personality**. Also called **anal character**. See also ANAL-AGGRESSIVE PERSONALITY; HOARDING ORIENTATION.

anal phase see ANAL STAGE.

anal-retentive phase in psychoanalytic theory, a phase of the ANAL STAGE marked by pleasure in retaining feces and thereby defying the parent, in which the sadistic instinct is linked to possession and control of the OBJECT. Fixation at this phase results in an adult ANAL PERSONALITY. See also ANAL-SADISTIC PHASE. Compare ANAL-EXPULSIVE PHASE.

anal sadism in psychoanalytic theory, the expression of aggressive impulses in the ANAL STAGE of psychosexual development, involving both the destruction of the OBJECT and its possession and control. It is manifested in the adult in the form of an ANAL-AGGRESSIVE PERSONALITY.

anal-sadistic phase in psychoanalytic theory, a phase of the ANAL STAGE in which the child manifests aggressive, destructive, and negative tendencies. One expression of these tendencies is withholding the feces in defiance of parental urging. See ANAL-AGGRESSIVE PERSONALITY. See also ANAL-EXPULSIVE PHASE; ANAL-RETENTIVE PHASE.

anal stage in psychoanalytic theory, the second stage of PSYCHOSEXUAL DEVELOPMENT, typically occurring during the 2nd year of life, in which the child's interest and sexual pleasure are focused on the expulsion and retention of feces and the sadistic instinct is linked to the desire to both possess and destroy the OBJECT. Fixation during this stage results in an ANAL PERSONALITY. Also called **anal phase**. See also ANAL-EXPULSIVE PHASE; ANAL-RETENTIVE PHASE; ANAL-SADISTIC PHASE.

analysand *n.* in psychoanalysis, a patient who is undergoing analysis.

analysis *n.* **1.** the division of any entity into its component parts, typically for the purpose of investigation or study. **2.** see PSYCHOANALYSIS. **—analytic** or **analytical** *adj.*

analysis of covariance (**ANCOVA**) an extension of the ANALYSIS OF VARIANCE that adjusts the dependent variable for the influence of a correlated variable (COVARIATE) that is not being investigated but may influence the study results. An analysis of covariance is appropriate in two types of cases: (a) when experimental groups are suspected to differ on a background-correlated variable in addition to the differences attributed to the experimental treatment and (b) where adjustment on a covariate can increase the precision of the experiment.

analysis of the resistance a basic procedure in psychoanalysis, in which the patient's tendency to maintain the REPRESSION of unconscious impulses and experiences is subjected to analytic scrutiny. The process of explaining RESISTANCES is believed to be a major contribution to self-understanding and positive change.

analysis of the transference in psychoanalysis, the interpretation of a patient's early relationships and experiences as they are reflected and expressed in his or her present relationship to the analyst. Also called **transference analysis**. See TRANSFERENCE; TRANSFERENCE RESISTANCE.

analysis of variance (**ANOVA**) any of several statistical procedures that isolate the joint and separate effects of independent variables upon a dependent variable and test them for statistical significance (i.e., to determine whether they are greater than they would be if obtained by chance alone). See also GENERAL LINEAR MODEL.

A

analyst *n.* generally, one who practices psychoanalysis. This is usually a PSYCHOANALYST in the tradition of Sigmund FREUD; however, the term is also applied to therapists adhering to the methods of Carl JUNG (see ANALYTIC PSYCHOLOGY) or Alfred ADLER (see INDIVIDUAL PSYCHOLOGY).

analytical intelligence in the TRIARCHIC THEORY OF INTELLIGENCE, the skills measured by conventional tests of intelligence, such as analysis, comparison, evaluation, critique, and judgment. Compare CREATIVE INTELLIGENCE; PRACTICAL INTELLIGENCE.

analytical psychotherapy 1. a short-term method of psychotherapy using psychoanalytic principles but with less depth of analysis, more active intervention on the part of the therapist, and less frequent sessions than are required for a true psychoanalysis. **2.** historically, an alternative method to psychoanalysis proposed by Viennese psychoanalyst Wilhelm Stekel (1868–1940).

analytic couch see COUCH.

analytic group psychotherapy a form of group psychotherapy based on the application of psychoanalytic concepts and techniques to three principal age groups: (a) PLAY-GROUP PSYCHOTHERAPY for preschool children, (b) ACTIVITY-INTERVIEW GROUP PSYCHOTHERAPY for children before adolescence, and (c) INTERVIEW GROUP PSYCHOTHERAPY for adolescents and adults. [developed by 20th-century Russian-born U.S. psychotherapist Samuel Richard Slavson]

analytic psychology the system of psychoanalysis proposed by Carl JUNG, in which the psyche is interpreted primarily in terms of philosophical values, primordial images and symbols, and a drive for self-fulfillment. Jung's basic concepts are (a) the EGO, which maintains a balance between conscious and unconscious activities and gradually develops a unique self through INDIVIDUATION; (b) the PERSONAL UNCONSCIOUS, made up of memories, thoughts, and feelings based on personal experience; (c) the COLLECTIVE UNCONSCIOUS, made up of ancestral images, or ARCHETYPES, that constitute the inherited foundation of an individual's intellectual life and personality; and (d) dynamic polarities, or tension systems, which derive their psychic energy from the LIBIDO and influence the development and expression of the ego: conscious versus unconscious values, introversion versus extraversion, sublimation versus repression, rational versus irrational. The object of life, and of Jungian therapy, is to achieve a creative balance among all these forces. Also called **analytical psychology**.

analytic rules the three rules laid down by Sigmund FREUD for conducting psychoanalytic therapy: the BASIC RULE of free association, which gives free reign to the unconscious to bring repressed impulses and experiences to the surface; the RULE OF ABSTINENCE, which discourages gratifications that might drain off energy that could be utilized in the therapeutic process; and the rule against ACTING OUT feelings and events instead of talking them out.

anamnesis *n.* a patient's account of his or her developmental, family, and medical history prior to the onset of a mental or physical disorder. Compare CATAMNESIS. [first suggested by Swiss-born U.S. psychiatrist Adolf Meyer (1866–1950) as an aid to diagnosis and exploration of possible causes of a patient's disorder]

anamnestic analysis psychoanalysis that emphasizes the patient's historical account of his or her problem with added material from family and friends. [introduced by Carl JUNG]

anancastic personality (**anankastic personality**) an older name for OBSESSIVE-COMPULSIVE PERSONALITY DISORDER.

anandria *n.* the absence of masculinity in a male.

anaphrodisiac *n.* a drug or other agent that functions as a sexual sedative to reduce or repress sexual desire. Among substances claimed to have this effect are potassium bromide, heroin, and camphor. Anaphrodisiacs also may be a cause of SEXUAL ANESTHESIA. See also CHEMICAL CASTRATION.

anaphylaxis *n.* hypersensitivity to the introduction of a substance (e.g., a food item such as peanuts or a drug such as penicillin) into body tissues, resulting from previous exposure to it. Symptoms, which may include breathing difficulties and wheezing, are sudden and severe, progressing rapidly to **anaphylactic shock**—pulmonary edema, heart arrhythmia, shock, loss of consciousness, and potential respiratory or cardiac arrest—if untreated. See also PSYCHOLOGICAL ANAPHYLAXIS. —**anaphylactic** *adj.*

anarthria *n.* inability to speak.

anatomically detailed doll a doll with anatomically correct genitalia that is used during an interview with a child to help a professional decide whether the child has been sexually abused. Also called **anatomically correct doll**.

anchor *n.* a reference point used when making a series of subjective judgments. For example, in an experiment in which participants gauge distances between objects, the experimenter introduces an anchor by informing the participants that the distance between two of the stimulus objects is a given value. That value then functions as a reference for participants in their subsequent judgments. Also called **anchor point**.

anchoring *n.* **1.** the assignment of set points (ANCHORS) for judgment scales. According to this theory, all judgments are relative to an implicit scale of comparison; for example, poverty is evaluated differently when people are given specific examples of either extreme or moderate poverty. **2.** the process in which one or more items in a list being learned serve as anchors with which the other items are associated. For instance, the first and last items in a list of words may serve as anchors, cuing the words in between.

ANCOVA acronym for ANALYSIS OF COVARIANCE.

androgen *n.* any of a class of steroid hormones that act as the principal male SEX HORMONES, the major one being TESTOSTERONE. Androgens are produced mainly by the testes and influence the development of masculine primary and secondary SEX CHARACTERISTICS. They are also secreted in small quantities by the cortex of the adrenal gland and can be produced synthetically. **—androgenic** *adj.*

androgen antagonist *n.* see ANTIANDROGEN.

androgenization *n.* the masculinizing effect of androgens, especially TESTOSTERONE, on body tissues and organs sensitive to them, as in the development of male sex characteristics.

androgynophilia *n.* **1.** sexual attraction to both males and females. See BISEXUAL BEHAVIOR. **2.** sexual attraction to someone who is androgynous in appearance.

androgynous personality a personality style in which an individual displays both stereotypical masculine and stereotypical feminine psychological characteristics (e.g., both assertiveness and sensitivity).

androgynous sex role 1. a mixture of SEX ROLES in which there is confusion or uncertainty about gender identity and behavior that may be labeled both masculine and feminine. A male may play a feminine role and prefer a partner of his own sex, or a female may play a masculine role and prefer a partner of her own sex. **2.** a sex role that does not conform to either stereotypical male or female sex roles, but rather combines positive elements of both.

androgyny *n.* **1.** the presence of male and female characteristics in one individual. **2.** the state of being neither distinguishably masculine or feminine in appearance, as in dress. See also HERMAPHRODITISM. **—androgyne** *n.* **—androgynous** *adj.*

anecdotal evidence evidence based on informal, uncontrolled personal observations.

Anectine *n.* a trade name for SUCCINYLCHOLINE.

anencephaly *n.* congenital absence of the cranial vault (the bones forming the rear of the skull), with cerebral hemispheres completely missing or reduced to small masses. Infants born with anencephaly are usually blind, deaf, unconscious, and unable to feel pain. Anencephaly is an example of a NEURAL TUBE DEFECT. **—anencephalic** *adj.*

anergia *n.* **1.** absence of energy. **2.** a state of passivity. Also called **anergy**. **—anergic** *adj.*

anesthesia (**anaesthesia**) *n.* the loss of sensitivity to stimuli, either in a particular area (local) or throughout the body and accompanied by loss of consciousness (general). It may be produced intentionally, for example via the administration of drugs (called **anesthetics**) or the use of techniques such as ACUPUNCTURE or hypnotic suggestion, or it may occur spontaneously as a result of injury or disease. **—anesthetic** *adj.*

anethopath *n.* a person lacking ethical or moral inhibitions. See also ANTISOCIAL PERSONALITY DISORDER. **—anethopathy** *n.*

aneuploidy *n.* the condition in which a cell or organism has fewer or more than the normal number of chromosomes, for example (in humans), 45 or 49, instead of the normal 46. Aneuploidy is often associated with neurological or cognitive defects. See AUTOSOME. **—aneuploid** *adj., n.*

aneurysm (**aneurism**) *n.* an enlargement (widening) at some point in an artery caused by the pressure of blood on weakened tissues, often at junctions where arteries split off from one another. **—aneurysmal** *adj.*

angakok *n.* an Inuit name for a SHAMAN or spiritual guide. The angakok is a central figure of Inuit spiritual life; present at major ceremonies, he foretells weather and the movement of game animals, cures illness, retrieves lost or stolen souls, and converses with other spiritual beings.

angel dust a street name for crystals of PCP (phencyclidine). The crystals are sometimes sprinkled onto oregano, parsley, or alfalfa and sold as marijuana.

Angell, James Rowland (1869–1949) U.S. psychologist. After studying at the University of Michigan under John DEWEY, Angell moved to Harvard University to study under William JAMES and Josiah Royce (1855–1916), before studying at various German universities, including the University of Halle. From 1894 through 1919 Angell taught at the University of Chicago, where he became professor of psychology, dean, and finally acting president of the university (1918–1919). He then became chair of the National Research Council, president of the Carnegie Corporation, and finally (in 1921) president of Yale University until his retirement in 1937. In all these positions, Angell used his considerable influence to promote the development of psychology as a science. He was a leading exponent of the school of FUNCTIONALISM, as outlined in his 1906 American Psychological Association presidential address. He argued that, rather than study the discrete elements of consciousness (e.g., memories, images, sensations) as Edward B. TITCHENER advocated, psychologists ought to study the evolutionary utility or functions of consciousness. Providing the foundation of the school of BEHAVIORISM, functionalism as Angell and others defined it has exerted widespread influence on psychology in the United States. Angell received many honors, including election to the National Academy of Sciences in 1920 and the American Academy of Arts and Sciences in 1932.

Angelman syndrome a congenital disorder, caused by a genetic abnormality on chromosome 15, characterized by abnormalities or im-

A

pairments in neurological, motor, and cognitive functioning, including severe learning disabilities, absence of speech, and a stiff, jerky gait and movements (see ATAXIA). Individuals with Angelman syndrome have happy dispositions and a propensity for paroxysms of inappropriate laughter. Craniofacial abnormalities, including a small or unusually flattened head, a large mouth, and a protruding jaw, are also common. The condition was formerly called **happy-puppet syndrome**. [Harry **Angelman** (1915–1996), British pediatrician]

anger *n.* an emotion characterized by tension and hostility arising from frustration, real or imagined injury by another, or perceived injustice. It can manifest itself in behaviors designed to remove the object of the anger (e.g., determined action) or behaviors designed merely to express the emotion (e.g., swearing). Anger is distinct from, but a significant activator of, AGGRESSION, which is behavior intended to harm someone or something. Despite their mutually influential relationship, anger is neither necessary nor sufficient for aggression to occur.

anger control therapy a treatment that makes use of therapist-guided progressive exposure to anger-provoking cues in conjunction with therapist modeling, client rehearsal, assertiveness training, and other forms of coping skills training. Practiced in both individual and group settings, the intervention is used with clients who have general difficulty with anger (e.g., intensity, frequency, or mode of expression) or with clients who have specific disorders. See also ANGER MANAGEMENT.

anger-in *n.* hostility turned inward, particularly as a source of depression. See also SELF-ACCUSATION.

anger management techniques used by individuals—sometimes in counseling or therapy—to control their inappropriate reactions to anger-provoking stimuli and to express their feelings of anger in appropriate ways that are respectful of others. Such techniques include using relaxation methods (breathing deeply, repeating a word or phrase, visualizing a relaxing experience) to reduce physiological responses to anger, replacing exaggerated or overly dramatic thoughts with more rational ones (see COGNITIVE RESTRUCTURING), communicating more calmly and thoughtfully about one's anger, and removing oneself from situations or circumstances that provoke anger or avoiding them altogether.

angst *n.* **1.** fear or anxiety (German). **2.** in EXISTENTIALISM, a state of anguish or despair in which a person recognizes the fundamental uncertainty of existence and understands the significance of conscious choice and personal responsibility.

anhedonia *n.* the inability to enjoy experiences or activities that normally would be pleasurable. It is one of two defining symptoms of a MAJOR DEPRESSIVE EPISODE (the other being a persistent depressed mood), but is also seen in other disorders, including schizophrenia. [first defined in 1897 by French psychologist Théodule Ribot (1839–1916)] **—anhedonic** *adj.*

anhypnia *n.* see INSOMNIA.

aniconia *n.* an absence of mental imagery.

anilides *pl. n.* a group of aniline derivatives developed as analgesics and antipyretics of which ACETAMINOPHEN is the only member in current use. The parent compound, **acetanilide**, was originally introduced in 1886 as an antipyretic, but its toxicity led to its disuse and the development of a number of derivatives, including **phenacetin** (**acetophenetidin**; no longer in clinical use) and acetaminophen.

anilingus *n.* the practice of applying the mouth to the anus as a form of sexual activity. Also called **aniliction**; **anililagnia**.

anima *n.* **1.** in the earlier writings of Carl JUNG, a person's innermost being, which is in closest contact with the UNCONSCIOUS and is contrasted with the PERSONA, or the externally directed part of a person. **2.** in Jung's later writings, (a) an ARCHETYPE that represents universal feminine characteristics or (b) the unconscious feminine aspect of the male psyche. Compare ANIMUS.

animal-assisted therapy the therapeutic use of pets to enhance individuals' physical, social, emotional, or cognitive functioning. Animal-assisted therapy may be used, for example, to help people receive and give affection, especially in developing communication and social skills. It may be most effective for people who have suffered losses or separation from loved ones. Also called **pet-assisted therapy**; **pet therapy**.

animal magnetism a hypothetical physical force that allegedly can have a curative effect when focused on ailing parts of the body, often through the use of a magnetized wand, magnetized rods, or a magnetized bath. See MESMERISM. [proposed by Austrian physician Franz Anton Mesmer (1734–1815), who claimed some success using this method]

animal phobia a persistent and irrational fear of a particular type of animal, such as snakes, cats, dogs, mice, or birds. The focus of fear is often anticipated harm or danger. The emotion of disgust may also play a role in the maintenance of certain animal phobias (e.g., mice). Situations in which the phobic animal may be encountered are often avoided or else endured with intense anxiety or distress. Animal phobias typically start in childhood. The *DSM–IV–TR* designation is SPECIFIC PHOBIA, animal type.

animatism *n.* the belief that within all entities, living and nonliving, there exist supernatural forces or powers.

animism *n.* the belief that natural phenomena or inanimate objects are alive or possess lifelike characteristics, such as intentions, desires, and feelings. **—animistic** *adj.*

A

animus *n.* in ANALYTIC PSYCHOLOGY, (a) an ARCHETYPE that represents universal masculine characteristics or (b) the unconscious masculine component of the female psyche. Compare ANIMA. [sense originated by Carl JUNG]

aniridia-oligophrenia-cerebellar ataxia syndrome a rare form of mental retardation in which the patient also suffers from lack of normal muscle control and has speech difficulty. Lenses and corneas may be normal, but the eyes lack irises and visual acuity is in a range between 20/100 and 20/200. Also called **Gillespie syndrome**.

Anna O. the pseudonym of Austrian social worker and feminist Bertha Pappenheim (1859–1936), who was a patient of Austrian physician Josef Breuer (1842–1925), a colleague of Sigmund FREUD. Breuer's treatment of her hysteria was written up in an early case study that was an important precursor to PSYCHOANALYSIS. See also TALKING CURE.

annihilation *n.* complete destruction. In psychoanalytic theory, annihilation is destruction of the self. In OBJECT RELATIONS THEORY, fear of annihilation (**annihilation anxiety**) is viewed as the earliest form of anxiety. Melanie KLEIN attributed it to the experience of the DEATH INSTINCT; British psychoanalyst Donald Winnicott (1896–1971) saw it as the anxiety that accompanies IMPINGEMENTS from the environment. **—annihilate** *vb.*

anniversary event the annual occurrence of a date marking a significant event or experience that may be positive or negative.

anniversary reaction a strong emotional response on the anniversary of a significant event. It most commonly involves depressive symptoms around the same time of the year that the death of a loved one or a severe disappointment or adverse event occurred.

annulment *n.* in psychoanalytic theory, a process in which disagreeable ideas or events are neutralized or made ineffective by converting them into daydreams and fantasies. Compare REPRESSION.

anodyne *n.* any agent or procedure that relieves pain, including analgesics (e.g., aspirin), anesthetics, or acupuncture.

anoetic *adj.* **1.** not involving or subject to intellectual or cognitive processes. Emotions are sometimes considered anoetic. **2.** describing a level of knowledge or memory in which there is no consciousness of knowing or remembering. **Anoetic consciousness** is a corresponding state of "unknowing knowing" in which one is aware of external stimuli but not of interpreting them. [defined by Estonian-born Canadian psychologist Endel Tulving (1927–)] **3.** lacking the capacity for understanding or concentrated thought. This meaning, originally applied to denote mental retardation, is no longer common. Compare AUTONOETIC; NOETIC. **—anoesis** *n.*

anomalous experience any of a variety of conscious states, often categorized as ALTERED STATES OF CONSCIOUSNESS, that are uncommon or that are believed to deviate from the usually accepted explanations of reality. Examples include OUT-OF-BODY EXPERIENCES, mystical experiences, lucid dreaming, and SYNESTHESIA.

anomaly *n.* anything that is irregular or deviates from the norm, often referring to a congenital or developmental defect. **—anomalous** *adj.*

anomia *n.* **1.** loss or impairment of the ability to name objects. All individuals with APHASIA exhibit anomia, and the extent of naming difficulty is a good general measure of aphasia severity. **2.** an obsolete term for a defective moral sense. [defined by U.S. physician Benjamin Rush (1745–1813)] **—anomic** *adj.*

anomic suicide a former name for a suicide in response to an unfavorable change in the person's financial or social situation. [first defined by French sociologist Émile Durkheim (1858–1917)]

anomie *n.* a sense of alienation and hopelessness in a society or group that is often a response to social upheaval. It may also be accompanied by changes in personal and social values. **—anomic** *adj.*

anorectant *n.* see APPETITE SUPPRESSANT. Also called **anorexiant**.

anorexia *n.* absence or loss of appetite for food or, less commonly, for other desires (e.g., sex), especially when chronic. It may be primarily a psychological disorder, as in ANOREXIA NERVOSA, or it may have physiological causes, such as hypopituitarism. **—anorectic** or **anorexic** *adj., n.*

anorexia mirabilis a CULTURE-BOUND SYNDROME found in medieval Europe, characterized by severe restriction of food intake associated with religious devotion and piety. Also called **holy anorexia**.

anorexia nervosa an eating disorder, occurring most frequently in adolescent girls, that involves persistent refusal of food, excessive fear of weight gain, refusal to maintain minimally normal body weight, disturbed perception of body image, and amenorrhea (absence of at least three menstrual periods). See also REVERSE ANOREXIA.

anorgasmia *n.* the inability to achieve orgasm. Also called **anorgasmy**. See also FEMALE ORGASMIC DISORDER; MALE ORGASMIC DISORDER. **—anorgasmic** *adj.*

anosmia *n.* absence or loss of the ability to smell, which may be general or limited to certain odors. General or total anosmia implies inability to smell all odorants on both sides of the nose, whereas partial anosmia implies an inability to smell certain odorants. **—anosmic** *adj.*

anosognosia *n.* a neurologically based failure to recognize the existence of a deficit or disorder, such as hearing loss, poor vision, or paralysis.

A

ANTON'S SYNDROME is an example of anosognosia for blindness.

ANOVA acronym for ANALYSIS OF VARIANCE.

anovulatory menstrual cycle a menstrual cycle that occurs without ovulation. It results from an imbalance between hormone production of the pituitary gland and the ovaries and is marked by irregular menstruation. An anovulatory menstrual cycle is most likely to be associated with menarche or menopause.

anoxemia *n.* the absence of oxygen in the blood, a condition that frequently results in loss of consciousness and brain damage. See also HYPOXEMIA. **—anoxemic** *adj.*

anoxia *n.* total lack of oxygen in the body tissues, including the brain. Consequences depend on the severity of the anoxia and the specific areas of the brain that are affected, but can include generalized cognitive deficits or more focal deficits in memory, perception, or EXECUTIVE FUNCTION. Anoxia sometimes is used as a synonym of HYPOXIA. **—anoxic** *adj.*

ANS abbreviation for AUTONOMIC NERVOUS SYSTEM.

Antabuse *n.* a trade name for DISULFIRAM.

antagonist *n.* a drug or other chemical agent that inhibits the action of another substance. For example, an antagonist may combine with the substance to alter and thus inactivate it (**chemical antagonism**); an antagonist may reduce the effects of the substance by binding to the same receptor without stimulating it, which decreases the number of available receptors (**pharmacological antagonism**); or an antagonist may bind to a different receptor and produce a physiological effect opposite to that of the substance (**physiological antagonism**). Compare AGONIST. **—antagonism** *n.* **—antagonistic** *adj.*

antecedent variable a variable (*a*) that precedes another variable (*b*) but that may or may not be causally related to variable *b*.

anterograde amnesia see AMNESIA.

anterograde memory the ability to retain events, experiences, and other information following a particular point in time. When this ability is impaired (i.e., by injury or disease), it becomes very difficult or even impossible to recall what happened from that moment forward, a condition known as anterograde AMNESIA. For example, an individual with deficits of anterograde memory resulting from a stroke might not remember the name of a new person introduced to him or her but would remember the name of a close childhood friend. Compare RETROGRADE MEMORY.

antiaging remedy any intervention that is hypothesized to slow down or reverse the effects of aging. Typically these interventions are pharmacological (e.g., antioxidants, vitamin C, growth hormones), but they also can be lifestyle changes (e.g., exercise).

antiandrogen *n.* a substance that reduces or blocks the physiological effects of androgens, the male sex hormones, on tissues normally responsive to these hormones. Examples include **bicalutamide** (U.S. trade name: **Casodex**), **finasteride** (U.S. trade name: **Propecia**), **flutamide** (U.S. trade name: **Eulexin**), and **nilutamide** (U.S. trade name: **Nilandron**).

antiandrogen therapy medical treatment using ANTIANDROGENS to correct the effects of excessive levels of male sex hormones. It may be used to control hair loss and cancer of the prostate in males and to reverse masculine traits (e.g., excessive facial hair) in females. More controversially, antiandrogens have been used in the treatment of repeat sex offenders (see CHEMICAL CASTRATION).

antianxiety medication see ANXIOLYTIC.

antibiotics *pl. n.* drugs that are used to destroy pathogenic or otherwise harmful microorganisms, especially bacteria. Antibiotics can be produced by or obtained from living cells (e.g., molds, yeasts, or bacteria) or manufactured as synthetic chemicals with effects similar to natural antibiotics. Some work by interfering with bacterial reproduction, while others may disrupt the normal life functions of the pathogen. Antibiotics are ineffective against viruses. Overuse and inappropriate use of antibiotics are contributing to the development of bacterial resistance to many commonly used antibiotics.

anticathexis *n.* in psychoanalytic theory, a process in which the EGO withdraws PSYCHIC ENERGY from certain unconscious wishes and ideas and uses it to strengthen other ideas and wishes capable of blocking their entrance into consciousness. The **anticathected** idea may be similar to the original idea or opposite but related to it: for example, philanthropy may neutralize an unconscious wish to hoard. Also called **countercathexis**. See also CATHEXIS.

anticholinergic drug any pharmacological agent that blocks or otherwise interferes with the release of the neurotransmitter acetylcholine and thus disrupts the transmission of impulses along parasympathetic routes. Because they act at MUSCARINIC RECEPTORS (a category of acetylcholine receptors), these agents are also known as **antimuscarinic drugs**. In large doses, they may also interfere with actions of histamine, serotonin, and norepinephrine. Natural anticholinergic drugs include ATROPINE and SCOPOLAMINE. A variety of synthetic anticholinergic drugs are used to treat neurological disorders, many as ANTIPARKINSONIAN DRUGS. They include BENZTROPINE, BIPERIDEN, PROCYCLIDINE, and TRIHEXYPHENIDYL, which are administered primarily to relieve the symptoms of muscular rigidity. Anticholinergic drugs are often used in combinations to control specific symptoms. TRICYCLIC ANTIDEPRESSANTS and some conventional ANTIPSYCHOTICS also have anticholinergic activity. Also called **parasympatholytic drugs**.

anticholinergic effects side effects that are

characteristic of ANTICHOLINERGIC DRUGS and are also associated with other agents (e.g., TRICYCLIC ANTIDEPRESSANTS, MONOAMINE OXIDASE INHIBITORS) that exert antagonist effects at MUSCARINIC RECEPTORS. They include dry mouth, blurred vision, urinary hesitancy or retention, and constipation. Also called **antimuscarinic effects**. See also ANTICHOLINERGIC SYNDROME.

anticholinergic ileus obstruction of the small bowel (ileum) due to paralysis of its muscle, resulting from administration of agents that block MUSCARINIC RECEPTORS in the bowel. Though rare, it may be caused by strongly ANTICHOLINERGIC DRUGS, such as tricyclic antidepressants and some older antipsychotics. Ileus may be fatal and requires medical intervention.

anticholinergic syndrome a disorder produced by anticholinergic drugs and due to their antagonistic effects at ACETYLCHOLINE RECEPTORS, marked by symptoms involving both the peripheral and central nervous systems. The former include dry mucous membranes, dry mouth, and flushed skin and face, while the latter include ataxia (unsteady gait), drowsiness, slurred speech, confusion and disorientation, hallucinations, and memory deficits, particularly of short-term memory. Tricyclic antidepressants, aliphatic phenothiazines, antiparkinsonian agents, and scopolamine are examples of drugs that can cause anticholinergic syndrome. This syndrome is often observed in patients receiving combinations of such drugs. See CENTRAL ANTICHOLINERGIC SYNDROME.

anticholinesterase *n.* see CHOLINESTERASE.

anticipation *n.* **1.** looking forward to a future event or state, sometimes with an affective component (e.g., pleasure, anxiety). **2.** the onset of a hereditary disease at earlier and earlier ages in successive generations.

anticipatory anxiety worry or apprehension about an upcoming event or situation because of the possibility of a negative outcome, such as danger, misfortune, or adverse judgment by others. The worry or apprehension is often accompanied by somatic symptoms of tension. Anticipatory anxiety is a common feature of PANIC DISORDER, in which the concern is over the possibility of experiencing future panic attacks.

anticipatory grief sorrow and anxiety experienced by someone who expects a loved one to die within a short period. The period of anticipatory grief can be regarded as having both stressful and constructive possibilities: It might cushion the emotional impact when the death actually occurs, but it could have the unfortunate consequence of leading a person to withdraw from the relationship, treating the other person as though he or she were already dead. See also COMPLICATED GRIEF; TRAUMATIC GRIEF. [introduced as a concept in 1944 by U.S. psychologist Erich Lindemann (1900–1974)]

anticipatory guidance counseling and educational services provided to individuals or families before they reach a turning point or significant developmental change in their lives. Examples include parental guidance before a child enters school and counseling of employees soon to reach retirement age.

anticipatory nausea nausea that occurs prior to chemotherapy (typically during the day before administration). Nausea and vomiting can also occur after an individual has received a few treatments, usually in response to triggers in the environment (e.g., odors and sights of the hospital room) that have been associated with the physical side effects of chemotherapy.

anticipatory regret a sense of the potential negative consequences of a decision that influences the choice made: For example, an individual may decide not to make an investment because of the feelings associated with an imagined loss. See PROSPECT THEORY.

anticonvulsant *n.* any drug used to reduce the frequency or severity of epileptic seizures or to terminate a seizure already underway. Until the advent of the HYDANTOINS in the 1930s, anticonvulsants consisted mainly of BROMIDES and BARBITURATES: PHENOBARBITAL was first used in the treatment of epilepsy in 1912 and remained the mainstay of treatment until the introduction of the hydantoin PHENYTOIN. Drugs now used to treat partial or tonic–clonic seizures include phenytoin, CARBAMAZEPINE, VALPROIC ACID, phenobarbital, and newer anticonvulsants, such as LAMOTRIGINE, GABAPENTIN, tiagabine, TOPIRAMATE, vigabatrin, and zonisamide. Ethosuximide and other SUCCINIMIDES may be used in managing absence seizures. The BENZODIAZEPINES are also effective antiseizure medications. Also called **antiepileptic**.

antidepressant *n.* any drug administered in the treatment of depression. Most antidepressants work by increasing the availability of monoamine neurotransmitters such as norepinephrine, serotonin, or dopamine, although they do so by different routes. The MONOAMINE OXIDASE INHIBITORS (MAOIs) work by inhibiting monoamine oxidase, one of the principal enzymes that metabolize these neurotransmitters. Most of the other antidepressants, including the TRICYCLIC ANTIDEPRESSANTS (TCAs) and the selective serotonin reuptake inhibitors (see SSRI), inhibit the reuptake of serotonin or norepinephrine (and to a much lesser degree dopamine) into the presynaptic neuron. Either process leaves more of the neurotransmitter free to bind with postsynaptic receptors, initiating a series of events in the postsynaptic neuron that is thought to produce the actual therapeutic effect.

antiepileptic *n.* see ANTICONVULSANT.

antiestrogen *n.* a substance that reduces or blocks the physiological effects of estrogens, the female sex hormones, on tissues normally responsive to these hormones. Examples include **tamoxifen** (U.S. trade name: **Nolvadex**), **toremifene** (U.S. trade name: **Fareston**), **fulvestrant** (U.S. trade name: **Faslodex**), and **selective estrogen receptor modulators** (SERMs), such as **raloxifene** (U.S. trade name: **Evista**), which have both inhibitory and facilitative effects upon different pathways mediated by estrogen receptors. Antiestrogens are variously used in the treatment or prevention of breast cancer and some estrogenically mediated effects of menopause and also in the treatment of some types of female infertility. Also called **estrogen antagonist**.

antiharassment policies policies and procedures adopted by an organization or institution to prevent and counter harassment due to gender, race, or sexual orientation. They typically include conducting awareness training designed to educate people about harassment, implementing disciplinary measures when necessary, and having formal grievance procedures.

antihistamine *n.* any drug or agent that inhibits the effects of HISTAMINE at central or peripheral histamine receptors. They may have sedative effects and are a common component of over-the-counter sleeping aids. Others (e.g., **diphenhydramine**, U.S. trade name: **Benadryl**; and **dimenhydrinate**, U.S. trade name: **Dramamine**) are used in the treatment of allergic reactions or motion sickness. The so-called **nonsedating antihistamines** have less ability to cross the BLOOD–BRAIN BARRIER and are used solely in the management of allergic responses. Also called **histamine antagonist**.

anti-intoxicant *n.* a theoretical drug that would have the effect of countering the intoxicating effects of alcohol. Also called **amethystic**.

antilibidinal ego in the OBJECT RELATIONS THEORY of British psychoanalyst W. Ronald D. Fairbairn (1889–1964), the portion of the EGO STRUCTURE that is similar to Sigmund FREUD'S SUPEREGO. The antilibidinal ego constitutes a nonpleasure-gratifying, self-deprecatory, or even hostile self-image; it is posited to develop out of the unitary ego present at birth when the infantile libidinal ego (similar to the ID) experiences deprivation at the hands of the parent and the infant suppresses his or her frustrated needs. Also called **internal saboteur**. See FAIRBAIRNIAN THEORY.

Antilirium *n.* a trade name for PHYSOSTIGMINE.

antimanic drugs see MOOD STABILIZER.

antimetabolite *n.* a substance that has a molecular structure so similar to that of another substance required for a normal physiological function that it may be accepted as the required molecule, thereby disrupting a normal metabolic process. For example, the anticoagulant bishydroxycoumarin functions as an antimetabolite by interfering with vitamin K in producing the blood-clotting agent prothrombin.

antimuscarinic drug see ANTICHOLINERGIC DRUG.

antinociceptive *adj.* describing or relating to any factor that increases tolerance for, or reduces sensitivity to, harmful stimuli, usually stimuli that cause pain. See also PAIN PERCEPTION.

antinodal behavior see NODAL BEHAVIOR.

antiparkinsonian drug any pharmacological agent that reduces the severity of symptoms of Parkinson's disease or drug-induced parkinsonism (common with the use of conventional ANTIPSYCHOTICS), including tremors, movement and gait abnormalities, and muscle rigidity. Antiparkinsonian agents include histamine antagonists (e.g., DIPHENHYDRAMINE), anticholinergic drugs (e.g., BENZTROPINE, TRIHEXYPHENIDYL), DOPAMINE-RECEPTOR AGONISTS (e.g., carbidopa, levodopa), and specific enzyme inhibitors.

antipsychiatry *n.* an international movement that emerged in the 1960s under the leadership of British psychiatrist Ronnie D. Laing (1927–1989), South African psychiatrist David Cooper (1931–1986), Italian psychiatrist Franco Basaglia (1924–1980), and U.S. psychoanalyst Thomas Szasz (1920–). Antipsychiatrists contested the scientific and practical validity of psychiatry and radically opposed what they understood as a hospital-centered medical specialty legally empowered to treat and institutionalize individuals with mental disorders. Indeed, many antipsychiatrists argued against the very existence of mental disorders themselves, advancing the notion that mental illnesses are not illnesses at all but rather alternative ways of behaving that alarm people. They viewed psychiatry as a form of social repression and a means to control deviance, and treatment as a disguised form of punishment. **—antipsychiatrist** *n.*

antipsychotic *n.* any pharmacological agent used to control the symptoms of schizophrenia and other disorders characterized by impaired reality testing, as evidenced by severely disorganized thought, speech, and behavior. Formerly called **major tranquilizers** and later **neuroleptics**, antipsychotics are commonly divided into two major classes: **conventional** (**first-generation**) **antipsychotics**, including the PHENOTHIAZINES and BUTYROPHENONES, and the newer **atypical** (**novel** or **second-generation**) **antipsychotics**, of which CLOZAPINE is the prototype. The latter class has fewer adverse side effects than the former, particularly the neurologically based EXTRAPYRAMIDAL SYMPTOMS but also the less serious yet unpleasant autonomic effects, such as dry mouth and blurred vision.

antipyretics *pl. n.* drugs that help control fever or other forms of hyperthermia (raised body temperature) by acting on the thermoregulatory center in the hypothalamus. They may also help the body to dissipate heat faster by dilating peripheral arteries. Aspirin and other nonopioid analgesics function as antipyretics.

A

antisocial *adj.* denoting or exhibiting behavior that sharply deviates from social norms and also violates other people's rights. Arson and vandalism are examples of antisocial behavior. Compare PROSOCIAL.

antisocial behavior aggressive, impulsive, and sometimes violent actions that violate the established rules, conventions, and codes of a society, such as the laws upholding personal and property rights. Compare PROSOCIAL BEHAVIOR.

antisocial personality disorder the presence of a chronic and pervasive disposition to disregard and violate the rights of others. Manifestations include repeated violations of the law, exploitation of others, deceitfulness, impulsivity, aggressiveness, reckless disregard for the safety of self and others, and irresponsibility, accompanied by lack of guilt, remorse, and empathy. The disorder has been known by various names, including **dyssocial personality**, **psychopathic personality**, and **sociopathic personality**. It is among the most heavily researched of the personality disorders and the most difficult to treat.

antispasmodic drug any pharmacological agent used in the management of spasms of smooth muscle. They are commonly used to treat gastrointestinal conditions such as IRRITABLE BOWEL SYNDROME.

antitussives *pl. n.* drugs that suppress coughing by affecting the cough-control center in the medulla oblongata of the brain. Because the cough center is sensitive to OPIOIDS, these drugs are effective in suppressing cough. Opioids used as antitussives include codeine and DEXTROMETHORPHAN. Also called **cough suppressants**.

antiviral drugs substances that interfere with the normal functioning of viruses. They may act by blocking host-cell enzyme systems required for viral reproduction, by blocking signals carried in messenger RNA, or by uncoating the nucleic acid molecule of the virus. Antiviral drugs are difficult to manage in clinical practice because chemicals that block viral processes may also interfere with the patient's normal cell functions. Antivirals occasionally interact with substances in human tissues to yield unexpected benefits, as with AMANTADINE, which can be used as an antiparkinsonian agent.

antivitamin *n.* a substance that interferes with the functions of vitamins. Most antivitamins are chemicals that are similar in structure to the vitamins they render ineffective. They are used mainly in studies and tests of vitamin deficiencies.

Anton's syndrome a rare disorder marked by the lack of awareness of blindness. The person genuinely believes he or she can see despite clinical evidence of loss of vision, such as difficulties in getting around, handling objects, and so forth. The condition is a type of visual ANOSOGNOSIA resulting from injury to the occipital lobe of the brain. [first described in 1899 by Gabriel **Anton** (1858–1933), Austrian physician]

antonym test an examination in which the respondent is presented with a word and asked to supply a word with the opposite meaning to it (e.g., being given "true" and replying "false"). Also called **opposites test**.

anxiety *n.* an emotion characterized by apprehension and somatic symptoms of tension in which an individual anticipates impending danger, catastrophe, or misfortune. The body often mobilizes itself to meet the perceived threat: Muscles become tense, breathing is faster, and the heart beats more rapidly. Anxiety may be distinguished from FEAR both conceptually and physiologically, although the two terms are often used interchangeably. The former is considered a disproportionate response to a vague, unidentifiable threat whereas the latter is an appropriate response to a clearly identifiable and specific threat. —**anxious** *adj.*

anxiety attack see PANIC ATTACK.

anxiety discharge any anxiety-reducing action or repetitive activity (e.g., exercise, knitting, weeding a garden) associated with normal daily living, viewed as an alternative to suppression of anxiety.

anxiety disorder any of a group of disorders that have as their central organizing theme the emotional state of fear, worry, or anxious apprehension. This category includes OBSESSIVE-COMPULSIVE DISORDER, PANIC DISORDER, various PHOBIAS, POSTTRAUMATIC STRESS DISORDER, and GENERALIZED ANXIETY DISORDER. Anxiety disorders have a chronic course, albeit waxing and waning in intensity, and are among the most common mental health problems in the United States.

anxiety disorder due to a general medical condition significant anxiety (e.g., generalized anxiety, panic attacks, obsessions, and compulsions) deemed to be caused directly by the physiological effects of a general medical condition. Anxiety may be caused by a number of such conditions, including endocrine disorders (e.g., hyperthyroidism), respiratory disorders (e.g., chronic obstructive pulmonary disease), cardiovascular disorders (e.g., arrhythmia), metabolic disorders (e.g., vitamin B_{12} deficiency), and neurological disorders (e.g., vestibular dysfunction).

anxiety disorder not otherwise specified clinically significant anxiety or phobic avoidance that does not meet the criteria for a specific anxiety disorder in *DSM–IV–TR*.

anxiety disturbance a condition characterized by a marked, persistent, and excessive anxiety that causes a significant degree of emotional distress, impairment in functioning (e.g., social, academic, occupational), or both. See ANXIETY DISORDER.

A

anxiety equivalent in psychoanalysis, a conscious, observable symptom of ANXIETY, such as trembling or nausea.

anxiety fixation in psychoanalysis, the maintenance or continuation of an anxiety reaction from an earlier developmental stage into a later one.

anxiety hierarchy a series of graduated anxiety-arousing stimuli centering on a specific source of anxiety in a specific individual. It is used in the treatment of phobias by SYSTEMATIC DESENSITIZATION: Patients proceed along the hierarchy from the least threatening situation toward the most threatening situation.

anxiety hysteria in psychoanalysis, a neurosis in which the anxiety generated by unconscious sexual conflicts is expressed in phobic symptoms, such as an irrational fear of dirt or open spaces, and in physical disturbances that are conversion symptoms. The term is now seldom used because it combines disorders that are now classified separately. See ANXIETY DISORDER; CONVERSION DISORDER. [defined by Sigmund FREUD]

anxiety management cognitive-behavioral, behavioral, or other techniques that aid in the reduction of anxiety, such as BIOFEEDBACK TRAINING, RELAXATION TECHNIQUES, or medication.

anxiety neurosis in psychoanalysis, a disturbance or neurosis in which the most prominent symptoms are persistent anxiety, feelings of impending disaster, and FREE-FLOATING FEAR accompanied by such symptoms as difficulty in making decisions, insomnia, loss of appetite, and heart palpitations. This term is now seldom used: The current classification of chronic anxiety of this nature is GENERALIZED ANXIETY DISORDER. Also called **anxiety state**. See also ANXIETY DISORDER.

anxiety nightmare a frightening dream that is sometimes taken to represent the fears of the dreamer.

anxiety object in psychoanalysis, an object upon which anxiety originally caused by another source is displaced. For example, a nonhuman object may be feared because it represents the father who caused the original anxiety. See LITTLE HANS.

anxiety reaction an emotional response characterized by marked apprehension and accompanied by somatic symptoms of tension.

anxiety-relief response in BEHAVIOR THERAPY, the repetition of reassuring or tranquilizing words (e.g., "calm") in anxiety-provoking situations.

anxiety scale any of numerous assessment instruments designed to measure the severity of anxiety symptoms. An important example is the TAYLOR MANIFEST ANXIETY SCALE. Such scales usually take the form of self-report tests but can also be based on clinician ratings or actual performance.

anxiety sensitivity fear of sensations associated with anxiety because of the belief that they will have harmful consequences. For example, an individual with high anxiety sensitivity is likely to regard feeling lightheaded as a sign of impending illness or fainting, whereas an individual with low anxiety sensitivity would tend to regard this sensation as simply unpleasant. Research indicates that high anxiety sensitivity is a personality risk factor for the development of PANIC ATTACKS and PANIC DISORDER.

anxiety state 1. see ANXIETY NEUROSIS. **2.** formerly, a traumatic neurosis precipitated by a wartime experience in which the ego-ideals of war conflict with customary ideals. [defined by Sigmund FREUD]

anxiolytic *n.* any of a class of drugs used in the control of anxiety, mild behavioral agitation, and insomnia. Formerly called **minor tranquilizers**, they can also be used as adjunctive agents in the treatment of depression and panic disorder. The most widely used anxiolytics are the BENZODIAZEPINES. See also AZAPIRONE; SEDATIVE, HYPNOTIC, AND ANXIOLYTIC DRUGS.

anxious–ambivalent attachment style an interpersonal style characterized by worry that a partner will break off a relationship or by hesitancy in forming deeply committed relationships despite a desire to do so. See also ATTACHMENT THEORY.

anxious–avoidant attachment in the STRANGE SITUATION, a form of INSECURE ATTACHMENT in which an infant explores only minimally and tends to avoid or be indifferent to the parent.

anxious–avoidant attachment style see AVOIDANT ATTACHMENT STYLE.

anxious depression a MAJOR DEPRESSIVE EPISODE accompanied by high levels of anxiety.

anxious–resistant attachment in the STRANGE SITUATION, a form of INSECURE ATTACHMENT in which an infant appears anxious in the parent's presence, distressed in the parent's absence, and angry upon the parent's return, often resisting contact with him or her.

aortic arch syndrome a disorder caused by progressive obliteration of the main branches of the aortic arch because of arteriosclerosis, aneurysm, or a related problem. Usually only one or two of the branches are involved, affecting blood flow to a local area. If the carotid or vertebral arteries are involved, the brain will be affected. The patient may experience fainting spells, epilepsy-like seizures, temporary blindness, paralysis on one side of the body, aphasia, memory disturbances, or a combination of symptoms. A typical effect is the **carotid-sinus syndrome**, in which the patient faints after turning the head. Collateral circulation may develop to compensate for some degree of interrupted blood flow, but progressive loss of vision may occur in the meantime.

APA **1.** abbreviation for AMERICAN PSYCHIATRIC ASSOCIATION. **2.** abbreviation for AMERICAN PSYCHOLOGICAL ASSOCIATION.

APAP *n.* see ACETAMINOPHEN.

apareunia *n.* **1.** the inability to perform sexual intercourse. **2.** abstinence from coitus.

apastia *n.* fasting or abstinence from food. Compare APHAGIA.

apathy *n.* indifference and lack of response to one's surroundings. Apathy is commonly associated with severe depression or schizophrenia. **—apathetic** *adj.*

apathy syndrome the pattern of emotional insulation (indifference, detachment) adopted by many prisoners-of-war and other victims of catastrophes in an effort to maintain their stability.

Apert's syndrome an inherited condition in which an abnormally shaped head due to premature closure of some of the cranial sutures is accompanied by mental retardation and syndactyly (partial or complete fusion of the digits). The syndactyly usually involves both hands and feet and typically results in fusion of the skin and bones, marked by "mitten hands" and "sock feet." Apert's syndrome may be complicated by CROUZON'S SYNDROME (and called **Apert–Crouzon syndrome**), in which case fusion of the digits is partial. Both syndromes are dominant traits (see ACROCEPHALOSYNDACTYLY). [Eugène **Apert** (1868–1940), French pediatrician]

aphagia *n.* inability to swallow or eat. Compare HYPERPHAGIA. **—aphagic** *adj.*

aphanisis *n.* an obsolete term indicating total extinction of sexual desire. [from Greek *aphanes*, "invisible": defined by British physician Ernest Jones (1879–1958)]

aphasia *n.* an acquired language impairment that results from neurological damage to the language areas of the brain, which are typically located in the left hemisphere. Common causes of damage include stroke, cerebral hemorrhage, brain tumors, and cortical degenerative disorders (e.g., Alzheimer's disease). Traditionally, a distinction has been made between expressive and receptive forms of aphasia, whereby individuals with the former primarily have difficulty producing spoken and written language and those with the latter primarily have difficulty comprehending spoken and written language. A more contemporary distinction, however, is commonly made between **fluent aphasias**, characterized by plentiful verbal output consisting of well articulated, easily produced utterances of relatively normal length and prosody (rhythm and intonation), and **nonfluent aphasias**, characterized by sparse, effortful utterances of short phrase length and disrupted prosody. Fluent aphasias are associated with posterior lesions that spare cortical regions critical for motor control of speech, whereas nonfluent aphasias are associated with anterior lesions that compromise motor and premotor cortical regions involved in speech production. Numerous types of aphasia exist, for example BROCA'S APHASIA and WERNICKE'S APHASIA. Also (but much less preferably) called **dysphasia**. **—aphasic** *adj.*

aphemia *n.* as originally defined by French physician Pierre Paul Broca (1824–1880), a motor APHASIA with nonfluency (i.e., lack of speech) but intact language functions, as evidenced by intact writing. This condition was later renamed BROCA'S APHASIA.

aphonia *n.* loss of the voice resulting from disease of or damage to the larynx or vocal tract.

aphrodisiac *n.* any agent that is thought to facilitate sexual desire. Substances with such a reputation include perfumes and other odors, foods such as raw oysters, and various drugs, particularly alkaloids such as yohimbine.

apnea (**apnoea**) *n.* temporary suspension of respiration. If the **apneic period** is a long one, the heart may be slowed and EEG (electroencephalogram) changes may occur. Apnea can occur during sleep (see SLEEP APNEA) and is also found in many disorders, such as major epilepsy and concussion. **—apneic** *adj.*

apodia *n.* the condition of being born with only one foot or with no feet. See also ACHEIRIA.

apomorphine *n.* a morphine derivative used as an expectorant and to induce vomiting.

a posteriori denoting conclusions derived from observations or other manifest occurrences: reasoning causes from facts. When applied to HYPOTHESIS TESTING, this concept means an **a posteriori test**, which is a statistical test planned after research data have been examined because certain patterns in the data warrant further study. Compare A PRIORI. [Latin, "from the latter"]

apotemnophilia *n.* see ACROTOMOPHILIA.

apparition *n.* a visual illusion that results from distortion of a perceived object. Often interpreted as threatening, apparitions may be associated with a neurological or toxic disorder, such as ALCOHOL-INDUCED PSYCHOTIC DISORDER.

Appelt–Gerken–Lenz syndrome see ROBERTS SYNDROME.

apperception *n.* **1.** the mental process by which a perception or an idea is assimilated into an individual's existing knowledge, thoughts, and emotions See also TENDENTIOUS APPERCEPTION. **2.** the act or process of perceiving something consciously. **—apperceive** *vb.* **—apperceptive** *adj.*

appersonation *n.* a delusion in which the individual believes him- or herself to be another person and assumes the characteristics of that other person. Also called **appersonification**.

appetite suppressant any agent that reduces desire for food and thus controls body weight, including the amphetamines and other stimu-

A

lants (e.g., PHENTERMINE, DIETHYLPROPION), SIBUTRAMINE, and serotonin agonists (fenfluramine, dexfenfluramine). Use of the latter compounds, particularly in combination with phentermine (so-called "phen-fen"), resulted in heart-valve defects, and this combination was removed from the market. Although appetite suppressants may result in short-term weight loss, there is no evidence that they achieve long-term weight reduction unless used in conjunction with a behavioral management program. Also called **anorectant**; **anorexiant**.

appetition system EXTRAVERSION as represented by an individual's relative sensitivity to appetitive (positive, rewarding) cues and stimuli and his or her processes for approaching them. Compare AVERSION SYSTEM. [proposed by Hans EYSENCK]

applied behavior analysis (**ABA**) the extension of SKINNER's behavioral principles (i.e., operant conditioning) to practical settings. Variations of applied behavior analysis may be used clinically (in the form of BEHAVIOR MODIFICATION or BEHAVIOR THERAPY) as treatment for abnormal or problematic behaviors.

applied psychology the application of the theories, principles, and techniques of psychology to practical concerns, such as problems of living or coping, education, vocational guidance, industry, ergonomics, consumer affairs, advertising, political campaigns, and environmental issues. It may be contrasted with theoretical psychology or academic psychology, in which the emphasis is on understanding for its own sake rather than the utility of the knowledge.

applied relaxation a technique in which clients are taught, in a step-wise fashion, to relax more and more rapidly over a series of sessions in order to master panic, anxiety, phobias, pain, and other symptoms. The goal is for clients to be able to relax in 20–30 seconds in situations in which their symptoms typically occur. See also PROGRESSIVE RELAXATION.

applied tension a technique in BEHAVIOR THERAPY that focuses on changing physiological responses (e.g., low blood pressure leading to fainting) by having the client practice muscle tensing and releasing during exposure to increasingly anxiety-evoking stimuli associated with a feared situation. The technique was developed and is still primarily used for blood, injury, and injection phobias.

appraisal *n.* the cognitive evaluation of the nature and significance of a phenomenon or event. In **appraisal theories** of emotion, such evaluations are seen as determinants of emotional experience. See COGNITIVE APPRAISAL THEORY. **—appraise** *vb.*

appraisal motive the desire to gain accurate information about the self. It leads people to seek highly diagnostic feedback (see DIAGNOSTICITY) and to reject flattery or other bias. Compare CONSISTENCY MOTIVE; SELF-ENHANCEMENT MOTIVE.

apprehension *n.* **1.** uneasiness or dread about an upcoming event or the future generally. Also called **apprehensiveness**. **2.** the act or capability of grasping something mentally. Compare COMPREHENSION. **—apprehend** *vb.* **—apprehensible** *adj.* **—apprehensive** *adj.*

approach *n.* a particular method or strategy used to achieve a goal or purpose, for example, a psychodynamic approach in psychological research and practice.

approach–approach conflict a situation involving a choice between two equally desirable but incompatible alternatives. Also called **double-approach conflict**. See also APPROACH–AVOIDANCE CONFLICT; AVOIDANCE–AVOIDANCE CONFLICT.

approach–avoidance conflict a situation involving a single goal or option that has both desirable and undesirable aspects or consequences. The closer an individual comes to the goal, the greater the anxiety, but withdrawal from the goal then increases the desire. See also APPROACH–APPROACH CONFLICT; AVOIDANCE–AVOIDANCE CONFLICT; DOUBLE APPROACH–AVOIDANCE CONFLICT.

approach gradient the variation in the strength of a drive as a function of the organism's proximity to its goal. For example, a rat's goal-directed behavior increases in intensity as it nears its goal of food. The approach gradient appears less steep than the AVOIDANCE GRADIENT. See also APPROACH–APPROACH CONFLICT; APPROACH–AVOIDANCE CONFLICT.

approach motivation expectation of reward (e.g., a positive emotional experience), which is a condition for goal-directed behavior.

approach response any behavior that brings an organism closer to a stimulus. See ADIENCE.

appropriate affect an expression of mood or feeling that is in harmony with, or naturally indicative of, the accompanying thought, action, reaction, or verbal expression.

appropriate death the death a person would choose if given the opportunity. The concept draws attention to the differing needs and values of individuals in the terminal phase of life. It challenges the tendency to treat the disease rather than the patient and the assumption that a "good death" has the same meaning for all people. PALLIATIVE CARE, especially as given in HOSPICES, attempts to protect individuality and offers a communication process and caring environment providing the maximum possible opportunity for the dying person to make personally meaningful decisions.

approximation conditioning see SHAPING.

apraxia *n.* loss or impairment of the ability to perform purposeful, skilled movements despite intact motor function and comprehension. The condition may be developmental or induced by neurological dysfunction and is believed to represent an impairment of the ability to plan, select, and sequence the motor execution of movements. There are several major types of apraxia, including **buccofacial** (or **orofacial**) **apraxia**, involving difficulty performing skilled facial movements; **ideational apraxia**, involving difficulty carrying out in the proper order a series of acts that comprise a complex task; **ideomotor apraxia**, involving difficulty imitating actions or gesturing to command; **limb kinetic** (or **melokinetic**) **apraxia**, involving difficulty making precise, coordinated but individual finger movements; and **speech** (or **verbal**) **apraxia**, involving difficulty coordinating the movements necessary for speaking. **—apraxic** *adj.*

A prime (symbol: A′) a measure of the sensitivity for correctly detecting or remembering a stimulus in a task or test. This measure is based on the nonparametric theory of signal detection, which does not make stringent assumptions about the distribution of responses. See SIGNAL DETECTION THEORY.

a priori denoting conclusions derived from premises or principles: deducing effects from prior assumptions. When applied to HYPOTHESIS TESTING, this concept means an **a priori test**, which is a statistical test explicitly planned before research data have been examined and trends observed. Compare A POSTERIORI. [Latin, "prior to"]

aprosody *n.* absence of the normal variations in the rhythm, stress, and pitch of speech, resulting in monotone speech. Unusual or abnormal variations are known as **dysprosody** (or **dysprosodia**). Also called **aprosodia**.

APS 1. abbreviation for AMERICAN PSYCHOLOGICAL SOCIETY. **2.** abbreviation for AMERICAN PSYCHOSOMATIC SOCIETY.

APsaA abbreviation for AMERICAN PSYCHOANALYTIC ASSOCIATION.

aptitude–treatment interaction (**ATI**) a phenomenon in which people with certain attributes (e.g., personality traits, cognitive styles) respond better to one treatment, whereas people different attributes respond better to another treatment. The influence of personal characteristics upon treatment outcome is of particular interest in educational and psychotherapeutic contexts, given the goal of finding the optimal instructional method or intervention for different types of people.

Aquachloral *n.* a trade name for CHLORAL HYDRATE.

arachidonic acid a long-chain, polyunsaturated fatty acid that is a component of cell membranes. When liberated from the membrane by the enzyme phospholipase A2, it is transformed into a series of compounds known as eicosanoids, which serve as precursors for prostaglandins, thromboxanes, and leukotrienes.

arachneophobia *n.* see SPIDER PHOBIA.

arachnophobia *n.* see SPIDER PHOBIA.

arbitrary inference a COGNITIVE DISTORTION in which a person draws a conclusion that is unrelated to or contradicted by the evidence.

archaic inheritance presumed phylogenetic influences in the development of the individual's mental processes, such as the RACIAL MEMORY and ARCHETYPES of Carl Jung's ANALYTIC PSYCHOLOGY. See PHYLOGENY.

archetype *n.* **1.** a perfect or typical example of something or the original model from which something is held to derive. See also PROTOTYPE. **2.** in ANALYTIC PSYCHOLOGY, a structural component of the mind that derives from the accumulated experience of humankind. These inherited components are stored in the COLLECTIVE UNCONSCIOUS and serve as a frame of reference with which individuals view the world and as one of the major foundations on which the structure of the personality is built. Examples are ANIMA, ANIMUS, PERSONA, SHADOW, supreme being, MAGNA MATER, and hero. Also called **archetypal image**; **primordial image**. **—archetypal** *adj.*

arctic hysteria see PIBLOKTO.

area postrema a highly vascularized region of the brain located in the basal wall of the lateral VENTRICLE. Brain capillaries in this area form a relatively permeable region of the BLOOD–BRAIN BARRIER, enabling the passage of toxic substances to the underlying CHEMORECEPTOR TRIGGER ZONE, which elicits a vomiting response.

arecoline *n.* a drug, related to MUSCARINE, that stimulates smooth muscles and glands that respond to postganglionic cholinergic agents. It is used in veterinary medicine to eliminate internal parasites and was formerly used in the management of schizophrenia.

argumentativeness *n.* a persistent tendency to dispute and argue. **—argumentative** *adj.*

Aricept *n.* a trade name for DONEPEZIL.

aripiprazole *n.* an ATYPICAL ANTIPSYCHOTIC agent that is thought to exert its effects by binding to the presynaptic D2 dopamine AUTORECEPTOR, thereby inhibiting the release of dopamine from the presynaptic terminal. It is used in the treatment of schizophrenia. U.S. trade name: **Abilify**.

arithmetic mean see MEAN.

Armed Forces Qualification Test (**AFQT**) a screening test developed in 1950 by the Department of Defense to determine a person's eligibility for acceptance into U.S. military service by assessing his or her mental ability qualification. Originally consisting of 100 multiple-choice items measuring vocabulary, arithmetic, spatial relations, and mechanical ability, the AFQT was used as a stand-alone test until 1976, when the ARMED SERVICES VOCATIONAL APTITUDE BATTERY (ASVAB) became the official screening instrument of all U.S. military branches.

A

Armed Services Vocational Aptitude Battery (**ASVAB**) a test battery developed in 1966 by the Department of Defense for use by the U.S. military as a standardized instrument for personnel selection and classification (specific job assignment); in 1976 it became the official testing instrument of all U.S. military branches. It currently consists of nine timed multiple-choice tests in the areas of word knowledge, paragraph comprehension, arithmetic reasoning, mathematics knowledge, general science, auto and shop information, mechanical comprehension, electronics information, and assembling objects. The first four tests are used to determine eligibility for service (see ARMED FORCES QUALIFICATION TEST); the remainder are used to determine interests and aptitudes. Although sometimes administered to high school students to assist in career planning, the ASVAB is a required part of the application process for all potential military recruits.

armoring *n.* a defense mechanism used to distance oneself by withholding the expression of emotion through BLOCKING of one's experience and expression of life-affirming emotions (sadness, joy, anger, grief, and fear).

Arnold–Chiari malformation a congenital deformity in which the MEDULLA OBLONGATA and CEREBELLUM protrude through the FORAMEN MAGNUM, so that the cerebellum overlaps the top of the spinal cord. HYDROCEPHALUS and MENINGOMYELOCELE are commonly associated with the different types of the deformity. [Julius **Arnold** (1835–1915), German pathologist; Hans **Chiari** (1851–1916), Austrian pathologist]

aromatherapy *n.* a type of therapy purported to improve psychological and physical health through the use of selected essential oils extracted from seeds, herbs, flowers, fruits, and trees. The fragrances of these oils are inhaled or the oils themselves are applied topically, using compresses, baths, or massages, in an effort to induce relaxation, reduce stress and emotional distress, and enhance well-being. So-called evidence supporting the effectiveness of aromatherapy is almost entirely anecdotal. See also COMPLEMENTARY AND ALTERNATIVE MEDICINE.

arousal *n.* **1.** a state of physiological activation or cortical responsiveness, associated with sensory stimulation and activation of fibers from the RETICULAR ACTIVATING SYSTEM. **2.** a state of excitement or energy expenditure linked to an emotion. Usually, arousal is closely related to a person's appraisal of the significance of an event or to the physical intensity of a stimulus. Arousal can either facilitate or debilitate performance. See also CATASTROPHE CUSP THEORY. **—arouse** *vb.*

arousal jag an increase of ACTIVATION followed by a more or less sudden decrease, often accompanied by LAUGHTER as a release of tension. The abrupt fall from elevated levels of AROUSAL to a lower, more appropriate level of arousal is thought to produce a pleasurable response. Common experiences that can produce an arousal jag include a roller-coaster ride or watching a scary movie. [introduced in 1970 by British-born Canadian psychologist Daniel E. Berlyne (1924–1976)]

arousal level the extent to which an organism is alert to stimuli.

arousal–performance relationship the pattern of association between cognitive or physiological AROUSAL (or both) and achievement at physical or cognitive tasks. Also called **anxiety–performance relationship**. See CATASTROPHE CUSP THEORY; INVERTED-U HYPOTHESIS; REVERSAL THEORY.

arousal phase see SEXUAL-RESPONSE CYCLE.

arousal regulation the controlling of cognitive and physiological activation using cognitive-behavioral methods. See AUTOGENIC TRAINING; PROGRESSIVE RELAXATION.

arousal training a technique in BEHAVIOR THERAPY that teaches clients to detect levels of physiological arousal and then to enhance or reduce these levels depending on therapeutic goals. This technique is often used in ANGER CONTROL THERAPY and BEHAVIORAL SEX THERAPY.

arousal transfer an increase in the intensity of one emotion that follows the experience of another emotion. For instance, the intensity of love may increase following an intense experience of fear or anger.

arranged marriage a marriage planned and contracted by the parents or other relatives of the partners or by significant figures (e.g., elders) in the partners' culture or social group. In cultures in which arranged marriages are the norm and in contrast to the concept of the "love match," marriage is typically seen as the union of two kinship groups and not merely of two individuals.

array *n.* any ordered arrangement of data, particularly a two-dimensional grouping of data into rows and columns (i.e., a MATRIX). The concept may be extended to more than two dimensions.

arrhythmia *n.* any variation from the normal rhythm of the heartbeat. Kinds of arrhythmia include tachycardia, any rate above 100 beats per minute; bradycardia, a rate of less than 60 beats per minute; premature beats; **atrial flutter**, in which one of the upper chambers contracts at a rate of as much as 400 times per minute; and **heart block**, marked by failure of the heart to contract because of the interruption or delay of an electrical stimulus needed to trigger the contraction. **—arrhythmic** *adj.*

Artane *n.* a trade name for TRIHEXYPHENIDYL.

arteriopathia hypertonica a form of arterial degeneration associated with hypertension. The muscle and elastic tissue of the walls of the arterial system increases and forms layers that are eventually replaced by connective-tissue fibers.

The condition can be both a cause and an effect of hypertension, leading to cerebrovascular accidents if not controlled by medication.

arteriosclerosis *n.* a group of diseases characterized by hardening and loss of elasticity of the walls of the arteries. A common type is ATHEROSCLEROSIS. **—arteriosclerotic** *adj.*

arteritis *n.* inflammation of an artery or more than one artery. A common form is **temporal** (or **giant cell**) **arteritis**, a chronic disease of older people that largely involves the carotid arterial system, especially the arteries of the temple and scalp. It is marked by the appearance of giant, multinucleate cells and granulomas in the affected arteries; symptoms include severe temporal-area headaches on both sides and visual disturbances, which may result in loss of sight in one eye. See also PANARTERITIS.

arthritis *n.* inflammation of a joint, causing pain, swelling, and stiffness. The most severe and disabling form is **rheumatoid arthritis**, associated with the body attacking its own cells as foreign (see AUTOIMMUNITY). The psychosocial effects of arthritis, which can be chronic, painful, recurrent, and debilitating, can include lifestyle changes, stress on personal relationships, and depression. **—arthritic** *adj.*

arthrogryposis multiplex congenita a congenital disorder, with evidence of hereditary factors in 30% of cases, marked by distorted joints in different body areas, clubfoot, and a greater than average incidence of mental retardation. In some cases arms are rotated inward, the hips are dislocated, and the muscles are small, weak, and hypotonic. The term itself means "crooked-joint disorder." Four separate types of the disease are known. Also called **arthrogryposis**.

articulation disorder any disorder of speech involving the substitution, omission, distortion, or addition of speech sounds. See also DYSARTHRIA; PHONOLOGICAL DISORDER; SPEECH AND LANGUAGE DISORDER.

artifact *n.* an experimental finding that is not a reflection of the true state of nature but rather the consequent of flawed design or analytic error.

artificial insemination (**AI**) the use of medical or surgical techniques to achieve conception by introducing sperm into the female reproductive system. In humans, this is done by introducing sperm from the donor (who masturbates to provide the semen) into the vagina or through the cervical opening, directly into the uterus. As with intercourse, artificial insemination may need to be done more than once for pregnancy to occur, but it is usually scheduled to coincide with the days of ovulation, to maximize success. Success rates of 75% are usual.

art therapy the use of artistic activities, such as painting and clay modeling, in psychotherapy and rehabilitation. The process of making art is seen as healing, an experience that provides the opportunity to express oneself imaginatively, authentically, and spontaneously; over time, this process can lead to personal fulfillment, emotional reparation, and transformation. The products made in art therapy are seen as a means of symbolic communication and a vehicle for developing new insights and understandings, resolving conflicts, solving problems, and formulating new perceptions to achieve positive changes, growth, and rehabilitation.

arugamama *n.* see MORITA THERAPY.

ASA abbreviation for acetylsalicylic acid. See ASPIRIN.

asana *n.* a yoga posture or position. Each asana is said to have both physical and psychological effects that may be therapeutic or cathartic.

ASC abbreviation for ALTERED STATE OF CONSCIOUSNESS.

Asch, Solomon E. (1907–1996) Polish-born U.S. psychologist. Asch emigrated with his family to the United States in 1920 and earned his doctorate from Columbia University in 1932; his dominant influences were the Gestalt psychologists, especially Max WERTHEIMER. Asch taught at various universities, including Swarthmore College, where for some 19 years he was part of a group of Gestalt psychologists that also included Wolfgang KÖHLER, and the University of Pennsylvania, where he remained from 1972 until his retirement. Asch is best known for his contributions to social psychology, especially for his classic 1952 text on that field. He was particularly successful in designing laboratory experiments that reflected the complexity of human social life. His experiments were among the first to show how social context could influence even such fundamental processes as perception. For example, in his famous studies of CONFORMITY, he showed that people's perception of a line's length could be influenced by the false reports of others around them. His work was widely influential; the famous conformity experiments of Stanley Milgram (1933–1984) grew directly out of Asch's work. Asch held many honors, including the Nicholas Murray Butler Medal from Columbia University and a Distinguished Scientific Contribution Award from the American Psychological Association. He was elected to the American Academy of Arts and Sciences in 1965.

ASD **1.** abbreviation for ACUTE STRESS DISORDER. **2.** abbreviation for AUTISTIC SPECTRUM DISORDER.

Asendin *n.* a trade name for AMOXAPINE.

asexual *adj.* lacking sexual characteristics or drive. **—asexuality** *n.*

as-if hypothesis an unproven hypothesis that is treated "as if" it were correct, usually because of its value as an explanatory model or its utility as a basis for experiment and research. Many of the hypothetical entities postulated by psychology and psychoanalysis are of this nature.

as-if personality a type of personality style in

A

which the individual behaves as if well adjusted, but in fact is doing only what is expected and is unable to behave in a genuine or spontaneous manner. This condition has reportedly been observed in individuals with schizophrenia before they exhibit psychotic symptoms, such as hallucinations or delusions. [first described in 1942 by U.S. psychologist Helene Deutsch (1884–1982)]

asitia *n.* repulsion at the thought or sight of food. See also ANOREXIA.

asocial *adj.* **1.** declining to engage, or incapable of engaging, in social interaction. See also SCHIZOID PERSONALITY DISORDER. **2.** lacking sensitivity or regard for social values or norms. See also ANTISOCIAL PERSONALITY DISORDER. **—asociality** *n.*

Asperger's disorder a pervasive developmental disorder associated with varying degrees of deficits in social and conversational skills, difficulties with transitions from one task to another or with changes in situations or environments, and preference for sameness and predictability of events. Obsessive routines and preoccupation with particular subjects of interest may be present, as may difficulty reading body language and maintaining proper social distance. Some people with Asperger's disorder have reported oversensitivity to sounds, tastes, smells, and sights, but the nature of such sensitivities is not well researched. In contrast to AUTISTIC DISORDER, language skills develop, and there is no clinically significant delay in cognitive or adaptive functioning other than in social interactions. By definition, people with Asperger's disorder have an IQ in the normal to superior range, and some may exhibit exceptional specific skills or talents. See also AUTISTIC SPECTRUM DISORDER. Also called **Asperger's syndrome**. [described in 1944 by Hans **Asperger** (1906–1980), Austrian psychiatrist]

asphyxophilia *n.* arousal and enjoyment obtained from being unable to breathe during sexual activity. As a PARAPHILIA, this may involve being choked or strangled by a partner.

aspirin *n.* acetylsalicylic acid: the most commonly used nonopioid ANALGESIC, which also has ANTIPYRETIC and anti-inflammatory properties and the ability to prevent formation of blood clots. Aspirin alleviates pain mainly by peripheral mechanisms (see NSAIDS); in controlling fever, it acts on the body's thermoregulatory center in the hypothalamus. Adverse effects include gastric irritation or ulceration with bleeding and occasional allergic reactions. Overdosage affects the central nervous system and other body systems (see SALICYLISM).

aspirin combinations drug mixtures that include ASPIRIN as one of the components, the others commonly being other analgesics (e.g., ACETAMINOPHEN, CODEINE, PROPOXYPHENE), stimulants (usually caffeine), or both. Aspirin combinations may also include a barbiturate (e.g., **butalbital**), a skeletal muscle relaxant (e.g., CARISOPRODOL, ORPHENADRINE), or other drugs. Because many of these preparations can be obtained without a doctor's prescription, individuals with the habit of regular self-medication are at risk of developing gastrointestinal symptoms (e.g., peptic ulcer) and other toxic reactions (see SALICYLISM; CAFFEINE INTOXICATION).

aspirin poisoning see SALICYLISM.

assault *n.* **1.** a violent attack on an individual. **2.** illegal conduct occurring when an individual either attempts to injure another person or threatens to do so, and has the capacity to carry out the threat. **—assaultive** *adj.*

assertiveness *n.* a style of communication in which individuals express their feelings and needs directly, while maintaining respect for others.

assertiveness training a method of teaching individuals to change verbal and nonverbal signals and behavioral patterns and to enhance interpersonal communication generally through techniques designed to help them express emotions, opinions, and preferences—positive and negative—clearly, directly, and in an appropriate manner. ROLE PLAY or BEHAVIOR REHEARSAL is often used to prepare clients to be appropriately assertive in real-life situations.

assessment *n.* **1.** in general, a judgment of the quality, worth, importance, or value of something or someone. **2.** see PSYCHOLOGICAL ASSESSMENT.

assignment therapy a technique used in group therapy to enhance cohesiveness and communication among the participants so as to obtain maximum therapeutic benefit. A sociometric test is administered to determine the patterns of intermember relations within the group as a whole, and these patterns are then used to assign individuals to smaller, more focused groups. [articulated by Romanian-born psychiatrist and philosopher Jacob L. Moreno (1889–1974)]

assisted death an action taken by one person to end the life of another, at the request of the latter. This action can take the form of either assisted suicide or ACTIVE EUTHANASIA. Assisted death differs from MERCY KILLING in that it is generally performed by a physician and is not in response to an acute situation. It is sometimes called **physician-assisted suicide**, which assumes a firm determination of the cause of death.

assisted living a form of congregate housing for older adults requiring long-term care services that include meals, personal care, and scheduled nursing care. Typically comprising private rooms or apartments, it encourages a degree of autonomy and independence in residents that is not provided for in NURSING HOMES.

assisted suicide suicide in which the person ending his or her own life is provided the means to do so (e.g., a prescription) by another. See ASSISTED DEATH.

assistive technology (AT) **1.** the field concerned with development and service provision of tools that improve the functioning of individuals with limitations or disabilities. See also BIOENGINEERING. **2.** any equipment or system designed to maintain or improve the functional capabilities of individuals with disabilities. **Assistive devices** (or **assistive technology devices**) range from simple low-technology items such as canes, walkers, and reachers to high-technology items such as voice-controlled computers and computerized speech-output devices. These devices are also occasionally referred to as **daily-living aids** or **independent-living aids**.

association *n.* **1.** a connection or relationship between items, particularly ideas, events, or feelings. Associations are established by experience and are fundamental to learning theory and BEHAVIORISM. **2.** the degree of statistical dependence between two or more phenomena. **3.** a group of individuals who gather occasionally for some common purpose. **—associative** *adj.* **—associational** *adj.*

association cortex any of various areas of the CEREBRAL CORTEX that are not involved principally in sensory or motor representations but may be involved in integrative functions. Also called **association area**.

association disturbance see DISTURBANCE OF ASSOCIATION.

Association for the Advancement of Psychology (**AAP**) an organization founded in 1974 for the purpose of promoting human welfare through the advancement of the profession and science of psychology. The AAP promotes the interests of psychologists through (a) representation before public and governmental bodies, (b) cooperation with other organizations and agencies in furtherance of the profession and science of psychology, and (c) the operation of a political committee known as Psychologists for Legislative Action Now (AAP/PLAN).

association-reaction time the elapsed time between stimulus and response in a word-association test.

associative anamnesis a psychiatric interview technique in which the client gives an autobiographical account of his or her history and difficulties, while the therapist listens for key words and expressions that are then used to establish an **associative linkage** that will bring the client closer to the unconscious roots of his or her disturbance. See also SECTOR THERAPY. [developed by Felix Deutsch (1884–1964)]

associative fluency the ability to make a wide range of connections when presented with an object, event, word, or concept. High associative fluency has been identified as an aspect of CREATIVITY that in many individuals is not positively correlated with high intelligence. See also CREATIVE THINKING; DIVERGENT THINKING.

associative learning the process of acquiring new and enduring information via the formation of bonds between elements. In different types of **associationistic learning theories**, these associated elements may be stimulus and response, mental representations of events, or elements in neural networks. Historically, the associationistic theories of Clark L. HULL and Kenneth W. SPENCE (1907–1967) are contrasted with the nonassociative and cognitive theory of Edward C. TOLMAN.

associative linkage see ASSOCIATIVE ANAMNESIS.

associative memory retrieval of a memory (e.g., of a stimulus, behavior, place, or past event) that occurs upon recall or presentation of something associated with it.

associative strength the strength of the link (association) between two or more items (e.g., between stimulus and response or between items in memory), as measured by the capacity of the first item to elicit the second.

associative thinking a largely uncontrolled cognitive activity in which the mind "wanders" without specific direction among elements based on their connections (associations) with one another, as occurs during reverie, daydreaming, and FREE ASSOCIATION.

assumption *n.* **1.** the premise or supposition that something is fact; that is, the act of taking something for granted. **2.** one or more conditions that need to be met in order for a statistical procedure to be fully justified from a theoretical perspective. For example, ANALYSIS OF VARIANCE assumes homogeneity of variance and independence of observations, among other criteria. If the assumptions were to be violated to an extreme extent, the results would be invalid.

assurance *n.* see REASSURANCE.

astasia *n.* severe impairment or complete loss of the ability to stand due to problems in motor coordination. **—astatic** *adj.*

astasia–abasia the ability to walk only with a wobbly, staggering gait, although control is normal while lying down. This is believed to be psychogenic in origin and may be manifested as a symptom of CONVERSION DISORDER. Also called **Blocq's disease**.

asthenia *n.* severe weakness or loss of strength, often associated with general fatigue or certain disorders. Asthenia was formerly thought to be a common symptom of a MAJOR DEPRESSIVE EPISODE but is no longer defined as such. **—asthenic** *adj.*

asthma *n.* a chronic disorder in which intermittent inflammation and narrowing of the bronchial passages produces wheezing, gasping, coughing, and chest tightness. Though the precipitating cause is usually an allergen, such as dust or pollen, environmental irritants, respiratory infection, anxiety, stress, and other agents may produce or aggravate symptoms. **—asthmatic** *adj.*

asymptomatic *adj.* not showing any symp-

A

toms. For example, hypertension is considered asymptomatic because usually it does not have any outright physical or behavioral symptoms and can be detected only by measuring the blood pressure.

AT abbreviation for ASSISTIVE TECHNOLOGY.

ataque de nervios a CULTURE-BOUND SYNDROME found among Latinos, characterized by shaking, uncontrollable shouting or crying, a sense of rising heat, loss of control, and verbal or physical aggression, followed by fainting or seizurelike episodes. Symptoms often occur following a stressful event related to the family, and most individuals quickly return to their previous level of functioning.

ataractics *pl. n.* agents that have a calming or quieting effect, producing a state of ATARAXY. The name was introduced as an alternative to TRANQUILIZER. Also called **ataraxics**.

Atarax *n.* a trade name for HYDROXYZINE.

ataraxy *n.* a state of mind that is characterized by perfect peace or detached serenity without loss of mental abilities or clouding of consciousness. Also called **ataraxia**. **—ataraxic** or **ataractic** *adj.*

ataxia *n.* inability to perform coordinated voluntary movements. Ataxia may be seen as a symptom of various disorders, such as multiple sclerosis or cerebral palsy, or it can occur in isolation. It can be heritable, as in FRIEDREICH'S ATAXIA, or acquired from injury or infection affecting the nervous system. When due to damage to the CEREBELLUM it is called CEREBELLAR ATAXIA and when due to loss of sensory feedback from the muscles and joints it is called SENSORY ATAXIA. **—ataxic** *adj.*

ataxic feeling a sense that the ability to coordinate muscular movement has been lost. The feeling may be psychogenic or caused by such psychotropic drugs as antipsychotics, benzodiazepines, and lithium.

ataxiophemia *n.* incoordination of the muscles used in speaking. It is essentially equivalent to DYSARTHRIA.

ateliosis *n.* **1.** incomplete development of the body or of any of its parts, as in infantilism or dwarfism. **2.** formerly, the persistence of infantile or childlike cognitive or emotional developmental stages. Also called **atelia**.

atherosclerosis *n.* a common form of ARTERIOSCLEROSIS resulting from accumulations of lipids such as cholesterol on the inner walls of arteries and their hardening into **atherosclerotic** (or **atheromatous**) **plaques**. **—atherosclerotic** *adj.*

athletic triad the combination of AMENORRHEA, disordered eating, and osteoporosis observed in some female athletes, particularly those in subjectively evaluated sports (e.g., gymnastics, diving) or endurance sports (e.g., cross-country running).

athymia *n.* **1.** absence of feeling or emotion. **2.** congenital absence of the THYMUS.

Ativan *n.* a trade name for LORAZEPAM.

atmosphere effect the tendency for particular behaviors to be stimulated by a particular environment or situation, even when inappropriate, such as gesturing when using the telephone or applauding a poor speech.

ATP *a*denosine *t*ri*p*hosphate: a nucleotide in living cells that is the source of chemical energy for biological processes. A bond between two of its three component phosphate groups is easily split by a particular enzyme, **ATPase** (**adenosine triphosphatase**), yielding energy when a cell requires it.

at risk vulnerable to a disorder or disease. Risk status for an individual is defined by genetic, physical, and behavioral factors or conditions. For example, children of people with schizophrenia may be considered at risk for schizophrenia, and heavy cigarette smokers are at risk for emphysema and lung cancer.

at-risk mental states psychological symptoms or mental processes that render individuals vulnerable to mental illnesses or to adverse behaviors, such as violence.

atrophy *n.* a wasting away of the body or a body part, as from lack of nourishment, inactivity, degenerative disease, or normal aging. **—atrophic** *adj.*

atropine *n.* an ANTICHOLINERGIC DRUG derived from certain plants, particularly belladonna (see BELLADONNA ALKALOIDS), and also produced synthetically. Its effects include increases in heart rate and rate of breathing, relaxation of smooth muscles, and reduction of secretions (e.g., saliva). It may be used to treat organophosphate poisoning and bradycardia (slowing of the heart rate), or as an adjunct to anesthesia, but is most commonly employed in eye examinations to dilate the pupil. Atropine is closely related, chemically and pharmacologically, to SCOPOLAMINE.

atropine-coma therapy (**ACT**) a now-abandoned method of treating tense, agitated, and anxious people with psychoses by administering atropine sulfate to induce coma.

attachment *n.* the close emotional bond between a human infant or a young nonhuman animal and its parent figure or caregiver, developed as a step in establishing a feeling of security and demonstrated by calmness while in their presence. Attachment also denotes the tendency to form such strong bonds with certain other individuals in infancy as well as the tendency in adulthood to seek emotionally supportive relationships.

attachment behavior **1.** behavior associated with the formation of and investment in significant relationships. **2.** infant behavior that results in the infant gaining proximity to or contact with his or her caregiver. Its manifestations include crying, smiling, calling, and clinging. See ATTACHMENT THEORY. [first described by John BOWLBY]

attachment bond the primary, enduring, special relationship that gradually develops between an infant and caregiver.

attachment disorder see REACTIVE ATTACHMENT DISORDER.

attachment style the characteristic way people relate to others in the context of intimate relationships, which is heavily influenced by SELF-WORTH and INTERPERSONAL TRUST. Theoretically, adults' degree of attachment security is related directly to how well they bonded to others as children. There are four distinct categories of adult attachment that have been identified: DISMISSIVE ATTACHMENT, FEARFUL ATTACHMENT, PREOCCUPIED ATTACHMENT, and SECURE ATTACHMENT.

attachment theory a theory that (a) postulates an evolutionarily advantageous need, especially in primates, to form close emotional bonds with significant others: specifically, a need for the young to maintain close proximity to and form bonds with their caregivers; and (b) characterizes the different types of relationships between human infants and caregivers. These relationships have been shown to affect the individual's later emotional development and emotional stability. See also INSECURE ATTACHMENT; SECURE ATTACHMENT; STRANGE SITUATION. [originally developed by John BOWLBY and later expanded by Canadian-born U.S. psychologist Mary D. Salter Ainsworth (1913–1999)]

attempted suicide a deliberate but, by implication, unsuccessful attempt to commit SUICIDE. Also called **suicide attempt**.

attendant care 1. nonmedical, in-home assistance with dressing, feeding, and other activities of daily living provided to individuals with a physical or developmental disability who otherwise are able to live independently. **2.** one-on-one direct supervision by a trained attendant of a juvenile who has been taken into custody in a nonsecure setting.

attending behavior any behavior engaged in by an individual while attentively listening to and observing a speaker, for example, exhibiting an open, interested posture and maintaining eye contact. Helpful attending behaviors, along with ACTIVE LISTENING, are considered cornerstones of a therapist's or counselor's general ability.

attention *n.* a state of awareness in which the senses are focused selectively on aspects of the environment and the central nervous system is in a state of readiness to respond to stimuli. Because human beings do not have an infinite capacity to attend to everything—focusing on certain items at the expense of others—much of the research in this field is devoted to discerning which factors influence attention and to understanding the neural mechanisms that are involved in the selective processing of information. For example, past experience affects perceptual experience (we notice things that have meaning for us), and some activities (e.g., reading) require conscious participation (i.e., intentional attention). However, attention can also be captured (i.e., directed unintentionally) by qualities of stimuli in the environment, such as intensity, movement, repetition, contrast, and novelty.

attentional control of consciousness the concept that SELECTIVE ATTENTION to an event can increase the likelihood of the event becoming conscious.

attentional dyslexia a form of acquired dyslexia (see ALEXIA) in which a person is able to read words but has difficulty identifying their constituent letters. This is thought to be caused by a failure of the letter-to-word binding system, resulting in the "migration" of letters between words. People with attentional dyslexia are able to read letters or words significantly better when they are presented in isolation than when presented together with others as part of a text.

attention-control training (**ACT**) a program that assists an individual to be more effective at maintaining appropriate attentional focus. It is achieved by assessment of the individual's attentional strengths and weaknesses, the attentional demands of the environment in which the individual's performance occurs, environmental and personal characteristics likely to induce stress and dictate behavior under pressure, and typical error patterns and situations in which they occur. This assessment leads to the planning of an intervention protocol, the purpose of which is to teach the individual to concentrate on all the task-relevant cues and ignore all the task-irrelevant cues in a given situation.

attention-deficit disorder (**ADD**) a former and still commonly used name for ATTENTION-DEFICIT/HYPERACTIVITY DISORDER.

attention-deficit/hyperactivity disorder (**ADHD**; **AHD**) in *DSM–IV–TR*, a behavioral syndrome characterized by the persistent presence (i.e., for 6 months or more) of six or more symptoms involving (a) inattention (e.g., failure to complete tasks or listen carefully, difficulty in concentrating, distractibility) or (b) impulsivity or hyperactivity (e.g., blurting out answers; impatience; restlessness; fidgeting; difficulty in organizing work, taking turns, or staying seated; excessive talking; running about; climbing on things). The symptoms, which impair social, academic, or occupational functioning, start to appear before the age of 7 and are observed in more than one setting. ADHD has been given a variety of names over the years, including the still commonly used **attention-deficit disorder** (**ADD**).

attention-deficit/hyperactivity disorder not otherwise specified in *DSM–IV–TR*, a disorder characterized by inattention, hyperactivity, or impulsivity that impair performance in educational or social situations but do not meet the diagnostic criteria for ATTENTION-DEFICIT/HYPERACTIVITY DISORDER (ADHD). It may, for example, be marked by significant problems in attention that start after the age of 7 or that are not among the criteria listed for a diagnosis of ADHD (e.g., daydreaming).

attention disorder a disturbance characterized by an inability to maintain focus on an activity or by difficulties in taking notice of, responding to, or being aware of the behavior, demands, or requests of other people. Previously, this term was frequently used interchangeably with MINIMAL BRAIN DYSFUNCTION, as impairments of attention are among the most common manifestations of brain damage. See also LEARNING DISABILITY.

attention-getting *adj.* describing a type of behavior, often inappropriate, that is used to gain attention. Childhood temper tantrums are an example of such behavior.

attention level the degree to which a task or event is likely to be reportable or conscious. Tasks with high attention-level demands are likely to interfere with each other when they must be done at the same time. See also DUAL-TASK COMPETITION.

attention load measure a method that uses competing cognitive tasks to assess the processing demands made by each task. The degradation in performance of one task is taken to be a measure of the attentional demands made by the other task.

attention overload a psychological condition that results from excessive demands on attention. The effect is temporary depletion of available attention and an inability to cope with tasks that demand attention. See also INFORMATION OVERLOAD.

attention span 1. the length of time an individual can concentrate on one specific task or other item of interest. **2.** the maximum number of distinct factors that can be comprehended from one brief exposure to an array of stimuli.

attenuated positive symptoms in schizophrenia, a reduction in hallucinations, delusions, bizarre behavior, or conceptual thought problems. See also POSITIVE SYMPTOM.

attenuated psychotic symptoms in schizophrenia and other PSYCHOTIC DISORDERS, an increase in reality-based perceptions and a reduction in symptoms, such as delusions, hallucinations, markedly incoherent speech, and disorientation.

attenuation *n.* **1.** the lessening or weakening in strength, value, or quality of a stimulus. **2.** in statistics, a reduction in the estimated size of an effect because of errors of measurement.

attitude *n.* a relatively enduring and general evaluation of an object, person, group, issue, or concept on a scale ranging from negative to positive. Attitudes provide summary evaluations of target objects and are often assumed to be derived from specific beliefs, emotions, and past behaviors associated with those objects. **—attitudinal** *adj.*

attitude–behavior consistency the extent to which behavior toward an ATTITUDE OBJECT is consistent with the attitude associated with that object. Positive attitudes are associated with approach behaviors; negative attitudes are associated with withdrawal behaviors.

attitude change any alteration in an attitude, which may result from active attempts by others to change the attitude or from processes initiated by the person holding the attitude.

attitude object any target of judgment that has an attitude associated with it. Attitude objects may be people, social groups, policy positions, abstract concepts, or physical objects.

attitude therapy a form of reeducative treatment that emphasizes current attitudes of the client in terms of the origins of these attitudes, the purpose such attitudes serve, and their distortions.

attitudinal group 1. an aggregation, or set, of individuals who are highly similar in their attitudes toward a given subject. **2.** any personal growth or therapy group in which the members are given the chance to express and exchange feelings and thoughts in an accepting environment.

attitudinal types in Carl Jung's ANALYTIC PSYCHOLOGY, two personality types defined by habitual EXTRAVERSION on the one hand and habitual INTROVERSION on the other. See INTROVERSION–EXTRAVERSION. See also FUNCTIONAL TYPES.

attraction *n.* **1.** the feeling of being drawn to one or more other individuals and desiring their company, usually but not necessarily always because of a personal liking for them. **2.** power of attraction: the extent to which any one individual is attractive to or liked by others. **—attractive** *adj.*

attraction relations patterns of liking–disliking, acceptance–rejection, and inclusion–exclusion among members of a group. Such patterns are also known as **sociometric structure**, particularly when assessed through the use of SOCIOMETRY.

attributable risk in EPIDEMIOLOGY, the incidence rate of a disease or disorder that can be considered to have been caused by exposure to a RISK FACTOR. A large portion of lung cancers can be attributed to tobacco use, constituting a substantial attributable risk for this disease.

attribution *n.* an inference regarding the cause of a person's behavior or an interpersonal event. The cause may be stable or unstable, internal or external, and controllable or uncontrollable, and the character of the reason affects motivation. See ATTRIBUTION THEORY; LEARNED HELPLESSNESS.

attributional style a person's characteristic

tendencies when inferring the cause of behavior or events. Three dimensions are often used to evaluate people's attributional styles: the internal–external dimension (whether they tend to attribute events to the self or to other factors), the stable–unstable dimension (whether they tend to attribute events to enduring or transient causes), and the global–specific dimension (whether they tend to attribute events to causes that affect many events or just a single event).

attribution of emotion see SCHACHTER–SINGER THEORY.

attribution theory the study of the processes by which people ascribe motives to their own and others' behavior. The motives ascribed may be either internal and personal (DISPOSITIONAL ATTRIBUTION) or external and circumstantial (SITUATIONAL ATTRIBUTION). According to U.S. social psychologist Harold H. Kelley (1921–2003), observers choose between the two types of ATTRIBUTION on the basis of three factors: consistency (how has the same individual (actor) behaved in the same situation in the past?); distinctiveness (how has the actor behaved in different situations?); and consensus (how do other people behave in the same situation?).

attribution therapy a form of therapy in which the therapist tries to change a client's views concerning the causes of events and behavior.

attrition *n.* in experimentation and other research, dropout or loss of participants.

A-type personality see TYPE A PERSONALITY.

atypical antipsychotic a class of ANTIPSYCHOTIC drugs that, compared to conventional (typical or first-generation) antipsychotics, produce fewer EXTRAPYRAMIDAL SYMPTOMS, are less likely to alter serum levels of PROLACTIN, and appear to be less likely to cause TARDIVE DYSKINESIA, all of which are significant adverse effects of the conventional drugs. They show some degree of activity as DOPAMINE-RECEPTOR ANTAGONISTS but also block the effects of serotonin or other neurotransmitters. Atypical antipsychotics are used in the treatment of schizophrenias, delusional disorders, dementias, and other disorders characterized by psychotic symptoms. They are also used as adjunctive agents in the treatment of some nonpsychotic conditions, such as obsessive-compulsive disorder, explosive disorder, or severe depression. The prototype of the group is CLOZAPINE; others in current clinical use include OLANZAPINE, RISPERIDONE, ILOPERIDONE, QUETIAPINE, ARIPIPRAZOLE, and ZIPRASIDONE. Also called **novel antipsychotic**; **second-generation antipsychotic**.

atypical autism see PERVASIVE DEVELOPMENTAL DISORDER NOT OTHERWISE SPECIFIED.

atypical conduct disorder in *DSM–III*, a diagnostic category for disorders that in *DSM–IV–TR* are classified as DISRUPTIVE BEHAVIOR DISORDER NOT OTHERWISE SPECIFIED.

atypical depression a MAJOR DEPRESSIVE EPISODE or, less commonly, DYSTHYMIC DISORDER characterized by ATYPICAL FEATURES.

atypical disorder in *DSM–III* and earlier editions, a residual category that included unusual or uncharacteristic variations of standard mental disorders. The equivalent *DSM–IV–TR* category is not otherwise specified.

atypical dissociative disorder in *DSM–III*, a residual category of dissociative disorders that in *DSM–IV–TR* is labeled DISSOCIATIVE DISORDER NOT OTHERWISE SPECIFIED.

atypical eating disorder in *DSM–III* and earlier editions, a residual category of disorders that in *DSM–IV–TR* is labeled EATING DISORDER not otherwise specified.

atypical features symptoms of a disorder other than the standard diagnostic criteria. For a MAJOR DEPRESSIVE EPISODE or DYSTHYMIC DISORDER, for example, they would include improvement of mood in response to positive events or HYPERSOMNIA.

atypical gender identity disorder in *DSM–III*, a residual category for disorders of gender identity that were not classifiable as any specific gender identity disorder. In *DSM–IV–TR* such disorders are designated GENDER IDENTITY DISORDER not otherwise specified.

atypical impulse-control disorder in *DSM–III* and earlier editions, a residual category of impulse-control disorders that in *DSM–IV–TR* is labeled impulse-control disorder not otherwise specified (see IMPULSE-CONTROL DISORDERS NOT ELSEWHERE CLASSIFIED).

atypical mental disorder see ATYPICAL DISORDER.

atypical, mixed, or other personality disorder in *DSM–III*, a category of personality disorders for which there is insufficient evidence for a more specific designation. Cases that involve features of several personality disorders without meeting the criteria for any one type are described as **mixed personality disorders**; **other personality disorders** are unclassified cases, such as masochistic, impulsive, or immature personality disorder.

atypical paraphilia in *DSM–III*, a residual category of paraphilias that in *DSM–IV–TR* is labeled PARAPHILIA NOT OTHERWISE SPECIFIED.

atypical pervasive developmental disorder in *DSM–III*, a diagnostic category for disorders that in *DSM–IV–TR* are classified as PERVASIVE DEVELOPMENTAL DISORDER NOT OTHERWISE SPECIFIED.

atypical psychosexual disorder a sexual problem that does not meet diagnostic criteria for sexual dysfunction or sexual deviancy. In *DSM–IV–TR* such disorders are categorized as SEXUAL DISORDER NOT OTHERWISE SPECIFIED.

atypical psychosexual dysfunction in *DSM–III*, a category that included psychosexual dysfunctions outside the standard specific categories. In *DSM–IV–TR* this is labeled SEXUAL DYSFUNCTION NOT OTHERWISE SPECIFIED.

atypical psychosis in *DSM–III*, any of various conditions involving psychotic symptoms that do not meet the criteria for any specific disorder. The equivalent *DSM–IV–TR* classification is PSYCHOTIC DISORDER NOT OTHERWISE SPECIFIED.

atypical specific developmental disorder in *DSM–III*, a residual category for disorders that in *DSM–IV–TR* are categorized as LEARNING DISORDER NOT OTHERWISE SPECIFIED or COMMUNICATION DISORDER NOT OTHERWISE SPECIFIED.

atypical stereotyped-movement disorder in *DSM–III* and earlier editions, a diagnostic category for disorders that in *DSM–IV–TR* are classified as TIC DISORDER NOT OTHERWISE SPECIFIED or STEREOTYPIC MOVEMENT DISORDER.

atypical tic disorder in *DSM–III*, a diagnostic category for tic disorders that in *DSM–IV–TR* are labeled TIC DISORDER NOT OTHERWISE SPECIFIED.

audible thought a type of hallucination in which one hears one's own thoughts as if they were projected by an inner voice.

audit *n.* an evaluation or review of the health care services proposed or rendered by a provider. See MEDICAL AUDIT; TREATMENT AUDIT.

auditory agnosia loss or impairment of the ability to recognize and understand the nature of verbal or nonverbal sounds. Subtypes are distinguished on the basis of the type of auditory stimulus the person has difficulty recognizing, for example, environmental sounds such as a dog barking or keys jingling (**nonverbal auditory agnosia** or **environmental sounds agnosia**), spoken words, or music.

Auditory Consonant Trigram (**ACT**) a memory test in which a three-letter nonsense syllable consisting only of consonants, such as *DCJ*, is presented verbally and the participant is asked to recall the sequence following delays of varying lengths (e.g., 9, 18, and 36 s). During the delay intervals, the participant performs a distractor task (e.g., counting backwards from a specified number by threes). See BROWN–PETERSON DISTRACTOR TECHNIQUE.

auditory hallucination the perception of sound in the absence of an auditory stimulus. Hallucinations may, for example, be of accusatory or laudatory voices or of strange noises and other nonverbal sounds. Auditory hallucinations occur frequently in schizophrenia and other psychotic disorders but may be associated with other conditions as well (e.g., delirium, dementia).

auditory memory span the number of simple items, such as words or numbers, that can be repeated in the same order by a person after hearing the series once. The auditory memory span indicates the capacity of a person's WORKING MEMORY. Also called **auditory span**. See also MEMORY SPAN.

auditory training helping people with hearing loss to better distinguish sounds and understand spoken language by teaching them how to make the most effective use of their residual hearing and to discern contextual clues related to situations and environments.

auditory verbal learning test a memory test that generally involves learning verbal material, usually single words, that is auditorily presented over repeated trials. Recall or recognition may be employed as a measure of learning over various delay periods.

augmentation strategy a mechanism to increase the effectiveness of pharmacological agents by the addition of other agents. Augmentation strategies are most commonly used in the treatment of depression.

aura *n.* a subjective sensation that precedes an epileptic seizure or migraine headache. It may include such phenomena as strange tastes or odors, flashes of light (a **visual aura**), numbness, and feelings of unreality or DÉJÀ VU.

autarchy *n.* **1.** in psychiatry, the period of infancy in which the child exerts autocratic power over others, including the parents who satisfy all his or her instinctual demands. **2.** more generally, supreme and absolute power. See also OMNIPOTENCE. **—autarchic** *adj.*

autassassinophilia *n.* a PARAPHILIA in which sexual arousal and the achievement of orgasm are facilitated by the belief that one is in danger of being killed. This often includes the individual staging a sexual encounter characterized by extreme MASOCHISM with the real potential for his or her own murder. Also called **autassassinatophilia**. Compare HOMICIDOPHILIA.

autemesia *n.* vomiting for which no organic cause can be identified.

authenticity *n.* **1.** in psychotherapy and counseling, a characteristic of the therapist or counselor who is considered to be genuine and caring. Authenticity is often demonstrated by a professional but down-to-earth attitude that the client senses to be a reflection of the true person and not simply of the therapist acting in his or her professional role. **2.** in EXISTENTIALISM, a mode of being that humans can achieve by accepting the burden of freedom, choice, and responsibility and the need to construct their own values and meanings in a meaningless universe. **—authentic** *adj.*

authoritarian *adj.* describing an individual, especially but not limited to one in a position of authority, who uses or favors restrictive, autocratic methods when interacting with others. See AUTHORITARIAN PERSONALITY. **—authoritarianism** *n.*

authoritarian conscience the type of conscience that is guided by (a) fear of an external authority or (b) the voice of an internalized external authority, such as the SUPEREGO. Compare HUMANISTIC CONSCIENCE. [defined by Erich FROMM]

authoritarian personality a personality pattern characterized by strict adherence to highly simplified conventional values, an attitude of great deference to authority figures while demanding subservience from those regarded as lower in status, and hostility toward people who deviate from conventional moral prescriptions.

authority complex a pattern of emotionally charged concepts of authority that are partially or completely repressed. To satisfy an unconscious need for authority, a person projects power onto certain other people (see PROJECTION) and experiences inferiority in the presence of these others. Therefore, reactions to authority often take the form of oversubmission.

autism *n.* **1.** abnormal preoccupation with the self and fantasy such that there is lack of interest in or ability to focus on external reality. **2.** a synonym for AUTISTIC DISORDER. **—autistic** *adj.*

autistic disorder a severe neurologically based pervasive developmental disorder characterized by markedly impaired social interactions and verbal and nonverbal communication; narrow interests; and repetitive behavior. Manifestations and features of the disorder appear before age 3 but vary greatly across children according to developmental level, language skills, and chronological age. They may include a lack of awareness of the feelings of others, impaired ability to imitate, absence of social play, abnormal speech, abnormal nonverbal communication, and a preference for maintaining environmental sameness.

autistic fantasy a DEFENSE MECHANISM in which a person deals with emotional conflict and stressors by indulging in excessive daydreaming as a substitute for human relationships or more active and direct problem solving.

autistic savant see SAVANT.

autistic spectrum disorder (**ASD**) any one of a group of disorders with an onset typically occurring during the preschool years and characterized by varying but often marked difficulties in communication and social interaction. The group includes the prototype AUTISTIC DISORDER as well as RETT SYNDROME, ASPERGER'S DISORDER, and CHILDHOOD DISINTEGRATIVE DISORDER. This term is synonymous with PERVASIVE DEVELOPMENTAL DISORDER but is now more commonly used, given its reflection of symptom overlap among the disorders. Also called **autism spectrum disorder**.

autistic thinking narcissistic, egocentric thought processes, such as fantasizing and daydreaming, that have little or no relation to reality. It is similar to dereistic thinking (see DEREISM), but the emphasis is on self-absorption rather than disconnection from reality. See AUTISM.

autoagonistophilia *n.* sexual arousal from being observed or filmed while engaging in sexual activity.

autoassassinatophilia *n.* see AUTASSASSINOPHILIA.

autobiographical memory **1.** a type of EPISODIC MEMORY comprising vivid recollections of significant instances in a person's life. Thus, remembering one's wedding day involves autobiographical memory while remembering a theater performance one attended involves episodic memory generally. Often, however, the two terms are used interchangeably. **2.** more broadly, memory for any information about the self, including not only personal experiences but also self-related factual knowledge, the SELF-SCHEMA, and so forth.

Autobiographical Memory Interview (**AMI**) a semistructured interview designed to assess memory for autobiographical information, impairment of which is often indicative of retrograde amnesia and potentially associated with a variety of neurological and psychiatric disorders. The AMI contains an Autobiographical Incidents Schedule, which queries specific, personally experienced events from childhood, early adult life, and the recent past; and a Personal Semantic Memory Schedule, which queries generic or semantic facts about the self, divided into childhood, early adult life, and recent information. [developed in 1989 by British neuropsychiatrist Michael D. Kopelman, British clinical psychologist Barbara A. Wilson, and British cognitive psychologist Alan D. Baddeley (1934–)]

autobiography *n.* in therapy or counseling, a technique in which a LIFE HISTORY, written by the client from his or her own point of view, is used to obtain information regarding the client's behavioral patterns and feelings. A **structured autobiography** is based on explicit questions or topic guidelines supplied by the therapist or counselor. An **unstructured autobiography** contains no guidelines. See also LIFE REVIEW.

autocentric *adj.* centered on or within the self. Compare ALLOCENTRIC.

autochthonous *adj.* **1.** native, indigenous, or original. **2.** denoting ENDOGENOUS processes and events that originate within the individual, independently of external influences. Compare ALLOCHTHONOUS.

autoenucleation *n.* an act of self-mutilation in which an individual excises an organ or tumor from his or her own body, as, for example, when a person with a psychotic disorder removes an eyeball (see ENUCLEATION). Also called **self-enucleation**.

autoerotic asphyxiation sexual pleasure obtained from being unable to breathe during masturbation. It may involve the person hanging him- or herself, a practice that has been found to result in a number of accidental deaths each year when the person is unable to get free of the rope.

A

autoeroticism *n.* **1.** the creation of sexual excitement and gratification by the self, whether it be through masturbation, other sexual behaviors (e.g., stimulating nongenital portions of the body), or thoughts (e.g., daydreams, fantasies). See also SECONDARY AUTOEROTICISM. [defined by British sexologist Havelock Ellis (1859–1939)] **2.** formerly, GENITAL AROUSAL IN SLEEP, which is now understood to be a normal component of one stage of sleep and is not associated with erotic dreams. Also called **autoerotism**. Compare ALLOEROTICISM. **—autoerotic** *adj.*

autoerythrocyte sensitization syndrome see GARDNER–DIAMOND SYNDROME.

autoflagellation *n.* sexual pleasure derived from striking, whipping, or beating oneself.

autogenic training a relaxation technique in which a quasi-hypnotic state is self-induced and deep relaxation is achieved through mental imagery, breath control, and exercises that focus attention on physical sensations, including warmth and heaviness of the limbs, a regular heartbeat, abdominal warmth, and cooling of the forehead. The aim is to reduce stress by gaining control of autonomic arousal associated with anxiety and to obtain an ideal performance state. [developed in the early 20th century by German neurologist Johannes Heinrich Schultz (1884–1970)]

autogenital stimulation any form of stimulation by a human or an animal of its own genitalia. It may take the form of pelvic thrusts, MASTURBATION, or self-stimulation preceding sexual intercourse. Autogenital stimulation may occur in the presence of members of the same or opposite sex or in the absence of other individuals.

autognosis *n.* knowledge of self.

autohypnosis *n.* see SELF-HYPNOSIS. **—autohypnotic** *adj.*

autohypnotic amnesia a Jungian term for repression, based on the observation that HYPNOTIC AMNESIA may be induced by a person under hypnosis.

autoimmunity *n.* a condition in which the body's immune system fails to recognize its own tissues as "self" and attempts to reject its own cells. It is a primary factor in the development of such diseases as rheumatoid arthritis and systemic lupus erythematosus (called **autoimmune disorders**). **—autoimmune** *adj.*

automasochism *n.* sexual pleasure derived from inflicting pain on oneself during masturbation or during sexual activity with a partner.

automated assessment see COMPUTERIZED ASSESSMENT.

automated clinical records a computerized database used for such purposes as monitoring patient care, providing data for administrative decisions, and assisting the clinician in understanding and treating patients.

automated desensitization the use of such devices as audiotapes, videotapes, and digitized media to facilitate the presentation of anxiety-provoking and relaxing stimuli during SYSTEMATIC DESENSITIZATION. It is especially helpful in situations where a client is reluctant to undergo desensitization in the presence of the therapist. See DEVICE FOR AUTOMATED DESENSITIZATION.

automatic anxiety see PRIMARY ANXIETY.

automatic drawing the act of drawing images or objects while in a hypnotic trance or in a situation in which attention is distracted. It may be used in HYPNOTHERAPY to provide a therapist with access to unconscious material from the client. See also AUTOMATIC WRITING.

automaticity *n.* the quality of a mental process that can be carried out rapidly and without effort or intention (an **automatic process**). See also CONSCIOUS PROCESS; UNCONSCIOUS PROCESS.

automatic obedience excessive, uncritical, or mechanical compliance with the requests, suggestions, or commands of others.

automatic speech **1.** speech that erupts involuntarily, or without conscious control. It sometimes occurs as a consequence of senility, Tourette's syndrome, or highly emotional states. **2.** speech that is uttered with little or no conscious consideration of the spoken material, such as the days of the week, numbers, the alphabet, and other well-learned material.

automatic thoughts **1.** instantaneous, habitual, but unconscious thoughts that affect a person's mood and actions. Helping clients become aware of the presence and impact of negative automatic thoughts and then test their validity is a central task of cognitive therapy. **2.** thoughts that have been so well learned and habitually repeated that they occur without cognitive effort. Also called **routinized thoughts**.

automatic writing the act of writing while one's attention is not focused on the task or of writing without conscious awareness, as during a hypnotic trance. It may be used in HYPNOTHERAPY to provide a therapist with access to unconscious material from the client. See also AUTOMATIC DRAWING.

automatism *n.* nonpurposeful behavior performed mechanically, without intention, and without conscious awareness. It may be motor or verbal and ranges from simple repetitive acts, such as lipsmacking or repeatedly using the same phrase (e.g., *as it were*), to complex activities, such as sleepwalking and automatic writing. Automatism is seen in several disorders, including CATATONIC SCHIZOPHRENIA and COMPLEX PARTIAL SEIZURES.

automatism defense a legal defense consisting of the claim that criminal intent (see MENS REA) is lacking as a result of the defendant's dissociated or unconscious state at the time the criminal act was committed. The defense is more common in the United Kingdom and Canada than in the United States.

A

automatization *n.* **1.** the development of a skill or habit to a point at which it becomes routine and requires little if any conscious effort or direction. **2.** the state of individuals who obey compulsive impulses so automatically that they may be described as automata.

automutilation *n.* sexual pleasure derived from mutilating parts of one's body or from fantasy about mutilated parts of one's body. It usually involves cutting some part of the body during masturbation.

autonecrophilia *n.* sexual pleasure derived from the fantasy that one is dead and that another person is having sexual relations with one's dead body.

autonepiophilia *n.* sexual pleasure derived from dressing as a baby, pretending to be a baby, or having a fantasy about being a baby.

autonoetic *adj.* describing a level of knowledge or memory in which one is aware not only of the known or remembered thing but also of one's personal experience in relation to that thing. **Autonoetic consciousness** is a corresponding level of consciousness in which one's knowledge of facts, concepts, and meanings is mediated through an awareness of one's own existence in time. Compare ANOETIC; NOETIC. [defined by Estonian-born Canadian psychologist Endel Tulving (1927–)]

autonomic dysfunction see DYSAUTONOMIA.

autonomic hyperactivity arousal of the AUTONOMIC NERVOUS SYSTEM (ANS), particularly its SYMPATHETIC NERVOUS SYSTEM functions, resulting in the physiological symptoms associated with anxiety and fear (e.g., sweating, palpitations, dry mouth, lightheadedness, upset stomach).

autonomic nervous system (**ANS**) the portion of the nervous system innervating smooth muscle and glands, including the circulatory, digestive, respiratory, and reproductive organs. It is divided into the SYMPATHETIC NERVOUS SYSTEM and PARASYMPATHETIC NERVOUS SYSTEM. **Autonomic responses** typically involve changes in involuntary bodily functions, such as heart rate, salivation, digestion, perspiration, pupil size, hormone secretion, bladder contraction, and engorgement of the penis and clitoris. The system is called autonomic because it was once thought to function independently of the central nervous system.

autonomic neuropathy see DYSAUTONOMIA.

autonomic restrictors people with GENERALIZED ANXIETY DISORDER (GAD), who have lower heart rate, blood pressure, skin conductance, and respiration rate than do people with other anxiety disorders.

autonomous depression 1. a MAJOR DEPRESSIVE EPISODE that does not occur in response to any obvious psychosocial stressor. See also ENDOGENOUS DEPRESSION. **2.** an obsolete name for depression characterized by agitation and self-criticism.

autonomy *n.* a state of independence and self-determination in an individual, a group, or a society. According to some theories, an inordinate focus on self-determination and achievement represents a risk factor for the development of MAJOR DEPRESSIVE DISORDER. See also FUNCTIONAL AUTONOMY. Compare HETERONOMY.

autonomy versus shame and doubt the second of ERIKSON'S EIGHT STAGES OF DEVELOPMENT, between the ages of 1½ and 3 years. During this stage, children acquire a degree of self-reliance and self-confidence if allowed to develop at their own pace but may begin to doubt their ability to control themselves and their world if parents are overcritical, overprotective, or inconsistent.

autopedophilia *n.* sexual pleasure derived from dressing as a child, pretending to be a child, or having a fantasy about being a child.

autophagy *n.* **1.** the chewing or eating of one's own flesh. **2.** the body's maintenance of nutrition by consumption of its own tissues, as in times of excessive fasting. Also called **autophagia**.

autoplasty *n.* **1.** adaptation to reality by modifying one's own behavioral patterns, rather than by altering one's environment. Autoplastic behavior can be negative and psychologically harmful, as in the development of neurotic behavior, or positive and psychologically healthy, as in the tendency toward more adaptive thinking and action following psychotherapeutic intervention. Also called **autoplastic development**. **2.** surgical repair using tissue from another part of the patient's body. Compare ALLOPLASTY. —**autoplastic** *adj.*

autopsychic delusion a delusion about one's personality. It is distinguished from **allopsychic delusions**, which refer to the outside world, and SOMATIC DELUSIONS, which refer to one's own body. [defined by German neurologist Carl Wernicke (1848–1905)]

autopsychosis *n.* a delusional condition in which the individual maintains distorted ideas about him- or herself, such as being the world's savior, the devil incarnate, or an unrecognized genius. —**autopsychotic** *adj.*

autoreceptor *n.* a molecule in the membrane of a presynaptic neuron that regulates the synthesis and release of a neurotransmitter by that neuron by monitoring how much transmitter has been released and "telling" the neuron.

autoscopophilia *n.* sexual pleasure derived from observing oneself disrobing, being nude, or watching oneself during sexual activity. It may involve viewing videos or pictures of these situations.

autoscopy *n.* seeing a double of oneself in external space. The image is generally short-lived and hazy, filmy, and colorless. Also called **auto-**

A

scopic phenomenon. See also DOPPELGANGER PHENOMENON; OUT-OF-BODY EXPERIENCE.

autosexuality *n.* any form of sexual arousal or stimulation that occurs without the participation of another person or animal, for example, masturbation, sexual dreams, or sexual fantasies.

autosomal aberration any disorder of structure, function, or both that is associated with an alteration in the structure or number of any of the pairs of chromosomes that are not sex chromosomes (see AUTOSOME). An example of such a disorder is DOWN SYNDROME. Also called **autosomal abnormality**; **autosomal anomaly**.

autosomal dominant see DOMINANT ALLELE.

autosomal recessive see RECESSIVE ALLELE.

autosomal trisomy of group G the condition in which either of the chromosome pairs 21 or 22 (known as group G) includes an additional autosome. The most common of these two autosome abnormalities is TRISOMY 21. See also DOWN SYNDROME.

autosome *n.* any chromosome that is not a SEX CHROMOSOME. A human normally has a total of 44 autosomes (arranged in 22 HOMOLOGOUS pairs) in the nucleus of each body cell, although irregular numbers may occur through the loss or addition of one or more autosomes. If a homologous pair of autosomes has an extra chromosome, the condition is called **trisomy**. If one member of a homologous pair is absent, the condition is called **monosomy**.

autosuggestibility *n.* susceptibility to being influenced by one's own suggestions, as in SELF-HYPNOSIS.

autosuggestion *n.* the process of making positive suggestions to oneself for such purposes as improving morale, inducing relaxation, or promoting recovery from illness. Also called **self-suggestion**. See also AUTOGENIC TRAINING; SUGGESTION.

autotomy *n.* SELF-MUTILATION or the cutting off by an individual of his or her body parts.

auxiliary ego in PSYCHODRAMA, a group member, other than the therapist, who assumes the role of a significant figure in the PROTAGONIST'S life.

auxiliary therapist a therapist who takes part in COTHERAPY.

ava *n.* see KAVA.

availability *n.* the presence of information in memory storage. Availability should be distinguished from **accessibility**, which refers to the ability of a portion of information to be retrieved.

availability heuristic *n.* a common strategy for making judgments about likelihood of occurrence in which the individual bases such judgments on the amount of information held in his or her memory about the particular type of event: The more information there is, the more likely the event is judged to be. Use of this strategy may lead to errors of judgment when information that is highly available in memory (e.g., about well-publicized events, such as plane crashes) leads people to believe that those kinds of events are more probable than they actually are, or when the relative unavailability of information (e.g., about less well-publicized causes of death, as from diabetes) leads people to believe that those kinds of events are less probable than they are. Compare REPRESENTATIVENESS HEURISTIC. See HEURISTIC.

Aventyl *n.* a trade name for NORTRIPTYLINE.

averse conditioning see AVERSIVE CONDITIONING.

aversion *n.* a physiological or emotional response indicating dislike for a stimulus. It is usually accompanied by withdrawal from or avoidance of the objectionable stimulus (an **aversion reaction**). **—aversive** *adj.*

aversion conditioning see AVERSIVE CONDITIONING.

aversion reaction a response expressed by avoiding a distasteful, threatening, or otherwise objectionable stimulus.

aversion system NEUROTICISM as represented by an individual's relative sensitivity to aversive (negative, punishing) cues and stimuli and his or her processes for avoiding them. Compare APPETITION SYSTEM. [proposed by Hans EYSENCK]

aversion therapy a form of BEHAVIOR THERAPY in which the client is conditioned to change or eliminate undesirable behavior or symptoms by associating them with noxious or unpleasant experiences, such as a bitter taste (for nail biting) or nausea (for alcoholism). Also called **aversive therapy**; **deterrent therapy**.

aversive conditioning the process by which a noxious or unpleasant stimulus is paired with an undesired behavior. This technique may be used therapeutically, as in AVERSION THERAPY. Also called **aversion conditioning**.

aversive control the use of an aversive outcome, such as punishment or negative reinforcement, to control behavior.

aversive stimulus any stimulus or occurrence that evokes AVOIDANCE BEHAVIOR or ESCAPE BEHAVIOR. Also called **aversive event**. See also AVOIDANCE CONDITIONING.

aversive therapy see AVERSION THERAPY.

aviophobia *n.* see FEAR OF FLYING.

avoidance *n.* the practice or an instance of keeping away from particular situations, environments, individuals, or things because of either (a) the anticipated negative consequences of such an encounter or (b) anxious or painful feelings associated with those things or events. Psychology brings several theoretical perspectives to the study of avoidance: its use as a means of coping; its use as a response to fear or shame; and its existence as a component in ANXIETY DISORDERS.

avoidance–avoidance conflict a situation involving a choice between two equally objectionable alternatives, for example, when an individual must choose between unemployment or a salary cut. Also called **double-avoidance conflict**. See also APPROACH–APPROACH CONFLICT; APPROACH–AVOIDANCE CONFLICT.

avoidance behavior any act that enables an individual to avoid or anticipate unpleasant or painful situations, stimuli, or events, including conditioned aversive stimuli. See AVOIDANCE CONDITIONING. Compare ESCAPE BEHAVIOR.

avoidance conditioning the establishment of behavior that prevents or postpones aversive stimulation. In a typical conditioning experiment a buzzer is sounded, then a shock is applied to the subject (e.g., a dog) until it performs a particular act (e.g., jumping over a fence). After several trials, the dog jumps as soon as the buzzer sounds, avoiding the shock. Also called **avoidance learning**; **avoidance training**. See also ESCAPE CONDITIONING.

avoidance gradient the variation in the strength of a drive as a function of the organism's proximity to an AVERSIVE STIMULUS. For example, a rat's withdrawal behavior increases in intensity as it nears a feared stimulus (e.g., an electric shock). The avoidance gradient appears steeper than the APPROACH GRADIENT. See also APPROACH–APPROACH CONFLICT; APPROACH–AVOIDANCE CONFLICT.

avoidance response a response in which an organism anticipates an aversive stimulus and consequently attempts to prevent contact with this stimulus. The avoidance response is a form of abient behavior (see ABIENCE). Also called **avoidance reaction**.

avoidant attachment in the STRANGE SITUATION, a form of INSECURE ATTACHMENT in which infants do not seek proximity to their parent after separation. Instead, the infant does not appear distressed by the separation and avoids the returning parent.

avoidant attachment style an adult interpersonal style characterized by a discomfort in being close to others. Also called **anxious–avoidant attachment style**. See also ANXIOUS–AVOIDANT ATTACHMENT; ATTACHMENT THEORY.

avoidant disorder of childhood or adolescence in *DSM–III*, a disorder lasting at least 6 months between the ages of 2½ and 18 and characterized by persistent, excessive retreating from strangers. It interferes with peer relationships, but satisfying relationships with family members may be intact. In *DSM–IV–TR*, this diagnostic category has been subsumed under SOCIAL PHOBIA. Also called **shyness disorder**. See also AVOIDANT PERSONALITY DISORDER.

avoidant marriage a long-lasting marriage in which the partners seldom argue because they have "agreed to disagree" and accept their differences of opinions with no apparent rancor.

avoidant paruresis inability to urinate in the presence of other people. Also called **bashful bladder syndrome**.

avoidant personality a personality trait characterized by feeling uncomfortable when psychologically close to others, resulting in a tendency not to form intimate relations.

avoidant personality disorder in *DSM–IV–TR*, a personality disorder characterized by (a) hypersensitivity to rejection and criticism, (b) a desire for uncritical acceptance, (c) social withdrawal in spite of a desire for affection and acceptance, and (d) low self-esteem. This pattern is long-standing and severe enough to cause objective distress and seriously impair the ability to work and maintain relationships. [first defined in 1969 by U.S. psychologist Theodore Millon (1929–)]

avolition *n.* failure to engage in goal-directed behavior, occasionally occurring in severe MAJOR DEPRESSIVE EPISODES.

awareness *n.* conscious realization, perception, or knowledge. See also SELF-AWARENESS.

awareness-training model an approach in psychology and education that stresses self-awareness, self-realization, exploration, and interpersonal sensitivity. The awareness-training model is associated with such writers as German-born U.S. psychologist Frederick (Fritz) S. Perls (1893–1970) and U.S. psychologist William C. Schutz (1925–2002).

awe *n.* the experience of admiration and elevation in response to physical beauty, displays of exceptional ability, or moral goodness. The awe-inspiring stimulus is experienced as "vast" and difficult to comprehend.

awfulizing *n.* an irrational thought pattern characterized by the tendency to overestimate the potential seriousness or negative consequences of events, situations, or perceived threats.

axis *n.* (*pl.* **axes**) **1.** in *DSM–IV–TR*, any of the dimensions that are helpful for describing individual behavior and thus facilitate CLINICAL ASSESSMENT. *DSM–IV–TR* uses a MULTIAXIAL CLASSIFICATION based on five axes: clinical disorders (Axis I), personality disorders and mental retardation (Axis II), GENERAL MEDICAL CONDITIONS (Axis III), psychosocial and environmental problems (Axis IV), and global assessment of functioning (Axis V). **2.** an imaginary line that bisects the body or an organ in a particular plane. For example, the **long** (or **cephalocaudal**) **axis** runs in the median plane, dividing the body into right and left halves. **3.** the second cervical vertebra, on which the skull rotates. **4.** a system made up of interrelated parts, as in the HYPOTHALAMIC–PITUITARY–ADRENOCORTICAL SYSTEM (or axis).

axon *n.* the long, thin, hollow, cylindrical extension of a NEURON that normally carries a nerve impulse away from the CELL BODY. An axon

A

often branches extensively and may be surrounded by a protective MYELIN SHEATH. Each branch of an axon ends in a **terminal button** (or **synaptic bouton**) from which an impulse is transmitted, through discharge of a NEUROTRANSMITTER, across a SYNAPSE to a neighboring neuron. Also called **nerve fiber**. **—axonal** *adj.*

ayahuasca *n.* a powerful hallucinogenic beverage made from the stems of a tropical South American woody vine, *Banisteriopsis caapi*, and the plant *Psychotria viridis*. It has been used for centuries by indigenous peoples of the Amazon for religious, spiritual, and medicinal purposes and more recently in the United States to evoke ANOMALOUS EXPERIENCES. The pharmacologically active ingredients are HARMINE and **harmaline** from *B. caapi* and dimethyltryptamine (see DMT)from *P. viridis*. In smaller doses, these ingredients have hallucinogenic and euphoric effects but in larger doses cause nausea and vomiting, TINNITUS, and collapse, followed by sedation. Also called **caapi**; **yagé**.

Ayurveda *n.* a holistic system of healing, originating and practiced primarily in the Indian subcontinent, that has spread to some extent in Western cultures. It includes diet and herbal remedies and emphasizes the use of body, mind, and spirit in disease prevention and treatment.

azapirone *n.* any of a class of nonbenzodiazepine ANXIOLYTICS of which the prototype is BUSPIRONE. They relieve anxiety by acting as PARTIAL AGONISTS at the 5-HT_{1A} serotonin receptor (see SEROTONIN-RECEPTOR AGONISTS). Other drugs in this class include gepirone, tandospirone, and ipsapirone. Azapirones produce less sedation than the BENZODIAZEPINES and they lack the abuse potential of these drugs. However, their onset of action is 2–3 weeks, and they cannot therefore be used to manage acute or paroxysmal anxiety. Also called **azapirodecanedione**.

azathioprine *n.* a drug used to suppress the immune response. It is the most widely used drug in support of organ transplantation and other potentially severe cases of immune reactions. U.S. trade name (among others): **Imuran**.

Bb

baah-ji *n.* see BAH-TSCHI.

baby blues a colloquial name for the transient depressive symptoms experienced by many women during the first 10 days after giving birth. It should be distinguished from POSTPARTUM DEPRESSION. Also called **maternity blues**; **postpartum blues**.

backup reinforcer in BEHAVIOR MODIFICATION, a reward given to a client or patient in return for tokens he or she has earned. See also TOKEN ECONOMY.

baclofen *n.* a skeletal MUSCLE RELAXANT that inhibits transmission of synaptic reflexes at the spinal cord level. It is often used in the treatment of reversible spasticity associated with multiple sclerosis or spinal cord injury. U.S. trade name: **Lioresal**.

bacterial endocarditis inflammation of the heart lining (endocardium) due to bacterial infection and causing damage to the heart valves and impaired pumping action of the heart. Fever and other systemic symptoms ensue, including embolism and heart failure. The infection can be acquired by unhygienic intravenous drug administration or abuse.

bad breast in the psychoanalytic theory of Melanie KLEIN, the internalized representation (see INTROJECTION) of the mother's breast as unsatisfying. According to Klein, the infant first experiences the mother and the nourishing breast as PART-OBJECTS with positive qualities—the GOOD BREAST—and negative qualities—the bad breast.

bad faith an individual's denial of his or her freedom as a human being or unwillingness to accept the undetermined and unforced nature of his or her actions. This often entails a denial of responsibility for the consequences of one's actions and choices or hiding the truth from oneself intentionally. See also EXISTENTIAL PSYCHOTHERAPY. [proposed by French existentialist philosopher Jean-Paul Sartre (1905–1980)]

bad is stronger than good the tendency for negative events, information, or feedback to have significantly more impact or influence on emotions, thoughts, or behavior than an equivalent positive event, information, or feedback.

bad me in the SELF-SYSTEM theory of U.S. psychoanalyst Harry Stack Sullivan (1892–1949), the internalized personification of impulses and behaviors that are considered to be negative by the self and, therefore, need to be hidden or disguised from others or from the self. In a child, for instance, the bad me may arise out of a sense of parental disapproval that in turn gives rise to anxiety and self-doubt. Compare GOOD ME. See also NOT ME.

bad object in the psychoanalytic theory of Melanie KLEIN, an introjected PART-OBJECT perceived as having negative qualities (see INTROJECTION). It is an early object representation that derives from SPLITTING of the object into parts containing negative qualities (i.e., the bad object) and positive qualities (i.e., the GOOD OBJECT).

bad trip an acute psychotic episode that is caused by ingestion of HALLUCINOGENS. The episode may also be marked by FLASHBACKS at a later date. See also HALLUCINOGEN INTOXICATION; HALLUCINOGEN-INDUCED MOOD DISORDER.

bah-tschi (**bah-tsi; baah-ji**) *n.* a CULTURE-BOUND SYNDROME found in Thailand, with symptoms similar to those of LATAH.

BAI abbreviation for BECK ANXIETY INVENTORY.

balance 1. *n.* a harmonious relationship or equilibrium of opposing forces or contrasting elements. See BALANCE THEORY; HOMEOSTASIS. **2.** *n.* the sense of equilibrium mediated by the VESTIBULAR SYSTEM of the inner ear. **3.** *vb.* to adjust forces to maintain something at a level from which it would ordinarily deviate.

balance theory a particular COGNITIVE CONSISTENCY THEORY specifying that people prefer elements within a cognitive system to be internally consistent with one another (i.e., balanced). Balanced systems are assumed to be more stable and psychologically pleasant than imbalanced systems. The theory has been primarily specified and tested within the context of systems involving three elements. These systems are sometimes referred to as **P-O-X triads**, in which P = person (i.e., self), O = other person, and X = some stimulus or event. See also COGNITIVE CONSISTENCY THEORY. [first proposed in 1946 by Austrian-born U.S. psychologist Fritz Heider (1896–1988)]

balance training a form of physical or occupational therapy for individuals who experience difficulty with **balance control** (maintaining balance when standing, walking, or performing other activities). It involves a series of exercises designed to enhance muscular control and improve interpretation of information from the senses and may make use of trainer bicycles, tricycles with body supports and foot attachments, stilts, pogo sticks, rocker boards, and a rubber bouncing tube used like a trampoline. Balance training is also used by many athletes to enhance fitness, coordination, and performance.

Bálint's syndrome a spatial and attentional disorder resulting from lesions in the parieto-occipital region of the brain. It consists of inability to visually guide the hand to an object (optic ataxia), inability to change visual gaze (**optic apraxia**), and inability to recognize multiple stimuli in a scene and understand their nature as a whole (simultanagnosia; see VISUAL AGNOSIA). [first described in 1909 by Rudolf **Bálint** (1874–1929), Hungarian physician]

B and D abbreviation for BONDAGE AND DISCIPLINE.

Bandura, Albert (1925–) Canadian-born U.S. psychologist. Born and raised in Alberta, Canada, Bandura received his PhD from the University of Iowa in 1952 under the direction of Arthur L. Benton (1909–2006). He then joined the faculty of Stanford University, where he remained throughout his career. Bandura is best known for his work on SOCIAL LEARNING THEORY. Early in his career, he studied the familial origins of antisocial aggression in adolescent boys, culminating in his first book, *Adolescent Aggression* (1959), and the later *Aggression: A Social Learning Analysis* (1973). These books showed that adolescents whose parents' behavior included hostile attitudes were more likely to display aggression, even when aggressive behavior was openly discouraged at home. Bandura and his colleagues went on to explore the role of OBSERVATIONAL LEARNING. In famous studies using a Bobo doll (an inflatable plastic toy), Bandura showed that, contrary to the predictions of then-dominant behaviorist theory, humans could learn through social MODELING in the absence of positive reinforcement. Bandura's subsequent work centered on various topics in the field of SOCIAL-COGNITIVE THEORY, especially self-regulatory processes and their role in motivation and behavior. Among his other important works are *Social Learning Theory* (1977), *Social Foundations of Thought and Action: A Social Cognitive Theory* (1986), and *Self-Efficacy: The Exercise of Control* (1997). Bandura served as president of the American Psychological Association and was elected to the American Academy of Arts and Sciences and the Institute of Medicine of the National Academy of Sciences.

bangungut *n.* a CULTURE-BOUND SYNDROME observed mainly among young, healthy, Filipino males. The individual is often overheard screaming or moaning during sleep, apparently experiencing a terrifying nightmare; this is followed by unexpected death. Also called **oriental nightmare-death syndrome**.

barbiturate abuse see SEDATIVE, HYPNOTIC, OR ANXIOLYTIC ABUSE.

barbiturate addiction see SEDATIVE, HYPNOTIC, OR ANXIOLYTIC DEPENDENCE.

barbiturate dependence see SEDATIVE, HYPNOTIC, OR ANXIOLYTIC DEPENDENCE.

barbiturate intoxication see SEDATIVE, HYPNOTIC, OR ANXIOLYTIC INTOXICATION.

barbiturates *pl. n.* a family of drugs, derived from barbituric acid, that depress activity of the central nervous system (see CNS DEPRESSANT) and were previously widely used as anxiolytics, sedatives, and hypnotics. They typically induce profound TOLERANCE and withdrawal symptoms and depress respiration: They can depress breathing completely—hence their use by individuals wishing to commit suicide. Barbiturates are commonly categorized according to their rates of action (including onset of effect, absorption, and excretion) as long acting, intermediate acting, short acting, or ultrashort acting. Their use became common in the 1930s, but they were rapidly supplanted in the 1970s by the BENZODIAZEPINES, which lack the lethality associated with overdose of the barbiturates. The group includes AMOBARBITAL, BUTABARBITAL, PENTOBARBITAL, PHENOBARBITAL, PRIMIDONE, and THIOPENTAL, among others. The prototype of the group, **barbital** was introduced into medical practice in 1903. See SEDATIVE, HYPNOTIC, AND ANXIOLYTIC DRUGS.

barbiturate withdrawal see SEDATIVE, HYPNOTIC, OR ANXIOLYTIC WITHDRAWAL.

barbiturate withdrawal delirium see SEDATIVE, HYPNOTIC, OR ANXIOLYTIC WITHDRAWAL DELIRIUM.

bar hustlers see MALE HOMOSEXUAL PROSTITUTION.

bariatrics *n.* a field of medicine that focuses on the study of overweight: its causes, prevention, and treatment.

barK abbreviation for BETA-ADRENERGIC RECEPTOR KINASE.

barricade incidents hostage and high-risk incidents, which require crisis management and negotiation capabilities.

barrier *n.* something that restricts, impedes, or blocks progress or the achievement of an ultimate objective or end. In psychological contexts barriers are mental, emotional, or behavioral limitations in individuals and groups.

barrier-free environment a built space that is free of obstacles to individuals with physical and cognitive disabilities and permits safe, uninhibited movements. Environmental barriers can include street curbs, revolving doors or doors too narrow to admit wheelchairs, inaccessible toilets and washbowls, and elevator buttons that cannot be read by people with visual impairment. See also UNIVERSAL DESIGN.

Barthel Index a form of FUNCTIONAL STATUS measurement that includes 10 items assessing an individual's ability to perform the ACTIVITIES OF DAILY LIVING independently. An individual is rated on a point scale regarding the degree of assistance required to perform each item, and the ratings are then combined to yield a total score.

B

[Dorothea W. **Barthel**, 20th-century U.S. psychologist]

Bartlett technique a study of memory based on the theory that memory should be viewed as constructive and reconstructive (see CONSTRUCTIVE MEMORY; RECONSTRUCTIVE MEMORY), rather than being simply reproductive. In the original 1932 study, British college students attempted to recall a particular Native American folk tale. Successive reproductions of the tale demonstrated that the students' own cultural knowledge and expectations intruded into the recall, rationalizing and eliminating unusual elements and structuring unrelated items of the tale into a more coherent and familiar framework. Also called **Bartlett tradition**. [Sir Frederic Charles **Bartlett** (1886–1969), British psychologist]

BAS abbreviation for BEHAVIORAL APPROACH SYSTEM.

basal ganglia a group of nuclei (neuron cell bodies) deep within the cerebral hemispheres of the brain that includes the CAUDATE NUCLEUS, PUTAMEN, GLOBUS PALLIDUS, SUBSTANTIA NIGRA, and SUBTHALAMIC NUCLEUS. The putamen and globus pallidus are together known as the **lenticular** (or **lentiform**) **nucleus**, the lenticular nucleus and caudate nucleus are together known as the **corpus striatum**, and the caudate nucleus and putamen are together called the **striatum**. The basal ganglia are involved in the generation of goal-directed voluntary movement. Also called **basal nuclei**.

baseline *n.* a stable level of performance used as a yardstick to assess the effects of particular manipulations or interventions. For example, experimental treatments are expected to modify behavior relative to BASELINE MEASURES. See also BEHAVIORAL BASELINE.

baseline assessment **1.** the measurement of characteristics of an individual or population prior to planned interventions in order to evaluate the intervention effects. **2.** the measurement of characteristics of humans and other animals at a particular point in development in order to evaluate natural changes in these characteristics over time.

baseline measures observations of participants' responses before the administration of any experimental intervention.

baseline performance the measured rate of a behavior before introduction of an intervention, which allows comparison and assessment of the effects of the intervention.

base rate the naturally occurring frequency of a phenomenon in a population. This rate is often contrasted with the rate of the phenomenon under the influence of some changed condition in order to determine the degree to which the change influences the phenomenon.

bases of an attitude the types of information from which an attitude is derived. Traditionally, researchers have distinguished between three categories of bases: The **affective basis** refers to the emotions, feelings, and moods associated with the ATTITUDE OBJECT; the **cognitive basis** refers to beliefs about attributes associated with the attitude object; and the **behavioral basis** refers to responses, such as past behaviors and future intentions, associated with the attitude object. Also called **components of an attitude**.

bashful bladder syndrome see AVOIDANT PARURESIS.

basic anxiety in EGO PSYCHOLOGY, a feeling of being helpless, abandoned, and endangered in a hostile world. According to German-born U.S. psychoanalyst Karen D. Horney (1885–1952), it arises from the infant's helplessness and dependence on his or her parents or from parental indifference. Defenses against basic anxiety and hostility may produce NEUROTIC NEEDS and NEUROTIC TRENDS, such as a submissive attitude, the need to exert power over others, or withdrawal from relationships. See also BASIC HOSTILITY.

basic conflict in EGO PSYCHOLOGY, the conflict between a person's dominant NEUROTIC TREND and his or her incompatible nondominant NEUROTIC NEEDS, which must be kept repressed. [first described by German-born U.S. psychoanalyst Karen D. Horney (1885–1952)]

basic emotion see PRIMARY EMOTION.

basic encounter a meaningful experience in one person's relating to another that is characterized by mutual trust and empathy. The development and occurrence of such encounters in therapy and counseling contexts is considered to be beneficial to the therapeutic process and outcome for the client. See also CLIENT-CENTERED THERAPY.

basic hostility in EGO PSYCHOLOGY, a feeling of hostility and resentment toward the parents that develops as a result of the BASIC ANXIETY that the infant feels at being dependent on them. To the extent that the infant fears the parents, basic hostility and anxiety are repressed and give rise to NEUROTIC NEEDS and NEUROTIC TRENDS. [defined by German-born U.S. psychoanalyst Karen D. Horney (1885–1952)]

BASIC ID see MULTIMODAL THERAPY.

basic mistake in the psychology of Alfred ADLER, a factor arising in early childhood that affects a person's lifestyle in later life and that may need to be corrected in order to resolve conflicts.

basic mistrust see BASIC TRUST VERSUS MISTRUST.

basic need see PHYSIOLOGICAL NEED.

Basic Nordic Sleep Questionnaire (**BNSQ**) a standardized questionnaire that uses a five-point quantitative scale, ranging from never (1) to every night (5), for measuring the frequency of occurrence during the previous 3 months of various sleep disturbances and complaints. The questionnaire was initially developed in 1988 by the Scandinavian Sleep Research Society for use in Denmark, Norway, Sweden, Finland, and Iceland (i.e., the Nordic countries).

B

basic rest–activity cycle (**BRAC**) cyclic alternations between activity and nonactivity during waking and sleep, thought typically to involve a 90-min cycle.

basic rule the fundamental rule of psychoanalysis that the patient must attempt to put all spontaneous thoughts, feelings, and memories into words without censorship, so that they can be analyzed to reveal unconscious wishes and emotions. Also called **fundamental rule**.

basic trust versus mistrust the first of ERIKSON'S EIGHT STAGES OF DEVELOPMENT, between birth and 18 months of age. During this stage, the infant either comes to view other people and himself or herself as trustworthy or comes to develop a fundamental distrust of his or her environment. The growth of basic trust, considered essential for the later development of self-esteem and positive interpersonal relationships, is attributed to a primary caregiver who is responsively attuned to the baby's individual needs while conveying the quality of trustworthiness, while the growth of basic distrust is attributed to neglect, lack of love, or inconsistent treatment.

BAT abbreviation for BEHAVIORAL APPROACH TASK.

bath therapy the use of water immersion in therapy. See also HYDROTHERAPY.

battered-child syndrome (**BCS**) the effects on a child of intentional and repeated physical abuse by parents or other caregivers. In addition to sustaining physical injuries, the child is at increased risk of experiencing longer-term problems, such as depression, POSTTRAUMATIC STRESS DISORDER, substance abuse, decreased self-esteem, and sexual and other behavioral difficulties. See also CHILD ABUSE.

battered-woman syndrome (**BWS**) the psychological effects of being physically abused by a spouse or domestic partner. The syndrome includes LEARNED HELPLESSNESS in relation to the abusive spouse, as well as symptoms of posttraumatic stress. See also CYCLE OF VIOLENCE.

battered women women who are physically abused by their spouses or domestic partners. Woman beating is considered to surpass rape as the most underreported act of violent assault in the United States. Data suggest that violence against women is common and occurs in all social classes and ethnic and religious groups, as well as between same-sex partners.

battering men's excuses rationalizations given by men who beat their spouses or domestic partners. These may include claims of provocation, or that beating a spouse or partner is acceptable in the batterer's culture, or that the batterer was angry.

battlefield recovery tasks stressful tasks associated with the aftermath of an armed conflict, such as recovering casualties and bodies and identifying and burying the dead.

battle inoculation training in simulated operational conditions (such as fire from real weapons) to prepare soldiers for deployment in combat. The battlefield performance of a soldier is directly related to the quality and amount of realistic unit and individual training that the soldier has received. Training must be related to the wartime mission of a unit and to the climatic conditions it can expect to face. Live-fire training prepares soldiers for the shock and noise of combat. Realistic training not only helps to inoculate soldiers to the stresses of operations (including combat) but also enables them to learn methods for coping with their reactions to these stresses. Previous operational experience (especially in combat) helps to prepare soldiers for future situations. See also STRESS TRAINING.

battle shock psychological impairment resulting from COMBAT STRESS REACTIONS. The expression was used in the Israeli Yom Kippur war to describe the condition of a combat STRESS CASUALTY who was unable to tolerate further military combat.

Bayesian approach the use of conditional probabilities as an aid in selecting between various options involving a degree of uncertainty, for example, in the delivery of health care services or utilization of limited resources. [Thomas **Bayes** (1702–1761), British mathematician and theologian]

Bayley Scales of Infant and Toddler Development scales for assessing the developmental status of infants and young children aged 1 month to 42 months. Test stimuli, such as form boards, blocks, shapes, household objects (e.g., utensils), and other common items, are used to engage the child in specific tasks of increasing difficulty and elicit particular responses. The Bayley scales currently have five components. Tasks from the **Mental scale** are designed to evaluate such functions as perception, memory, and learning; those from the **Motor scale** measure gross and fine motor abilities, such as crawling, sitting, grasping, and object manipulation. The **Behavior Rating scale** (formerly called the **Infant Behavior Record**) contains detailed descriptions of specific categories of behavior that are graded on a 5-point scale. It supplements the Mental and Motor scales and provides an assessment of overall attention and arousal, orientation and engagement, emotional regulation, and motor quality. The final two components, the **Social–Emotional scale** and the **Adaptive Behavior scale**, use questionnaires to obtain parent or caregiver perceptions of their child's development. The Bayley scales were originally published in 1969 and subsequently revised in 1993; the most recent version is the **Bayley–III**, published in 2005. [developed by Nancy **Bayley** (1899–1994), U. S. psychologist]

BBBG syndrome see TELECANTHUS-HYPOSPADIAS SYNDROME.

B-cognition *n.* see BEING COGNITION.

BCS abbreviation for BATTERED-CHILD SYNDROME.

BDD abbreviation for BODY DYSMORPHIC DISORDER.

BDI abbreviation for BECK DEPRESSION INVENTORY.

BDS abbreviation for BLESSED DEMENTIA SCALE.

beast fetishism a PARAPHILIA involving contact with animal furs or hides, which serve as an APHRODISIAC.

beating fantasy in the CLASSICAL PSYCHOANALYSIS of Sigmund FREUD, a male or female child's fantasy of being beaten by his or her father or mother. For both sexes, the fantasy is interpreted as an expression of the child's oedipal desires toward the father and is said to be based on the child's belief that the father beats the mother in the PRIMAL SCENE.

Beck Anxiety Inventory (BAI) a self-report, 21-item measure used to assess the severity of anxiety in adults and to discriminate anxiety from depression. [Aaron T. **Beck** (1921–), U.S. psychiatrist]

Beck Depression Inventory (BDI) a self-report questionnaire designed to assess the severity of depressive symptoms in adolescents and adults. Extensively used in both clinical and research settings, it consists of 21 item groups, each of which includes four statements of increasing severity. Each group reflects a symptom or attitude associated with depression (e.g., loss of energy, self-dislike), and each statement has a numerical value from 0 to 3. Participants choose the statement within each group that most accurately reflects how they have felt within the past two weeks. The BDI was originally published in 1961; the most recent version is the **BDI–II**, published in 1996. [Aaron T. **Beck** and colleagues]

Beck Hopelessness Scale (BHS) a scale of 20 true–false statements used to measure an individual's attitudes about the future, loss of motivation, and expectations in order to predict suicide risk. [Aaron T. **Beck**]

Beck Scale for Suicide Ideation (BSS) a measure of the necessity for detailed questioning about a patient's intentions, administered to patients who are considered to be at risk of suicide. [Aaron T. **Beck**]

Beck therapy a COGNITIVE BEHAVIOR THERAPY, with individuals or groups, in which the therapist collaborates with the client to design in-session and homework tasks to test the validity of maladaptive thoughts and perceptions. Clients identify the negative thought or perception, label it (e.g., overgeneralization, polarized thinking), test its validity, devise alternative explanations, discuss the implications of these alternatives, and complete homework to practice the alternatives. [Aaron T. **Beck**]

bed-wetting *n.* the involuntary discharge of urine during sleep. Bed-wetting is considered problematic if it occurs in children older than 4 or 5 years of age; it is twice as common in boys. Also called **sleep enuresis**. See also ELIMINATION DISORDER; ENURESIS.

before–after design an experimental design in which one or more groups of participants are measured both prior to and following administration of the treatment or manipulation. Also called **pre–post design**; **pretest–posttest design**.

behavior *n.* **1.** an organism's activities in response to external or internal stimuli, including objectively observable activities, introspectively observable activities (see COVERT BEHAVIOR), and unconscious processes. **2.** more restrictively, any action or function that can be objectively observed or measured in response to controlled stimuli. Historically, behaviorists contrasted objective behavior with mental activities, which were considered subjective and thus unsuitable for scientific study. See BEHAVIORISM. **—behavioral** *adj.*

behavioral approach system (BAS) a brain system theorized to underlie incentive motivation by activating approach behaviors in response to stimuli related to positive reinforcement. It has been suggested that the BAS is associated as well with the generation of positive affective responses, and that a strong or chronically active BAS tends to result in extraversion. Also called **behavioral activation system**. Compare BEHAVIORAL INHIBITION SYSTEM. [described by British psychologist Jeffrey Alan Gray (1934–2004)]

behavioral approach task (BAT) an observational assessment technique in which an individual approaches a feared situation until he or she is unable to go further. The BAT is used to assess levels of avoidance and fear of specific situations associated with phobias. It may also be used to corroborate information obtained in the CLINICAL INTERVIEW and to measure treatment progress and outcome. Variables that can be measured using the BAT include physical symptoms (e.g., increased heart rate), escape or avoidance strategies, and subjective ratings of fear. Also called **behavioral approach test**; **behavioral avoidance test**.

behavioral assessment the systematic study and evaluation of an individual's behavior using a wide variety of techniques, including direct observation, interviews, and self-monitoring. When used to identify patterns indicative of disorder, the procedure is called **behavioral diagnosis** and is essential in deciding upon the use of specific behavioral or cognitive-behavioral interventions.

behavioral avoidance test see BEHAVIORAL APPROACH TASK.

behavioral baseline a STEADY STATE of behavior against which the effects of introducing an

B

INDEPENDENT VARIABLE may be compared. For example, a child may throw between six and eight tantrums per week over the course of several weeks. This level of tantrums could then serve as a behavioral baseline to assess the effectiveness of a treatment regime. Also called **behavior baseline**.

behavioral clinic see MENTAL HEALTH CLINIC.

behavioral congruence consistency between the aims, attitudes, and values professed by an individual or group and observable behaviors. In personality research, behavioral congruence occurs when individuals' SELF-RATINGS are consistent with their actions.

behavioral contagion the rapid copying of the behavior of one or a few people by others in the vicinity, often in response to a salient rewarding or threatening stimulus. After the initiators first perform the behavior, the action is quickly adopted and copied by the others in an almost compulsive manner, with little analysis of the situation. Also called **behavior contagion**. See also CONTAGION; EMOTIONAL CONTAGION; MASS CONTAGION.

behavioral contract an agreement between therapist and client in which the client agrees to carry out certain behaviors, usually between sessions but sometimes during the session as well. Also called **behavior contract**. See also CONTRACT; CONTINGENCY CONTRACT.

behavioral contrast in clinical practice, an increase in the occurrence of a behavior in a nontreatment setting when a decrease in that behavior has been achieved in a treatment setting. For example, an intervention decreases tantrums in school, but the rate of tantrums increases at home, where the intervention is not in use.

behavioral counseling a system of counseling in which the primary focus is on changing client behavior through SELF-MANAGEMENT, OPERANT CONDITIONING, and related techniques. Specific behaviors are targeted for modification, and intervention strategies and environmental changes are then established in order to bring about the desired modification.

behavioral couples therapy a COUPLES THERAPY that focuses on interrupting negative interaction patterns through instruction, modeling, rehearsal, feedback, positive behavior exchange, and structured problem solving. This therapy can be conducted with individual couples or in a couples group format. When practiced with legally married partners, it is called **behavioral marital therapy**, though some practitioners use this term interchangeably with behavioral couples therapy. See also COMMUNICATION SKILLS TRAINING; INTEGRATIVE BEHAVIORAL COUPLES THERAPY.

behavioral criterion an aspect of actual (rather than self-reported) behavior that must exist in a person for an accurate diagnosis to be made. Also called **behavior criterion**.

behavioral deficit the lack of certain age-specific aspects of behavior in an individual, who is therefore not developmentally on target. Also called **behavior deficit**.

behavioral diagnosis see BEHAVIORAL ASSESSMENT.

behavioral diary a tool used to collect data in which the research participant keeps a record of events at the time they occur.

behavioral disorder see BEHAVIOR DISORDER.

behavioral economics the application of economic principles (e.g., the law of supply and demand) to the prediction, analysis, and potential modification of behavior. For example, substance abuse may be discussed in terms of the price of and demand for the substance in question.

behavioral endocrinology the study of the relationships between behavior and the functioning of the endocrine glands and neuroendocrine cells (see NEUROENDOCRINOLOGY). A variety of endocrine glands, including the hypothalamus, the pituitary gland, and the adrenal glands, have been shown to affect behavior. For example, gonadal secretion of sex hormones affects sexual behavior, and secretion of corticosteroids by the adrenal glands affects physiological and behavioral responses to stress.

behavioral family therapy a family treatment that is characterized by behavioral analysis of presenting problems and a focus on overt behavior change through application of learning-based behavioral principles and techniques of BEHAVIOR THERAPY. Techniques used to modify targeted behavior patterns include behavioral contracts, instruction, modeling, and rehearsal.

behavioral genetics the study of familial or hereditary behavior patterns and of the genetic mechanisms of behavior traits. Also called **behavior genetics**.

behavioral group therapy a form of GROUP THERAPY that applies learning-based behavioral principles and techniques, including modeling, rehearsal, social reinforcement, SYSTEMATIC DESENSITIZATION, and other methods of BEHAVIOR THERAPY, in the context of a group. See also COGNITIVE BEHAVIORAL GROUP THERAPY.

behavioral health an interdisciplinary subspecialty of BEHAVIORAL MEDICINE that promotes a philosophy of health emphasizing individual responsibility in the maintenance of one's own health and in the prevention of illness and dysfunction by means of self-initiated activities (jogging, exercising, healthy eating, no smoking, etc.). [proposed by U.S. psychologist Joseph D. Matarazzo (1925–)]

behavioral hierarchy see BEHAVIOR HIERARCHY.

behavioral homeostasis an organism's tendency to maintain stability or equilibrium through various behavioral processes. For example, temperature regulation is achieved via shivering, sweating, or panting, and satiety is achieved by the initiation and then cessation of feeding behavior. Also called **behavior homeostasis**. See also HOMEOSTASIS.

behavioral homology functional similarity (i.e., common behavior) across species, suggestive of a shared ancestral origin. Also called **behavior homology**.

behavioral immunogen a behavior or lifestyle associated with a decreased risk of illness and with longer life. Examples of behavioral immunogens are moderate consumption of alcohol, regular exercise, adequate sleep, and a healthy diet. Compare BEHAVIORAL PATHOGEN.

behavioral incident a single, separate behavioral event with a clearly defined start and finish (e.g., brushing one's teeth), which may be combined with other events to form a BEHAVIORAL SEQUENCE.

behavioral inhibition a temperamental predisposition characterized by restraint in engaging with the world combined with a tendency to scrutinize the environment for potential threats and to avoid or withdraw from unfamiliar situations or people. [first described by U.S. psychologists Jerome Kagan (1929–) and J. Steven Reznick (1951–)]

behavioral inhibition system (**BIS**) a brain system theorized to underlie behavioral inhibition by activating avoidance behaviors in response to perceived threats. It has been suggested that the BIS is associated as well with the generation of negative affective responses, and that a strong or chronically active BIS tends to result in introversion. Compare BEHAVIORAL APPROACH SYSTEM. [described by British psychologist Jeffrey Alan Gray (1934–2004)]

behavioral integration **1.** the combination of separate individual behaviors into a synchronized or coordinated behavioral unit. **2.** a model for environmentally sound behavior that specifies the relevant cognitions and affects and their interactions. Also called **behavior integration**.

behavioral interview an approach to clinical interviewing that focuses on relating a problem behavior to antecedent stimuli and the consequences of reinforcement.

behavioral marital therapy see BEHAVIORAL COUPLES THERAPY.

behavioral medicine a field that applies behavioral theories and methods to the prevention and treatment of medical and psychological disorders. Areas of application include chronic illness, lifestyle issues (e.g., tobacco, drugs, alcohol, obesity), SOMATOFORM DISORDERS, and the like. Behavioral medicine is a multidisciplinary field in which physicians, psychologists, psychiatrists, social workers, and others work together; it includes strong integration of biological, psychosocial, behavioral, and interpersonal perspectives in developing biopsychosocial models of illness and disease and interventions to treat and manage diseases, promote good health, and maintain healthy behaviors. See also BEHAVIORAL HEALTH.

behavioral model a conceptualization of psychological disorders in terms of overt behavior patterns produced by learning and the influence of REINFORCEMENT CONTINGENCIES. Treatment techniques, including SYSTEMATIC DESENSITIZATION and MODELING, focus on modifying ineffective or maladaptive patterns.

behavioral neurochemistry the study of the relationships between behavior and biochemical influences, including the effects of drugs on metabolic processes within the brain and the roles of different NEUROTRANSMITTERS and neuroregulatory substances.

behavioral neuroscience a branch of NEUROSCIENCE and BIOLOGICAL PSYCHOLOGY that seeks to understand and characterize the specific neural circuitry and mechanisms underlying behavioral propensities or capacities.

behavioral pathogen a behavior or lifestyle that may increase the risk of developing illness or disability and may reduce life expectancy. Examples of behavioral pathogens are smoking, drug abuse, poor diet, unprotected sexual activity, and a sedentary lifestyle. Compare BEHAVIORAL IMMUNOGEN.

behavioral pattern see BEHAVIOR PATTERN.

behavioral pediatrics a multidisciplinary specialty in psychology that is often part of PEDIATRIC PSYCHOLOGY, clinical child psychology, and HEALTH PSYCHOLOGY. In prevention and intervention, practitioners address such problems as habit disorders, oppositional behavior, sleep and eating disorders, and physical health problems (e.g., traumatic brain injury). In the medical literature, it is also called **developmental-behavioral pediatrics**.

behavioral pharmacology a branch of pharmacology concerned with the physiological and behavioral mechanisms by which drugs operate, encompassing not only the effects of drugs on behavior but also how behavioral factors contribute to the actions of drugs and the ways in which they are used.

behavioral phenotype a pattern of motor, cognitive, linguistic, and social abnormalities that is consistently associated with a biological disorder. In some cases, the behavioral phenotype may constitute a discrete psychiatric disorder; in others, the abnormalities are usually not regarded as symptoms of a psychiatric disorder.

behavioral plasticity the degree to which a person's behavior can be influenced and modified by social experience and learning. High plasticity leaves ample room for change, whereas low plasticity involves inflexible behavior patterns.

behavioral procedure any psychological procedure based on the principles and techniques of

BEHAVIOR THEORY. It may be used in basic research or in applied settings. See APPLIED BEHAVIOR ANALYSIS.

behavioral profile an overall representation of the behavioral characteristics of a participant in a test or experiment, obtained not only from the scores on each individual characteristic but also from the general pattern of these scores. The scores on each characteristic are often made more directly comparable by using percentiles or standard scores of one type or another.

behavioral psychology an approach to understanding psychological phenomena that focuses on observable aspects of behavior and makes use of BEHAVIOR THEORY for explanation. See also BEHAVIORISM.

behavioral psychotherapy see BEHAVIOR THERAPY.

behavioral rehearsal see BEHAVIOR REHEARSAL.

behavioral relaxation training a form of relaxation training and BEHAVIOR THERAPY that emphasizes labeling of sensations, modeling, reinforcement, and therapist feedback. See also PROGRESSIVE RELAXATION.

behavioral repertoire see REPERTOIRE.

behavioral risk factor any specific behavior or pattern of behaviors that increases an individual's likelihood of developing a disorder, disease, or syndrome (e.g., overeating or smoking).

behavioral segment see BEHAVIOR SEGMENT.

behavioral self-control training a technique in BEHAVIOR THERAPY that uses self-monitoring, self-evaluation, self-reinforcement, coaching, behavioral contracts, and relapse prevention techniques to help clients achieve active coping strategies, to increase their sense of mastery, and to decrease undesired habits (e.g., nail biting). See also BEHAVIORAL WEIGHT CONTROL THERAPIES.

behavioral sequence a combination of BEHAVIORAL INCIDENTS directed toward a particular goal or outcome (e.g., getting ready for work in the morning).

behavioral sex therapy a form of SEX THERAPY that focuses on behavioral analysis of presenting problems and on changes to behavioral sequences that hinder healthy sexual functioning through BEHAVIOR THERAPY methods. Behavioral sequences can include those that are relationship-based (e.g., communication behaviors) or specifically sexually based (e.g., avoidance of sexual stimuli).

behavioral sleep medicine (**BSM**) a growing clinical specialty area combining aspects of health psychology and sleep disorders medicine. Practitioners include psychologists, physicians, nurse practitioners, and other health-care professionals certified in the discipline who seek to understand the cognitive and behavioral factors that contribute to the development and maintenance of adult and pediatric sleep disorders and who use this knowledge to provide empirically validated, nonpharmacological interventions. For example, a BSM practitioner would help a client with insomnia to fall asleep faster, wake up less frequently, and sleep more efficiently using specialized behavioral and cognitive techniques that normalize the person's sleep schedule and condition him or her to see the bedroom as a restful place.

behavioral technology experimentally established procedures (influenced by scientific behavior analysis) that are designed to produce behavioral change.

behavioral teratology the study of impairments in behavior that are produced by embryonic or fetal exposure to teratogens, that is, toxic substances that affect the developing organism (see TERATOGEN).

behavioral toxicity an adverse behavioral change produced by psychotropic drugs, for example, insomnia, sedation, impaired psychomotor activity, or changes in mental status.

behavioral toxicology the study of the behavioral impact of toxic exposure. There is increasing evidence that many toxins produce subtle behavioral changes, often in neurosensory functioning, at levels far below thresholds for detectable neurological damage. Perhaps the best known example is lead, which is now banned from gasoline and interior paint in many countries because of its low-level, behavioral-toxicological effects on developing children.

behavioral weight control therapies interventions that use the principles and techniques of BEHAVIOR THERAPY to help clients change eating and exercise habits to achieve and maintain a healthy weight. Practiced in group or individual sessions, these techniques include self-monitoring, behavioral contracts, environmental change (e.g., eating seated and only in a specific room), and reinforcement (e.g., social or monetary). See also BEHAVIORAL SELF-CONTROL TRAINING.

behavior analysis the decomposition of behavior into its component parts or processes. This approach to psychology is based on the experimental analysis of behavior, in which behavior is the subject matter for research rather than an indicator of underlying psychological entities or processes. Emphasis is placed on interactions between behavior and the environment. See APPLIED BEHAVIOR ANALYSIS. [originally developed by B. F. SKINNER]

behavior change **1.** a systematic approach to changing behavior through the use of OPERANT CONDITIONING. **2.** any alteration or adjustment of behavior that affects a patient's functioning, brought about by psychotherapeutic or other interventions or occurring spontaneously.

behavior checklist a list of behaviors that are to be recorded each time they are observed by an experimental investigator or participant or by a clinician.

behavior clinic see MENTAL HEALTH CLINIC.

behavior-constraint theory the concept that an individual may acquire LEARNED HELPLESSNESS when repeated efforts fail to gain control over excessive or undesirable environmental stimuli.

behavior contract see BEHAVIORAL CONTRACT.

behavior control 1. the use of any type of psychological manipulation, such as threats or promises, to steer individual or group behavior in a desired direction. **2.** the misuse of invasive or intrusive treatments (e.g., drugs or aversive conditioning) to achieve control over the lives of individuals, including patients.

behavior criterion see BEHAVIORAL CRITERION.

behavior deficit see BEHAVIORAL DEFICIT.

behavior determinant any factor that produces a behavioral effect.

behavior disorder any persistent and repetitive pattern of behavior that violates societal norms or rules or that seriously impairs a person's functioning. The term is used in a very general sense to cover a wide range of disorders or other syndromes. Also called **behavioral disorder**. See also ATTENTION-DEFICIT/HYPERACTIVITY DISORDER; DISRUPTIVE BEHAVIOR DISORDER; PRIMARY BEHAVIOR DISORDER.

behavior disorders of childhood and adolescence observable behaviors in young people that deviate from the norm. The term is often used in SPECIAL EDUCATION and school placement.

behavior dysfunctions classification the classification of personal problems on the basis of behaviors rather than symptoms or hypothetical constructs. Such a classification leads the clinician to work on helping the patient change behaviors rather than treating syndromes or diseases.

behavior episode a unit or sequence of activity with a relatively well-defined start and end. Also called **behavior unit**.

behavior field any set of stimuli or conditions, or accumulation of factors, that produces a behavioral effect.

behavior hierarchy a ranking of possible responses based on the relative probabilities of their being elicited, with more probable behaviors ranked higher than less probable behaviors. Also called **behavioral hierarchy**.

behavior integration see BEHAVIORAL INTEGRATION.

behaviorism *n.* an approach to psychology, formulated in 1913 by John B. WATSON, based on the study of objective, observable facts rather than subjective, qualitative processes, such as feelings, motives, and consciousness. To make psychology a naturalistic science, Watson proposed to limit it to quantitative events, such as stimulus–response relationships, effects of conditioning, physiological processes, and a study of human and animal behavior, all of which can best be investigated through laboratory experiments that yield objective measures under controlled conditions. Historically, behaviorists held that mind was not a proper topic for scientific study since mental events are subjective and not independently verifiable. With its emphasis on activity as an adaptive function, behaviorism is seen as an outgrowth of FUNCTIONALISM. See DESCRIPTIVE BEHAVIORISM; METHODOLOGICAL BEHAVIORISM; NEOBEHAVIORISM; RADICAL BEHAVIORISM.

behaviorist *n.* a person who espouses the principles of BEHAVIORISM and whose activities are consciously guided by those principles. See also BEHAVIOR ANALYSIS; BEHAVIOR MODIFICATION.

behavior modification the use of OPERANT CONDITIONING, BIOFEEDBACK, MODELING, AVERSIVE CONDITIONING, RECIPROCAL INHIBITION, or other learning techniques as a means of changing human behavior. For example, behavioral modification is used in clinical contexts to improve adaptation and alleviate symptoms and in industrial and organizational contexts to encourage employees to adopt safe work practices. The term is often used synonymously with BEHAVIOR THERAPY.

behavior observation a recording or evaluation (or both) of the ongoing behavior of one or more research participants by one or more observers. Observations may be made—using charts, checklists, rating scales, etc.—either directly as the behavior occurs or from such media as film, videotape, or audiotape.

behavior pattern a complex arrangement of two or more responses that occur in a prescribed order. Behavior patterns are also referred to as **chains of behavior**, highlighting their nature as a complex linking of simpler segments of behavior. They may be formed via the OPERANT CONDITIONING of various segments presented in the appropriate order. Also called **behavioral pattern**.

behavior problem a pattern of disruptive behavior that generally falls within social norms and does not seriously impair a person's functioning.

behavior rating a rating of the degree to which a participant shows each of several behaviors in a given situation.

behavior rehearsal a technique used in BEHAVIOR THERAPY or COGNITIVE BEHAVIOR THERAPY for modifying or enhancing social or interpersonal skills. The therapist introduces effective interpersonal strategies or behavior patterns to be practiced and rehearsed by the client until these are ready to be used in a real-life situation. The technique is also commonly used in ASSER-

TIVENESS TRAINING. Also called **behavioral rehearsal**.

behavior reversal a method of BEHAVIOR MODIFICATION in which the client, supervised by the therapist, practices desirable responses to interpersonal conflicts, which are often opposite to his or her usual behavior.

behavior sampling the process of recording a set of observations of a participant's behavior during a designated time frame. Behavior sampling may be conducted over multiple periods of observation in either natural or laboratory settings, with or without the awareness of the participant.

behavior segment a distinct response or BEHAVIOR EPISODE that, when linked with other responses, forms a BEHAVIOR PATTERN or chain. Also called **behavioral segment**.

behavior shaping see SHAPING.

behavior system 1. the different activities that can be undertaken to reach the same goal or carry out the same function, for example, communication is achieved through writing, speaking, or gestures. **2.** the expression of important motives (e.g., hunger, sex, aggression), which varies between cultures and among individuals within the same culture who have had different training and experiences. Also called **activity system**.

behavior theory the assumption that behavior, including its acquisition, development, and maintenance, can be adequately explained by principles of learning. Behavior theory attempts to describe environmental influences on behavior, often using controlled studies of animals. Behavior theory encompasses historical approaches to formal theorizing, such as those of C. L. HULL and K. W. SPENCE, and the operant theory of B. F. SKINNER, as well as contemporary approaches to behavior. Also called **general behavior theory**.

behavior therapy a form of psychotherapy that applies the principles of learning, OPERANT CONDITIONING, and PAVLOVIAN CONDITIONING to eliminate symptoms and modify ineffective or maladaptive patterns of behavior. The focus of this therapy is upon the behavior itself and the CONTINGENCIES and environmental factors that reinforce it, rather than exploration of the underlying psychological causes of the behavior. A wide variety of techniques are used in behavior therapy, such as BEHAVIOR REHEARSAL, BIOFEEDBACK, MODELING, and SYSTEMATIC DESENSITIZATION. Also called **behavioral psychotherapy**; **conditioning therapy**.

being-beyond-the-world *n.* in existential psychology, the potential for human beings to transcend the limitations of BEING-IN-THE-WORLD, usually through selfless love. See also DASEIN. [introduced by Swiss psychologist Ludwig Binswanger (1881–1966)]

being cognition 1. (**B-cognition**) in the HUMANISTIC PSYCHOLOGY of Abraham MASLOW, an exceptional type of cognition that can be distinguished from one's everyday perception of reality (**deficiency cognition** or **D-cognition**). Being cognition takes one of two forms: In the first, a person is aware of the whole universe and the interrelatedness of everything within it, including the perceiver; in the second, a person becomes entirely focused on a single object (e.g., a natural phenomenon, a work of art, or a loved person) to the extent that the rest of the universe, including the perceiver, seems to disappear. According to Maslow, self-actualizers (see SELF-ACTUALIZATION) frequently experience being cognitions. See also PEAK EXPERIENCE; TIMELESS MOMENT. **2.** awareness of the inner core of one's existence, that is, one's self or identity.

being-in-the-world *n.* in theories and clinical approaches derived from EXISTENTIALISM, the particular type of being characteristic of humans, in contrast to the type of being of animals, inanimate objects, or abstractions. The term is roughly synonymous with DASEIN, the term used by German philosopher Martin Heidegger (1889–1976). The word "being" is meant to emphasize that human existence is an activity more than a state or condition. Similarly, "world" is meant to convey a much richer and more meaningful ground for human life than would be conveyed by a more sterile term, such as "environment." Being-in-the-world is by its very nature oriented toward meaning and growth; while it characterizes the type of being of all humans, it is also unique for every person, and can be seen to be offering an explanation of what in other psychological traditions might be called IDENTITY or SELF. Compare BEING-BEYOND-THE-WORLD.

being love (**B-love**) in Abraham MASLOW'S HUMANISTIC PSYCHOLOGY, a form of love characterized by mutuality, genuine concern for another's welfare and pleasure, and reduced dependency, selfishness, and jealousy. B-love is one of the qualities Maslow ascribes to self-actualizers (see SELF-ACTUALIZATION). Compare DEFICIENCY LOVE.

being motivation see METAMOTIVATION.

being–not being a paraphrase of the fundamental question that, according to German philosopher Martin Heidegger (1889–1976), motivates human beings, namely, the worry or concern about dying and not being here any longer. See also DASEIN.

being psychology a psychological perspective that deals with "persons insofar as they are ends-in-themselves." It is concerned with the sacred, the unique, and the incomparable in people and things. [developed by Abraham MASLOW]

being values see METANEEDS.

belief–desire reasoning the process by which one explains and predicts another's behavior on the basis of one's understanding of the other's desires and beliefs. Belief–desire reasoning is the basis for THEORY OF MIND. See also MINDBLINDNESS.

belladonna alkaloids substances obtained from the shrub *Atropa belladonna* (commonly known as belladonna or deadly nightshade). They were known to the ancient Hindus and were used in the Middle Ages as poisons (the genus is named for Atropos, eldest of the mythological Fates, who cuts the thread of life). Their pharmacology was unknown until the 1860s, when they were found to affect heart rate, salivary secretion, and other body functions. ATROPINE and SCOPOLAMINE are the best known examples.

belladonna delirium delirium due to the effects on the central nervous system of large doses of belladonna alkaloids, such as atropine and scopolamine. Symptoms, in addition to delirium, include hallucinations and overactive coordinated limb movements.

bell and pad a device used in treatments aimed at controlling nocturnal enuresis (bed-wetting) in children. If the child urinates, an electric circuit is closed via the wetted pad and a bell rings, awakening the child.

bell curve the characteristic curve obtained by plotting a graph of a NORMAL DISTRIBUTION. With a large rounded peak tapering off on either side, it resembles a cross-sectional representation of a bell. Also called **bell-shaped curve**.

belle indifférence see LA BELLE INDIFFÉRENCE.

Bell's mania see LETHAL CATATONIA. [Luther Vose **Bell** (1806–1862), U.S. physician]

below average denoting a range of intellectual functioning that is just below the average range, roughly between 80 and 90 on most IQ scales, and is inconsistent with the presence of mental retardation. Such a range may also be described as **low normal** or **dull normal**, but below average is now the preferred term.

Bem Sex Role Inventory (**BSRI**) a MASCULINITY–FEMININITY TEST in which participants rate themselves on 60 traits regarded as characteristically masculine or feminine. Masculinity and femininity are treated as independent variables; people with high scores for both types of traits (e.g., assertiveness plus warmth) are classified as androgynous (see ANDROGYNY), and people with low scores for both feminine and masculine traits are classified as undifferentiated. [Sandra **Bem** (1944–), U.S. psychologist]

Benadryl *n.* a trade name for DIPHENHYDRAMINE.

benchmark *n.* a measure of best performance for a particular process or outcome, which can be used as a reference to improve performance in other settings.

Bender Visual–Motor Gestalt Test a visuoconstructive test in which the participant first copies line drawings of 16 geometric figures onto blank pieces of paper (Copy Phase) and then redraws them from memory (Recall Phase). All reproductions are scored on a 5-point scale, ranging from 0 (no resemblance) to 4 (nearly perfect). The test is appropriate for individuals aged 4 years and older and is used to assess visual–motor functioning and perceptual ability as well as to diagnose neuropsychological impairment. It is sometimes also used, albeit controversially, in conjunction with other personality tests to determine the presence of emotional and psychological disturbances, such as schizophrenia. Originally developed in 1938, the test (often shortened to **Bender–Gestalt**) is now in its second edition (published in 2003). [Lauretta **Bender** (1897–1987), U.S. psychiatrist]

benign *adj.* **1.** in mental health, denoting a disorder or illness that is not serious and has a favorable prognosis. **2.** denoting a disease condition that is relatively mild, transient, or not associated with serious pathology. See also NEOPLASM. Compare MALIGNANT.

benign stupor 1. a state of unresponsiveness, immobility, and indifference to one's surroundings that is unlikely to be permanent. **2.** PSYCHOMOTOR RETARDATION and apathy that often occur in severe MAJOR DEPRESSIVE EPISODES.

benny *n.* (*pl.* **bennies**) slang for an amphetamine tablet. See AMPHETAMINES.

Benzedrine *n.* a trade name for AMPHETAMINE.

Benzedrine dependence see AMPHETAMINE DEPENDENCE.

benzene a volatile solvent that, when chronically inhaled, can cause kidney failure and death. See INHALANT. See also INHALANT ABUSE; INHALANT DEPENDENCE.

benzisoxazoles *pl. n.* a class of ATYPICAL ANTIPSYCHOTICS that include RISPERIDONE and ILOPERIDONE.

benzodiazepine *n.* any of a family of drugs that depress central nervous system activity (CNS DEPRESSANTS) and also produce sedation and relaxation of skeletal muscles. Benzodiazepines include the prototype CHLORDIAZEPOXIDE and the common sedatives DIAZEPAM and ALPRAZOLAM. They are commonly used in the treatment of generalized anxiety and insomnia and are useful in the management of acute withdrawal from alcohol and in seizure disorders. Clinically introduced in the 1960s, they rapidly supplanted the barbiturates, largely due to their significantly lower toxicity in overdose. Members of the group show considerable variation in ABUSE POTENTIAL: Prolonged use can lead to tolerance and psychological and physical dependence.

benzodiazepine agonists drugs that facilitate the binding of benzodiazepines to subunits of the benzodiazepine receptor complex (see $GABA_A$ RECEPTOR).

benzodiazepine antagonists agents that prevent the binding of benzodiazepines and related chemicals to the benzodiazepine receptor site on the $GABA_A$ RECEPTOR complex. Benzodiazepine antagonists in clinical use include FLUMAZENIL.

benzothiadiazides *pl. n.* see THIAZIDE DIURETICS.

benztropine *n.* an ANTICHOLINERGIC DRUG used in the management of adverse side effects of conventional or first-generation antipsychotic drugs and as an adjunct in the treatment of Parkinson's disease. U.S. trade name: **Cogentin**.

berdache *n.* see TWO-SPIRIT.

bereavement *n.* a feeling of loss, especially over the death of a friend or loved one. The bereaved person may experience emotional pain and distress (see GRIEF; TRAUMATIC GRIEF) and may or may not express this distress to others (see MOURNING; DISENFRANCHISED GRIEF); individual grief and mourning responses vary. Bereavement may also signify a change in social status (e.g., from wife to widow). **—bereaved** *adj.*

bereavement program any of a variety of treatment services (e.g., support groups, GRIEF COUNSELING) offered to individuals coping with the death of a loved one.

bereavement therapy therapy or counseling provided to individuals who are experiencing loss and grief following the death of a loved one. The therapy may include issues of separation, grieving, and carrying on with life. See also GRIEF COUNSELING.

Bernoulli distribution see BINOMIAL DISTRIBUTION. [Jacques **Bernoulli** (1654–1705), Swiss mathematician and scientist]

Bernoulli trial see BINOMIAL DISTRIBUTION. [Jacques **Bernoulli**]

Berry syndrome see TREACHER COLLINS SYNDROME. [reported in 1889 by George Andreas **Berry** (1853–1929), British physician]

berserk 1. *adj.* destructive or violent. **2.** *n.* one who is destructive or violent. The term is derived from an Old Norse word literally meaning "bearshirt," used to describe ancient Norse warriors who wore bearskins during battle and fought with great strength and fury.

bestiality *n.* see ZOOERASTY.

best interests of the child a standard used by courts to make child custody decisions in divorce proceedings, namely that the potential for the child to lead a happy and successful life should be given greater weight than the rights of either parent.

beta (symbol: β) *n.* the probability of a TYPE II ERROR.

beta-adrenergic blocking agent see ADRENERGIC BLOCKING AGENT.

beta-adrenergic receptor a receptor that binds NOREPINEPHRINE. There are two main types, designated β1 and β2. The former mediate stimulation of heart muscle, causing a faster and stronger heartbeat. The latter are associated with relaxation of smooth muscle, causing (for example) dilation of blood vessels and widening of airways. Also called **beta adrenoceptor**; **beta adrenoreceptor**; **beta receptor**. Compare ALPHA-ADRENERGIC RECEPTOR.

beta-adrenergic receptor kinase (**barK**) a CYCLIC AMP-dependent enzyme that is responsible for inactivating BETA-ADRENERGIC RECEPTORS, thereby inhibiting the ability of these receptors to activate SECOND MESSENGERS within the cell. BarK is a member of a family of G PROTEIN-coupled receptor kinases that function only when receptors are occupied by an agonist.

beta-adrenoreceptor blocking agent see ADRENERGIC BLOCKING AGENT.

beta alcoholism one of five types of alcoholism defined by U.S. physician Elvin M. Jellinek (1890–1963), the others being ALPHA ALCOHOLISM, GAMMA ALCOHOLISM, DELTA ALCOHOLISM, and EPSILON ALCOHOLISM. It is characterized by serious medical complications (e.g., liver damage, gastritis, nutritional deficiency) associated with undisciplined drinking but does not involve physical or psychological dependence.

beta-amyloid (**β-amyloid**) *n.* a protein that accumulates—via aberrant processing of **amyloid precursor protein** (**APP**)—in the brains of patients with Alzheimer's disease, forming SENILE PLAQUES and contributing to neuronal impairment and eventual loss. Significant progress has been made recently toward developing therapies that target this processing pathway and several promising pharmacological agents are now in advance-stage clinical trials.

beta blocker see ADRENERGIC BLOCKING AGENT.

beta coefficient see BETA WEIGHT.

beta-endorphin *n.* a neuropeptide involved in pain and hunger that produces its analgesic effects by binding to OPIOID RECEPTORS and disinhibiting dopamine pathways. See ENDOGENOUS OPIOID; ENDORPHIN.

beta error see TYPE II ERROR.

beta level the probability of failing to reject the NULL HYPOTHESIS when it is in fact false, that is, making a TYPE II ERROR.

beta wave in electroencephalography, the type of BRAIN WAVE (frequency 13–30 Hz) associated with alert wakefulness and intense mental activity. Also called **beta rhythm**.

beta weight (symbol: β) in REGRESSION ANALYSIS, the multiplicative constant that reflects a variable's contribution to the prediction of a criterion, given the other variables in the prediction equation (e.g., b in $y = a + bx$). Also called **beta coefficient**.

betel nut the seed of the areca palm (*Areca catechu*), which is chewed as a stimulant by local populations of India and the islands of the Indian and Pacific Oceans. It contains the drug ARECOLINE.

bethanechol *n.* a CHOLINERGIC DRUG used to stimulate movement in the bladder in the management of such conditions as lower MOTOR

NEURON disease and postoperative or postpartum urinary retention. U.S. trade name: **Urecholine**.

betrayal trauma theory a conceptual model for explaining why some children are unable to access memories of prior sexual or physical abuse. According to the theory, this sort of REPRESSION occurs when the perpetrator of the abuse is an adult on whom the child is emotionally dependent and it develops out of the child's need to preserve the ATTACHMENT BOND; hence the child is unable to access the stored memories of the abuse while the need for attachment is still strong. [first proposed in 1991 by U.S. cognitive psychologist Jennifer J. Freyd]

between-groups design see BETWEEN-SUBJECTS DESIGN.

between-groups variance the variation in experimental scores that is attributable only to membership in different groups and exposure to different experimental conditions. It is reflected in the ANALYSIS OF VARIANCE by the degree to which the several group means differ from one another and is compared with WITHIN-GROUP VARIANCE to obtain an F RATIO.

between-subjects design any of a large number of experimental designs in which each person, or other sampling unit, experiences only one experimental condition (treatment) and therefore contributes only a single final score to enter into the analysis. Compare WITHIN-SUBJECTS DESIGN.

bewildered *adj.* confused or puzzled, especially when presented with conflicting situations or statements. See also DISORIENTATION. **—bewilderment** *n.*

beyond reasonable doubt the standard of proof required in a criminal trial. In order to convict a defendant, a jury must be convinced of the defendant's guilt "beyond any reasonable doubt," meaning there is no justifiable, rational cause for jury members to doubt the defendant's guilt. This standard is considered to be equivalent to a moral certainty but is less than an absolute certainty.

bhang *n.* the mildest preparation of CANNABIS, consisting of the whole *Cannabis sativa* plant, dried and powdered.

BHS abbreviation for BECK HOPELESSNESS SCALE.

BIA abbreviation for BODY IMAGE ASSESSMENT.

bias *n.* **1.** partiality: an inclination or predisposition for or against something. See also PREJUDICE. **2.** a tendency or preference, such as a RESPONSE BIAS or TEST BIAS. **3.** in research, systematic and directional error arising during SAMPLING, data collection, data analysis, or data interpretation. **4.** in statistics, the difference between the expected value of a statistic and the actual value that is obtained. **—biased** *adj.*

biastophilia *n.* a PARAPHILIA involving sexual arousal and excitement based on surprising or attacking a stranger sexually.

bibliotherapy *n.* a form of therapy that uses structured reading material. Bibliotherapy is often used as an adjunct to psychotherapy for such purposes as reinforcing specific in-session concepts or strategies or enhancing lifestyle changes. Carefully chosen readings are also used by some individuals as SELF-HELP tools to foster personal growth and development, for example, by facilitating communication and open discussion of problems or enhancing self-concept.

bicalutamide *n.* see ANTIANDROGEN.

bicameralism *n.* a highly controversial theory of primitive human mentality (posited to predate the development of consciousness) in which cognitive functions are separated into one section of the brain that "speaks" or "orders," specifically through auditory hallucination, and another section that "listens" or "obeys." The concept, proposed by U.S. psychologist John Jaynes in his 1976 publication *The Origins of Consciousness in the Breakdown of the Bicameral Mind*, has not received significant attention in neuropsychological research, although analogies have been drawn to neurological models describing the differing functions of the right and left hemispheres of the brain.

bicuculline *n.* an alkaloid derived from the plant *Dicentra cucullaria* that acts as a competitive GABA ANTAGONIST at $GABA_A$ RECEPTORS and has strong convulsant effects. It has no modern clinical applications but may be used experimentally in laboratory animals for various research purposes.

Biemond's syndrome a disorder that combines mental retardation, growth impairment, abnormalities in the iris (a hole, split, or cleft), and excess fingers or toes. [A. **Biemond** (1902–), French physician]

bigamy *n.* the crime of marrying someone when already married to someone else. In cultures that permit individuals to have more than one spouse this practice should be referred to as POLYGAMY and not bigamy. Compare MONOGAMY. **—bigamist** *n.* **—bigamous** *adj.*

Big Five personality model a model of the primary dimensions of individual differences in personality. The dimensions are usually labeled EXTRAVERSION, NEUROTICISM, AGREEABLENESS, CONSCIENTIOUSNESS, and OPENNESS TO EXPERIENCE, though the labels vary somewhat among researchers. See also FIVE-FACTOR PERSONALITY MODEL. [described by (among others) U.S. psychologists Lewis R. Goldberg (1932–) and Gerard T. Saucier]

bigorexia *n.* see MUSCLE DYSMORPHIA.

bilis *n.* a CULTURE-BOUND SYNDROME found among Latino groups, who attribute it to extremely strong anger or rage. Symptoms include abrupt nervous tension, headache, screaming, stomach disturbances, vomiting, loss of weight, tremors, chronic tiredness, and—in extreme cases—loss of consciousness or death. The extreme anger is said to disturb the center of balance of hot and cold in the body, which upsets the material and spiritual aspects of the person. Also called **colera**; **muina**.

B

bill of rights in health care, a document stating the entitlements a patient has with respect to providers, institutions, and THIRD-PARTY PAYERS. See PATIENTS' RIGHTS.

bimodal distribution a set of scores that has two modes (represented by two peaks in their graphical distribution), reflecting a tendency for scores to cluster around two separate values. See also UNIMODAL DISTRIBUTION.

binary choice in decision making, a choice between two alternatives.

binary variable a variable that may take on only two values, for example, male versus female, or 0 versus 1 in computer code.

binding hypothesis a theory, proposing that the neural mechanism responsible for drawing together disparate information from separate cortical areas and "binding" it into unified percepts is temporal synchrony: that is, the simultaneous firing of action potentials from individual neurons—each coding different properties—is the means by which they are organized into a single representation. Recently, some individuals have emphasized feature binding as essential to consciousness, providing a requisite coherence of mental contents.

Binet, Alfred (1857–1911) French psychologist. Although he had no formal training in psychology, Binet became a pioneer investigator of SUGGESTION and the thought processes of mentally gifted individuals and those with mental retardation. Opposing James McKeen Cattell's (1860–1944) reduction of mental abilities to sensory and motor capacities, as measured by "brass instruments," Binet developed a variety of verbal and numerical test items in 1905, with the assistance of French psychologist Théodore Simon (1873–1961). These were used to determine a child's mental age and to identify pupils with mental retardation who might not be able to succeed in an ordinary academic curriculum. Later revisions of the Binet–Simon Scale led ultimately to the development of the STANFORD–BINET INTELLIGENCE SCALE, which is in wide use today. See also IQ.

binge drinking 1. a single occasion of intense, extremely heavy drinking that often results in intoxication. **2.** a pattern of alcohol consumption characterized by the setting aside of repeated periods of time for intense, extremely heavy drinking, with or without sobriety in between.

binge-eating disorder a disorder marked by recurring episodes of binge eating (i.e., discrete periods of uncontrolled consumption of abnormally large quantities of food) and distress associated with this behavior. There is an absence of distinct inappropriate compensatory behaviors (e.g., vomiting, laxative misuse, excessive exercise, fasting). In *DSM–IV–TR* it is classified as EATING DISORDER not otherwise specified. Compare BULIMIA NERVOSA.

binomial distribution the distribution of the outcomes in a sequence of **Bernoulli trials**, experiments of chance that are independent of one another and each have one of two possible outcomes (0 or 1; success or failure), with a fixed probability of each outcome on each trial. Also called **Bernoulli distribution**.

Binswanger's disease a progressive VASCULAR DEMENTIA characterized by DEMYELINATION and multiple INFARCTIONS of subcortical white matter associated with hypertension and subsequent arteriosclerosis. Symptoms include loss of cognitive functioning, memory impairment, and changes in mood and behavior. Also called **subcortical arteriosclerotic encephalopathy**. [Otto Ludvig **Binswanger** (1852–1929), German neurologist]

bioavailability *n.* the quantity of an administered drug that is available for distribution within the body to the target organ or site after absorption into the bloodstream.

biochemical approach 1. the study of behavioral patterns, including mental disorders, from the standpoint of chemical changes. An example of this approach is the view that a mental disorder can be explained in terms of an excess or deficiency of certain substances in the nervous system, such as serotonin. **2.** the use of psychotropic drugs in the treatment of mental disorders. See PSYCHOPHARMACOTHERAPY.

biochemical defect any of numerous chemical imbalances or aberrations in the brain that may be associated with neurological or psychiatric disorder. Such disorders may be related to the production of specific NEUROTRANSMITTERS or the availability of other biochemical substances necessary for brain function.

biochemical marker a variation in the chemical activity of an organism that accompanies a disorder, irrespective of whether it directly causes the disorder; an example is demonstrated in the DEXAMETHASONE SUPPRESSION TEST. See also BIOLOGICAL MARKER; CLINICAL MARKER.

biodata *pl. n.* see BIOGRAPHICAL DATA.

biodynamics *n.* the study of dynamic processes within living organisms. See DYNAMIC.

bioecological model a paradigm that treats human development as a process that continues both through the life span and across successive generations, thus according importance to historical continuity and change as forces indirectly affecting human development through their impact on proximal processes.

bioenergetics *n.* a form of alternative psychotherapy that combines work with the body and the mind in treating emotional problems. Bioenergetics proposes that body and mind are functionally identical: What happens in the mind reflects what is happening in the body, and vice versa. It uses exercises and postural changes in an attempt to relieve chronic muscular tensions and rigidity attributed to emotional stress and unresolved emotional conflicts. The approach was developed by U.S. physician Alexander Lowen (1910–2008) and is based on the work of Austrian psychoanalyst Wilhelm Reich (1897–1957).

bioequivalence *n.* a measure comparing the relative BIOAVAILABILITY of two forms or preparations of a drug. In bioequivalent drug preparations, the same proportion of unchanged, active drug reaches the systemic circulation. Bioequivalence may be a clinical issue when comparing two preparations of a drug (i.e., immediate-release versus delayed-release) or when comparing trademarked drugs and their generic counterparts. **—bioequivalent** *adj.*

bioethics *n.* the study of ethics and values relevant to the conduct of clinical practice and research in medicine and the life sciences. **—bioethical** *adj.*

biofeedback *n.* information about bodily processes and systems provided by an organism's receptors to enable it to maintain a physiologically desirable internal environment and make adjustments as necessary.

biofeedback training a technique by which a person learns to control a normally involuntary autonomic response (e.g., blood pressure, heart rate, or alpha rhythm in the brain) by watching the output of a device that monitors the response continuously (e.g., a blood pressure monitor, an electrocardiograph, or an electroencephalograph). Biofeedback training is sometimes used to treat stress disorders, such as migraine headaches and hypertension. It is also used as an adjunctive treatment for other disorders, such as insomnia, substance abuse, attention-deficit/hyperactivity disorder, and epilepsy. See also ALPHA WAVE.

biogenesis *n.* the origin of living things from other living things. **Biogenetics** is the scientific study of the principles and processes governing the production of living organisms from other living organisms, including the mechanisms of heredity. **—biogenetic** *adj.*

biogenic *adj.* **1.** produced by living organisms or biological processes. **2.** necessary for the maintenance of life.

biogenic amine any of a group of amines (chemical compounds that contain one or more amino groups [$-NH_2$]) that affect bodily processes and nervous system functioning. Biogenic amines are divided into subgroups (e.g., catecholamines, indoleamines) and include the neurotransmitters dopamine, epinephrine, histamine, norepinephrine, and serotonin.

biogenic amine hypothesis any of a variety of hypotheses, such as the CATECHOLAMINE HYPOTHESIS and DOPAMINE HYPOTHESIS, that consider abnormalities in the physiology and metabolism of biogenic amines essential to the etiology of certain mental disorders.

biographical data information gathered by a therapist or medical professional about a client's history and behavioral patterns, primarily from the client but sometimes—when permitted by the client or deemed necessary—from individuals who know or are related to the client. Also called **biodata**.

Biographical Evaluation and Screening of Troops a program used for the selection and classification of military personnel. Formerly called the **Air Force Medical Evaluation Test (AFMET)**, it is used to identify individuals who are unlikely to complete the Air Force basic training or who might find it difficult to function in a military system.

bioinformational theory a general theory of emotional–motivational organization, integrating cognitive and psychophysiological levels of analysis. It is concerned with how emotions are elicited and displayed and with how they interact; specifically, information about emotions is contained in associative memory networks that include action information (motor programs) and connections to subcortical motivation circuits. Emotions are viewed as context-specific action or response dispositions activated by input that modifies concepts in the emotion network. The model, originally forwarded in the 1970s as a theory of emotional imagery, was derived from research on fear and anxiety but has since evolved and acquired diverse applications across a variety of behavioral and emotional phenomena.

biological clock the mechanism within an organism that controls the periodicity of BIOLOGICAL RHYTHMS, even in the absence of any external cues. Also called **internal clock**.

biological determinism the concept that psychological and behavioral characteristics are entirely the result of constitutional and biological factors. Environmental conditions serve only as occasions for the manifestation of such characteristics. Compare ENVIRONMENTAL DETERMINISM. See DETERMINISM; GENETIC DETERMINISM; NATURE–NURTURE.

biological drive an innate motivational state produced by depletion or deprivation of a needed substance (e.g., water, oxygen) in order to impel behavior that will restore physiological equilibrium. See also DRIVE.

biological factor any physical, chemical, genetic, or neurological condition associated with psychological disturbances.

biological family a person's blood relations as opposed to relations acquired through marriage, adoption, or fostering.

biological marker a variation in the physiological processes of an organism that accompanies a disorder, irrespective of whether it directly causes the disorder. Also called **biomarker**. See also BIOCHEMICAL MARKER; CLINICAL MARKER.

biological measures assessments or other

B

markers of processes or outcomes that are drawn from bodily activity or other natural biological systems or events. Such measures include assessments of cardiopulmonary, endocrine, nervous-system, and immune-system activity.

biological perspective an approach to abnormal psychology that emphasizes physiologically based causative factors, such as the SENILE PLAQUES in Alzheimer's disease, and consequently tends to focus primarily upon BIOLOGICAL THERAPIES.

biological psychology the science that deals with the area of overlap between psychology and biology and with the reciprocal relations between biological and psychological processes. It includes such fields as BEHAVIORAL NEUROSCIENCE, clinical NEUROSCIENCE, COGNITIVE NEUROSCIENCE, BEHAVIORAL ENDOCRINOLOGY, and PSYCHONEUROIMMUNOLOGY, and involves reciprocal interactions between the neural, endocrine, and immune systems as they affect and are affected by behavior. It was formerly known as **physiological psychology**. Also called **biopsychology**.

biological rhythm any periodic variation in a living organism's physiological or psychological function, such as energy level, sexual desire, or menstruation. Such rhythms are usually linked to cyclical changes in environmental cues, such as daylength or passing of the seasons, and tend to be daily (circadian rhythm) or annual (circannual rhythm). They also can vary with individuals and with the period of the individual's life. Also called **biorhythm; endogenous rhythm**; **internal rhythm**; **life rhythm**.

biological therapy any form of treatment for mental disorders that attempts to alter physiological functioning, including various drug therapies, ELECTROCONVULSIVE THERAPY, and PSYCHOSURGERY. Also called **biomedical therapy**.

biology *n.* the study of living organisms and life processes. **—biological** *adj.* **—biologist** *n.*

biomechanics *n.* the application of the principles of mechanics to the study of the structure and function of biological systems, which includes the study of the physical stresses and strains on organisms while at rest and in motion. **—biomechanical** *adj.*

biomedical therapy see BIOLOGICAL THERAPY.

bion *n.* a hypothetical microscopic vesicle charged with sexual energy, postulated by Austrian psychoanalyst Wilhelm Reich (1897–1957) as the ultimate source of the orgasm. See also ORGONE; ORGONE THERAPY.

biopsychology *n.* see BIOLOGICAL PSYCHOLOGY.

biopsychosocial *adj.* denoting a systematic integration of biological, psychological, and social approaches to the study of mental health and specific mental disorders.

biosocial theory any approach that explains personality or human behavior in terms of biological predispositions that are influenced by social or environmental factors.

biostatistics *n.* **1.** data compiled about a population, including rates of birth, disease, and death. See also DEMOGRAPHY. **2.** a branch of statistics concerned with the application of statistical methods to biological processes, especially in medicine and epidemiology. Also called **biometrics**. **—biostatistical** *adj.* **—biostatistician** *n.*

biosynthesis *n.* **1.** the production of chemical compounds by living organisms from nutrients by means of enzyme-catalyzed reactions. **2.** the production of molecules of biological or medical interest, either in the laboratory or commercially, for example, by recombinant DNA technology. **—biosynthetic** *adj.*

biotaxis *n.* **1.** the classification of living organisms by their anatomical features and traits. **2.** the ability of living cells to orient themselves with respect to their environment. See NEUROBIOTAXIS. **—biotactic** *adj.*

biotransformation *n.* the metabolic process by which a substance (e.g., a drug) is changed from one chemical to another by means of a chemical reaction within a living system. The metabolites, or products, of this change may be active or inactive within the system.

biperiden *n.* a synthetic ANTICHOLINERGIC DRUG closely related to TRIHEXYPHENIDYL but having greater affinity for NICOTINIC RECEPTORS than for MUSCARINIC RECEPTORS, compared with trihexyphenidyl. It is used to manage symptoms of Parkinson's disease and parkinsonian symptoms induced by antipsychotic drugs. U.S. trade name: **Akineton**.

biphasic sleep see POLYPHASIC SLEEP.

bipolar *adj.* denoting something with two opposites or extremities, such as BIPOLAR DISORDERS. **—bipolarity** *n.*

bipolar concept the notion, often applied to MOOD and AFFECT, that a particular phenomenon can accurately be described by reference to a dimension characterized by opposing attributes, such as happiness versus sadness. It is contrasted with a **unidimensional concept**, which is characterized by the extent of one particular attribute, such as a greater or lesser degree of sadness.

bipolar disorder any of a group of MOOD DISORDERS in which symptoms of mania and depression alternate. *DSM–IV–TR* distinguishes between **bipolar I disorder**, in which the individual has experienced one or more MANIC EPISODES or MIXED EPISODES and usually (but not necessarily) one or more MAJOR DEPRESSIVE EPISODES, and **bipolar II disorder**, characterized by one or more major depressive episodes and at least one HYPOMANIC EPISODE. Also categorized as bipolar disorders in *DSM–IV–TR* are CYCLOTHYMIC DISORDER and **bipolar disorder not oth-**

erwise specified, which does not meet the criteria for more specific bipolar disorders. In *DSM–III* the bipolar disorders were grouped into the types **depressive**, **manic**, and **mixed**, according to the nature of the current or most recent episode. The former official name for bipolar disorders, **manic-depressive illness**, is still in frequent use.

bipolar factor in FACTOR ANALYSIS, a factor (variable) characterized as having a neutral aspect at a relatively central position on a spectrum ranging from positive to negative extremes at either end, for example, attitudes toward work ranging from strong engagement to neutrality to sheer boredom.

bipolar rating scale a rating scale anchored at each end by opposite terms (e.g., very fast to very slow). It is distinguished from a **unipolar rating scale** (e.g., very fast to not at all fast, or very slow to not at all slow).

birth control voluntary regulation of the number and spacing of offspring, including the prevention of conception using INTRAUTERINE DEVICES, ORAL CONTRACEPTIVES, spermicides, the RHYTHM METHOD, male contraceptive devices, surgical methods of sterilization (e.g., salpingectomy, vasectomy), and the termination of pregnancy by induced ABORTION.

birth defect see CONGENITAL DEFECT.

birth order the ordinal position of a child in the family (first-born, second-born, youngest, etc.). There has been much psychological research into how birth order affects personal adjustment and family status, but the notion that it has strong and consistent effects on psychological outcomes is not supported. Early interest in birth order appears in the work of British scientist Francis Galton (1822–1911) and Sigmund FREUD, but it was Alfred ADLER who first proposed that birth order is an important factor in personality development. Current family-structure research sees birth order not so much as a causal factor but rather as an indirect variable that follows more process-oriented variables (e.g., parental discipline, sibling interaction, and genetic and hormonal makeup) in importance.

birth trauma the psychological shock of being born, due to the sudden change from the security of the womb to being bombarded with stimuli from the external world. Sigmund FREUD viewed birth as the child's first anxiety experience and the prototype of separation anxiety. To Austrian psychoanalyst Otto Rank (1884–1939), who first proposed the idea of birth trauma, it was the crucial factor in causing neuroses. See also PRIMAL ANXIETY; PRIMAL TRAUMA.

BIS abbreviation for BEHAVIORAL INHIBITION SYSTEM.

biserial correlation a measure of the association between a CONTINUOUS VARIABLE and a DICHOTOMOUS VARIABLE.

bisexual behavior behavior of a person who is attracted sexually to both sexes and is usually able to achieve orgasm in contact with members of either sex.

bisexuality *n.* **1.** sexual attraction to or sexual behavior with both men and women. Although much psychological research demonstrates the existence of a continuum of sexual attraction within most individuals, equal responsiveness to both sexes over the life span is rare, appearing to be more common in women than in men. Same-sex attractions and behaviors generally occur after those to the opposite sex for bisexual women, whereas bisexual men typically experience their first homosexual attractions and behavior before or at the same age as their first heterosexual experiences. Anthropological studies note that bisexuality is present in many cultures. **2.** the existence of both male and female genitals in the same organism. See HERMAPHRODITISM; INTERSEXUALITY. **—bisexual** *adj., n.*

biting stage see ORAL-BITING PHASE.

bivariate *adj.* characterized by two variables or attributes. See also MULTIVARIATE; UNIVARIATE.

bizarre behavior behavior that is odd, strange, or unexpected, particularly if it is out of the ordinary for a given person. It may be a symptom of brain damage or a mental disorder, especially a psychotic disorder, such as schizophrenia.

bizarre delusion a belief that is clearly fantastic and implausible but is nonetheless maintained with conviction. For example, an individual with schizophrenia may believe that external forces are removing the thoughts from his or her mind (see THOUGHT WITHDRAWAL).

blacking out see FALLING OUT.

blackout *n.* **1.** total loss of consciousness produced, for example, by sudden lowering of the blood supply to the brain or by decreased oxygen supply. **2.** amnesia produced by alcoholic intoxication. Also called **alcoholic blackout**.

blaming the victim a social psychological phenomenon in which individuals or groups attempt to cope with the bad things that have happened to others by assigning blame to the victim of the trauma or tragedy. Victim blaming serves to create psychological distance between the blamer and the victim, may rationalize a failure to intervene if the blamer was a bystander, and creates a psychological defense for the blamer against feelings of vulnerability.

blank hallucination a HALLUCINATION involving a sense of floating in space, changes in equilibrium or body size, or other hazy sensations, occurring mostly in response to stress or when falling asleep. In psychoanalytic theory, a blank hallucination is thought to repeat an early defensive mechanism by reproducing the soothing experience of suckling at the breast.

blank screen in psychoanalysis, the metaphorical backdrop onto which the patient projects his or her feelings and fantasies during the TRANSFERENCE process. The screen is the psychoanalyst, who is described as blank because he or she must remain passive and neutral to enable the patient to feel free to give voice to his or her innermost thoughts.

blended family see STEPFAMILY.

Blessed Dementia Scale (BDS) a behavioral rating scale used in the assessment of DEMENTIA severity. It is administered to a caregiver and has subscales measuring changes in the performance of everyday tasks, changes in daily activities and habits, and changes in personality and motivation. [developed in 1968 by Gary **Blessed**, British psychogeriatrician; Bernard E. Tomlinson, British neuropathologist; and Martin Roth, British psychiatrist]

Bleuler's theory a theory proposing a basic underlying symptomatology for SCHIZOPHRENIA. It defined four FUNDAMENTAL SYMPTOMS required for a diagnosis of the condition; the more obvious manifestations of schizophrenia (e.g., delusions, hallucinations) were regarded as accessory symptoms (see SECONDARY SYMPTOMS) because they are shared with other disorders. [Eugen **Bleuler** (1857–1939), Swiss psychiatrist]

blind *adj.* **1.** denoting a lack of sight. See BLINDNESS. **2.** denoting a lack of awareness. In research, a blind procedure may be employed deliberately to enhance experimental control: A **single blind** is a procedure in which participants are unaware of the experimental conditions under which they are operating; a **double blind** is a procedure in which both the participants and the experimenters interacting with them are unaware of the particular experimental conditions; and a **triple blind** is a procedure in which the participants, experimenters, and data analysts are all unaware of the particular experimental conditions.

blind analysis a study or interpretation of data or conditions without specific knowledge or previous information about the topic being examined. For example, a clinical psychologist might diagnose a patient without having information concerning any previous psychological diagnoses.

blind judgment an evaluation made without knowledge of information that might influence one's assessment of the situation. Such an approach is used to eliminate conscious or unconscious bias. Blind judgments are often used in clinical experiments, for example, judging patients' current level of depression in the absence of information about which, if any, treatment they have received; and in scholarly peer review of manuscripts, in which the author's institutional affiliation is not disclosed to the reviewer.

blindness *n.* **1.** profound, near-total, or total impairment of the ability to perceive visual stimuli. According to the World Health Organization's international classification (1977), blindness is defined as visual acuity worse than 20/400 in the better eye with best correction or a visual field less than 10% in the widest meridian in the better eye. In the United States, the criterion for **legal blindness** is visual acuity of 20/200 or worse in the better eye with best correction or a visual field of 20% or less in the widest meridian of the better eye. **2.** absence of usable vision with the exception of light perception. See also FUNCTIONAL BLINDNESS; LOW VISION; VISUAL IMPAIRMENT. **—blind** *adj.*

blind review a review of a manuscript or grant proposal to evaluate its quality and suitability for publication or funding by a person who does not know the identity of the author.

blindsight *n.* the capacity of some individuals with blindness in parts or all of the visual field to detect and localize visual stimuli presented within the blind field region. Discrimination of movement, flicker, wavelength, and orientation may also be present. However, these visual capacities are not accompanied by awareness: They have been demonstrated only in experimental conditions, when participants are forced to guess. Blindsight therefore does not help individuals to compensate for their loss of vision.

blind spot a lack of insight or awareness—often persistent—into a specific area of one's behavior or personality, typically because recognition of one's true feelings and motives would be painful. In classical psychoanalysis, it is regarded as a defense against recognition of repressed impulses or memories that would threaten the patient's EGO. See SCOTOMIZATION.

blind walk a TRUST EXERCISE used in a group setting (e.g., an ENCOUNTER GROUP) to help members develop mutual trust. Half of the group close their eyes; the other half become their partners and lead the "blind" people through various events and experiences. Roles are then reversed, and finally all members discuss their reactions to the experience.

BLM (BLMS) abbreviation for BUCCOLINGUAL MASTICATORY SYNDROME.

bloating *n.* a feeling of distension in the abdomen, which may be a feature of IRRITABLE BOWEL SYNDROME and is also frequently encountered as a symptom of SOMATIZATION DISORDER. Also called **abdominal bloating**.

block 1. *n.* an abrupt, involuntary interruption in the flow of thought or speech in which the individual is suddenly aware of not being able to perform a particular mental act, such as finding the words to express something he or she wishes to say. Also called **mental block**. See RETRIEVAL BLOCK; TIP-OF-THE-TONGUE PHENOMENON. **2.** *n.* in psychotherapy, an obstacle to progress that is perceived as a barrier that cannot be crossed. **3.** *n.* any physical, biochemical, or psychological barrier or obstacle that obstructs or impedes a process, function, or activity. **4.** *n.* in an experimental block design, any of the relatively homogeneous subsets or levels into which the entire sample of participants is subdivided. **5.** *vb.* to subdivide the participants into such subsets.

blocking *n.* a process in which one's flow of thought or speech is suddenly interrupted (see BLOCK). Also called **thought deprivation**; **thought obstruction**.

Blocq's disease see ASTASIA–ABASIA. [Paul O. **Blocq** (1860–1896), French physician]

blood–brain barrier a semipermeable barrier formed by cells lining the blood capillaries that supply the brain and other parts of the central nervous system. It prevents large molecules, including many drugs, passing from the blood to the fluid surrounding brain cells and to the cerebrospinal fluid, and thus protects the brain from potentially harmful substances. Ions and small molecules, such as water, oxygen, carbon dioxide, and alcohol, can cross relatively freely. Entry is also possible for lipid-soluble compounds, such as anesthetics, which diffuse through plasma membranes. Several anatomical features contribute to the barrier. Cells lining the capillary walls are joined together by tight junctions, which block the passage of molecules through the intercellular spaces found in capillaries elsewhere. Also, the brain capillaries lack pores, called fenestrations, which normally promote the passage of fluid and solutes. Furthermore, the brain capillaries are tightly enveloped in a sheath formed by star-shaped glial cells, called astrocytes. The barrier formed by these features helps maintain a constant environment in which the brain can function, but it also means that many potentially useful drugs cannot enter the brain from the bloodstream. See also AREA POSTREMA.

blood phobia a persistent and irrational fear of blood, specifically of seeing blood. An individual confronting blood experiences a subjective feeling of disgust and fears the consequences of the situation, such as fainting. In certain diagnostic classifications, such as *DSM–IV–TR*, the broader term **blood-injection-injury phobia** is used instead. Blood phobia rarely is called **hematophobia** or **hemophobia**.

blood poisoning a severe or significant bacterial infection of the bloodstream, usually by microorganisms invading from an infection site elsewhere in the body. Blood poisoning may be characterized by fever, chills, and skin eruptions. A particularly hazardous complication is spread of the infection to tissues of the nervous system. Also called **bacteremia**; **septicemia**. See also SEPSIS.

B-love *n.* see BEING LOVE.

blow 1. *n.* slang for COCAINE. **2.** *vb.* to inhale cocaine or to smoke marijuana. See also COCAINE INTOXICATION; CANNABIS INTOXICATION.

blow job slang for oral stimulation of the penis by a partner, which may occur as a part of FOREPLAY or may be continued to the point of orgasm.

blues *pl. n.* a colloquial name for depressive symptoms, especially sadness or ANHEDONIA. See also BABY BLUES.

blunted affect a disturbance in which emotional responses to situations and events are dulled.

blushing *n.* an involuntary reddening of the face, sometimes associated with feelings of embarrassment, self-consciousness, modesty, or shame.

BMI abbreviation for BODY MASS INDEX.

B-motivation *n.* see METAMOTIVATION.

BNSQ abbreviation for BASIC NORDIC SLEEP QUESTIONNAIRE.

board certified denoting a physician or other health care professional who has passed an examination set by a specialty board and has been certified as a specialist in that area. A board-certified (or **boarded**) individual is known as a **diplomate**.

boarding home see ADULT HOME; GROUP HOME; HALFWAY HOUSE.

boarding-out system a system in which patients with psychoses are cared for in private homes.

body awareness the perception of one's physical self or body at any particular time.

body boundaries a component of the body image consisting of the definiteness or indefiniteness of the boundary of the body. Barrier responses in RORSCHACH INKBLOT TESTS, such as "turtle with shell" and "man in armor," indicate a definite body boundary, while PENETRATION RESPONSES, such as "person bleeding" and "torn coat," indicate indefinite boundaries.

body buffer zone the physical distance a person prefers to maintain between him- or herself and one or more other individuals to avoid feeling uncomfortable. This zone varies depending on the relationship with the others; it is smaller, for example, when there is a close relationship. It also varies according to culture.

body-build index an index of constitutional types. Individuals are grouped according to the formula: (height × 100)/(transverse chest diameter × 6). **Mesomorphs**, who are muscular, fall within one standard deviation of the mean; **leptomorphs** one standard deviation or more above the mean; and broadly built **eurymorphs** one standard deviation or more below the mean. [proposed by Hans Jürgen EYSENCK]

body cognitions beliefs or attitudes about the features of one's appearance. Characteristically negative and self-defeating thoughts are related to subjective dissatisfaction.

body concept the thoughts, feelings, and perceptions that constitute the way an individual views his or her body: that is, the conceptual image of one's body. Compare BODY PERCEPT. See BODY IMAGE.

body disfigurement an objective defect of appearance related to a congenital malformation, physical injury, or any disease process that modifies the physical integrity of the individual.

B

body distortion a tendency to overestimate one's body size or to have bizarre perceptual experiences. See also BODY-SIZE OVERESTIMATION; BODY-IMAGE DISTORTION.

body dysmorphia an extreme disparagement of some aspect of appearance that is not supported by the objective evidence. There may be a mild defect in the body feature or, in extreme cases, there may be no objective evidence of any malformation or oddity of appearance. See also BODY DYSMORPHIC DISORDER; MUSCLE DYSMORPHIA.

body dysmorphic disorder (**BDD**) in *DSM–IV–TR*, a SOMATOFORM DISORDER characterized by excessive preoccupation with an imagined defect in physical appearance or markedly excessive concern with a slight physical anomaly, formerly called **dysmorphophobia**. The preoccupation is typically accompanied by frequent checking of the defect. BDD shares features of OBSESSIVE-COMPULSIVE DISORDER, such as obsessions with appearance and associated compulsions (e.g., mirror-checking), and causes significant distress or impairment in social, occupational, or other important areas of functioning.

body ego in psychoanalytic theory, the part of the EGO that develops out of self-perceptions of the body. It is the core of the ego around which all perceptions of the self are grouped, including individual memories, sensations, ideas, wishes, strivings, and fantasies.

body esteem the degree of positiveness with which individuals regard the various parts of their body and the appearance of those parts.

body ideal the BODY TYPE considered most attractive or most appropriate to one's age and sex by a particular individual, culture, or generation. See BODY IMAGE.

body image the mental picture one forms of one's body as a whole, including both its physical and functional characteristics (BODY PERCEPT) and one's attitudes toward these characteristics (BODY CONCEPT). Also called **body identity**. See also BODY SCHEMA.

Body Image Assessment (**BIA**) a measure of body image in which a participant is shown silhouettes of figures that increase incrementally in size from very thin to very overweight and is asked to choose the one that represents his or her actual figure and the one that represents his or her ideal figure. In addition to the BIA for adults, there are three other forms of the instrument: BIA-O for obese adults, BIA-C for younger children, and BIA-P for preadolescents. [originally developed in 1985 by U.S. psychologist Donald A. Williamson (1950–) and colleagues]

body-image avoidance behavioral manifestations of excessive concern with one's appearance, evidenced by such behaviors as avoiding social functions and engaging in cover-up activities (e.g., wearing bulky and loose-fitting clothing) to obscure and hide aspects of the body with which one is dissatisfied.

body-image distortion distortion in the subjective image or mental representation of one's own body appearance, size, or movement. The term is usually applied to overestimation of body size or used to define the perceptual experiences of individuals with psychoses. Also called **body-image disturbance**. See also ANOREXIA NERVOSA; BODY DISTORTION. Compare BODY DYSMORPHIC DISORDER.

body-image ideals personal standards of optimal appearance for various body features: idealized features as opposed to actual attributes of appearance.

body language the expression of feelings and thoughts, which may or may not be verbalized, through posture, gesture, facial expression, or other movements. For example, anger is usually indicated by a facial expression in which there are downward lines in the forehead, cheeks, and mouth, and the fist may be clenched. Although body language is often called NONVERBAL COMMUNICATION, such movements may be unintentional, and many investigators therefore believe the term "communication" is often inappropriate in this context.

body mass index (**BMI**) a widely used measure of adiposity or obesity based on the following formula: weight (kg) divided by height squared (m^2).

body memory a sensory recollection of trauma in the form of pain, arousal, tension, or discomfort, usually unaccompanied by words or images. Body memory is frequently the result of trauma occurring during the period of CHILDHOOD AMNESIA, leading to a sensorimotor, rather than cognitive, encoding of the traumatic event. See also SENSORIMOTOR MEMORY.

body–mind problem see MIND–BODY PROBLEM.

body narcissism 1. an exaggerated preoccupation or fascination with one's own body and its erogenous zones. See also NARCISSISM. **2.** in psychoanalytic theory, the PRIMARY NARCISSISM of the young infant.

body percept the mental image one forms of the physical characteristics of one's own body, that is, whether one is slim or stocky, strong or weak, attractive or unattractive, tall or short. Compare BODY CONCEPT. See BODY IMAGE.

body rocking see ROCKING.

body schema the cognitive organization of one's appearance, including internal image, thoughts, and feelings. See BODY PERCEPT.

body-size overestimation the specific tendency to overestimate the size of body features (e.g., width of waist, hips, or thighs) in relation to objective size measurements. It was once thought to be an essential feature of ANOREXIA NERVOSA. See BODY DISTORTION; BODY-IMAGE DISTORTION.

B

body therapies a group of physical therapies that seek the relief of psychological tensions and other symptoms through body manipulation, relaxation, massage, breathing exercises, and changes in posture and position of body parts. The therapies are based on the theory that the body and its functioning embody an individual's basic personality and way of life. See also BODYWORK.

body type a classification of individuals according to body build or physique. Some have theorized an association between aspects of physique and psychological traits, proposing a variety of CONSTITUTIONAL TYPES and SOMATOTYPES.

bodywork *n.* an adjunctive treatment (see ADJUNCTIVE THERAPY) that may be recommended in addition to psychotherapy. It typically includes massage, movement, and exercises involving touch.

bond 1. *n.* a relationship between two or more individuals that signifies trust and alliance. In a social context, the existence of such an ATTACHMENT enables individuals to provide emotional support for each other (see also PAIR BOND). In psychotherapy, the bond of a THERAPEUTIC ALLIANCE between therapist and client is considered beneficial to the treatment. **2.** *n.* a chemical bond, such as an ionic or covalent bond, by which atoms are bound into a molecule. **3.** *vb.* to form a bond of either of these types.

bondage *n.* physical restraint of one person by another to arouse sexual pleasure in one or both partners.

bondage and discipline (B and D) a phase of sexual BONDAGE that is accompanied by such acts as whipping or spanking. Because of the potential physical danger, the partners usually agree on a signal, called a safe word, to be used when the erotic activity exceeds the pleasurable limits.

bonding *n.* the process in which ATTACHMENTS or other close relationships are formed between individuals, especially between mother and infant. An early, positive relationship between a mother and a newborn child is considered to be essential in establishing unconditional love on the part of the parent, as well as security and trust on the part of the child. In subsequent development, bonding establishes friendship and trust (see BOND).

bone pointing see VOODOO DEATH.

booster sessions in therapy, particularly COGNITIVE BEHAVIOR THERAPY, occasional periodic sessions, after the main sessions are officially ended, in order to reinforce progress or troubleshoot obstacles to continuance of positive changes made during the therapy.

bootstrapping *n.* any process or operation in which a system uses its initial resources to develop more powerful and complex processing routines, which are then used in the same fashion, and so on cumulatively. In statistics, it denotes a method for estimating the variability of a parameter associated with a batch of data, such as the standard error. A number of samples of equal size are obtained from the original data by sampling with replacement, the parameter is calculated for each, and the individual parameters are combined to provide an estimate of the overall parameter for the entire sample. **—bootstrap** *vb.*

borderline 1. *adj.* pertaining to any phenomenon difficult to categorize because it straddles two distinct classes, showing characteristics of both. Thus, BORDERLINE INTELLIGENCE is supposed to show characteristics of both the average and subaverage categories. See also BORDERLINE DISORDER; BORDERLINE STATE. **2.** *n.* an inappropriate designation for someone with BORDERLINE PERSONALITY DISORDER or its symptoms.

borderline disorder 1. BORDERLINE PERSONALITY DISORDER or, more broadly, any personality disorder. **2.** historically, any psychological condition that lies between normality and neurosis, between normality and psychosis, or between normal intelligence and mental retardation. See also BORDERLINE INTELLIGENCE.

borderline intelligence a level of measured intellectual performance between average and significantly subaverage intelligence. Some researchers define it as an IQ between 68 and 83, others as any IQ in the 70s, but it is most often associated with IQs in the range 70–75. IQs in the borderline range, especially above 75, do not justify a basis for diagnosis of mental retardation. Also called **borderline intellectual functioning**; **borderline mental retardation**.

borderline personality disorder in *DSM–IV–TR*, a personality disorder characterized by a long-standing pattern of instability in mood, interpersonal relationships, and self-image that is severe enough to cause extreme distress or interfere with social and occupational functioning. Among the manifestations of this disorder are (a) self-damaging behavior in such areas as gambling, sex, spending, overeating, and substance use; (b) intense but unstable relationships; (c) uncontrollable temper outbursts; (d) uncertainty about self-image, gender, goals, and loyalties; (e) shifting moods; (f) self-defeating behavior, such as fights, suicidal gestures, or self-mutilation; and (g) chronic feelings of emptiness and boredom. An alternative name for this disorder, **unstable personality disorder**, was proposed in the *DSM–III* task force.

borderline psychosis see BORDERLINE STATE.

borderline schizophrenia historically, a condition in which an individual inconsistently displays symptoms of schizophrenia (e.g., only under circumstances of high stress) but is in touch with reality most of the time. In *DSM–II*, this condition was included within the diagnostic category of latent schizophrenia.

borderline state any condition in which an in-

B

dividual's presenting symptoms are difficult to classify. Historically, borderline state (or **borderline psychosis**) more specifically referred to a condition in which an individual may become psychotic if exposed to unfavorable circumstances but has not currently lost touch with reality.

boredom *n.* a state of weariness or ennui resulting from a lack of engagement with stimuli in the environment. **—bored** *adj.*

Börjeson–Forssman–Lehmann syndrome a disorder characterized by MICROCEPHALY, severe mental retardation, short stature, and hypogonadism. Affected individuals have severe to profound mental retardation and little or no pubic hair, even as adults. The syndrome is related to an X-linked recessive mutant gene (locus Xq26–27). [Mats Gunnar **Börjeson** (1922–), Hans Axel **Forssman** (1912–1994), and J. O. Orla **Lehmann** (1927–), Swedish physicians]

Boston Naming Test (BNT) a 60-item fluency test of word retrieval used to evaluate dysphasia (see APHASIA). Line drawings of objects—ranging in difficulty from the commonly encountered (e.g., tree, bed) to the rarely encountered (e.g., sphinx, abacus)—are presented, and the participant provides the name of each object. [originally developed in 1978 by U.S. neuropsychologist Edith F. Kaplan (1924–2009), U.S. clinical psychologist Harold Goodglass (1920–2002), and U.S. neuropsychologist Sandra Weintraub (1946–)]

BOT abbreviation for BRUININKS–OSERETSKY TEST OF MOTOR PROFICIENCY.

bottoming out a state of despair characterized by financial ruin, suicide attempts, or shattered family and other intimate interpersonal relationships that is frequently experienced by people with severe depression or addiction disorders (e.g., substance abusers and pathological gamblers).

bottom-up analysis an inductive approach to problem solving that begins with specific instances or empirical data and works up to a more abstract level of analysis, such as a general principle or hypothesis. See INDUCTIVE REASONING. Compare TOP-DOWN ANALYSIS.

bouffée délirante see ACUTE DELUSIONAL PSYCHOSIS.

Boulder model see SCIENTIST-PRACTITIONER MODEL.

boulimia *n.* see BULIMIA.

boundary *n.* **1.** a psychological demarcation that protects the integrity of an individual or group or that helps the person or group set realistic limits on participation in a relationship or activity. **2.** in psychotherapy, an important limit that is usually set by the therapist as part of the GROUND RULES in treatment. Boundaries may involve areas of discussion (e.g., the therapist's personal life is off limits) or physical limits (e.g., rules about touching), which are guided by ethical codes and standards. Respect for boundaries by both the therapist and client is an important concept in the therapeutic relationship.

boundary ambiguity uncertainty that arises in a family system when an individual's status, role, or family membership is brought into question, most often as a result of separation, divorce, and remarriage. See PERMEABLE FAMILY.

boundary issues **1.** ethical issues relating to the proper limits of a professional relationship between a provider of services (e.g., a physician or a psychotherapist) and his or her patient or client, such that the trust and vulnerability of the latter are not abused (see BOUNDARY). A particular area of concern is PROFESSIONAL–CLIENT SEXUAL RELATIONS. **2.** in health care, issues relating to the demarcations between different areas and levels of expertise and questions of who is best qualified to give certain types of treatment or advice.

boundary system in GENERAL SYSTEMS THEORY, the semipermeable boundaries between living systems, permitting information to flow in either direction but posing the question of how much interpenetration and interdependence is feasible in a given social system. See also EGO BOUNDARY.

bounded rationality decision making in which the processes used are rational within the constraints imposed by (a) limitations in the individual's knowledge; (b) human cognitive limitations generally; and (c) empirical factors arising from the complex, real-life situations in which decisions have to be made. The concept was introduced by U. S. economist and psychologist Herbert Simon (1916–2001) as a corrective to the assumption of classical economic theory that individuals can and will make ideally informed and rational decisions in pursuit of their own self-interest.

bound energy in psychoanalytic theory, PSYCHIC ENERGY that is located within the ego and focused on the individual's external reality. Bound energy is associated with the SECONDARY PROCESSES and is contrasted with the FREE ENERGY of the id.

bowel disorder any disorder of the small or large intestine, which frequently occurs as a response to stress and anxiety, (e.g., chronic constipation, IRRITABLE BOWEL SYNDROME).

bowel incontinence see FECAL INCONTINENCE.

Bowen family systems theory see FAMILY SYSTEMS THEORY.

Bowlby, Edward John Mostyn (1907–1990) British psychiatrist. Bowlby received his MD in 1933 from University College in London and trained as a psychoanalyst. Influenced by the studies of IMPRINTING in animals that Austrian ethologist Konrad Lorenz (1903–1989) conducted, Bowlby integrated psychoanalytic ideas with evolutionary biology and cognitive psychology to create his ATTACHMENT THEORY. He argued that the attachment of human infants to their caregivers and their distress at being separated from them have an evolutionary advantage: They increase the infants' likelihood of survival by keeping them close to their caregivers. Patterns of attachment (secure and insecure) established in early childhood affect later emotional development and emotional stability in the child and adult. Bowlby's work has been very influential in developmental psychology since the 1970s, initiating a rich body of research on the importance of early attachment patterns to psychological well-being.

boxer's dementia a chronic, slowly progressive DEMENTIA resulting from scattered hemorrhages in the brain produced by repeated blows to the head. Affected individuals are often described as "punch-drunk." Common symptoms include poorly articulated speech (see DYSARTHRIA), poor balance, impaired memory and concentration, and involuntary movements. The term is often applied to the more advanced cases, while **boxer's traumatic encephalopathy** refers to all types of cases. Also called **dementia pugilistica**.

BPRS abbreviation for BRIEF PSYCHIATRIC RATING SCALE.

BPS abbreviation for BRITISH PSYCHOLOGICAL SOCIETY.

BRAC abbreviation for BASIC REST–ACTIVITY CYCLE.

Brachmann–de Lange syndrome see AMSTERDAM DWARF DISEASE; DE LANGE'S SYNDROME. [described in 1916 by Winfried **Brachmann** (1888–c. 1915), German physician, and in 1933 by Cornelia **de Lange** (1871–1950), Dutch pediatrician]

bradyarthria *n.* see BRADYLALIA.

bradycardia *n.* see ARRHYTHMIA.

bradykinesia *n.* abnormal slowness in the execution of voluntary movements. Also called **bradykinesis**. Compare HYPOKINESIS. **—bradykinetic** *adj.*

bradylalia *n.* abnormal slowness or hesitation in speech. Also called **bradyarthria**; **bradylogia**.

bradylogia *n.* see BRADYLALIA.

bradyrhythmia *n.* slowness of the rhythms of the heart.

braid cutting a hair fetish in which a person's hair is cut as part of sexual activity.

brain *n.* the enlarged, anterior part of the CENTRAL NERVOUS SYSTEM within the skull. The young adult human brain weighs about 1,450 g, and its outer layer (the CEREBRAL CORTEX) contains over 10 billion nerve cells. The brain develops by differentiation of the embryonic NEURAL TUBE along an anterior–posterior axis to form three main regions—the FOREBRAIN, MIDBRAIN, and HINDBRAIN—that can be further subdivided on the basis of anatomical and functional criteria. The cortical tissue is concentrated in the forebrain, and the midbrain and hindbrain structures are often considered together as the BRAINSTEM. Also called **encephalon**. See also BRAIN LOCALIZATION THEORY; EVOLUTION OF THE BRAIN; SPLIT BRAIN.

brain biorhythm a BIOLOGICAL RHYTHM involving recurring periods of altered excitability or activity of the brain. Some practitioners claim to be able to predict an individual's brain biorhythms from his or her birthdate, and to use this information to improve performance.

brain concussion mild injury to the brain, due to trauma or jarring, that disrupts brain function but is typically followed by spontaneous recovery. Concussion usually involves at least brief unconsciousness, although it may be diagnosed in the absence of unconsciousness. The symptoms may include memory loss, headache, irritability, inappropriate emotional reactions, and changes in behavior. Concussions may be classified by severity based on the period of unconsciousness or the extent of memory loss for events before and after the trauma. See HEAD INJURY.

brain damage injury to the brain. It can have various causes, including prenatal infection, birth injury, head injury, toxic agents, BRAIN TUMOR, brain inflammation, severe seizures, certain metabolic disorders, vitamin deficiency, intracranial hemorrhage, stroke, and surgical procedures. Brain damage is manifested by impairment of cognitive, motor, or sensory skills mediated by the brain.

brain death the cessation of neurological signs of life. Medical criteria for brain death include absence of reflex response or response to noxious stimuli, fixed pupils, and absence of electroencephalogram (EEG) activity. The absence of EEG activity alone is not a final diagnostic sign, but brain death cannot be diagnosed if there is any sign of EEG activity.

brain disorder **1.** any condition marked by disruption of the normal functioning of the brain. **2.** an older (*DSM–I*) term for an acute or chronic mental disorder caused by or associated with impairment of brain function and characterized by mild to severe impairment of cognition and mood. Also called **brain syndrome**.

brain fag a CULTURE-BOUND SYNDROME originating in west Africa and most often experienced by high school or college students. Symptoms typically include difficulties with concentration, memory, and understanding information; feelings of pain, tightness, and burning around the head and neck; blurred vision; and tiredness associated with excessive thinking.

brain graft the surgical transplantation or implantation of brain tissue to replace a damaged part or compensate for a defect.

brain growth the increase in size, mass, and complexity of the brain. In humans, the brain grows very rapidly in the fetus and during the early postnatal years, reaching its maximum

B

mass at about 20 years, after which there is a slow decline. Some regions of the brain grow more rapidly than others, well into the teenage years.

brain imaging study of the anatomy or activity of the brain through the intact skull by noninvasive computerized techniques, such as MAGNETIC RESONANCE IMAGING, COMPUTED TOMOGRAPHY, and POSITRON EMISSION TOMOGRAPHY. See also NUCLEAR IMAGING.

brain lesion any damage to an area of brain tissue caused by injury, disease, surgery, tumor, stroke, or infection. Also called **cerebral lesion**.

brain localization theory any of various theories that different areas of the brain serve different functions. Since the early 19th century, opinion has varied between notions of highly precise localization and a belief that the brain, or large portions of it, function as a whole. In 1861 French physician Paul Broca (1824–1880) deduced from localized brain lesions that the speech center of the brain is in the left frontal lobe (see BROCA'S AREA). Since then, many techniques, including localized electrical stimulation of the brain, electrical recording from the brain, and BRAIN IMAGING, have added information about localization of function in the brain. For many investigators, however, the concept of extreme parcellation of functions has given way to concepts of distributed control by collective activity of different regions. See also MASS ACTION.

brain mapping the creation of a visual representation of the brain in which different functions are assigned to different brain regions. Mapping may be based on a variety of sources of information, including effects of localized brain lesions, recording electrical activity of the brain, and BRAIN IMAGING during various behavioral states. See also BRAIN LOCALIZATION THEORY.

brain plasticity 1. the capacity of the brain to compensate for losses in brain tissue caused by injury or disease. **2.** the capacity of the brain to change as a function of experience. The term plasticity in this sense was first used by William JAMES in 1890.

brain reserve an ability of the adult brain to tolerate pathological changes without overt signs of disturbance that stems from the capacity of remaining neurons in the central nervous system to compensate for damaged or destroyed tissue. In other words, a person with a high brain reserve can sustain a greater amount of brain injury or deterioration before manifesting symptoms than a person with low brain reserve can. Implicit to this concept is the notion of a critical threshold level of functioning neurons below which normal activities can no longer be maintained and symptoms of disorder appear. The validity of this hypothesis has been difficult to establish empirically, but the concept nonetheless has been influential within neurology and cognitive science since it was first proposed to explain the observation that many individuals with Alzheimer's disease who had extensive SENILE PLAQUES and NEUROFIBRILLARY TANGLES in their brains nonetheless showed few decrements in their intellectual abilities. This same discrepancy has since been observed in different types of dementia, Parkinson's disease, and other disorders. Indeed, the lack of a direct relationship between the degree of brain pathology and the clinical manifestation of that damage makes it difficult to diagnose these conditions in their early stages during which degenerative alterations of cerebral anatomy have begun accumulating and intervention would be most effective. Various operational definitions of brain reserve capacity are used in studies, including overall brain volume, component structure volumes, head circumference, cerebral glucose metabolism, cortical thickness, the number of brain neurons, the density of their interconnections, regional cerebral blood flow, neural transmission speed, and various parameters of the sensory EVOKED POTENTIAL. The term brain reserve at times is used interchangeably with COGNITIVE RESERVE, despite the differing theoretical emphases of the two concepts. Also called **neural reserve**. See also FUNCTIONAL PLASTICITY.

brain scan any of a variety of techniques designed either to reveal structural or functional abnormalities of the diseased brain or to measure activity of the healthy brain. See BRAIN IMAGING.

brain splitting surgical separation of the cerebral hemispheres of the brain. See COMMISSUROTOMY; SPLIT BRAIN.

brainstem *n.* the part of the brain that connects the cerebrum with the spinal cord. It includes the MIDBRAIN, PONS, and MEDULLA OBLONGATA and is involved in the autonomic control of visceral activity, such as salivation, respiration, heartbeat, and digestion.

brainstorming *n.* a problem-solving strategy in which ideas are generated spontaneously and uninhibitedly, usually in a group setting, without any immediate critical judgment about their potential value. See also CREATIVE THINKING; DIVERGENT THINKING. **—brainstorm** *vb.*

brain trauma physical injury to the brain. It can be produced by, for example, a blow to the head, a gunshot wound, or a cerebrovascular accident. See BRAIN CONCUSSION; HEAD INJURY.

brain tumor any abnormal tissue growth (see NEOPLASM) within the confines of the skull. Damage may occur by the destruction of healthy tissue or through increased INTRACRANIAL PRESSURE as there is little room for the tumor to grow within the skull without compressing healthy tissue and interfering with the flow of blood and nutrients into the brain. Brain tumors can occur at any age, producing initial symptoms of headache, nausea, or sudden vomiting without apparent cause. As the tumor progresses, the patient may experience disturbances of vision, hearing, and smell, loss of coordination, changes in mental status, weakness, and paralysis. Seizures sometimes are caused by a tumor.

brainwashing *n.* a broad class of intense and often coercive tactics intended to produce profound changes in attitudes, beliefs, and emotions. Targets of such tactics have typically been prisoners of war and members of religious cults. See also PSYCHOLOGICAL KIDNAPPING.

brain waves spontaneous, rhythmic electrical impulses emanating from different areas of the brain. Electroencephalographic brain-wave recordings are used to study SLEEP STAGES and cognitive processes. According to their frequencies, brain waves are classified as ALPHA WAVES (8–12 Hz), BETA WAVES (13–30 Hz), DELTA WAVES (1–3 Hz), GAMMA WAVES (31–80 Hz), or THETA WAVES (4–7 Hz). The first substantial account of brain waves was given in 1929 by German neuropsychiatrist Hans Berger (1873–1944).

brain-wave therapy an alternative or adjunctive therapy in which ALPHA WAVES and THETA WAVES are stimulated because they are posited to have a vital role in learning and memory and, hence, in therapeutic INSIGHT.

brain weight the weight of a brain, which is about 1,450 g for a young adult human. Brain weights for elephants and whales may exceed 7,000 g and 9,000 g, respectively. Human brain sizes usually increase until around the age of 20, then gradually diminish. Brain weight correlates significantly ($r = .4$) with intelligence. See also BRAIN GROWTH.

bravery *n.* see COURAGE.

Brazelton Neonatal Behavioral Assessment Scale an instrument used in both research and clinical settings to assess the neurological and behavioral status of newborns and infants up to 2 months old, as indicated by their responses to various stimuli (a light directed to the eye, a moving ball, a rattle, etc.). The Brazelton scale currently contains 14 neurologically and 26 behaviorally oriented items; the former are graded on a 4-point scale of intensity of response, and the latter on a 9-point scale. Originally developed in 1973, the Brazelton Neonatal Behavioral Assessment Scale was revised in 2000. Also called **Neonatal Behavioral Assessment Scale** (**NBAS**). [Thomas Berry **Brazelton** (1918–), U.S. pediatrician]

breakdown *n.* see NERVOUS BREAKDOWN.

breakthrough *n.* **1.** a significant, sometimes sudden, forward step in therapy, especially after an unproductive plateau. **2.** a major or significant advance in knowledge, research, or treatment.

breast envy in the psychoanalytic theory of Melanie KLEIN, the idea that infants envy the nourishing capacity and creative power of the mother's breast. Such envy may later be transformed into PENIS ENVY.

breathing-related sleep disorder in *DSM–IV–TR*, a primary SLEEP DISORDER marked by excessive sleepiness or insomnia arising from sleep disruption due to breathing difficulties during sleep, for example, SLEEP APNEA. See DYSSOMNIA.

breathing retraining a technique used in BEHAVIOR THERAPY and COGNITIVE BEHAVIOR THERAPY, particularly in the treatment of hyperventilation in anxiety and panic disorders. The technique teaches clients slow diaphragmatic breathing through various methods, including therapist modeling and corrective feedback. See also PROGRESSIVE RELAXATION; STRESS MANAGEMENT.

breathwork *n.* see REBIRTHING.

bridge to reality see REMOTIVATION.

bridging *n.* a method used in MULTIMODAL THERAPY in which the therapist first focuses on the client's preferred aspect of treatment (e.g., cognitions) before moving to another aspect (e.g., sensations) that the therapist believes may be more effective.

brief group therapy group psychotherapy conducted on a short-term (time- or session-limited) or CRISIS-INTERVENTION basis and focused clearly upon a specific treatment goal. See TIME-LIMITED PSYCHOTHERAPY.

brief intensive group cognitive behavior therapy a form of COGNITIVE BEHAVIOR THERAPY conducted in a group setting over a relatively brief period of time but in lengthy sessions (e.g., all day) and often on consecutive days (e.g., weekends). The therapy is typically used to treat anxiety disorders, particularly panic disorder.

Brief Psychiatric Rating Scale (**BPRS**) a system of evaluating the presence and severity of clinical psychiatric signs on the basis of 24 factors, such as bizarre behavior, hostility, emotional withdrawal, and disorientation. Each factor is rated on a 7-point scale ranging from "not present" to "extremely severe," based on the judgments of trained observers. [introduced in its original version in 1962 by U.S. psychiatrist John E. Overall and U.S. clinical psychologist Donald R. Gorman]

brief psychodynamic psychotherapy a collection of time-limited PSYCHODYNAMIC PSYCHOTHERAPY approaches intended to enhance client self-awareness and understanding of the influence of the past on present behavior. One particularly important issue is identified as the central focus for the treatment, thus creating a structure and establishing a goal for the sessions. Rather than allowing the client to associate freely and discuss unconnected issues, as occurs in more traditional psychoanalytic practice, the brief psychodynamic therapist is expected to be fairly active in keeping the session focused on the main issue. The number of sessions varies from one approach to another, but brief psychodynamic therapy is typically considered to be no more than 20–25 sessions. Also called **short-term psychodynamic psychotherapy**. [originally developed by Hungarian psychoanalyst Franz Alexander (1891–1964) and his colleague Thomas French]

B

brief psychotherapy any form of psychotherapy intended to achieve change during a short period (generally 10–20 sessions). Brief psychotherapies rely on active techniques of inquiry, focus, and goal setting and tend to be symptom specific. They may be applied on an individual or group level and are used in the treatment of a variety of behavioral and emotional problems. There are numerous different types, such as brief COGNITIVE BEHAVIOR THERAPY, brief PLAY THERAPY, BRIEF PSYCHODYNAMIC PSYCHOTHERAPY, FOCAL PSYCHOTHERAPY, and INTERPERSONAL PSYCHOTHERAPY. Also called **short-term psychotherapy**.

brief psychotic disorder in *DSM–IV–TR*, a disturbance involving the sudden onset of at least one psychotic symptom (e.g., incoherence or loosening of associations, delusions, hallucinations, or grossly disorganized or catatonic behavior). The condition is often accompanied by emotional turmoil and lasts from 1 day to 1 month, with complete remission of all symptoms and a full return to previous levels of functioning. It may develop following a period of extreme stress, such as the loss of a loved one; in *DSM–III*, brief psychotic disorder involving a precipitating stressor was termed **brief reactive psychosis**.

brief stimulus therapy (**BST**) ELECTROCONVULSIVE THERAPY (ECT) in which the electric current is modified significantly to decrease the duration of stimulus needed to produce a seizure. Some researchers and clinicians claim that this technique not only achieves satisfactory clinical results comparable to those of standard ECT but also diminishes the duration of confusion or memory impairment. Also called **brief stimuli therapy**; **brief stimulus technique**.

bright light therapy see PHOTOTHERAPY.

Briquet's syndrome a former name for SOMATIZATION DISORDER. [Paul **Briquet** (1796–1881), French physician, who provided the first systematic description of its characteristics in 1859]

British Psychological Society (**BPS**) a professional organization, founded in 1901, that is the representative body for psychologists and psychology in the United Kingdom. By royal charter, it is charged with national responsibility for the development, promotion, and application of psychology for the public good.

Broca's aphasia one of eight classically identified APHASIAS, characterized by nonfluent conversational speech and slow, halting speech production. Auditory comprehension is relatively good for everyday conversation, but there is considerable difficulty with complex syntax or multistep commands. It is associated with injury to BROCA'S AREA of the brain. [Pierre Paul **Broca** (1824–1880), French physician]

Broca's area a region of the posterior portion of the inferior frontal convolution of a CEREBRAL HEMISPHERE that is associated with the production of speech. It is located on the left hemisphere of right-handed people and of most left-handed individuals. [discovered in the 1860s and studied and researched by Pierre Paul **Broca**]

Brodmann's area an area of cerebral cortex characterized by variation in the occurrence and arrangement of cells from that of neighboring areas. These areas are identified by numbers and in many cases have been associated with specific brain functions, such as area 17 (striate cortex or primary visual cortex), areas 18 and 19 (prestriate cortex), area 4 (motor area), and area 6 (premotor area). Brodmann's original map of 1909 identified 47 different cortical areas, but investigators have refined the mapping to identify more than 200 distinctive cortical areas. Also called **Brodmann's cytoarchitectonic area**. [Korbinian **Brodmann** (1868–1918), German neurologist]

brofaromine *n.* an antidepressant drug that is a reversible MONOAMINE OXIDASE INHIBITOR (RIMA) and relatively selective for MONOAMINE OXIDASE A. It therefore lacks many of the food interactions that limit the use of irreversible nonselective MAO inhibitors. Brofaromine is not currently available in the United States. European trade name: **Consonar**.

bromazepam *n.* a BENZODIAZEPINE used for the treatment of anxiety. It has a short to intermediate duration of action (serum HALF-LIFE up to 30 hours) and a slow onset of action due to its low lipid solubility (see BLOOD–BRAIN BARRIER). Bromazepam is not currently available in the United States. Canadian trade name: **Lectopam**.

bromide *n.* a class of drugs formerly used as anticonvulsants and as sedatives in the treatment of anxiety. Because of their toxicity and the frequency of adverse side effects, bromides were largely supplanted by phenobarbital in the early 20th century. Bromide intoxication was a recognized complication, manifested in early stages by cognitive impairment and emotional disturbances and in later stages by psychosis, coma, and death.

bromocriptine *n.* a DOPAMINE-RECEPTOR AGONIST used to relieve the symptoms of PARKINSON'S DISEASE and, due to its ability to inhibit release of the pituitary hormone PROLACTIN, to treat GALACTORRHEA. It is also used to treat amenorrhea, infertility, prolactin-secreting adenomas, and parkinsonism, including drug-induced EXTRAPYRAMIDAL SYMPTOMS of conventional (typical or first-generation) antipsychotic agents. U.S. trade name: **Parlodel**.

bronchodilator medications drugs administered to widen the airways in the treatment of asthma, bronchitis, and related respiratory disorders. They include METHYLXANTHINES and SYMPATHOMIMETIC DRUGS.

brooding compulsion an irresistible drive to mentally review trivial details or ponder abstract concepts as a means of reducing distress or preventing some dreaded event or situation. This is a common symptom of OBSESSIVE-COMPULSIVE DISORDER.

brotherliness *n.* the feeling of human unity or solidarity, as expressed in productive involvement with others, care for their well-being, and concern for society as a whole. According to Erich FROMM, brotherliness represents the positive or ideal resolution of the search for ROOTEDNESS.

Brown, Roger (1925–1997) U.S. psychologist. Brown earned his doctorate at the University of Michigan in 1952 with a study of the social psychology of the AUTHORITARIAN PERSONALITY. He then joined the faculty of Harvard University, where he remained throughout his career except for a relatively brief interlude (1957–1962) at the Massachusetts Institute of Technology. His most important contributions to psychology were in the fields of social psychology and psycholinguistics. At Harvard, Brown became involved with the research group of U.S. development psychologist Jerome Bruner (1915–) studying cognitive processes and he became interested in the relationship between language and mind. His *Words and Things* (1957) is considered a classic in the field of psycholinguistics. Arguably his most important contribution to that field was his intensive study of language development in three children, published as *A First Language: The Early Stages* (1973). Brown is also noted for devising successful scientific experiments to study cognitive problems not previously thought amenable to scientific inquiry, such as the TIP-OF-THE-TONGUE PHENOMENON, and he coined the term FLASHBULB MEMORY. Among Brown's other important writings are the two editions of his widely used textbook *Social Psychology* (1965; 1986). He was elected to the American Academy of Arts and Sciences and the National Academy of Sciences and received the Distinguished Scientific Contribution Award from the American Psychological Association.

Brown–Peterson distractor technique a technique used in memory studies in which participants are allowed a brief period for remembering during which REHEARSAL is minimized. Typically, three items (e.g., words) are presented, after which the participant is asked to count backward for a certain time (as a distractor) before attempting to recall the presented items. [John A. **Brown**; Lloyd R. **Peterson** (1922–) and Margaret Jean **Peterson** (1930–), U.S. psychologists]

brucine *n.* an alkaloid obtained from the *Brucea* genus of shrubs that is an antagonist at receptor sites for the inhibitory neurotransmitter GLYCINE. Brucine is also found (with strychnine) in NUX VOMICA; it resembles strychnine but is less potent.

Bruck–de Lange type see DE LANGE'S SYNDROME. [described in 1889 by F. **Bruck**, German physician, and in 1934 by Cornelia **de Lange** (1871–1950), Dutch pediatrician]

Bruininks–Oseretsky Test of Motor Proficiency (**BOT**) a set of standardized tests to assess FINE MOTOR and GROSS MOTOR skills in children aged 4 to 21 years. Its 53 items are grouped into eight subtests: fine motor precision, fine motor integration, manual dexterity, bilateral coordination, balance, running speed and agility, upper-limb coordination, and strength. The BOT, originally published in 1978 as a revision of the 1923 **Oseretsky Tests of Motor Proficiency**, is now in its second edition (published in 2005). [Robert H. **Bruininks** (1942–), U.S. psychologist; N. I. **Oseretsky**, 20th-century Russian psychologist]

brujeria *n.* see ROOTWORK.

Brushfield–Wyatt syndrome a form of mental retardation associated with several other anomalies, including an extensive port-wine birthmark, paralysis on the side opposite to the causal lesion, and cerebral tumor. [Thomas **Brushfield** (1858–1937), British physician]

bruxism *n.* persistent grinding, clenching, or gnashing of teeth, usually during sleep. It can be associated with feelings of tension, anger, frustration, or fear. Also called **bruxomania**; **stridor dentium**.

BSRI abbreviation for BEM SEX ROLE INVENTORY.

BSS abbreviation for BECK SCALE FOR SUICIDE IDEATION.

BST abbreviation for BRIEF STIMULUS THERAPY.

B-type personality see TYPE B PERSONALITY.

buccal intercourse see OROGENITAL ACTIVITY.

buccolingual masticatory syndrome (**BLM**; **BLMS**) a movement disorder associated with the use of conventional ANTIPSYCHOTIC agents and characterized by involuntary movements of the tongue and musculature of the mouth and face. Patients may involuntarily chew, protrude the tongue, or make grimacing or pursing movements of the lips and cheeks. Also called **buccal–lingual masticatory syndrome**; **oral–lingual dyskinesia**. See also TARDIVE DYSKINESIA.

buffer **1.** *n.* see BUFFER ITEM. **2.** *n.* a temporary store in memory. For example, SHORT-TERM MEMORY is a buffer. **3.** *vb.* see BUFFERING.

buffering *n.* the protection against stressful experiences that is afforded by an individual's social support. **—buffer** *vb.*

buffer item an irrelevant item interspersed between others in a test or experiment. For example, a buffer item may be a question that is not scored and is introduced only to separate or disguise other items.

bufotenin a naturally occurring, mildly hallucinogenic substance found on the skin of a species of toad (genus *Bufo*) and in plants of the genus *Anadenanthera*; it is also reported to be a component of the urine of certain patients with schizophrenia. Bufotenin is related chemically to LSD, PSILOCIN, and DMT. See also HALLUCINOGEN.

B

buggery *n.* SODOMY or ANAL INTERCOURSE.

bulimia *n.* insatiable hunger for food. It may have physiological causes, such as a brain lesion or endocrine disturbance, or be primarily a psychological disorder (see BINGE-EATING DISORDER; BULIMIA NERVOSA). See also HYPERBULIMIA; HYPERPHAGIA. **—bulimic** *adj., n.*

bulimia nervosa an EATING DISORDER involving recurrent episodes of binge eating (i.e., discrete periods of uncontrolled consumption of abnormally large quantities of food) followed by inappropriate compensatory behaviors (e.g., self-induced vomiting, misuse of laxatives, fasting, excessive exercise). Compare BINGE-EATING DISORDER.

bullying *n.* persistent threatening and aggressive physical behavior or verbal abuse directed toward other people, especially those who are younger, smaller, weaker, or in some other situation of relative disadvantage.

buprenorphine *n.* an OPIOID ANALGESIC with both agonist and antagonist activity at opioid receptors, used for the treatment of moderate to severe pain and also for the management of opioid dependence. Because of its ability to partially block the mu OPIOID RECEPTOR, it can attenuate the euphoria and other subjective and physiological effects associated with opioids, and therefore may be useful in both opioid withdrawal and as a substitute for illicit opioids in long-term maintenance treatment of opioid dependence. U.S. trade name: **Buprenex**.

bupropion *n.* an aminoketone agent commonly used in the treatment of depression. It is also appropriate as an adjuvant to behavioral treatment for smoking cessation. It is occasionally used in combination with other antidepressants to augment antidepressant response (see AUGMENTATION STRATEGY), and has also been used in the treatment of attention-deficit/hyperactivity disorder. Bupropion is available in both immediate-release and extended-release preparations. U.S. trade names: **Wellbutrin**; **Zyban**.

burned out 1. describing an individual who is mentally or physically exhausted or overwhelmed. See BURNOUT. **2.** historically, describing individuals with chronic schizophrenia who are apathetic, withdrawn, and show progressive deterioration, with little hope of significant improvement, personal growth, or adaptive functioning.

burnout *n.* physical, emotional, or mental exhaustion, especially in one's job or career, accompanied by decreased motivation, lowered performance, and negative attitudes toward oneself and others. It results from performing at a high level until stress and tension, especially from extreme and prolonged physical or mental exertion or an overburdening workload, take their toll. The word was first used in this sense in 1975 by U.S. psychologist Herbert J. Freudenberger (1926–1999) in referring to workers in clinics with heavy caseloads. Burnout is most often observed in professionals who work closely with people (e.g., social workers, teachers, correctional officers) in service-oriented vocations and experience chronic high levels of STRESS. It can be particularly acute in therapists or counselors doing TRAUMA work, who feel overwhelmed by the cumulative secondary trauma of witnessing the effects. Burnout is also experienced by athletes when continually exposed to stress associated with performance without commensurate rewards or rest. See also OVERTRAINING SYNDROME.

buspirone *n.* a nonbenzodiazepine anxiolytic of the AZAPIRONE class. Both it and its primary metabolic product, 6-hydroxybuspirone, produce relief of subjective symptoms of anxiety without the sedation, behavioral disinhibition, and risk of dependence associated with the benzodiazepines. Its use has been limited due to its relative lack of efficacy compared with benzodiazepines. U.S. trade name: **BuSpar**.

butabarbital *n.* an intermediate-acting BARBITURATE used in the treatment of insomnia and for daytime and preoperative sedation. Like other barbiturates, it is a nonselective CNS DEPRESSANT and therefore quite toxic in overdose. Because tolerance to its sedative and hypnotic effects accrues much more rapidly than tolerance to its CNS depressant effects, its THERAPEUTIC INDEX drops and its potential lethality increases as the dose is increased. These factors, plus its potential for abuse, have caused a decline in its clinical use. U.S. trade name: **Butisol Sodium**.

butorphanol *n.* a synthetic OPIOID that acts as a mixed agonist–antagonist: It is an agonist at kappa OPIOID RECEPTORS but an antagonist at mu opioid receptors. It is used clinically for the management of moderate to severe pain, including migraine headaches, and as a preoperative medication. It is available in an injectable preparation and an intranasal spray, but the ease of use of the latter has made it a common drug of abuse. As with other opioid agents, butorphanol may cause respiratory depression, nausea, and dependence. U.S. trade name: **Stadol**.

butyrophenone *n.* any of a class of HIGH-POTENCY ANTIPSYCHOTICS used primarily in the treatment of schizophrenia, mania, and severe agitation. They are associated with numerous EXTRAPYRAMIDAL SYMPTOMS, as well as NEUROLEPTIC MALIGNANT SYNDROME and TARDIVE DYSKINESIA. The prototype is HALOPERIDOL.

butyrylcholinesterase (**BuChE**) *n.* see CHOLINESTERASE.

buzz group a subdivision of a group that has been broken up so that each member may be involved in more direct and active discussion to ascertain his or her feelings or opinions. The results are then typically conveyed to the primary (i.e., entire) group by a spokesperson. Also called **buzz session**.

B-values *pl. n.* see METANEEDS.

BWS abbreviation for BATTERED-WOMAN SYNDROME.

Cc

caapi *n.* see AYAHUASCA.

cachexia *n.* an extreme state of poor health, physical wasting away, and malnutrition, usually associated with chronic illnesses, such as cancer and pulmonary tuberculosis.

cacoethes *n.* an irresistible, and sometimes irrational, desire or compulsion.

cafard *n.* a CULTURE-BOUND SYNDROME found in Polynesia, with symptoms similar to those of AMOK. Also called **cathard**.

Cafergot *n.* a trade name for ERGOTAMINE.

caffeine *n.* a CNS STIMULANT found in coffee, tea, cola, cocoa, chocolate, and certain prescribed and over-the-counter medications. It is an antagonist of the neuromodulator ADENOSINE. Caffeine belongs to the METHYLXANTHINE group of alkaloids, and its effects include rapid breathing, increased pulse rate and blood pressure, and diminished fatigue. Precise effects vary with the amount ingested and the tolerance of the individual. Moderate doses produce an improved flow of thought and clearness of ideas, together with increased respiratory and vaso-motor activity; large doses may make concentration or continued attention difficult and cause insomnia, headaches, and confusion in some individuals (see CAFFEINE INTOXICATION; SUBSTANCE-INDUCED ANXIETY DISORDER). Because of its stimulant effects, caffeine is used in KEEP-AWAKE PILLS and in certain analgesics and cold remedies containing ingredients that usually cause drowsiness. See also ASPIRIN COMBINATIONS.

caffeine intoxication intoxication due to recent consumption of large amounts of caffeine (typically over 250 mg), in the form of coffee, tea, cola, or medications, and involving at least five of the following symptoms: restlessness, nervousness, excitement, insomnia, flushed face, diuresis (increased urination), gastrointestinal complaints, muscle twitching, rambling thought and speech, rapid or irregular heart rhythm, periods of inexhaustibility, or psychomotor agitation. Brewed coffee contains 100–150 mg caffeine per cup; tea contains about 50 mg, and cola about 35 mg. Also called **caffeinism**.

CAGE *n.* a screening instrument to detect alcohol dependence. It consists of the following four questions: (a) Have you ever felt you should *C*ut down on your drinking? (b) Have people *A*nnoyed you by criticizing your drinking? (c) Have you ever felt bad or *G*uilty about your drinking? (d) Have you ever used a drink as an *E*ye-opener?

calcium-channel blocker any of a class of drugs, the prototype of which is **verapamil**, used in the treatment of hypertension and abnormal heart rhythms (arrhythmias). Calcium-channel blockers inhibit the flow of calcium ions into the smooth-muscle cells of blood vessels and the cells of heart muscle, which need calcium to contract, thus inducing prolonged relaxation of the muscles.

calcium-deficiency disorders diseases caused by a deficiency of calcium in the tissues. Absorption of calcium from food and its deposition in bone is facilitated by vitamin D, and deficiency of this vitamin is the usual cause of **rickets**, a disease of childhood marked by deformed bones and teeth and lax muscles, and **osteomalacia**, the adult form of rickets. **Osteoporosis**, in which the bones become brittle and break easily, is caused by resorption (loss) of calcified bone, due to disease or aging (it is common in postmenopausal women). **Tetany** (muscle spasms) is due to a deficiency of calcium in the blood.

calendar method of birth control attempting to avoid pregnancy by not having intercourse during the middle days of the woman's menstrual cycle, when ovulation occurs. However, because ovulation is not completely regular, and sperm have been found to stay active for up to 3 days in the uterus, this method is not very successful. See also RHYTHM METHOD.

California Psychological Inventory (**CPI**) a self-report inventory designed to evaluate adult and adolescent personality characteristics, interpersonal behavior, and social interaction. It currently consists of 434 true–false statements (a 260-statement short form is also available) that produces scores on 20 scales divided into four measurement classes: (a) poise, ascendancy, self-assurance, and interpersonal adequacy; (b) socialization, responsibility, intrapersonal values, and character; (c) achievement potential and intellectual efficacy; and (d) intellectual and interest modes. Originally published in 1957, the CPI is now in its third edition (published 1996). Also called **California Psychological Inventory Test**. [devised by U.S. psychologist Harrison G. Gough (1921–) at the University of California, Berkeley]

California Verbal Learning Test (**CVLT**) a word-list learning test consisting of 16 items belonging to one of four categories. Currently in its second edition (**CVLT–II**), the test assesses immediate FREE RECALL following each of five learning trials as well as an interference trial. Free recall and CUED RECALL are also assessed following a short-term delay (immediately after the interference trial) and a long-term (20-min) delay. Finally, long-term recognition is assessed using distractors that vary in their likelihood of eliciting false positive errors. In addition to the adult version, a 9-item version has been developed for use with individuals with memory impairment (**CVLT–II short form**). There is also a 15-item version for children aged 5–16, **California Verbal Learning Test for Children** (**CVLT–C**).

call boy see MALE HOMOSEXUAL PROSTITUTION.

call girl *n.* a female prostitute who does not work out of a brothel or by soliciting in the street. Instead, her services are ordered by telephone, and she may then be collected by the client or come to the client's home or hotel. Call girls typically charge higher prices than other types of prostitutes.

CAM abbreviation for COMPLEMENTARY AND ALTERNATIVE MEDICINE.

camisole *n.* see STRAITJACKET.

camphorated tincture of opium see PAREGORIC.

Campral *n.* a trade name for ACAMPROSATE.

camptocormia *n.* a condition in which the back is bent forward at a sharp angle (30–90°). In some cases it may be a rare manifestation of CONVERSION DISORDER and may be accompanied by back pain, tremors, or both.

campus crisis center a campus organization created to provide support and advice for students experiencing personal difficulty or trauma in their school, college, or university. Substance abuse, rape, depression, academic failure, and suicidal tendencies are typical of the problems or traumas encountered by students. A campus crisis center may offer such services as counseling, a hotline, or an escort service for students returning to housing late at night.

Canadian Psychological Association (**CPA**) a professional organization representing psychologists in Canada, organized in 1939 and incorporated in 1950. Its objectives are to lead, advance, and promote psychology as a science and profession for the benefit of humanity; to provide leadership in psychology in Canada; to promote the advancement, dissemination, and application of psychological knowledge; and to develop standards and ethical principles for education, training, science, and practice in psychology.

canalization *n.* **1.** in evolutionary genetics, the containment of variation of certain characters within narrow bounds so that expression of underlying genetic variation is repressed. It is a developmental mechanism that maintains a constant PHENOTYPE over a range of different environments in which the organism might normally occur. **2.** in neurology, the hypothetical process by which repeated use of a neural pathway leads to greater ease of transmission of impulses and hence its establishment as permanent. **3.** in psychology, the channeling by an organism of its needs into fixed patterns of gratification, for example, food preferences and recreational preferences.

cancer *n.* any one of a group of diseases characterized by the unregulated, abnormal growth of cells to form malignant tumors (see NEOPLASM), which invade neighboring tissues; the abnormal cells are generally capable of spreading via the bloodstream or lymphatic system to other body areas or organs by the process of **metastasis**. Causes of cancer are numerous but commonly include viruses, environmental toxins, diet, and inherited gentic variations. Cancers are generally classified as **carcinomas** if they involve the epithelium (e.g., cancers of the lungs, stomach, or skin) and **sarcomas** if the affected tissues are connective (e.g., bone, muscle, or fat). More than 150 different kinds of cancer have been identified in humans, based on cell types, rate of growth, and other factors. Because cancers can be disfiguring and life-threatening, psychological counseling is often helpful for patients. —**cancerous** *adj.*

cancer phobia a persistent and irrational fear of cancer. Fear of developing cancer may be a symptom of OBSESSIVE-COMPULSIVE DISORDER; it may also be classified as a SPECIFIC PHOBIA, other type. The belief that one has cancer based on the misinterpretation of bodily symptoms is classified as HYPOCHONDRIASIS.

Candlelighters Childhood Cancer Foundation an organization that links children with cancer and their families to SUPPORT GROUPS in which they can share feelings and exchange information.

cannabinoid *n.* any of a class of about 60 substances in the CANNABIS plant that includes those responsible for the psychoactive properties of the plant. The most important cannabinoid is TETRAHYDROCANNABINOL.

cannabis *n.* any of three related plant species (*Cannabis sativa, C. indica*, or *C. ruderalis*) whose dried flowering or fruiting tops or leaves are widely used as a recreational drug, known as **marijuana**. The principal psychoactive agent in these plants, delta-9-TETRAHYDROCANNABINOL (THC), is concentrated in the resin, most of which is in the plants' flowering tops. When smoked, THC is rapidly absorbed into the blood and almost immediately distributed to the brain, causing the rapid onset of subjective effects that last 2–3 hours. These effects include a sense of euphoria or well-being, easy laughter, perceptual distortions, impairment of concentration and short-term memory, and craving for food. Adverse effects of anxiety or panic are not uncommon, and hallucinations may occur with high doses (see also CANNABIS-INDUCED PSYCHOTIC DISORDER; CANNABIS INTOXICATION). Tolerance to the effects of THC develops with repeated use, but reports of CANNABIS DEPENDENCE are rare.

The most potent marijuana preparation is HASHISH, which consists of pure resin. A less potent preparation is sinsemilla, also called GANJA; it is made from the plants' flowering tops. The weakest preparation is BHANG. Also called **hemp**.

cannabis abuse in *DSM–IV–TR*, a pattern of CANNABIS use manifested by recurrent significant adverse consequences related to its repeated ingestion. This diagnosis is preempted by the diagnosis of CANNABIS DEPENDENCE: If the criteria for cannabis abuse and cannabis dependence are both met, only the latter diagnosis is given. See also SUBSTANCE ABUSE.

cannabis dependence in *DSM–IV–TR*, a cluster of cognitive, behavioral, and physiological symptoms indicating continued use of cannabis despite significant cannabis-related problems. There is a pattern of repeated cannabis ingestion resulting in tolerance, withdrawal symptoms (chiefly motor agitation) if use is suspended, and an uncontrollable drive to continue use. See CANNABIS ABUSE. See also SUBSTANCE DEPENDENCE.

cannabis-induced psychotic disorder a rare disorder marked by persecutory delusions associated with CANNABIS INTOXICATION, sometimes accompanied by marked anxiety, emotional lability, depersonalization, and subsequent amnesia for the episode. The disorder usually remits within a day, although it may persist for a few days. Hallucinations occur rarely. Also called **cannabis psychosis**.

cannabis intoxication a reversible syndrome that occurs during or shortly after the ingestion or smoking of CANNABIS. It consists of clinically significant behavioral or psychological changes (e.g., enhanced sense of well-being, intensification of perceptions, a sense of slowed time), as well as one or more signs of physiological involvement (e.g., increased pulse rate, conjunctivitis, dry mouth and throat). See also SUBSTANCE INTOXICATION.

cannabis psychosis see CANNABIS-INDUCED PSYCHOTIC DISORDER.

cannibalism *n.* **1.** the consumption of human flesh. **2.** a pathological urge to devour human flesh, occasionally observed in schizophrenia and similar mental disturbances, such as WINDIGO. In classical psychoanalytic theory, cannibalistic impulses are associated with fixation at the ORAL-BITING PHASE of PSYCHOSEXUAL DEVELOPMENT. **—cannibalistic** *adj.*

Capgras syndrome a condition characterized by a delusional belief that the self or known individuals have been replaced by doubles or impostors. This type of MISIDENTIFICATION SYNDROME may be associated with paranoid schizophrenia, a neurological disorder, or a mood disorder. Also called **illusion of doubles**. [Jean Marie Joseph **Capgras** (1873–1950), French psychiatrist]

capitation *n.* a method of payment for health care services in which a provider or health care facility is paid a fixed amount for each person served under a risk contract. Capitation is the characteristic payment method of HMOs. **—capitated** *adj.*

carbamate *n.* any of a class of ACETYLCHOLINESTERASE INHIBITORS (e.g., RIVASTIGMINE) used in the treatment of dementia. Carbamates can delay the progression of certain dementias, slowing declines in cognitive function and in activities of daily living. They are preferred to earlier generations of acetylcholinesterase inhibitors because of their relatively benign side effects, relative lack of liver toxicity, and improved dosing schedule (they need to be administered only once or twice a day).

carbamazepine (**CBZ**) *n.* a drug that is related to the TRICYCLIC ANTIDEPRESSANTS, used mainly as an ANTICONVULSANT but also as a MOOD STABILIZER in mania. U.S. trade name (among others): **Tegretol**.

carbidopa *n.* see SINEMET.

carbon dioxide therapy a form of inhalation therapy, now no longer in use, that was occasionally applied (in conjunction with psychotherapy) to patients with anxiety, conversion, or psychophysiological symptoms. [first used in the 1920s by Hungarian-born U.S. psychiatrist Ladislaus Joseph Meduna (1896–1964) to induce unconsciousness as a means of interrupting pathological brain circuits]

carbonic anhydrase inhibitor any of a group of drugs that interfere with the action of the enzyme carbonic anhydrase in the body. Although their primary role was originally as diuretics, via their ability to block reabsorption of sodium bicarbonate from the proximal renal tubule, thus improving urine excretion and electrolyte balance, their use has been supplanted by less toxic diuretics. At present, **acetazolamide** (the prototype; U.S. trade name: **Diamox**) and other carbonic anhydrase inhibitors are used primarily for the management of glaucoma and acute mountain sickness. The drugs are also used as adjunctive agents in the management of epilepsy. Acetazolamide inhibits epileptic seizures and decreases the rate of cerebrospinal fluid formation.

carbon tetrachloride a volatile solvent that, when inhaled, can produce euphoria, disorientation and depersonalization, and other behavioral effects similar to those produced by the major sedatives. Continued use can lead to the rapid development of persisting dementia, as well as a variety of physical problems. See also INHALANT; INHALANT ABUSE; INHALANT DEPENDENCE; INHALANT INTOXICATION.

carcinoma *n.* see CANCER.

cardiac neurosis an anxiety reaction precipitated by a heart condition, the suspicion of having a heart condition, or the fear of developing coronary disease. In some cases a cardiac neurosis develops when the patient detects a harmless heart murmur, palpitations, or a chest pain due to emotional stress. In other cases it may be caused or aggravated by a physician's examination (see IATROGENIC ILLNESS). Cardiac anxiety is a common symptom of PANIC DISORDER; it may also be a focus in HYPOCHONDRIASIS.

cardiac psychology a specialization within HEALTH PSYCHOLOGY that focuses solely on physical and behavioral health and disease related to the cardiovascular system.

cardiac psychosis a disorganization of thought processes that is associated with an acute state of fear and anxiety following a heart attack.

cardinal trait a basic and pervasive characteristic or PERSONALITY TRAIT that dominates an individual's total behavior. [defined by Gordon Willard ALLPORT]

cardiomyopathy *n.* any disease involving the heart muscle, particularly when the specific cause is uncertain.

cardiophobia *n.* an excessive fear of the heart or, more specifically, of having or developing a heart condition. See CARDIAC NEUROSIS.

cardiovascular disease any disease, congenital or acquired, that affects the heart and blood vessels. Cardiovascular diseases include HYPERTENSION, congestive heart failure, myocardial INFARCTION, ARTERIOSCLEROSIS, and CORONARY HEART DISEASE.

card-sorting test a test in which the participant is asked to sort randomly mixed cards into specific categories. Such tests may be used to determine frontal lobe functioning, learning ability, discriminatory powers, or clerical aptitude.

CARE acronym for COMMUNICATED AUTHENTICITY, REGARD, EMPATHY.

care-and-protection proceedings court intervention on behalf of a child when the parents or caregivers do not adequately provide for the child's welfare.

caregiver *n.* **1.** a person who attends to the needs of and provides assistance to someone else who is not fully independent, such as an infant or an ill adult. **2.** in health care, any individual involved in the process of identifying, preventing, or treating an illness or disability. **—caregiving** *adj.*

caregiver burden the stress and other psychological symptoms experienced by family members and other nonprofessional caregivers in response to looking after individuals with mental or physical disabilities, disorders, or diseases. See also BURNOUT; COMPASSION FATIGUE.

carezza (**karezza**) *n.* a form of coitus in which the man does not reach orgasm. It is sometimes used as a means of birth control, but if combined with meditation it is similar to the COITUS RESERVATUS technique. Carezza techniques are derived from principles of Hindu Tantrism, and in this sense were first described by U.S. gynecologist Alice B. Stockham in 1896. Also called **coitus prolongatus**.

carisoprodol *n.* a drug belonging to the PROPANEDIOLS, a group originally developed as anxiolytics. Carisoprodol is now used as a MUSCLE RELAXANT and is increasingly seen as an intoxicant drug of abuse. U.S. trade name: **Soma**.

carnal *adj.* relating to the physical desires and appetites of the body, particularly sexual ones. **Carnal knowledge** is a mainly legal term for sexual intercourse.

carotid-sinus syndrome see AORTIC ARCH SYNDROME.

carphology *n.* see FLOCCILLATION.

carryover effect the effect on the current performance of a research participant of the experimental conditions that preceded the current conditions.

Cartesian dualism the position taken by French philosopher, mathematician, and scientist René Descartes (1596–1650) that the world comprises two distinct and incompatible classes of substance: res extensa, or extended substance, which extends through space; and res cogitans, or thinking substance, which has no extension in space. The body (including the brain) is composed of extended and divisible substance, whereas the mind is not. For Descartes, this means that the mind would continue to exist even if the material body did not. He accepted that there is interaction between mind and body, holding that in some activities the mind operates independently of bodily influences, whereas in others the body exerts an influence. Similarly, in some bodily activities there is influence from the mind, while in others there is not. Descartes proposed that the locus for the interaction of the mind and body is the point in the pineal gland in the brain termed the conarium. However, to the question of how such incompatible substances can interact at all, Descartes had no answer. See DUALISM; GHOST IN THE MACHINE; MIND–BODY PROBLEM.

carve out to eliminate coverage for specific health care services (e.g., mental health or substance abuse) from a health care plan and contract for those services from a separate provider. **—carve-out** *n.*

Casanova complex a man's desire to have a large number of lovers, leading to very active pursuit of women and attempts to seduce or entice women into having sexual intercourse without any emotional relationship or commitment. The complex is named for Giovanni Jacopo **Casanova** (1725–1798), an Italian adventurer noted for his sexual conquests.

case *n.* **1.** an instance of a disease or disorder, usually at the level of the individual patient. In a **borderline case**, the symptoms resemble those of a disease or disorder but do not fully meet the criteria. See also PROBAND. **2.** a person about whom data are collected or who is the recipient of assistance (e.g., from a health care professional or lawyer). **3.** a specific instance, occurrence, or example or a type thereof.

case advocate see ADVOCATE.

case-finding *n.* the process of identifying individuals who need treatment for mental disorders by administering screening tests, locating individuals who have contacted social agencies or mental health facilities, obtaining referrals from general practitioners, or via triage after a disaster.

case history a record of information relating to a person's psychological or medical condition used as an aid to diagnosis and treatment. It usually contains test results, interviews, professional evaluations, and sociological, occupational, and educational data.

case load the amount of work required of a psychotherapist, psychiatrist, doctor, social worker, or counselor during a particular period, as computed by the number of clients assigned to him or her and the comparative difficulty of their cases.

case management a system of managing and coordinating the delivery of health care in order to improve the continuity and quality of care as well as reducing costs. Case management is usually a function of a hospital's UTILIZATION REVIEW department.

case manager a health care professional, usually a nurse or social worker, who works with patients, providers, and health insurance plans to coordinate the continuity and cost-effectiveness of services.

case report a collection of data relating to a person's psychological or medical condition.

case study an in-depth investigation of a single individual, family, or other social unit. Multiple types of data (psychological, physiological, biographical, environmental) are assembled in order to understand the subject's background, relationships, and behavior.

casework *n.* the tasks carried out by a professional, usually a social worker known as a **caseworker**, who provides or oversees services being delivered, including counseling or therapy. Casework includes identifying and assessing the needs of the individual and his or her family and providing or coordinating and monitoring the provision of support and services. These services may include private counseling, treatment in a hospital or other institution, or such concrete services as arranging for public assistance, housing, and other aid. Also called **social casework**.

cassina *n.* a perennial evergreen shrub, *Ilex vomitoria*, that grows wild in eastern North America, particularly Virginia and the Carolinas. The leaves contain caffeine and have been used by Native Americans to prepare a tealike beverage known as the "black drink" for medicinal, ceremonial, and social purposes. Also called **yaupon**; **youpon**.

castration *n.* surgical removal of the testes (see ORCHIDECTOMY); less commonly it can indicate removal of the ovaries (see OVARIECTOMY). In either men or women, inactivation of these glands can also be accomplished with radiation, by illness, or with drugs (see CHEMICAL CASTRATION).

castration anxiety fear of injury to or loss of the genitals. In the PREGENITAL PHASE posited by psychoanalytic theory, the various losses and deprivations experienced by the infant boy may give rise to the fear that he will also lose his penis. See also CASTRATION COMPLEX.

castration complex in psychoanalytic theory, the whole combination of the child's unconscious feelings and fantasies associated with being deprived of the PHALLUS, which in boys means the loss of the penis and in girls the belief that it has already been removed. It derives from the discovery that girls have no penis and is closely tied to the OEDIPUS COMPLEX.

casualty *n.* **1.** a person or group harmed, psychologically or physically, by such negative life experiences as accidents, abuse, warfare, and disasters. **2.** an individual whose psychological well-being declines, rather than improves, as a result of his or her experiences in a change-promoting group.

CAT acronym for computerized axial tomography (see COMPUTED TOMOGRAPHY).

catalepsy *n.* a state of sustained unresponsiveness in which a fixed body posture or physical attitude is maintained over a long period of time. It is seen in cases of CATATONIC SCHIZOPHRENIA, EPILEPSY, and other disorders. Also called **catatonic rigidity**; **cerea flexibilitas**; **flexibilitas cerea**; **waxy flexibility**. See also EPIDEMIC CATALEPSY. **—cataleptic** *adj.*

catalogia *n.* see VERBIGERATION.

catalytic agent in group psychotherapy, a member who stimulates emotional reactions in other members.

catamite *n.* a boy who participates in PEDERASTY.

catamnesis *n.* the medical history of a patient following the onset of a mental or physical disorder, either after the initial examination or after discharge from treatment (in the latter case it is also known as **follow-up history**). Compare ANAMNESIS.

cataphasia *n.* **1.** a language disorder characterized by repetition of a single word. **2.** see VERBIGERATION.

cataplexy *n.* a sudden loss of muscle tone that may be localized, causing (for example) loss of grasp or head nodding, or generalized, resulting in collapse of the entire body. It is a temporary condition usually precipitated by an extreme emotional stimulus (e.g., an uncontrollable fit of laughter, overwhelming anxiety, excitement, or anger). See NARCOLEPSY. **—cataplectic** *adj.*

Catapres *n.* a trade name for CLONIDINE.

catastrophe cusp theory a theory concerning the interaction of COGNITIVE ANXIETY and physiological arousal. Under conditions of high cognitive anxiety, as physiological arousal increases, performance will increase to a certain point, but past this point a catastrophic drop in performance will occur. To regain an optimal level of performance, a substantial lowering of physiological arousal is necessary.

C

catastrophic illness a severe illness, acute or chronic, that is likely to result in serious disability or death. Treatment is typically prolonged, intense, and costly.

catastrophic reaction **1.** a breakdown in the ability to cope with a threatening or traumatic situation. The individual experiences acute feelings of inadequacy, anxiety, frustration, and helplessness. **2.** highly emotional behavior (extreme anxiety, sudden crying, aggressive or hostile behavior, etc.) sometimes observed in individuals who have suffered brain damage, including those with APHASIA. The origin of this behavior remains unclear, although U.S. neurologist D. Frank Benson (1928–1996) ascribed such reactions to individuals' frustration, embarrassment, or agitation at their struggle to communicate or perform tasks they had previously performed with ease. Also called **catastrophic behavior**. [first described by German-born U.S. psychologist Kurt Goldstein (1878–1965)]

catastrophic stress an overwhelming reaction to a traumatic event that is beyond the limits of normal life. Traumatic events, such as rape, torture, genocide, or severe war-zone experiences, are filtered through cognitive and emotional processes before being appraised as extreme threats.

catastrophize *vb.* to exaggerate the negative consequences of events or decisions. People are said to be catastrophizing when they think that the worst possible outcome will occur from a particular action or in a particular situation or when they feel as if they are in the midst of a catastrophe in situations that may be serious and upsetting but are not necessarily disastrous. The tendency to catastrophize can unnecessarily increase levels of anxiety and lead to maladaptive behavior.

catathymic crisis see ISOLATED EXPLOSIVE DISORDER.

catatonia *n.* a state of muscular rigidity or other disturbance of motor behavior, such as CATALEPSY, extreme overactivity, or adoption of bizarre postures. It is most frequently observed in CATATONIC SCHIZOPHRENIA. Also called **catatonic state**. **—catatonic** *adj.*

catatonic excitement periods of extreme restlessness and excessive and apparently purposeless motor activity, often as a symptom of CATATONIC SCHIZOPHRENIA.

catatonic rigidity see CATALEPSY.

catatonic schizophrenia in *DSM–IV–TR*, a relatively rare subtype of schizophrenia characterized by abnormal motor activity, specifically motor immobility (see CATALEPSY; CATATONIC STUPOR) or excessive motor activity (see CATATONIC EXCITEMENT). Other common features include extreme NEGATIVISM (apparently motiveless resistance to all instructions or maintenance of a rigid posture against attempts to be moved) or MUTISM; peculiarities of voluntary movement, such as POSTURING or stereotyped movements; and ECHOLALIA or ECHOPRAXIA. The *DSM–III* designation was **catatonic type schizophrenic disorder**.

catatonic state see CATATONIA.

catatonic stupor a state of significantly decreased reactivity to environmental stimuli and events and reduced spontaneous movement, often as a symptom of CATATONIC SCHIZOPHRENIA.

catchment area the geographic area served by a health care program (e.g., a community mental health center).

cat-cry syndrome see CRI DU CHAT SYNDROME.

catechetical method a form of instruction or means of persuasion that uses a skillfully devised series of questions, the answers to which gradually lead the person being questioned to accept the conclusions desired by the questioner. Also called **catechetical procedure**. See SOCRATIC DIALOGUE.

catecholamine *n.* any of a class of BIOGENIC AMINES formed by a catechol molecule and an amine group. Derived from tyrosine, catecholamines include dopamine, epinephrine and norepinephrine, which are the predominant neurotransmitters in the SYMPATHETIC NERVOUS SYSTEM.

catecholamine hypothesis the hypothesis that deficiencies in the catecholamine neurotransmitters norepinephrine, epinephrine, and dopamine at receptor sites in the brain lead to a state of physiological and psychological depression, and that an excess of such neurotransmitters at these sites is responsible for the production of mania. The catecholamine hypothesis underlay the development of the early tricyclic antidepressants in the late 1950s, as it had been known that these compounds inhibited the reuptake of norepinephrine into presynaptic neurons. Despite numerous shortcomings, the catecholamine hypothesis, and the related MONOAMINE HYPOTHESIS, became the dominant hypotheses in the biological treatment of depression in the last half of the 20th century.

categorical data numerical values that indicate counts or observations in specific categories, for example, the number of people in a particular town who are male and the number who are female. Categorical data are similar to NOMINAL DATA, and the two terms are often used interchangeably.

categorical intrusion in a memory recall test, the recall by the participant of one or more items that were not presented for memorization but are from the same semantic category (e.g., names, animals, foods) as the presented items.

categorical scale see NOMINAL SCALE.

categorical thought in Jean PIAGET's theory of cognitive development, ABSTRACT THINKING that involves the use of general concepts and classifications. It is particularly lacking in young children, who tend to think concretely (see CONCRETE THINKING). See also ABSTRACT ATTITUDE.

categorical variable a variable defined by membership in a group, class, or category, rather than by rank or by scores on more continuous scales of measurement.

Category Test a nonverbal problem-solving task that requires abstract reasoning, concept formation, and mental flexibility. The participant is presented with six subtests each comprising a different set of stimuli organized according to a specific principle and each stimulus within each set associated with a particular number. The participant must respond by choosing a number and, using feedback about response accuracy, determine the principle of organization underlying the set of stimuli within a particular subtest. Once the principle is correctly identified, the participant can solve each item correctly within the subtest. A final subtest contains items from the previous six. The Category Test is part of the HALSTEAD–REITAN NEUROPSYCHOLOGICAL BATTERY. Also called **Halstead Category Test**. [designed in 1947 by U.S. psychologist Ward Halstead (1908–1969)]

cathard *n.* see CAFARD.

catharsis *n.* **1.** in psychoanalytic theory, the discharge of affects connected to traumatic events that had previously been repressed by bringing these events back into consciousness and reexperiencing them. See also ABREACTION. **2.** more generally, the release of strong, pent-up emotions. [from Greek, literally: "purgation, purification"] **—cathartic** *adj.*

cathected *adj.* see CATHEXIS.

cathectic discharge see AFFECTIVE DISCHARGE.

cathexis *n.* in psychoanalytic theory, the investment of PSYCHIC ENERGY in an OBJECT of any kind, such as a wish, fantasy, person, goal, idea, social group, or the self. Such objects are said to be **cathected** when an individual attaches emotional significance (positive or negative AFFECT) to them. See also ANTICATHEXIS; DECATHEXIS; EGO CATHEXIS; HYPERCATHEXIS; OBJECT CATHEXIS.

cathinone *n.* see KHAT.

cat's-eye syndrome a rare chromosomal disorder caused by the presence of a small additional section of chromosome material, possibly from chromosome 14, resulting in a set of birth defects that include an imperforate anus and a cleft iris that produces a cat's-eye appearance. Affected individuals show normal or near normal mental development (some may have mild mental retardation). Also called **extra-small acrocentric chromosome syndrome**; **partial trisomy 6 syndrome**; **Schachenmann's syndrome**; **Schmid–Fraccaro syndrome**.

Cattell–Horn theory of intelligence a theory proposing that there are two main kinds of intellectual abilities nested under general intelligence: *g-c*, or **crystallized intelligence** (or **ability**), which is the sum of one's knowledge and is measured by tests of vocabulary, general information, etc.; and *g-f*, or **fluid intelligence** (or **ability**), which is the set of mental processes that is used in dealing with relatively novel tasks and is used in the acquisition of *g-c*. In later versions of the theory, other abilities have been added, such as *g-v*, or visual intelligence (or ability), which is the set of mental processes used in handling visual-spatial tasks, such as mentally rotating a geometric figure or visualizing what pieces of paper would look like were they folded. [Raymond Bernard **Cattell** (1905–1998), British-born U.S. personality psychologist who originally developed the theory in the 1940s; John L. **Horn** (1928–2006), U.S. psychologist who subsequently contributed to the theory beginning in the 1960s]

Cattell inventory any of several self-report inventories based on a study of personality traits by FACTOR ANALYSIS. The best known of these inventories is the SIXTEEN PERSONALITY FACTOR QUESTIONNAIRE. [Raymond **Cattell**]

Cattell's personality trait theory an approach to personality description based on the identification of traits through FACTOR ANALYSIS and their classification into SURFACE TRAITS and the 16 SOURCE TRAITS that underlie them. [Raymond **Cattell**]

caudate nucleus one of the BASAL GANGLIA, so named because it has a long extension, or tail.

causal analysis an attempt to draw dependable inferences about cause-and-effect relationships from data not obtained from true (randomized) experiments. Such analyses differ in the degree to which they are statistically complex and the degree to which causal inferences are, in fact, justified.

causal inference the reasoned process of concluding that one variable is the cause of another.

causal latency 1. the temporal separation of a cause from its effect. Not all causes need have immediate effects; indeed, there may be a lengthy interval between a cause and the effect it produces. Causal latency may be expected to increase when there are other factors in a situation that may influence the cause-and-effect relationship. Some causes studied in psychology and the other social sciences are REMOTE CAUSES, in that they require the presence or activity of other factors or conditions before their effects become manifest. Remote causes may be expected to have large causal latencies. See DELAYED EFFECT. **2.** in the statistical procedure known as PATH ANALYSIS, the quality of a variable that has a measurable statistical effect on prediction only when other predictor variables are also included in the prediction model. Although the statistical relationships identified in such analyses are not, strictly speaking, causal, the language of causality is commonly employed. See CAUSAL PATH.

C

causation *n.* the empirical relation between two events, states, or variables such that one (the cause) is held or known to bring about the other (the effect). **—causal** *adj.*

CBCL abbreviation for CHILD BEHAVIOR CHECKLIST.

CBT abbreviation for COGNITIVE BEHAVIOR THERAPY.

CBZ abbreviation for CARBAMAZEPINE.

CCRT abbreviation for CORE CONFLICTUAL RELATIONSHIP THEME.

CCU 1. abbreviation for CONTINUING CARE UNIT. **2.** abbreviation for critical care unit (see INTENSIVE CARE UNIT).

CD abbreviation for COMMUNICATION DEVIANCE.

CDC abbreviation for CENTERS FOR DISEASE CONTROL AND PREVENTION.

CDI abbreviation for CHILDREN'S DEPRESSION INVENTORY.

CEFT abbreviation for CHILDREN'S EMBEDDED FIGURES TEST.

ceiling effect a situation in which a large proportion of participants perform as well as, or nearly as well as, possible on a task or other evaluative measure, thus skewing the distribution of scores and making it impossible to discriminate differences among the many individuals at that high level. For example, a test whose items are too easy for those taking it would show a ceiling effect because most people would obtain or be close to the highest possible score of 100. Compare FLOOR EFFECT.

Celexa *n.* a trade name for CITALOPRAM.

celibacy *n.* **1.** the state of being unmarried, especially as the result of a religious vow. **2.** abstinence from sexual activity. See also CHASTITY. **—celibate** *adj., n.*

cell body the part of a NEURON (nerve cell) that contains the nucleus and most organelles. Also called **perikaryon**; **soma**. See also AXON.

cenesthopathy *n.* a general feeling of illness or lack of well-being that is not identified with any particular part of the body.

censor *n.* in psychoanalytic theory, the mental agency, located in the PRECONSCIOUS, that is responsible for REPRESSION. The censor is posited to determine which of one's wishes, thoughts, and ideas may enter consciousness and which must be kept unconscious because they violate one's conscience or society's standards. The censor is also posited to be responsible for the distortion of wishes that occurs in dreams (see DREAM CENSORSHIP). The idea was introduced in the early writings of Sigmund FREUD, who later developed it into the concept of the SUPEREGO. **—censorship** *n.*

census tract a small, generally homogeneous geographic area with boundaries established to facilitate the collection and reporting of census data. Community demographic data are frequently used in the assessment of the area's characteristics and needs, including mental health needs. See also CATCHMENT AREA.

centered *adj.* **1.** describing the state of an organism that is perfectly integrated with its environment. [defined by German-born U.S. neurologist Kurt Goldstein (1878–1965)] **2.** denoting a state of mind characterized by having a firm grip on reality, knowing who one is and what one wants out of life, and being prepared to meet most eventualities in an efficient manner.

Center for Epidemiologic Studies Depression Scale (**CES-D**) a 20-item self-administered rating scale used to determine an individual's depression quotient. The test provides a quantitative measure of different depressive feelings and behaviors during the previous week. [developed in 1971 by Lenore Sawyer Radloff (1935–) while a researcher at the National Institute of Mental Health]

Centers for Disease Control and Prevention (**CDC**) an agency founded in 1946 (now one of the 13 major operating components of the U.S. Department of Health and Human Services) that stands at the forefront of public health efforts to prevent and control infectious and chronic diseases, injuries, workplace hazards, disabilities, and environmental health threats. The CDC works with public health partners, both nationally and internationally, to monitor health, detect and investigate health problems, conduct research to enhance and implement prevention, promote healthy behaviors and safe and healthful environments, and develop and advocate sound public health policies.

Centers for Medicare and Medicaid Services (**CMS**) a federal government agency within the Department of Health and Human Services that is responsible for the administration of the MEDICARE and MEDICAID programs, as well as the State Children's Health Insurance Program. Formerly known as the **Health Care Financing Administration** (HCFA), the CMS consists of three business offices: the Center for Beneficiary Choices, the Center for Medicare Management, and the Center for Medicaid and State Operations.

central anticholinergic syndrome a syndrome observed in patients receiving combinations of agents with psychopharmacological effects and due to the additive ANTICHOLINERGIC EFFECTS on the central nervous system of, among others, tricyclic antidepressants, the weaker phenothiazines, and antiparkinsonian agents. The symptoms include anxiety, disorientation, short-term memory loss, visual distortions or hallucinations, and agitation. See also ANTICHOLINERGIC SYNDROME.

central conflict the intrapsychic struggle between the healthy constructive forces of the real self and the obstructive, neurotic forces of the idealized self-image. [first described by German-born U.S. psychiatrist Karen Horney (1885–1952)]

central dyslexia any form of acquired dyslexia characterized by difficulties with the pronunciation and comprehension of written words. Unlike PERIPHERAL DYSLEXIA, the visual analysis system is intact, and the damage is to other, higher level pathways and systems involved in reading (e.g., the semantic system).

central executive see WORKING MEMORY.

centralism *n.* the concept that behavior is a function of the central nervous system mediated by the brain. See CENTRALIST PSYCHOLOGY. Compare PERIPHERALISM.

centralist psychology **1.** a psychological approach that focuses on behavior as a function of the higher brain centers, as opposed to peripheralist psychology (see PERIPHERALISM), which focuses on the effects of the receptors, glands, and muscles on behavior. Centralist psychology is essentially equivalent to CENTRALISM. **2.** more generally, the idea that mental activity or mind occurs in or is a function of the brain alone.

central limit theorem the statistical principle that a linear combination of values (including the mean of those values) tends to be normally distributed over repeated samples as the sample sizes increase, whether or not the population from which the observations are drawn is normal in distribution.

central nervous system (**CNS**) the entire complex of NEURONS, AXONS, and supporting tissue that constitute the brain and spinal cord. The CNS is primarily involved in mental activities and in coordinating and integrating incoming sensory messages and outgoing motor messages. Compare PERIPHERAL NERVOUS SYSTEM.

central organizing trait see CENTRAL TRAIT.

central pain pain that is caused by a disorder of the central nervous system, such as a brain tumor or infection or injury of the spinal cord.

central processing dysfunction impairment in the analysis, storage, synthesis, and symbolic use of information. Because these processes involve memory tasks, the dysfunction is believed to be related to difficulties in learning.

central tendency the middle or center point of a DISTRIBUTION, estimated by a number of different statistics (e.g., MEAN and MEDIAN).

central trait any of a cluster of traits (e.g., compassion, ambition, sociability, helpfulness) that comprise the basic pattern of an individual's personality. [defined by Gordon W. ALLPORT]

centrifugal *adj.* directed away from the center. For example, a **centrifugal nerve** carries impulses from the central nervous system to a peripheral region of the body. Compare CENTRIPETAL.

centripetal *adj.* **1.** directed toward the center. For example, a **centripetal nerve** carries nerve impulses from the periphery to the central nervous system. Compare CENTRIFUGAL. **2.** in psychiatry, characterizing treatment or approaches that focus inward on minute changes in feelings and impulses, as in psychoanalysis.

cephalic index the ratio of the maximum breadth of the head to its maximum length, multiplied by 100. The average, or medium, cephalic index for humans is between 75 and 81 (**mesocephalic**). A measure below 75 indicates a narrow head that is long in proportion to its width (**dolichocephalic**); a measure above 81 indicates a head that is wide in proportion to its length (**brachycephalic**). Compare CRANIAL INDEX. [defined by Swedish anatomist Anders Retzius (1796–1860)]

cephalization *n.* **1.** the evolutionary tendency for important structures (brain, major sense organs, etc.) to develop at the anterior (front) end of organisms. **2.** the evolutionary tendency for the brain to increase in size. See ENCEPHALIZATION; EVOLUTION OF THE BRAIN.

cerea flexibilitas see CATALEPSY.

cerebellar ataxia poor muscular coordination (see ATAXIA) due to damage in the CEREBELLUM. Individuals cannot integrate voluntary movements and therefore find it difficult to stand or walk, feed themselves, and perform complex activities (e.g., playing the piano).

cerebellar cortex the GRAY MATTER, or unmyelinated nerve cells, covering the surface of the CEREBELLUM.

cerebellum *n.* (*pl.* **cerebella**) a portion of the HINDBRAIN dorsal to the rest of the BRAINSTEM. The cerebellum modulates muscular contractions to produce smooth, accurately timed movements; it helps maintain equilibrium by predicting body positions ahead of actual body movements, and it is required for some kinds of motor conditioning.

cerebral arteriosclerosis a hardening of the arteries that supply the brain. See ARTERIOSCLEROSIS.

cerebral atrophy degeneration and shrinkage of the brain, usually due to aging, disease, or injury. It is marked by enlargement of the surface clefts and inner cavities (VENTRICLES) of the brain. In normal aging there may be few or no cognitive effects, but cerebral atrophy may be secondary to more serious disorders, such as cerebrovascular disease, encephalitis, Alzheimer's disease, or head injury. Also called **brain atrophy**.

cerebral cortex the layer of GRAY MATTER that covers the outside of the CEREBRAL HEMISPHERES in the brain and is associated with higher cognitive functions, such as language, learning, perception, and planning. It consists mostly of NEOCORTEX, which has six main layers of cells; regions of cerebral cortex that do not have six layers are known as ALLOCORTEX. Differences in the cell structure of the layers led to the recognition of distinct areas, called BRODMANN'S AREAS, many of which are known to serve different functions.

cerebral dominance **1.** the control of lower brain centers by the cerebrum or cerebral cortex. **2.** the controlling or disproportionate influence on certain aspects of behavior by one CEREBRAL HEMISPHERE (e.g., language is typically left-lateralized in right-handed people). See DOMINANCE; HEMISPHERIC LATERALIZATION.

cerebral dysfunction any impairment in cerebral processes, including disturbances of memory, language, attention, or executive functioning.

cerebral edema an abnormal accumulation of fluid in the intercellular spaces of brain tissues, which may be caused by injury, disease, cerebrovascular accident, or tumor. The condition results in swelling and a rise in INTRACRANIAL PRESSURE; if uncorrected, this may be followed by herniation of cerebral tissue through weakened areas. It may be reversible unless the damage extends to the brainstem, where the effects can be fatal. The increase in intracranial pressure may result in headaches and visual disorders. Cerebral edema can also cause dementia that recedes when the defect is corrected.

cerebral electrotherapy (**CET**) the application of low-voltage pulses of direct electrical current to the brain, occasionally used in the treatment of depression, anxiety, and insomnia. See ELECTRONARCOSIS.

cerebral embolism the presence of a small mass of material in the blood vessels of the brain (see EMBOLISM), which blocks or impedes the flow of blood to a part of the brain, resulting in an acute or chronic neurological deficit. See EMBOLIC STROKE; STROKE.

cerebral gigantism see SOTOS SYNDROME.

cerebral hemisphere either half (left or right) of the cerebrum. The hemispheres are separated by a deep longitudinal fissure but they are connected by commissural, projection, and association fibers so that each side of the brain normally is linked to functions of tissues on either side of the body. See also HEMISPHERIC LATERALIZATION.

cerebral hemorrhage any bleeding into the brain tissue due to a damaged blood vessel. The cause may be cerebrovascular disease, a ruptured aneurysm, a penetrating injury or blow to the head, or other factors. The neurological effects vary with the extent of the hemorrhage. Also called **intracerebral hemorrhage**. See HEMORRHAGIC STROKE; STROKE.

cerebral hyperplasia an abnormal increase in the volume of brain tissue, usually due to a proliferation of new, normal cells. Although neurons do not proliferate after the central nervous system has reached maturity, cells of the GLIA do continue to multiply into adulthood; in some cases neuroglial cell growth is associated with HYDROCEPHALUS.

cerebral infarction the death of brain tissue due to an interruption of blood flow caused by rupture of a blood vessel, blockage of a blood vessel by a clot, or a narrowing (stenosis) of a blood vessel.

cerebral ischemia a condition in which brain tissue is deprived of an adequate blood supply and thus lacks oxygen and nutrients. It is usually marked by loss of normal function of the affected area and may be accompanied by CEREBRAL EDEMA. A brief interruption in blood supply—a TRANSIENT ISCHEMIC ATTACK (TIA)—usually causes no serious damage. An interruption lasting more than several minutes may result in CEREBRAL INFARCTION. See CEREBROVASCULAR ACCIDENT; STROKE.

cerebral palsy (**CP**) a set of nonprogressive movement and posture disorders that results from trauma to the brain occurring prenatally, during the birth process, or before the age of 5. Symptoms include spasticity, uncontrolled movements, paralysis, unsteady gait, and speech abnormalities (see DYSARTHRIA) but may be accompanied by disorders of any other brain function, resulting in cognitive changes, seizures, visual defects, tactile impairment, hearing loss, and mental retardation. CP is commonly classified into the following types: **spastic**, the most common, resulting from damage to the motor cortex, corticospinal tract, or pyramidal tract; **dyskinetic**, resulting from damage to the basal ganglia; **ataxic**, resulting from damage to the cerebellum; and **mixed**, in which more than one type is evident.

cerebral syphilis a condition that results when untreated syphilis involves the cerebral cortex and surrounding meningeal membranes, causing GENERAL PARESIS. The condition, which usually develops about 10 years after the initial infection, is marked by irritability, memory impairment, inability to concentrate, headaches, insomnia, and behavioral deterioration.

cerebral trauma any damage to the brain, which may be temporary or permanent, following a blow to the head of sufficient severity to produce a concussion, contusion, or laceration.

cerebration *n.* any kind of conscious thinking, such as pondering or problem solving. **—cerebrate** *vb.*

cerebrocranial defect a deformity or dysfunction involving the cerebrum and the eight bones of the skull that form a protective layer around it. An example is the premature closing of the sutures of the skull, resulting in a displacement of cerebral tissues.

cerebrotonia *n.* the personality type that, according to SHELDON'S CONSTITUTIONAL THEORY

OF PERSONALITY, is associated with an ectomorphic (linear, fragile) physique (see ECTOMORPH). Cerebrotonia is characterized by a tendency toward introversion, restraint, inhibition, love of privacy and solitude, and sensitivity. **—cerebrotonic** *adj.*

cerebrovascular accident (**CVA**) a disorder of the brain arising from CEREBROVASCULAR DISEASE, such as CEREBRAL HEMORRHAGE, CEREBRAL EMBOLISM, or cerebral THROMBOSIS, resulting in temporary or permanent alterations in cognition, motor and sensory skills, or levels of consciousness. This term is often used interchangeably with STROKE. Also called **cerebral vascular accident**.

cerebrovascular disease a pathological condition of the blood vessels of the brain. It may manifest itself as symptoms of STROKE or a TRANSIENT ISCHEMIC ATTACK. Also called **cerebral vascular disease**. See also CEREBROVASCULAR ACCIDENT.

cerebrovascular insufficiency failure of the cardiovascular system to supply adequate levels of oxygenated blood to the brain tissues. The condition usually arises when one of the four main arteries supplying the brain, namely the two carotid and two vertebral arteries, is interrupted. It may also result from generalized ARTERIOSCLEROSIS or the inability of the heart to maintain adequate blood flow to the brain. Also called **cerebral vascular insufficiency**.

cerebrum *n.* the largest part of the brain, forming most of the FOREBRAIN and lying in front of and above the cerebellum. It consists of two CEREBRAL HEMISPHERES bridged by the CORPUS CALLOSUM. Each hemisphere is divided into four main lobes: the FRONTAL LOBE, OCCIPITAL LOBE, PARIETAL LOBE, and TEMPORAL LOBE. The outer layer of the cerebrum—the CEREBRAL CORTEX—is intricately folded and composed of GRAY MATTER. Also called **telencephalon**.

certifiable *adj.* **1.** describing people who, because of mental illness, may be a danger to themselves or others and are therefore eligible to be institutionalized. See CERTIFICATION LAWS; COMMITMENT LAWS. **2.** having met the requirements to be formally recognized by the relevant licensing or sanctioning body.

certification *n.* **1.** the formal process by which an external agency affirms that a person has met predetermined standards and has the requisite knowledge and skills to be considered competent in a particular area. Certification applies to individuals and ACCREDITATION applies to institutions. See also CREDENTIALING. **2.** the legal proceedings in which appropriate mental health care professionals formally confirm that a person has a mental disorder, which may result in COMMITMENT of that person. **—certificated** *adj.*

certification laws 1. legislation governing the admission of individuals to mental institutions, including commitment proceedings as well as a review of case records to determine whether health care is necessary and whether the institution and type of care are appropriate. **2.** state laws governing the right of an individual to describe himself or herself as a psychologist.

cervical angina see PSEUDOANGINA.

Cesamet *n.* a trade name for NABILONE.

CES-D abbreviation for CENTER FOR EPIDEMIOLOGIC STUDIES DEPRESSION SCALE.

CET abbreviation for CEREBRAL ELECTROTHERAPY.

CFS abbreviation for CHRONIC FATIGUE SYNDROME.

chain of behavior see BEHAVIOR PATTERN.

chakra *n.* in oriental philosophy, one of the seven energy centers in the body. The chakras roughly correspond with the endocrine system. Each chakra symbolizes different, ascending human needs and has a sound (MANTRA) and color associated with it. Focused awareness and contemplation of the chakras may be practiced in YOGA and in other therapeutic approaches and traditions.

challenge 1. *n.* an obstacle appraised as an opportunity rather than a threat. A threat becomes a challenge when the individual judges that his or her coping resources are adequate not only to overcome the stress associated with the obstacle but also to improve the situation in a measurable way. **2.** *vb.* to pose or face with an obstacle or threat.

challenged *adj.* describing an individual with a DISABILITY or HANDICAP. The word is often considered to be euphemistic.

challenging behavior behavior that is dangerous, or that interferes in participation in preschool, educational, or adult services, and often necessitates the design and use of special interventions. The term is used principally in human services in the United Kingdom and within educational services in the United States and most typically refers to behaviors of people with mental retardation or related conditions.

CHAMPUS acronym for CIVILIAN HEALTH AND MEDICAL PROGRAM OF THE UNIFORMED SERVICES.

change agent 1. a specific causative factor or element or an entire process that results in change, particularly in the sense of improvement. In psychotherapy research, a change agent may be a component or process in therapy that results in improvement in the behavior or psychological adaptation of a patient or client. **2.** an individual who instigates or implements change within an organization or group, such as a mental health professional who takes an active role in social policy planning, social action, and social engineering directed to improving community mental health.

change score a score based on two or more measurements made on the same person over time. The simplest change score is postscore minus prescore. More complex change scores can also be used to index, for example, the linearity of change over three, four, five, or more occasions of measurement.

C

character *n.* **1.** the totality of an individual's attributes and PERSONALITY TRAITS, particularly his or her characteristic moral, social, and religious attitudes. Character is often used synonymously with PERSONALITY. **2.** see CHARACTER TYPE.

character analysis 1. in psychoanalysis, the treatment of a CHARACTER DISORDER. **2.** see CHARACTEROLOGY.

character development the gradual development of moral concepts, conscience, religious values or views, and social attitudes as an essential aspect of personality development.

character disorder formerly, in psychoanalysis, an alternative name for PERSONALITY DISORDER.

characteristic *n.* **1.** a quality of a person, especially any of the enduring qualities that define an individual's nature or personality in relation to others. **2.** any distinguishing feature of an organism, object, place, process, condition, or event.

characterization *n.* a description of psychological aspects of an individual, including ascriptions of personality traits, characteristics, or motives. **—characterize** *vb.*

character neurosis in psychoanalysis, a former name, used interchangeably with **neurotic character**, for PERSONALITY DISORDER.

characterology *n.* **1.** formerly, the branch of psychology concerned with character and personality. Also called **character analysis**. **2.** a pseudoscience in which character is "read" by external signs, such as hair color or facial type.

character strength a positive trait, such as kindness, teamwork, or hope, that is morally valued in its own right and contributes to the fulfillment of the self and others. Also called **human strength**. See POSITIVE PSYCHOLOGY.

character structure the organization of the traits and attributes that make up a person's CHARACTER.

character traits in trait conceptions of personality functioning, dispositional tendencies having to do with values, motives, and the regulation of behavior in accord with moral and ethical standards.

character type 1. see PERSONALITY TYPE. **2.** in psychoanalytic theory, a personality type defined by the kinds of DEFENSE MECHANISM used (e.g., a PHOBIC CHARACTER) or FIXATION at a particular stage in PSYCHOSEXUAL DEVELOPMENT (e.g., an ORAL PERSONALITY).

Charles Bonnet syndrome complex visual hallucinations without delusions or the loss of insightful cognition, typically seen in older adults who have severe visual impairment. Such hallucinations are usually nonthreatening and often pleasant and are not indicative of mental illness or psychological disorder. Also called **Bonnet syndrome**. [Charles **Bonnet** (1720–1793), Swiss naturalist and philosopher]

chart 1. *n.* a graphic representation of data. **2.** *vb.* to create such a representation.

chastity *n.* the state of abstaining from illicit sexual intercourse or—by extension—from all sexual activity. In religious usage it also includes the concept of not having sexual urges or impure thoughts. See also CELIBACY. **—chaste** *adj.*

chat *n.* see KHAT.

chatterbox effect the conversational behavior of many people with hydrocephalus and mental retardation or with spina bifida. The person may appear quite fluent and sociable in conversations but does not communicate in a meaningful manner, may tend to fabricate information as long as it seems interesting to the listener, and may be unable later to recall what was discussed. Also called **cocktail-party syndrome**.

CHD abbreviation for CORONARY HEART DISEASE.

cheilophagia (**chilophagia**) *n.* the repeated biting of one's own lips.

chemical antagonism see ANTAGONIST.

chemical castration the administration of ANTIANDROGENS for the purposes of managing advanced prostate cancer or, more controversially, to reduce sexual drive in repeat sex offenders. Research has shown that a minority of sex offenders will offend again after chemical castration, indicating that sex drive is not the only cause of sexual offenses.

chemical dependence see SUBSTANCE DEPENDENCE.

chemoreceptor trigger zone (**CTZ**) a cluster of cells in the MEDULLA OBLONGATA that is sensitive to certain toxic chemicals and reacts by causing vomiting. The trigger zone is particularly sensitive to narcotics and responds by producing dizziness, nausea, and vomiting, the precise effects depending on the agent and the dosage. See also AREA POSTREMA.

chemotherapy *n.* the use of chemical agents to treat diseases, particularly cancer, in which case it is contrasted with RADIATION THERAPY. **—chemotherapeutic** *adj.* **—chemotherapist** *n.*

chi (**qi**) *n.* in oriental philosophy, life-force energy (from Chinese, "energy"). Blockages in chi are believed to create illness. The equivalent Hindu concept is **prana** (Sanskrit, literally: "breath of life"). See also ACUPUNCTURE.

chibih *n.* see SUSTO.

Chicago school a school of psychology that emerged at the University of Chicago in the early 20th century, associated with psychologists John DEWEY, James R. ANGELL, and Harvey Carr (1873–1954). Their approach, called FUNCTIONALISM, was related to the ACT PSYCHOLOGY of Franz Brentano (1838–1917); it was an attempt to modify the subject matter of psychology by introducing the Darwinian idea that mental activities subserve an adaptive biological action function that should be the focus of psychology.

child abuse harm to a child caused by a parent or other caregiver. The harm may be physical (violence), sexual (violation or exploitation), psychological (causing emotional distress), or neglect (failure to provide needed care). See also BATTERED-CHILD SYNDROME.

child advocacy any organized and structured interventions on behalf of children by professionals or institutions, often in relation to such issues as special parenting needs, child abuse, and adoption or foster care.

child analysis the application of psychoanalytic principles (considerably modified from those of CLASSICAL PSYCHOANALYSIS) to the treatment of children. In his first and most famous case, Sigmund FREUD analyzed 5-year-old LITTLE HANS by having the child answer questions through his father, but Freud never directly analyzed a child patient. Pioneers in the field are Melanie KLEIN, who developed the PSYCHOANALYTIC PLAY TECHNIQUE to achieve a deep analysis of the child's unconscious, and Anna FREUD, whose method was more pedagogical and encouraged EGO DEVELOPMENT. See also PLAY THERAPY.

Child Behavior Checklist (**CBCL**) a standardized instrument used to assess the behavioral problems and competencies of children between the ages of 4 and 18 years (a separate version is available for assessing the behavior of children ages 2 to 3). The CBCL is administered to parents, who describe their children's behavior by assigning a rating to each of the more than 100 items on the checklist. The items assessed range from "internalizing behaviors" (e.g., fearful, shy, anxious, inhibited) to "externalizing behaviors" (e.g., aggressive, antisocial, undercontrolled). [developed in 1983 by U.S. psychologists Thomas M. Achenbach (1940–) and Craig S. Edelbrock (1951–)]

child care 1. the daytime care of children by a nursery or childminder while parents are at work. **2.** the full-time residential care of children who have no other home or whose home life is seriously troubled.

child care facilities facilities licensed to provide regular out-of-home care to children during the working day. Child care facilities may be privately run but may also be associated with firms, churches, or social agencies. Such a facility is often referred to as a **day care center**.

child custody the care, protection, and supervision of a child. In certain legal proceedings, such as divorce or separation, the court may grant custody to one or both parents following a CHILD CUSTODY EVALUATION.

child custody evaluation a procedure, often conducted by clinical psychologists, that involves evaluating parenting behavior, analyzing parents' capacity to address children's needs, and providing the court with a recommendation regarding CHILD CUSTODY arrangements. See PRIMARY CARETAKER STANDARD.

child find in the U.S. educational system, an organized screening and identification program, directed by each state's Department of Education, that identifies preschool children in need of particular services and evaluates their readiness for school entry as well as their risk for developmental disabilities.

child-focused family a family in which the children's needs are paramount, sometimes to a point where they dominate the FAMILY CONSTELLATION and the parents' needs become secondary. Also called **child-centered family**.

child guidance a mental health approach for children that focuses not only on treatment but also on the prevention of possible future disorders by offering instruction, information, and therapeutic aid to the child and his or her family. Child guidance services and treatment are typically provided by specialized **child-guidance clinics**. The child-guidance movement emerged in the early 20th century and was at its strongest from the 1940s to 1970s.

childhood *n.* **1.** the period between the end of infancy (about 2 years of age) and the onset of puberty, marking the beginning of ADOLESCENCE (10–12 years of age). This period is sometimes divided into (a) early childhood, from 2 years through the preschool age of 5 or 6 years; (b) middle childhood, from 6 to 8–10 years of age; and (c) late childhood or PREADOLESCENCE, which is identified as the 2-year period before the onset of puberty. **2.** the period between 3 or 4 years of age and about 7 years of age. In this context, childhood represents the period after weaning and before children can fend for themselves. [defined by U.S. anthropologist Barry Bogin (1950–)]

childhood amnesia the inability to recall events from early childhood (see EARLY MEMORY). Childhood amnesia has been attributed to the facts that (a) cognitive abilities necessary for encoding events for the long term have not yet been fully developed and (b) parts of the brain responsible for remembering personal events have not yet matured. Also called **infantile amnesia**.

childhood autism see AUTISTIC DISORDER.

childhood depression a MAJOR DEPRESSIVE EPISODE that occurs in childhood. Defining symptoms may differ from those of major depressive episodes in adults in that irritable mood is more characteristic than depressed mood, and failure to make expected weight gains often replaces an actual weight loss.

childhood disintegrative disorder in *DSM–IV–TR*, a PERVASIVE DEVELOPMENTAL DISORDER characterized by a significant loss of two or more of the following: previously acquired language skills, social skills or adaptive behavior, bowel or bladder control, play, or motor skills. This regression in functioning follows a period of normal development and occurs between the ages of 2 and 10. Impairments in social interaction and communication are also evident.

C

childhood disorder any social, emotional, behavioral, or educational disorder of childhood.

childhood fears fears occurring at different stages of childhood, such as fear of strangers, which usually develops around 8 months of age, and fear of heights, which emerges after the child learns to crawl. The content of fear changes for children from 2 to 6 years of age, with fears of darkness, animals, doctors, ghosts, monsters, and storms being common occurrences that usually pass in a few months or years without treatment.

childhood neurosis in Freudian theory, the development of psychological symptoms in childhood in response to efforts of defense against conflict.

childhood psychosis a PSYCHOTIC DISORDER with onset in childhood: In *DSM–IV–TR*, the defining features of psychotic disorders are essentially equivalent across all age groups. Historically, the term has been used much more widely to denote any of a variety of disorders or mental conditions of children that result in severe functional impairment, encompassing, for example, mental retardation and PERVASIVE DEVELOPMENTAL DISORDERS.

childhood schizophrenia SCHIZOPHRENIA with onset prior to age 12: In *DSM–IV–TR*, the defining features of schizophrenia are essentially equivalent across all age groups. Historically, the term has been used more widely to denote schizophrenic behavior that appears early in life, encompassing PERVASIVE DEVELOPMENTAL DISORDERS and AUTISTIC DISORDER in particular.

child molestation child SEXUAL ABUSE: any sexual behavior toward a child by an adult. See also EMOTIONAL INCEST; RITUAL ABUSE.

child neglect the denial of attention, care, or affection considered essential for the normal development of a child's physical, emotional, and intellectual qualities, usually due to indifference, disregard, or impairment of the child's caregivers. See also PARENTAL REJECTION.

child pornography pornographic material featuring children. This may include written stories, pictures, or videos of naked children or of children engaging in sexual activity. Child pornography is illegal in the United States, and production or circulation of such materials is usually vigorously prosecuted.

child psychotherapy psychotherapy for children up to the age at which they reach puberty. The focus may be on emotions, cognitions, or behavior. The level of parental involvement is typically dependent upon the age of the child, type of problem, or approach used. The child may be treated concurrently in group or family therapy.

children in need of supervision (**CHINS**) children who commit offenses that may lead the court to act in service to them when they cannot be adequately controlled by parents or guardians. The child will typically appear before the court and receive some form of sanction. The crimes that lead to a CHINS classification are "status offenses," such as truancy, running away from home, and misbehavior at school.

Children's Depression Inventory (**CDI**) a self-report questionnaire, based on the BECK DEPRESSION INVENTORY, designed to assess the severity of depression in children aged between 7 and 17 years. Intended primarily as a research tool, the CDI comprises 27 items that each consist of three statements reflecting different levels of severity of a particular symptom. For each item, the participant chooses the statement that best describes himself or herself during the previous two weeks. [originally published in 1977 by U.S. clinical psychologist Maria Kovacs (1944–)]

Children's Embedded Figures Test (**CEFT**) a version of the EMBEDDED FIGURES TEST of cognitive style that is designed for children aged 5 to 12 years. Participants are required to detect a simple shape within 25 increasingly complex figures or colored backgrounds. [developed in 1971 by U.S. clinical psychologist Stephen A. Karp (1928–) and Norma Konstadt]

Children's Manifest Anxiety Scale (**CMAS**) a 53-item modification of the TAYLOR MANIFEST ANXIETY SCALE that is appropriate for children. Originally developed in 1956 by U.S. psychologists Alfred Castaneda (1923–), Boyd R. McCandless (1915–1975), and David S. Palermo (1929–2011), the CMAS was subsequently revised in 1978 by U.S. educational psychologists Cecil R. Reynolds (1952–) and Bert O. Richmond (1929–). This **Revised Children's Manifest Anxiety Scale** (**RCMAS**) comprises 37 yes–no items measuring the nature and level of anxiety symptoms in children and adolescents aged between 6 and 19 years.

Children's Personality Questionnaire (**CPQ**) a 140-item self-report inventory for children aged 8 to 12 years that is based on CATTELL'S PERSONALITY TRAIT THEORY. It assesses 14 dimensions of personality (e.g., shy versus bold, self-assured versus apprehensive, sober versus enthusiastic) conceptualized as useful in evaluating, understanding, and predicting personal adjustment, social development, and academic performance. [originally developed in 1959 by U.S. educator Rutherford Burchard Porter (1909–2002) and British-born U.S. personality psychologist Raymond Bernard Cattell (1905–1998)]

child support a legally enforceable requirement that parents meet the economic and educational needs of their children. This includes providing the financial means to meet these needs.

child visitation in the context of divorce or situations in which children have been legally placed in the care of another (e.g., foster care), the permission granted by the court allowing a noncustodial parent some time to visit the child, provided this contact remains in the best interests of the child. Also called **visitation rights**.

chilophagia see CHEILOPHAGIA.

chimeric stimulation a procedure, used by Roger SPERRY in the split-brain technique (see COMMISSUROTOMY), for studying the functions of the two cerebral hemispheres of the brain. In a typical experiment participants are shown an image of a **chimeric face**, consisting of the left half of one person's face joined to the right half of another person's face. In participants with a severed corpus callosum (i.e., a SPLIT BRAIN), one hemisphere perceives only one face, while the other hemisphere perceives the other, suggesting that there are two separate spheres of conscious awareness located in the two hemispheres. See also RIGHT-HEMISPHERE CONSCIOUSNESS.

chiropractic *n.* an alternative health care system concerned with the relationship between the structure of the body (particularly the spine) and disease processes. Treatment comprises noninvasive drug-free methods, primarily manipulations and adjustments to the body, theorized to restore proper nerve functioning and to promote health. See also COMPLEMENTARY AND ALTERNATIVE MEDICINE. **—chiropractor** *n.*

chi-square distribution (**χ^2 distribution**) the distribution of the sum of a set of independent squared normal random deviates. If p independent variables are involved, the distribution is said to have p DEGREES OF FREEDOM. The CHI-SQUARE TEST is based upon it.

chi-square test a measure of how well a theoretical probability distribution fits a set of data. If values $x_1, x_2, \ldots x_p$ are observed $o_1, o_2, \ldots o_p$ times and are expected by theory to occur $e_1, e_2, \ldots, e_p$ times, then chi-square is calculated as $(o_1 - e_1)^2/e_1 + (o_2 - e_2)^2/e_2 + \ldots$ Tables of chi-square for different degrees of freedom can be used to indicate the probability that the theory is correct. Also called **chi-square procedure**.

chloral hydrate a short-acting depressant of the central nervous system, first synthesized in 1832 and formerly widely used clinically, chiefly as a hypnotic. It is occasionally still used to induce sleep, but its use is limited by its potential toxicity. U.S. trade name: **Aquachloral**. See also KNOCKOUT DROPS.

chlordiazepoxide *n.* the first commercially available BENZODIAZEPINE anxiolytic. Developed in 1957 and in clinical use in the early 1960s, it became one of the most heavily prescribed medications ever developed. It is characterized by extensive metabolism in the liver and possesses a number of metabolic products, giving it a lengthy HALF-LIFE and a consequent long-acting anxiolytic effect. Its use in the management of anxiety and insomnia has been largely supplanted by benzodiazepines with less complicated metabolism and more predictable half-lives, but it remains in common use to protect against the effects of alcohol withdrawal. It is available in oral and injectable form. Because of erratic absorption, intramuscular administration is not advised. U.S. trade name: **Librium**.

chloride channel see ION CHANNEL.

chlorpromazine (**CPZ**) *n.* the first synthesized ANTIPSYCHOTIC agent, introduced into clinical use in Europe in 1952 and in Canada and the United States in 1954. It was initially used to reduce presurgical anxiety and deepen conscious sedation during surgical procedures; its antipsychotic effects were discovered serendipitously. This low-potency PHENOTHIAZINE provided a degree of behavioral control and management of positive psychotic symptoms previously unavailable and ushered in the modern era of psychopharmacological treatment. However, although effective in managing the acute symptoms of schizophrenia, acute mania, and other psychoses, chlorpromazine caused a number of unwanted adverse effects, including neuromuscular rigidity and other EXTRAPYRAMIDAL SYMPTOMS, sedation, ORTHOSTATIC HYPOTENSION, cognitive slowing, and long-term association with TARDIVE DYSKINESIA. Although chlorpromazine has been largely supplanted by newer antipsychotic agents, it is still used as a referent for dose equivalency of other antipsychotics. It has also been used in lower doses to treat nausea, vomiting, and intractable hiccups. U.S. trade name: **Thorazine**.

chlorprothixene *n.* a low-potency antipsychotic of the THIOXANTHENE class, similar in its effects to other thioxanthenes. U.S. trade names: **Taractan**; **Taractin**.

choice *n.* a decision-making problem in which a person has to indicate a preference for one of a set of alternatives. See also BINARY CHOICE. **—choose** *vb.*

choice behavior the selection of one of many available options or behavioral alternatives.

choleric type a type of temperament characterized by irritability and quick temper, as described by Roman physician Galen (129–199 CE).

cholesterol *n.* a steroid derivative abundant in animal tissues, found especially in foods rich in animal fats. Cholesterol is a constituent of plasma membranes, the precursor of other steroids (e.g., the sex hormones), and a component of plasma lipoproteins, especially low-density lipoproteins (LDLs), which are believed to play an important role in forming atherosclerotic plaques (see ATHEROSCLEROSIS).

cholinergic drug any pharmacological agent that stimulates activity in the PARASYMPATHETIC NERVOUS SYSTEM because it potentiates the activity of ACETYLCHOLINE or has effects similar to this neurotransmitter. Cholinergic drugs include such alkaloids as PHYSOSTIGMINE and PILOCARPINE; BETHANECHOL; and anticholinesterases (CHOLINESTERASE inhibitors; e.g., EDROPHONIUM, NEOSTIGMINE, and PYRIDOSTIGMINE); they are used for such purposes as treating myasthenia gravis, glaucoma, and urinary retention. Also called **parasympathetic drug**; **parasympathomimetic drug**.

cholinesterase (**ChE**) *n.* an enzyme that splits ACETYLCHOLINE into choline and acetic acid, thus inactivating the neurotransmitter after its release at a synaptic junction. Cholinesterase occurs in two forms: **acetylcholinesterase** (**AChE**), found in nerve tissue and red blood cells; and **butyrylcholinesterase** (**BuChE**, or **pseudocholinesterase** [**PChE**]), found in blood plasma and other tissues. Drugs that block the ability of this enzyme to degrade acetylcholine are called **cholinesterase inhibitors** (**ChEIs**, or ACETYLCHOLINESTERASE INHIBITORS [AChEIs], or **anticholinesterases**). Some ChEIs are used clinically as NOOTROPICS to slow the progression of dementia in Alzheimer's disease; there is speculation that agents acting on both forms of the enzyme may be beneficial in reducing the formation of the plaques and NEUROFIBRILLARY TANGLES associated with the disease.

chorea *n.* irregular and involuntary jerky movements of the limbs and facial muscles. Chorea is associated with various disorders, including HUNTINGTON'S DISEASE and **Sydenham's chorea** (formerly known as **Saint Vitus's dance**), which occurs as a complication of a streptococcal infection (e.g., rheumatic fever). —**choreal** *adj.* —**choreic** *adj.*

choreomania *n.* an uncontrollable urge to dance, especially in a frenzied, convulsive manner. Major outbreaks of choreomania occurred in the European dance epidemics of the Middle Ages. Also called **dancing madness**; **dancing mania**.

chorion *n.* the outermost of the membranes that surround and protect the developing embryo. In most mammals (including humans) a section of it forms the embryonic part of the placenta. —**chorionic** *adj.*

chorionic villus sampling (**CVS**) a method of diagnosing diseases and genetic and chromosomal abnormalities in a fetus. Samples of cells of the chorionic villi, the microscopic projections in the protective membrane surrounding the fetus, are obtained for analysis of bacteria, metabolites, or DNA. Unlike AMNIOCENTESIS, this procedure can be carried out in the first trimester of pregnancy.

Chotzen's syndrome an inherited condition in which an abnormally shaped head due to premature closing of one or more of the cranial sutures, usually involving the coronal suture, is accompanied by webbing of the fingers and toes. Mental retardation may be associated with the disorder, but affected children often have average intelligence. The trait is transmitted by an autosomal dominant gene (see ACROCEPHALOSYNDACTYLY). Also called **acrocephalosyndactyly Type III**; **Saethre–Chotzen syndrome**. [F. **Chotzen**, German physician]

chrematisophilia *n.* sexual arousal obtained by paying for sex, as opposed to having sexual relations with a willing partner who is not a prostitute.

chromosomal aberration **1.** an abnormal change in the structure of a chromosome. **2.** a congenital defect that can be attributed to an abnormal chromosome. See AUTOSOMAL ABERRATION; SEX-CHROMOSOMAL ABERRATION.

chromosome *n.* a usually invisible strand or filament composed of nucleic acid (mainly DNA in humans) and proteins that carries the genetic, or hereditary, traits of an individual. Located in the cell nucleus, chromosomes are visible, through a microscope, only during cell division. The normal human complement of chromosomes totals 46, or 23 pairs (44 AUTOSOMES and 2 SEX CHROMOSOMES), which contain more than 30,000 genes (see GENOME). Each parent contributes one chromosome to each pair, so a child receives half its chromosomes from its mother and half from its father. —**chromosomal** *adj.*

chromosome 4, deletion of short arm a chromosomal disorder involving absence of a portion of chromosome 4, resulting in microcephaly (small head), visual defects, severe mental retardation, and indifference to painful stimuli. Until 1965 the condition was considered a variation of CRI DU CHAT SYNDROME, involving chromosome 5, although the cat-cry effect was rarely noted.

chromosome 5, deletion of short arm see CRI DU CHAT SYNDROME.

chromosome 18, deletion of long arm a chromosomal disorder characterized by microcephaly (small head), deafness, and mental retardation associated with the absence of part of the long arm of chromosome 18. Reduced muscle tone and nystagmus (involuntary eye movements) are other neurological effects observed in affected individuals.

chromosome abnormality an abnormality that is evidenced by either an abnormal number of chromosomes or some alteration in the structure of one or more chromosomes.

chromosome disorder any disorder caused by a defect in the structure or number of one or more chromosomes. Such disorders can result from AUTOSOMAL ABERRATIONS or SEX-CHROMOSOMAL ABERRATIONS.

chromosome-13 trisomy a chromosomal syndrome involving an extra chromosome 13, resulting in the birth of an infant with a variety of defects, including mental retardation; cleft lip and palate; polydactyly (extra fingers or toes); cerebral anomalies; and ocular abnormalities such as missing or very small eyes, cataracts, and defects in the iris. Also called **D trisomy**; **Patau's syndrome**; **trisomy 13**; **trisomy 13–15**.

chronic *adj.* denoting conditions or symptoms that persist or progress over a long period of time and are resistant to cure. Compare ACUTE.

chronic adjustment disorder see ADJUSTMENT DISORDER.

chronic alcoholism habitual, long-term dependence on alcohol (see ALCOHOL DEPENDENCE). See also GAMMA ALCOHOLISM.

chronically accessible constructs mental contents (e.g., ideas or categories) that are frequently used and therefore come to mind particularly readily.

chronically suicidal describing an individual with a history of multiple suicide attempts or episodes that include serious thoughts about or plans for committing suicide. Such a history often occurs in individuals with BORDERLINE PERSONALITY DISORDER.

chronic anxiety a persistent, pervasive state of apprehension that may be associated with aspects of a number of anxiety disorders. These include uncontrollable worries in GENERALIZED ANXIETY DISORDER, fear of a panic attack in PANIC DISORDER, and obsessions in OBSESSIVE-COMPULSIVE DISORDER.

chronic brain disorder any disorder caused by or associated with brain damage and producing permanent impairment in one or more areas of brain function (cognitive, motor, sensory, and emotional). Such disorders may arise from trauma, stroke, infection, degenerative diseases, or many other conditions. In older literature, these disorders are also referred to as **chronic brain syndrome**.

chronic care long-term care and treatment of patients with long-standing health care problems.

chronic fatigue syndrome (**CFS**) an illness characterized by often disabling fatigue, decrease in physical activity, and flulike symptoms, such as muscle weakness, swelling of the lymph nodes, headache, sore throat, and sometimes depression. The condition is typically not diagnosed until symptoms have been ongoing for several months and it can last for years. The cause is unknown, although certain viral infections can set off the illness.

chronic illness illness that persists for a long period. Chronic illnesses include many major diseases and conditions, such as heart disease, cancer, diabetes, and arthritis. Disease management is important when dealing with chronic illness; this includes ensuring adherence to treatment and maintaining quality of life.

chronicity *n.* **1.** the state of being CHRONIC. **2.** see SOCIAL BREAKDOWN SYNDROME.

chronic mania a manic state that persists indefinitely.

chronic mental illness a mental illness that continues for a prolonged period of time.

chronic mood disorder a mood disorder, such as DYSTHYMIC DISORDER or CYCLOTHYMIC DISORDER, in which symptoms rarely remit.

chronic motor or vocal tic disorder in *DSM–IV–TR*, a TIC DISORDER characterized by motor or vocal tics (but not both) for a period of more than 1 year, during which any period without tics lasts for no more than 3 months. The disorder has an onset before the age of 18. Compare TOURETTE'S DISORDER.

chronic myofascial pain (**CMP**) a MUSCULOSKELETAL DISORDER characterized by pain and stiffness that is restricted to certain locations on the body, called "trigger points." It is nonprogressive, nondegenerative, and noninflammatory. Chronic myofascial pain is sometimes referred to as **myofascial pain syndrome** (**MPS**), especially in older literature.

chronic obstructive pulmonary disease (**COPD**) a group of lung diseases, most commonly chronic bronchitis and emphysema, that are characterized by limited airflow with varying degrees of lung-tissue damage and alveolar (air-sac) enlargement. Marked by coughing, wheezing, and shortness of breath, COPD is caused by cigarette smoking, exposure to other irritants and pollutants, lung infections, or genetic factors. Individuals with COPD frequently experience depression, anxiety, and problems with sexual function; they also sometimes have cognitive and neuropsychological difficulties that may be associated with chronic deficiencies of oxygen to the brain. In addition to medical treatments, behavioral interventions (e.g., those that promote smoking cessation and exercise), psychotherapy, and treatment with psychoactive drugs can benefit patients with this condition. Also called **chronic obstructive lung disease**.

chronic pain pain that may have been caused by actual tissue damage, disease, or emotional trauma but continues to occur despite all medical and pharmacological efforts at treatment. Cognitive factors and beliefs influence the course of rehabilitation and the subjective experience of pain and may lead to maladaptive avoidance behaviors and family problems if left unattended.

chronic posttraumatic stress disorder a form of POSTTRAUMATIC STRESS DISORDER that is diagnosed when the symptoms persist over a period of more than 2 years, regardless of when they first appeared.

chronic psychosis **1.** a delusional or hallucinatory state that persists indefinitely. **2.** a former name for CHRONIC SCHIZOPHRENIA. **3.** historically, any irreversible disorder of cognition, mood or affect, and behavior.

chronic schizophrenia schizophrenia of any type—paranoid, disorganized, catatonic, or undifferentiated—in which the symptoms persist for an extended period and are generally resistant to treatment. It is contrasted with ACUTE SCHIZOPHRENIC EPISODES, in which the symptoms are florid (blatant) but transient.

C

chronic tic disorder any TIC DISORDER that lasts for more than a year. See CHRONIC MOTOR OR VOCAL TIC DISORDER; TOURETTE'S DISORDER.

chronobiology *n.* the branch of biology concerned with BIOLOGICAL RHYTHMS, such as the sleep–wake cycle.

chronological age (**CA**) the amount of time elapsed since an individual's birth, typically expressed in terms of months and years. Also called **calendar age**; **life age**.

chronotaraxis *n.* a condition of time confusion in which the individual tends to underestimate or overestimate the passage of time or is confused about the time of day or day of the week.

chronotaxis *n.* see DISCHRONATION.

chronotherapy *n.* a treatment for CIRCADIAN RHYTHM SLEEP DISORDERS that systematically moves bedtime progressively later by intervals (phase delays) until it approaches the desired bedtime.

chunking *n.* **1.** the process by which the mind sorts information into small, easily digestible units (**chunks**) that can be retained in SHORT-TERM MEMORY. As a result of this RECODING, one item in memory (e.g., a keyword or key idea) can stand for multiple other items (e.g., a short list of associated points). The capacity of short-term memory is believed to be constant for the number of individual units it can store (see SEVEN PLUS OR MINUS TWO), but the units themselves can range from simple chunks (e.g., individual letters or numbers) to complex chunks (e.g., words or phrases). The exact number of chunks remembered can depend on the size of each chunk or the subunits contained within each chunk. **2.** the associated principle that effective communication between humans depends on sorting information into units that do not exceed the mind's capacity to chunk them (the **chunking limit**). This has implications for the content and layout of written documents, diagrams and visual aids, websites, and so on. For example, any list of more than nine bullet points should normally be subdivided into two or more shorter lists. [coined by U.S. cognitive psychologist George Armitage Miller (1920–) in 1956]

cigarette smoking a common form of substance abuse. See NICOTINE; NICOTINE DEPENDENCE; TOBACCO.

Cinderella syndrome behavior in childhood based on the child's belief of being a "Cinderella," or a victim of parental rejection, neglect, or abuse.

cingulate gyrus a long strip of CEREBRAL CORTEX on the medial surface of each cerebral hemisphere. The cingulate gyrus arches over and generally outlines the location of the CORPUS CALLOSUM, from which it is separated by the callosal sulcus. It is a component of the LIMBIC SYSTEM. Also called **callosal gyrus**; **cingulate cortex**; **gyrus cinguli**.

cingulotomy *n.* a procedure used in the treatment of chronic pain in which electrodes are used to destroy portions of the cingulum bundle. It is also, albeit rarely, used in the treatment of some chronic mental disorders (e.g., OBSESSIVE-COMPULSIVE DISORDER) that have not responded to other, nonsurgical forms of treatment. Also called **cingulumotomy**.

circadian dysrhythmia a disruption of the normal cycles of wakefulness and sleep. See CIRCADIAN RHYTHM SLEEP DISORDER.

circadian rhythm any variation in physiological or behavioral activity that repeats at approximately 24-hour intervals, such as the SLEEP–WAKE CYCLE. Also called **diurnal rhythm**. See also BIOLOGICAL RHYTHM.

circadian rhythm sleep disorder in *DSM–IV–TR*, a sleep disorder that is due to a mismatch between the sleep–wake schedule required by a person's environment and his or her circadian sleep–wake pattern, resulting in excessive sleepiness or insomnia. In the **delayed sleep-phase type**, sleep onset and awakening times are later than is socially typical or appropriate and the person is unable to fall asleep and wake up at a desired earlier time. In the **jet-lag type**, which affects people who repeatedly travel across two or more time zones, sleepiness and alertness occur at times inappropriate to the local time. In the **shift-work type**, sleep disruption is produced by recurrent changes in work shifts; it is characterized by insomnia during the major sleep period or excessive sleepiness during the major wake period. This disorder was formerly called **sleep–wake schedule disorder**. See DYSSOMNIA. See also DISORDERS OF THE SLEEP–WAKE CYCLE SCHEDULE.

circle of support a group of people who provide support for an individual. For a person with a developmental disability, the circle often includes family members, friends, acquaintances, coworkers, and sometimes service providers or coordinators, who meet on a regular basis and help the individual accomplish personal goals. These goals are selected based on extensive and recurrent review of the person's past and current preferences and interests; they are addressed one stage at a time.

circuit resistance training a series of different exercises set out in a specific order, with a specific time or number of repetitions for each exercise. The type and order of exercises will be set according to their use as rehabilitation—health-related exercise for individuals with spinal cord injuries, diabetes, obesity, and other conditions—or as fitness training for athletes.

circular behavior any action that stimulates a similar action in others, such as yawning or laughing. Also called **circular response**.

circular questioning a technique used in

some methods of family therapy to yield information about the dynamics and relationships in a family. For example, one family member may be asked to answer a question about who in the family is most depressed; subsequent family members each respond to the same question. This method of questioning everyone in the "circle" is intended to elicit the various perspectives within the group.

circumlocution *n.* **1.** a mode of speaking characterized by difficulty or inability in finding the right words to identify or explain an object that has been perceived and recognized. It involves the use of a variety of words or phrases that indirectly communicate the individual's meaning. Circumlocution can be a manifestation of ANOMIA caused by damage to the left posterior temporal lobe of the brain, but in some cases it is an indication of disorganized thought processes, as in schizophrenia. See CIRCUMSTANTIALITY. **2.** a style of speaking used consciously by healthy individuals to convey meaning indirectly, so that the meaning is inferred by the listener.

circumplex model of personality and emotion a type of model for determining the degree of similarity between personality traits and emotions by depicting in a circular form the relations and interactions between those traits and emotions. Elements adjacent to one another on the circle are highly similar (positively correlated); the similarity (and correlation) between elements declines as the distance between them on the circle increases. Certain elements may be completely unrelated to each other (a correlation of 0). Elements opposite each other on the circle are highly dissimilar (negatively correlated) and represent dimensional extremes (e.g., agreeableness versus contrariness, joy versus sorrow, pessimism versus optimism).

circumscribed belief a narrowly defined delusional belief held by some people with paranoia or brain damage who otherwise seem to function entirely normally. For example, such people may believe they are being persecuted by the CIA, be convinced that they are Jesus, or suspect that the interviewer has hidden hostility toward them. The delusional belief system is generally highly consistent and resistant to disproof and appears to function separately from other beliefs held by the same person.

circumstantiality *n.* circuitous, indirect speech in which the individual digresses to give unnecessary and often irrelevant details before arriving at the main point. An extreme form, arising from disorganized associative processes, may occur in schizophrenia, obsessional disorders, and certain types of dementia. Circumstantiality differs from TANGENTIALITY in that the main point is never lost but rather accompanied by a large amount of nonessential information.

cirrhosis *n.* a chronic liver disease marked by widespread formation of fibrous tissue and loss of normal liver function. In most cases, it is a consequence of alcohol abuse, although it may also be due to congenital defects involving metabolic deficiencies, exposure to toxic chemicals, or infections (e.g., hepatitis). **—cirrhotic** *adj.*

CISD abbreviation for CRITICAL-INCIDENT STRESS DEBRIEFING.

cissa *n.* a craving for unusual foods or nonnutritive substances while pregnant. See also PICA.

citalopram *n.* an antidepressant of the SSRI class. It exerts its action by blocking the presynaptic serotonin TRANSPORTER, preventing reabsorption of serotonin into the presynaptic neuron and thereby increasing levels of available serotonin in the SYNAPTIC CLEFT without increasing overall levels of serotonin in the brain. U.S. trade name: **Celexa**.

cittosis *n.* an abnormal desire for unusual foods or nonnutritive substances. See CISSA; PICA.

civil commitment a legal procedure that permits a person who is not charged with criminal conduct to be certified as mentally ill and to be institutionalized involuntarily.

Civilian Health and Medical Program of the Uniformed Services (CHAMPUS) the medical insurer that since 1967 has provided and paid for health care to U.S. military retirees and families and surviving family members of deceased military sponsors. Many new benefits have been added since the program was first established. The current program is called TRICARE.

CJD abbreviation for CREUTZFELDT–JAKOB DISEASE.

CL abbreviation for COMPARISON LEVEL.

claims review an evaluation of the appropriateness of a claim for payment for a medical or mental health service rendered. It will consider whether the claimant is eligible for reimbursement, whether the charges are consistent with customary fees or published institutional rates, and whether the service was necessary.

CLAlt abbreviation for COMPARISON LEVEL FOR ALTERNATIVES.

clang association an association of words by similarity of sound rather than meaning. Clang association occurs as a pathological disturbance in manic states and schizophrenia. Also called **clanging**.

clarification *n.* a therapist's formulation, in clearer terms and without indicating approval or disapproval, of a client's statement or expression of feelings. Clarification goes further than restatement and REFLECTION OF FEELING but stops short of interpretation.

classical *adj.* denoting a style, mode of operation, or function that was typical or standard at some time in the past. In psychology, it was applied to PAVLOVIAN CONDITIONING to contrast it with newly recognized OPERANT CONDITIONING when the distinction between the two forms of learning was pointed out by B. F. SKINNER in 1938.

classical conditioning see PAVLOVIAN CONDITIONING.

classical depression a MAJOR DEPRESSIVE EPISODE characterized by intense sadness, difficulty in concentrating, PSYCHOMOTOR RETARDATION, decreased appetite, insomnia, and weight loss, as well as psychotic features (i.e., delusions or hallucinations). It is often thought to be prototypical of DEPRESSIVE DISORDERS.

classical paranoia as conceptualized in the 19th century by German physician Karl Ludwig Kahlbaum (1828–1899) and later refined by German psychiatrist Emil Kraepelin (1856–1926), a rare disorder characterized by elaborate, fixed, and systematic DELUSIONS, usually of a persecutory, grandiose, or jealous character, that develop insidiously, cannot be accounted for by any psychiatric disorder, and exist in the context of preserved logical and orderly thinking. The basic definition of DELUSIONAL DISORDER in *DSM–IV–TR* retains much of the original concept of Kahlbaum and Kraepelin.

classical psychoanalysis 1. psychoanalytic theory in which major emphasis is placed on the LIBIDO, the stages of PSYCHOSEXUAL DEVELOPMENT, and the ID instincts or drives. The prototypical theory of this kind is that of Sigmund FREUD. Also called **classical theory**; **drive theory**. **2.** psychoanalytic treatment that adheres to Sigmund Freud's basic procedures, using dream interpretation, free association, and analysis of RESISTANCE, and to his basic aim of developing insight into the patient's unconscious life as a way to restructure personality. Also called **orthodox psychoanalysis**.

classical test theory (**CTT**) a body of psychometric theory of measurement that partitions observed scores into two components—TRUE SCORES and ERROR SCORES—and estimates error variance by calculating INTERNAL CONSISTENCY reliability, RETEST RELIABILITY, and ALTERNATE-FORMS RELIABILITY. Among the key benefits of CTT—the principal framework for test development prior to the 1970s—are that it is relatively simple to execute and that it can be applied to a broad range of measurement situations. Among its major limitations are that examinee characteristics cannot be separated from test characteristics and that the measurement statistics derived from it are fundamentally concerned with how people perform on a given test as opposed to any single item on that test. These inherent limitations of CTT prompted the development of ITEM RESPONSE THEORY and other models that are not subject to these limitations, that more accurately detect BIAS, and that offer enhanced reliability assessment and increased precision in ability measurement.

classical theory see CLASSICAL PSYCHOANALYSIS.

classic categorical approach a method for classifying disorders founded on the assumption that there are clear-cut differences between disorders.

classification *n.* in clinical psychology and psychiatry, the grouping of mental disorders on the basis of their characteristics or symptoms. See also DSM–IV–TR; INTERNATIONAL CLASSIFICATION OF DISEASES; NOSOLOGY. **—classify** *vb.*

classification table a table (usually two-dimensional) in which the number of cases in a sample are arranged on the basis of their joint membership in the row and column classes of the table.

classroom-behavior modification an instructor's use of basic learning techniques, such as conditioning, to alter the behavior of the students within a learning environment. Specifically, classroom behavior modification may utilize such methods as adjusting classroom seating, providing a flexible time deadline for assignments, or altering the lesson requirements. Direct intervention, however, is the most effective modification procedure, using cognitive-behavioral techniques to address inappropriate classroom behavior. Such procedures are most useful for students with learning disabilities, attention-deficit/hyperactivity disorder, and other special needs.

claustrophobia *n.* a persistent and irrational fear of enclosed places (e.g., elevators, closets, tunnels) or of being confined (e.g., in an airplane or the backseat of a car). The focus of fear is typically on panic symptoms triggered in these situations, such as feelings of being unable to breathe, choking, sweating, and fears of losing control or going crazy. **—claustrophobic** *adj.*

clavus *n.* a sharp sensation as if a nail were being driven into the head.

clay therapy a form of therapy in which children manipulate clay, often used in physical rehabilitation, in stimulating individuals with mental retardation, and in the assessment and treatment of various disorders. The clay can be a metaphor for feelings, yet at the same time it serves as a tangible item that is visible, changeable, and under the child's control. A child can look at the clay, focus on it, manipulate it, squeeze it, and pound it, which can help reduce anxiety, enable the acting out of hostile emotions, and provide opportunities for gratification, achievement, and acceptance.

clearance (**CL**) *n.* the rate of elimination of a drug from the body in relation to its concentration in a body fluid, as expressed by the equation CL = rate of elimination/C, where C is the concentration of the drug in the body fluid. Clearance is additive, that is, drugs are eliminated by various mechanisms (renal, hepatic, etc.) at differing rates; thus, total clearance is the sum of clearance from each individual organ system.

clear sensorium see SENSORIUM.

Clérambault's syndrome a form of EROTIC

PARANOIA in which a person has EROTIC DELUSIONS that someone else, who is typically older and of higher social status, is in love with him or her. The person continues to hold this belief despite having little contact with the other person and no reciprocation of feelings. The condition is more common in females than in males. Also called **de Clérambault's syndrome**. [first described in 1922 by Gaëtan Gatian de **Clérambault** (1872–1934), French physician]

client *n.* a person receiving treatment or services, especially in the context of counseling or social work. See PATIENT–CLIENT ISSUE.

client abuse harm to clients caused by therapists and counselors who exploit their clients' vulnerability and their own position of influence and trust to engage in inappropriate, unprofessional behavior. Client abuse, which sometimes takes the form of sexual involvement with a client, is usually grounds for legal and professional action against the practitioner. See also PROFESSIONAL ETHICS; PROFESSIONAL STANDARDS.

client-centered therapy a form of psychotherapy developed by Carl ROGERS in the early 1940s. According to Rogers, an orderly process of client self-discovery and actualization occurs in response to the therapist's consistent empathic understanding of, acceptance of, and respect for the client's FRAME OF REFERENCE. The therapist sets the stage for personality growth by reflecting and clarifying the ideas of the client, who is able to see himself or herself more clearly and come into closer touch with his or her real self. As therapy progresses, the client resolves conflicts, reorganizes values and approaches to life, and learns how to interpret his or her thoughts and feelings, consequently changing behavior that he or she considers problematic. It was originally known as **nondirective counseling** or **nondirective therapy**, although this term is now used more broadly to denote any approach to psychotherapy in which the therapist establishes an encouraging atmosphere but avoids giving advice, offering interpretations, or engaging in other actions to actively direct the therapeutic process. Also called **client-centered psychotherapy**; **person-centered psychotherapy**; **Rogerian therapy**.

client characteristics aspects of a client that define his or her physical and personality attributes as well as the problems and symptoms that the client brings into therapy for resolution and healing.

client education interventions aimed at giving clients information intended to change their cognitions, beliefs, affect, and behaviors. This educational process can take place in formal groups (psychoeducational groups) or as a routine part of initiating psychotherapy.

client obligations see CONTRACT.

client–patient issue see PATIENT–CLIENT ISSUE.

client rights the rights of patients or clients to be fully informed of the benefits or risks of treatment procedures and to make informed decisions to accept or reject treatment.

client satisfaction the extent to which a person seeking mental health services is content with the results.

client self-monitoring see SELF-MONITORING.

client–treatment matching the selection of therapies and psychotherapists most appropriate for the clients' needs and characteristics (e.g., ethnicity, gender, personality traits). Client–treatment matching is assumed to enhance therapeutic outcomes.

climacteric *n.* the biological stage of life in which reproductive capacity declines and finally ceases. In women this period, which results from changes in the levels of estrogens and progesterone and is known as **menopause** (popularly, **change of life**), occurs between 45 and 55 years of age and lasts 2–3 years. During this time, menstrual flow gradually decreases and finally ceases altogether, and various physical and potentially psychological changes occur, typically manifest as hot flashes, night sweats, and emotional lability, joint pains, and depression may occur in varying combinations and degrees. Some men undergo a similar period about 10 years later than is typical for women (see MALE CLIMACTERIC).

climax *n.* see ORGASM.

clinging behavior a form of ATTACHMENT BEHAVIOR in which a child of 6 months or older clings to the primary caregiver and becomes acutely distressed when left alone. Clinging behavior reaches a maximum in the 2nd and 3rd years and then slowly subsides.

clinic *n.* **1.** a health care facility for the diagnosis and treatment of emergency and ambulatory patients. **2.** a brief instructional program or session with diagnostic, therapeutic, or remedial purpose in the areas of mental or physical health or education.

clinical *adj.* **1.** of or relating to the diagnosis and treatment of psychological, medical, or other disorders. Originally involving only direct observation of patients, clinical methods have now broadened to take into account biological and statistical factors in treating patients and diagnosing disorders. **2.** relating to or occurring in a clinic.

clinical assessment the systematic evaluation and measurement of psychological, biological, and social factors in a person presenting with a possible psychological disorder. See also DYNAMIC ASSESSMENT.

clinical counseling counseling that addresses a client's personal or emotional difficulties. The counseling encompasses general goals for the client, for example, greater self-acceptance, better reality orientation, improved decision-making ability, and greater effectiveness in interpersonal relationships. The counselor's responsibilities include gathering and interpretating data, identifying the client's major problems, and formulating and (sometimes) implementing a treatment plan.

C

clinical diagnosis the process of identifying and determining the nature of a mental disorder through the study of the symptom pattern, review of medical records, investigation of background factors, and, where indicated, administration of psychological tests.

clinical efficacy the effectiveness of clinical interventions based on the evidence of controlled studies. Such studies typically include random assignment to control groups and treatment manuals that guide therapist actions.

clinical evidence information about clients or patients that is relevant to clinical diagnosis and therapy, obtained either directly, through questioning (see CLINICAL INTERVIEW), or indirectly, through observation of their behavior in a clinical setting, their CASE HISTORIES, and the like.

clinical health psychology a specialty field in HEALTH PSYCHOLOGY that applies biopsychosocial theory, research, and practice principles to promote physical health and to help resolve the immediate problems of patients with medical conditions and related family difficulties. Biofeedback, relaxation training, hypnotherapy, and coping skills are among the many methods used by **clinical health psychologists**, who are also active in health policy and in developing and implementing models of preventive intervention.

clinical interview a type of directed conversation initially used with children but now applied in a variety of contexts, including human factors research and diagnostic evaluation and treatment planning of patients by mental health professionals. In a clinical interview, the investigator may utilize certain standard material but essentially determines which questions to ask based on the responses given by the participant to previous ones. This technique is largely spontaneous and enables the interviewer to adapt questions to the patient's understanding and ask additional questions to clarify ambiguities and enhance understanding.

clinical investigation 1. examination of an individual by means of interviews, testing, behavioral observation, or document analysis. **2.** an in-depth analysis of an individual's life experiences and personal history.

clinical judgment analysis, evaluation, or prediction of disordered behavior, symptoms, or other aspects of psychological functioning. It includes assessing the appropriateness of particular treatments and the degree or likelihood of clinical improvement. These conclusions are derived from the expert knowledge of mental health professionals, as opposed to conclusions drawn from actuarial tables or statistical methods.

clinical judgment research empirical studies of the factors influencing the judgments mental health practitioners make with regard to assessment, treatment, predictions (e.g., dangerousness, suicidality), and prognosis in therapeutic and legal settings. Factors researched include individual differences of the practitioner (e.g., values, gender, sexual orientation), social contexts, and complex cognitive thought processes involved in judgment.

clinical marker an observable sign indicative of disorder or predictive of an upcoming event of special interest. See also BIOCHEMICAL MARKER; BIOLOGICAL MARKER.

clinical method 1. the process by which a clinical psychologist, psychiatrist, or other mental health or medical professional arrives at a conclusion, judgment, or diagnosis about a client or patient in a clinical situation. **2.** the process of collecting data in a natural situation (e.g., home, office, school) rather than in the formal setting of a laboratory.

clinical neuropsychology an applied specialty in NEUROPSYCHOLOGY that comprises neuropsychological assessment and rehabilitation, which are critical in cases of neuropsychological injury that results in a range of impairments that disrupt an individual's abilities to function.

clinical practice guidelines systematically developed statements to assist providers, as well as clients or patients, in making decisions about appropriate medical or mental health care for specific clinical conditions.

clinical prediction the process of examining such factors as signs, symptoms, and case history to determine the CLINICAL DIAGNOSIS and likely progress of patients. Clinical prediction can be contrasted with statistical prediction, in which formal statistical methods combine numerical information for the same purposes. See CLINICAL JUDGMENT.

clinical psychology the branch of psychology that specializes in the research, assessment, diagnosis, evaluation, prevention, and treatment of emotional and behavioral disorders. The **clinical psychologist** is a doctorate-level professional who has received training in research methods and techniques for the diagnosis and treatment of various psychological disorders (see also PSYCHOLOGIST). Clinical psychologists work primarily in health and mental health clinics, in research, or in group and independent practices. They also serve as consultants to other professionals in the medical, legal, social-work, and community-relations fields. Clinical psychologists comprise approximately one third of the psychologists working in the United States and are governed by the code of practice of the American Psychological Association.

clinical psychopharmacology a branch of pharmacology concerned with how drugs affect the brain and behavior and specifically with the clinical evaluation and management of drugs developed for the treatment of mental disorders. See also PSYCHOPHARMACOTHERAPY.

clinical risk assessment a clinician-based prediction of the likelihood that an individual will pose a threat to others or engage in a certain behavior (e.g., violence) within a given period. Unlike ACTUARIAL RISK ASSESSMENT, a specific formula or weighting system using empirically derived predictors is not applied. Instead, clinicians make predictions of dangerousness or violent behavior based primarily on their own experience, reasoning, and judgment; their observations, examination, and psychological testing of the client; and information obtained from client life histories.

clinical social work a field devoted to providing individual, family, and group treatment from a psychosocial perspective in such areas as health, mental health, family and child welfare, and correction. Clinical social work additionally involves client-centered advocacy that assists clients with information, referral, and in dealing with local, state, and federal agencies.

clinical sociology a multidisciplinary, practice-oriented specialization in the field of sociology that seeks to effect social change through analysis, applied sociological theory, and problem-focused intervention.

clinical sport psychology a specialty within clinical psychology focused on individuals involved in sport. Clinical sport psychologists help athletes with performance enhancement and consistency and with clinical issues (e.g., depression, eating disorders).

clinical study see CLINICAL TRIAL.

clinical trial a research study designed to compare a new treatment or drug with an existing standard of care or other control condition (see CONTROL GROUP). Trials are generally designed to answer scientific questions and to find better ways to treat individuals who have a specific disease or disorder. Also called **clinical study**.

clinical type an individual whose pattern of symptoms or behaviors is consistent with a recognizable disorder of clinical psychology and psychiatry.

clinical utility the extent to which clinical interventions can be applied successfully and cost-effectively in real clinical settings. It is one of a proposed set of guidelines for evaluating clinical interventions.

clinical validation the act of acquiring evidence to support the accuracy of a theory by studying multiple cases with specific procedures for diagnosis or treatment.

clinician *n.* a medical or mental health care professional who is directly involved in the care and treatment of patients, as distinguished from one working in other areas, such as research or administration.

clitoridectomy *n.* the surgical removal of all or part of the clitoris, usually as an ethnic or religious rite. It is a highly controversial practice and the most common form of FEMALE GENITAL MUTILATION.

clitoris *n.* a small body of erectile tissue situated anterior to the vaginal opening. It is homologous to the penis but usually much smaller. **—clitoral** *adj.*

cloaca *n.* the common cavity, occurring in early mammalian embryos, into which the intestinal, urinary, and reproductive canals open. The proximity of these functions and the pleasure involved in them are a major factor in Sigmund FREUD's psychosexual theory. [Latin, literally: "sewer", "drain"] **—cloacal** *adj.*

cloacal theory a theory, sometimes held by young children, that combines the vagina and the anus into a single orifice and includes the belief that birth takes place through the anus and is a form of defecation. See PRIMAL FANTASY.

clomipramine *n.* a TRICYCLIC ANTIDEPRESSANT drug used for the treatment of obsessive-compulsive disorder (OCD) as well as depression and panic disorder. Clomipramine is a more potent inhibitor of serotonin reuptake than other tricyclic antidepressants, and its active metabolite inhibits norepinephrine reuptake; it thus is classified as a mixed serotonin–norepinephrine reuptake inhibitor. Because of its tricyclic structure, it has the same adverse side effects and toxicity as other tricyclic antidepressants, and it has been largely supplanted by the SSRIS, one of which—FLUVOXAMINE—is also used for the treatment of OCD. U.S. trade name: **Anafranil**.

clonazepam *n.* a highly potent BENZODIAZEPINE originally developed to treat absence seizures but now used for the treatment of panic disorder and other anxiety disorders and as a MOOD STABILIZER. Because it has a slow onset of action, long HALF-LIFE, and slow rate of CLEARANCE, it needs to be taken less frequently (twice a day) than some other benzodiazepines. U.S. trade name: **Klonopin**.

clonidine *n.* a drug used for the treatment of hypertension. It functions by direct stimulation of ALPHA-ADRENERGIC RECEPTORS in the brainstem to restrict the flow of impulses in peripheral sympathetic nerves supplying the arteries, thus causing them to relax (widen); most of the other commonly prescribed antihypertensive drugs act as beta blockers or as diuretics. Clonidine has been used as an adjunctive agent in the management of alcohol and opioid withdrawal, as a nonstimulant treatment for attention-deficit/hyperactivity disorder, and in the management of clozapine-induced sialorrhea (i.e., drooling). It has also been tried in patients with bipolar disorder resistant to other drug treatments, but with limited effectiveness. U.S. trade name (among others): **Catapres**.

clonus *n.* a type of involuntary movement caused by a rapid succession of alternate muscular contractions and relaxations. Although some forms of clonus, such as hiccups, are considered normal, most such movements are abnormal; for example, clonus occurs as part of a TONIC–CLONIC SEIZURE. More severe forms are associated with spinal cord damage, poisoning (e.g., from strychnine), or an infection (e.g., syphilis).

Clopixol *n.* a trade name for ZUCLOPENTHIXOL.

clorazepate *n.* a long-acting BENZODIAZEPINE used in the treatment of anxiety, alcohol withdrawal, and PARTIAL SEIZURES. U.S. trade name (among others): **Tranxene.**

closed-ended question a question that provides respondents with alternative answers from which to select their response. Also called **fixed-alternative question**; **multiple-choice question**. Compare OPEN-ENDED QUESTION.

closed group a counseling or therapy group consisting of only those members who constituted the original group. New members may not join during the course of therapy. Compare OPEN GROUP.

closed head injury a head injury, such as a concussion, in which the head strikes against an object but the skull is not broken open or pierced. Compare OPEN HEAD INJURY.

closed marriage a marriage that changes little over the years and that involves relatively little change in the individual partners. A closed marriage relies on the legal bond between the parties to enforce permanence and sexual exclusivity. Also called **static marriage**. Compare OPEN MARRIAGE.

closedmindedness *n.* see DOGMATISM.

closet homosexual a gay man or lesbian who does not reveal his or her sexual orientation to others, particularly to family members, parents, or employers. Compare COMING OUT.

closing *n.* ending a session in psychotherapy or counseling. Approaches to closing vary among therapists: Some allow the client to initiate the end of the session; others initiate it themselves.

closure *n.* **1.** the act, achievement, or sense of completing or resolving something. In psychotherapy, for example, a client achieves closure with the recognition that he or she has reached a resolution to a particular psychological issue or relationship problem. **2.** one of the GESTALT PRINCIPLES OF ORGANIZATION. It states that people tend to perceive incomplete forms (e.g., images, sounds) as complete, synthesizing the missing units so as to perceive the image or sound as a whole—in effect closing the gap between the incomplete and complete forms. Also called **law of closure**; **principle of closure**. See also GOODNESS OF CONFIGURATION; PRÄGNANZ.

clouded sensorium see SENSORIUM.

clouding of consciousness a mental state involving a reduced awareness of the environment, inability to concentrate, and confusion. Also called **mental fog**.

cloverleaf skull see KLEEBLATTSCHÄDEL SYNDROME.

clozapine *n.* an ATYPICAL ANTIPSYCHOTIC agent of the DIBENZODIAZEPINE class: the first of the atypical antipsychotics to be used clinically and released into the U.S. market in 1990. Although regarded by some as the most effective of all antipsychotic drugs, clozapine has problematic side effects that have limited its use. Among others, these adverse effects may include weight gain, sedation, and—importantly—AGRANULOCYTOSIS, which may occur in 1–2% of patients treated with the drug. Use of clozapine therefore requires frequent monitoring of white blood cell counts in patients and is generally reserved for patients who have responded suboptimally to other antipsychotic agents. U.S. trade name: **Clozaril.**

club drugs substances used by teenagers and young adults at bars, dance clubs, or all-night parties known as "raves." Such substances include MDMA (Ecstasy); GHB and FLUNITRAZEPAM (see also DATE-RAPE DRUG); KETAMINE; METHAMPHETAMINE; and LSD. Chronic abuse can have severe physiological or psychological repercussions (or both) and, when combined with the intake of alcohol, might also prove fatal.

clumsy child syndrome an outdated and pejorative name for DEVELOPMENTAL DYSPRAXIA or DEVELOPMENTAL COORDINATION DISORDER.

cluster analysis a method of data analysis in which individuals (cases) are grouped together into clusters based on their strong similarity with regard to specific attributes.

cluster evaluation **1.** a type of program evaluation, either a FORMATIVE EVALUATION or a SUMMATIVE EVALUATION, carried out at several sites. Each site has the same EVALUATION OBJECTIVES, which are assessed in a coordinated effort by different evaluators in a continuous process. Information so obtained is then shared to enable common PROGRAM OUTCOMES to be assessed and to identify elements that contributed to the failures or successes of the program. **2.** a strategy for accumulating information in evaluation research that involves combining and reconciling studies with somewhat different conclusions. This approach suggests criteria for determining when data from dissimilar studies can be pooled. **3.** an approach in which individual evaluators in separate projects collaborate with an overarching evaluator.

cluster headache a headache, typically limited to the area around one eye, that lasts between 15 min and 3 hr and occurs in bouts, or "clusters," every day (sometimes twice or more a day or every other day) for a period of up to 3 months, followed by a headache-free period of months or years.

clustering *n.* **1.** the tendency for items to be consistently grouped together in the course of recall. This grouping typically occurs for related items. It is readily apparent in memory tasks in which items from the same category, such as animals, are recalled together. **2.** in statistics, the process by which a CLUSTER ANALYSIS is conducted. **—cluster** *n.*, *vb.*

cluster sampling a survey sampling method in which the complete population is first subdivided into groups, or clusters, and random samples are then drawn from certain clusters. A common example would be sampling voters in a large jurisdiction (e.g., a state) by identifying clusters on the basis of close geographical proximity (e.g., counties) and then drawing samples from the county clusters (e.g., towns and cities).

cluster suicides a statistically high occurrence of suicides within a circumscribed geographic area, social group, or time period. Such clusters typically occur among adolescents who imitate the suicide of a high-status peer or among dispersed individuals, all exposed to the same or similar media coverage, who imitate the suicide of a widely admired role model. Compare MASS SUICIDE.

cluttering *n.* rapid speech that is confused, jumbled, and imprecise, often occurring during a MANIC EPISODE.

CMAS abbreviation for CHILDREN'S MANIFEST ANXIETY SCALE.

CME abbreviation for CONTINUING MEDICAL EDUCATION.

CMHC abbreviation for COMMUNITY MENTAL HEALTH CENTER.

CMI abbreviation for CORNELL MEDICAL INDEX.

CMP abbreviation for CHRONIC MYOFASCIAL PAIN.

CMS abbreviation for CENTERS FOR MEDICARE AND MEDICAID SERVICES.

CNS abbreviation for CENTRAL NERVOUS SYSTEM.

CNS abnormality any defect in structure or function of the tissues of the brain and spinal cord, that is, the central nervous system (CNS).

CNS depressant any of a group of drugs that, at low doses, depress the inhibitory centers of the brain. At somewhat higher doses, they depress other neural functions, slow reaction times, and lower respiration and heart rate. At still higher doses, they can induce unconsciousness, coma, and death. Examples of CNS depressants are ALCOHOL, BARBITURATES, BENZODIAZEPINES, INHALANTS, and MEPROBAMATE. See also SEDATIVE, HYPNOTIC, AND ANXIOLYTIC DRUGS.

CNS stimulant any of a group of drugs that, at low to moderate doses, heighten wakefulness and alertness, diminish fatigue, and provoke feelings of energy and well-being. At higher doses, the more powerful stimulants can produce agitation, panic excitement, hallucinations, and paranoia. In general, stimulants exert their effects by enhancing CATECHOLAMINE neurotransmission and increasing activity in the SYMPATHETIC NERVOUS SYSTEM. COCAINE and the AMPHETAMINES are examples of stimulants thought to activate the reward system (nucleus accumbens, limbic, and frontal cortex) by potentiating dopaminergic neurotransmission. CAFFEINE and NICOTINE are CNS stimulants with different mechanisms of action at ADENOSINE receptors and NICOTINIC RECEPTORS, respectively. In non-Western cultures, BETEL NUT, COCA leaves, GUARANA, KHAT, and numerous other substances are used as stimulants. Some stimulants are used clinically in mental health, and in psychiatric contexts are often referred to as **psychostimulants**. These drugs include the amphetamines and related or similarly acting compounds (e.g., METHYLPHENIDATE, PEMOLINE, MODAFINIL), used for the treatment of attention-deficit/hyperactivity disorder, narcolepsy, depression, and organic brain syndromes and as appetite suppressants. Caffeine and ephedrine are ingredients of over-the-counter "alertness" medications.

coaching *n.* specialized instruction and training provided to enable individuals to acquire or enhance particular skills, as in LIFE COACHING, or to improve performance, as in athletic coaching or academic coaching.

coca *n.* a shrub, *Erythroxylum coca*, that is indigenous to Peru, Bolivia, and other South American countries and cultivated in India, Sri Lanka, and Indonesia. The leaves have been used for centuries as the source of COCAINE.

cocaine *n.* a drug, obtained from leaves of the COCA shrub, that stimulates the central nervous system (see CNS STIMULANT), with the effects of reducing fatigue and increasing well-being. These are followed by a period of depression as the initial effects diminish. The drug acts by blocking the reuptake of the neurotransmitters DOPAMINE, SEROTONIN, and NOREPINEPHRINE. The psychoactive properties of the coca plant were recognized by the Peruvian Incas before 4000 BCE, and in the 1880s the possible therapeutic uses of cocaine were investigated. Sigmund FREUD observed that the drug functioned as a topical anesthetic. See also CRACK; FREEBASE.

cocaine abuse in *DSM–IV–TR*, a pattern of cocaine use manifested by recurrent significant adverse consequences related to the repeated ingestion of the substance. This diagnosis is preempted by the diagnosis of COCAINE DEPENDENCE: If the criteria for cocaine abuse and cocaine dependence are both met, only the latter diagnosis is given. See also SUBSTANCE ABUSE.

Cocaine Anonymous a voluntary organization of men and women who seek to recover from cocaine addiction by using a TWELVE-STEP PROGRAM. See also SELF-HELP GROUP.

cocaine dependence in *DSM–IV–TR*, a cluster of cognitive, behavioral, and physiological symptoms indicating continued use of cocaine despite significant cocaine-related problems. There is a pattern of repeated cocaine ingestion resulting in tolerance, withdrawal symptoms if use is suspended, and an uncontrollable drive to continue use. See also COCAINE ABUSE; SUBSTANCE DEPENDENCE.

cocaine intoxication a reversible syndrome due to the recent ingestion of cocaine. It includes clinically significant behavioral or psychological changes (e.g., agitation, aggressive behavior, elation, grandiosity, impaired judgment, talkativeness, hypervigilance), as well as one or more physiological signs (e.g., rapid heartbeat, elevated blood pressure, perspiration or chills, nausea and vomiting). Large doses, especially when taken intravenously, may produce confusion, incoherence, apprehension, transient paranoid ideas, increased sexual interest, and perceptual disturbances (e.g., a sensation of insects crawling on the skin). An hour or so after these effects subside, the user may experience tremulousness, anxiety, irritability, fatigue, and depression. See also SUBSTANCE INTOXICATION.

cocaine intoxication delirium a reversible syndrome that develops over a short period of time (usually hours to days) following the heavy ingestion of cocaine. It includes disturbance of consciousness (e.g., reduced ability to focus, sustain, or shift attention), accompanied by changes in cognition (e.g., memory deficit, disorientation, or language disturbance) in excess of those usually associated with COCAINE INTOXICATION. See also SUBSTANCE INTOXICATION DELIRIUM.

cocaine withdrawal a characteristic withdrawal syndrome that develops after cessation of (or reduction in) prolonged, heavy consumption of cocaine. The essential characteristic is depressed mood, sometimes severe, and there may also be fatigue, disturbed sleep, increased appetite, vivid and unpleasant dreams, or PSYCHOMOTOR RETARDATION or agitation, or all of these features. Marked withdrawal symptoms (see CRASH) often follow an episode of intense, high-dose use. See also SUBSTANCE WITHDRAWAL.

Cockayne's syndrome a hereditary disorder involving dwarfism, microcephaly (small head), mental retardation, visual disorders, hypersensitivity to sunlight, and progressive neurological deterioration. Early psychomotor development is slow, and most affected individuals show an IQ of less than 50. Affected individuals eventually become blind and deaf and typically do not live past the age of 20. Also called **Cockayne–Neill dwarfism**. [reported in 1936 by Edward Alfred **Cockayne** (1880–1956), British physician, and in about 1950 by Catherine A. **Neill** (1922–2006), British-born U.S. pediatrician]

cocktail-party syndrome see CHATTERBOX EFFECT.

cocoa *n.* a product derived from the cacao plant (*Theobroma cacao*) by roasting and grinding the beans (seeds) and removing the oils. The pharmacologically active ingredients are THEOBROMINE (typically about 1–3% of dry weight) and CAFFEINE.

coconsciousness *n.* **1.** in early psychology, the relationship among multiple selves, or mental processes, that are simultaneously available but separated by a "diaphanous veil" from everyday awareness. [defined by William JAMES] **2.** in contemporary philosophy, the unity of consciousness. **—coconscious** *adj.*

cocounseling *n.* the counseling of peers by each other, as opposed to one-way professionally led counseling.

codeine *n.* an OPIATE derived from morphine, with which it shares many properties—it is a potent analgesic (used alone or in combination with other analgesics, e.g., aspirin) and it induces euphoria. However, its addiction potential is substantially less than that of heroin. See OPIOID ANALGESIC.

code of ethics a set of standards and principles of professional conduct, such as the *Ethical Principles of Psychologists and Code of Conduct* of the American Psychological Association. See ETHICS; STANDARDS OF PRACTICE.

codependency *n.* **1.** the state of being mutually reliant, for example, a relationship between two individuals who are emotionally dependent on one another. **2.** a dysfunctional relationship pattern in which an individual is psychologically dependent on (or controlled by) a person who has a pathological addiction (e.g., alcohol, gambling). **—codependent** *adj.*

Co-Dependents Anonymous a SELF-HELP GROUP for individuals who seek to improve problematic codependent relationships with others (see CODEPENDENCY) by using a TWELVE-STEP PROGRAM.

coefficient *n.* **1.** a number that functions as a measure of some property. For example, the CORRELATION COEFFICIENT is a measure of the degree of linear relatedness. **2.** in algebra, a scalar that multiplies a variable in an equation. For example, in the equation $y = bx$, the scalar quantity b is said to be a coefficient.

coercive behavior behavior designed to force others to do one's bidding, often masked as filial devotion or as marital or parental concern and sometimes expressed in undisguised form (e.g., "If you don't do what I say, I'll kill myself").

coexistence hypothesis a theoretical explanation of the MISINFORMATION EFFECT stating that when misleading information is introduced after a witnessed event, it exists in competition with the original memory of the event. The false information is more accessible due to the RECENCY EFFECT and is more likely to be retrieved upon questioning, leading to erroneous reporting of the event. Compare ALTERATION HYPOTHESIS.

cofacilitator *n.* a therapist or student in training who assists in leading a therapy group. The cofacilitator may act as an observer or as one who balances the approach of the other group leader.

coffee *n.* a product derived from evergreen trees of the genus *Coffea*, which grow wild or are cultivated in tropical regions worldwide, including Brazil, Columbia, and Ethiopia. Of more than 100 species of *Coffea*, two are commercially important sources of coffee beans (seeds), used in beverages. They are *C. arabica* and *C. robusta*, whose beans contain significant concentrations (about 1% and 2%, respectively) of the stimulant CAFFEINE.

Cogentin *n.* a trade name for BENZTROPINE.

Cognex *n.* a trade name for TACRINE.

cognition *n.* **1.** all forms of knowing and awareness, such as perceiving, conceiving, remembering, reasoning, judging, imagining, and problem solving. Along with affect and conation, it is one of the three traditionally identified components of mind. **2.** an individual percept, idea, memory, or the like. **—cognitional** *adj.* **—cognitive** *adj.*

cognitive–affective crossfire a state of conflict between a person's cognitive responses to feedback about the self and his or her affective responses. In particular, an individual's thoughts (cognitions) may favor information that confirms his or her existing SELF-CONCEPT (see CONSISTENCY MOTIVE), whereas the same individual's emotional reactions (affects) may favor pleasant or positive views of the self (see SELF-ENHANCEMENT MOTIVE).

cognitive–affective personality system a theoretical conception of personality structure in which personality is viewed as a complex system that features a large number of highly interconnected cognitions and emotional tendencies. [developed by U.S. personality psychologists Walter Mischel (1930–) and Yuichi Shoda]

cognitive aids external representations that support various mental processes. Examples are reminders, checklists, and other prompts provided to prevent forgetting of critical tasks.

cognitive-analytic therapy a time-limited integrative, collaborative psychotherapy that emphasizes SCHEMAS and integrates principles and techniques from PSYCHODYNAMIC PSYCHOTHERAPY and COGNITIVE BEHAVIOR THERAPY.

cognitive anxiety the level of worry and apprehension an individual experiences in a particular situation.

cognitive appraisal theory the theory that cognitive evaluation is involved in the generation of each and every emotion (see APPRAISAL). This concept is more appropriately expressed in the COGNITIVE–MOTIVATIONAL–RELATIONAL THEORY, as the latter recognizes that cognition is only one of three simultaneously operating processes that contribute to the generation of any emotion. See also CORE RELATIONAL THEMES. [proposed by U.S. psychologist Richard S. Lazarus (1922–2002)]

cognitive arousal theory of emotion see SCHACHTER–SINGER THEORY.

cognitive balance theory see BALANCE THEORY.

cognitive behavioral couples therapy couples therapy that uses BEHAVIORAL COUPLES THERAPY techniques yet also focuses on the reciprocal influence of the partners' idiosyncratic patterns of ideas about each other and about couples in general. Interfering ideas are made conscious and explicit, and then modified to improve the couple's relationship using techniques modified from COGNITIVE BEHAVIOR THERAPY. Compare INTEGRATIVE BEHAVIORAL COUPLES THERAPY.

cognitive behavioral group therapy a type of group psychotherapy that uses techniques and methods of COGNITIVE BEHAVIOR THERAPY, such as modeling, restructuring thoughts, relaxation training, and communication skills training, to achieve behaviorally defined goals. Groups can include clients with diverse issues or can be limited to clients with specific problems (e.g., agoraphobia, anger). See also BECK THERAPY.

cognitive behavior modification see COGNITIVE BEHAVIOR THERAPY.

cognitive behavior theory any theory deriving from general behavioral theory that considers cognitive or thought processes as significant mediators of behavioral change. A central feature in the theoretical formulations of the process is that the human organism responds primarily to cognitive representations of its environments rather than to the environments themselves. The theory has led to popular therapeutic procedures that incorporate cognitive behavior techniques to effect changes in self-image as well as behaviors.

cognitive behavior therapy (**CBT**) a form of psychotherapy that integrates theories of cognition and learning with treatment techniques derived from COGNITIVE THERAPY and BEHAVIOR THERAPY. CBT assumes that cognitive, emotional, and behavioral variables are functionally interrelated. Treatment is aimed at identifying and modifying the client's maladaptive thought processes and problematic behaviors through COGNITIVE RESTRUCTURING and behavioral techniques to achieve change. Also called **cognitive behavior modification**; **cognitive behavioral therapy**.

cognitive click a moment in psychotherapy in which it becomes suddenly clear to the client that his or her thinking is incorrect and therefore that he or she must change his or her attitudes and beliefs.

cognitive closure 1. the state in which an individual recognizes that he or she has achieved understanding of something. **2.** the final stage in figuratively seeing the total picture and how all pieces of it fit together.

cognitive complexity the state or quality of a thought process that involves numerous constructs, with many interrelationships among them. Such processing is often experienced as difficult or effortful.

C

cognitive conditioning a process in which a stimulus is repeatedly paired with an imagined or anticipated response or behavior. Cognitive conditioning has been used as a therapeutic technique, in which case the stimulus is typically aversive. For example, the client imagines that he or she is smoking a cigarette and gives himself or herself a pinch; the procedure is repeated until the thought produces the effect of discouraging the behavior. See also COGNITIVE REHEARSAL.

cognitive consistency theory any of a broad class of theories postulating that attitude change is a result of the desire to maintain consistency among elements of a cognitive system. See also BALANCE THEORY; COGNITIVE DISSONANCE THEORY; CONGRUITY THEORY.

cognitive consonance in COGNITIVE DISSONANCE THEORY, a situation in which two cognitive elements are consistent with one another, that is, one cognitive element follows from or is implied by the other.

cognitive control the set of processes that organize, plan, and schedule mental operations. See also CONTROL PROCESSES; EXECUTIVE.

cognitive coping strategy any COPING STRATEGY in which mental activity is used to counter the problem or situation. Examples include thinking out the cause of the problem, working out how others might handle it, diverting one's attention to something less stressful or anxiety-provoking (e.g., remembering happy times, solving mathematical problems), and meditation or prayer.

cognitive decline reduction in one or more cognitive abilities, such as memory, awareness, judgment, and mental acuity, across the adult life span. The presence and degree of decline varies with the cognitive ability being measured: Fluid abilities often show greater declines than crystallized abilities (see CATTELL–HORN THEORY OF INTELLIGENCE). Cognitive decline is a part of normal healthy aging, but a severe decline could be symptomatic of disease: It is the primary symptom of disease-induced dementia (e.g., ALZHEIMER'S DISEASE).

cognitive deconstruction a mental state characterized by lack of emotion, the absence of any sense of future, a concentration on the here-and-now, and focus on concrete sensation rather than abstract thought. People may cultivate this state to escape from emotional distress or troublesome thoughts.

cognitive defect any impairment in perceptual, learning, memory, linguistic, or thinking abilities. Multiple significant cognitive defects are characteristic of DEMENTIA.

cognitive deficit performance on intellectual and other mentally based tasks (e.g., those involving memory), as measured by individually administered standardized assessments (verbal and nonverbal cognitive measures), that is substantially below that expected given the individual's chronological age and formal educational experience.

cognitive derailment the often abrupt shifting of thoughts or associations so that they do not follow one another in a logical sequence. Cognitive derailment is a symptom of schizophrenia; the term is essentially equivalent to THOUGHT DERAILMENT. See DERAILMENT. See also COGNITIVE SLIPPAGE.

cognitive development the growth and maturation of thinking processes of all kinds, including perceiving, concept formation, remembering, problem solving, imagining, and reasoning.

cognitive developmental theory any theory that attempts to explain the mechanisms underlying the growth and maturation of thinking processes. Explanations may be in terms of stages of development in which the changes in thinking are relatively abrupt and discontinuous, or the changes may be viewed as occurring gradually and continuously over time.

cognitive discrimination the ability to make distinctions between concepts and to distinguish between examples and nonexamples of a particular concept.

cognitive disorder any disorder that involves impairment of the EXECUTIVE FUNCTIONS, such as organization, regulation, and perception. These fundamental abilities can affect performance in many cognitive areas, including speed, reasoning, planning, judgment, decision making, emotional engagement, perseveration, impulse control, temper control, awareness, attention, language, learning, memory, and timing.

cognitive dissonance an unpleasant psychological state resulting from inconsistency between two or more elements in a cognitive system. It is presumed to involve a state of heightened arousal and to have characteristics similar to physiological drives (e.g., hunger). Thus, cognitive dissonance creates a motivational drive in an individual to reduce the dissonance (see DISSONANCE REDUCTION). See also COGNITIVE CONSONANCE. [first described by Leon FESTINGER]

cognitive dissonance theory a theory proposing that people have a fundamental motivation to maintain consistency among elements in their cognitive systems. When inconsistency occurs, people experience an unpleasant psychological state that motivates them to reduce the dissonance in a variety of ways (see DISSONANCE REDUCTION). See also COGNITIVE CONSONANCE; NEW-LOOK THEORY OF COGNITIVE DISSONANCE; SELF-CONSISTENCY PERSPECTIVE OF COGNITIVE DISSONANCE THEORY. [first proposed by Leon FESTINGER]

cognitive distortion faulty or inaccurate thinking, perception, or belief. An example is OVERGENERALIZATION. Cognitive distortion is a normal psychological process that can occur in all people to a greater or lesser extent.

cognitive dysfunction any disruption in mental activities associated with thinking, knowing, and remembering.

cognitive electrophysiology see ELECTROENCEPHALOGRAPHY.

cognitive enhancers see NOOTROPIC.

cognitive faculty a specific aspect or domain of mental function, such as language, object recognition, or face perception.

cognitive flooding a method used in psychotherapy, mainly to treat phobias, in which the client is encouraged to focus on negative or aversive mental images to generate emotional states similar to those experienced when faced with a feared object or situation. The simulated fear is then seen to be manageable and associated with images that will reduce the original fear. See also IMPLOSIVE THERAPY.

cognitive generalization **1.** the ability to apply knowledge, concepts, or cognitive skills acquired in one context or domain to problems in another. See GENERALIZATION. **2.** a general principle of human cognition, such as association or categorization, that applies across cognitive faculties or domains.

cognitive hypothesis testing problem-solving behavior in which the individual derives a set of rules (hypotheses) that are then sampled and tested until the one rule is discovered that consistently results in correct solutions to the problem.

cognitive interview a structured technique developed for enhancing eyewitness recollection in criminal investigation. It relies on principles of cognition and memory retrieval, such as reporting everything (however seemingly irrelevant), recalling events in different order, and changing perspectives. See also AIDED RECALL.

cognitive learning the acquisition and retention of a mental representation of information and the use of this representation as the basis for behavior.

cognitive learning theory any theory postulating that learning requires central constructs and new ways of perceiving events. An example is the purposive behaviorism of Edward C. TOLMAN. Cognitive theory is usually contrasted with behavioral learning theories, which suggest that behaviors or responses are acquired through experience.

cognitive load the relative demand imposed by a particular task, in terms of mental resources required. Also called **mental load**; **mental workload**. See also COGNITIVE OVERLOAD.

cognitive map a mental understanding of an environment, formed through trial and error as well as observation. The concept is based on the assumption that an individual seeks and collects contextual clues, such as environmental relationships, rather than acting as a passive receptor of information needed to achieve a goal. Human beings and other animals have well-developed cognitive maps that contain spatial information enabling them to orient themselves and find their way in the real world; symbolism and meaning are also contained in such maps. See also MENTAL MAP. [introduced by Edward Chace TOLMAN]

cognitive mediation the processing that is presumed to occur in the mind between arrival of a stimulus and initiation of the response.

cognitive model a theoretical view of thought and mental operations, which provides explanations for observed phenomena and makes predictions about an unknown future. People are continually creating and accessing internal representations (models) of what they are experiencing in the world for the purposes of perception, comprehension, and behavior selection (action).

cognitive–motivational–relational theory an extension of the COGNITIVE APPRAISAL THEORY that puts equal emphasis on three processes involved in the generation of an emotion: (a) appraisal (the cognitive process), (b) the central role of the individual's strivings, intentions, and goals (the motivational process), and (c) the relevance of external events to these strivings (the relational process). [proposed by U.S. psychologist Richard S. Lazarus (1922–2002)]

cognitive neuropsychology the study of the structure and function of the brain as it relates to perception, reasoning, remembering, and all other forms of knowing and awareness. Cognitive neuropsychology focuses on examining the effects of brain damage on thought processes—typically through the use of in-depth SINGLE-CASE EXPERIMENTAL DESIGN—so as to construct models of normal cognitive functioning.

cognitive neuroscience a branch of NEUROSCIENCE and BIOLOGICAL PSYCHOLOGY that focuses on the neural mechanisms of cognition. Although overlapping with the study of the mind in COGNITIVE PSYCHOLOGY, cognitive neuroscience, with its grounding in such areas as experimental psychology, neurobiology, physics, and mathematics, specifically examines how mental processes occur in the brain, but the two perspectives continually exert significant influence on each other.

cognitive operations the mental manipulation of MENTAL REPRESENTATIONS. See also SYMBOLIC PROCESS; THINKING.

cognitive overload the situation in which the demands placed on a person by mental work (the COGNITIVE LOAD) are greater than the person's mental abilities can cope with. See also SENSORY OVERLOAD; STIMULUS OVERLOAD.

cognitive penetrability the capacity of a mental process to be influenced by an individual's knowledge, beliefs, or goals. Reflex behavior is said to be **cognitively impenetrable**.

cognitive plan in problem solving, a mental

outline of the steps to be undertaken to solve a problem or complete a task.

cognitive process any of the mental functions assumed to be involved in the acquisition, storage, interpretation, manipulation, transformation, and use of knowledge. These processes encompass such areas as attention, perception, learning, and problem solving and are commonly understood through several basic theories, including the SERIAL PROCESSING approach, the PARALLEL PROCESSING approach, and a combination theory, which assumes that cognitive processes are both serial and parallel, depending on the demands of the task. This term is often used synonymously with MENTAL PROCESS.

cognitive processing therapy (**CPT**) a treatment approach, based on INFORMATION PROCESSING theory, that deals with the client's conceptualizations of the self, others, and events. It is often used in the treatment of posttraumatic stress disorder resulting from sexual assault to facilitate the expression of affect and the appropriate accommodation of the traumatic event with more general cognitive schemas regarding one's self and the world.

cognitive psychology the branch of psychology that explores the operation of mental processes related to perceiving, attending, thinking, language, and memory, mainly through inferences from behavior. The cognitive approach, which developed in the 1940s and 1950s, diverged sharply from contemporary BEHAVIORISM in (a) emphasizing unseen knowledge processes instead of directly observable behaviors and (b) arguing that the relationship between stimulus and response was complex and mediated rather than simple and direct. Its concentration on the higher mental processes also contrasted with the focus on the instincts and other unconscious forces typical of psychoanalysis. More recently, cognitive psychology has been influenced by approaches to INFORMATION PROCESSING and information theory developed in computer science and artificial intelligence. See also COGNITIVE SCIENCE.

cognitive rehabilitation specific REHABILITATION interventions designed to address problems in mental processing that are associated with chronic illness, brain injury, or trauma, such as stroke. Rehabilitation may include relearning specific mental abilities, strengthening unaffected abilities, or substituting new abilities to compensate for lost ones.

cognitive rehearsal a therapeutic technique in which a client imagines those situations that tend to produce anxiety or self-defeating behavior and then repeats positive coping statements or mentally rehearses more appropriate behavior.

cognitive reserve a capacity of the adult brain to sustain the effects of disease or injury without manifesting clinical symptoms of dysfunction that stems from the active acquisition and differential use of numerous sophisticated cognitive strategies to process information, solve problems, and perform tasks. In other words, individuals with high cognitive reserve have developed a variety of efficient neural networks and neural pathways to cope with brain pathology such that they can sustain a greater degree of underlying neurological damage than individuals with low cognitive reserve before becoming symptomatic. The size of this hypothesized supply of mental abilities and mechanisms, and thus the degree of protection against dementia and other neurological disorders it conveys, is believed to depend on the intellectual challenges a person experiences throughout life: more mental stimulation creates more reserve. Possible mechanisms by which this might occur include: (a) Knowledge can enhance memory in the form of richer and more elaborate encoding and more effective retrieval cues facilitated by a superior organizational structuring of information; (b) knowledge can result in easier access to relevant information and better organized representations of the problem, resulting in enhanced problem solving skills; (c) knowledge of past consequences of various alternatives can provide an effortless means of making accurate predictions regarding future consequences; (d) knowledge can enable reliance on previously compiled efficient algorithms, rather than on slow and controlled processes; and (e) knowledge of prior solutions to familiar problems can reduce online processing requirements. Commonly used indirect measures of cognitive reserve include number of years of education, literacy level, vocabulary knowledge, occupational complexity, estimated premorbid intelligence, and frequency and range of participation in mentally stimulating leisure activities (e.g., reading, writing, doing crossword puzzles, playing board or card games, playing music) or complex mental activities generally. It is important to distinguish cognitive reserve from the closely related BRAIN RESERVE, which posits that brain-based anatomical differences among people convey differential abilities to tolerate neuronal damage or loss before developing cognitive impairment. Despite the different emphases of the two terms, many researchers use them interchangeably.

cognitive response an evaluative response to attitude-relevant information. Cognitive responses include inferences generated about the information, assessments of its validity, and other evaluative reactions that may or may not be cognitive in nature (e.g., emotional responses). Positive cognitive responses are associated with the formation or bolstering of positive attitudes; negative cognitive responses are associated with the formation or bolstering of negative attitudes. See also ELABORATION.

cognitive restructuring a technique used in COGNITIVE THERAPY and COGNITIVE BEHAVIOR THERAPY to help the client identify his or her self-defeating beliefs or cognitive distortions, refute them, and then modify them so that they are adaptive and reasonable.

cognitive science an interdisciplinary approach to understanding the mind and mental processes that combines aspects of cognitive psychology, the philosophy of mind, epistemology, neuroscience, anthropology, psycholinguistics, and computer science.

cognitive self-guidance system the use of private, self-directed speech to guide problem-solving behavior. [proposed by Lev VYGOTSKY]

cognitive self-management the use of self-talk, imagery, or both to direct one's behavior in demanding or stressful situations.

cognitive set the predetermined way an individual construes a situation, which is based on a group of concepts, related to the self and other things, that determines a person's view of the world and influences his or her ability to negotiate living.

cognitive sign principle the belief that, through learning, stimuli come to signal outcomes or events in the environment. Edward C. TOLMAN offered cognitive sign learning as an alternative to the ideas of other behavioral theorists, such as Clark L. HULL, who postulated that stimuli become directly associated with responses.

cognitive slippage a mild form of disconnected thought processes or LOOSENING OF ASSOCIATIONS. Cognitive slippage may be seen in patients with a range of physical and mental disorders; it is a common characteristic of individuals with schizophrenia. [coined by Paul Everett MEEHL]

cognitive specificity hypothesis the belief that specific feeling states, such as depression and anxiety, are linked to particular kinds of automatic thoughts. [proposed by U.S. psychiatrist Aaron T. Beck (1921–)]

cognitive stage in some theories of cognitive development, especially that of Jean PIAGET, a plane of cognition that is characterized by a particular, qualitatively different level of thinking than preceding or later stages.

cognitive structure **1.** a mental framework, pattern, or SCHEMA that maintains and organizes a body of information relating to a particular topic. When a need arises for the cognitive structure, as in a college test, the individual is thought to engage in a memory search in which the stored cognitive structure is retrieved and applied to the present requirements. **2.** a unified structure of facts, beliefs, and attitudes about the world or society. See COGNITIVE MAP; CONCEPTUAL SYSTEM; FRAME OF REFERENCE.

cognitive style a person's characteristic mode of perceiving, thinking, remembering, and problem solving. Cognitive styles might differ in preferred elements or activities, such as group work versus working individually, more structured versus less defined activities, or visual versus verbal ENCODING. Other dimensions along which cognitive styles vary include REFLECTIVITY–IMPULSIVITY and ABSTRACT ATTITUDE versus CONCRETE ATTITUDE. Also called **learning style**; **thinking style**. Many use the term **learning style** interchangeably with cognitive style, whereas others use the former more specifically to mean a person's characteristic cognitive, affective, and psychological behaviors that influence his or her preferred instructional methods and interactions with the learning environment. See also THEORY OF MENTAL SELF-GOVERNMENT.

cognitive system a set of cognitions that are organized into a meaningful complex with implied or stated relationships between them. See also COMPLEX OF IDEAS.

cognitive task a task requiring mental processes related to such activities as perceiving, attending, problem solving, thinking, or remembering.

cognitive theory any theory of mind that focuses on mental activities, such as perceiving, attending, thinking, remembering, evaluating, planning, language, and creativity, especially one that suggests a model for the various processes involved.

cognitive therapy (CT) a form of psychotherapy based on the concept that emotional and behavioral problems in an individual are, at least in part, the result of maladaptive or faulty ways of thinking and distorted attitudes toward oneself and others. The objective of the therapy is to identify these faulty cognitions and replace them with more adaptive ones, a process known as COGNITIVE RESTRUCTURING. The therapist takes the role of an active guide who attempts to make the client aware of these distorted thinking patterns and who helps the client correct and revise his or her perceptions and attitudes by citing evidence to the contrary or by eliciting it from the client. See also COGNITIVE BEHAVIOR THERAPY. [developed by U.S. psychiatrist Aaron T. Beck (1921–)]

cognitive triad a set of three beliefs thought to characterize MAJOR DEPRESSIVE EPISODES. These are negative beliefs about the self, the world, and the future. Also called **negative triad**.

cognitive unconscious unreportable mental processes, collectively. There are many sources of evidence for a cognitive unconscious, including regularities of behavior due to habit or AUTOMATICITY, inferred grammatical rules, the details of sensorimotor control, and implicit knowledge after brain damage (see TACIT KNOWLEDGE). It is often contrasted with the psychoanalytically derived notion of the dynamic UNCONSCIOUS, which involves material that is kept out of consciousness to avoid anxiety, shame, or guilt.

cognitive vulnerability a set of beliefs or attitudes thought to make a person vulnerable to depression. Examples include PERFECTIONISM, DEPENDENCE, and SOCIOTROPY.

cognitivism *n.* adherence to the principles of COGNITIVE PSYCHOLOGY, especially as opposed to those of BEHAVIORISM.

cognizance need the drive to acquire knowledge through questions, exploration, and study. [proposed by U.S. psychologist Henry Alexander Murray (1893–1988)]

cohabitation *n.* the state or condition of living together as sexual and domestic partners without being married. See COMMON-LAW MARRIAGE; DOMESTIC PARTNERSHIP; SAME-SEX MARRIAGE. **—cohabit** *vb.* **—cohabitee** *n.*

coherence *n.* meaningful interconnections between distinct psychological entities. For example, a system of independent beliefs that is logically consistent from one belief to another would be described as **coherent**.

cohesion *n.* the unity or solidarity of a group, as indicated by the strength of the bonds that link group members to the group as a whole, the sense of belongingness and community within the group, the feelings of attraction for specific group members and the group itself experienced by individuals, and the degree to which members coordinate their efforts to achieve goals. According to Leon FESTINGER, cohesion reflects the degree to which group members are attracted to the group, which in turn depends on their liking for each other or the group's prestige or activities. The higher the cohesion, the stronger the members' motivation to adhere to the group's standards. Group cohesion is frequently considered essential to effective GROUP THERAPY. Also called **cohesiveness**; **group cohesion**. **—cohesive** *adj.*

cohort *n.* a group of people who have experienced a significant life event (e.g., marriage) during the same period of time. The term usually refers to a **birth cohort**, or generation.

cohort sampling a SAMPLING method in which one or more COHORTS are selected for observation.

coil *n.* see INTRAUTERINE DEVICE.

coital anorgasmia failure of a woman to reach orgasm during penile–vaginal intercourse. Studies show that roughly half of women do not have coital orgasms in the absence of concurrent clitoral stimulation. Sex therapists do not consider this a dysfunction; if the woman can have orgasm with her partner in other ways, and enjoys intercourse, there is no requirement that both happen simultaneously.

coital position any of various postures that may be assumed by sexual partners during intercourse.

coitus *n.* an act of sexual union, usually the insertion of the penis into the vagina followed by ejaculation. Variations include **coitus a tergo**, in which the penis is inserted from the rear; and **coitus inter femora** (**interfemoral sex**), in which the penis is inserted between the pressed thighs of the female. Also called **coition**; **intercourse**; **sexual intercourse**. See also ANAL INTERCOURSE; CAREZZA. **—coital** *adj.*

coitus analis see ANAL INTERCOURSE.

coitus a tergo see COITUS.

coitus in ano see ANAL INTERCOURSE.

coitus inter femora see COITUS.

coitus interruptus the withdrawal of the penis during intercourse, prior to orgasm, with orgasm occurring external to the vagina. This is done mainly to reduce the likelihood of conception but is not very effective, as some semen is often released prior to orgasm.

coitus intra mammas coitus in which the penis is inserted between the breasts of the female.

coitus prolongatus see CAREZZA.

coitus reservatus sexual intercourse in which the man suppresses the ejaculation of semen. Coitus reservatus has been practiced for generations in eastern Asia, by the application of opium paste to the glans penis to reduce its sensitivity. In the Oneida community (a 19th-century Methodist commune in the northeastern United States), young men were encouraged to practice coitus reservatus with menopausal women until they were able to achieve a state of male continence. See also CAREZZA.

coke *n.* slang for COCAINE.

cola nut see KOLA NUT.

cold cognition a mental process or activity that does not involve feelings or emotions. For instance, reading a list of nonsense syllables or factoids (brief pieces of invented or inaccurate information) typically involves cold cognition.

cold emotion a reaction to some stimulants (e.g., epinephrine) that entails the physiological responses of emotional arousal without an identifiable affective root.

coldness *n.* a psychological characteristic featuring a relative absence of empathy toward and emotional support of others.

cold turkey the abrupt cessation of the use of drugs, particularly opiates, without cushioning the impact by the use of methadone or tranquilizers. The name refers specifically to the chills and gooseflesh experienced during OPIOID WITHDRAWAL.

coleadership *n.* leadership by two equal therapists or counselors, often used in GROUP THERAPY.

colera *n.* see BILIS.

colitis *n.* inflammation of the colon, the main part of the large intestine. Colitis may be caused or aggravated by emotional disturbances, such as depression or anxiety.

collaborative care 1. collaboration between two or more disciplines or practitioners to assess a client's problem or problems, develop a treatment plan, and monitor progress. **2.** collaboration across agencies to coordinate services to a particular client or client group.

collaborative empiricism an approach to psychotherapy in which the therapist and client work together as equal partners in addressing issues and fostering change through mutual understanding, communication, and respect. The therapist views the client as a peer who is capable of objective analyses and conclusions.

collaborative family health care a form of interdisciplinary practice that asserts that health events occur simultaneously on biological, psychological, and social levels and that offers treatment incorporating individual, family, community, and cultural influences. Collaborative clinicians share decision making and responsibility with patients and their families and integrate clinical expertise from relevant disciplines to provide patients with comprehensive and coordinated care.

collaborative filtering 1. in therapeutic and social interactions, the cooperative screening out of unproductive information and ideas during a discussion. **2.** any process of acquiring from other people the information needed to make a choice or decision, whether by asking them individually (word of mouth) or by polling them in large numbers.

collaborative therapy 1. any form of therapy employing COLLABORATIVE EMPIRICISM. **2.** COUPLES THERAPY conducted by two therapists, each seeing one partner but conferring from time to time. Also called **collaborative marriage therapy**; **collaborative marital therapy**.

collective experience in group psychotherapy, the common body of emotional experience that develops out of the individual members' identification with each other's problems and mutual support and empathy. [first described by 20th-century Russian-born U.S. psychotherapist Samuel Richard Slavson]

collective formation 1. generally, the initial constitution of a social aggregate or group, particularly when a group forms naturally as individuals interact with one another frequently. **2.** in the psychoanalytic theory of Sigmund FREUD, the human tendency to form and interact in groups, as when a multiplicity of individuals take the same object as the EGO-IDEAL.

collective hypnotization the act of hypnotizing a group of people at the same time. Also called **group hypnosis**.

collective hysteria the spontaneous outbreak of atypical thoughts, feelings, or actions in a group or social aggregate. Manifestations may include psychogenic illness, collective hallucinations, and bizarre actions. Instances of epidemic manias and panics, such as listeners' reactions to the Orson Welles broadcast based on H. G. Wells's *War of the Worlds* in 1938, have been attributed to contagious hysteria (see CONTAGION) rather than conventional, individualistic disorders. Also called **group hysteria**; **mass hysteria**.

collective method any method that relies on groups rather than single individuals to solve problems, perform tasks, make decisions, and so on. In psychological treatment, for example, the collective method is seen in the use of GROUP THERAPY, ENCOUNTER GROUPS, and the like.

collective neurosis an archaic name for any fairly mild and transient disorder (e.g., hysteria, an obsession or phobia, anxiety) exhibited by an entire group of people rather than by a single individual. Compare COLLECTIVE PSYCHOSIS. See COLLECTIVE HYSTERIA.

collective psychosis an archaic name for any grossly distorted reaction (e.g., hallucination, depression, delusion) exhibited by an entire group of people rather than by a single individual. Compare COLLECTIVE NEUROSIS. See COLLECTIVE HYSTERIA.

collective self the part of the self (or self-concept) that derives from one's relationships with other people and memberships in groups or categories, ranging from family to nationality or race. The collective self is distinguished from the PUBLIC SELF and the PRIVATE SELF. Also called **social identity**. See also SOCIAL SELF.

collective suicide see MASS SUICIDE.

collective unconscious the part of the UNCONSCIOUS that, according to Carl JUNG, is common to all humankind and contains the inherited accumulation of primitive human experiences in the form of ideas and images called ARCHETYPES. It is the deepest and least accessible part of the unconscious mind. See also PERSONAL UNCONSCIOUS; RACIAL MEMORY.

collectivism *n.* **1.** the tendency to view oneself as a member of a larger (family or social) group, rather than as an isolated, independent being. **2.** a social or cultural tradition, ideology, or personal outlook that emphasizes the unity of the group or community rather than each person's individuality. Asian, African, and South American societies tend to put more value on collectivism than do Western societies, in so far as they stress cooperation, communalism, constructive interdependence, and conformity to cultural roles and mores. Compare INDIVIDUALISM. **—collectivist** *adj.*

collegial model any collaborative approach that encourages equal participation by all interactants while minimizing status differences. In research, for example, this approach enjoins researchers to involve participants fully in the research process; in therapeutic settings the model requires therapists to treat clients as equals.

collusion *n.* in psychotherapy, the process in which a therapist consciously or unconsciously participates with a client or third party to avoid an issue that needs to be addressed. **—collusional** *adj.*

collusional marriage a marriage in which one partner instigates or engages in inordinate, deficient, irregular, or illegal conduct, and the other covertly endorses it or covers it up, while ostensibly being in the role of passive victim or martyr. See also MARITAL SKEW.

coma *n.* a profound state of unconsciousness characterized by little or no response to stimuli, absence of reflexes, and suspension of voluntary activity. Common causes include severe brain injury, intracranial tumor, encephalitis, cerebral hemorrhage or embolism, diabetes, and drug or alcohol intoxication. Also called **comatose state**. See also GLASGOW COMA SCALE.

coma therapy a treatment for schizophrenia, developed in the 1930s but rarely used after 1960, in which hypoglycemia was induced by intramuscular injection of insulin to produce a temporary coma. Inductions might last for 15 to 60 min, and a full course of coma treatment typically involved numerous coma inductions over a given period. Also called **insulin-coma therapy**; **insulin-shock therapy**.

combat stress reactions (**CSR**) psychological reactions to traumatic events in military operations, which can range from mild to severe and are normal reactions to the abnormal events. In World War I such reactions were known as SHELL SHOCK, whereas in World War II the terms **battle fatigue**, **combat fatigue**, **combat hysteria**, and **combat neurosis** were widely used. In *DSM–IV–TR* they are categorized as POSTTRAUMATIC STRESS DISORDERS. See also STRESS CASUALTY.

combat stress reduction measures designed to develop skills to reduce COMBAT STRESS REACTIONS. Stress reduction entails remediation procedures, regulatory techniques, and preventive strategies (psychological coping techniques).

combination therapy the application of two or more distinct therapeutic approaches by the same therapist to a client's presenting problem. It is distinct from ADJUNCTIVE THERAPY, which involves multiple practitioners.

combined therapy 1. psychotherapy in which the client is engaged in two or more treatments with the same or different therapists. For example, COUPLES THERAPY may include group therapy with several other couples in addition to individual therapy or CONJOINT THERAPY for each couple. **2.** treatment using a combination of psychotherapy and medication. See also ADJUNCTIVE THERAPY; ADJUVANT THERAPY.

combined treatment see COMBINED THERAPY.

coming out revealing that one is gay, lesbian, bisexual, or transgender. Such a declaration can sometimes lead to problems with the individual's family, employers, or friends and can therefore be a difficult step, even for those who accept and are comfortable with their sexual orientation. Also called **coming out of the closet**.

commissure *n.* a structure that forms a bridge or junction between two anatomical areas, particularly the two cerebral hemispheres or the halves of the spinal cord. Examples include the two key landmarks in brain mapping: the **anterior commissure**, a bundle of myelinated fibers that joins the TEMPORAL LOBES and contains fibers of the olfactory tract; and the **posterior commissure**, a bundle of myelinated fibers that connects regions in the midbrain and DIENCEPHALON. See also CORPUS CALLOSUM; GRAY COMMISSURE; WHITE COMMISSURE. **—commissural** *adj.*

commissurotomy *n.* surgical transection or severing of a COMMISSURE, especially surgical separation of the cerebral hemispheres of the brain by severing the CORPUS CALLOSUM (called **callosectomy**, **callosotomy**, or **corpuscallosotomy**) and often the anterior commissure. This procedure is used clinically to treat severe epilepsy and has been used experimentally in animals to study the functions of each hemisphere. Because commissurotomy allows each hemisphere to function relatively independently, considerable information has been obtained about HEMISPHERIC LATERALIZATION in humans and animals. Research in this area was pioneered by Roger SPERRY, who—by directing stimuli to one or the other hemisphere—provided compelling evidence that the two hemispheres have different roles (see also CHIMERIC STIMULATION). Also called **split-brain procedure**; **split-brain technique**.

commitment *n.* confinement to a mental institution by court order following certification by appropriate psychiatric or other mental health authorities. The process may be voluntary but is generally involuntary. See CERTIFICATION LAWS. See also CIVIL COMMITMENT; CRIMINAL COMMITMENT; OBSERVATION COMMITMENT; TEMPORARY COMMITMENT; VOLUNTARY ADMISSION.

commitment laws legislation governing the holding of a patient in a mental hospital involuntarily upon certification. See CERTIFICATION LAWS.

commitment therapy see ACCEPTANCE AND COMMITMENT THERAPY.

common factors in psychotherapy, variables that are common to various therapies with individuals, such as THERAPEUTIC ALLIANCE and length of treatment, as opposed to factors that are unique to a particular therapy, such as the use of interpretation. THERAPEUTIC FACTORS are similar, but typically apply to therapies with groups.

common-law marriage a relationship between an unmarried but long-term cohabiting couple that is considered legally equivalent to marriage. Most states in the United States do not recognize common-law marriages, although cohabitees may be regarded as equivalent to married partners for some purposes.

common trait in the personality theory of Gordon W. ALLPORT, any of a number of enduring characteristics that describe or determine an individual's behavior across a variety of situations and that are common to many people and similarly expressed. Common traits, such as assertiveness, thus serve as a basis for comparison of one person to another and are distinct from PERSONAL DISPOSITIONS.

communal relationship a relationship in which interaction is governed primarily by consideration of the other's needs and wishes. This contrasts with an **exchange relationship**, in which the people involved are concerned mainly with receiving as much as they give. See also SOCIAL EXCHANGE THEORY. [discussed by U.S. social psychologists Margaret Clark and Judson Mills]

communicated authenticity, regard, empathy (**CARE**) qualities of a psychotherapist regarded by some theorists as necessary for therapy to be effective and, ultimately, successful. CARE is considered essential to CLIENT-CENTERED THERAPY.

communication *n.* the transmission of information, which may be by verbal (oral or written) or nonverbal means (see NONVERBAL COMMUNICATION). Humans communicate to relate and exchange ideas, knowledge, feelings, and experiences and for many other interpersonal and social purposes. Communication is studied by cognitive and experimental psychologists, and COMMUNICATION DISORDERS are treated by mental and behavioral health therapists and by speech and language therapists.

communication apprehension anxiety related to initiating or maintaining conversation with others. This is a common feature of SOCIAL PHOBIA. See also PUBLIC-SPEAKING ANXIETY.

communication deviance (**CD**) lack of clarity in communication, making it hard to follow and difficult for the listener to share a common focus of attention and meaning with the speaker. Communication deviance is thought to be a long-term trait within families that may engender inefficient patterns of thinking and information processing. It is also thought to be associated with schizophrenia and other psychological disorders.

communication disorder any of a group of disorders characterized by difficulties with speech and language. In *DSM–IV–TR* communication disorders include EXPRESSIVE LANGUAGE DISORDER, MIXED RECEPTIVE-EXPRESSIVE LANGUAGE DISORDER, PHONOLOGICAL DISORDER, STUTTERING, and COMMUNICATION DISORDER NOT OTHERWISE SPECIFIED.

communication disorder not otherwise specified in *DSM–IV–TR*, a communication disorder that does not meet the diagnostic criteria for any of the specific disorders of this category. An example is a VOICE DISORDER.

communication skills training an intervention that teaches individuals to express themselves clearly and directly and to listen in an active and empathic way, using such techniques as feedback and modeling, in group, family, or work contexts. Training sessions typically focus on a specific theme (e.g., active listening, problem solving, or conflict resolution) after which homework is assigned. Initially developed for couples and families, the training is now used with such populations as people with developmental impairment and with teams in industry settings.

communion principle a theory that the first requisite of individual and group psychotherapy is a sense of unity and mutuality between client and therapist, thus enabling both parties to feel that they are engaged in a common enterprise to bring about improvement for the client.

communities for people with mental retardation service settings that consist of clusters of houses in which adults with mental retardation who can function somewhat independently participate in work and daily routines with people without disabilities. With the help of staff members, these adults manage the houses independently—planning meals, purchasing and preparing food, and participating in household maintenance chores—and enjoy leisure activities with their peers. In many instances staff live in the community as well.

community action group a group of citizens organized to campaign against specific problems within the local community, such as inadequate delivery of health services, homelessness, or crime.

community care in psychiatry, psychology, and rehabilitation, comprehensive community-based services and supports for people with developmental or physical disabilities. These facilities or services include halfway houses, group homes, sheltered workshops and supported work arrangements, supervised and supportive residences for people with multiple disabilities or mental retardation, special education or integrated education programs for children and young people, in-home treatment and family support, personal-care or home-care assistance, case management or service coordination, cooperative living, and hospital-based or free-standing clinics.

community-centered approach a concerted, coordinated approach to such problems as mental disorder, delinquency, and substance abuse on the part of agencies and facilities in the local community or catchment area. The community-centered approach holds that since these problems developed in the community, efforts at prevention and treatment should be community-based rather than being the province primarily of state institutions or federal agencies. See COMMUNITY MENTAL HEALTH CENTER; COMMUNITY MENTAL HEALTH PROGRAM; COMMUNITY SERVICES.

C

community inclusion the practice of accepting and encouraging the presence and participation of people with disabilities, in particular developmental disabilities, in the full range of social, educational, work, and community activities.

community integration the practice of assisting people with disabilities, especially developmental disabilities, to participate in community activities. Those with such disabilities are encouraged to attend community functions, engage in social interactions with peers and community members without disabilities, and join formal and informal community groups.

community mental health activities undertaken in the community, rather than in institutional settings, to promote mental health. The community approach focuses primarily on the total population of a single catchment area and involves overall planning and demographic analyses. It emphasizes preventive services as distinguished from therapeutic services (e.g., by identifying sources of stress within the community) and seeks to provide a continuous, comprehensive system of services designed to meet all mental health-related needs in the community. Mental health is approached indirectly through consultation and education, with emphasis on such strategies as BRIEF PSYCHOTHERAPY and CRISIS INTERVENTION and on using such workers as paraprofessionals and indigenous mental health workers.

community mental health center (**CMHC**) a community-based facility or group of facilities providing a full range of prevention, treatment, and rehabilitation services, sometimes organized as a practical alternative to the largely custodial care given in mental hospitals. Typical services are full diagnostic evaluation; outpatient individual and group psychotherapy; emergency inpatient treatment; specialized clinics for people with substance abuse and for disturbed children and families; aftercare (foster homes, halfway houses, home visiting); vocational, educational, and social rehabilitation programs for current and former patients; consultation to physicians, members of the clergy, courts, schools, health departments, and welfare agencies; and training for all types of mental health personnel. Also called **comprehensive mental health center**.

community mental health program an integrated program designed to meet the overall mental health needs of a particular community, including inpatient, outpatient, and emergency treatment; special facilities for treating children and patients with alcohol and drug dependence; and educational, counseling, rehabilitation, research, and training programs. See COMMUNITY-CENTERED APPROACH; COMMUNITY MENTAL HEALTH CENTER.

community mental health services see COMMUNITY SERVICES.

community mental health training training for mental health professionals in order to facilitate programs and services offered to the community.

community needs assessment see NEEDS ASSESSMENT.

Community Notification Act see MEGAN'S LAW.

community prevention and intervention organized efforts by professionals, indigenous nonprofessionals, and others to implement preventive programs as well as systems for intervention in dealing constructively with problems in the community, such as substance abuse, homelessness, child abuse, juvenile delinquency, cigarette smoking, and a high suicide rate. These efforts are typically most effective where the residents are themselves involved in dealing with such problems through existing community groups, such as neighborhood councils, block committees, service groups, social and fraternal organizations, and community educational and self-help programs.

community psychology the branch of psychology concerned with person–environment interactions and the way society affects individual and community functioning. Community psychology focuses on social issues, social institutions, and other settings that influence individuals, groups, and organizations. Community researchers examine the ways that individuals interact with each other, social groups (e.g., clubs, churches, schools, families), and the larger culture and environment. Research findings and methods are applied with regard to poverty, substance abuse, violence, school failure, and many other social issues. See COMMUNITY-CENTERED APPROACH; COMMUNITY SERVICES.

community residence a residential setting, usually serving 3 to 15 people and located in a regular house, with live-in or shift staffing. Community residences, some of which provide clinical services in addition to supervision, personal assistance, and training in everyday living skills, represent the most common out-of-home residential setting for people with mental retardation or developmental disabilities.

community services the complex of community-based services and facilities designed to maintain health and welfare, including mental health clinics, public health and adoption services, family services, vocational training facilities, rehabilitation centers, and living facilities (e.g., halfway houses, home care, and foster-family care). Also called **community mental health services**. See COMMUNITY CARE; COMMUNITY-CENTERED APPROACH.

community social worker a social worker who maintains liaison between local, state, and federal government officials and the public on matters affecting the physical and psychological health of the community. For example, community social workers may try to raise the social consciousness of the community regarding recreational facilities, adequate housing, local employment problems, and environmental obstacles to the mobility of people with physical impairment.

community speech and hearing center see SPEECH, LANGUAGE, AND HEARING CENTER.

comorbidity *n.* the simultaneous presence in an individual of two or more mental or physical illnesses, diseases, or disorders. **—comorbid** *adj.*

companionate love a type of LOVE characterized by strong feelings of intimacy and affection for another person but not accompanied by strong passion or emotional arousal in the other's presence. In these respects, companionate love is distinguished from PASSIONATE LOVE. From the perspective of Robert J. Sternberg's TRIANGULAR THEORY OF LOVE, the relationship is high in intimacy and commitment.

comparable groups two or more representative samples drawn from the same population for the purpose of observation or experiment.

comparison level (**CL**) in SOCIAL EXCHANGE THEORY, the standard by which an individual evaluates the quality of any social relationship in which he or she is currently engaged. The CL derives from the average of all outcomes experienced by the individual in previous similar relationships or observed by the individual in similar relationships of others. In most cases, individuals whose prior relationships yielded positive rewards with few costs will have higher CLs than those who experienced fewer rewards and more costs in prior relationships. If the reward-to-cost ratio of the current relationship falls below the CL, the individual will experience dissatisfaction. [proposed in 1959 by U.S. social psychologists Harold H. Kelley (1921–2003) and John W. Thibaut (1917–1986)]

comparison level for alternatives (**CLAlt**) in SOCIAL EXCHANGE THEORY, a standard used by individuals making decisions about whether to remain in a relationship. According to this theory, such decisions are based on a comparison of the outcomes (reward-to-cost ratios) of the current relationship with the possible outcomes of available alternative relationships. If the latter is higher, the relationship will become unstable and may not last. [proposed in 1959 by U.S. social psychologists John Thibaut (1917–1986) and Harold H. Kelley (1921–2003)]

comparison stimulus (**Co**) one of a number of stimuli to be compared with a standard stimulus.

compartmentalization *n.* a DEFENSE MECHANISM in which thoughts and feelings that seem to conflict or to be incompatible are isolated from each other in separate and apparently impermeable psychic compartments. In the classical psychoanalytic tradition, compartmentalization produces fragmentation of the EGO, which ideally should be able to tolerate ambiguity and ambivalence. See also ISOLATION. **—compartmentalize** *vb.*

compassion *n.* a strong feeling of SYMPATHY with another person's feelings of sorrow or distress, usually involving a desire to help or comfort that person. **—compassionate** *adj.*

Compassionate Friends a voluntary organization that offers support, friendship, and understanding to parents and siblings grieving the death of a child. See SELF-HELP GROUP.

compassion fatigue the BURNOUT and stress-related symptoms experienced by caregivers and other helping professionals in reaction to working with traumatized people over an extended period of time. See also POSTTRAUMATIC STRESS DISORDER. [defined by U.S. psychologist Charles R. Figley (1944–)]

Compazine *n.* a trade name for PROCHLORPERAZINE.

compensation *n.* **1.** substitution or development of strength or capability in one area to offset real or imagined lack or deficiency in another. This may be referred to as **overcompensation** when the substitute behavior exceeds what might actually be necessary in terms of level of compensation for the lack or deficiency. Compensation may be a conscious or unconscious process. In his classical psychoanalytic theory, Sigmund FREUD described compensation as a DEFENSE MECHANISM that protects the individual against the conscious realization of such lacks or deficiencies. The idea of compensation is central to Alfred ADLER's theory of personality, which sees all human striving as a response to feelings of inferiority (see also INFERIORITY COMPLEX). However, many psychologists emphasize the positive aspects of compensation in mitigating the effects of a weakness or deficiency (see COMPENSATORY MECHANISM). For example, it can be regarded as an important component of successful aging because it reduces the negative effects of cognitive and physical decline associated with the aging process. **2.** in Jean PIAGET's theory of cognitive development, a mental process in which one realizes that for any operation there exists another operation that compensates for the effects of the first, that is, a change in one dimension can compensate for changes in another. Also called **reciprocity**. **—compensate** *vb.* **—compensatory** *adj.*

compensatory mechanism a cognitive process that is used to offset a cognitive weakness. For example, someone who is weaker in spatial abilities than in verbal abilities might use compensatory mechanisms to attempt to solve spatial problems, such as mentally rotating a geometric figure by using verbal processes. The underlying theory is that intelligence partly consists of finding ways to compensate for the skills that one has lost over time or in which one was not adept in the first place. See also COMPENSATION.

compensatory reflex a response that is opposite to, and therefore compensates for, another response. For example, a compensatory response to the suppression of pain by opioid drugs would be an increase in pain sensitivity, that is, with extended use, more of the drug is needed to achieve the same effect.

compensatory self-enhancement a strategy for self-presentation or boosting self-esteem in which people respond to bad feedback in one sphere by focusing on or emphasizing their positive traits in an unrelated sphere. The positive traits seem to offset the unwelcome implications of the bad feedback. Also called **self-affirmation**.

competence *n.* **1.** the ability to exert control over one's life, to cope with specific problems effectively, and to make changes to one's behavior and one's environment, as opposed to the mere ability to adjust or adapt to circumstances as they are. Affirming, strengthening, or achieving a client's competence is often a basic goal in psychotherapy. **2.** one's developed repertoire of skills, especially as it is applied to a task or set of tasks. A distinction is sometimes made between competence and performance, which is the extent to which competence is realized in one's actual work on a problem or set of problems. **3.** in law, the capacity to comprehend the nature of a transaction and to assume legal responsibility for one's actions. See COMPETENCY TO STAND TRIAL; INCOMPETENCE. **—competent** *adj.*

competence motivation the drive to interact effectively with the environment and develop personal skill and capability in solving problems and performing tasks, such mastery being reinforced by a sense of control and positive self-esteem.

competency evaluation evaluation of the defendant by a psychologist to determine his or her competency to stand trial.

competency to stand trial the capacity to be tried in court as determined by a person's ability, at the time of trial, to understand and appreciate the criminal proceedings against him or her, to consult with an attorney with a reasonable degree of understanding, and to make and express choices among available options. It is a component of ADJUDICATIVE COMPETENCE. See DUSKY STANDARD. See also INCOMPETENCY PLEA.

competing response training a technique in BEHAVIOR THERAPY that involves two sequential stages: (a) identification of habit occurrence, including antecedents and warning signs; and (b) creation and practice, in session and through homework, of a competing (i.e., alternative) response to the problem behavior. The competing response should be physically incompatible with the behavioral habit, inconspicuous, and easy to practice. This technique is typically used with habit disorders and is also used in ANGER MANAGEMENT training. See also ALTERNATIVE BEHAVIOR COMPLETION.

complementary and alternative medicine (CAM) a group of therapies and health care systems that fall outside the realm of conventional Western medical practice. These include but are not limited to ACUPUNCTURE, CHIROPRACTIC, MEDITATION, AROMATHERAPY, HOMEOPATHY, NATUROPATHY, TOUCH THERAPY, REFLEXOLOGY, REIKI, and the use of certain dietary supplements. Complementary medicine is used as an adjunct to conventional treatment; alternative medicine stands alone and replaces conventional treatment.

completion test a type of test in which the participant is usually required to supply a missing phrase, word, or letter in a written text. In nonverbal completion tests, a missing number, symbol, or representation must be supplied.

complex *n.* a group or system of related ideas or impulses that have a common emotional tone and exert a strong but usually unconscious influence on the individual's attitudes and behavior. The term, introduced by Carl JUNG to denote the contents of the PERSONAL UNCONSCIOUS, has taken on an almost purely pathological connotation in popular usage, which does not necessarily reflect usage in psychology. Primary examples from CLASSICAL PSYCHOANALYSIS and its offshoots are Jung's power complex, Sigmund FREUD'S CASTRATION COMPLEX and OEDIPUS COMPLEX, and Alfred ADLER'S INFERIORITY COMPLEX.

complex behavior an activity that requires many decisions and actions in rapid order or simultaneously. Dancing in a ballet is an example of a complex behavior.

Complex Figure Test a nonverbal memory test for a complex design. The individual is first asked to copy a complex design without being forewarned about a later memory test. This is followed by immediate and delayed recall trials in which the individual is asked to reproduce the complex figure from memory. A comparison of performance on the copy and recall trials allows the examiner to estimate the contribution of visuospatial and visuomotor processes, task strategy, and memory abilities to the individual's performance. The **Children's Complex Figure Test** is a version of this test for children. Also called **Rey Complex Figure Test (RCFT)**; **Rey–Osterrieth Complex Figure Test**.

complexity hypothesis a hypothesis that conscious events result from neural systems in the DYNAMIC CORE that have high levels of complexity, a mathematical quantity defined as a joint function of neuronal integration and differentiation. [proposed by Italian–U.S. psychologist Giulio Tononi (1960–) and U.S. neuroscientist Gerald M. Edelman (1929–)]

complex motives simultaneous, multiple desires to achieve one or more goals. For example, desires may be compatible and oriented toward the same goal (e.g., working hard due to a desire for success as well as a desire for money) or incompatible and oriented toward opposing goals (e.g., desiring to achieve success through work while simultaneously desiring to relax by not working).

complex of ideas a set of related ideas closely associated with emotions, memories, and other psychic factors so that when one of the ideas is recalled, other aspects of the complex are recalled with it. See also COGNITIVE SYSTEM.

complex partial seizure a PARTIAL SEIZURE that is characterized by complex psychological symptoms, repetitive motor activities, and specific sensory experiences. During the seizure the individual is in an impaired or altered, often trancelike, state of consciousness, typically accompanied by FALSE MEMORIES (e.g. déjà vu), and may experience such emotions as fear, anxiety, or (less commonly) sadness or pleasure. Stereotyped motor behavior includes grimacing, sucking, chewing, and swallowing, and there may also be visual or olfactory hallucinations. Complex partial seizures are most commonly associated with abnormal discharges from neurons in the temporal lobe and were formerly called **temporal lobe seizures**. Also called **psychomotor seizure**.

compliance *n.* **1.** submission to the demands, wishes, or suggestions of others. See also CONFORMITY. **2.** in pharmacotherapy, see ADHERENCE. **3.** a change in a person's behavior in response to a direct request. A variety of techniques have been developed to enhance compliance with requests. Although some techniques may enhance compliance by producing ATTITUDE CHANGE, behavioral change is the primary goal of these techniques. **—compliant** *adj.* **—comply** *vb.*

compliant character a submissive personality whose prime motive is to seek affection from others. German-born U.S. psychoanalyst Karen D. Horney (1885–1952) defined the development of such a character as one of three basic NEUROTIC TRENDS used as a defense against BASIC ANXIETY. Compare AGGRESSIVE CHARACTER; DETACHED CHARACTER.

complicated grief a response to death (or, sometimes, to other significant loss or trauma) that deviates significantly from normal expectations. Three different types of complicated grief are posited: chronic grief, which is more intense, prolonged, or both; delayed grief; and absent grief. The most often observed form of complicated grief is the pattern in which the immediate response to the loss is exceptionally devastating and in which the passage of time does not moderate the emotional pain or restore competent functioning. The concept of complicated grief was intended to replace the earlier terms abnormal grief and pathological grief.

complication *n.* an additional disease, disorder, or condition that occurs or develops during the course of another disease or disorder or during a medical procedure. See also COMORBIDITY.

component evaluation an approach in program evaluation that examines the separate elements comprising a HUMAN SERVICE DELIVERY SYSTEM or intervention program. The unit of analysis in the evaluation shifts from the program level to components or links between components and subsequent PROGRAM OUTCOMES.

component instinct in psychoanalytic theory, a fundamental element of the SEXUAL INSTINCT that has a specific source in one part of the body (e.g., the oral instinct) and a particular aim (e.g., instinct to master). The component instincts are posited to function independently during the early stages of PSYCHOSEXUAL DEVELOPMENT and later to fuse together during the GENITAL STAGE, which begins at puberty. Also called **partial instinct**; **part instinct**.

composite figure in psychoanalytic theory, a person or object in a dream whose image is created from the features or qualities of two or more individuals or objects (actual or existing in fantasy or imagination) by the process of CONDENSATION.

compos mentis in law, mentally competent, that is, neither mentally deficient nor legally insane. See COMPETENCE. Compare NON COMPOS MENTIS.

comprehension *n.* the act or capability of understanding something, especially the meaning of a communication. Compare APPREHENSION. **—comprehend** *vb.*

comprehensive assessment service a team of professionals, often affiliated with a health care system or hospital, who perform multiple assessments of patients. The team's purposes are to identify specific health conditions and behavioral factors affecting an individual's growth and development and to enhance the value of the individual's referral to subsequent specialized educational or developmental services.

comprehensive functional assessment an assessment that is broad in scope, often implemented by an interdisciplinary team, and most frequently focuses on a person with mental retardation or a related condition. It typically incorporates findings regarding specific developmental strengths and individual preferences, specific functional and adaptive social skills that the individual needs to learn, the nature of any presenting disabilities and their causes, and the need for a wide range of services.

comprehensive mental health center see COMMUNITY MENTAL HEALTH CENTER.

compression *n.* in neurology, pressure on the brain, spinal cord, or a nerve. Compression inside the skull raises INTRACRANIAL PRESSURE and may be caused by, for example, edema, hydrocephalus, or a tumor. Symptoms include motor disorders and disturbances of sensation, memory, or consciousness.

compromise formation in psychoanalytic theory, the conscious form of a repressed wish or idea that has been modified or disguised, as in a

C

dream or symptom, so as to be unrecognizable. Thus it represents a compromise between the demands of the ego's defenses and the unconscious wish.

compulsion *n.* a type of behavior (e.g., hand washing, checking) or a mental act (e.g., counting, praying) engaged in to reduce anxiety or distress. Typically the individual feels driven or compelled to perform the compulsion to reduce the distress associated with an OBSESSION or to prevent a dreaded event or situation. For example, individuals with an obsession about contamination may wash their hands until their skin is cracked and bleeding. Compulsions may also take the form of rigid or stereotyped acts based on idiosyncratic rules that do not have a rational basis (e.g., having to perform a task in a certain ritualized way). Compulsions do not provide pleasure or gratification and are disproportionate or irrelevant to the feared situation they are used to neutralize. See COUNTERCOMPULSION; OBSESSIVE-COMPULSIVE DISORDER. **—compulsive** *adj.*

compulsion to repeat see REPETITION COMPULSION.

compulsive character a personality pattern characterized by rigid, perfectionistic standards, an exaggerated sense of duty, and meticulous, obsessive attention to order and detail. Individuals of this type are usually humorless, parsimonious, stubborn, inhibited, rigid, and unable to relax. Also called **compulsive personality**.

compulsive disorder any disorder in which the individual feels forced to perform acts that are against his or her wishes or better judgment. The act may be associated with an experience of pleasure or gratification (e.g., compulsive gambling, drinking, or drug taking) or with the reduction of anxiety or distress (e.g., rituals in OBSESSIVE-COMPULSIVE DISORDER). See INTERMITTENT EXPLOSIVE DISORDER; KLEPTOMANIA; PARAPHILIA; PATHOLOGICAL GAMBLING; PYROMANIA; SUBSTANCE ABUSE; TRICHOTILLOMANIA. See also IMPULSE-CONTROL DISORDER.

compulsive drinker an individual who has an uncontrollable urge to drink excessively: an ALCOHOLIC. See ALCOHOL DEPENDENCE.

compulsive eating an irresistible drive to overeat, in some cases as a reaction to frustration or disappointment. See also BINGE-EATING DISORDER; BULIMIA NERVOSA; FOOD ADDICTION.

compulsive exerciser an individual who feels it is necessary to participate in moderate to high-level physical activity on a regular basis.

compulsive gambling see PATHOLOGICAL GAMBLING.

compulsive laughter persistent, inappropriate, and apparently uncontrollable laughter of which the individual may be unaware. See also INAPPROPRIATE AFFECT.

compulsiveness *n.* a behavior pattern associated with OBSESSIVE-COMPULSIVE DISORDER or OBSESSIVE-COMPULSIVE PERSONALITY DISORDER. See COMPULSION.

compulsive orderliness overconcern with everyday arrangements, such as a clean desk or dust-free house, with unbearable anxiety if there is any variation. See OBSESSIVE-COMPULSIVE DISORDER; OBSESSIVE-COMPULSIVE PERSONALITY DISORDER.

compulsive personality see COMPULSIVE CHARACTER.

compulsive personality disorder see OBSESSIVE-COMPULSIVE PERSONALITY DISORDER.

compulsive repetition the irresistible drive to perform needless acts, such as checking and rechecking a door to see whether it has been locked. See COMPULSION; OBSESSIVE-COMPULSIVE DISORDER.

compulsive stealing see KLEPTOMANIA.

compunction *n.* distress or guilt associated with wrongdoing or with an anticipated action or result.

computed tomography (**CT**) a radiographic technique for quickly producing detailed, three-dimensional images of the brain or other soft tissues. An X-ray beam is passed through the tissue from many different locations, and the different patterns of radiation absorption are analyzed and synthesized by a computer. Because a **CT scan** produces many slice-by-slice pictures of the head, chest, or abdomen, it is possible to locate abnormalities, such as lesions or tumors, without exploratory surgery. Also called **computer-assisted tomography**; **computerized axial tomography** (**CAT**); **computerized tomography**. See also MAGNETIC RESONANCE IMAGING.

computer addiction see INTERNET ADDICTION.

computer anxiety strong apprehension about computers and computer use that is disproportionate to the actual threat posed by these machines. The anxiety may be related to fear of the unknown or fear of the possible outcome of trying to use a computer (e.g., failure, frustration, embarrassment, or disappointment). If the anxiety is sufficient to cause significant distress and impairment, it may be classified as a SPECIFIC PHOBIA, situational type. Also called **computer phobia**.

computer-assisted diagnosis see COMPUTERIZED DIAGNOSIS.

computerized assessment the process of using a computer to obtain and evaluate psychological information about a person. The computer presents questions or tasks and then makes diagnoses and prognoses based on a comparison of the participant's responses or performance to databases of previously acquired information on many other individuals. Also called **automated assessment**.

computerized diagnosis the use of computer programs for cataloging, storing, comparing, and evaluating psychological and medical data as an aid to CLINICAL DIAGNOSIS. In view of the many possible variables involved in a particular type of disorder, computerized diagnosis makes use of information based on thousands of similar or related sets of signs and symptoms of previous patients, as well as information on diagnoses and effective treatments stored in databases. Also called **computer-assisted diagnosis**. See PROBLEM-ORIENTED RECORD.

computerized therapy the use of a specially programmed computer to provide therapy, under the auspices of a trained therapist. Computers have been used for assessment, history taking, diagnosis, patient education, and intervention. Computer therapy software operates through a series of if–then statements, which determine how the computer responds to explicit input by the individual.

computer phobia see COMPUTER ANXIETY.

computer simulation in cognitive psychology, a technique in which a model of cognitive processes is implemented as a computer program. This is generally to investigate specific theories of cognitive processing rather than to explore the more general issues that are the province of artificial intelligence.

Comrey Personality Scales (**CPS**) an inventory of individual differences in eight personality traits constructed primarily through FACTOR ANALYSIS and yielding scores on eight scales: trust versus defensiveness, orderliness versus lack of compulsion, social conformity versus rebelliousness, activity versus lack of energy, emotional stability versus neuroticism, extraversion versus introversion, masculinity versus femininity, and empathy versus egocentrism. Designed for individuals aged 16 years and over, it consists of 180 statements to which participants respond using a 7-point LIKERT SCALE format, ranging from "never" to "always" or from "definitely not" to "definitely." [developed in 1970 by Andrew Laurence **Comrey** (1923–), U.S. psychologist]

conation *n.* the proactive (as opposed to habitual) part of motivation that connects knowledge, affect, drives, desires, and instincts to behavior. Along with COGNITION and affect, conation is one of the three traditionally identified components of mind. The behavioral basis of attitudes is sometimes referred to as the **conative component**. See also BASES OF AN ATTITUDE.

conative *adj.* characterized by volition or self-activation toward a goal.

concentration-camp syndrome a variant form of POSTTRAUMATIC STRESS DISORDER suffered by survivors of concentration camps. Persistent stress symptoms in concentration-camp victims consist of severe anxiety, defenses against anxiety, an obsessive ruminative state, psychosomatic reactions, depression, and SURVIVOR GUILT produced by remaining alive while so many others died.

concentration difficulty a common symptom of a MAJOR DEPRESSIVE EPISODE in which the ability to concentrate and think clearly is diminished.

concentrative meditation a type of MEDITATION that focuses on a single stimulus (e.g., breathing); a specific image (e.g., a YANTRA); a specific sound, syllable, word, or phrase (see MANTRA); or a specific thought. It is the opposite of INSIGHT in that thoughts unrelated to the stimulus do not enter the consciousness. See also TRANSCENDENTAL MEDITATION. Compare MINDFULNESS MEDITATION.

concept formation the process by which a person abstracts a common idea or concept from particular examples, such as learning what dogs are by experience of various different dogs. Also called **concept acquisition**. See also ABSTRACTION.

concept-formation test any test used in studying the process of concept formation and in assessing the level of concept acquisition achieved by a specific individual.

conceptual disorder a disturbance in the thinking process or in the ability to formulate abstract ideas from generalized concepts.

conceptual disorganization irrelevant, rambling, or incoherent verbalizations, frequently including NEOLOGISMS and stereotyped expressions. It is one of the major signs of disorganized thought processes. See also SCHIZOPHRENIC THINKING.

conceptualization *n.* the process of forming concepts or ideas, particularly those of an abstract nature, out of experience or learned material using thought processes and verbalization. See also ABSTRACT CONCEPTUALIZATION; ABSTRACTION; CONCEPT FORMATION. **—conceptualize** *vb.*

conceptual system the organization of a person's cognitive abilities, emotional awareness, experience, and philosophical or religious orientation into a system for understanding events, data, or experience. See also COGNITIVE STRUCTURE; FRAME OF REFERENCE.

conceptual tempo the pace that is typical of a person's approach to cognitive tasks, for example, a hasty rather than a deliberate approach to observing, thinking, and responding. Conceptual tempo is an aspect of COGNITIVE STYLE. See also REFLECTIVITY–IMPULSIVITY.

Concerta *n.* a trade name for METHYLPHENIDATE.

concordance *n.* **1.** the state or condition of being in harmony or agreement. **Affective concordance** is said to exist, for instance, when facial gestures mirror internal states of feeling, such as frowning when perplexed or annoyed, or, in another context, when two or more individuals related through some condition or activity experience the same or similar emotional reactions. **2.** in TWIN STUDIES, the presence of a given trait or disorder in both members of the pair. Evidence for genetic factors in the production of the trait or disorder comes from the comparison of concordance rates between identical and fraternal twins. Compare DISCORDANCE.

C

concordance rate the percentage of pairs of twins or other blood relatives who exhibit a particular trait or disorder. Also called **concordance ratio**. See also TWIN STUDY.

concrete attitude a COGNITIVE STYLE that is directed to specific objects and immediate stimuli. A person who exhibits a concrete attitude tends not to make abstract comparisons and will not usually respond to abstract qualities, concepts, or categories. Compare ABSTRACT ATTITUDE. [defined by German-born U.S. neurologist Kurt Goldstein (1878–1965)]

concrete intelligence the ability to understand and manipulate objects. It is often contrasted with ABSTRACT INTELLIGENCE and SOCIAL INTELLIGENCE.

concrete thinking thinking focused on immediate experiences and specific objects or events. It is characteristic of young children and may also be seen in people with schizophrenia and people who have suffered a brain injury, especially frontal-lobe damage. Compare ABSTRACT THINKING.

concretism *n.* in the ANALYTIC PSYCHOLOGY of Carl JUNG, a type of thought or feeling that is dependent on immediate physical sensation and displays little or no capacity for abstraction. In some traditional societies, such thinking may manifest itself in fetishism and belief in magic. In the modern world, it may display itself as an inability to think beyond the obvious material facts of a situation.

concretization *n.* **1.** inability to think abstractly in which there is an overemphasis on details and immediate experience. It occurs in such conditions as dementia and schizophrenia. **2.** in general usage, the process of being specific or of giving an example of a concept or relationship.

concurrent review an analysis of admissions to a psychiatric hospital or clinic carried out while care is being provided. It comprises certification of the necessity for admission (see ADMISSION CERTIFICATION) and assessment of the need for care to be continued (see CONTINUED-STAY REVIEW).

concurrent therapy **1.** the use of two treatments at the same time. **2.** in COUPLES THERAPY and FAMILY THERAPY, the simultaneous treatment of spouses or other family members in individual or group therapy, either by the same therapist or different therapists. See also COMBINED THERAPY.

concurrent validity the extent of correspondence between two measurements at about the same point in time: specifically, the assessment of one test's validity by comparison of its results with a separate but related measurement, such as a standardized test, at the same point in time. See also CONTENT VALIDITY; CRITERION VALIDITY.

concussion *n.* see BRAIN CONCUSSION.

condensation *n.* the fusion of several meanings, concepts, or emotions into one image or symbol. Condensation is particularly common in dreams, in which, for example, one person may exhibit the characteristics of several or one behavior may represent several feelings or reactions.

conditional discharge the release of a patient from a psychiatric facility with imposition of certain conditions and limitations (such as periodically reporting to a supervisor or taking medications), during which time the patient is still under commitment.

conditional positive regard an attitude of acceptance and esteem expressed by others on a conditional basis, that is, depending on the acceptability of the individual's behavior and the other's personal standards. In his theory of personality, Carl ROGERS proposed that while the need for positive regard is universal, conditional regard works against sound psychological development and adjustment in the recipient. Compare UNCONDITIONAL POSITIVE REGARD.

conditional probability the probability that an event will occur given that another event is known to have occurred.

conditioned *adj.* relating to or describing behavior whose occurrence, form of display, or both is a result of experience. The two main classes of experience resulting in conditioned behavior are OPERANT CONDITIONING and PAVLOVIAN CONDITIONING.

conditioned emotional response (**CER**) any negative emotional response, typically fear or anxiety, that becomes associated with a neutral stimulus as a result of PAVLOVIAN CONDITIONING.

conditioned reinforcement see SECONDARY REINFORCEMENT.

conditioned response (**CR**) in PAVLOVIAN CONDITIONING, the learned or acquired response to a conditioned stimulus. Also called **conditioned reflex**.

conditioned stimulus (**CS**) a neutral stimulus that is repeatedly associated with an UNCONDITIONED STIMULUS until it acquires the ability to elicit a response that it previously did not. In many (but not all) cases, the response elicited by the conditioned stimulus is similar to that elicited by the unconditioned stimulus. A light, for example, by being repeatedly paired with food (the unconditioned stimulus), eventually comes to elicit the same response as food (i.e., salivation) when presented alone. Also called **conditional stimulus**.

conditioning *n.* the process by which certain kinds of experience make particular actions more or less likely. See INSTRUMENTAL CONDI-

TIONING; OPERANT CONDITIONING; PAVLOVIAN CONDITIONING.

conditioning therapy see BEHAVIOR THERAPY.

conditions not attributable to a mental disorder in *DSM–III* and earlier editions, a residual category of conditions that in *DSM–IV–TR* is labeled OTHER CONDITIONS THAT MAY BE A FOCUS OF CLINICAL ATTENTION.

conditions of worth the state in which an individual considers love and respect to be conditional on meeting the approval of others. This belief derives from the child's sense of being worthy of love on the basis of parental approval: As the individual matures, he or she may continue to feel worthy of affection and respect only when expressing desirable behaviors. [proposed by Carl ROGERS]

condom *n.* a sheath, usually made of latex rubber, placed over the erect penis to prevent pregnancy and to avoid sexually transmitted diseases.

conduct *n.* the behavior of an individual, either generally or on a specific occasion, usually as it conforms to or violates social norms.

conduct disorder in *DSM–IV–TR*, a persistent pattern of behavior that involves violating the basic rights of others and ignoring age-appropriate social standards. Specific behaviors include lying, theft, arson, running away from home, aggression, truancy, burglary, cruelty to animals, and fighting. This disorder is distinguished from OPPOSITIONAL DEFIANT DISORDER by the increased severity of the behaviors and their occurrence independently of an event occasioning opposition. ATTENTION-DEFICIT/HYPERACTIVITY DISORDER frequently coexists with or is misdiagnosed as conduct disorder.

confabulation *n.* the falsification of memory in which gaps in recall are filled by fabrications that the individual accepts as fact. It is not typically considered to be a conscious attempt to deceive others. Confabulation occurs most frequently in KORSAKOFF'S SYNDROME and to a lesser extent in other conditions associated with organically derived amnesia. In forensic contexts, eyewitnesses may resort to confabulation if they feel pressured to recall more information than they can remember. **—confabulate** *vb.*

confederate *n.* **1.** in an experimental situation, an aide of the experimenter who poses as a participant but whose behavior is rehearsed prior to the experiment. The real participants are sometimes referred to as NAIVE PARTICIPANTS. See also ACTIVE DECEPTION. **2.** in parapsychology, an individual who assists a supposed PSYCHIC by covertly providing him or her with information about a client's concerns, preferences, background, or situation, thus creating or strengthening the illusion of the psychic's paranormal abilities.

confidence interval a range of values (an interval) used for estimating the value of a population parameter from data obtained in a SAMPLE, with a preset, fixed probability that the interval will include the true value of the population parameter being estimated. Most research is done on samples, but it is done in order to draw inferences about the entire relevant population. Compare POINT ESTIMATE.

confidence level the probability that a CONFIDENCE INTERVAL contains the true value of an experimental variable under investigation. It is expressed as a percentage that indicates the statistical likelihood that the value of the variable obtained using a SAMPLE is an accurate reflection of the actual value in the entire POPULATION. For example, a survey of 100 individuals in a small town of 1,000 people might indicate that 20% of respondents intend to enroll in a distance learning class within the next month. If the confidence level for this research is 95%, this indicates that if the entire town were surveyed then the results obtained would be within 5% of the value obtained with the sample (i.e., anywhere between 16 and 24% of respondents would enroll in a class). In other words, the researcher is 95% certain that his or her results for the sample are accurate for the entire population and thus would be obtained were the research to be repeated with additional samples.

confidence limits the upper and lower end points of a CONFIDENCE INTERVAL; that is, the values between which the value of the parameter is anticipated with a known probability to be.

confidentiality *n.* a principle of PROFESSIONAL ETHICS requiring providers of mental health care or medical care to limit the disclosure of a patient's identity, his or her condition or treatment, and any data entrusted to professionals during assessment, diagnosis, and treatment. Similar protection is given to research participants and survey respondents against unauthorized access to information they reveal in confidence. See INFORMED CONSENT; TARASOFF DECISION. **—confidential** *adj.*

configuration *n.* **1.** an arrangement of elements or components in a particular pattern or figure. See GOODNESS OF CONFIGURATION. **2.** the usual English translation of GESTALT. **—configurational** *adj.*

configurational analysis an integrative psychodynamic model for case formulation, psychotherapy, and outcome evaluation. Maladaptive states of mind in the context of the client's problems, topics of concern, defenses, identity, and relationships are the focus of assessment and therapy. [developed by 21st-century U.S. psychiatrist Mardi Horowitz]

confirmation *n.* the fulfillment of an expectancy that reinforces the behavior that led to the fulfillment.

confirmation bias the tendency to gather evidence that confirms preexisting expectations, typically by emphasizing or pursuing supporting evidence while dismissing or failing to seek contradictory evidence.

confirmatory data analysis statistical data analysis designed to address one or more specific research questions. Compare EXPLORATORY DATA ANALYSIS.

confirmatory factor analysis one of a set of procedures used in FACTOR ANALYSIS to demonstrate that a group of variables possess a theoretically expected factor structure. In other words, confirmatory factor analysis provides formal statistical tests of a priori hypotheses about the specific underlying (latent) variables thought to explain the data obtained on a set of observed (manifest) variables. Unlike exploratory factor analysis, in which all measured variables relate to all latent factors, confirmatory factor analysis imposes explicit restrictions so that the measured variables relate with some (or usually just one) latent factors but do not relate with others.

conflict *n.* the occurrence of mutually antagonistic or opposing forces, including events, behaviors, desires, attitudes, and emotions. This general term has more specific meanings within different areas of psychology. For example, in psychoanalytic theory it refers to the opposition between incompatible instinctual impulses or between incompatible aspects of the mental structure (i.e., the ID, EGO, and SUPEREGO) that may be a source of NEUROSIS if it results in the use of defense mechanisms other than SUBLIMATION. In interpersonal relations conflict denotes the disagreement, discord, and friction that occur when the actions or beliefs of one or more individuals are unacceptable to and resisted by others.

conflict-free sphere in EGO PSYCHOLOGY, an area of the ego that develops and functions without giving rise to internal conflict. Functions ordinarily controlled by the conflict-free sphere include speech, motility, and other autonomous ego functions. Also called **conflict-free area**.

conflict of interest a situation in which individuals or groups are drawn to the pursuit of goals or outcomes that are incompatible with the goals they are supposed to be pursuing. For example, psychologists who are employed by a health agency may find that their obligation to help their clients is incompatible with the agency's requirement to minimize treatment costs. See also DOUBLE-AGENTRY.

conformity *n.* the adjustment of one's opinions, judgments, or actions so that they match either (a) the opinions, judgments, or actions of other people or (b) the normative standards of a social group or situation. Conformity includes the temporary COMPLIANCE of individuals, who agree publicly with the group but do not accept its position as their own, as well as the CONVERSION of individuals, who fully adopt the group position. Compare ANTICONFORMITY; NONCONFORMITY. See also MAJORITY INFLUENCE; PEER PRESSURE.

confound *n.* in an experiment using a FACTORIAL DESIGN, a variable that is conceptually distinct but empirically inseparable from one or more other variables. **Confounding** makes it impossible to differentiate that variable's effects in isolation from its effects in conjunction with other variables. These indistinguishable effects are themselves called **aliases**.

confrontation *n.* **1.** an argument or hostile disagreement. **2.** the act of directly facing, or being encouraged or required to face, a difficult situation, realization, discrepancy, or contradiction involving information, beliefs, attitudes, or behavior. Confrontational techniques may be used therapeutically, for example, to reveal and invite self-examination of inconsistencies in a client's reported and actual behavior, but they have a potential for disruptive as well as constructive effects. **3.** in INDIVIDUAL PSYCHOLOGY, a statement or question calculated to motivate the client to make a decision or face the reality of a situation. **—confrontational** *adj.*

confrontational methods methods intended to change behavior in which individuals are aggressively forced to confront their failures and weaknesses. Such methods are used, for example, in residential drug programs staffed by ex-addicts. Similar but less aggressive methods are used in ENCOUNTER GROUPS as a means of increasing awareness and modifying behavior. Research has not supported the efficacy of confrontational approaches, and many patients respond negatively.

confusion *n.* a disturbance of consciousness characterized by bewilderment, inability to think clearly or act decisively, and DISORIENTATION for time, place, and person. Also called **mental confusion**.

confusional psychosis a form of CYCLOID PSYCHOSIS in which disturbances of cognitive processes are prominent and accompanied by a labile (highly changeable) emotional state characterized alternately by manifest anxiety, with the individual often misidentifying other people, and by mutism and greatly decreased movement. The latter differs from CATATONIC STUPOR in that self-care and spontaneity are preserved and negativism is absent. [defined by German psychiatrist Karl Leonhard (1904–1988)]

confusional state a state of impaired mental functioning in which awareness is retained but with loss of cognitive coherence and orientation to time, place, and sometimes identity. It may be accompanied by rambling or incoherent speech, visual hallucinations, and PSYCHOMOTOR disturbances. It can arise from a wide variety of causes, including brain lesions, trauma, toxicity, medications, neurotransmitter imbalances, sleep disturbances, Alzheimer's disease, sedation, or fever.

congenital *adj.* denoting a condition or disorder that is present at birth. Also called **connate**.

congenital acromicria see DOWN SYNDROME.

congenital anomaly see CONGENITAL DEFECT.

congenital defect any abnormality present at birth, regardless of the cause. It may be caused by faulty fetal development (e.g., spina bifida, cleft palate), hereditary factors (e.g., Huntington's disease), chromosomal aberration (e.g., Down syndrome), maternal conditions affecting the developing fetus (e.g., fetal alcohol syndrome), metabolic defects (e.g., phenylketonuria), or injury to the brain before or during birth (e.g., some cases of cerebral palsy). A congenital defect may not be apparent until several years after birth (for example, an allergy or a metabolic disorder) or even until after the individual has reached adulthood (e.g., Huntington's disease). Also called **birth defect**; **congenital anomaly**.

congenital hypothyroidism a condition of motor and mental retardation associated with a deficiency of thyroid hormone. More than a dozen causes, mostly hereditary metabolic defects, have been identified with the disorder. The prognosis varies with the degree of thyroid deficiency during fetal and early infant life, but early and adequate thyroid-hormone therapy generally reverses signs and symptoms.

congenital rubella syndrome a complex of congenital defects in infants whose mothers were infected by the rubella virus early in pregnancy. The defects may include deaf-mutism, cataracts, heart disease, cerebral palsy, microcephaly (small head), and mental retardation. Neurological abnormalities occur in about 80% of affected individuals, and brain weight is usually subnormal. Psychomotor retardation, marked by general lack of response to stimuli, and intellectual impairment are common. In developed nations rubella vaccination has resulted in a massive decline in the occurrence of this syndrome.

congenital sensory neuropathy with anhidrosis a disorder marked by the absence of pain perception. Severe injuries, such as multiple fractures, may go untreated because they cause no pain. Affected individuals tend to show delayed intellectual development, with IQs below 80. Skin biopsies show normal but nonfunctional sweat glands.

congruence *n.* **1.** in general, agreement, harmony, or conformity. **2.** in the phenomenological personality theory of Carl ROGERS, (a) the need for a therapist to act in accordance with his or her true feelings rather than with a stylized image of a therapist or (b) the conscious integration of an experience into the self. **—congruent** *adj.*

congruity theory a COGNITIVE CONSISTENCY THEORY that focuses on the role of persuasive communications in attitude change. Congruity theory is similar to BALANCE THEORY in that it postulates that people tend to prefer elements within a cognitive system to be internally consistent with one another. Accordingly, if the person receiving a persuasive communication has a negative attitude to the content of the message but a positive attitude to the source of the message, or vice versa, then he or she will be motivated to revise both of these attitudes in some degree in order to restore congruity. Congruity theory differs from balance theory in that it takes into account gradations of evaluation of elements and therefore makes more precise predictions regarding the magnitude of change required to restore congruity among elements. [first proposed by U.S. psychologists Charles OSGOOD and Percy Tannenbaum (1927–2009)]

conjoint marital therapy see CONJOINT THERAPY.

conjoint therapy therapy in which the partners in a relationship or members of a family are treated together in joint sessions by one or more therapists, instead of being treated separately. The technique is commonly applied in resolving marital disputes, when it is also known as **conjoint marital therapy**. Also called **conjoint counseling**. See also COUPLES THERAPY; FAMILY THERAPY.

conjunctive motivation the drive to achieve true and lasting (rather than temporary or substitute) satisfaction. Compare DISJUNCTIVE MOTIVATION. [defined by U.S. psychiatrist Harry Stack Sullivan (1892–1949)]

connate *adj.* see CONGENITAL.

Conners' Comprehensive Behavior Rating Scales (**Conners' CBRS**) a questionnaire that assesses a variety of emotional, behavioral, and academic problems in those 6 to 18 years of age and aids in the identification of certain disorders. It includes a 203-item parent form, a 204-item teacher form, and a 179-item self-report, and provides evaluations in nine areas: emotional distress, aggressive behaviors, language and math difficulties, hyperactivity/impulsivity, social problems, separation fears, perfectionist and compulsive behaviors, violence potential, and physical symptoms. [originally developed in 2008 by U.S. clinical psychologist C. Keith **Conners**]

Conners' Rating Scales (**CRS**) a questionnaire used to assess ATTENTION-DEFICIT/HYPERACTIVITY DISORDER and diagnose the most common comorbid disorders in those 6 to 18 years of age. It includes a 110-item parent form, a 115-item teacher form, and a 99-item self-report, and provides evaluations in seven areas: inattention, hyperactivity/impulsivity, learning problems, executive functioning, aggression, peer relations, and family relations. Participants respond to items—such as "argues with adults" for parents, "talks excessively" for teachers, and "I break the rules" for self-report—using the four rating options of "not at all," "just a little," "pretty much," or "very much." This widely used instrument was originally published in 1989 and subsequently revised in 1997 (**Conners' Rating**

C

Scales–Revised; CRS-R) and in 2008 (**Conners' Third Edition; Conners 3**). [C. Keith **Conners**]

Conradi's disease a congenital disorder marked by short limbs, anomalies of the head and face, cataracts, dry skin, and, in some cases, degenerating cartilage at the ends of the long bones. In the RHIZOMELIC form of the disease mental retardation is common. However, it is rarely present in the **Conradi–Hunermann** form of the disease. [Erich **Conradi**, 20th-century German physician]

conscience *n.* an individual's sense of right and wrong or of transgression against moral values. In psychoanalysis, conscience is the SUPEREGO, or ethical component of personality, which acts as judge and critic of one's actions and attitudes. More recent biopsychological approaches suggest that the capacity of conscience may be genetically determined, and research on brain damage connects behavioral inhibitions to specific brain regions (e.g., the PREFRONTAL CORTEX). Psychosocial approaches emphasize the role of conscience in the formation of groups and societies.

conscientiousness *n.* the tendency to be organized, responsible, and hardworking, construed as one end of a dimension of individual differences (conscientiousness versus lack of direction) in the BIG FIVE PERSONALITY MODEL. It is also a dimension in the FIVE-FACTOR PERSONALITY MODEL. **—conscientious** *adj.*

conscious 1. (**Cs**) *n.* in the classical psychoanalytic theory of Sigmund FREUD, the region of the psyche that contains thoughts, feelings, perceptions, and other aspects of mental life currently present in awareness. The content of the conscious is thus inherently transitory and continuously changing. Compare PRECONSCIOUS; UNCONSCIOUS. **2.** *adj.* relating to or marked by awareness or consciousness.

conscious access hypothesis the notion that the primary function of consciousness is to mobilize and integrate brain functions that are otherwise separate and independent.

conscious memory see DECLARATIVE MEMORY; EXPLICIT MEMORY.

conscious moment the present moment, often thought to be about 3 s in duration. This theoretical measurement approximates to the decay time for conscious sensory images.

consciousness *n.* **1.** the phenomena that humans report experiencing, including mental contents ranging from sensory and somatic perception to mental images, reportable ideas, inner speech, intentions to act, recalled memories, semantics, dreams, hallucinations, emotional feelings, "fringe" feelings (e.g., a sense of knowing), and aspects of cognitive and motor control. Operationally, these **contents of consciousness** are generally assessed by the ability to report an event accurately (see REPORTABILITY). **2.** any of various subjective states of awareness in which conscious contents can be reported. Consciousness most often refers to the ordinary waking state (see WAKEFULNESS), but it may also refer to the state of sleeping or to an ALTERED STATE OF CONSCIOUSNESS. In cognitive theory, consciousness appears to have a global-access function, presenting an endless variety of focal contents to executive control and decision making. In medicine and brain science, the distinctive electrical activity of the brain, as recorded on an electroencephalogram, is often used to identify conscious states (see BRAIN WAVES). **Sensory consciousness** of the perceptual world depends on the posterior sensory area of the brain. **Abstract consciousness** refers to abstract ideas, judgments, specific intentions, expectations, and events of FRINGE CONSCIOUSNESS; it may involve the FRONTAL CORTEX in addition to sensory cortex. The distinction between sensory and abstract experiences was originally made by Greek philosopher Plato (c. 427–c. 347 BCE). See also HIGHER ORDER CONSCIOUSNESS.

consciousness-altering substance any of a large class of psychoactive compounds that affect conscious experience and perception. These substances are related to neurotransmitters (e.g., serotonin) and include LSD, CANNABIS, and alcoholic beverages. See also ALTERED STATE OF CONSCIOUSNESS.

consciousness of freedom the sense of choice people tend to have in making decisions and controlling actions. It may be the intuitive basis for the widespread belief in free will.

consciousness raising a process, often used in group discussion, directed toward greater awareness of (a) oneself, for example, one's condition, needs, values, and goals; or (b) a political or social issue, such as discrimination against a particular group of people.

conscious process a mental operation of which a person is aware and often in control. Compare UNCONSCIOUS PROCESS. See also AUTOMATICITY.

conscious resistance in psychoanalysis, the patient's deliberate withholding of unconscious material that has newly risen into consciousness. This withholding tends to occur because of shame, fear of rejection, or distrust of the analyst. See RESISTANCE. Compare ID RESISTANCE; REPRESSION-RESISTANCE.

conscious state see CONSCIOUSNESS.

consensual validation the process by which a therapist helps a client check the accuracy of his or her perception or the results of his or her experience by comparing it with those of others, often in the context of GROUP THERAPY.

consensus trance a continuous state of culture-induced trance in which individuals are hypothesized to exist. According to this idea, feelings, impressions, and images considered to be part of conscious reality are the result of powerful, repeated suggestions instilled in people since birth.

consent *n.* voluntary assent or approval given by an individual: specifically, permission granted by an individual for medical or psychological treatment, participation in research, or both. Individuals should be fully informed about the treatment or study and its risks and potential benefits (see INFORMED CONSENT).

conservation withdrawal a response to emotional or physical stressors (or both) in which a person tends to withdraw from family and friends, become fatigued, and have less energy and strength for activities. A means of conserving energy and recouping psychological and physical strength, this response resembles symptoms experienced as part of a MAJOR DEPRESSIVE EPISODE.

conservatorship *n.* a legal arrangement by which an individual is appointed by a court to protect the interests and property of a person who cannot be declared incompetent (see INCOMPETENCE) but is unable by reason of a physical or mental condition to take full responsibility for managing his or her own affairs.

consistency motive the desire to get feedback that confirms what one already believes about one's self. This contributes to maintaining a stable, unchanging SELF-CONCEPT, whether positive or negative. Compare APPRAISAL MOTIVE; SELF-ENHANCEMENT MOTIVE. See also SELF-VERIFICATION HYPOTHESIS.

consistency principle the theory that healthy and well-adjusted people strive to be consistent in their behavior, opinions, and attitudes.

Consonar *n.* a trade name for BROFAROMINE.

conspecific 1. *adj.* belonging to the same species. **2.** *n.* a member of the same species.

constancy law see PRINCIPLE OF CONSTANCY.

constant error a systematic error in some particular direction. Constant error is computed as the average positive or negative difference between the observed and actual values along a dimension of interest. For example, if a weight of 1 kg is judged on average to be 1.5 kg, the constant error is 500 g. See also ABSOLUTE ERROR; RANDOM ERROR.

constellation *n.* in cognitive psychology, a group of ideas with a common theme or association. **—constellatory** *adj.*

constitution *n.* **1.** the sum of an individual's innate characteristics. **2.** more broadly, the basic psychological and physical makeup of an individual, due partly to heredity and partly to life experience and environmental factors. **—constitutional** *adj.*

constitutional disorder a condition, disease, behavior, or constellation of behaviors arising from or inherent within some aspect of the individual's physical makeup or physiological characteristics.

constitutional factor a basic physiological tendency that is believed to contribute to personality, temperament, and the etiology of specific mental and physical disorders. These factors include hereditary predispositions and physiological characteristics (circulatory, musculoskeletal, glandular, etc.).

constitutional psychopathic inferior a former name for an individual with ANTISOCIAL PERSONALITY DISORDER. The term **psychopathic inferior** was introduced in 1888 by German physician Robert Koch (1843–1910) and included by German psychiatrist Emil Kraepelin (1856–1928) in his classification of mental disorders (1893). U.S. psychiatrist Adolf Meyer (1866–1950) added the word *constitutional* in the sense of deep-seated (but not congenital).

constitutional type a classification of individuals based on physique and other biological characteristics or on a hypothetical relationship between physical and psychological characteristics, such as temperament, personality, and a tendency to develop a specific type of mental disorder. See KRETSCHMER TYPOLOGY; SHELDON'S CONSTITUTIONAL THEORY OF PERSONALITY.

constraint question one of a series of questions that narrow the field of inquiry, particularly in psychotherapy.

construal *n.* a person's perception and interpretation of attributes and behavior of the self or others. See also INDEPENDENT SELF-CONSTRUAL; INTERDEPENDENT SELF-CONSTRUAL.

construct *n.* **1.** a complex idea or concept formed from a synthesis of simpler ideas. **2.** an explanatory model based on empirically verifiable and measurable events or processes—an **empirical construct**—or on processes inferred from data of this kind but not themselves directly observable—a **hypothetical construct**. Many of the models used in psychology are hypothetical constructs. See also AS-IF HYPOTHESIS; HEURISTIC. **3.** in the study of social cognition, an element of knowledge (a **cognitive construct**).

constructional apraxia an inability, because of brain damage, to copy an object or assemble it from its component parts. Tests for the condition include drawing from a model, reconstructions of puzzles, and building a particular structure using wooden sticks or blocks. See APRAXIA.

constructive alternativism in the personality construct theory of U.S. psychologist George A. Kelly (1905–1967), the capacity to view the world from multiple perspectives, that is, to envision a variety of alternative constructs.

constructive coping any instrumental approach to stress management that is generally considered to be adaptive or otherwise positive. Examples include planning and strategizing, seeking help and support from others, REFRAMING the situation, and meditating. Constructive coping strategies are task relevant and action oriented, and are divided into one of three categories: PROBLEM-FOCUSED COPING, EMOTION-FOCUSED COPING, and APPRAISAL-focused coping. They rely on realistic assessments of stressors and available coping resources; indeed, their use is associated with better physical and mental health outcomes than the use of other strategies (e.g., ACTIVE COPING, PASSIVE COPING, DEFENSE MECHANISMS). Research suggests that constructive coping is likely to be used when stressors are of high intensity or when there is little negative emotional arousal generated in the context of the stressful experience or event.

constructive hypothesis of consciousness the hypothesis that the function of consciousness is to construct experience in a flexible way depending on the context and available mental contents. [originated by Austrian-born U.S. psychologist George A. Mandler (1924–)]

constructive memory a form of remembering marked by the use of general knowledge stored in one's memory to construct a more complete and detailed account of an event or experience. See BARTLETT TECHNIQUE; RECONSTRUCTIVE MEMORY.

constructive thinking the ability to solve problems in everyday life with minimal stress.

Constructive Thinking Inventory (**CTI**) a self-report measure of experiential intelligence, yielding scores on such dimensions as superstitious thinking, categorical thinking, naive optimism, and defensiveness. Designed for individuals aged 18 to 80 years, it consists of 108 self-statements about thoughts and behavior to which participants respond using a 5-point LIKERT SCALE format, ranging from "definitely false" to "definitely true." [originally developed in 1989 by U.S. psychologist Seymour Epstein (1924–)]

constructivism *n.* the theoretical perspective, central to the work of Jean PIAGET, that people actively build their perception of the world and interpret objects and events that surround them in terms of what they already know. Thus, their current state of knowledge guides processing, substantially influencing how (and what) new information is acquired. Also called **constructionism**. See also SOCIAL CONSTRUCTIVISM.

constructivist psychotherapy 1. a form of individual psychotherapy, derived from CONSTRUCTIVISM, that focuses on meaning-making to help clients reconceptualize their problems in a more life-enhancing way using story, myth, poetry, and other linguistic and nonverbal forms. **2.** a group of psychotherapies all of which rely on a philosophy of interpersonal and social processes of meaning-making. Such therapies are typically derived from constructivism and encompass developments in existential, humanistic, and family therapy. See also NARRATIVE THERAPY. [developed by U.S. clinical psychologist George Kelly (1905–1967)]

constructivist theory of emotion any theory holding that emotions are not INNATE but constructed through social and cultural experience. See SOCIAL CONSTRUCTIVISM.

construct validation the process of establishing the CONSTRUCT VALIDITY of an instrument. The process usually requires the simultaneous examination of CONVERGENT VALIDITY, DISCRIMINANT VALIDITY, and CONTENT VALIDITY.

construct validity the degree to which a test or instrument is capable of measuring a theoretical construct, trait, or ability (e.g., intelligence).

consultant *n.* **1.** a mental health care or medical specialist called upon to provide professional advice or services in terms of diagnosis, treatment, or rehabilitation. **2.** in the United Kingdom, a hospital doctor of the most senior rank in his or her field.

consulting *n.* the use of the particular skill, experience, and expertise of an individual or group to advise individuals, groups, or organizations.

consulting psychology the branch of psychology that provides expert psychological guidance to business and industry, federal and state agencies, the armed forces, educational and scientific groups, religious groups, and volunteer and public service organizations. **Consulting psychologists** specialize in a variety of approaches—clinical, community, school, education, and industrial and organizational—and offer a wide variety of services, the most common of which are individual assessment, individual and group-process consultation, organizational development, education and training, employee selection and appraisal, research and evaluation test construction, management coaching, and change management.

consumer *n.* an individual who purchases (or otherwise acquires) and uses goods or services. In the context of medical and mental health care, consumers are those who purchase or receive health care services.

consumer counseling counseling for individuals that focuses on good decision making in personal money management.

consumer empowerment a practice in which the end-users of services increase their exercise of service choice and their influence over how, when, and by whom services are developed, delivered, and changed.

consumerism *n.* a movement to protect the rights of the consumer with regard to the quality and safety of available products and services (including psychotherapeutic and medical care). Consumers of mental health care have a number of clearly defined rights, including the right to know, to confidentiality, to choice, to determination of treatment, to nondiscrimination, to treatment review, and to accountability of treating professionals. **—consumerist** *adj.*

contact comfort the positive effects experienced by infants or young animals when in close contact with soft materials. The term originates from the classic experiments of U. S. psychologist Harry Harlow (1905–1981), in which young rhesus monkeys exposed both to an artificial cloth mother without a bottle for feeding and to an artificial wire mother with a bottle for feeding spent more time on the cloth mother and, when frightened, were more readily soothed by the presence of the cloth mother than the wire mother.

contact desensitization a variation of SYSTEMATIC DESENSITIZATION involving PARTICIPANT MODELING instead of relaxation training: used especially in the treatment of anxiety. The therapist demonstrates appropriate behaviors, beginning with those in the weakest anxiety-provoking situation for the client, and then assists the client in performing such behaviors. For example, in working with a client who is afraid of spiders, the therapist might first sit near a spider, then touch the spider, and then pick it up while the client observes. The client, with the guidance and assistance of the therapist, would then perform the same activities in the same order.

contagion *n.* in social theory, the spread of behaviors, attitudes, and affect through crowds and other types of social aggregation from one member to another. Early analyses of contagion suggested that it resulted from the heightened suggestibility of members and likened the process to the spread of contagious diseases. Subsequent studies have argued that contagion is sustained by relatively mundane interpersonal processes, such as social comparison (see SOCIAL COMPARISON THEORY), IMITATION, SOCIAL FACILITATION, CONFORMITY, and UNIVERSALITY. Also called **social contagion**. See also COLLECTIVE HYSTERIA; MASS CONTAGION.

containment *n.* in OBJECT RELATIONS THEORY, the notion that either the mother or the analyst aids growth and alleviates anxieties by acting as a "container," or "holding environment," for the projected aspects of the child's or patient's psyche (see PROJECTION). For instance, the infant, overwhelmed by distress and having no context to understand the experience, is held and soothed by the parent, who thus creates a safe context for the child and endows the experience with meaning.

contamination *n.* **1.** in testing and experimentation, the process of permitting knowledge, expectations, or other factors about the variable under study to influence the collection and interpretation of data about that variable. **2.** the mixing together of two or more discrete percepts, such as might occur on the RORSCHACH INKBLOT TEST or the MACHOVER DRAW-A-PERSON TEST. **3.** the creation of a NEOLOGISM by combining a part of one word with a part of another, usually resulting in a word that is unintelligible.

contamination obsession an intense preoccupation with disease, dirt, germs, mud, excrement, sputum, and so forth, based on a feeling that the world is disgusting, decaying, and dying. In extreme cases, it is regarded as a symptom of schizophrenia.

contemporaneity *n.* in psychotherapy, the principle of focusing on immediate experience. See also HERE AND NOW.

contempt *n.* an emotion characterized by negative regard for anything or anybody considered to be inferior, vile, or worthless. **—contemptuous** *adj.*

content *n.* in psychology, the thoughts, images, and sensations that occur in conscious experience. Contents are contrasted with the mental processes or the neural structures that underlie them.

contentiousness *n.* a tendency toward disputes and strife: quarrelsomeness. Contentiousness may be observed in MANIA and in the early stages of predominantly persecutory DELUSIONAL DISORDERS when individuals perceive that they are being treated unfairly.

content psychology an approach to psychology that is concerned with the role of conscious experience and the CONTENT of that experience. The term is mainly applied to early STRUCTURALISM. Compare ACT PSYCHOLOGY.

contents of consciousness see CONSCIOUSNESS.

content-thought disorder a type of thought disturbance, typically found in schizophrenia and some other mental disorders (e.g., OBSESSIVE-COMPULSIVE DISORDER, MANIA), characterized by multiple fragmented, bizarre delusions.

content validity the extent to which a test measures a representative sample of the subject matter or behavior under investigation. For example, if a test is designed to survey arithmetic skills at a third-grade level, content validity will indicate how well it represents the range of arithmetic operations possible at that level.

context *n.* **1.** generally, the conditions or circumstances in which a particular phenomenon occurs. **2.** in studies of cognition, the environment in which a stimulus event occurs, especially as this influences memory, learning, judgment, or other cognitive processes. **3.** in laboratory tasks involving the recognition of stimuli, the setting in which a target stimulus is presented, including any distractors or maskers. **—contextual** *adj.*

context shifting in conversation or therapy, a tendency to change subjects abruptly, generally to avoid anxiety-laden issues.

context-specific learning learning that has occurred in a particular place, or context, and is displayed only in that context and not when testing occurs in another context.

contextualism *n.* **1.** the theory that memory and learning are not the result only of linkages between events, as in the associationist doctrine, but are due to the meaning given to events by the context surrounding the experiences. **2.** a worldview asserting that the environment in which an event occurs intrinsically informs the event and its interpretation.

contextualize *vb.* to interpret an event within a preexisting mental framework. See CONTEXT. **—contextualization** *n.*

continence *n.* the ability to control sexual urges or the urge to defecate or urinate. **—continent** *adj.*

contingencies of self-worth particular areas of life in which people invest their SELF-ESTEEM, such that feedback regarding their standing or abilities in these domains has a crucial impact on their SELF-CONCEPT. Research indicates that people choose to stake their self-esteem in different domains, so that for some people material or professional success is vital to their sense of self-worth, whereas for others this is much less important than being well liked or sexually attractive.

contingency *n.* a conditional, probabilistic relation between two events. When the probability of Event B given Event A is 1.0, a perfect **positive contingency** is said to exist. When Event A predicts with certainty the absence of Event B, a perfect **negative contingency** is said to exist. Probabilities between –1.0 and 1.0 define a continuum from negative to positive contingencies, with a probability of zero indicating no contingency. Contingencies may be arranged via dependencies or they may emerge by accident (see ACCIDENTAL REINFORCEMENT). See also REINFORCEMENT CONTINGENCY.

contingency contract a mutually agreed-upon statement between a teacher and student, a parent and child, or a client and therapist regarding the change or changes desired, typically specifying behaviors and their positive and negative consequences.

contingency management in BEHAVIOR THERAPY, a technique in which a reinforcement, or reward, is given each time the desired behavior is performed. This technique is particularly common in substance abuse treatment.

contingency table a two-dimensional table in which the number of cases that are simultaneously in a given spot in a given row and column of the table are specified. For example, the ages and geographical locations of a sample of individuals applying for a particular job may be displayed in a contingency table, such that there are X number of individuals under 25 from New York City, Y number of individuals under 25 from Los Angeles, Z number of individuals between the ages of 25 and 35 from New York City, and so on.

continued-stay review (**CSR**) a UTILIZATION REVIEW in which an internal or external auditor determines if continued inpatient care is medically necessary or if the current health care facility is still the most appropriate to provide the level of care required by the patient. See also CONCURRENT REVIEW; EXTENDED-STAY REVIEW.

continuing bond the emotional attachment that a bereaved person continues to maintain with the deceased long after the death. The increasingly influential continuing-bond approach focuses on ways in which the emotional and symbolic relationship with the deceased can be reconstructed and integrated into the individual's life. See also BEREAVEMENT; GRIEF; MOURNING; OBJECT LOSS.

continuing care unit (**CCU**) a hospital unit to which a patient with a catastrophic or chronic illness is transferred for additional care after the acute hospitalization period. Compare INTENSIVE CARE UNIT. See also CONVALESCENT CENTER; SKILLED NURSING FACILITY.

continuing medical education (**CME**) postdoctoral educational activities that serve to develop or extend the knowledge, skills, and professional qualities that a physician uses to provide health care services.

continuity *n.* the quality or state of being unending or connected into a continuous whole. For example, the traditional concept of continuity of care implies the provision of a full range of uninterrupted medical and mental health care services to a person throughout his or her lifespan, from birth to death, as needed.

continuity hypothesis 1. the assumption that successful DISCRIMINATION LEARNING or problem solving results from a progressive, incremental, continuous process of trial and error. Responses that prove unproductive are extinguished, whereas every reinforced response results in an increase in ASSOCIATIVE STRENGTH, thus producing the gradual rise of the learning curve. Problem solving is conceived as a step-by-step learning process in which the correct response is discovered, practiced, and reinforced. Compare DISCONTINUITY HYPOTHESIS. **2.** the contention that psychological processes of various kinds (e.g., learning, childhood development) take place either in small steps or continuously, rather than in jumps from one identifiable stage to another. Also called **continuity theory**.

continuous amnesia ongoing memory loss for all events after a particular period of time, up to and including the present.

continuous bath treatment see HYDROTHERAPY.

continuous group see OPEN GROUP.

continuous operations (**CONOPS**) operations conducted without interruption, which require strict discipline, planning, time management, and coordination. They may cause sleep loss and affect ability to perform operational tasks.

continuous performance test (**CPT**) any test that measures sustained attention and concentration, usually by requiring responses to an auditory or verbal target stimulus while ignoring nontarget stimuli.

C

continuous rating scale a scale on which ratings are assigned along a continuum (e.g., a line) rather than according to categories. Such ratings are made by making a mark on the scale to indicate the "placement" of the rating or by assigning a numerical value to indicate the magnitude of response.

continuous recognition task a memory task in which a series of items is presented, with some items presented on multiple occasions in the series. The participant responds to each item by indicating whether it is old (seen previously in the series) or new (not seen earlier in the series).

continuous variable a RANDOM VARIABLE that can take on an infinite number of values; that is, a variable measured on a continuous scale, as opposed to a CATEGORICAL VARIABLE. Also called **continuous random variable**.

continuum approach an approach based on the view that behavior ranges over a continuum from effective functioning to severe abnormality. It assumes that differences between people's behavior are a matter of degree rather than kind.

contraception *n.* the prevention of conception, that is, the natural fertilization of the female ovum by the male spermatozoa. See BIRTH CONTROL. **—contraceptive** *n., adj.*

contract *n.* an explicit written agreement between parties or individuals. A contract between a client and therapist may detail (a) both the client's and the therapist's obligations, (b) the provisions for benefits or privileges to be gained through achievements, and (c) the specified consequences of failures (e.g., missing sessions). See also BEHAVIORAL CONTRACT; CONTINGENCY CONTRACT.

contracture *n.* an abnormal shortening or tightening of a muscle, which can result in permanent disability due to difficulty in stretching the muscle. A contracture often follows a disorder or injury that makes movement painful or is a consequence of prolonged, enforced inactivity (e.g., a coma).

contrarian *n.* a person who tends to disagree with someone or argue against something, regardless of the validity of the topic under discussion.

contrast *n.* **1.** that state in which the differences between one thing, event, or idea and another are emphasized by a comparison of their qualities. This may occur when the stimuli are juxtaposed (simultaneous contrast) or when one immediately follows the other (successive contrast). In making judgments, for example, meeting a person in a social context that includes physically attractive people could lead to a more negative evaluation of the attractiveness of that person than would have been the case otherwise. The evaluation of the person's attractiveness has been contrasted away from the social context. **2.** in the ANALYSIS OF VARIANCE, a comparison among group means using one DEGREE OF FREEDOM.

contrasuggestibility *n.* a tendency to do or say the opposite of what has been suggested or requested.

contributing cause a cause that is not sufficient to bring about an end or event but that helps in some way to bring about that end or event. A contributing cause may be a necessary condition or it may influence events more indirectly by affecting other conditions that make the event more likely.

control *n.* **1.** authority, power, or influence over events, behaviors, situations, or people. **2.** the regulation of all extraneous conditions and variables in an experiment so that any change in the DEPENDENT VARIABLE can be attributed solely to manipulation of the INDEPENDENT VARIABLE. In other words, the results obtained will be due solely to the experimental condition or conditions and not to any other factors.

control analysis psychoanalytic treatment conducted by a trainee under the guidance of a qualified PSYCHOANALYST, who helps the trainee to decide the direction of the treatment and to become aware of his or her COUNTERTRANSFERENCE. Also called **supervised analysis; supervisory analysis**.

control condition see CONTROL GROUP.

control group a group of participants in an experiment that are exposed to the **control conditions**, that is, the conditions of the experiment not involving a treatment or exposure to the INDEPENDENT VARIABLE. Compare EXPERIMENTAL GROUP.

controlled drinking a controversial approach to alcoholism treatment formerly advocated by some behaviorists as a viable alternative to total abstinence. The development of treatment programs based on social learning approaches and training in self-regulation and coping skills did not consistently materialize, and, since the 1980s, research has not supported controlled drinking as an efficacious or ethical primary goal of intervention.

Controlled Oral Word Association (COWA) a test that requires participants to name all the words that they can beginning with specific letters (most commonly F, A, and S). The words cannot include proper names and cannot consist of previously used words with a suffix. The most widely utilized word fluency task, COWA is used to measure EXECUTIVE FUNCTIONS. Also called **FAS Test**. [originally developed in 1968 by U.S. neuropsychologist Arthur Lester Benton (1909–2006)]

controlled processing in cognitive psychology, attentive processing: that is, processing that requires control, effort, and intention. See ATTENTION.

control-mastery theory 1. a perspective, underlying an integrative form of psychotherapy, that focuses on changing a client's unconscious and maladaptive beliefs developed in childhood due to thwarted attempts to achieve attachment and safety in the client's family. The client is seen to have an inherent motivation toward health that results in testing these beliefs through TRANSFERENCE and through passive-into-active behaviors; when such testing is productive, the client is then free to pursue adaptive goals. [developed by U.S. psychiatrist Joseph Weiss] **2.** an integrative approach to child development that focuses on thoughts, feelings, and behaviors resulting from children's needs for attachment and safety in the family.

control processes 1. in the theory of memory proposed by U.S. cognitive psychologists Richard C. Atkinson (1930–) and Richard M. Shiffrin (1942–), those processes that manipulate information in short-term memory, such as REHEARSAL or RECODING. **2.** those processes that organize the flow of information in an INFORMATION-PROCESSING system. See also COGNITIVE CONTROL; EXECUTIVE.

control variable a variable that is purposely not changed during an experiment in order to minimize its effects on the outcome. Because control variables are outside factors related in some way to the other variables under investigation, their influence may potentially distort research results.

contusion *n.* a bruise. For example, various kinds of HEAD INJURY can result in cerebral contusion.

convalescent center an EXTENDED CARE facility for patients whose recovery from disease or injury has reached a stage where full-time hospital inpatient services are no longer required. Convalescent centers generally provide professional personnel, including an available physician and 24-hour nursing service, rehabilitation services, and an authorized system of dispensing medications. See also CONTINUING CARE UNIT; SKILLED NURSING FACILITY.

convenience sampling the process of obtaining a sample because it is convenient for the purpose, regardless of whether it is representative of the population being investigated.

conventional antipsychotic see ANTIPSYCHOTIC.

conventionalism *n.* a personality trait marked by excessive concern with and inflexible adherence to social customs and traditional or accepted values and standards of behavior. The term is also used to refer specifically to one of the traits associated with the AUTHORITARIAN PERSONALITY.

convergent production the capacity to produce the right answer to a question or to choose the best solution to a problem. It is one of the abilities recognized in Joy P. GUILFORD's theory of intelligence (see GUILFORD DIMENSIONS OF INTELLIGENCE). Compare DIVERGENT PRODUCTION.

convergent thinking critical thinking in which an individual uses linear, logical steps to analyze a number of already formulated solutions to a problem to determine the correct one or the one that is most likely to be successful. Compare DIVERGENT THINKING.

convergent validity a form of CONSTRUCT VALIDITY based on the degree to which the measurement instrument in question exhibits high correlation with conceptually similar instruments. See also DISCRIMINANT VALIDITY.

conversion *n.* **1.** an unconscious process in which anxiety generated by psychological conflicts is transformed into physical symptoms. Traditionally, this process was presumed to be involved in CONVERSION DISORDER, but current *DSM–IV–TR* diagnostic criteria for the disorder do not make such an implication. **2.** in a therapeutic context, the movement of clients away from their initial interpretations to one recommended by their therapists. **3.** actual change in an individual's beliefs, attitudes, or behaviors that occurs as a result of SOCIAL INFLUENCE. Unlike COMPLIANCE, which is outward and temporary, conversion occurs when the targeted individual is personally convinced by a persuasive message or internalizes and accepts as his or her own the beliefs expressed by other group members. Also called **private acceptance**. See also CONFORMITY. **—convert** *vb.*

conversion anesthesia a SENSORY CONVERSION SYMPTOM marked by the absence of sensation in certain areas of the body that cannot be accounted for by any identifiable organic pathology or defect. See GLOVE ANESTHESIA; STOCKING ANESTHESIA.

conversion disorder in *DSM–IV–TR,* a SOMATOFORM DISORDER in which patients present with one or more symptoms or deficits affecting voluntary motor and sensory functioning that suggest a physical disorder but for which there is instead evidence of psychological involvement. These **conversion symptoms** are not intentionally produced or feigned and are not under voluntary control. They include paralysis, loss of voice, blindness, seizures, GLOBUS PHARYNGEUS, disturbance in coordination and balance, and loss of pain and touch sensations (see MOTOR CONVERSION SYMPTOMS; SENSORY CONVERSION SYMPTOMS).

conversion hysteria a former name for CONVERSION DISORDER.

conversion nonepileptic seizure a form of PSYCHOGENIC NONEPILEPTIC SEIZURE (PNES) that is a result of a diagnosed CONVERSION DISORDER. It is not associated with abnormal electrical activity on an electroencephalogram. Most PNESs are conversion nonepileptic seizures. Also called **conversion seizure**.

conversion paralysis a PSYCHOGENIC DISORDER in which there is an apparent loss of function of the muscles of a limb or a portion of the body for which no neurological cause can be identified. Unlike organic paralysis, reflexes may be intact, muscle tone may be normal, and the paralyzed limb may be moved inadvertently when the patient's attention is elsewhere. This is one of the possible symptoms of CONVERSION DISORDER.

conversion seizure see CONVERSION NONEPILEPTIC SEIZURE.

conversion symptom see CONVERSION DISORDER.

conversion therapy a highly controversial and generally discredited therapy based on the belief that individuals of same-sex sexual orientation may become heterosexual. Also called **reorientation therapy**; **reparative therapy**.

convulsant *n.* any substance that causes or otherwise results in convulsions, usually by blocking inhibitory neurotransmission.

convulsion *n.* an involuntary, generalized, violent muscular contraction, in some cases tonic (contractions without relaxation), in others clonic (alternating contractions and relaxations of skeletal muscles).

convulsive disorder any form of EPILEPSY that involves recurrent GENERALIZED SEIZURES or PARTIAL SEIZURES with convulsions.

convulsive therapy any treatment that is based on the induction of a generalized seizure by electrical or chemical means. See ELECTROCONVULSIVE THERAPY.

Coolidge Assessment Battery (**CAB**) a self-administered rating-scale instrument used to measure *DSM–IV–TR* personality (Axis II) disorders, as well as five major clinical (Axis I) disorders and EXECUTIVE FUNCTION. Developed in 1999, it comprises 225 items to which participants respond using a 4-point LIKERT SCALE ranging from strongly false (1) to strongly true (4). The CAB is a more comprehensive successor to the **Coolidge Axis II Inventory**. [Frederick L. Coolidge (1948–), U.S. neuropsychologist]

COPD abbreviation for CHRONIC OBSTRUCTIVE PULMONARY DISEASE.

coping *n.* the use of cognitive and behavioral strategies to manage the demands of a situation when these are appraised as taxing or exceeding one's resources or to reduce the negative emotions and conflict caused by stress. See also COPING STRATEGY. **—cope** *vb.*

coping behavior a characteristic and often automatic action or set of actions taken in dealing with stressful or threatening situations. Coping behaviors can be both positive (i.e., adaptive), for example, taking time to meditate or exercise in the middle of a hectic day; or negative (i.e., maladaptive, avoidant), for example, not consulting a doctor when symptoms of serious illness appear or persist. See also COPING MECHANISM; COPING STRATEGY.

coping imagery a DESENSITIZATION technique in which relaxation is accompanied by images that have proved successful in controlling anxiety in situations that had previously aroused fear. See also COPING-SKILLS TRAINING. [developed by U.S. psychologist Joseph R. Cautela (1927–1999)]

coping mechanism any conscious or unconscious adjustment or adaptation that decreases tension and anxiety in a stressful experience or situation. Modifying maladaptive coping mechanisms is often the focus of psychological interventions. See also COPING BEHAVIOR; COPING STRATEGY.

coping potential an individual's evaluation of the prospects of successfully managing environmental demands or personal commitments. Coping potential differs from COPING in that it deals with prospects of successful management (rather than with actual deployment of resources).

coping-skills training therapy or educational interventions to increase an individual's ability to manage a variety of often uncomfortable or anxiety-provoking situations, ranging from relatively normal or situational problems (e.g., test taking, divorce) to diagnosed disorders (e.g., phobias). The types of skills taught are tailored to the situation and can involve increasing cognitive, behavioral, and affective proficiencies.

coping strategy an action, a series of actions, or a thought process used in meeting a stressful or unpleasant situation or in modifying one's reaction to such a situation. Coping strategies typically involve a conscious and direct approach to problems, in contrast to DEFENSE MECHANISMS. See also COPING BEHAVIOR; COPING MECHANISM; EMOTION-FOCUSED COPING; PROBLEM-FOCUSED COPING.

coping style the characteristic manner in which an individual confronts and deals with stress, anxiety-provoking situations, or emergencies.

coprolagnia (**koprolagnia**) *n.* a PARAPHILIA in which the sight, or even the thought, of excrement may result in sexual pleasure.

coprolalia *n.* spontaneous, unprovoked, and uncontrollable use of obscene or profane words and expressions, particularly those related to feces. It is a symptom that may be observed in individuals with a variety of neurological disorders, particularly TOURETTE'S DISORDER. See also LATAH. Also called **coprophrasia**.

coprophagia *n.* the eating of feces. Also called **coprophagy**.

coprophemia (**koprophemia**) *n.* the use of obscenities as a PARAPHILIA, for example to stimulate sexual excitement. See SCATOPHILIA.

coprophilia *n.* literally, the love of FECES, which is manifested in behavior as an excessive or pathological preoccupation with the bodily product itself or with objects and words that represent it. In classical psychoanalytic theory, these tendencies are held to represent a fixation during the ANAL STAGE of development. See also PARAPHILIA NOT OTHERWISE SPECIFIED.

coprophrasia *n.* see COPROLALIA.

C

core conflictual relationship theme a method of research, case formulation, and PSYCHODYNAMIC PSYCHOTHERAPY that emphasizes central relationship patterns in clients' stories. Three components are analyzed: the wishes, needs, or intentions of the client with regard to the other person; the other person's expected or actual reaction to these; and the client's emotion, behavior, or symptoms as they relate to the other person's reaction. [developed by U.S. psychologist Lester Luborsky (1920–2009)]

core gender identity in psychoanalytic theory, an infant's sense of himself or herself as male or female, typically solidifying in the second year of life. See also GENDER IDENTITY.

core relational themes 1. in the COGNITIVE APPRAISAL THEORY of emotions, a person's judgments of the specific significance of particular events to himself or herself, resulting in the generation of specific emotional states (e.g., anger, joy, envy, or shame) in that person. Any core relational theme has three components: goal relevance, ego involvement, and COPING POTENTIAL. See PRIMARY APPRAISAL; SECONDARY APPRAISAL. **2.** repetitive patterns of relating to others that are presumed to be determined by relationships with parents and other influential individuals in early life. These relational themes can include dependent patterns and distrustful patterns, among others.

Coricidin *n.* a trade name for DEXTROMETHORPHAN.

Cornelia de Lange's syndrome see DE LANGE'S SYNDROME.

Cornell Medical Index (**CMI**) a psychological test originally designed for screening military personnel in World War II and later adapted for other purposes, such as diagnosing psychosomatic disorders on the basis of pathological mood and anxiety. The test is now rarely used. Also called **Cornell Selective Index**.

coronary heart disease (**CHD**) a cardiovascular disorder characterized by restricted flow of blood through the coronary arteries supplying the heart muscle. The cause is usually ATHEROSCLEROSIS of the coronary arteries and often leads to fatal myocardial INFARCTION. Behavioral and psychosocial factors are frequently involved in the development and prognosis of the disease. Also called **coronary artery disease**.

coronary-prone behavior actions or patterns of actions believed to be associated with an increased risk of coronary heart disease. The preferred term for such a behavior pattern is now TYPE A BEHAVIOR.

corpse phobia see NECROPHOBIA.

corpus callosum a large tract of nerve fibers running across the longitudinal fissure of the brain and connecting the cerebral hemispheres: It is the principal connection between the two sides of the brain. The largest of the interhemispheric commissures, it is known as the **great commissure**.

correctional psychology a branch of FORENSIC PSYCHOLOGY concerned with the application of counseling and clinical techniques to criminal and juvenile offenders in penal and correctional institutions (e.g., reformatories, training schools, penitentiaries). **Correctional psychologists** also participate professionally in court activities, probation departments, parole boards, prison administration, supervision of inmate behavior, and programs for the rehabilitation of offenders.

corrective emotional experience a concept from psychoanalysis positing that clients achieve meaningful and lasting change through new interpersonal affective experiences with the therapist, particularly with regard to situations that clients were unable to master as children. This concept has been debated both within and outside psychoanalytic treatment circles. [advocated by Hungarian psychoanalyst Franz Alexander (1891–1964)]

correlation *n.* the degree of a relationship (usually linear) between two attributes.

correlational design a research method that attempts to identify and describe the relationship between two variables without directly manipulating them. Correlational designs are often used in clinical and other applied areas of psychology and do not allow for inferences regarding cause and effect; that is, a change in one particular variable employed in the research cannot be said with any certainty to result in a change in the other.

correlational study a study of the relationship between two or more variables.

correlation coefficient (symbol: r) a numerical index reflecting the degree of relationship (usually linear) between two attributes scaled so that the value of +1 indicates a perfect positive relationship, –1 a perfect negative relationship, and 0 no relationship. The most commonly used type of correlation coefficient is the PRODUCT–MOMENT CORRELATION.

correlation matrix a square symmetric MATRIX in which the correlation coefficient between the ith and jth variables in a set of variables is displayed in the intersection of the ith row and the jth column of the matrix. The diagonal elements of a correlation matrix are all equal to 1.

correspondence training a BEHAVIOR THERAPY intervention for children and adolescents in which the clients are tangibly or socially reinforced either for verbally promising to do something and then following through or for doing a desired behavior and then verbally reporting on the activity. Promises and reports can be made to either an adult or a peer.

cortex *n.* (*pl.* **cortices**) the outer or superficial layer or layers of a structure, as distinguished from the central core. In mammals, the cortex of a structure is identified with the name of the gland or organ, for example, the ADRENAL CORTEX, CEREBELLAR CORTEX, or CEREBRAL CORTEX. Compare MEDULLA. —**cortical** *adj.*

cortical amnesia a form of amnesia due to organic causes, such as a stroke or brain injury.

cortical dementia DEMENTIA arising from degeneration of the cortical areas of the brain, rather than the subcortical (deeper) areas. The most common dementia of this type is ALZHEIMER'S DISEASE. Compare SUBCORTICAL DEMENTIA.

cortical lesion a pathological change in the CEREBRAL CORTEX of the brain, which may be congenital or acquired and due to any cause.

cortical undercutting a former psychosurgical procedure—a type of prefrontal LOBOTOMY—used in controlling severe emotional and mental disturbance. In this procedure the skull was opened and long association fibers severed. The object was to prevent frontal lobe damage, which affects thinking processes.

corticosteroid *n.* any of the steroid hormones produced by the ADRENAL CORTEX. They include the GLUCOCORTICOIDS (e.g., CORTISOL), which are involved in carbohydrate metabolism; and the MINERALOCORTICOIDS (e.g., aldosterone), which have a role in electrolyte balance and sodium retention. Also called **adrenocorticoid**.

corticosteroid therapy medical treatment that involves the use of CORTICOSTEROID drugs. Both MINERALOCORTICOIDS and GLUCOCORTICOIDS may be used as replacement therapy in patients whose secretion of the natural hormones is deficient, either through disease or surgical removal of one or both adrenal glands. However, glucocorticoids are most widely used as anti-inflammatory agents; they are also used in the treatment of asthma, dermatologic conditions, and seasonal rhinitis.

corticotropin *n.* a hormone secreted by the anterior pituitary gland, particularly when a person experiences stress. It stimulates the release of various other hormones (primarily CORTICOSTEROIDS) from the adrenal cortex, the outer layer of the adrenal gland. Also called **adrenocorticotropic hormone** (**ACTH**); **adrenocorticotropin**.

corticotropin-releasing factor (**CRF**) a neuropeptide produced by the hypothalamus that is important in the control of the hypothalamic–pituitary–adrenal response to stress (see HYPOTHALAMIC–PITUITARY–ADRENOCORTICAL SYSTEM). It controls the daily rhythm of corticotropin (ACTH) release by the pituitary gland and is also involved in a number of behaviors, such as anxiety, food intake, learning, and memory. Also called **ACTH-releasing factor**; **corticotropin-releasing hormone** (**CRH**).

cortisol *n.* a CORTICOSTEROID hormone whose GLUCOCORTICOID activity increases blood sugar levels. Blood levels of cortisol in humans vary according to sleep–wake cycles (being highest around 9:00 a.m. and lowest at midnight) and other factors; for example, they increase with stress and during pregnancy but decrease during diseases of the liver and kidneys. Since 1963, cortisol and its synthetic analogs have been administered in the treatment of chronic inflammatory and autoimmune disorders. Also called **hydrocortisone**.

cortisone *n.* a CORTICOSTEROID that is produced naturally by the adrenal cortex or synthetically. Cortisone is biologically inactive but is converted to the active hormone CORTISOL in the liver and other organs. It is used therapeutically in the management of disorders due to corticosteroid deficiency.

cosmic identification a feeling of identification with the universe, which is most often seen in patients with SCHIZOID PERSONALITY DISORDER or BORDERLINE DISORDERS. The patient cannot distinguish between that which is himself or herself and the outside world. Also called **magic omnipotence**. See also MYSTIC UNION; OCEANIC FEELING.

cost analysis a systematic determination of the costs associated with the implementation of a program's services. These include direct personnel, material, and administrative costs, calculated from the perspective of a given purchaser (e.g., government agency, client), budgetary category, and time period. Once determined, these costs are utilized further in COST–BENEFIT ANALYSIS or COST-EFFECTIVENESS ANALYSIS.

cost–benefit analysis an analytic procedure that attempts to determine and compare the economic efficiency of different programs. Costs and benefits are reduced to their monetary value and expressed in a **cost–benefit** (or **benefit–cost**) **ratio**.

cost containment a program goal that seeks to control the costs involved in managing and delivering the PROGRAM OUTCOME. In health administration, a range of fiscal strategies is used to prevent health care costs from increasing. See also COST ANALYSIS.

cost-effectiveness analysis a measure of PROGRAM EFFICACY or economic efficiency expressed in terms of the cost of achieving a unit of PROGRAM OUTCOME. The analysis is most appropriate when programs have one main identifiable evaluation outcome, when future costs are not confounded with changes in outcome, or when outcomes are not directly reducible to monetary payoffs.

Cotard's syndrome a psychotic condition characterized by severe depression and intense nihilistic delusions (see NIHILISM) in which individuals insist that their bodies or parts thereof, and in some cases the whole of reality, have disintegrated or ceased to exist. [first reported in 1880 by Jules **Cotard** (1840–1887), French neurologist, who called it **délire de négation** ("delirium of negation")]

cotherapy *n.* therapy by two therapists working with a client, pair of clients (e.g., a couple), family, or group to enhance understanding and change behavior and relationships during treatment. Also called **dual-leadership therapy**.

couch *n.* in psychoanalysis, the article of furniture on which the patient reclines. The use of the couch is based on the theory that this posture will facilitate FREE ASSOCIATION, encourage the patient to direct attention to his or her inward world of feeling and fantasy, and enable the patient to uncover his or her unconscious mind. The expression "on the couch" is sometimes used popularly to indicate psychoanalytic treatment. Also called **analytic couch**.

cough suppressants see ANTITUSSIVES.

counseling *n.* professional assistance in coping with personal problems, including emotional, behavioral, vocational, marital, educational, rehabilitation, and life-stage (e.g., retirement) problems. The COUNSELOR makes use of such techniques as ACTIVE LISTENING, guidance, advice, discussion, CLARIFICATION, and the administration of tests.

counseling process the interpersonal process engaged in by COUNSELOR and client as they attempt to define, address, and resolve specific problems of the client in face-to-face interviews. See also COUNSELING.

counseling psychology the branch of psychology that specializes in facilitating personal and interpersonal functioning across the life span. Counseling psychology focuses on emotional, social, vocational, educational, health-related, developmental, and organizational concerns—such as improving well-being, alleviating distress and maladjustment, and resolving crises—and addresses issues from individual, family, group, systems, and organizational perspectives. The **counseling psychologist** has received professional education and training in one or more COUNSELING areas, such as educational, vocational, employee, aging, personal, marriage, or rehabilitation counseling. In contrast to a clinical psychologist (see CLINICAL PSYCHOLOGY), who usually emphasizes origins of maladaptations, a counseling psychologist emphasizes adaptation, adjustment, and more efficient use of the individual's available resources.

counseling relationship the interaction between counselor and client in which the relationship is professional yet also characterized by empathic warmth and AUTHENTICITY, with the counselor bringing professional training, experience, and personal insight to bear on the problems revealed by the client. The relationship is considered to be of central importance in bringing about desired change.

counseling services professional help provided by a government, social service, or mental health agency to individuals, families, and groups. Services are typically provided by licensed counselors, psychologists, social workers, and nurses. See also COUNSELING.

counselor *n.* an individual professionally trained in counseling, psychology, social work, or nursing who specializes in one or more counseling areas, such as vocational, rehabilitation, educational, substance abuse, marriage, relationship, or family counseling. A counselor provides professional evaluations, information, and suggestions designed to enhance the client's ability to solve problems, make decisions, and effect desired changes in attitude and behavior.

counteraction need the drive to overcome difficult challenges rather than accept defeat. It is motivated by the desire for power, knowledge, prestige, or creative achievement. [defined by U.S. psychologist Henry Alexander Murray (1893–1988)]

counterattitudinal role play a technique used in PSYCHODRAMA or ROLE PLAY in which the individuals taking part are directed to express opinions contrary to those in which they believe.

counterbalancing *n.* the process of arranging a series of experimental conditions or treatments in such a way as to minimize the influence of other factors, such as practice or fatigue, on experimental effects. A simple form of counterbalancing would be to administer experimental conditions in the order AB to half the participants and in the order BA to the other half.

countercathexis *n.* see ANTICATHEXIS.

countercompulsion *n.* a COMPULSION that is secondarily developed to resist the original compulsion when the latter cannot be continued. The new compulsion then replaces the original so that the compulsive behavior can continue. See OBSESSIVE-COMPULSIVE DISORDER.

counterconditioning *n.* an experimental procedure in which an animal, already conditioned to respond to a stimulus in a particular way, is trained to produce a different response to the same stimulus that is incompatible with the original response. This same principle underlies many of the techniques used in BEHAVIOR THERAPY to eliminate unwanted behavior.

counterfactual thinking imagining ways in which events in one's life might have turned out differently. This often involves feelings of regret or disappointment (e.g., *If only I hadn't been so hasty*) but may also involve a sense of relief, as at a narrow escape (e.g., *If I had been standing three feet to the left ...*).

counterfeit role a false (i.e., inaccurate or deceptive) role. See also ROLE PLAY.

counteridentification *n.* in psychoanalysis, a form of COUNTERTRANSFERENCE in which the psychoanalyst identifies with the patient. —**counteridentify** *vb.*

counterphobic character a personality that takes pleasure in pursuing risky or dangerous activities that other people would normally find anxiety-provoking. In psychoanalytic theory, this is explained as a manic defense that achieves satisfaction from the feeling of mastering anxiety.

countershock *n.* a mild electric shock administered to a patient undergoing ELECTROCONVULSIVE THERAPY (ECT) for 1 min after the convulsive shock. The countershock is intended to relieve some of the common aftereffects of ECT, such as postconvulsion confusion or amnesia.

countersuggestion *n.* in psychotherapy, a suggestion by the therapist that contradicts or opposes a previous suggestion or a particular fixed idea. This strategy is used to decrease the influence of the previous suggestion or idea, provide an alternative, or both.

countertransference *n.* the therapist's unconscious reactions to the patient and to the patient's TRANSFERENCE. These thoughts and feelings are based on the therapist's own psychological needs and conflicts and may be unexpressed or revealed through conscious responses to patient behavior. The term was originally used to describe this process in psychoanalysis but has since become part of the common lexicon in other forms of psychodynamic psychotherapy and in other therapies. In CLASSICAL PSYCHOANALYSIS, countertransference is viewed as a hindrance to the analyst's understanding of the patient, but to some modern analysts and therapists it may serve as a source of insight into the patient's impact on other people. In either case, the analyst or therapist must be aware of, and analyze, countertransference so that it does not interfere with the therapeutic process. See also CONTROL ANALYSIS.

couples counseling COUNSELING in which guidance and advice focuses on issues confronting relationships between partners. Couples counseling is short-term and problem oriented; it may include a variety of approaches to such difficult areas as shared responsibilities, expectations for the future, and loyalties. Compare COUPLES THERAPY.

couples therapy therapy in which both partners in a committed relationship are treated at the same time by the same therapist or therapists. Couples therapy is concerned with problems within and between the individuals that affect the relationship. For example, one partner may have an undiagnosed, physiologically based depression that is affecting the relationship, and both partners may have trouble communicating effectively with one another. Individual sessions may be provided separately to each partner, particularly at the beginning of therapy; most of the course of therapy, however, is provided to both partners together. Couples therapy for married couples is known as **marital therapy**.

courage *n.* the ability to meet a difficult challenge despite the physical, psychological, or moral risks involved in doing so. Examples of acts of courage include saving another's or one's own life against a meaningful threat; coping with a painful, debilitating, or terminal illness; overcoming a destructive habit; and voicing an unpopular opinion. Also called **bravery**; **valor**. —**courageous** *adj.*

C

course *n.* the length of time a disorder, illness, or treatment typically lasts, its natural progression, and (if applicable) its recurrence over time.

course modifier a pattern that develops in a disorder (e.g., recurrence, seasonal variation) that helps to predict its future course or may serve to alter its usual course.

courtesan fantasy see HETAERAL FANTASY.

court-ordered treatment any assessment, treatment, consultation, or other service for defendants, plaintiffs, or criminal offenders that is mandated by a judge or magistrate.

couvade *n.* **1.** a custom in some cultures in which the father takes to bed before or after his child is born, as if he himself suffered the pain of childbirth. **2.** abdominal pain or other somatic symptoms appearing in male partners of pregnant women, usually presumed to be PSYCHOGENIC in origin. Also called **couvade syndrome**.

covariance *n.* a scale-dependent measure of the relationship between two variables.

covariate *n.* a correlated variable that is often controlled or held constant through the ANALYSIS OF COVARIANCE. Also called **concomitant variable**.

coverage *n.* health care benefits and services provided within a given HEALTH PLAN.

cover memory see SCREEN MEMORY.

covert behavior behavior that is not directly observable and can only be inferred or self-reported. For example, imagining something is covert behavior.

covert conditioning a technique of BEHAVIOR THERAPY that relies on the use of imagination and assumes that overt and covert behaviors are associated, that each affects the other, and that both forms of behavior depend on the laws of learning. The individual imagines performing a desired behavior in a problematic real-life situation, rewards himself or herself for mentally engaging in the behavior, and finally achieves an actual change in behavior. Also called **covert behavioral reinforcement**. [developed in 1966 by U.S. psychologist Joseph R. Cautela (1927–1999)]

covert desensitization a form of DESENSITIZATION therapy in which an individual is helped to overcome a fear or anxiety by learning to relax while recollecting the anxiety-producing stimulus in his or her imagination. A hierarchy is devised with a sequence of items that range from the least to the most anxiety-producing aspects of the stimulus. The client then uses relaxation techniques while progressively imagining items on the hierarchy until able to imagine the stimulus without feeling anxious. Compare IN VIVO DESENSITIZATION. See also SYSTEMATIC DESENSITIZATION.

C

covert extinction a COVERT CONDITIONING procedure in which the client first imagines performing an unwanted behavior and then imagines failing to be rewarded or to receive REINFORCEMENT for the behavior. See also COVERT POSITIVE REINFORCEMENT.

covert modeling a COVERT CONDITIONING procedure in which the client pictures a role model, imagines behaving as this person might, and then visualizes specific favorable consequences of the behavior. See also COVERT POSITIVE REINFORCEMENT.

covert negative reinforcement in BEHAVIOR THERAPY, a technique in which the client first imagines an aversive event and then switches to imagining engaging in the target behavior. For example, a client might imagine that he or she is alone at a restaurant, feeling insecure and unhappy, and then switches the imaginary scene to one in which he or she is asking another person for a date and that person says yes. Compare COVERT POSITIVE REINFORCEMENT.

covert positive reinforcement in BEHAVIOR THERAPY, a technique in which a person imagines performing a desired behavior that is followed by a pleasant consequence and subsequently rehearsing the behavior in the hope that it will eventually be adopted. Also called **covert reinforcement**. Compare COVERT NEGATIVE REINFORCEMENT.

covert rehearsal a technique in which either rote or elaborate repetitive rehearsing in one's mind of words or behaviors is used to improve memory or to prepare for overt speech or behavior. See also BEHAVIOR REHEARSAL.

covert reinforcement see COVERT POSITIVE REINFORCEMENT.

covert response any generally unobservable response, such as a thought, image, emotion, or internal physiological reaction, the existence of which is typically inferred or measured indirectly. For example, covert preparation for physical responses can be observed in an electric brain potential called the LATERALIZED READINESS POTENTIAL and in electromyographic measures of muscle activity. Also called **implicit response**. Compare OVERT RESPONSE.

covert self an individual's perception of his or her true nature.

covert sensitization a BEHAVIOR THERAPY technique for reducing an undesired behavior in which the client imagines performing the undesired behavior (e.g., overeating) and then imagines an unpleasant consequence (e.g., vomiting).

covert speech talking to oneself. Covert speech is usually seen as the externalization of a person's inner voice: Some explanations have equated it with thought itself.

COWA abbreviation for CONTROLLED ORAL WORD ASSOCIATION.

CP abbreviation for CEREBRAL PALSY.

CPA abbreviation for CANADIAN PSYCHOLOGICAL ASSOCIATION.

CPI abbreviation for CALIFORNIA PSYCHOLOGICAL INVENTORY.

CPQ abbreviation for CHILDREN'S PERSONALITY QUESTIONNAIRE.

CPR fees abbreviation for CUSTOMARY, PREVAILING, AND REASONABLE FEES.

CPS abbreviation for COMREY PERSONALITY SCALES.

CPT 1. abbreviation for COGNITIVE PROCESSING THERAPY. **2.** abbreviation for CONTINUOUS PERFORMANCE TEST.

CPZ abbreviation for CHLORPROMAZINE.

crack *n.* a dried mixture of COCAINE and baking soda that can be smoked. It contains a relatively small, inexpensive amount of cocaine, which produces a rapid and short-lived high, thus increasing the drug's accessibility.

cracking facades the process of encouraging people to reveal their true selves. It is associated with Carl ROGERS's encounter-group work.

cramp *n.* a painful muscle spasm (contraction).

cranial bifida a congenital disorder manifested by a horseshoe-shaped depression of the medial (middle) plane of the forehead. A median-cleft palate, a cleft of the nose ranging from a notch to complete division, and widely spaced eyes are present. Because of a failure of the two sides of the head to fuse normally during prenatal development, the corpus callosum, the nerve tract connecting the two sides of the brain, may be defective. Mental retardation is common.

cranial electrical stimulation see ELECTROSLEEP THERAPY.

cranial index the ratio of the maximum breadth of the skull to its maximum length, multiplied by 100. Compare CEPHALIC INDEX.

cranial nerve any of the 12 pairs of nerves that arise directly from the brain and are distributed mainly to structures in the head and neck. Some of the cranial nerves are sensory, some are motor, and some are mixed (i.e., both sensory and motor). Cranial nerves are designated by Roman numerals, as follows: I, olfactory nerve; II, optic nerve; III, oculomotor nerve; IV, trochlear nerve; V, trigeminal nerve; VI, abducens nerve; VII, facial nerve; VIII, vestibulocochlear nerve; IX, glossopharyngeal nerve; X, vagus nerve; XI, accessory nerve; XII, hypoglossal nerve.

craniofacial dysostosis see CROUZON'S SYNDROME.

craniostenosis *n.* a skull deformity caused by premature closing of the cranial sutures. The condition restricts normal development of brain structures and usually results in mental retardation.

craniotomy *n.* the surgical opening of the skull, a procedure that may be performed, for example, to administer surgical treatment or to release pressure when the brain is expanding due to HYDROCEPHALUS or CEREBRAL EDEMA. Craniotomy is one of the oldest types of surgery: Evidence of it has been found in prehistoric skulls in nearly every part of the world.

crank *n.* a street name for smokable METHAMPHETAMINE.

crash *n.* **1.** the withdrawal symptoms, usually dominated by feelings of severe depression, that occur following a lengthy period of amphetamine intoxication. The user may sleep for several days more or less continuously, displaying signs of exhaustion and irritation during waking periods. See AMPHETAMINE WITHDRAWAL. **2.** the period following the "rush" or "high" produced by intravenous cocaine. As feelings of euphoria wear off, they are replaced by irritability, depression, and anxiety, as well as strong craving for another dose. See COCAINE WITHDRAWAL.

creative arts therapy therapeutic interventions that use artistic endeavors or mediums, such as music, poetry, dance, and drama, to facilitate communication and emotional expression, enhance self-awareness, and foster health and change. See also ART THERAPY; DANCE THERAPY; DRAMA THERAPY; MUSIC THERAPY; POETRY THERAPY.

creative dramatics the use, especially with children, of spontaneous drama-oriented play ("pretending") as a therapeutic technique designed to enhance creativity and imagination, improve communication and social skills, and foster health. The emphasis in creative dramatics is not on the end product (e.g., performance) but rather on the creative process itself.

creative imagination the faculty by which new, uncommon ideas are produced, especially when this does not seem explicable by the mere combination of existing ideas. The operations of the creative imagination are sometimes explained by the interaction of dormant or unconscious elements with active, conscious thoughts. See also CREATIVE THINKING; CREATIVITY; DIVERGENT THINKING; IMAGINATION.

creative intelligence in the TRIARCHIC THEORY OF INTELLIGENCE, the set of skills used to create, invent, discover, explore, imagine, and suppose. This set of skills is alleged to be relatively (although not wholly) distinctive with respect to analytical and practical skills. Compare ANALYTICAL INTELLIGENCE; PRACTICAL INTELLIGENCE.

creative synthesis the combination of several ideas, images, or associations into a new whole, especially when this differs fundamentally from any of its components. [coined by Wilhelm WUNDT]

creative thinking the mental processes leading to a new invention, solution, or synthesis in any area. A creative solution may use preexisting objects or ideas but creates a new relationship between the elements it utilizes. Examples include new machines, social ideas, scientific theories, and artistic creations. Compare CRITICAL THINKING. See also DIVERGENT THINKING.

creativity *n.* the ability to produce or develop original work, theories, techniques, or thoughts. A creative individual typically displays originality, imagination, and expressiveness. Analyses have failed to ascertain why one individual is more creative than another, but creativity does appear to be a very durable trait. See also CREATIVE IMAGINATION; CREATIVE THINKING; DIVERGENT THINKING. **—creative** *adj.*

creativity test any psychological test designed to identify CREATIVITY or DIVERGENT THINKING. Existing tests focus on a variety of factors, such as an individual's FLUENCY with words and ideas or ability to generate original associations; tasks may involve finding solutions to practical problems, suggesting different endings to stories, or listing unusual uses for objects. See also TORRANCE TESTS OF CREATIVE THINKING.

credentialing *n.* the administrative process of reviewing a health care provider's qualifications, practice history, and medical CERTIFICATION or license to determine if criteria for clinical privileges are met. See also PROFESSIONAL LICENSING.

creeping commitment see ESCALATION OF COMMITMENT.

Creutzfeldt–Jakob disease (**CJD**) a rapidly progressive neurological disease characterized by DEMENTIA, involuntary muscle movements (especially MYOCLONUS), ATAXIA, visual disturbances, and seizures. Vacuoles form in the gray matter of the brain and spinal cord, giving it a spongy appearance; the prion is thought to cause misfolding of other proteins, leading to the cellular pathology. **Classical CJD** occurs sporadically worldwide and typically affects individuals who are middle-aged or older. A small proportion (about 10%) of cases are inherited. Early symptoms are muscular incoordination (ataxia), with abnormalities of gait and speech, followed by worsening dementia and myoclonus. Death occurs usually within 1 year of the onset of symptoms. **Variant CJD** (**vCJD**) was first reported in Great Britain in the 1990s. It causes similar symptoms but typically affects younger people, who are believed to have acquired the disease by eating meat or meat products from cattle infected with bovine spongiform encephalopathy (BSE). Also called **Jakob–Creutzfeldt disease**; **subacute spongiform encephalopathy** (**SSE**). [Hans Gerhard **Creutzfeldt** (1885–1964) and Alfons **Jakob** (1884–1931), German neuropathologists]

cri du chat syndrome a chromosomal disorder involving deletion of the short arm of chromosome 5, which results in severe mental retardation, walking and talking difficulty or inability, and an anomaly of the epiglottis and larynx that causes a high-pitched wailing cry like

C

that of a cat. Almost all affected individuals have very small heads (see MICROCEPHALY). The defect seems to be hereditary. Also called **cat-cry syndrome**; **chromosome 5, deletion of short arm**; **crying-cat syndrome**; **Lejeune syndrome**; **monosomy 5p**.

criminal commitment the confinement of people in mental institutions either because they have been found NOT GUILTY BY REASON OF INSANITY or in order to establish their COMPETENCY TO STAND TRIAL as responsible defendants.

criminal intent see MENS REA.

criminally insane describing defendants who are judged to be suffering from a mental illness or defect that absolves them of legal responsibility for the criminal acts they are alleged to have committed. The term is now seldom used.

criminal psychopath a person with ANTISOCIAL PERSONALITY DISORDER who repeatedly violates the law.

criminal responsibility a defendant's ability to formulate a criminal intent (see MENS REA) at the time of the crime with which he or she is charged, which must be proved in court before the person can be convicted. Criminal responsibility may be excluded for reason of INSANITY (see DURHAM RULE; IRRESISTIBLE IMPULSE RULE; MCNAUGHTEN RULE) or mitigated for a number of other reasons (see DIMINISHED CAPACITY; DIMINISHED RESPONSIBILITY).

criminal type a classification of individuals who repeatedly engage in criminal or illegal acts, supposedly because of a genetic predisposition to do so.

crisis *n.* (*pl.* **crises**) **1.** a situation (e.g., a traumatic change) that produces significant cognitive or emotional stress in those involved in it. **2.** a turning point for better or worse in the course of an illness.

crisis center a facility established for emergency therapy or referral, sometimes staffed by medical and mental health professionals and paraprofessionals. See DROP-IN CENTER.

crisis counseling immediate drop-in, phone-in, or on-site professional counseling provided following a trauma or sudden stressful event, often for emergency situations or in the aftermath of a disaster. See DISASTER COUNSELING; HOTLINE.

crisis intervention 1. the brief ameliorative, rather than specifically curative, use of psychotherapy or counseling to aid individuals, families, and groups who have undergone a highly disruptive experience, such as an unexpected bereavement or a disaster. Crisis intervention may prevent more serious consequences of the experience, such as POSTTRAUMATIC STRESS DISORDER. **2.** psychological intervention provided on a short-term, emergency basis for individuals experiencing mental health crises, such as an ACUTE PSYCHOTIC EPISODE or ATTEMPTED SUICIDE.

crisis intervention service any of the services provided (usually by governmental or social agencies) during emergencies, disasters, and for personal crises. Such services include hot lines, drop-in services, and on-site intervention at the scene of a disaster.

crisis management the organization and mobilization of resources to overcome the difficulties presented by a sudden and unexpected threat. The psychological stress produced by a crisis can reduce the information-processing capacities of those affected, which should be taken into account by crisis managers when considering possible solutions.

crisis team a group of professionals and paraprofessionals trained to help individuals cope with psychological reactions during and following emergencies or mental health crises, for example, natural disasters or suicide threats or attempts.

crisis theory the body of concepts that deals with the nature, precipitants, prevention, intervention, and resolution of, as well as the behavior associated with, a crisis.

criteria of evaluation the criteria used to specify or measure program impact or, often, PROGRAM OUTCOME as stated in the EVALUATION OBJECTIVES of a study.

criterion *n.* (*pl.* **criteria**) **1.** a standard against which a judgment, evaluation, or comparisons can be made. **2.** a test score or item against which other tests or items can be validated. For example, a well-validated test of creativity might be used as the criterion to select new tests of creativity.

criterion-based content analysis (**CBCA**) a form of STATEMENT VALIDITY ANALYSIS in which children's statements in instances of alleged abuse are analyzed in terms of key content criteria, in order to evaluate their truth.

criterion group a group tested for traits its members are already known to possess, usually for the purpose of validating a test. For example, a group of children with diagnosed visual disabilities may be given a visual test to assess its VALIDITY as a means of evaluating the presence of visual disabilities.

criterion-referenced testing an approach to testing based on the comparison of a person's performance with an established standard or criterion. The criterion is fixed, that is, each person's score is measured against the same criterion and is not influenced by the performance of others. See NORM-REFERENCED TESTING.

criterion score a predicted score on an attribute or variable that is derived from REGRESSION ANALYSIS.

criterion validity an index of how well a test correlates with a criterion, that is, an established standard of comparison. Criterion validity is divided into two types: CONCURRENT VALIDITY and PREDICTIVE VALIDITY.

critical care unit (**CCU**) see INTENSIVE CARE UNIT.

critical-incident stress debriefing (**CISD**) a systematic and programmed process designed to help individuals who witness or work at the scene of a critical incident or disaster (e.g., firefighters). The process uses basic stress counseling techniques; formal training in CISD is provided in workshops for personnel in emergency services as well as for mental health professionals. [developed by U.S. psychologist Jeffrey T. Mitchell (1948–)]

critical life event an event in life that requires major ADJUSTMENT and adaptive behavior. Such events may be regarded in retrospect as unusually formative or pivotal in shaping attitudes and beliefs. Common critical life events include bereavement, divorce, and unemployment. See also LIFE EVENTS.

critical period an early stage in life when an organism is especially open to specific learning, emotional, or socializing experiences that occur as part of normal development and will not recur at a later stage. For example, the first 3 days of life are thought to constitute a critical period for IMPRINTING in ducks, and there may be a critical period for language acquisition in human infants. See also SENSITIVE PERIOD.

critical point a point in the course of psychotherapy at which the client sees his or her problem clearly and decides on an appropriate course of action to handle or resolve it.

critical thinking a form of directed, problem-focused thinking in which the individual tests ideas or possible solutions for errors or drawbacks. It is essential to such activities as examining the validity of a hypothesis or interpreting the meaning of research results. Compare CREATIVE THINKING. See CONVERGENT THINKING.

critical value the value of either end point of the critical region; that is, either of the values of the test statistic above and below which the NULL HYPOTHESIS will be rejected.

critical variable a variable required to bring about a particular result or to make a particular prediction.

Cronbach, Lee J. (1916–2001) U.S. psychologist. Cronbach received his doctorate in education from the University of Chicago in 1940. He held faculty positions at a number of universities, spending the longest periods at the University of Illinois (1948–1964) and Stanford University (from 1964 until his retirement). Cronbach is best known for his contributions to the fields of educational psychology and psychological testing. He developed a measure of test reliability that became known as CRONBACH'S ALPHA; he also contributed importantly to the topic of test VALIDITY. His widely cited paper "Construct Validity in Psychological Tests" (1955, coauthored by Paul MEEHL) helped to establish validity as a keystone of psychological testing. Cronbach was particularly influential in the field of education in California, where he headed a faculty consortium involved in evaluating education in the state. His book *Designing Educational Evaluations* (1982) summarized his ideas resulting from the work of the consortium. Cronbach also made important contributions to the field of instruction, with research focusing on the need to match student aptitude with the appropriate learning environment. This work is summarized in *Aptitudes and Instructional Methods* (1977, coauthored with R. E. Snow). Cronbach's honors included the Distinguished Scientific Contribution Award of the American Psychological Association and membership in the American Academy of Arts and Sciences. He served as president of the American Psychological Association in 1956.

Cronbach's alpha an index of INTERNAL CONSISTENCY reliability, that is, the degree to which a set of items that comprise a measurement instrument tap a single, unidimensional construct. Also called **alpha coefficient**; **coefficient alpha**. [Lee J. CRONBACH]

cross-addiction *n.* see CROSS-TOLERANCE.

cross-cultural approach in the social sciences, a research method in which specific social practices, such as courtship behavior, child-rearing practices, or therapeutic attitudes and techniques, are studied and compared across a number of different cultures. Also called **cross-cultural method**. See also CROSS-CULTURAL PSYCHOLOGY.

cross-cultural counseling see MULTICULTURAL THERAPY.

cross-cultural psychology a branch of psychology that studies similarities and variances in human behavior across different cultures and identifies the different psychological constructs and explanatory models used by these cultures. It may be contrasted with CULTURAL PSYCHOLOGY, which tends to adopt a systemic, within-culture approach. Also called **ethnopsychology**.

cross-cultural testing testing individuals with diverse cultural backgrounds and experiences using a method and materials that do not favor certain individuals over others. Typically, CULTURE-FAIR TESTS are administered with nonverbal instructions and content, avoid objects indigenous to a particular culture, and do not depend on speed.

cross-cultural treatment treatment in situations in which therapist and client differ in terms of race, ethnicity, gender, language, or lifestyle. Mental health providers should be attentive to cultural differences with clients for the following (among other) reasons: (a) Social and cultural beliefs influence diagnosis and treatment, (b) diagnosis differs across cultures, (c) symptoms are expressed differently across cul-

C

tures, (d) diagnostic categories reflect majority cultural values, and (e) most providers are from the majority culture.

cross-dressing *n.* the process or habit of putting on the clothes of the opposite sex. It is done for a variety of reasons, for example, as part of a performance, as social commentary, or as a preliminary stage in sex-reversal procedures (see also TRANSSEXUALISM). Although synonymous with transvestism, cross-dressing is distinct from TRANSVESTIC FETISHISM.

cross-gender behavior the process or habit of assuming the role of the opposite sex by adopting the clothes, hair style, and manner of speaking and gesturing that society considers characteristic of the opposite sex. See CROSS-DRESSING.

cross-lagged panel design a longitudinal experimental design used to increase the plausibility of causal inference in which two variables, A and B, are measured at time 1 (A_1, B_1) and at time 2(A_2, B_2). Comparison of **cross-lagged panel correlations** between A_1B_2 and B_1A_2 may suggest a preponderance of causal influence of A over B or of B over A.

crossover design an experimental design in which different treatments are applied to the same sampling units (e.g., individuals) during different periods.

cross-sectional design an experimental design in which individuals of different ages or developmental levels are directly compared, for example, in a **cross-sectional study** comparing 5-year-olds with 10-year-olds. Compare LONGITUDINAL DESIGN.

cross-situational consistency the degree to which a psychological attribute, such as a personal disposition or a cognitive style, is displayed in the same, or a functionally equivalent, manner in different social environments.

cross-tabulation *n.* a method of arranging or presenting data (e.g., values, levels) in tabular form to show the mutual influence of one variable or variables on another variable or variables.

cross-tolerance *n.* the potential for a drug, often a CNS DEPRESSANT, to produce the diminished effects of another drug of the same type when tissue tolerance for the effects of the latter substance has developed. Thus, a person with alcohol dependence can substitute a barbiturate or another sedative to prevent withdrawal symptoms, and vice versa. Similarly, cross-tolerance exists among most of the hallucinogens, except marijuana. Also called **cross-addiction**.

cross-validation *n.* a model-evaluation approach in which the VALIDITY of a model is assessed by applying it to new data (i.e., data that were not used in developing the model). For example, a test's validity may be confirmed by administering the same test to a new sample in order to check the correctness of the initial validation. Cross-validation is necessary because chance and other factors may have inflated or biased the original validation.

Crouzon's syndrome a condition in which a wide skull with a protrusion near the anterior fontanel (on top of the head, at the front) is associated with a beaked nose and ocular abnormalities. The latter may include atrophy, divergent strabismus, and blindness. Mild to moderate mental retardation is typical. Other neurological disorders may result from intracranial pressure. Also called **craniofacial dysostosis**. See also APERT'S SYNDROME. [described in 1912 by Octave **Crouzon** (1874–1938), French neurologist]

crutch *n.* **1.** a device, usually made of metal or wood, designed to aid people with disabilities or other problems affecting the lower limbs by providing support in walking. The simplest type of crutch consists of two long parallel shafts that taper to a single point at the bottom and fit under the armpit at the top; a crosspiece in the middle functions as a handgrip. In contrast, arm crutches consist of a single shaft with a handgrip and a cuff that fits either the forearm or the upper arm. **2.** colloquially, a nonspecific coping or support mechanism, which may be of a psychological, medicinal, or other nature.

crying-cat syndrome see CRI DU CHAT SYNDROME.

cryotherapy *n.* the use of cold for therapeutic effect; for example, abnormal tissue is destroyed by freezing it. Cryotherapy is commonly used in sports medicine, though its effects on motor control remain unclear. It is possible that cryotherapy elevates the pain threshold.

cryptophasia *n.* secret or incomprehensible language, especially the peculiar communication patterns that are sometimes developed between twins and are understandable only to them.

cryptophoric symbolism a type of REPRESENTATION expressed indirectly in the form of a metaphor. For example, a person may describe a difficult relationship in terms of an illegible map or a stuck door. In METAPHOR THERAPY patients are encouraged to alter their attitudes or perceptions by finding new metaphors. Also called **metaphoric symbolism**. [described by U.S. psychotherapist Richard Royal Kopp (1942–)]

cryptophthalmos syndrome a familial or hereditary disorder in which a child is born with skin covering the eyes. The anomaly may occur on one side or both. The eyes are usually present under the facial skin and lack eyelids, eyelashes, and, usually, tear ducts, and the individual may be able to discern light and colors. Hearing loss is common, as are ear anomalies. This syndrome often occurs with mental retardation.

crystal healing a pseudoscientific medical practice in which the alleged power of certain crystals to affect the human energy field is used to treat physical or mental ailments. See also FAITH HEALING; PSYCHIC HEALING.

crystallized intelligence (**crystallized ability**) see CATTELL–HORN THEORY OF INTELLIGENCE.

Cs abbreviation for CONSCIOUS.

CSR **1.** abbreviation for COMBAT STRESS REACTIONS. **2.** abbreviation for CONTINUED-STAY REVIEW.

CT **1.** abbreviation for COGNITIVE THERAPY. **2.** abbreviation for COMPUTED TOMOGRAPHY.

CTD abbreviation for cumulative trauma disorder (see REPETITIVE STRAIN INJURY).

CTI abbreviation for CONSTRUCTIVE THINKING INVENTORY.

CTZ abbreviation for CHEMORECEPTOR TRIGGER ZONE.

cube model a three-dimensional model of the information cues that determine causal attributions. The cues are consistency (the extent to which observed behavior agrees with previous behavior), distinctiveness (the contextual, or situational, variability surrounding the behavior), and consensus (the extent to which others act similarly in the same situations). See ATTRIBUTION THEORY.

cuddling behavior holding close, a form of ATTACHMENT BEHAVIOR between individuals that is intended to convey affection or give comfort. In developmental psychology, it typically refers to such behavior between a parent or caregiver and a child.

cue *n.* a stimulus that serves to guide behavior, such as a RETRIEVAL CUE.

cue-controlled relaxation a technique in which a client is taught to associate a cue word with the practice of relaxing. See also APPLIED RELAXATION.

cued panic attack in *DSM–IV–TR,* a PANIC ATTACK that occurs almost invariably upon exposure to, or in anticipation of, a specific situational trigger. For example, an individual with social phobia may have a panic attack as a result of just thinking about an upcoming presentation. Also called **situationally bound panic attack**. See also SITUATIONALLY PREDISPOSED PANIC ATTACK. Compare UNCUED PANIC ATTACK.

cued recall a type of memory task in which an item to be remembered is presented for study along with a CUE and the participant subsequently attempts to recall the item when given the cue.

cue exposure a BEHAVIOR THERAPY technique in which a client is exposed to stimuli that induce cravings for substances (e.g., alcohol, tobacco), while the therapist uses other techniques to reduce or eliminate the craving. This technique is most frequently used in substance abuse and smoking cessation programs. See also EXPOSURE THERAPY.

culpability *n.* **1.** responsibility for an adverse outcome. **2.** in law, the state of being found criminally responsible for one's actions and subject to legal sanctions. See CRIMINAL RESPONSIBILITY. **—culpable** *adj.*

cultural bias the tendency to interpret and judge phenomena in terms of the distinctive values, beliefs, and other characteristics of the society or community to which one belongs. This sometimes leads people to form opinions and make decisions about others in advance of any actual experience with those others (see PREJUDICE). Cultural bias has become a significant concern in many areas, including PSYCHOMETRICS and CLINICAL PSYCHOLOGY. See also CULTURE-FAIR TEST; CULTURE-FREE TEST.

cultural deprivation **1.** lack of opportunity to participate in the cultural offerings of the larger society due to such factors as economic deprivation, substandard living conditions, or discrimination. See PSEUDORETARDATION. **2.** lack of culturally stimulating phenomena in one's environment.

cultural determinism the theory or premise that individual and group character patterns are produced largely by a given society's economic, social, political, and religious organization. See also DETERMINISM; SOCIAL DETERMINISM.

cultural-familial mental retardation mental retardation, usually mild, that occurs in the absence of any known organic cause and is therefore attributed to hereditary or early (preschool) environmental factors. Hereditary factors include natural variation, in the absence of genetic anomalies, in intellectual abilities among members of populations. Also called **familial retardation**; **sociocultural mental retardation**.

cultural psychology an interdisciplinary extension of general psychology concerned with those psychological processes that are inherently organized by culture. It is a heterogeneous class of perspectives that focus on explaining how human psychological functions are culturally constituted through various forms of relations between people and their social contexts. As a discipline, cultural psychology relates to cultural anthropology, sociology, semiotics, language, philosophy, and culture studies. Within psychology, cultural psychology relates most closely to cross-cultural, social, developmental, and cognitive issues. It may be contrasted with CROSS-CULTURAL PSYCHOLOGY, which tends to examine multiple cultures in order to identify the similarities and variances among them.

cultural relativism the view that attitudes, behaviors, values, concepts, and achievements must be understood in the light of their own cultural milieu and not judged according to the standards of a different culture. In psychology, the relativist position questions the universal application of psychological theory, research, therapeutic techniques, and clinical approaches, since those used or developed in one culture may not be appropriate or applicable to another. Compare CULTURAL UNIVERSALISM.

cultural specificity of emotions the finding that the elicitors and the expressions of emotions differ dramatically in members of different cultures and societies. Compare UNIVERSALITY OF EMOTIONS.

cultural test bias partiality of a test in favor of individuals from certain backgrounds at the expense of individuals from other backgrounds. The partiality may be in the content of the items, in the format of the items, or in the very act of taking a test itself. For example, suppose a verbal comprehension exam was delivered on a computer and incorporated passages, pictures, and questions drawn from American literature. The exam is likely to favor individuals who grew up in American families that could afford to have computers and a variety of books at home. In contrast, poorer individuals who emigrated to America and were without computers or many books in the home might find that the exam had some degree of cultural test bias. See also TEST BIAS.

cultural universalism the view that the values, concepts, and behaviors characteristic of diverse cultures can be viewed, understood, and judged according to universal standards. Such a view involves the rejection, at least in part, of CULTURAL RELATIVISM. Also called **cultural absolutism**.

culture-bound syndrome a pattern of mental illness and abnormal behavior that is unique to a small ethnic or cultural population and does not conform to Western classifications of psychiatric disorders. Culture-bound syndromes include, among others, AMOK, AMURAKH, BANGUNGUT, HSIEH-PING, IMU, JUMPING FRENCHMEN OF MAINE SYNDROME, KORO, LATAH, MAL DE PELEA, MYRIACHIT, PIBLOKTO, SUSTO, VOODOO DEATH, and WINDIGO. Also called **culture-specific syndrome**.

culture conflict 1. tension or competition between different cultures. It often results in the weakening of a minority group's adherence to cultural practices and beliefs as these are superseded by those of a dominant or adjoining culture. Also called **intergroup culture conflict**. **2.** the conflicting loyalties experienced by individuals who endorse the cultural beliefs of their subgroup but are also drawn to the practices and beliefs of the dominant culture. Also called **internal culture conflict**. See CULTURE SHOCK.

culture-fair test a test based on common human experience and considered to be relatively unbiased with respect to special background influences. Unlike some standardized intelligence assessments, which may reflect predominantly middle-class experience, a culture-fair test is designed to apply across social lines and to permit equitable comparisons among people from different backgrounds. Nonverbal, nonacademic items are used, such as matching identical forms, selecting a design that completes a given series, or drawing human figures. Studies have shown, however, that any assessment reflects certain socioethnic norms in some degree, and hence may tend to favor people with certain backgrounds rather than others. For example, an item that included the phrase "bad rap" could be unclear, as the phrase could refer to unjust criticism or to rap music that was either not very good or rather good, depending on an individual's common use of the word "bad." See also CROSS-CULTURAL TESTING.

culture-free test an intelligence test designed to eliminate cultural bias completely by constructing questions that contain either no environmental influences or no environmental influences that reflect any specific culture. However, the creation of such a test is probably impossible, and psychometricians instead generally seek to develop a CULTURE-FAIR TEST.

culture shock feelings of inner tension or conflict experienced by an individual or group that has been suddenly thrust into an alien culture or that experiences loyalties to two different cultures.

culture-specific syndrome see CULTURE-BOUND SYNDROME.

cumulative frequency distribution a table with three columns, where the first column (labelled X) lists the possible values for a variable, the second column (labeled f, for frequency) lists the number of scores that occur at each of the possible values given in the first column, and the third column (labeled CF, for cumulative frequency) gives the running total of each of the values in the second column. For example, a teacher administers a test and the students' scores are 1 F, 2 Ds, 4 Cs, 3 Bs, and 2 As. In a cumulative frequency distribution, the first column (X) represents exam scores, with F, D, C, B, and A listed from the bottom to the top. In the second column (f) are the values of 1, 2, 4, 3, and 2 to indicate 1 F, 2 Ds, 4 Cs, 3 Bs, and 2 As. In the final column (CF) are running totals of the second column from the bottom up, listing 1, 3, 7, 10, and 12 to indicate the summed total of scores at each of the grades, with the total number of scores listed at the top (i.e., there are 12 total scores in this cumulative frequency distribution). This type of table is useful in DESCRIPTIVE STATISTICS to depict the number of scores at or below each score level. Also called **cumulative distribution**; **cumulative frequency table**.

cumulative trauma disorder (**CTD**) see REPETITIVE STRAIN INJURY.

cunnilingus *n.* stimulation of the external female genital organs (i.e., the clitoris and vulva) with the mouth or tongue. Also called **cunnilinctio**; **cunnilinction**; **cunnilinctus**; **cunnilingam**. See also OROGENITAL ACTIVITY.

curare *n.* any of various toxic plant extracts, especially extracts from plants of the genus

Strychnos. Curare and related compounds exert their effects by blocking the activity of ACETYLCHOLINE at neuromuscular junctions, resulting in paralysis. Curare has a long ethnopharmacological history among indigenous peoples of the Amazon and Orinoco river basins, where it was applied to the tips of arrows to paralyze prey. It was brought to Europe in the 16th century by explorers of South America, but was not introduced into clinical use until the 1930s, when it was used to treat patients with tetanus and other spastic disorders. It has also been used in experiments showing that stimulus–response associations can be formed in paralyzed animals. The development of neuromuscular blocking agents with more predictable pharmacological profiles led to the abandonment of curare as a clinical agent.

curative factors model a model that seeks to identify those elements present in therapeutic groups that aid and promote personal growth and adjustment. U.S. psychologist Irwin Yalom (1931–) identified 10–15 curative factors, including the installation of hope, UNIVERSALITY, the imparting of information, altruism, and interpersonal learning.

curiosity *n.* the impulse or desire to investigate, observe, or gather information, particularly when the material is novel or interesting. This drive appears spontaneously in animals and in young children, who use sensory exploration and motor manipulation to inspect, bite, handle, taste, or smell practically everything in the immediate environment. **—curious** *adj.*

current material information about a client's present feelings, interpersonal relationships, and life events that is used in understanding that person's PSYCHODYNAMICS, especially by contrasting it with data from past experiences.

Cushing's syndrome a group of signs and symptoms related to a chronic overproduction of corticosteroid hormones, mainly CORTISOL, by the adrenal cortex. The condition occurs most commonly in women and is usually associated with a tumor of the adrenal or pituitary gland. Cushing's syndrome is characterized by a "moon face" due to fat deposits, "buffalo hump" fat pads on the trunk, hypertension, glucose intolerance, and psychiatric disturbances. [Harvey W. **Cushing** (1869–1939), U.S. surgeon]

custodial care 1. care rendered to a patient with prolonged mental or physical disability that includes assisted daily living (e.g., the regular feeding and washing of bedridden patients) but typically not mental health services themselves. **2.** confinement in such institutions as prisons and military correctional facilities that place restrictions on individuals' liberty under the rules of law and that protect and monitor the individual or protect others from the individual's violent and harmful tendencies or potential.

custodial case a court case concerning who should maintain legal custody of a child. See CHILD CUSTODY.

customary, prevailing, and reasonable fees (**CPR fees**) a criterion invoked in reimbursing health care providers. It is determined by profiling the prevailing fees in a geographic area. Also called **usual, customary, and reasonable** (**UCR**) **fees**.

cutoff point a numerical value that divides a DISTRIBUTION into two distinct parts.

cutting *n.* the act of cutting one's wrists or the inside of one's forearms, often accompanied by a sense of heightened arousal and little sensation of pain. This occurs most frequently in the context of BORDERLINE PERSONALITY DISORDER and occasionally in MAJOR DEPRESSIVE EPISODES.

CVLT abbreviation for CALIFORNIA VERBAL LEARNING TEST.

CVLT–C abbreviation for California Verbal Learning Test for Children. See CALIFORNIA VERBAL LEARNING TEST.

CVLT–II abbreviation for California Verbal Learning Test–II. See CALIFORNIA VERBAL LEARNING TEST.

CVS abbreviation for CHORIONIC VILLUS SAMPLING.

cycle of violence a conceptual framework for understanding the persistence of battering relationships. The cycle has three phases: (a) a "honeymoon phase," in which the batterer treats the battered partner lovingly; (b) a "tension build-up phase," in which the batterer begins to display irritability and anger toward the battered partner; and (c) the violence phase, in which battering occurs. The phases are then proposed to recycle. As a battering relationship persists over time, the honeymoon phases shorten, and the tension-building and violence phases lengthen. Also called **cycle of abuse**. [proposed in 1979 by U.S. clinical and forensic psychologist Lenore Walker (1942–)]

cyclic *adj.* characterized by alternating phases. Also called **cyclical**.

cyclical vomiting syndrome recurrent, severe episodes of vomiting that may last for hours or days but are separated by intervals of completely normal health. Stress may be an important precipitant of cyclical vomiting, which occurs frequently in children.

cyclic AMP (**cAMP**; **cyclic adenosine monophosphate**) a SECOND MESSENGER that is involved in the activities of DOPAMINE, NOREPINEPHRINE, and SEROTONIN in transmitting signals at nerve synapses. Also called **adenosine 3′,5′-monophosphate**.

cyclic illness 1. any disorder characterized by alternating phases. **2.** bipolar I disorder (see BIPOLAR DISORDER) in which both MAJOR DEPRESSIVE EPISODES and MANIC EPISODES occur alternately.

cyclobenzaprine *n.* a drug used for the treatment of acute skeletal muscle spasm (see MUSCLE

RELAXANT). Structurally related to the tricyclic antidepressants, it has many features in common with them, including sedation and significant ANTICHOLINERGIC EFFECTS. Low doses are moderately effective in treating FIBROMYALGIA SYNDROME. Because of its resemblance to the tricyclic drugs, cyclobenzaprine should not be taken concurrently with MONOAMINE OXIDASE INHIBITORS. U.S. trade name: **Flexeril**.

cycloid psychosis an atypical and controversial psychiatric disorder with three forms: **motility**, **confusional**, and **anxiety–happiness**. Symptoms, which resemble those of both a SCHIZOAFFECTIVE DISORDER and a PSYCHOTIC DISORDER NOT OTHERWISE SPECIFIED, follow a phasically recurring course and may change rapidly. [as modified in 1957 by German psychiatrist Karl Leonhard (1904–1988) from the original 1924 conceptualization of German neuropsychiatrist Karl Kleist (1879–1960)]

cyclosporine (**cyclosporin**) *n.* an immunosuppressive agent used primarily to prevent rejection of organ transplants but also used in the treatment of some autoimmune disorders, such as inflammatory bowel disease and severe atopic dermatitis. It is extensively metabolized by the CYTOCHROME P450 3A4 enzyme, and accordingly has numerous potential interactions with psychotropic drugs metabolized via the same enzyme (e.g., clonidine, nefazodone, St. John's wort). Depression, anxiety, and other psychological disturbances are rare side effects. U.S. trade name (among others): **Sandimmune**.

cyclothymic disorder in *DSM–IV–TR*, a MOOD DISORDER characterized by periods of hypomanic symptoms and periods of depressive symptoms that occur over the course of at least 2 years (1 year in children and adolescents), during which any symptom-free periods must last no longer than 2 months. The symptoms are those of a MAJOR DEPRESSIVE EPISODE or a HYPOMANIC EPISODE, but the number, duration, and severity of these symptoms do not meet the full criteria for a major depressive episode or a hypomanic episode. It often is considered to be a mild BIPOLAR DISORDER. Also called **cyclothymia**.

Cylert *n.* a trade name for PEMOLINE.

cyproheptadine *n.* a drug that acts as a ANTIHISTAMINE and SEROTONIN ANTAGONIST and is used for the the treatment of allergic symptoms (e.g., runny nose and watery eyes), appetite stimulation, and relief of migraine headaches. U.S. trade name (among others): **Periactin**.

cystathionine synthetase deficiency see HOMOCYSTINURIA.

cystathioninuria *n.* an inherited disorder of amino acid metabolism marked by deficiency of the enzyme cystathionase. The effects include vascular, skeletal, and ocular abnormalities. Mental retardation occurs in less than 50% of cases, often accompanied by behavioral disorders. Also called **gamma-cystathionase deficiency**.

cytochrome P450 (**CYP**) a group of proteins located in liver and other cells that, in combination with other oxidative enzymes, is responsible for the metabolism of various chemicals, including many psychotropic drugs. Approximately 50 cytochrome P450 enzymes (so named because their reduced forms show a spectroscopic absorption peak at 450 nm) are currently identified as being active in humans, of which cytochromes belonging to the CYP2D6 subclass, CYP2C variants, and CYP3A4/5 subclass predominate. Cytochromes are mainly active in Phase I DRUG METABOLISM; by donating an atom of oxygen, they tend to make parent drugs more water soluble and therefore more easily excreted. Because numerous drugs are metabolized via the same cytochrome, these enzymes are important in DRUG INTERACTIONS.

Cytomel *n.* a trade name for LIOTHYRONINE.

Dd

DA abbreviation for DOPAMINE.

Da Costa's syndrome an anxiety state identified in soldiers during the American Civil War (1861–1865) in which heart palpitations were the most prominent symptom. It is now recognized as a form of PANIC DISORDER observed in soldiers during the stress of combat and marked by fatigue, heart palpitations, chest pain, and breathing difficulty. Also called **neurocirculatory asthenia**; **soldier's heart**. See also EFFORT SYNDROME. [Jacob Méndes **Da Costa** (1833–1900), U.S. surgeon]

DAD abbreviation for DEVICE FOR AUTOMATED DESENSITIZATION.

DAH test abbreviation for Machover Draw-a-House Test. See MACHOVER DRAW-A-PERSON TEST.

Dalmane *n.* a trade name for FLURAZEPAM.

DALYs acronym for DISABILITY ADJUSTED LIFE YEARS.

dance therapy the use of various forms of rhythmic movement—classical, modern, folk, or ballroom dancing; exercises to music; and the like—as a therapeutic technique to help individuals achieve greater body awareness and social interaction and enhance their psychological and physical functioning. See also MOVEMENT THERAPY. [pioneered in 1942 by U.S. dance professional Marian Chace (1896–1970)]

dancing mania see CHOREOMANIA.

dangerousness *n.* the state in which individuals become likely to do harm either to themselves or to others, representing a threat to their own or other people's safety. **—dangerous** *adj.*

dantrolene *n.* a MUSCLE RELAXANT whose primary action is directly on skeletal muscles; it also indirectly affects the central nervous system as a secondary action. Dantrolene is used in the treatment of muscular spasm associated with spinal cord injury, stroke, cerebral palsy, and multiple sclerosis, as well as with NEUROLEPTIC MALIGNANT SYNDROME. U.S. trade name: **Dantrium**.

DAP test abbreviation for MACHOVER DRAW-A-PERSON TEST.

darkness fear see FEAR OF DARKNESS.

Darvocet *n.* a trade name for the analgesic combination PROPOXYPHENE and ACETAMINOPHEN. In 2010, Darvocet was withdrawn from the U.S. market.

Darvon *n.* a trade name for PROPOXYPHENE. In 2010, Darvon was withdrawn from the U.S. market.

Dasein *n.* in the thought of German philosopher Martin Heidegger (1889–1976), the particular kind of being manifest in humans. It is their being as *Dasein* that allows humans access to the larger question of being in general, since our access to the world is always through what our own being makes possible. The term is commonly used in EXISTENTIAL PSYCHOLOGY and related therapeutic approaches. See BEING-IN-THE-WORLD. [German, literally: "being there"]

Dasein analysis a method of EXISTENTIAL PSYCHOTHERAPY emphasizing the need to recognize not only one's BEING-IN-THE-WORLD but also what one can become (see DASEIN). Through examination of such concepts as intentionality and intuition, Dasein analysis attempts to help clients not to adapt to others or eliminate anxiety (which tends to submerge individuality and encourage outer conformity), but rather to accept themselves and realize their potential. [developed by Swiss psychiatrist Medard Boss (1903–1990)]

DAT abbreviation for dementia of the Alzheimer's type. See ALZHEIMER'S DISEASE; DEMENTIA.

data reduction the process of reducing a set of measurements or variables into a smaller, more manageable, more reliable, or better theoretically justified set or form. For example, a researcher may conduct a FACTOR ANALYSIS on a set of 50 items on well-being and satisfaction to determine whether the information could be summarized more efficiently on underlying dimensions of relationship satisfaction, degree of meaning in life, job satisfaction, and general health.

date rape sexual assault by an acquaintance, date, or other person known to the victim, often involving alcohol or DATE-RAPE DRUGS that may hinder the victim's ability to withhold consent. Also called **acquaintance rape**.

date-rape drug a drug that is surreptitiously administered to impair consciousness or memory for the purpose of sexual exploitation of the victim. Such drugs are commonly introduced into alcoholic beverages in social settings. Common date-rape drugs include barbiturates, high-potency benzodiazepines (FLUNITRAZEPAM, TRIAZOLAM), and the illicit substance GHB (gamma-hydroxybutyrate). The U.S. Congress passed the Drug-Induced Rape Prevention and Punishment Act in 1996, making it a federal crime to give an unaware person a controlled substance with the intent of committing a violent crime.

Daubert test a test used in U.S. federal courts to determine if expert scientific testimony is admissible under Federal Rules of Evidence 702. It generally takes place during a Daubert hearing, at which judges evaluate whether the testimony is both relevant and reliable, considering such factors as testability, error rate, evidence of peer review, and general acceptance within the scientific community.

Daubert v. Merrell Dow Pharmaceuticals Inc. a case resulting in an influential 1993 U.S. Supreme Court ruling that Federal Rules of Evidence should be the standard to determine whether expert scientific testimony is admissible. The court noted that judges should evaluate the validity of the scientific testimony according to whether the research reported (a) is peer-reviewed, (b) is testable (i.e., capable of being falsified), (c) has known error rates, and (d) is generally accepted within the scientific community.

Dauerschlaf *n.* a type of therapy in which prolonged sleep is induced with drugs (e.g., barbiturates). Dauerschlaf (German, "perpetual sleep") has been used in the treatment of substance dependence, status epilepticus, and acute psychotic episodes. Its efficacy and use have been the subject of extreme controversy, and it is now rarely encountered clinically.

day camp a facility that provides recreational, educational, or therapeutic services to children on a short-term, day-by-day basis as opposed to long-term camps that require overnight accommodation.

day care center 1. a nonresidential facility that provides health and social services in a community setting for adults who are unable to perform many ordinary tasks without supervision or assistance. See ADULT DAY CARE. **2.** see CHILD CARE FACILITIES.

daydream *n.* a waking fantasy, or reverie, in which wishes, expectations, and other potentialities are played out in imagination. Part of the stream of thoughts and images that occupy most of a person's waking hours, daydreams may be unbidden and apparently purposeless or simply fanciful thoughts, whether spontaneous or intentional. Researchers have identified at least three ways in which individuals' daydreaming styles differ: positive-constructive daydreaming, guilty and fearful daydreaming, and poor attentional control. These styles are posited to reflect the daydreamer's overall tendencies toward positive emotion, negative emotion, and other personality traits. Among the important positive functions that daydreams may serve are the release of strong affect, the gaining of self-insight when reviewing past experiences or rehearsing for future situations, the generation of creative solutions, and the production of greater empathy for others.

day habilitation a HOME AND COMMUNITY-BASED SERVICE provided for a person with mental retardation or a related condition. This service provides productive daily schedules of activity based on individualized service and support planning, including clinical services, companion services, socialization, recreation, vocational development, and lifestyle enrichment. In practice, these services may be delivered on a person-by-person basis or in small groups in any location during daytime hours.

day hospital a nonresidential facility where individuals with mental disorders receive a full range of treatment and support services during the day and return to their homes at night. Specific service offerings vary across facilities but generally include psychological evaluation, individual and group psychotherapy, social and occupational rehabilitation, and SOMATIC THERAPY. Staff members are multidisciplinary, comprising psychiatrists, psychologists, social workers, vocational counselors, and others.

daymare *n.* an attack of acute anxiety, distress, or terror, which is similar to a NIGHTMARE but occurs in a period of wakefulness and is precipitated by waking-state fantasies.

day treatment a program of coordinated interdisciplinary assessment, treatment, and rehabilitation services provided by professionals and paraprofessionals for people with disabilities, mental or physical disorders, or substance abuse problems, usually at a single location for 6 or more hours. Services also address skill and vocational development and may include adjustment programs or SHELTERED WORKSHOPS.

dc (**d/c**) in pharmacology, abbreviation for discontinue.

D-cognition *n.* see BEING COGNITION.

DDAVP *n.* a trade name for DESMOPRESSIN.

deadly catatonia see LETHAL CATATONIA.

deadly nightshade see BELLADONNA ALKALOIDS.

deaf-blind *adj.* lacking or having severely compromised vision and hearing concomitantly. People with deaf-blind impairment encounter significant—sometimes lifelong—challenges in communication, development, and education. Solutions involving tactile devices are often appropriate (e.g., braille). There is a large number of known causes, including MENINGITIS, CONGENITAL RUBELLA SYNDROME, and USHER SYNDROME. **—deaf-blindness** *n.*

deafness *n.* the partial or complete absence or loss of the sense of hearing. The condition may be hereditary or acquired by injury or disease at any stage of life, including in utero. The major kinds are conduction deafness, due to a disruption in sound vibrations before they reach the nerve endings of the inner ear; and sensorineural deafness, caused by a failure of the nerves or brain centers associated with the sense of hearing to transmit or interpret properly the impulses from the inner ear. Some individuals experience both conduction and sensorineural deafness, a form called **mixed deafness**. **—deaf** *adj.*

deaggressivization *n.* in psychoanalytic theory, the NEUTRALIZATION of the aggressive drive so that its energy can be diverted to various tasks and wishes of the EGO. See also SUBLIMATION.

death *n.* **1.** the permanent cessation of physical and mental processes in an organism. In the United States in the early 1980s, the American Medical Association and the American Bar Association drafted and approved the Uniform Determination of Death Act, in which death is defined as either the irreversible cessation of core physiological functioning (i.e., spontaneous circulatory and respiratory functions) or the irreversible loss of cerebral functioning (i.e., BRAIN DEATH). Given the emergence of sophisticated technologies for cardiopulmonary support, brain death is more often considered the essential determining factor, particularly within the legal profession. See also ASSISTED DEATH; DYING PROCESS; THANATOLOGY. **2.** the degeneration or disintegration of a biological cell. See NECROSIS.

death anxiety emotional distress and insecurity aroused by reminders of mortality, including one's own memories and thoughts. Classical psychoanalytic theory asserted that the unconscious cannot believe in its own death, therefore THANATOPHOBIA was a disguise for some deeper fear. Existentialists later proposed that death anxiety is at the root of all fears, though often disguised. A mass of research using self-report scales (see DEATH-ANXIETY SCALES) suggests that most people have a low to moderate level of death anxiety. See also EDGE THEORY; TERROR MANAGEMENT THEORY.

death-anxiety scales questionnaires that yield scores for the level of self-reported concern about death. Some scales distinguish between several types of concern, such as fear of pain or fear of nonbeing. See also THANATOPHOBIA.

death education learning activities or programs designed to educate people about death, dying, coping with grief, and the various emotional effects of bereavement. Death education is typically provided by certified thanatologists from a wide array of mental and medical health personnel, educators, clergy, and volunteers. Individual or group sessions provide information, discussion, guided experiences, and exploration of attitudes and feelings.

death instinct in psychoanalytic theory, a drive whose aim is the reduction of psychical tension to the lowest possible point, that is, death. It is first directed inward as a self-destructive tendency and is later turned outward in the form of the AGGRESSIVE INSTINCT. In the DUAL INSTINCT THEORY of Sigmund FREUD, the death instinct, or THANATOS, stands opposed to the LIFE INSTINCT, or EROS, and is believed to be the drive underlying such behaviors as aggressiveness, sadism, and masochism. Also called **destructive instinct**. See also DESTRUDO; MORTIDO; NIRVANA PRINCIPLE.

death phobia see THANATOPHOBIA.

death wish 1. in psychoanalytic theory, a conscious or unconscious wish that another person, particularly a parent, will die. According to Sigmund FREUD, such wishes are a major source of guilt, desire for self-punishment, and depression. **2.** an unconscious desire for one's own death, as manifested in self-destructive or dangerous behaviors. See also DEATH INSTINCT.

Debré–Sémélaigne syndrome see KOCHER–DEBRÉ–SÉMÉLAIGNE SYNDROME.

debriefing *n.* the process of giving participants in a completed research project a fuller explanation of the study in which they participated than was possible before or during the research.

debt counseling counseling specifically aimed at helping individuals with financial problems. The help and advice given includes budgeting, credit-card usage, debt consolidation, and awareness of difficulties in managing money. Debt counseling may be part of the counseling or therapy for other problems or it may be carried out by financial planners and accountants.

Decadron *n.* a trade name for DEXAMETHASONE.

decarceration *n.* **1.** the process of removing offenders from correctional facilities, often to community facilities. **2.** see DEINSTITUTIONALIZATION.

decatastrophizing *n.* a technique, used in treating people with irrational or exaggerated fears, that explores the reality of the situation rather than imagined or anticipated events.

decathexis *n.* in psychoanalytic theory, the withdrawal of LIBIDO from objects (i.e., other people) in the external world. Compare CATHEXIS.

decentering *n.* **1.** any of a variety of techniques aimed at changing centered thinking to open-minded thinking. A person with centered thinking is focused on only one salient feature at a time, to the total exclusion of other important characteristics. **2.** dissolution of unity between self and identity. **—decenter** *vb.*

decentralization *n.* the trend to relocate patients with chronic mental illness from long-term institutionalization, usually at government hospitals, to outpatient care in community-based, residential facilities. **—decentralize** *vb.*

deception by commission see ACTIVE DECEPTION.

deception by omission see PASSIVE DECEPTION.

deception clue a behavioral indication that an individual is not telling the truth. Deception clues include inconsistencies between voluntary and involuntary behavior and unusual or exaggerated physiological or expressive responses to knowledge that only a guilty person possesses. To date, behavioral scientists have discovered no

D

behavioral or physiological response that, by itself, shows a 1:1 relation to deception.

decisional competence the ability of a defendant to make the decisions normally faced by defendants in a criminal defense (e.g., deciding among various plea agreements). See also COMPETENCY EVALUATION; COMPETENCY TO STAND TRIAL; DUSKY STANDARD.

decision making the cognitive process of choosing between two or more alternatives, ranging from the relatively clear cut (e.g., ordering a meal at a restaurant) to the complex (e.g., selecting a mate). Psychologists have adopted two converging strategies to understand decision making: (a) statistical analysis of multiple decisions involving complex tasks and (b) experimental manipulation of simple decisions, looking at elements that recur within these decisions.

decision-making model of counseling an approach that envisions counseling as a process with three stages: the problem definition phase, the work phase, and the action phase. The problem definition phase includes considering alternative definitions of the problem and committing to one of these. During the work phase the problem is examined from different perspectives to identify facts as well as the thoughts and feelings of the client. The counselor helps the client to look at issues, answers, and solutions in new ways. The action phase deals with finding alternative solutions and choosing one to test in the home environment.

decision–redecision method a technique used in TRANSACTIONAL ANALYSIS that allows clients to reexperience decision moments in their childhood and choose to redecide. These decision moments resulted from such self-injunctions as "Don't be you," "Don't feel," "Don't be a child," and so forth, and have associated habitual patterns of emotion.

decisive moment in psychotherapy, that moment at which a client makes a momentous decision, such as revealing a secret or deciding to make a major change in his or her life.

declarative memory the ability to retain information about facts or events over a significant period of time and to consciously recall such **declarative knowledge**, typically in response to a specific request to remember. It is one of two major divisions in memory proposed in 1980 by U.S. neuroscientist and biological psychologist Larry R. Squire (1941–), and generally is divided into two subtypes: EPISODIC MEMORY and SEMANTIC MEMORY. This form of memory is selectively impaired in AMNESIA and is known as EXPLICIT MEMORY in other theoretical classifications. Compare NONDECLARATIVE MEMORY.

de Clérambault's syndrome see CLÉRAMBAULT'S SYNDROME.

decompensation *n.* a breakdown in an individual's DEFENSE MECHANISMS, resulting in progressive loss of normal functioning or worsening of psychiatric symptoms.

deconditioning *n.* a technique in BEHAVIOR THERAPY in which learned responses, such as phobias, are "unlearned" (deconditioned). For example, a person with a phobic reaction to flying might be deconditioned initially by practicing going to the airport when not actually taking a flight and using breathing techniques to control anxiety. See also DESENSITIZATION.

decontextualization *n.* **1.** the process of examining, considering, or interpreting something separately from the context within which it is embedded. Decontextualization may occur consciously (e.g., with the aim of subjecting a constituent element of some phenomenon or process to closer, individual study) or unconsciously. Either mode may result on the one hand in greater clarity but on the other in oversimplification and inaccuracies in comprehension. **2.** in perception, the process of turning implicit or contextual events into objects of conscious perception or belief. **—decontextualize** *vb.*

dedifferentiation *n.* loss of specialization or of advanced organizational and functional abilities. This may occur, for example, when mature cells within an organism regress to a more general, simplified state, as is sometimes seen in the progression of certain cancers, or as a form of thought disorganization seen in schizophrenia.

deductive reasoning the form of logical reasoning in which a conclusion is shown to follow necessarily from a sequence of premises, the first of which stands for a self-evident truth or agreed-upon data. In the empirical sciences, deductive reasoning underlies the process of deriving predictions from general laws or theories. Compare INDUCTIVE REASONING. See also LOGIC; TOP-DOWN ANALYSIS.

deep depression a severe MAJOR DEPRESSIVE EPISODE characterized by PSYCHOMOTOR RETARDATION, guilt, SUICIDAL IDEATION, and psychotic features. RUMINATION is frequent, and risk of suicide is high.

deep dyslexia a form of acquired dyslexia (see ALEXIA) characterized by semantic errors (e.g., reading *parrot* as *canary*), difficulties in reading abstract words (e.g., *idea, usual*) and function words (e.g., *the, and*), and an inability to read pronounceable nonwords. See also PHONOLOGICAL DYSLEXIA; SURFACE DYSLEXIA. [first described in 1973 by British neuropsychologists John C. Marshall and Freda Newcombe (1925–2001)]

deep processing cognitive processing of a stimulus that focuses on its meaningful properties rather than its perceptual characteristics. It is considered that processing at this semantic level, which usually involves a degree of ELABORATION, produces stronger, longer-lasting memories than SHALLOW PROCESSING. See also SEMANTIC ENCODING. [proposed in 1972 by Canadian psychologists Fergus I. M. Craik (1935–) and Robert S. Lockhart]

deep sleep the stage of the sleep cycle in which arousal thresholds are highest and consciousness is taken to be least likely. In deep sleep, DELTA WAVES are prominent in the electroencephalogram. See SLOW-WAVE SLEEP.

deep trance in hypnosis and shamanistic practices, a state in which participants are minimally responsive to environmental cues except for suggestions consistent with their beliefs. See TRANCE.

Deese paradigm a laboratory memory task used to study false recall. It is based on the report in 1959 that, after presentation of a list of related words (e.g., *snore, rest, dream, awake*), participants mistakenly recalled an unpresented but strongly associated item (e.g., *sleep*). Following renewed research into the technique, it is now generally referred to as the **Deese–Roediger–McDermott paradigm**. [James **Deese** (1921–1999), U.S. psychologist; Henry L. **Roediger** III (1947–) and Kathleen B. **McDermott** (1968–), U.S. cognitive psychologists]

defect *n.* a fault or error in something that prevents it from functioning correctly. **—defective** *adj.*

defective delinquent an outdated legal name for an individual who engages in repeated criminal behavior and is considered to be below average in intelligence.

defectology *n.* in Russian psychology, the area of abnormal psychology and learning disabilities. More specifically, defectology is concerned with the education of children with sensory, physical, cognitive, or neurological impairment. Russian defectology offers services to roughly the same population as special education and school psychology in the United States. It is based on the view that the primary problem of a disability is not the organic impairment itself but its social implications. [originally defined by Lev VYGOTSKY]

defect orientation 1. in interdisciplinary team or other individual service-planning processes, an emphasis that focuses on the impairments, limitations, deficits, or defects in functioning of individuals with disabilities, but that excludes corresponding assessment of and emphasis on their skills, abilities, and strengths. **2.** see DEFECT THEORY. Compare DEVELOPMENTAL ORIENTATION.

defect theory the proposition that the cognitive processes and behavioral development of people with mental retardation are qualitatively different from those of their peers without mental retardation. Also called **defect orientation**; **difference hypothesis**. Compare DEVELOPMENTAL THEORY.

defense interpretation in psychoanalysis, an interpretation of the ways in which the patient protects himself or herself from anxiety. Such an interpretation aims to make the patient aware of his or her defenses and to uncover the source of the anxiety in intrapsychic conflict.

defense mechanism in classical psychoanalytic theory, an unconscious reaction pattern employed by the EGO to protect itself from the anxiety that arises from psychic conflict. Such mechanisms range from mature to immature, depending on how much they distort reality: DENIAL is very immature because it negates reality, whereas SUBLIMATION is one of the most mature forms of defense because it allows indirect satisfaction of a true wish. In more recent psychological theories, defense mechanisms are seen as normal means of coping with everyday problems, but excessive use of any one, or the use of immature defenses (e.g., DISPLACEMENT or REPRESSION), is still considered pathological. Also called **escape mechanism**. See also AVOIDANCE; DENIAL; PROJECTION; REGRESSION; SUBLIMATION; SUBSTITUTION. [proposed in 1894 by Sigmund FREUD]

defense reflex a sudden response elicited by a painful or unexpected stimulus. The term is applied to a variety of responses, ranging from an acceleration in heart rate in reaction to a startling auditory stimulus, through flight, fight, or freezing elicited by perceived threat, to complex psychological responses. Also called **defense response**.

defensive behavior 1. aggressive or submissive behavior in response to real or imagined threats of bodily or psychic (particularly emotional) harm. A cat, for example, may exhibit defensive aggression by spitting and hissing, arching its back, and raising the hair along the back of the neck in anticipation of a physical threat. A human might unconsciously fend off criticism by putting forth self-justifying excuses or by expressing an emotional reaction (e.g., crying) to limit another's disapproval or anger. **2.** in psychoanalytic theory, behavior characterized by the use or overuse of DEFENSE MECHANISMS operating at an unconscious level.

defensive identification the process by which a victim of abuse psychologically identifies with the perpetrator of abuse, or with the group with which the perpetrator is identified, as a defensive strategy against continuing feelings of vulnerability to further victimization.

defensiveness *n.* a tendency to be sensitive to criticism or comment about one's deficiencies and to counter or deny such criticisms. **—defensive** *adj.*

deficiency *n.* a lack or shortage of something. A deficiency may, for example, be a relative or absolute lack of a skill, of a biological substrate or process, or of resources that enable specific functions or actions to be performed.

deficiency cognition see BEING COGNITION.

deficiency love (**D-love**) in Abraham MASLOW's humanistic psychology, a type of love that is fulfillment-oriented (e.g., based on a need for belonging, self-esteem, security, or power) and characterized by dependency, possessiveness, lack of mutuality, and little concern for the other's true welfare. Compare BEING LOVE.

deficiency motivation in Abraham MASLOW's humanistic psychology, the type of motivation operating on the lower four levels of his hierarchy of needs (see MASLOW'S MOTIVATIONAL HIERARCHY). Deficiency motivation is characterized by the striving to correct a deficit that may be physiological or psychological in nature. Compare METAMOTIVATION.

D

deficiency need any need created by lack of a substance required for survival (e.g., food, water) or of a state required for well-being (e.g., security, love).

deficit *n.* a lack of an essential element in something that prevents it from functioning correctly.

defusion *n.* in psychoanalytic theory, the separation of INSTINCTS that usually operate together. Defusion is posited to lead to various neuroses. Compare FUSION. **—defused** *adj.*

degeneracy *n.* **1.** a state in which a person has declined or reverted to a much earlier state of development in physical, mental, or moral qualities. **2.** the state of possessing few if any of the moral standards considered normal in one's society. Degeneracy is often popularly used with special reference to sexual offenses. **3.** in biology, reversion to a less highly organized and simpler stage of development. **—degenerate** *adj.*

degeneration *n.* **1.** deterioration or decline of organs or tissues, especially of neural tissue, to a less functional form. **2.** deterioration or decline of moral values. **—degenerate** *vb.*

degrees of freedom (symbol: *df*; ν) the number of elements that are allowed to vary in a statistical calculation, or the number of scores minus the number of mathematical restrictions. If the MEAN of a set of scores is fixed, then the number of degrees of freedom is one less than the number of scores. For example, if four individuals have a mean IQ of 100, then there are three degrees of freedom, because knowing three of the IQs determines the fourth IQ. See also CHI-SQUARE DISTRIBUTION.

dehumanization *n.* any process or practice that is thought to reduce human beings to the level of nonhuman animals or mechanisms, especially by denying them autonomy, individuality, and a sense of dignity. **—dehumanize** *vb.*

dehydration *n.* lack of water in the body tissues. Dehydration may be absolute, as measured in terms of the difference from normal body-water content, or relative, as considered in terms of fluid needed to maintain effective osmotic pressure. The physiological lag between water loss through excretion and the development of thirst sensations that stimulate replacement of the water is called **voluntary dehydration**.

dehydration reactions metabolic and psychological disturbances occurring when the body's water supply falls far below its normal quota. Early symptoms are apathy, irritability, drowsiness, inability to concentrate, and anxiety. Dehydration reactions may progress to delirium, spasticity, blindness, deafness, stupor, and death if more than 10% of body weight is lost.

dehypnosis *n.* in hypnosis, the process of eliminating the belief that hypnotic fantasies are actual.

deindividuation *n.* an experiential state characterized by loss of self-awareness, altered perceptions, and a reduction of inner restraints that results in the performance of unusual, atypical behavior. It can be caused by a number of factors, such as a sense of anonymity or of submersion in a group (see GROUP IDENTIFICATION).

deinstitutionalization *n.* the joint process of moving people with developmental or psychiatric disabilities from structured institutional facilities to their home communities and developing comprehensive community-based residential, day, vocational, clinical, and supportive services to address their needs. See COMMUNITY CARE. **—deinstitutionalize** *vb.*

déjà raconté the feeling that a long-forgotten event, now recalled, has been told before (French, "already told"). Some theorists believe that the illusion arises from the need for reassurance that a threatening experience was previously mastered and can therefore be mastered again. See also FALSE MEMORY.

déjà vu the feeling that a new event has already been experienced or that the same scene has been witnessed before (French, "already seen"). The feeling of familiarity may be due to a neurological anomaly, to resemblance between the present and the past scenes, or to the fact that a similar scene has been pictured in a daydream or night dream. See FALSE MEMORY.

de Lange's syndrome a congenital disorder that occurs in two forms, both of which include moderate to severe mental retardation and are associated with autosomal dominant inheritance or duplication of the long arm of chromosome 3. One form, the **Bruck–de Lange type**, features a short, broad neck, broad shoulders, short and thick extremities, and muscular hypertrophy, which gives the child the appearance of a small professional wrestler. The other, **Brachmann–de Lange type**, is also known as AMSTERDAM DWARF DISEASE or Amsterdam type of retardation, because the disorder was identified among patients in the Amsterdam area. Also called **Cornelia de Lange's syndrome**. [Cornelia **de Lange** (1871–1950), Dutch physician]

delayed auditory feedback (**DAF**) a technique of feedback in which speakers listen through headphones to their own speech, which is heard a short time after it is spoken. It is one of several techniques that may be used to induce greater fluency and clearer articulation in those with various speech and language disorders, particularly in those who stutter. Paradoxically, however, the delay in DAF has also been found to cause DYSFLUENCY in normally fluent speakers.

delayed development slower than expected developmental increases in physical, emotional, social, or cognitive abilities or capacities. A child with delayed development may hold attitudes, exhibit habits, or engage in behaviors consistent with an earlier developmental level.

delayed effect an effect that is not observed for some period of time after the event or factor that is held to have caused it. Usually the precipitating event exerts an indirect influence by starting a process or chain of events that ultimately has a demonstrable effect. See CAUSAL LATENCY; REMOTE CAUSE.

delayed posttraumatic stress disorder a form of POSTTRAUMATIC STRESS DISORDER that is diagnosed when the symptoms first appear more than 6 months after exposure to the traumatic stressor.

delayed speech the failure of speech to develop at the expected age. It may be due to DEVELOPMENTAL DELAY, hearing loss, brain injury, mental retardation or other psychological disorders, or emotional disturbance.

delay of gratification forgoing immediate reward in order to obtain a larger, more desired, or more pleasurable reward in the future. Compare IMMEDIATE GRATIFICATION.

deliberate psychological education (**DPE**) a curriculum that is designed to affect personal, ethical, aesthetic, and philosophical development in adolescents and young adults, through a balance of real and role-taking experiences and reflective inquiry. Counselors act as psychological educators or developmental instructors.

delibidinization *n.* see DESEXUALIZATION.

délire de négation see COTARD'S SYNDROME.

délire du toucher the compulsion to touch objects, which may be associated with OBSESSIVE-COMPULSIVE DISORDER or may be a complex tic in TOURETTE'S DISORDER.

deliriant *n.* a substance capable of inducing a state of acute DELIRIUM, commonly associated with restlessness or agitation. An acute delirium may result from excess ingestion of anticholinergic drugs (see CENTRAL ANTICHOLINERGIC SYNDROME) or withdrawal from alcohol and certain other substances.

delirium *n.* a state of disturbed consciousness in which attention cannot be sustained, the environment is misperceived, and the stream of thought is disordered. The individual may experience changes in cognition (which can include disorientation, memory impairment, or disturbance in language), perceptual disturbances, hallucinations, illusions, and misinterpretation of sounds or sights. The episode develops quickly and can fluctuate over a short period. Delirium may be caused by a variety of conditions including, but not limited to, infections, cerebral tumors, substance intoxication and withdrawal, head trauma, and seizures.

delirium of persecution DELIRIUM in which the predominant symptoms include intense mistrust and hallucinations that one is being threatened.

delirium tremens (**DTs**) a potentially fatal alcohol withdrawal syndrome involving extreme agitation and anxiety, fearfulness, paranoia, visual and tactile hallucinations, tremors, sweating, and increased heart rate, body temperature, and blood pressure.

delta alcoholism one of the five types of alcoholism defined by U.S. physician Elvin M. Jellinek (1890–1963), the others being ALPHA ALCOHOLISM, BETA ALCOHOLISM, GAMMA ALCOHOLISM, and EPSILON ALCOHOLISM. It is characterized by physical and psychological dependence, tolerance, inability to abstain, and withdrawal symptoms if use is suspended. Delta alcoholism is similar to gamma alcoholism but distinguished by the person's inability to abstain, as opposed to his or her complete loss of control over drinking.

delta receptor see OPIOID RECEPTOR.

delta-9-tetrahydrocannabinol *n.* see CANNABIS.

delta wave the lowest frequency BRAIN WAVE recorded in electroencephalography. Delta waves are large, regular-shaped waves that have a frequency of 1–3 Hz. They are associated with deep, often dreamless, sleep (**delta-wave sleep**) and indicate a synchronization of cells of the cerebral cortex. Also called **delta rhythm**; **slow wave**. See NREM SLEEP; STAGE 3 SLEEP; STAGE 4 SLEEP.

delusion *n.* an improbable, often highly personal, idea or belief system, not endorsed by one's culture or subculture, that is maintained with conviction in spite of irrationality or evidence to the contrary. Delusions may be transient and fragmentary, as in DELIRIUM, or highly systematized and elaborate, as in DELUSIONAL DISORDERS, though most of them fall between these two extremes. Common types include DELUSIONAL JEALOUSY, DELUSIONS OF BEING CONTROLLED, DELUSIONS OF GRANDEUR, DELUSIONS OF PERSECUTION, DELUSIONS OF REFERENCE, nihilistic delusions (see NIHILISM), and SOMATIC DELUSIONS. Data suggest delusions are not primarily logical errors but are derived from emotional material. Delusions have come to represent one of the most important factors in systems for classifying diagnostic categories. Some researchers believe that delusions may be the most important symptom of schizophrenia. See also BIZARRE DELUSION; ENCAPSULATED DELUSION; FRAGMENTARY DELUSION; SYSTEMATIZED DELUSION.

delusional disorder in *DSM–IV–TR*, any one of a group of psychotic disorders with the essential feature of one or more nonbizarre DELUSIONS that persist for at least 1 month but are not due to schizophrenia. The delusions are nonbizarre in that they feature situations that could conceivably occur in real life (e.g., being followed, poisoned, infected, deceived by one's government, etc.). Seven types of delusional disorder are specified, according to the theme of the delusion: **erotomanic type**, **grandiose type**, **jealous type**, **persecutory type**, **somatic type**, **mixed type**, and **unspecified type**. In *DSM–III*, delusional disorder was called **paranoid disorder**.

delusional jealousy a fixed delusion that a spouse or partner is unfaithful. The individual is constantly on the watch for indications that this false belief is justified, manufactures evidence if it is not to be found, and completely disregards facts that contravene the conviction. This type of delusion was formerly called **amorous** (or **conjugal**) **paranoia**. Also called **morbid jealousy**; **Othello syndrome** or **delusion**; **pathological jealousy**.

delusional mania a MANIC EPISODE characterized by delusions. Delusional mania is now more often described as a **manic episode with psychotic features**.

delusional misidentification see MISIDENTIFICATION.

delusional misidentification syndrome see MISIDENTIFICATION SYNDROME.

delusional system a more or less logically interconnected group of DELUSIONS held by the same person. Delusions that are tightly logical, but based on a false premise, are characteristic of persecutory type DELUSIONAL DISORDER. Also called **delusion system**.

delusion of being controlled the false belief that external forces, such as machines or other people, are controlling one's thoughts, feelings, or actions.

delusion of grandeur the false attribution to the self of great ability, knowledge, importance or worth, identity, prestige, power, accomplishment, or the like. Also called **grandiose delusion**. See also MEGALOMANIA.

delusion of influence **1.** the false supposition that other people or external agents are covertly exerting powers over oneself. **Idea of influence** is used synonymously, but with the implication that the condition is less definite, of shorter duration, or less severe. **2.** the false belief that one's intentions or actions directly control external events or the thoughts and behavior of other people.

delusion of negation see NIHILISM.

delusion of observation the false belief that one is being watched by others. Also called **observation delusion**.

delusion of persecution the false conviction that others are threatening or conspiring against one. Also called **persecutory delusion**.

delusion of poverty a false belief in which the individual insists that he or she is, or will soon be, entirely destitute.

delusion of reference the false conviction that the actions of others and events occurring in the external world have some special meaning or significance (typically negative) in relation to oneself. See also IDEA OF REFERENCE.

delusion of sin a delusion in which the individual is convinced of having committed unpardonable sins, for example, being to blame for wars, droughts, and other catastrophes. Such a delusion is frequently accompanied by intense fear of punishment.

delusion system see DELUSIONAL SYSTEM.

demand *n.* a requirement or urgent need, particularly any internal or external condition that arouses a DRIVE in an organism.

demand characteristics in an experiment or research project, cues that may influence or bias participants' behavior, for example, by suggesting the outcome or response that the experimenter expects or desires. Such cues can distort the findings of a study.

demandingness *n.* insistence upon attention, help, or advice from others. It is commonly associated with depression. See also DEPENDENCE. **—demanding** *adj.*

demandment *n.* any self-constructed and often self-defeating and unconscious imperative that converts important desires and goals into absolute demands: "Because I am not performing well, as I *absolutely must,* I am a terrible person." See RATIONAL EMOTIVE BEHAVIOR THERAPY. [defined by U.S. psychotherapist Albert Ellis (1913–2007)]

démence précoce see DEMENTIA PRAECOX.

dementia *n.* a generalized, pervasive deterioration of cognitive functions, such as memory, language, and EXECUTIVE FUNCTIONS, due to any of various causes. The loss of intellectual abilities is severe enough to interfere with an individual's daily functioning and social and occupational activity. In *DSM–IV–TR*, dementias are categorized according to the cause, which may be Alzheimer's disease, cerebrovascular disease (see VASCULAR DEMENTIA), Pick's disease (mainly affecting the frontal and temporal lobes), Parkinson's disease (see also LEWY BODY DEMENTIA), Huntington's disease, HIV infection (see AIDS DEMENTIA COMPLEX), Creutzfeldt–Jakob disease, head injury, alcoholism (see ALCOHOL-INDUCED PERSISTING DEMENTIA), or substance abuse (see SUBSTANCE-INDUCED PERSISTING DEMENTIA). Brain tumor, HYPOTHYROIDISM, HEMATOMA, or other conditions, which may be treatable, can also cause dementia. The age of onset varies with the cause but is usually late in life. When occurring after the age of 65 it is termed **senile dementia** and when appearing before 65 it is called **presenile dementia**. However, dementia should not be confused with AGE-ASSOCIATED MEMORY IMPAIRMENT, which has a much less deleterious impact on day-to-day functioning.

dementia of the Alzheimer's type (**DAT**) see ALZHEIMER'S DISEASE.

dementia praecox the original, now obsolete, name for SCHIZOPHRENIA, first used in 1896 by German psychiatrist Emil Kraepelin (1856–1926). It is derived from **démence précoce** (French, "early deterioration of the mind"), coined in 1857 by Austrian-born French psychiatrist Bénédict A. Morel (1809–1873), this name reflecting the belief that the symptoms of the disorder arose in adolescence or before and involved incurable degeneration. Swiss psychiatrist Eugen Bleuler (1857–1939) questioned both of these views and in 1911 renamed the disorder schizophrenia.

Dementia Rating Scale (**DRS**) a neuropsychological assessment instrument used to measure cognitive status in adults with cognitive impairments due to brain pathologies. It comprises 36 tasks of varying difficulty (e.g., repeating a series of numbers, naming objects present in the immediate environment, copying designs from stimulus cards onto blank pieces of paper) that are presented to participants in a fixed order. The scale evaluates performance on five subscales: attention, initiation–perseveration, construction, conceptualization, and memory. Originally developed in 1973 by U.S. neuropsychologist Steven Mattis and published commercially in 1988, the DRS subsequently was revised in 2001 (**DRS–2**).

dementia syndrome of depression see PSEUDODEMENTIA.

Demerol *n.* a trade name for MEPERIDINE.

democratic parenting a parenting style, derived from the ideas of Alfred ADLER, in which the parent guides the child's development in an accepting but steady manner and fosters a climate in which cooperation, fairness, equality, and mutual respect between parent and child are assumed.

demographic pattern a significant pattern revealed by a statistical study of population variables, such as marriages, births, infant mortality, income, or geographical distribution of the use of medical or mental health services.

demography *n.* the statistical study of human populations in regard to various factors and characteristics, including geographical distribution, sex and age distribution, size, structure, and growth trends. Such analyses are used in many types of study, including epidemiological studies. **—demographer** *n.* **—demographic** *adj.*

demonic possession the supposed invasion of the body by an evil spirit or devil that gains control of the mind or soul, producing mental disorder, illness, or criminal behavior. Many forms of physical and psychological illness were formerly attributed to such possession, notably EPILEPSY, SCHIZOPHRENIA, and TOURETTE'S DISORDER. The traditional remedy for possession was ritual EXORCISM.

demonomania *n.* a morbid preoccupation with demons and demonic possession, including the belief that one is possessed by or under the control of an evil spirit or demon.

demoralization *n.* a breakdown of values, standards, and mores in an individual or group, such as may occur in periods of rapid social change, extended crises (e.g., war, economic depression), or personal traumas. A demoralized person may be disorganized and feel lost, bewildered, and insecure. **—demoralize** *vb.*

demoralization hypothesis the idea that effective psychotherapy depends on the therapist overcoming the client's state of demoralization, which can be achieved by encouraging the client to confide, explaining his or her symptoms, and providing a therapeutic ritual through which these may be resolved. Such an approach is held to be a common factor underlying the success of various therapies. [proposed by U.S. psychologist Jerome D. Frank (1909–2005)]

demotivation *n.* negative imagery or self-talk that emphasizes why one cannot do well in a task and thus discourages any attempt to perform it.

demyelination *n.* the loss of the MYELIN SHEATH that covers nerve fibers.

dendrite *n.* a branching, threadlike extension of the CELL BODY that increases the receptive surface of a neuron. **—dendritic** *adj.*

dendrophilia *n.* a PARAPHILIA characterized by sexual attraction to trees. The person may have actual sexual contact with trees, may venerate them as phallic symbols, or both. Also called **dendrophily**.

denervation *n.* removal or interruption of the nerves that supply a part of the body.

denial *n.* a DEFENSE MECHANISM in which unpleasant thoughts, feelings, wishes, or events are ignored or excluded from conscious awareness. It may take such forms as refusal to acknowledge the reality of a terminal illness, a financial problem, an addiction, or a partner's infidelity. Denial is an unconscious process that functions to resolve emotional conflict or reduce anxiety. Also called **disavowal**. **—deny** *vb.*

dental phobia a persistent and irrational fear of dentists or of dental treatment, resulting in the avoidance of dental care or marked distress and anxiety during dental visits. It may be related to a prior negative dental experience, fear of pain, perceived lack of control, or feelings of helplessness or embarrassment.

deoxyribonucleic acid see DNA.

Depacon *n.* a trade name for valproate sodium. See VALPROIC ACID.

Depakene *n.* a trade name for VALPROIC ACID.

Depakote *n.* a trade name for DIVALPROEX SODIUM.

dependence *n.* **1.** the state of having some reliance on or ASSOCIATION with another entity or event. For example, in statistics two variables are said to have "linear dependence" if one variable is formed from another variable in an analysis, as would occur if including IQ, formed from mental age over actual age, in an analysis that already has age as a variable. **2.** a state in which assistance from others is intuitively expected or actively sought for emotional or financial support, protection, security, or daily care. The dependent person leans on others for guidance, decision making, and nurturance. Whereas some degree of dependence is natural in interpersonal relations, excessive, inappropriate, or misdirected reliance on others is often a focus of psychological treatment. Personality, social, and behavioral psychology, as well as psychoanalytic theory, all contribute different perspectives to the study and treatment of pathological dependence. **3.** see SUBSTANCE DEPENDENCE. **—dependent** *adj.*

Dependency Court in the United States, a court dealing with all issues concerned with child abuse and neglect; such issues are brought to the attention of the court by a government agency (typically Child Protective Services), that intervenes on behalf of the child by filing a petition alleging abuse or neglect.

dependency need any personal need that must be satisfied by others, including the need for affection, love, shelter, physical care, food, warmth, protection, and security. Such needs are considered universal and normal for both sexes and at all ages. It is also recognized that dependence can be maladaptive (e.g., excessive and overencouraged) and generate a variety of issues surrounding attachment. See also CODEPENDENCY; MORBID DEPENDENCY.

dependent personality disorder in *DSM–IV–TR*, a personality disorder manifested in a long-term pattern of passively allowing others to take responsibility for major areas of life and of subordinating personal needs to the needs of others, due to lack of self-confidence and self-dependence. It was formerly known as **passive-dependent personality**.

dependent variable (DV) the outcome that is observed to occur or change after the occurrence or variation of the INDEPENDENT VARIABLE in an experiment, or the effect that one wants to predict or explain in correlational research. Dependent variables may or may not be related causally to the independent variable. Also called **criterion variable**; **outcome variable**; **response variable**.

depersonalization *n.* a state of mind in which the self appears unreal. Individuals feel estranged from themselves and usually from the external world, and thoughts and experiences have a distant, dreamlike character. In its persistent form, depersonalization is observed in such disorders as depression, hypochondriasis, dissociative states, temporal-lobe epilepsy, and early schizophrenia. The extreme form is called **depersonalization syndrome**.

depersonalization disorder a DISSOCIATIVE DISORDER characterized by one or more episodes of DEPERSONALIZATION severe enough to impair social and occupational functioning. Onset of depersonalization is rapid and usually manifested in a sensation of self-estrangement, a feeling that one's extremities are changed in size, a sense of being mechanical, perceiving oneself at a distance, and, in some cases, a feeling that the external world is unreal (DEREALIZATION).

depersonification *n.* **1.** treatment of another person as something other than the unique individual that he or she really is. For example, parents may treat their child as an extension of themselves, which leads to the child having a distorted sense of self. **2.** in psychoanalytic theory, a stage in the maturation of the SUPEREGO that follows INTROJECTION of parental IMAGOES and leads to integration of parental values as abstract ideas. **—depersonify** *vb.*

deployment psychology a branch of MILITARY PSYCHOLOGY devoted to understanding and addressing the unique mental and behavioral health needs of members of the armed forces and their families during and after members' posting to combat zones and other operational environments. Although relatively scarce to date, research in this area focuses on (a) the psychosocial effects on military personnel and their families of combat exposure and of injuries sustained in combat, including disfigurement, amputation, sensory loss, TRAUMATIC BRAIN INJURY, and other severe wounds; (b) barriers to accessing mental health care in the military and the efficacy of existing prevention and intervention programs; (c) the psychology of trauma and promotion of RESILIENCE among military personnel and their families; and (d) the process of readjusting to family, community, and general civilian life for returning military personnel. Similarly, clinical services focus on (a) treating posttraumatic stress disorder, anxiety disorder, adjustment disorder, depression, substance abuse, and other mental health disorders common among returning military personnel; (b) mitigating the negative effects of these disorders on the families of those affected; (c) mitigating the stress experienced by families while military personnel are deployed; (d) teaching effective coping skills—such as anger management, conflict resolution, and communication techniques—to returning soldiers and their families to better prepare them to handle interpersonal difficulties that may arise; and (e) utilizing STRESS-INOCULATION TRAINING and other strategies during deployment to enhance the psychological well-being of soldiers and thus prevent the subsequent development of serious problems.

Depo-Provera *n.* a trade name for medroxyprogesterone acetate, an ANTIANDROGEN used in the treatment of sex offenders. See CHEMICAL CASTRATION.

deprenyl *n.* see SELEGILINE.

depressant *n.* any agent that diminishes or retards any function or activity of a body system or organ, especially a CNS DEPRESSANT.

depression *n.* **1.** a fluctuation in normal mood ranging from unhappiness and discontent to an extreme feeling of sadness, pessimism, and despondency. **2.** in psychiatry, any of the DEPRESSIVE DISORDERS. **—depressed** *adj.*

depression after delivery a less common name for POSTPARTUM DEPRESSION.

depressive anxiety in psychoanalytic theory, anxiety provoked by fear of one's own hostile feelings toward others. It is based on the theory that depression is hostility turned inward.

depressive disorder in *DSM–IV–TR*, any of the MOOD DISORDERS that typically have sadness as one of their symptoms. They include DYSTHYMIC DISORDER, MAJOR DEPRESSIVE DISORDER, and DEPRESSIVE DISORDER NOT OTHERWISE SPECIFIED. See UNIPOLAR DEPRESSION.

depressive disorder not otherwise specified in *DSM–IV–TR*, a mood disorder with depressive symptoms that does not meet the criteria for either of the specific DEPRESSIVE DISORDERS (i.e., major depressive disorder or dysthymic disorder). This category includes MINOR DEPRESSIVE DISORDER and PREMENSTRUAL DYSPHORIC DISORDER.

depressive episode see MAJOR DEPRESSIVE EPISODE.

depressive neurosis a former name for DYSTHYMIC DISORDER.

depressive personality disorder a personality disorder (in the appendix of *DSM–IV–TR*) characterized by glumness, pessimism, a lack of joy, the inability to experience pleasure, and motor retardation. Feelings of loss, a sense of giving up, and an orientation to pain are notable. There are vegetative signs, despair regarding the future, and a disheartened outlook.

depressive position in the OBJECT RELATIONS THEORY of Melanie KLEIN, the stage of infant development that reaches its peak at about 6 months of age. In the depressive position the infant begins to perceive the GOOD OBJECT and BAD OBJECT as a single whole and feels guilt for having attacked the good object during the preceding PARANOID-SCHIZOID POSITION. In this—Klein's most mature—phase of primary psychological organization, the infant fears that he or she will lose or destroy the good object and attempts to make REPARATION for earlier hostility.

depressive reaction see REACTIVE DEPRESSION.

depressive spectrum the range of severity and disparate symptoms that characterize DEPRESSIVE DISORDERS. The underlying concept is that depression is a range of related disorders, rather than a single diagnostic entity.

deprivation *n.* **1.** the removal, denial, or unavailability of something needed or desired. See CULTURAL DEPRIVATION; MATERNAL DEPRIVATION. **2.** in CONDITIONING, reduction of access to or intake of a REINFORCER. **—deprive** *vb.*

deprivation dwarfism stunting of physical growth in infancy and early childhood due to such nonorganic factors as maternal separation or emotional neglect. See also FAILURE TO THRIVE.

deprogramming *n.* the process by which people who have adopted profoundly new sets of attitudes, beliefs, and values have their original attitudes, beliefs, and values restored. Deprogramming techniques are typically used on people who have left or been removed from highly coercive social groups, such as religious cults. See also BRAINWASHING.

depth interview an interview designed to reveal deep-seated feelings, attitudes, opinions, and motives by encouraging the individual to express himself or herself freely without fear of disapproval or concern about the interviewer's reactions. Such interviews may be conducted, for example, in counseling and as part of qualitative market research. They tend to be relatively lengthy, unstructured, one-on-one conversations.

depth-oriented brief therapy a form of brief psychotherapy that applies principles of CONSTRUCTIVIST PSYCHOTHERAPY in a time-limited fashion.

depth psychology a general approach to psychology and psychotherapy that focuses on unconscious mental processes as the source of emotional disturbance and symptoms, as well as personality, attitudes, creativity, and lifestyle. A typical example is CLASSICAL PSYCHOANALYSIS, but others include Carl JUNG'S ANALYTIC PSYCHOLOGY and Alfred ADLER'S INDIVIDUAL PSYCHOLOGY.

depth therapy any form of psychotherapy, brief or extended, that involves identifying and working through unconscious conflicts and experiences that underlie and interfere with behavior and adjustment. Compare SURFACE THERAPY.

Deracyn *n.* a trade name for ADINAZOLAM.

derailment *n.* a symptom of thought disorder, often occurring in individuals with schizophrenia, marked by frequent interruptions in thought and jumping from one idea to another unrelated or indirectly related idea. It is usually manifested in speech (**speech derailment**) but can also be observed in writing. Derailment is essentially equivalent to LOOSENING OF ASSOCIATIONS. See COGNITIVE DERAILMENT; THOUGHT DERAILMENT.

derangement *n.* **1.** disturbance in the regular order or normal functioning of something. **2.** loosely, mental illness or mental disturbance.

derealization *n.* a state characterized by a sense of unreality; that is, an alteration in the perception of external reality so that it seems strange or unreal ("This can't be happening"), often due to trauma or stress. It may also occur as a feature of

SCHIZOPHRENIA or of certain DISSOCIATIVE DISORDERS. See also DEPERSONALIZATION.

dereflection *n.* a common technique used to allay anxiety or stop inappropriate behavior by diverting attention to a different topic and away from the self. It is used to reduce excessive self-concern, shyness, and worry about the self and is a central component in MORITA THERAPY.

dereism *n.* mental activity that is not in accord with reality, experience, or logic. It is similar to AUTISTIC THINKING. Also called **dereistic thinking**.

derivative insight an insight into a problem that is achieved by the client without interpretation by the therapist.

derived need a need developed through association with or generalization from a PRIMARY NEED.

dermatoglyphics *n.* the study of the patterns of lines on the skin of the fingers, palms, and soles. The technique is used in the diagnosis of certain kinds of chromosomal abnormalities based on observations that some patterns are associated with certain types of birth defects or disorders. For example, people with Down syndrome have a single crease across the palm and a single crease on the skin of the little (fifth) finger.

dermatological disorder any disorder or disease of the skin. See also PSYCHOCUTANEOUS DISORDER.

DES 1. abbreviation for DIETHYLSTILBESTROL. **2.** abbreviation for DYSEXECUTIVE SYNDROME.

descriptive approach see TOPOGRAPHIC MODEL.

descriptive behaviorism an approach to the study of behavior espoused by B. F. SKINNER, who felt that psychology should limit itself to a description of behaviors of organisms, the conditions under which they occur, and their effects on the environment. It requires that theoretical explanations in terms of underlying biological or hypothetical psychological processes be avoided. See BEHAVIORISM; RADICAL BEHAVIORISM.

descriptive statistic a numerical index used to describe (summarize) a particular feature of the data, such as a MEAN or STANDARD DEVIATION.

descriptive study a research method in which the primary goal is to reveal patterns and illustrate connections in the phenomena under investigation, without manipulating variables or seeking to establish cause and effect. For example, a survey undertaken to ascertain the political party preferences of a group of voters would be a descriptive study because it is intended simply to identify attitudes rather than systematically infer or analyze influencing factors.

desensitization *n.* a reduction in emotional or physical reactivity to stimuli that is achieved by such means as gaining insight into its nature or origin, CATHARSIS, or DECONDITIONING techniques. See also COVERT DESENSITIZATION; IN VIVO DESENSITIZATION; SYSTEMATIC DESENSITIZATION.

desertion *n.* see ABANDONMENT.

desexualization *n.* in psychoanalytic theory, the elimination or NEUTRALIZATION of a sexual aim. Also called **delibidinization**. See also SUBLIMATION. **—desexualize** *vb.*

designer drug any of various synthetic opioids, usually with heroin-like effects, designed with chemical structures that circumvent existing legal definitions of controlled substances and hence avoid restrictions on their use. These drugs tend to be abused by young middle-class people. See also CLUB DRUGS.

design fluency test any of a group of tests in which participants must generate (within a given time) a series of figures that have specific criteria. The tests were developed to provide clinical information regarding nonverbal capacity for flexibility and planning similar to VERBAL FLUENCY TESTS. For example, participants may be required to produce figures made from five lines and must devise new ways to put the lines together in an organized manner to make new figures or designs. Also called **figural fluency test**.

desipramine *n.* a TRICYCLIC ANTIDEPRESSANT and the principal metabolic product of IMIPRAMINE, produced in the body by the demethylation of imipramine in the liver. Desipramine is a stronger inhibitor of norepinephrine reuptake than of serotonin reuptake relative to imipramine. In general, it is less sedating and has fewer ANTICHOLINERGIC EFFECTS than imipramine and was frequently used to treat behavior disorders and insomnia in children. However, like all tricyclic antidepressants, it has fallen into relative disuse as safer medications have become available. U.S. trade name: **Norpramin**.

desmopressin *n.* a synthetic analog of the pituitary hormone VASOPRESSIN that, among other functions, stimulates water retention and raises blood pressure. Desmopressin is used in the form of a nasal spray to treat nocturnal enuresis (bedwetting) and DIABETES INSIPIDUS. It possesses more antidiuretic activity (i.e., prevents excessive water loss from the body) and less potential to raise blood pressure than vasopressin. U.S. trade name (among others): **DDAVP**.

desocialization *n.* gradual withdrawal from social contacts and interpersonal communication, with absorption in private thought processes and adoption of idiosyncratic and often bizarre behavior.

Desoxyn *n.* a trade name for METHAMPHETAMINE.

despair *n.* **1.** the emotion or feeling of hopelessness, that is, that things are profoundly wrong and will not change for the better. Despair is one of the most negative and destructive of human affects and behaviors, and as such is a primary area for psychotherapeutic intervention. **2.** in ERIKSON'S EIGHT STAGES OF DEVELOPMENT, see INTEGRITY VERSUS DESPAIR.

despondency *n.* a state characterized by both APATHY and depressed mood. **—despondent** *adj.*

destiny neurosis see FATE NEUROSIS.

destructive behavior the expression of anger, hostility, or aggression by damaging or destroying external objects or oneself (see SELF-DESTRUCTIVENESS).

destructive instinct see DEATH INSTINCT.

destructiveness *n.* a tendency toward the expression of aggressive behavior by destroying, damaging, or defacing objects. See also SELF-DESTRUCTIVENESS.

destrudo *n.* the energy associated with THANATOS, the DEATH INSTINCT. Destrudo contrasts with LIBIDO, the energy of EROS, the LIFE INSTINCT. See also MORTIDO. [defined by Austrian-Italian psychoanalyst Edoardo Weiss (1889–1970)]

desurgency *n.* a personality trait characterized by anxiety, brooding, and seclusion. [defined by British-born U.S. personality psychologist Raymond Bernard Cattell (1905–1998)]

desymbolization *n.* the process of depriving symbols, especially words, of their accepted meanings and substituting distorted, neologistic, autistic, or concrete ideas for them.

desynchronization *n.* in electroencephalography, the replacement of ALPHA WAVES by fast, low-amplitude, irregular waveforms, often because of an external stimulus, usually one that alerts the individual. See ALPHA BLOCKING.

Desyrel *n.* a trade name for TRAZODONE.

DET *di*ethyl*t*ryptamine: a synthetic HALLUCINOGEN belonging to the indolealkylamine family, to which LSD, PSILOCIN, and DMT also belong.

detached character a personality characterized by extreme self-sufficiency and lack of feeling for others. German-born U.S. psychoanalyst Karen D. Horney (1885–1952) identified the development of such a character as one of three basic NEUROTIC TRENDS used as a defense against BASIC ANXIETY. Compare AGGRESSIVE CHARACTER; COMPLIANT CHARACTER.

detachment *n.* **1.** a feeling of emotional freedom resulting from a lack of involvement in a problem or with another situation or person. **2.** objectivity: that is, the ability to consider a problem on its merits alone. Also called **intellectual detachment**. **3.** in developmental psychology, the child's desire to have new experiences and develop new skills. This occurs at about 2 years of age, as the child begins to outgrow the period of total attachment to and dependence on the parent or caregiver.

detailed inquiry a phase of a CLINICAL INTERVIEW during which the therapist gains an understanding of the patient by asking direct questions on many diverse topics, ranging from mundane questions about everyday life to highly detailed questions, for example, about particular reactions to specific events.

deterioration *n.* progressive impairment or loss of basic functions, such as emotional, judgmental, intellectual, muscular, and memory functions.

deterioration effect an adverse effect or negative outcome from participating in psychotherapy.

deterioration index a pattern of subtest scores on the WECHSLER ADULT INTELLIGENCE SCALE viewed as suggestive of neurological deficit and used in measuring the degree of reduced performance that can be attributed to aging. Also called **deterioration quotient**. See also DON'T-HOLD FUNCTIONS; HOLD FUNCTIONS.

deterioration of attention inconstant and shifting attention and impaired ability to concentrate on external reality.

determination *n.* **1.** a mental attitude characterized by a strong commitment to achieving a particular goal despite barriers and hardships. **2.** the act or process of making a decision, reaching a conclusion, or ascertaining the characteristics or exact nature of something, or the end result of such a process.

determinism *n.* the philosophical position that all events, physical or mental, including human behavior, are the necessary results of antecedent causes or other entities or forces. Determinism, which requires that both the past and the future are fixed, manifests itself in psychology as the position that all human behaviors result from specific efficient causal antecedents, such as biological structures or processes, environmental conditions, or past experience. The relationships between these antecedents and the behaviors they produce can be described by generalizations much like the laws that describe regularities in nature. Determinism contrasts with belief in **free will**, which implies that individuals can choose to act in some ways independent of antecedent events and conditions. Those who advocate free-will positions often adopt a position of "soft determinism," which holds that free will and responsibility are compatible with determinism. Others hold that free will is illusory, a position known as "hard determinism." Of contemporary psychological theories, BEHAVIORISM takes most clearly a hard determinist position. See also GENETIC DETERMINISM. **—determinist** *adj., n.* **—deterministic** *adj.*

deterrent therapy see AVERSION THERAPY.

detoxification *n.* a therapeutic procedure, popularly known as **detox**, that reduces or eliminates toxic substances in the body. These procedures may be metabolic (by converting the toxic substance to a less harmful agent that is more easily excreted) or they may require induced vomiting, gastric lavage (washing), or dialysis, depending upon the nature of the poison and other factors. Examples are the use of methadone in opioid intoxication, tranquilizers to ease alcohol withdrawal, and lavage and artificial respiration in barbiturate poisoning.

detoxification center a clinic, hospital unit, or other facility devoted to the alleviation of the toxic effects of drug or alcohol overdose and to the management of acute withdrawal symptoms. These centers may focus on either medical or nonmedical procedures, depending on the severity of the syndromes handled. See ALCOHOL WITHDRAWAL; SUBSTANCE WITHDRAWAL.

detoxification effects see SUBSTANCE WITHDRAWAL.

Detussin *n.* a trade name for a combination of HYDROCODONE and pseudoephedrine.

devaluation *n.* a DEFENSE MECHANISM that involves denying the importance of something or someone, including the self. **—devalue** *vb.*

developmental assessment the evaluation of a child's level of physical, cognitive, emotional, and social development, as assessed by specific developmental scales.

developmental-behavioral pediatrics see BEHAVIORAL PEDIATRICS.

developmental coordination disorder in *DSM–IV–TR*, a motor skills disorder characterized by marked impairment in the development of motor coordination. Performance in activities that require motor coordination is substantially below that expected given the child's chronological age and measured intelligence. Significant impairment of academic performance or daily living activities is also observed. However, the difficulties are not due to mental retardation or PERVASIVE DEVELOPMENTAL DISORDERS. See also DEVELOPMENTAL DYSPRAXIA.

developmental delay delay in the age at which developmental milestones are achieved by a child or delay in the development of communication, social, and daily living skills. It most typically refers to delays in infants, toddlers, and preschool children that are meaningful but do not constitute substantial handicap. Children with developmental delays are often eligible for early intervention or preschool services to ameliorate these delays.

developmental disability a developmental level or status that is attributable to a cognitive or physical impairment, or both, originating before the age of 22. Such an impairment is likely to continue indefinitely and results in substantial functional or adaptive limitations. Examples of developmental disabilities include, but are not limited to, mental retardation, pervasive developmental disorders, learning disorders, developmental coordination disorder, communication disorders, cerebral palsy, epilepsy, blindness, deafness, mutism, and muscular dystrophy. Also called **developmental disorder**.

developmental dyslexia a form of DYSLEXIA that is apparent during an early developmental age or phase and manifested as difficulty in learning to read and spell single words.

developmental dysphasia language difficulty or delayed language acquisition believed to be associated with brain damage or cerebral maturation lag. It is characterized by defects in expressive language and articulation (**expressive dysphasia**) and in more severe cases by defects in comprehension of language (**receptive dysphasia**). Also called **developmental aphasia**.

developmental dyspraxia DYSPRAXIA present since birth and manifested during an early developmental age or phase as difficulty in performing coordinated movements. In *DSM–IV–TR* this condition is equivalent to DEVELOPMENTAL COORDINATION DISORDER. Compare ACQUIRED DYSPRAXIA.

developmental expressive writing disorder see DISORDER OF WRITTEN EXPRESSION.

developmental hyperactivity a condition shown by children who are within or above the average range intellectually but display high activity levels as an integral part of their behavior.

developmental immaturity the status of a child who exhibits a delay (usually temporary) in reaching developmental landmarks without clinical or historical evidence of damage to the central nervous system. The child may appear younger than his or her chronological age in physical development, gross and fine motor abilities, language development, social awareness, or any combination of these. See also DEVELOPMENTAL DELAY; DEVELOPMENTAL RETARDATION.

developmental language disorder in *DSM–III*, a diagnostic category comprising two types of disorder in which the development of language skills is impaired: an expressive type and a receptive type. The equivalent *DSM–IV–TR* classifications for these types are EXPRESSIVE LANGUAGE DISORDER and MIXED RECEPTIVE-EXPRESSIVE LANGUAGE DISORDER, respectively.

developmental levels the stages into which the human life span is typically divided: (a) neonatal period; (b) infancy; (c) early, middle, and late childhood; (d) adolescence; and (e) early, middle, and late adulthood.

developmental orientation 1. in interdisciplinary team or other individual service-planning processes, an emphasis on the skills, abilities, and strengths of people with disabilities in relation to expected developmental attainments and performance of children or young people without disabilities. **2.** see DEVELOPMENTAL THEORY. Compare DEFECT ORIENTATION.

developmental pharmacokinetics the study of how pharmacological agents are processed (see PHARMACOKINETICS) in infants and children.

developmental psychopathology the scientific study of the origins and progression of psychological disorders as related to the typical processes of human growth and maturation. Central to this field is the belief that studying departures from developmental NORMS will enhance understanding of those norms, which will in turn enhance the conceptualization and treatment of mental illness.

developmental retardation abnormally slow growth in any or all areas—intellectual, motor, perceptual, linguistic, or social. See also DEVELOPMENTAL DELAY; DEVELOPMENTAL IMMATURITY.

Developmental Test of Visual–Motor Integration (**VMI**) a measure of visuomotor development that requires the participant to copy onto blank pieces of paper geometric designs increasing in difficulty from a straight line to complex figures. The VMI is used to identify problems with visual perception, motor coordination, and visual–motor integration. It is available in two versions: the Short Format, containing 15 designs and appropriate for children aged 2 to 8 years, and the Full Format, containing 24 designs and appropriate for children through age 18. [originally developed in 1967 by U.S. psychologists Keith E. Beery (1932–2010) and Norman A. Buktenica (1930–)]

developmental theory 1. any theory based on the continuity of human development and the importance of early experiences in shaping the personality. Examples are the psychoanalytic theory of PSYCHOSEXUAL DEVELOPMENT, ERIKSON'S EIGHT STAGES OF DEVELOPMENT, learning theories that stress early conditioning, and role theories that focus on the gradual acquisition of different roles in life. **2.** the proposition that mental retardation is due to slower than normal development of cognitive processes and is not qualitatively different from the cognitive processes of other people. Also called **developmental orientation**. Compare DEFECT THEORY.

developmental therapy a method of treatment for children and adolescents with emotional, social, or behavioral problems. A series of graded experiences is used to help clients to function better in various areas, such as interacting with others or managing anger.

developmental toxicology the study of the effects of toxic (poisonous) substances on the normal development of infants and children: specifically, the study of the adverse effects of certain drugs administered to them or to which they may have been exposed in the uterus.

developmental trauma disorder (**DTD**) a new diagnosis, proposed for inclusion in the upcoming fifth edition of the *Diagnostic and Statistical Manual of Mental Disorders*, for children who have been exposed in early life to multiple adverse interpersonal events, such as sexual or physical abuse, parental substance abuse, domestic or community violence, neglect, and abandonment. These experiences, termed **complex trauma**, have a pervasive and long-range influence on children's emotional, cognitive, behavioral, and psychobiological functioning that many clinicians believe is not adequately captured by POSTTRAUMATIC STRESS DISORDER or any other existing diagnosis. Six domains of potential impairment related to complex trauma exposure have been delineated: (a) affect regulation; (b) information processing; (c) self-concept; (d) behavioral control; (e) interpersonal relationships; and (f) biological processes. This multifaceted dysregulation can disrupt typical maturation, potentially leading to wide-ranging developmental delays and to persistently altered attributions and expectancies about the self, relationships, and others.

D

deviance *n.* **1.** any behavior that differs significantly from what is considered appropriate or typical for a social group. Also called **deviancy**. **2.** in statistics, a measure of the GOODNESS OF FIT between a smaller nested model and a fuller model that has all of the same parameters plus more. The difference or deviance between these models follows a CHI-SQUARE DISTRIBUTION, with the DEGREES OF FREEDOM equal to the number of parameters that are added by the fuller model. If the deviance reveals a SIGNIFICANT DIFFERENCE, then the larger model is needed. If the deviance is not significant, then the smaller, more parsimonious model is retained as more appropriate.

deviant sexuality see SEXUAL DEVIANCE.

deviant verbalization see SCHIZOPHRENIC THINKING.

deviation *n.* a significant departure or difference. This conceptually broad term has a variety of applications in psychology and related fields but most commonly refers to behavior that is significantly different from the accepted standard or norm, or to the arithmetical difference between one of a set of values and some fixed amount, generally the mean of the set or the value predicted by a model. See STANDARD DEVIATION.

deviation IQ the absolute measure of how far an individual differs from the mean on an individually administered IQ test. This is the approach now most commonly used in standard IQ tests. A reported deviation IQ is a standard score on an IQ test that has a mean of 100 and a standard deviation specific to that of the test administered, usually 15 or 16 for intelligence tests. The test scores represent a deviation from the mean score rather than a quotient, as was typical in the early days of IQ testing.

device for automated desensitization (**DAD**) a computerized system for applying DESENSITIZATION therapy to the treatment of focused phobic behavior. The device administers visual or audio instructions for muscle relaxation and visualization of feared stimuli arranged in a hierarchical order. See also CO-

VERT DESENSITIZATION; SYSTEMATIC DESENSITIZATION.

devil's trumpet see JIMSONWEED.

Dewey, John (1859–1952) U.S. philosopher, educator, and psychologist. After receiving his doctorate in 1884 under George S. Morris (1840–1889) at Johns Hopkins University, Dewey taught for a decade each at the universities of Michigan and Chicago before moving to Columbia University, where he spent the rest of his career. Dewey wrote the first scientific text on psychology in the United States *(Psychology,* 1886) and went on to develop the functionalist, or instrumentalist, approach, in conjunction with William JAMES, James Rowland ANGELL, and others. Dewey's 1896 essay, "The Reflex Arc Concept in Psychology," is considered to be the debut of FUNCTIONALISM in psychology. Dewey's work also had a great impact in the fields of education and philosophy. In keeping with his functionalist views, he held that education must relate to the child's own experience, involve the child's participation, and develop a spirit of inquiry leading to the solution of real rather than merely academic problems. In philosophy, Dewey is famous as one of the founders of the American school of PRAGMATISM, together with William James, Charles S. Peirce (1839–1914), and George Herbert Mead (1863–1931). See also INSTRUMENTALISM; PROGRESSIVE EDUCATION.

dexamethasone *n.* a synthetic analog of CORTISOL, with similar biological action. It is used to treat nausea and vomiting and as an anti-inflammatory agent. U.S. trade name (among others): **Decadron**.

dexamethasone suppression test (**DST**) a test of the ability of dexamethasone, a synthetic analogue of CORTISOL, to inhibit the secretion of CORTICOTROPIN and hence suppress levels of cortisol in the blood. In the test, dexamethasone is administered and, after a waiting period, cortisol levels are assessed. In normal individuals cortisol levels will be suppressed by dexamethasone. If cortisol is still elevated, the individual is categorized as a nonsuppressor. The test is used primarily to aid in the diagnosis of Cushing's syndrome. Dexamethasone nonsuppression was thought at one time to be a good indication that the individual has, or is likely to develop, MAJOR DEPRESSIVE DISORDER, but it does not reliably predict this condition. Because of this, and the development of less invasive and less costly diagnostics, the DST has been generally abandoned as a clinical maneuver in depression.

dexamphetamine *n.* see DEXTROAMPHETAMINE.

Dexedrine *n.* a trade name for DEXTROAMPHETAMINE.

dextroamphetamine *n.* a sympathomimetic agent and CNS STIMULANT that is the dextrorotated form of the amphetamine molecule. It is used in the treatment of narcolepsy and attention-deficit/hyperactivity disorder. Like all AMPHETAMINES, it is prone to abuse and dependence. Also called **dexamphetamine**. U.S. trade names (among others): **Dexedrine**; **Adderall** (in combination with AMPHETAMINE).

dextromethorphan *n.* a synthetic OPIOID used clinically as a cough suppressant. Its mechanism of action is unknown, but it is known to bind to NMDA RECEPTORS. Dextromethorphan is a common ingredient in over-the-counter cough and cold preparations and is increasingly used as a drug of abuse, particularly among adolescents. Because it is metabolized extensively by the CYTOCHROME P450 (CYP) 2D6 liver enzyme, it is used in pharmacology as a comparison when calculating the degree to which certain drugs inhibit CYP enzymes. It should not be taken by individuals who are taking MONOAMINE OXIDASE INHIBITORS, and it should be used with caution by those taking inhibitors of the CYP2D6 enzyme (i.e., fluoxetine, paroxetine) because unexpectedly high plasma concentrations of either drug may occur (see ENZYME INHIBITION). Examples of some common U.S. proprietary products that include dextromethorphan are **Coricidin**, **NyQuil**, **Robitussin**, **Tylenol PM**, and **Vicks 44**.

dhat *n.* in *DSM–IV–TR*, a CULTURE-BOUND SYNDROME specific to India. Dhat involves severe anxiety and hypochondriacal concerns about the discharge of semen, whitish discoloration of the urine, and feelings of weakness and exhaustion. It is similar to SHEN-K'UEI.

DHE 45 *n.* a trade name for DIHYDROERGOTAMINE.

diabetes insipidus a metabolic disorder marked by a deficiency of VASOPRESSIN (antidiuretic hormone), which promotes the reabsorption of water from the kidney tubules. The patient experiences excessive thirst and excretes large amounts of urine, but without the high level of sugar found in the urine of people with diabetes mellitus. See also NEPHROGENIC DIABETES INSIPIDUS.

diabetes mellitus a metabolic disorder caused by ineffective production or utilization of the hormone insulin. Because of the insulin disruption, the patient is unable to oxidize and utilize carbohydrates in food. Glucose accumulates in the blood, causing weakness, fatigue, and the appearance of sugar in the urine. Fat metabolism is also disrupted so that end products of fat metabolism (ketones) accumulate in the blood.

diacetylmorphine *n.* the chemical name for HEROIN. A synthetic analog of MORPHINE (produced by substituting acetyl groups for hydroxyl groups at two positions on the morphine molecule), it is, like morphine and CODEINE, a pure opioid agonist, activating receptors for endorphins and enkephalins (see ENDOGENOUS OPIOID). Diacetylmorphine is characterized by a rapid onset of action and a duration of action similar to that of morphine; however, it is three times more potent than morphine. In Great Britain and Canada it is used clinically in the management of severe pain, for example, in terminally ill patients, but it is not legally available in the United States due to concerns about its potential for abuse. Also called **diamorphine**. See OPIOID ANALGESIC.

diadochokinesis *n.* the ability to rapidly perform repetitive muscular movements, such as finger tapping or pursing and retracting the lips. This ability is often examined during clinical assessments of motor behavior.

diagnosis (**Dx**) *n.* (*pl.* **diagnoses**) **1.** the process of identifying and determining the nature of a disease or disorder by its signs and symptoms, through the use of assessment techniques (e.g., tests and examinations) and other available evidence. **2.** the classification of individuals on the basis of a disease, disorder, abnormality, or set of characteristics. Psychological diagnoses have been codified for professional use, notably in the DSM–IV–TR. **—diagnostic** *adj.*

diagnosis-related groups (**DRGs**) an inpatient or hospital classification used as a financing tool to reimburse health care providers. Each of the DRGs (of which there are currently over 500) has a preset price based on diagnosis, age and sex of patient, therapeutic procedure, and length of stay.

Diagnostic and Statistical Manual of Mental Disorders see DSM–IV–TR.

diagnostic baseline the entry or pretreatment levels of condition- or disease-related symptoms used in identifying or treating diseases or disorders. Such levels are often used to assign patients or participants in a study to correlational groups. See also BASELINE.

diagnostic center a facility equipped with skilled personnel and appropriate laboratory and other equipment for evaluating the condition of a patient and determining the cause of his or her physical or psychological disorder. The diagnostic center may be a part of a larger health care facility or a separate institution.

diagnostic formulation a comprehensive evaluation of a patient, including a summary of his or her behavioral, emotional, and psychophysiological disturbances. Diagnostic formulation includes the most significant features of the patient's total history; the results of psychological and medical examinations; a tentative explanation of the origin and development of his or her disorder; the diagnostic classification of the disorder; a therapeutic plan, including basic and adjunctive treatments; and a prognostic evaluation based on carrying out this plan.

diagnostic interview an interview in which a psychologist or other mental health professional explores a patient's presenting problem, current situation, and background, with the aim of formulating a diagnosis and prognosis as well as developing a treatment program.

Diagnostic Interview Schedule (**DIS**) a STRUCTURED INTERVIEW assessing an individual's current and past symptoms of a variety of psychiatric disorders, including depression, schizophrenia, and alcohol and substance dependence. Designed to be an objective diagnostic instrument requiring a minimum of clinical judgment, the DIS consists of a predetermined set of questions that are asked in a specific order. It was originally developed in the late 1970s by the NATIONAL INSTITUTE OF MENTAL HEALTH for use in the EPIDEMIOLOGIC CATCHMENT AREA SURVEY. The **Diagnostic Interview Schedule for Children** (**DISC**) is also available.

diagnosticity *n.* the informational value of an interaction, event, or feedback for someone seeking self-knowledge. Information with high diagnosticity has clear implications for the SELF-CONCEPT, whereas information with low diagnosticity may be unclear, ambiguous, or inaccurate. The impulse to seek highly diagnostic information about the self is called the APPRAISAL MOTIVE.

diagnostic overshadowing the failure, when assessing an individual with multiple disabilities, to discern the presence of one disability because its features are attributed to another, primary disability. In particular, it refers to the failure to recognize a psychiatric condition or mental disorder in a person with mental retardation, because characteristics of that condition are erroneously attributed to the mental retardation. See also DUAL DIAGNOSIS.

diagnostic test any examination or assessment measure that may help reveal the nature and source of an individual's physical, mental, or behavioral problems or anomalies. In medical research, for example, a diagnostic test would be expected to show SENSITIVITY (i.e., correctly identifying individuals with a certain illness) and SPECIFICITY (i.e., correctly identifying those who do not have a specific illness).

dialectic *n.* **1.** in general language, any investigation of the truth of ideas through juxtaposition of opposing or contradictory opinions. **2.** the conversational mode of argument attributed to Greek philosopher Socrates (c. 470–399 BCE), in which knowledge is sought through a process of question and answer. **—dialectical** *adj.*

dialectical behavior therapy a flexible, stage-based therapy that combines principles of BEHAVIOR THERAPY, COGNITIVE BEHAVIOR THERAPY, and MINDFULNESS. Dialectical behavior therapy concurrently promotes acceptance and change, especially with difficult-to-treat patients. [developed by U.S. clinical psychologist Marsha Linehan (1943–)]

dialogue (**dialog**) *n.* **1.** in general, an exchange of ideas between two or more people. **2.** in GESTALT THERAPY, a technique in which the client engages in an imaginary conversation (a) with a body part from which he or she feels alienated; (b) with a person, such as his or her mother or father, who is pictured sitting in an empty chair (see EMPTY-CHAIR TECHNIQUE); or (c) with an object associated with a dream. The technique often elicits strong feelings. Also called **dialogue technique**.

dialysis dementia an aluminum-induced brain disease affecting patients undergoing long-term dialysis. Major symptoms are progressive mental deterioration, personality changes, and speech impairment, with such neurological signs as seizures, DYSARTHRIA, dysnomia (difficulty in naming objects), and DYSPRAXIA.

D

diamorphine *n.* see DIACETYLMORPHINE.

dianetics *n.* a controversial therapeutic technique claiming to treat, according to its founder, "all inorganic mental ills and all inorganic psychosomatic ills, with assurance of complete cure." Dianetics has been largely discredited within the fields of psychology and psychiatry. [introduced in 1950 by L(afayette) Ron(ald) Hubbard (1911–1986), U.S. writer and subsequent founder of Scientology]

diaphragm *n.* **1.** a muscular sheet that separates the thoracic and abdominal cavities. **2.** a cup-shaped contraceptive device made from a layer of thick latex rubber fitted over a round or spiral spring. The diaphragm is filled with a contraceptive jelly and inserted in the vagina so that it forms a barrier between the cervix and any spermatozoa that enter the vagina during coitus. The spring holds it in place. The diaphragm has been used by women since 1882. **—diaphragmatic** *adj.*

diathesis *n.* a susceptibility to acquiring (not inheriting) certain diseases or disorders (e.g., allergies, arthritic diathesis). Compare GENETIC PREDISPOSITION.

diathesis–stress model the theory that mental and physical disorders develop from a genetic or biological predisposition for that illness (diathesis) combined with stressful conditions that play a precipitating or facilitating role. Also called **diathesis–stress hypothesis**; **diathesis–stress paradigm**; **diathesis–stress theory**. See also STRESS–VULNERABILITY MODEL.

diazepam *n.* a long-acting BENZODIAZEPINE that is used for the management of alcohol withdrawal and as an ANTICONVULSANT, ANXIOLYTIC, and MUSCLE RELAXANT. It is broken down in the liver to produce a number of metabolites (metabolic products) of varying HALF-LIVES, including the active compounds desmethyldiazepam (nordiazepam) and OXAZEPAM. Its complex metabolism and lengthy half-life make diazepam unsuitable for use in older adults and those with liver disease. U.S. trade name (among others): **Valium**.

diazepam-binding inhibitor (**DBI**) an endogenous NEUROPEPTIDE that binds to molecular receptors for BENZODIAZEPINES. It counters the effectiveness of these drugs, thus increasing anxiety, and may be involved in the development of drug dependence.

dibenzodiazepine *n.* any member of a class of chemically related compounds that include CLOZAPINE, the first ATYPICAL ANTIPSYCHOTIC introduced into clinical medicine. This class is structurally similar to the DIBENZOXAZEPINES.

dibenzothiazepine *n.* any member of a class of chemically related compounds that include QUETIAPINE, an atypical antipsychotic. This class is structurally similar to the DIBENZODIAZEPINES and the DIBENZOXAZEPINES.

dibenzoxazepine *n.* any member of a class of chemically related compounds that include LOXAPINE, one of the older antipsychotics that does not belong to the phenothiazine class. This class is structurally similar to the DIBENZODIAZEPINES.

dichotomous thinking the tendency to think in terms of bipolar opposites, that is, in terms of the best and worst, without accepting the possibilities that lie between these two extremes. This has been found to be especially common among individuals with MAJOR DEPRESSIVE EPISODES, and is sometimes thought to be a risk factor for MAJOR DEPRESSIVE DISORDER. Also called **polarized thinking**.

dichotomous variable a variable that can have only two values (typically, 0 or 1) to designate membership in one of two possible categories, for example, female versus male, Republican versus Democrat.

didactic analysis see TRAINING ANALYSIS.

didactic group therapy an early form of group psychotherapy based on the theory that institutionalized individuals will respond most effectively to the active guidance of a professional leader. In one form of didactic group therapy the group members bring up their own problems and the therapist leads the discussion, often giving his or her own interpretations. In another form, the therapist presents a short lecture based on printed material designed to stimulate the members to break through their resistances and express themselves. The didactic approach is also used in self-help groups.

didactic teaching 1. a technique in which behavioral and therapeutic concepts and techniques are explained to clients, and instructions are given in both verbal and written form. Such instruction is common in many forms of therapy, with the exception of long-term PSYCHODYNAMIC PSYCHOTHERAPY and PSYCHOANALYSIS. **2.** a component of many courses in undergraduate and graduate psychology courses and multidisciplinary psychotherapy training.

diencephalic amnesia amnesia caused by lesions of the DIENCEPHALON. Causes include infarction of the paramedian artery, trauma, diencephalic tumors, and WERNICKE–KORSAKOFF SYNDROME.

diencephalon *n.* the posterior part of the FOREBRAIN that includes the thalamus, epithalamus, and hypothalamus. —**diencephalic** *adj.*

dietary neophobia avoidance of new foods. A nonpathological form is commonly seen in children who display a reluctance to try unfamiliar food. Acceptance of novel diets may be facilitated through observation of others eating similar foods or, in some cases, by simply observing others eating familiar foods.

diethylpropion *n.* a CNS STIMULANT used as an appetite suppressant in the treatment of obesity. See also ANALEPTICS. U.S. trade name: **Tenuate**.

diethylstilbestrol (**DES**) *n.* a synthetic, nonsteroidal compound with the activity of estrogen. It was formerly widely prescribed to pregnant women to prevent miscarriages or premature deliveries, but such use was discontinued in the early 1970s due to the health risks associated with DES, including increased risk of reproductive abnormalities and cancer in female offspring. It is still used clinically to treat selected cases of breast cancer or prostate cancer, but this is very rare.

diethyltryptamine *n.* see DET.

dieting *n.* the deliberate restriction of the types or amounts of food one eats, usually in an effort to lose weight or to improve one's health. Dieting is viewed by some medical and mental health professionals as a solution to obesity and by others as a primary pathology associated with EATING DISORDERS.

difference hypothesis see DEFECT THEORY.

difference score (symbol: *D*) an index of dissimilarity or change between observations from the same individual across time, based on the measurement of a construct or attribute on two or more separate occasions. For example, it would be helpful to calculate a difference score for a person's weight at the beginning of a diet and exercise program and the final weight six months later. Also called **change score**; **gain score**.

differential diagnosis 1. the process of determining which of two or more diseases or disorders with overlapping symptoms a particular patient has. **2.** the distinction between two or more similar conditions by identifying critical symptoms present in one but not the other.

differential emotions theory a theory proposing the existence of a large but limited set of specific emotions that appear without social learning at the age when the emotions can first play an adaptive role in the behavior of the child. [associated with the work of U.S. psychologist Carroll E. Izard (1923–)]

differential psychology the branch of psychology that studies the nature, magnitude, causes, and consequences of psychological differences between individuals and groups, as well as the methods for assessing these differences.

differential reinforcement in conditioning, the REINFORCEMENT of only selected behavior. For example, one might reinforce lever presses that are more than 1 s in duration, but not reinforce those that are less than 1 s in duration.

differential reinforcement of alternative behavior (**DRA**) the REINFORCEMENT of a particular behavior as a means of decreasing another, targeted behavior. It combines EXTINCTION of the targeted response with competition from the reinforced alternative.

differential reinforcement of other behavior (**DRO**) a procedure in which REINFORCEMENT occurs if a particular response does not occur for a fixed period of time. It is used to decrease the rate of the targeted response. Also called **omission training**.

differential validity 1. the accuracy of a battery of tests in discriminating between a person's subsequent success in two or more different criterion tasks. **2.** differences in validity coefficients across groups. For example, the correlation between test scores and job performance may differ for males and females.

differentiation of self the ability to distinguish and maintain personal thoughts, feelings, goals, and identity in the presence of emotional and societal pressures to do otherwise, especially in family systems.

Digit Span an attentional subtest in the WECHSLER ADULT INTELLIGENCE SCALE that assesses the ability of an individual to repeat a series of digits of increasing length. **Digit Span Forward** assesses the number of digits an individual is able to repeat immediately following their presentation, in the exact order they were presented. **Digit Span Backward** assesses the number of digits an individual is able to repeat immediately following their presentation, but in reverse order. The former is regarded as a measure of IMMEDIATE MEMORY; the latter provides a measure of WORKING MEMORY.

Digit Symbol a performance subtest in the WECHSLER ADULT INTELLIGENCE SCALE that measures the time taken to indicate digits associated with abstract symbols using a substitution key. It is a measure of fluid abilities (see CATTELL–HORN THEORY OF INTELLIGENCE) and performance and is negatively correlated with adult age.

dihydrocodeine *n.* see OPIOID ANALGESIC; OPIOID.

dihydroergotamine *n.* a semisynthetic derivative of the ergot alkaloid ERGOTAMINE, used in the treatment of acute migraine headache. It is a potent VASOCONSTRICTOR due to its ability to antagonize ALPHA-ADRENERGIC RECEPTORS in blood-vessel walls as well as serotonin and dopamine receptors. U.S. trade names: **DHE 45**; **Migranal**.

dihydroindolone *n.* any member of a class of chemically related compounds whose molecular structure incorporates an indole nucleus similar to that of serotonin. The group includes MOLINDONE, a conventional ANTIPSYCHOTIC.

dihydromorphine *n.* a semisynthetic OPIOID ANALGESIC used primarily in research on OPIOID RECEPTORS. It is also a metabolite (metabolic product) of dihydrocodeine. See also OPIOID.

Dilantin *n.* a trade name for PHENYTOIN.

dildo *n.* an artificial penis, made usually of rubber or plastic but occasionally of wood or other materials. A dildo is used in autoerotic practices and other sexual activities. Also called **olisbos**; **lingam**; **godemiche**. See also VIBRATOR.

D

dimenhydrinate *n.* a nonprescription ANTIHISTAMINE at H_1 receptors that is commonly taken to suppress symptoms of motion sickness. U.S. trade name (among others): **Dramamine**.

dimensional theory of emotion any theory postulating that emotions have two or more fundamental dimensions. There is universal agreement among theories on two fundamental dimensions—pleasantness–unpleasantness (hedonic level) and arousal–relaxation (level of activation)—but considerable differences in labeling others.

dimensions of consciousness dimensions along which the overall quality of awareness can vary, including mood, involvement with inner or outer events, changes in immediate memory, sensation and perception, self-awareness, and identification with events outside of oneself.

dimethoxymethylamphetamine *n.* see DOM.

dimethyltryptamine *n.* see DMT.

diminished capacity a legal defense in which a mental abnormality, due either to intoxication or mental defect, is claimed to have limited the defendant's ability to form the requisite criminal intent (see MENS REA) for the crime with which he or she is charged.

diminished responsibility a form of AFFIRMATIVE DEFENSE in which evidence of mental abnormality is presented to mitigate or reduce a defendant's accountability for an act. It is distinct from an INSANITY DEFENSE, which takes an all-or-none perspective with regard to CRIMINAL RESPONSIBILITY. Also called **limited responsibility**. See also PARTIAL INSANITY.

diminutive visual hallucination see LILLIPUTIAN HALLUCINATION.

DIMS abbreviation for DISORDERS OF INITIATING AND MAINTAINING SLEEP.

diphenhydramine *n.* a sedating ANTIHISTAMINE at H_1 receptors that also possesses activity at cholinergic and other receptor sites. It is used generally to suppress allergic responses and, in mental health, as a sedative and hypnotic or to suppress the parkinsonian symptoms induced by conventional antipsychotic drugs. U.S. trade name (among others): **Benadryl**.

diphenylbutylpiperidine *n.* any member of a class of chemically related compounds that include the conventional antipsychotic PIMOZIDE.

diphenylmethanes *pl. n.* a class of sedating ANTIHISTAMINE at H_1 receptors that are used primarily as ANXIOLYTICS. They also prevent cardiac fibrillation and have local anesthetic effects. The prototype is HYDROXYZINE.

diploid *adj.* denoting or possessing the normal number of chromosomes, which in humans is 46: 22 HOMOLOGOUS pairs of AUTOSOMES plus the male or female set of XY or XX SEX CHROMOSOMES. Compare HAPLOID.

diplomate *n.* see BOARD CERTIFIED.

dipsomania *n.* formerly, episodic binge drinking. See EPSILON ALCOHOLISM. **—dipsomaniac** *n.*

direct aggression aggressive behavior directed toward the source of the frustration or anger. Compare DISPLACED AGGRESSION.

direct-contact group see FACE-TO-FACE GROUP.

direct coping active, focused confrontation and management or resolution of stressful or otherwise problematic situations.

direct dyslexia a form of acquired dyslexia (see ALEXIA) characterized by an ability to read words aloud but an inability to understand what is being read.

directed analysis see FOCUSED ANALYSIS.

directed attention see SELECTIVE ATTENTION.

directed facial action studies studies in which participants are instructed to contract specific facial muscles to produce prototypical emotional facial expressions without any verbal reference being made to the emotions themselves (e.g., "anger," "frown"). These studies have reported that facial configurations of negative emotions produce distinctive patterns of autonomic physiological activity.

directed movement movement targeted toward achieving a specific goal.

directedness *n.* the sense of unified purpose that provides the mature individual with enduring motivation, continuity, and orientation to the future. [first described by G. W. ALLPORT]

directed reverie in individual and group therapy, a technique in which the therapist directs the client to reexperience a dream or something that happened in early life by creating and then describing a mental image of that dream or event. See also GUIDED AFFECTIVE IMAGERY.

directed thinking controlled, purposeful thinking that is focused on a specific goal, such as the solution to a problem, and guided by the requirements of that goal. See also CRITICAL THINKING.

directional test see ONE-TAILED TEST.

directive *n.* a command, suggestion, or order specifying the type of action that should be performed. In therapeutic contexts, a directive is a specific statement by the therapist that enjoins the client to act, feel, or think in a particular way when he or she confronts a particular problem or situation. The use of directives in therapy depends a great deal on the particular mode of therapy; in some modes (e.g., psychoanalysis) directives occur rarely if at all, whereas in others (e.g., behavior therapy) they occur more frequently.

directive counseling an approach to counseling and psychotherapy in which the therapeutic process is directed along lines considered relevant by the counselor or therapist. Directive counseling is based on the assumption that the professional training and experience of the counselor or therapist equip him or her to manage the therapeutic process and to guide the client's behavior. Therapy is considered to progress along primarily intellectual lines in contrast to the approaches of PSYCHODYNAMIC PSYCHOTHERAPY, which emphasizes unconscious motivation and affective dynamics. Also called **directive psychotherapy**.

directive group psychotherapy a type of group psychotherapy designed to help members adjust to their environment through educational tasks, group guidance, group counseling, and therapeutic recreation. [developed by 20th-century Russian-born U.S. psychotherapist Samuel Richard Slavson]

directive play therapy a controlled approach to PLAY THERAPY in which the therapist is actively involved, structuring a child's activities by providing selected play materials and encouraging the child to use them in the enactment of "pretend" situations and the expression of feelings. Compare NONDIRECTIVE PLAY THERAPY.

directive therapy an approach to psychotherapy in which the therapeutic process is directed along lines considered relevant by the therapist. Directive therapy is based on the assumption that the professional training and experience of the therapist equip him or her to manage the therapeutic process and to guide the client's behavior. Therapy is considered to progress along primarily intellectual lines in contrast to the approaches of PSYCHODYNAMIC PSYCHOTHERAPY, which emphasizes unconscious motivation and affective dynamics.

director *n.* in a PSYCHODRAMA, the therapist who establishes the scenario or ROLE PLAY and manages the interactions therein.

direct suggestion 1. a technique in SUPPORTIVE PSYCHOTHERAPY in which attempts are made to alleviate emotional distress and disturbance in an individual through reassurance, encouragement, and direct instructions. **2.** a technique in HYPNOTHERAPY in which a client under hypnosis is directed to follow instructions of the therapist either in the session or in his or her daily life.

dirt phobia a persistent and irrational fear of dirt, often accompanied by a fear of contamination and a hand-washing compulsion. Fear of dirt is a common obsession associated with OBSESSIVE-COMPULSIVE DISORDER. Also (rarely) called **rupophobia**.

DIS abbreviation for DIAGNOSTIC INTERVIEW SCHEDULE.

disability *n.* a lasting physical or mental impairment that significantly interferes with an individual's ability to function in one or more central life activities, such as self-care, ambulation, communication, social interaction, sexual expression, or employment. For example, an individual who cannot see has visual disability. See also HANDICAP. **—disabled** *adj.*

disability adjusted life years (**DALYs**) a measure of the impact of disease or injury on the length and quality of a person's life. It takes into account the potential loss of years due to premature mortality and the value of years lived with disability. One DALY represents one lost year of "healthy" life.

disability evaluation an evaluation of the effect of an impairment (i.e., a loss of function) on an individual's capabilities, particularly in terms of his or her capacity for gainful employment.

Disability Rating Scale (**DRS**) a rating scale, used primarily in rehabilitation facilities to monitor the rehabilitative progress of individuals with moderate to severe brain damage, that measures arousal and awareness, cognitive ability, dependence on others, and psychosocial adaptability. Each of the 8 items on the scale (eye opening, communication ability, motor response, feeding, toileting, grooming, level of functioning in self-care, and employability) is assigned a value from 0 to either 3, 4, or 5. These values are then added together to obtain a total score, which may range from 0 (no disability) to 29 (extreme vegetative state). [originally developed in 1982 by psychiatrist Maurice Rappaport (1926–2008) and colleagues]

disadvantaged *adj.* denoting individuals, families, or communities deprived of equal access to society's resources, especially the necessities of life or the advantages of education and employment.

disaster counseling counseling offered to victims and their families, emergency workers, and witnesses during or immediately following a traumatic event. Individual therapists and counselors and mental health teams are specially trained (e.g., by the American Red Cross) to respond in disaster situations. Disaster counseling may include defusing, debriefing (e.g., CRITICAL-INCIDENT STRESS DEBRIEFING), and other counseling techniques to help traumatized people cope with stress. One aim of the counseling might be to reduce the potential for POST-TRAUMATIC STRESS DISORDER, which may develop after the event.

disavowal *n.* see DENIAL.

discharge *n.* **1.** in clinical psychology, the abrupt reduction in psychic tension that occurs in symptomatic acts, dreams, or fantasies. **2.** in neurophysiology, the firing or activity of a neuron or group of neurons, resulting in an ACTION POTENTIAL. **3.** in hospitals and other mental and physical health facilities, the dismissal of a patient from treatment or other services.

discharge of affect the reduction of an emotion by giving it active expression, for example, by crying. [described by Sigmund FREUD]

discharge procedure the process of releasing a patient from a mental hospital or psychiatric unit. Common steps in the process include a final clinical interview and evaluation, instructions regarding prescribed medication (if relevant), and discussion of follow-up treatment and services.

discharge rate the ratio of the number of patients discharged from a hospital or other institution in a given period to the number admitted. Also called **improvement rate**; **recovery ratio**.

dischronation *n.* an aspect of DISORIENTATION in which there is confusion about time. Also called **chronotaxis**.

discipline *n.* **1.** training that is designed to establish desired habits of mind and behavior. **2.** control of conduct, usually a child's, by means of punishment or reward. **3.** a field of study.

discomfort anxiety tension and consequent low frustration tolerance that arise from irrational beliefs about perceived threats to well-being. For example, one may experience discomfort anxiety when one has the AWFULIZING belief "I can't stand it when things don't go my way." [proposed in 1979 by U.S. psychologist Albert Ellis (1913–2007)]

discomfort disturbance a low tolerance to either discomfort or frustration that may make people overreact to unpleasant life experiences, frustration, or their own negative feelings. [proposed by U.S. psychologist Albert Ellis (1913–2007)]

discomfort–relief quotient see DISTRESS–RELIEF QUOTIENT.

discontinuity hypothesis in GESTALT PSYCHOLOGY, the viewpoint that emphasizes the role of sudden insight and perceptual reorganization in successful DISCRIMINATION LEARNING and problem solving. According to this view, a correct answer is only recognized when its relation to the issue as a whole is discovered. Also called **discontinuity theory**. Compare CONTINUITY HYPOTHESIS. See also AHA EXPERIENCE; EUREKA TASK.

discordance *n.* **1.** the state or condition of being at variance. **Affective discordance** may be observed, for example, during psychotherapy when a client relates a particularly disturbing experience without any facial or vocal indication of distress. **2.** in TWIN STUDIES, dissimilarity between a pair of twins with respect to a particular trait or disease. Compare CONCORDANCE. **—discordant** *adj.*

discrete data data that are not on a continuous scale but are limited to specific categories or values, which may be ordered or not ordered. See CATEGORICAL DATA; DISCRETE VARIABLE.

discrete measure a measure of a discrete (i.e., discontinuous, distinct, and limited) value, for example, the grade level of a student.

discrete variable a RANDOM VARIABLE that is not continuous but takes on only a relatively small number of distinct values. Also called **discrete random variable**. Compare CONTINUOUS VARIABLE.

discriminability *n.* the quality that enables an object or person to be readily distinguished from something or someone else.

discriminant analysis a MULTIVARIATE statistical method that combines information from a set of predictor variables in order to allow maximal discrimination among a set of predefined groups.

discriminant function any of a range of statistical techniques to situate an item that could belong to any of two or more variables in the correct set, with minimal probability of error.

discriminant validity a form of CONSTRUCT VALIDITY demonstrated by showing that measures of constructs that are conceptually unrelated do not correlate in the data. See also CONVERGENT VALIDITY.

discriminating power a measure of the ability of a test to distinguish between two groups being measured.

discrimination index see INDEX OF DISCRIMINATION.

discrimination learning a conditioning or learning experience in which an individual must learn to make choices between seemingly identical or similar alternatives in order to reach a goal. Also called **discriminative learning**.

discussion group any group set up to explore problems and questions in a variety of vocational, educational, guidance, therapeutic, and community settings. In schools, a discussion group is usually an instructional technique; in psychiatric and other therapeutic settings, the focus is emotional and interpersonal; in vocational, guidance, and community settings, the objective may be to stimulate decision-making processes and to channel recommendations to a study or action group.

disease *n.* a definite pathological process with organic origins, marked by a characteristic set of symptoms that may affect the entire body or a part of the body and that impairs functioning.

disease course the progress of a pathological condition or process from inception, manifestation, and DIAGNOSIS through treatment and resolution.

disease model 1. any of several theories concerning the causes and course of a pathological condition or process. **2.** see MEDICAL MODEL.

disease of adaptation any of a group of illnesses, including high blood pressure and heart attacks, that are associated with or partly caused by long-term defective physiological or psychological reactions to stress. [named and defined by Austrian physician Hans Selye (1907–1982)]

disease phobia a persistent and irrational fear of disease in general or of a particular disease, formerly called **nosophobia**. Fear of disease may be a SPECIFIC PHOBIA or a feature of HYPOCHONDRIASIS or OBSESSIVE-COMPULSIVE DISORDER. Also called **pathophobia**.

disenfranchised grief grief that society (or some element of it) limits, does not expect, or may not allow a person to express. Examples include the grief of parents for stillborn babies, of teachers for the death of students, and of nurses for the death of patients. People who have lost an animal companion are often expected to keep their sorrow to themselves. Disenfranchised grief may isolate the bereaved individual from others and thus impede recovery. Also called **hidden grief**. See also GRIEF COUNSELING; GRIEFWORK; MOURNING.

disengaged family a family whose members are mutually withdrawn from each other psychologically and emotionally.

disengagement theory a theory proposing that old age involves a gradual withdrawal of the individual from society and of society from the individual. According to this theory, those happiest in old age have turned their attention inward toward the self and away from involvement in the outside world. Empirical research has shown, however, that this mutual withdrawal is not an inevitable component of old age and that a **continuity theory** of aging is most likely, in which older people are happiest when they are able to maintain their preferred level of social involvement. Compare ACTIVITY THEORY. [developed by 20th century U.S. psychologist Elaine Cumming and William E. Henry]

disequilibrium *n.* **1.** a loss of physical balance, as in PARKINSON'S DISEASE and ATAXIAS due to cerebellar disorder or injury. **2.** emotional imbalance, as in individuals with extreme mood swings or LABILE AFFECT. **3.** in developmental psychology, a state of tension between cognitive processes competing against each other. In contrast to Jean PIAGET, some theorists believe that disequilibrium is the optimal state for significant cognitive advances to occur.

disfigurement *n.* a blemish or deformity that mars the appearance of the face or body. Disfigurement can result from severe burn scars; mutilations due to wounds, accidents, or radical surgery; and a wide variety of congenital anomalies, some of which are at least partially reparable. The psychological effects of disfigurement are often devastating, especially since they are due in part to the negative and often humiliaating reactions of others in a society that places a high value on physical attractiveness. Among these effects are damage to the self-image, loss of self-esteem, feelings of inferiority, self-consciousness, shame, resentment, hypersensitivity, withdrawal, antisocial behavior, and paranoid reactions. See also FACIAL DISFIGUREMENT.

disgust *n.* a strong aversion, for example, to the taste, smell, or touch of something deemed revolting, or toward a person or behavior deemed morally repugnant. **—disgusting** *adj.*

dishabituation *n.* the reappearance or enhancement of a habituated response (i.e., one that has been weakened following repeated exposure to the evoking stimulus) due to the presentation of a new stimulus. Dishabituation can be interpreted as a signal that a given stimulus can be discriminated from another habituated stimulus and is a useful method for investigating perception in nonverbal individuals or animals. Compare HABITUATION.

disinhibition *n.* **1.** diminution or loss of the normal control exerted by the cerebral cortex, resulting in poorly controlled or poorly restrained emotions or actions. Disinhibition may be due to the effects of alcohol, drugs, or brain injury, particularly to the frontal lobes. **2.** in conditioning experiments, the reappearance of responding, which has stopped occurring as a result of exposure to EXTINCTION, when a new stimulus is presented.

disintegration *n.* a breakup or severe disorganization of some structure or system of functioning, for example, of psychic and behavioral functions.

disintegration of personality fragmentation of the personality to such an extent that the individual no longer presents a unified, predictable set of beliefs, attitudes, traits, and behavioral responses. The most extreme examples of disintegrated, disorganized personality are found in the schizophrenias.

disjunctive motivation striving for substitute or temporary (rather than true and lasting) satisfaction. Compare CONJUNCTIVE MOTIVATION. [defined by U.S. psychiatrist Harry Stack Sullivan (1892–1949)]

dismissive attachment an adult attachment style that combines a positive INTERNAL WORKING MODEL OF ATTACHMENT of oneself, characterized by a view of oneself as competent and worthy of love, and a negative internal working model of attachment of others, characterized by one's view that others are untrustworthy or undependable. Individuals with dismissive attachment are presumed to discount the importance of close relationships and to maintain rigid self-sufficiency. Compare FEARFUL ATTACHMENT; PREOCCUPIED ATTACHMENT; SECURE ATTACHMENT.

disorder *n.* a group of symptoms involving abnormal behaviors or physiological conditions, persistent or intense distress, or a disruption of physiological functioning. See also MENTAL DISORDER.

disorder of written expression in *DSM–IV–TR,* a LEARNING DISORDER in which writing skills are substantially below those expected, given the person's chronological age, formal education experience, and measured intelligence. The writing difficulties, which may involve errors in grammar, punctuation, and paragraph organization, often combined with extremely poor handwriting and spelling errors, significantly interfere with academic achievement and activities of daily living that require writing skills. Also called **developmental expressive writing disorder**.

disorders of excessive somnolence (**DOES**) one of four basic types of SLEEP DISORDERS, differentiated from the other types by the presence of excessive sleepiness for at least 1 month. The equivalent classification in *DSM–IV–TR* is PRIMARY HYPERSOMNIA. Diagnosis can involve observation in a SLEEP LABORATORY, in which such criteria as nocturnal awakenings, sleep time, sleep continuity, SLEEP LATENCY, percentage of time in STAGE 2 SLEEP, and percentage of time in STAGE 3 SLEEP and STAGE 4 SLEEP are measured.

disorders of infancy, childhood, or adolescence not otherwise specified in *DSM–IV–TR,* disorders with an onset during infancy, childhood, or adolescence that do not meet *DSM–IV–TR* criteria for any specific disorder.

disorders of initiating and maintaining sleep (**DIMS**) one of four basic types of SLEEP DISORDERS, differentiated from the other types by the presence of INSOMNIA, that is, persistent inability to fall asleep or stay asleep. The equivalent classification in *DSM–IV–TR* is PRIMARY INSOMNIA. Diagnosis can involve observation in a SLEEP LABORATORY, in which such criteria as nocturnal awakenings, sleep time, sleep efficiency, breathing patterns, percentage of time in STAGE 2 SLEEP, percentage of time in STAGE 3 SLEEP and STAGE 4 SLEEP, minutes of REM SLEEP, and REM SLEEP LATENCY are measured.

disorders of the self in SELF PSYCHOLOGY, narcissistic problems resulting from insufficient response by others (such as parents) to one's needs. According to this view, an individual's self-cohesion, self-esteem, and vitality derive from and are maintained by the empathic responsiveness of others; lack of this response can lead to deficiencies or inabilities in loving other people and a focus on oneself. [defined by Austrian psychoanalyst Heinz Kohut (1913–1981)]

disorders of the sleep–wake cycle schedule one of four basic types of SLEEP DISORDERS, differentiated from the other types in that it results from a mismatch between one's internal CIRCADIAN RHYTHM and one's actual sleep schedule. The equivalent classification in *DSM–IV–TR* is CIRCADIAN RHYTHM SLEEP DISORDER. Rotating work-shift schedules and jet lag are two common causes of this disorder. Diagnosis can involve observation in a SLEEP LABORATORY, in which such criteria as nocturnal awakening, sleep time, sleep efficiency, breathing patterns, body temperature, minutes of REM SLEEP, and REM SLEEP LATENCY are measured.

disorganization *n.* loss or disruption of orderly or systematic structure or functioning. For example, thought disorganization is an inability to integrate thought processes; behavior disorganization is a disruption of behavior.

disorganized attachment in the STRANGE SITUATION, a form of INSECURE ATTACHMENT in which infants show no coherent or consistent behavior during separation from and reunion with their parent. Also called **disoriented attachment**.

disorganized behavior behavior that is self-contradictory or inconsistent. It may include childlike silliness, unpurposeful or aimless behavior, unpredictable agitation, or extreme emotional reaction (e.g., laughing after a catastrophe). A typical example is dressing in clothing inappropriate for the weather (e.g., wearing several layers on a warm summer day). Disorganized behavior is commonly seen in individuals with schizophrenia.

disorganized development disruption in the normal course of ATTACHMENT in children in which the child does not learn how to deal with separation from or reunion with a parent. As infants, these children react to their parents with fear or apprehension and do not know how to seek them out when stressed (see DISORGANIZED ATTACHMENT).

disorganized schizophrenia in *DSM–IV–TR,* a subtype of schizophrenia characterized primarily by random and fragmented speech and behavior and by flat or inappropriate affect, frequently associated with grimaces, mannerisms, laughter, and extreme social withdrawal. It tends to be the most severe of the schizophrenia subtypes and is often associated with poor premorbid personality and early and insidious onset. In *DSM–III,* it was called **disorganized type schizophrenic disorder**; historically, and in other classifications, this subtype is known as **hebephrenia** or **hebephrenic schizophrenia**.

disorganized speech incoherent speech. This may be speech in which ideas shift from one subject to another, seemingly unrelated, subject, sometimes described as LOOSENING OF ASSOCIATIONS. Other types of disorganized speech include responding to questions in an irrelevant way, reaching illogical conclusions, and making up words. See METONYMIC DISTORTION; NEOLOGISM; PARALOGIA.

disorientation *n.* a state of impaired ability to identify oneself or to locate oneself in relation to time, place, or other aspects of one's surroundings. Long-term disorientation can be characteristic of organic neurological and psychological disorders; temporary disorientation can be caused by alcohol or drugs or can occur in situations of acute stress, such as fires or earthquakes. See also CONFUSION; TIME DISORIENTATION. **—disoriented** *adj.*

disoriented attachment see DISORGANIZED ATTACHMENT.

dispersion *n.* the degree to which a batch of scores deviate from the mean. Also called **spread**.

displaced aggression the direction of hostility away from the source of frustration or anger and toward either the self or a different person or object. Displaced aggression may occur, for example, when circumstances preclude direct confrontation with the responsible person or institution because that person or institution is perceived as too powerful to attack without fear of reprisal. See DISPLACEMENT. Compare DIRECT AGGRESSION.

displacement *n.* the transfer of feelings or behavior from their original object to another person or thing. In psychoanalytic theory, displacement is considered to be a DEFENSE MECHANISM in which the individual discharges tensions associated with, for example, hostility and fear by taking them out on a neutral, nonthreatening or less threatening target. Thus, an angry child might hurt a sibling instead of attacking the father; a frustrated employee might criticize his or her spouse instead of the boss; or a person who fears his or her own hostile impulses might transfer that fear to knives, guns, or other objects that might be used as a weapon. See also DISPLACED AGGRESSION; DRIVE DISPLACEMENT; SCAPEGOATING. **—displace** *vb.*

displacement behavior a behavior in which an individual substitutes one type of action for another when the first action is unsuccessful or when two competing motivations are present that lead to incompatible actions. Also called **displacement activity**.

displacement of affect see TRANSPOSITION OF AFFECT.

disposition *n.* a recurrent behavioral or affective tendency that distinguishes an individual from others. See also PERSONAL DISPOSITION.

dispositional attribution the ascription of one's own or another's actions, an event, or an outcome to internal or psychological causes specific to the person concerned, such as moods, attitudes, decisions and judgments, abilities, or effort. Also called **internal attribution**; **personal attribution**. Compare SITUATIONAL ATTRIBUTION.

dispositional hearing a proceeding held in juvenile court cases after the court finds that an offense has been committed. It is similar to the sentencing hearing or penalty phase in an adult criminal court.

disruptive behavior behavior that chronically threatens and intimidates others or violates social norms. The term is typically applied to the behavior of children, but it can also be used to describe adult behavior. According to *DSM–IV–TR* criteria, children exhibiting disruptive behavior are diagnosed with one of the DISRUPTIVE BEHAVIOR DISORDERS, whereas those older than 18 years of age are diagnosed with ANTISOCIAL PERSONALITY DISORDER.

disruptive behavior disorder a psychiatric disorder in which the primary symptom involves DISRUPTIVE BEHAVIOR (e.g., violation of social rules and rights of others, defiance, hostile behavior) that is severe enough to produce significant impairment in social or occupational functioning. In *DSM–IV–TR*, disruptive behavior disorders include CONDUCT DISORDER, OPPOSITIONAL DEFIANT DISORDER, and DISRUPTIVE BEHAVIOR DISORDER NOT OTHERWISE SPECIFIED.

disruptive behavior disorder not otherwise specified in *DSM–IV–TR*, a pattern of behavior involving violation of social rules or the basic rights of others, aggression, or defiance that results in clinically significant impairment but does not conform to the full *DSM–IV–TR* criteria of other, specific disruptive behavior disorders.

dissociated state a reaction to a traumatic event in which the individual splits the components of the event into those that can be faced in the present and those that are too harmful to process. The latter components are repressed and can be recalled later in life if triggered by a similarly traumatic event, introspection, or psychotherapy. In the healthily functioning psyche, consciousness, memory, identity, and perception of the self and the environment are integrated rather than split into separate components. See also DISSOCIATIVE DISORDERS.

dissociation *n.* **1.** an unconscious DEFENSE MECHANISM in which conflicting impulses are kept apart or threatening ideas and feelings are separated from the rest of the psyche. See COMPARTMENTALIZATION; DISSOCIATIVE DISORDERS. **2.** in research, a method used to differentiate processes, components, or variables. For instance, it might involve discovering a variable that influences short-term memory but not long-term memory. See DOUBLE DISSOCIATION.

dissociative amnesia in *DSM–IV–TR*, a DISSOCIATIVE DISORDER characterized by failure to recall important information about one's personal experiences, usually of a traumatic or stressful nature, that is too extensive to be explained by normal forgetfulness. Recovery of memory often occurs spontaneously within a few hours and is usually connected with removal from the traumatic circumstances with which the amnesia was associated. In *DSM–III* this disorder was called **psychogenic amnesia**.

dissociative anesthetic an anesthetic agent capable of producing amnesia, analgesia, and sedation without inducing loss of consciousness.

dissociative barriers in dissociative disorders, the barriers to full conscious access by individuals to their recollections of a traumatic event. The trauma is presumed to be implicated in the development of the disorder, and the dissociative barriers are theorized to serve a protective function, allowing the traumatized person to avoid knowledge of horrific life events.

dissociative disorder not otherwise specified in *DSM–IV–TR*, a residual category of disorders that do not meet the diagnostic criteria for any of the specific DISSOCIATIVE DISORDERS. It includes DISSOCIATIVE TRANCE DISORDER, DEREALIZATION without depersonalization, DISSOCIATED STATES resulting from brainwashing or other forms of coercion, and GANSER SYNDROME.

dissociative disorders in *DSM–IV–TR*, any of a group of disorders characterized by a sudden, gradual, transient, or chronic disruption in the normal integrative functions of consciousness, memory, or perception of the environment. Such disruption may last for minutes or years, depending on the type of disorder. Included in this category are DISSOCIATIVE AMNESIA, DISSOCIATIVE FUGUE, DISSOCIATIVE IDENTITY DISORDER, DEPERSONALIZATION DISORDER, and DISSOCIATIVE DISORDER NOT OTHERWISE SPECIFIED.

dissociative fugue in *DSM–IV–TR*, a DISSOCIATIVE DISORDER in which the individual suddenly and unexpectedly travels away from home or a customary place of daily activities and is unable to recall some or all of his or her past. Symptoms also include either confusion about personal identity or assumption of a new identity. No other signs of mental disorder are present, and the fugue state can last from hours to months. Travel can be brief or extended in duration, and there may be no memory of travel once the individual is brought back to the prefugue state. In *DSM–III* this disorder was called **psychogenic fugue**.

dissociative hysteria a former name for a DISSOCIATIVE DISORDER.

dissociative identity disorder in *DSM–IV–TR*, a DISSOCIATIVE DISORDER characterized by the presence in one individual of two or more distinct identities or personality states that each recurrently take control of the individual's behavior. It is typically associated with severe physical and sexual abuse, especially during childhood. An increase in reported cases has been seen in the United States in recent years, and research suggests that there may be a hereditary component. In *DSM–III* this disorder was called **multiple personality disorder**.

dissociative pattern a pattern of behavior consistent with DISSOCIATIVE DISORDERS, as evidenced by disruption in the normal integrative functions of consciousness, memory, or perception of the environment.

dissociative process a process of disruption of the normal integrative functions of consciousness, memory, or perception of the environment. It typically occurs as a result of a traumatic or profoundly disturbing event, such as physical or sexual abuse, wartime experience, or involvement in an accident in which someone else died. See also DISSOCIATIVE DISORDERS.

dissociative stupor a profound decrease in or absence of voluntary movement and responsiveness to external stimuli, apparently resulting from acute STRESS.

dissociative trance disorder a DISSOCIATIVE DISORDER characterized by involuntary alterations in consciousness, identity, awareness or memory, and motor functioning that result in significant distress or impairment. The two subtypes of the disorder are distinguished by the individual's identity state. In **possession trance**, the individual's usual identity is replaced by a new identity perceived to be an external force, such as a ghost, another person, or a divine being, and there is loss of memory for the episode of trance. In **trance disorder**, individuals retain their usual identity but have an altered perception of their milieu. These types of dissociative experiences are common in various cultures and may be part of customary religious practice; they should not be regarded as pathological unless considered abnormal within the context of that cultural or religious group. Also called **possession trance disorder**; **trance and possession disorder** (**TPD**). See DISSOCIATIVE DISORDER NOT OTHERWISE SPECIFIED. See also AMOK; ATAQUE DE NERVIOS; LATAH; PIBLOKTO.

dissonance *n.* see COGNITIVE DISSONANCE.

dissonance reduction the process by which a person reduces the uncomfortable psychological state that results from inconsistency among elements of a cognitive system (see COGNITIVE DISSONANCE). Dissonance can be reduced by making one or more inconsistent elements consistent with other elements in the system, by decreasing the perceived importance of an inconsistent element, or by adding new consistent elements to the system. Finally, SELF-AFFIRMATION THEORY postulates that merely affirming some valued aspect of the self, even if it is not directly relevant to the inconsistency, can reduce dissonance.

distance therapy any type of psychotherapy in which sessions are not conducted face-to-face because of problems of mobility, geographical isolation, or other limiting factors. Distance therapy includes interventions by telephone, audioconference, or videoconference (known collectively as **telepsychotherapy**) and the Internet (see E-THERAPY).

distorting-mirror procedure a method of documenting accuracy of body-size perception by using a mirror distorted to represent an appearance that is either smaller or larger than one's actual dimensions. Accuracy of image perception is determined by comparison with objective size level.

distorting-photograph procedure a procedure for documenting accuracy of body-size perception by using a photograph distorted to provide an image of an individual that is smaller or larger than actual size. Discrepancy between the size of the selected image and that of an accurate image is used as an index of perceptual accuracy of body size.

distorting-video procedure a method of documenting accuracy of body-size perception by using a video image modified to be smaller or larger than one's actual size.

distortion *n.* **1.** either the unconscious process of altering emotions and thoughts that are unacceptable in the individual's psyche or the conscious misrepresentation of facts, which often serves the same underlying purpose of disguising that which is unacceptable to or in the self. **2.** in psychoanalytic theory, the outcome of the DREAM-WORK that modifies forbidden thoughts and wishes to make them more acceptable to the EGO. Such distortion of the dream WISH through the use of substitutes and symbols means that only an act of INTERPRETATION can uncover the true meaning of the dream.

distractibility *n.* difficulty in maintaining attention or a tendency to be easily diverted from the matter at hand. Excessive distractibility is frequently found in children with learning disorders or ATTENTION-DEFICIT/HYPERACTIVITY DISORDER and in people experiencing MANIC EPISODES or HYPOMANIC EPISODES.

distractible speech a speech pattern in which the individual shifts rapidly from topic to topic in response to external or internal stimuli. It is a common symptom in mania. See also FLIGHT OF IDEAS.

distraction *n.* **1.** the process of interrupting attention. **2.** a stimulus or task that draws attention away from the task of primary interest.

distress *n.* **1.** the negative stress response, involving excessive levels of stimulation: a type of stress that results from being overwhelmed by demands, losses, or perceived threats. It has a detrimental effect by generating physical and psychological maladaptation and posing serious health risks for individuals. This generally is the intended meaning of the word STRESS. Compare EUSTRESS. **2.** a negative emotional state in which the specific quality of the emotion is unspecified or unidentifiable. For example, STRANGER ANXIETY in infants is more properly designated **stranger distress** because the infant's negative behavior, typically crying, allows no more specific identification of the emotion. **—distressing** *adj.*

distress–relief quotient the ratio of verbal expressions of distress to those of relief, used as an index of improvement in counseling and psychotherapy. Also called **discomfort–relief quotient; relief–discomfort quotient; relief–distress quotient**.

distribution *n.* the relation between the values that a variable may take and the relative number of cases taking on each value. A distribution may be simply an empirical description of that relationship or a mathematical (probabilistic) specification of the relationship.

distributive analysis and synthesis an approach to psychotherapy, developed within PSYCHOBIOLOGY. In the first stage, a systematic analysis is made from information gained from the client about past and present experience and distributed into such categories as symptoms and complaints, assets and liabilities, and pathological or immature reactions. In the second stage this study is used as a prelude to a constructive synthesis built on the client's own strengths, goals, and abilities. [developed by Swiss-born U.S. psychiatrist Adolf Meyer (1866–1950)]

disturbance in executive functioning see EXECUTIVE DYSFUNCTION.

disturbance of association interruption of a logical chain of culturally accepted thought, leading to apparently confused and haphazard thinking that is difficult for others to comprehend. It is one of the FUNDAMENTAL SYMPTOMS of schizophrenia described by Swiss psychiatrist Eugen Bleuler (1857–1939). See also SCHIZOPHRENIC THINKING; THOUGHT DISORDER.

disulfiram *n.* a drug used as an aversive agent in managing alcohol abuse or dependence. Disulfiram inhibits the activity of acetaldehyde dehydrogenase, an enzyme responsible for the metabolism of alcohol (ethanol) in the liver. Consumption of alcohol following administration of disulfiram results in accumulation of acetaldehyde, a toxic metabolic product of ethanol, with such unpleasant effects as nausea, vomiting, sweating, headache, a fast heart rate, and palpitations. Because of the serious nature of some of these effects (which can include damage to the liver and heart), careful INFORMED CONSENT is required before use of disulfiram. Disulfiram by itself is rarely effective in managing alcoholism and should be administered only in concert with a carefully designed behavioral regimen. U.S. trade name: **Antabuse**.

disuse theory of aging the theory that some decline in psychological abilities with aging may be due to the lack of use of those abilities. According to this theory, as adults grow older, they engage their minds less and less with the types of tasks that are found on most psychological tests.

diuretic *n.* a substance that increases the flow of urine. Diuretics may be endogenous agents (e.g., dopamine) or prescription or nonprescription drugs (e.g., THIAZIDE DIURETICS). Many diuretics (including thiazides) work by inhibiting or blocking the reabsorption of sodium and potassium ions from the kidney filtrate, so that less water is reabsorbed across the kidney tubules. Others, called osmotic diuretics, increase the osmolality of the filtrate. Both mechanisms result in increased urine volume. Some diuretics may produce adverse effects with psychological implications, for example, lassitude, weakness, vertigo, sexual impotence, headaches, polydipsia (intense thirst), irritability, or excitability.

diurnal enuresis see ENURESIS.

diurnal mood variation a feature of some BIPOLAR DISORDERS and DEPRESSIVE DISORDERS in which daily, predictable fluctuations in mood occur. Typically, this pattern consists of an elevation of mood during the daytime and evening hours and a depression of mood during the overnight and morning hours. See also SEASONAL AFFECTIVE DISORDER.

divagation *n.* rambling, digressive speech, writing, or thought. See also DISORGANIZED SPEECH.

divalproex sodium an ANTICONVULSANT drug, derived from VALPROIC ACID, originally used in the treatment of absence seizures and now used primarily for the stabilization of mania and for prophylaxis in individuals with bipolar disorder. It has also been used in the treatment of various other conditions, including autism, migrainous and other forms of head pain, other chronic pain syndromes, and mood symptoms associated with borderline personality disorder. Liver damage and reduction in blood platelets (thrombocytopenia) may occur with use of the drug, and monitoring of blood count and liver function should be carried out, particularly in the early course of treatment and particularly in children, as most fatalities due to liver failure have occurred in children. Because of its possible association with NEURAL TUBE DEFECTS, divalproex sodium should not be prescribed during pregnancy. The drug has significant interactions with antidepressants, antipsychotics, anxiolytics, and numerous other classes of medication. U.S. trade name: **Depakote**.

divergent production the capacity to produce novel solutions to a problem. It is one of the abilities recognized in Joy P. GUILFORD's theory of intelligence (see GUILFORD DIMENSIONS OF INTELLIGENCE). Compare CONVERGENT PRODUCTION.

divergent thinking creative thinking in which an individual solves a problem or reaches a decision using strategies that deviate from commonly used or previously taught strategies. This term is often used synonymously with LATERAL THINKING. Compare CONVERGENT THINKING.

diversion program a program that may be available in some circumstances for individuals who have been arrested but have not been tried and sentenced. After the defendant has been formally charged with a crime and has entered a plea, he or she may be sent to a diversion program (e.g., for drug treatment) instead of proceeding to trial; the charges are dropped if the individual successfully completes the program. Also called **deferred prosecution**.

divided consciousness a state in which two or more mental activities appear to be carried out at the same time, for example, listening, planning questions, and taking notes during an interview. To the extent that the activities require consciousness and attention, they will tend to degrade each other. See also DUAL-TASK COMPETITION.

divorce *n.* the legal dissolution of marriage, leaving the partners free to remarry. See also EMOTIONAL DIVORCE. **—divorcee** *n.*

divorce counseling counseling provided to individuals and their family members to help them cope with the problems resulting from divorce. The counseling can be conducted with the entire family or with one parent and children to provide group support and encourage a sense of belonging and identity during the transitional period. In either a family or individual context, family members may be encouraged to let go of the past and learn to deal with their present emotions. Spouses seen either individually or together may explore what their own contributions to the breakup may have been so as to decrease blame and increase probability of future relationship success.

divorce mediation counseling aimed at resolving issues for couples facing separation or divorce. The mediator remains neutral and impartial while assisting in negotiations to come to an agreed settlement over such issues as financial arrangements, child custody and visitation, and child support. Divorce mediation attempts to avoid confrontation and undue litigation prior to final settlement.

dizygotic twins (**DZ twins**) twins, of the same or different sexes, that have developed from two separate ova fertilized by two separate sperm. DZ twins are genetically as much alike as ordinary full siblings born as singletons, with each individual inheriting a random half of each parent's genes. On average, DZ twins are approximately half as genetically similar to one another as MONOZYGOTIC TWINS. For every 1,000 pregnancies there are, on average, 7–12 DZ twins. Also called **fraternal twins**. See also TWIN STUDY.

D-love *n.* see DEFICIENCY LOVE.

DLPFC abbreviation for DORSOLATERAL PREFRONTAL CORTEX.

DMT *di*methyl*t*ryptamine: a HALLUCINOGEN belonging to the indolealkylamine family, to which LSD, PSILOCIN, and DET also belong.

DNA *d*eoxyribo*n*ucleic *a*cid: one of the two types of nucleic acid found in living organisms, which is the principal carrier of genetic information in chromosomes and, to a much lesser extent, in mitochondria (an organelle that is the main site of energy production in cells). Certain segments of the DNA molecules constitute the organism's genes. Structurally, DNA consists of two intertwined, helically coiled strands of nucleotides—the **double helix**. The nucleotides each contain one of four bases: adenine, guanine, cytosine, or thymine. Each base forms hydrogen bonds with the adjacent base on the other, sister strand, producing consecutive **base pairs** arranged rather like the "rungs" on a helical ladder. Adenine (A) is always paired with thymine (T), and guanine (G) with cytosine (C). DNA can undergo self-replication in such a way that each strand serves as the template for the assembly of a complementary matching strand, resulting in two molecules exactly like the original helix in terms of base pairing. The sequence of bases in the DNA of genes contains information according to the GENETIC CODE. Each gene specifies the manufacture of a particular protein or ribosome. Because of DNA's ability to conserve its base sequence when replicating, the genetic instructions it carries are also conserved, both during cell division within a single organism and for that organism's offspring following reproduction. Compare RNA. See also RECOMBINANT DNA.

DNR abbreviation for do not resuscitate. See INFORMED CONSENT.

doctor *n.* an individual, usually an MD, PhD, or PsyD, trained and licensed to deliver medical or mental health care services.

DOES abbreviation for DISORDERS OF EXCESSIVE SOMNOLENCE.

dogmatism *n.* **1.** the tendency to act in a blindly certain, assertive, and authoritative manner in accord with a strongly held set of beliefs. **2.** a personality trait characterized by the tendency to act in a blindly certain, assertive, and authoritative manner in accord with a strongly held set of beliefs that are presumed to be resistant to change. These belief systems contain elements that are isolated from one another and thus may contradict one another. Dogmatic people tend to be intolerant of those who hold different beliefs. See ROKEACH DOGMATISM SCALE. [first proposed by U.S. psychologist Milton Rokeach (1918–1988)] **—dogmatic** *adj.*

doll play in PLAY THERAPY, the use of dolls and figurines, which may represent individuals familiar to the child, to facilitate the expression of feelings, to enact stories that express emotional needs, or to reveal significant family relationships. Also called **projective doll play**.

Dolophine *n.* a trade name for METHADONE.

DOM *d*imeth*o*xy*m*ethylamphetamine: a synthetic HALLUCINOGEN that is also called **STP**—*s*erenity, *t*ranquillity, and *p*eace, which the substance is said to induce. It is a member of the phenylisopropylamine family, to which MDA and MDMA also belong.

domestic partnership two people who live together in a stable, intimate relationship and share the responsibilities of a household in the same way that a married couple would. Some states and companies in the United States and some other countries provide legal and economic rights to domestic partners (e.g., insurance and death benefits) that are similar to those granted to married couples. See COMMON-LAW MARRIAGE; SAME-SEX MARRIAGE.

domestic violence any action by a person that causes physical harm to one or more members of his or her family unit. For example, it can involve battering of one partner by another, violence against children by a parent, or violence against elders by younger family members. See also BATTERED WOMEN; CHILD ABUSE; ELDER ABUSE.

dominance *n.* **1.** the exercise of major influence or control over others. **2.** the tendency for one hemisphere of the brain to exert greater influence than the other over certain functions, such as language or handedness. The two hemispheres contribute differently to many functions; researchers therefore use the terms **hemispheric specialization** or HEMISPHERIC LATERALIZATION in preference to dominance (or **hemispheric dominance**). **3.** in genetics, the ability of one allele to determine the PHENOTYPE of a HETEROZYGOUS individual. See DOMINANT ALLELE; DOMINANT TRAIT. **—dominant** *adj.*

dominance hierarchy 1. any ordering of motives, needs, or other psychological or physical responses based on priority or importance. An example is MASLOW'S MOTIVATIONAL HIERARCHY. **2.** in social psychology, a system of stable linear variations in prestige, status, and authority among group members.

dominance need the need to dominate, lead, or otherwise control others. It is motivated by the desire for power, knowledge, prestige, or creative achievement. [proposed by U.S. psychologist Henry Alexander Murray (1893–1988)]

dominance–submission a key dimension of interpersonal behavior, identified through FACTOR ANALYSIS, in which behavior is differentiated along a continuum ranging from extreme dominance (active, talkative, extraverted, assertive, controlling, powerful) to extreme subordination (passive, quiet, introverted, submissive, weak). Also called **ascendance–submission**.

dominant allele the version of a gene (see ALLELE) whose effects are manifest in preference to another version of the same gene (the RECESSIVE ALLELE) when both are present in the same cell. Hence, the trait determined by a dominant allele (the **dominant trait**) is apparent even when the allele is carried on only one of a pair of HOMOLOGOUS chromosomes. The term **autosomal dominant** is used to describe such patterns of inheritance in which characteristics are conveyed by dominant alleles. For example, Huntington's disease is an autosomal dominant disorder.

dominant complex an emotional disturbance that dominates or controls one's conduct.

dominant trait in genetics, a trait, such as a particular eye color, that is manifest in preference to an alternative version of the same trait (i.e., the RECESSIVE TRAIT) when the individual concerned carries both dominant and recessive versions of the gene determining the trait. See DOMINANT ALLELE.

dominatrix *n.* a woman who takes the dominant role in sexual activity, often associated with BONDAGE AND DISCIPLINE or SADOMASOCHISM.

donepezil *n.* an ACETYLCHOLINESTERASE INHIBITOR used as a NOOTROPIC in the management of mild to moderate dementia. By inhibiting the degradation of acetylcholine in the SYNAPTIC CLEFT, donepezil increases available levels of acetylcholine in the basal nucleus of Meynert, thought to be associated with improved memory and other aspects of cognitive functioning. U.S. trade name: **Aricept**.

dong quai an herbal agent derived from the plant *Angelica sinensis,* native to mountainous regions of China, Korea, and Japan, with extensive folk use in Asia, America, and western Europe for a variety of conditions but particularly as a remedy for AMENORRHEA, DYSMENORRHEA, and other menstrual irregularities. It also is reputed to ameliorate the physical and psychological symptoms associated with premenstrual syndrome and menopause. The limited research that has been done on dong quai is inconclusive, providing conflicting results on its effectiveness for any of these uses. Side effects include abdominal bloating, diarrhea and other gastrointestinal disturbances, fever, photosensitivity, and increased bleeding. Additionally, the plant contains numerous phytoestrogens (see ESTROGEN) and coumarin-like compounds and may therefore interact with pharmaceutical estrogenic compounds and prescribed blood thinners.

Don Juan a man who ruthlessly seduces women, concerned only with sexual conquest, after which he abruptly loses interest in them (**Don Juanism**). The original Don Juan was a legendary Spanish libertine, the subject of literature and Mozart's opera *Don Giovanni.* In contrast to men with a CASANOVA COMPLEX, who adore women, a Don Juan may think of women as prey. See also SATYRIASIS; EROTOMANIA.

don't-hold functions cognitive abilities, such as those involved in digit–symbol association (see DIGIT SYMBOL), that often deteriorate with adult aging as observed on intellectual or cognitive tests (e.g., the WECHSLER ADULT INTELLIGENCE SCALE).

dopa (**DOPA**) *n.* 3,4-*d*ihydr*o*xy*p*henyl*a*lanine: an amino acid that is a precursor to DOPAMINE and other catecholamines. See also LEVODOPA.

dopa decarboxylase the intermediate enzyme in the metabolism of catecholamines from the dietary amino acid tyrosine. Tyrosine is transformed to L-DOPA by TYROSINE HYDROXYLASE. L-Dopa is in turn converted to DOPAMINE by dopa decarboxylase, which also transforms a number of other aromatic amino acids. Dopamine is the final product in DOPAMINERGIC neurons; in adrenergic neurons, dopamine is transformed by the enzyme dopamine beta-hydroxylase to NOREPINEPHRINE and subsequently—in specialized cells in the adrenal medulla and other sites, via the action of the enzyme phenylethanolamine *N*-methyltransferase—to EPINEPHRINE. Also called **aromatic L-amino acid decarboxylase**.

dopamine (**DA**) *n.* a CATECHOLAMINE neurotransmitter that has an important role in motor behavior and is implicated in numerous mental conditions (see CATECHOLAMINE HYPOTHESIS; DOPAMINE HYPOTHESIS). It is found in DOPAMINERGIC neurons in the brain and elsewhere. Dopamine is synthesized from the dietary amino acid tyrosine, which in the first, rate-limiting stage of the reaction is converted to L-dopa (3,4-dihydroxy-L-phenylalanine; see LEVODOPA) by the enzyme TYROSINE HYDROXYLASE. L-Dopa is then transformed into dopamine by the enzyme DOPA DECARBOXYLASE. In nondopaminergic neurons and the adrenal medulla, dopamine is further metabolized to form norepinephrine and epinephrine, respectively. Destruction of the dopaminergic neurons in the SUBSTANTIA NIGRA is responsible for the symptoms of Parkinson's disease (e.g., rigidity, tremor). Blockade of the actions of dopamine in other brain regions accounts for the therapeutic activities of antischizophrenic drugs.

dopamine hypothesis the influential theory that schizophrenia is caused by an excess of dopamine in the brain, due either to an overproduction of dopamine or a deficiency of the enzyme needed to convert dopamine to norepinephrine (adrenaline). There is some supporting pharmacological and biochemical evidence for this hypothesis, and it is still widely discussed and promoted, particularly in a revised form that postulates the involvement in schizophrenia of both an increased mesolimbic and a decreased prefrontal dopaminergic activity. See also GLUTAMATE HYPOTHESIS.

dopamine receptor a receptor molecule that is sensitive to DOPAMINE and chemically related compounds. Dopamine receptors are located in parts of the nervous system, such as the BASAL GANGLIA, and also in blood vessels of the kidneys and mesentery, where binding of dopamine to its receptors results in widening (dilation) of the arteries. There are several subtypes of dopamine receptors, designated D1, D2, and so on.

dopamine-receptor agonists drugs or other agents that bind to and directly activate DOPAMINE RECEPTORS, producing physiological effects that mimic those of the neurotransmitter DOPAMINE. BROMOCRIPTINE is an example. Because PARKINSONISM is associated with a deficiency of dopamine in the brain, drugs that help to maintain adequate levels of dopamine are valuable in treating the disorder. Dopamine-receptor agonists are used to manage some of the drug-induced parkinsonian symptoms associated with use of antipsychotic drugs; they are also used in the treatment of Parkinson's disease, GALACTORRHEA, and prolactin-secreting tumors of the pituitary gland. Also called **dopaminergic agents**. Compare DOPAMINE-RECEPTOR ANTAGONISTS.

dopamine-receptor antagonists substances that reduce the effects of the neurotransmitter DOPAMINE by competitively binding to, and thus blocking, DOPAMINE RECEPTORS. Classically, the clinical use of dopamine antagonists in mental health has been to modulate the symptoms of schizophrenia and other psychotic conditions. Most conventional (typical or first-generation) ANTIPSYCHOTIC drugs are thought to act via antagonism of the postsynaptic dopamine D2 receptor. Most second-generation (atypical) antipsychotics possess some degree of antagonistic activity at that receptor. Other dopamine-receptor antagonists are used to prevent or treat nausea and vomiting. Compare DOPAMINE-RECEPTOR AGONISTS.

dopaminergic *adj.* responding to, releasing, or otherwise involving dopamine. For example, a **dopaminergic neuron** is any neuron in the brain or other parts of the central nervous system for which dopamine serves as the principal neurotransmitter. Three major tracts of dopamine-containing neurons are classically described: the mesolimbic–mesocortical tract (see MESOCORTICAL SYSTEM; MESOLIMBIC SYSTEM), in which excess dopamine activity is hypothesized to be associated with positive and negative symptoms of schizophrenia; the NIGROSTRIATAL TRACT, which is involved in motor functions and Parkinson's disease; and the tuberoinfundibular pathway, a local circuit in the hypothalamus that is involved in the regulation of the pituitary hormone prolactin.

dopaminergic agents see DOPAMINE-RECEPTOR AGONISTS.

Dopar *n.* a trade name for LEVODOPA.

Doppelganger phenomenon the delusion that one has a double or twin, who looks and acts the same as oneself (German, "double walker"). See also AUTOSCOPY.

Dora case one of Sigmund FREUD's earliest and most celebrated cases, reported in *Fragment of an Analysis of a Case of Hysteria* (1905). The study of this woman's multiple symptoms (headaches, loss of speech, suicidal thoughts, amnesic episodes) contributed to his theory of REPRESSION and the use of DREAM ANALYSIS as an analytic tool.

Doral *n.* a trade name for QUAZEPAM.

Doriden *n.* a trade name for GLUTETHIMIDE.

dorsal stream a series of specialized visual regions in the cerebral cortex of the brain that originate in the striate cortex (primary visual cortex) of the occipital lobe and project forward and upward into the parietal lobe. Known informally as the "where" or "how" pathway, it is involved in processing object motion and location in space. Compare VENTRAL STREAM.

dorsolateral prefrontal cortex (DLPFC) a region of the brain located near the front and to both sides of the PREFRONTAL CORTEX (BRODMANN'S AREAS 9 and 46) in mammals, involved in WORKING MEMORY and attentional control. Damage to this region in humans results in an inability to select task-relevant information and to shift attention based on external cues.

dose–response relationship a principle relating the potency of a drug to the efficacy of that drug in affecting a target symptom or organ system. **Potency** refers to the amount of a drug necessary to produce the desired effect; **efficacy** refers to the drug's ability to act at a target receptor or organ to produce the desired effect. Dose–response curves may be graded, suggesting a continuous relationship between dose and effect, or quantal, where the desired effect is an either–or phenomenon, such as prevention of arrhythmias. There is considerable variability among individuals in response to a given dose of a particular drug.

dotting test a pencil-and-paper motor test in which the participant makes as many dots as possible in a given time period, either randomly (**tapping test**) or within small circles (**aiming test**).

double *n.* in PSYCHODRAMA, an individual, one of the AUXILIARY EGOS, who speaks or acts out the presumed inner thoughts of the PROTAGONIST (i.e., the person presenting the problem to be explored). The technique is known as **doubling**.

double-agentry *n.* the situation in which the therapist's allegiance to the patient is in conflict with demands from the institution or from other professionals. See CONFLICT OF INTEREST.

double approach–avoidance conflict a complex conflict situation arising when a person is confronted with two goals or options that each have significant attractive and unattractive features. See also APPROACH–AVOIDANCE CONFLICT.

double-approach conflict see APPROACH–APPROACH CONFLICT.

double-avoidance conflict see AVOIDANCE–AVOIDANCE CONFLICT.

double bind a situation in which an individual receives contradictory messages from another person or from two different people. For example, a parent may respond negatively when his or her child approaches or attempts to engage in affectionate behavior, but then, when the child turns away or tries to leave, reaches out to encourage the child to return. Double-binding communication was once considered a causative factor in schizophrenia. [proposed by British anthropologist Gregory Bateson (1904–1980)]

double blind see BLIND.

double consciousness a condition in which two distinct, unrelated mental states coexist within the same person. This may occur, for example, in an individual with a DISSOCIATIVE IDENTITY DISORDER. Also called **dual consciousness**.

double dissociation a research process for

demonstrating the action of two separable psychological or biological systems, such as differentiating between types of memory or the function of brain areas. One experimental variable is found to affect one of the systems, whereas a second variable affects the other. The differentiating variables may be task-related, pharmacological, neurological, or individual differences. [described by German-born U.S. psychologist Hans-Lukas Teuber (1916–1977)]

double insanity see FOLIE À DEUX.

double technique in PSYCHODRAMA, a procedure in which one of the participants, usually the therapist, sits behind a member of the group and speaks for that member saying what he or she believes the person is thinking. Also called **priming-the-pump technique**.

doubling *n.* see DOUBLE.

doubt *n.* **1.** lack of confidence or uncertainty about something or someone, including the self. Doubt may center on everyday concerns (Can I accomplish this task?), issues of daily living (Can I change this ingrained habit?), or the very meaning of life itself (see EXISTENTIAL ANXIETY). It is a perception, typically with a strong affective component, that is frequently a focus during psychotherapeutic intervention. **2.** in ERIKSON'S EIGHT STAGES OF DEVELOPMENT, see AUTONOMY VERSUS SHAME AND DOUBT.

doubting mania extreme and obsessive feelings of uncertainty about even the most obvious matters. Doubting mania is a common obsession associated with OBSESSIVE-COMPULSIVE DISORDER and often results in checking rituals (e.g., repeatedly looking to see if the door is locked) as a means of reducing doubt-related anxiety. [named by French psychiatrist Jean-Pierre Falret (1794–1870)]

downers *pl. n.* slang for SEDATIVE, HYPNOTIC, AND ANXIOLYTIC DRUGS.

Down syndrome a chromosomal disorder characterized by an extra chromosome 21 (in some cases, 22) and manifested by a round flat face and eyes that seem to slant (the disorder was formerly known as **mongolism**). Brain size and weight are below average; affected individuals usually have mild to severe mental retardation and have been characterized as having docile, agreeable dispositions. Muscular movements tend to be slow, clumsy, and uncoordinated. In many cases growth is retarded, the tongue is thick, and the fingers are stubby. Affected individuals may have heart defects and respiratory insufficiencies or anomalies that are often corrected during infancy by surgery. However, lifespan is reduced compared to the general population, and affected individuals typically show early onset of ALZHEIMER'S DISEASE. Down syndrome is one of the most common organic causes of mental retardation. Also called **Down's syndrome**; **Langdon Down's disease**; **congenital acromicria**. See also AUTOSOMAL TRISOMY OF GROUP G; TRISOMY 21. [described in 1866 by John Langdon Haydon **Down** (1828–1896), British physician]

downward drift hypothesis see DRIFT HYPOTHESIS.

doxepin *n.* a TRICYCLIC ANTIDEPRESSANT, among the most sedating and most anticholinergic of these agents. Although it currently has little use as an antidepressant, it may be used in relatively low doses as a hypnotic or in the management of neuromuscular or musculoskeletal pain. It is also available as a topical treatment for management of dermatologic conditions. U.S. trade name (among others): **Sinequan**.

doxylamine *n.* an ethanolamine antihistamine (see ANTIHISTAMINE) with significant sedative properties, which is included in numerous nonprescription sleep aids. Like all antihistamines, it may lose its efficacy with repeated use. Overdose is characterized by symptoms of anticholinergic toxicity, including raised temperature, a rapid heart rate, and delirium.

DPE abbreviation for DELIBERATE PSYCHOLOGICAL EDUCATION.

d prime (symbol: d′) a measure of an individual's ability to detect signals; more specifically, a measure of sensitivity or discriminability derived from SIGNAL DETECTION THEORY that is unaffected by response biases. It is the difference (in standard deviation units) between the means of the NOISE and signal+noise distributions. The assumptions underlying the validity of d′ as a bias-free measure are that the probability distributions upon which decisions are based are Gaussian (normal) and have equal variances. If this is true, then d′ completely describes the **receiver-operating characteristic curve**, the relationship between hit and false-alarm rates of yes responses in a detection, discrimination, or recognition task. In practice, d′ has proved to be sufficiently bias-free to be the "best" measure of psychophysical performance. It is essentially a STANDARDIZED SCORE and is computed as the difference between the (Gaussian) standard scores for the false-alarm rate and the hit rate. A value of $d' = 3$ is close to perfect performance; a value of $d' = 0$ is chance ("guessing") performance.

Dramamine *n.* a trade name for DIMENHYDRINATE.

drama therapy in GROUP THERAPY, the use of theater techniques to gain self-awareness and increase self-expression. See also PSYCHODRAMA.

dramatics *n.* **1.** the use of drama as a rehabilitation technique, using published or original scripts with patients as performers. See also PSYCHODRAMA. **2.** see CREATIVE DRAMATICS.

dramatization *n.* **1.** the use of ATTENTION-GETTING behavior as a defense against anxiety. An example of dramatization is the exaggeration of the symptoms of an illness to make it appear more important than the occurrence of the same illness in another person. **2.** in psychoanalytic theory, the expression of repressed wishes or impulses in dreams. **—dramatize** *vb.*

dread *n.* **1.** intense fear or fearful anticipation. **Existential dread** (see EXISTENTIALISM) refers to a profound, deep-seated psychic or spiritual condition of insecurity and despair in relation to the human condition and the meaning of life. See also ANGST. **2.** in psychoanalysis, anxiety elicited by a specific threat, such as going out on a dark night, as contrasted with anxiety that does not have a specific object.

dream *n.* a mental state that occurs in sleep and is characterized by a rich array of sensory, motor, emotional, and cognitive experiences. Dreams occur most often, but not exclusively, during periods of REM SLEEP. They are characterized by (a) vivid imagery, especially visual imagery, and a strong sense of movement; (b) intense emotion, especially fear, elation, or anger; (c) delusional acceptance of the dream as a waking reality; and (d) discontinuity in time and space and incongruity of character and plot. Despite the vivid intensity of dreams, it can be difficult to remember them to any extent unless promptly awakened from REM sleep, but even then much content cannot be accurately retrieved. Because the reports of dream content have little apparent relation to the physical or mental stimuli impinging on the sleeper and few dream events seem ever to have occurred, as it were, in vivo, the research tools of experimental psychology cannot be used effectively to study the phenomenon. Thus, assumptions about how a dream is produced and what it means are strongly dependent on theories about waking cognitive events and processes. Diverse theories have arisen from varied sources throughout history, including certain cultural beliefs in communication with the supernatural; the suggestion of Greek physician Hippocrates (c. 460–c. 377 BCE) that dreams provide early evidence of disease; FREUD's interpretation of dreams as a struggle in which the part of the mind representing social strictures (the SUPEREGO) plays out a conflict with the sexual impulses (the LIBIDO) while the rational part of the mind (the EGO) is at rest; JUNG's view that dreams provide evidence of the biological inheritance of universal symbols (ARCHETYPES); and ADLER's view that inferiority feelings are played out in dreams. The discovery in the early 1950s of REM sleep initiated the scientific study of dreaming as a neurocognitive process, a recent product of which is the ACTIVATION–SYNTHESIS HYPOTHESIS. See also DREAM CENSORSHIP; DREAM STATE; DREAM-WORK; LATENT CONTENT; MANIFEST CONTENT; NIGHTMARE. **—dreamlike** *adj.* **—dreamy** *adj.*

dream analysis a technique, originally used in psychoanalysis but now also used in other psychotherapies, in which the content of dreams is interpreted to reveal underlying motivations or symbolic meanings and representations (i.e., LATENT CONTENT). Dream analysis is aided by such techniques as FREE ASSOCIATION. Also called **dream interpretation**.

dream anxiety disorder see NIGHTMARE DISORDER.

dream censorship in psychoanalytic theory, the disguising in dreams of unconscious wishes that would be disturbing to the EGO if allowed conscious expression. According to the classic psychoanalytic theory of Sigmund FREUD, the thoroughness of dream disguise varies directly with the strictness of the censorship. See CENSOR.

dream content the images, ideas, and impulses expressed in a dream. See LATENT CONTENT; MANIFEST CONTENT.

dream ego in the ANALYTIC PSYCHOLOGY of Carl JUNG, a fragment of the conscious EGO that is active during the dream state.

dream function the purpose or function of dreaming. In the classical psychoanalytic theory of Sigmund FREUD, the dream functions as a disguised fulfillment of a repressed WISH or as mastery of a traumatic experience. In the ANALYTIC PSYCHOLOGY of Carl JUNG, it is a reflection of fundamental personality tendencies.

dream imagery endogenous visual experiences during dreams, sometimes taken to represent daytime experiences or dilemmas.

dream incorporation the integration of an ACCIDENTAL STIMULUS in the content of a dream.

dream induction see DREAM SUGGESTION.

dream interpretation see DREAM ANALYSIS.

dream state (**D-state**) the state of sleep during which dreaming takes place most often, characterized by rapid eye movements (see REM SLEEP) and patterns on the electroencephalogram that most closely resemble those of wakefulness. It usually occurs four or five times during the night and is physiologically distinct from DEEP SLEEP and wakefulness. Studies indicate that about 20% of sleeping time is spent in the dream state. The lower brainstem appears to be the area most involved in originating the dream state, under the control of genetically and light-regulated diurnal rhythms (see PGO SPIKES; PONTINE SLEEP). See also TWILIGHT STATE.

dream stimulus any of the stimuli that may initiate a dream, such as external stimulation, internal sensory stimulation, mental images, feelings, or memories. Compare ACCIDENTAL STIMULUS.

dream suggestion a specialized hypnotic technique in which the client is instructed to dream about a problem or its source, either during the hypnotic state or posthypnotically, during natural sleep. The technique is sometimes used as an aid in HYPNOTHERAPY. Also called **dream induction**.

dream-work *n.* in psychoanalytic theory, the transformation of the LATENT CONTENT of a dream into the MANIFEST CONTENT experienced by the dreamer. This transformation is effected by such processes as CONDENSATION, SYMBOLISM, DISPLACEMENT, and DRAMATIZATION.

dreamy state a brief altered state of consciousness similar to a dream, during which the individual experiences visual, olfactory, or auditory hallucinations.

D

dressing behavior dressing in accordance with social expectations for one's gender, which is an important factor in GENDER IDENTITY. Studies of transvestites and transsexuals indicate that they often cross-dressed (or were cross-dressed) in childhood and adolescence. See CROSS-DRESSING.

DRGs abbreviation for DIAGNOSIS-RELATED GROUPS.

drift hypothesis a sociological concept purporting to explain the higher incidence of schizophrenia in urban poverty centers, suggesting that during the preclinical phase people tend to drift into poverty and social isolation. Also called **downward drift hypothesis**.

drinking bouts see EPSILON ALCOHOLISM.

drive *n.* **1.** a generalized state of readiness precipitating or motivating an activity or course of action. Drive is hypothetical in nature, usually created by deprivation of a needed substance (e.g., food), the presence of negative stimuli (e.g., pain, cold), or the occurrence of negative events. Drive is said to be necessary for the stimuli or events to serve as REINFORCERS. **2.** in the psychoanalytic theory of Sigmund FREUD, a concept used to understand the relationship between the psyche and the soma (mind and body); drive is conceived as a having a somatic source but creating a psychic effect. Freud identified two separate drives as emerging from somatic sources: LIBIDO and AGGRESSION. See also MOTIVATION; OBJECT RELATIONS.

drive discrimination the ability of an organism to differentiate between various psychological, emotional, and physiological needs and to direct responses accordingly, for example, drinking when thirsty, eating when hungry. [defined by Edward C. TOLMAN]

drive displacement the activation of one drive when another drive is thwarted; for example, eating chocolate when one is prohibited from smoking a cigarette.

drive theory see CLASSICAL PSYCHOANALYSIS.

dromomania *n.* an abnormal drive or desire to travel that involves spending beyond one's means and sacrificing job, partner, or security in the lust for new experiences. People with dromomania not only feel more alive when traveling but also start planning their next trip as soon as they arrive home. Fantasies about travel occupy many of their waking thoughts and some of their dreams. The condition was formerly referred to as **vagabond neurosis**.

dronabinol *n.* see TETRAHYDROCANNABINOL.

droperidol *n.* an antipsychotic agent of the BUTYROPHENONE class that is used in premedication for surgery and to maintain surgical anesthesia. It is occasionally used for the emergency treatment of acute psychotic agitation. Because of its extremely rapid onset of action, it has few other mental health applications. U.S. trade name: **Inapsine**.

drop-in center a facility, often associated with a substance-abuse program, where professional support and advice can be obtained without an advance appointment. A drop-in center also serves as a gathering place providing social, educational, and recreational activities.

dropout *n.* **1.** a student who leaves school before graduating. **2.** a patient or client who terminates treatment before it is completed.

drowsiness *n.* a state of low alertness in which the BRAIN WAVE pattern found during waking alternates with DELTA WAVES. See also HYPERSOMNIA; SOMNOLENCE.

DRS **1.** abbreviation for DEMENTIA RATING SCALE. **2.** abbreviation for DISABILITY RATING SCALE.

drug *n.* any substance, other than food, that influences motor, sensory, cognitive, or other bodily processes. Drugs generally are administered for experimental, diagnostic, or treatment purposes but also tend to be used recreationally to achieve particular effects.

drug abuse see SUBSTANCE ABUSE.

drug abuse treatment see SUBSTANCE ABUSE TREATMENT.

drug addiction see SUBSTANCE DEPENDENCE.

drug culture the activities and way of life of those people who habitually use one or more kinds of drugs of abuse, usually illicit drugs such as hashish, cocaine, heroin, LSD, or other substances that produce altered states of consciousness.

drug dependence see SUBSTANCE DEPENDENCE.

drug education the process of informing individuals or groups about the effects of various chemical agents on the human body, usually with a special emphasis on the effects of mind-altering substances.

drug holiday discontinuance of a therapeutic drug for a limited period in order to control dosage and side effects and to evaluate the patient's behavior with and without it. Formerly commonly recommended for children taking METHYLPHENIDATE, drug holidays on weekends or school vacations were thought to prevent growth suppression that was tentatively associated with this agent. Drug holidays are infrequent in modern clinical practice.

drug-induced lactation see GALACTORRHEA.

drug-induced parkinsonism see PARKINSONISM.

drug-induced psychosis a psychotic state resulting from use or abuse of a variety of therapeutic or illicit substances. Well-described drug-induced psychoses may result from excessive or chronic use of amphetamines, cocaine, or other stimulants; cannabis; LSD, PCP (phencyclidine), or other hallucinogens; and other illicit substances. A variety of medications may produce psychotic symptoms, including anticholinergic drugs at therapeutic doses in susceptible individuals. In *DSM–IV–TR*, it is categorized as SUBSTANCE-INDUCED PSYCHOTIC DISORDER.

drug interactions the effects of administering two or more drugs concurrently, which alters the pharmacological action of one or more of them. Pharmacokinetic interactions alter the absorption, distribution, metabolism, and excretion of the drugs; they may induce or inhibit the elimination of drugs, leading to unexpected increases or decreases in their concentrations in the body. Pharmacodynamic interactions affect the drugs' activities at target organs or receptor sites; they may be synergistic, enhancing the effectiveness of a drug at a target receptor or organ (see DRUG SYNERGISM), or antagonistic, in which the presence of one drug reduces the effectiveness of another (see ANTAGONIST).

drug metabolism the process by which a drug is transformed in the body (in the liver and other organs), usually from a more lipid-soluble form, which makes it more readily absorbed into the body, to a more water-soluble form, which facilitates its excretion. Two phases of drug metabolism are recognized. In **Phase I metabolism**, the drug is oxidized, reduced, or hydrolyzed—that is, oxygen is added, oxygen is removed, or hydrogen is added, respectively (see CYTOCHROME P450). In **Phase II metabolism**, functional groups (specific clusters of atoms) are added to drug molecules (e.g., by GLUCURONIDATION).

drug screening instrument a brief interview, such as CAGE, or a brief self-report instrument, such as MAST, that is designed to identify individuals who should be assessed thoroughly for the possibility of substance abuse.

drug synergism an enhancement of efficacy occurring when two or more drugs are administered concurrently, so that their combined pharmacological or clinical effects are greater than those occurring when the drugs are administered individually. Drug synergism can be metabolic, when the administration of one agent interferes with the metabolism of another, or it can be pharmacological, when the administration of two or more agents results in enhanced receptor binding or other activity at target sites. The enhanced antimicrobial activity of two antibiotics administered together is an example of positive synergism; negative synergism can be seen when the administration of a nontoxic agent with a toxic drug worsens the toxicity of the latter.

drug therapy see PHARMACOTHERAPY.

drug tolerance see TOLERANCE.

drug withdrawal see SUBSTANCE WITHDRAWAL.

D sleep abbreviation for dreaming sleep (see DREAM STATE) or desynchronized sleep, that is, REM SLEEP. Compare S SLEEP.

DSM–IV–TR the text revision of the fourth edition of the *Diagnostic and Statistical Manual of Mental Disorders*, prepared by the Task Force on *DSM–IV* of the American Psychiatric Association and published in 2000. The classification presents descriptions of diagnostic categories (which appear as entries in this dictionary) without favoring any particular theory of etiology. It is largely modeled on the INTERNATIONAL CLASSIFICATION OF DISEASES (9th edition, 1978), developed by the World Health Organization and modified for use in the United States (*ICD–9–CM*), but contains greater detail and a method of coding on different axes (see AXIS; MULTIAXIAL CLASSIFICATION). Previous editions were published in 1952 (*DSM–I*), 1968 (*DSM–II*), 1980 (*DSM–III*), and 1994 (*DSM–IV*). Over that period, the number of identified disorders has increased from about 100 to more than 300. An updated edition (*DSM-V*) is expected in 2013.

DST abbreviation for DEXAMETHASONE SUPPRESSION TEST.

D-state abbreviation for DREAM STATE, as opposed to the S-state (sleeping state) and the W-state (waking state).

DTD abbreviation for DEVELOPMENTAL TRAUMA DISORDER.

D trisomy see CHROMOSOME-13 TRISOMY.

DTs abbreviation for DELIRIUM TREMENS.

dual-action antidepressants see MIXED-FUNCTION ANTIDEPRESSANTS.

dual consciousness see DOUBLE CONSCIOUSNESS.

dual diagnosis the identification of two distinct disorders that are present in the same person at the same time, for example, the coexistence of depression or anxiety disorder and a substance-abuse disorder (e.g., alcohol or drug dependence). See also COMORBIDITY.

dual instinct theory in psychoanalytic theory, the view that human life is governed by two antagonistic forces: the LIFE INSTINCT, or EROS, and the DEATH INSTINCT, or THANATOS. This was a late theoretical formulation by Sigmund FREUD, who held that "the interaction of the two basic instincts with or against each other gives rise to the whole variegation of the phenomena of life" (*Beyond the Pleasure Principle*, 1920).

dualism *n.* the position that reality consists of two separate substances, defined by French philosopher René Descartes (1596–1650) as thinking substance (mind) and extended substance (matter). In the context of the MIND–BODY PROBLEM, dualism is the position that the mind and the body constitute two separate realms or substances. Dualistic positions raise the question of how mind and body interact in thought and behavior. Compare MONISM. See also CARTESIAN DUALISM. **—dualist** *adj., n.* **—dualistic** *adj.*

dual-leadership therapy see COTHERAPY.

dual personality a condition in which the personality is divided into two relatively independent and generally contrasting systems. See DISSOCIATIVE IDENTITY DISORDER.

dual process theory 1. the theory that the response made by an individual to a stimulus that permits behavioral control involves two stages: (a) a decision as to whether or not to respond and (b) a choice between alternative responses. **2.** in theories of memory, the operation of two different cognitive processes (for example, recollection and familiarity) in recognition memory.

dual relationship see MULTIPLE RELATIONSHIP.

dual-store model of memory the concept that memory is a two-stage process, comprising SHORT-TERM MEMORY, in which information is retained for a few seconds, and LONG-TERM MEMORY, which permits the retention of information for hours to many years. William JAMES called these stages PRIMARY MEMORY and SECONDARY MEMORY, respectively. Also called **dual memory theory**.

dual-task competition a phenomenon observed in experimental techniques examining performance in which participants are asked to do two tasks (e.g., speeded reaction time and mental arithmetic) simultaneously. Such tasks require effort (see EFFORTFULNESS) and tend to compete against each other, so that their performances degrade. The decrease in performance is often taken as a measure of mental capacity limits (see CENTRAL LIMITED CAPACITY).

Duchenne smile a smile characterized by bilaterally symmetrical upturning of the lips and activation of the orbicularis oculi muscles surrounding the eyes, which creates a crow's-foot effect at the corners of the eyes. Duchenne smiles are believed to be authentic smiles, as opposed to posed, voluntary smiles that lack the orbicularis oculi component. [Guillaume Benjamin Armand **Duchenne** (1806–1875), French neurologist]

dull normal see BELOW AVERAGE.

dummy *n.* in double-blind drug trials (see BLIND), an inert substance that appears identical in all aspects (e.g., dosage form, method of administration) to the active drug under investigation, thereby helping to preserve experimental blinds for both patients and clinical investigators. Since a dummy is completely inert it has no pharmacological activity, unlike an ACTIVE PLACEBO, which may produce side effects.

dummy variable coding a method of assigning numerical values (often 0 and 1) to a CATEGORICAL VARIABLE in such a way that the variable reflects class membership.

durable power of attorney a legal document that designates someone to make health care decisions, financial decisions, or both for an individual if that person becomes incapacitated or otherwise incapable of making decisions on his or her own.

Duragesic *n.* a trade name for FENTANYL.

duration of untreated illness in schizophrenia, the length of time that the illness is present before antipsychotic drug treatment or other forms of therapy are initiated. Such periods are studied to determine the effect of untreated schizophrenia on symptom severity and the likelihood that specific treatments will be effective.

Durham rule a 1954 ruling by the U.S. Court of Appeals in a case involving a defendant named Durham. It stated that "an accused is not criminally responsible if his unlawful act was the product of mental disease or mental defect." This rule has been replaced by the AMERICAN LAW INSTITUTE MODEL PENAL CODE INSANITY TEST. Also called **Durham decision**; **Durham test**; **product rule**.

Dusky standard an influential 1960 U.S. Supreme Court ruling establishing that defendants' COMPETENCY TO STAND TRIAL must be related to their ability to understand and appreciate the criminal proceedings against them and to whether they can reasonably assist their own counsel by making choices among available options (e.g., pleas).

duty to protect the obligation of mental health professionals to protect third parties from harm or violence that may result from the actions of their clients. This obligation may involve, but is not necessarily restricted to, a DUTY TO WARN. See TARASOFF DECISION.

duty to warn the obligation of mental health professionals to warn third parties whom their clients intend to harm. See also DUTY TO PROTECT; TARASOFF DECISION.

Dx abbreviation for DIAGNOSIS.

dyad (**diad**) *n.* **1.** a pair of individuals in an interpersonal situation, such as mother and child, husband and wife, cotherapists, or patient and therapist. **2.** two individuals who are closely interdependent, particularly on an emotional level (e.g., twins reared together, mother and infant, or a very close married couple). **—dyadic** *adj.*

dyadic relationship 1. any committed, intimate two-person relationship. **2.** in psychotherapy and counseling, the working relationship between therapist and patient or counselor and client.

dyadic session a meeting of a therapist with only one particular client, as opposed to a couple or a family.

dyadic therapy see INDIVIDUAL THERAPY.

dying phobia see THANATOPHOBIA.

dying process a progressive and nonreversible loss of vital functions that results in the end of life. The transition from health to death can be swift or extended, predictable or unpredictable, depending on the specific life-threatening condition, the vigor of the patient, and the treatment available (see also END OF LIFE). See also STAGES OF GRIEF.

dynamic *adj.* **1.** pertaining to force. **2.** continuously changing or in flux. **3.** describing systems of psychology that emphasize motivation, mental processes, and the complexities of force and interaction. See also PSYCHODYNAMICS.

dynamic assessment 1. an approach to CLINICAL ASSESSMENT that follows the same basic principles as DYNAMIC TESTING, including not only tests but also other forms of assessment, such as projects, essays, and performances. **2.** an assessment that has the goal of elaborating on the complex reasons for dysfunctions, especially with regard to conflicts.

dynamic core a theoretical construct involving a subset of neurons in the thalamocortical system of the brain that support conscious experience. The specific subset of neurons involved may vary dynamically from moment to moment, but the dynamic core always maximizes high integration and differentiation of information. See COMPLEXITY HYPOTHESIS. [proposed by U.S. neuroscientist Gerald M. Edelman (1929–) and Italian–U.S. psychologist Giulio Tononi (1960–)]

dynamic effect law the theory that GOAL-DIRECTED BEHAVIORS become habitualized as they effectively attain the goal. [proposed by British-born U.S. psychologist Raymond B. Cattell (1905–1998)]

dynamic formulation the ongoing attempt to organize the clinical material elicited about a client's behavior, traits, attitudes, and symptoms into a structure that helps the therapist understand the client and plan his or her treatment more effectively.

dynamic model in psychoanalytic theory, the view that the psyche can be explained in terms of underlying, unconscious drives and instincts that mold the personality, motivate behavior, and produce emotional disorder. Compare ECONOMIC MODEL; TOPOGRAPHIC MODEL. See also METAPSYCHOLOGY.

dynamic psychotherapy see PSYCHODYNAMIC PSYCHOTHERAPY.

dynamic resignation see NEUROTIC RESIGNATION.

dynamic system a system in which a change in one part influences all interrelated parts. Such a system is described by a set of quantitative variables changing continuously and interdependently in time in accordance with laws captured by some set of equations. The motion on a pendulum is a simple example. Dynamic system models provide an important alternative to symbolic models as a way to understand many psychological phenomena (e.g., coordinated movements, developmental phenomena, and decision making).

dynamic systems theory a theory that attempts to explain behavior and personality in terms of constantly changing, self-organizing interactions among multiple organismic and environmental factors that operate on multiple timescales and multiple levels of analysis.

dynamic testing a psychometric approach that attempts to measure not only the products or processes of learning but also the potential to learn. It focuses on the difference between actual ability and potential, that is, the extent to which developed abilities reflect latent capacity. It attempts to quantify the process of learning rather than the products of that process. This is done by presenting progressively more challenging tasks and providing continuous feedback on performance in an atmosphere of teaching and guidance toward the right answer. [introduced by Lev VYGOTSKY]

dynamic trait a personality trait that involves motivation or putting the individual into action. It is one of three classes of SOURCE TRAITS in CATTELL'S PERSONALITY TRAIT THEORY, the others being ABILITY TRAITS and TEMPERAMENT TRAITS.

dynamic unconscious see UNCONSCIOUS. Compare COGNITIVE UNCONSCIOUS.

dysaesthesia *n.* see DYSESTHESIA.

dysarthria *n.* any of a group of MOTOR SPEECH DISORDERS caused by muscular impairment originating in the central or peripheral nervous system. Respiration, articulation, phonation, resonance, and prosody may be affected. There are four main types: dyskinetic, spastic, peripheral, and mixed. **Dyskinetic dysarthria** includes **hypokinetic dysarthria**, in which prosody is affected in terms of rate and rhythm, and **hyperkinetic dysarthria**, in which articulation is poor due to difficulties in controlling the rate and range of movement in ongoing speech. In **spastic dysarthria**, all speech parameters are affected, respiration is poor, intonation patterns are restricted, and spasticity in the vocal cords causes hoarseness. **Peripheral dysarthria** is characterized by continual breathiness during phonation, with audible inspiration, distortion of consonants, and, often, a need to speak in short phrases. **Mixed dysarthria** occurs in those who have impairment in more than one motor system, possibly caused by tumors, degenerative conditions, or trauma. —**dysarthric** *adj.*

dysautonomia *n.* dysfunction of the autonomic nervous system, including impairment, failure, or overactivity of sympathetic or parasympathetic functioning. The dysfunction may be local or generalized, acute or chronic, and is associated with a number of disorders. Also called **autonomic dysfunction**; **autonomic neuropathy**.

dysbulia *n.* **1.** difficulty in thinking, maintaining attention, or maintaining a train of thought. **2.** lack of willpower or weakness of volition.

dyscalculia *n.* an impaired ability to perform simple arithmetic operations that results from a congenital deficit. It is a developmental condition, whereas ACALCULIA is acquired.

dyscheiria (**dyschiria**) *n.* see ACHEIRIA.

dyscontrol *n.* an impaired ability to direct or regulate one's functioning in volition, emotion, behavior, cognition, or some other area, which often entails inability to resist impulses and leads to abnormal behaviors without significant provocation.

D

dysesthesia (**disesthesia; dysaesthesia**) *n.* abnormalities of any sense but particularly that of touch.

dysexecutive syndrome (**DES**) a collection of symptoms that involve impaired executive control of actions (see EXECUTIVE DYSFUNCTION), caused by damage to the frontal lobes of the brain. Individuals can perform routine tasks but cannot deal with new tasks or situations. They have difficulty in initiating and switching actions; for example, they cannot prevent an inappropriate but highly automated action from occurring or change their actions to appropriate ones. A questionnaire called the **Dysexecutive Questionnaire** (**DEX**) can be used to assess the severity of the impairment.

dysfluency *n.* any disturbance in the normal flow or patterning of speech, marked by repetitions, prolongations, and hesitations. See also STUTTERING.

dysfunction *n.* any impairment, disturbance, or deficiency in behavior or operation. **—dysfunctional** *adj.*

dysfunctional family a family in which relationships or communication are impaired and members are unable to attain closeness and self-expression. Members of a dysfunctional family often develop symptomatic behaviors, and often one individual in the family presents as the IDENTIFIED PATIENT.

dysfunctions associated with sleep, sleep stages, or partial arousals one of four basic types of SLEEP DISORDERS, differentiated from the other types by the presence of physiological activations at inappropriate times during sleep rather than abnormalities in the mechanisms involved in the timing of sleep and wakefulness. This type of sleep disorder includes NIGHTMARE DISORDER, SLEEP TERROR DISORDER, and SLEEP-WALKING DISORDER; in *DSM–IV–TR* these are classified as PARASOMNIAS.

dysgeusia *n.* abnormalities of the sense of taste. These gustatory distortions may occur during pregnancy, prior to an epileptic seizure, or as a symptom of psychosis or an eating disorder. See also HYPOGEUSIA.

dyskinesia *n.* any involuntary (unintended) movement, such as a tic or spasm. The term also is used more imprecisely to denote distorted or impaired voluntary movement. Also called **dyskinesis**. **—dyskinetic** *adj.*

dyslexia *n.* a neurologically based learning disability manifested as severe difficulties in reading, spelling, and writing words and sometimes in arithmetic. Dyslexia is characterized by impairment in the ability to process sounds, that is, to make connections between written letters and their sounds; written work is often characterized by letter or word reversals. It can be either acquired (see ALEXIA) or developmental (see DEVELOPMENTAL DYSLEXIA), is independent of intellectual ability, and is unrelated to disorders of speech and vision that may also be present. It is not the result of lack of motivation, sensory impairment, inadequate instructional or environmental opportunities, emotional disturbances, or other such factors. Investigators have proposed various subtypes of dyslexia—DEEP DYSLEXIA, SURFACE DYSLEXIA, WORD-FORM DYSLEXIA, PHONOLOGICAL DYSLEXIA, and NEGLECT DYSLEXIA, among others—but there is no universally accepted system of classification. See also READING DISABILITY; READING DISORDER. **—dyslexic** *adj.*

dyslogia *n.* see ALOGIA.

dysmenorrhea *n.* difficult or painful menstruation. The cause may be an obstruction in the cervix or vagina that traps menstrual blood, or the condition may be secondary to an infection or tumor. More than three fourths of cases are a primary, or functional, form of the disorder for which no organic cause can be found. Dysmenorrhea may be characterized by cramplike pains in the lower abdomen, headache, irritability, depression, and fatigue. Kinds of dysmenorrhea include **congestive dysmenorrhea**, marked by congestion of the uterus; **inflammatory dysmenorrhea**, associated with inflammation; **membranous dysmenorrhea**, marked by loss of membrane tissue from the uterus; **obstructive dysmenorrhea**, associated with mechanical interference of menstrual flow; and **essential dysmenorrhea**, for which there is no obvious cause. **—dysmenorrheic** *adj.*

dysmnesia *n.* an impairment of memory, which may occur as a discrete episode or persist as a chronic condition and may be caused by any of a number of problems, such as DELIRIUM, acute or chronic brain disorders, or brain injury. Also called **dysmnesic syndrome**. **—dysmnesic** *adj.*

dysmorphism *n.* an abnormality in the shape or structure of some part of the body.

dysmorphophobia *n.* see BODY DYSMORPHIC DISORDER.

dysnomia–auditory retrieval disorder a speech and language disorder marked by problems in object naming and word retrieval and deficits in auditory memory. Affected children may have difficulty remembering meaningful information (expressed, for example, as sentences or stories) in a sequential fashion, even though they may have good language skills and normal or high verbal output. The memory deficit may mimic some forms of ATTENTION-DEFICIT/HYPERACTIVITY DISORDER, but behavior is rarely a problem (although frustration may be seen). Although increasingly supported by the research literature, the disorder is not classified in *DSM–IV–TR*.

dysorexia *n.* any distortion of normal appetite or disturbance in normal eating behavior. See also EATING DISORDER.

dysorthographia *n.* an impairment in the ability to spell.

dyspareunia *n.* painful sexual intercourse, particularly in women. The term is sometimes used for inability to enjoy intercourse, but *DSM–IV–TR* treats lack of enjoyment of intercourse without pain as FEMALE SEXUAL AROUSAL DISORDER or male erectile disorder (see IMPOTENCE). If there are no medical causes for the pain, the diagnosis is FUNCTIONAL DYSPAREUNIA.

dyspepsia *n.* abdominal pain or discomfort that may be caused by ULCERS, gastroesophageal reflux (acid reflux) disease, gallstones, and, rarely, stomach or pancreatic cancer, although in a majority of cases the cause is unknown. **Functional** (or **nonulcer**) **dyspepsia** describes the condition when other medical illnesses with similar symptoms have been excluded; it may be experienced, for example, after eating too much or too quickly or eating during stressful situations. In common parlance, dyspepsia is known as **indigestion**.

dysphagia spastica a somatic or, more often, psychological symptom in which the act of swallowing is painful or difficult because of throat-muscle spasms. In psychological cases, it is a symptom of SOMATIZATION DISORDER.

dysphemia *n.* a disorder of phonation, articulation, or hearing associated with emotional or mental disturbance and, frequently, a predisposition to a neurological disorder. **—dysphemic** *adj.*

dysphonia *n.* any dysfunction in the production of sounds, especially speech sounds, which may affect pitch, intensity, or resonance. See also SPASMODIC DYSPHONIA; VOICE DISORDER.

dysphoria *n.* a mood characterized by generalized discontent and agitation. **—dysphoric** *adj.*

dysphoria nervosa **1.** a less common name for PSYCHOMOTOR AGITATION. **2.** convulsive or spasmodic muscle contractions.

dyspnea *n.* shortness of breath or difficulty in breathing. When not accounted for by high altitude, exertion, or any identifiable organic cause, the condition is referred to as **functional dyspnea**.

dysponesis *n.* in biofeedback, a state of habitual tension that generates hypertension, migraine headaches, bruxism (teeth grinding), or related disorders.

dyspraxia *n.* an impaired ability to perform skilled, coordinated movements that is neurologically based and not due to any muscular or sensory defect. See ACQUIRED DYSPRAXIA; DEVELOPMENTAL DYSPRAXIA. See also APRAXIA. **—dyspraxic** *adj.*

dyssocial behavior a former name for behavior associated with delinquent or criminal activities, such as gangsterism, racketeering, prostitution, or illegal gambling. Also called **sociopathic behavior**, it was attributed to distorted moral and social influences, frequently aggravated by a broken home or a deprived environment. Such behavior is now regarded as an aspect of ANTISOCIAL PERSONALITY DISORDER.

dyssocial personality an obsolete name for ANTISOCIAL PERSONALITY DISORDER.

dyssomnia *n.* any of various SLEEP DISORDERS marked by abnormalities in the amount, quality, or timing of sleep. In *DSM–IV–TR* dyssomnias include PRIMARY INSOMNIA, PRIMARY HYPERSOMNIA, NARCOLEPSY, CIRCADIAN RHYTHM SLEEP DISORDER, BREATHING-RELATED SLEEP DISORDER, and **dyssomnia not otherwise specified**, which may be due to excessive noise, light, or other environmental factors, ongoing sleep deprivation, EKBOM'S SYNDROME, or nocturnal MYOCLONUS.

dysthymia *n.* **1.** see DYSTHYMIC DISORDER. **2.** any depressed mood that is mild or moderate in severity. **—dysthymic** *adj.*

dysthymic disorder a DEPRESSIVE DISORDER characterized by a depressed mood for most of the day, occurring more days than not, that persists for at least 2 years (1 year in children or adolescents). During this depressed mood, at least two of the following must also be present: increased or decreased appetite, insomnia or hypersomnia, diminished energy, low self-esteem, difficulty in concentrating or making decisions, and hopelessness. It is distinguished from MAJOR DEPRESSIVE DISORDER in that the symptoms are less severe but more enduring: There are no MAJOR DEPRESSIVE EPISODES during the first 2 years (or, in children or adolescents, 1 year) of the disorder. Also called **dysthymia**.

DZ twins abbreviation for DIZYGOTIC TWINS.

Ee

EAP abbreviation for EMPLOYEE ASSISTANCE PROGRAM.

Early and Periodic Screening, Diagnosis, and Treatment (**EPSDT**) surveillance or search for indications or early manifestations of a disease or disorder, regularly carried out at specific intervals. In the United States, an EPSDT program of preventive health care services (e.g., for vision, hearing, and dental problems) and mental health and behavioral screenings (e.g., for such issues as substance abuse) is provided for children and young adults insured through Medicaid.

early experience experience acquired in the first 5 years of life, which is believed to have a significant influence on a child's subsequent cognitive, social, and emotional development. Whereas theorists in the early and middle part of the 20th century believed that early experience permanently determined a child's development, more recent research indicates that later experience can modify the effects of early experience.

early infantile autism see AUTISTIC DISORDER.

early intervention a collection of specialized services provided to children from birth to 3 years of age with identified conditions placing them at risk of developmental disability or with evident signs of developmental delay. Services are designed to minimize the impact of the infant's or toddler's condition, and in addition to stimulatory, social, therapeutic, and treatment programs may include family training, screening, assessment, or health care.

early intervention program see INFANT DEVELOPMENT PROGRAM.

early memory adult recollection of childhood events, which typically goes back only to the age of 3 or so, even though the capacity to learn is present at birth. The absence of earlier childhood memories, referred to as CHILDHOOD AMNESIA, has been noted since the time of Sigmund FREUD. Explanations include neural immaturity, absence of language or adult SCHEMAS to organize event memory, or different coding dimensions in infancy.

eating compulsion an irresistible impulse leading to abnormal eating behavior. This is a primary symptom of a number of eating disorders, such as BULIMIA NERVOSA and FOOD ADDICTIONS. See also COMPULSIVE EATING.

eating disorder any disorder characterized primarily by a pathological disturbance of attitudes and behaviors related to food. *DSM–IV–TR* categorizes eating disorders as ANOREXIA NERVOSA, BULIMIA NERVOSA, or **eating disorder not otherwise specified**, which does not meet the diagnostic criteria for either of the specific eating disorders and includes BINGE-EATING DISORDER. Other eating-related disorders include PICA and RUMINATION DISORDER, which are usually diagnosed in infancy or early childhood and in *DSM–IV–TR* are classified as FEEDING AND EATING DISORDERS OF INFANCY OR EARLY CHILDHOOD.

EBP abbreviation for EVIDENCE-BASED PRACTICE.

EBV abbreviation for EPSTEIN–BARR VIRUS.

ECA Survey abbreviation for EPIDEMIOLOGIC CATCHMENT AREA SURVEY.

ECF abbreviation for extended care facility. See EXTENDED CARE.

echinacea *n.* an herbal agent derived from any of nine related plant species native to the United States and southern Canada, with *Echinacea purpurea* being the most commonly used and perhaps the most potent. Echinacea traditionally has been used in the belief that it stimulates the immune system. It is approved by Commission E, a committee of 24 interdisciplinary health care professionals formed in 1978 by the German Federal Institute for Drugs and Medical Devices, for use in the treatment or prevention of fevers and colds, cough and bronchitis, urinary tract and other infections, inflammation of the mouth and pharynx, and—as an external application—to promote healing of wounds and burns. Some studies have shown, however, that taking echinacea has no clinical or significant effects on whether people become infected with a cold or, in those who develop colds, on the severity or duration of their symptoms. Although echinacea is generally considered safe and there are no known reports of toxicity, some people may experience hypersensitivity reactions to echinacea, such as rashes, increased asthma, and ANAPHYLAXIS.

écho des pensées an AUDITORY HALLUCINATION in which an individual hears his or her own thoughts repeated in spoken form. Also called **thought echoing**.

echoencephalography *n.* a method of mapping brain anatomy for diagnostic purposes by using ultrasonic waves. The waves are transmitted through the skull using an instrument called an **echoencephalograph**, and echoes of the waves from intracranial structures are recorded to produce a visual image called an **echoencephalogram**.

echographia *n.* pathological writing that involves copying words and phrases without understanding them.

echoic memory the retention of auditory information for a brief period (2–3 s) after the end of the stimulus. Also called **auditory sensory memory**.

echolalia *n.* mechanical repetition of words and phrases uttered by another individual. It is often a symptom of a neurological or developmental disorder, particular catatonic schizophrenia or autism. Also called **echophrasia**.

echo phenomenon ECHOLALIA, ECHOPRAXIA, or both. [first described by German psychiatrist Emil Kraepelin (1856–1926)]

echophrasia *n.* see ECHOLALIA.

echopraxia *n.* mechanical repetition of another person's movements or gestures. It is often a symptom of a neurological disorder, particularly catatonic schizophrenia.

eclectic behaviorism an approach to BEHAVIOR THERAPY that does not adhere to one theoretical model but applies, as needed, any of several techniques, including PAVLOVIAN CONDITIONING, MODELING, OPERANT CONDITIONING, self-control mechanisms, and COGNITIVE RESTRUCTURING.

eclectic counseling any COUNSELING theory or practice that incorporates and combines doctrines, findings, and techniques selected from diverse theoretical systems.

eclectic psychotherapy any PSYCHOTHERAPY that is based on a combination of theories or approaches or uses concepts and techniques from a number of different sources, including the integrated professional experiences of the therapist. The more formalized **prescriptive eclectic psychotherapy** involves the use of a combination of psychotherapy approaches that is specifically sequenced in terms of formats, methods, and processes in order to improve outcome.

eclima *n.* increased appetite or insatiable hunger, often associated with BULIMIA NERVOSA. Also called **eclimia**. See also HYPEROREXIA; HYPERPHAGIA.

ecobehavioral assessment an observational research method used in APPLIED BEHAVIOR ANALYSIS to measure moment-to-moment effects of multiple environmental events on an individual's specific behaviors. These events include the behavior of others, task demands, time of day, and situational changes.

ecological perspective a concept of COMMUNITY PSYCHOLOGY in which a community (or any other social entity) is viewed in terms of the interrelations between people, roles, organizations, local events, resources, and problems. It accounts for complex reciprocal interactions of individuals and their environment. The premise of the ecological perspective is that intervention should contribute to the development of the entire community.

ecological studies research that evaluates the influence of environmental factors on individual behavior and mental health.

ecological systems theory an evolving body of theory and research concerned with the processes and conditions that govern the course of human development in the actual environments in which human beings live. Generally, ecological systems theory accords equal importance to the concept of environment as a context for development (in terms of nested systems ranging from micro- to macro-) and to the role of biopsychological characteristics of the individual person. The current, still evolving, paradigm is now referred to as the BIOECOLOGICAL MODEL. See also ECOSYSTEMIC APPROACH. [originally conceptualized by Russian-born U.S. developmental psychologist Urie Bronfenbrenner (1917–2005)]

ecomania *n.* a morbid preoccupation with and pathological attitude toward members of one's family, characterized by irritable and domineering behavior. It is often a factor in DOMESTIC VIOLENCE and the CYCLE OF VIOLENCE. Also called **oikomania**.

economic model in psychoanalytic theory, the view that the psyche can be explained in terms of the amounts and distributions of PSYCHIC ENERGY associated with particular mental states and processes. Compare DYNAMIC MODEL; TOPOGRAPHIC MODEL.

ecopathology *n.* the identification of people as abnormal by other members of their community. Behavior considered normal in some communities (i.e., conforming to the attitudes and beliefs of community members) may be regarded as eccentric or even psychotic in other communities.

ecosystemic approach an approach to therapy that emphasizes the interaction between the individual or family and larger social contexts, such as schools, workplaces, and social agencies. The approach emphasizes interrelatedness and interdependency and derives from diverse fields, including psychology, sociology, anthropology, economics, and political science. FAMILY THERAPY, in particular, has made use of this approach in designing interventions for complex families and systems. See also ECOLOGICAL SYSTEMS THEORY. [developed in psychology by Russian-born U.S. developmental psychologist Uri Bronfenbrenner (1917–2005)]

ECS abbreviation for electroconvulsive shock. See ELECTROCONVULSIVE THERAPY.

ecstasy *n.* a state of intense pleasure and elation, including some mystical states, orgasm, aesthetic experiences, and drug-induced states. Such extreme euphoria also occasionally occurs in the context of a HYPOMANIC EPISODE or a MANIC EPISODE. Also called **ecstatic state**. —**ecstatic** *adj.*

Ecstasy *n.* the popular name for MDMA.

ECT abbreviation for ELECTROCONVULSIVE THERAPY.

ECT-induced amnesia amnesia that is a byproduct of ELECTROCONVULSIVE THERAPY (ECT). Although ECT is effective in the relief of depression, memory deficits often arise, especially when the current is applied to both sides of the brain. Memory can be severely compromised in the hours or days following treatment, but new learning typically returns to normal by 6 months after treatment. Some impairment in the retrieval of events that occurred close to the time of treatment may remain.

ectomorph *n.* a constitutional type (SOMATOTYPE) in SHELDON'S CONSTITUTIONAL THEORY OF PERSONALITY characterized by a thin, long, fragile physique, which—according to this theory—is highly correlated with CEREBROTONIA. Also called **ectomorphic body type**. **—ectomorphic** *adj.* **—ectomorphy** *n.*

ectopic pregnancy a pregnancy that develops outside the uterus, most commonly in a fallopian tube (a tubal pregnancy). Also called **eccyesis**; **extrauterine pregnancy**; **paracyesis**.

ED_{50} (**ED-50**) abbreviation for effective dose 50 (see EFFECTIVE DOSE). See also THERAPEUTIC RATIO.

edema *n.* an excess accumulation of fluid in body cells, organs, or cavities. The cause may be a loss of fluid through the walls of the blood vessels as a symptom of a circulatory disorder or the interruption of flow of cerebrospinal fluid due to blockage of a passageway or failure of tissues to absorb the excess. See also CEREBRAL EDEMA. **—edematous** *adj.*

edge theory a theory proposing that DEATH ANXIETY has a survival function that emerges when individuals perceive themselves to be in life-threatening situations. Edge theory attempts to resolve the apparent discrepancy between other theoretical claims that DEATH ANXIETY is a major motivational force and empirical studies that reveal only low to moderate levels of death anxiety in the general population. It suggests that death anxiety is the subjective or experiential side of a holistic preparation to deal with danger (symbolic of standing at the edge of the void). Heightened arousal is turned on by anxiety surges in emergency situations; psychological difficulties arise when the emergency response has permeated the individual's everyday functioning. See also TERROR MANAGEMENT THEORY. [introduced by U.S. psychologist Robert J. Kastenbaum (1932–)]

edrophonium *n.* an anticholinesterase (see CHOLINERGIC DRUG) characterized by a rapid onset and short duration of action. It is the drug of choice in the diagnosis of myasthenia gravis, and it may also be used in surgical anesthesia to reverse the effects of neuromuscular blocking agents. U.S. trade names: **Enlon**; **Reversol**.

educable mentally retarded (**EMR**) formerly, describing people with mild or high-moderate mental retardation (IQ 50 to 70 or 80), who are capable of achieving approximately a fifth-grade academic level.

educational counseling the COUNSELING specialty concerned with providing advice and assistance to students in the development of their educational plans, choice of appropriate courses, and choice of college or technical school. Counseling may also be applied to improve study skills or provide assistance with school-related problems that interfere with performance, for example, learning disabilities. Educational counseling is closely associated with VOCATIONAL COUNSELING because of the relationship between educational training and occupational choice. Also called **educational guidance**; **student counseling**. See also COUNSELING PSYCHOLOGY.

educational diagnosis 1. the process of analytically examining a learning problem, which may involve identification of cognitive, perceptual, emotional, and other factors that influence academic performance or school adjustment. **2.** the conclusion reached as a result of the analytical examination of a learning problem.

educational retardation 1. slowness or delay of student progress in acquiring knowledge due to a physical, emotional, intellectual, or mental disability. **2.** a slowness or delay that is specific to a certain subject or educational setting.

educational therapy individualized treatment interventions for people with learning disabilities or emotional or behavioral problems that significantly interfere with learning. Educational therapy integrates educational techniques and therapeutic practices to promote academic achievement and the attainment of basic skills while building self-esteem and confidence, fostering independence, and aiding personal development. It is usually conducted by a professionally trained **educational therapist**.

Edwards Personal Preference Schedule (**EPPS**) a personality inventory for college students and adults in which the strength of 15 "manifest needs" is assessed on a forced-choice basis. The needs are: achievement, order, deference, autonomy, exhibition, affection, succorance, sympathy, change, endurance, heterosexuality, aggression, intraception, abasement, and affiliation. [developed in the 1950s by Allen L. **Edwards** (1914–1994), U.S. psychologist, based on the needs described in the personality theory of U.S. psychologist Henry A. Murray (1893–1988)]

Edwards syndrome see TRISOMY 17–18. [John Hilton **Edwards** (1928–), British geneticist]

EE abbreviation for EXPRESSED EMOTION.

EEG abbreviation for ELECTROENCEPHALOGRAPHY or electroencephalogram.

effectance *n.* the state of having a causal effect on objects and events in the environment, commonly used in the term **effectance motivation**.

effective dose (**ED**) the minimum amount of a drug that is required to produce a specified effect. It is usually expressed in terms of **median effective dose**, or **effective dose 50** (**ED_{50}, ED-50**), the dose at which 50% of the nonhuman animal test population has a positive response. In psychotherapy, this criterion is also used to express the number of sessions that are needed for 50% of patients to show a clinically significant change. See also THERAPEUTIC RATIO.

effectiveness evaluation the assessment of the degree of success of a program in achieving a project's goals. The process requires the determination of EVALUATION OBJECTIVES, methods, and CRITERIA OF EVALUATION and the presentation of findings. See also IMPACT ANALYSIS; PROGRAM OUTCOME.

effect size the magnitude, often in standardized units, of an effect (influence of independent variables) in a study. It is often an indicator of the strength of a relationship, the magnitude of mean differences among several groups, or the like. See also STATISTICAL SIGNIFICANCE.

effect-size correlation (symbol: $r_{\text{effect size}}$) the correlation between scores on the DEPENDENT VARIABLE and the contrast weights (i.e., predicted values) without removing any other sources of variation in the data.

effeminacy *n.* female behavior or appearance in a male, which is regarded as not fitting the male GENDER ROLE expectations of society. **—effeminate** *adj.*

Effexor *n.* a trade name for VENLAFAXINE.

efficacy *n.* **1.** competence in behavioral performance, especially with reference to a person's perception of his or her performance capabilities, or PERCEIVED SELF-EFFICACY. **2.** in pharmacology, see DOSE–RESPONSE RELATIONSHIP.

efficiency *n.* **1.** a measure of the ability of an organization, work unit, or individual employee to produce the maximum output with a minimum investment of time, effort, and other inputs. Given the same level of output, efficiency increases as the time, effort, and other inputs taken to produce that level decrease. Also called **industrial efficiency**; **organizational efficiency**. **2.** in statistics, the degree to which an ESTIMATOR uses all the information in a sample to estimate a particular parameter. **—efficient** *adj.*

effortfulness *n.* a sense of effort, or consciousness of effort: a feature of many psychological tasks that can be judged reliably by participants. Effortful tasks compete against each other under dual-task conditions (see DUAL-TASK COMPETITION), indicating that effortfulness correlates with demands on mental resources. Novel skills often begin in an effortful and conscious way and become less effortful and more automatic with practice. Because the sense of effort lacks conscious sensory qualities, it can be considered an experience of FRINGE CONSCIOUSNESS. It is believed to involve increased brain activity in the DORSOLATERAL PREFRONTAL CORTEX. **—effortful** *adj.*

effortful processing mental activity that requires deliberation and control and involves a sense of effort, or overcoming resistance. Compare AUTOMATICITY.

effort syndrome the former name for an anxiety reaction now classified as PANIC DISORDER: The symptoms are those of a PANIC ATTACK. This syndrome has been given many names, including cardiac neurosis, hyperkinetic heart syndrome, irritable heart, soldier's heart, Da Costa's syndrome, neurocirculatory asthenia, and hyperventilation syndrome.

EFPPA abbreviation for EUROPEAN FEDERATION OF PROFESSIONAL PSYCHOLOGISTS' ASSOCIATIONS.

EFT abbreviation for EMBEDDED FIGURES TEST.

egersis *n.* intense or extreme wakefulness.

ego *n.* **1.** the SELF, particularly the conscious sense of self (Latin, "I"). In its popular and quasi-technical sense, ego refers to all the psychological phenomena and processes that are related to the self and that comprise the individual's attitudes, values, and concerns. **2.** in psychoanalytic theory, the component of the personality that deals with the external world and its practical demands. The ego enables the individual to perceive, reason, solve problems, test reality, and adjust the instinctual impulses of the ID to the behests of the SUPEREGO. See also ANTILIBIDINAL EGO; BODY EGO; SUPPORTIVE EGO.

ego-alien *adj.* see EGO-DYSTONIC.

ego analysis psychoanalytic techniques directed toward discovering the strengths and weaknesses of the EGO and uncovering its defenses against unacceptable impulses. Ego analysis is a short form of psychoanalysis: It does not attempt to penetrate to the ultimate origin of impulses and repressions. See also EGO STRENGTH; EGO WEAKNESS.

ego anxiety in psychoanalytic theory, anxiety caused by the conflicting demands of the EGO, ID, and SUPEREGO. Thus, ego anxiety refers to internal rather than external demands. Compare ID ANXIETY. See also SIGNAL ANXIETY.

ego boundary **1.** the concept that individuals are able to distinguish between self and not-self. Someone who is said to lack clear ego boundaries blurs the distinction between himself or herself and others by identifying with them too easily and too much. **2.** in psychoanalysis, the boundary between the EGO and the ID (the INTERNAL BOUNDARY) or between the ego and external reality (the EXTERNAL BOUNDARY).

ego-boundary loss a condition in which the person lacks a clear sense of where his or her own body, mind, and influence end and where these characteristics in other animate and inanimate objects begin.

ego cathexis in psychoanalytic theory, the concentration of PSYCHIC ENERGY onto the self, taking one's own ego as a LOVE OBJECT. Ego cathexis is thus a form of NARCISSISM. Also called **ego libido**. See CATHEXIS. Compare OBJECT CATHEXIS.

E

egocentric speech speech that is apparently not directed to others or in which there is no attempt to exchange thoughts or take into account another person's point of view. According to Jean PIAGET, a child's use of egocentric speech prevails until the 7th or 8th year of age and then disappears as the child develops social speech geared to others' needs. According to Lev VYGOTSKY, however, egocentric speech is in part vocalized social speech geared to solving problems and develops into INNER LANGUAGE. Also called **private speech**.

egocentrism *n.* **1.** the tendency to emphasize one's personal needs and focus on one's individual concerns rather than those of the social unit or group to which one belongs. Also called **egocentricity**. See also IDIOCENTRIC. Compare SOCIOCENTRISM. **2.** in Jean PIAGET's theory of cognitive development, the tendency to perceive the situation from one's own perspective, believing that others see things from the same point of view as oneself and that events will elicit the same thoughts, feelings, and behavior in others as in oneself. **—egocentric** *adj.*

ego control a personality characteristic consisting of the tendency to inhibit the expression of emotional and motivational impulses, ranging from undercontrol to overcontrol of such impulses.

ego-coping skills adaptive techniques developed by an individual to deal with personal problems and environmental stresses.

ego defect in psychoanalytic theory, the absence of limitation of an EGO FUNCTION. The prime function of the ego is perception of reality and adjustment to it. An ego defect can be either the target of treatment or a deficiency that slows recovery.

ego defense in psychoanalytic theory, protection of the EGO from anxiety arising from threatening impulses and conflicts as well as external threats through the use of DEFENSE MECHANISMS.

ego depletion a state marked by reduction in the self's capacity for volition (initiative, choice, and self-regulation), especially in the context of SELF-REGULATORY RESOURCES THEORY. Ego depletion is typically temporary and is restored by rest, positive emotions, or other means.

ego development **1.** the infant's emerging consciousness of being a separate individual distinct from others, particularly the parents. **2.** in CLASSICAL PSYCHOANALYSIS, the process in which a part of the ID is gradually transformed into the EGO as a result of environmental demands. It involves a preconscious stage, in which the ego is partly developed, and a subsequent conscious stage, in which such ego functions as reasoning, judging, and reality testing come to fruition and help to protect the individual from internal and external threats. Also called **ego formation**. See also ID-EGO.

ego-dystonic *adj.* in psychoanalytic theory, describing impulses, wishes, or thoughts that are unacceptable or repugnant to the EGO or self. Also called **ego-alien**. Compare EGO-SYNTONIC.

ego-dystonic homosexuality the condition of being distressed about an inability to be aroused by the opposite sex. There is a sustained pattern of same-sex arousal that the person explicitly states has been unwanted and persistently distressing. The condition is frequently accompanied by feelings of loneliness, shame, anxiety, and depression. In *DSM–IV–TR* it is categorized as a SEXUAL DISORDER NOT OTHERWISE SPECIFIED.

ego formation see EGO DEVELOPMENT.

ego functions in psychoanalytic theory, the various activities of the EGO, including perception of the external world, self-awareness, problem solving, control of motor functions, adaptation to reality, memory, and reconciliation of conflicting impulses and ideas. The ego is frequently described as the executive agency of the personality, working in the interest of the REALITY PRINCIPLE. See also SECONDARY PROCESS.

ego-ideal *n.* in psychoanalytic theory, the part of the EGO that is the repository of positive identifications with parental goals and values that the individual genuinely admires and wishes to emulate, such as integrity and loyalty, and which acts as a model of how he or she wishes to be. As new identifications are incorporated in later life, the ego-ideal may develop and change. In his later theorizing, Sigmund FREUD incorporated the ego-ideal into the concept of the SUPEREGO. Also called **self-ideal**.

ego identity **1.** in psychoanalytic theory, the experience of the self as a recognizable, persistent entity resulting from the integration of one's unique EGO-IDEAL, life roles, and ways of adjusting to reality. **2.** the gradual acquisition of a sense of continuity, worth, and integration that Erik ERIKSON believed to be the essential process in personality development. See ERIKSON'S EIGHT STAGES OF DEVELOPMENT. See also IDENTITY.

ego instinct in psychoanalytic theory, instincts, such as hunger, that are directed toward self-preservation. In Sigmund FREUD's early theory, the energy of the ego instincts is used by the EGO to defend against the SEXUAL INSTINCTS.

ego integration in psychoanalytic theory, the process of organizing the various aspects of the personality, such as drives, attitudes, and aims, into a balanced whole.

ego integrity versus despair see INTEGRITY VERSUS DESPAIR.

egoism *n.* a personality characteristic marked by selfishness and behavior based on self-interest with disregard for the needs of others. See also EGOTISM. **—egoistic** *adj.*

egoistic helping a form of HELPING behavior in which the goal of the helper is to increase his or her positive feelings or to receive some other benefit. See also ALTRUISTIC BEHAVIOR.

egoistic suicide a type of suicide associated with an extreme sense of alienation. Lacking significant attachments to family members and others, the person withdraws from society and comes to feel his or her life is meaningless. [associated with the work of French sociologist Émile Durkheim (1858–1917)]

ego libido see EGO CATHEXIS.

egomania *n.* extreme, pathological preoccupation with oneself, often characterized by an exaggerated sense of one's abilities and worth. This includes the tendency to be totally self-centered, callous with regard to the needs of others, and interested only in the gratification of one's own impulses and desires. See also EGOPATHY. **—egomaniac** *n.*

egopathy *n.* hostile attitudes and actions stemming from an exaggerated sense of self-importance, often manifested by a compulsion to deprecate others. See also EGOMANIA.

ego psychology in psychoanalysis, an approach that emphasizes the functions of the EGO in controlling impulses and dealing with the external environment. This is in contrast to ID PSYCHOLOGY, which focuses on the primitive instincts of sex and hostility. Ego psychology differs from CLASSICAL PSYCHOANALYSIS in proposing that the ego contains a CONFLICT-FREE SPHERE of functioning and that it has its own store of energy with which to pursue goals that are independent of instinctual wishes. Ego psychology theories extend beyond classic psychoanalytic drive theory by combining a biological and psychological view of the individual's development with a recognition of the complex influences of sociocultural dimensions on individual functioning. The scope of psychoanalysis is thereby broadened from the study of unconscious events and psychopathology to exploration of adaptive processes within the matrix of interpersonal, familial, and sociocultural forces.

ego resiliency a personality characteristic consisting of the ability to vary, in an adaptive manner, the degree to which one inhibits or expresses emotional impulses, depending on social demands.

ego resistance see REPRESSION-RESISTANCE.

ego-splitting *n.* **1.** in psychoanalytic theory, the EGO's development of opposed but coexisting attitudes toward a phenomenon, whether in the normal, neurotic, or psychotic person. In the normal context, ego-splitting can be seen in the critical attitude of the self toward the self; in neuroses, contrary attitudes toward particular behaviors are fundamental; and in psychoses, ego-splitting may produce an "observing" part of the individual that sees and can report on delusional phenomena. **2.** in the OBJECT RELATIONS THEORY of Melanie KLEIN, fragmentation of the EGO in which parts that are perceived as bad are split off from the main ego.

ego state in psychoanalytic theory, an integrated state of mind that determines the individual's relationships to the environment and to other people.

ego strength in psychoanalytic theory, the ability of the EGO to maintain an effective balance between the inner impulses of the ID, the SUPEREGO, and outer reality. An individual with a **strong ego** is thus one who is able to tolerate frustration and stress, postpone gratification, modify selfish desires when necessary, and resolve internal conflicts and emotional problems before they lead to NEUROSIS. Compare EGO WEAKNESS.

ego stress any situation, external or internal, that challenges the individual and produces stress (tension, anxiety, etc.) requiring adaptation by the EGO. Ego stress is sometimes expressed as such defensive reactions as DISSOCIATION, SOMATIZATION, or panic.

ego structure in psychoanalytic theory, the organization of the EGO.

ego suffering in psychoanalytic theory, the guilt feelings produced in the EGO by the aggressive forces in the SUPEREGO when it disapproves of the ego.

ego-syntonic *adj.* compatible with the ego or conscious SELF-CONCEPT. Thoughts, wishes, impulses, and behavior are said to be ego-syntonic when they form no threat to the ego and can be acted upon without interference from the superego. Compare EGO-DYSTONIC. [first described in 1914 by Sigmund FREUD]

egotheism *n.* identification of oneself with a deity. See also JEHOVAH COMPLEX; MESSIAH COMPLEX.

egotism *n.* excessive conceit or excessive preoccupation with one's own importance. See also EGOISM. **—egotistic** *adj.*

ego transcendence the feeling that one is beyond concern with the self and is thus able to perceive reality with less egocentric bias and greater objectivity.

ego weakness in psychoanalytic theory, the inability of the EGO to control impulses and tolerate frustration, disappointment, or stress. The individual with a **weak ego** is thus one who suffers from anxiety and conflicts, makes excessive use of DEFENSE MECHANISMS or uses immature defense mechanisms, and is likely to develop neurotic symptoms. Compare EGO STRENGTH.

Einfühlung *n.* German for EMPATHY.

either–or thinking a less common name for DICHOTOMOUS THINKING.

ejaculation *n.* the automatic expulsion of semen and seminal fluid through the penis resulting from involuntary and voluntary contractions of various muscle groups. See ORGASM. See also PREMATURE EJACULATION; RETROGRADE EJACULATION. **—ejaculatory** *adj.*

E

ejaculatio retardata excessively delayed ejaculation during sexual intercourse, usually due to psychogenic factors, aging, or the use of drugs, but also voluntary. Also called **male continence**.

Ekbom's syndrome a sense of uneasiness, twitching, or restlessness that occurs in the legs when at rest (i.e., sitting or lying) or after retiring for the night. The cause is unknown but it has been associated with a deficiency of iron, vitamin B_{12}, or folic acid; nerve damage associated with rheumatoid arthritis, kidney failure, or diabetes; and the use of such drugs as lithium, anticonvulsants, antidepressants, and beta blockers. Also called **restless-legs syndrome**; **tachyathetosis**; **Wittmaack–Ekbom syndrome**. [Karl-Axel **Ekbom** (1907–1977), Swedish physician]

elaboration *n.* **1.** the process of interpreting or embellishing information to be remembered or of relating it to other material already known and in memory. The levels-of-processing model of memory holds that the level of elaboration applied to information as it is processed affects both the length of time that it can be retained in memory and the ease with which it can be retrieved. See ACTIVATION–ELABORATION. See also CHUNKING; DEEP PROCESSING; RECODING. **2.** the process of scrutinizing and thinking about the central merits of attitude-relevant information. This process includes generating inferences about the information, assessing its validity, and considering the implications of evaluative responses to the information. See also COGNITIVE RESPONSE. **—elaborate** *vb.*

elation *n.* a state of extreme joy, exaggerated optimism, and restless excitement. In extreme or prolonged forms, it is a symptom of a number of disorders; in particular, it may be drug-induced or a symptom of acute MANIA, but it is also found in GENERAL PARESIS, schizophrenia, and psychosis with brain tumor. **—elated** *adj.*

Elavil *n.* a trade name for AMITRIPTYLINE.

Eldepryl *n.* a trade name for SELEGILINE.

elder abuse harm to an older adult caused by another individual. The harm can be physical (violence), sexual (nonconsensual sex), psychological (causing emotional distress), material (improper use of belongings or finances), or neglect (failure to provide needed care).

elder care the provision of health-related services, supportive personal care, supervision, and social services to an older adult requiring assistance with daily living because of physical disabilities, cognitive impairments, or other conditions. Elder care may be home based (via specialized programs) or community based (via ASSISTED LIVING, RESIDENTIAL CARE, or a SKILLED NURSING FACILITY).

elder neglect the failure of a responsible caregiver to provide needed care to an older adult. Extreme neglect in the form of abandonment can occur when the caregiver deserts the older adult in need. See ELDER ABUSE.

elective mutism see SELECTIVE MUTISM.

Electra complex the female counterpart of the OEDIPUS COMPLEX, involving the daughter's love for her father, jealousy toward the mother, and blame of the mother for depriving her of a penis. Although Sigmund FREUD rejected the phrase, using the term "Oedipus complex" to refer to both boys and girls, many modern textbooks of psychology propagate the mistaken belief that Electra complex is a Freudian term. The name derives from the Greek myth of Electra, daughter of Agamemnon and Clytemnestra, who seeks to avenge her father's murder by persuading her brother Orestes to help her kill Clytemnestra and her lover Aegisthus. [defined by Carl JUNG]

electrical stimulation the stimulation of brain cells or sensory or motor neurons by electrical or electronic devices. This is usually accomplished with the use of an electrode on a research animal but also occasionally on human volunteers undergoing brain surgery.

electrical transcranial stimulation see ELECTROSLEEP THERAPY.

electric shock method the use of electricity in treating humans. See ELECTROCONVULSIVE THERAPY; ELECTROTHERAPY.

electrocardiographic effect a change in the electrical activity of the heart as recorded by an electrocardiogram, especially one associated with administration of a drug. Prolongation of segments of the cardiac cycle, particularly the Q-T interval (the period of ventricular contraction), may be observed with excess doses of numerous antipsychotics and tricyclic antidepressants. A malignant form of electrocardiographic change is an arrhythmia known as **torsades de pointes** (French, literally "twisting of the points"), so called because of its characteristic outline on an electrocardiograph tracing. Torsades de pointes syndrome may result from drug interactions increasing the serum concentration of certain drugs or from an abnormal reaction to single drugs (e.g., pimozide) in susceptible individuals.

electroconvulsive therapy (**ECT**) a controversial treatment in which a seizure is induced by passing a controlled, low-dose electric current (an **electroconvulsive shock**; **ECS**) through one or both temples. The patient is prepared by administration of an anesthetic and injection of a muscle relaxant. An electric current is then applied for a fraction of a second through electrodes placed on the temples and immediately produces a two-stage seizure (tonic and clonic). ECT may be bilateral or unilateral (usually of the right hemisphere). Now a somewhat rare procedure, it is sometimes used with patients with severe endogenous depression who fail to respond to antidepressant drugs. Benefits are temporary, and the mechanisms of therapeutic action are unknown. Also called **electroconvulsive shock therapy** (**EST**); **electroshock therapy** (**EST**). See also BRIEF STIMULUS THERAPY; ECT-INDUCED AMNESIA. [introduced in 1938 by Italian psychiatrists Ugo Cerletti (1877–1963) and Lucio Bini (1908–1964)]

electrocorticography (**ECoG**) *n.* a method of studing the electrical activity of the brain using electrodes placed directly on the cerebral cortex, rather than on the scalp as in ELECTROENCEPHALOGRAPHY. The resulting record of brain-wave patterns is called an **electrocorticogram**.

electrodiagnosis *n.* the application of an electric current to nerves and muscles for diagnostic purposes. See ELECTROENCEPHALOGRAPHY; ELECTROMYOGRAPHY.

electroencephalography (**EEG**) *n.* a method of studying BRAIN WAVES using an instrument (**electroencephalograph**) that amplifies and records the electrical activity of the brain through electrodes placed at various points on the scalp. The resulting record (**electroencephalogram** [**EEG**]) of the brain-wave patterns is frequently used in studying sleep, monitoring the depth of anesthesia, diagnosing epilepsy and other brain disorders or dysfunction, and studying normal brain function. Also called **cognitive electrophysiology**.

electromyography (**EMG**) *n.* the recording (via an instrument called an **electromyograph**) of the electrical activity of muscles through electrodes placed in or on different muscle groups. This procedure is used in the diagnosis of neuromuscular diseases, such as myasthenia gravis or amyotrophic lateral sclerosis. A print-out of the electric potentials is called an **electromyogram** (**EMG**).

electronarcosis *n.* a form of ELECTROTHERAPY in which the amount of electricity, the duration of the shock, or both is sufficient to generate the tonic phase of a seizure but either limits or prevents the clonic phase. Electronarcosis is a generally less effective alternative to standard ELECTROCONVULSIVE THERAPY (ECT) and more likely to cause side effects. The technique has also been used to induce relaxation and sleep. See ELECTROSLEEP THERAPY.

electronystagmography *n.* a neurological test that measures movements of the eye muscles, used to confirm the presence of NYSTAGMUS. A graphical recording of eye movements is generated and is used to evaluate dizziness, vertigo, and the function of the auditory nerve.

electroshock therapy (**EST**) see ELECTROCONVULSIVE THERAPY.

electrosleep therapy a former treatment for depression, chronic anxiety, and insomnia by inducing a state of relaxation or sleep through low-voltage **electrical transcranial stimulation** (**ETS**; or **cranial electrical stimulation**, **CES**), a technique developed in the Soviet Union in the 1940s.

electrostimulation *n.* an aversive, or negative-reinforcement, technique involving administration of an electric shock. See also AVERSION THERAPY.

electrotherapy *n.* any therapeutic measure that involves the application of an electric current to the body.

Elephant Man's disease see VON RECKLINGHAUSEN'S DISEASE.

elevated mood a heightened mood characterized by feelings of EUPHORIA, ELATION, and well-being.

elevator phobia a persistent and irrational fear of elevators, which may represent fear of height (ACROPHOBIA), fear of being enclosed (CLAUSTROPHOBIA), or fear of having panic symptoms in people with AGORAPHOBIA.

elfin facies see WILLIAMS SYNDROME.

elimination by aspects a theory of decision making holding that a choice is reached through a series of eliminations. At each stage, the decision maker selects an attribute or aspect perceived to be important and eliminates alternatives lacking that attribute. The next most important attribute is then selected, and the process continues until only one alternative is left. [introduced in 1972 by Israeli psychologist Amos Tversky (1937–1996)]

elimination disorder any disorder related to defecation or urination, usually occurring in children (or individuals of equivalent mental age), that is not due to the use of substances or a general medical condition. In *DSM–IV–TR*, this class of disorders includes ENCOPRESIS and ENURESIS.

elimination drive the urge to expel feces or urine from the body. Psychological factors have considerable effects on these drives; for example, tension and fright may precipitate involuntary voiding of both the bladder and bowel.

ellipsis *n.* in psychoanalysis, a form of PARAPRAXIS involving the omission of significant ideas in FREE ASSOCIATION or DREAMS. Efforts are made to recover these ideas during analysis. **—elliptical** *adj.*

Ellis–van Creveld syndrome an autosomal recessive disorder (see RECESSIVE ALLELE) marked by polydactyly (extra fingers or toes); poorly formed hair, teeth, and nails; and skeletal anomalies. Associated abnormalities may include genital anomalies and mental retardation. A high incidence of the disorder is seen among the Old Order Amish of Pennsylvania. Also called **chon-**

droectodermal dysplasia. [Richard White Bernard **Ellis** (1902–1966), British physician; Simon **van Creveld** (1894–1971), Dutch pediatrician]

elopement *n.* **1.** the act of secretly leaving home to marry without parental consent. **2.** the departure of a patient from a psychiatric hospital or unit without permission. **3.** in law enforcement, slang for the escape of an inmate.

E

emancipation disorder a disorder of early adulthood in which the individual experiences conflict between a desire for freedom from parental control and the responsibilities of independence. Symptoms may include indecisiveness, homesickness, excessive dependence on peers, and paradoxical overdependence on parental advice. Also called **emancipation disorder of adolescence and early adulthood**.

emancipatory striving efforts to free oneself from the influence or domination of parents and to achieve a sense of independence and self-dependence. Emancipatory striving is particularly evident during adolescence.

emasculation *n.* castration or, by extension, the reduction or removal of a man's sense of MASCULINITY, as by depriving him of a culturally sanctioned male role. **—emasculate** *vb.*

embarrassment *n.* a SELF-CONSCIOUS EMOTION in which a person feels awkward or flustered in other people's company or because of the attention of others, as, for example, when being observed engaging in actions that are subject to mild disapproval from others. It often has an element of self-deprecating humor and is typically characterized by nervous laughter, a shy smile, or blushing. **—embarrassed** *adj.*

Embedded Figures Test (**EFT**) a test that consists of finding and tracing a simple form embedded within a complex figure, in some cases further complicated by an irregularly colored background. The test, for use with individuals aged 10 years and over, was designed to evaluate cognitive style, particularly FIELD DEPENDENCE and FIELD INDEPENDENCE: Those demonstrating ability in the test are defined as field-independent people, who tend to follow active, participant approaches to learning, whereas those who have difficulties in performing the test are defined as field-dependent people, who often use spectator approaches and are also more open and responsive to other people's behavior. The EFT is also employed in neuropsychological contexts, as poor performance on the test may indicate a lesion or injury in the cerebral cortex. Also called **Hidden Figures Test**. [originally developed in 1950 by U.S. psychologist Herman Allen Witkin (1916–1979)]

embodiment *n.* the claim that much human thinking is a metaphorical extension of experiences of the body and its immediate surroundings. [attributable to U.S. cognitive linguist George Philip Lakoff (1941–)]

embolic stroke a STROKE caused by a blood clot, cholesterol, fibrin, or other material breaking away from the wall of an artery or the heart and traveling up the arterial tree to lodge suddenly in a smaller cerebral artery (see CEREBRAL EMBOLISM). Embolic strokes account for approximately 30% of all strokes and are abrupt in onset.

embolism *n.* the interruption of blood flow due to blockage of a vessel by an **embolus**, material formed elsewhere and carried by the bloodstream to become lodged at the site of obstruction. The embolus may be a blood clot, air bubble, fat globule, or other substance, such as a clump of bacteria or tissue cells. An embolus usually occurs at a point where a blood vessel branches or narrows. The symptoms are those associated with a disruption of the normal flow of fresh blood to a part of an organ and include pain, numbness, and loss of body warmth in the affected area. An embolus in a coronary artery may cause a fatal heart attack, whereas in the brain the result is an EMBOLIC STROKE.

EMDR abbreviation for EYE-MOVEMENT DESENSITIZATION AND REPROCESSING.

emergence *n.* **1.** in philosophy of mind, the notion that conscious experience is the result of, but cannot be reduced to, brain processes. **2.** the idea that higher order phenomena are derived from lower order phenomena but exhibit characteristics not predictable from those lower order phenomena. See EPIGENETIC THEORY.

emergency psychotherapy psychological treatment of individuals who have undergone a traumatic experience (e.g., a road accident) and are in a state of acute anxiety, panic, or shock or are suicidal. Therapists may call on a very broad range of techniques depending on the immediate needs of the client. See also CRISIS INTERVENTION.

emergency reaction see FIGHT-OR-FLIGHT RESPONSE.

emergency services in health care, services provided to an individual in response to perceived need for immediate medical or psychological treatment.

emergency theory of emotions the theory that the emotional and visceral changes controlled by the AUTONOMIC NERVOUS SYSTEM are designed to prepare individuals for fight or flight during an emergency (see FIGHT-OR-FLIGHT RESPONSE).

emergent evolution the theory that new phenomena evolve from an interaction of ancestral events but cannot be reduced to them.

emergentism *n.* the view that complex phenomena and processes have EMERGENT PROPERTIES that arise from interactions of the more basic processes that underlie them but cannot be deduced or explained from the nature and logic of these processes. Compare REDUCTIONISM.

emergent property a characteristic of a complex system that is not implicit in or predictable from an analysis of the components or elements that make it up and that, thus, often arises unexpectedly. For example, it has been said that conscious experience is not predictable by analysis of the neurophysiological and biochemical complexity of the brain.

emetic therapy the use of drugs that produce aversive states when combined with problem behaviors or stimuli. Side effects of the drugs used and other issues with regard to this form of treatment limit its application. See AVERSION THERAPY.

EMG abbreviation for ELECTROMYOGRAPHY.

emotion *n.* a complex reaction pattern, involving experiential, behavioral, and physiological elements, by which the individual attempts to deal with a personally significant matter or event. The specific quality of the emotion (e.g., FEAR, SHAME) is determined by the specific significance of the event. For example, if the significance involves threat, fear is likely to be generated; if the significance involves disapproval from another, shame is likely to be generated. Emotion typically involves FEELING but differs from feeling in having an overt or implicit engagement with the world. **—emotional** *adj.*

emotional abuse nonphysical abuse: a pattern of behavior in which one person deliberately and repeatedly subjects another to acts that are detrimental to behavioral and affective functioning and overall mental well-being. Researchers have yet to formulate a universally agreed upon definition of the concept, but have identified a variety of forms emotional abuse may take, including verbal abuse, intimidation and terrorization, humiliation and degradation, exploitation, harassment, rejection and withholding of affection, isolation, and excessive control. Also called **psychological abuse**.

emotional adjustment the condition or process of personal acceptance of and adaptation to one's circumstances, which may require modification of attitudes and the expression of emotions that are appropriate to a given situation.

emotional blocking the inhibition of thought, speech, or other responses due to extreme emotion, often associated with extreme fear. See also BLOCKING.

emotional charge strong emotion, such as anger, conceived as being bottled up under pressure and ready to explode. The concept also involves the idea that emotions are negatively or positively charged.

emotional cognition the ability to recognize and interpret the emotions of others, notably from such cues as facial expression and voice tone, and to interpret one's own feelings correctly. Impairment of emotional cognition is associated with a range of psychological conditions, notably ASPERGER'S DISORDER.

emotional conflict a state of disharmony between incompatible intense emotions, such as love and hate or the desire for success and fear of failure, that causes distress to the individual.

emotional contagion the rapid spread of an emotion from one or a few individuals to others. For example, fear of catching a disease can spread rapidly through a community. See also BEHAVIORAL CONTAGION; CONTAGION; MASS CONTAGION.

emotional content themes or characteristics of feelings that tend to elicit strong emotions, especially as they are portrayed in various forms of communication (reading material, motion pictures, etc.) or as they are manifested in specific situations.

emotional control self-regulation of the influence that one's emotions have on one's thoughts and behavior.

emotional dependence dependence on others for emotional support, comfort, and nurturance.

emotional deprivation lack of adequate interpersonal attachments that provide affirmation, love, affection, and interest, especially on the part of the primary caregiver during a child's developmental years.

emotional deterioration an emotional state characterized by carelessness toward oneself, indifference to one's surroundings, including other people, and inappropriate emotional reactions.

emotional development a gradual increase in the capacity to experience, express, and interpret the full range of emotions and in the ability to cope with them appropriately. For example, infants begin to smile and frown around 8 weeks of age and to laugh around 3 or 4 months, and older children begin to learn that hitting others is not an acceptable way of dealing with anger. Expressions of delight, fear, anger, and disgust are evident by 6 months of age, and fear of strangers from 8 months. Expressions of affection and jealousy are seen between 1 and 2 years of age, and expressions of rage in the form of temper tantrums appear a year or so later. Cortical control, imitation of others, hormonal influences, home atmosphere, and conditioning play major roles in emotional development. Also called **affective development**.

emotional disorder 1. any psychological disorder characterized primarily by maladjustive emotional reactions that are inappropriate or disproportionate to reality. Also called **emotional illness**. See also MOOD DISORDER. **2.** loosely, any mental disorder.

emotional disposition a tendency to have a particular type or class of affective experience (e.g., POSITIVE AFFECT or NEGATIVE AFFECT).

emotional dissemblance lack of correspondence between an individual's internal AFFECTIVE STATE and its outward expression.

emotional divorce a marital relationship in

which the partners live separate lives, with an absence of normal interaction between them.

emotional expression **1.** an outward manifestation of an intrapsychic state. For example, a high-pitched voice is a sign of AROUSAL, blushing is a sign of EMBARRASSMENT, and so on. See also AFFECT DISPLAY. **2.** an emotional response in which the individual attempts to influence his or her relation to the world through the intermediacy of others, rather than directly. For example, a sad face and slumped posture elicit nurturing from others. Expressions differ from ACTION TENDENCIES, which influence the world directly, and from FEELINGS, which are intrapsychic experiences of the significance of a transaction.

emotional flatness see FLAT AFFECT.

emotional flooding a lay term, not used in current psychological or medical literature, for an influx of great and uncontrollable emotion that may be overwhelming to the person who experiences it.

emotional handicap (**EH**) a fear-, anxiety-, or other emotionally based condition that results in maladaptive behavior—ranging from withdrawal and isolation to acting out and aggression—and adversely affects a student's academic and social functioning. For example, the inability to form or sustain satisfactory relationships with peers or teachers would constitute an emotional handicap.

emotional illness see EMOTIONAL DISORDER.

emotional immaturity **1.** a tendency to express emotions without restraint or disproportionately to the situation. Compare EMOTIONAL MATURITY. **2.** a lay term for MALADJUSTMENT.

emotional incest a form of child SEXUAL ABUSE consisting of nonphysical sexualized interactions between parent figures and a child in their care. Emotional incest may involve the parent commenting on the child's sexual attractiveness, the parent's own arousal to the child, or the size or shape of the child's secondary sexual characteristics (e.g., breasts, pubic hair), or implying that the child is sexually active (e.g., calling a child a slut).

emotional inoculation the imagining, practicing, or COGNITIVE REHEARSAL of an anxiety-producing experience. Rehearsal lowers anxiety by allowing the individual to anticipate reactions and plan responses.

emotional insight the client's awareness of the emotional forces, such as internal conflicts or traumatic experiences, that underlie his or her symptoms. This form of insight is considered a prerequisite to change in many therapeutic approaches.

emotional instability a tendency to exhibit unpredictable and rapid changes in emotions.

emotional insulation a defense mechanism characterized by seeming indifference and detachment in response to frustrating situations or disappointing events. The extreme of emotional insulation is found in states of complete apathy and catatonic stupor; in lesser forms it appears as **emotional isolation**.

emotional intelligence a type of intelligence that involves the ability to process emotional information and use it in reasoning and other cognitive activities, proposed by U.S. psychologists Peter Salovey (1958–) and John D. Mayer (1953–). According to Mayer and Salovey's 1997 model, it comprises four abilities: to perceive and appraise emotions accurately; to access and evoke emotions when they facilitate cognition; to comprehend emotional language and make use of emotional information; and to regulate one's own and others' emotions to promote growth and well-being. Their ideas were popularized in a best-selling book by U.S. psychologist and science journalist Daniel J. Goleman (1946–), who also altered the definition to include many personality variables. See also EMOTIONAL INTELLIGENCE QUOTIENT.

emotional intelligence quotient an index of EMOTIONAL INTELLIGENCE. Popular writers and the media sometimes abbreviate the term to **EQ** (for emotional quotient, nominally similar to IQ).

emotional isolation see EMOTIONAL INSULATION.

emotionality *n.* the degree to which an individual experiences and expresses emotions, irrespective of the quality of the emotional experience.

emotional maturity a high and appropriate level of emotional control and expression. Compare EMOTIONAL IMMATURITY.

emotional processing theory a theory proposing a hypothetical sequence of fear-reducing changes that is evoked by emotional engagement with the memory of a significant event, particularly a trauma. The theory is based on the concept of a **fear structure**, a type of mental framework for reacting to threat that includes information about a feared stimulus (e.g., a snake), about physiological and behavioral responses (e.g., rapid heartbeat, sweating), and about the meaning of the stimulus and response elements (e.g., the snake is poisonous and will bite me and I am afraid of it). Although most fear structures accurately represent legitimate threats, others become distorted: Individuals do not reflect sufficiently upon the event initially and thus do not successfully evoke and cope with the associated emotions, so that harmless stimuli become seen as dangerous and act to trigger excessive physiological reactions, deliberate avoidance of memories of the event, emotional withdrawal, and other maladaptive behaviors. The existence of such erroneous fear structures originally was proposed in response to the difficulties of traditional learning theories in explaining intrusion symptoms and fear in POSTTRAUMATIC STRESS DISORDER. According to this conceptualization, which has since been expanded to other anxiety disorders, treatment (i.e., PROLONGED EXPOSURE THERAPY) should be designed to provide information that is incompatible with the pathological elements of a specific fear structure. Thus the repetitive exposure to the event memory in a safe environment in which the threat is not realized gradually decreases emotional responding until the fear structure changes to accommodate this new, more accurate information (e.g., If I am not anxious, the situation cannot be so bad). [proposed in 1986 by U.S. psychologists Edna B. Foa (1937–) and Michael J. Kozak (1952–)]

emotional quotient see EMOTIONAL INTELLIGENCE QUOTIENT.

emotional reeducation PSYCHOTHERAPY focused on modifying the client's attitudes, feelings, and reactions by helping the client gain greater insight into emotional conflicts and self-defeating behavior arising from affective disturbance or disorder. Typical objectives are an increase in self-confidence, sociability, and self-reliance. The methods used include group discussions, personal counseling, relationship therapy, and self-exploration.

emotional regulation the ability of an individual to modulate an EMOTION or set of emotions. Techniques of conscious emotional regulation can include learning to construe situations differently in order to manage them better, changing the target of an emotion (e.g., anger) in a way likely to produce a more positive outcome, and recognizing how different behaviors can be used in the service of a given emotional state. Emotional regulation typically increases across the life span.

emotional release the CATHARSIS or sudden outpouring of emotions that have been pent up or suppressed.

emotional response an emotional reaction, such as happiness, fear, or sadness, to a given stimulus.

emotional security the feeling of safety, confidence, and freedom from apprehension. In the approach of German-born U.S. psychoanalyst Karen D. Horney (1885–1952), the need for emotional security is the underlying determinant of personality and behavior; in the approach of U.S. psychoanalyst Harry Stack Sullivan (1892–1949), it is itself determined primarily by interpersonal relations. See also SECURITY OPERATIONS.

emotional stability predictability and consistency in emotional reactions, with absence of rapid mood changes.

emotional stress the feeling of psychological strain and uneasiness produced by situations of danger, threat, and loss of personal security or by internal conflicts, frustrations, loss of self-esteem, and grief. Also called **emotional tension**.

emotional stupor a form of affective stupor marked by depression or intense anxiety and accompanied by mutism.

emotional support the verbal and nonverbal processes by which one communicates care and concern for another, offering reassurance, empathy, comfort, and acceptance. It may be a major factor contributing to the effectiveness of SELF-HELP GROUPS, within which members both provide and receive emotional support.

emotional tension see EMOTIONAL STRESS.

emotion-focused coping a strategy for managing stress in which a person focuses on regulating his or her negative emotional reactions to a stressor. Rather than taking actions to change the stressor itself, the individual tries to control feelings using a variety of cognitive and behavioral tools, including meditation and other relaxation techniques, prayer, positive REFRAMING, wishful thinking and other AVOIDANCE techniques, self-blame, seeking SOCIAL SUPPORT (or conversely engaging in SOCIAL WITHDRAWAL), and talking with others (including mental health care professionals). It has been proposed that emotion-focused coping is used primarily when a person appraises a stressor as beyond his or her capacity to change. Compare PROBLEM-FOCUSED COPING. [identified in 1984 by Richard S. Lazarus (1922–2002) and Susan Folkman (1938–), U.S. psychologists]

emotion-focused couples therapy a form of COUPLES THERAPY that is based on the premise that relationship problems are most often due to thwarted fulfillment of emotional needs, particularly the need for attachment. This intervention involves isolating the conflict regarding thwarted needs, interrupting the negative interaction cycle, reframing the conflict, and accepting the emotional experience of one's partner as valid.

emotion-focused therapy an integrative INDIVIDUAL THERAPY that focuses on emotion as the key determinant of personality development and of psychotherapeutic change. In sessions, the therapist helps the client to become aware of, make sense of, accept, and regulate emotions as a way of resolving problems and promoting growth. Techniques are drawn from CLIENT-CENTERED THERAPY, GESTALT THERAPY, and COGNITIVE BEHAVIOR THERAPY. A principal proponent of this approach is South African-born Canadian psychologist Leslie S. Greenberg (1945–).

emotive *adj*. related to or arousing emotion.

emotive imagery in behavior therapy and cognitive behavior therapy, a procedure in which the client imagines emotion-arousing scenes while relaxing in a comfortable, protective setting. See RECIPROCAL INHIBITION.

emotive technique any of various therapeutic techniques designed to encourage clients to express their thoughts and feelings in an intense and animated manner so as to make these more obvious and available for discussion in therapy.

Emotive techniques are used, for example, in RATIONAL EMOTIVE BEHAVIOR THERAPY in attempts to dispute irrational beliefs in order to move from intellectual to emotional insight.

empathy *n.* understanding a person from his or her frame of reference rather than one's own, so that one vicariously experiences the person's feelings, perceptions, and thoughts. Empathy does not, of itself, entail motivation to be of assistance, although it may turn into SYMPATHY or personal distress, which may result in action. In psychotherapy, therapist empathy for the client can be a path to comprehension of the client's cognitions, affects, or behaviors. **—empathic** or **—empathetic** *adj.* **—empathize** *vb.*

empathy–altruism helping a theory that explains ALTRUISTIC BEHAVIORS as resulting from feelings of empathy and compassion toward others.

empathy training 1. a systematic procedure to increase empathetic feeling and communications in an individual. **2.** help given to convicted abusers to enable them to envision their victims' feelings and become sensitive to the pain they have caused, with the aim of decreasing the likelihood that they will commit similar crimes in the future.

empirical-criterion keying a method for developing personality inventories, in which the items (presumed to measure one or more traits) are created and then administered to a criterion group of people known to possess a certain characteristic (e.g., antisocial behavior, significant anxiety, exaggerated concern about physical health) and to a control group of people without the characteristic. Only those items that demonstrate an ability to distinguish between the two groups are chosen for inclusion in the final inventory.

empirically derived test a test developed using content, criterion, or construct validation procedures or a combination of these.

empirically keyed test a test in which answers are coded in such a way as to maximize CRITERION VALIDITY, CONSTRUCT VALIDITY, or both. See also EMPIRICAL-CRITERION KEYING.

empiric-risk figure in genetic counseling, a percentage representing the risk for common disorders, such as schizophrenia and depression, when there is evidence of genetic factors of unknown mechanism. The figure is based upon reports of frequency of occurrence in large series of families (in addition to the approximately 3% risk of mental retardation or birth defects that every couple takes when having a child).

employee assistance program (EAP) a designated formal function within an organization that is responsible for helping individual employees with personal problems that affect their job performance (e.g., substance abuse, family difficulties, or emotional problems). EAP services range from screening, assessment, and referral of employees to community resources, through direct clinical treatment by psychologists or other mental health professionals.

employment counseling counseling designed to help an individual with issues related to work, such as job seeking, work compatibility, outside pressures interfering with job performance, termination of employment, and work efficiency. Within an organization, employment counseling is often provided through an EMPLOYEE ASSISTANCE PROGRAM.

empowerment *n.* the promotion of the skills, knowledge, and confidence necessary to take greater control of one's life, as in certain educational or social schemes. In psychotherapy, the process involves helping clients become more active in meeting their needs and fulfilling their desires. Empowerment provides a client with a sense of achievement and realization of his or her own abilities and ambitions. See also ENABLING. **—empower** *vb.*

empty-chair technique a technique originating in GESTALT THERAPY in which the client conducts an emotional dialogue with some aspect of himself or herself or some significant person in his or her life (e.g., a parent), who is imagined to be sitting in an empty chair during the session. The client then exchanges chairs and takes the role of that aspect or of that other person. This technique is now sometimes also referred to as the **two-chair technique**.

empty speech fluent speech that lacks information or meaningful content.

EMR abbreviation for EDUCABLE MENTALLY RETARDED.

enabler *n.* a person, often an intimate partner or good friend, who passively permits or unwittingly encourages negative behavior in an individual, such as abusing a child or maintaining an addiction. Often, the enabler is aware of the destructiveness of the negative behavior but feels powerless to prevent it.

enabling *n.* **1.** a process whereby someone unwittingly or knowingly contributes to continued maladaptive or pathological behavior in another person, such as one with substance dependence. **2.** the process of encouraging or allowing individuals to meet their own needs and achieve desired ends. A therapist attempts to enable clients to believe in themselves, have the confidence to act on their desires, and affirm their ability to achieve. See also EMPOWERMENT.

enaction *n.* the process of putting something into action. The word is preferred to terms like execution, which have computing or machine-based connotations. Enaction thus involves guidance and support; it does not imply complete automation. Much of the literature on process modeling states that models should be **enactable**.

enactment *n.* the acting out of an important life event, rather than expressing it in words. See also PSYCHODRAMA.

enantiodromia *n.* in the approach of Carl JUNG, the "necessary opposition" that governs psychic life, as in the interplay between conscious and unconscious, introverted and extraverted tendencies, and the EGO and SHADOW.

encapsulated delusion a delusion that does not significantly affect the person's functioning or everyday behavior.

encapsulation *n.* the process of separating or keeping separate, particularly the ability of some people experiencing delusions to maintain high levels of functioning and prevent their delusions from pervading everyday behavior and cognitive states.

encephalization *n.* a larger than expected brain size for a species, given its body size. For example, an average person weighing 140 lb has an actual brain weight of 2.9 lb instead of the predicted 0.6 lb. This enlargement is the result of evolutionary advancement, with the brains of higher species increasing in anatomical complexity as cognitive functions are transferred from more primitive brain areas to the cerebral cortex.

encephalofacial angiomatosis see STURGE–WEBER SYNDROME.

encoding *n.* the conversion of a sensory input into a form capable of being processed and deposited in memory. Encoding is the first stage of memory processing, followed by RETENTION and then RETRIEVAL.

encopresis *n.* repeated defecation in inappropriate places (clothing, floor, etc.) that occurs after the age of 4 and is not due to a substance (e.g., a laxative) or to a general medical condition. Encopresis may or may not be accompanied by constipation and is often associated with poor toilet training and stressful situations. Compare FECAL INCONTINENCE.

encounter group a group of individuals in which constructive insight, sensitivity to others, and personal growth are promoted through direct interactions on an emotional and social level. The leader functions as a catalyst and facilitator rather than as a therapist and focuses on here-and-now feelings and interaction, rather than on theory or individual motivation.

encounter movement a trend toward the formation of small groups in which various techniques, such as CONFRONTATION, GAMES, and REENACTMENT, are used to stimulate awareness, personality growth, and productive interactions. The movement gained popularity in the 1960s but diminished at the end of the 20th century.

endemic *adj.* occuring in a specific region or population, particularly with reference to a disease or disorder. Compare EPIDEMIC; PANDEMIC.

endocarditis *n.* inflammation of the **endocardium**, the inner lining of the heart, and often the heart valves. It is typically caused by bacterial or fungal infections. Primary diagnostic symptoms include fever, new or changing heart murmur, and minute hemorrhages (particularly in the extremities and conjunctiva of the eye).

endocathection *n.* the inward focusing of PSYCHIC ENERGY and withdrawal from external pursuits. Compare EXOCATHECTION. See CATHEXIS. [defined by U.S. psychologist Henry Alexander Murray (1893–1988)]

endocrine gland any ductless gland that secretes hormones directly into the bloodstream to act on distant targets. Such glands include the PITUITARY GLAND, ADRENAL GLAND, THYROID GLAND, gonads (testis and ovary), and ISLETS OF LANGERHANS.

endocrine system the set of ENDOCRINE GLANDS, which synthesize and secrete HORMONES into the bloodstream.

endocrinology *n.* the study of the morphology, physiology, biochemistry, and pathology of the ENDOCRINE GLANDS. See also NEUROENDOCRINOLOGY. **—endocrinological** *adj.* **—endocrinologist** *n.*

end of life the variable period during which individuals and their families, friends, and caregivers face issues and decisions related to the imminent prospect of death. The end-of-life concept is a way of considering the total context of an approaching death, rather than medical factors only. End-of-life issues include decisions relating to the nature of terminal care (hospice or traditional), whether to resuscitate, the distribution of property and assets, funeral and memorial arrangements, and leave taking and possible reconciliations with family and friends. See also ADVANCE DIRECTIVE; INFORMED CONSENT.

endogenous *adj.* originating within the body as a result of normal biochemical or physiological processes (e.g., ENDOGENOUS OPIOIDS) or of predisposing biological or genetic influences (e.g., ENDOGENOUS DEPRESSION). Compare EXOGENOUS. **—endogenously** *adv.*

endogenous depression depression that occurs in the absence of an obvious psychological stressor and in which a biological or genetic cause is implied. Compare REACTIVE DEPRESSION.

endogenous opioid a substance produced in the body that has the analgesic and euphoric effects of morphine. Three families of endogenous opioids are well known: the **enkephalins**, ENDORPHINS, and **dynorphins**. All are NEUROPEPTIDES that bind to OPIOID RECEPTORS in the central nervous system; they are mostly inhibitory, acting like opiates to block pain. They bind relatively nonselectively to opioid receptors, although enkephalins bind preferentially to the delta opioid receptors and dynorphins to kappa receptors. Recently, three other endogenous opioid peptides have been identified: **orphanin** (**nociceptin**) and **endomorphins 1** and **2**. Also called **opioid neurotransmitter**.

E

endogenous smile a spontaneous or reflexive smile that is observed when an infant, early in life, is in a state of REM SLEEP. Characterized by a simple turning up of the corners of the mouth, such smiles are seen from birth and are not elicited by social stimulation.

endomorph *n.* in SHELDON'S CONSTITUTIONAL THEORY OF PERSONALITY, a constitutional type characterized by a soft, round physique, which—according to this theory—is highly correlated with VISCEROTONIA. Also called **endomorphic body type**. **—endomorphic** *adj.* **—endomorphy** *n.*

endophenotype *n.* a type of BIOLOGICAL MARKER that is simpler to detect than genetic sequences and that may be useful in researching vulnerability to a wide range of psychological and neurological disorders. Endophenotypes may be a useful link between genetic sequences and their external emotional, cognitive, or behavioral manifestations.

endopsychic *adj.* pertaining to unconscious material or intrapsychic processes (i.e., processes occurring within the mind). Compare EXOPSYCHIC.

endopsychic structure in psychoanalysis, the internal structure of the mind or psyche. In Sigmund FREUD's formulation the mind is divided into three components: the ID, EGO, and SUPEREGO. See STRUCTURAL MODEL.

endorphin *n.* any of a class of NEUROPEPTIDES, found mainly in the pituitary gland, that function as ENDOGENOUS OPIOIDS. The best known is BETA-ENDORPHIN; the others are **alpha-endorphin** and **gamma-endorphin**. The production of endorphins during intense physical activity is one explanation for the runner's high or exercise high, as well as for an athlete's ability to feel little or no pain during a competition.

end-stage renal disease the terminal stage of chronic kidney failure, indicating the necessity for the individual with the disease to undergo replacement therapy (hemodialysis, peritoneal dialysis, or kidney transplant) in order to survive. The psychological effects of living with the condition and its treatment can include depression arising from a sense of lost or limited personal control due to dependence on a dialysis machine, to dialysis-related diet restrictions, and the like. Body-image problems caused by transplantation can develop as well.

enelicomorphism *n.* see ADULTOMORPHISM.

enema *n.* the injection of a liquid into the rectum via the anus to empty the bowel. It is also used for introducing radiopaque contrast media into the bowel for radiography and also for ADMINISTRATION of certain drugs in solution for absorption through the rectal mucosa.

enema addiction a dependence upon enemas to empty the bowel. Enema addiction may develop through the repeated use of enemas, which reduce rectal sensitivity to the presence of feces in the bowel. This condition is often associated with EATING DISORDERS in which enemas are routinely used for purging. See also KLISMAPHILIA; LAXATIVE ADDICTION.

enervate *vb.* **1.** to weaken or deprive of energy. **2.** to surgically remove a nerve or a part of a nerve. **—enervation** *n.*

engendering psychology the project of developing an approach to psychological issues that is sensitive to questions of gender. See FEMINIST PSYCHOLOGY; WOMAN-CENTERED PSYCHOLOGY. [introduced by U.S. psychologist Florence L. Denmark (1932–)]

engulfment *n.* **1.** extreme distress and anxiety related to feelings of being taken over by an external force. **2.** fear of close interpersonal relationships because of a perceived loss of independence and selfhood. This fear is common in those with feelings of personal insecurity, who experience relationships as overwhelming threats to personal identity. It may also be associated with BORDERLINE PERSONALITY DISORDER. [first described by British psychiatrist R. D. Laing (1927–1989)]

Enlon *n.* a trade name for EDROPHONIUM.

enmeshment *n.* a condition in which two or more people, typically family members, are involved in each other's activities and personal relationships to an excessive degree, thus limiting or precluding healthy interaction and compromising individual AUTONOMY and IDENTITY.

enriched environment an environment that offers many opportunities to engage in activity and provides plenty of sensory and intellectual stimulation. See ENRICHMENT.

enrichment *n.* **1.** enhancement or improvement by the addition or augmentation of some desirable property, quality, or component. For example, the Instrumental Enrichment program was originally designed to help pupils with mental retardation improve their metacognitive and cognitive skills; job enrichment policies are designed to enhance quality of worklife and thus employees' interest in and attitude toward work tasks; and MARRIAGE-ENRICHMENT GROUPS are intended to enhance the interpersonal relationships of married couples. **2.** the provision of opportunities to increase levels of behavioral or intellectual activity in an otherwise unstimulating (i.e., impoverished) environment. For example, the provision of play materials and opportunities for social contacts has been shown to enhance the development of young children.

enthusiasm *n.* a feeling of excitement or passion for an activity, cause, or object. **—enthusiastic** *adj.*

entitlement *n.* **1.** rights or benefits legally bestowed on a person or group, for example, by legislation or contract. **2.** unreasonable claims to special consideration, especially as a disturbance of self-concept in NARCISSISTIC PERSONALITY DISORDER. The exploitiveness–entitlement dimension of narcissism may be particularly useful for explaining why people with narcissistic personality disorder report higher rates of interpersonal transgressions in their daily lives.

entitlement program a program of the U.S. government that provides financial assistance and welfare benefits to individuals who meet requirements set by law, for example, people with mental or physical disabilities. Entitlement programs are administered through MEDICARE, MEDICAID, SOCIAL SECURITY disability insurance, and similar funding sources.

entity theory the belief that psychological attributes, such as level of intelligence, are fixed, essential qualities rather than attributes that develop gradually. [formulated by U.S. personality psychologist Carol S. Dweck (1946–) in her analysis of cognition, personality, and motivation]

entrapment *n.* a pathological condition in which swelling of surrounding tissue places excessive pressure on a nerve. Fibers located on the surface of the nerve usually bear the brunt of the compression, while interior fibers tend to be less affected. Repeated or long-term entrapment can cause nerve damage and muscle weakness.

enucleation *n.* the removal of an entire organic structure, such as a tumor or a bodily organ, without damaging the surrounding structure. Enucleation often refers to the removal of an eyeball in which the optic nerve and connective eye muscles have been severed so that the eye can be removed wholly and cleanly. See also AUTOENUCLEATION.

enuresis *n.* repeated involuntary urination in inappropriate places (clothing, floor, etc.) that occurs after the chronological age when continence is expected (generally 5 years old) and is not due to a substance (e.g., a diuretic) or to a general medical condition. Enuresis may occur during the day (**diurnal enuresis**), night (**nocturnal enuresis**), or both and is frequently associated with delayed bladder development, poor toilet training, and stressful situations. See also BED-WETTING. Compare URINARY INCONTINENCE.

environmental approach a therapeutic approach in which efforts are directed either toward reducing external pressures (e.g., employment or financial problems) that contribute to emotional difficulties or toward modifying aspects of the individual's living or working space to improve functioning.

environmental assessment the evaluation of situational and environmental variables that have an influence on behavior, based on the theory that disordered functioning may be rooted partly in the social system, or particular social context, rather than wholly in the individual and his or her personal characteristics. In an organizational context, for example, measures of manager support and availability of resources to accomplish a job would likely be used in the environmental assessment of employee job satisfaction.

environmental constraint any circumstance of a person's situation or environment that discourages the development of skills and abilities, independence, social competence, or adaptive behavior or inhibits the display of skills previously acquired. For example, living in a COMMUNITY RESIDENCE where staff prepare all the meals would act as an environmental constraint for someone who has learned how to make sandwiches, since it would provide no opportunity to display this ability.

environmental deprivation an absence of conditions that stimulate intellectual and behavioral growth and development, such as educational, recreational, and social opportunities. Environmental deprivation is often associated with social isolation and may be so severe that it causes PSEUDORETARDATION.

environmental determinism the view that psychological and behavioral characteristics are largely or completely the result of environmental conditions. Biological factors are considered to be of minor importance, exerting little if any influence. Compare BIOLOGICAL DETERMINISM; GENETIC DETERMINISM. See DETERMINISM; NATURE–NURTURE.

environmentalism *n.* **1.** the concept that the environment and learning are the chief determinants of behavior. They are, therefore, the major cause of interpersonal variations in ability and adjustment; accordingly, behavior is largely modifiable. Compare HEREDITARIANISM. See also NATURE–NURTURE. **2.** a social movement and position that emphasizes the ecological relationship between humans and the natural environment and strives to protect the environment as an essential resource. **—environmentalist** *n.*

environmental load theory the theory that humans have a limited ability to handle environmental stimuli. The limit is determined by the amount of information inputs that can be processed by the central nervous system. When the environmental load exceeds the individual's capacity for processing, the central nervous system reacts by ignoring some of the inputs. See also COGNITIVE OVERLOAD; INFORMATION OVERLOAD; SENSORY OVERLOAD; STIMULUS OVERLOAD.

environmental manipulation a method of improving the well-being of people by changing their living conditions, for example, by placing an abused or delinquent child in a foster home or by transferring an adult patient from a mental institution to an ADULT HOME or a HALFWAY HOUSE.

environmental stress any kind of STRESS caused by factors in the environment.

environmental stress theory the concept that autonomic and cognitive factors combine to form an individual's appraisal of stressors in

E

the environment as threatening or nonthreatening. Stressors perceived as threatening may lead to stress reactions involving physiological, emotional, and behavioral elements, which in turn may elicit strategies designed to cope with and potentially adapt to the threat.

environmental therapy therapy that includes and addresses the client's interaction with his or her physical or social surroundings (or both) in an effort to promote greater cognitive, affective, and behavioral health. See MILIEU THERAPY; THERAPEUTIC COMMUNITY.

envy 1. *n.* a NEGATIVE EMOTION of discontent and resentment generated by desire for the possessions, attributes, qualities, or achievements of another (the target of the envy). Unlike JEALOUSY, with which it shares certain similarities and with which it is often confused, envy need involve only two individuals: the envious person and the person envied. **2.** *vb.* to feel such discontent or resentment. **—envious** *adj.*

enzyme *n.* a protein that acts as a biological catalyst, accelerating the rate of a biochemical reaction without itself becoming permanently altered. Many enzymes require other organic molecules (coenzymes) or inorganic ions (cofactors) to function normally. Most enzymes are named according to the type of reaction they catalyze; for example, glucosidases convert glucosides to glucose; acetylcholinesterase (see CHOLINESTERASE) splits and inactivates molecules of the neurotransmitter acetylcholine.

enzyme induction the ability of drugs or other substances to increase the activity of enzymes, especially hepatic (liver) enzymes, that are responsible for the metabolism of those drugs or other substances. The CYTOCHROME P450 hepatic enzymes, which are responsible for the metabolism of numerous psychotropic compounds, are susceptible to induction. Barbiturates, some anticonvulsants, and steroids may induce hepatic enzymes, usually resulting in a decrease in activity of the drug or other substances metabolized via the same enzyme system. Substances contained in cigarette smoke, charbroiled meat, and environmental pollutants are also capable of enzyme induction.

enzyme inhibition the ability of drugs or other substances to impair or arrest the ability of enzymes, especially liver (hepatic) enzymes, to metabolize those drugs or other substances. The CYTOCHROME P450 enzymes that are responsible for the metabolism of numerous psychotropic drugs are susceptible to inhibition by psychotropics or other substances. Many of the SSRIs (selective serotonin reuptake inhibitors) inhibit the activity of enzymes for which they are SUBSTRATES, leading to increased concentrations of the SSRIs or other drugs that are metabolized by the same enzyme. Enyzme inhibition can be competitive, when a drug partially inhibits an enzyme by competing for the same binding site as the substrate (the compound on which the enzyme acts), or irreversible, when a drug binds so completely to an enzyme that it fundamentally alters the enzyme and even partial metabolism of other substances cannot take place.

eonism *n.* the adoption by a male of a female role, or vice versa, as in TRANSVESTISM. Eonism is named for Charles Eon de Beaumont, a French political adventurer, who died in 1810 after posing as a woman for many years.

epena *n.* a hallucinogenic snuff prepared from the bark of South American trees of the genus *Virola* and used in Colombia, Brazil, and Venezuela. The bark is scraped from the trees and boiled to extract a red resin that is dried, ground, and mixed with wood ash. The active agents, which include dimethyltryptamine (see DMT), produce effects that are comparable to those of LSD. Also called **nyakwana**; **parica**; **yakee**.

ephebophilia *n.* sexual attraction to and arousal by adolescent children, usually early adolescents who are just going through puberty.

ephedra *n.* a bushy shrub (*Ephedra sinica*), known to Chinese herbalists as ma huang, that is indigenous to arid regions of the world, particularly Mongolia and northern China. The leaves contain significant amounts of the alkaloid stimulants **ephedrine** and **pseudoephedrine** and are traditionally made into a tisane and drunk as a stimulating beverage. Both ephedrine and pseudoephedrine are strong sympathomimetic agents and therefore increase blood pressure, alertness, and anxiety, as well as causing peripheral symptoms of sympathetic activity (e.g., tremor, sweating). These agents also relax smooth muscle, hence the plant and its active components have often been used as a remedy for asthma or other respiratory complaints. In addition, ephedra has been combined into many dietary supplements that are reputed to aid weight loss, increase energy, and enhance athletic performance. There is, however, little evidence of ephedra's effectiveness for these uses except for modest, short-term weight loss without any clear health benefit. It is toxic and potentially fatal, particularly in high doses or when combined with other stimulants, such as CAFFEINE. In 2004 the U.S. Food and Drug Administration banned the sale of products containing ephedra, the first U.S. government ban of a dietary supplement.

ephedrine *n.* see EPHEDRA.

EPI 1. abbreviation for extrapyramidal involvement. See EXTRAPYRAMIDAL SYMPTOMS. **2.** abbreviation for EYSENCK PERSONALITY INVENTORY.

epidemic *adj.* generally prevalent: affecting a significant number of people, particularly with reference to a disease or disorder not ordinarily present in a specific population or present at a much higher rate than is typical. Compare ENDEMIC; PANDEMIC.

epidemic catalepsy a situation in which CATALEPSY occurs in a number of individuals at the same time as a result of identification or imitation.

Epidemiologic Catchment Area Survey (**ECA Survey**) a telephone survey of mental disorders carried out in two waves from 1980 to 1985 using *DSM–III* and the DIAGNOSTIC INTERVIEW SCHEDULE (DIS). More than 20,000 people were surveyed in households, group homes, and long-term care institutions across the United States to obtain information on the prevalence and incidence of mental disorders, the use of services for mental health problems, and the extent to which those with mental disorders are underserved.

epidemiology *n.* the study of the incidence and distribution of specific diseases and disorders. The **epidemiologist** also seeks to establish relationships to such factors as heredity, environment, nutrition, or age at onset. Results of epidemiological studies are intended to find clues and associations rather than necessarily to show causal relationships. See also INCIDENCE; PREVALENCE; RELATIVE RISK. **—epidemiologic** or **epidemiological** *adj.*

epigenesis *n.* **1.** the theory that characteristics of an organism, both physical and behavioral, arise from an interaction between genetic and environmental influences rather than from one or the other. See also NATURE–NURTURE. **2.** in genetics, the occurrence of a heritable change in gene function that is not the result of a change in the base sequence of the organism's DNA. **3.** in the theory of Erik ERIKSON, the emergence of different goals at each stage of ego and social development. See ERIKSON'S EIGHT STAGES OF DEVELOPMENT. **—epigenetic** *adj.*

epigenetic theory the concept that mind and consciousness developed when living organisms reached a high level of complexity. See EMERGENCE.

epilepsy *n.* a group of chronic brain disorders associated with disturbances in the electrical discharges of brain cells and characterized by recurrent SEIZURES, with or without clouding or loss of consciousness. **Symptomatic epilepsy** is due to known conditions, such as brain inflammation, brain tumor, vascular disturbances, structural abnormality, brain injury, or degenerative disease; **idiopathic epilepsy** is of unknown origin or is due to nonspecific brain defects. Types of seizure vary depending on the nature of the abnormal electrical discharge and the area of the brain affected (see ABSENCE SEIZURE; GENERALIZED SEIZURE; PARTIAL SEIZURE; TONIC–CLONIC SEIZURE). Epilepsy was formerly known as **falling sickness**. Also called **seizure disorder**. **—epileptic** *adj.*

epileptic cry a momentary cry produced by sudden contraction of the chest and laryngeal muscles during the tonic phase of a TONIC–CLONIC SEIZURE. Also called **initial cry**.

epileptic furor see FUROR.

epileptiform seizure an episode that resembles an epileptic seizure but is unrelated to epilepsy. See also NONEPILEPTIC SEIZURE.

epileptoidism *n.* see EPILEPTOID PERSONALITY.

epileptoid personality a personality pattern that includes such traits as irritability, selfishness, uncooperativeness, and aggressiveness. This personality pattern is believed by some to be associated with epilepsy. Also called **epileptoidism**.

epinephrine *n.* a CATECHOLAMINE neurotransmitter and adrenal hormone that is the end product of the metabolism of the dietary amino acid tyrosine. It is synthesized primarily in the adrenal medulla by methylation of norepinephrine, which itself is formed from DOPAMINE by the action of the enzyme dopamine β-hydroxylase. As a hormone, it is secreted in large amounts when an individual is stimulated by fear, anxiety, or a similar stressful situation. As a neurotransmitter, it is the primary stimulant of both ALPHA-ADRENERGIC RECEPTORS and BETA-ADRENERGIC RECEPTORS. Thus it increases the heart rate and force of heart contractions, relaxes bronchial and intestinal smooth muscle, and produces varying effects on blood pressure as it acts both as a vasodilator and vasoconstrictor. Also called **adrenaline**.

epiphany *n.* a sudden perception of the essential nature of oneself, others, or reality.

epiphenomenalism *n.* the position that bodily (physical) events produce mental events, such as thoughts and feelings, but that mental events do not have causal power to produce bodily (physical) events. Thus, causality between the mental and the physical proceeds in one direction only. A more radical form of the same position would add that mental events lack causal efficacy to produce anything, including other mental events. An example of this radical position is the claim that consciousness is merely a side effect of the functioning of the brain, with no causal connection to it. See also MIND–BODY PROBLEM; REDUCTIONISM. [coined by British philosopher and psychologist James Ward (1843–1925)]

epiphora *n.* excessive secretion of tears, which is most commonly due to an organic condition causing an insufficient drainage of tears but may be associated with emotional stress, such as chronic anxiety or fear.

episode *n.* a noteworthy isolated event or series of events. An episode of an illness is an isolated occurrence, which may be repeated.

episodic amnesia a loss of memory only for certain significant events. Episodic amnesia may also involve a transient ability to recall an event followed by periods of inability to access the memory.

episodic buffer see WORKING MEMORY.

episodic disorder any disorder characterized by the appearance of symptoms in discrete, often brief, periods or episodes.

episodic memory the ability to remember personally experienced events that happened at a particular time and place. As defined in 1972 by Estonian-born Canadian psychologist Endel Tulving (1927–), episodic memory supplements SEMANTIC MEMORY as a form of DECLARATIVE MEMORY. Although Tulving's original description of episodic memory required recollecting the three 'Ws' of an event—what, where, and when—it has since been revised to include a sense of self-awareness and a subjective conscious experience as well (termed AUTONOETIC consciousness). In other words, in addition to recalling the facts of a past event, an individual also has to engage in "mental time travel" and remember that he or she was the one who lived the event. The hippocampus plays a key role in episodic memory formation and retrieval. Indeed, atrophy of this area and structures in the associated HIPPOCAMPAL FORMATION is a hallmark feature of Alzheimer's disease, although episodic memory also declines considerably with normal aging. See also AUTOBIOGRAPHICAL MEMORY.

epistemological loneliness a profound sense of alienation or separation from others.

epistemophilia *n.* the love of knowledge: the impulse to investigate and inquire. See also CURIOSITY.

EPPS abbreviation for EDWARDS PERSONAL PREFERENCE SCHEDULE.

EPQ abbreviation for Eysenck Personality Questionnaire. See EYSENCK PERSONALITY INVENTORY.

EPS abbreviation for EXTRAPYRAMIDAL SYMPTOMS.

EPSDT abbreviation for EARLY AND PERIODIC SCREENING, DIAGNOSIS, AND TREATMENT.

epsilon alcoholism the least common of the five types of alcoholism defined by U.S. physician Elvin M. Jellinek (1890–1963), the others being ALPHA ALCOHOLISM, BETA ALCOHOLISM, GAMMA ALCOHOLISM, and DELTA ALCOHOLISM. It is characterized by periodic drinking bouts or binges interspersed with dry periods lasting weeks or months.

Epstein–Barr virus (**EBV**) a herpes virus that is the cause of infectious mononucleosis. It is commonly found in the extracellular oral fluids of those who have been exposed to the disease. The virus has also been isolated from the cells of patients with certain cancers (e.g., Burkitt's lymphoma). [Michael Anthony **Epstein** (1921–) and Yvonne M. **Barr** (1932–), British pathologists]

EQ abbreviation for EMOTIONAL INTELLIGENCE QUOTIENT.

equal-interval scale see INTERVAL SCALE.

equipotentiality *n.* U.S. psychologist Karl S. LASHLEY's generalization that large areas of cerebral cortex have equal potential to perform particular functions, being equally involved in learning and certain other complex processes, such that intact cortical areas can assume to some extent the functions of damaged or destroyed areas. Proposed in 1929 following experimental observations of the effects of different brain lesions on rats' ability to learn a complex maze, the concept has been challenged by subsequent research showing that areas of cortex have relatively specific functions. See also MASS ACTION.

equity theory see SOCIAL EXCHANGE THEORY.

equivalence *n.* a relationship between two or more items (e.g., stimuli or variables) that permits one to replace another.

equivocal sign see SOFT SIGN.

erectile dysfunction the lack or loss of ability to achieve an erection. Causes of erectile dysfunction may be psychological or physical, including the effects of medications or drug abuse. If a man normally experiences a nocturnal erection or is able to induce an erection by masturbation, but cannot achieve or maintain an erection during sexual intercourse, the dysfunction is assumed to be due largely or solely to psychological factors and in *DSM–IV–TR* is called MALE ERECTILE DISORDER. See also PRIMARY ERECTILE DYSFUNCTION; SECONDARY ERECTILE DYSFUNCTION.

eremophilia *n.* a pathological desire to be alone.

erethism *n.* **1.** an abnormally high degree of sensitivity to sensory stimulation in some or all parts of the body. It is associated with a number of conditions and is a major symptom of mercury poisoning. See also MAD HATTER'S DISEASE. **2.** any abnormally high degree of sensitivity, excitability, or irritability in response to stimulation, such as emotional erethism.

erg *n.* **1.** a term used by British-born U.S. psychologist Raymond B. Cattell (1905–1998) in preference to drive or instinct, to denote a type of innate DYNAMIC TRAIT that directs an individual toward a goal and provides the motivational energy to obtain it. Examples include curiosity, self-assertion, gregariousness, protectiveness, and hunger. **2.** in physics, a unit of work or energy.

ergasiology *n.* see PSYCHOBIOLOGY.

ergic trait a dynamic trait that motivates an individual to achieve an objective.

ergomania *n.* a compulsion to work and keep busy. Also called **workaholism**. See WORKAHOLIC.

ergonovine *n.* see ERGOT DERIVATIVES; OXYTOCICS.

ergot alkaloids pharmacologically active substances derived from the parasitic fungus *Claviceps purpurea*, which grows naturally on rye and other grains. Although highly toxic, ergot alkaloids have been used for centuries by midwives to induce abortion or labor. A number have been isolated, including lysergic acid, and the compounds are sometimes utilized as adrenoreceptor blocking agents (see ERGOT DERIVATIVES). Epidemics of ergot poisoning (**ergotism**) were widespread until relatively modern times in Europe; symptoms included peripheral vasoconstriction (rarely gangrene) and changes in mental functioning, including visual hallucinations. Because of the pharmacological relationship between ergot and LSD (lysergic acid diethylamide), the hallucinogenic effects are similar to those of LSD.

ergotamine *n.* an alkaloid drug (an ERGOT DERIVATIVE) used in the treatment of vascular headaches, including migraines. The exact nature of its therapeutic action is unknown, but ergotamine is believed to constrict the dilated cranial blood vessels responsible for the headache symptoms. U.S. trade name (among others): **Cafergot**.

ergot derivatives a group of ADRENERGIC BLOCKING AGENTS with selective inhibitory activity, derived from ERGOT ALKALOIDS. Ergot derivatives act on the central nervous system in a complex manner and, in various forms and doses, can both stimulate and depress higher brain centers. A circulatory effect is vasoconstriction. Some of these agents, including ERGOTAMINE, are used in the control of migraine headaches, sometimes combined with other drugs (e.g., caffeine). The derivative ergonovine is used as an OXYTOCIC.

Erhard Seminar Training (**est**; **EST**) a controversial group therapy technique and personal development training system introduced in 1971. It purports to be consciousness-expanding, borrowing from business-world motivation techniques and various theories of psychology. It was renamed **Landmark Forum** in 1985. [Werner **Erhard** (born John Paul Rosenberg; 1935–), U.S. consultant and lecturer]

Ericksonian psychotherapy a form of psychotherapy in which the therapist works with the client to create, through hypnosis (specifically through indirect suggestion) and suggestive metaphors, real-life experiences intended to activate previously dormant, intrapsychic resources. Also called **Ericksonian hypnotherapy**. [Milton H. **Erickson** (1902–1980), U.S. psychiatrist and psychologist]

Erikson, Erik H. (1902–1994) German-born U.S. psychologist. Originally called Erik Homburger, he lived from 1927 to 1933 in Vienna, where he underwent training in PSYCHOANALYSIS with Anna FREUD for 3 years. When the Nazis rose to power, Erikson emigrated with his wife Joan to the United States, where he spent the bulk of his career at Harvard University. Erikson is best known as a personality theorist and preeminent figure in the field of EGO PSYCHOLOGY. His theory of the eight stages of the life cycle (see ERIKSON'S EIGHT STAGES OF DEVELOPMENT) contained the development of self-identity as its central theme; he coined the term IDENTITY CRISIS to describe the crucial developmental process of ADOLESCENCE. Erikson argued for the importance of researching individual life histories in personality theory, opposing the trend toward the use of aggregate statistics in his field. Erikson's most influential works include *Childhood and Society* (1950) and *Identity: Youth and Crisis* (1968), as well as two psychobiographies, *Young Man Luther* (1958) and *Ghandi's Truth* (1969). See also EPIGENESIS; PSYCHOBIOGRAPHY; PSYCHOHISTORY.

Erikson's eight stages of development the theory of psychosocial development proposed by Erik ERIKSON, in which EGO IDENTITY is gradually achieved by facing positive goals and negative risks during eight stages of development across the lifespan. The stages are: (a) infancy: BASIC TRUST VERSUS MISTRUST; (b) toddler: AUTONOMY VERSUS SHAME AND DOUBT; (c) preschool age: INITIATIVE VERSUS GUILT; (d) school age: INDUSTRY VERSUS INFERIORITY; (e) adolescence: IDENTITY VERSUS IDENTITY CONFUSION; (f) young adulthood: INTIMACY VERSUS ISOLATION; (g) middle age: GENERATIVITY VERSUS STAGNATION; and (h) older adulthood: INTEGRITY VERSUS DESPAIR.

erogenous zone an area or part of the body sensitive to stimulation that is a source of erotic or sexual feeling or pleasure. Among the primary zones are the genitals, buttocks and anus, the breasts (especially the nipples), and the mouth.

Eros *n.* the god of love in Greek mythology (equivalent to the Roman Cupid), whose name was chosen by Sigmund FREUD to designate a theoretical set of strivings oriented toward sexuality, development, and increased life activity (see LIFE INSTINCT). In Freud's DUAL INSTINCT THEORY, Eros is seen as involved in a dialectic process with THANATOS, the striving toward reduced psychical tension and life activity (see DEATH INSTINCT). See also LIBIDO.

erotica *pl. n.* literature, illustrations, motion pictures or other artistic material likely to arouse sexual response. The term is sometimes used interchangeably with PORNOGRAPHY. However, the distinction is often made that erotica, unlike pornography, does not involve violence, coercion, or exploitative sexuality, instead depicting sexuality in a positive manner.

erotic-arousal pattern the sequence of actions or stimuli that produces sexual response. The actions or stimuli vary with different species: In humans they may involve dress, perfume, music, and foreplay.

erotic asphyxiation sexual pleasure associated with restriction of breathing during sexual activity. See ASPHYXOPHILIA; AUTOEROTIC ASPHYXIATION.

erotic delusion the false perception or belief that one is loved by or has had a sexual affair with a public figure or other individual. Also called **erotomanic delusion**. See CLÉRAMBAULT'S SYNDROME; DELUSIONAL DISORDER; EROTIC PARANOIA; SIMENON'S SYNDROME.

E

erotic instinct 1. in psychoanalytic theory, the sex drive or LIBIDO. **2.** EROS, or the LIFE INSTINCT.

eroticism *n.* **1.** the quality of being sexually arousing or pleasurable or the condition of being sexually aroused. **2.** a preoccupation with or susceptibility to sexual excitement. **3.** the use of sexually arousing themes, images, or suggestions in entertainment or the arts. **4.** in psychoanalytic theory, the pleasurable sensations associated not only with stimulation of the genitals but also with nongenital parts of the body, such as the mouth or anus (see ANAL EROTICISM; ORAL EROTICISM). Also called **erotism**. See also AUTOEROTICISM; EROTIZATION. **—erotic** *adj.*

eroticization *n.* see EROTIZATION.

erotic paranoia a disorder in which the individual experiences EROTIC DELUSIONS. Also called **erotomanic-type delusional disorder**. See DELUSIONAL DISORDER. See also CLÉRAMBAULT'S SYNDROME; SIMENON'S SYNDROME.

erotic plasticity the degree to which sexual desire and sexual behavior are shaped by social, cultural, and situational factors. See BEHAVIORAL PLASTICITY.

erotic pyromania see PYROLAGNIA.

erotic type see LIBIDINAL TYPES.

erotism *n.* see EROTICISM.

erotization *n.* the investment of bodily organs and biological functions or other not specifically sensual or sexual activities with sexual pleasure and gratification. Common examples are the erotization of certain areas of the body, such as the oral or anal EROGENOUS ZONES; organs, such as the nipple or skin; functions, such as sucking, defecation, urination, or scopophilic activities (looking at nudity or sexual activity); and olfactory sensations associated with sex. Theoretically, almost any interest or activity can be erotized by the individual; for example, activities such as dancing and eating are not infrequently seen as erotic or as having erotic components. Also called **eroticization**; **libidinization**; **sexualization**. **—erotize** *vb.*

erotogenesis *n.* in psychoanalytic theory, the origination of erotic impulses from sources that may include the anal, oral, and genital zones. See EROTIZATION.

erotogenic *adj.* denoting or relating to any stimulus that evokes or excites sexual feelings or responses. Also called **erotogenetic**.

erotogenic masochism see PRIMARY MASOCHISM.

erotographomania *n.* an obsession with erotic writing that is accompanied by a pathological compulsion to write about sexual matters or draw sexual images, typically expressed through anonymous love letters or graffiti.

erotolalia *n.* speech that contains sexual obscenities, particularly as used to enhance gratification during sexual intercourse.

erotomania *n.* **1.** a preoccupation with sexual activities, thoughts, and fantasies. **2.** the false belief that one is loved by another person. See EROTIC DELUSION. **3.** compulsive, insatiable sexual activity with the opposite sex. Also called **aidoiomania**. See DON JUAN; NYMPHOMANIA; SATYRIASIS. **—erotomanic** *adj.*

erotomanic delusion see EROTIC DELUSION.

erotophonophilia *n.* see LUST MURDER.

ERP abbreviation for EVENT-RELATED POTENTIAL.

error *n.* **1.** in experimentation, any change in a DEPENDENT VARIABLE not attributable to the manipulation of an INDEPENDENT VARIABLE. **2.** in statistics, a deviation of an observed score from a true score, where true score is often defined by the MEAN of the particular group or condition in which the score being assessed for error occurs, or from the score predicted by a model.

error of measurement any deviation or departure of a measurement from its true value.

error rate the rate at which errors are made, for example, the proportion of an experimenter's data recordings that are wrong.

error score in CLASSICAL TEST THEORY, the difference between a person's observed measurement or score and his or her expected measurement or score.

error term the element of a statistical equation that indicates what is unexplained by the INDEPENDENT VARIABLES. Also called **disturbance term**; **residual term**.

error variance unexplained variability in a score that is produced by extraneous factors, such as measurement imprecision, and is not attributable to the INDEPENDENT VARIABLE or other controlled experimental manipulations.

erythema multiforme major see STEVENS–JOHNSON SYNDROME.

Esalen Institute an alternative educational center in California, founded in 1962, where enhancement of well-being is approached through a number of meditative and new-age therapies. Therapists and members of the general public participate in seminars, workshops, experiential programs, and other events that are designed to promote self-exploration and enhance relationships with others.

escalation of commitment continued commitment and increased allocation of resources to a failing course of action, often in the hope of recouping past losses associated with that course of action. It is often associated with expenditures and decision making in the development of new products, when a company increases the allocation of resources to a failing product, regardless of the low probability of its success, in an attempt to recover some of its initial investment. Also called **creeping commitment**.

escape behavior any response designed to move away from or eliminate an already present aversive stimulus. Escape behavior may be mental (through fantasy or daydreams) or behavioral (physical withdrawal from a noxious stimulus or a conditioned response, as when an animal taps a lever in order to terminate a shock). See also ACTIVE AVOIDANCE. Compare AVOIDANCE BEHAVIOR.

escape from freedom a false solution to the individual's problems of loneliness and isolation, in which he or she seeks refuge in social conformity. See also IDENTITY NEED. [defined by Erich FROMM]

escape from reality a defensive reaction involving the use of fantasy as a means of avoiding conflicts and problems of daily living. See also FLIGHT FROM REALITY.

escape into illness see FLIGHT INTO ILLNESS.

escape mechanism see DEFENSE MECHANISM.

escapism *n.* the tendency to escape from the real world to the delight or security of a fantasy world. Escapism may reflect a periodic, normal, and common impulse, as might be seen in harmless DAYDREAMS, or it may be evidence of or accompany other symptoms of neurosis or more serious mental pathology. **—escapist** *adj.*

Eskalith *n.* a trade name for LITHIUM.

espanto *n.* see SUSTO.

essential dysmenorrhea see DYSMENORRHEA.

essential hypertension high blood pressure (see HYPERTENSION) that is not secondary to another disease and for which no obvious cause can be found. It accounts for at least 85% of all cases of hypertension; predisposing factors include obesity, cigarette smoking, genetic factors, and psychological influences (e.g., an aggressive personality or stressful environment). See also TYPE A PERSONALITY.

est (**EST**) abbreviation for ERHARD SEMINAR TRAINING.

EST 1. abbreviation for electroshock therapy or electroconvulsive shock therapy. See ELECTROCONVULSIVE THERAPY. **2.** see EST.

estazolam *n.* a high-potency BENZODIAZEPINE used for the short-term treatment of insomnia (see HYPNOTIC). U.S. trade name: **ProSom**.

esteem need any desire for achievement, reputation, or prestige that is necessary for a sense of personal value and the development of SELF-ESTEEM. Comprising the fourth level of MASLOW'S MOTIVATIONAL HIERARCHY, esteem needs thus are dependent upon the admiration and approval of others.

estimate 1. *n.* a best guess of the value of a parameter of a DISTRIBUTION on the basis of a set of empirical observations. **2.** *vb.* to assign a value to a parameter in this way.

estimator *n.* a quantity calculated from the values in a sample according to some rule and used to give an estimate of the value in a population. For example, the sample mean is an estimator for the population mean; the value of the sample mean is the estimate.

estrangement *n.* **1.** a state of increased distance or separation from oneself or others. See ALIENATION. **2.** a significant decrease or discontinuation of contact with individuals with whom one formerly had close relationships, such as a spouse or family member, due to apathy or antagonism. **—estranged** *adj.*

estrogen *n.* any of a class of steroid hormones that are produced mainly by the ovaries and act as the principal female SEX HORMONES, inducing estrus in female mammals and secondary female sexual characteristics in humans. The estrogens occurring naturally in humans are estradiol, estrone, and estriol, secreted by the ovarian follicle, corpus luteum, placenta, testes, and adrenal cortex. Estrogens are also produced by certain plants; these **phytoestrogens** may be used in the manufacture of synthetic steroid hormones. Estrogens are used therapeutically in ESTROGEN REPLACEMENT THERAPY and oral contraceptives and to treat certain menstrual disorders and some types of breast and prostate cancers.

estrogen antagonist see ANTIESTROGEN.

estrogen replacement therapy the administration of natural or synthetic estrogens, such as estradiol or ethinyl estradiol, for the relief of symptoms associated with menopause, surgical removal of the ovaries, or failure of the ovaries to develop. Although estrogen replacement therapy is an extremely common therapy in menopausal women, recent studies have questioned its material long-term benefits. See HORMONE REPLACEMENT THERAPY.

estrone *n.* an ESTROGEN produced by ovarian follicles and other tissues. It is used therapeutically in the treatment of menopausal and other estrogen-deficiency disorders (see ESTROGEN REPLACEMENT THERAPY) and in certain cases of vaginitis.

eszopiclone *n.* a nonbenzodiazepine HYPNOTIC used for the short-term treatment of insomnia. Like the related drug ZALEPLON, it is relatively selective for a specific subunit on the $GABA_A$ RECEPTOR complex. Side effects include excessive sedation or confusion, dry mouth, and a bitter taste. U.S. trade name: **Lunesta**.

ethanol *n.* a substance formed naturally or synthetically by the fermentation of glucose and found in beverages such as beers, wines, and distilled liquors. It is the most frequently used and abused CNS DEPRESSANT in many cultures. When consumed its primary effects are on the central nervous system, mood, and cognitive functions. In small doses, it can produce feelings of warmth, well-being, and confidence. As more is consumed, there is a gradual loss of self-control, and speech and control of limbs become difficult; at high consumption levels, nausea and vomiting, loss of consciousness, and even fatal respiratory arrest may occur. Ethanol has been mistakenly identified as a stimulant, since its stimulating effect derives from an associated loss of cortical inhibition. Also called **alcohol**; **ethyl alcohol**. See also ALCOHOL ABUSE; ALCO-

E

HOL DEPENDENCE; ALCOHOL INTOXICATION; ALCOHOL WITHDRAWAL.

ethchlorvynol *n.* an alcohol derivative introduced in the 1950s as a nonbarbiturate sedative. Ethchlorvynol is an effective, rapidly acting hypnotic, but because of its toxicity in overdose, as well as its ability to induce enzymes involved in drug metabolism (see ENZYME INDUCTION) and its association with blood disorders, it has become clinically obsolete. It is at times a substance of abuse. U.S. trade name: **Placidyl**.

E

ether *n.* a drug introduced into medicine as a general anesthetic in the mid-1800s. The effects of ether include a progressive series of physical and psychological reactions, beginning with a feeling of suffocation, bodily warmth, visual and auditory aberrations, and a feeling of stiffness and inability to move the limbs. A second stage may be marked by some resistance to the sense of suffocation of the anesthetic, but the muscles relax, blood pressure and pulse increase, and pupils dilate. In the third stage, pulse and blood pressure return to normal, pupils contract, and reflexes are absent. If additional ether is administered beyond the third stage, there is danger of paralysis of the medullary centers, followed by shock and death. In clinical practice, ether has been replaced by safer anesthetics.

e-therapy *n.* an Internet-based form of DISTANCE THERAPY used to expand access to clinical services typically offered face-to-face. This therapy can be conducted in real-time messaging, in chat rooms, and in e-mail messages. Also called **online therapy**.

ethical code see CODE OF ETHICS.

ethical conflict see BOUNDARY ISSUES; CONFLICT OF INTEREST; DOUBLE-AGENTRY.

ethics *n.* **1.** the branch of philosophy that investigates both the content of moral judgments (i.e., what is right and what is wrong) and their nature (i.e., whether such judgments should be considered objective or subjective). The study of the first type of question is sometimes termed **normative ethics** and that of the second **metaethics**. Also called **moral philosophy**. **2.** the principles of morally right conduct accepted by a person or a group or considered appropriate to a specific field (e.g., medical ethics, ethics of animal research). See CODE OF ETHICS; PROFESSIONAL ETHICS. **—ethical** *adj.*

ethnopsychology *n.* see CROSS-CULTURAL PSYCHOLOGY.

ethnopsychopharmacology *n.* the branch of pharmacology that deals with issues related to ethnic and cultural variations in the use of and response to psychoactive agents across divergent groups, as well as the mechanisms responsible for such differences. **—ethnopsychopharmacological** *adj.*

ethnotherapy *n.* therapy sensitive to the distinct cultural features of a client from an ethnic minority and the various ways in which the client relates to others, expresses himself or herself, and deals with problems. See also MULTICULTURAL THERAPY.

ethosuximide *n.* see SUCCINIMIDE.

ethotoin *n.* see HYDANTOIN.

ethyl alcohol see ETHANOL.

etiology *n.* **1.** the causes and progress of a disease or disorder. **2.** the branch of medical and psychological science concerned with the systematic study of the causes of physical and mental disorders. **—etiological** *adj.*

Etrafon *n.* a trade name for a combination of the tricyclic antidepressant AMITRIPTYLINE and the antipsychotic PERPHENAZINE, used for the treatment of concurrent anxiety and depression.

E trisomy see TRISOMY 17–18.

euergasia *n.* normal mental or psychobiological functioning. Also called **orthergasia**. [defined by U.S. psychiatrist Adolf Meyer (1866–1950)]

eugenics *n.* a social and political philosophy, based loosely on the evolutionary theory of Charles Darwin (1809–1882) and the research on hereditary genius of Francis Galton (1822–1911), that seeks to eradicate genetic defects and improve the genetic makeup of populations through selective human breeding. **Positive eugenics** is directed toward promoting reproduction by individuals with superior traits, whereas **negative eugenics** is directed toward preventing reproduction by individuals with undesirable traits. The eugenic position is groundless and scientifically naive, in that many conditions associated with disability or disorder, such as syndromes that increase risk of MENTAL RETARDATION, are inherited recessively and occur unpredictably. Nevertheless, the philosophy gained popularity in the United Kingdom and United States, where eugenic policies, such as sterilization of women with mental retardation, persisted into the latter half of the 20th century. Attitudes toward genetics in the 21st century are often influenced by individual and community concerns about prior eugenic abuses.

eunuch *n.* a male who has been castrated before puberty and who therefore develops the secondary SEX CHARACTERISTICS of a female, such as a higher voice and absence of facial hair. See also CASTRATION.

euphenics *n.* interventions that aim to improve the outcome of a genetic disease by altering the environment to minimize expression of the disease. For example, people with PHENYLKETONURIA can reduce or prevent its expression by eliminating major sources of phenylalanine (e.g., soft drinks sweetened with aspartame) from their diet.

euphoria *n.* an elevated mood of well-being and happiness. An exaggerated degree of euphoria that does not reflect the reality of one's situation is a frequent symptom of MANIC EPISODES and HYPOMANIC EPISODES. **—euphoric** *adj.*

euphoriant *n.* a substance capable of inducing a subjective sense of well-being and happiness.

euphorogenic *adj.* describing an event or medication that generates a state of EUPHORIA.

eureka task a problem-solving task designed to investigate the phenomenon of sudden INSIGHT into a problem's solution. The route to solving the problem is usually not obvious, and usually requires a mental leap of some kind beyond the sorts of solutions used for everyday problems. See also AHA EXPERIENCE; DISCONTINUITY HYPOTHESIS.

European Federation of Professional Psychologists' Associations (**EFPPA**) a federation of national psychology associations founded in 1981 to provide a forum for European cooperation in a wide range of fields of academic training, psychology practice, and research.

eustress *n.* the positive stress response, involving optimal levels of stimulation: a type of stress that results from challenging but attainable and enjoyable or worthwhile tasks (e.g., participating in an athletic event, giving a speech). It has a beneficial effect by generating a sense of fulfillment or achievement and facilitating growth, development, mastery, and high levels of performance. Compare DISTRESS. [first described by Canadian physician Hans Selye (1907–1982)]

euthanasia *n.* the act or process of terminating a life to prevent further suffering. Voluntary euthanasia requires the consent of a competent person who has established a valid ADVANCE DIRECTIVE or made his or her wishes otherwise clearly known. Euthanasia is distinguished from the much more widely accepted practice of forgoing invasive treatments, as permitted under natural-death laws throughout the United States. Traditionally, a distinction between PASSIVE EUTHANASIA (withholding treatment) and ACTIVE EUTHANASIA (taking directly lethal action) has been made. In current practice, however, the term euthanasia typically is used to mean active euthanasia only. See also ASSISTED DEATH.

euthymia *n.* a mood of well-being and tranquillity. The term often is used to refer to a state in patients with a bipolar disorder that is neither manic nor depressive but in between, associated with adaptive behavior and enhanced functioning. **—euthymic** *adj.*

evaluability-assessment data information sought to identify problematic areas of program evaluation. **Evaluability assessment** comprises a review of expectations for program performance and questions to be answered by evaluation data, followed by a study of program implementation to identify designs, measurements, and analyses that are possible.

evaluation objective any of the purposes of an evaluation of a program. For example, the purpose of FORMATIVE EVALUATIONS is to consider implementation problems, program integrity, and program monitoring, whereas the purpose of SUMMATIVE EVALUATIONS is to focus on program impact, program effectiveness, and cost analysis.

evaluation research the use of scientific principles and methods to assess the effectiveness of social interventions and programs, including those related to mental health, education, and safety (e.g., crime prevention, automobile accident prevention). Evaluation research is thus a type of applied research.

evaluative reasoning a form of CRITICAL THINKING that involves appraisal of the effectiveness, validity, meaning, or relevance of any act, idea, feeling, technique, or object.

evaluator *n.* an individual whose role is to evaluate and provide advice about the progress of a therapy or sensitivity group, a project team, an institution, or an individual.

evasion *n.* **1.** a form of PARALOGIA in which an idea that is logically next in a chain of thought is replaced by another idea closely but not accurately or appropriately related to it. **2.** elusion or avoidance.

evenly hovering attention see FREE-FLOATING ATTENTION.

event-related potential (**ERP**) a specific pattern of electrical activity produced in the brain when a person is engaged in a cognitive act, such as discriminating one stimulus from another. There are a number of different ERP components, including the highly researched P3 component, and different cognitive operations have been associated with the amplitude and latency of each. Because ERPs provide specific information about the precise timing and (given appropriate caveats) location of mental events, they can yield data about cognitive operations not readily derived from behavioral measures and also serve as an important bridge between psychological function and neural structures. Although the terms are sometimes used synonymously, ERPs are distinct from EVOKED POTENTIALS, which are associated with more elementary sensory stimulation.

everyday creativity the ability to think divergently and demonstrate flexibility and originality in one's daily work and leisure activities. Examples include redecorating a room at home or devising a novel solution to a business problem. Also called **ordinary creativity**. Compare EXCEPTIONAL CREATIVITY.

everyday intelligence the intellectual skills used in everyday living (e.g., activities such as price comparison shopping and using a map to travel unfamiliar streets). Everyday intelligence refers not to a psychometrically validated construct but to a loosely conceptualized kind of intelligence relevant to the problems people face on a daily basis.

evidence-based practice (**EBP**) the integration of the best available scientific research from laboratory and field settings with clinical expertise so as to provide effective psychological services that are responsive to a patient's culture, preferences, and characteristics (e.g., functional status, level of social support, strengths). In uniting researchers and practitioners, EBP ensures that the research on psychological assessment, case formulation, intervention strategies, therapeutic relationships and outcomes, and specific problems and patient populations is both clinically relevant and internally valid. Clinical decisions should be made in collaboration with the patient, based on relevant data, and with consideration for the probable costs, benefits, and available resources and options. The ultimate goal of EBP is to promote empirically supported principles that can be used to enhance public health.

eviration *n.* **1.** castration or emasculation. **2.** the delusion of a man that he has been turned into a woman.

evocative therapy therapy based on the idea that behavior is aroused by underlying factors. Once the factors underlying a maladaptive or unwanted behavior have been identified, dispositional and environmental changes can be made to affect those factors and therefore alter the behavior. [originated by U.S. psychologist Jerome D. Frank (1910–2005)]

evoked potential (**EP**) a specific pattern of electrical activity produced in a particular part of the nervous system, especially the brain, in response to external stimulation, such as a flash of light or a brief tone. Different modalities and types of stimuli produce different types of sensory potentials, and these are labeled according to their electrical polarity (positive- or negative-going) and timing (by serial order or in milliseconds). Although the terms are sometimes used synonymously, EPs are distinct from EVENT-RELATED POTENTIALS, which are associated with higher level cognitive processes. Also called **evoked response** (**ER**).

evolutionary psychology an approach to psychological inquiry that views human cognition and behavior in a broadly Darwinian context of adaptation to evolving physical and social environments and new intellectual challenges. It differs from SOCIOBIOLOGY mainly in its emphasis on the effects of natural selection on INFORMATION PROCESSING and the structure of the human mind.

evolution of the brain the concept that the brains of complex animals have evolved over many millions of years from a network of simple nerve fibers connecting various body areas, as in primitive multicellular animals. At a more advanced stage, a neural axis developed to connect and integrate neurons serving the periphery and to house cell bodies; this axis became a spinal cord. Still later, collections of neurons with control functions developed at the head end of the spinal cord, as in the brains of higher invertebrates, birds, fish, and reptiles. From those concentrations of brain tissue evolved the FOREBRAIN, with its highly convoluted CEREBRAL CORTEX, of mammals, especially prominent in whales, great apes, and *Homo sapiens*. See also CEPHALIZATION; ENCEPHALIZATION.

evolved mechanism a subsystem of the brain (or mind) that is a product of natural selection and is generally seen as having evolved as a result of its success in solving a problem related to survival or reproduction during the evolution of a species. For example, the elements of the brain's visual system that enable organisms to perceive objects in three-dimensional space (despite the fact that vision involves the projection of light onto a two-dimensional surface, the retina) would be seen as an evolved mechanism that solved the problem of determining the distance between oneself and objects in the environment.

exact replication repetition of an experiment in which the goal is to duplicate as closely as possible the conditions of the original experiment. See REPLICATION.

exaggeration *n.* the act of embellishing or overstating a quality or characteristic of a person, thing, or situation. It is often a defensive reaction in which the individual justifies questionable attitudes or behavior through overstatement, such as dramatizing the oppressive acts of a parent as a means of justifying rebellious behavior.

exaltation *n.* an extreme state of EUPHORIA and PSYCHOMOTOR AGITATION, accompanied by a lack of restraint. It occurs in some MANIC EPISODES.

examination *n.* a test, observation, or other means of investigation carried out on a patient to evaluate physical or mental health or detect the presence or absence of signs or symptoms of diseases, disorders, or conditions. See also MENTAL EXAMINATION; NEUROLOGICAL EVALUATION; PSYCHOLOGICAL EXAMINATION.

examination anxiety see TEST ANXIETY.

exceptional child a child who is substantially above or below the average in some significant respect. Often applied to a child who shows marked deviations in intelligence, the term may also be used to indicate the presence of a special talent or an unusual emotional or social difficulty. See also GIFTEDNESS; SLOW LEARNER.

exceptional creativity the capability of individuals to make unique and important contributions to society through their work and the products of their work. Exceptional creativity, as measured by creative output, seems to peak at different points in the adult life span depending on the field of activity. Also called **creative genius**. Compare EVERYDAY CREATIVITY.

excitability *n.* **1.** the tendency of some individuals to be readily aroused to emotional responses. **2.** in neurophysiology, the capacity of neurons and some muscle cells to respond electrically to external stimulation with a sudden, transient increase in their ionic permeability and a change in the electric potential across their cell membrane. —**excitable** *adj.*

excitation-transfer theory the theory that emotional responses can be intensified by AROUSAL from other stimuli not directly related to the stimulus that originally provoked the response. According to this theory, when a person becomes aroused physiologically, there is a subsequent period of time when the person will experience a state of residual arousal yet be unaware of it. If additional arousing stimuli are presented during this time, the individual will experience more arousal, and thus greater response, to those succeeding stimuli than if there had been no residual arousal. See also AROUSAL TRANSFER. [originally proposed in 1971 by psychologist Dolf Zillman]

excitatory–inhibitory processes **1.** processes in which the transmission of neuronal signals is activated or inhibited by the effects of neurotransmitters on the postsynaptic membrane. **2.** antagonistic functions of the nervous system defined by Ivan Petrovich PAVLOV. **3.** the stimulation of the cortex and the subsequent facilitation of the processes of learning, memory, and action (excitatory processes) and central nervous system processes that inhibit or interfere with perceptual, cognitive, and motor activities (inhibitory processes). Individuals with predominant inhibitory processes are theorized to be predisposed to a higher degree of INTROVERSION, whereas individuals with predominant excitatory processes are theorized to be predisposed to a higher degree of EXTRAVERSION. [proposed by Hans EYSENCK]

excitement *n.* an emotional state marked by enthusiam, eagerness or anticipation, and general arousal.

excitement phase see SEXUAL-RESPONSE CYCLE.

excrement *n.* see FECES.

executive *n.* a theoretical superordinate mechanism in some models of cognition—particularly those in cognitive science, cognitive neuropsychology, and artificial intelligence—that organizes, initiates, monitors, and otherwise controls information-processing activities and other mental operations. A similar concept is that of the **central executive** (see WORKING MEMORY).

executive area a region of the brain hypothesized to account for higher order brain functions, such as thinking and reasoning (see EXECUTIVE FUNCTIONS). The FRONTAL LOBE is commonly referred to as an executive area.

executive dysfunction impairment in the ability to think abstractly and to plan, initiate, sequence, monitor, and stop complex behavior. Related especially to disorders of the frontal lobe or associated subcortical pathways, it is one of the multiple COGNITIVE DEFICITS characteristic of ALCOHOL-INDUCED PERSISTING DEMENTIA and SUBSTANCE-INDUCED PERSISTING DEMENTIA. Also called **disturbance in executive functioning**.

executive functions higher level cognitive processes that organize and order behavior, such as judgment, abstraction and concept formation, logic and reasoning, problem solving, planning, and sequencing of actions. Deficits in executive functioning are seen in various disorders, including Alzheimer's disease and schizophrenia. In the latter, for example, major deficits in such cognitive abilities as selecting goals or task-relevant information and eliminating extraneous information are apparent and are a focus of neurorehabilitative treatment. Also called **central processes**; **higher order processes**.

executive self the AGENT to which regulation and implementation of voluntary actions is ordinarily attributed. The concept of an executive self has acquired considerable scientific plausibility, being associated with well-studied functions of the PREFRONTAL CORTEX of the brain. However, there is a class of false attributions of executive control (see ILLUSION OF AGENCY).

Exelon *n.* a trade name for RIVASTIGMINE.

exercise addiction the condition of being dependent on or devoted to physical exercise. Stopping exercise will cause the addicted person to experience withdrawal symptoms. Also called **exercise dependence**. See NEGATIVE EXERCISE ADDICTION; POSITIVE EXERCISE ADDICTION.

exercise–behavior model an adaptation of the HEALTH–BELIEF MODEL that identifies the relationships of the following to likelihood of exercising: (a) personal predispositions, (b) sociodemographic variables, (c) perceived cost and benefits of exercising, and (d) perceived self-efficacy and locus of control.

exercise obsession see NEGATIVE EXERCISE ADDICTION.

exercise therapy the prevention or treatment of disorders and chronic disease using regular, repetitive physical activity that enhances fitness and mobility. This type of therapy is designed to improve the functional capacity of body structures and has been demonstrated to have beneficial effects for a wide variety of conditions, for example the alleviation of symptoms of depression and multiple sclerosis and the reduction in risk of developing cardiovascular disease and osteoporosis. More generally, there is widespread research evidence for a positive relationship between regular exercise and several indices of mental health and physical well-being.

exhaustion death see LETHAL CATATONIA.

exhaustion delirium a state of DELIRIUM occurring under conditions of extreme fatigue, which result from prolonged and intense overexertion, particularly when coupled with other forms of stress, such as prolonged insomnia, starvation, excessive heat or cold, or toxic states. It is typically associated with the extreme physical effort required of those who engage in prolonged duration sports or of others facing extreme environmental conditions, as well as with debilitating diseases.

exhibitionism *n.* **1.** the disposition or tendency to draw attention to oneself, particularly through conspicuous behavior. See also ATTENTION-GETTING. **2.** a PARAPHILIA in which the genitals are repeatedly exposed to unsuspecting strangers as a means of achieving sexual excitement, but without any attempt at further sexual activity with the stranger. **—exhibitionist** *n.*

existential analysis a type of psychoanalysis, or a phase in EXISTENTIAL PSYCHOTHERAPY, that places an emphasis on conscious perception and experience over unconscious motivation and drive in the search for meaning. The therapist typically takes an active, often confrontational, role by posing difficult questions and noting maladaptive decision making. The approach to "being" is future- or growth-oriented, and the goal is the development and encouragement of highly conscious decision making on the part of the client. Also called **existential psychoanalysis**.

existential anxiety a general sense of anguish or despair associated with an individual's recognition of the inevitability of death and associated search for purpose and meaning in life, in light of the finitude of past choices and the unknowns inherent to future choices.

existential–humanistic therapy a form of psychotherapy that focuses on the entire person, rather than just behavior, cognition, or underlying motivations. Emphasis is placed on the client's subjective experiences, free will, and ability to decide the course of his or her own life. Also called **humanistic–existential therapy**.

existentialism *n.* a philosophical and literary movement that emerged in Europe in the period between the two World Wars and became the dominant trend in Continental thought during the 1940s and 1950s. Existentialism is notoriously difficult to sum up in a single definition—partly because many who might be identified with the movement reject the label, and partly because the movement is itself, in many ways, a rejection of systematization and classification. The origins of existentialism have been traced to a range of thinkers, including French philosopher and mathematician Blaise Pascal (1623–1662), Danish philosopher Søren Kierkegaard (1813–1855), German philosopher Friedrich Nietzsche (1844–1900), and Russian novelist Fyodor Dostoevsky (1821–1881). However, the first fully developed philosophy of existentialism is usually taken to be the "existential phenomenology" elaborated by German philosopher Martin Heidegger (1889–1976) in the 1910s and 1920s. Heidegger's concept of DASEIN was a key influence on the work of the French philosopher and author Jean-Paul Sartre (1905–1980), who is usually seen as the existentialist thinker *par excellence*. In the immediate postwar years Sartre popularized both the term "existentialism" and most of the ideas now associated with it. Existentialism represents a turning away from systematic philosophy, with its emphasis on metaphysical absolutes and principles of rational certainty, and toward an emphasis on the concrete existence of a human being "thrown" into a world that is merely "given" and contingent. Such a being encounters the world as a subjective consciousness, "condemned" to create its own meanings and values in an "absurd" and purposeless universe. The human being must perform this task without benefit of a fixed essence or inherent nature, and in the absence of any possibility of rational certainty. However, by accepting the burden of this responsibility, and refusing the "bad faith" of religion and other spurious rationalizations, he or she can achieve AUTHENTICITY. Various forms of EXISTENTIAL PSYCHOLOGY have taken up the task of providing explanations, understandings of human behavior, and therapies based on existentialist assumptions about human existence. They have emphasized such constructs as ALIENATION, authenticity, and freedom, as well as the difficulties associated with finding meaning and overcoming anxiety. **—existential** *adj.* **—existentialist** *n., adj.*

existential living the capacity to live fully in the present and respond freely and flexibly to new experience without fear. Existential living is considered to be a central feature of the FULLY FUNCTIONING PERSON. [defined in psychology by Carl ROGERS]

existential neurosis a pathological condition characterized by feelings of despair and anxiety that arise from living inauthentically, that is, from failing to take responsibility for one's own life and to make choices and find meaning in living. See AUTHENTICITY.

existential psychoanalysis see EXISTENTIAL ANALYSIS.

existential psychology a general approach to psychological theory and practice that derives from EXISTENTIALISM. It emphasizes the subjective meaning of human experience, the uniqueness of the individual, and personal responsibility reflected in choice. Such an approach was pioneered by Swiss psychologist Ludwig Binswanger (1881–1966). See BEING-IN-THE-WORLD. See also HUMANISTIC PSYCHOLOGY.

existential psychotherapy a form of psychotherapy that deals with the HERE AND NOW of the client's total situation rather than with the client's past or underlying dynamics. It emphasizes the exploration and development of meaning in life, focuses on emotional experiences and decision making, and stresses a person's responsibility for his or her own existence. See also LOGOTHERAPY.

exocathection *n.* a concentration of PSYCHIC ENERGY on practical, worldly affairs rather than personal matters. Compare ENDOCATHECTION. See CATHEXIS. [defined by U.S. psychologist Henry Alexander Murray (1893–1988)]

exogenous *adj.* originating outside the body: referring, for example, to drugs (exogenous chemicals) or to phenomena, conditions, or disorders resulting from the influence of external factors (e.g., EXOGENOUS STRESS). Compare ENDOGENOUS. **—exogenously** *adv.*

exogenous depression see REACTIVE DEPRESSION.

exogenous stress stress arising from external situations, such as natural catastrophes, excessive competition at work, or climbing a precipitous mountain.

exopsychic *adj.* characterizing mental activity that purportedly produces effects outside the individual. Compare ENDOPSYCHIC.

exorcism *n.* the act or practice in which supposed evil spirits are expelled from a person believed to be possessed, or a place thought to be haunted, by means of certain rites, ceremonies, prayers, and incantations. It was formerly widely believed that such spirits were the major cause of mental disease and other disorders and that exorcism was therefore a suitable form of treatment. The Roman Catholic Church still makes use of ritual exorcism in certain very restricted circumstances. **—exorcise** *vb.* **—exorcist** *n.*

exotic psychosis see HYSTERICAL PSYCHOSIS.

expanded consciousness a purported sense that one's mind has been opened to a new kind of awareness or to new concepts, associated particularly with meditation or drug use. See also ALTERED STATE OF CONSCIOUSNESS.

expansive delusion a less common name for a DELUSION OF GRANDEUR.

expansive mood a mood that reflects feelings of GRANDIOSITY.

expansiveness *n.* a personality trait manifested by loquaciousness, overfriendliness, hyperactivity, and lack of restraint.

ex-patient club in psychiatry, an ongoing group organized by a former mental patient or by a hospital as part of its aftercare program. The objective is to provide social and recreational experience, to promote readjustment and rehabilitation, and to maintain improvement through group support and, in some cases, group therapy. See also MENTAL PATIENT ORGANIZATION.

expectancy *n.* the internal state resulting from experience with predictable relationships between stimuli or between responses and stimuli. This basic meaning becomes slightly more specific in some fields. For example, in cognitive psychology it refers to an attitude or MENTAL SET that determines the way in which a person approaches a situation, and in motivation theory it refers to an individual's belief that his or her actions can produce a particular outcome (e.g., attainment of a goal). **—expectant** *adj.*

expectant analysis the orthodox technique of psychoanalysis, in which the analyst awaits the gradual, free-floating unfolding of the patient's psyche. Compare FOCUSED ANALYSIS.

expected frequency **1.** a frequency predicted from a theoretical model and contrasted with an observed frequency. **2.** a frequency that would occur on the basis of chance alone.

expected value the mean value of a random variable or one of its functions as derived by mathematical calculation.

experience *n.* **1.** a conscious event: an event that is lived through, or undergone, as opposed to one that is imagined or thought about. **2.** the present contents of CONSCIOUSNESS. **—experiential** *adj.*

experiential family therapy a therapist who emphasizes intuition, feelings, and underlying processes in treating families and who deemphasizes theoretical frameworks. The work is often characterized by the use of the therapist's own feelings and self-disclosures in interactions with clients. Notable experiential family therapists have included U.S. psychiatrists Carl A. Whitaker (died 1995) and Virginia M. Satir (1916–1988).

experiential history the social, environmental, and behavioral components of an individual's background from birth to death.

experiential knowledge understanding and expertise that emerge from life experience, rather than from professional training. Members of SELF-HELP GROUPS draw upon experiential knowledge in supporting and helping each other.

experiential psychotherapy a broad family of psychotherapies originating in the 1950s and 1960s and falling under the umbrella of existential–humanistic psychology. A core belief of the approach is that true change occurs through the client's direct, active "experiencing" of what the client is undergoing and feeling at any given point in therapy, both on the surface and at a deeper level. Experiential therapists typically engage clients very directly with regard to accessing and expressing their inner feelings and experiencing both present and past life scenes, and they offer clients perspectives for integrating such experiences into realistic and healthy self-concepts. Experiential psychotherapy has its antecedents in the work of U.S. psychiatrists Carl A. Whitaker (1912–1995) and Thomas P. Malone (died 2000), U.S. psychologist Carl ROGERS, U.S. philosopher and psychologist Eugene T. Gendlin (1926–), and others.

experimental attrition see ATTRITION.

experimental control see CONTROL.

experimental group a group of participants in an experiment who are exposed to a particular manipulation of the INDEPENDENT VARIABLE (i.e., a particular TREATMENT LEVEL or, more briefly, a particular treatment). Compare CONTROL GROUP. The responses of the experimental group are compared to the responses of a CONTROL GROUP, other experimental groups, or both.

experimental hypothesis a premise that describes what a researcher in a scientific study hopes to demonstrate if certain experimental conditions are met.

experimental psychology the scientific study of behavior, motives, or cognition in a laboratory or other experimental setting in order to predict, explain, or control behavior or other psychological phenomena. Experimental psychology aims at establishing quantified relationships and explanatory theory through the analysis of responses under various controlled conditions and the synthesis of adequate theoretical accounts from the results of these observations.

experimental treatment 1. in research, the conditions applied to one or more groups that are expected to cause change in some outcomes. **2.** an intervention or regimen that has shown some promise as a cure or ameliorative for a disease or condition but is still being evaluated for efficacy, safety, and acceptability.

experimental variable an INDEPENDENT VARIABLE: a variable under investigation that is manipulated by the experimenter to determine its relationship to or influence upon some DEPENDENT VARIABLE.

experimenter bias any unintended errors in the experimental process or the interpretation of its results that are attributable to an experimenter's preconceived beliefs about results.

expert testimony evidence given in court by an EXPERT WITNESS. Unlike other testimony, this evidence may include the witness's opinions about certain facts in order to help the trier of fact to make a decision. See ULTIMATE OPINION TESTIMONY.

expert witness an individual who is qualified to testify regarding scientific, technical, or professional matters and provide an opinion concerning the evidence or facts presented in a court of law. Eligibility to testify as an expert witnesses is based on the person's special skills or knowledge as judged by the court. In U.S. federal courts, eligibility criteria are established by the Federal Rules of Evidence 702–706. Mental health professionals often serve as expert witnesses in such complex issues as insanity pleas and child custody cases. See DAUBERT TEST; DAUBERT V. MERRELL DOW PHARMACEUTICALS INC.

expiation *n.* atonement for wrongdoing that represents acknowledgment, relieves or reduces feelings of guilt, and moves toward righting the situation.

explanatory style an individual's unique style of describing and explaining some phenomenon, event, or personal history.

explicit attitude a relatively enduring and general evaluative response of which a person is consciously aware. Compare IMPLICIT ATTITUDE.

explicit behavior see OVERT BEHAVIOR.

explicit memory long-term memory that can be consciously recalled: general knowledge or information about personal experiences that an individual retrieves in response to a specific need or request to do so. This term, proposed in 1985 by Canadian psychologist Peter Graf and U.S. psychologist Daniel Schacter, is used interchangeably with DECLARATIVE MEMORY but typically with a performance-based orientation—that is, a person is aware that he or she possesses certain knowledge and specifically retrieves it to complete successfully a task overtly eliciting that knowledge (e.g., a multiple-choice exam). Compare IMPLICIT MEMORY.

explicit process 1. a cognitive event that can be described accurately and that is available to introspection, especially one that involves a defined meaning. **2.** an occasional synonym for CONSCIOUS PROCESS. Compare IMPLICIT PROCESS.

exploitative orientation in the existential psychoanalysis of Erich FROMM, a character pattern marked by the use of stealth, deceit, power, or violence to obtain what the individual wants. The character type is plagiaristic rather than spontaneously or resourcefully creative. Also called **exploitative character**. Compare HOARDING ORIENTATION; MARKETING ORIENTATION.

exploratory data analysis data analysis designed to generate new research questions or insights rather than to address specific preplanned research questions. Compare CONFIRMATORY DATA ANALYSIS.

explosive personality a personality with a pattern of frequent outbursts of uncontrolled anger and hostility out of proportion to any provocation. See INTERMITTENT EXPLOSIVE DISORDER.

ex post facto research research that uses existing data collected previously for another purpose or that is conducted following the occurrence of an event of interest. Ex post facto research does not permit the systematic manipulation of variables (i.e, is nonexperimental) but nonetheless is used to identify potential causal relationships. [from Latin *ex post facto*, "after the event"]

exposure therapy a form of BEHAVIOR THERAPY that is effective in treating anxiety disorders. Exposure therapy involves systematic confrontation with a feared stimulus, either in vivo (live) or in the imagination, and may encompass any of a number of behavioral interventions, including DESENSITIZATION, FLOODING, IMPLOSIVE THERAPY, and extinction-based techniques. It works by (a) HABITUATION, in which repeated exposure reduces anxiety over time by a process of EXTINCTION; (b) disconfirming fearful predictions; (c) deeper processing of the feared stimulus; and (d) increasing feelings of SELF-EFFICACY and mastery.

expressed emotion (**EE**) negative attitudes, in the form of criticism, hostility, and emotional overinvolvement, demonstrated by family members toward a person with a mental disorder. High levels of expressed emotion have been shown to be associated with poorer outcomes in mood, anxiety, and schizophrenic disorders and increased likelihood of relapse. [first described in a study (1972) by British psychiatrists George W. Brown, Jim L. T. Birley, and John K. Wing]

expression *n.* an external manifestation of an internal condition or characteristic. For example, **gene expression** is the process by which the instructions encoded in DNA are used to create observable products, such as proteins (and by extension demonstrable physical attributes, such as hair or eye color). The term, however, is most often used in reference to the communication of a thought, behavior, or emotion, as in EMOTIONAL EXPRESSION or FACIAL EXPRESSION.

expressive language disorder a developmental disorder characterized by impairment in acquiring the ability to use language effectively for communicating with others despite normal language comprehension. Manifestations include below-average vocabulary skills, difficulty producing complete sentences, and problems recalling words.

expressive therapy 1. a form of PSYCHOTHERAPY in which the client is encouraged to talk through his or her problems and to express feelings openly and without restraint. Compare SUPPRESSIVE THERAPY. **2.** any of a variety of therapies that rely on nonverbal methods (e.g., art, dance, movement) to facilitate change.

extended care a health care service provided at a residential facility where 24-hour nursing care and rehabilitation therapy are available, usually following an acute hospitalization. A facility that provides such a service is known as an **extended care facility** (**ECF**). See also CONTINUING CARE UNIT; CONVALESCENT CENTER; SKILLED NURSING FACILITY.

extended family 1. a family unit consisting of parents and children living in one household with certain other individuals united by kinship (e.g., grandparents, cousins). **2.** in modern Western societies, the NUCLEAR FAMILY together with various other relatives who live nearby and keep in regular touch.

extended-family therapy GROUP THERAPY involving not only the nuclear family but also other family members, such as aunts, uncles, grandparents, and cousins. See also FAMILY THERAPY.

extended-release preparation see SLOW-RELEASE PREPARATION.

extended-stay review a review of a continuous hospital stay that has equaled or exceeded the period defined by a hospital or third-party UTILIZATION REVIEW. See also CONTINUED-STAY REVIEW.

extended suicide MURDER–SUICIDE in which both the murder and the suicide reflect the suicidal process. The individual first kills those perceived as being a part of his or her identity or extended self and then commits suicide.

exteriorization *n.* **1.** the act of relating one's inner feelings and attitudes to external, objective reality. **2.** the outward expression of one's private and personal ideas.

external attribution see SITUATIONAL ATTRIBUTION.

external boundary in psychoanalytic theory, the boundary between the EGO and external reality, as opposed to the INTERNAL BOUNDARY between ego and ID. Also called **outer boundary**.

external control the belief that one's experiences and behavior are determined by circumstances, luck, other people, or other external factors. See EXTERNALIZERS; LOCUS OF CONTROL. Compare INTERNAL CONTROL.

externalization *n.* **1.** a DEFENSE MECHANISM in which one's thoughts, feelings, or perceptions are attributed to the external world and perceived as independent of oneself or one's own experiences. A common expression of this is PROJECTION. **2.** the process of learning to distinguish between the self and the environment during childhood. **3.** the process by which a drive, such as hunger, is aroused by external stimuli, such as food, rather than by internal stimuli.

externalizers *pl. n.* people who believe that their behavior and reactions to conditions or situations around them are determined largely or entirely by events beyond their control, that is, they have an external LOCUS OF CONTROL. Compare INTERNALIZERS.

externalizing behavior see EXTERNALIZING–INTERNALIZING.

externalizing–internalizing 1. a broad classification of children's behaviors and disorders based on their reactions to stressors. Externalizing behaviors and disorders are characterized primarily by actions in the external world, such as acting out, antisocial behavior, hostility, and aggression. Internalizing behaviors and disorders are characterized primarily by processes within the self, such as anxiety, SOMATIZATION, and depression. [proposed by U.S. psychologist Thomas M. Achenbach (1940–)] **2.** see EXTERNALIZATION; INTERNALIZATION.

external locus of control see LOCUS OF CONTROL.

external validity the extent to which the results of research or testing can be generalized beyond the sample that generated the results to other individuals or situations. For example, if research has been conducted only with male participants, it cannot be assumed that similar results will apply to female participants. The more specialized the sample, the less likely will it be that the results are highly generalizable.

extinction *n.* **1.** in PAVLOVIAN CONDITIONING: (a) a procedure in which pairing of stimulus events is discontinued, either by presenting the CONDITIONED STIMULUS alone or by presenting the conditioned stimulus and the UNCONDITIONED STIMULUS independently of one another; or (b) the result of this procedure, which is a gradual decline in the probability and magnitude of the CONDITIONED RESPONSE. **2.** in OPERANT CONDITIONING: (a) a procedure in which reinforcement is discontinued, that is, the reinforcing stimulus is no longer presented; or (b) the result of this procedure, which is a decline in the rate of the formerly reinforced response. **—extinguish** *vb.*

extirpation *n.* see ABLATION.

extraception *n.* an attitude of skepticism, objectivity, and adherence to the facts. [defined by U.S. psychologist Henry Alexander Murray (1893–1988)]

extrapsychic *adj.* pertaining to that which originates outside the mind or that which occurs between the mind and the environment. Compare INTRAPSYCHIC.

extrapsychic conflict CONFLICT arising between the individual and the environment, as contrasted with INTRAPSYCHIC CONFLICT.

extrapunitive *adj.* referring to the punishment of others: tending to direct anger, blame, or hostility away from the self toward the external factors, such as situations and other people, perceived to be the source of one's frustrations. Compare INTROPUNITIVE.

extrapyramidal dyskinesia any of various distortions of voluntary movement (DYSKINESIAS), such as tremors, spasms, tics, rigidity, or gait disturbances, associated with some lesion of the EXTRAPYRAMIDAL TRACT. These dyskinesias can occur in neurological disorders or as a side effect of antipsychotic drugs, which produce such conditions as AKATHISIA and TARDIVE DYSKINESIA.

extrapyramidal symptoms (**EPS**) a group of adverse drug reactions attributable to dysfunction of the EXTRAPYRAMIDAL TRACT of the central nervous system, such as rigidity of the limbs, tremor, and other Parkinson-like signs; dystonia (abnormal facial and body movements); and akathisia (restlessness). Extrapyramidal symptoms are among the most common side effects of the HIGH-POTENCY ANTIPSYCHOTICS and have also been reported with use of other drugs (e.g., SSRIS). Also called **extrapyramidal syndrome** (**EPS**).

extrapyramidal tract a motor portion of the central nervous system that includes the BASAL GANGLIA and some closely related structures (e.g., the SUBTHALAMIC NUCLEUS) and descending pathways to the midbrain. It regulates muscle tone and body posture and coordinates opposing sets of skeletal muscles and movement of their associated skeletal parts. Also called **extrapyramidal motor system**; **extrapyramidal system**.

extra-small acrocentric chromosome syndrome see CAT'S-EYE SYNDROME.

extra sum of squares principle a basic approach for model comparison in the GENERAL LINEAR MODEL in which the value of an additional parameter in the model is assessed in terms of the reduction in the SUM OF SQUARES error that its addition accomplishes.

extraterrestrial kidnapping see ALIEN ABDUCTION.

extrauterine pregnancy see ECTOPIC PREGNANCY.

extraversion (**extroversion**) *n.* one of the elements of the Big Five and FIVE-FACTOR PERSONALITY MODELS, characterized by an orientation of one's interests and energies toward the outer world of people and things rather than the inner world of subjective experience. Extraversion is a broad personality trait and, like INTROVERSION, exists on a continuum of attitudes and behaviors. Extroverts are relatively more outgoing, gregarious, sociable, and openly expressive. Extroversion is also one of the three personality dimensions, along with PSYCHOTICISM and NEUROTICISM, of EYSENCK'S TYPOLOGY. **—extraversive** *adj.* **—extraverted** *adj.* **—extravert** *n.*

extrinsic motivation an external incentive to engage in a specific activity, especially motivation arising from the expectation of punishment or reward (e.g., studying to avoid failing an examination). Compare INTRINSIC MOTIVATION.

extrinsic reward a reward for behavior that is not a natural consequence of that behavior. For example, winning a trophy for finishing first in a race and receiving praise or money in the work setting are extrinsic rewards. Compare INTRINSIC REWARD.

extroversion *n.* see EXTRAVERSION.

eye contact a direct look exchanged between two people who are interacting. Maintaining eye contact is considered essential to communication between therapist and client during face-to-face interviews. This communication behavior is used as a variable in some social-psychological studies to represent the degree of interpersonal intimacy. Social-psychological studies of eye contact generally find that people typically look more at the other person when listening to that person than when they themselves are talking, that they tend to avoid eye contact when they are embarrassed, that women are apt to maintain more eye contact than are men, and that the more intimate the relationship, the greater is the eye contact. Also called **mutual gaze**.

eyelash sign a reaction of eyelid movement to the stimulus of stroking the eyelashes. It can be used as part of a diagnostic test for LOSS OF CON-

SCIOUSNESS due to a functional or psychogenic disorder. If the loss of consciousness is due to a neurological disease or injury, the reflex will not occur.

eye-movement desensitization and reprocessing (**EMDR**) a treatment methodology used to reduce the emotional impact of trauma-based symptomatology associated with anxiety, nightmares, flashbacks, or intrusive thought processes. The therapy incorporates simultaneous visualization of the traumatic event while concentrating on the rapid lateral movements of a therapist's finger. [developed in the late 1980s by U.S. psychologist Francine Shapiro]

eye-roll sign a physiological index believed to show susceptibility to hypnosis. The participant is directed to roll his or her eyes upward as far as possible and at the same time lower the eyelids slowly. Hypnotizability or depth of hypnosis is believed to be a function of the amount of white sclera that becomes visible below the cornea.

eyewitness memory an individual's recollection of an event, often a crime or accident of some kind, that he or she personally saw or experienced. The reliability of eyewitness testimony is a major issue in FORENSIC PSYCHOLOGY.

Eysenck, Hans Jurgen (1916–1997) German-born British psychologist. An emigré from Germany because of his unwillingness to join the Nazi party, Eysenck earned his doctorate in psychology at University College, London, in 1940. He founded the Department of Psychology at the Institute of Psychiatry, Maudsley Hospital, University of London, where he remained throughout his career. He is best known for contributions to personality theory, popularizing the terms "introvert" and "extravert" (see EYSENCK'S TYPOLOGY), and developing a number of personality tests, such as the EYSENCK PERSONALITY INVENTORY. Eysenck was often controversial, most notably for his claim that patients undergoing Freudian psychoanalysis and other psychodynamic therapies were no more likely to improve than patients who had no therapy. He favored behavioral treatments for emotional and behavioral disorders. Eysenck also advocated the controversial view that racial differences in intelligence are genetically based, publishing *Race, Intelligence, and Education* in 1971; in later years, however, he acknowledged the mitigating influences of environment.

Eysenck Personality Inventory (**EPI**) a self-report personality test for use with adolescents and adults. It comprises 57 yes–no questions that are designed to measure two major personality dimensions of EYSENCK'S TYPOLOGY—introversion–extraversion and neuroticism—and includes a Lie scale intended to detect response distortion. It was a modification and replacement of the **Maudsley Personality Inventory** (**MPI**), a personality test containing 24 items measuring neuroticism and 24 measuring extraversion that was developed in 1959 by Hans EYSENCK while working at the Maudsley Hospital, London, England. The EPI has been revised and expanded since its initial publication in 1963 to become the **Eysenck Personality Questionnaire** (**EPQ**), the most recent version of which (the **EPQ–R**) includes 90 questions and measures the additional personality dimension of PSYCHOTICISM. [Hans Eysenck and British psychologist Sybil B. G. **Eysenck**]

Eysenck's typology a system for classifying personality types in which individual differences are described according to three dimensions: PSYCHOTICISM, EXTRAVERSION, and NEUROTICISM (referred to as **PEN**). Also called **PEN typology**. See also FACTOR THEORY OF PERSONALITY. [Hans EYSENCK]

Ff

fabrication *n.* **1.** the act of concocting or inventing a whole or part of a story, often with the intention to deceive. **2.** a story concocted in this way.

fabulation *n.* random speech that includes the recounting of imaginary incidents by a person who believes these incidents are real. See also DELUSION. [first described by Swiss-born U.S. psychiatrist Adolf Meyer (1866–1950)]

face-to-face group any group whose members are in personal contact and, as a result, are able to perceive each other's needs and responses and carry on direct interaction. Examples include T-GROUPS and psychotherapy groups. Also called **direct-contact group**.

face validity apparent validity: the extent to which the items or content of a test or other assessment instrument appear to be appropriate for measuring something, regardless of whether they really are.

facial disfigurement any distortion, malformation, or abnormality of the facial features due to injury, disease, or congenital anomaly. Because of a common tendency to assign traits to individuals on the basis of facial features, people with facial disfigurements are particularly vulnerable to social, psychological, and economic discrimination and unfavorable stress effects. See DISFIGUREMENT.

facial electromyography a technique for measuring the endogenous electrical activity of any muscle or muscle group in the face by the appropriate placement of electrodes (see ELECTROMYOGRAPHY). This procedure is usually carried out to detect implicit, invisible facial movements related to emotion or speech.

facial expression a form of nonverbal signaling using the movement of facial muscles. As well as being an integral part of communication, facial expression also reflects an individual's emotional state. British naturalist Charles Darwin (1809–1882) suggested that facial expressions are innate reactions that possess specific survival value; for example, a baby's smile evokes nurturing responses in parents. Although controversial, this theory has been supported by cross-cultural research and studies of blind children, which indicate that certain facial expressions are spontaneous and universally correlated with such primary emotions as surprise, fear, anger, sadness, and happiness. Physical conditions can produce characteristic facial expressions, such as the masklike countenance in parkinsonism, and the face can be a mirror of emotional disorder, as evidenced by the anguished look of those who are depressed.

facial feedback hypothesis the hypothesis that sensory information provided to the brain from facial muscle movements is a major determinant of intrapsychic feeling states, such as fear, anger, joy, contempt, and so on. This idea was introduced by British naturalist Charles Darwin (1809–1882) and developed by U.S. psychologists Sylvan S. Tomkins (1911–1991) and Carroll E. Izard (1923–).

facies *n.* FACIAL EXPRESSION, which is often considered to be a guide to an individual's emotions or state of health.

facilitated communication 1. communication that is made more effective or efficient (e.g., easier to understand or faster), often with the aid of a technological device or process. Examples include the captioning of TV broadcasts for the benefit of viewers with hearing loss (close-captioned television) and the use of speech synthesizers by people who are unable to talk. **2.** a controversial method of communication in which a person with a severe developmental disability (e.g., AUTISM) is assisted by a **facilitator** in typing letters, words, phrases, or sentences using a typewriter, computer keyboard, or alphabet facsimile. Facilitated communication involves a graduated manual prompting procedure, with the intent of supporting a person's hand sufficiently to make it more feasible to strike the keys he or she wishes to strike, without influencing the key selection. The procedure is often claimed to produce unexpected literacy, revealed through age-normative or superior communication content, syntax, and fluency. Scientific research findings, however, indicate that the content of the communication is being determined by the facilitator via nonconscious movements. [developed in the 1970s by Australian educator Rosemary Crossley (1945–)]

facilitation *n.* **1.** the strengthening or increased occurrence of a response resulting from environmental support for the response. See also SOCIAL FACILITATION. **2.** in neuroscience, the phenomenon in which the threshold for propagation of the action potential of a neuron is lowered due to repeated signals at a SYNAPSE or the summation of subthreshold impulses. **—facilitate** *vb.*

facilitator *n.* **1.** a professionally trained or lay member of a group who fulfills some or all of the functions of a group leader. The facilitator encourages discussion among all group members, without necessarily entering into the discussion. **2.** see FACILITATED COMMUNICATION.

FACM abbreviation for FUNCTIONAL ANALYTIC CAUSAL MODEL.

fact giver a person who assumes the role of providing information during a GROUP THERAPY discussion of a particular topic.

factitious disorder in *DSM–IV–TR*, any of a group of disorders in which the patient intentionally produces or feigns physical or psychological symptoms solely so that he or she may assume the SICK ROLE (compare MALINGERING). Four subtypes are recognized: **factitious disorder with predominantly psychological signs and symptoms** (e.g., depression, suicidal thoughts following the [unconfirmed] death of a spouse, hallucinations, delusions), in which the symptoms often become aggravated if the individual is aware of being observed and very often do not respond to treatment or follow traditional courses; **factitious disorder with predominantly physical signs and symptoms** (e.g., pain, vomiting, blackouts, seizures, infections), the most severe form of which is MUNCHAUSEN SYNDROME; **factitious disorder with combined psychological and physical signs and symptoms**; and FACTITIOUS DISORDER NOT OTHERWISE SPECIFIED.

factitious disorder by proxy see MUNCHAUSEN SYNDROME BY PROXY.

factitious disorder not otherwise specified in *DSM–IV–TR*, a FACTITIOUS DISORDER that does not meet the criteria for one of the four specific subtypes. An example is **factitious disorder by proxy** (commonly known as MUNCHAUSEN SYNDROME BY PROXY), in which a caretaker, very often a mother, will intentionally produce symptoms (usually physical) in the person being cared for, solely to play a role in the illness, its treatment, or both (i.e., to assume the sick role by proxy).

factor *n.* **1.** anything that contributes to a result or has a causal relationship to a phenomenon, event, or action. **2.** an underlying influence that accounts in part for variations in individual behavior. **3.** in ANALYSIS OF VARIANCE, an independent variable. **4.** in FACTOR ANALYSIS, an underlying, unobservable LATENT VARIABLE thought (together with other factors) to be responsible for the interrelations among a set of variables.

factor analysis a broad family of mathematical procedures for reducing a set of intercorrelations among MANIFEST VARIABLES to a smaller set of unobserved LATENT VARIABLES (factors). For example, a number of tests of mechanical ability might be intercorrelated to enable factor analysis to reduce them to a few factors, such as fine motor coordination, speed, and attention. This technique is often used to examine the common influences believed to give rise to a set of observed measures (measurement structure) or to reduce a larger set of measures to a smaller set of linear composites for use in subsequent analysis (data reduction).

factorial design an experimental design in which two or more independent variables are simultaneously manipulated or observed in order to study their joint and separate influences on a dependent variable. See also SIMPLE FACTORIAL DESIGN; TWO-BY-TWO FACTORIAL DESIGN; TWO-FACTOR DESIGN.

factor loading the correlation between a manifest variable and a latent variable (factor) in FACTOR ANALYSIS. The factor loading reflects the degree to which a manifest variable is said to be "made up of" the factor whose loading is being examined.

factor rotation in FACTOR ANALYSIS, the repositioning of factors (latent variables) to a new, more interpretable configuration by a set of mathematically specifiable TRANSFORMATIONS. Factor rotation is possible because for any one factor solution that fits the data to a specific degree there will exist an infinite number of equally good solutions, each represented by a different factor loading matrix. Rotations can be orthogonal (e.g., varimax, quarimax), in which the rotated factors are uncorrelated, or oblique, in which the rotated factors are correlated.

factor theory of personality an approach to the discovery and measurement of personality components through FACTOR ANALYSIS. The components are identified primarily by a statistical study of the differences between people as revealed by tests covering various aspects of behavior. The factor-analytic method is central to such personality models as the BIG FIVE PERSONALITY MODEL, CATTELL'S PERSONALITY TRAIT THEORY, and EYSENCK'S TYPOLOGY.

fact seeker a person who takes the role of seeking further information in relation to specific topics, for example, during a GROUP THERAPY discussion.

faculty *n.* **1.** in cognitive psychology, see COGNITIVE FACULTY. **2.** more generally, any intrinsic mental or physical power, such as reason, sight, or will. **3.** the body of the teaching, research, and administrative staff of an educational institution.

FAE abbreviation for fetal alcohol effects (see FETAL ALCOHOL SYNDROME).

failure to grow see FAILURE TO THRIVE.

failure to thrive (**FTT**) significantly inadequate gain in weight and height by an infant. It reflects a degree of growth failure due to inadequate release of growth hormone and, despite an initial focus on parental neglect and emotional deprivation, is currently believed to have multifactorial etiology, including biological, nutritional, and environmental contributors. The condition is associated with poor long-term developmental, growth, health, and socioemotional outcomes.

Fairbairnian theory the psychoanalytic approach of British psychoanalyst W. Ronald D. Fairbairn (1889–1964), which forms a part of OBJECT RELATIONS THEORY. Fairbairn saw personality structure developing in terms of object relationships, rather than in terms of Sigmund FREUD'S ID, EGO, and SUPEREGO. Fairbairn proposed the existence of an ego at birth, which then splits apart during the PARANOID-SCHIZOID POSITION to form the structures of personality. In response to frustrations and excitement experienced in the relationship with the mother, the ego is split into (a) the central ego, which corresponds to Freud's concept of the ego; (b) the libidinal ego, which corresponds to the id; and (c) the ANTILIBIDINAL EGO, which corresponds to the superego.

faith healing **1.** the treatment of physical or psychological illness by means of religious practices, such as PRAYER or "laying on of hands." Believers hold that this may be effective even when those being prayed for have no knowledge of the fact and no faith themselves. Also called **faith cure**; **religious healing**; **spiritual healing**. **2.** any form of unorthodox medical treatment whose efficacy is said to depend upon the patient's faith in the healer or the healing process (see PLACEBO EFFECT). In such cases any beneficial effects may be attributed to a psychosomatic process rather than a paranormal or supernatural one. See also MENTAL HEALING; PSYCHIC HEALING.

falling out a CULTURE-BOUND SYNDROME found in the United States and the Caribbean. Symptoms include sudden collapse, sometimes preceded by feelings of dizziness or "swimming" in the head. Although their eyes are usually open, patients claim to be unable to see; they usually hear and understand what is occurring around them but feel powerless to move. The condition may correspond to CONVERSION DISORDER or DISSOCIATIVE DISORDER. Also called **blacking out**.

false belief an internal cognitive representation that has no basis in reality.

false dementia a condition that mimics the symptoms of DEMENTIA but is a normal response to certain environmental conditions, such as sensory deprivation, restricted movement, or institutionalization with prolonged medication.

false memory a distorted recollection of an event or, most severely, recollection of an event that never happened at all. False memories are errors of commission, because details, facts, or events come to mind, often vividly, but the remembrances fail to correspond to prior events. Even when people are highly confident that they are remembering "the truth" of the original situation, experimental evidence shows that they can be wrong. For example, one quarter of adults in a particular experiment who were told an untrue story about being lost in a mall as a child—ostensibly obtained from their family members—adopted the belief, sometimes embellishing the reports with vivid sensory detail (e.g., the clothes that the rescuer was wearing). The phenomenon is of particular interest in legal cases, specifically those involving eyewitness memories and **false memory syndrome** (**FMS**), in which adults seem to recover memories of having been physically or sexually abused as children, with such recoveries often occurring during therapy. The label is controversial, as is the evidence for and against recovery of abuse memories; false memory syndrome is not an accepted diagnostic term, and some have suggested using the more neutral phrase RECOVERED MEMORY. Also called **illusory memory**; **paramnesia**; **pseudomemory**.

false negative a case that is incorrectly excluded from a group by the test used to determine inclusion. In diagnostics, for example, a false negative is an individual who, in reality, has a particular condition but whom the diagnostic instrument indicates does not have the condition.

false positive a case that is incorrectly included in a group by the test used to determine inclusion. In diagnostics, for example, a false positive is an individual who, in reality, does not have a particular condition but whom the diagnostic instrument indicates does have the condition.

false pregnancy see PSEUDOCYESIS.

false self in the OBJECT RELATIONS THEORY of British psychoanalyst Donald Winnicott (1896–1971), the self that develops as a defense against IMPINGEMENTS and in adaptation to the environment. This contrasts with the TRUE SELF, which develops in an environment that adapts to the infant and allows him or her to discover and express his or her true impulses.

familial factor an element or condition in a family, inherited or not, that accounts for a certain disease, disorder, or trait.

familial hormonal disorder a syndrome associated with mental deficiency, deafness, and ataxia. Urinary gonadotropins, estrogen, pregnandiol, and 17-ketosteroids are markedly reduced in the patients, who seldom exceed a mental age of 5 years. Development of genitalia is impaired, and female patients may never experience menstruation. The disease is believed to be hereditary. [first observed in 1919 by W. Koennicke]

familial microcephaly see MICROCEPHALY.

familial retardation see CULTURAL-FAMILIAL MENTAL RETARDATION.

familial study a study in which some measure or measures of an attribute or condition (e.g., a disorder, intelligence, suicidal behavior) among people of a known genetic relationship are correlated. The extent to which performance on a given measure varies as a function of genetic similarity is used as an indication of the HERITABILITY of that measure.

familial Turner syndrome see NOONAN'S SYNDROME.

familism *n.* a cultural value common in collectivist or traditional societies that emphasizes strong interpersonal relationships within the EXTENDED FAMILY together with interdependence, collaboration, and the placing of group interests ahead of individual interests. **—familistic** *adj.*

family *n.* a kinship unit consisting of a group of individuals united by blood or by marital, adoptive, or other intimate ties. Although the family is the fundamental social unit of most human societies, its form and structure vary widely. See BIOLOGICAL FAMILY; EXTENDED FAMILY; NUCLEAR FAMILY; PERMEABLE FAMILY; STEPFAMILY. **—familial** *adj.*

family constellation the total set of relationships within a particular family, as characterized by such factors as the number and birth order of members and their ages, roles, and patterns of interaction. The term is associated with Alfred ADLER.

family counseling counseling of parents or other family members by psychologists, social workers, licensed counselors, or other professionals, who provide information, emotional support, and practical guidance on problems faced in the family context, such as raising a child with visual or hearing impairment, adoption, public assistance, family planning, and substance abuse. See also GENETIC COUNSELING.

family group psychotherapy therapeutic methods that treat a family as a system rather than concentrating on individual family members. The various approaches include psychodynamic, behavioral, systemic, and structural, but all regard the interpersonal dynamics within the family as more important than individual intrapsychic factors. See also FAMILY THERAPY.

family interaction method a study technique for investigating family behavior by observing the interaction of its members in a controlled situation, such as a clinic or laboratory.

family mediation a structured process in which a neutral third party, typically an attorney or a mental health practitioner with training in negotiation, helps individuals or families to resolve conflicts and reach agreements in such areas as divorce and child custody.

family method in behavior genetics, the study of the frequency of a trait or disorder by determining its occurrence in relatives who share the same genetic background.

family of origin the family in which an individual was raised, which may or may not be his or her BIOLOGICAL FAMILY.

family pattern a characteristic quality of the relationship between the members of a particular family (e.g., between parents and children). Family patterns vary widely in emotional tone and in the attitudes of the members toward each other. Some families are warm, others cool; some are extremely close and symbiotic, in others the members keep each other at a distance; some are open to friends and relatives, others are not; in some, one or more children are accepted and loved, in others one or more children are distanced or otherwise rejected. Such patterns or elements of such patterns may range from unconscious to fully realized. See also PATHOGENIC FAMILY PATTERN.

family psychology a basic and applied specialty in psychology that focuses on interactions within the family and developmentally influential contexts (neighborhood, schools, etc.). Research and clinical intervention in this specialty are taught in doctoral psychology programs, either within a specified family curriculum or more often within broader programs, such as clinical research and applied clinical and counseling programs.

family romance a common childhood fantasy in which a child imagines that he or she is not the child of his or her biological parents but the offspring of a noble or royal personage. Sigmund FREUD saw this as rooted in the OEDIPUS COMPLEX. See FOSTER-CHILD FANTASY.

family sculpting a technique in FAMILY THERAPY in which the therapist asks one or more members of the family to physically arrange the other family members (and lastly themselves) in relation to one another in terms of posture, space, and attitude so as to portray the arranger's perception of the family, either in general or with regard to a particular situation or conflict. This technique often reveals family dynamics visually in a way that may not be adequately captured in verbal descriptions by family members.

family support services partial, periodic, or intermittent services provided to one or more family members of a person with a developmental disability for the purpose of enhancing their ability to care for the person or alleviating stress associated with family living. Examples include day and overnight respite (see RESPITE CARE), parent training, behavioral consultation, parent education, transportation to appointments, and sibling services (e.g., counseling).

family systems theory a broad conceptual model underlying various family therapies. Family systems theory focuses on the relationships between and among interacting individuals in the family and combines core concepts from GENERAL SYSTEMS THEORY, cybernetics, family development theory, OBJECT RELATIONS THEORY, and SOCIAL LEARNING THEORY. Family systems theory stresses that therapists cannot work only with individual family members to create constructive family changes but must see the whole family to effect systemic and lasting changes. Also called **Bowen family systems theory; family systems model**. [developed by U.S. psychiatrist Murray Bowen (1913–1990)]

family therapy a form of PSYCHOTHERAPY that

F

focuses on the improvement of interfamilial relationships and behavioral patterns of the family unit as a whole, as well as among individual members and groupings, or subsystems, within the family. Family therapy includes a large number of treatment forms with diverse conceptual principles, processes and structures, and clinical foci. Some family therapy approaches (e.g., OBJECT RELATIONS THEORY) reflect extensions of models of psychotherapy with individuals in the interpersonal realm, whereas others (e.g., STRUCTURAL FAMILY THERAPY) evolved in less traditional contexts. Most approaches emphasize contexts in which clinical problems arise. This accompanying systemic view potentially allows clinical attention to all levels of the organization of behavior, for example from individual unconscious and conscious dynamics, to the family, and to the community. Family therapy models vary enormously in terms of length, past versus present orientation, techniques used, and treatment goals. See also CONJOINT THERAPY; COUPLES THERAPY; FAMILY GROUP PSYCHOTHERAPY; FAMILY SYSTEMS THEORY.

Fanapt *n.* a trade name for ILOPERIDONE.

fanaticism *n.* excessive and often irrational zeal or devotion, for example, to a cause or a set of extreme beliefs. **—fanatic** *adj., n.*

fantasy *n.* **1.** any of a range of mental experiences and processes marked by vivid imagery, intensity of emotion, and relaxation or absence of logic. Fantasizing is normal and common and often serves a healthy purpose of releasing tension, giving pleasure and amusement, or stimulating creativity. It can also be indicative of pathology, as in delusional thinking or significant disconnection from reality. **2.** in psychoanalytic theories, a figment of the imagination: a mental image, night DREAM, or DAYDREAM in which a person's conscious or unconscious wishes and impulses are fulfilled (see WISH-FULFILLMENT). Followers of Melanie KLEIN use the spelling PHANTASY to denote specifically unconscious wishes. **—fantasize** *vb.*

fantasy play pretend or make-believe play that includes an as-if orientation to actions, objects, and peers. It often involves playing a distinct role, such as mother, teacher, or doctor. Fantasy play involves taking a stance that is different from reality and using a mental representation of a situation as part of an enactment. See also SYMBOLIC PLAY.

FAR abbreviation for FETUS AT RISK.

FAS abbreviation for FETAL ALCOHOL SYNDROME.

fascination *n.* **1.** profound interest in, attraction to, or enchantment with a person, object, activity, or phenomenon. **2.** in psychoanalytic theory, an infant's primitive attempt to master what is perceived (e.g., a light) by identifying with it. **—fascinate** *vb.*

fate neurosis in psychoanalytic theory, a compulsive, unconscious, and self-punitive need to arrange life experiences in such a way that failure and defeat are inevitable. Also called **destiny neurosis**.

father–daughter incest sexual relations between father and daughter, which is the most common form of INCEST.

father figure see FATHER SURROGATE.

father fixation in psychoanalytic theory, an abnormally strong emotional attachment to the father. See FIXATION.

father-ideal *n.* in psychoanalytic theory, the father component of the EGO-IDEAL, which is formed through identification with the parents.

father surrogate a substitute for a person's biological father, who performs typical paternal functions and serves as an object of identification and attachment. Father surrogates may include such individuals as adoptive fathers, stepfathers, older brothers, teachers, and others. Also called **father figure**; **surrogate father**.

fatigue *n.* **1.** a state of tiredness and diminished functioning. Fatigue is typically a normal, transient response to exertion, stress, boredom, or inadequate sleep but also may be unusually prolonged and indicative of disorder (e.g., chronic fatigue syndrome, anemia, hypothyroidism). **2.** reduced response of a receptor cell or sense organ resulting from excessive stimulation.

fatigue checklist a list of the symptoms of fatigue, including (a) an increased need to sleep, (b) trouble finding the energy to start new tasks, (c) poor endurance for completing a task that has been started, (d) difficulty in concentrating on any task, and (e) weakness or fatigability of muscles during physical effort.

fatigue effect a decline in performance on a prolonged or physically demanding research task that is generally attributed to the participant becoming tired or bored with the task.

fatigue studies research on factors that cause both mental and physical fatigue. Physiological and psychological studies are conducted in numerous and varied contexts, such as job stress, caregiving, chronic illness, and ergonomic design.

F distribution a theoretical PROBABILITY DISTRIBUTION widely used in the ANALYSIS OF VARIANCE and other statistical tests of hypotheses about population variances. It is the ratio of the variances of two independent random variables each divided by its DEGREES OF FREEDOM.

fear *n.* an intense emotion aroused by the detection of imminent threat, involving an immediate alarm reaction that mobilizes the organism by triggering a set of physiological changes. These include rapid heartbeat, redirection of blood flow away from the periphery toward the gut, tensing of the muscles, and a general mobilization of the organism to take action (see FEAR RESPONSE; FIGHT-OR-FLIGHT RESPONSE). According to some theorists, fear differs from ANXIETY in that it has an object (e.g., a predator, financial ruin) and is a proportionate response to the objective threat, whereas anxiety typically lacks an object or is a more intense response than is warranted by the perceived threat. See also FRIGHT.

feared self in analyses of self-concept, a mental representation of psychological attributes that one might possess in the future, in which thoughts about the acquisition of these attributes elicits a sense of anxiety or dread.

fearful attachment an adult attachment style characterized by a negative INTERNAL WORKING MODEL OF ATTACHMENT of oneself and of others. Individuals with fearful attachment doubt both their own and others' competence and efficacy and are presumed not to seek help from others when distressed. Compare DISMISSIVE ATTACHMENT; PREOCCUPIED ATTACHMENT; SECURE ATTACHMENT.

fear of commitment feelings of anxiety and uncertainty related to the decision to become bound to a course of action. Such feelings are commonly aroused by the decision to become emotionally or legally committed to a long-standing relationship with another person and often stem from problems with intimacy and attachment; in an extreme form, fear of commitment may lead to social maladjustment.

fear of darkness normal or pathological fear of darkness or night. Fear of darkness is associated with feelings of helplessness and a sense of unfamiliarity because things look different in the dark. The fear first occurs at about 3 years of age but may develop into a SPECIFIC PHOBIA in which darkness is associated with danger and threat (this phobia is also known variously as **achluophobia**, **nictiphobia**, **noctiphobia**, **nyctophobia**, and **scotophobia**, although these names are now seldom used).

fear of failure persistent and irrational anxiety about failing to measure up to the standards and goals set by oneself or others. This may include anxiety over academic standing, losing a job, sexual inadequacy, or loss of face and self-esteem. Fear of failure may be associated with PERFECTIONISM and is implicated in a number of psychological disorders, including some ANXIETY DISORDERS and EATING DISORDERS. A pathological fear of failure has been called **kakorrhaphiophobia**, but this name is now seldom used.

fear of flying a persistent and irrational fear of flying in an airplane or other airborne vehicle, also called **aviophobia** (although this name is now seldom used). In *DSM–IV–TR*, fear of flying is classified as a SPECIFIC PHOBIA, situational type.

fear of public speaking see SOCIAL PHOBIA.

fear of rejection a persistent and irrational fear of being socially excluded or ostracized, which is often a feature of SOCIAL PHOBIA.

fear of strangers see STRANGER ANXIETY.

fear of success a fear of accomplishing one's goals or succeeding in society, or a tendency to avoid doing so. Fear of success was originally thought to be experienced primarily by women, because striving for success was held to place a woman in conflict between a general need for achievement and social values that tell her not to achieve "too much." It is now thought that men and women are equally likely to experience fear of success. Also called **fear of success syndrome**; **Horner effect**. See also JONAH COMPLEX. [first proposed in 1969 by U.S. psychologist Matina Horner (1939–)]

fear response a response to a threat in which the threatened organism attempts to guard vulnerable vital organs and to protect the integrity of the self. In addition to these protective functions, the fear response is aimed at removing the person or animal from the threatening situation, either by overt withdrawal or by coping behaviors, such as shutting the eyes to avoid seeing the fear stimulus. Physiological responses vary depending on the situation and the proximity of the threat. See also FIGHT-OR-FLIGHT RESPONSE.

fear structure see EMOTIONAL PROCESSING THEORY.

Fear Survey Schedule (**FSS**) a questionnaire designed to measure fear, phobic behavior, and generalized anxiety. It is currently available in numerous versions, with the 72-item **FSS–III** being the most commonly used, particularly in SYSTEMATIC DESENSITIZATION. These items consist of fear- or anxiety-producing objects or situations, grouped into six classes (animal fears, social fears, etc.), to which participants respond on a scale from 0 ("Not at all") to 4 ("Very much") regarding their degree of discomfort. [originally published in 1964 by South African-born U.S. psychologist Joseph Wolpe (1915–1997) and U.S. clinical psychologist Peter J. Lang (1930–)]

feasibility standards criteria used to judge the practical, feasible, and cost-effective nature of any enterprise or project. For example, the feasibility of an evaluation research study is determined on the basis of its pragmatic implementation, its political viability among various stakeholders, and the cost of the resources necessary to carry out the research. See also ACCURACY STANDARDS; PROPRIETY STANDARDS; UTILITY STANDARDS.

feasibility test an investigation conducted prior to a study in order to establish properties of response measures and to determine the successfulness of the study's design. It is used to establish the validity of response measures, to provide early information on the probable level of effects, or to try out new methodologies. See also EVALUABILITY-ASSESSMENT DATA; FEASIBILITY STANDARDS.

feature abstraction a hypothetical process by which people learn from their experience with exemplars of different categories which features might be used to define membership in these categories.

febrile delirium DELIRIUM associated with or caused by fever.

fecal incontinence the involuntary passage of flatus and feces in inappropriate places (clothing, floor, etc.) resulting from loss of bowel control and due to an injury or organic condition. Also called **bowel incontinence**. Compare ENCOPRESIS.

feces *n.* waste matter expelled from the bowels. In psychoanalytic theory, a child's interest in feces is one of the earliest expressions of curiosity and withholding feces is one of the earliest expressions of the drive for aggression and independence. Also called **excrement**; **fecal matter**. See also ANAL-EXPULSIVE PHASE; ANAL-RETENTIVE PHASE; ANAL PERSONALITY; ANAL-SADISTIC PHASE; SPHINCTER CONTROL. **—fecal** *adj.*

fecundity *n.* **1.** in biology, a measure of the number of offspring produced by an individual organism over a given time. **2.** in demography, the general capacity of a human population to have offspring. A below-average capacity is termed **subfecundity**. **—fecund** *adj.*

Federation of Behavioral, Psychological, and Cognitive Sciences an association of scientific societies with interests in basic research on problems of behavior, psychology, language, education, and knowledge systems and their psychological, behavioral, and physiological bases. The federation was incorporated in 1980; its efforts focus on legislative and regulatory advocacy, education, and the communication of information to scientists.

feeblemindedness *n.* an obsolete name for MENTAL RETARDATION or LEARNING DISABILITY.

feedback *n.* information about a process or interaction provided to the governing system or agent and used to make adjustments that eliminate problems or otherwise optimize functioning. It may be stabilizing NEGATIVE FEEDBACK or amplifying POSITIVE FEEDBACK. The term's origins in engineering and cybernetics lend it a distinct connotation of input–output models that is not as strictly applicable to the wide variety of usages found in psychology, such as BIOFEEDBACK, INFORMATION FEEDBACK, and social feedback.

feedback evaluation see FORMATIVE EVALUATION.

feeding and eating disorders of infancy or early childhood in *DSM–IV–TR*, a category of disorders characterized by pathological feeding or eating behaviors that are usually first diagnosed in infancy, childhood, or adolescence. They include PICA, RUMINATION DISORDER, and FEEDING DISORDER OF INFANCY OR EARLY CHILDHOOD.

feeding disorder of infancy or early childhood in *DSM–IV–TR*, a disorder with an onset before the age of 6 (but typically within the 1st year following birth) characterized by persistent failure to eat adequately that results in significant failure to gain weight or significant loss of weight over a period of 1 month or more. There is no apparent cause.

feeding problem a form of behavior disorder in children that is characterized by refusal to eat, persistent failure to eat adequate amounts or types of food, or failure to hold down the food ingested. It is not due to a gastrointestinal or other medical condition or lack of available food, and it is not an EATING DISORDER. Also called **feeding disturbance**. See also RUMINATION DISORDER.

fee-for-service *adj.* denoting the traditional method of payment for health care services, in which physicians or other providers set their own fees for services, and patients or insurance companies pay all or a percentage of these charges. This is the system of reimbursement used by indemnity insurance plans.

feeling *n.* **1.** a self-contained phenomenal experience. Feelings are subjective, evaluative, and independent of the sensory modality of the sensations, thoughts, or images evoking them. They are inevitably evaluated as pleasant or unpleasant but they can have more specific intrapsychic qualities, so that, for example, the AFFECTIVE TONE of fear is experienced as different from that of anger. The core characteristic that differentiates feelings from cognitive, sensory, or perceptual intrapsychic experiences is the link of AFFECT to APPRAISAL. Feelings differ from EMOTIONS in being purely mental, whereas emotions are designed to engage with the world. **2.** any experienced sensation, particularly a tactile or temperature sensation (e.g., pain or coldness).

feeling of unreality see DEPERSONALIZATION.

feeling tone see AFFECTIVE TONE.

feeling type in Carl JUNG'S ANALYTIC PSYCHOLOGY, a FUNCTIONAL TYPE characterized by a dominance of feeling or affects. Feeling types evaluate their experiences and the world in terms of how these make them feel. The feeling type is one of Jung's two RATIONAL TYPES, the other being the THINKING TYPE. See also INTUITIVE TYPE; SENSATION TYPE.

felbamate *n.* an ANTICONVULSANT drug, structurally related to MEPROBAMATE, that is thought to work by both enhancing the effects of the inhibitory neurotransmitter GAMMA-AMINOBUTYRIC ACID (see GABA AGONISTS) and inhibiting the effects of the excitatory amino acid GLUTAMATE (see NMDA RECEPTOR). Due to the increased incidence of aplastic anemia and hepatitis associated with this drug, it is less commonly used than other anticonvulsants; it is generally reserved for patients with severe epilepsy who respond inadequately to other treatments. U.S. trade name: **Felbatol**.

Feldenkrais method a process of body movements that are designed to enhance psychological functioning. The method is used by certified practitioners and may be interpreted in numerous ways, but always involves a dynamic interaction between bodily movements and psychological awareness. [Moshe **Feldenkrais** (1904–1984), physicist and engineer]

fellatio *n.* the use of the mouth in sexual stimulation of the penis. Also called **fellation**; **oral coitus**; **penilingus**. See also OROGENITAL ACTIVITY. **—fellate** *vb.*

felt need a consciously experienced need that may relate to a sense of deprivation or a discrepancy with an affective ideal.

felt sense in FOCUSING therapy, the subjective qualities of the contents of CONSCIOUSNESS. See FRINGE CONSCIOUSNESS. [defined by Austrian-born U.S. psychologist Eugene T. Gendlin (1926–)]

female circumcision see FEMALE GENITAL MUTILATION.

female genital mutilation (**FGM**) any nontherapeutic procedure performed to modify or remove any part of the external genitalia of prepubertal or adolescent girls. It is a traditional practice in certain countries, with the highest prevalence in Africa, and variously associated with cultural norms of femininity, chastity, and religious observance. Female genital mutilation takes one of four forms: excision of the clitoral hood only; excision of the entire clitoris (CLITORIDECTOMY) and often the labia minora; excision of the clitoris, labia minora, and most of the labia majora, and the sewing together of the remaining tissue, leaving only a small vaginal opening (INFIBULATION); and any other injurious procedure, such as incising or burning of the clitoris, cutting of the vagina, and insertion of substances to cause vaginal bleeding. Female genital mutilation is sometimes called **female** (or **clitoral**) **circumcision** and—more recently—**female genital cutting** (**FGC**), terms that downplay its potential adverse medical, psychological, and sexual consequences. These may include (but are not limited to) severe pain, excessive bleeding, infection, gynecological and obstetrical complications, disordered sleeping and eating habits, mood changes, impaired cognition (e.g., poor concentration and difficulty learning), reduced sexual sensitivity, less frequent orgasm, and decreased enjoyment of sexual intercourse.

femaleness *n.* the quality of being female in the anatomical and physiological sense by virtue of possessing the female complement of a pair of X CHROMOSOMES. Compare FEMININITY.

female orgasmic disorder in *DSM–IV–TR*, a condition in which a woman recurrently or persistently has difficulty obtaining orgasm or is unable to reach orgasm at all following sexual stimulation and excitement, causing marked distress or interpersonal difficulty. Female orgasmic disorder is the second most frequently reported women's sexual problem. Cognitive behavior therapy has been shown to be an effective treatment and involves promoting attitude and sexually relevant thought changes and anxiety reduction using such exercises as directed masturbation, sensate focus, and systematic desensitization.

female sexual arousal disorder in *DSM–IV–TR*, a condition in which a woman recurrently or persistently is unable to attain or maintain adequate vaginal lubrication and swelling during sexual excitement, causing marked distress or interpersonal difficulty. It is a prevalent sexual problem for women and has a complex etiology involving a variety of physiological and psychological factors.

femininity *n.* possession of social-role behaviors that are presumed to be characteristic of a girl or woman, as contrasted with FEMALENESS, which is genetically determined. **—feminine** *adj.*

femininity complex in psychoanalytic theory, a man's envy of women's procreative powers that has its roots in the young boy's envy of the mother's body. Some psychoanalysts see the femininity complex as the male counterpart to the female CASTRATION COMPLEX and PENIS ENVY. [first used in 1930 by German psychoanalyst Felix Boehm (1881–1958)]

femininity phase in the OBJECT RELATIONS THEORY of Melanie KLEIN, a period during the early phases of the OEDIPUS COMPLEX in which both boys and girls are posited to adopt a feminine attitude toward the father and desire a child by him. Klein saw this as turning to the father as an object of desire and away from the mother as the child's first object.

feminist family therapy an intervention model, informed by FEMINIST THERAPY, used by therapists to reorganize the family so that no one is entrapped in dysfunctional roles or patterns of interaction that are based on the politics of power, particularly with regard to patriarchal roles.

feminist psychology an approach to psychological issues that emphasizes the role of the female perspective in thought, action, and emotion in the life of the individual and in society. It is seen by its proponents as an attempt to counterbalance traditional male-oriented and male-dominated psychology, as well as a model for similar approaches for other less represented groups. See also ENGENDERING PSYCHOLOGY; WOMAN-CENTERED PSYCHOLOGY.

feminist therapy an eclectic approach to psychotherapy based conceptually in feminist political analyses and feminist scholarship on the psychology of women and gender. In this orientation, the ways in which gender and gendered experiences inform people's understanding of their lives and the development of the distress that serves as a catalyst for seeking therapy are central. Race, class, sexual orientation, age cohort, and ability, as they interact with gender, are explored. Feminist therapy attempts to create an egalitarian therapy relationship in which intentional efforts are made by the therapist to empower the client and define the client as an authority equal in value to the therapist. Feminist therapy can be indicated for both female and male clients.

feminization *n.* the process of acquiring FEMININITY, regardless of the sex of the individual. —**feminize** *vb.*

fenfluramine *n.* a sympathomimetic agent, structurally related to the AMPHETAMINES, that functions as a SEROTONIN-RECEPTOR AGONIST and was formerly used for management of obesity (see APPETITE SUPPRESSANT). It was withdrawn from the U.S. market in 1997 due to the incidence of heart-valve abnormalities associated with its use.

fentanyl *n.* a highly potent OPIOID ANALGESIC that is used for anesthesia during surgery, for the management of severe cancer pain in patients resistant to other opioids, and (as a lozenge or sucker) for the relief of severe anxiety in children prior to surgical procedures. Its toxicity is similar to that of other opioids, with respiratory and circulatory depression predominating. It is known as **China white** in illicit use. Analogs of fentanyl in current use include SUFENTANIL, **alfentanil** (U.S. trade name: **Alfenta**), and **remifentanil** (U.S. trade name: **Ultiva**). U.S. trade names: **Sublimaze** (injectable form); **Actiq** and **Oralet** (oral forms); **Duragesic** (transdermal form, i.e., applied to the skin).

fertility *n.* **1.** in biology, the potential of an individual to have offspring. Although most frequently applied to females, it may also refer to reproductive capacity in males. **2.** in demography, the number of live children born to an individual or a population. Compare FECUNDITY.

fertilization *n.* the fusion of a sperm and an egg cell to produce a ZYGOTE.

Festinger, Leon (1919–1989) U.S. psychologist. Festinger earned his doctorate at the University of Iowa under Kurt LEWIN in 1942. He was hired as a statistician for the remainder of World War II and was involved in the training and selection of Air Force pilots. After the war he held brief appointments at the Massachusetts Institute of Technology, the University of Michigan, and the University of Minnesota before settling at Stanford University in 1955 for 13 years; he completed his career at the New School for Social Research in New York City. Festinger's research interests in social psychology included such phenomena as group COHESION, CONFORMITY, and SOCIAL COMPARISON THEORY. He is best known, however, for his series of experiments that tested his COGNITIVE DISSONANCE THEORY. Festinger argued that DISSONANCE REDUCTION was capable of explaining phenomena that traditional behaviorist theories of reinforcement could not, such as why low or infrequent rewards could result in persistent behavior. His most influential writings include his books, *A Theory of Cognitive Dissonance* (1957) and *Conflict, Decision, and Dissonance* (1964). Festinger was elected to the National Academy of Sciences and the American Academy of Arts and Sciences and received the Distinguished Scientific Contribution Award of the American Psychological Association in 1959.

fetal alcohol syndrome (**FAS**) a group of adverse fetal and infant health effects associated with heavy maternal alcohol intake during pregnancy. It is characterized by low birth weight and retarded growth, craniofacial anomalies (e.g., microcephaly), neurobehavioral problems (e.g., hyperactivity), and cognitive abnormalities (e.g., language acquisition deficits); mental retardation may be present. Children showing some (but not all) features of this syndrome are described as having **fetal alcohol effects** (**FAE**).

fetal distress the condition of a fetus during late pregnancy or labor whose life or health is threatened, most commonly by an inadequate supply of oxygen via the placenta. Signs of fetal distress include abnormal heart rate, elevated blood acidity, and absence of movement. This term has been criticized as imprecise and nonspecific, and the alternative **nonreassuring fetal status** (**NRFS**) is recommended by many instead.

fetal hypoxia a significant reduction in oxygen to the human fetus, which is believed to be a risk factor for severe mental illness, such as schizophrenia. See also HYPOXIA.

fetal–maternal exchange the exchange of substances between mother and fetus, via the placenta, during gestation. The fetus is thereby supplied with nutrients and oxygen, and its waste products (e.g., carbon dioxide, urea) are eliminated. Substances of low molecular weight cross the placental barrier easily, but large molecules (e.g., proteins) do not, therefore the fetus manufactures its own proteins from amino acids supplied by the mother. Some drugs (e.g., alcohol, opioids) as well as disease agents (e.g., the rubella virus) may cross the placental barrier and produce congenital defects.

fetal response a response of a fetus to environmental conditions. For example, there is an increase in the fetal heart rate when the mother smokes, and some investigators claim that there is an increase in activity when the mother is undergoing severe emotional stress. See PRENATAL INFLUENCE.

fetish *n.* **1.** a material object (e.g., a shoe, an undergarment) or nonsexual part of the body (e.g., a foot, lock of hair) that arouses sexual interest or excitement. **2.** any object, idea, or behavior that is the focus of irrational devotion or abnormally excessive attention, for example, punctuality or the pursuit of wealth. **3.** in anthropology, an object, such as a talisman or amulet, that is believed to embody a supernatural spirit or exert magical force.

fetishism *n.* a type of PARAPHILIA in which inanimate objects—commonly undergarments, stockings, rubber items, shoes, or boots—are repeatedly or exclusively used in achieving sexual excitement. Objects designed for use in stimulating the genitals (e.g., vibrators) are not considered to be involved in fetishism. Fetishism occurs primarily among males and may compete or interfere with sexual contact with a partner. See also PARTIALISM. —**fetishistic** *adj.*

fetus *n.* an animal embryo in the later stages of development. In humans, the fetal period is from the end of the eighth week after fertilization until birth. —**fetal** *adj.*

fetus at risk (**FAR**) a fetus that has a significant risk of being born with a mental or physical disorder because of known influences from the parents or other family members (e.g., a mother with diabetes or hypertension). The risk of a mental disorder in a child born into a family with no history of mental disorder is relatively small, but the risk may be as much as 50% in certain cases, for example, if the disorder is a SEX-LINKED recessive trait inherited from the mother's side of the family and the parents are related. See also FETAL DISTRESS.

FFM abbreviation for FIVE-FACTOR PERSONALITY MODEL.

FGM abbreviation for FEMALE GENITAL MUTILATION.

fibromyalgia syndrome a syndrome of uncertain origin that is characterized by widespread musculoskeletal pain and chronic fatigue. Pain may be triggered by pressure on numerous tender points on the body. Other commonly associated symptoms are muscle stiffness, headaches, sleep disturbance, and depression. Symptoms overlap with those of CHRONIC FATIGUE SYNDROME, and fibromyalgia syndrome often occurs simultaneously with other disorders, such as IRRITABLE BOWEL SYNDROME and migraine. The condition was formerly called **fibromyositis–fibromyalgia syndrome**. See also CHRONIC MYOFASCIAL PAIN.

fiction *n.* **1.** in psychology, an unproven or imaginary concept that may be accepted by an individual as if it were true for pragmatic reasons. See AS-IF HYPOTHESIS. **2.** see GUIDING FICTION. —**fictional** *adj.*

fictional finalism in the psychoanalytic theory of Alfred ADLER, the belief that human beings are more strongly motivated by the goals and ideals—realizable or unattainable—that they create for themselves and more influenced by future possibilities than by past events such as childhood experiences. This is in strong contrast to the emphasis of classical Freudian psychoanalytic theory. See also GUIDING FICTION; INDIVIDUAL PSYCHOLOGY.

fidelity *n.* **1.** faithfulness to a person, group, belief, or the like. **2.** the degree of accuracy of a measuring instrument. **3.** the degree of accuracy of sound or visual reproduction in an electronic device (e.g., a sound system or television).

fidgetiness *n.* a state of increased motor activity, which is associated with anxiety, tics, chorea, or boredom.

field dependence a COGNITIVE STYLE in which the individual consistently relies more on external referents (environmental cues) than on internal referents (bodily sensation cues). The opposite tendency, relying more on internal than external referents, is called FIELD INDEPENDENCE. Discovered during experiments conducted in the 1950s to understand the factors that determine perception of the upright in space, field dependence–independence typically is measured using the ROD-AND-FRAME TEST.

field independence a COGNITIVE STYLE in which the individual consistently relies more on internal referents (body sensation cues) than on external referents (environmental cues). Field-independent people tend to be able to disregard deceptive environmental cues, particularly in tasks requiring the performance of simple actions or the identification of familiar elements in unfamiliar contexts. Compare FIELD DEPENDENCE.

field of consciousness the total awareness of an individual at a given time. See CONSCIOUSNESS.

field properties the environmental factors that surround and influence a living organism.

field research studies conducted outside the laboratory, in a "real-world" setting, which typically involve observing or interacting with participants in their typical environments over an extended period of time. Field research has the advantages of ecological validity, the opportunity to understand how and why behavior occurs in a natural social environment; it has the disadvantages of loss of environmental control and ability to do precise experimental manipulations. Thus, field research is often said to have more EXTERNAL VALIDITY and less INTERNAL VALIDITY than laboratory-based research.

field theory in psychology, a systematic approach describing behavior in terms of patterns of dynamic interrelationships between individuals and the psychological, social, and physical situation in which they exist. This situation is known as the **field space** or LIFE SPACE, and the dynamic interactions are conceived as forces with positive or negative VALENCES. [proposed by Kurt LEWIN]

field theory of personality a theory in which personality is understood in terms of dynamic interrelations among a field of intrapsychic forces. See FIELD THEORY. [devised by Kurt LEWIN]

field work 1. a less common name for FIELD RESEARCH. **2.** in clinical practice education, a practicum in which the student supplements and applies classroom theory by taking responsibility for actual cases under the tutelage of experienced, qualified supervisors.

fight-or-flight response a pattern of physiological changes elicited by activity of the SYMPATHETIC NERVOUS SYSTEM in response to threatening or otherwise stressful situations that leads to mobilization of energy for physical activity (e.g., attacking or avoiding the offending stimulus), either directly or by inhibiting physiological activity that does not contribute to energy mobilization. Specific sympathetic responses involved in the reaction include increased heart rate, respiratory rate, and sweat gland activity; elevated blood pressure; decreased digestive activity; pupil dilation; and a routing of blood flow to skeletal muscles. In the EMERGENCY THEORY OF EMOTIONS, such changes are the basis of all human emotions. Also called **emergency reaction**; **emergency syndrome**. [first described by U.S. physiologist Walter B. Cannon (1871–1945)]

F

figure-drawing test any test in which the participant draws a human figure, used as a measure of intellectual development or as a projective technique. See MACHOVER DRAW-A-PERSON TEST.

filial anxiety fear and apprehension in children caused by their relationships with their parents, often in anticipation of caregiving responsibility by adult children of older parents.

filicide *n.* the intentional killing of one's children, a very rare event that is sometimes thought to be caused by severe MAJOR DEPRESSIVE DISORDER.

final free recall an unexpected test of memory given at the end of a memory assessment session, asking the individual to recall all of the materials that were studied and tested in the session.

finasteride *n.* see ANTIANDROGEN.

fine motor describing activities or skills that require coordination of small muscles to control small, precise movements, particularly in the hands and face. Examples of **fine motor skills** include handwriting, drawing, cutting, and manipulating small objects. Compare GROSS MOTOR.

Finger Localization Test a 60-item NEUROPSYCHOLOGICAL TEST consisting of three parts: (1) The participant is asked to identify which finger is touched by the examiner; (2) the participant is blindfolded or otherwise prevented from using vision and then asked to identify which finger is touched; and (3) the participant again is blindfolded or otherwise prevented from using vision and then asked to identify which two fingers are simultaneously touched. Each hand is tested in each part of the test, which is scored for the number of correct identifications and currently appears in a variety of forms and as part of several neuropsychological test batteries. Also called **Tactile Finger Recognition**. [originally developed in 1983 by U.S. neuropsychologist Arthur Lester Benton (1909–2006) and colleagues]

Finger Tapping Test a measure of fine motor speed in which the individual taps an index finger as quickly as possible against a response key. The test is part of the HALSTEAD–REITAN NEUROPSYCHOLOGICAL BATTERY. It was originally called the **Finger Oscillation Test**.

fire-setting behavior a tendency to set fires. Compare PYROMANIA.

FIRO theory acronym for FUNDAMENTAL INTERPERSONAL RELATIONS ORIENTATION THEORY.

first admission a patient admitted for the first time to a mental institution.

first-episode schizophrenia the first time that the criteria for a diagnosis of SCHIZOPHRENIA are met in an individual, a situation that poses a number of specific treatment challenges that the practitioner must address, such as denial and grief in the patient and his or her family. It is helpful to study specific impairments, underlying neurological deficits, and course of treatment response in such patients, since there is hypothetically no confounding of results due to previous administration of antipsychotic drugs.

first-generation antipsychotic see ANTIPSYCHOTIC.

first-impression bias see PRIMACY EFFECT.

first-line medication a drug that is the first choice for treating a particular condition because it is considered a very effective treatment for that condition with the least likelihood of causing side effects. A first-line medication may be a class of drugs (e.g., SSRIS for depression) as well as a single drug.

first-order factor in FACTOR ANALYSIS, any of the factors that are derived from the correlation (or covariance) among the MANIFEST VARIABLES, as opposed to SECOND-ORDER FACTORS, which are determined from the correlation (or covariance) among the factors.

first-person perspective the point of view of the subjective observer. Compare SECOND-PERSON PERSPECTIVE; THIRD-PERSON PERSPECTIVE.

first-rank symptoms symptoms originally proposed by German psychiatrist Kurt Schneider (1887–1967) for the differential diagnosis of schizophrenia. They are audible thoughts; hearing voices arguing or commenting on one's actions; thought withdrawal, diffusion, and other disturbances; delusional perceptions; somatic passivity (experiencing external forces as influencing or controlling one's body); and other external impositions on feelings, inputs, and actions. It is now known that these symptoms can also occur in other psychotic disorders, in mood disorders, and in neurological disorders.

fishbowl technique a procedure used in a GROWTH GROUP in which participants form two concentric circles. The individuals in the inner group engage in a discussion or other form of interaction while the members of the outer group observe. When the interaction has concluded, the outer group provides information and feedback to the inner group. Later, the groups may exchange places and repeat the exercise.

Fisher's r to Z transformation a mathematical transformation of the PRODUCT–MOMENT CORRELATION coefficient (r) to a new statistic (Z)

whose sampling distribution is the normal distribution. It is used for testing hypotheses about correlations and constructing CONFIDENCE INTERVALS on correlations. [Sir Ronald Aylmer **Fisher** (1890–1962), British statistician and geneticist]

fissure *n.* a cleft, groove, or indentation in a surface, especially any of the deep grooves in the cerebral cortex.

fit 1. *n.* the degree to which values predicted by a model correspond with empirically observed values. **2.** *n.* a lay term for an epileptic SEIZURE. **3.** *n.* a colloquial name for an emotional outburst. **4.** *adj.* see FITNESS.

fitness *n.* **1.** a set of attributes that people have or are able to achieve relating to their ability to perform physical work and to carry out daily tasks with vigor and alertness, without undue fatigue, and with ample energy to enjoy leisure pursuits. **2.** in biology, the extent to which an organism or population is able to produce viable offspring in a given environment, which is a measure of that organism's or population's adaptation to that environment. **—fit** *adj.*

fitness for duty evaluation (**FFDE**) a psychological assessment of an employee's present mental state and functioning to estimate the employee's future functioning and determine whether that individual is able to safely and effectively perform his or her job duties. An FFDE is also used to determine if mental illness or emotional stress experienced by a person has interfered with his or her job performance. It is routinely conducted on police officers after they have had a traumatic experience in the line of duty. Also called **fit for duty evaluation**.

fitness for trial see COMPETENCY TO STAND TRIAL.

five-factor personality model (**FFM**) a model of personality in which five dimensions of individual difference—EXTRAVERSION, NEUROTICISM, CONSCIENTIOUSNESS, AGREEABLENESS, and OPENNESS TO EXPERIENCE—are viewed as core personality structures. Unlike the BIG FIVE PERSONALITY MODEL, which views the five personality dimensions as descriptions of behavior and treats the five-dimensional structure as a taxonomy of individual differences, the FFM also views the factors as psychological entities with causal force. The two models are frequently and incorrectly conflated in the scientific literature, without regard for their distinctly different emphases. [proposed by U.S. psychologists Robert R. McCrae (1949–) and Paul T. Costa, Jr. (1942–)]

fixation *n.* **1.** an obsessive preoccupation with a single idea, impulse, or aim, as in an IDÉE FIXE. **2.** in psychoanalytic theory, the persistence of an early psychosexual stage (see PSYCHOSEXUAL DEVELOPMENT) or inappropriate attachment to an early psychosexual object or mode of gratification, such as anal or oral activity. **—fixate** *vb.*

fixed belief see IDÉE FIXE.

fixed-effects model a statistical procedure for analyzing data from experimental designs that use FIXED FACTORS, independent variables whose levels are specifically selected by the researcher for study rather than randomly chosen from a wide range of possible values. For example, a researcher may wish to investigate the effects of the available dosages of a certain drug on symptom alleviation. Fixed-effects models generally are intended to make inferences solely about the specific levels of the independent variables actually used in the experiment. See also MIXED-EFFECTS MODEL.

fixed factor a factor (INDEPENDENT VARIABLE) in an experimental design whose levels are specified by the researcher rather than randomly generated within some range of permissible values. As a rule, one should not generalize results of studies of this type beyond the specific levels of the factors used in the experiment.

fixed idea see IDÉE FIXE.

fixed model see FIXED-EFFECTS MODEL; FIXED FACTOR.

flagellation *n.* whipping another person or oneself or submitting to whipping. Flagellation may be a form of penitence (as a religious ritual) or a means of achieving sexual excitement. Flagellation is a common practice among those who engage in BONDAGE AND DISCIPLINE. Also called **flagellantism**.

flashback *n.* **1.** the reliving of a traumatic event after the initial adjustment to the trauma appears to have been made. Flashbacks are part of POSTTRAUMATIC STRESS DISORDER: Forgotten memories are reawakened by words, sounds, smells, or scenes that are reminiscent of the original trauma (e.g., when a backfiring car elicits the kind of anxiety that a combat veteran experienced when he or she was the target of enemy fire). **2.** the spontaneous recurrence of the perceptual distortions and disorientation to time and place experienced during a previous period of hallucinogen intoxication. Flashbacks may occur months or even years after the last use of the drug and are associated particularly with LSD.

flashbulb memory a vivid, enduring memory associated with a personally significant and emotional event. Such memories have the quality of a photograph taken the moment the individual experienced the emotion, including such details as where the individual was or what he or she was doing. [first described in 1977 by U.S. psychologists Roger BROWN and James Kulick (1940–) in their study of people's recollection of public events, such as U.S. President John F. Kennedy's assassination]

flat affect total or near absence of appropriate emotional responses to situations and events. See also SHALLOW AFFECT.

Flexeril *n.* a trade name for CYCLOBENZAPRINE.

flexibilitas cerea see CATALEPSY.

flight from reality a defensive reaction involving withdrawal into inactivity, detachment, or fantasy as an unconscious defense against anxiety-provoking situations. This may be expressed as a number of defensive behaviors, such as RATIONALIZATION, daydreaming, or substance abuse. It may include a retreat into psychotic behavior as a means of avoiding real or imagined problems. Also called **retreat from reality**. See also ESCAPE FROM REALITY. Compare FLIGHT INTO FANTASY; FLIGHT INTO REALITY.

flight into disease see FLIGHT INTO ILLNESS.

F

flight into fantasy a defensive reaction in which individuals experiencing disturbing thoughts and impulses retreat into fantasy (e.g., through DAYDREAMS) as a means of avoiding harming themselves or others by acting on these impulses. In this way they can maintain control over their impulses. Compare FLIGHT FROM REALITY; FLIGHT INTO REALITY.

flight into health in psychotherapy, an abrupt "recuperation" by a prospective client after or during intake interviews and before entry into therapy proper or, more commonly, by a client in ongoing therapy in order to avoid further confrontation with cognitive, emotional, or behavioral problems. Psychoanalytic theory interprets the flight into health as an unconscious DEFENSE MECHANISM. Also called **transference cure**; **transference remission**.

flight into illness 1. a tendency to focus on or exaggerate minor physical complaints as an unconscious means of avoiding stressful situations and feelings. **2.** in psychotherapy, the sudden development of neurotic or physical symptoms by a client or prospective client. Psychoanalytic theory interprets this as an unconscious DEFENSE MECHANISM that is used to avoid examination of a deeper underlying conflict. Also called **escape into illness**; **flight into disease**.

flight into reality a defensive reaction in which an individual becomes overinvolved in activity and work as an unconscious means of avoiding threatening situations or painful thoughts and feelings. Compare FLIGHT FROM REALITY; FLIGHT INTO FANTASY.

flight of ideas a rapid, continuous succession of superficially related thoughts and ideas, manifest as hurried speech with frequent abrupt shifts in topic. A common symptom of a MANIC EPISODE, such disturbed thinking occasionally is seen in other disorders as well, including schizophrenia.

flippancy *n.* inappropriate levity when addressing a serious problem or an anxiety-provoking subject, often as a defensive strategy for limiting discussion. **—flippant** *adj.*

floating-limb response in standard hypnotic inductions, a positive response to the suggestion to allow the hand and arm to float upward. See also KOHNSTAMM TEST.

floccillation *n.* aimless grasping and plucking at clothing or bedding, typically associated with dementia, delirium, and high fever. It is sometimes a sign of extreme exhaustion and is considered a serious symptom, often associated with a poor prognosis. Also called **carphology**.

flooding *n.* a technique in BEHAVIOR THERAPY in which the individual is exposed directly to a maximum-intensity anxiety-producing situation or stimulus, either in the imagination but most often in reality, without any attempt made to lessen or avoid anxiety or fear during the exposure. For an individual with claustrophobia, for example, this would entail spending extended periods of time in a small room. Flooding techniques aim to diminish or extinguish the undesired behavior and are used primarily in the treatment of individuals with phobias and similar disorders. It is distinct from SYSTEMATIC DESENSITIZATION, which involves a gradual, step-by-step approach to encountering the feared situation or stimulus while attempting throughout to maintain a nonanxious state. See also IMPLOSIVE THERAPY.

floor effect a situation in which a large proportion of participants perform as poorly as, or nearly as poorly as, possible on a task or other evaluative measure, thus skewing the distribution of scores and making it impossible to discriminate differences among the many individuals at that low level. For example, a test whose items are too difficult for those taking it would show a floor effect because most people would obtain or be close to the lowest possible score of 0. Compare CEILING EFFECT.

flourishing *n.* a condition denoting good mental and physical health: the state of being free from illness and distress but, more important, of being filled with vitality and functioning well in one's personal and social life. Compare LANGUISHING. **—flourish** *vb.*

flow *n.* a state of optimal experience arising from intense involvement in an activity that is enjoyable, such as playing a sport, performing a musical passage, or writing a creative piece. Flow arises when one's skills are fully utilized yet equal to the demands of the task, intrinsic motivation is at a peak, one loses self-consciousness and temporal awareness, and one has a sense of total control, effortlessness, and complete concentration on the immediate situation (the here and now).

flowing consciousness the pleasurable sense of FLOW and effortlessness that accompanies skilled, nonconflictual activities.

fluency *n.* in cognitive psychology, the ability to generate ideas, words, mental associations, or potential solutions to a problem with ease and rapidity. It is usually considered to be an important dimension of CREATIVITY. See ASSOCIATIVE FLUENCY. **—fluent** *adj.*

fluent speech speech that is essentially normal in quantity, stress, pitch, rhythm, and intonation.

fluid–crystallized intelligence theory an occasional synonym of CATTELL–HORN THEORY OF INTELLIGENCE.

fluid intelligence (**fluid ability**) see CATTELL–HORN THEORY OF INTELLIGENCE.

flumazenil *n.* a drug used for the emergency reversal of symptoms of BENZODIAZEPINE overdose and in anesthesia to reverse benzodiazepine-induced sedation. It acts by displacing benzodiazepine (which acts as a GABA AGONIST) from binding sites on the GABA receptor complex (see BENZODIAZEPINE ANTAGONISTS; $GABA_A$ RECEPTOR). Because it is a short-acting agent, multiple doses may be required. It is not effective in managing benzodiazepine dependence, because its rapid action may precipitate a sudden withdrawal syndrome, nor does it antagonize the central nervous system effects of other GABA agonists (e.g., barbiturates) or reverse their effects. U.S. trade name: **Romazicon**.

flunitrazepam *n.* a BENZODIAZEPINE that is legally prescribed in some countries (but not the United States) for the short-term treatment of insomnia and as a preanesthetic medication. It is also used as a drug of abuse for its sedating and disinhibiting effects. When combined with alcohol, like many other CNS DEPRESSANTS, it can cause serious problems (see DATE-RAPE DRUG). Trade name: **Rohypnol**.

fluoxetine *n.* an antidepressant that is the prototype of the SSRIS (selective serotonin reuptake inhibitors). It acts by inhibiting the serotonin TRANSPORTER, preventing reuptake of serotonin into the terminal button (see AXON) of the presynaptic neuron. This presumably results in higher levels of available neurotransmitter to interact with postsynaptic receptors. Fluoxetine differs from other SSRIs in that it and its biologically active metabolic product, norfluoxetine, have a prolonged HALF-LIFE of 5–7 days after a single dose; thus it takes around 30 days (20–35 days) for the drug to reach steady-state concentrations. Like other SSRIs, it should not be used with monoamine oxidase inhibitors. U.S. trade names: **Prozac**; **Sarafem**.

fluphenazine *n.* a HIGH-POTENCY ANTIPSYCHOTIC of the piperazine PHENOTHIAZINE class. It is as potent as HALOPERIDOL and has similar side effects, with neuromuscular and extrapyramidal symptoms predominating. Like haloperidol, it is also available in an oil-based injectable form. These so-called depot preparations are injected intramuscularly and are very slowly absorbed, allowing periods of several weeks between doses. U.S. trade name: **Prolixin**.

flurazepam *n.* a BENZODIAZEPINE derivative used in the short-term treatment of insomnia. U.S. trade name: **Dalmane**.

flutamide *n.* see ANTIANDROGEN.

fluvoxamine *n.* a potent SSRI (selective serotonin reuptake inhibitor). Although its mechanism of action and antidepressant efficacy match those of other SSRIs, it is marketed largely as an agent for treating obsessive-compulsive disorder (see also CLOMIPRAMINE). U.S. trade name: **Luvox**.

fly agaric the highly poisonous mushroom *Amanita muscaria*, so called because it was once used as an insecticide to kill flies. MUSCARINE was the first active ingredient to be identified, but it is now known that IBOTENIC ACID and its metabolite **muscimol**, which is similar in structure to the inhibitory neurotransmitter GAMMA-AMINOBUTYRIC ACID (GABA) and acts as a GABA AGONIST, are the principal active components. Effects on humans are initially stimulating, ranging from euphoria through hallucinations to hyperactivity or excitement, and then sedating, inducing deep sleep. Symptoms of poisoning include dizziness, abdominal pains, vomiting, muscle cramps, and movement difficulties; at higher doses these symptoms may be followed by unconsciousness, asphyxiation, coma, and potentially death. Fly agaric has been variously identified as the substance taken by Norse berserkers before battle, as the plant SOMA worshipped in ancient times, and, in fiction, as the mushroom eaten by Alice before she perceived objects larger than life in Lewis Carroll's *Alice in Wonderland*.

fMRI abbreviation for FUNCTIONAL MAGNETIC RESONANCE IMAGING.

FMS abbreviation for false memory syndrome; see FALSE MEMORY.

focal degeneration the development of a lesion or dysfunction in a specific area of the brain due to a degenerative process, such as dementia. The lesion may remain limited in focus or spread into neighboring regions.

focal psychotherapy a form of BRIEF PSYCHOTHERAPY in which a single problematic area (e.g., excessive anxiety) is made the target of the entire course of treatment. The therapist continually redirects the process so as to avoid deviations from this specifically identified aim, for example, by preventing discussion of material he or she deems irrelevant to the intended therapeutic goal.

focal therapy see FOCUSED ANALYSIS.

focused analysis a modification of orthodox psychoanalysis in which interpretations are focused on a specific area of the patient's problem or pathology (e.g., a particular symptom, a particular aspect of the TRANSFERENCE). Also called **directed analysis**; **focal therapy**. Compare EXPECTANT ANALYSIS.

focus group a small group of people, typically 8–12 in number, who share common characteristics (e.g., working parents with 5- to 8-year-old children) and are selected to discuss a topic of which they have personal experience (e.g., their children's reading abilities and school performance). A leader conducts the discussion and keeps it on target. Originally used in marketing to determine consumer response to particular products, focus groups are now used for determining typical reactions, adaptations, and solutions to any number of issues, events, or topics.

focusing *n.* in EXPERIENTIAL PSYCHOTHERAPY, a process in which the therapist guides a client to focus silently on his or her body-centered experience of a problem or symptom in a relaxed and nonjudgmental way, often with eyes closed. The client then invites his or her mind to explore intuitively what the issue is about, without attempting to analyze or control thought processes. The method is believed to lead the client to deeper feelings and greater insight about and peace with the problem or symptom. [developed by Austrian-born U.S. psychologist Eugene T. Gendlin (1926–)]

focus of convenience in the personality theory of U.S. psychologist George A. Kelly (1905–1967), the set of phenomena to which a given theory best applies.

folie à cinq a rare psychotic disorder in which five people, usually members of the same family, share similar or identical delusions (French, "insanity of five"). It is an example of SHARED PSYCHOTIC DISORDER.

folie à deux a rare psychotic disorder in which two intimately related individuals simultaneously share similar or identical delusions (French, "double insanity"). It is the most common form of SHARED PSYCHOTIC DISORDER.

folie à quatre a rare psychotic disorder in which four people, usually members of the same family, share similar or identical delusions (French, "insanity of four"). It is an example of SHARED PSYCHOTIC DISORDER.

folie à trois a rare psychotic disorder in which three intimately related people simultaneously share similar or identical delusions (French, "triple insanity"). It is an example of SHARED PSYCHOTIC DISORDER.

follow-up counseling 1. the measures taken by a counselor or clinician in helping a client with ongoing problems or new manifestations of the original problems. **2.** an evaluation of a client's progress and the effectiveness of counseling to date.

follow-up history see CATAMNESIS; POSTTREATMENT FOLLOW-UP.

follow-up study a long-term study designed to examine the degree to which effects seen shortly after the imposition of a therapeutic intervention persist over time. Follow-up studies are also used for the long-term study of participants in a laboratory experiment to examine the degree to which effects of the experimental conditions are lasting.

Folstein Mini-Mental State Examination see MINI-MENTAL STATE EXAMINATION.

food addiction an eating disturbance characterized by a preoccupation with one's body image and weight, obsessive thoughts about food, the use of food as a source of pleasure, and COMPULSIVE EATING. In addition, the individual may experience symptoms of withdrawal during attempts to reduce food intake or abstain from particular types of food. See also BINGE-EATING DISORDER; BULIMIA NERVOSA.

food faddism any dietary practice based on exaggerated and often incorrect beliefs about the effects of food or nutrition on health, particularly for the prevention or cure of illness. This is often expressed as strange or inappropriate eating habits and the adoption of cult diets; it may lead to unhealthy weight loss or side effects arising from poor nutrition. It is sometimes associated with eating disorders, such as ANOREXIA NERVOSA.

foot anesthesia see STOCKING ANESTHESIA.

foot fetishism see RETIFISM.

foramen magnum a large opening at the base of the skull through which the spinal cord and the left and right vertebral arteries, as well as other tissues, pass between the neck and the interior of the skull.

forced treatment therapy administered to an individual with a mental disorder without his or her INFORMED CONSENT, for example, court-ordered administration of psychotropic drugs to a person to restore his or her competency to stand trial or the INVOLUNTARY HOSPITALIZATION of a person considered dangerous to him- or herself or others. Many question the ethical acceptability of the practice, citing its infringement of autonomy and the RIGHT TO REFUSE TREATMENT and its lack of scientifically demonstrated effectiveness, with such controversy intensifying in recent decades. Also called **coercive treatment**.

forebrain *n.* the part of the brain that develops from the anterior section of the NEURAL TUBE in the embryo, containing the CEREBRUM and the DIENCEPHALON. The former comprises the cerebral hemispheres with their various regions (e.g., BASAL GANGLIA, AMYGDALA, HIPPOCAMPUS); the latter comprises the THALAMUS and HYPOTHALAMUS. Also called **prosencephalon**.

foreclosure *n.* in development, see IDENTITY FORECLOSURE. See also IDENTITY VERSUS IDENTITY CONFUSION.

foreconscious *n.* see PRECONSCIOUS.

forensic assessment systematic evaluation by a mental health practitioner of a defendant, witness, or offender for the purpose of informing the court about such issues as COMPETENCY TO STAND TRIAL, CRIMINAL RESPONSIBILITY, and RISK ASSESSMENT.

forensic neuropsychology the application of CLINICAL NEUROPSYCHOLOGY to issues of both civil and criminal law, particularly those relating to claims of brain injury.

forensic psychiatry the branch of psychiatry concerned with abnormal behavior and mental disorders as they relate to legal issues, hearings, and trials. Major areas of concern include insanity pleas (see INSANITY DEFENSE) and the legal definition of INSANITY, procedures to commit individuals to mental hospitals, and questions of CRIMINAL RESPONSIBILITY, COMPETENCY TO STAND TRIAL, GUARDIANSHIP, CONSERVATORSHIP, and CONFIDENTIALITY. Also called **legal psychiatry**.

forensic psychology the application of psychological principles and techniques to situations involving the civil and criminal legal systems. Its functions include assessment and treatment services, provision of ADVOCACY and EXPERT TESTIMONY, and research and policy analysis. Also called **legal psychology**. See also CORRECTIONAL PSYCHOLOGY.

foreplay *n.* activity engaged in prior to COITUS, marked by psychological as well as physical stimulation. The purpose of foreplay, which includes kissing, stroking, fantasizing, and similar activities, is to encourage sexual arousal in the participants. It may last from a few minutes to several hours.

forgetting *n.* the failure to remember material previously learned. Forgetting typically is a normal phenomenon that plays an important adaptive role in restricting access to information that is likely to be needed in current interactions with the environment, but may also be pathological, as, for example, in amnesia.

forgiveness *n.* willfully putting aside feelings of resentment toward an individual who has committed a wrong, been unfair or hurtful, or otherwise harmed one in some way. Forgiveness is not equated with reconciliation or excusing another, and it is not merely accepting what happened or ceasing to be angry. Rather, it involves a voluntary transformation of one's feelings, attitudes, and behavior toward the individual, so that one is no longer dominated by resentment and can express compassion, generosity, or the like toward the individual. Forgiveness is often considered an important process in psychotherapy or counseling.

formal thought disorder disruptions in the form or structure of thinking. Examples include DERAILMENT and TANGENTIALITY. It is distinct from THOUGHT DISORDER, in which the disturbance relates to thought content.

formative evaluation a process that is concerned with helping to improve or guide the development of a program through the use of qualitative or quantitative research methodology. Ideally, the formative evaluator will repeatedly interact, often informally, with the program personnel from the outset of the work to clarify goals, monitor implementation, and assess staff and resource requirements. Also called **feedback evaluation**. See also PROCESS EVALUATION; SUMMATIVE EVALUATION.

formative spirituality see TRANSCENDENCE THERAPY.

formative tendency the general drive toward self-improvement, growth, and SELF-ACTUALIZATION hypothesized by Carl ROGERS in his CLIENT-CENTERED THERAPY.

formication *n.* an acutely distressing sensation of ants or other insects crawling on the skin. It is a tactile (haptic) hallucination that occurs in cocaine abuse and delirious states associated with acute alcoholic hallucinosis, meningitis, rheumatic fever, scarlet fever, diphtheria, and other infectious disorders. See also ACAROPHOBIA.

formicophilia *n.* sexual interest and pleasure derived from small animals, insects, or snails, which sometimes involves having these creatures placed on the genitals.

fornication *n.* voluntary sexual intercourse between any two people who are not married to each other. The legal definition varies in different areas.

fornix *n.* (*pl.* **fornices**) any arch-shaped structure, especially the long tract of white matter in the brain arching between the HIPPOCAMPUS and the HYPOTHALAMUS, projecting chiefly to the MAMMILLARY BODIES.

foster care temporary care provided to children in settings outside their family of origin and by individuals other than their natural or adoptive parents, under the supervision of a public child welfare agency. Foster care is intended to keep children whose parents are unavailable or incapable of proper care safe from harm, with the ultimate goal being to find a secure and permanent home. Typically, a child is placed with a family approved for foster care and paid a fee for such by a public child welfare agency. Although these FOSTER HOME arrangements are most common, children may also be placed in group homes or other institutions. See also ADULT FOSTER CARE.

foster-child fantasy the childhood belief or fantasy that the parents are actually adoptive or foster parents. See FAMILY ROMANCE.

foster home 1. a home for the temporary placement of children whose parents are unavailable or incapable of proper care. **2.** a home in which a person with a mental or physical impairment is placed by a social agency for purposes of care and sustenance. The foster family is usually paid by the agency, and the placement may be temporary or permanent. See ADULT FOSTER CARE.

fostering *n.* the process of providing care in a family environment to children or others to whom one is not related. See ADULT FOSTER CARE; FOSTER CARE.

foster placement see FOSTER CARE.

Four As see FUNDAMENTAL SYMPTOMS.

fragile X syndrome a genetic condition that differentially affects males and causes a range of developmental problems including learning disabilities and mental retardation. The disorder is so named because of alterations in the *FMR1* gene, on the arm of the X chromosome, that abnormally expand and destabilize it. Males with fragile X syndrome have characteristic physical features that become more apparent with age, such as large ears, prominent jaw and forehead, a long and narrow face, and enlarged testicles. Both males and females with fragile X may exhibit hyperactivity and attention deficits, while some males also show autistic behavior.

fragmentary delusion a disorganized, undeveloped DELUSION or a series of disconnected delusions that is inconsistent and illogical. Also called **unsystematized delusion**. Compare SYSTEMATIZED DELUSION.

fragmentation *n.* division or separation into pieces or fragments. For example, fragmentation of thinking (typically termed LOOSENING OF ASSOCIATIONS) is a disturbance in which thoughts become disjointed to such an extent as to no longer be unified, complete, or coherent; fragmentation of personality (typically termed PERSONALITY DISINTEGRATION) occurs when an individual no longer presents a unified, predictable set of beliefs, attitudes, traits, and behavioral responses.

F

frame-of-orientation need the need to develop or synthesize one's major assumptions, ideas, and values into a coherent worldview. The term was introduced by Erich FROMM, who distinguished between frames of reference based on reason and those based on subjective distortions, superstition, or myth.

frame of reference 1. in social psychology, the set of assumptions or criteria by which a person or group judges ideas, actions, and experiences. A frame of reference can often limit or distort perception, as in the case of PREJUDICE and STEREOTYPES. **2.** in cognitive psychology, a set of parameters defining either a particular mental SCHEMA or the wider COGNITIVE STRUCTURE by which an individual perceives and evaluates the world. See also CONCEPTUAL SYSTEM; PERCEPTUAL SET.

framing *n.* the process of defining the context or issues surrounding a question, problem, or event in a way that serves to influence how the context or issues are perceived and evaluated. Also called **framing effect**. See also REFRAMING.

framing effect 1. see ATMOSPHERE EFFECT. **2.** see FRAMING.

Franschetti–Zwahlen–Klein syndrome see TREACHER COLLINS SYNDROME. [Adolphe **Franschetti** (1896–1968), Swiss ophthalmologist]

fraternal twins see DIZYGOTIC TWINS.

F ratio (symbol: *F*) in an ANALYSIS OF VARIANCE or a MULTIVARIATE ANALYSIS OF VARIANCE, the ratio of explained to unexplained variance; that is, the ratio of BETWEEN-GROUPS VARIANCE to WITHIN-GROUP VARIANCE. Also called **F statistic**; **F value**.

free association a basic process in PSYCHOANALYSIS and other forms of PSYCHODYNAMIC PSYCHOTHERAPY, in which the patient is encouraged to verbalize without censorship or selection whatever thoughts come to mind, no matter how embarrassing, illogical, or irrelevant. The object is to allow unconscious material, such as traumatic experiences or threatening impulses, and otherwise inhibited thoughts and emotions to come to the surface where they can be interpreted. Free association is also posited to help the patient discharge some of the feelings that have given this material excessive control over him or her. See BASIC RULE; VERBALIZATION.

free-association test a test in which participants are offered a stimulus word and are expected to respond as quickly as possible with a word they associate with the stimulus.

freebase 1. *n.* a highly concentrated, chemically altered form of COCAINE that is prepared by treating cocaine with ether. It is ingested by smoking. **2.** *vb.* to smoke this form of cocaine.

Freedom From Distractibility Index an index historically calculated on the WECHSLER INTELLIGENCE SCALE FOR CHILDREN that measures short-term attention and concentration. In recent years, this index has been renamed the WORKING MEMORY INDEX to be more consistent with contemporary research and the adult versions of the Wechsler scales.

freedom to withdraw the right of a research participant to drop out of an experiment at any time.

free energy in psychoanalytic theory, PSYCHIC ENERGY that is located in the ID, is mobile, and is associated with PRIMARY PROCESSES. Compare BOUND ENERGY.

free-floating anxiety 1. a diffuse, chronic sense of uneasiness and apprehension not directed toward any specific situation or object. It may be a characteristic of a number of anxiety disorders, in particular GENERALIZED ANXIETY DISORDER. **2.** in psychoanalysis, general feelings of distress that have been set free from the original circumstances that caused them.

free-floating attention in psychoanalysis and in other forms of psychodynamic psychotherapy, the analyst's or therapist's state of evenly suspended attention during the therapeutic session. This attention does not focus on any one thing the client says, but allows the analyst or therapist to listen to all the material being presented and tune into the client's affects and unconscious ideas. Also called **evenly hovering attention**.

free-floating emotion a diffuse, generalized emotional state that does not appear to be associated with any specific cause. A common example is FREE-FLOATING ANXIETY.

free-floating fear a generalized sense of fear that is not directed toward a particular object or situation.

free radical an atom or molecule that has at least one "unpaired" electron in its outer shell. This makes it highly reactive and able to engage in rapid chain reactions that destabilize the molecules around it, thus causing the formation of more free radicals. Free radicals can damage cells and have been implicated in aging, inflammation, and the progression of various pathological conditions, including cancer.

free recall a type of memory task in which a list of items is presented one at a time and participants attempt to remember them in any order. The first and last items presented are best remembered: Proponents of the DUAL-STORE MODEL OF MEMORY attribute this to the fact that the last items are still in SHORT-TERM MEMORY, and hence recoverable, while the first items received the most REHEARSAL and were transferred to LONG-TERM MEMORY.

Fregoli's phenomenon a MISIDENTIFICATION SYNDROME in which an individual identifies a persecutor successively in different people known to him or her (e.g., a neighbor, doctor, attendant), on the delusional assumption that the persecutor is capable of changing faces. [first identified in 1927 and named for Italian actor Leopoldo **Fregoli** (1867–1936), who was renowned for his ability to alter his appearance]

frenzy *n.* a temporary state of wild excitement and mental agitation, at times including violent behavior. It has been associated with MANIA and is sometimes considered synonymous with this term.

frequency distribution a plot of the frequency of occurrence of scores of various sizes, arranged from lowest to highest score.

Freud, Anna (1895–1982) Austrian-born British psychoanalyst. The youngest daughter of Sigmund FREUD, Anna Freud trained first as an elementary school teacher and then as a psychoanalyst in Vienna. She made many original contributions to both the theory and practice of psychoanalysis, particularly through her studies of DEFENSE MECHANISMS (*The Ego and the Mechanisms of Defense*, 1936). She was a pioneer in the field of CHILD ANALYSIS, especially through her work at the Hampstead Clinic in England, to which she moved after the Nazis invaded Austria in 1938. Although an orthodox psychoanalyst in many respects, she devoted more attention than most to the topic of normal development; this research resulted in her 1965 book, *Normality and Pathology in Childhood*. Anna Freud held numerous administrative posts during her career; among them, she served as chair of the prestigious Vienna Psychoanalytic Society in the 1920s and 1930s, until it disbanded at the time of the Nazi invasion. See also METAPSYCHOLOGICAL PROFILE.

Freud, Sigmund (1856–1939) Austrian neurologist and psychiatrist, who invented the technique of PSYCHOANALYSIS. Freud earned a doctorate in medicine in 1881 from the University of Vienna, where he studied under psychologist Franz Brentano (1838–1917) and physiologist Ernst Brüecke (1819–1892). He began his professional life as a neurologist, making significant contributions to that field, but turned his full attention to the psychological approach to mental disorders, such as hysteria, after witnessing demonstrations of hypnosis in Paris by French physician Jean-Martin Charcot (1825–1893). After discarding hypnosis as a technique limited to removal of symptoms, Freud developed the method of FREE ASSOCIATION, which led to recognition of UNCONSCIOUS sexual conflicts and REPRESSION as the major factors in neuroses. These concepts became the cornerstones of the new discipline that he called psychoanalysis. This discipline focused on such procedures as (a) the interpretation of dreams in terms of hostile or sexual feelings stemming from childhood, (b) analysis of resistances and the relationship between therapist and patient, and (c) a study of the patient's present symptomatology in terms of psychosexual development and early experiences. The goal of this process, which takes many months or years, was not merely to eliminate symptoms, but to restructure the patient's entire psyche. Freud also applied his psychoanalytic method to the study of historical figures, such as Leonardo da Vinci, and to the exploration of primitive cultures, drawing a parallel between the "childhood" of the individual and the childhood of the human race. To disseminate his views, which were regarded as highly controversial at the time (and have remained so), he taught many disciples, was instrumental in establishing the first psychoanalytic association, and published a series of books, including *The Interpretation of Dreams* (1900), *Three Essays on the Theory of Sexuality* (1905), *Totem and Taboo* (1913), *Beyond the Pleasure Principle* (1920), and *The Ego and the Id* (1923). See also FREUDIAN THEORY OF PERSONALITY; NEO-FREUDIAN. —**Freudian** *adj.*

Freudian approach (**Freudianism**) see PSYCHOANALYSIS.

Freudian slip in the popular understanding of psychoanalytic theory, an unconscious error or oversight in writing, speech, or action that is held to be caused by unacceptable impulses breaking through the EGO's defenses and exposing the individual's true wishes or feelings. See PARAPRAXIS; SLIP OF THE TONGUE; SYMPTOMATIC ACT. [Sigmund FREUD]

Freudian theory of personality the general psychoanalytic concept that character and personality are the product of experiences and FIXATIONS stemming from the early stages of PSYCHOSEXUAL DEVELOPMENT. See PSYCHOANALYSIS. [Sigmund FREUD]

Friedreich's ataxia a hereditary, progressive form of ATAXIA (muscular incoordination) that results from the degeneration of nerves in the spinal cord and nerves that connect the spinal cord to the arms and legs. Symptoms typically appear in childhood or early adolescence and may include clumsiness, balance problems, difficulty walking, unsteady gait, slurred speech, hearing and vision loss, and rapid involuntary eye movements. [Nikolaus **Friedreich** (1825–1882), German neurologist]

friendship *n.* a voluntary relationship between two or more people that is relatively long-lasting and in which those involved tend to be concerned with meeting the others' needs and interests as well as satisfying their own desires. Friendships frequently develop through shared experiences in which the people involved learn that their association with one another is mutually gratifying.

fright *n.* the emotional reaction that arises in the face of a dangerous or potentially dangerous situation or encounter. Fright differs from FEAR in that the danger is usually immediate, physical, concrete, and overwhelming. Physiological changes in the body associated with fright include trembling, widening of the eyes, and drawing away from the fear-producing stimulus.

frigidity *n.* a woman's impairment of sexual desire or inability to achieve orgasm. This obsolescent term has largely been abandoned in favor of female SEXUAL DYSFUNCTION. **—frigid** *adj.*

fringe consciousness aspects of experience that lack focal perceptual qualities (e.g., color, texture, taste) but are nevertheless reported with a high degree of confidence and accuracy. Fringe experiences vary widely, from feelings of EFFORTFULNESS and the TIP-OF-THE-TONGUE PHENOMENON to mystical feelings.

fringe–focus structure a model of consciousness in which the conscious contents typically have a focal component, with clear and discriminable sensory features, and a "fringe-conscious" component.

Fröhlich's syndrome a disorder caused by underfunctioning of the anterior lobe of the pituitary gland (**hypopituitarism**). Major symptoms are underdeveloped genital organs and secondary sexual characteristics, general sluggishness, obesity, and in some cases polyuria (frequent urination), polydipsia (frequent consumption of liquids), and mild mental retardation. Also called **adiposogenital dystrophy**; **adiposogenitalism**; **Launois–Cleret syndrome**. [Alfred **Fröhlich** (1871–1953), Austrian neurologist]

Fromm, Erich (1900–1980) German psychoanalyst. Fromm earned a doctorate at the University of Heidelberg in 1922 before training as a psychoanalyst in Berlin and Munich. The bulk of his career was spent in the United States. Fromm developed a broad cultural, yet personal, approach focused on (a) the search for meaning, (b) the development of personality and socially productive relationships, and (c) the enrichment of life through character, the need to belong, the development of individuality, and the replacement of a commercial MARKETING ORIENTATION with a sane society. This enrichment of life, he believed, should be built around cooperation, caring, and the ability to love. These concepts were vividly expressed in such books as *Man for Himself* (1947), *The Sane Society* (1955), and *The Art of Loving* (1956).

frontal cortex the CEREBRAL CORTEX of the frontal lobe. See also PREFRONTAL CORTEX.

frontal lobe one of the four main lobes of each cerebral hemisphere of the brain, lying in front of the central sulcus. It is concerned with motor and higher order EXECUTIVE FUNCTIONS. See also PREFRONTAL LOBE.

frontal lobe syndrome deterioration in personality and behavior resulting from lesions in the frontal lobe. Typical symptoms include loss of initiative, inability to plan activities, difficulty with abstract thinking, perseveration, impairments in social judgment and impulse control, and mood disturbances such as apathy or mania.

frontal lobotomy see LOBOTOMY.

frotteurism *n.* in *DSM–IV–TR*, a PARAPHILIA in which an individual deliberately and persistently seeks sexual excitement by rubbing against other people. This may occur as apparently accidental contact in crowded public settings, such as elevators or lines. The person displaying this type of behavior is called a **frotteur** or a **rubber**. Also called **frottage**.

frustration *n.* **1.** the thwarting of impulses or actions that prevents individuals from obtaining something they have been led to expect based on past experience, as when a hungry animal is prevented from obtaining food that it can see or smell or when a child is prevented from playing with a visible toy. Internal forces can include motivational conflicts and inhibitions; external forces can include the actions of other individuals, admonitions of parents or others, and the rules of society. **2.** the emotional state an individual experiences when such thwarting occurs. **3.** in psychoanalytic theory, the damming up of PSYCHIC ENERGY, which then seeks an outlet in wish-fulfilling fantasies and dreams or in various neurotic symptoms. **—frustrate** *vb.*

frustration–aggression hypothesis the theory, advanced in 1939 by U.S. social scientist John Dollard (1900–1980) and colleagues, that (a) frustration always produces an aggressive urge and (b) aggression is always the result of prior frustrations. U.S. psychologist Neal MILLER, one of the proponents of this theory, later noted that frustration can lead to several kinds of actions, but maintained that the urge to aggression will become more dominant as the thwarting continues. In 1989 U.S. psychologist Leonard Berkowitz (1926–) proposed that the frustration must be decidedly unpleasant in order to evoke an aggressive urge. Also called **aggression–frustration hypothesis**.

frustration–regression hypothesis the theory that frustration often leads to behavior characteristic of a much earlier period of life (see REGRESSION). [proposed in 1941 by U.S. psychologists Roger G. Barker (1903–1990), Tamara Dembo (1902–1993), and Kurt LEWIN]

frustration tolerance the ability of an individual to delay gratification or to preserve relative equanimity on encountering obstacles. The growth of adequate frustration tolerance generally occurs as part of a child's cognitive and affective development but may also be strengthened to more adaptive levels later in life through therapeutic intervention.

FSS abbreviation for FEAR SURVEY SCHEDULE.

F statistic see F RATIO.

F test any of a class of statistical tests, notably including the widely used ANALYSIS OF VARIANCE, that rely on the assumption that the test statistic—the F RATIO—follows the F DISTRIBUTION when the null hypothesis is true. F tests are tests of hypotheses about population variances.

FTT abbreviation for FAILURE TO THRIVE.

fugue *n.* **1.** see DISSOCIATIVE FUGUE. **2.** a brief period in which an individual appears to be in a semiconscious state, sometimes engaging in routine activity, and subsequently has no memory for events during that period. This condition is typically associated with epilepsy but may occur in other conditions, such as alcohol intoxication and catatonic excitement.

fulfillment *n.* the actual or felt satisfaction of needs and desires, or the attainment of aspirations. See also WISH-FULFILLMENT. **—fulfill** *vb.*

full inclusion the practice of providing children with disabilities with services in their home school and of educating them in a regular classroom on a permanent, full-time basis. See also LEAST RESTRICTIVE ENVIRONMENT; MAINSTREAMING.

fully functioning person a person with a healthy personality, who experiences freedom of choice and action, is creative, and exhibits the qualities of EXISTENTIAL LIVING. [as defined in the CLIENT-CENTERED THERAPY of Carl ROGERS]

function *n.* **1.** in biology, an activity of an organ or an organism that contributes to the organism's FITNESS, such as the secretion of a sex hormone by a gonad to prepare for reproduction or the defensive behavior of a female with young toward an intruder. **2.** (symbol: f) a mathematical procedure that relates one number, quantity, or entity to another according to a defined rule. For example, if $y = 2x + 1$, y is said to be a function of x. This is often written $y = f(x)$. Here y is the dependent variable and x is the independent variable.

functional *adj.* **1.** denoting or referring to a disorder for which there is no known organic or structural basis. In psychology and psychiatry, functional disorders are improperly considered equivalent to PSYCHOGENIC disorders. **2.** based on or relating to use rather than structure.

functional activities actions associated with basic daily home and work requirements: an umbrella term encompassing both ACTIVITIES OF DAILY LIVING and INSTRUMENTAL ACTIVITIES OF DAILY LIVING.

functional age an individual's age as determined by measures of functional capability indexed by age-normed standards. Functional age is distinct from CHRONOLOGICAL AGE and represents a combination of physiological, psychological, and social age. In older adults it is calculated by measuring a range of variables that correlate closely with chronological age, such as eyesight, hearing, mobility, cardiopulmonary function, concentration, and memory. Following the passing of the Age Discrimination in Employment Act, functional age, rather than chronological age, has been made a criterion for employment in some jobs. The functional age of a child is measured in terms of the developmental level he or she has reached. It may be compared with his or her chronological age as a means of gauging the existence and extent of any impairment or developmental problem.

functional amnesia loss of memory for events one has personally experienced in the absence of any identifiable neurological pathology. While loss of EPISODIC MEMORY about oneself is the hallmark of functional amnesia, in some cases SEMANTIC MEMORY about the self may also be lost, as when a person forgets who he or she is. Functional amnesia is thought to arise as a defense against anxiety and distress or as a way of escaping from specific situations.

functional analysis 1. the detailed analysis of a behavior to identify contingencies that sustain the behavior. **2.** a synthesis of a client's behavior problems and the variables that are associated with or hypothesized to cause them.

functional analytic causal model (FACM) a vector diagram of a functional analysis of an individual client that visually presents a clinician's conjectures or theories about the client's maladaptive behaviors, the objectives of those behaviors, and the variables affecting them. Use of FACM graphically organizes and elucidates contingencies affecting the design of therapeutic interventions and provides an alternative or supplement to clinical case conceptualization.

functional autonomy 1. the ability of a person to perform independently the various tasks required in daily life, a core concept in such areas as rehabilitation and successful aging. For example, decline in functional autonomy is a major component of symptoms in severe dementia. Very few INSTRUMENTAL ACTIVITIES OF DAILY LIVING remain, and there is a gradual loss of self-care, or basic ACTIVITIES OF DAILY LIVING. **2.** as defined in 1973 by Gordon Willard ALLPORT, a general principle of motivation stating that during the performance of purposeful, goal-oriented behavior, various derivative drives emerge as independent units from the original drive that inspired the behavior. For example, studying motivated by the desire to obtain high grades may be gradually replaced by the desire for (and therefore pursuit of) knowledge for its own sake.

functional behavioral assessment (FBA) 1. an assessment approach that identifies the functions fulfilled by a particular maladaptive or problematic behavior by examining the circumstances and consequences associated with its occurrence. The circumstances (called antecedents), behavior, and consequences are typically defined in measurable terms, and combinations of particular types of antecedents and consequences may be presented systematically as part of the assessment. Thus circumstances and consequences (i.e., motivational factors) associated with increases or decreases in the particular behavior can be identified. Results of these assessments provide information of immediate utility in designing interventions or treatments to address the behavior. **2.** any of a wide variety of assessment methods used in APPLIED BEHAVIOR ANALYSIS.

F

functional blindness visual deterioration without any apparent change or disease affecting the structural integrity of the visual system: one of the most frequent symptoms in SOMATIZATION DISORDER. In addition to loss of acuity, visual functional phenomena may include photophobia, burning eyes, painful eyes, tired eyes, monocular diplopia (double vision), and severe concentric visual field constriction in one or both eyes. Despite the symptoms, the pupils continue to react to light, and the patient automatically avoids objects that would cause injury. Complete functional blindness is rare. The condition was formerly known as **hysterical blindness** or **psychic blindness**.

functional brain imaging the use of BRAIN IMAGING techniques to localize areas of cognitive activation. See FUNCTIONAL MAGNETIC RESONANCE IMAGING; POSITRON EMISSION TOMOGRAPHY.

functional communication training a BEHAVIOR THERAPY technique used with children and adults diagnosed with developmental impairments, such as autism or mental retardation, who are exhibiting aggressive, self-injurious, or highly disruptive behavior. The technique assesses the function that the negative behavior serves and uses positive reinforcement to replace it with more appropriately adaptive communication or behavior that meets the same need.

functional deafness loss of hearing that is not associated with any known structural abnormality.

functional disorder a disorder for which there is no known organic basis. In psychology and psychiatry, functional disorders are improperly considered equivalent to PSYCHOGENIC DISORDERS.

functional dyspareunia a sexual dysfunction of men or women in which there is recurrent and persistent genital pain during coitus. It does not include conditions caused exclusively by a physical disorder or due to lack of lubrication, FUNCTIONAL VAGINISMUS, or another mental disorder.

functional dyspepsia see DYSPEPSIA.

functional dyspnea see DYSPNEA.

functional encopresis see ENCOPRESIS.

functional enuresis see ENURESIS.

functional family therapy a type of FAMILY THERAPY that focuses on both family interaction patterns and on the benefits family members may derive from problem behavior. Using reframing and COGNITIVE BEHAVIOR THERAPY methods, functional family therapy focuses primarily on at-risk and behaviorally troubled youth and their families.

Functional Independence Measure (FIM) an instrument used in rehabilitation to evaluate specific routine motor, cognitive, and self-care skills and provide a measure of FUNCTIONAL STATUS. It consists of 18 items related to eating, grooming, bathing, dressing, toileting, bladder and bowel management, transfers, locomotion, comprehension, expression, social interaction, problem solving, and memory that are each rated on a 7-point scale ranging from "dependent" to "independent."

functionalism *n.* a general psychological approach that views mental life and behavior in terms of active adaptation to environmental challenges and opportunities. Functionalism was developed at the University of Chicago by psychologists John DEWEY, James R. ANGELL, and Harvey A. Carr (1878–1954) at the beginning of the 20th century as a revolt against the atomistic point of view of STRUCTURALISM, which limited psychology to the dissection of states of consciousness and the study of mental content rather than mental activities. This focus reveals the debt of functionalism to evolutionary concepts, to the ACT PSYCHOLOGY of German psychologist Franz Brentano (1838–1917), and to the approach detailed by William JAMES. Functionalism emphasized the causes and consequences of human behavior; the union of the physiological with the psychological; the need for objective testing of theories; and the applications of psychological knowledge to the solution of practical problems, the evolutionary continuity between animals and humans, and the improvement of human life. Also called **functional psychology**. See also CHICAGO SCHOOL.

functional limitation restriction or lack of ability in performing an action or activity that arises as a result of a disability. For example, a person who is unable to move safely about his or her home or community or is otherwise unable to travel independently has a functional limitation with regard to mobility.

functional magnetic resonance imaging (fMRI; functional MRI) a form of MAGNETIC RESONANCE IMAGING used to localize areas of cognitive activation, based on the correlation between brain activity and blood property changes linked to local changes in blood flow to the brain. During periods of cognitive activation, blood flow is always increased to a greater extent than oxygen extraction. In consequence, the proportion of oxygenated hemoglobin in the red blood cells transiently increases in an active region, leading to a local increase in the signal detected by fMRI.

functional pain pain with no known organic cause.

functional plasticity the ability of the brain to adapt to loss of or damage to tissue by transferring all or part of the functions previously performed by those injured areas to other regions. The degree to which the brain is able to do this successfully is called **functional reserve** and is thought to depend on several factors, including age and the physical status of the brain.

functional psychosis 1. a psychotic state for which no specific neurological or other physical pathology has been demonstrated. **2.** an obsolete name for any severe mental disorder for which no specific neurological or other physical pathology has been demonstrated.

functional reorganization changes that occur after a brain injury to enable other areas of the brain to take over all or part of the functions performed by the injured area.

functional status a measure of an individual's ability to perform ACTIVITIES OF DAILY LIVING and INSTRUMENTAL ACTIVITIES OF DAILY LIVING independently, used as an assessment of the severity of that individual's disability.

functional types in Carl JUNG'S ANALYTIC PSYCHOLOGY, four personality types based on functions of the ego. Jung identified four functions, one of which typically dominates the conscious ego while the others remain unconscious. The individuated person (see INDIVIDUATION) will have integrated all the functions into his or her conscious personality. The functional types are: (a) the FEELING TYPE; (b) the THINKING TYPE; (c) the SENSATION TYPE; and (d) the INTUITIVE TYPE. See QUATERNITY. See also ATTITUDINAL TYPES.

functional vaginismus a sexual dysfunction characterized by recurrent and persistent involuntary spasms of the musculature of the outer third of the vagina, which interfere with coitus and are not caused exclusively by a physical disorder or due to another mental disorder.

function pleasure the pleasure that results from doing something well and that motivates people to do their best at a task even when there is no other reward.

fundamental attribution error in ATTRIBUTION THEORY, the tendency to overestimate the degree to which an individual's behavior is determined by his or her abiding personal characteristics, attitudes, or beliefs and, correspondingly, to minimize the influence of the surrounding situation on that behavior (e.g., financial or social pressures). There is evidence that this tendency is more common in some societies than in others. Also called **correspondence bias**; **overattribution bias**. [identified by U.S. psychologist Lee D. Ross]

fundamental interpersonal relations orientation theory (**FIRO theory**) a theory explaining the pattern of interactions among members of a group in terms of three interpersonal needs of the group members: the need for inclusion (i.e., to belong to and be accepted by the group), the need for control (i.e., to direct the group's activities), and the NEED FOR AFFECTION. [proposed by U.S. psychologist William Schutz (1925–2002)]

fundamental lexical hypothesis see LEXICAL HYPOTHESIS.

fundamental need see PHYSIOLOGICAL NEED.

fundamental rule see BASIC RULE.

fundamental symptoms according to Swiss psychiatrist Eugen Bleuler (1857–1939), the four primary symptoms of schizophrenia: abnormal *a*ssociations in thinking, *a*utistic behavior and thinking, abnormal *a*ffect (including flat and inappropriate affect), and *a*mbivalence. These symptoms are also known as the **Four As**. Compare SECONDARY SYMPTOMS.

furor *n.* a sudden outburst of rage or excitement during which an irrational act of violence may be committed. In rare cases of epilepsy, the occurrence of furor takes the place of a tonic–clonic or complex partial seizure; this is known as **furor epilepticus** or **epileptic furor**. See also EXPLOSIVE PERSONALITY; INTERMITTENT EXPLOSIVE DISORDER; ISOLATED EXPLOSIVE DISORDER.

fusion *n.* the blending into one unified whole of two or more components or elements. This general meaning is applied in a variety of different psychological contexts. In perception, for example, it may denote a blending of sounds received by the two ears (**binaural fusion**) or of images falling on the two retinas (**binocular fusion**), while in psychoanalytic theory it denotes instinctual fusion, the merging of different INSTINCTS, as in the union of sexual and aggressive drives in SADISM. The term is also sometimes applied to a state in which the normal differentation between the self and the environment seems to recede or disappear, so that the individual experiences a sense of being united with other individuals or with nature. **—fuse** *vb.*

future-mindedness *n.* the ability to engage in means–ends thinking about the future, that is, to think ahead to what the future may hold and how it might come to pass.

future orientation a time perspective that is focused on the future, especially on how to achieve one's future goals.

future shock the personal confusion and social disorientation that accompany very rapid technological and social change. [defined by U.S. futurist Alvin Toffler (1928–)]

F value see F RATIO.

Gg

g symbol for GENERAL FACTOR.

GA abbreviation for GAMBLERS ANONYMOUS.

GABA abbreviation for GAMMA-AMINOBUTYRIC ACID.

GABA agonists compounds that exert an agonistic (augmentative) effect at gamma-aminobutyric acid (GABA) receptor sites (see $GABA_A$ RECEPTOR; $GABA_B$ RECEPTOR) or on the action of GABA. Several classes of GABA receptor agonists exist. Direct GABA agonists (e.g., muscimol) act at the GABA binding-site on the receptor; indirect GABA agonists facilitate, in various ways, the release or activity of GABA. Of the indirect GABA agonists, the BENZODIAZEPINES, which act as allosteric modulators (see ALLOSTERIC MODULATION) at the GABA receptor complex, are in the most common clinical use.

GABA antagonists substances that exert an antagonistic (inhibitive) effect at gamma-aminobutyric acid (GABA) receptor sites (see $GABA_A$ RECEPTOR; $GABA_B$ RECEPTOR) or on the action of GABA. Like GABA AGONISTS, GABA antagonists can be direct or indirect. Direct GABA antagonists block the GABA receptor; the best known of these is BICUCULLINE, which acts as a competitive antagonist for GABA at its receptor site. Indirect GABA antagonists include PICROTOXIN, which is a noncompetitive antagonist at the $GABA_A$ receptor complex and blocks the effects of GABA on the receptor complex.

gabapentin *n.* a drug used for the treatment of seizures (see ANTICONVULSANT) and for the relief of pain associated with shingles. Its mechanism of action is unknown: It is a chemical analog of the neurotransmitter gamma-aminobutyric acid (GABA) and may be involved in the increased synthesis or release of GABA. Gabapentin is currently being investigated for the treatment of certain psychological disorders: It may be of some use in managing mania associated with BIPOLAR DISORDERS, but this has not yet been conclusively established and gabapentin has been reported to induce excitation or increase the frequency of episodes in bipolar disorders. Side effects are primarily sedation, dizziness, ATAXIA, and fatigue; abrupt withdrawal may precipitate seizures. U.S. trade name: **Neurontin**.

$GABA_A$ receptor one of the two main types of receptor protein that bind the neurotransmitter GAMMA-AMINOBUTYRIC ACID (GABA), the other being the $GABA_B$ RECEPTOR. It is located at most synapses of most neurons that use GABA as a neurotransmitter. The predominant inhibitory receptor in the central nervous system (CNS), it functions as a chloride channel (see ION CHANNEL). GABA AGONISTS, such as the barbiturates and benzodiazepines, enhance the binding of GABA to $GABA_A$ receptors, allowing for increased conductance of chloride through the ion channel and thereby hyperpolarizing the neuron and inhibiting its activity. GABA ANTAGONISTS, such as bicuculline and picrotoxin, block the inhibitory effects of GABA at this receptor. Many other substances, including alcohol (ethanol), are thought to exert at least part of their effect via interaction at the $GABA_A$ receptor.

$GABA_B$ receptor one of the two main types of receptor protein that bind the neurotransmitter GAMMA-AMINOBUTYRIC ACID (GABA), the other being the $GABA_A$ RECEPTOR. $GABA_B$ receptors, which are G PROTEIN-coupled receptors, are less plentiful in the brain than $GABA_A$ receptors and do not have binding sites for benzodiazepine or barbiturate GABA agonists. Activation of $GABA_B$ receptors results in relatively long-lasting neuronal inhibition, but few psychotropic substances exert their effect at these receptors: BACLOFEN is a relatively selective agonist at $GABA_B$ receptors and is used clinically as a skeletal-muscle relaxant.

GAD abbreviation for GENERALIZED ANXIETY DISORDER.

GAF scale abbreviation for GLOBAL ASSESSMENT OF FUNCTIONING SCALE.

GAI abbreviation for GUIDED AFFECTIVE IMAGERY.

galactorrhea *n.* abnormal expression of breast milk, which may occur either in women at times other than when nursing or in men. Lactation is stimulated by the pituitary hormone PROLACTIN, and the neurotransmitter dopamine normally acts to inhibit the release of prolactin. Therefore administration of DOPAMINE-RECEPTOR ANTAGONISTS (e.g., conventional antipsychotics), which inhibit the effects of dopamine, may cause galactorrhea. Pituitary tumors or injury to the pituitary gland, causing excessive secretion of prolactin, may also result in galactorrhea. The dopamine-receptor agonist BROMOCRIPTINE may be used to treat the condition.

galantamine *n.* an inhibitor of the enzyme acetylcholinesterase that is used for the treatment of mild to moderate Alzheimer's disease (see NOOTROPIC). Although galantamine and other ACETYLCHOLINESTERASE INHIBITORS do not reverse symptoms of dementia, they have been demonstrated to temporarily slow progression of the disease. U.S. trade name: **Razadyne**.

Gamblers Anonymous (**GA**) an organization of men and women who share experiences, strength, and hope with each other to recover from compulsive gambling, following the TWELVE-STEP PROGRAM. See PATHOLOGICAL GAMBLING.

gambler's fallacy a failure to recognize the independence of chance events, leading to the mistaken belief that one can predict the outcome of a chance event on the basis of the outcomes of past chance events. For example, a person might think that the more often a tossed coin comes up heads, the more likely it is to come up tails in subsequent tosses, although each coin toss is independent of the other, and the true probability of the outcome of any toss is still just 0.5.

gambling *n.* see PATHOLOGICAL GAMBLING.

game *n.* **1.** in psychotherapy, a situation in which members of a group take part in some activity designed to elicit emotions or stimulate revealing interactions and interrelationships. In PLAY THERAPY games are often used as a projective or observational technique. **2.** in TRANSACTIONAL ANALYSIS, a recurrent and often deceitful ploy adopted by an individual in his or her dealings with others. **3.** in GESTALT THERAPY, an exercise or experiment designed to increase self-awareness, for example, acting out frightening situations or participating in the HOT-SEAT TECHNIQUE.

gamma alcoholism one of the five types of alcoholism defined by U.S. physician Elvin M. Jellinek (1890–1963), the others being ALPHA ALCOHOLISM, BETA ALCOHOLISM, DELTA ALCOHOLISM, and EPSILON ALCOHOLISM. It is characterized by physical and psychological dependence, tolerance, loss of control over drinking, and withdrawal symptoms if use is suspended. Jellinek considered gamma alcoholism the predominant form of alcoholism in the United States. Although similar to delta alcoholism, gamma alcoholism is distinguished by the person's complete loss of control, as opposed to his or her inability to abstain.

gamma-aminobutyric acid (**GABA**) a major inhibitory NEUROTRANSMITTER in the mammalian nervous system and found widely distributed in both invertebrate and vertebrate nervous systems. It is synthesized from the amino acid GLUTAMIC ACID. See also $GABA_A$ RECEPTOR; $GABA_B$ RECEPTOR.

gamma-aminobutyric acid agonists see GABA AGONISTS.

gamma-aminobutyric acid antagonists see GABA ANTAGONISTS.

gamma-cystathionase deficiency see CYSTATHIONINURIA.

gamma-hydroxybutyrate *n.* see GHB.

gamma wave in electroencephalography, a type of low-amplitude BRAIN WAVE ranging from 31 to 80 Hz (with power peaking near 40 Hz) and associated with higher-level cognitive activities, such as memory storage. Also called **gamma rhythm**.

gamonomania *n.* an abnormally strong desire or urge to marry.

ganglionic blocking agents drugs that inhibit the action of the neurotransmitter ACETYLCHOLINE at synapses in the ganglia of the AUTONOMIC NERVOUS SYSTEM (autonomic ganglia). Among other effects, this causes a decrease in heart rate and a lowering of blood pressure, and these drugs were formerly widely used in the treatment of hypertension. However, because of the severity of their side effects, this use is now rare. See MECAMYLAMINE.

G

ganja *n.* one of the more potent forms of CANNABIS, made from the dried flowering tops of female plants. Smokers of this substance reportedly experience respiratory disorders at a rate twice that of the average for cannabis smokers.

Ganser syndrome a condition in which psychotic illness is simulated or a DISSOCIATED STATE occurs purportedly as a result of an unconscious effort by the individual to escape from an intolerable situation. It is typically seen in psychiatric hospitals and, historically, in prisons (it is referred to in the older literature as **prison psychosis**). The most prominent feature is the giving of approximate answers to simple or familiar questions (e.g., "3 + 3 = 7"; "a horse has five legs"). Some other features include clouding of consciousness, inattentiveness or drowsiness, conversion symptoms (e.g., CONVERSION PARALYSIS), hallucinations, and, frequently, loss of memory for events subsequent to the episode. The syndrome has been variously categorized as a MALINGERING process, a psychotic disorder, and a consequence of a head injury. In *DSM–IV–TR*, it is classified as a DISSOCIATIVE DISORDER NOT OTHERWISE SPECIFIED. Also called **pseudodementia**. [first described in 1898 by Sigbert **Ganser** (1853–1931), German psychiatrist]

Gardner–Diamond syndrome a condition in which an individual bruises easily (purpura simplex) and black and blue patches (ecchymoses) tend to enlarge and result in pain in the affected tissue. Also called **autoerythrocyte sensitization syndrome**; **painful bruising syndrome**; **psychogenic purpura**. [Louis Klein **Diamond** (1902–1995) and Frank H. **Gardner** (1919–), U.S. physicians]

gargoylism *n.* the facial appearance of people with HURLER'S SYNDROME. The features include an abnormally long and narrow skull due to premature closure of the sagittal suture, a broad nose bridge, an open mouth with a large protruding tongue, thick lips, and clouded corneas.

GAS abbreviation for GENERAL ADAPTATION SYNDROME.

gasoline intoxication a euphoric reaction induced by inhalation of gasoline vapor. It also results in headache, weakness, depression of the central nervous system, confusion, nausea, and respiratory disorders. See INHALANT; INHALANT ABUSE.

gate-control theory the hypothesis that the subjective experience of pain is modulated by large nerve fibers in the spinal cord that act as gates, such that pain is not the product of a simple transmission of stimulation from the skin or some internal organ to the brain. Rather, sensations from noxious stimulation impinging on pain receptors have to pass through these spinal gates to the brain in order to emerge as pain perceptions. The status of the gates, however, is subject to a variety of influences (e.g., drugs, injury, emotions, possibly even instructions coming down from the brain itself), which can operate to shut them, thus inhibiting pain transmission, or cause them to be fully open, thus facilitating transmission. [first proposed in 1965 by Canadian psychologist Ronald Melzack (1929–) and British neuroscientist Patrick D. Wall (1925–2001)]

gatekeeper *n.* a health care professional, usually a PRIMARY CARE PROVIDER associated with a MANAGED CARE organization, who determines a patient's access to health care services and whose approval is required for referrals to specialists.

gateway drug any chemical substance whose chronic use leads to the subsequent use of more harmful substances that have significant potential for abuse and dependence. For example, alcohol, tobacco, and CANNABIS are often considered a gateway to such drugs as HEROIN, COCAINE, LSD, and PCP. Introduced in the 1950s, the concept has become the most popular framework for understanding drug use among adolescent populations, guiding prevention efforts and even shaping governmental policy.

Gaussian distribution see NORMAL DISTRIBUTION. [Karl Friedrich **Gauss** (1777–1855), German mathematician]

gay 1. *adj.* denoting individuals, especially males, who are sexually attracted to and aroused by members of their own sex. **2.** *n.* a gay individual. See also HOMOSEXUALITY.

gay bashing see HOMOPHOBIA.

GBBB syndrome see TELECANTHUS-HYPOSPADIAS SYNDROME.

GCS abbreviation for GLASGOW COMA SCALE.

GDS 1. abbreviation for GERIATRIC DEPRESSION SCALE. **2.** abbreviation for GLOBAL DETERIORATION SCALE. **3.** abbreviation for GORDON DIAGNOSTIC SYSTEM.

gelasmus *n.* spasmodic laughter in individuals with certain psychogenic disorders, schizophrenia, and some diseases of the brain (especially of the medulla oblongata). When occurring as an aspect of a psychomotor seizure, this type of spasmodic laughter is termed **gelastic epilepsy**.

Gemeinschaftsgefühl *n.* SOCIAL INTEREST or community spirit (German, literally: "feeling for community"): a spirit of equality, belonging, and unity.

gender *n.* the condition of being male, female, or neuter. In a human context, the distinction between gender and sex reflects usage of these terms: Sex usually refers to the biological aspects of maleness or femaleness, whereas gender implies the psychological, behavioral, social, and cultural aspects of being male or female (i.e., masculinity or femininity). See also SEX ROLE.

gender assignment classification of an infant at birth as either male or female. Children born with ambiguous genitalia are usually assigned a gender by parents or physicians. See also GENDER REASSIGNMENT.

gender coding assigning particular traits or behaviors exclusively or predominantly to males or females.

gender concept an understanding of the socially constructed distinction between male and female, based on biological sex but also including the roles and expectations for males and females of a culture. Children begin to acquire concepts of gender, including knowledge of the activities, toys, and other objects associated with each gender and of how they view themselves as male or female in their culture, possibly from as early as 18 months of age.

gender dysphoria discontent with the physical or social aspects of one's own sex. See also DYSPHORIA; GENDER IDENTITY DISORDER.

gender identification the process of identifying oneself as male or female and adopting the roles and values of that gender. See also GENDER CONCEPT; GENDER SCHEMA.

gender identity a recognition that one is male or female and the internalization of this knowledge into one's self-concept. Although the dominant approach in psychology for many years had been to regard gender identity as residing in individuals, the importance of societal structures, cultural expectations, and personal interactions in its development is now recognized as well. Indeed, significant evidence now exists to support the conceptualization of gender identity as influenced by both environmental and biological factors. See also GENDER ROLE.

gender identity disorder in *DSM–IV–TR*, a disorder characterized by clinically significant distress or impairment of functioning due to cross-gender identification (i.e., a desire to be or actual insistence that one is of the opposite sex) and persistent discomfort arising from the belief that one's sex or gender is inappropriate to one's true self (see TRANSSEXUALISM). The disorder is distinguished from simple dissatisfaction or nonconformity with gender roles. In children, the disorder is manifested as aversion to physical aspects of their sex and rejection of traditional gender roles. In adolescents and adults, it is manifested as the persistent belief that one was born the wrong sex and preoccupation with altering primary and secondary sex characteristics. The category **gender identity disorder not otherwise specified** is used to classify gender-related disorders distinct from gender identity disorder, such as GENDER DYSPHORIA related to congenital INTERSEXUALITY, stress-related cross-dressing behavior (see TRANSVESTISM), or preoccupation with castration or penectomy (removal of the penis).

gender nonconformity behavior that differs from that of others of the same sex or from cultural expectations of male and female behavior. It sometimes is a developmental marker of adult sexual orientation.

gender orientation see SEXUAL ORIENTATION.

gender reassignment **1.** the changing of an individual's gender label because of incorrect gender assignment at birth, due to the presence of anomalous genitalia (as in INTERSEXUALITY). **2.** see SEX REASSIGNMENT.

gender role the pattern of behavior, personality traits, and attitudes that define masculinity or femininity in a particular culture. It frequently is considered the external manifestation of the internalized GENDER IDENTITY, although the two are not necessarily consistent with one another.

gender schema the organized set of beliefs and expectations that guides one's understanding of maleness and femaleness.

gender stereotype a relatively fixed, overly simplified concept of the attitudes and behaviors considered normal and appropriate for a person in a particular culture, based on his or her biological sex. Research indicates that these STEREOTYPES are prescriptive as well as descriptive. Gender stereotypes often support the social conditioning of gender roles.

gender typing expectations about people's behavior that are based on their biological sex or the process through which children acquire and internalize such expectations.

gene *n.* the basic unit of heredity, responsible for storing genetic information and transmitting it to subsequent generations. The observable characteristics of an organism (i.e., its PHENOTYPE) are determined by numerous genes, which contain the instructions necessary for the functioning of the organism's constituent cells. Each gene consists of a section of DNA, a large and complex molecule that, in higher organisms, is arranged to form the CHROMOSOMES of the cell nucleus. Instructions are embodied in the chemical composition of the DNA, according to the GENETIC CODE. In classical genetics, a gene is described in terms of the trait that it determines and is investigated largely by virtue of the variations brought about by its different forms, or ALLELES. At the molecular level, most genes encode proteins, which carry out the functions of the cell or act to regulate the expression of other genes. A minority encode vital components of the cell's protein-assembling apparatus, such as ribosomes. Recent advances in genetic technology and the work of the HUMAN GENOME PROJECT have done much to illuminate the mechanism of gene action and have pinpointed genes responsible for various inherited diseases. This will greatly enhance knowledge of physical and mental disease in coming decades. See also DOMINANT ALLELE; RECESSIVE ALLELE.

gene–environment interaction an interaction between one or more genes and factors in the environment, such as may be needed to trigger the onset of a disease, condition, or characteristic.

gene–gene interaction an interaction between two or more genes, such as may be responsible for the development of a disease, condition, or characteristic.

gene knockout the deliberate inactivation of a particular gene in order to understand better the function of that gene. Using GENETIC ENGINEERING, scientists replace a normal gene (in an organism such as a mouse) with a defective gene and assess the impact of the defect on the organism.

gene linkage the tendency for genes or GENETIC MARKERS that are located physically close to each other on a chromosome to be inherited together. Linkage data can provide high-risk family members with estimates of their individual risk for the disease or condition conveyed by the gene.

general ability a measurable ability believed to underlie skill in handling all types of intellectual tasks. See also GENERAL FACTOR.

general ability tests tests designed to measure the GENERAL FACTOR of intelligence. They usually require, among other things, understanding and applying relations among relatively abstract stimuli, such as geometric forms.

general adaptation syndrome (**GAS**) the physiological consequences of severe stress. The syndrome has three stages: alarm, resistance, and exhaustion. The first stage, the **alarm reaction** (or **alarm stage**), comprises two substages: the **shock phase**, marked by a decrease in body temperature, blood pressure, and muscle tone and loss of fluid from body tissues; and the **countershock phase**, during which the sympathetic nervous system is aroused and there is an increase in adrenocortical hormones, triggering a defensive reaction, such as the FIGHT-OR-FLIGHT RESPONSE. The **resistance stage** (or **adaptation stage**) consists of stabilization at the increased physiological levels. High blood pressure can develop into hypertension, with risk of cardiovascular disturbance. Resources may be depleted, and permanent organ changes produced. The **exhaustion stage** is characterized by breakdown of acquired adaptations to a prolonged stressful situation; it is evidenced by sleep disturbances, irritability, severe loss of concentration, restlessness, trembling that disturbs motor coordination, fatigue, jumpiness, low startle threshold, vulnerability to anxiety attacks, depressed mood, and crying spells. [first described by Austrian-born Canadian physician Hans Seyle (1907–1982)]

general arousal level of energy expenditure, proposed as one of the two dimensions in terms of which all human behavior can be explained (see AROUSAL), the other being approach–withdrawal.

general factor (symbol: *g*) a hypothetical source of individual differences in GENERAL ABILITY, which represents individuals' abilities to perceive relationships and to derive conclusions from them. The general factor is said to be a basic ability that underlies the performance of different varieties of intellectual tasks, in contrast to SPECIFIC FACTORS, which are alleged each to be unique to a single task. Even theorists who posit multiple mental abilities have often suggested that a general factor may underlie these (correlated) mental abilities. [postulated in 1904 by British psychologist Charles Spearman (1863–1945)]

G

generalizability *n.* the accuracy with which results or findings can be transferred to situations or people other than those originally studied.

generalization *n.* **1.** the process of deriving a concept, judgment, principle, or theory from a limited number of specific cases and applying it more widely, often to an entire class of objects, events, or people. See INDUCTIVE REASONING. **2.** a judgment or principle derived and applied in this way. **—generalize** *vb.*

generalized anxiety disorder (**GAD**) excessive anxiety and worry about a range of events and activities (e.g., world events, finances, health, appearance, activities of family members and friends, work, or school) accompanied by such symptoms as restlessness, fatigue, impaired concentration, irritability, muscle tension, and disturbed sleep. The anxiety occurs on more days than not and is experienced as difficult to control.

generalized seizure a seizure in which abnormal electrical activity involves the entire brain rather than a specific focal area. The two most common forms are ABSENCE SEIZURES and some TONIC–CLONIC SEIZURES.

general linear model a large class of statistical techniques, including REGRESSION ANALYSIS, ANALYSIS OF VARIANCE, and correlational analysis, that describe the relationship between a DEPENDENT VARIABLE and one or more INDEPENDENT VARIABLES. Most statistical techniques employed in the behavioral sciences can be subsumed under the general linear model.

general medical condition a disorder that has known physical causes and observable physical psychopathology. Examples include hypertension and diabetes. Such disorders are classified on Axis III of the *DSM–IV–TR* (see AXIS).

General Neuropsychological Deficit Scale a scale that combines a series of tests from the HALSTEAD–REITAN NEUROPSYCHOLOGICAL BATTERY to generate an overall estimate of cognitive impairment: The higher the score, the greater the impairment.

general paresis dementia associated with advanced neurosyphilitic infection of the brain (neurosyphilis), a condition that is now extremely rare because syphilis is usually diagnosed and treated in its early stages. The first symptoms of general paresis appear 5–30 years after the primary infection. Psychological signs are irritability, confusion, fatigue, and forgetfulness, followed by headaches, confabulation, and deterioration in behavior and judgment. If untreated with antibiotics, physical signs gradually develop, including sagging facial muscles, vacant expression, slurred speech, and poor handwriting, followed by inability to dress, paralysis, convulsions, loss of bladder and bowel control, and gradual deterioration to a vegetative state. General paresis was formerly known as **general paralysis of the insane**, **dementia paralytica**, **paralytic dementia**, and **paretic psychosis**. Also called **general paralysis**.

general psychology the study of the basic principles, problems, and methods underlying the science of psychology, including such areas as the physiological basis of behavior, human growth and development, emotions, motivation, learning, the senses, perception, thinking processes, memory, intelligence, personality theory, psychological testing, behavior disorders, social behavior, and mental health. The study is viewed from various perspectives, including physiological, historical, theoretical, philosophical, and practical.

general systems theory an interdisciplinary conceptual framework focusing on wholeness, pattern, relationship, hierarchical order, integration, and organization. It was designed to move beyond the reductionistic and mechanistic tradition in science (see REDUCTIONISM) and integrate the fragmented approaches and different classes of phenomena studied by contemporary science into an organized whole. An entity or phenomenon should be viewed holistically as a set of elements interacting with one another (i.e., as a system), and the goal of general systems theory is to identify and understand the principles applicable to all systems. The impact of each element in a system depends on the role played by other elements in the system and order arises from interaction among these elements. Also called **systems theory**. [formulated by Austrian biologist Ludwig von Bertalanffy (1901–1972)]

generativity versus stagnation the seventh stage of ERIKSON'S EIGHT STAGES OF DEVELOPMENT. Generativity is the positive goal of middle adulthood, interpreted in terms not only of procreation but also of creativity and fulfilling one's full parental and social responsibilities toward the next generation, in contrast to a narrow interest in the self, or self-absorption. Also called **generativity versus self-absorption**.

generic name the nonproprietary name for a pharmaceutical compound. In the United States, the name is adopted by the United States Adopted Name Council and, if recognized by the United States Pharmacopoeia (USP), becomes the official name of the compound. Compare PROPRIETARY DRUG; TRADEMARK.

generosity *n.* the quality of freely giving one's support or resources to others in need. See also KINDNESS. **—generous** *adj.*

gene splicing the technique of inserting genetic material, in the form of DNA, into an existing DNA molecule. This is commonly performed in GENETIC ENGINEERING when genetic material from one organism is introduced into another organism, usually of a different species. The resultant RECOMBINANT DNA may create new sources of drugs or similar organic substances from microorganisms or correct genetic defects in organisms.

gene therapy the insertion of segments of healthy DNA into human body cells to correct defective segments responsible for disease development. A carrier molecule called a vector is used to deliver the therapeutic gene to the patient's target cells, restoring them to a normal state of producing properly functioning proteins. Though experimental, current gene therapy holds significant promise as an effective treatment for a variety of pathological conditions, including neurodegenerative disorders. It is, however, not without its share of problems: (a) difficulties integrating therapeutic DNA into the genome and the rapidly dividing nature of many cells have prevented any long-term benefits; (b) avoiding the stimulation of the immune system response to foreign objects; and (c) conditions that arise from mutations in a single gene are the best candidates for gene therapy, yet some the most commonly occurring disorders (e.g., heart disease, high blood pressure, Alzheimer's disease, arthritis, diabetes) are caused by the combined effects of variations in many genes. Additionally, there are ethical, legal, and social concerns associated with the practice. See also GENETIC ENGINEERING.

genetic code the instructions in genes that "tell" the cell how to make specific proteins. The code resides in the sequence of bases occurring as constituents of the genetic material, DNA or RNA. These bases are represented by the letters A, T, G, and C (which stand for adenine, thymine, guanine, and cytosine, respectively). In messenger RNA, uracil (U) replaces thymine. Each unit, or codon, of the code consists of three consecutive bases. Hence, there are 64 possible triplet combinations of the four bases, which specify the amino acids that make up each protein molecule.

genetic counseling an interactive method of educating a prospective parent about genetic risks, benefits and limitations of genetic testing, reproductive risks, and options for surveillance and screening related to diseases with potentially inherited causes. Genetic counseling is most often provided by geneticists or **genetic counselors**, who are trained to discuss hereditary disease with individuals, take PEDIGREES, and help individuals and families make decisions about the options open to them with regard to genetic disease. Genetic testing may or may not be a part of genetic counseling. Genetic counselors also assess the psychological implications of risk notification to the individual being counseled and the need for further psychological counseling following disclosure of test results. Also called **genetic guidance**. See also PRETEST COUNSELING; POSTTEST COUNSELING.

genetic determinism the doctrine that human and nonhuman animal behavior and mental activity are largely (or completely) controlled by the genetic constitution of the individual and that responses to environmental influences are for the most part innately determined. See BIOLOGICAL DETERMINISM; DETERMINISM; NATURE–NURTURE.

genetic disorder any disease or condition that is due to an abnormality of a gene or chromosome (see MUTATION). Also called **inherited disorder**.

genetic engineering techniques by which the genetic contents of living cells or viruses can be deliberately altered, either by modifying the existing genes or by introducing novel material (e.g., a gene from another species). This is undertaken for many different reasons, including basic research on genetic mechanisms, the large-scale production of particular gene products (e.g., medically useful proteins), and the genetic modification of crop plants. There have also been attempts to modify defective human body cells in the hope of treating certain genetic diseases. However, considerable public concern focuses on the effects and limits of genetic engineering of plants and animals, including humans. See also GENE SPLICING; RECOMBINANT DNA.

geneticism *n.* the concept that behavior is inborn, as in Sigmund FREUD's theory of instincts and psychosexual development. See also GENETIC DETERMINISM.

geneticist *n.* a health professional who specializes in the study of GENETICS. A geneticist may be a member of the staff of a medical services department of a hospital, medical college, or research institution.

genetic map a chromosome map of a species that shows the position of its known genes, GENETIC MARKERS, or both relative to each other. In humans, genetic mapping entails examining the pattern of inheritance of numerous traits or other markers, over many generations, to establish the degree of GENE LINKAGE.

genetic marker a gene or segment of DNA with an identifiable location on a chromosome and whose inheritance can be readily tracked through different generations. Because DNA segments that lie near each other on a chromosome tend to be inherited together, markers are often used to determine the inheritance of a gene that has not yet been identified but whose approximate location is known.

genetic predisposition a tendency for certain physical or mental traits to be inherited, including physical and mental conditions and disorders. Schizophrenia, for example, is a mental disorder with a genetic predisposition that affects less than 1% of the general population but increasingly larger percentages of distant relatives, siblings, and identical twins of individuals affected. Also called **hereditary predisposition**.

G

genetics *n.* the branch of biology that is concerned with the mechanisms and phenomena of heredity and the laws that determine inherited traits. See also BEHAVIORAL GENETICS; BIOGENESIS.

genetotropic disease any disease due to an inherited enzyme defect or deficiency. Phenylketonuria and other inborn errors of metabolism are examples of such disorders.

genital *adj.* relating to the sex organs. The external genital organs are the penis and scrotum for men and the vulva for women. The internal genital organs are the vagina, uterus, and ovaries for women and the testicles and prostate for men.

genital arousal in sleep penile erection in men and clitoral enlargement and vaginal lubrication in women that occur during REM SLEEP (in which dreams occur). It is the result of an increase in pelvic blood flow and occurs with all dream content; it is not associated only with sexual dreams. The phenomenon is used as part of the diagnostic procedures for male erection problems, as absence of nocturnal penile tumescence is a measure of physical problems involved in ERECTILE DYSFUNCTION.

genital character see GENITAL PERSONALITY.

genital eroticism the arousal of sexual excitement by stimulation of the genital organs.

genital herpes a HERPES INFECTION that involves the genitals, caused by herpes simplex Type 2. Although genital herpes is usually transmitted by sexual contact, some epidemiologists believe that because of extreme human susceptibility to the virus it is possible for transmission to occur through other means (e.g., hand-to-hand contact), especially in cities or other areas of high population density.

genitalia *pl. n.* the reproductive organs of the male or female. The **male genitalia** include the penis, testes and related structures, prostate gland, seminal vesicles, and bulbourethral glands. The **female genitalia** consist of the vagina, uterus, ovaries, fallopian tubes, and related structures. The **external genitalia** comprise the vulva in females and the penis and testicles in males. Also called **genitals**.

genital intercourse sexual intercourse involving insertion of the penis into the vagina, as opposed to other forms of sexual activity.

genitality *n.* the capacity to experience erotic sensation in the genital organs, starting with childhood masturbation and culminating in adult sexuality.

genitalization *n.* **1.** in psychoanalytic theory, the focusing of the genital libido on nonsexual objects that resemble or symbolize the sex organs, such as knives, shoes, or locks of hair. See also FETISH. **2.** in psychoanalytic theory, the achievement of a GENITAL PERSONALITY. **—genitalize** *vb.*

genital love in psychoanalytic theory, sexually mature love of another person achieved during the GENITAL STAGE of PSYCHOSEXUAL DEVELOPMENT. See also GENITAL PERSONALITY.

genital mutilation the destruction or physical modification of the external genitalia, especially when done for cultural reasons (as in circumcision or FEMALE GENITAL MUTILATION) or as a form of self-punishment.

genital personality in psychoanalytic theory, the sexually mature, adult personality that ideally develops during the last stage (the GENITAL STAGE) of PSYCHOSEXUAL DEVELOPMENT. Individuals who have reached this stage of development are posited to have fully resolved their OEDIPUS COMPLEX and to exhibit a mature sexuality that involves true intimacy and expresses equal concern for their own and their partner's satisfaction. Also called **genital character**. See also GENITAL LOVE.

genital stage in psychoanalytic theory, the final stage of PSYCHOSEXUAL DEVELOPMENT, ideally reached in puberty, when the OEDIPUS COMPLEX has been fully resolved and erotic interest and activity are focused on intercourse with a sexual partner. Also called **genital phase**. See also GENITAL LOVE; GENITAL PERSONALITY.

genital stimulation a complex set of factors associated with sexual arousal in mammals, including integration of male and female genital reflexes, odors, hormone secretions, sights, sounds, and tactile and kinesthetic cues. Each factor contributes to genital stimulation, which still may occur in the absence of one or more of the cues.

genital zones the external reproductive or-gans and adjacent areas that are capable of producing genital sensations. See also EROGENOUS ZONE.

genome *n.* all of the genetic material contained in an organism or cell. Mapping of the estimated 20,000–25,000 genes in human DNA was one of several goals of the HUMAN GENOME PROJECT.

genotype *n.* the genetic composition of an individual organism as a whole or at one or more specific positions on a chromosome. Compare PHENOTYPE. **—genotypic** *adj.*

genotype–environment effects the effects of genetic constitution on experience, based on the proposal that an individual's GENOTYPE influences which environments he or she encounters and the type of experiences he or she has. Three types of genotype–environment effects are proposed: passive (through environments provided by biologically related parents); evocative (through responses elicited by individuals from others); and active (through the selection of different environments by different individuals). [proposed by U.S. psychologists Sandra Scarr (1936–) and Kathleen McCartney (1955–)]

genotype–phenotype correlation a correlation between the location or nature of a mutation in a gene and the expression of that mutation in the individual, based on observations of affected individuals and their genotypes. Attempts at such correlations are made to elucidate which characteristics of a mutation affect the age of onset or severity of diseases with a genetic etiology.

Geodon *n.* a trade name for ZIPRASIDONE.

geophagy *n.* the eating of dirt or clay. It is most commonly seen in individuals with mental retardation, young children, and occasionally in pregnant women. It is usually a symptom of PICA but in some cultures it is an accepted practice.

Geriatric Depression Scale (**GDS**) an assessment instrument specifically designed for use with adults aged 65 years and over. It is self-administered and comprises a series of 30 yes–no questions (e.g., "Do you often get bored?", "Is it easy for you to make decisions?", "Do you enjoy getting up in the morning?") about depressive symptoms that excludes somatic disturbances often experienced by older adults. [originally developed in 1982 by psychologist T. L. Brink (1949–), psychiatrist Jerome A. Yesavage, and colleagues]

geriatric disorder any disease or chronic condition that occurs commonly, but not exclusively, among older people. Examples of geriatric disorders include glaucoma, arthritis, and Alzheimer's disease and other dementias.

geriatrician *n.* a physician, psychologist, or other health care provider who specializes in the biopsychosocial treatment and management of older adults. See also GERIATRICS.

geriatric psychology see GEROPSYCHOLOGY.

geriatric psychopharmacology the branch of pharmacology that deals with issues related to the use of and response to psychoactive agents in older adults, as well as the mechanisms responsible. Metabolic changes associated with aging can affect a drug's biological activity and may increase the sensitivity of the patient's central nervous system to drugs.

geriatric psychotherapy the use of therapy to treat the mental disorders of older adults. Geriatric psychotherapy requires an understanding of age-related and cohort-related differences in symptoms and behavior.

geriatric rehabilitation the process of restoring, to the fullest extent possible, the functional abilities of older adults following an illness or injury that resulted in loss of the ability to live independently.

geriatrics *n.* the branch of medicine that deals with the diagnosis and treatment of disorders in older adults. **—geriatric** *adj.*

geriatric screening a program or system administered by a hospital, community center, county health center, or other such agency to provide qualified staff who evaluate the needs of older adults by providing physical examinations and care, psychological evaluations, and financial counseling.

gerontology *n.* the scientific interdisciplinary study of old age and the aging process. Those involved in gerontology include psychologists, biologists, sociologists, medical scientists, medical practitioners, geriatric service providers, and scholars from the humanities and social sciences. **—gerontological** *adj.* **—gerontologist** *n.*

gerophilia *n.* sexual attraction to much older partners. Also called **gerontophilia**.

geropsychology *n.* a branch of psychology dealing with enhancing the welfare and mental health of older adults via the provision of various psychological services. Also called **geriatric psychology**. **—geropsychological** *adj.* **—geropsychologist** *n.*

Gesamtvorstellung *n.* the act of holding in mind the entire content of a sentence before the first word is spoken. [German, literally: "complete concept"; coined by Wilhelm WUNDT]

Geschwind's theory the hypothesis that excessive intrauterine exposure to ANDROGENS inhibits development of the THYMUS gland and left cerebral hemisphere, explaining why autoimmune disorders tend to be associated with learning disabilities (including DYSLEXIA) and are more frequent in males than in females. [proposed in 1984 by U.S. neuroscientists Norman **Geschwind** (1926–1984) and Albert Galaburda (1948–)]

gestalt *n.* an entire perceptual configuration (from German: "shape," "configuration," "totality," "form"), made up of elements that are integrated and interactive in such a way as to confer properties on the whole configuration that are not possessed by the individual elements. See PERCEPTUAL ORGANIZATION. See also GESTALT PRINCIPLES OF ORGANIZATION; GESTALT PSYCHOLOGY.

gestaltism *n.* the belief system of GESTALT PSYCHOLOGY.

gestalt principles of organization principles of perception, derived by the Gestalt psychologists, that describe the tendency to perceive and interpret certain configurations at

G

the level of the whole, rather than in terms of their component features. See also GOODNESS OF CONFIGURATION; PRÄGNANZ.

Gestalt psychology a psychological approach that focuses on the dynamic organization of experience into patterns or configurations (from German *Gestalt* [pl. *Gestalten*]: "shape," "form," "configuration," "totality"). This view was espoused by German psychologists Wolfgang KÖHLER, Kurt KOFFKA, and Max WERTHEIMER in the early 20th century as a revolt against STRUCTURALISM, which analyzed experience into static, atomistic sensations, and also against the equally atomistic approach of BEHAVIORISM, which attempted to dissect complex behavior into elementary conditioned reflexes. Gestalt psychology holds, instead, that experience is an organized whole of which the pieces are an integral part. A crucial demonstration (1912) is that of Wertheimer with two successively flashed lights, which gave the illusion of motion between them rather than of individually flashing lights. Later experiments gave rise to principles of perceptual organization (see, for example, CLOSURE; PRÄGNANZ), which were then applied to the study of learning, insight, memory, social psychology, and art.

gestalt therapy a form of PSYCHOTHERAPY in which the central focus is on the totality of the client's functioning and relationships in the HERE AND NOW, rather than on investigation of past experiences and developmental history. One of the themes is that growth occurs by assimilation of what is needed from the environment and that psychopathology arises as a disturbance of contact with the environment. Gestalt techniques, which can be applied in either a group or an individual setting, are designed to bring out spontaneous feelings and self-awareness and promote personality growth. Examples of such techniques are ROLE PLAY, the EMPTY-CHAIR TECHNIQUE, and the HOT-SEAT TECHNIQUE. [first proposed in the 1940s by German-born U.S. psychiatrist Frederick (Fritz) S. Perls (1893–1970)]

GHB *g*amma-*h*ydroxy*b*utyrate: a potent CNS DEPRESSANT that is a metabolic product of the inhibitory neurotransmitter GAMMA-AMINOBUTYRIC ACID (GABA). It is currently used for treatment of narcolepsy and management of alcohol withdrawal, and in some countries (although not the United States) has been used as an intravenous general anesthetic. It is commonly encountered as a drug of abuse that produces euphoria and sedation and purportedly enhances sexual arousal. Its ability to induce amnesia or unconsciousness has led it to be characterized as a DATE-RAPE DRUG. Signs of severe toxicity may occur at levels greater than 40–60 mg/kg, and deaths have been reported, usually when the substance is mixed with alcohol. Withdrawal syndromes, characterized by anxiety, tremor, confusion, and rarely seizures, have also been reported. U.S. trade name: **Xyrem**.

ghost sickness a CULTURE-BOUND SYNDROME found in Native American communities and attributed to ghosts or sometimes witchcraft. Symptoms include recurring nightmares, weakness, loss of appetite, fear, anxiety, hallucinations, confusion, and a sense of suffocation.

giftedness *n.* the state of possessing a great amount of natural ability, talent, or intelligence, which usually becomes evident at a very young age. Giftedness in intelligence is often categorized as an IQ of two standard deviations above the mean or higher (130 for most IQ tests), obtained on an individually administered IQ test. Many schools and service organizations now use a combination of attributes as the basis for assessing giftedness, including one or more of the following: high intellectual capacity, academic achievement, demonstrable real-world achievement, creativity, task commitment, proven talent, leadership skills, and physical or athletic prowess. The combination of several attributes, or the prominence of one primary attribute, may be regarded as a threshold for the identification of giftedness. Unfortunately, many schools and program administrators have created policies that require multiple indicators for identifying and teaching gifted individuals, and—as a group—these people have received less attention and fewer special services than individuals with disabilities who require SPECIAL EDUCATION. **—gifted** *adj.*

gigolo *n.* a man who is paid to be a woman's social companion or escort, or to provide sexual services for her, or both.

Gilles de la Tourette's syndrome see TOURETTE'S DISORDER.

Gillespie syndrome see ANIRIDIA-OLIGOPHRENIA-CEREBELLAR ATAXIA SYNDROME. [described in 1965 by F. D. **Gillespie** (1927–), U.S. ophthalmologist]

Gindler method a series of exercises involving breathing, gentle touch, and posturing intended to foster personal growth and enhance sensory awareness. [Elsa **Gindler** (1885–1961), German gymnastics teacher]

ginkgo *n.* a tree, *Ginkgo biloba*, that is indigenous to Asia but now cultivated widely. An extract of the leaves has been used for centuries by Chinese herbalists and is reputed to possess medicinal and psychotropic properties. It is also a popular dietary supplement primarily used to improve mental acuity, although clinical evidence supporting this effect is largely lacking. The active compounds in ginkgo extract have anticoagulant properties, and ginkgo has been investigated as a treatment for vascular disorders, both peripheral and cerebral (e.g., vascular dementia), the latter with equivocal results. Gingko may also have neuroprotective properties and currently is under investigation as a treatment for the symptoms of Alzheimer's disease, with results suggesting a potential cognition stabilizing effect. Data, however, suggest continual long-term use of ginkgo may be associated with excessive bleeding or spontaneous hemorrhage. Additionally, there are several known and potential interactions of ginkgo with other agents, including anticoagulants, anticonvulsants, MONOAMINE OXIDASE INHIBITORS, and NSAIDS. Ginkgo may also lower seizure thresholds and should not be used by people who have a history of seizures.

ginseng *n.* the root of various plants of the genus *Panax*, valued for its medicinal properties, particularly in Oriental cultures. It has a reputation as an aphrodisiac and is also used to enhance overall physical and mental well-being, enhance strength, boost energy, and relieve stress, but there is little clinical evidence supporting its effectiveness for any of these purposes. Some studies, however, have suggested that ginseng may help regulate blood glucose levels, which has prompted investigation of its potential use as a treatment for diabetes, and may improve immune function. Side effects of ginseng use are infrequent but may include nausea and vomiting, diarrhea, insomnia, headaches, nosebleeds, and blood pressure abnormalities. Additionally, ginseng may interact with anticoagulants, caffeine, MONOAMINE OXIDASE INHIBITORS, and oral hypoglycemics.

Glasgow Coma Scale (**GCS**) a rating scale, with scores ranging from 3 to 15, that is used to assess levels of consciousness following a head injury. It is the sum of three ratings: eye-opening response (graded 1–4), motor response (1–6), and verbal response (1–5). Scores of 8 or below are indicative of severe brain injury and coma, scores of 9 to 12 are indicative of moderate injury, and scores of 13 or higher are indicative of mild injury. [originally developed in 1974 by neurologists Graham M. Teasdale and Bryan J. Jennett at the University of Glasgow, Scotland]

Glasgow Outcome Scale (**GOS**) a rating scale to assess social activity and independent functioning after traumatic brain injury. The five categories of the original scale are death, persistent vegetative state, severe disability, moderate disability, and good recovery. An extended GOS that divides each of the latter three levels into an upper and lower degree of disability is also available. [originally developed in 1975 by neurologist Bryan J. Jennett and psychiatrist Michael R. Bond at the University of Glasgow, Scotland]

glia *n.* nonneuronal tissue in the nervous system that provides structural, nutritional, and other kinds of support to neurons. It may consist of very small cells (microglia) or relatively large ones (macroglia). The latter include astrocytes, ependymal cells, and the two types of cells that form the MYELIN SHEATH around axons: oligodendrocytes in the central nervous system and Schwann cells in the peripheral nervous system. Also called **neuroglia**. **—glial** *adj.*

global amnesia loss of memory for recent events (retrograde amnesia) combined with an inability to remember new information (anterograde amnesia). It is a very rare condition of unknown etiology. See also TRANSIENT GLOBAL AMNESIA.

Global Assessment of Functioning Scale (**GAF scale**) a scale used for treatment planning and outcome evaluation on Axis V of *DSM–IV–TR*'s multiaxial evaluation system. Scores (1–100) reflect the clinician's judgment of a patient's overall level of psychological, social, and occupational functioning at the time of assessment. The GAF scale is also used to measure the highest level of such functioning in the past year.

Global Deterioration Scale (**GDS**) a seven-point scale used to indicate the severity of a primary degenerative DEMENTIA, such as ALZHEIMER'S DISEASE, in an older adult, based on caregivers' observations of behaviors in the individual. The scale ranges from no cognitive decline (1) to very severe cognitive decline (7). [developed in 1982 by U.S. geriatric psychiatrist Barry Reisberg (1947–)]

globus pallidus one of the BASAL GANGLIA. It is the main output region of the basal ganglia: Its output neurons terminate on thalamic neurons, which in turn project to the cerebral cortex.

globus pharyngeus a sensation of having a lump in the throat for which no medical cause can be identified. It can be a symptom of CONVERSION DISORDER and was formerly called **globus hystericus**.

glossolalia *n.* unintelligible utterances that simulate coherent speech, which may have meaning to the utterer but do not to the listener. Glossolalia is found in religious ecstasy ("speaking in tongues"), hypnotic or mediumistic trances, and occasionally in schizophrenia. See also NEOLOGISM.

glove anesthesia a SENSORY CONVERSION SYMPTOM in which there is a functional loss of sensitivity in the hand and part of the forearm (i.e., areas that would be covered by a glove). See also STOCKING ANESTHESIA.

glucocorticoid *n.* any CORTICOSTEROID hormone that acts chiefly on carbohydrate metabolism. Glucocorticoids include cortisol, corticosterone, and cortisone.

glucuronidation *n.* a metabolic process by which drugs or other substances are combined with glucuronic acid to form more water-soluble compounds, which are more readily excreted by the kidneys or in bile. Glucuronidation is the most prevalent of the Phase II reactions of DRUG METABOLISM.

glue sniffing a form of substance abuse in which the fumes of certain adhesives, particularly plastic model glue, are inhaled for their stimulant effect and euphoria. TOLUENE is the ingredient with psychoactive effects; other hydrocarbons used for this purpose include XYLENE and BENZENE. See INHALANT; INHALANT ABUSE.

glutamate *n.* a salt or ester of the amino acid

G

GLUTAMIC ACID that serves as the predominant excitatory NEUROTRANSMITTER in the brain. Glutamate plays a critical role in cognitive, motor, and sensory functions; its role in the pathogenesis of schizophrenia is the subject of investigation. It exerts its effects by binding to GLUTAMATE RECEPTORS on neurons. Excessive activity of glutamate at these receptors is associated with damage to nerve tissue (neurotoxicity) and cell death, possibly the result of calcium ions flooding into the cell following overstimulation of NMDA RECEPTORS.

glutamate hypothesis the theory that decreased activity of the excitatory neurotransmitter glutamate is responsible for the clinical expression of schizophrenia. The hypothesis developed from observations that administration of NMDA receptor antagonists, such as PCP (phencyclidine) and KETAMINE, produce psychotic symptoms in humans and is supported by a number of recent studies. See also DOPAMINE HYPOTHESIS.

G

glutamate receptor any of various receptors that bind and respond to the excitatory neurotransmitter glutamate. Glutamate receptors are found on the surface of most neurons. There are two main divisions of glutamate receptors: the ionotropic and metabotropic. Ionotropic glutamate receptors are further divided into three classes: NMDA RECEPTORS, AMPA RECEPTORS, and kainate receptors. Metabotropic glutamate receptors (mGlu or mGluR) are subdivided into several classes denoted by subscript numbers (i.e., $mGlu_1$, $mGlu_2$, etc.).

glutamic acid an AMINO ACID that is regarded as nonessential in diets but is important for normal brain function. It is converted into GAMMA-AMINOBUTYRIC ACID in a reaction catalyzed by the enzyme glutamic acid decarboxylase and requiring pyridoxal phosphate, formed from vitamin B_6 (pyridoxine), as a coenzyme.

glutamic acid decarboxylase the enzyme responsible for the formation of the neurotransmitter GAMMA-AMINOBUTYRIC ACID (GABA) from GLUTAMIC ACID.

glutethimide *n.* one of the nonbarbiturate sedatives introduced in the early 1950s. Structurally similar to and pharmacologically interchangeable with the BARBITURATES, glutethimide offered no advantages for treatment of anxiety or insomnia. Now rarely used clinically, it is sometimes encountered as a drug of abuse. U.S. trade name: **Doriden**.

glycine *n.* an AMINO ACID that serves as one of the two major inhibitory neurotransmitters in the central nervous system (particularly the spinal cord), the other being GAMMA-AMINOBUTYRIC ACID (GABA). Glycine synthesis occurs via two different pathways; in the most important of these, glycine is synthesized from the amino acid serine in a single reaction catalyzed by the enzyme serine hydroxymethyltransferase. Also called **aminoacetic acid**.

glycosaminoglycan *n.* see MUCOPOLYSACCHARIDOSIS.

goal-directed behavior behavior that is oriented toward attaining a particular goal. It is typically identifiable by observing that the animal or person ceases search behavior and engages in detour behavior when it encounters obstacles to the goal.

goal-limited adjustment therapy see SECTOR THERAPY.

goal object that which an individual is seeking to attain, particularly the final, ultimate goal following a series of subgoals.

goal orientation **1.** the tendency to physically or mentally position oneself toward a goal. **2.** the characteristic of individuals who tend to direct their behaviors toward attaining goals, particularly long-term goals.

goal response the final response in a chain of behavior directed toward obtaining a goal. In conditioning, it specifically refers to the response given to a positive reinforcing stimulus.

goal stimulus a proprioceptive or other interoceptive stimulus arising from GOAL-DIRECTED BEHAVIOR.

go-around *n.* a technique used in group psychotherapy in which each member in turn is requested to react to another member, a discussion theme, or a described or enacted situation.

godemiche *n.* see DILDO.

goldenseal *n.* a shrub, *Hydrastis canadensis*, with medicinal properties. Indigenous to the eastern United States, it has a long history as a folk remedy to control uterine bleeding, and its leaves are commonly used as a poultice and antibacterial agent. There are few clinical studies evaluating the efficacy of goldenseal but its active ingredients, the alkaloids **berberine** and **hydrastine**, have been studied extensively. Berberine has been shown to have antimicrobial properties and may also be effective in preventing the growth of cancer cells. Hydrastine has vasoconstrictive and abortifacient effects and has been shown to induce labor in pregnant women when taken orally. At recommended doses, goldenseal appears to have minimal adverse effects (e.g., irritation of the mouth, throat, and stomach; tingling of the skin) but at higher doses it may cause hypertension and increase heart rate; it has also been associated with seizures and other evidence of overstimulation of the central nervous system, and at very high doses may be toxic, potentially causing paralysis, respiratory failure, and death.

Goltz syndrome a congenital disorder marked by eye anomalies, absent or extra digits, and skin lesions, particularly nodules of herniated subcutaneous fat in thin skin areas. About 5% of affected individuals tested have been found to have mental retardation. Also called **focal dermal hypoplasia**; **Goltz–Gorlin syndrome**.

[Robert William **Goltz** (1923–) and Robert James **Gorlin** (1923–2006), U.S. physicians]

gonad *n.* either of the primary male and female sex organs, that is, the testis or the ovary. **—gonadal** *adj.*

gonadal dysgenesis see TURNER'S SYNDROME.

gonadotropin *n.* any of several hormones that stimulate functions of the gonads. Gonadotropins include follicle-stimulating hormone and luteinizing hormone, produced by the anterior PITUITARY GLAND in response to GONADOTROPIN-RELEASING HORMONE, and chorionic gonadotropin, which is produced by the placenta (see HUMAN CHORIONIC GONADOTROPIN). Also called **gonadotropic hormone**. See also HUMAN MENOPAUSAL GONADOTROPIN. **—gonadotropic** *adj.*

gonadotropin-releasing hormone (**GnRH**) a hypothalamic hormone that controls the release of luteinizing hormone and follicle-stimulating hormone from the anterior pituitary gland. See also RELEASING HORMONE.

gonorrhea *n.* a sexually transmitted disease caused by the bacterium *Neisseria gonorrhoeae* (the gonococcus). The primary focus of infection is the genital tract; untreated, it can lead to sterility. The bacterium can later infect the eyes and cause **gonococcal conjunctivitis**, a serious condition that can lead to blindness. See also URETHRITIS.

good breast in the psychoanalytic theory of Melanie KLEIN, the internalized representation (see INTROJECTION) of the mother's breast as nourishing and satisfying. According to Klein, the infant first experiences the mother and the nourishing breast as PART-OBJECTS with positive qualities—the good breast—and negative qualities—the BAD BREAST.

good enough mother in the OBJECT RELATIONS THEORY of British psychoanalyst Donald Winnicott (1896–1971), the ordinary, devoted mother who provides an adequate or good enough environment for the growth of the infant's ego to express its TRUE SELF. The good enough mother begins mothering by adapting entirely to the infant and providing an environment free of IMPINGEMENTS, but later gradually creates small failures of adaptation to teach the infant to tolerate the frustrations of reality.

good enough parent a parent who cares for his or her child in any way that is adequate for proper development. [proposed by U.S. psychologist Sandra Scarr (1936–)]

good gestalt the quality possessed by an arrangement of stimuli that is complete, orderly, and clear with a high degree of GOODNESS OF CONFIGURATION. Although this is related to the principle of PRÄGNANZ, it is distinct in that the arrangement of stimuli need not be the simplest one possible. See also GESTALT; GESTALT PRINCIPLES OF ORGANIZATION.

good me in the SELF-SYSTEM theory of U.S. psychoanalyst Harry Stack Sullivan (1892–1949), the child's PERSONIFICATION of behaviors and impulses that meet with the approval of the parents. The good me is posited to develop as a part of the socialization process and to protect the child from anxiety about himself or herself. Compare BAD ME. See also NOT ME.

goodness of configuration the quality of a shape or form that has high levels of simplicity, regularity, symmetry, or continuity. Gestalt psychologist Wolfgang KÖHLER speculated that the mind tends to perceive more goodness of configuration than may actually exist in a shape. See also CLOSURE; GESTALT PRINCIPLES OF ORGANIZATION; PRÄGNANZ.

goodness of fit any index that reflects the degree to which values predicted by a model agree with empirically observed values.

good object in the OBJECT RELATIONS THEORY of Melanie KLEIN, an introjected PART-OBJECT that is perceived as benevolent and satisfying (see INTROJECTION). It is an early object representation that derives from of the object SPLITTING into parts containing positive and negative qualities. The good object forms the core of the infant's immature ego. Compare BAD OBJECT.

Gordon Diagnostic System (**GDS**) an assessment device that aids in the diagnosis of attention deficits. It provides information about an individual's ability to sustain attention and exert self-control on a continuous performance test. The GDS is a microprocessor-based, portable unit that administers a series of tasks in the form of games. [Michael **Gordon** (1952–), U.S. psychologist]

GOS abbreviation for GLASGOW OUTCOME SCALE.

G protein any of a class of proteins that are coupled to the intracellular portion of a type of membrane RECEPTOR (**G-protein-coupled receptors**) and are activated when the receptor binds an appropriate ligand (e.g., a neurotransmitter) on the extracellular surface. G proteins thus have a role in signal transduction, being involved, for example, in indirect chemical NEUROTRANSMISSION. They work in conjunction with the nucleotides guanosine diphosphate (GDP) and guanosine triphosphate (GTP) and serve to transmit the signal from the receptor to other cell components (e.g., ion channels) in various ways, for example by controlling the synthesis of SECOND MESSENGERS within the cell.

Graefenberg spot (**G-spot**) an area on the anterior wall of the vagina, about 4 cm (1–2 in.) into the vagina. Some women experience pleasure from stimulation of this area and may have an ejaculation from a gland there. However, it is not clear how many women have this gland, or find this area to be especially responsive during sexual activity, and some research suggests that the ejaculation may be urine, expelled from the bladder. [Ernst **Graefenberg** (1881–1957), German gynecologist]

grandiose delusion see DELUSION OF GRANDEUR.

grandiosity *n.* an exaggerated sense of one's greatness, importance, or ability. In extreme form, it may be regarded as a DELUSION OF GRANDEUR.

grand mal see TONIC–CLONIC SEIZURE.

grand mean a mean (numerical average) of a group of means.

graphoanalysis *n.* see GRAPHOPATHOLOGY.

graphology *n.* the study of the physical characteristics of handwriting, particularly as a means of inferring the writer's psychological state or personality characteristics. For example, it is sometimes used in personnel selection as a predictor of job performance. Graphology is based on the premise that writing is a form of expressive behavior, although there is little empirical evidence for its validity. Also called **handwriting analysis**. **—graphological** *adj.* **—graphologist** *n.*

graphomania *n.* a pathological impulse to write. In its most severe form, it may degenerate into GRAPHORRHEA.

graphopathology *n.* the interpretation of personality disorders by studying handwriting. Also called **graphoanalysis**.

graphorrhea *n.* the writing of long lists of incoherent, meaningless words, which sometimes occurs in the context of a MANIC EPISODE.

graphospasm *n.* a rare name for WRITER'S CRAMP.

grasp reflex an involuntary grasping by an individual of anything that touches the palm. This reflex is typical of infants but in older individuals it may be a sign of FRONTAL LOBE damage.

gratification *n.* the state of satisfaction following the fulfillment of a desire or the meeting of a need. See DELAY OF GRATIFICATION; IMMEDIATE GRATIFICATION.

gratification of instincts see SATISFACTION OF INSTINCTS.

Graves' disease a disorder characterized by enlargement and overactivity of the thyroid gland and marked by a swelling in the neck (goiter), abnormal protrusion of the eyeballs (exophthalmos), and rapid pulse and other symptoms of THYROTOXICOSIS. Also called **exophthalmic goiter**. [Robert J. **Graves** (1796–1853), Irish physician]

gray matter any area of neural tissue that is dominated by CELL BODIES and is devoid of myelin, such as the CEREBRAL CORTEX and the H-shaped PERIAQUEDUCTAL GRAY of the spinal cord. Compare WHITE MATTER.

Great Mother see MAGNA MATER.

greeting behavior a form of ATTACHMENT BEHAVIOR that in humans begins to manifest itself clearly at about 6 months of age, when the infant responds to the arrival of a parent or caregiver.

Greig syndrome see HYPERTELORISM. [David M. **Greig** (1864–1936), Scottish physician]

grief *n.* the anguish experienced after significant loss, usually the death of a beloved person. Grief is often distinguished from BEREAVEMENT and MOURNING. Not all bereavements result in a strong grief response; nor is all grief given public expression (see DISENFRANCHISED GRIEF). Grief often includes physiological distress, SEPARATION ANXIETY, confusion, yearning, obsessive dwelling on the past, and apprehension about the future. Intense grief can become life-threatening through disruption of the immune system, self-neglect, and suicidal thoughts. Grief may also take the form of regret for something lost, remorse for something done, or sorrow for a mishap to oneself.

grief counseling the provision of advice, information, and psychological support to help individuals whose ability to function has been impaired by someone's death, particularly that of a loved one or friend. It includes counseling for the grieving process and practical advice concerning arrangements for the funeral and burial of the loved one. Grief counseling is sometimes offered by staff in specialized agencies (e.g., hospices) or it may be carried out in the context of other counseling. See also BEREAVEMENT THERAPY.

griefwork *n.* the theoretical process through which bereaved people gradually reduce or transform their emotional connection to the person who has died and thereby refocus appropriately on their own ongoing lives. It is not necessary to sever all emotional connections with the dead person. Instead, adaptive griefwork will help transform the relationship symbolically, as a CONTINUING BOND that provides a sense of meaning and value conducive to forming new relationships.

grisi siknis a CULTURE-BOUND SYNDROME found in Nicaragua and characterized by headache, anxiety, anger, and the sudden onset of an episode of hyperactivity and potentially dangerous behavior in the form of running or fleeing. There is ensuing exhaustion, sleep, and amnesia for the episode. The syndrome, which has some similarities to PIBLOKTO, is usually classified as a DISSOCIATIVE TRANCE DISORDER.

grooming *n.* a basic function of self-care that includes cleaning and maintaining one's body, hair, clothes, and general appearance. In animals, grooming has both hygienic functions, such as picking parasites or dirt from the fur, and social functions, including the provision of reward through activation of ENDOGENOUS OPIOIDS in the recipients. Training or retraining in grooming can be a central aspect in the rehabilitation of individuals with mental or physical impairments.

gross motor describing activities or skills that use large muscles to move the trunk or limbs and control posture to maintain balance. Examples of **gross motor skills** include waving an arm, walking, hopping, and running. Compare FINE MOTOR.

grounded theory a set of procedures for the systematic analysis of unstructured qualitative data so as to derive by induction a theory that explains the observed phenomena.

ground rules in psychotherapy, the elements of the contract for therapy, including but not limited to the fee; the time, location, and frequency of the sessions; and therapist confidentiality.

group *n.* **1.** in social psychology, two or more interdependent individuals who influence one another through social interaction. Common features of groups include joint activities that either focus on the task at hand or concern the interpersonal relations between group members, structures involving roles and norms, a degree of cohesiveness, and shared goals. Also called **social group**. **2.** a collection of participants in a research study whose responses are to be compared to the responses of one or more other collections of research participants. Participants in a particular group all experience the same experimental conditions or receive the same treatment, which differs from the experimental conditions or treatments participants in other groups experience or receive. **3.** in the psychology of perception, a configuration of individual objects that are perceived to form a unified whole, or GESTALT.

group analysis the study of the pathological behavior of a group.

group-analytic psychotherapy a type of group psychotherapy that focuses on the communication and interaction processes taking place in the group as a whole. Interventions make use of group rather than individual forces as the principal therapeutic agent. Also called **therapeutic group analysis**. [originated in the 1940s by Sigmund Heinrich Foulkes (1898–1976)]

group climate the relative degree of acceptance, tolerance, and freedom of expression that characterizes the relationships within a counseling or therapy group. Interpersonal behavioral boundaries are generally freer and broader than in social contexts, and the meaning of interpersonal behavior is often the specific focus of group discussion.

group cohesion see COHESION.

group consciousness 1. the awareness of the group, its members, and their commonalities exhibited by individual members of the group. Just as SELF-CONSCIOUSNESS pertains to awareness of the self, so group consciousness pertains to awareness of the collective. **2.** a group's total awareness of itself, suggested in some cases to be greater than the sum of individual members' awareness.

group counseling a method of providing guidance and support for clients organized as a group, as opposed to individual counseling. Group counseling can be used, for example, to assist high school students in choosing a college or to assist employees of an organization in stating dissatisfactions and proposing solutions to managers and employers.

group difference any observed variation between groups of participants in an experiment when considering each group as a single entity.

group dynamics 1. the dynamic rather than static processes, operations, and changes that occur within social groups, which affect patterns of affiliation, communication, conflict, conformity, decision making, influence, leadership, norm formation, and power. The term, as used by Kurt LEWIN, emphasizes the power of the fluid, ever-changing forces that characterize interpersonal groups. Also called **group process**. **2.** the field of psychology devoted to the study of groups and group processes. **3.** a conceptual and clinical orientation in group psychotherapy that explicitly recognizes and explores group-level processes in the treatment group.

group experience in group psychotherapy and group counseling, the interactions that give the client an opportunity to gain insight into his or her problems by sharing with and learning from other members. The group experience is particularly valuable in helping clients understand how they are perceived by other people. When group therapy or counseling is given in addition to individual intervention, it allows the therapist or counselor to observe the client's emotional difficulties as revealed in group interactions.

group G monosomy a rare chromosomal disorder involving the absence of all or part of a G-group chromosome (i.e., chromosome 21 or 22). Affected individuals have short spadelike hands and severe mental retardation. Because of varied effects, more than one chromosomal defect may be involved. Chromosome 21 is often involved in translocations and aberrations related to DOWN SYNDROME.

group health plan see INDEMNITY PLAN.

group home a residential facility that offers housing and personal care services, such as meals, supervision, and transportation. Also called **group residence**.

group hypnosis see COLLECTIVE HYPNOTIZATION.

group identification 1. the act or process of associating oneself so strongly with a group and its members that one imitates and internalizes the group's distinctive features (actions, beliefs, standards, objectives, etc.). This process can lead not only to an enhanced sense of group belonging, group pride, and group commitment but also to autostereotyping, in which one accepts as self-descriptive certain stereotypical qualities attributed to the group as a whole, and a reduced sense of individuality (see DEINDIVIDUATION). **2.** in the psychoanalytic theory of Sigmund FREUD, the process by which individuals become emotionally attached to social groups. Just as children bond with and imitate their parents, adults bond with, and take on the characteristics of, their groups. **3.** more rarely, the act of considering another group's perspective or outlook even though one is not a member of that group.

group marriage a family pattern found in some indigenous cultures and certain minority religious groups in which several men and women live together, sharing the burdens of the household, the rearing of children, and a common sexual life. See also POLYGAMY.

group medical practice the practice of medicine by a group of physicians, typically various specialists, associated not only for administrative reasons but also for such clinical purposes as cooperative diagnosis, treatment, and prevention. Also called **group practice**.

G

group practice see GROUP MEDICAL PRACTICE.

group process 1. see GROUP DYNAMICS. **2.** the interpersonal component of a group session, in contrast to the content (such as decisions or information) generated during the session.

group relations theory the view that behavior is influenced not only by one's unique pattern of traits but also by one's need to conform to social demands and expectations. Social determinants become particularly evident in group therapy, which tends to challenge attitudes, such as prejudices, that are based on conformity and restricted thinking. [proposed by Gordon W. ALLPORT]

group residence see GROUP HOME.

group sex sexual activity among a group of heterosexual people, gay men, or lesbians, who usually meet with the express purpose of obtaining maximum satisfaction through such means as observing each other, experimenting with different techniques, and exchanging partners.

group superego in psychoanalytic theory, the portion of the SUPEREGO acquired from peer groups as opposed to the part derived from parental IDENTIFICATIONS.

group therapy treatment of psychological problems in which two or more participants interact with each other on both an emotional and a cognitive level, in the presence of one or more psychotherapists who serve as catalysts, facilitators, or interpreters. The approaches of groups vary, but in general they aim to provide an environment in which problems and concerns can be shared in an atmosphere of mutual respect and understanding. Group therapy seeks to enhance self-respect, deepen self-understanding, and improve interpersonal relationships. Also called **group psychotherapy**. Compare INDIVIDUAL THERAPY.

GROW, INC. a mutual-help organization developed to provide help for individuals with depression, anxiety, and other mental health problems. Using a TWELVE-STEP PROGRAM, it offers a "caring and sharing" community to help members attain emotional maturity, personal responsibility, and recovery from mental illness. GROW, INC., originated in Australia.

growth group a group that focuses on the growth and development of its individual members. See also ENCOUNTER GROUP; MARATHON GROUP; T-GROUP.

growth motivation see METAMOTIVATION.

growth principle the concept that in an atmosphere free of coercion and distortion an individual's creative and integrative forces will lead to fuller adaptation, insight, self-esteem, and realization of potential. [formulated by Carl ROGERS]

G-spot abbreviation for GRAEFENBERG SPOT.

guanfacine *n.* a drug used for the treatment of hypertension. It acts as an agonist at ALPHA-ADRENERGIC RECEPTORS, directly stimulating α_2-adrenoreceptors to restrict the flow of impulses in peripheral sympathetic nerves supplying the arteries, thus causing them to relax (widen); most of the other commonly prescribed antihypertensive drugs act as beta blockers or as diuretics. Guanfacine is also a sedating agent that is occasionally used as an adjunct in the treatment of attention-deficit/hyperactivity disorder and similar behavior disorders in children, although it is not officially approved by the U.S. Food and Drug Administration for these conditions and may cause excess sedation and hypotension (low blood pressure). The drug has also been investigated for the management of posttraumatic stress disorder, Tourette's disorder, and Alzheimer's disease. U.S. trade name: **Tenex**.

guarana *n.* a shrub (*Paullinia cupana*) indigenous to the Brazilian Amazon, the seeds of which were originally thought to contain **guaranine**, a METHYLXANTHINE compound that is essentially indistinguishable from CAFFEINE. It is now known that guarana in fact contains a significant amount of caffeine, which is its primary active ingredient, as well as lesser amounts of the methylxanthines **theophylline** (the active ingredient in tea) and THEOBROMINE. Used as a stimulant and appetite suppressant, guarana is available in many over-the-counter preparations in the United States and other Western nations. At recommended doses it appears to have the same mild adverse effects known to be associated with other sympathomimetic stimulants (e.g., restlessness, increased urination, gastrointestinal distress) but may interact with medications, particularly MONOAMINE OXIDASE INHIBITORS. Additionally, additive effects and potential toxicity may occur when guarana is combined with other caffeine-containing products, and there is growing concern that use of guarana-containing products may cause such serious adverse events as chest pain, irregular heartbeat, seizures, coma, and possibly death.

guardian ad litem an individual appointed by

the court to represent in a lawsuit someone who is incapacitated, either by age or by mental or physical disability. The individual's status as guardian ad litem is temporary and is dissolved upon resolution of that lawsuit.

guardianship *n.* a legal arrangement that places the care of a person and his or her property in the hands of another. When people are deemed incompetent by the court, and therefore unable to make decisions about their own care or to manage their own affairs, a **guardian** is appointed by the court to manage their property, make personal decisions on their behalf, and provide for their care and well-being. See also CONSERVATORSHIP.

guided affective imagery (**GAI**) in psychotherapy, the drawing out of emotional fantasies, or waking dreams, a technique used to ease CATHARSIS and work on emotions that are present but painful for the client to discuss. The therapist suggests concentration on past images that would bring up the emotional state or, in some cases, images of desired future successes. The technique is often used in BRIEF PSYCHOTHERAPY and GROUP THERAPY. Also called **guided imagery**. See also VISUALIZATION.

guiding fiction a personal principle that serves as a guideline by which an individual can understand and evaluate his or her experiences and determine his or her lifestyle. In individuals considered to be in good or reasonable mental health, the guiding fiction is assumed to approach reality and be adaptive. In those who are not, it is assumed to be largely unconscious, unrealistic, and nonadaptive. [term originally used by Alfred ADLER]

Guilford, Joy Paul (1897–1987) U.S. psychologist. Guilford received his doctorate in psychology from Cornell University, studying under Edward B. TITCHENER, Karl Dallenbach (1887–1971), and Gestalt psychologists Kurt KOFFKA and Harry Helson (1898–1977). After teaching at the University of Nebraska, he moved in 1940 to the University of Southern California, where he remained for the rest of his career. Guilford is best known for his contributions to psychometrics, publishing the first edition of the widely used *Psychometric Methods* in 1936, and also for his use of FACTOR ANALYSIS in studying personality and intelligence. Important works on these topics include *Personality* (1959) and *The Nature of Human Intelligence* (1967). Countering the view that intelligence could be characterized by a single, immutable rating, such as the IQ, Guilford argued that intelligence was multifaceted and that its components could be improved through education. He developed an important model, known as the structure of intellect model, to classify the many components of intelligence that he and other researchers had named. Among his honors were the Distinguished Scientific Contributions Award from the American Psychological Association and the Gold Medal of the American Psychological Foundation.

Guilford dimensions of intelligence three dimensions of intelligence postulated to underlie individual differences in scores on intelligence tests, namely, contents, operations, and products. Each mental ability represents a combination of these three facets. For example, a verbal-analogies test would represent a combination of cognition (operation) of verbal (content) relations (product). The number of mental abilities initially proposed by Guilford was 120; this was later increased to 150. The validity of this theory was subsequently called into question by the work of U.S. psychologist John L. Horn (1928–2006), which suggested that the existence of the proposed factors is not supported by research results. [Joy Paul GUILFORD]

Guilford–Zimmerman Temperament Survey (**GZTS**) a personality inventory for use with individuals aged 16 years and over, measuring 10 traits identified by FACTOR ANALYSIS: ascendance, sociability, friendliness, thoughtfulness, personal relations, masculinity, objectivity, general activity, restraint, and emotional stability. It comprises 300 descriptive statements (e.g., "You tend to lose your temper") to which participants respond "yes," "no," or "?". [originally developed in 1949 by U.S. psychologists Joy Paul GUILFORD and Wayne S. **Zimmerman** (1916–)]

guilt *n.* a SELF-CONSCIOUS EMOTION characterized by a painful sense of having done (or thought) something that is wrong and often by a readiness to take action designed to undo or mitigate this wrong. **—guilty** *adj.*

guilty but mentally ill (**GBMI**) a court judgment that may be made in some states when defendants plead insanity (see INSANITY DEFENSE). Defendants found guilty but mentally ill are treated in a mental hospital until their mental health is restored; they then serve the remainder of their sentence in the appropriate correctional facility.

Gulf War syndrome a collection of unexplained symptoms experienced by some veterans of the 1991 Gulf War. Symptoms may include headaches, fatigue, joint pain, skin rashes, and memory loss.

gynecomastia *n.* abnormal development of breast tissue in males. In young men the condition usually occurs on both sides, whereas in men over 50 gynecomastia tends to be unilateral. Gynecomastia may occur as a result of hormonal imbalance related to a tumor or as a side effect of therapy with ANTIANDROGENS or with DOPAMINE-RECEPTOR ANTAGONISTS, which include many antipsychotic drugs. Dopamine inhibits the release from the anterior pituitary of the hormone PROLACTIN; therefore, inhibition of dopaminergic activity may result in excess secretion of prolactin, leading to engorgement of breast tissue and possibly expression of breast milk (see GALACTORRHEA). Gynecomastia may also be observed (though rarely) with administration of SSRIS.

gynecomimesis *n.* sexual interest and arousal obtained by a man from impersonating a woman.

gynemimetophilia *n.* sexual interest in and arousal by men who are cross-dressing and playing the role of women.

gyrator treatment a form of alternative psychiatric treatment used in the late 18th and early 19th centuries for patients diagnosed as "torpid and melancholic" and whose condition was attributed to depletion of blood in the brain. The patient was placed in a revolving device in the belief that the rotation would drive out the illness by inducing vertigo, perspiration, and nausea and would restore the blood supply to the brain by centrifugal force. Also called **rotation treatment**. [devised by U.S. physician Benjamin Rush (1745–1813)]

GZTS abbreviation for GUILFORD–ZIMMERMAN TEMPERAMENT SURVEY.

Hh

habilitation *n.* the process of enhancing the independence, well-being, and level of functioning of an individual with a disability or disorder by providing appropriate resources, such as treatment or training, to enable that person to develop skills and abilities he or she had not had the opportunity to acquire previously. Compare REHABILITATION.

habit *n.* a well-learned behavior or automatic sequence of behaviors that is relatively situation-specific and over time has become motorically reflexive and independent of motivational or cognitive influence, that is, it is performed with little or no conscious intent. For example, the habit of hair twirling may eventually occur without the individual's conscious awareness. **—habitual** *adj.*

habit disorder any repetitive maladaptive behavior that may interfere with social, educational, or other important areas of functioning. In *DSM–IV–TR*, this has been subsumed under the diagnostic category of STEREOTYPIC MOVEMENT DISORDER.

habit formation the process by which, through repetition or conditioning, animals or humans acquire a behavior that becomes regular and increasingly easy to perform.

habit-forming drug a drug with ABUSE POTENTIAL.

habit regression the act of returning to a previously discontinued habit or pattern of behavior, often as a result of emotional distress.

habit reversal a technique of BEHAVIOR THERAPY in which the client must learn a new correct response to a stimulus and stop responding to a previously learned cue. Habit reversal is used in behavioral conditioning, for example, to control such unwanted habits as overeating, smoking, hair pulling (trichotillomania), and nail biting.

habit tic a brief, recurrent movement of a psychogenic nature, as contrasted with TICS of organic origin. Examples are grimacing, blinking, and repeatedly turning the head to one side.

habituation *n.* **1.** in general, the process of growing accustomed to a situation or pattern of behavior. **2.** the weakening of a response to a stimulus, or the diminished effectiveness of a stimulus, following repeated exposure to the stimulus. Compare DISHABITUATION. **3.** the process of becoming psychologically dependent on the use of a particular drug, such as cocaine, but without the increasing tolerance and physiological dependence that are characteristic of addiction. **4.** the elimination of extraneous responses that interfere with learning a skill through repetition and practice.

hair pulling see TRICHOTILLOMANIA.

halazepam *n.* a BENZODIAZEPINE used for the management of anxiety disorders and the short-term treatment of insomnia. As with most of the long-acting benzodiazepines, halazepam is metabolized to the active intermediate compound, desmethyldiazepam (nordiazepam), which has a very long HALF-LIFE (and therefore duration of action). This allows halazepam to be taken only once a day but also is associated with its accumulation in older adults and others with reduced ability to metabolize the long-acting benzodiazepines. U.S. trade name: **Paxipam**.

Halcion *n.* a trade name for TRIAZOLAM.

Haldol *n.* a trade name for HALOPERIDOL.

half-life (symbol: $t_{½}$) *n.* in pharmacokinetics, the time necessary for the concentration in the blood of an administered drug to fall by 50%. Half-life is a function of the rate of CLEARANCE of a drug and its VOLUME OF DISTRIBUTION in various body systems; it is expressed by the equation $t_{½}$ = (0.7 × volume of distribution)/clearance. Clinically, half-life varies among individuals as a result of age, disease states, or concurrent administration of other drugs. Half-life is useful in predicting the duration of effect of a drug and the time required for a drug to reach a state of equilibrium (steady state) in the body, that is, when the amount of drug administered is equal to that excreted. Generally, steady state is predicted to be achieved after 4–5 half-lives of a drug; for example, if a drug has a measured half-life of 8 hours (and its dosing schedule remains the same), steady state would be anticipated within 32–40 hours.

half-show *n.* a form of child psychotherapy in which a psychological problem is presented as a puppet-show drama, which is stopped at a crucial moment. The child is then asked to suggest how the story should end.

halfway house a transitional living arrangement for people, such as individuals recovering from alcohol or substance abuse, who have completed treatment at a hospital or rehabilitation center but still require support to assist them in restructuring their lives.

Hall, Granville Stanley (1844–1924) U.S. psychologist. Hall is best known as a founder and organizer of psychology in the United States. He received what was probably the first PhD in psychology in America (Harvard, 1878). He founded the first U.S. psychology journal, the

American Journal of Psychology (1887), as well as several other journals, and became the first president of the American Psychological Association, which he helped to organize, in 1892. As an early advocate of child study, he gathered information on children's interests and attitudes through the use of questionnaires, stimulated interest in child guidance, and published widely read texts on *Adolescence* (1904), human development, and educational problems. His research was underpinned throughout by an interest in evolutionary theory and a belief that the development of individual humans recapitulated the development of the human race (recapitulation theory). He became the first president of the newly founded Clark University in 1889 but maintained an active research and writing career and was mentor to a number of graduate students who rose to prominence within psychology. As a side interest, Hall introduced Sigmund FREUD, Carl JUNG, and other leading European psychoanalysts to the American public by inviting them to a special conference celebrating Clark University's 20th anniversary in 1909. See also STORM-AND-STRESS PERIOD.

Hallermann–Streiff syndrome a congenital disorder marked by craniofacial anomalies, including a small, beaked nose, small eyes, and low-set ears. In many affected individuals, the skull sutures are slow to close and may remain open into puberty. Mental retardation is present in about 15% of these individuals. [reported in 1948 by Wilhelm **Hallermann** (1901–1976), German physician, and in 1950 by Enrico Bernardo **Streiff** (1908–1988), Swiss ophthalmologist]

hallucination *n.* a false sensory perception that has a compelling sense of reality despite the absence of an external stimulus. It may affect any of the senses, but AUDITORY HALLUCINATIONS and VISUAL HALLUCINATIONS are most common. Hallucination is typically a symptom of a PSYCHOTIC DISORDER, particularly schizophrenia, but also may result from substance use, neurological abnormalities, and other conditions. It is important to distinguish hallucinations from ILLUSIONS, which are misinterpretations of real sensory stimuli.

hallucinogen *n.* a substance capable of producing a sensory effect (visual, auditory, olfactory, gustatory, or tactile) in the absence of an actual stimulus. Because they produce alterations in perception, cognition, and mood, hallucinogens are also called **psychedelic drugs** (from the Greek, meaning "mind-manifesting"). Hallucinogens are a group of heterogeneous compounds, many of which are naturally occurring; others are produced synthetically. Many hallucinogens are structurally similar to one of several neurotransmitters, which may be used as a mechanism of categorization. For example, serotonin-like hallucinogens include the indolealkylamines, exemplified by lysergic acid diethylamide (see LSD), PSILOCIN, DMT, DET, and BUFOTENIN; catecholamine-like hallucinogens include the PHENYLETHYLAMINES and their derivatives, such as MESCALINE, DOM, MDA, and MDMA. Both classes in general produce visual hallucinations via activity on subtypes of SEROTONIN RECEPTORS. Other hallucinogens include PCP and various natural substances, including AYAHUASCA. See HALLUCINOGEN ABUSE; HALLUCINOGEN DEPENDENCE. —**hallucinogenic** *adj.*

hallucinogen abuse in *DSM–IV–TR*, a pattern of HALLUCINOGEN use manifested by recurrent significant adverse consequences related to the repeated ingestion of hallucinogens. This diagnosis is preempted by the diagnosis of HALLUCINOGEN DEPENDENCE: If the criteria for hallucinogen abuse and hallucinogen dependence are both met, only the latter diagnosis is given. See also SUBSTANCE ABUSE.

hallucinogen-affective disorder see HALLUCINOGEN-INDUCED MOOD DISORDER.

hallucinogen dependence in *DSM–IV–TR*, a cluster of cognitive, behavioral, and physiological symptoms indicating continued use of hallucinogens despite significant hallucinogen-related problems. There is a pattern of repeated hallucinogen ingestion resulting in tolerance, withdrawal symptoms (agitation, mood lability, and craving) if use is suspended, and an uncontrollable drive to continue use. See also HALLUCINOGEN ABUSE; SUBSTANCE DEPENDENCE.

hallucinogen hallucinosis see HALLUCINOGEN-INDUCED PSYCHOTIC DISORDER.

hallucinogen-induced mood disorder a prominent and persistent disturbance of mood experienced during and after HALLUCINOGEN INTOXICATION. It may be characterized by depression or anxiety, self-reproach, feelings of guilt, and tension. Also called **hallucinogen-affective disorder**.

hallucinogen-induced psychotic disorder prominent hallucinations, delusions, or both due to HALLUCINOGEN INTOXICATION that are not recognized by the individual as having been induced by hallucinogens. The hallucinations and delusions exceed those usually associated with such intoxication, being sufficiently severe to warrant clinical attention. Also called **hallucinogen hallucinosis**.

hallucinogen intoxication a reversible syndrome due to the recent ingestion of a specific hallucinogen. Clinically significant behavioral or psychological changes include marked anxiety or depression, DELUSION OF REFERENCE, difficulty focusing attention, fear of losing one's mind, paranoia, and impaired judgment. These are accompanied by one or more signs of physiological involvement, for example, subjective intensification of perceptions, hallucinations, SYNESTHESIAS, pupillary dilation, increased heart rate, sweating, palpitations, blurring of vision, tremors, or incoordination. See also SUBSTANCE INTOXICATION.

hallucinosis *n.* a pathological condition characterized by prominent and persistent hallucinations without alterations of consciousness, particularly when due to the direct physiological effects of a substance or associated with neurological factors.

haloperidol *n.* a HIGH-POTENCY ANTIPSYCHOTIC of the BUTYROPHENONE class, in use in Europe in the 1950s and in the United States from 1965. Haloperidol and other high-potency antipsychotics were preferred over lower potency PHENOTHIAZINES because of their lack of cardiovascular and ANTICHOLINERGIC EFFECTS; however, they were associated more with EXTRAPYRAMIDAL SYMPTOMS and TARDIVE DYSKINESIA than lower potency agents. The increased safety profile of the second-generation ATYPICAL ANTIPSYCHOTICS has led to a decline in use of haloperidol, although it is still used individually and in conjunction with newer agents. Some argue that few differences exist between the newer agents and haloperidol if the latter is used in much lower doses than has been customary. U.S. trade name: **Haldol**.

Halstead–Reitan Impairment Index see IMPAIRMENT INDEX. [Ward C. **Halstead** (1908–1969) and Ralph M. **Reitan** (1922–), U.S. psychologists]

Halstead–Reitan Neuropsychological Battery (**HRNB**) a set of tests designed to diagnose and localize brain damage by providing a comprehensive assessment of cognitive functioning. The battery includes five core subtests and five optional subtests purportedly measuring elements of language, attention, motor dexterity, sensory–motor integration, abstract thinking, and memory. Additionally, the MINNESOTA MULTIPHASIC PERSONALITY INVENTORY and either the WECHSLER ADULT INTELLIGENCE SCALE or the WECHSLER INTELLIGENCE SCALE FOR CHILDREN are often administered as well. There is a version of the HRNB for adults, for children aged 5 to 8 years, and for children aged 9 to 14 years. [Ward C. **Halstead** and Ralph M. **Reitan**]

Hamilton Rating Scale for Depression (**HAM-D**; **HRSD**) an interview-based, clinician-administered measure of the severity of depressive symptoms, such as DYSPHORIA, insomnia, and weight loss. It is the most widely used measure of the effectiveness of antidepressant medication in clinical trials, and its use is most appropriately restricted to individuals in whom depression has been diagnosed, rather than as a general measure of depressive symptoms. A 38-item self-report version, the **Hamilton Depression Inventory** (**HDI**), was developed in 1995. Also called **Hamilton Depression Scale**. [originally published in 1960 by Max **Hamilton** (1912–1988), British psychiatrist]

Hand–Christian–Schüller syndrome a rare disturbance of lipid metabolism marked by the presence of large phagocytic blood cells and an accumulation of cholesterol plus a triad of symptoms: membranous bone defects, diabetes insipidus, and protrusion of the eyes. Growth and mental development are retarded in half of affected individuals. Also called **Schüller–Christian–Hand disease**. [Alfred **Hand** (1868–1949), U.S. pediatrician; Henry A. **Christian** (1876–1951), U.S. physician; Arthur **Schüller** (1874–1958), Austrian neurologist]

handicap 1. *n.* any disadvantage or characteristic that limits or prevents a person from performing various physical, cognitive, or social tasks or from fulfilling particular roles within society. For example, a nonaccessible building entry or exit for a person in a wheelchair would be considered a handicap, as would the person's inability to walk. The term generally is considered pejorative nowadays and its use has fallen into disfavor. See also DISABILITY. **2.** *vb.* to place an individual or group of individuals at a disadvantage, or to hinder or impede progress. **—handicapped** *adj.*

handicapping strategy see SELF-HANDICAPPING.

hand-washing obsession a persistent and irrational preoccupation with washing the hands, also called **ablutomania** (although this name is now seldom used). It is characteristic of OBSESSIVE-COMPULSIVE DISORDER. See OBSESSION.

handwriting analysis see GRAPHOLOGY.

Hans *n.* see LITTLE HANS.

haploid *adj.* describing a nucleus, cell, or organism that possesses only one representative of each chromosome, as in a sperm or egg cell. In most organisms, including humans, fusion of the haploid sex cells following fertilization restores the normal DIPLOID condition of body cells, in which the chromosomes occur in pairs. Hence for humans, the **haploid number** is 23 chromosomes, that is, half the full complement of 46 chromosomes.

happiness *n.* an emotion of joy, gladness, satisfaction, and well-being. **—happy** *adj.*

haptic hallucination see TACTILE HALLUCINATION.

hard drug a colloquial name for a drug of abuse, especially one that produces PHYSICAL DEPENDENCE. See SUBSTANCE ABUSE; SUBSTANCE DEPENDENCE.

hardiness *n.* an ability to adapt easily to unexpected changes combined with a sense of purpose in daily life and of personal control over what occurs in one's life. Hardiness dampens the effects of a stressful situation through information gathering, decisive actions, and learning from the experience. A hardy athlete, for example, is less prone to MORBIDITY or injury. **—hardy** *adj.*

hard of hearing having difficulty in distinguishing sounds at normal levels of intensity.

hard-wired *adj.* in neurophysiology, referring to fixed, inflexible NEURAL CIRCUITS.

harmaline *n.* see AYAHUASCA.

harmine *n.* a naturally occurring hallucinogen derived from the plant *Peganum harmala*, native to the Middle East, and *Banisteriopsis caapi*, native to the South American tropics. Harmine is a potent MONOAMINE OXIDASE INHIBITOR and is a principal ingredient in AYAHUASCA, a psychoactive beverage.

harm reduction a theoretical approach in programs designed to reduce the adverse effects of risky behaviors (e.g., alcohol use, drug use, indiscriminate sexual activity), rather than to eliminate the behaviors altogether. Programs focused on alcohol use, for example, do not advocate abstinence but attempt instead to teach people to anticipate the hazards of heavy drinking and learn to drink safely.

hashish *n.* the most potent CANNABIS preparation. It contains the highest concentration of delta-9-TETRAHYDROCANNABINOL (THC) because it consists largely of pure resin from one of the species of the *Cannabis* plant from which it is derived.

H

hate *n.* a hostile emotion combining intense feelings of detestation, anger, and often a desire to do harm. Also called **hatred**.

hate crime a crime of violence that is motivated by bias or hatred against the group to which the victims of the crimes belong. Examples of hate crimes are killing a man because he is (or is thought to be) gay and bombing a place of worship of a religious minority.

HCBS abbreviation for HOME AND COMMUNITY-BASED SERVICES.

HCFA abbreviation for Health Care Financing Administration. See CENTERS FOR MEDICARE AND MEDICAID SERVICES.

HD abbreviation for HUNTINGTON'S DISEASE.

HDI abbreviation for Hamilton Depression Inventory. See HAMILTON RATING SCALE FOR DEPRESSION.

head banging the act or habit of repeatedly striking the head on a crib, wall, or other object, observed in infants and young children as a stereotyped behavior (see STEREOTYPY) or during a temper tantrum. See also STEREOTYPIC MOVEMENT DISORDER.

head injury any physical injury to the scalp or skull or any brain damage that may result. Head injuries are usually caused by blunt force, such as a blow to the head, but may result from significant acceleration or deceleration in the absence of physical contact (an **acceleration–deceleration injury**). They are commonly classified as either closed, in which the head strikes an object (e.g., a concussion), or open (penetrating), in which a foreign object passes through the skull and enters the brain (e.g., a gunshot wound). A variety of transient or permanent neuropsychological consequences may result, including emotional, behavior, and personality changes; disturbances of EXECUTIVE FUNCTIONS; memory and attention difficulties; and sensory and motor deficits. Also called **head trauma**.

headshrinking *n.* the shrinking of severed heads, usually human, through the application of heat or herbal liquids, as practiced among various indigenous societies, mainly in southeast Asia and South America. The heads are used for various ritual purposes, including healing rituals. The slang SHRINK (short for **headshrinker**), meaning a psychiatrist or psychologist, is probably derived from this practice.

healing group broadly, any of a variety of groups formed for the purpose of improving or promoting the mental and emotional health and well-being or interpersonal relationships of the members, as in GROUP THERAPY, SELF-HELP GROUPS, ENCOUNTER GROUPS, and CONSCIOUSNESS-RAISING groups.

health activities questionnaire any questionnaire designed to measure an individual's current repertoire of health-related behaviors. There is an increased emphasis on prevention in health care, and many inventories exist to measure an individual's compliance with physical activity, dietary control, preventive inoculations, and screening for potential health problems, such as mammography and prostate or colon cancer testing.

health anxiety excessive or inappropriate anxiety about one's health, based on misinterpretation of symptoms (e.g., pain, gastrointestinal distress) as indicative of serious illness. Health anxiety is regarded as a less severe form of HYPOCHONDRIASIS.

health–belief model a model that identifies the relationships of the following to the likelihood of taking preventive health action: (a) individual perceptions about susceptibility to and seriousness of a disease, (b) sociodemographic variables, (c) environmental cues, and (d) perceptions of the benefits and costs. See also EXERCISE–BEHAVIOR MODEL.

health care services and delivery related to the health and well-being of individuals and communities, including preventive, diagnostic, therapeutic, rehabilitative, maintenance, monitoring, and counseling services. In its broadest sense, health care relates to both physical and mental health and is provided by medical and mental health professionals. See also MENTAL HEALTH CARE; MENTAL HEALTH SERVICES.

Health Care Financing Administration (HCFA) see CENTERS FOR MEDICARE AND MEDICAID SERVICES.

health education **1.** instruction in the care and hygiene of the human body, with emphasis on how to prevent illness. **2.** any type of education regarding physical, mental, and emotional health. Conducted in school, institutional, and community settings, this education may cover stress management, smoking cessation, nutrition and fitness, reproductive health, self-esteem, relationship issues, health risks, personal safety (e.g., self-defense and rape prevention), and minority health issues.

health insurance a contractual relationship in

which an insurance company undertakes to reimburse the insured for health care expenses in exchange for a premium. Such payment protections might include, for example, medical expense, outpatient mental health, accident, dental, disability income, and accidental death and dismemberment insurances.

health locus of control the perceived source of control over health, that is, either personal behaviors or external forces.

health maintenance organization see HMO.

Health Opinion Survey see KRANTZ HEALTH OPINION SURVEY.

health plan an organized program that provides a defined set of health care benefits. Health plans may be HMOs, PPOs, insured plans, self-insured plans, or other plans that cover health care services.

health professional an individual who has received advanced training or education in a health-related field, such as direct patient care, administration, or ancillary services.

health psychology the subfield of psychology that focuses on (a) the examination of the relations between behavioral, cognitive, psychophysiological, and social and environmental factors and the establishment, maintenance, and detriment of health; (b) the integration of psychological and biological research findings in the design of empirically based interventions for the prevention and treatment of illness; and (c) the evaluation of physical and psychological status before, during, and after medical and psychological treatment.

health risk appraisal the perception by individuals of the extent to which they believe that they are susceptible to a health threat. See also PERCEIVED RISK; PERCEIVED SUSCEPTIBILITY.

health visitor a health professional, usually associated with a VISITING NURSE association, who visits families where health supervision is needed, for example, to ensure that children are not abused or neglected.

hearing mute an obsolescent and pejorative name for an individual who is unable or unwilling to speak but is able to hear.

heart attack sudden, severe chest pain that occurs when one of the coronary arteries becomes blocked. The condition may result in a myocardial infarction (i.e., death of a section of heart muscle), depending upon the extent of damage to the surrounding muscle.

heart rate in emotion changes in heart rate associated with particular emotional states. It is usually held that heart rate increases in states of fear, anger, and scorn and decreases in states of attentiveness, positive emotional reaction, and interest. However, the actual relation between heart rate and emotion is complex and largely mediated by the energy demands of the bodily musculature of the organism in an emotional state. Thus, a frightened animal that reacts with tonic immobility (death feigning) and limpness will show a reduction in heart rate in its reaction to a threat, whereas an animal that is immobile but poised for flight typically shows acceleration of heart rate. States of laughter, although pleasurable, are typically associated with an accelerated heart rate owing to the involvement of large muscle groups in the act of laughing.

heatstroke *n.* a serious condition caused by a breakdown of the body's temperature-regulation ability following exposure to excessive heat. Since the body is no longer able to cool itself by sweating, the skin feels hot and dry and the person may experience convulsions or seizures and potentially lose consciousness. The elevated body temperature may cause brain damage or death. Emergency treatment involving cooling the patient must be started immediately.

hebephrenia *n.* see DISORGANIZED SCHIZOPHRENIA.

hebetude *n.* a state of severe emotional dullness, lethargy, and lack of interest.

hedonic contingency hypothesis a theory of affect and information processing postulating that people consider the hedonic implications of information when determining whether to elaborate information. When people are in positive mood states, they tend to be highly attentive to the impact information will have on their mood. If the information is seen as uplifting, they will engage in extensive ELABORATION to maintain their positive mood, but if it is seen as unpleasant, they will engage in little elaboration. When people are in negative mood states, they tend to elaborate information with little attention to its hedonic consequences because such information is unlikely to make their mood more negative and might make it more positive. [originally proposed by U.S. social psychologists Duane T. Wegener (1966–) and Richard E. Petty (1951–)]

hedonic level the degree of pleasantness or unpleasantness aroused by an interaction or a thought.

hedonic psychology a psychological perspective that focuses on the spectrum of experiences ranging from pleasure to pain and includes biological, social, and phenomenological aspects and their relationship to motivation and action.

hedonics *n.* the branch of psychology concerned with the study of pleasant and unpleasant sensations and thoughts, especially in terms of their role in human motivation.

height phobia see ACROPHOBIA.

hellebore *n.* any plant of the genus *Veratrum* but particularly *Veratrum viride*, a poisonous plant indigenous to North America that has a history of use by Native Americans for various medicinal purposes. It contains more than 20 alkaloids, including **veratrine**, which has analgesic properties when used topically but produces prolonged muscle contractions when ingested. The hellebore alkaloids were also used medicinally in England as well as America in the 18th and 19th centuries in the treatment of numerous conditions, including seizures, neuralgia, headaches, and respiratory problems. They have been used more recently to lower blood pressure but generally are avoided because of their potential toxicity. The name "hellebore" is also given to poisonous ornamental plants of the Eurasian genus *Helleborus*.

helping *n.* a type of PROSOCIAL BEHAVIOR that involves one or more individuals acting to improve the status or well-being of another or others. Although much helping behavior is typically in response to a small request that involves little individual risk, all helping behavior incurs some cost to the individual providing it. Also called **helpfulness**. See also ALTRUISM; ALTRUISTIC BEHAVIOR; EGOISTIC HELPING.

helping professions those professions that provide health and education services to individuals and groups, including occupations in the fields of psychology, psychiatry, counseling, medicine, nursing, social work, physical and occupational therapy, teaching, and education.

helping relationship a relationship in which at least one of the parties intends to promote the growth, development, maturity, or improved functioning of the other. The parties may be either individuals or groups. [defined in 1961 by Carl ROGERS]

helplessness *n.* a state of incapacity, vulnerability, or powerlessness defined by low problem-focused COPING POTENTIAL and low future expectancy. It results from the realization that one cannot do much to improve a negative situation and that the situation is not going to get better on its own; it often involves anxiety and dependence on others. A recognition of one's helplessness in a situation can lead one to withdraw and become sad or demoralized. See also LEARNED HELPLESSNESS. **—helpless** *adj.*

helplessness theory the theory that LEARNED HELPLESSNESS explains the development of or vulnerability to depression. According to this theory, people repeatedly exposed to stressful situations beyond their control develop an inability to make decisions or engage effectively in purposeful behavior.

help-seeking behavior actions directed toward searching for or requesting help from others via formal or informal mechanisms, especially through mental health services. See TREATMENT-SEEKING BEHAVIOR.

hematoma *n.* an abnormal accumulation of blood as a result of vessel leakage or rupture. In the brain, hematomas can cause substantial behavioral deficits, and even death, by increasing INTRACRANIAL PRESSURE. Although some may spontaneously reabsorb and disappear, others must be surgically evacuated.

hemeraphonia *n.* a psychogenic speech disorder in which the person is unable to vocalize during the day but may be able to speak normally at night.

hemianopia *n.* a visual defect marked by loss of vision in half the normal visual field. Hemianopia may result from a lesion in the optic chiasm or the optic radiations. Also called **hemianopsia**; **hemiopia**. **—hemianopic** *adj.* **—hemianoptic** *adj.*

hemicrania *n.* pain or aching on only one side of the head, characteristic of a typical migraine.

hemidecortication *n.* surgical removal of the CEREBRAL CORTEX on one side of the brain.

hemispherectomy *n.* surgical removal of either one of the cerebral hemispheres of the brain.

hemispheric lateralization the processes whereby some functions, such as handedness or language, are controlled or influenced more by one cerebral hemisphere than the other and each hemisphere is specialized for particular ways of working. Researchers now prefer to speak of hemispheric lateralization or **hemispheric specialization** for particular functions, rather than **hemispheric dominance** or **lateral dominance** (see DOMINANCE).

hemlock *n.* see SORCERY DRUGS.

hemorrhage *n.* bleeding; any loss of blood from an artery or vein. A hemorrhage may be external, internal, or within a tissue, such as the skin; a bruise is a sign of bleeding within the skin. A hemorrhage from a ruptured artery is bright red in color and erupts in spurts that coincide with heart contractions; it is generally more serious than hemorrhage from a vein, which shows as a relatively slow, steady flow of dark red blood. Brain hemorrhages may arise from head injuries or ANEURYSMS, causing widespread damage in some cases (see CEREBRAL HEMORRHAGE). **—hemorrhagic** *adj.*

hemorrhagic stroke a STROKE resulting from rupture of a cerebral vessel, causing intracranial bleeding. Intracerebral hemorrhage accounts for approximately 10% of strokes and tends to occur deep in the basal ganglia, internal capsule, and brainstem.

hemothymia *n.* a lust for blood and a morbid desire to commit murder. See also HOMICIDOMANIA.

hemp *n.* see CANNABIS.

henbane *n.* a poisonous plant, *Hyoscyamus niger*, native to the Mediterranean and southern Europe and a source of the anticholinergic alkaloids ATROPINE, hyoscyamine, and SCOPOLAMINE. Although traditionally used in small doses as an analgesic, sedative, and smooth muscle relaxant, henbane in larger quantities is highly toxic, producing effects similar to those of poisoning with BELLADONNA ALKALOIDS, including delirium, hallucinations, convulsions, coma, and possibly death. It has long been associated in folklore with witchcraft and magic and even enjoyed a reputation for a time as an aphrodisiac.

heparitinuria *n.* see SANFILIPPO'S SYNDROME.

hepatitis *n.* inflammation of the liver, marked by diffuse or patchy areas of dead liver cells in the liver lobules. Symptoms range from mild, flulike symptoms to liver failure, which can be fatal. Jaundice and orange bile pigment (bilirubin) coloring of the urine are usual signs. The causes include viruses, alcohol and drug abuse, infectious mononucleosis, and other infectious agents. The different forms of viral hepatitis are identified by letters, indicating the virus responsible. **Hepatitis A** is contracted by ingesting contaminated food or water, while **hepatitis B** is usually transmitted by transfusions of contaminated blood, through group use of dirty hypodermic needles, or by sexual contact with an infected person. The **hepatitis C** virus (HCV) is one of the most important causes of chronic liver disease in the United States, having similar modes of transmission to hepatitis B.

herbal Ecstasy an over-the-counter stimulant purchased through mail-order catalogs and often confused with MDMA.

here and now the immediate situation. In psychotherapy, it comprises the cognitive, affective, and behavioral material arising at any given point in a session, as well as the relationship between the therapist and client at the corresponding point in time. When the **here-and-now approach** is used in psychotherapy, the emphasis is placed on understanding present feelings and interpersonal reactions as they occur in an ongoing treatment session, with little or no emphasis on or exploration of past experience or underlying reasons for the client's thoughts, emotions, or behavior. The approach is often used in PSYCHODYNAMIC PSYCHOTHERAPY with regard to the therapeutic relationship, GESTALT THERAPY, and many forms of FAMILY THERAPY to heighten the client's awareness.

hereditarianism *n.* the view that genetic inheritance is the major influence on behavior. Opposed to this view is the belief that environment and learning account for the major differences between people. The question of heredity versus environment or "nature versus nurture" continues to be controversial, especially as it applies to human intelligence. See GENETIC DETERMINISM; NATURE–NURTURE. **—hereditarian** *adj.*

hereditary hyperuricemia (**hereditary choreoathetosis**) see LESCH–NYHAN SYNDROME.

hereditary predisposition see GENETIC PREDISPOSITION.

heredity *n.* the transmission of traits from parents to their offspring. Study of the mechanisms and laws of heredity is the basis of the science of GENETICS. Heredity depends upon the character of the genes contained in the parents' CHROMOSOMES, which in turn depends on the particular GENETIC CODE carried by the DNA of which the chromosomes are composed.

heredity–environment controversy see NATURE–NURTURE.

heritability *n.* **1.** the capacity to be inherited. **2.** an estimate of the contribution of inheritance to a given trait or function. Heritabilities can range from 0, indicating no contribution of heritable factors, to 1, indicating total contribution of heritable factors. The heritability of intelligence is believed to be roughly .5, although research indicates that heritability tends to increase with age and may rise to .7 or above in adulthood. Heritability is determined using a variety of behavior-genetic methods, such as studies of identical twins raised apart or ADOPTION STUDIES in which IQs of children are compared to the IQs of both their biological and their adoptive parents. Heritability is not the same as genetic contribution, because heritability is sensitive only to sources of individual differences. Moreover, a trait can be heritable and yet modifiable. For example, intelligence is heritable in some degree, but also has risen in recent generations. Also called **heritability estimate**.

hermaphroditism *n.* the condition of possessing both male and female sex organs (in humans, for example, possessing both ovarian and testicular tissue). Hermaphroditism is very rare and should not be confused with the more common PSEUDOHERMAPHRODITISM, in which the gonads are of one sex but the external genitalia are either ambiguous or of the opposite sex. See also INTERSEXUALITY. **—hermaphrodite** *n.*

hero *n.* in PSYCHODRAMA, the person (PROTAGONIST) who is portraying a problem.

heroin *n.* a highly addictive OPIOID that is a synthetic analog of MORPHINE and three times more potent. In many countries, including Great Britain and Canada, it is used clinically for pain management (see DIACETYLMORPHINE), but it is not legally available in the United States due to concerns about its potential for abuse. Its rapid onset of action leads to an intense initial high, followed by a period of euphoria and a sense of well-being. As a street drug, heroin is commonly injected intravenously or subcutaneously ("skin popping"). Injection using shared needles is a common mechanism of transmission of HIV, hepatitis, and other disease agents. It can also be insufflated (snorted) or smoked.

heroin abuse in *DSM–IV–TR,* a pattern of heroin use manifested by recurrent significant adverse consequences related to the repeated ingestion of the substance. This diagnosis is preempted by the diagnosis of HEROIN DEPENDENCE: If the criteria for heroin abuse and heroin dependence are both met, only the latter diagnosis is given.

heroin dependence in *DSM–IV–TR,* a cluster of cognitive, behavioral, and physiological symptoms indicating continued use of heroin despite significant heroin-related problems. There is a pattern of repeated heroin ingestion resulting in tolerance, characteristic withdrawal symptoms if use is suspended (see OPIOID WITHDRAWAL), and an uncontrollable drive to continue use.

heroin intoxication a reversible syndrome that develops following recent ingestion of heroin, characterized by euphoria, PSYCHOMOTOR RETARDATION, drowsiness, and impaired attention or memory.

heroin withdrawal see OPIOID WITHDRAWAL.

herpes infection a disease produced by one of the strains of herpes virus. A herpes infection may be manifested as chicken pox, cold sores, shingles, ulceration of the cornea, encephalitis, stomatitis, or vulvovaginitis (GENITAL HERPES). The major strains are **herpes varicella-zoster**, which causes both chicken pox and shingles; **herpes simplex Type 1**, the cause of cold sores; and **herpes simplex Type 2**, the cause of genital herpes. See also PERINATAL HERPES-VIRUS INFECTION.

hetaeral fantasy a fantasy in which a woman plays the role of a courtesan. In the male version of the fantasy, the man possesses a courtesan. Also called **courtesan fantasy**.

heteroeroticism *n.* an attraction toward the opposite sex, as in heterosexuality. Also called **heteroerotism**. Compare HOMOEROTICISM. **—heteroerotic** *adj.*

heterohypnosis *n.* a state of suggestibility induced in one person by another. Compare SELF-HYPNOSIS.

heterolalia *n.* see HETEROPHEMY.

heteronomous superego in psychoanalytic theory, a SUPEREGO that demands that the individual behave in whatever manner is expected at the moment in order to secure the approval of others.

heteronomy *n.* a state of dependence on others and lack of self-determination. Compare AUTONOMY.

heterophemy *n.* the act of saying or writing a word or phrase other than the words intended. Often, the substitution conveys the opposite meaning to what the individual intended. Also called **heterolalia**; **heterophasia**; **heterophemia**. See also FREUDIAN SLIP; SLIP OF THE TONGUE.

heterophilia *n.* love of, or attraction to, members of the opposite sex.

heterosexism *n.* prejudice against any non-heterosexual form of behavior, relationship, or community, in particular the denigration of gay men and lesbians. Whereas HOMOPHOBIA generally refers to an individual's fear or dread of gay men or lesbians, heterosexism denotes a wider system of beliefs, attitudes, and institutional structures that attach value to heterosexuality and denigrate same-sex behavior and orientation.

heterosexual anxiety persistent and irrational anxiety that is related to heterosexual relationships, for example, a feeling that one is not sexually attractive in appearance or performance.

heterosexuality *n.* sexual attraction to or activity between members of the opposite sex. **—heterosexual** *adj.*

heterosociality *n.* relationships on a social (rather than a sexual or romantic) level between people of opposite sexes.

heterozygous *adj.* possessing two different forms of a gene (i.e., different ALLELES) at a given genetic locus on each of a pair of HOMOLOGOUS chromosomes. One allele is inherited from the mother, and the other from the father. In such individuals, the DOMINANT ALLELE is expressed, and the RECESSIVE ALLELE is not. Compare HOMOZYGOUS. **—heterozygote** *n.*

heuristic *n.* **1.** in cognition, a strategy for solving a problem or making a decision that provides an efficient means of finding an answer but cannot guarantee a correct outcome. By contrast, an algorithm guarantees a solution to a problem (if there is one) but may be much less efficient. Also called **cognitive heuristic**. See also AVAILABILITY HEURISTIC; REPRESENTATIVENESS HEURISTIC. **2.** in the social sciences, a conceptual device, such as a model or working hypothesis, that is intended to explore or limit the possibilities of a question rather than to provide an explanation of the facts. See also AS-IF HYPOTHESIS; CONSTRUCT.

HGPRT abbreviation for HYPOXANTHINE–GUANINE PHOSPHORIBOSYLTRANSFERASE.

5-HIAA abbreviation for 5-HYDROXYINDOLEACETIC ACID.

hidden observer the phenomenon whereby highly hypnotizable people (see HYPNOTIC SUSCEPTIBILITY) who are asked to block certain stimuli (e.g., pain) can sometimes register the blocked pain or other sensation via hand signals, as if a dissociated observer is simultaneously taking part in events that are disavowed by the dominant observer. Such individuals can later recall auditory, visual, or tactile stimuli to which they appeared oblivious at the time.

hidden variable an undiscovered causative variable. When a relationship is found between variables *A* and *B*, variable *A* may erroneously be thought to be the cause of *B*. However, the cause of *B* may be a hidden variable *C* (sometimes called a third variable) that is correlated with variable *A*.

hierarchical model of personality a model of either within-person psychology dynamics or individual differences in personality in which some psychological constructs are viewed as high-level variables that organize or govern the functioning of lower-level variables. For example, a hierarchical model of personality traits might view the construct SOCIABILITY as being at a lower level in a hierarchy than the construct EXTRAVERSION: Sociability would be seen as a form or example of the higher level trait of extraversion.

hierarchy of motives (**hierarchy of needs**) see MASLOW'S MOTIVATIONAL HIERARCHY.

high *n.* slang for the subjective feelings of intoxication experienced following ingestion of psychoactive drugs.

high blood pressure see HYPERTENSION.

higher level skill a work method or skill that can be applied to many tasks rather than one particular task.

higher mental process any of the more complex types of cognition, such as thinking, judgment, imagination, memory, and language.

higher order consciousness a type of CONSCIOUSNESS that goes beyond sensory contents (see SENSORY CONSCIOUSNESS) to include abstract ideas, language-dependent thinking, and self-consciousness. [proposed by U.S. neuroscientist Gerald M. Edelman (1929–) and others]

higher order interaction in the ANALYSIS OF VARIANCE, the joint effect of three or more independent variables on the dependent variable.

higher response unit any integration of simple responses into a more complex response.

higher states of consciousness see TRANSPERSONAL PSYCHOLOGY.

high-potency antipsychotic any of various conventional ANTIPSYCHOTICS that have either a relatively high degree of affinity for the dopamine D2 receptor or significant EXTRAPYRAMIDAL SYMPTOMS. High-potency antipsychotics include FLUPHENAZINE, HALOPERIDOL, thiothixene (see THIOXANTHENES), TRIFLUOPERAZINE, and PIMOZIDE.

high risk significantly heightened vulnerability to a disorder or disease. An individual's risk status is influenced by genetic, physical, and behavioral factors or conditions. For example, children of a parent with bipolar disorder have a much greater risk of developing the disorder than other children, and individuals who engage in unprotected sex are at high risk of contracting HIV and other sexually transmitted diseases.

highway hypnosis a colloquial name for accident proneness resulting from a state of drowsy inattention experienced during long-distance driving on monotonous roads.

Hilgard, Ernest R. (1904–2001) U.S. psychologist. Hilgard earned his doctorate in psychology in 1930 from Yale University, where he studied under Raymond Dodge (1871–1942). He taught at Yale until 1933, when he accepted a joint appointment in psychology and education at Stanford University. Throughout his career Hilgard was a masterful synthesizer and organizer of research in the fields of conditioning, learning theory, and hypnosis. His early research led to publication of the classic text *Conditioning and Learning* (1940) with Donald G. Marquis (1908–1973). Hilgard's subsequent *Theories of Learning* (1948) also became a standard text in the field. Later in his career Hilgard's research interests focused on hypnosis, culminating in a number of books including *Hypnotic Susceptibility* (1965) and *Divided Consciousness* (1977). After his retirement, Hilgard became increasingly interested in the history of psychology and published *Psychology in America: A Historical Survey* (1987). His many honors included the Award for Distinguished Scientific Contributions from the American Psychological Association, the Gold Medal Award from the American Psychological Foundation, and membership in the National Academy of Sciences, the American Academy of Arts and Sciences, and the American Philosophical Society.

hindbrain *n.* the posterior of three bulges that appear in the embryonic brain as it develops from the NEURAL TUBE. The bulge eventually becomes the MEDULLA OBLONGATA, PONS, and CEREBELLUM. Also called **rhombencephalon**.

hindsight bias the tendency, after an event has occurred, to overestimate the extent to which the outcome could have been foreseen.

hippocampal formation a region of the brain located in the medial temporal lobe and concerned with the consolidation of long-term memory. It comprises the dentate gyrus, hippocampus, and subiculum and communicates with areas of neocortex via the entorhinal cortex.

hippocampus *n.* (*pl.* **hippocampi**) a seahorse-shaped part of the forebrain, in the basal medial region of the TEMPORAL LOBE, that is important for DECLARATIVE MEMORY and learning. Because of its resemblance to a ram's horn, 19th-century neuroanatomists named it **Ammon's horn** (**cornu ammonis**; CA) for the horn of the ram that represented the Egyptian deity Ammon. Parts of the hippocampus were then labeled **CA1**, **CA2**, **CA3**, and **CA4**; these designations are still used for the different regions of the hippocampus. See HIPPOCAMPAL FORMATION; PAPEZ CIRCUIT. —**hippocampal** *adj.*

hippotherapy *n.* the therapeutic use of horses to help people with physical and developmental disabilities improve their balance, coordination, posture, and mobility. During each 30-minute hippotherapy session, the client sits or lies on the horse, and a therapist evaluates and positively influences the client's neuromuscular responses to the animal's movement while an equine handler adjusts its gait, tempo, and direction. One or two sidewalkers next to the horse accompany the client for safety purposes. The therapists who conduct such sessions are specially trained physical, occupational, and speech and language therapists who offer hippotherapy as part of their broader, occupation-specific spectrum of therapeutic activities. The handlers themselves are hippotherapy-certified. The therapy is most commonly used for people with autism, cerebral palsy, Down syndrome, multiple sclerosis, muscular dystrophy, spina bifida, spinal cord injury, stroke, and traumatic brain injury. In addition to its physical benefits, it often improves the client's affect, self-confidence, communication skills, spatial awareness, SENSORY INTEGRATION, and social interaction. It is a type of ANIMAL-ASSISTED THERAPY.

histamine *n.* a compound that is synthesized from the amino acid histidine by the enzyme histidine decarboxylase. Most histamine in humans is localized in peripheral tissues, where it is involved in allergic reactions or the inflammatory response to injury, causing dilation of blood vessels. In the brain, histamine acts as a neurotransmitter to modulate such functions as arousal, appetite, and regulation of autonomic functions. **Histamine receptors** can be divided into three categories, designated H_1, H_2, and H_3 receptors. Many antidepressants and antipsychotics may block histamine receptors in the brain, causing sedation and other side effects.

H

histamine antagonist see ANTIHISTAMINE.

historical method the technique of analyzing, counseling, or otherwise offering therapy by focusing on a client's personal history.

historical psychoanalysis see PSYCHOHISTORY.

history taking the process of compiling the history of a patient or research participant from the individual directly and from other sources, such as the patient's family, hospitals or clinics, psychiatrists or psychologists, neurologists, social workers, and others who have direct knowledge of the individual. See ANAMNESIS.

histrionic personality disorder in *DSM–IV–TR,* a personality disorder characterized by a pattern of long-term (rather than episodic) self-dramatization in which individuals draw attention to themselves, crave activity and excitement, overreact to minor events, experience angry outbursts, and are prone to manipulative suicide threats and gestures. Such individuals appear to others to be shallow, egocentric, inconsiderate, vain, demanding, dependent, and helpless. The disorder was formerly known as **hysterical personality disorder**.

HIV *h*uman *i*mmunodeficiency *v*irus: a parasitic agent in blood, semen, and vaginal fluid that destroys a class of lymphocytes with a crucial role in the immune response. HIV infection can occur by various routes—unprotected sexual intercourse, administration of contaminated blood products, sharing of contaminated needles and syringes by intravenous drug users, or transmission from an infected mother to her child in utero or through breast feeding—and is characterized by a gradual deterioration of immune function that can progress to AIDS. Because the diagnosis of HIV infection is stigmatizing and can result in considerable emotional stress and social ostracism, counseling is available in which guidance, advice, and information are provided to individuals on topics related to HIV infection and AIDS, including managing the myriad associated psychological and social issues.

HIV/AIDS counseling see AIDS COUNSELING.

Hi-Wa itck a CULTURE-BOUND SYNDROME found in Mohave American Indian populations that would be categorized as a mood disorder by *DSM–IV–TR* standards. Symptoms include depression, insomnia, loss of appetite, and sometimes suicide associated with unwanted separation from a loved one; it generally affects the young wife of an older Mohave male.

HM the initials of a patient who became amnesic after undergoing bilateral temporal lobectomy in 1953 for the relief of intractable seizures. The case of HM, who was a patient of U.S. neurologist William Beecher Scoville (1906–1984), demonstrated the critical role of the HIPPOCAMPUS and surrounding structures in the process of memory formation and storage. The analysis of his memory disorder has also contributed greatly to understanding of the existence of various forms of memory mediated by distinct neural systems.

HMO *h*ealth *m*aintenance *o*rganization: a health plan that offers a range of services through a specified network of health professionals and facilities to subscribing members for a fixed fee. Members select a PRIMARY CARE PROVIDER who coordinates all care and is required to use approved providers for all services. Services may need further approval from the HMO utilization program. The HMO is reimbursed through fixed, periodic prepayments (capitated rates) by, or on behalf of, each member for a specified period of time. HMOs may subcapitate, or CARVE OUT, certain services, such as mental health, to other groups. See CAPITATION.

hoarding *n.* a COMPULSION, characteristic of OBSESSIVE-COMPULSIVE DISORDER, that involves the persistent collection of useless or trivial items (e.g., old newspapers, garbage, magazines) and an inability to organize or discard these. The accumulation of items (usually in piles) leads to the obstruction of living space, causing distress or impairing function. Any attempt or encouragement by others to discard hoards causes extreme anxiety. **—hoard** *vb., n.*

hoarding orientation in the existential psychoanalysis of Erich FROMM, a character pattern in which the individual doubts that personal needs can ever be completely satisfied and bases his or her sense of security on what he or she can save and own. The character is thought to be rigid, stubborn, and obsessively orderly. Also called **hoarding character**. See also ANAL PERSONALITY. Compare EXPLOITATIVE ORIENTATION; MARKETING ORIENTATION.

hold functions cognitive abilities—such as those involved in vocabulary and verbal knowledge, object assembly, and picture completion—that typically remain stable or improve with adult aging as observed on intellectual or cognitive tests (e.g., the WECHSLER ADULT INTELLIGENCE SCALE).

holding environment in the OBJECT RELATIONS THEORY of British psychoanalyst Donald Winnicott (1896–1971), that aspect of the mother experienced by the infant as the environment that literally—and figuratively, by demonstrating highly focused attention and concern—holds him or her comfortingly during calm states. This is in contrast to the mother who is experienced as the object of the infant's excited states.

holiday syndrome sadness, anxiety, and pessimism that tend to occur during major holiday periods. Severe depression, serious injuries, suicides, and fatal accidents tend to increase during the holiday season. Also called **holiday blues**.

holistic education a form of psychotherapy, derived from the approach of HOLISTIC MEDICINE, in which the therapist serves as a teacher and the client as student. The therapist aims to create conditions within which the student may choose to learn. For maximum growth, all aspects of the client's physical, spiritual, emotional, and intellectual life should be explored and developed. [developed by U.S. psychologist William C. Schutz (1925–2002)]

holistic healing a health care concept based on the premise that body, mind, and spirit function as a harmonious unit and that an adverse effect on one also adversely affects the others, requiring treatment of the whole to restore the harmonious balance.

holistic medicine a branch of medicine that, in the prevention and treatment of disease, focuses on the whole person—including physical, mental, spiritual, social, and environmental aspects—rather than on disease symptoms alone. Major features of holistic medicine include patient education about behavioral and attitudinal changes that promote and maintain good health and well-being, and patient self-help and participation in the healing process through diet, exercise, and other measures. It is often practiced in tandem with both conventional medicine (e.g., medication, surgery) and with COMPLEMENTARY AND ALTERNATIVE MEDICINE.

holistic psychology an approach to psychology based on the view that psychological phenomena must be studied as wholes, or that individuals are biological, psychological, and sociocultural totalities that cannot be fully explained in terms of individual components or characteristics. Holistic psychology is not a specific school but a perspective that informs the theories, methodologies, and practice of certain approaches, such as HUMANISTIC PSYCHOLOGY and CLIENT-CENTERED THERAPY.

holographic brain theory a brain theory suggesting that neuronal processes operate by means of fieldlike states of wave interference similar to holograms. Also called **holonomic brain theory**. [originated by Austrian-born U.S. neurophysiologist Karl Harry Pribram (1919–)]

holy anorexia see ANOREXIA MIRABILIS.

home and community-based services (**HCBS**) care or services provided in a patient's place of residence or in a noninstitutional setting located in the community. The aim is to help individuals of all ages with disabilities to live in the community, thereby avoiding more costly residential placements. In the United States, the primary means by which such services are funded is the **Home and Community-Based Services Waiver** (or **Medicaid Waiver**) program. Through this waiver, the federal government reimburses states for a percentage of their spending on designated community services, such as DAY HABILITATION, RESIDENTIAL HABILITATION, and service coordination. These services are defined in a flexible manner; they can be tailored to the specific needs of individuals enrolled in the waiver, allowing appropriate services to be provided to people with greatly varying requirements.

home care patient care in the home for people with physical or mental disabilities, including older adults with dementia or physical infirmity. Home care is an alternative to institutionalization, enabling the patient to live in familiar surroundings and preserve family ties. Such services as nursing care, administration of medication, therapeutic baths, physical therapy, and occupational therapy are provided by visiting professionals or paraprofessionals connected with clinics, hospitals, or health agencies. Also called **home health care**.

home health aide a specially trained person who works with a SOCIAL SERVICES agency or a local VISITING NURSE association to provide personal care services, such as bathing, light meal preparation, and dressing, to people with disabilities.

home health care see HOME CARE.

homeopathy *n.* a system of medicine based on the belief that "like cures like." Small, highly diluted quantities of substances are given to cure symptoms when the same substances given at higher or more concentrated doses would actually cause those symptoms. Homeopathy is considered a form of COMPLEMENTARY AND ALTERNATIVE MEDICINE. Compare ALLOPATHY. [first given practical application by German physician Christian Friedrich Samuel Hahnemann (1755–1843)] **—homeopathic** *adj.*

homeostasis *n.* **1.** the regulation by an organism of all aspects of its internal environment, including body temperature, salt–water balance, acid–base balance, and blood sugar level. This involves monitoring changes in the external and internal environments by means of RECEPTORS and adjusting bodily processes accordingly. [first described by U.S. physiologist Walter Bradford Cannon (1871–1945)] **2.** maintenance of a

H

stable balance, evenness, or symmetry. **—homeostatic** *adj.*

home-service agency a group, which may be a public health, social service, or voluntary organization, that provides HOME HEALTH AIDES for people with mental or physical disabilities. The personnel generally are paraprofessionals who are recruited, trained, and supervised by another agency, such as the VISITING NURSE association or a hospital with a home-care unit.

home visit a visit to an individual at home by a professional or paraprofessional, such as a psychologist, physician, nurse, social worker, or rehabilitation therapist, for crisis intervention, aftercare, or other assistance in solving personal problems.

homework *n.* tasks assigned to a client to be performed between sessions of therapy. Assignments may require reading, research, or practicing new behaviors (e.g., attending a lecture, speaking to a specific person).

homicidomania *n.* a mental or emotional disturbance characterized by a desire to kill others, often including actual attempts to do so.

homicidophilia *n.* sexual interest and arousal obtained from murder. In the extreme form, this PARAPHILIA results in what are called LUST MURDERS, or cases of murder and rape. Less extreme cases may consist of the use of murder fantasies or murder-related pornographic materials during masturbation.

homocystinuria *n.* a genetic metabolic disorder characterized by a deficiency of an enzyme needed to convert L-homocystine to L-cystathionine. Mental retardation often occurs, along with a shuffling, ducklike gait and, in some instances, seizures or hemiplegia. Brain abnormalities are often due to arterial or venous thromboses. Also called **cystathionine synthetase deficiency**.

homoeroticism *n.* an erotic desire for people of one's own sex. Also called **homoerotism**. **—homoerotic** *adj.*

homogeneity *n.* see LINEAR SYSTEM.

homogenitality *n.* an interest in the genitalia of one's own sex.

homologous *adj.* **1.** exhibiting resemblance based on common ancestry. **2.** describing chromosomes that are identical in terms of their visible structure and location of gene segments, although they may carry different ALLELES. DIPLOID organisms, such as humans, possess homologous pairs of chromosomes (see AUTOSOME) in the nuclei of their body cells. **3.** describing any segment of a nucleic acid (DNA or RNA) or protein whose sequence of, respectively, bases or amino acids is similar to that of another segment.

homophile *n.* a person who loves others of his or her own sex, that is, a gay man or a lesbian.

homophobia *n.* dread or fear of gay men and lesbians, associated with prejudice and anger focused on them. This results in discrimination on such issues as employment, housing, and legal rights and may also lead to violence (**gay bashing**). Extreme homophobia may lead to murder.

homosexual behavior 1. sexual impulses, feelings, or relations directed toward members of one's own sex. **2.** sexual acts, such as mutual genital caressing, cunnilingus, fellatio, and anal intercourse, that are practiced by gay men and lesbians but also may be practiced by heterosexual couples.

homosexuality *n.* sexual attraction or activity between members of the same sex. Although the term can refer to such sexual orientation in both men and women, current practice distinguishes between gay men and lesbians, and homosexuality itself is now commonly referred to as same-sex sexual orientation or activity. **—homosexual** *adj., n.*

homosexual love a sexual relationship with a member of one's own sex involving the full range of erotic, emotional, and sexual feelings.

homosexual marriage see SAME-SEX MARRIAGE.

homosexual panic a sudden, acute anxiety attack precipitated by (a) the unconscious fear that one might be gay or lesbian or will act out gay or lesbian impulses, (b) the fear of being sexually attacked by a person of the same sex, or (c) loss of or separation from a same-sex partner.

homovanillic acid (**HVA**) the end product of the catabolism of the neurotransmitter dopamine, produced by the action either of catechol-*O*-methyltransferase (COMT) on 3,4-dihydroxyphenylacetic acid (DOPAC) or of aldehyde dehydrogenase on 3-methoxy-4-hydroxyphenylacetaldehyde (MHPA). Levels of homovanillic acid are typically reduced in individuals with Parkinson's disease.

homozygous *adj.* possessing identical forms of a gene (i.e., identical ALLELES) at a given genetic locus on each of a pair of HOMOLOGOUS chromosomes. Either autosomal dominant (see DOMINANT ALLELE) or autosomal recessive (see RECESSIVE ALLELE) conditions are expressed when the individual is homozygous for that condition. Compare HETEROZYGOUS. **—homozygote** *n.*

homunculus *n.* (*pl.* **homunculi**) **1.** a putative process or entity in the mind or the nervous system whose operations are invoked to explain some aspect of human behavior or experience. **2.** in neuroanatomy, a figurative representation, in distorted human form, of the relative sizes of motor and sensory areas in the brain that correspond to particular parts of the body. For example, the brain area devoted to the tongue is much larger than the area for the forearm, so the homunculus has a correspondingly larger tongue. **3.** a completely formed minute human figure (Latin, "little man") thought by some 16th- and 17th-century theorists to exist in the spermatozoon and simply to expand in size in the transition from zygote to embryo to infant to adult.

This idea is an example of "preformism" and is contrary to the epigenetic principle of cumulative development and successive differentiation. **—homuncular** *adj.*

honesty *n.* in psychotherapy, the ability of an individual to express true feelings and communicate immediate experiences, including conflicting, ambivalent, or guilt-ridden attitudes. **—honest** *adj.*

ho'oponopono *n.* in Hawaiian culture, a type of group process, similar to family therapy, in which the 'OHANA or a similar group addresses its personal and family problems in order to restore harmony within the group.

hope *n.* an emotion characterized by the expectation that one will have positive experiences (or that a potentially threatening or negative situation will not materialize or will ultimately result in a favorable state of affairs) and by the belief that one can influence one's experiences in a positive way. See also OPTIMISM.

hopelessness *n.* the feeling that one will not experience positive emotions or an improvement in one's condition. Hopelessness is common in severe MAJOR DEPRESSIVE EPISODES and other DEPRESSIVE DISORDERS and is often implicated in attempted and completed suicides. **—hopeless** *adj.*

Hopkins Symptom Checklist (**HSCL**) a 58-item self-report inventory designed to identify symptom patterns along five dimensions that yield a total distress score: obsessive-compulsive behavior, anxiety, depression, somatization, and interpersonal sensitivity. Developed at Johns Hopkins University in the 1970s, the HSCL provided a much-needed standard for self-report measurement of psychological distress and, ultimately, provided a sound foundation for the development of more comprehensive and sophisticated outcome measures that followed. See also SYMPTOM CHECKLIST-90-REVISED.

Hopkins Verbal Learning Test (**HVLT**) a standardized brief individual test used to assess verbal learning and memory (specifically, immediate recall, delayed recall, and delayed recognition) in individuals aged 16 years and over. The examiner reads aloud 12 nouns, and participants must first repeat them (both immediately and 25 min following their presentation) and then identify them from among a verbally presented list of distractor words. Originally published in 1991, the HVLT subsequently was revised in 2001 (**HVLT–R**). [developed by U.S. medical psychologist Jason Brandt (1954–) and U.S. clinical psychologist Ralph H. B. Benedict (1960–) at Johns Hopkins University, Baltimore]

hormic psychology a school of psychology, originating in the 1920s, that emphasizes goal seeking, striving, and foresight, with the instincts serving as the primary motivation for behavior. It is particularly concerned with explaining social psychological phenomena in terms of INSTINCTIVE BEHAVIOR. [introduced by British-born U.S. psychologist William McDougall (1871–1938)]

hormone *n.* a substance secreted into the bloodstream by an ENDOCRINE GLAND or other tissue or organ to regulate processes in distant target organs and tissues. These secretions include the posterior and anterior pituitary hormones (see PITUITARY GLAND); the CORTICOSTEROIDS and EPINEPHRINE, secreted by the adrenal glands; and the SEX HORMONES released by the reproductive glands. Other organs that secrete hormones include the hypothalamus and the stomach. **—hormonal** *adj.*

hormone replacement therapy (**HRT**) **1.** the administration of female sex hormones—usually an estrogen (see ESTROGEN REPLACEMENT THERAPY) or a combined estrogen–progestin preparation—to postmenopausal women to relieve menopausal symptoms. The use of HRT for other purposes is controversial, since long-term use may increase the risk of breast cancer, cardiovascular disease, stroke, and other conditions associated with the aging process. **2.** the administration of any other hormone to treat a hormone deficiency, for example, thyroid hormone to treat hypothyroidism.

Horner effect see FEAR OF SUCCESS. [Matina **Horner** (1939–), U.S. psychologist]

horticultural therapy the use of gardening as an auxiliary intervention for therapeutic or rehabilitational purposes. It is typically used for individuals with physical or mental illness or disability but may also be used to improve the social, educational, psychological, and physical well-being of older adults as well as those recovering from injury. Also called **horticulture therapy**.

HOS abbreviation for Health Opinion Survey. See KRANTZ HEALTH OPINION SURVEY.

hospice *n.* a place or form of care for terminally ill individuals, often those with life expectancies of less than a year as determined by medical personnel. Instead of curing disease and prolonging life, the emphases of the hospice concept are patient comfort, psychological well-being, and pain management. Care is provided by medical, volunteer, and family caregivers, either in special facilities or in the patient's home. See also TERMINAL CARE.

hospitalitis *n.* the state of mind of patients who are so dependent psychologically on hospital life that their symptoms suddenly recur when they learn that they are about to be discharged.

hospital phobia a persistent and irrational fear of hospitals. In *DSM–IV–TR*, hospital phobia is classified as a form of SPECIFIC PHOBIA, situational type.

hostile-detached marriage an unstable marriage in which there are short but hostile disagreements between the partners.

hostile-engaged marriage an unstable marriage in which the partners have long and fre-

H

quent arguments without the balance of love and humor found in long-lasting VOLATILE MARRIAGES.

hostile work environment a situation in which the workplace is made intimidating, abusive, or offensive to an employee as a consequence of another's conduct within it (e.g., inappropriate comments, remarks, or gestures, unwanted sexual attention) or characteristics of the setting (e.g., displays of distasteful, insulting, or otherwise inappropriate material). See also MERITOR SAVINGS BANK V. VINSON; SEXUAL HARASSMENT.

hostility *n.* the overt expression of intense animosity or antagonism in action, feeling, or attitude. **—hostile** *adj.*

H

hot cognition an enlightened comprehension of the self, others, and events that engenders strong emotional reactions. See also ABREACTION.

hot flash a typical menopausal symptom, caused by decreased levels of estrogen, experienced as a sudden rush of heat to the neck, face, and possibly other parts of the body that may last from 30 s to 5 min. It may begin with a sudden tingling in the fingers, toes, cheeks, or ears, and in some women it is followed by a sensation of cold. Fifty percent of women experience hot flashes around the time of menopause.

hotline *n.* a telephone line maintained by trained personnel for the purpose of providing a crisis intervention service. See TELEPHONE COUNSELING.

hot-seat technique a technique of GESTALT THERAPY in which a client sits in a chair next to the therapist, who encourages the client through direct prompting and questioning to relive stressful experiences and openly express feelings of discomfort, guilt, or resentment. The technique aims to generate a new, more vivid awareness, which leads the client to find his or her own solutions to problems or emotional difficulties. In a GROUP THERAPY variation of the hot-seat technique, an individual member expresses to the therapist his or her interest in dealing with a particular issue, and the focus moves away from the group into an extended interaction between the group member and group leader for a limited period of time. During the one-on-one interaction, the other group members remain silent; afterward, they give feedback on how they were affected, what they observed, and how their own experiences are similar to those on which the individual member worked. Compare EMPTY-CHAIR TECHNIQUE.

HRNB abbreviation for HALSTEAD–REITAN NEUROPSYCHOLOGICAL BATTERY.

HRSD abbreviation for HAMILTON RATING SCALE FOR DEPRESSION.

HRT abbreviation for HORMONE REPLACEMENT THERAPY.

HSCL abbreviation for HOPKINS SYMPTOM CHECKLIST.

hsieh-ping *n.* a CULTURE-BOUND SYNDROME observed in China and Taiwan, characterized by temporary trancelike states in which the individual supposedly becomes possessed by ancestral spirits. It is often accompanied by tremors, DISORIENTATION, DELIRIUM, and visual or auditory hallucinations.

5-HT abbreviation for 5-hydroxytryptamine. See SEROTONIN.

hubris *n.* arrogant pride or presumption. In Greek tragedy, hubris is specifically the overweening pride that leads to the destruction of the protagonist. **—hubristic** *adj.*

Hull, Clark Leonard (1884–1952) U.S. psychologist. Hull earned his doctorate in 1918 at the University of Wisconsin under Joseph Jastrow (1863–1944). He was the originator of the influential drive-reduction theory, which states that all behavior, including conditioning and learning, is initiated by needs and directed to need reduction. Activities that reduce need reinforce specific responses called habits; for example, when a hungry rat obtains food by inadvertently pushing a lever, it learns to repeat that response. Hull's most important work was his widely cited *Principles of Behavior: An Introduction to Behavior Theory* (1943). Together with B. F. SKINNER and Edward Chace TOLMAN, he is considered one of the founders of NEOBEHAVIORISM. He spent the bulk of his career at Yale University, where he was mentor to numerous graduate students who became prominent psychologists.

human channel capacity the limit on the amount of information that may be processed simultaneously by the human information-processing system.

Human Genome Project an international project to map each human gene and determine the complete sequence of base pairs in human DNA. The project began in 1990 and was completed in 2003. It has yielded vast amounts of valuable information about the genes responsible for various diseases, which may lead to the development of effective genetic screening tests and, possibly, treatments. However, controversy surrounds the attempts by some biotechnology companies to patent certain human DNA sequences with the potential for commercial exploitation.

human-growth movement see HUMAN-POTENTIAL MOVEMENT.

human immunodeficiency virus see HIV.

humanistic conscience the type of conscience that is guided by individual standards and not by fear of external authority. Compare AUTHORITARIAN CONSCIENCE. [defined by Erich FROMM]

humanistic–existential therapy see EXISTENTIAL–HUMANISTIC THERAPY.

humanistic perspective the assumption in

psychology that people are essentially good and constructive, that the tendency toward SELF-ACTUALIZATION is inherent, and that, given the proper environment, human beings will develop to their maximum potential. The humanistic perspective arose from the contributions of Gordon ALLPORT, Abraham MASLOW, and Carl ROGERS, who advocated a personality theory based on the study of healthy individuals as opposed to people with mental disorders.

humanistic psychology an approach to psychology that flourished particularly in academia between the 1940s and the early 1970s and that is most visible today as a family of widely used approaches to psychotherapy and counseling. It derives largely from ideas associated with EXISTENTIALISM and PHENOMENOLOGY and focuses on individuals' capacity to make their own choices, create their own style of life, and actualize themselves in their own way. Its approach is holistic, and its emphasis is on the development of human potential through experiential means rather than analysis of the unconscious or behavior modification. Leading figures associated with this approach include Abraham MASLOW, Carl ROGERS, and Rollo MAY. Also called **humanistic theory**. See also HUMAN-POTENTIAL MOVEMENT.

humanistic therapy any of a variety of psychotherapeutic approaches that reject psychoanalytic and behavioral approaches; seek to foster personal growth through direct experience; and focus on the development of human potential, the HERE AND NOW, concrete personality change, responsibility for oneself, and trust in natural processes and spontaneous feeling. Some examples of humanistic therapy are CLIENT-CENTERED THERAPY, GESTALT THERAPY, EXISTENTIAL PSYCHOTHERAPY, and EXPERIENTIAL PSYCHOTHERAPY.

humanity *n.* compassion in one's personal relations with specific others, shown by kindness, nurturance, charity, and love.

human-potential movement an approach to psychotherapy and psychology based on the quest for personal growth, development, interpersonal sensitivity, and greater freedom and spontaneity in living. The ideas of German-born U.S. psychiatrist Frederick (Fritz) S. Perls (1893–1970) were an influential force in the development of the human-potential movement, which derives its general perspective from HUMANISTIC PSYCHOLOGY. GESTALT THERAPY, SENSITIVITY TRAINING, and ENCOUNTER GROUPS are representative of this approach. Also called **human-growth movement**.

human relations training techniques designed to promote awareness in an individual of the feelings and needs of others and to promote constructive interactions. See also SENSITIVITY TRAINING; T-GROUP.

human service delivery system a complex, interrelated set of services aimed at providing physical and mental health programs.

human strength see CHARACTER STRENGTH.

humiliation *n.* a feeling of shame due to being disgraced or deprecated. The feeling sometimes leads to severe depression and deterioration of the individual's sense of SELF-ESTEEM. Humiliation of the partner is frequently found in sexual sadism and sexual masochism.

humility *n.* the quality of being humble, characterized by a low focus on the self, an accurate (not over- or underestimated) sense of one's accomplishments and worth, and an acknowledgment of one's limitations, imperfections, mistakes, gaps in knowledge, and so on.

hunger drive a DRIVE or arousal state induced by food deprivation, precipitating food-seeking behavior.

Hunter's syndrome an X-linked recessive disease, the most common MUCOPOLYSACCHARIDOSIS. As in HURLER'S SYNDROME, there is an excess of mucopolysaccharides in the tissues. The child shows normal development until the 2nd year and may learn some words and sentences and achieve toilet training. Hyperkinetic behavior and a clumsy gait develop after the age of 2; physical activity slows down around the age of 5. Mental retardation appears in the 2nd year. Also called **mucopolysaccharidosis Type II**. [Charles **Hunter** (1872–1955), U.S. physician]

Huntington's disease (**HD**) a progressive hereditary disease associated with degeneration of nerve cells in the BASAL GANGLIA and CEREBRAL CORTEX. It is characterized by abnormalities of gait and posture, motor incoordination, and involuntary jerking motions (CHOREA) as well as DEMENTIA, mood disturbances, and personality and behavioral changes. The age of onset is usually between 30 and 50, but there is a juvenile form of the disease in which symptoms first appear before the age of 20. Huntington's disease is inherited as an autosomal dominant trait (see DOMINANT ALLELE); the single gene responsible is located on chromosome 4. Also called **Huntington's chorea**. [George **Huntington** (1850–1916), U.S. physician]

Hurler's syndrome an autosomal recessive disease marked by mucopolysaccharide levels in tissues more than 10 times normal (see MUCOPOLYSACCHARIDOSIS), combined with elevated levels of polysaccharides and GARGOYLISM. Mental development begins normally but slows after the early months and reaches a plateau around 2 years of age. The child may learn a few words, but not sentences, and toilet training is seldom achieved. Also called **Pfaundler–Hurler syndrome**; **mucopolysaccharidosis Type I**. [Gertrud **Hurler** (1889–1965), Austrian pediatrician]

HVA abbreviation for HOMOVANILLIC ACID.

HVLT abbreviation for HOPKINS VERBAL LEARNING TEST.

hwa-byung *n.* a CULTURE-BOUND SYNDROME specific to Korea and characterized by a range of symptoms that are attributed to the suppression of anger (Korean, literally "anger disease"). Symptoms include a feeling of a mass in the throat, chest, or abdomen, a sensation of heat in the body, headaches, palpitations, indigestion, insomnia, fatigue, panic, dysphoria, fear of impending death, anorexia, generalized aches and pains, and poor concentration. Also called **suppressed anger syndrome**; **wool-hwa-byung**.

hyalophagia *n.* the eating of glass, typically a symptom of PICA.

H

hybristophilia *n.* sexual interest in and attraction to those who commit crimes. In some cases, this may be directed toward people in prison for various types of criminal activities.

hydantoin *n.* any of a group of drugs developed primarily to control epileptic seizures. They were introduced in 1938 after careful studies of chemicals capable of suppressing electroshock convulsions without also causing adverse effects on the central nervous system. Hydantoin molecules are similar in structure to barbiturates but have the advantage of not altering the threshold for minimal seizures. The prototype of the hydantoins is PHENYTOIN (previously called diphenylhydantoin). Other hydantoins include **mephenytoin** (U.S. trade name: **Mesantoin**) and **ethotoin** (U.S. trade name: **Peganone**), but these are rarely used.

hydrocephalus *n.* a condition caused by excessive accumulation of cerebrospinal fluid in the ventricles of the brain, resulting in raised INTRACRANIAL PRESSURE, with such symptoms as headache, vomiting, nausea, poor coordination, gait imbalance, urinary incontinence, slowing or loss of development, lethargy, drowsiness, or irritability or other changes in personality or cognition, including memory loss. Hydrocephalus commonly occurs due to obstruction of cerebrospinal fluid from head injury, brain tumor, or hemorrhage. The pressure can sometimes be relieved by surgery, in which the excess fluid is shunted into the bloodstream. In infants, hydrocephalus often produces enlargement of the skull. Also called **hydrocephaly**. **—hydrocephalic** *adj.*

hydrocodone *n.* a mild to moderately potent, orally administered OPIOID ANALGESIC used in the treatment of moderate to moderately severe pain. It is more effective when combined with ACETAMINOPHEN or an NSAID (e.g., aspirin) and is generally marketed in combination with such agents. It is also often marketed in combination with a cough suppressant for the symptomatic relief of cough due to colds or nasal congestion. U.S. trade names (among others): **Detussin** (in combination with pseudephedrine); **Vicadin** (in combination with acetaminophen).

hydrocortisone *n.* see CORTISOL.

hydrophobia *n.* **1.** a persistent and irrational fear of water, resulting in avoidance of activities involving water, such as swimming, drinking, or washing one's hands. **2.** a former name for rabies. **—hydrophobic** *adj.*

hydrotherapy *n.* the therapeutic use of water to promote recovery from disease or injury. Hydrotherapy includes such treatments as baths, streams of water (douches), and aquatic sports or exercise.

6-hydroxydopamine (**6-OHDA**) *n.* a dopamine analog used in nonhuman animal studies for its ability to destroy catecholamine-containing nerve cell bodies. 6-OHDA does not cross the blood–brain barrier, but when administered into the central nervous system it causes permanent degeneration of catecholamine-containing neurons. Destruction of dopamine-containing neurons in the NIGROSTRIATAL TRACT with 6-OHDA results in symptoms that clinically resemble Parkinson's disease.

5-hydroxyindoleacetic acid (**5-HIAA**) the main metabolic product of SEROTONIN. Some individuals with depression have low levels of 5-HIAA in the cerebrospinal fluid and exhibit a preferential response to CLOMIPRAMINE.

5-hydroxytryptamine (**5-HT**) *n.* see SEROTONIN.

5-hydroxytryptophan (**5-HTP**) *n.* a naturally occurring precursor of the neurotransmitter SEROTONIN. It is produced from the essential amino acid tryptophan (see TRYPTOPHAN HYDROXYLASE) and is converted in the brain to 5-hydroxytryptamine, or serotonin. Administration of 5-HTP increases the production of serotonin in the brain, and the agent is being investigated for potential use in the treatment of certain forms of MYOCLONUS (severe muscle spasms). 5-HTP is currently available as a dietary supplement for the relief of (among other conditions) headache, depression, fibromyalgia, and CEREBELLAR ATAXIA (causing difficulty in standing and walking) and for appetite suppression. However, reports of a serious, potentially fatal reaction (eosinophilia-myalgia syndrome) have led to cautions regarding its use as a natural remedy.

hydroxyzine *n.* a sedating antihistamine of the DIPHENYLMETHANE class. It is used for the relief of pre- and postoperative pain, obstetric pain, anxiety, dermatitis, and emesis (vomiting). Although also appropriate for the management of alcohol withdrawal, it is rarely used for this purpose in modern clinical practice. Hydroxyzine has significant ANTICHOLINERGIC EFFECTS. U.S. trade names: **Atarax**; **Vistaril**.

hygiene *n.* **1.** the science of health and how to maintain it. **2.** a condition or practice that promotes cleanliness and good health. **—hygienic** *adj.* **—hygienist** *n.*

hyoscine *n.* see SCOPOLAMINE.

hypalgesia *n.* see HYPOALGESIA.

hyperactivity *n.* a condition characterized by spontaneous gross motor activity or restlessness that is excessive for the age of the individual. Although a prominent feature of ATTENTION-DEFICIT/HYPERACTIVITY DISORDER, it is not diagnostic of any particular entity and must be correlated with other findings to identify the appropriate diagnosis. See also DEVELOPMENTAL HYPERACTIVITY; PURPOSELESS HYPERACTIVITY. **—hyperactive** *adj.*

hyperaggressivity *n.* an increased tendency to express anger and hostility in action, as in violent and assaultive behavior. See also EXPLOSIVE PERSONALITY.

hyperbulimia *n.* inordinate appetite and excessive intake of food. It is observed, for example, in certain psychological disorders and in patients with hypothalamic lesions. See also BULIMIA; HYPERPHAGIA. **—hyperbulimic** *adj.*

hypercalcemia *n.* high concentrations of calcium in the blood.

hypercathexis *n.* in psychoanalytic theory, an excess of PSYCHIC ENERGY invested in an OBJECT. Compare HYPOCATHEXIS. See CATHEXIS.

hypercritical *adj.* having an excessive tendency to scrutinize and find fault.

hyperemia *n.* the presence of an increased amount of blood in a part of the body. In some parts, this condition causes a flushed appearance. See also BLUSHING.

hyperesthesia *n.* extreme sensitivity in any of the senses, especially abnormal sensitivity to touch. **—hyperesthetic** *adj.*

hyperexcitability *n.* a tendency to overreact to stimuli, often occurring during a MANIC EPISODE. **—hyperexcitable** *adj.*

hyperfunction *n.* excessive activity of a body function, part, or organ.

hyperglycemia *n.* an excess of glucose in the blood. In DIABETES MELLITUS, hyperglycemia results from a relative or absolute lack of insulin needed to remove the excess glucose from the blood. Signs range from pain or sensory loss to failure of reflexes and coma. **—hyperglycemic** *adj.*

hyperhedonia *n.* a pathological increase in the feeling of pleasure derived from any act or event. Compare ANHEDONIA; HYPHEDONIA.

hyperhidrosis *n.* excessive sweating, which may occur under various circumstances and is not necessarily related to environmental, physical, or psychological factors. In severe cases, the skin in the affected areas may become macerated and vulnerable to infections. Also called **hyperidrosis**.

hypericin *n.* a psychoactive compound that is thought to be the most pharmacologically active agent in ST. JOHN'S WORT.

hyperingestion *n.* excessive intake of food, fluid, or drugs through the mouth, particularly when intake is greater than the maximum safe level.

hyperkinesis *n.* **1.** excessive involuntary movement. **2.** restlessness or HYPERACTIVITY. Also called **hyperkinesia**. **—hyperkinetic** *adj.*

hyperlipidemia *n.* the presence in the blood of excessive amounts of lipids (e.g., cholesterol, triglycerides), which may predispose to atherosclerosis.

hyperlogia *n.* see LOGORRHEA.

hypermania *n.* an extreme manic state marked by constant activity, erratic behavior, DISORIENTATION, and incoherent speech. See also LETHAL CATATONIA. **—hypermanic** *adj.*

hypermnesia *n.* **1.** an extreme degree of retentiveness and recall, with unusual clarity of memory images. In forensic contexts, eyewitnesses have demonstrated increased recall after undergoing hypnotic induction to help retrieve memories, but such memories have been ruled inadmissible in some U.S. courts. See also CIRCUMSTANTIALITY. **2.** remembering more over time rather than less, in contrast to forgetting. See REMINISCENCE.

hypermotility *n.* abnormally increased or excessive activity or movement, particularly in the digestive tract. The cholinergic nervous system dominates the upper portion of the gastrointestinal tract, while the adrenergic system controls the lower portion. Gastrin and serotonin stimulate digestive-tract motility, while secretin and glucagon inhibit contractions. Hypermotility is associated with gastric neuropathy, colitis, and IRRITABLE BOWEL SYNDROME.

hyperobesity *n.* a state of being extremely overweight, sometimes defined as weighing in excess of 45 kg (100 lb) above the accepted ideal body weight for one's height, age, and body build. See also MORBID OBESITY. **—hyperobese** *adj.*

hyperorexia *n.* a pathologically increased appetite. See also BULIMIA. Compare HYPOPHAGIA.

hyperphagia *n.* pathological overeating, particularly when due to a metabolic disorder or to a brain lesion. Compare APHAGIA; HYPOPHAGIA. **—hyperphagic** *adj.*

hyperphilia *n.* sexual arousal by and response to a particular activity or type of stimulus that is above the normal range.

hyperphrasia *n.* see LOGORRHEA.

hyperphrenia *n.* an obsolescent name for a state of increased mental activity combined with concentration difficulty and distractibility, a common pattern in MANIC EPISODES.

hyperplasia *n.* an abnormal increase in the size of an organ or tissue caused by the growth of an excessive number of new, normal cells. **—hyperplastic** *adj.*

hyperpnea *n.* an abnormal increase in the rate and depth of breathing, which may be deep, labored, and rapid.

hyperpraxia *n.* a less common name for PSYCHOMOTOR AGITATION.

hyperprosexia *n.* an exaggerated fixation of attention on an idea or stimulus (e.g., the creaking of a door) to the exclusion of other stimuli. Hyperprosexia is a feature of COMPULSIVE DISORDERS. Also called **hyperprosessis**.

hypersensitivity *n.* an excessive responsiveness of the immune system to certain foreign substances, including various drugs. Hypersensitivity reactions may be immediate, involving an acute allergic reaction leading to ANAPHYLAXIS, or more delayed, involving dangerous and sometimes fatal reductions in the number of certain white blood cells (see AGRANULOCYTOSIS) in response to treatment with some antipsychotic drugs (CLOZAPINE is a classic example). Drug hypersensitivity can also result in serum-sickness-type reactions or in an immune vasculitis, such as STEVENS–JOHNSON SYNDROME, as seen after administration of some ANTICONVULSANT drugs.

hypersexuality *n.* extreme frequency of sexual activity, or an inordinate desire for sexual activity. Hypersexuality may be associated with lesions of the AMYGDALA or HIPPOCAMPUS as demonstrated in nonhuman animal experiments, but direct proof of this in humans is lacking. See NYMPHOMANIA; SATYRIASIS. **—hypersexual** *adj.*

hypersomnia *n.* excessive sleepiness during daytime hours or abnormally prolonged episodes of nighttime sleep. This can be a feature of certain DYSSOMNIAS (e.g., NARCOLEPSY) or other sleep or mental disorders, or it can be associated with neurological dysfunction or damage, with a general medical condition, or with substance use. Hypersomnia may, however, occur in the absence of any known cause or of an association with another condition (see PRIMARY HYPERSOMNIA). See also DISORDERS OF EXCESSIVE SOMNOLENCE. Compare HYPOSOMNIA.

hypersthenia *n.* a condition of excessive strength and tension associated with hyperactivity of the lymphatic system. **—hypersthenic** *adj.*

hypertelorism *n.* an abnormally large distance between two body organs or areas. **Ocular hypertelorism** (**Greig's syndrome**), in which the eyes are farther apart than normal, is often associated with mental retardation or other neurological conditions involving cranial anomalies. See also MEDIAN-CLEFT-FACE SYNDROME.

hypertension *n.* high blood pressure: a circulatory disorder characterized by persistent arterial blood pressure that exceeds readings higher than an arbitrary standard, which usually is 140/90. In the majority of cases there is no obvious cause (see ESSENTIAL HYPERTENSION). In a few people high blood pressure can be traced to a known cause, such as tumors of the adrenal gland, chronic kidney disease, hormone abnormalities, the use of oral contraceptives, or pregnancy. This is called **secondary hypertension**; it is usually cured if its cause is removed or is corrected. Compare HYPOTENSION. **—hypertensive** *adj.*

hyperthymia *n.* emotional response that is disproportionate to the stimulus, frequently occurring in MANIC EPISODES and HYPOMANIC EPISODES.

hyperthyroidism *n.* overactivity of the thyroid gland, resulting in excessive production of thyroid hormones and a consequent increase in metabolic rate. Manifestations include nervousness, excessive activity, and weight loss and other physical problems. Compare HYPOTHYROIDISM. See THYROTOXICOSIS.

hypertrophy *n.* overgrowth of an organ or part due to an increase in the size of its constituent cells. **—hypertrophic** *adj.*

hyperventilation *n.* abnormally rapid and deep breathing, usually due to anxiety or emotional stress. This lowers the carbon dioxide level of the blood and produces such symptoms as light-headedness, palpitation, numbness and tingling in the extremities, perspiration, and in some cases fainting (these features are known as **hyperventilation syndrome**). Also called **overbreathing**.

hypervigilance *n.* a state of abnormally heightened alertness, particularly to threatening or potentially dangerous stimuli.

hypesthesia (**hypaesthesia**) *n.* severely diminished sensitivity in any of the senses, especially the touch sense. Also called **hypoesthesia** (**hypoaesthesia**).

hyphedonia *n.* a pathological diminution in pleasure from experiences that normally would produce pleasure. Compare HYPERHEDONIA.

hyphenophilia *n.* sexual interest and arousal derived from touching skin, fur, hair, leather, or fabrics.

hypnagogic *adj.* describing or relating to a state of drowsiness or light sleep that occurs just before falling fully asleep.

hypnagogic reverie 1. dream activity or fantasies occuring during the period of drowsiness and fading awareness that immediately precedes the onset of sleep. **2.** the state of being hypnotized.

hypnalgia *n.* literally, dream pain: pain experienced during sleep or in a dream.

hypnoanalysis *n.* a modified and shortened form of psychoanalytic treatment, or a technique incorporated into full analysis, in which hypnosis is used (a) to help patients overcome RESISTANCES, (b) to enhance the TRANSFERENCE process, and (c) to recover memories and release repressed material. The material so brought forth is meant to be incorporated into the patient's consciousness for exploration and, ultimately, for interpretation by the therapist. However, this form of therapy is controversial because many psychologists and psychoanalysts question the veracity of repressed memories recovered during a hypnotic state.

hypnodontics *n.* the use of HYPNOSUGGESTION in dentistry as a means of relaxing tense patients, relieving anxiety, reinforcing or replacing anesthesia, and correcting such habits as bruxism (grinding the teeth).

hypnodrama *n.* a technique of PSYCHODRAMA in which a hypnotic state is induced and the client, or PROTAGONIST, is encouraged to act out his or her relationships and traumatic experiences with the aid of AUXILIARY EGOS. Hypnodrama might be used to overcome a client's resistance to dramatizing his or her problems in conscious psychodrama and to stimulate the revival of past incidents and emotional scenes in their full intensity. The technique is rarely used now. [introduced in 1959 by Romanian-born U.S. psychiatrist Jacob Levi Moreno (1889–1974)]

hypnogenic *adj.* **1.** sleep-producing. **2.** hypnosis-inducing.

hypnogenic spot a putative point on the body that, when touched, may induce hypnosis if the individual is highly susceptible. Such an effect is probably the result of AUTOSUGGESTION.

hypnoid state 1. a state of light hypnosis. **2.** a state resembling hypnosis. Also called **hypnoidal state**.

hypnophrenosis *n.* any type of sleep disturbance. See also SLEEP DISORDER.

hypnopompic *adj.* relating to the drowsy, semiconscious state between deep sleep and waking.

hypnosis *n.* (*pl.* **hypnoses**) the procedure, or the state induced by that procedure, whereby a hypnotist suggests that a subject experience various changes in sensation, perception, cognition, emotion, or control over motor behavior. Subjects appear to be receptive, to varying degrees, to suggestions to act, feel, and behave differently than in a normal waking state. The exact nature of the psychological state and of the use and effectiveness of hypnotic procedures as therapy remain the subject of much debate and, consequently, of ongoing psychological research. As a specifically psychotherapeutic intervention, hypnosis is referred to as HYPNOTHERAPY. See also ALTERED STATE OF CONSCIOUSNESS; HETEROHYPNOSIS; POSTHYPNOTIC SUGGESTION; SELF-HYPNOSIS; WAKING HYPNOSIS.

hypnosuggestion *n.* the application of direct hypnotic suggestion in therapy. It is used to relieve such problems as insomnia, intractable pain, cigarette smoking, anorexia nervosa, and various types of crises (e.g., combat situations, panic, and dissociative amnesia).

hypnotherapy *n.* the use of hypnosis in psychological treatment, either in BRIEF PSYCHOTHERAPY directed toward alleviation of symptoms and modification of behavior patterns or in long-term RECONSTRUCTIVE PSYCHOTHERAPY aimed at personality adaptation or change. Hypnotherapy may use one or a combination of techniques, typically involving the administration by a properly trained professional of therapeutic suggestions to patients or clients who have been previously exposed to a HYPNOTIC INDUCTION procedure. Although discussions of its clinical applications engender controversy, there has been scientific evidence that hypnotherapy can be applied with some success to a wide range of clinical problems (e.g., hypertension, asthma, insomnia, bruxism); chronic and acute pain management; habit modification (e.g., overeating, smoking); mood and anxiety disorders (e.g., some phobias); and personality disorders. There is also some positive evidence demonstrating the effectiveness of hypnosis as an ADJUNCTIVE THERAPY. See also AGE REGRESSION; AUTOMATIC WRITING; DIRECT SUGGESTION; DREAM SUGGESTION; ERICKSONIAN PSYCHOTHERAPY; HYPNOANALYSIS; HYPNOTIC REGRESSION.

hypnotic 1. *n.* a drug that helps induce and sustain sleep by increasing drowsiness and reducing motor activity. In general, hypnotics differ from SEDATIVES only in terms of the dose administered, with higher doses used to produce sleep or anesthesia and lower doses to produce sedation or relieve anxiety. BENZODIAZEPINES are among the most widely prescribed hypnotics; antihistamines and other agents are used to lesser degrees. Newer, nonbenzodiazepine hypnotics, such as ESZOPICLONE, ZOLPIDEM, and ZALEPLON, are achieving clinical currency because of their relative infrequency of adverse side effects. **2.** *adj.* pertaining to hypnosis or sleep.

hypnotic amnesia suggested forgetfulness for designated events. In highly hypnotizable individuals (see HYPNOTIC SUSCEPTIBILITY), there can be spontaneous forgetfulness for the entire hypnotic experience.

hypnotic induction a process by which an individual comes under the influence of verbal suggestions, or any other stimuli that are believed by the individual to induce suggestibility, during HYPNOSIS. The process depends on the individual's HYPNOTIC SUSCEPTIBILITY and often involves fixation of attention and relaxation.

hypnotic regression a therapeutic technique in which an individual under hypnosis is induced to relive a previous experience that may be contributing to current emotional difficulties. There are two types: AGE REGRESSION and past life regression.

hypnotic rigidity a condition of apparent muscular rigidity induced by suggestion during hypnosis.

hypnotic susceptibility the degree to which an individual is able to enter into HYPNOSIS. Although many individuals can enter at least a light trance, people vary greatly in their ability to achieve a moderate or DEEP TRANCE. Also called **hypnotizability**. See also STANFORD HYPNOTIC SUSCEPTIBILITY SCALE.

hypnotic trance see TRANCE.

hypnotism *n.* **1.** the act of inducing HYPNOSIS. **2.** the state of hypnosis.

hypnotizability *n.* see HYPNOTIC SUSCEPTIBILITY. **—hypnotizable** *adj.*

hypoactive sexual desire disorder in *DSM–IV–TR,* persistent and distressing deficiency or absence of sexual interest and desire to engage in sexual activity. This may be global, involving all forms of sexual activity, or situational, limited to one partner or one type of sexual activity. It also may be lifelong or result from some life event or relationship issue.

hypoactivity *n.* abnormally slowed or deficient motor or other activity.

hypoageusia *n.* see HYPOGEUSIA.

H

hypoalgesia *n.* diminished sensitivity to pain. Also called **hypalgesia**.

hypocathexis *n.* in psychoanalytic theory, an abnormally low investment of PSYCHIC ENERGY in an OBJECT. Compare HYPERCATHEXIS. See CATHEXIS.

hypochondria *n.* morbid concern with the state of one's health, including unfounded beliefs of ill health. If severe and disabling, this preoccupation is classified as a mental disorder (see HYPOCHONDRIASIS). **—hypochondriac** or **hypochondriacal** *adj.* **—hypochondriac** *n.*

hypochondriasis *n.* in *DSM–IV–TR,* a SOMATOFORM DISORDER characterized by a preoccupation with the fear or belief that one has a serious physical disease based on the incorrect and unrealistic interpretation of bodily symptoms. This fear or belief persists for at least 6 months and interferes with social and occupational functioning in spite of medical reassurance that no physical disorder exists.

hypodermic injection see SUBCUTANEOUS INJECTION.

hypodontia *n.* see RIEGER'S SYNDROME.

hypoesthesia (**hypoaesthesia**) *n.* see HYPESTHESIA.

hypofrontality *n.* a condition of reduced activation or inadequate functioning of the cortex of the frontal lobes of the brain. In theory, this is a factor in schizophrenia but it is not well established, either as a characteristic phenomenon or as a cause.

hypofunction *n.* reduced function or activity, especially of an organ, such as a gland.

hypogeusia *n.* diminished sensitivity to taste. See also DYSGEUSIA. **—hypogeusic** *adj.*

hypoglycemia *n.* the condition of having a low blood-sugar level, due to interference with the formation of sugar in the blood or excessive utilization of sugar. In infants the major symptoms are tremors, cyanosis, seizures, apathy, weakness, respiratory problems, and failure to develop intellectually; the infantile idiopathic form may be due to a single recessive gene. In adults the major symptoms are debility, profuse sweating, nervousness, and dizziness. The adult form may be a psychophysiological reaction (**functional hyperinsulinism**) or it may result from inadequate intake of carbohydrates or insulin overdosage in those with DIABETES MELLITUS. **—hypoglycemic** *adj.*

hypokinesis *n.* abnormal slowness in the initiation of voluntary movement. Also called **hypokinesia**. Compare BRADYKINESIA. **—hypokinetic** *adj.*

hypolipemia *n.* the presence in the blood of an abnormally low level of lipids.

hypomania *n.* see HYPOMANIC EPISODE. **—hypomanic** *adj.*

hypomanic episode a period of elevated, expansive, or irritable mood lasting at least 4 days and accompanied by at least three of the following (four if the mood is irritable): inflated self-esteem, a decreased need for sleep, increased speech, racing thoughts, distractibility, increase in activity or PSYCHOMOTOR AGITATION, and increased involvement in risky activities (e.g., foolish investments, sexual indiscretions), all of which affect functioning and are noticeable by others but do not cause marked impairment. One or more hypomanic episodes are characteristic of bipolar II disorder (see BIPOLAR DISORDER), and hypomanic symptoms are a feature of CYCLOTHYMIC DISORDER. Also called **hypomania**.

hypomenorrhea *n.* a condition of diminished menstrual flow or menstruation of abnormally short duration.

hypomotility *n.* abnormally decreased or deficient activity or movement.

hypophagia *n.* pathologically reduced food intake. Compare HYPERPHAGIA.

hypophilia *n.* sexual arousal by and response to a particular activity or type of stimulus that is below the normal range.

hypophrasia *n.* impaired or slow speech, a feature of severe PSYCHOMOTOR RETARDATION that sometimes occurs in a MAJOR DEPRESSIVE EPISODE.

hypopituitarism *n.* see FRÖHLICH'S SYNDROME.

hypoplasia *n.* underdevelopment of an organ or tissue, usually due to an inadequate number of cells or diminished size of cells forming the structure. When applied to an entire body, hypoplasia usually refers to a dwarf of the species. **—hypoplastic** *adj.*

hypoprosexia *n.* an abnormal lack of attentive ability. Also called **hypoprosessis**.

hyposexuality *n.* an abnormally low level of sexual behavior. Hyposexual individuals may show no sex drive or interest in sexual activity. **—hyposexual** *adj.*

hyposomnia *n.* a reduction in a person's sleep time, often as a result of INSOMNIA or some other sleep disturbance. See also SLEEP DISORDER. Compare HYPERSOMNIA.

hypospadias *n.* a congenital anomaly in which the urethra opens below its normal anatomical position. In males, hypospadias is usually manifested by a urethral opening on the underside of the penis. In females, the urethra may open into the vagina.

hypotaxia *n.* poor motor coordination. **—hypotaxic** *adj.*

hypotension *n.* abnormally low blood pressure, causing dizziness and fainting. Compare HYPERTENSION. See also ORTHOSTATIC HYPOTENSION. **—hypotensive** *adj.*

hypothalamic–pituitary–adrenocortical system (**HPA system**) a neuroendocrine system that is involved in the physiological response to stress. Outputs from the amygdala to the hypothalamus stimulate the release of CORTICOTROPIN-RELEASING FACTOR (CRF). CRF elicits the release from the anterior pituitary of CORTICOTROPIN, which in turn regulates the production and release of stress hormones (e.g., cortisol) from the adrenal cortex into the bloodstream.

hypothalamic syndrome any of various disorders arising from injuries to the HYPOTHALAMUS. These may involve disturbances of eating, drinking, sleep, water balance, and temperature or development of secondary sexual characteristics.

hypothalamus *n.* (*pl.* **hypothalami**) part of the DIENCEPHALON of the brain, lying ventral to the THALAMUS, that contains nuclei with primary control of the autonomic (involuntary) functions of the body. It also helps integrate autonomic activity into appropriate responses to internal and external stimuli. **—hypothalamic** *adj.*

hypothermia *n.* the state of having an abnormally low body temperature. It can be caused by absence of normal reflexes such as shivering, sometimes associated with disease or a disorder of the brain, or by exposure to extreme cold. **Accidental hypothermia** is most likely to affect older people, who are less able to cope with the cooling effect of environmental temperatures in the winter months. Symptoms include listlessness, drowsiness, apathy, and indifference to progressive frostbite, progressing (if untreated) to coma and death. **—hypothermic** *adj.*

hypothesis *n.* (*pl.* **hypotheses**) an empirically testable proposition about some fact, behavior, relationship, or the like, usually based on theory, that states an expected outcome resulting from specific conditions or assumptions.

hypothesis testing the process of using any of a collection of statistical tests to assess the likelihood that an experimental result might have been the result of a chance or random process.

hypothymia *n.* an obsolescent name for a restricted range of affect, occurring in severe cases of MAJOR DEPRESSIVE EPISODE.

hypothyroidism *n.* underactivity of the thyroid gland, resulting in underproduction of thyroid hormones and a consequent decrease in metabolic rate. Manifestations include fatigue, weakness, and weight gain and other physical problems. Compare HYPERTHYROIDISM. See also CONGENITAL HYPOTHYROIDISM.

hypoxanthine–guanine phosphoribosyltransferase (**HGPRT**) an enzyme whose deficiency in the human body leads to symptoms of LESCH–NYHAN SYNDROME. It was the first enzyme found to be associated with an inherited disorder involving maladaptive behavior and mental retardation. Also called **hypoxanthine phosphoribosyltransferase**.

hypoxemia *n.* a deficiency of oxygen in the blood. The most reliable method for measuring the degree of hypoxemia is blood gas analysis to determine the partial pressure of oxygen in the arterial blood. Insufficient oxygenation of the blood may lead to HYPOXIA. Compare ANOXEMIA.

hypoxia *n.* reduced oxygen in the body tissues, including the brain. This can result in widespread brain injury depending on the degree of oxygen deficiency and its duration. Signs and symptoms of hypoxia vary according to its cause, but generally include shortness of breath, rapid pulse, fainting, and mental disturbances (e.g., delirium, euphoria). See also ANOXIA. **—hypoxic** *adj.*

hypoxyphilia *n.* erotic self-strangulation. See ASPHYXOPHILIA; AUTOEROTIC ASPHYXIATION.

hysteria *n.* the historical name for the condition classified in *DSM–IV–TR* as SOMATIZATION DISORDER. Although technically outdated, it is often used as a lay term for any psychogenic disorder characterized by such symptoms as paralysis, blindness, loss of sensation, and hallucinations and often accompanied by suggestibility, emotional outbursts, and histrionic behavior. Sigmund FREUD interpreted hysterical symptoms as defenses against guilty sexual impulses (e.g., a paralyzed hand cannot masturbate), but other conflicts are now recognized. Freud also included dissociative conditions in his concept of hysteria, but these are now regarded as separate disorders. The name derives ultimately from the Greek *husteros*, "uterus," based on the early and erroneous belief that such disorders were unique to women and originated in uterine disorders. **—hysterical** *adj.*

hysterical amnesia an older name, now rarely encountered, for a disorder characterized by inability to recall traumatic or anxiety-provoking events, such as experiences associated with guilt, failure, or rejection. See DISSOCIATIVE AMNESIA.

hysterical blindness see FUNCTIONAL BLINDNESS.

hysterical disorder an outdated name for any disorder characterized by involuntary psychogenic dysfunction of the sensory, motor, or visceral activities of the body. See CONVERSION DISORDER; SOMATIZATION DISORDER.

hysterical paralysis a former name for CONVERSION PARALYSIS.

hysterical personality disorder see HISTRIONIC PERSONALITY DISORDER.

hysterical psychosis an old name for a condition in which psychotic symptoms (e.g., hallucinations, delusions, and bizarre and sometimes violent behavior) appear suddenly in a person with HISTRIONIC PERSONALITY DISORDER (formerly referred to as hysterical personality disorder), usually in response to a stressful precipitating life event. Symptoms are of short duration, lasting 2 weeks or less, and there is a full return to the previous level of functioning. In *DSM–III*, hysterical psychosis was subsumed under the diagnostic category of brief reactive psychosis (see BRIEF PSYCHOTIC DISORDER). Currently, however, hysterical psychosis is not widely considered a distinct clinical entity; it is not listed in the *DSM–IV–TR*. Also called **dissociative psychosis**.

hysteriform *adj.* characterized by symptoms that resemble those associated with HYSTERIA. The term is not in current usage.

H

Ii

IAAP abbreviation for INTERNATIONAL ASSOCIATION OF APPLIED PSYCHOLOGY.

IADLs abbreviation for INSTRUMENTAL ACTIVITIES OF DAILY LIVING.

iatrogenesis *n.* the process of producing an IATROGENIC ILLNESS. Also called **iatrogeny**.

iatrogenic *adj.* denoting or relating to a pathological condition that is caused inadvertently by treatment, particularly the actions of a health care professional. For example, an **iatrogenic addiction** is a dependence on a substance, most often a painkiller, originally prescribed by a physician to treat a physical or psychological disorder.

iatrogenic illness a disorder that is induced or aggravated by the attending clinician, therapist, or physician. It may be due to the behavior of the clinician (e.g., his or her comments or expressions, the manner in which the patient is examined) or a result of the treatment given (e.g., an infection acquired during the course of the treatment).

iatrogenic schizophrenia see TARDIVE DYSMENTIA.

iatrogeny *n.* see IATROGENESIS.

ibogaine *n.* a hallucinogenic agent found in the root of the African forest plant *Tabernanthe iboga*. It is used mainly by adherents of the Bwiti (or Bouiti) religion in rituals or as a stimulant, although data suggest that ibogaine may have potential clinical use in the treatment of substance dependence and management of withdrawal symptoms. Although its mechanism of action is unknown, ibogaine may function as a low-affinity blocker of the ion channels associated with NMDA RECEPTORS.

ibotenic acid an agent that enhances the action of the excitatory neurotransmitter GLUTAMATE: It is an agonist at NMDA RECEPTORS. Ibotenic acid and its metabolic product, muscimol (a GABA AGONIST), are found in some mushrooms of the genus *Amanita* (see FLY AGARIC).

IBS abbreviation for IRRITABLE BOWEL SYNDROME.

ICD abbreviation for INTERNATIONAL CLASSIFICATION OF DISEASES.

ice *n.* slang for illicitly manufactured METHAMPHETAMINE, a common drug of abuse, especially the free-base, concentrated, smokable form of methamphetamine. It has an intense, persistent action; chronic use may lead to serious psychiatric, metabolic, cardiovascular, and neuromuscular changes.

ICF abbreviation for INTERMEDIATE CARE FACILITY.

iconomania *n.* a pathological impulse to collect and worship images.

ICU abbreviation for INTENSIVE CARE UNIT.

id *n.* in psychoanalytic theory, the component of the personality that contains the instinctual, biological drives that supply the psyche with its basic energy or LIBIDO. Sigmund FREUD conceived of the id as the most primitive component of the personality, located in the deepest level of the unconscious; it has no inner organization and operates in obedience to the PLEASURE PRINCIPLE. Thus the infant's life is dominated by the desire for immediate gratification of instincts, such as hunger and sex, until the EGO begins to develop and operate in accordance with reality. See also PRIMARY PROCESS; STRUCTURAL MODEL.

id anxiety in psychoanalytic theory, anxiety deriving from instinctual drives. This is the main cause of PRIMARY ANXIETY (automatic anxiety). Compare EGO ANXIETY.

idealism *n.* **1.** in philosophy, the position that reality, including the natural world, is not independent of mind. Positions range from strong forms, holding that mind constitutes the things of reality, to weaker forms holding that reality is correlated with the workings of the mind. There is also a range of positions as to the nature of mind, from those holding that mind must be conceived of as absolute, universal, and apart from nature itself to those holding that mind may be conceived of as individual minds. See ABSOLUTE IDEALISM; IDEALISTIC MONISM; SUBJECTIVE IDEALISM. See also MIND–BODY PROBLEM. **2.** commitment to moral, political, or religious ideals. Compare MATERIALISM. **—idealist** *n.* **—idealistic** *adj.*

idealization *n.* **1.** the exaggeration of the positive attributes and minimization of the imperfections or failings associated with a person, place, thing, or situation, so that it is viewed as perfect or nearly perfect. **2.** in psychoanalytic theory, a DEFENSE MECHANISM that protects the individual from conscious feelings of ambivalence toward the idealized OBJECT. Idealization of the parents and other important figures plays a role in the development of the EGO-IDEAL. **—idealize** *vb.*

ideal observer a hypothetical person whose sensory and perceptual systems operate without error or bias. The concept of the ideal observer is used most commonly within the context of psychophysical testing, particularly SIGNAL DETECTION THEORY. Performance of the ideal observer can be simulated and compared with actual human performance.

ideal self in models of self-concept, a mental representation of an exemplary set of psychological attributes that one strives or wishes to possess.

idea of influence see DELUSION OF INFLUENCE.

idea of reference the sense that events or the actions of others (e.g., talking, whispering, or smiling) relate particularly to oneself. In an extreme degree, it is a DELUSION OF REFERENCE.

ideation *n.* the process of forming ideas and images. **—ideate** *vb.* **—ideational** *adj.*

idée fixe 1. a firmly held, irrational idea or belief that is maintained despite evidence to the contrary. It may take the form of a delusion and become an obsession. Also called **fixed belief**; **fixed idea**. **2.** a subconscious unit of mental processing (see AUTOMATISM) that has become split off or dissociated from consciousness and, as a result, interferes with the normal processing of information. In some theories, this is considered a primary mechanism for the symptoms of HYSTERIA. [proposed by French psychologist Pierre Janet (1859–1947)]

id-ego *n.* in psychoanalytic theory, the undifferentiated structure of the infant's personality before the EGO develops enough maturity to separate from the ID. The concept is based on Sigmund FREUD's view that the newborn infant is all id and the ego develops out of it in response to the demands of reality. See EGO DEVELOPMENT.

identical twins see MONOZYGOTIC TWINS.

identification *n.* **1.** the process of associating the self closely with other individuals and their characteristics or views. This process takes many forms: The infant feels part of his or her mother; the child gradually adopts the attitudes, standards, and personality traits of the parents; the adolescent takes on the characteristics of the peer group; the adult identifies with a particular profession or political party. Identification operates largely on an unconscious or semiconscious level. **2.** in psychoanalytic theory, a DEFENSE MECHANISM in which the individual incorporates aspects of his or her OBJECTS inside the EGO in order to alleviate the anxiety associated with OBJECT LOSS or to reduce hostility between himself or herself and the object.

identification transference in GROUP THERAPY, the client's identification with other members of the group and desire to emulate them. [first described by Russian-born U.S. psychotherapist Samuel Richard Slavson (1890–1981)]

identification with the aggressor an unconscious mechanism in which an individual identifies with someone who poses a threat or an opponent who cannot be mastered. The identification may involve adopting the aggression, or emulating other characteristics, of the aggressor. This has been observed in cases of hostage taking and in other extreme situations, such as concentration camps. In psychoanalytic theory, it occurs on a developmental level when the male child identifies with his rival, the father, toward the end of the OEDIPAL PHASE. It was first described by Anna FREUD in 1936. See also STOCKHOLM SYNDROME.

identified patient a member of a structured group (especially a family) who exhibits the symptoms of a mental disorder and for whom treatment may be sought by the other group members. Clinical investigation may reveal that there is a complex and seriously maladaptive behavioral pattern among members of the group as a whole but that the psychological stigma has fallen primarily on one person, the identified patient. Also called **symptom bearer**; **symptom wearer**. See also DYSFUNCTIONAL FAMILY.

identity *n.* **1.** an individual's sense of self defined by (a) a set of physical and psychological characteristics that is not wholly shared with any other person and (b) a range of social and interpersonal affiliations (e.g., ethnicity) and social roles. Identity involves a sense of continuity: the feeling that one is the same person today that one was yesterday or last year (despite physical or other changes). Such a sense is derived from one's body sensations; one's body image, and the feeling that one's memories, purposes, values, and experiences belong to the self. Also called **personal identity**. **2.** in cognitive development, awareness that an object remains the same even though it may undergo many transformations. For example, a piece of clay may be made to assume various forms but is still the same piece of clay.

identity confusion uncertainty regarding one's identity, which often occurs during adolescence but may also occur at a later stage of life. See IDENTITY VERSUS IDENTITY CONFUSION.

identity crisis a phase of life marked by role experimentation, changing, conflicting, or newly emerging values, and a lack of commitment to one's usual roles in society (especially in work and family relationships). Erik ERIKSON claimed that it is natural and desirable for adolescents to go through a period of identity crisis and that greater maturity results from the experience. The concept has been expanded to refer to adult MIDLIFE CRISIS and other periods marked by change or experimentation with the SELF. See EGO IDENTITY.

identity diffusion 1. lack of stability or focus in the view of the self or in any of the elements of an individual's IDENTITY. **2.** in the EGO PSYCHOLOGY of Erik ERIKSON, a possible outcome of the IDENTITY VERSUS IDENTITY CONFUSION stage in which the individual emerges with an uncertain sense of identity and confusion about his or her wishes, attitudes, and goals.

identity disorder 1. in *DSM–III*, a chronic disturbance, usually of late adolescence, in which feelings of uncertainty and distress are generated by such identity issues as long-term goals, career choice, sexual orientation and behavior, group loyalty, moral values, and religious identification. In *DSM–IV–TR*, this is categorized as an **identity problem** within the section **Other Conditions That May Be a Focus of Clinical Attention. 2.** see DISSOCIATIVE IDENTITY DISORDER; GENDER IDENTITY DISORDER.

identity foreclosure premature commitment to an identity: the unquestioning acceptance by individuals (usually adolescents) of the role, values, and goals that others (e.g., parents, close friends, teachers, athletic coaches) have chosen for them. The individual's commitment to the foreclosed identity—for example, that of an athlete—occurs without exploring its value or contemplating alternative roles that might be more appropriate for him or her. See also SEPARATION–INDIVIDUATION.

identity need in the theory of Erich FROMM, the need to achieve a sense of uniqueness, individuality, and selfhood. Psychological autonomy and the severing of INCESTUOUS TIES are considered essential for healthy individuality. Unhealthy, spurious individuality is expressed in conformity, a manifestation of the ESCAPE FROM FREEDOM. Compare ROOTEDNESS.

identity style an adolescent's characteristic mode of approaching problems and decisions that are relevant to his or her personal identity or sense of self. Differences in style reflect differences in the social-cognitive processes that individuals use to construct a sense of identity. Three basic identity styles are recognized: informational, normative, and diffuse-avoidant. Information-oriented individuals actively seek out, evaluate, and use self-relevant information. They are skeptical about their self-constructions and willing to test and revise aspects of their self-identity when confronted with discrepant feedback. Normative individuals deal with identity questions and decisional situations by conforming to the prescriptions and expectations of significant others. Diffuse-avoidant-oriented individuals are reluctant to face up to and confront personal problems and decisions.

identity theory the theory that mental states are identical with brain states. In **token identity theory**, identical mental and brain states occur within the individual. **Type identity theory** extends this to theorize that when two or more people share a mental state (e.g., the belief that ice is cold) they also have the same brain state. Also called **central state theory**; **identity theory of the mind**. See also EPIPHENOMENALISM; MATERIALISM; MIND–BODY PROBLEM; PHYSICALISM; REDUCTIONISM.

identity versus identity confusion the fifth of ERIKSON'S EIGHT STAGES OF DEVELOPMENT, marked by an identity crisis that occurs during adolescence. During this stage the individual may experience a psychosocial MORATORIUM, a period of time that permits experimentation with social roles. The individual may "try on" different roles and identify with different groups before forming a cohesive, positive identity that allows him or her to contribute to society; alternatively, the individual may identify with outgroups to form a negative identity, or may remain confused about his or her sense of identity, a state Erikson calls IDENTITY DIFFUSION.

idiocentric 1. *adj.* denoting internality to the self, particularly an orientation toward or focus on personal needs and interests. **2.** *n.* an individual who is dispositionally predisposed to put his or her personal interests and motivations before the interests and goals of other people and other groups. Just as societies based on INDIVIDUALISM stress the rights of the individual over the group, so idiocentrics emphasize their personal needs and are emotionally detached from groups and communities. They are more likely to describe themselves in terms of personal qualities and traits rather than memberships and roles. See also EGOCENTRISM; INDIVIDUALISM. Compare ALLOCENTRIC. **—idiocentrism** *n.*

I

idiogamist *n.* a person who is capable of full sexual response only with his or her spouse and is sexually incapable or inadequate with other partners. An idiogamist is usually a man who cannot obtain or maintain penile erection with any partner other than his wife (or, sometimes, women who resemble his wife).

idiogenesis *n.* origin without evident cause, particularly the origin of an IDIOPATHIC disease.

idioglossia *n.* the omission, substitution, and distortion of so many sounds that speech is rendered unintelligible. It is often associated with mental retardation. Also called **idiolalia**.

idiographic *adj.* relating to the description and understanding of an individual case, as opposed to the formulation of NOMOTHETIC general laws describing the average case. U.S. psychologists Kenneth MacCorquadale (1919–1986) and Paul MEEHL identified these as two contrasting traditions in explaining psychological phenomena. An **idiographic approach** involves the thorough, intensive study of a single person or case in order to obtain an in-depth understanding of that person or case, as contrasted with a study of the universal aspects of groups of people or cases. In those areas of psychology in which the individual person is the unit of analysis (e.g., in personality, developmental, or clinical psychology), the idiographic approach has appeal because it seeks to characterize a particular individual, emphasizing that individual's characteristic traits (see IDIOGRAPHIC TRAIT) and the uniqueness of the individual's behavior and adjustment, rather than to produce a universal set of psychological constructs that might be applicable to a population.

idiographic trait a personality trait that is observed in only one individual or one member of a population or that is seldom found in the same form among individuals or members. Also called **unique trait**.

idiolalia *n.* see IDIOGLOSSIA.

idiopathic *adj.* without known cause or of spontaneous origin: usually denoting diseases, such as some forms of epilepsy, whose ETIOLOGY is obscure.

idiosyncratic intoxication a condition characterized by sudden and extreme changes in personality, mood, and behavior following the ingestion of an amount of alcohol usually considered to be too little to account for the degree of the changes. It may include extreme excitement, impulsive and aggressive behavior (at times to the point of extreme violence), persecutory ideas, disorientation, and hallucinations. The episode ends when the individual falls into a deep sleep, after which there is often complete loss of memory for it. Some researchers believe that the condition may be related to stress or may be due in part to a psychomotor seizure triggered by alcohol. Also called **mania a potu**; **pathological intoxication**. See also FUROR.

idiosyncratic reaction an unexpected reaction to a drug resulting in effects that may be contrary to the anticipated results. Idiosyncratic reactions can result in various symptoms, but generally refer to an extreme sensitivity or an extreme insensitivity to a particular agent. Such reactions may be genetically mediated.

idiot savant (*pl.* **idiots savants** or, less often, **idiot savants**) see SAVANT. [French, "learned idiot"]

id psychology in psychoanalysis, an approach that focuses on the unorganized, instinctual impulses contained in the ID that seek immediate pleasurable gratification of primitive needs. The id is believed to dominate the lives of infants and is frequently described as blind and irrational until it is disciplined by the other two major components of the personality: the EGO and the SUPEREGO. Compare EGO PSYCHOLOGY.

id resistance in psychoanalysis, a form of RESISTANCE to therapy that is motivated by unconscious ID impulses, whose underlying motive is the REPETITION COMPULSION. Compare REPRESSION-RESISTANCE; SUPEREGO RESISTANCE.

IDS abbreviation for INTEGRATED DELIVERY SYSTEM.

IEP abbreviation for INDIVIDUALIZED EDUCATION PROGRAM.

IFSP abbreviation for INDIVIDUAL FAMILY SERVICE PLAN.

if...then profiles a methodology for describing personal dispositions in which within-person variations across social contexts are charted in terms of the behaviors evoked by particular situations. [developed by U.S. personality psychologists Walter Mischel (1930–) and Yuichi Shoda]

IHS abbreviation for INDIAN HEALTH SERVICE.

iich'aa *n.* a CULTURE-BOUND SYNDROME found in Navaho communities, with symptoms similar to those of AMOK.

I–It *adj.* describing a relationship in which a subject ("I") treats something or someone else exclusively as an impersonal object ("It") to be used or controlled. German Jewish philosopher Martin Buber (1878–1965), who originated the term, maintained that this type of relationship between people stands in the way of human warmth, mutuality, trust, and group cohesiveness. Compare I–THOU.

ikota *n.* see MYRIACHIT.

Illinois Test of Psycholinguistic Abilities (ITPA) a norm-referenced test for children aged 5–13 years and designed to measure spoken and written linguistic abilities considered important in communication and learning disorders. It currently consists of 12 subtests: spoken analogies, spoken vocabulary, morphological closure, syntactic sentences, sound deletion, rhyming sequences, sentence sequencing, written vocabulary, sight decoding, sound decoding, sight spelling, and sound spelling. First published in 1961 as an experimental edition, the ITPA is now in its third edition (published in 2001). [originally developed by U.S. psychologists Samuel Alexander Kirk (1904–1996) and James Jerome McCarthy (1927–) at the University of Illinois]

illness behavior behaviors, attitudes, and emotions exhibited by individuals during the course of a physical or mental illness. It includes the perception of feeling ill, the expression of illness-related concerns to others, changes in functioning, and utilization of health care services.

illogicality *n.* a tendency to make unwarranted or faulty inferences, often characteristic of delusional thinking and speech. **—illogical** *adj.*

illumination *n.* a moment of insight, for example into the nature and processes of an interpersonal relationship, the solution to a problem, or understanding of an event. See also AHA EXPERIENCE; EPIPHANY.

illuminism *n.* an exalted hallucinatory state in which the person carries on conversations with imaginary, often supernatural, beings.

illusion *n.* **1.** a false perception. Illusions of the senses, such as visual (or optical) illusions, result from the misinterpretation of sensory stimuli. For example, parallel railroad tracks appear to meet in the distance. Many illusions are quite normal occurrences, although they may also occur in delirium, schizophrenia, and in those taking mind-altering drugs. Visual illusions may also occur as a result of a pathological condition. **2.** a distortion in memory, such as DÉJÀ VU. **—illusory** *adj.*

illusion of agency the illusion of controlling an action that is not actually under one's control. Also called **illusion of will**. [defined by U.S. psychologist Daniel M. Wegner (1948–)]

illusion of control a false belief that external

events result from or are governed by one's own actions or choices. See POSITIVE ILLUSION.

illusion of doubles see CAPGRAS SYNDROME.

illusion of orientation misidentification of environmental or other stimuli, such as confusion about one's location or the identity of people, due to impaired consciousness, for example, during DELIRIUM.

illusory correlation 1. the appearance of a relationship that in reality does not exist. **2.** an overestimation of the degree of relationship (i.e., correlation) between two variables. For example, if an unusual action occurred at the same time that an adolescent was present, the assumption that the action was carried out by the adolescent would be an illusory correlation.

illusory memory see FALSE MEMORY.

iloperidone *n.* an ATYPICAL ANTIPSYCHOTIC agent of the benzisoxazole class that is active at a range of receptors. It acts as an antagonist at postsynaptic serotonin 5-HT_{2A} receptors as well as at dopamine D2 receptors. It is thought also to act as a PARTIAL AGONIST at postsynaptic dopamine D2 receptors. This blend of agonist and antagonist properties, plus its wide-ranging receptor activity, is thought to confer antipsychotic activity without the negative side effects commonly associated with antipsychotics. U.S. trade name: **Fanapt**.

im abbreviation for *i*ntra*m*uscular.

image *n.* **1.** a likeness or cognitive representation of an earlier sensory experience recalled without external stimulation. For example, remembering the shape of a horse or the sound of a jet airplane brings to mind an image derived from earlier experiences with these stimuli. **2.** a representation of an object produced by an optical system.

imageless thought thinking that occurs without the aid of IMAGES or sensory content. The so-called Würzburg school (late 19th century) upheld the existence of imageless thought on the basis of introspective reports, for example, experimental participants' stated ability to name a piece of fruit without picturing it. Edward Bradford TITCHENER and others in the structural school opposed this view (see STRUCTURALISM).

imagery *n.* **1.** cognitive generation of sensory input from the five senses, individually or collectively, which is recalled from experience or self-generated in a nonexperienced form. **2.** mental IMAGES considered collectively, or the particular type of imagery characteristic of an individual, such as VISUAL IMAGERY.

imagery technique the use of imagined scenes as a therapeutic technique, often in HYPNOTHERAPY but also in therapies that use breathing and relaxation techniques to reduce anxiety. For example, an anxious client may be directed to imagine a placid scene recalled from memory, such as sitting, relaxed and calm, on a beach. The technique may be used by an individual in stressful situations, for example, by a nervous passenger in an aircraft. See also GUIDED AFFECTIVE IMAGERY.

imaginal exposure a type of EXPOSURE THERAPY used for treating individuals with anxiety disorders (e.g., PHOBIAS, OBSESSIVE-COMPULSIVE DISORDER) or posttraumatic stress disorder. Vivid imagery evoked through speech is used by the therapist to expose the client mentally to an anxiety-evoking stimulus. Compare IN VIVO EXPOSURE.

Imaginary *n.* the realm of images: one of three aspects of the psychoanalytic field defined by French psychoanalyst Jacques Lacan (1901–1981). The Imaginary is that state of being in which the infant has no sense of being a subject distinct from other people or the external world and no sense of his or her place in human culture. After the infant's entry into the SYMBOLIC (the world of language, culture, and morality), he or she can return to the wholeness of the Imaginary only in fantasy. See also REAL.

I

imaginary audience the belief of an adolescent that others are constantly focusing attention on him or her, scrutinizing behaviors, appearance, and the like. The adolescent feels as though he or she is continually the central topic of interest to a group of spectators (i.e., an audience) when in fact this is not the case (i.e., an imaginary audience). It is an early adolescent construct reflective of acute self-consciousness.

imaginary companion a fictitious person, animal, or object created by a child or adolescent. The individual gives the imaginary companion a name, talks, shares feelings, and pretends to play with it, and may use it as a scapegoat for his or her misdeeds. The phenomenon is considered an elaborate but common form of SYMBOLIC PLAY. Also called **invisible playmate**.

imagination *n.* the faculty that produces ideas and images in the absence of direct sensory data, often by combining fragments of previous sensory experiences into new syntheses. See also CREATIVE IMAGINATION. **—imaginary** *adj.* **—imagine** *vb.*

imagination inflation the increased likelihood of a person judging that an event has actually occurred (e.g., during that person's childhood) when the person imagines the event before making such a judgment.

imaging *n.* **1.** the process of scanning the brain or other organs or tissues to obtain an optical image. Techniques used include COMPUTED TOMOGRAPHY, POSITRON EMISSION TOMOGRAPHY (PET), anatomical MAGNETIC RESONANCE IMAGING (aMRI), and FUNCTIONAL MAGNETIC RESONANCE IMAGING (fMRI). The imaging may be either static or dynamic. See also BRAIN IMAGING; NUCLEAR IMAGING. **2.** in therapy, the use of suggested mental images to control body function, including the easing of pain. See also IMAGERY TECHNIQUE; VISUALIZATION.

imago *n.* an unconscious mental image of another person, especially the mother or father, that influences the way in which an individual relates to others. The imago is typically formed in infancy and childhood and is generally an idealized or otherwise not completely accurate representation. The term was originally used by Sigmund FREUD and the early psychoanalysts, and its meaning has carried over into other schools of psychology and psychotherapy.

imago therapy a type of therapy for relationship problems based on the theory that people carry unconscious composite images (see IMAGO) of the character traits and behaviors of their primary childhood caretakers that impel them to select certain partners and to behave in ways that are meant to heal earlier emotional wounds but that actually create relationship problems. Structured exercises, either in groups (for individuals or couples) or in COUPLES THERAPY, reveal the imago and help individuals learn to become less defensive and more compassionate toward partners as well as themselves.

imbecility *n.* formerly, a low to moderate level of intellectual disability characterized by an IQ between 25 and 50–55 and social and practical skills similar to those of 2- to 7-year-olds. This level of intellectual disability is now described as SEVERE MENTAL RETARDATION or MODERATE MENTAL RETARDATION (depending on the degree).

imipramine *n.* a TRICYCLIC ANTIDEPRESSANT (TCA) with a tertiary amine molecular structure. It was originally synthesized in the hopes of creating an effective antipsychotic, but was observed to be ineffective in reducing psychotic symptoms. It did, however, seem to help individuals with severe depression and was subsequently marketed as an antidepressant. It is considered the prototype TCA and, like all tricyclic agents, its use as an antidepressant has been largely supplanted by less toxic drugs. It continues, however, to have a therapeutic role as a sedative and adjunct in the management of neuromuscular or musculoskeletal pain. U.S. trade name: **Tofranil**.

imitation *n.* the process of copying the behavior of another person, group, or object, intentionally or unintentionally. It is a basic form of learning that accounts for many human skills, gestures, interests, attitudes, role behaviors, social customs, and verbal expressions, but can also take pathological form, as in ECHOLALIA and ECHOPRAXIA. **—imitate** *vb.*

immaturity *n.* a state of incomplete growth or development (e.g., neural immaturity). The term, however, is often used to describe childish, maladaptive, or otherwise inappropriate behaviors, particularly when indicative of a lack of age-relevant skills.

immediate experience current experience and impressions of that experience without any analysis (see MEDIATE EXPERIENCE). See also CONTEMPORANEITY.

immediate gratification the experience of satisfaction or receipt of reward as soon as a response is made. See also PLEASURE PRINCIPLE. Compare DELAY OF GRATIFICATION.

immediate memory a type or stage of memory in which an individual recalls information recently presented, such as a street address or telephone number, although this information may be forgotten after its immediate use. Immediate memory is frequently tested in assessing intelligence or cerebral impairment. See also SHORT-TERM MEMORY.

immobilizing activity see LIBIDO-BINDING ACTIVITY.

immune system a complex system in vertebrates that helps protect the body against pathological effects of foreign substances (antigens), such as viruses and bacteria. The organs involved include the bone marrow and THYMUS, in which lymphocytes—the principal agents responsible for specific immune responses—are produced, together with the spleen, lymph nodes, and other lymphoid tissues and various chemicals that mediate the immune response. The immune system interacts with both the nervous system and the endocrine system. See also PSYCHONEUROIMMUNOLOGY.

Imodium *n.* a trade name for LOPERAMIDE.

impact analysis a quantitative analytic procedure used to assess the net success or failure of a program, usually through controlled experimentation. It is appropriate only if the program's objectives are specifiable and measurable, the program is well implemented for its intended participants, and the outcome measures are reliable and valid. Also called **impact assessment**. See also OUTCOME EVALUATION; SUMMATIVE EVALUATION.

impaired judgment difficulty in forming evaluative opinions or reaching conclusions concerning available evidence, often about people and courses of action. Impaired judgment may lead to seemingly irrational actions and risk-taking behaviors. It has been thought of as both a diagnostic and a predictive criterion for delirium, dementia, and substance-related disorders, but its diagnosis and measurement are hindered by the lack of an agreed operational definition. Various fields have contributed research to this, including developmental and industrial psychology, experimental psychology (perception), medicine, and legal decision making.

impairment *n.* any departure from the body's typical physiological or psychological functioning.

impairment index a measure of impairment on a series of cognitive tests. The best known such index is the **Halstead–Reitan Impairment Index**, which reflects the percentage of tests in the impaired range; the higher the percentage, the greater the likelihood of brain damage.

impenetrability *n.* the state of certain cognitive capacities, such as syntax, that are claimed to be inherently walled off from conscious access and not available to introspective analysis.

imperative *n.* in psychoanalytic theory, a demand of the SUPEREGO that represents the commanding voice of parental or social rule, and operates on an unconscious level to direct the behavior of the individual.

impersonation *n.* **1.** the deliberate assumption of another person's identity, usually as a means of gaining status or other advantage. See also IMPOSTOR SYNDROME. **2.** the imitation of another person's behavior or mannerisms, which is sometimes done for its corrective or therapeutic effect on one's own behavior (e.g., to gain insight).

impingement *n.* **1.** in the OBJECT RELATIONS THEORY of British psychoanalyst Donald Winnicott (1896–1971), an experience in the infant's maternal environment that is felt to be disturbing. Such experiences are posited to lead to the development of a FALSE SELF because the infant may develop through a series of reactions to impingements rather than becoming aware of his or her true tendencies and capacities by discovering the environment on his or her own terms. **2.** in perception, impact or contact with a sensory receptor. **—impinge** *vb.*

implanted memory the apparent recollection of an event that never occurred because someone has convinced the person that it did occur. There have been allegations that some psychotherapists have implanted memories in their clients by leading questioning. See FALSE MEMORY SYNDROME.

implicit attitude an ATTITUDE of which a person has little or no conscious awareness. Compare EXPLICIT ATTITUDE.

implicit behavior **1.** behavior that cannot be observed directly, such as a cognitive process or emotional reaction. **2.** behavior that cannot be observed without the aid of instruments, such as subtle physiological responses. **3.** behavior of which the individual is not consciously aware.

implicit cognition an idea, perception, or concept that may be influential in the cognitive processes or the behavior of an individual, even though the person is not explicitly aware of it. See COGNITION.

implicit knowledge see TACIT KNOWLEDGE.

implicit learning learning of a cognitive or behavioral task that occurs without intention to learn or awareness of what has been learned. Implicit learning is evidenced by improved task performance rather than as a response to an explicit request to remember. See also IMPLICIT MEMORY. Compare EXPLICIT MEMORY.

implicit measure of personality any measure that does not ask people to report explicitly on their psychological characteristics but instead employs subtle indices capable of tapping mental content that individuals may not wish to express or perhaps are not even aware they possess because the mental content is not explicitly represented in consciousness. Measures of the time it takes individuals to answer questions, irrespective of the content of their answers, are one commonly employed implicit measure.

implicit memory memory for a previous event or experience that is produced indirectly, without an explicit request to recall the event and without awareness that memory is involved. For instance, after seeing the word *store* in one context, a person would complete the word fragment *st_r_* as *store* rather than *stare*, even without remembering that *store* had been recently encountered. Implicit memory can exist when conscious or EXPLICIT MEMORY fails, as occurs in amnesia and brain disease. This term, proposed in 1985 by Canadian psychologist Peter Graf and U.S. psychologist Daniel Schacter, is used interchangeably with NONDECLARATIVE MEMORY. Compare EXPLICIT MEMORY.

implicit personality theory any set of tacit assumptions about the interrelations of personality traits, used in everyday life when people infer the presence of one trait on the basis of observing another.

implicit process **1.** a cognitive event that cannot be described accurately, even under optimal conditions. **2.** an occasional synonym for UNCONSCIOUS PROCESS. Compare EXPLICIT PROCESS.

implosive therapy a technique in BEHAVIOR THERAPY that is similar to FLOODING but distinct in generally involving imagined stimuli and in attempting to enhance anxiety arousal by adding imaginary exposure cues believed by the therapist to be relevant to the client's fear. Also called **implosion therapy**. [developed by U.S. psychologists Thomas G. Stampfl (1923–2005) and Donald J. Levis (1936–)]

impostor syndrome **1.** the tendency to attribute achievements and success to external factors rather than internal factors, associated with a persistent belief in one's lack of ability despite consistent objective evidence to the contrary. As a result, the individual may feel like a fraud and have low self-esteem and identity problems. Also called **impostor phenomenon**. **2.** a personality pattern characterized by PATHOLOGICAL LYING, which takes the form of fabricating an identity or a series of identities in an effort to gain recognition and status. See IMPERSONATION.

impotence *n.* the inability of a man to complete the sex act due to partial or complete failure to achieve or maintain erection. This condition is called MALE ERECTILE DISORDER in *DSM–IV–TR* and ERECTILE DYSFUNCTION in clinical contexts. The most common causes of drug-induced impotence are antidepressants and antihypertensives. It is not clearly understood how the use of antidepressants results in impotence and other forms of sexual dysfunction: Possible mechanisms include inhibition of NITRIC OXIDE or effects on serotonin (particularly the 5-HT_2 SEROTONIN RECEPTOR), dopamine, acetylcholine, and norepinephrine. Impotence may also denote premature ejaculation, limited interest in sex, orgasm without pleasure, or coitus without ejaculation. See also ORGASTIC IMPOTENCE; PRIMARY ERECTILE DYSFUNCTION; SECONDARY ERECTILE DYSFUNCTION. **—impotent** *adj.*

impoverished *adj.* **1.** describing a stimulus that is lacking in complexity or information value. **2.** deficient in or deprived of qualities or lacking in richness because something essential is missing. An **impoverished environment** offers few opportunities to engage in activity and does not provide adequate sensory and intellectual stimulation. See also INTELLECTUAL IMPOVERISHMENT. **—impoverishment** *n.*

impression *n.* **1.** the presumed effect on the brain of stimulation. **2.** a vague or unanalyzed judgment or reaction.

impression formation the process in which an individual develops a PERCEPTUAL SCHEMA of some object, person, or group. Early research on impression formation demonstrated that the accuracy of impressions was frequently poor; more recent studies have focused on the roles played in the process by such factors as the perceiver's cognitive processes (e.g., how readily some types of ideas come to mind) and feelings (e.g., anger can predispose the perceiver to stereotype an individual).

impression management behaviors that are designed to control how others perceive one's SELF, especially by guiding them to attribute desirable traits to the self. Typically, it is assumed that people attempt to present favorable images of themselves as a means of obtaining social rewards and enhancing self-esteem. Impression management has been offered as an alternative explanation for some phenomena that have traditionally been interpreted in terms of COGNITIVE DISSONANCE THEORY. Some psychologists distinguish impression management from SELF-PRESENTATION by proposing that impression management involves only deliberate, conscious strategies.

imprinting *n.* **1.** a simple yet profound and highly effective learning process that occurs during a CRITICAL PERIOD in the life of some animals. It was first described in 1873 by British naturalist Douglas A. Spalding (1840–1877) when he observed that newly hatched chicks tended to follow the first moving object, human or animal, that caught their attention. The term itself was introduced by Austrian ethologist Konrad Lorenz (1903–1989) in 1937. Some investigators believe that such processes are instinctual; others regard them as a form of PREPARED LEARNING. **2.** in conditioning, the process of establishing a stimulus as a REINFORCER by presenting it in the appropriate context. The stimulus thus established is called an **imprinted stimulus**.

improvement rate see DISCHARGE RATE.

improvisation *n.* in PSYCHODRAMA, the spontaneous acting out of problems and situations without prior preparation.

IMPS abbreviation for INPATIENT MULTIDIMENSIONAL PSYCHIATRIC SCALE.

impulse *n.* **1.** a sudden and compelling urge to act immediately, often resulting in action without deliberation for a purpose that cannot be recalled. Also called **impulsion**. See also IMPULSE-CONTROL DISORDER; IMPULSIVE. **2.** see NERVE IMPULSE. **3.** in psychoanalytic theory, the movement of PSYCHIC ENERGY associated with instinctual drives, such as sex and hunger.

impulse control the ability to resist an impulse, desire, or temptation and to regulate its translation into action. See also IMPULSE-CONTROL DISORDER.

impulse-control disorder a disorder characterized by a failure to resist impulses, drives, or temptations to commit acts that are harmful to oneself or to others. Impulse-control disorders include those in the *DSM–IV–TR* category IMPULSE-CONTROL DISORDERS NOT ELSEWHERE CLASSIFIED. Other disorders that may involve problems of impulse control include substance-use disorders, paraphilias, conduct disorders, and mood disorders.

impulse-control disorders not elsewhere classified in *DSM–IV–TR*, a class of IMPULSE-CONTROL DISORDERS not classified in other categories (such as substance-use disorders). This class includes PATHOLOGICAL GAMBLING, KLEPTOMANIA, PYROMANIA, INTERMITTENT EXPLOSIVE DISORDER, and TRICHOTILLOMANIA, all of which have their own specific sets of diagnostic criteria, together with **impulse-control disorders not otherwise specified**, which do not meet the criteria for any of the specific disorders. All these disorders have the following common features: (a) failure to resist an impulse or a drive or a temptation to perform an act that is harmful to the individual or others; (b) mounting tension before committing the act; and (c) pleasure or relief during the act, with or without regret and self-reproach afterward.

impulsion *n.* see IMPULSE.

impulsive *adj.* describing or displaying behavior characterized by little or no forethought, reflection, or consideration of the consequences, which may involve taking risks. See also REFLECTIVITY–IMPULSIVITY; SELF-CONTROL. **—impulsiveness** or **impulsivity** *n.*

impulsive character a personality pattern marked by a tendency to act hastily and without due reflection.

imu *n.* a CULTURE-BOUND SYNDROME resembling LATAH, observed among the Ainu and Sakhalin women of Japan. It is characterized by an extreme STARTLE RESPONSE involving automatic movements, imitative behavior, infantile reactions, and obedience to command. See also JUMPING FRENCHMEN OF MAINE SYNDROME; MYRIACHIT.

Imuran *n.* a trade name for AZATHIOPRINE.

inaccessibility *n.* unresponsiveness to external stimuli, most commonly associated with the state of withdrawal sometimes seen in autism and schizophrenia. **—inaccessible** *adj.*

inappetence *n.* impaired appetite or desire, a frequent symptom of depression.

inappropriate affect emotional responses that are not in keeping with the situation or are incompatible with expressed thoughts or wishes, for example, smiling when told about the death of a friend. Extreme inappropriate affect is a defining characteristic of DISORGANIZED SCHIZOPHRENIA.

Inapsine *n.* a trade name for DROPERIDOL.

inattention *n.* a state in which there is a lack of concentrated or focused attention or in which attention drifts back and forth. See also SELECTIVE INATTENTION.

inattentional blindness failure to notice and remember otherwise perceptible stimuli in the visual background while the focus of attention is elsewhere. Research into inattentional blindness has led some to conclude that there is no conscious perception of the world without attention. [defined by U.S. psychologists Arien Mack (1931–) and Irvin Rock (1922–1995)]

inborn error of metabolism any biochemical disorder caused by a genetic defect. It is often expressed as a defect or deficiency in the structure or enzymatic function of a protein molecule or in the transport of a vital substance across a cell membrane. Examples of such errors include diabetes mellitus, gout, phenylketonuria, and Tay–Sachs disease. Also called **metabolic anomaly**.

incendiarism *n.* compulsive or intentional fire setting. See FIRE-SETTING BEHAVIOR; PYROMANIA.

incentive motivation 1. an inducement, such as the expectation of a reward or punishment, that serves as an INTERVENING VARIABLE to influence response strength. **2.** more generally, any motivation induced by a positive reinforcer.

incentive theory the theory that motivation arousal depends on the interaction between environmental incentives (i.e., stimulus objects)—both positive and negative—and an organism's psychological and physiological states (e.g., drive states).

incest *n.* sexual activity between people of close blood relationship (e.g., brother and sister) that is prohibited by law or custom. In some societies sexual intercourse between cousins, uncles and nieces, or aunts and nephews is prohibited; in others it is permitted. Incest taboos of some kind are found in practically every society. **—incestuous** *adj.*

incest barrier in psychoanalytic theory, an EGO DEFENSE against incestuous impulses and fantasies. The barrier is the result of the INTROJECTION of social laws and customs. These internal and external prohibitions free the LIBIDO to make an external OBJECT CHOICE.

incest taboo social prohibition against sexual intercourse between people of close blood relationship. See INCEST.

incestuous ties in psychoanalytic theory, the condition in which an individual remains psychologically dependent on the mother, family, or symbolic substitute to the extent that healthy involvement with others and with society is inhibited or precluded. According to Erich FROMM, who introduced the term, incestuous ties represent the negative resolution of the search for ROOTEDNESS. See also IDENTITY NEED.

incidence *n.* the rate of occurrence of new cases of a given event or condition, such as a disorder, disease, symptom, or injury, in a particular population in a given period. An **incidence rate** is normally expressed as the number of cases per some standard proportion (1,000 or 100,000 are commonly used) of the entire population at risk per year. See also PREVALENCE.

incidental stimulus an unintentional or coincidental stimulus that may occur during an experiment or in another situation, which may elicit an unplanned response from the participants or result in the distortion of research findings.

inclusion *n.* the practice of teaching students with disabilities in the same classroom as other students to the fullest extent possible, via the provision of appropriate supportive services. See also FULL INCLUSION.

inclusion–exclusion criteria in clinical research, criteria used for determining which individuals are eligible to participate in a particular study. Inclusion criteria might specify, for example, age range, whereas exclusion criteria might specify, for example, the existence of more than one illness or psychological disorder.

incoherence *n.* inability to express oneself in a clear and orderly manner, most commonly manifested as disjointed and unintelligible speech. This may be an expression of disorganized and impaired thinking. **—incoherent** *adj.*

incompatible response a response or action that conflicts with another or occurs simultaneously with another. For example, a state of anxiety is incompatible with a state of relaxation.

incompatible response method a technique used to break bad habits in which an undesirable response is replaced by a more acceptable one that cannot coexist with the undesirable response.

incompetence *n* **1.** in law, the inability of a defendant to participate meaningfully in criminal proceedings, which include all elements of the criminal justice system, from initial interrogation to sentencing. Defendants who do not have the ability to communicate with attorneys or understand the proceedings may be ruled incompetent to stand trial (see COMPETENCY TO STAND TRIAL). See also DUSKY STANDARD. **2.** in law, the inability to make sound judgments regarding one's transactions or personal affairs. See LEGAL CAPACITY. Also called **incompetency**. **—incompetent** *adj.*

incompetency plea the plea, in a court of law, that the defendant, because of mental illness, mental defect, or other reasons, does not understand the nature and object of the proceedings, cannot appreciate or comprehend his or her own condition in relation to the proceedings, or is unable, for some other reason, to assist the attorney in his or her own defense. See also COMPETENCY TO STAND TRIAL.

incomplete-sentence test see SENTENCE-COMPLETION TEST.

incongruence *n.* lack of consistency or appropriateness, as in INAPPROPRIATE AFFECT or as when one's subjective evaluation of a situation is at odds with reality. **—incongruent** *adj.*

incontinence *n.* **1.** an inability to control basic body functions, particularly urination and defecation (see FECAL INCONTINENCE; URINARY INCONTINENCE). Incontinence is often caused by bodily and neurological injury or damage or organic abnormalities and changes. **2.** an inability to restrain sexual impulses. **—incontinent** *adj.*

incorporation *n.* in psychoanalytic theory, the fantasy that one has ingested an external OBJECT, which is felt to be physically present inside the body. According to the theory, it first occurs in the ORAL STAGE, when the infant fantasizes that he or she has ingested the mother's breast. Incorporation is often confused with IDENTIFICATION and INTROJECTION. **—incorporate** *vb.*

incorporation dream a dream whose content is wholly or partially taken in from concurrent sensory stimulation. See ACCIDENTAL STIMULUS.

incremental validity an increase in the accuracy level of decisions made on the basis of a test over the level of accuracy obtained had the test not been employed.

incubation *n.* **1.** the provision of warmth and protection for eggs that develop outside the female's body. In birds, incubation can be undertaken by either or both parents and is essential for hatching of the eggs. **2.** the gradual generation of a solution to a problem at an unconscious or semiconscious level, often after an attempt at a conscious, deliberate solution has failed. **3.** the maintenance of an artificial environment for a premature or hypoxic infant. **—incubate** *vb.* **—incubator** *n.*

incubation of anxiety the increase in a conditioned anxiety response that occurs with repeated unreinforced presentation of a CONDITIONED STIMULUS. For example, a person with a spider phobia might become more afraid of spiders each time he or she encounters one, even if no encounter is paired with a traumatic event, such as the spider biting. [first proposed by Hans EYSENCK as the basis of his conditioning theory of neurosis]

indemnity plan a system of HEALTH INSURANCE in which the insurer pays for the costs of covered services after care has been given. Such plans typically offer participants considerable freedom to choose their own health care providers and are contrasted with **group health plans**, which provide service benefits through GROUP MEDICAL PRACTICES.

independence *n.* **1.** complete lack of relationship between two or more events, sampling units, or variables such that none is influenced by any other and that changes in any one have no implication for changes in any other. **2.** in probability theory, the condition in which the probability of an event does not depend on the probability of some other event. If A and B are independent events, then $\Pr(A/B) = \Pr(A)$. **—independent** *adj., n.*

independent events either of two events whose occurrence does not influence the occurrence of the other.

independent living 1. the ability of an individual to perform—without assistance from others—all or most of the daily functions typically required to be self-sufficient, including those tasks essential to personal care (see ACTIVITIES OF DAILY LIVING) and to maintaining a home and job. **2.** a philosophy and civil reform movement promoting the rights of people with disabilities to determine the course of their lives and be full, productive members of society with access to the same social and political freedoms and opportunities as individuals without disabilities. Central to the philosophy are the concepts of self-determination and self-worth, peer support, consumer-controlled assistance and support services, and political and social reform. **Centers for Independent Living** (**CILs**), nonresidential, nonprofit organizations that are staffed and operated by individuals with disabilities, encourage self-sufficiency and self-determination in all aspects of life for individuals with disabilities by providing information and referral services, peer counseling, and independent living training (e.g., assistance with such things as ASSISTIVE TECHNOLOGY, budgeting, meal preparation, transportation arrangements, employment searches, and access to housing and health care). CILs also advocate on behalf of individuals with disabilities to achieve legislative and social change.

independent-living program 1. a system of community-based services and support designed to help individuals with disabilities achieve their highest level of personal functioning without the need to depend on others. Independent-living programs are administered by state vocational rehabilitation agencies. See also INDEPENDENT LIVING. **2.** a federally funded, state-administered program to prepare foster care youth who are 16–21 years old for the transition to independence.

independent measures measures that are unrelated to each other.

independent practice association (**IPA**) an organized form of prepaid medical practice in which a group of private physicians join together in an association and are reimbursed on a FEE-FOR-SERVICE basis or a CAPITATION basis.

independent self-construal a view of the self (SELF-CONSTRUAL) that emphasizes one's unique traits and accomplishments and downplays one's embeddedness in a network of social relationships. Compare INTERDEPENDENT SELF-CONSTRUAL.

independent variable (**IV**) the variable in an experiment that is specifically manipulated or is observed to occur before the occurrence of the dependent, or outcome, variable. Independent variables may or may not be causally related to the DEPENDENT VARIABLE. In statistical analysis, an independent variable is likely to be referred to as a PREDICTOR VARIABLE. See also TREATMENT.

Inderal *n.* a trade name for PROPRANOLOL.

index of discrimination an index of the sensitivity of a test or test item to differences between individuals. Also called **discrimination index**.

index variable a variable that is not a determinant or true causal factor but represents or symbolizes the complex process or processes under study.

Indian Health Service (**IHS**) the principal federal health care provider and health advocate for Native Americans, providing services to approximately 1.5 million American Indians and Alaska Natives belonging to more than 557 federally recognized peoples in 35 states. It is an agency within the U.S. Department of Health and Human Services.

indicator variable a variable used with the GENERAL LINEAR MODEL for quantitatively indicating the class of a qualitative attribute.

indirect agonist a substance that acts to increase the activity of an AGONIST at a receptor in ways other than direct action at the receptor site. Indirect agonists may exert their effect by increasing the metabolism or release of agonist compounds or by displacing other substances that impair full binding of an agonist to its receptor site.

indirect associations a symptom of schizophrenia in which the association between ideas is not apparent and not expressed, such that the person's statements seem bizarre and incoherent to others. See also LOOSENING OF ASSOCIATIONS.

indirect method of therapy a method of conducting therapy, particularly exemplified by CLIENT-CENTERED THERAPY, in which the therapist does not attempt to direct the client's communication or evaluate the client's remarks, although he or she may refer back to the client's remarks or restate them (see RESTATEMENT).

individual accountability the extent to which a particular person can be held responsible for his or her actions and the consequences of those actions. In groups, ACCOUNTABILITY is influenced by anonymity and the extent to which the contributions of each member of the group are clearly identifiable.

individual differences traits or other characteristics by which individuals may be distinguished from one another. This is the focus of DIFFERENTIAL PSYCHOLOGY, for which the term **individual differences psychology** increasingly is used.

Individual Family Service Plan (**IFSP**) a plan of services and supports for children up to 3 years of age and their families. Under the U.S. requirements for early intervention programs, the IFSP content must address the child's developmental status and the concerns of parents, define services to be provided and their desired outcomes, and (if appropriate) contain transition steps to preschool services. Also called **Individualized Family Service Plan**.

individualism *n.* **1.** a social or cultural tradition, ideology, or personal outlook that emphasizes the individual and his or her rights, independence, and relationships with other individuals. Compare COLLECTIVISM. **2.** in ethical and political theory, the view that individuals have intrinsic value. Once granted, this implies that the unique values, desires, and perspectives of individuals should also be valued in their own right. Thus, individualism often manifests itself as an approach to life that emphasizes the essential right to be oneself and to seek fulfillment of one's own needs and desires. **—individualist** *n.* **—individualistic** *adj.*

individuality *n.* the uniqueness of each individual's personality.

individualized education program (**IEP**) a plan for providing specialized educational services and procedures that meet the unique needs of a child with a disability. Each IEP must be documented in writing, tailored to a particular child, and implemented in accordance with the requirements of U.S. federal law. The IEP must be created by a team of individuals that includes, but is not restricted to, parents, teachers, a representative of the school system, and an individual who will evaluate the child's needs and monitor progress. Additionally, the IEP must contain certain information, such as the child's current academic performance, annual achievement objectives for the child, a discussion of the particular special education and related services that will be provided for the child and their duration and location, and a means of measuring and informing the parents of the child's progress.

individual psychology 1. the psychological theory of Alfred ADLER, which is based on the idea that throughout life individuals strive for a sense of mastery, completeness, and belonging and are governed by a conscious drive to overcome their sense of inferiority by developing to their fullest potential, obtaining their life goals, and creating their own styles of life, as opposed to the view that human beings are dominated by "blind," irrational instincts operating on an unconscious level. Also called **Adlerian psychology**. **2.** historically, a synonym for DIFFERENTIAL PSYCHOLOGY.

individual psychotherapy see INDIVIDUAL THERAPY.

Individual Service Plan (ISP) the core plan of services and supports for a person with a developmental disability, constructed by professionals, paraprofessionals, the focal person (depending on his or her abilities), and others concerned (e.g., parents and advocates). The ISP incorporates relevant comprehensive functional assessment findings, stipulates desired and preferred outcomes, and identifies the full range of services and supports to be provided in order to achieve each outcome. In certain instances ISPs may be drawn up for individuals with psychiatric conditions, emotional disturbances, or behavior disorders.

individual therapy treatment of psychological problems that is conducted on a one-to-one basis. One therapist sees one client at a time, tailoring the process to his or her unique needs in the exploration of contributory factors and alleviation of symptoms. Also called **dyadic therapy**; **individual psychotherapy**. Compare GROUP THERAPY.

individuation *n.* **1.** in psychology, the physiological, psychological, and sociocultural processes by which a person attains status as an individual human being and exerts him- or herself as such in the world. **2.** in the psychoanalytic theory of Carl JUNG, the gradual development of a unified, integrated personality that incorporates greater and greater amounts of the UNCONSCIOUS, both personal and collective, and resolves any conflicts that exist, such as those between introverted and extraverted tendencies. Also called **self-realization**. **3.** a phase of development, occurring between the 18th and 36th months, in which infants become less dependent on their mothers and begin to satisfy their own wishes and fend for themselves. [postulated by Hungarian-born U.S. psychiatrist Margaret Schonberger Mahler (1897–1985)]

indoctrination *n.* the social inculcation of beliefs, especially by those in positions of power or authority. Such beliefs are characterized by their inflexibility. **—indoctrinate** *vb.*

indolealkylamines *pl. n.* see HALLUCINOGEN.

induced hallucination a hallucination that is evoked in one individual by another, typically by hypnotic suggestion in highly susceptible individuals.

induced psychotic disorder see SHARED PSYCHOTIC DISORDER.

inductive reasoning the form of reasoning in which inferences and general principles are drawn from specific observations and cases. Inductive reasoning is a cornerstone of the scientific method (Baconian method) in that it underlies the process of developing hypotheses from particular facts and observations. See also BOTTOM-UP ANALYSIS; GENERALIZATION. Compare DEDUCTIVE REASONING.

industrial and organizational psychology (I/O psychology) the branch of psychology that studies human behavior in the work environment and applies general psychological principles to work-related issues and problems, notably in such areas as personnel selection, personnel training, employee evaluation, working conditions, accident prevention, job analysis, job satisfaction, leadership, team effectiveness, and work motivation. I/O psychologists conduct empirical research aimed at understanding individual and group behavior within organizations and use their findings to improve organizational effectiveness and the welfare of employees. Also called **business psychology**; **employment psychology**; **industrial psychology**; **management psychology**; **occupational psychology**; **organizational psychology**; **work psychology**. See also OCCUPATIONAL HEALTH PSYCHOLOGY.

industrial psychopath an individual in a work setting who displays a pattern of behavior regarded as typical of ANTISOCIAL PERSONALITY DISORDER. Such individuals act without regard for others and use manipulation to effectively manage both supporters and detractors, often resulting in career advancement. This type of individual is most likely to find success in organizations undergoing rapid changes.

industriousness *n.* see PERSISTENCE.

industry versus inferiority the fourth of ERIKSON'S EIGHT STAGES OF DEVELOPMENT, occurring from ages 6 to 11 years, during which the child learns to be productive and to accept evaluation of his or her efforts or becomes discouraged and feels inferior or incompetent.

ineffability *n.* **1.** the quality of certain kinds of feelings or experiences that are difficult to describe explicitly. The sense of something being ineffable is often attributed to spiritual, aesthetic, or affective states. **2.** an irrepressible sense of well-being that is difficult to convey to others, often described by patients experiencing a MANIC EPISODE. **—ineffable** *adj.*

inertia principle see PRINCIPLE OF INERTIA.

infancy *n.* the earliest period of postnatal life, in humans generally denoting the time from birth through the first year. **—infant** *n.*

infant and preschool tests individually administered tests designed to assess the development of infants (from birth to 18 months) and preschool children (from 18 to 60 months). Important tests include the BAYLEY SCALES OF INFANT AND TODDLER DEVELOPMENT and the WECHSLER PRESCHOOL AND PRIMARY SCALE OF INTELLIGENCE.

infant at risk an infant whose development may be threatened by complications at the time of birth, such as conditions that reduce the supply of oxygen to brain tissue, or by conditions after birth, such as malnutrition during the first months of life.

infant consciousness sensory and higher order awareness as developed early in life, including prenatally. See ONTOGENY OF CONSCIOUS EXPERIENCE.

infant development program a coordinated program of stimulatory, social, therapeutic, and treatment services provided to children from birth to 3 years of age with identified conditions placing them at risk of developmental disability or with evident developmental delays. Younger children are more likely to have syndromes posing risk of mental retardation or physical and sensory disability, whereas older children are likely to have developmental delays identified by the age of 1½ to 2 years. Services can include assessment, stimulation, parent or family training, and assistance to families in identifying and accessing appropriate community services. Also called **early intervention program**.

infantile amnesia see CHILDHOOD AMNESIA.

infantile autism see AUTISTIC DISORDER.

infantile osteopetrosis a rare hereditary disorder in which the bones, including the skull bones, are abnormally dense and brittle. It is sometimes accompanied by retinal degeneration and cranial-nerve palsy. Mental retardation has been reported in more than 20% of affected children, with sensory deprivation a possible contributing factor.

infantile sexuality in psychoanalytic theory, the concept that PSYCHIC ENERGY or LIBIDO concentrated in various organs of the body throughout infancy gives rise to erotic pleasure. This is manifested in sucking the mother's breast during the ORAL STAGE of development, in defecating during the ANAL STAGE, and in self-stimulating activities during the early GENITAL STAGE. The term and concept, first enunciated by Sigmund FREUD, proved highly controversial from the start, and it is more in line with subsequent thought to emphasize the sensual nature of breast-feeding, defecation, and discovery of the body in childhood and the role of the pleasurable feelings so obtained in the origin and development of sexual feelings.

infantile speech speech or verbalizations using the sounds and forms characteristic of infants or very young children beyond the stage when such speech is normal.

infantilism *n.* behavior, physical characteristics, or mental functioning in older children or adults that is characteristic of that of infants or young children. See REGRESSION.

infantilization *n.* the encouragement of infantile or childish behavior in a more mature individual.

infant massage therapy the systematic gentle touching, stroking, and kneading of the body of a baby. Therapeutic benefits include helping the baby relax and inducing sounder, longer sleep.

infarction *n.* **1.** an area of dead tissue resulting from obstruction of a supplying artery. Infarction of brain tissue can have effects ranging from mild to severe, depending on the extent of the dead tissue and its location in the brain (see CEREBRAL INFARCTION). A **myocardial infarction** (heart attack) involves death of a segment of the heart muscle, usually due to obstruction of a coronary artery, and is a common cause of death. **2.** a sudden shortfall in the blood supply to a particular tissue, organ, or part resulting from obstruction of a supplying artery, due, for example, to THROMBOSIS or EMBOLISM. Also called **infarct**. See STROKE.

infecundity *n.* inability to produce offspring.

inferential statistics a broad class of statistical techniques that allows inferences about characteristics of a population to be drawn from a sample of data from that population while controlling (at least partially) the extent to which errors of inference may be made. These techniques include approaches for testing hypotheses and estimating the value of parameters.

inferior function in the ANALYTIC PSYCHOLOGY of Carl JUNG, one of the three nondominant, unconscious functions of the personality that are dominated by the SUPERIOR FUNCTION in a particular FUNCTIONAL TYPE.

inferiority *n.* in ERIKSON'S EIGHT STAGES OF DEVELOPMENT, see INDUSTRY VERSUS INFERIORITY.

inferiority complex a basic feeling of inadequacy and insecurity, deriving from actual or imagined physical or psychological deficiency, that may result in behavioral expression ranging from the "withdrawal" of immobilizing timidity to the overcompensation of excessive competition and aggression. See also SUPERIORITY COMPLEX.

infertility *n.* inability to produce offspring due to a low fertility level in the male partner (about 40% of cases), the female partner (about 60% of cases), or both. Infertility is caused by physical problems: No evidence clearly shows a psychological cause, although maternal stress has been suggested as a factor. Many patients can be treated successfully. See also ARTIFICIAL INSEMINATION; IN VITRO FERTILIZATION. **—infertile** *adj.*

infibulation *n.* the removal of the entire clitoris and most of the labia and sewing together of the remaining tissue, leaving a small opening for menstruation and urination. It is practiced in some cultures as the most severe form of FEMALE GENITAL MUTILATION, usually being done in early childhood or in the prepubertal years.

influencing machine the subject of a DELUSION OF PERSECUTION in which the individual feels controlled by a machine that serves as the instrument of persecution.

information feedback responses that inform an individual about the correctness, physical effect, or social or emotional impact of his or her behavior or thinking. The concept is similar to the principle behind "knowledge of results," namely, that immediate feedback is beneficial to learning. In interpersonal relations and psychotherapy, information feedback gives an individual insight into other people's experience of him or her. In BEHAVIOR THERAPY, information feedback is intended to help change and shape behavior directly.

I

information overload the state that occurs when the amount or intensity of environmental stimuli exceeds the individual's processing capacity, thus leading to an unconscious or subliminal disregard for some environmental information.

information processing (**IP**) **1.** the manipulation of data by computers to accomplish some goal, such as problem solving or communication. **2.** in cognitive psychology, the flow of information through the human nervous system, involving the operation of perceptual systems, memory stores, decision processes, and response mechanisms. **Information processing psychology** is the approach that concentrates on understanding these operations.

informed consent voluntary agreement to participate in a research or therapeutic procedure on the basis of the participant's or patient's understanding of its nature, its potential benefits and possible risks, and available alternatives. Supported by court decisions, the principle of informed consent has provided a foundation for do not resuscitate (DNR) orders, ADVANCE DIRECTIVES, and the natural-death acts that have been passed into law throughout the United States.

ingenuity *n.* cleverness at solving routine problems of daily life (at work, home, etc.): everyday CREATIVITY. —**ingenious** *adj.*

INH abbreviation for isonicotinic acid hydrazide. See ISONIAZID.

inhalant *n.* any of a variety of volatile substances that can be inhaled to produce intoxicating effects. Anesthetic gases (e.g., ether, chloroform, NITROUS OXIDE), industrial solvents (e.g., TOLUENE, gasoline, trichloroethylene, various aerosol propellants), and organic nitrites (e.g., AMYL NITRITE) are common inhalants. Anesthetic gases may cause asphyxiation, and chloroform has been associated with damage to the liver and kidneys. Industrial solvents are generally toxic, being associated with damage to the kidneys, liver, and both central and peripheral nervous systems. Organic nitrites are less toxic but may cause ARRHYTHMIAS in individuals with heart conditions. See also INHALATION OF DRUGS.

inhalant abuse in *DSM–IV–TR*, a pattern of inhalant use manifested by recurrent significant adverse consequences related to the repeated ingestion of these substances. This diagnosis is preempted by the diagnosis of INHALANT DEPENDENCE: If the criteria for inhalant abuse and inhalant dependence are both met, only the latter diagnosis is given. See also SUBSTANCE ABUSE; SUBSTANCE DEPENDENCE.

inhalant dependence in *DSM–IV–TR*, a cluster of cognitive, behavioral, and physiological symptoms indicating continued use of inhalants despite significant inhalant-related problems. There is a pattern of repeated inhalant ingestion resulting in tolerance, withdrawal symptoms if use is suspended, and an uncontrollable drive to continue use. See INHALANT ABUSE. See also SUBSTANCE ABUSE; SUBSTANCE DEPENDENCE.

inhalant intoxication a reversible syndrome resulting from the recent ingestion of inhalants. It includes clinically significant behavioral or psychological changes (e.g., confusion, belligerence, assaultiveness, apathy, impaired judgment, and impaired social or occupational functioning), as well as one or more signs of physiological involvement (e.g., dizziness, visual disturbances, involuntary eye movements, incoordination, slurred speech, unsteady gait, tremor). At higher doses, lethargy, PSYCHOMOTOR RETARDATION, generalized muscle weakness, depressed reflexes, stupor, or coma may develop. See also SUBSTANCE INTOXICATION.

inhalation of drugs a means of administering a drug—in the form of a gas or aerosol—via the mouth or the nose (insufflation), enabling it to reach the body tissues rapidly. Anesthetics for major surgery are administered by inhalation, which permits almost instant contact with the blood supplying the alveoli (air sacs) of the lungs. Inhalation (oral or nasal) is also a means of self-administration of abused substances, including cannabis, nicotine, cocaine, and volatile hydrocarbons (see INHALANT). Oral inhalation is used for nicotine (smoking) and amyl or butyl nitrite, and the nasal route ("snorting") for cocaine, heroin, amphetamines, and other street drugs.

inhibited female orgasm in *DSM–III*, the dysfunction now called FEMALE ORGASMIC DISORDER.

inhibited male orgasm in *DSM–III*, the dysfunction now called MALE ORGASMIC DISORDER.

inhibitedness *n.* the tendency to constrain one's actions and emotional experiences, particularly in social settings, or to withdraw entirely from social interactions in such settings. —**inhibited** *adj.*

inhibited sexual desire in *DSM–III*, the dysfunction now called HYPOACTIVE SEXUAL DESIRE DISORDER.

inhibited sexual excitement in *DSM–III*, a psychosexual disorder characterized by recurrent and persistent inhibition of sexual excitement during sexual activity that is judged to be adequate in focus, intensity, and duration. In *DSM–IV–TR* this general diagnosis was replaced by FEMALE SEXUAL AROUSAL DISORDER and MALE ERECTILE DISORDER.

inhibition *n.* **1.** the process of restraining one's impulses or behavior, either consciously or unconsciously, due to such factors as lack of confidence, fear of consequences, or moral qualms. **2.** in psychoanalysis, an unconscious mechanism in which the SUPEREGO controls instinctive impulses that would threaten the EGO if allowed conscious expression. For example, inhibited sexual desire may result from unconscious feelings of guilt implanted by parents. See also RECIPROCAL INHIBITION. **3.** in conditioning, the active blocking or delay of a response to a stimulus. **—inhibit** *vb.* **—inhibited** *adj.*

inhibitor *n.* a mechanism or stimulus that slows or suppresses an activity, process, or behavior.

inhibitory process any phenomenon in human or animal behavior that prevents or blocks actions that are problematic for the individual. See EXCITATORY–INHIBITORY PROCESSES.

initial insomnia difficulty in falling asleep, usually due to tension, anxiety, or depression. Some people with INSOMNIA due to anxiety become so worried about being unable to fall asleep or about the effects of loss of sleep that they cannot relax sufficiently to induce sleep. Initial insomnia may be a symptom of a MAJOR DEPRESSIVE EPISODE. Compare MIDDLE INSOMNIA; TERMINAL INSOMNIA.

initial interview in psychotherapy, the first interview with a client, which has some or all of the following goals: to establish a positive relationship; to listen to the client's problem described in his or her own words; to make a tentative diagnosis; and to formulate a plan for diagnostic tests, possible treatment, or referral.

initiative versus guilt the third of ERIKSON'S EIGHT STAGES OF DEVELOPMENT, which occurs during the child's 3rd through 5th years. In planning, launching, and initiating all forms of fantasy, play, and other activity, the child learns to believe in his or her ability to successfully pursue goals. However, should these pursuits often fail or be criticized, the child may develop instead a feeling of self-doubt and guilt.

injection *n.* see ADMINISTRATION; INTRAMUSCULAR INJECTION; INTRAVENOUS INJECTION; SUBCUTANEOUS INJECTION.

inkblot test see RORSCHACH INKBLOT TEST.

innate *adj.* denoting a capability or characteristic existing in an organism from birth, that is, belonging to the original or essential constitution of the body or mind. Innate processes should be distinguished from those that develop later in infancy and childhood under maturational control. Also called **inborn**; **native**; **natural**.

innate behavior behavior that appears to be developed and expressed with no specific training or experience and thus has a strong genetic basis. It is generally accepted that most behavior is neither purely innate nor purely due to learning or experience. See EPIGENESIS; NATURE–NURTURE.

inner audience the imaginary hearer of silent, spontaneous inner speech, often associated in psychoanalytic and psychodynamic theory with parental figures.

inner boundary see INTERNAL BOUNDARY.

inner conflict see INTRAPSYCHIC CONFLICT.

inner dialogue a mental debate that an individual may engage in about any issue. In some systems of psychotherapy, clients are encouraged to express the inner dialogue aloud in words during sessions.

inner-directed *adj.* describing or relating to an individual who is self-motivated and not easily influenced by the opinions, values, or pressures of other people. Compare OTHER-DIRECTED; TRADITION-DIRECTED. [introduced by U.S. sociologist David Riesman (1909–2002)]

inner estrangement the feeling that external objects are unfamiliar and unreal. [defined by Austrian psychoanalyst Paul Federn (1871–1950)]

inner language 1. the visual, auditory, and kinesthetic mental imagery of words and concepts. **2.** speech spoken to oneself without vocalization. According to Lev VYGOTSKY, inner language follows EGOCENTRIC SPEECH and represents the child's recruitment of language in his or her reasoning efforts. Also called **inner speech**. See also INTERNALIZED SPEECH; VERBAL THOUGHT.

innovative therapies loosely, psychological treatments that are new and different from traditional therapies. Relatively current examples include the EMPTY-CHAIR TECHNIQUE and PARADOXICAL TECHNIQUES.

Inocybe *n.* a genus of mushrooms, some species of which are poisonous because they contain the toxic alkaloid MUSCARINE. Symptoms of poisoning include salivation, perspiration, and lacrimation (tears); at higher doses these symptoms may be followed by abdominal pains, severe nausea and vomiting, diarrhea, visual disturbances, labored breathing, and bradycardia (slowed heart rate), which may potentially result in death from cardiac or respiratory failure. Treatment is with ATROPINE.

inositol *n.* a compound (similar to glucose) that occurs in many foods and is sometimes classed as a vitamin. It is a component of cell-membrane phospholipids and plasma lipoproteins, and phosphorylated derivatives (see INOSITOL PHOSPHATES) function as SECOND MESSENGERS in cells.

inositol phosphates derivatives of INOSITOL that contain one or more phosphate groups, some of which are SECOND MESSENGERS in cells, serving to relay signals from receptors at the cell surface to other parts of the cell. The most studied of these second messengers is **inositol 1,4,5-trisphosphate** (**IP_3**). The action of LITHIUM salts, used to treat bipolar disorders, may be linked to their inhibition of the enzyme **inositol monophosphatase**, which is involved in the recycling of inositol from the inositol phosphates. It has been hypothesized that this inhibition thus leads to a deficiency of inositol and a corresponding excess of inositol phosphates.

inpatient *n.* a person who has been formally admitted to a hospital for a period of at least 24 hours for observation, care, diagnosis, or treatment, as distinguished from an OUTPATIENT or an emergency-room patient.

I

Inpatient Multidimensional Psychiatric Scale (**IMPS**) an interview-based rating instrument used to assess attitudes and behaviors of individuals with psychoses, typically administered on admission to mental institutions. It yields information on symptom severity and is used to classify patients into psychotic types, such as hostile–paranoid, excited–hostile, excited–grandiose, and so forth. The scale was originally published in 1962 as a revision of the 1953 **Multidimensional Scale for Rating Psychiatric Patients**. [developed by U.S. psychometrician Maurice Lorr (1910–1998) and U.S. psychologists C. James Klett (1926–), Douglas M. McNair (1927–2008), and Julian J. Lasky (1918–2012)]

inpatient services diagnostic and treatment services available to hospitalized patients and usually unavailable or only partially available in outpatient facilities. Examples are continuous supervision; medical treatment and nursing care; and specialized treatment techniques, such as rehabilitational, occupational, movement, or recreation therapy, as well as social work services.

input–output mechanism a simple model of INFORMATION PROCESSING in which a given input automatically produces a given output. An input–output mechanism is a closed system in which information is subjected to a fixed sequence of preset operations and there is no interaction with the environment during throughput. Some behaviorist theories have been criticized as reducing the human organism to an input–output mechanism.

insanity *n.* in law, a condition of the mind that renders a person incapable of being responsible for his or her criminal acts. Defendants who are found to be NOT GUILTY BY REASON OF INSANITY therefore lack CRIMINAL RESPONSIBILITY for their conduct. Whether a person is insane, in this legal sense, is determined by judges and juries, not psychologists or psychiatrists. Numerous legal standards for determining criminal responsibility, the central issue in an INSANITY DEFENSE, have been used at various times in many jurisdictions. These include the DURHAM RULE, the AMERICAN LAW INSTITUTE MODEL PENAL CODE INSANITY TEST, and the MCNAUGHTEN RULE. See also PARTIAL INSANITY. **—insane** *adj.*

insanity defense in criminal law, the defense plea that an individual lacks CRIMINAL RESPONSIBILITY for his or her conduct. See also AMERICAN LAW INSTITUTE MODEL PENAL CODE INSANITY TEST; DIMINISHED RESPONSIBILITY; DURHAM RULE; MCNAUGHTEN RULE.

Insanity Defense Reform Act (**IDRA**) legislation passed by the U.S. Congress in 1984 that modified existing laws relating to INSANITY DEFENSE cases. One modification involved removing the volitional component of the AMERICAN LAW INSTITUTE MODEL PENAL CODE INSANITY TEST, so that "conforming one's conduct to the requirements of the law" was no longer a factor in judging insanity. Another modification involved shifting the burden of proof (responsibility for convincing the court beyond a reasonable doubt of the truth of an allegation) in insanity defense cases from the prosecution to the defense.

insect phobia see ACAROPHOBIA; ANIMAL PHOBIA; SPECIFIC PHOBIA.

insecure attachment in the STRANGE SITUATION, one of several patterns of generally negative parent–child relationship in which the child fails to display confidence when the parent is present, sometimes shows distress when the parent leaves, and reacts to the returning parent by avoidance (see AVOIDANT ATTACHMENT) or with ambivalence (see AMBIVALENT ATTACHMENT). See also ANXIOUS–AVOIDANT ATTACHMENT; ANXIOUS–RESISTANT ATTACHMENT; DISORGANIZED ATTACHMENT.

insecurity *n.* a feeling of inadequacy, lack of self-confidence, and inability to cope, accompanied by general uncertainty and anxiety about one's goals, abilities, or relationships with others. **—insecure** *adj.*

insensible *adj.* **1.** denoting or relating to a state of nonresponsiveness and unconsciousness. **2.** lacking emotional response. **—insensibility** *n.*

insight *n.* **1.** the clear and often sudden discernment of a solution to a problem by means that are not obvious and may never become so, even after one has tried hard to work out how one has arrived at the solution. There are many different theories of how insights are formed and of the kinds of insights that exist. For example, in the 1990s, U.S. psychologists Robert Sternberg (1949–) and Janet Davidson proposed a theory in which there are three main kinds of insights: (a) selective encoding insights, which are used to distinguish relevant from irrelevant information; (b) selective comparison insights, which are used to distinguish what information already stored in long-term memory is relevant for one's purposes; and (c) selective combination insights, which are used to put together the information available so as to formulate a solution to a given problem. **2.** in psychotherapy, an awareness of underlying sources of emotional, cognitive, or behavioral difficulty in oneself or another person. See also AHA EXPERIENCE; EPIPHANY.

insight learning a cognitive form of learning involving the mental rearrangement or restructuring of the elements in a problem to achieve a sudden understanding of the problem and arrive at a solution. Insightful learning was described by Wolfgang KÖHLER in the 1920s, based on his observations of apes stacking boxes or using sticks to retrieve food, and was offered as an alternative to trial-and-error learning.

insight therapy any form of psychotherapy based on the theory that a client's problems cannot be resolved without his or her gaining self-understanding and thus becoming aware of their origins. This approach (characteristic, for example, of PSYCHOANALYSIS and PSYCHODYNAMIC PSYCHOTHERAPY) contrasts with therapies directed toward removal of symptoms or behavior modification.

insomnia *n.* difficulty in initiating or maintaining a restorative sleep that results in fatigue, the severity or persistence of which causes clinically significant distress or impairment in functioning. Such sleeplessness may be caused by a transient or chronic physical condition or psychological disturbance. Also called **agrypnia**; **ahypnia**; **ahypnosia**; **anhypnia**. See DISORDERS OF INITIATING AND MAINTAINING SLEEP; INITIAL INSOMNIA; INTERMITTENT INSOMNIA; MIDDLE INSOMNIA; PRIMARY INSOMNIA; PSEUDOINSOMNIA; TERMINAL INSOMNIA. **—insomniac** *n.*

inspectionalism *n.* see VOYEURISM.

inspiration *n.* **1.** in cognitive psychology, a sudden INSIGHT or leap in understanding that produces new, creative ideas or approaches to a problem. See AHA EXPERIENCE; DISCONTINUITY HYPOTHESIS. See also CREATIVE IMAGINATION; CREATIVE THINKING; DIVERGENT PRODUCTION. **2.** the process of being aroused or stimulated to do something, or the quality of being so aroused, as in *Her speech gave us the inspiration we needed.* **—inspirational** *adj.* **—inspire** *vb.* **—inspired** *adj.*

instability *n.* in psychology, a tendency toward lack of self-control, erratic behavior, and rapidly changing or excessive emotions. Also called **lability**. **—unstable** *adj.*

instant gratification the meeting or satisfying of one's needs or wishes without delay. Therapy may be important to help reduce the desire for instant gratification when postponing needs and tolerating delays would be realistic or in the best interests of the client.

instigation therapy BEHAVIOR THERAPY in which the therapist provides a positive model and reinforces the client's progress toward self-regulation and self-evaluation.

instinct *n.* **1.** an innate, species-specific biological force that impels an organism to do something, particularly to perform a certain act or respond in a certain manner to specific stimuli. See also HORMIC PSYCHOLOGY. **2.** in psychoanalytic theory, a basic biological drive (e.g., hunger, thirst, sex, aggression) that must be fulfilled in order to maintain physical and psychological equilibrium. Sigmund FREUD classified instincts into two types: those derived from the LIFE INSTINCT and those derived from the DEATH INSTINCT. See also COMPONENT INSTINCT; DESTRUDO; EROTIC INSTINCT; LIBIDO; SATISFACTION OF INSTINCTS; SEXUAL INSTINCT. **3.** in popular usage, any inherent or unlearned predisposition (behavioral or otherwise) or motivational force. **—instinctive** or **instinctual** *adj.*

instinctive behavior stereotyped, unlearned, largely stimulus-bound adaptive behavior limited in its expression by the inherent properties of the nervous system and genetic factors. It is species-specific and involves complex activity patterns rather than simple reflexes.

instinctive drift the tendency of learned, reinforced behavior to gradually return to a more innate behavior. For example, racoons trained to drop coins into a container will eventually begin to dip the coins into the container, pull them back out, rub them together, and dip them in again. The learned behavior of dropping coins becomes more representative of the innate behavior of food washing. Also called **instinctual drift**. [proposed in 1961 by U.S. psychologists Keller Breland (1915–1965) and Marian Breland (1920–2001)]

instinctive knowledge unlearned and generally unalterable behavior, observable when a new stimulus (i.e., one not previously encountered) elicits an affective response indicative of genetic influences. An example is fear of and flight from certain predators in the absence of previous exposure to these animals.

instinctual aim see AIM OF THE INSTINCT.

instinctual drive see INSTINCT.

instinctual fusion see FUSION.

instinctual impulse see INSTINCT. See also IMPULSE.

instinctualization of smell **1.** the capacity of smell to play a part in COPROPHILIA or anal fixations. **2.** the role of body odors as arousal factors in sexual foreplay. See also COMPONENT INSTINCT.

institution *n.* **1.** an established practice, tradition, behavior, or system of roles and relationships, such as marriage, that is considered normative within a society. Sociologists usually distinguish between four main types of institution: political institutions (e.g., monarchy), economic institutions (e.g., capitalism), cultural institutions (e.g., religion and accepted forms of artistic expression), and kinship institutions (e.g., the extended family). **2.** a building or building complex in which individuals are cared for or confined for extended periods of time, especially a psychiatric hospital or a prison. —**institutional** *adj.*

institutional care medical or mental health care services received by an inpatient in a hospital, nursing home, or other residential institution.

institutionalism *n.* see SOCIAL BREAKDOWN SYNDROME.

institutionalization *n.* **1.** placement of an individual in an institution for therapeutic or correctional purposes. **2.** an individual's gradual adaptation to institutional life over a long period, especially when this is seen as rendering him or her passive, dependent, and generally unsuited to life outside the institution. —**institutionalize** *vb.*

institutional neurosis see SOCIAL BREAKDOWN SYNDROME.

I

institutional review board (**IRB**) a committee named by an agency or institution to review research proposals originating within that agency for ethical acceptability.

instructional treatments educational interventions that have been designed, implemented, and evaluated by an instructor to increase learning or various kinds of performance.

instrumental activities of daily living (**IADLs**) activities essential to an individual's ability to function autonomously, including cooking, doing laundry, using the telephone, managing money, shopping, getting to places beyond walking distance, and the like. See also ACTIVITIES OF DAILY LIVING.

instrumental behavior behavior that is learned and elicited via positive or negative reinforcement of target (rather than instinctive) responses. The term is used synonymously with OPERANT BEHAVIOR, usually for describing behavior during CONDITIONING procedures that involves long sequences of activity, such as solving a puzzle box.

instrumental conditioning any form of CONDITIONING in which the correct response is essential for REINFORCEMENT. Instrumental conditioning is similar to OPERANT CONDITIONING and usually involves complex activities in order to reach a goal, such as when a rat is trained to navigate a maze to obtain food. It contrasts with PAVLOVIAN CONDITIONING, in which reinforcement is given regardless of the response. Also called **instrumental learning**; **Type II conditioning**; **Type R conditioning**.

instrumental dependence the tendency to rely on others for accomplishing tasks.

insulin-coma therapy see COMA THERAPY.

insulin-shock therapy see COMA THERAPY.

intake interview 1. the initial interview with a client by a therapist or counselor to obtain both information regarding the issues or problems that have brought the client into therapy or counseling and preliminary information regarding personal and family history. **2.** the initial interview with a patient who is being admitted into a psychiatric hospital, day treatment, or inpatient substance abuse facility. Intake interviews are also common in government-funded mental health services, such as those provided at community mental health centers, in determining eligibility and appropriateness of the client for services offered. An intake interview may be carried out by a specialist who may not necessarily treat the patient, but the information obtained is used to determine the best course of treatment and the appropriate therapist to provide it.

integrated care a consistent, systematic, and coordinated set of HEALTH CARE services that are developed, managed, and delivered to individual patients over a range of organizations and by a variety of associated professionals and other care providers. The approach seeks to reduce fragmented care (i.e., diagnosis and treatment by multiple unconnected and minimally communicating doctors and caregivers); to improve clinical outcomes, quality of life, patient satisfaction, effectiveness and efficiency (ideally using EVIDENCE-BASED PRACTICE guidelines); and to reduce costs. The complexities underlying development of such approaches include establishing a common philosophy of assessment and treatment, developing partnership relationships, linking and planning information systems, coordinating patient flow among providers, and so forth. The efficacy of integrated care is often viewed and measured from two perspectives: that of the patient and that of the organizations and individual service providers. Although primarily associated with medicine proper, services may include mental health components (e.g., psychosocial assessment and treatment). Also called **integrated medicine**. See also INTEGRATED DELIVERY SYSTEM.

integrated delivery system (**IDS**) a health care provider organization that is completely integrated operationally and clinically and that offers a full range of health care services, including physician, hospital, and adjunct services. IDSs began to develop in the early 1980s and multiplied rapidly in the 1990s. They come in varying formats, one of the more typical being an alliance between hospitals and individual physicians or GROUP MEDICAL PRACTICES. An IDS is a MANAGED CARE organization.

integrated model in evaluation research, an administrative relationship, used in FORMATIVE EVALUATION, between the program director and multiple production units, each made up of writers, designers, and evaluators who are all involved in program development as well as program evaluation. Members of these units do not necessarily share equal importance or equal access to the program director. Also called **dependent model**. Compare SEGREGATED MODEL.

integrated personality a personality in which the constituent traits, behavioral patterns, motives, and so forth are used effectively and with minimal effort or without conflict. Those with integrated personalities are thought essentially to know themselves and to be able to enjoy and live life fully. Also called **well-integrated personality**.

integrated therapy see INTEGRATIVE PSYCHOTHERAPY.

integration *n.* the coordination or unification of parts into a totality. This general meaning has been incorporated into a wide variety of psychological contexts and topics. For example, the integration of personality denotes the gradual bringing together of constituent traits, behavioral patterns, motives, and so forth to form an organized whole that functions effectively and with minimal effort or without conflict.

integrative behavioral couples therapy couples therapy that uses techniques of BEHAVIORAL COUPLES THERAPY but also focuses on each person's emotional acceptance of his or her partner's genuine incompatibilities, which may or may not be amenable to change. It is based on the conviction that focusing on changing incompatibilities leads to a resistance to change when change is possible or that this focus results in unnecessary frustration for both partners when change is not possible.

integrative medicine the combination of conventional medical treatments and complementary therapies that have demonstrated scientific merit with regard to safety and efficacy. See also COMPLEMENTARY AND ALTERNATIVE MEDICINE.

integrative psychotherapy psychotherapy that selects models or techniques from various therapeutic schools to suit the client's particular problems. For example, PSYCHODYNAMIC PSYCHOTHERAPY and GESTALT THERAPY may be combined through the practice of INTERPRETATION of material in the HERE AND NOW. The Society for the Exploration of Psychotherapy Integration (SEPI), founded in 1983, reflects the growing interest in, and the rapid development and use of, such combined therapeutic techniques. Also called **integrated therapy**; **psychotherapy integration**. See also ECLECTIC PSYCHOTHERAPY.

integrity *n.* the quality of moral consistency, honesty, and truthfulness with oneself and others.

integrity group psychotherapy a type of GROUP THERAPY in which openness and honesty are expected from all participants, and experienced members of the group serve as models of sincerity and involvement. [developed by U.S. psychologist O. Hobart Mowrer (1907–1982)]

integrity versus despair the eighth and final stage of ERIKSON'S EIGHT STAGES OF DEVELOPMENT, which occurs during old age. In this stage the individual reflects on the life he or she has lived and may develop either integrity—a sense of satisfaction in having lived a good life and the ability to approach death with equanimity—or despair—a feeling of bitterness about opportunities missed and time wasted, and a dread of approaching death. Also called **ego integrity versus despair**.

intellect *n.* **1.** the INTELLECTUAL FUNCTIONS of the mind considered collectively. **2.** an individual's capacity for abstract, objective reasoning, especially as contrasted with his or her capacity for feeling, imagining, or acting. **—intellectual** *adj.*

intellectual detachment see DETACHMENT.

intellectual disability increasingly the preferred term for MENTAL RETARDATION.

intellectual function any of the mental functions involved in acquiring, developing, and relating ideas, concepts, and hypotheses. Memory, imagination, and judgment can also be considered intellectual functions. Also called **intellectual operation**. See HIGHER MENTAL PROCESS.

intellectual impoverishment diminished intellectual capacity, such as problem-solving ability and concentration. This condition is observed in many people with chronic schizophrenia, senility, or depression and in individuals living in a deprived, unstimulating environment. See also POVERTY OF IDEAS.

intellectual insight in psychotherapy, an objective, rational awareness of experiences or relationships. Some theorists posit that intellectual insight by itself does not advance the therapeutic process and may even impede it because little or no feeling (i.e., emotional content) is involved.

intellectual subaverage functioning an IQ more than two standard deviations below the mean obtained on an intelligence test. Also called **significantly subaverage intellectual functioning**.

intelligence quotient see IQ.

intelligence test an individually administered, standardized test used to determine a person's level of intelligence by measuring his or her ability to solve problems, form concepts, reason, acquire detail, and perform other intellectual tasks. It comprises mental, verbal, and performance tasks of graded difficulty that have been standardized by use on a representative sample of the population. Examples of intelligence tests include the STANFORD–BINET INTELLIGENCE SCALE and the WECHSLER ADULT INTELLIGENCE SCALE. Also called **intelligence scale**. See IQ.

intensive care syndrome a type of psychotic condition observed in some individuals in intensive care who are immobilized in an isolated, unfamiliar environment that may have the effect of sensory deprivation. Variable factors may include the mental and physical condition of the individual prior to the need for intensive care, the age of the individual, medical or surgical complications, and behavioral effects of drugs administered.

intensive care unit (**ICU**) a hospital unit in which critically ill patients receive intensive and continuous nursing, medical care, and supervision that includes the use of sophisticated monitoring and resuscitative equipment. ICUs are often organized for the care of specific groups of patients, such as neonatal ICUs or pulmonary ICUs. Also called **critical care unit** (**CCU**). Compare CONTINUING CARE UNIT.

intensive psychotherapy broad, thorough, and prolonged psychological treatment of an individual's concerns and problems. The qualifier "intensive" indicates both the nature of the discussions, which typically involve extensive examination of the individual's life history and conflicts, and the duration of the therapy. Compare BRIEF PSYCHOTHERAPY; COUNSELING.

intent analysis analysis of social interaction in which verbal content is classified according to intent (providing support, seeking approval, etc.).

intentional accident see PURPOSIVE ACCIDENT.

intentional forgetting inaccessibility of a memory that is due to REPRESSION or to an unconscious wish to forget. See also FORGETTING.

intentionality *n.* a characteristic of an individual's acts that requires the individual (a) to have goals, desires, and standards; (b) to select behaviors that are in the service of attaining the goal (e.g., means to an end); and (c) to call into conscious awareness a desired future state. Investigators differ as to whether (a) alone, (a) and (b) but not (c), or (a), (b), and (c) are required for intentionality to be attributable to an individual. The concept of intentionality, as developed by German philosopher and psychologist Franz Brentano (1838–1917), has been very influential in ACT PSYCHOLOGY, PHENOMENOLOGY, and related approaches in hermeneutics.

intention movement a physical behavior that precipitates another physical response, such that the first behavior may signal the second. For example, when two people are talking, one may exhibit certain postural behaviors (e.g., changing stance, shifting weight) predictive of terminating the interaction, before actually ending the conversation and walking away.

interactional model of anxiety a model of anxiety proposing that STATE ANXIETY is determined by the interaction of factors relating to the situation (**situational factors**) and factors relating to the individual (**person factors**).

interaction effect the joint effect of two or more independent variables on a dependent variable above and beyond the sum of their individual effects: The independent variables combine to have a different (and multiplicative) effect, such that the value of one is contingent upon the value of another. This indicates that the relationship between the independent variables changes as their values change. Interaction effects contrast with—and may obscure—MAIN EFFECTS. Compare ADDITIVE EFFECT.

interactionism *n.* **1.** the position that mind and body are distinct, incompatible substances that nevertheless interact, so that each has a causal influence on the other. This position is particularly associated with French philosopher René Descartes (1596–1650). See CARTESIAN DUALISM; MIND–BODY PROBLEM. **2.** a set of approaches, particularly in personality psychology, in which behavior is explained not in terms of personality attributes or situational influences but by references to interactions that typify the behavior of a certain type of person in a certain type of setting. **—interactionist** *adj.*

interaction-process analysis (**IPA**) a technique used to study the emotional, intellectual, and behavioral interactions among members of a group, for example, during GROUP THERAPY. It requires observers to classify every behavior displayed by a member of a group into one of 12 mutually exclusive categories, such as "asks for information" or "shows tension." [developed by U.S. social psychologist Robert Freed Bales (1916–2004)]

interactive group psychotherapy see INTERPERSONAL GROUP PSYCHOTHERAPY.

intercourse *n.* see COITUS.

interdependence *n.* **1.** dependence of two or more people, things, situations, or other entities on each other. **2.** a state in which factors rely on or react with one another such that one cannot change without affecting the other. Also called **interdependency**. **—interdependent** *adj., n.*

interdependent self-construal a view of the self (SELF-CONSTRUAL) that emphasizes one's embeddedness in a network of social relationships and downplays one's unique traits or accomplishments. Compare INDEPENDENT SELF-CONSTRUAL.

interdisciplinary approach a manner of dealing with psychological, medical, or other scientific questions in which individuals from different disciplines or professions collaborate to obtain a more thorough, detailed understanding of the nature of the questions and consequently develop more comprehensive answers. For example, an interdisciplinary approach to the treatment or rehabilitation of an individual who is ill, disabled, or experiencing distress or pain uses the talents and experiences of therapists from a number of appropriate medical and psychological specialties. Also called **multidisciplinary approach**.

interdisciplinary team a health care team that consists of professionals from different therapeutic disciplines, paraprofessionals, a focal person, and concerned family members. Teams establish treatment priorities and goals and plan and provide treatment. Effective teams increase treatment benefits by conducting comprehensive assessment, sharing information, and adopting complementary treatment approaches.

interfemoral sex see COITUS.

intergluteal sex coitus in which the penis is placed between the cheeks of the buttocks, without entry into the vagina or anus.

interjudge reliability see INTERRATER RELIABILITY.

interlocking pathologies unconscious and dysfunctional ways of acting that are present in a couple or other intimate dyad or in a family or other close social unit.

intermarriage *n.* **1.** marriage between two individuals belonging to different racial, ethnic, or religious groups. **2.** marriage between two closely related individuals, as in a consanguineous marriage. **—intermarry** *vb.*

intermediate care facility (**ICF**) a facility providing an appropriate level of nursing and other medical care to individuals who do not require the degree of care and treatment provided by a hospital or SKILLED NURSING FACILITY but need more than room and board.

intermediate need in MASLOW'S MOTIVATIONAL HIERARCHY, a DEFICIENCY NEED that is psychologically based, such as the need for self-esteem, love, or security.

intermetamorphosis syndrome a MISIDENTIFICATION SYNDROME characterized by delusions that particular people have been transformed both physically and psychologically into other people.

intermission *n.* an asymptomatic period, for example, between MANIC EPISODES, MAJOR DEPRESSIVE EPISODES, or both.

intermittent explosive disorder an impulse-control disorder consisting of multiple episodes in which the individual fails to resist aggressive impulses and commits assaultive acts or destroys property. These aggressive acts are significantly out of proportion to any precipitating factors, are not caused by any other mental disorder or a general medical condition, and are not substance-induced. In *DSM–IV–TR* this disorder is included in the category IMPULSE-CONROL DISORDERS NOT ELSEWHERE CLASSIFIED. Compare ISOLATED EXPLOSIVE DISORDER.

intermittent insomnia periods of INSOMNIA occurring several times a night.

internal attribution see DISPOSITIONAL ATTRIBUTION.

internal boundary in psychoanalytic theory, the boundary between EGO and ID. Also called **inner boundary**. Compare EXTERNAL BOUNDARY.

internal conflict see INTRAPSYCHIC CONFLICT.

internal consistency the degree to which all the items on a test measure the same thing. See INTERRATER RELIABILITY.

internal control the belief that one is responsible for the consequences of one's behavior and that one can take action to deal with any problems, threats, or challenges. Higher internal control is thought to be associated with better mental health. See INTERNALIZERS; LOCUS OF CONTROL. Compare EXTERNAL CONTROL.

internal frustration in psychoanalytic theory, denial of gratification of instinctual impulses due to internal factors (e.g., the SUPEREGO), as opposed to external factors.

internalization *n.* **1.** the unconscious mental process by which the characteristics, beliefs, feelings, or attitudes of other individuals or groups are assimilated into the self and adopted as one's own. **2.** in psychoanalytic theory, the process of incorporating an OBJECT relationship inside the psyche, which reproduces the external relationship as an intrapsychic phenomenon. For example, through internalization the relationship between father and child is reproduced in the relationship between SUPEREGO and EGO. Internalization is often mistakenly used as a synonym for INTROJECTION. **—internalize** *vb.*

internalized speech silent speech in which one argues with oneself over a course of action, rehearses what one is going to do, or reassures oneself when feeling threatened. See also INNER LANGUAGE; SELF-TALK.

internalizers *pl. n.* people who assume that the LOCUS OF CONTROL over their lives is within themselves (i.e., under their own control) and who characteristically try harder to change themselves and their environment. This involves being more perceptive, gathering more information and remembering it better, and using more facts and care in making decisions about how to cope. Internalizers may be less likely to follow orders blindly; they are more likely to realize there are choices to be made and to rely on their own judgment. Compare EXTERNALIZERS.

internalizing behavior see EXTERNALIZING–INTERNALIZING.

internal locus of control see LOCUS OF CONTROL.

internal object an image or representation of a person (particularly someone significant to the individual, such as a parent) that is experienced as an internalized "presence" within the mind. In her development of OBJECT RELATIONS THEORY, Melanie Klein saw the psyche as being made up of internal objects whose relations to each other and to the individual determine his or her personality and symptoms. See also PART-OBJECT.

internal saboteur see ANTILIBIDINAL EGO.

internal validity the degree to which a study or experiment is free from flaws in its internal structure and its results can therefore be taken to represent the true nature of the phenomenon.

internal working model of attachment a cognitive construction or set of assumptions about the workings of relationships, such as expectations of support or affection. The earliest relationships may form the template for this internal model, which may be positive or negative. See also ATTACHMENT THEORY. [originally proposed by John BOWLBY]

International Association of Applied Psychology (**IAAP**) the oldest international association of professional psychologists, founded in 1920 to promote the science and practice of applied psychology and to facilitate interaction and communication among those who work in applied psychology around the world.

International Classification of Diseases (**ICD**) a system of categories of disease conditions compiled by the World Health Organization (WHO) in conjunction with 10 WHO collaborating centers worldwide. Based on a formal classification system developed in 1893 that was known as the *Bertillon Classification or International List of Causes of Death,* the ICD is now in its 10th revision. The **ICD-10**, published in 1992 as the *International Statistical Classification of Diseases and Related Health Problems*, uses a four-character alphanumeric coding system to classify diseases and disorders and their subtypes. Such standardization permits international statistical analyses and comparisons of mortality data, although the ICD is often used in epidemiological studies and by systems of payment for health care. See also DSM–IV–TR.

International Council of Psychologists a professional organization founded in 1941 to advance psychology and its applications by facilitating communication and strengthening bonds between psychologists worldwide. In 1981, ICP was recognized as a nongovernmental organization in consultative status with the United Nations Economic and Social Council.

International Pilot Study of Schizophrenia (**IPSS**) a 1973 diagnostic study sponsored by the World Health Organization, involving psychiatrists in 9 countries and a total of 1,119 patients assigned to a schizophrenic or nonschizophrenic category. The most discriminating of 13 symptoms were lack of insight, auditory hallucinations, verbal hallucinations, ideas of reference, and delusions of reference. The project used the PRESENT STATE EXAMINATION. See also FIRST-RANK SYMPTOMS.

Internet addiction a behavioral pattern characterized by excessive or obsessive online and offline computer use that leads to distress and impairment. The condition, though controversial, has attracted increasing attention in the popular media and among healthcare professionals; it has been proposed for inclusion in the next edition of the *Diagnostic and Statistical Manual of Mental Disorders* (see DSM–IV–TR). Expanding research has identified various subtypes, including those involving excessive gaming, sexual preoccupations, and e-mail and text messaging.

interneuron *n.* any neuron that is neither sensory nor motor but connects other neurons within the central nervous system. Also called **connector**; **connector neuron**; **internuncial neuron**.

interpersonal *adj.* pertaining to actions, events, and feelings between two or more individuals. For example, **interpersonal skill** is an aptitude enabling a person to carry on effective relationships with others, such as an ability to communicate thought and feeling or to assume appropriate social responsibilities.

interpersonal conflict disagreement or discord between people with respect to goals, values, or attitudes. See also EXTRAPSYCHIC CONFLICT.

interpersonal distance the distance that individuals choose to maintain between themselves and others. Studies show that most individuals maintain a smaller interpersonal distance for friends than for strangers.

interpersonal group psychotherapy a group approach to the treatment of psychological, behavioral, and emotional problems that emphasizes the curative influence of interpersonal learning, including the analysis of group events, experiences, and relationships, rather than the review of issues that are external to the group. Also called **interactive group psychotherapy**.

interpersonal process recall (**IPR**) a method used for understanding the processes of psychotherapy and for the training of counselors and therapists. It involves videotaping or audiotaping counseling or psychotherapy sessions, which are later reexperienced and analyzed by the counselor or therapist in the presence of a supervisor, who questions and discusses the thoughts and feelings of the counselor or therapist and client. [developed by U.S. counseling psychologist Norman I. Kagan (1931–1994)]

interpersonal psychotherapy (**IPT**) a time-limited form of psychotherapy, originally based on the INTERPERSONAL THEORY of U.S. psychiatrist Harry Stack Sullivan (1892–1949), positing that relations with others constitute the primary force motivating human behavior. A central feature of IPT is the clarification of the client's interpersonal interactions with significant others, including the therapist. The therapist helps the client explore current and past experiences in detail, relating not only to interpersonal reaction but also to environmental influences generally on personal adaptive and maladaptive thinking and behavior.

interpersonal reconstructive psychotherapy an INTEGRATIVE PSYCHOTHERAPY and method of symptom analysis that blends psychodynamic and cognitive behavior techniques and focuses on presenting problems and symptoms as they relate to long-term interpersonal difficulties. Interventions are active and focused on attachment-based factors that maintain current problems. [approach developed by U.S. clinical psychologist Lorna Smith Benjamin]

interpersonal relations 1. the connections and interactions, especially ones that are socially and emotionally significant, between two or more people. **2.** the pattern or patterns observable in an individual's dealings with other people.

interpersonal theory in psychoanalysis, the theory of personality developed by U.S. psychoanalyst Harry Stack Sullivan (1892–1949), which is based on the belief that people's interactions with other people, especially SIGNIFICANT OTHERS, determine their sense of security, sense of self, and the dynamisms that motivate their behavior. For Sullivan, personality is the product of a long series of stages in which the individual gradually develops "good feeling" toward others and a sense of a GOOD ME toward himself or herself. The individual also learns how to ward off anxiety and correct distorted perceptions of other people; learns to verify his or her ideas through CONSENSUAL VALIDATION; and above all seeks to achieve effective interpersonal relationships on a mature level.

interpersonal trust the confidence a person or group of people has in the reliability of another person or group, specifically the degree to which people feel they can depend on others to do what they say they will do. The key factor is not the intrinsic honesty of the other people but their predictability.

interpretation *n.* in psychotherapy, explanation by the therapist in terms that are meaningful to the client of the client's issues, behaviors, or feelings. Interpretation typically is made along the lines of the particular conceptual framework or dynamic model of the form of therapy. In psychoanalysis, for example, the analyst uses the constructs of psychoanalytic theory to interpret the patient's early experiences, dreams, character defenses, and resistance. Although interpretation exists to some extent in almost any form of therapy, it is a critical procedural step in psychoanalysis and in other forms of PSYCHODYNAMIC PSYCHOTHERAPY.

interpretive response a reply by a therapist intended to summarize or illuminate the essential meaning of or motive underlying a statement made by a client during therapy. See also INTERPRETATION.

interpretive therapy any form of active, directive psychotherapy in which the therapist elicits the client's conflicts, repressions, dreams, and resistances, which are then interpreted or explained to the client in the light of his or her experiences. See also INTERPRETATION.

interrater agreement the degree to which a group of raters (people, instruments, tests) rate an attribute in the same way (e.g., assign the same score or category to the same case). Although often used synonymously with INTERRATER RELIABILITY, interrater agreement refers only to the degree to which raters agree on (typically) categorical assignments.

interrater reliability the consistency with which different examiners produce similar ratings in judging the same abilities or characteristics in the same target person or object. Although often used synonymously with INTERRATER AGREEMENT, this is a more specific term linked conceptually with CLASSICAL TEST THEORY and possessing an underlying TRUE SCORE sense. It usually refers to continuous measurement assignments. Also called **interjudge reliability**.

interrole conflict the form of ROLE CONFLICT that occurs when individuals have more than one role within a group and the expectations and behaviors associated with one role are not consistent with the expectations and behaviors associated with another. Compare INTRAROLE CONFLICT.

I

intersexuality *n.* a modern term for HERMAPHRODITISM and pseudohermaphroditism: the condition of possessing the sexual characteristics of both sexes. An individual who exhibits such characteristics is called an **intersex**. Also called **intersexualism**. See also HERMAPHRODITISM; PSEUDOHERMAPHRODITISM. **—intersexual** *adj.*

intersubjectivity *n.* the property of being accessible in some way to more than one mind, implying a communication and understanding among different minds and the possibility of converting subjective, private experiences into objective, public ones. **—intersubjective** *adj.*

interval *n.* in statistics, a range of scores or values. See CONFIDENCE INTERVAL.

interval data numerical values that indicate magnitude but lack a "natural," meaningful zero point. Interval data represent exact quantities of the variables under consideration, and when arranged consecutively have equal differences among adjacent values (regardless of the specific values selected) that correspond to genuine differences between the physical quantities being measured. Temperature is an example of interval data: the difference between 50°F and 49°F is the same as the difference between 40°F and 39°F, but a temperature of 0°F does not indicate that there is no temperature. See also RATIO DATA.

interval scale a scale marked in equal intervals so that the difference between any two consecutive values on the scale is equivalent regardless of the two values selected. Interval scales lack a true, meaningful zero point, which is what distinguishes them from RATIO SCALES.

intervening variable 1. a hypothetical entity that is influenced by an INDEPENDENT VARIABLE and that in turn influences a DEPENDENT VARIABLE. **2.** more specifically, an unseen process or event, inferred to occur within the organism between a stimulus event and the time of response, that affects the relationship between the stimulus and response. Also called **mediating variable**; **mediator variable**.

intervention *n.* **1.** action on the part of a therapist to deal with the issues and problems of a client. The selection of the intervention is guided by the nature of the problem, the orientation of the therapist, the setting, and the willingness and ability of the client to proceed with the treatment. Also called **psychological intervention**. **2.** a technique in addictions counseling in which significant individuals in a client's life meet with him or her, in the presence of a trained counselor, to express their observations and feelings about the client's addiction and related problems. The session, typically a surprise to the client, may last several hours, after which the client has a choice of seeking a recommended treatment immediately (e.g., as an inpatient) or ignoring the intervention. If the client chooses not to seek treatment, participants state the interpersonal consequences; for example, a drug-abusing adult living at home may be requested to move out, or the client's employment may be terminated. **3.** a similar confrontation between an individual and family and friends, but outside of the formal structure of counseling or therapy, usually over similar issues and with the goal of urging the confronted individual to seek help with an attitudinal or behavioral problem.

interventionist *n.* a physician, behavioral scientist, therapist, or other professional who modifies the conditions or symptoms of a patient.

interview *n.* a directed conversation in which a researcher, therapist, clinician, employer, or the like (the **interviewer**) intends to elicit specific information from an individual (the **interviewee**) for purposes of research, diagnosis, treatment, or employment. Interviews may be either highly structured, including set questions, or unstructured, varying with material introduced by the interviewee. See also CLINICAL INTERVIEW.

interview group psychotherapy a type of GROUP THERAPY for adolescents and adults. A balanced therapeutic group is selected on the basis of common problems and personal characteristics, and participants are encouraged to reveal their attitudes, symptoms, and feelings. See also ANALYTIC GROUP PSYCHOTHERAPY. [developed by Russian-born U.S. psychotherapist Samuel Richard Slavson (1890–1981)]

in the closet see CLOSET HOMOSEXUAL.

intimacy *n.* an interpersonal state of extreme emotional closeness such that each party's personal space can be entered by any of the other parties without causing discomfort to that person. Intimacy characterizes close, familiar, and usually affectionate or loving personal relationships and requires the parties to have a detailed knowledge or deep understanding of each other. —**intimate** *adj.*

intimacy problem difficulty in forming close relationships and becoming intimate with others, whether physically or psychologically, which might involve difficulties with sexual contact, self-disclosure, trust, or commitment to a lasting relationship. See also FEAR OF COMMITMENT.

intimacy versus isolation the sixth of ERIKSON'S EIGHT STAGES OF DEVELOPMENT, which extends from late adolescence through courtship and early family life to early middle age. During this period, individuals must learn to share and care without losing themselves; if they fail, they will feel alone and isolated. The development of a cohesive identity in the previous stage provides the opportunity to achieve true intimacy.

intoxicant *n.* a substance capable of producing transient alterations in mental function. The nature of the intoxication depends on the psychoactive properties of the intoxicant. In general, mild intoxication is marked by minor perceptual changes or a sense of euphoria or well-being; more pronounced intoxication involves such changes as behavioral disinhibition, perceptual distortions, hallucinations, or delirium; and severe intoxication is marked by loss of motor control and cognitive and autonomic function, possibly progressing to coma or death.

intoxication *n.* see INTOXICANT; SUBSTANCE INTOXICATION.

intraconscious personality a phenomenon of DISSOCIATIVE IDENTITY DISORDER in which one personality functioning on a subconscious level is aware of the thoughts and outer world of another personality functioning on a conscious level.

intracranial pressure (**ICP**) the pressure within the skull. Excessive intracranial pressure can cause brain damage and impede blood flow within the brain, with a range of effects that may include memory loss, balance problems, dementia, coma, and death. Causes of raised ICP include hydrocephalus, hemorrhage, hematomas, brain tumors, and head injuries.

intrafamily dynamics the changes in the relationships among the members of a family within a period of time, together with the influences operating in their interactions with each other that bring about these changes.

intramuscular injection (**im injection**) the injection of a substance into a muscle by means of a hypodermic syringe, usually into the muscle of the upper arm, thigh, or buttock. The choice of muscle area is important in order to avoid damage to a nerve or blood vessel. See ADMINISTRATION.

intrapersonal *adj.* describing factors operating or constructs occurring within the person, such as attitudes, decisions, self-concept, self-esteem, or self-regulation.

intrapersonal conflict see INTRAPSYCHIC CONFLICT.

intrapsychic *adj.* pertaining to impulses, ideas,

conflicts, or other psychological phenomena that arise or occur within the psyche or mind.

intrapsychic ataxia lack of coordination of feelings, thoughts, and volition (e.g., laughing when depressed). The concept was introduced in 1904 by Austrian psychiatrist Erwin Stransky (1878–1962) in association with schizophrenia, but it has subsequently been seen in other disorders as well. Also called **mental ataxia**. See also INAPPROPRIATE AFFECT.

intrapsychic conflict in psychoanalytic theory, the clash of opposing forces within the psyche, such as conflicting drives, wishes, or agencies. Also called **inner conflict**; **internal conflict**; **intrapersonal conflict; psychic conflict**.

intrarole conflict the form of ROLE CONFLICT caused by incompatibility among the behaviors and expectations associated with a single role. These inconsistencies may result from the inherent complexity of the role itself, the ambiguity of the role, or a superordinate group's lack of consensus in defining the role and its demands. Compare INTERROLE CONFLICT.

intrasubject replication design see SINGLE-CASE EXPERIMENTAL DESIGN.

intrauterine device (**IUD**) a device made of plastic or other material (e.g., copper or rubber) that is inserted into the cervix as a contraceptive device. Usually having a **coil** design or the shape of a T, Y, or other configuration, it interferes with implantation of an embryo in the wall of the uterus.

intravenous drug usage a form of drug use in which the drug is injected directly into a vein with a needle and syringe. The opioids, especially HEROIN, are often injected intravenously to enhance their effects. Poor hygiene results in dirty needles or syringes, use of which increases the risk of acquiring serious blood-borne disorders, including HEPATITIS and HIV infection.

intravenous injection (**iv injection**) the injection of a substance into a vein by means of a hypodermic syringe. This technique is used when rapid absorption of a drug is needed, when the substance would be irritating to the skin or to muscle tissue, or when it cannot be administered through the digestive tract. It is a dangerous route of administration because of its rapid onset of pharmacological action, which may cause a potentially fatal reaction. Slow intravenous injection, called **intravenous** (**iv**) **infusion**, is used for blood transfusions, parenteral administration of nutrients (i.e., directly into the bloodstream, bypassing the digestive tract), or continuous administration of drugs. See also ADMINISTRATION.

intrinsic activity **1.** the magnitude of a response to a drug regardless of dosage. **2.** a measure of the efficacy of a drug-receptor complex in producing a pharmacological effect. Also called **intrinsic efficacy**. **3.** the inborn readiness of babies to be inquisitive and to make contact with their environment. According to Jean PIAGET'S theory of cognitive development, cognitive structures, by their very nature, seek to be active, predisposing the child to learn from experience with the environment.

intrinsic behavior **1.** a type of behavior expressed through a specific organ (e.g., smiling, the knee-jerk reflex). **2.** behavior that is inherently rewarding. For example, reading a book is pleasurable for some individuals and so is intrinsically rewarding.

intrinsic motivation an incentive to engage in a specific activity that derives from the activity itself (e.g., a genuine interest in a subject studied), rather than because of any external benefits that might be obtained (e.g., course credits). Compare EXTRINSIC MOTIVATION.

intrinsic reward a positively valued outcome that is implicit in an activity, such as the pleasure or satisfaction gained from developing a special skill. Intrinsic rewards originate directly from the task performance and do not originate from other people. Compare EXTRINSIC REWARD.

I

introception *n.* a personality trait reflecting the extent to which a person is attentive to understanding the needs, motives, and experiences of him- or herself and others. **—introceptive** *adj.*

introjection *n.* **1.** a process in which an individual unconsciously incorporates aspects of reality external to himself or herself into the self, particularly the attitudes, values, and qualities of another person or a part of another person's personality. Introjection may occur, for example, in the mourning process for a loved one. **2.** in psychoanalytic theory, the process of internalizing the qualities of an external OBJECT into the psyche in the form of an internal object or mental REPRESENTATION, which then has an influence on behavior. This process is posited to be a normal part of development, as when introjection of parental values and attitudes forms the SUPEREGO, but may also be used as a DEFENSE MECHANISM in situations that arouse anxiety. Compare IDENTIFICATION; INCORPORATION. **—introject** *vb.* **—introjective** *adj.*

introjective depression self-critical depression: intense sadness and DYSPHORIA stemming from punitive, relentless feelings of self-doubt, self-criticism, and self-loathing that often are related to the internalization of the attitudes and values of harsh and critical parental figures. The individual with introjective depression becomes involved in numerous activities in an attempt to compensate for his or her excessively high standards, constant drive to perform and achieve, and feelings of guilt and shame over not having lived up to expectations. Compare ANACLITIC DEPRESSION.

introjective personality according to some psychoanalytic theories, a line of personality development that is focused on achievement and evaluation and—if the personality fails to develop properly—may result in feelings of worthlessness, failure, and psychopathological self-criticism. Compare ANACLITIC PERSONALITY.

intromission *n.* the act of sending or putting in something, especially the insertion of the penis into the vagina. See also PENETRATION. **—intromissive** *adj.*

intropunitive *adj.* referring to the punishment of oneself: tending to turn anger, blame, or hostility internally, against the self, in response to frustration. Compare EXTRAPUNITIVE. **—intropunitiveness** *n.*

introspection *n.* the process of attempting to access directly one's own internal psychological processes, judgments, perceptions, or states. **—introspective** *adj.*

introversion *n.* orientation toward the internal private world of one's self and one's inner thoughts and feelings, rather than toward the outer world of people and things. Introversion is a broad personality trait and, like EXTRAVERSION, exists on a continuum of attitudes and behaviors. Introverts are relatively more withdrawn, retiring, reserved, quiet, and deliberate; they may tend to mute or guard expression of positive affect, adopt more skeptical views or positions, and prefer to work independently. See also INTROVERSION–EXTRAVERSION. [concept originated by Carl JUNG for the study of personality types] **—introversive** *adj.* **—introvert** *n.* **—introverted** *adj.*

introversion–extraversion the range, or continuum, of self-orientation from INTROVERSION, characterized by inward and self-directed concerns and behaviors, to EXTRAVERSION, characterized by outward and social-directed concerns and behaviors. See also EYSENCK'S TYPOLOGY; FIVE-FACTOR PERSONALITY MODEL. [concept originated by Carl JUNG for the study of personality types]

intrusive thoughts mental events that interrupt the flow of ongoing and task-related thoughts in spite of persistent efforts to avoid them. They are a common aspect of such disorders as posttraumatic stress and obsessive-compulsive disorder. Also called **TUITs** (**task-unrelated images and thoughts**).

intuition *n.* immediate insight or perception as contrasted with conscious reasoning or reflection. Intuitions have been characterized alternatively as quasi-mystical experiences or as the products of instinct, feeling, minimal sense impressions, or unconscious forces. **—intuit** *vb.* **—intuitive** *adj.*

intuitive judgment a decision reached on the basis of subjective feelings that cannot easily be articulated and may not be fully conscious. See INTUITION.

intuitive knowledge knowledge that appears to be based on subjective judgment or gut feeling rather than on specific learning. Intuitive knowledge is probably based on nonconsciously recalled information, such as IMPLICIT MEMORY or PROCEDURAL MEMORY, both of which are forms of knowing that are not necessarily accompanied by verbal awareness of knowing.

intuitive sociogram see SOCIOGRAM.

intuitive type in Carl JUNG'S ANALYTIC PSYCHOLOGY, a FUNCTIONAL TYPE characterized by an ability to adapt "by means of unconscious indications" and "a fine and sharpened perception and interpretation of faintly conscious stimuli." The intuitive type is one of Jung's two IRRATIONAL TYPES; the other is the SENSATION TYPE. See also FEELING TYPE; THINKING TYPE.

invalidate *vb.* to show the lack of VALIDITY of a proposition, hypothesis, or theory.

inventory *n.* a list of items, often in question form, used in describing and studying behavior, interests, and attitudes.

inventory test 1. in educational assessment, a type of achievement test that contains questions in the major areas of instruction so that an overview or profile of the individual's achievement may be obtained. **2.** in personality research, a test designed to provide a broad overview of personality patterns in a variety of areas.

inverse agonist see AGONIST.

Inversine *n.* a trade name for MECAMYLAMINE.

inversion *n.* in sexual psychology, an old name for same-sex sexual behavior or orientation or the assumption of the role of the opposite sex.

inversion of affect see REVERSAL OF AFFECT.

inverted Oedipus complex see NEGATIVE OEDIPUS COMPLEX.

inverted-U hypothesis a proposed correlation between motivation (or AROUSAL) and performance such that performance is poorest when motivation or arousal is at very low or very high states. This function is typically referred to as the **Yerkes–Dodson law**. Emotional intensity (motivation) increases from a zero point to an optimal point, increasing the quality of performance; increase in intensity after this optimal point leads to performance deterioration and disorganization, forming an inverted U-shaped curve. The optimal point is reached sooner (i.e., at lower intensities) the less well learned or more complex the performance; increases in emotional intensity supposedly affect finer skills, finer discriminations, complex reasoning tasks, and recently acquired skills more readily than routine activities. However, the correlation is considered weak; at best, the inverted U-function represents an entire family of curves in which the peak of performance takes place at different levels of arousal.

investment *n.* see CATHEXIS. **—invest** *vb.*

investment model a theory explaining commitment to a relationship in terms of one's satisfaction with, alternatives to, and investments in the relationship. According to the model, commitment is a function not only of a comparison of the relationship to the individual's expectations, but also the quality of the best available alternative and the magnitude of the individual's investment in the relationship; the investment of resources serves to increase commitment by increasing the costs of leaving the relationship. Although originally developed in the context of romantic associations and friendships, the investment model has since been extended to a variety of other areas, including employment and education.

in vitro referring to biological conditions or processes that occur or are made to occur outside the living body, usually in a laboratory dish (Latin, literally: "in glass"). Compare IN VIVO.

in vitro fertilization (**IVF**) a procedure in which an ovum (egg) is removed from a woman's body, fertilized externally with sperm, and then returned to the uterus. It is used to treat the most difficult cases of INFERTILITY, but success rates for the procedure are not high.

in vivo 1. referring to biological conditions or processes that occur or are observed within the living organism. Compare IN VITRO. **2.** denoting a condition or process that approximates a real-life environment, often created for an experiment or research study. [Latin, literally: "in life"]

in vivo desensitization a technique used in BEHAVIOR THERAPY, usually to reduce or eliminate phobias, in which the client is exposed to the stimuli that induce anxiety. The therapist, in discussion with the client, produces a hierarchy of anxiety-invoking events or items relating to the anxiety-producing stimulus or phobia. The client is then exposed to the actual stimuli in the hierarchy, rather than being asked to imagine them. Success depends on the client overcoming anxiety as the events or items are encountered. Compare COVERT DESENSITIZATION. See also SYSTEMATIC DESENSITIZATION. [first developed by U.S. psychologist Mary Cover Jones (1896–1987)]

in vivo exposure a type of EXPOSURE THERAPY, generally used for treating individuals with PHOBIAS, OBSESSIVE-COMPULSIVE DISORDER, and other anxiety disorders, in which the client directly experiences anxiety-provoking situations or stimuli in real-world conditions. For example, a client who fears flying could be accompanied by a therapist to the airport to simulate boarding a plane while practicing anxiety-decreasing techniques, such as deep breathing. Compare IMAGINAL EXPOSURE.

involuntary civil commitment COMMITMENT of an individual to a mental facility against his or her wishes. For individuals to be committed in this way, it must be established in court that the individuals pose a threat to themselves or others.

involuntary errors errors that are made in spite of one knowing that they are mistakes, for example, slips of the tongue and place-losing errors.

involuntary hospitalization the confinement of a person with a serious mental disorder or illness to a mental hospital by medical authorization and legal direction (as in INVOLUNTARY CIVIL COMMITMENT). Individuals so hospitalized may be considered dangerous to themselves or others, may fail to recognize the severity of their illness and the need for treatment, or may be unable to have their daily living and treatment needs otherwise met in the community or survive without medical attention. Compare VOLUNTARY ADMISSION.

involuntary treatment the treatment of people diagnosed with a mental illness against their will. See FORCED TREATMENT.

involutional depression a largely obsolete name for a MAJOR DEPRESSIVE EPISODE occurring during late middle age or menopause.

ion *n.* an atom or molecule that has acquired an electrical charge by gaining or losing one or more electrons. **—ionic** *adj.*

Ionamin *n.* a trade name for PHENTERMINE.

ion channel a group of proteins forming a channel that spans a cell membrane, allowing the passage of ions between the extracellular environment and the cytoplasm of the cell. Ion channels are selective; allow passage of ions of a particular chemical nature, size, or electrostatic charge; and may be ungated (i.e., always open) or gated, opening and closing in response to chemical, electrical, or mechanical signals. Ion channels are important in the transmission of neural signals between neurons at a SYNAPSE. The opening of **sodium channels** in the membrane of a postsynaptic neuron permits an influx of sodium ions (Na^+) into the neuron, which produces an **excitatory postsynaptic potential**, that is, an increased probability that the postsynaptic neuron will initiate an ACTION POTENTIAL and hence fire a nerve impulse. The opening of **potassium channels** or **chloride channels** allows potassium ions (K^+) to leave the postsynaptic neuron or chloride ions (Cl^-) to enter it, either of which produces an **inhibitory postsynaptic potential**, that is, a decreased probability that the postsynaptic neuron will initiate an action potential and hence fire a nerve impulse.

I/O psychology abbreviation for INDUSTRIAL AND ORGANIZATIONAL PSYCHOLOGY.

ip abbreviation for *i*ntra*p*eritoneal.

IPA 1. abbreviation for INDEPENDENT PRACTICE ASSOCIATION. **2.** abbreviation for INTERACTION-PROCESS ANALYSIS.

IPR abbreviation for INTERPERSONAL PROCESS RECALL.

iproniazid *n.* a MONOAMINE OXIDASE INHIBITOR developed in the 1950s for the treatment of tuberculosis and later found to have therapeutic value in the treatment of mood disorders. Iproniazid was found to elevate the mood of tuberculosis patients, and clinical trials led to its widespread use as an antidepressant. However, it has now been replaced by other less toxic antidepressant drugs.

ipsative *adj.* referring back to the self. For example, ipsative analyses of personal characteristics involve assessing multiple psychological attributes and conducting within-person analyses of the degree to which an individual possesses one attribute versus another.

IPSS abbreviation for INTERNATIONAL PILOT STUDY OF SCHIZOPHRENIA.

IPT abbreviation for INTERPERSONAL PSYCHOTHERAPY.

IQ *i*ntelligence *q*uotient: a standard measure of an individual's intelligence level based on psychological tests. In the early years of intelligence testing, IQ was calculated by dividing the MENTAL AGE by the CHRONOLOGICAL AGE and multiplying by 100 to produce a **ratio IQ**. This concept has now mostly been replaced by the DEVIATION IQ, computed as a function of the discrepancy of an individual score from the mean (or average) score. The mean IQ is customarily 100, with slightly more than two thirds of all scores falling within plus or minus 15 points of the mean (usually one standard deviation). More than 95% of all scores fall between 70 (two standard deviations below the mean) and 130 (two standard deviations above the mean). Some tests yield more specific IQ scores, such as a VERBAL IQ, which measures VERBAL INTELLIGENCE, and **performance IQ**, which measures NONVERBAL INTELLIGENCE. Discrepancies between the two can be used diagnostically to detect learning disabilities or specific cognitive deficiencies. Additional data are often derived from IQ tests, such as performance speed, freedom from distractibility, verbal comprehension, and PERCEPTUAL ORGANIZATION indices. There are critics who consider the concept of IQ (and other intelligence scales) to be flawed. They point out that the IQ test is more a measure of previously learned skills and knowledge than of underlying native ability and that many participants are simply not accustomed to sitting still and following orders (conditions that such tests require), although they function well in the real world. Critics also refer to cases of misrepresentation of facts in the history of IQ research. Nevertheless, these problems seem to apply to the interpretation of IQ scores rather than the validity of the scores themselves.

IRB abbreviation for INSTITUTIONAL REVIEW BOARD.

irkunii *n.* see MYRIACHIT.

ironic mental control the phenomenon whereby the attempt to suppress some mental content from consciousness results in an unexpectedly high level of awareness of that very content. [defined by U.S. psychologist Daniel M. Wegner (1948–)]

ironic monitoring process a component of mental processing that keeps suppressed mental content active and available outside of awareness.

irrational *adj.* **1.** lacking in reason or sound judgment: illogical or unreasonable. **2.** lacking in usual mental clarity.

irrational belief an illogical, erroneous, or distorted idea, firmly held despite objective contradictory evidence. See also COGNITIVE DISTORTION. [attributed to U.S. psychologist Albert Ellis (1913–2007)]

irrationality *n.* the state, condition, or quality of lacking rational thought. The term is typically used in relation to cognitive behavior (e.g., thinking, decision making) that is illogical.

irrational type in Carl JUNG'S ANALYTIC PSYCHOLOGY, one of the two major categories of FUNCTIONAL TYPE: It comprises the INTUITIVE TYPE and the SENSATION TYPE. Compare RATIONAL TYPE.

irreflexive affect see AFFECT.

irrelevant language a language composed of sounds, phrases, or words that are usually understood only by the speaker, as observed in some individuals with schizophrenia or autistic disorder.

irresistible impulse rule formerly, a rule commonly used in U.S. courts of law for determining INSANITY, according to which defendants were judged to be insane and therefore absolved of CRIMINAL RESPONSIBILITY if they were unable to control their conduct, even if they were aware that it was wrong. This rule is no longer used.

irreversible decrement model the view that physical and psychological changes associated with aging are caused by biological deterioration and thus are not amenable to training or intervention.

irritability *n.* **1.** a state of excessive, easily provoked anger, annoyance, or impatience. **2.** in physiology, the ability of a cell or tissue to respond to stimuli (e.g., neural irritability). **—irritable** *adj.*

irritable bowel syndrome (**IBS**) a common functional disorder of the intestines characterized by abdominal pain or discomfort (e.g., bloating) and changes in bowel habits, with some people experiencing increased constipation, others increased diarrhea, and others alternating between the two. As yet there is no known cause (psychogenic or organic), though stress and emotional factors are currently thought to play a role. Also called **mucous colitis**.

IRT abbreviation for ITEM RESPONSE THEORY.

ischemia *n.* deficiency of blood in an organ or tissue, due to functional constriction or actual obstruction of a blood vessel. See CEREBRAL ISCHEMIA. **—ischemic** *adj.*

islets of Langerhans clusters of endocrine cells within the pancreas. The A (or alpha) cells secrete glucagon, the B (or beta) cells secrete insulin, and the D (or delta) cells secrete somatostatin. Together these hormones play a key role in regulating blood sugar and carbohydrate metabolism. [Paul **Langerhans** (1847–1888), German anatomist]

isocarboxazid *n.* an irreversible MONOAMINE OXIDASE INHIBITOR (MAOI) whose use is limited by its unpleasant side effects (sedation, ORTHOSTATIC HYPOTENSION, weight gain, etc.) and potentially dangerous interactions with tyramine-containing foodstuffs (e.g., cheese). U.S. trade name: **Marplan**.

isolate 1. *n.* an individual who remains apart from others, either as a result of choosing to minimize his or her contact with others or through rejection and ostracism by other individuals or groups. **2.** *n.* in the psychology of groups, a group member with no, very few, or very superficial social and personal relations with other group members. **3.** *n.* in SOCIOMETRY, any individual who is infrequently or never mentioned when group members report on whom they like in their group. In measures of peer acceptance among children, an isolate (or **neglected child**) is a child who has low social impact and is usually referred to negatively but is not actively disliked by other children. Compare REJECTED CHILD. **4.** *vb.* see ISOLATION.

isolated explosive disorder an IMPULSE-CONTROL DISORDER characterized by a single, discrete episode in which the individual commits a violent, catastrophic act, such as shooting strangers during a sudden fit of rage. The episode is out of all proportion to any precipitating stress, is not due to any other mental disorder or to a general medical condition, and is not substance-induced. Also called **catathymic crisis**. Compare INTERMITTENT EXPLOSIVE DISORDER.

isolation *n.* **1.** the condition of being separated from other individuals. See LONELINESS; SOCIAL ISOLATION. **2.** in psychoanalytic theory, a DEFENSE MECHANISM that relies on keeping unwelcome thoughts and feelings from forming associative links with other thoughts and feelings, with the result that the unwelcome thought is rarely activated. See also COMPARTMENTALIZATION. **3.** in ERIKSON'S EIGHT STAGES OF DEVELOPMENT, see INTIMACY VERSUS ISOLATION. **—isolate** *vb.*

isolation of affect in psychoanalytic theory, a DEFENSE MECHANISM in which the individual screens out painful feelings by recalling a traumatic event without experiencing the emotion associated with it.

isomers *pl. n.* forms of molecules that are identical in chemical composition but differ in the spatial orientation of their atoms (i.e., they are **stereoisomers**). **Enantiomers** are stereoisomers that exist in pairs as mirror images. The two enantiomers of a pair rotate the plane of polarized light in opposite directions: L forms produce leftward or counterclockwise rotation (**levorotation**), while D forms produce rightward or clockwise rotation (**dextrorotation**). In general, L forms tend to have biological activity.

isomorphism *n.* **1.** a one-to-one structural correspondence between two or more different entities or their constituent parts. **2.** the concept, especially in GESTALT PSYCHOLOGY, that there is a structural correspondence between perceptual experience and psychoneural activity in the brain. **—isomorph** *n.* **—isomorphic** *adj.*

isoniazid *n.* a drug of choice for the treatment of tuberculosis. Use of the drug can cause a form of neuritis by blocking the function of pyridoxine (vitamin B_6) in metabolizing glutamic acid to form the neurotransmitter GAMMA-AMINOBUTYRIC ACID. Isoniazid is a precursor of the monoamine oxidase inhibitor IPRONIAZID and was reputed to have some antidepressant activity, though it is not clinically used in this role. Also called **isonicotinic acid hydrazide (INH)**.

isophilia *n.* feelings of affection or affectionate behavior toward members of one's own sex, but without the genital component characteristic of same-sex sexual behavior. [first described by U.S. psychiatrist Harry Stack Sullivan (1892–1949)]

isopropyl alcohol an isomer of propyl alcohol used as an ingredient in cosmetics (e.g., hand lotion) as well as in medications for external use. It also may be used as an antiseptic. If ingested, it has initial effects similar to those of ETHANOL, but it is extremely toxic.

Isopto Carpine a trade name for PILOCARPINE.

Isopto Eserine a trade name for PHYSOSTIGMINE.

isotretinoin *n.* an analog of vitamin A used in the treatment of severe acne that is resistant to other therapies. It is highly teratogenic (see TERATOGEN) and therefore should not be used in pregnancy. More controversially, the use of isotretinoin has been linked with psychological disturbances, such as depression, psychosis, and suicide. The mechanism responsible for these side effects is unknown. U.S. trade name (among others): **Accutane**.

ISP abbreviation for INDIVIDUAL SERVICE PLAN.

I statement a communication tool in which the first person pronoun is used in talking about relationship issues. Therapists may coach clients to use "I" instead of "you" in statements, for example, "I am bothered by your habit" rather than "You have a bad habit" (which is a **you statement**). I statements tend to reduce the negativity and blame directed toward the other person and put the ownership of the issue with the speaker, not the listener.

item analysis a set of procedures used to evaluate the statistical merits of individual items comprising a psychological measure or test. These procedures may be used to select items for a test from a larger pool of initial items or to evaluate items on an established test.

item difficulty the difficulty of a test item for a particular group as determined by the proportion of individuals who correctly respond to the item.

item response theory (**IRT**) a psychometric theory of measurement based on the concept that the probability that an item will be correctly answered is a function of an underlying trait or ability that is not directly observable, that is, a latent trait (see LATENT TRAIT THEORY). Item response theory models differ in terms of the number of parameters contained in the model.

item scaling the assignment of a test item to a scale position on some dimension, often the dimension of difficulty level.

item validity the extent to which an individual item in a test or experiment measures what it purports to measure.

item weighting a numerical value assigned to a test item that expresses its percentage of the total score of the test. For example, an essay question may be assigned a value of 40, representing 40 out of 100 possible points.

I–Thou *adj.* denoting a relationship in which a subject ("I") treats someone or something else as another unique subject ("Thou") and in which there is complete personal involvement. German Jewish philosopher Martin Buber (1878–1965), who introduced the term, held that this type of relationship between individuals is characterized by mutual openness to, and recognition of, the unique personhood of the other. The I–Thou relationship is transformative for both people. Buber held that a person's relationship with God is the ultimate I–Thou relationship, because God is quintessentially Thou. In forms of EXISTENTIAL–HUMANISTIC THERAPY especially, I–Thou moments are prized and denote a significant contact and understanding between client and therapist. Compare I–IT.

itinerancy *n.* see PEREGRINATION.

ITPA abbreviation for ILLINOIS TEST OF PSYCHOLINGUISTIC ABILITIES.

IUD abbreviation for INTRAUTERINE DEVICE.

iv abbreviation for *i*ntra*v*enous. See INTRAVENOUS INJECTION.

IVF abbreviation for IN VITRO FERTILIZATION.

Jj

Jacobson relaxation method see PROGRESSIVE RELAXATION.

James, William (1842–1910) U.S. psychologist and philosopher. After earning his medical degree in 1868 from Harvard Medical School, James served as professor of physiology, philosophy, and psychology at Harvard University. Arguably the most influential psychologist of his time, he taught many students who contributed to the development of American psychology, including Mary Whiton Calkins, G. Stanley Hall, Robert S. Woodworth, and Edward L. Thorndike. He also wrote a best-selling textbook, *Principles of Psychology* (1890), that helped shape the field of psychology in its early decades. Embracing Darwinian evolutionary theory, he promoted a functionalist approach to psychology, emphasizing the usefulness of psychological phenomena, such as habits, emotions, and consciousness, in helping organisms survive. James also made lasting contributions to the psychology of religion in his *Varieties of Religious Experience* (1902) and to psychical research as a means of uncovering unconscious factors in mental life. In addition, James is one of the founders, with John DEWEY and Charles S. Peirce (1839–1914), of PRAGMATISM, America's most important contribution to philosophy. See JAMES–LANGE THEORY; FUNCTIONALISM; SELF; STREAM OF ACTION; STREAM OF CONSCIOUSNESS.

JAS abbreviation for JENKINS ACTIVITY SURVEY.

JCAHO abbreviation for JOINT COMMISSION ON ACCREDITATION OF HEALTHCARE ORGANIZATIONS.

jealousy *n.* a NEGATIVE EMOTION in which an individual resents a third party for appearing to take away (or be likely to take away) the affections of a loved one. Jealousy requires a triangle of social relationships between three individuals: the one who is jealous, the partner with whom the jealous individual has or desires a relationship, and the rival who represents a preemptive threat to that relationship. Romantic relationships are the prototypical source of jealousy, but any significant relationship (with parents, friends, and so on) is capable of producing it. It differs from ENVY in that three people are always involved. See also DELUSIONAL JEALOUSY. **—jealous** *adj.*

Jehovah complex a form of MEGALOMANIA in which the individual suffers from delusions of grandeur and identifies with qualities associated with God.

Jenkins Activity Survey (JAS) a self-administered, multiple-choice survey that attempts to duplicate the clinical assessment of the TYPE A BEHAVIOR pattern by means of an ob-jective psychometric procedure. It measures characteristics of this behavior pattern, such as extreme competitiveness, striving for achievement and personal recognition, aggressiveness, haste, impatience, and explosiveness. [Carlyle David **Jenkins** (1928–), U.S. psychologist]

jimsonweed *n.* a poisonous annual weed, *Datura stramonium*, of the nightshade family that grows wild in temperate and subtropical areas of North America and the rest of the world and contains several potent anticholinergic agents, including the alkaloids SCOPOLAMINE and ATROPINE. It has been taken in small doses to treat asthma, whooping cough, muscle spasms, and other conditions and has also been applied externally for pain relief. Poisoning results in such symptoms as hyperthermia, flushing, dry mucous membranes, nausea and vomiting, rapid heartbeat, visual disturbances, hallucinations, delirium, coma, and potentially death; there is often amnesia for the period of intoxication. The name is a corruption of "Jamestown weed," the name given to the plant by early settlers of Virginia. Also called **devil's trumpet**.

jinjinia bemar see KORO.

jiryan *n.* a CULTURE-BOUND SYNDROME found in India, with symptoms similar to those of SHEN-K'UEI.

Jocasta complex in psychoanalytic theory, an abnormally close or incestuous attachment of a mother to her son. It is named for Jocasta, the mother and wife of Oedipus in Greek mythology. Compare OEDIPUS COMPLEX.

joie de vivre a sense of enjoyment or pleasure in life that is absent in ANHEDONIA. [French, "joy of living"]

Joint Commission on Accreditation of Healthcare Organizations (JCAHO) a national, private, nonprofit organization, founded in 1951, whose purpose is to encourage the attainment of uniformly high standards of institutional medical care. The Joint Commission evaluates and accredits hospitals and health care organizations that provide MANAGED CARE (including HMOS, PPOS, and INTEGRATED DELIVERY SYSTEMS), HOME CARE, long-term care, behavioral health care, laboratory services, and ambulatory care services.

Jonah complex in the humanistic psychology of Abraham MASLOW, inhibition of becoming fully self-actualized—that is, of fulfilling one's potential—for fear of facing new challenges and situations. It is named for the biblical prophet Jonah, who attempted to evade the mission imposed on him by God. See also FEAR OF SUCCESS.

jouissance *n.* in the theory of French psychoanalyst Jacques Lacan (1901–1981), enjoyment or pleasure that goes beyond mere satisfaction of an INSTINCT. Such pleasure is seen as a subversive and destabilizing force. [French, literally: "enjoyment," "pleasure"]

joy *n.* a feeling of extreme gladness, delight, or exultation of the spirit arising from a sense of well-being or satisfaction. Joy promotes confidence and an increase in energy, which in turn tend to promote positive feelings about the self.

judgment *n.* the capacity to recognize relationships, draw conclusions from evidence, and make critical evaluations of events and people.

J

jumping Frenchmen of Maine syndrome a CULTURE-BOUND SYNDROME resembling LATAH, observed in lumberjacks of French Canadian descent living in Quebec and Maine. It is characterized by an extreme STARTLE RESPONSE involving yelling, imitative speech and behavior, involuntary jumping, flinging of the arms, and command obedience. Also called **jumper disease of Maine**; **jumping disease**. See also IMU; MYRIACHIT.

Jung, Carl Gustav (1875–1961) Swiss psychiatrist and psychoanalyst. Jung studied natural science and medicine at the University of Basel in Switzerland, earning a medical degree (c. 1899). He then moved to Zürich to work at the Bürghölzi Mental Hospital with the prominent Swiss physician Eugen Bleuler (1857–1939), who specialized in the schizophrenic disorders. A wide-ranging student of medicine, archeology, mysticism, and philosophy, Jung associated himself with the psychoanalytic school of Sigmund FREUD because it recognized the influence of the UNCONSCIOUS. However, after 5 years he broke with Freud over Freud's theories of infantile sexuality, his emphasis on instinctual impulses, and his limitation of mental contents to personal experiences. In contrast, Jung held that we are molded by our ancestral as well as personal history, and motivated by moral and spiritual values more than by psychosexual drives. On this basis he constructed a theory of ANALYTIC PSYCHOLOGY. An important aspect of this theory was its emphasis on personality dynamics, viewed in terms of opposing forces, such as conscious versus unconscious values, introversive versus extraversive tendencies, and rational versus irrational processes. For Jung, healthy personality development consisted in constructively resolving these conflicts and achieving a new integration. For conflicts that persist and generate emotional disturbances, Jung advocated a form of therapy aimed at eliciting unconscious forces to help individuals solve their problems and realize their potential. This process usually involves the study of dreams and drawings and the exploration of new activities that will express the individual's personality, but does not utilize the Freudian couch or the method of FREE ASSOCIATION. The popular MYERS–BRIGGS TYPE INDICATOR is based on Jungian principles. See also ANAMNESTIC ANALYSIS; ANIMA; ANIMUS; COMPLEX; FUNCTIONAL TYPES; INDIVIDUATION; INTROVERSION–EXTRAVERSION; SELF; SHADOW; TELEOLOGY. **—Jungian** *adj.*

Jungian psychology the psychoanalytical theory and approach to psychotherapy of Carl JUNG. See ANALYTIC PSYCHOLOGY.

Jungian typology a theory of personality that classifies individuals into types according to (a) attitudes of INTROVERSION and EXTRAVERSION (see ATTITUDINAL TYPES) and (b) the dominant functions of the psyche (see FUNCTIONAL TYPES). [Carl JUNG]

junkie *n.* slang for a drug addict, especially a heroin addict. See HEROIN DEPENDENCE.

junk science invalid research findings admitted into court. Junk science is a cause of concern because judges, attorneys, and juries often lack the scientific training to identify unsound research.

justification *n.* **1.** in clinical psychology, the defensive intellectualization of behavior, as in making an excuse for an action, cognition, or affect that one knows to be or is considered to be wrong or indefensible. **2.** in epistemology, a concept of intellectual responsibility regarding the norms of belief about ideas, actions, emotions, claims, theories, and so forth.

juvenile justice system the courts and other government entities involved in the adjudication of cases involving minors (usually identified as individuals aged under 18). Fundamentally, it differs from the criminal justice system for adults in its belief that young people are more amenable to treatment than adults. Consequently, there is greater emphasis on rehabilitation, and greater efforts are made than in the adult system to reduce the stigmatization associated with being labeled a criminal.

juvenile transfer hearing a formal presentation and assessment of facts during which the court decides whether a minor should be transferred to an adult court for adjudication.

juvenilism *n.* a sexual attraction to children or adolescents. See EPHEBOPHILIA; PEDOPHILIA.

Kk

kainate receptor see GLUTAMATE RECEPTOR.

kairos *n.* in EXISTENTIAL PSYCHOLOGY, the moment of heightened awareness at which a person gains INSIGHT into the meaning of an important event. See also AHA EXPERIENCE; EPIPHANY. [from Greek, "fitness, opportunity, time"]

Kalischer syndrome see STURGE–WEBER SYNDROME.

Kallmann's syndrome a hereditary disorder characterized by hypogonadism (sometimes in the form of underdeveloped male sexual organs), mental retardation, color blindness, complete ANOSMIA (absence of the sense of smell), and unintentional muscle movements. Kallmann's syndrome is transmitted as an X-linked dominant trait. [Franz Josef **Kallmann** (1897–1965), German-born U.S. psychiatrist and geneticist]

Kanner's syndrome see AUTISTIC DISORDER. [Leo **Kanner** (1894–1981), Austrian-born U.S. child psychiatrist]

Kansas v. Hendricks a case resulting in a controversial 1997 U.S. Supreme Court decision that upheld the INVOLUNTARY CIVIL COMMITMENT of an offender after he had already completed his sentence for a sex crime. The court ruled that laws permitting confinement of sex offenders in mental hospitals after they have served their criminal sentences are not unconstitutional if the offender remains a threat.

kappa receptor see OPIOID RECEPTOR.

karezza *n.* see CAREZZA.

kat *n.* see KHAT.

katasexuality *n.* a sexual preference for dead people or human beings with animal-like characteristics. See NECROPHILIA.

Katz Index of Activities of Daily Living an observer-based measure of the FUNCTIONAL STATUS of older adults and individuals with chronic disorders. An individual is rated regarding the degree of assistance required to perform six basic functions: bathing, dressing, feeding, toileting, transferring, and continence. Baseline measurements provide useful feedback when compared to periodic or subsequent measurements. Also called **Katz Index of Independence in Activities of Daily Living**. [originally developed in 1963 by Sidney **Katz**, 20th-century U.S. physician and geriatrician]

kava *n.* an extract of the root of *Piper methysticum*, a shrub indigenous to certain southern Pacific islands, where it has an established use as a mild intoxicant, sedative, and analgesic agent. The primary active ingredients of the plant are kavain, dihydrokavain, methysticin, and dihydromethysticin—alkaloids that have anticonvulsant and muscle relaxant properties and also produce sedation without clouding of consciousness. Kava is now widely available in Western countries as an herbal supplement promoted for relaxation (e.g., to relieve stress, anxiety, and tension) and as a remedy for sleeplessness and menopausal symptoms, among other uses. However, the ability of these supplements to provide such benefits has not been definitively determined, and they have in fact been shown to be ineffective for treating menopausal symptoms. Additionally, in 2002 the U.S. Food and Drug Administration issued a consumer advisory warning of the potential risk of rare but serious reactions—including hepatitis, cirrhosis, and liver failure—associated with use of kava-containing supplements. Kava has also been associated with depression of the central nervous system or coma (particularly in combination with prescribed anxiolytics), and other less serious adverse reactions (e.g., skin rash) have been reported as well. There are several known and potential interactions of kava with other agents (see DRUG INTERACTIONS), including anticoagulants, MONOAMINE OXIDASE INHIBITORS, and drugs metabolized by the CYTOCHROME P450 3A4 enzyme (e.g., clonidine, nefazodone, St. John's wort). Also called **ava**; **kava kava**.

K complex a characteristic brief, high-amplitude pattern of electrical activity recorded from the brain during the early stages of sleep. K complexes and SLEEP SPINDLES commonly occur during stage 2 sleep as a normal phenomenon (see SLEEP STAGES) but they may also be associated with nocturnal epileptic seizures.

keep-awake pills a popular name for stimulant pills that contain CAFFEINE as the active ingredient and can be obtained without a doctor's prescription. A keep-awake pill usually contains approximately 100 mg caffeine, equivalent to the amount of caffeine in one cup of regular coffee or two cups of strong tea.

Kegel exercises exercises designed to help women build strength and gain control of the pelvic-floor muscles. These exercises are used in the treatment of VAGINISMUS and play a role in increasing sexual pleasure. The muscle increases abdominal pressure by contracting, drawing the anus toward the pubis, as when an individual tightens control of the urinary sphincter. The exercises are therefore also used in the treatment of stress incontinence. [developed in 1948 by A. H. **Kegel**, 20th-century U.S. gynecologist]

Kemadrin *n.* a trade name for PROCYCLIDINE.

kernicterus *n.* a congenital disorder associated with excessive levels of orange bile pigment (bilirubin) in the newborn infant. It is characterized by severe jaundice and has the potential of causing severe damage to the central nervous system. Kernicterus is often a complication of RH BLOOD-GROUP INCOMPATIBILITY.

ketamine *n.* a drug that is closely related to PCP (phencyclidine). It acts as an antagonist at NMDA RECEPTORS and was formerly used as a DISSOCIATIVE ANESTHETIC. Disorientation and perceptual distortions may result from its use, which have limited its utility in surgical anesthesia but have made it a sought-after and common drug of abuse. It is ingested (in the form of tablets, capsules, or powder) by drug users for its hallucinogenic effects. U.S. trade name: **Ketalar**.

ketoconazole *n.* an antifungal agent that has been suggested as a treatment for depression resistant to conventional drugs, due to its ability to inhibit the biosynthesis of steroids. No large-scale clinical data support this. Ketoconazole is a potent inhibitor of numerous CYTOCHROME P450 enzymes (particularly CYP3A4), and has significant interactions with psychotropic drugs that utilize this metabolic path. Its numerous interactions and propensity to cause liver damage limit its use. U.S. trade name: **Nizoral**.

K

khat (**chat**; **kat**; **qat**) *n.* an herbal CNS STIMULANT obtained from the leaves and other parts of an evergreen shrub, *Catha edulis*, indigenous to northeast Africa and the Arabian peninsula. The leaves are traditionally chewed to produce mild stimulant effects (e.g., mental alertness, suppression of appetite and the need for sleep, general sense of well-being); they can also be used to make a tea. The substance responsible for khat's psychoactive properties is **cathinone**, a compound that is structurally similar to amphetamine. As with amphetamines, physiological tolerance and dependence and a variety of adverse reactions (e.g., behavioral disorganization and psychosis) may occur with continued or high-dose use. The use of khat has spread beyond its traditional boundaries to the United States and other Western countries. In many of those places, however, khat is illegal; it is classified by the U.S. Drug Enforcement Administration as a Schedule I controlled substance (see SCHEDULED DRUG).

KHOS abbreviation for KRANTZ HEALTH OPINION SURVEY.

Kiddie Schedule for Affective Disorders and Schizophrenia (**KSADS**) see SCHEDULE FOR AFFECTIVE DISORDERS AND SCHIZOPHRENIA.

kindness *n.* benevolent and helpful action intentionally directed toward another person. Kindness is motivated by the desire to help another, not to gain explicit reward or to avoid explicit punishment. See ALTRUISM. **—kind** *adj.*

kinesics technique the analysis of the BODY LANGUAGE (e.g., facial expressions) of a person. The technique is used particularly during the interviewing of a suspect.

kinesiology *n.* **1.** the study of the mechanics of body movement, especially their relationship to anatomical characteristics and physiological functions. **2.** a discipline that encompasses all the sport sciences as well as the professional skills for the application of sport and exercise knowledge. **—kinesiological** *adj.* **—kinesiologist** *n.*

kinesiotherapy *n.* the application of progressive physical exercise and activities to treat individuals with FUNCTIONAL LIMITATION or to aid those interested in improving or maintaining general physical and emotional health, formerly called **corrective therapy**. A **kinesiotherapist** (formerly a **corrective therapist**) is a certified professional who develops a specific treatment plan for each individual, determining appropriate therapeutic exercises and physical-education activities and directing their implementation.

kinetic information in clinical assessment and therapy, the observed gestures, postures, and other body-language clues used in making an evaluation of a client or patient.

Kinsey, Alfred (1894–1956) U.S. zoologist and sex researcher. Kinsey earned a doctorate of science at Harvard University in 1920 and then moved to Indiana University, where he remained for his entire teaching and research career, eventually serving as director of the Institute for Sex Research. His dissertation and early research involved studies of the gall wasp, but he is best known for his later scientific studies of human sexual behavior. Fifteen years of interviews with thousands of people culminated in two volumes that pioneered the field of SEXOLOGY: *Sexual Behavior in the Human Male* (1948) and *Sexual Behavior in the Human Female* (1953). These presented, for the first time, statistics on a range of human sexual behaviors, including such controversial issues as extramarital intercourse, masturbation, and homosexuality. Kinsey is also well known for developing what became known as the **Kinsey (Six) scale** (from 0 to 6), which provided an index of an individual's relative position on a continuum from homosexual to heterosexual.

Kinsey Institute for Research in Sex, Gender, and Reproduction a private nonprofit corporation affiliated with Indiana University whose mission is to promote interdisciplinary research and scholarship in the fields of human sexuality, gender, and reproduction. It was founded in 1947 by Alfred KINSEY, who served as its first director and carried out much of his pioneering research into human sexual behavior there.

Kirton Adaption–Innovation Inventory (**KAI**) a questionnaire, used chiefly in organizational settings, that is designed to measure creativity, cognitive style, and the degree to which individuals are adaptive, innovative, or a range of both in their approach to problem solving. It comprises 33 items (32 scored, 1 unscored) requiring participants to rate how difficult it is for them to be the person described (e.g., a person who is thorough) using a 17-point LIKERT SCALE format, ranging from "very hard" to "very easy." [originally developed in 1976 by Michael J. **Kirton**, British psychologist]

kissing behavior the activity of making contact with the lips, usually as a sign of friendship or affection. The kiss may involve lip contact with any part of the body and with varying degrees of pressure. Mouth-to-mouth kissing may include extension of the tongues (French kiss). Kissing behavior possibly is related to the licking behavior manifested by animals. It is not observed in all cultures.

Kleeblattschädel syndrome a type of birth defect characterized by a three-lobed skull caused by upward and lateral bulging of the brain through skull sutures. Affected individuals also have hydrocephalus, severe mental retardation, and abnormally short limbs. Also called **cloverleaf skull**. [from German *Kleeblatt*, "cloverleaf," and *Schädel*, "skull"]

Klein, Melanie (1882–1960) Austrian-born British psychoanalyst. Although she had no formal medical education, Klein trained as a psychoanalyst in Budapest under Hungarian psychoanalyst Sandor Ferenczi (1873–1933). Klein was a pioneer in CHILD ANALYSIS. She was the first therapist to use play as an analytic and treatment technique; she also suggested that the OEDIPUS COMPLEX, paranoid attitudes, and the SUPEREGO originate in very early infancy. While Klein's ideas were not readily accepted by the psychoanalytic establishment on the European continent, they found fertile soil in England. Ernest Jones (1879–1958), president of the British Psycho-Analytical Society, invited her to England, where her work was sufficiently well received for her to remain there for the rest of her life. Klein's theories differed from those of Anna FREUD, another pioneer of child analysis. While Anna Freud emphasized the development of the child's ego, Klein emphasized oedipal conflicts and the primary object relationship with the mother (see OBJECT RELATIONS THEORY). She also developed controversial ideas about the similarities between infant mental life and adult neuroses and psychoses. Through her work on the PARANOID-SCHIZOID POSITION, she contributed to knowledge of schizoid defense mechanisms. See also BAD BREAST; BAD OBJECT; DEPRESSIVE POSITION; EGO-SPLITTING; GOOD BREAST; GOOD OBJECT.

Kleinian *adj.* denoting or in accordance with the theories and methods of the school of psychoanalysis founded by Melanie KLEIN, including such concepts as INTERNALIZATION, OBJECT RELATIONS, the DEPRESSIVE POSITION, IDEALIZATION, and the PARANOID-SCHIZOID POSITION.

kleptolagnia *n.* a morbid urge to steal, considered by some theorists to be associated with sexual excitement. However, this association is controversial, and many consider the urge to be unrelated to sexual issues.

kleptomania *n.* an IMPULSE-CONTROL DISORDER characterized by a repeated failure to resist impulses to steal objects that have no immediate use or intrinsic value to the individual, accompanied by feelings of increased tension before committing the theft and either pleasure or relief during the act. The stealing is not done out of anger or in response to a delusion or hallucination and is not better accounted for by another disorder, such as conduct disorder or a manic episode. In *DSM–IV–TR*, kleptomania is included in the category IMPULSE-CONTROL DISORDERS NOT ELSEWHERE CLASSIFIED. **—kleptomaniac** *n.*

Klinefelter's syndrome a disorder in which males are born with an extra X chromosome, resulting in small testes, absence of sperm, enlarged breasts, mental retardation, and abnormal behavior. Also called **XXY syndrome**. [Harry F. **Klinefelter** (1912–1990), U.S. physician]

Klippel–Feil syndrome a congenital condition characterized by a short neck, low hairline, and a reduced number of vertebrae, some of which may be fused into a single mass. The condition is often accompanied by deafness and mental retardation. [Maurice **Klippel** (1858–1942), French neurologist; André **Feil** (1884–?), French neurologist]

klismaphilia *n.* interest in, and arousal from, the use of enemas in sexual activity. See PARAPHILIA NOT OTHERWISE SPECIFIED.

Klonopin *n.* a trade name for CLONAZEPAM.

knockout drops a popular name for a combination of CHLORAL HYDRATE (formerly in common use as a sedative but now rarely employed clinically) and alcohol, used surreptitiously to produce a sudden loss of consciousness. This combination was called a **Mickey Finn** and might be considered an early example of a DATE-RAPE DRUG.

Kocher–Debré–Sémélaigne syndrome a disorder of infants and children marked by weakness and overgrowth of muscles associated with cretinism and mental retardation in some cases. Also called **Debré–Sémélaigne syndrome**. [reported in 1892 by Emil Theodor **Kocher** (1841–1917), Swiss surgeon, and in the 1930s by Robert **Debré** (1882–1978), French pediatrician, and Georges **Sémélaigne**, 20th-century French pediatrician]

Koffka, Kurt (1886–1941) German experimental psychologist. After obtaining his PhD at the University of Berlin in 1908 under Carl Stumpf (1848–1936), Koffka worked with Wolfgang KÖHLER and Max WERTHEIMER on studies that led to the founding of GESTALT PSYCHOLOGY. Following a number of research and teaching positions in Germany, in the mid-1920s Koffka

K

took a series of teaching positions in the United States before settling into a research professorship at Smith College in Northampton, Massachusetts, in 1927. He spent the remainder of his career there, eventually becoming chief spokesperson for Gestalt psychology through articles and books that explained the theory and its applications. His most important writings include *Growth of the Mind* (1924) and *Principles of Gestalt Psychology* (1935). Koffka's research centered on visual perception, and his work contributed significantly to the understanding of visual phenomena. More broadly, Gestalt psychology presented a holistic view of the mind that contrasted sharply with the reductionist view offered by BEHAVIORISM, another prominent and contemporaneous school of psychology. See also HOLISM; REDUCTIONISM.

Köhler, Wolfgang (1887–1967) German experimental psychologist. Köhler earned a doctorate at the University of Berlin in 1909, studying under the psychologist Carl Stumpf (1848–1936) and the physicist Max Planck (1858–1947). He subsequently joined Max WERTHEIMER and Kurt KOFFKA in developing GESTALT PSYCHOLOGY. In 1913 Köhler became director of the Anthropoid Station at Tenerife for 7 years. During this time he published his book *The Mentality of Apes* (1917), which included his famous studies of insight in nonhuman primates. He demonstrated persuasively that even chimpanzees can "get an idea" in order to solve a problem, such as piling up boxes or putting sticks together to retrieve a piece of fruit placed out of their reach (see INSIGHT LEARNING). Köhler returned to Germany in 1920, ultimately becoming director of the Psychological Institute at Berlin, the most prestigious position for an experimental psychologist in Germany. When the Nazis came to power in the 1930s and began summarily dismissing Jewish and other professors from German universities, Köhler tried for 2 years to resist their policies within the institute but eventually gave up in frustration, moving to the United States. He became a professor at Swarthmore College in Pennsylvania for the remainder of his career. Apart from his book on apes, his most famous work includes *Gestalt Psychology* (1929) and *The Place of Value in the World of Facts* (1938). See also GOODNESS OF CONFIGURATION.

Kohnstamm test a demonstration frequently used in preparing an individual for hypnosis. The participant is asked first to stand next to a wall and press an arm tightly against it for a minute or two, thus numbing it, and then to step away, whereupon the arm spontaneously rises (an occurrence known as **Kohnstamm's phenomenon**). This demonstrates to the participant how it feels to yield passively to an external force, as in hypnosis. [Oskar **Kohnstamm** (1871–1917), German physician]

kola nut (**cola nut**) the seed of a tree, *Cola acuminata* or *Cola nitida*, that is native to tropical Africa and is cultivated in South America and the West Indies. The active ingredient is CAFFEINE, which comprises about 1.5% of the dry weight of the nut. Kola was discovered for the Western world in 1667 by a Congo missionary, Father Carli, who observed that local tribesmen chewed the nut before meals.

koprolagnia *n.* see COPROLAGNIA.

koprophemia *n.* see COPROPHEMIA.

koro *n.* a CULTURE-BOUND SYNDROME observed primarily in males in China and southeast Asia. It is an acute anxiety reaction in which the male suddenly fears that his penis is shrinking and will disappear into his abdomen, bringing death. (In females, the fear is focused on the vulva and nipples.) Individuals may also experience shame if they associate the fear with immoral sexual behavior. Also called **jinjinia bemar**; **rok-joo**; **shook yong**; **shuk yang**; **suk-yeong**; **suo yang**.

Korsakoff's syndrome a syndrome occurring primarily in cases of severe, chronic alcoholism. It is caused by thiamine (vitamin B_1) deficiency and damage to the MAMMILLARY BODIES. Patients with Korsakoff's syndrome demonstrate dense anterograde and retrograde amnesia (see AMNESIA) that are thought to be due to lesions in the anterior or dorsomedial nuclei (or both) of the thalamus. The selective and acute nature of the memory disorder in Korsakoff's syndrome sets it apart from alcoholic dementia (see ALCOHOL-INDUCED PERSISTING DEMENTIA), a syndrome characterized by more global impairments in intellectual functioning that evolve gradually over time. Korsakoff's syndrome often follows an episode of WERNICKE'S ENCEPHALOPATHY (see WERNICKE–KORSAKOFF SYNDROME). Also called **Korsakoff's disease**; **Korsakoff's psychosis**. [first described in 1887 by Sergei **Korsakoff** (1853–1900), Russian neurologist]

Kraepelin's disease a disorder that is characterized by depressive symptoms accompanied by psychotic features but does not meet the criteria for a MAJOR DEPRESSIVE EPISODE. [first described by Emil W. M. G. **Kraepelin** (1856–1926), German psychiatrist]

Kraepelin's theory the concept of DEMENTIA PRAECOX, the disorder now known as SCHIZOPHRENIA. Kraepelin's theory emphasized the progressive intellectual deterioration (dementia) and the early onset (praecox) of the disorder. [first presented in 1898 by Emil **Kraepelin**]

Krantz Health Opinion Survey (**KHOS**) a questionnaire to measure patient attitudes toward treatment and preferences for different approaches in health care. Participants indicate whether they agree or disagree with each of 16 statements (e.g., "I usually ask the doctor or nurse lots of questions about the procedures during a medical exam"), which are keyed so that high scores represent favorable attitudes toward self-directed care. Also called **Health Opinion Survey** (**HOS**). [developed in 1980 by David S.

Krantz (1949–), U.S. medical psychologist, and colleagues at the Uniformed University of the Health Sciences, Bethesda, Maryland]

Kretschmer typology a controversial classification of individuals based on a "clear biological affinity" between specific physiques and specific personality tendencies. According to this classification, the short, stocky (pyknic type) tends to be jovial and subject to mood swings; the frail (asthenic type) is likely to be introversive and sensitive; the muscular (athletic type) is usually energetic and aggressive; and the disproportioned (dysplastic type) presents a combination of traits but tends toward the asthenic. These tendencies were attributed to endocrine secretions. [formulated in the 1920s by German psychiatrist Ernst **Kretschmer** (1888–1964)]

KSADS abbreviation for Kiddie Schedule for Affective Disorders and Schizophrenia. See SCHEDULE FOR AFFECTIVE DISORDERS AND SCHIZOPHRENIA.

kymograph *n.* an instrument for recording temporal data in psychological or physiological research by tracing the variations of a particular parameter on a sheet of paper attached to a revolving drum. The resulting trace on the paper is a **kymogram**. Computer-output systems have largely replaced such instruments.

K

Ll

LAAM L-alpha-acetyl-methadol: a long-acting OPIOID AGONIST that is a chemical analog of METHADONE. A strong agonist at the mu OPIOID RECEPTOR, it is used in the management of opioid dependence because of its ability to suppress physical withdrawal symptoms and block the reinforcing effects of opioids. It has a longer HALF-LIFE (about 72 hours) than methadone and therefore needs to be taken only three times a week, which is a major advantage over methadone (which is taken daily). However, its possible adverse effects on heart rate and interactions with other drugs have limited its clinical use.

labeling *n.* in psychological assessment, classifying a patient according to a certain diagnostic category. Patient labeling may be incomplete or misleading, because not all cases conform to the sharply defined characteristics of the standard diagnostic categories.

labeling theory the sociological hypothesis that describing an individual in terms of particular behavioral characteristics may have a significant effect on his or her behavior, as a form of SELF-FULFILLING PROPHECY. For example, describing an individual as deviant and then treating him or her as such may result in mental disorder or delinquency. Also called **societal-reaction theory**. See also PRIMARY DEVIANCE.

la belle indifférence inappropriate lack of concern about the seriousness or implications of one's physical symptoms, often seen in CONVERSION DISORDER.

labile *adj.* **1.** liable to change. **2.** lacking emotional stability. See LABILE AFFECT. **3.** describing the early stage of memory formation that can be easily disrupted by factors influencing brain activity. **—lability** *n.*

labile affect highly variable, suddenly shifting emotional expression.

laconic speech see POVERTY OF SPEECH.

lacrimation *n.* crying, especially excessive crying.

lacuna *n.* (*pl.* **lacunae**) a gap or break, such as a gap in memory. **—lacunar** *adj.*

lacunar amnesia see LOCALIZED AMNESIA.

lalling *n.* an infantile form of speech characterized by the omission or substitution of sounds, particularly the substitution of the [l] sound for other sounds that are more difficult for the speaker to produce, for example, saying "lellow" for *yellow*. Lalling is considered a speech disorder when it persists beyond the age at which accurate articulation should have been acquired. See also PHONOLOGICAL DISORDER.

lalopathy *n.* any form of speech disorder.

lamotrigine *n.* an ANTICONVULSANT drug used as an adjunct in the treatment of adults with partial seizures and some generalized seizures and for maintenance treatment of bipolar disorder. Although ineffective in treating acute manic episodes, it has gained acceptance as a single-drug treatment for acute bipolar depression and rapid-cycling bipolar II disorder. Lamotrigine is presumed to exert its anticonvulsant and mood-stabilizing effects by inhibiting the release of GLUTAMATE from presynaptic neurons. Serious skin reactions, including STEVENS–JOHNSON SYNDROME, have been reported at the start of therapy, particularly in children. U.S. trade name: **Lamictal**.

Landmark Forum see ERHARD SEMINAR TRAINING.

Langdon Down's disease see DOWN SYNDROME.

language deficit an absence, loss, or delay in the normal speech and language development of a child due to some neurological dysfunction.

language disability any significant difficulty with or impairment of language development or function. When the difficulty or impairment is restricted to a specific aspect of language development or a specific language function, it is termed **specific language disability**. When the difficulty or impairment is more pervasive and not restricted to a particular aspect or function, the term **general language disability** is used.

language disorder see SPEECH AND LANGUAGE DISORDER.

language pathology see SPEECH AND LANGUAGE PATHOLOGY.

language retardation delayed acquisition of language skills, manifested, for example, by single word utterances or unintelligible sounds, due to neurological causes.

language therapy see SPEECH AND LANGUAGE THERAPY.

languishing *n.* the condition of absence of mental health, characterized by ennui, apathy, listlessness, and loss of interest in life. Compare FLOURISHING. **—languish** *vb.*

Lanterman Developmental Disabilities Act Californian legislation, introduced in 1969, that sets forth the rights and responsibilities of people with developmental disabilities and the structure of the system for planning, coordinating, and delivering services and supports to them. This act is noteworthy because, unlike similar statutes in most U.S. states, it has been interpreted judicially as establishing an entitlement to services. In a 1993 class action decision, reduction in the use of institutional settings and movement of institutional residents to community settings was ordered, as were specific changes to processes for individual planning of services and supports.

lapsus linguae see SLIP OF THE TONGUE.

Lariam *n.* a trade name for MEFLOQUINE.

Larodopa *n.* a trade name for LEVODOPA.

laryngeal cancer a malignant growth of the upper respiratory tract that affects mainly men over the age of 40 and accounts for about 4,200 deaths each year in the United States. The risk of laryngeal cancer increases with cigarette smoking, drinking alcoholic beverages, and living in urban areas; the incidence among cigarette smokers is approximately seven times that of the general population. Early symptoms include hoarseness or a feeling of soreness or a "lump" in the throat. As the cancer progresses, it interferes with breathing and swallowing. Treatment usually includes surgery or radiation, or both, the appropriate procedure depending upon the cancer site and the extent of its growth. If it is possible to correct the problem by excising only one vocal cord, the patient is trained to speak with the remaining vocal cord. If it is necessary to remove the entire larynx, the patient is trained to speak with the aid of an electronic device or by a technique of swallowing air into the esophagus and forcing it out again while the lips and teeth are manipulated to form speech sounds. However, the vocabulary of words that can be produced in this manner is limited.

Lashley, Karl Spencer (1890–1958) U.S. psychologist. Lashley earned his PhD in zoology and genetics at Johns Hopkins University in 1914. His dominant influences were the zoologist Herbert S. Jennings (1868–1947), behaviorist John B. WATSON, and neuropsychologist Shepherd I. Franz (1874–1933). Lashley taught at a number of universities before joining the faculty of Harvard University, where he taught from 1935 until his retirement in 1955. From 1942 until 1955 he also served as director of the Yerkes Laboratories of Primate Biology in Florida. Lashley was most influential in the fields of animal learning, comparative psychology, and neurophysiology. Perhaps most famous is the work summarized in his classic *Brain Mechanisms and Intelligence* (1929). In it, he showed that if portions of a rat's brain were damaged (through lesions or partial ablations), any disruption in learning or ability was only temporary; in time the brain could recover its functions unless very large portions were damaged. In essence, healthy portions of the brain could adapt and take over the work of damaged portions. Lashley used his research to counter cerebral localization theory, which asserted that when specific portions of the brain were damaged, the disrupted functions were definitively gone because brain function was extremely localized. Lashley's honors included election to the National Academy of Sciences and the American Academy of Arts and Sciences. See also LAW OF EQUIPOTENTIALITY; MASS ACTION.

Lasthenie de Ferjol syndrome a type of PATHOMIMICRY consisting of life-threatening hemorrhages caused by secretly self-inflicted wounds. It is linked with the pathology of mourning and introjection: Patients with this disorder have all experienced traumatic losses. The syndrome takes its name from a short story by French writer Jules Barbey D'Aurevilly (1808–1889).

latah (**lattah**) *n.* a CULTURE-BOUND SYNDROME first observed in Malaysia and Indonesia, although similar syndromes have been found in many other parts of the world. The condition primarily affects middle-aged women and is characterized by an exaggerated startle reaction. Its major symptoms, besides fearfulness, are imitative behavior in speech (see ECHOLALIA) and body movements (see ECHOPRAXIA), a compulsion to utter profanities and obscenities (see COPROLALIA), command obedience, and disorganization. See also IMU; JUMPING FRENCHMEN OF MAINE SYNDROME; MYRIACHIT.

late luteal phase dysphoric disorder see PREMENSTRUAL DYSPHORIC DISORDER.

latency stage in psychoanalytic theory, the stage of PSYCHOSEXUAL DEVELOPMENT in which overt sexual interest is sublimated and the child's attention is focused on skills and peer activities with members of his or her own sex. This stage is posited to last from about the resolution of the OEDIPUS COMPLEX, at about age 6, to the onset of puberty during the 11th or 12th year. Also called **latency**; **latency period**; **latency phase**; **latent stage**.

latent content **1.** the hidden or disguised meanings, wishes, and ideas beneath the MANIFEST CONTENT of any utterance or other form of communication. **2.** in psychoanalytic theory, the unconscious wishes seeking expression in dreams or fantasies. This unconscious material is posited to encounter censorship (see CENSOR) and to be distorted by the DREAM-WORK into symbolic representations in order to protect the EGO. Through DREAM ANALYSIS, the latent content may be uncovered. See also DREAM CENSORSHIP.

latent homosexuality gay or lesbian tendencies that have never been expressed overtly and are usually unrecognized (i.e., repressed) and actively denied by the individual. Also called **unconscious homosexuality**.

latent need a need that is assumed to be present in a person and determines behavior but is not in that person's conscious awareness.

latent stage see LATENCY STAGE.

L

latent trait theory a general psychometric theory contending that observed traits, such as intelligence, are reflections of more basic unobservable traits (i.e., latent traits). Several quantitative models (e.g., ITEM RESPONSE THEORY and FACTOR ANALYSIS) have been developed to allow for the identification and estimation of these latent traits from manifest observations.

latent variable a hypothetical, unobservable characteristic that is thought to underlie and explain observed, manifest attributes that are directly measurable. The values of latent variables are inferred from patterns of interrelationships among the MANIFEST VARIABLES.

late-onset schizophrenia a psychotic state that starts after middle age (typically after age 45). It is believed that late-onset schizophrenia is distinct from early-onset schizophrenia.

late paraphrenia any delusional disorder with onset after age 60. Late paraphrenia is used as a diagnostic entity in Europe and Britain, but is not listed in the *DSM–IV–TR*. Also called **late-onset paraphrenia**.

lateralization *n.* the relationship between handedness, eye dominance, footedness, and HEMISPHERIC LATERALIZATION. Observed more frequently in humans than in other primates, lateralization is manifested in the way tasks are performed and can also be extrapolated from the effects of localized brain damage. Directional confusion and DYSLEXIA are among disorders diagnosed through lateralization tests.

lateralized readiness potential (**LRP**) an EVENT-RELATED POTENTIAL that is a measure of the difference in activation between the left and right motor areas of the brain. This potential is taken to indicate preparation to respond with one hand or the other, since each hand is controlled by the contralateral hemisphere.

lateral thinking creative thinking that deliberately attempts to reexamine basic assumptions and change perspective or direction in order to provide a fresh approach to solving a problem. This term is often used synonymously with DIVERGENT THINKING. [defined by Maltese-born British psychologist Edward de Bono (1933–)]

later life adjustment adaptation to stress caused by events associated with life as an older adult, including chronic disease, familial loss, and lifestyle changes.

lattah *n.* see LATAH.

laudanum *n.* a mixture of alcohol and opium once commonly used as an analgesic and anesthetic. The mixture was introduced around 1530 by German alchemist and physician Paracelsus (1493–1541) and was widely consumed as an intoxicating beverage in 18th-century England.

laughing gas see NITROUS OXIDE.

laughter *n.* vocal expression of the emotions of amusement, enjoyment, or derision, characterized by inspiratory and expiratory movements occurring in rapid succession. Laughter is pleasurable because it serves to release tension built up when people listen to an amusing story or watch an amusing event. Laughter may also result when states of threat occur in a safe context (see AROUSAL JAG) or from an abrupt resolution of a cognitive incongruity. In psychoanalytic theory, laughter may be viewed as a defense against crying or embarrassment. Unrestrained or paroxysmal **laughing spells** have been found to precipitate cataplectic attacks, to be a common manifestation in manias, and to be an occasional symptom of psychomotor seizure among children, termed gelastic epilepsy. Spasmodic laughter, or GELASMUS, is also found in schizophrenia, hysteria, and organic (especially bulbar and pseudobulbar) diseases of the brain, as well as in CHOREOMANIA. **—laugh** *vb.*

Launois–le Cleret syndrome see FRÖHLICH'S SYNDROME.

Laurence–Moon–Biedl syndrome an autosomal recessive disorder that may be characterized by some degree of obesity, extra fingers or toes, below average intelligence, and ocular abnormalities, particularly of the retina. A common finding is progressive cone and rod degeneration and night blindness. Hypogonadism (small testicles) and hearing difficulty are often associated with the disorder. More than 75% of affected individuals tested have mental retardation. Also called **Laurence–Moon–Biedl–Bardet syndrome**; **retinodiencephalic degeneration**. [John Zachariah **Laurence** (1830–1874), British ophthalmologist; Robert C. **Moon** (1844–1914), U.S. ophthalmologist; Artur **Biedl** (1869–1933), Austrian physician]

law of constancy in psychoanalytic theory, see PRINCIPLE OF CONSTANCY.

law of equipotentiality the principle that intact areas of ASSOCIATION CORTEX can take over some functions of areas that have been destroyed, that is, different areas can function virtually equivalently. Based on behavioral studies of rats with cortical lesions, the law has subsequently been challenged by research involving more specific behavioral tests, which has shown that areas of association cortex have relatively specific functions. Also called **principle of equipotentiality**. See also MASS ACTION. [proposed in 1929 by Karl S. LASHLEY]

laxative addiction a dependence on the use of laxatives to induce bowel movements. The addiction is a vicious cycle, in which the use of laxatives gradually reduces bowel activity so that further use becomes the only way to avoid constipation. Laxative addiction is often associated with EATING DISORDERS in which laxatives are routinely used for purging. See also ENEMA ADDICTION; KLISMAPHILIA.

lay analysis psychoanalytic therapy performed by a person who has been trained in psychoanalytic theory and practice but is not a physician (i.e., a layperson). This is to be distinguished from psychoanalysis performed by a fully accredited PSYCHIATRIST.

LCU abbreviation for LIFE-CHANGE UNIT.

LD 1. abbreviation for LEARNING DISABILITY. **2.** abbreviation for LEARNING DISORDER. **3.** abbreviation for LETHAL DOSE.

L data life data: information about an individual gathered from his or her *l*ife record or life history. See also O DATA; Q DATA; T DATA.

LE abbreviation for LUPUS ERYTHEMATOSUS.

leaderless group discussion (**LGD**) an exchange of opinions, ideas, and information related to some topic by the members of a leaderless group. Such discussions are used in training and educational settings to provide participants with insights into their own and others' behaviors in open, unstructured group situations.

leaderless group therapy a form of GROUP THERAPY in which leaderless meetings are held either (a) on an occasional or regularly scheduled basis as an adjunct to the traditional therapist-led process or (b) on an entirely self-directed basis in which a group always meets without a designated leader.

leakage *n.* the unintended revelation that a person has a feeling or motive different from the one intended to be communicated to others. It may be manifested, for example, by frequent speech pauses when a person describes an event untruthfully. See VERBAL LEAKAGE. See also DECEPTION CLUE.

learned helplessness a phenomenon in which repeated exposure to uncontrollable stressors results in individuals failing to use any control opions that may later become available. Essentially, individuals learn that they lack behavioral control over environmental events, which, in turn, undermines the motivation to make changes or attempt to alter situations. Learned helplessness was first described in 1967 by U.S. psychologists J. Bruce Overmier (1938–) and Martin E. P. Seligman (1942–) following experiments in which animals exposed to a series of unavoidable electric shocks (see AVERSIVE STIMULUS) later failed to learn to escape these shocks when tested in a different apparatus, whereas animals exposed to shocks that could be terminated by a response did not show interference with escape learning in another apparatus. A SYNDROME with three features developed: (a) a motivational deficit characterized by a failure to respond when challenged with further aversive events; (b) an associative deficit characterized by impairment of learning from successful coping; and (c) an emotional deficit characterized by apparent underreactivity to painful events—although later research revealed by assaying corticoid levels that the animals were very stressed. In the 1970s Seligman extended the concept from nonhuman animal research to clinical depression in humans (see HELPLESSNESS THEORY). Subsequent researchers have noted a robust fit between the concept and POST-TRAUMATIC STRESS DISORDER.

learned optimism an acquired explanatory style that attributes causes for negative events to factors that are more external, unstable, and specific: that is, problems are believed to be caused by other people or situational factors, the causes are seen as fleeting in nature, and are localized to one or a few situations in one's life. According to LEARNED HELPLESSNESS theory, the manner in which individuals routinely explain the events in their lives can drain or enhance motivation, reduce or increase persistence, and enhance vulnerability to depression or protect against it, making learned optimism a putative mechanism by which therapy ameliorates depression.

learning *n.* the process of acquiring new and relatively enduring information, behavior patterns, or abilities, characterized by modification of behavior as a result of practice, study, or experience.

learning disabilities specialist an individual, usually working within an interdisciplinary team of school professionals, who is trained to identify and assist students with problems associated with learning disabilities.

learning disability (**LD**) any of various conditions with a neurological basis that are marked by substantial deficits in acquiring certain scholastic or academic skills, particularly those associated with written or expressive language. Learning disabilities include learning problems that result from perceptual disabilities, brain injury, and MINIMAL BRAIN DYSFUNCTION but exclude those that result from visual impairment or hearing loss, mental retardation, emotional disturbance, or environmental, cultural, or economic factors. For diagnostic purposes, learning disability is the condition that exists when a peron's actual performance on achievement testing is substantially (typically two standard deviations) below that expected for his or her established intelligence, age, and grade.

learning disorder (**LD**) in *DSM–IV–TR*, any neurologically based information-processing disorder characterized by achievement that is substantially below that achievement expected for the age, education, and intelligence of the individual, as measured by standardized tests in reading, mathematics, and written material. In standard practice, a discrepancy of two standard deviations must exist between general intelligence testing scores (as measured by a standard-normed IQ test) and achievement scores (as measured by a standard-normed achievement test). A discrepancy of between one and two deviations can be considered a learning disorder if some other special feature is present, such as a cognitive-processing disorder, a relevant mental disorder, a prominent medical disability, or exceptional absence from formal education. Major types of learning disorders are DISORDER OF WRITTEN EXPRESSION, MATHEMATICS DISORDER,

NONVERBAL LEARNING DISORDER, and READING DISORDER. This term essentially is synonymous with LEARNING DISABILITY.

learning disorder not otherwise specified in *DSM–IV–TR*, a learning disorder that does not meet the diagnostic criteria for any of the specific disorders of this category but nevertheless causes significant impairment of academic achievement, for example, because of problems in all three areas of reading, writing, and mathematics.

learning goal in the analysis of personality and goal-directed motivation of U.S. personality psychologist Carol Dweck (1946–), a goal to acquire mastery of a task or subject matter. Also called **mastery goal**.

learning paradigm in abnormal psychology, the theory that abnormal behavior is learned through the same processes as other forms of behavior.

Learning Potential Assessment Device (LPAD) a test that dynamically assesses individuals' learning potential. First used primarily for individuals with mental retardation, it has since been used for participants displaying a wide variety of skill levels. The test exists in individual and group versions; it is dynamic in that the examinee receives feedback about his or her performance while actually taking the test. The LPAD is intended primarily for clinical use, yielding interpretive data to help the examiner understand the examinee's pattern of strengths and weaknesses. [devised in 1985 by Romanian-born psychologist Reuven Feuerstein (1921–) and colleagues]

L

learning style see COGNITIVE STYLE.

least effort principle the basic behavioral hypothesis that an organism will choose a course of action that appears to require the smallest amount of effort or expenditure of energy.

least restrictive alternative the U.S. legal directive that less treatment rather than more (e.g., community care versus hospitalization) is the most desirable objective in treating people with chronic mental disorder. The principal consideration is combining safety concerns with the minimum level of restrictions on personal liberty. This position was emphasized in two decisions of U.S. Court of Appeals Judge David L. Bazelon (1910–1993) in 1966: *Rouse v. Cameron* and *Lake v. Cameron*.

least restrictive environment (LRE) in the United States, an educational setting that gives a student with disabilities the opportunity to receive instruction within a classroom that meets his or her learning needs and physical requirements. According to the Individuals With Disabilities Education Act, students with disabilities should be educated with students who do not have disabilities to the maximum extent possible, depending on the nature or severity of their disabilities. See also FULL INCLUSION; MAINSTREAMING.

least squares criterion the principle that one should estimate the values of the parameters of a model in such a way that will minimize the squared error of predictions from the model.

least squares regression see STEPWISE REGRESSION.

leaving the field the act of removing oneself from a situation when confronted with seemingly insurmountable obstacles, insoluble conflicts, or intensely frustrating problems. It may involve physical withdrawal, escape into PSYCHOGENIC illness, or some other behavior, such as distraction or changing the subject during a conversation.

lécheur *n.* a man or woman who performs CUNNILINGUS or FELLATIO. A female lécheur is more properly called a **lécheuse**. See also ORO-GENITAL ACTIVITY.

Lectopam *n.* a trade name for BROMAZEPAM.

left hemisphere the left half of the cerebrum, the part of the brain concerned with sensation and perception, motor control, and higher level cognitive processes. The two CEREBRAL HEMISPHERES differ somewhat in function; for example, in most people the left hemisphere has greater responsibility for speech. See HEMISPHERIC LATERALIZATION. Compare RIGHT HEMISPHERE.

left-hemisphere consciousness the claim by U.S. cognitive neuropsychologist Michael Gazzaniga that the hemisphere of the brain that controls speech (the left hemisphere in most people) is the seat of consciousness. Others, including Roger SPERRY, have proposed that both hemispheres are independently conscious (see RIGHT-HEMISPHERE CONSCIOUSNESS).

legal capacity the ability to acquire the knowledge and understanding necessary to make a rational choice regarding any issue that has legal implications (e.g., entering into contracts, making a will, standing trial). See also COMPETENCY TO STAND TRIAL.

legal psychiatry see FORENSIC PSYCHIATRY.

legal psychology see FORENSIC PSYCHOLOGY.

legasthenia *n.* a controversial syndrome in which the primary symptom is difficulty in synthesizing letters into words and analyzing words into their component letters, despite adequate intellectual and perceptual ability.

legibility *n.* the ease with which an environment can be cognitively represented, which determines one's ability to navigate or find one's way within an environment or setting. Landmarks, the overall shape or configuration of street grids, and building layout can significantly influence legibility. See also COGNITIVE MAP. **—legible** *adj.*

Lejeune syndrome see CRI DU CHAT SYNDROME.

length of stay (LOS) the length of an inpatient's continuous stay in a hospital. A UTILIZATION REVIEW will normally compare the LOS under review with regional norms, as expressed by the average LOS for the relevant diagnosis.

lesbianism *n.* female–female sexual orientation or behavior. The name is derived from Lesbos, an Aegean island where the poet Sappho (c. 600 BCE) wrote glowing accounts of erotic activities between women. Also called **Sapphism**. See also HOMOSEXUALITY. **—lesbian** *adj., n.*

Lesch–Nyhan syndrome an X-linked recessive disorder associated with deficiency of the enzyme HYPOXANTHINE–GUANINE PHOSPHORIBOSYLTRANSFERASE, overproduction of uric acid, and a tendency to compulsions involving self-mutilation by biting the lips and fingers. Affected individuals have mental retardation, with IQs generally below 50. Motor development deteriorates after the first 6 to 8 months of life, marked by spasticity, chorea (involuntary jerky movements), and athetosis (sinuous involuntary movements). Also called **hereditary choreoathetosis**; **hereditary hyperuricemia**. [described in 1964 by Michael **Lesch** (1939–) and William L. **Nyhan** (1926–), U.S. pediatricians]

lethal catatonia a form of acute maniacal excitement that in some cases leads to unexplained death. Also called **Bell's mania**; **deadly catatonia**; **exhaustion death**. See also HYPERMANIA. [first described in 1849 by U.S. physician Luther Vose Bell (1806–1862)]

lethal dose (**LD**) the minimum amount of a drug that is required to cause death. It is generally expressed in terms of the **median lethal dose** (**LD_{50}**; **LD-50**), the amount required to cause death (within a specified time frame) in 50% of nonhuman animals to which the drug is administered. See also THERAPEUTIC RATIO.

lethality *n.* the degree of dangerousness or likelihood of death associated with a particular course of action. The word is often used when comparing methods of committing suicide. **—lethal** *adj.*

lethality scale a set of criteria used to predict the probability of a suicide or attempted suicide occurring. A variety of such scales exist, most including gender, prior suicide attempts, and psychiatric diagnosis and history.

lethargy *n.* low energy level and lack of motivated behavior, often occurring in depression. **—lethargic** *adj.*

leucotomy *n.* see LOBOTOMY.

leukotomy (**leucotomy**) *n.* see LOBOTOMY.

leuprolide *n.* an analog of GONADOTROPIN-RELEASING HORMONE that opposes the action of androgens and estrogens through inhibition of GONADOTROPIN secretion. It is used for the treatment of uterine tumors, some forms of precocious puberty, and advanced prostate cancer. Because of its potent antiandrogen effects, it has been used controversially to perform CHEMICAL CASTRATION in repeat sex offenders. U.S. trade name (among others): **Lupron**.

level of significance see SIGNIFICANCE LEVEL.

levels of consciousness levels of awareness ranging from alert wakefulness, through relaxed wakefulness, drowsiness, sleep, and deep sleep to coma. Levels of consciousness can be indexed either behaviorally or by means of electroencephalographic or brain imaging methods.

levodopa (**L-dopa**) *n.* the naturally occurring form of dihydroxyphenylalanine (see DOPA), a precursor of the neurotransmitter dopamine. Synthetic levodopa is used in the treatment of Parkinson's disease (see DOPAMINE-RECEPTOR AGONISTS), usually in combination with carbidopa (see SINEMET). U.S. trade names: **Dopar**; **Larodopa**.

Levo-Dromoran *n.* a trade name for LEVORPHANOL.

levomepromazine *n.* see METHOTRIMEPRAZINE.

Levoprome *n.* a trade name for METHOTRIMEPRAZINE.

levorphanol *n.* an OPIOID ANALGESIC produced by manipulation of the morphine molecule. Levorphanol is approximately four to six times more potent as an analgesic than morphine and possesses similar risks of dependence and respiratory depression. U.S. trade name: **Levo-Dromoran**.

Lewin, Kurt (1890–1947) German-born U.S. psychologist. Lewin earned his PhD from the University of Berlin in 1916, studying under psychologist Carl Stumpf (1848–1936). He was heavily influenced by the nascent GESTALT PSYCHOLOGY as well as by the philosophy of Ernst Cassirer (1874–1945). The early part of Lewin's career was spent at the University of Berlin, but in 1933, with the rise of the Nazis in Germany, Lewin (a Jew) emigrated to the United States. He spent nearly a decade at the University of Iowa's Child Welfare Research Station, moving to the Massachusetts Institute of Technology's new Center for Group Dynamics in 1944. He was a founding member of the Society for the Psychological Study of Social Issues (SPSSI) and the Commission on Community Interrelations of the American Jewish Congress. Lewin is known for both his theoretical and experimental accomplishments. He developed a comprehensive and holistic FIELD THEORY, explaining human behavior as a function of various internal and external forces that together interact in a dynamic field. His book *Principles of Topological Psychology* (1936) attempted to formalize and mathematize field theory. His empirical studies have been even more influential. Particularly well known are his social psychological experiments on the styles of democratic leaders versus authoritarian leaders, on frustration and regression in children, on group COHESION, and on GROUP DYNAMICS, a term he coined in 1939. Opposing the trend to view science as value-free, Lewin promoted what he called action research, a type of socially engaged research, such as his research on intergroup relations with the Com-

L

mission on Community Interrelations. See also LIFE SPACE; SENSITIVITY TRAINING; T-GROUP.

Lewy body dementia a specific type of DEMENTIA associated with the presence of abnormal proteins called **Lewy bodies** in the brain. It is characterized by hallucinations and delusions occurring early in the disease process, marked day-to-day fluctuations in cognition, and spontaneous PARKINSONISM. [Frederich Heinrich **Lewy** (1885–1950), German neurologist]

lexical hypothesis the supposition that any significant individual difference, such as a central personality trait, will be encoded into the natural-language lexicon; that is, there will be a term to describe it in any or all of the languages of the world. Also called **fundamental lexical hypothesis**.

LGD abbreviation for LEADERLESS GROUP DISCUSSION.

libidinal development see PSYCHOSEXUAL DEVELOPMENT.

libidinal stage in psychoanalytic theory, any of the various defined stages of PSYCHOSEXUAL DEVELOPMENT, principally the ORAL STAGE, the ANAL STAGE, the PHALLIC STAGE, and the GENITAL STAGE.

libidinal transference in psychoanalysis, the TRANSFERENCE of the patient's LIBIDO, or feelings of love, from his or her parents onto his or her therapist.

libidinal types in psychoanalytic theory, a personality classification based on the distribution of LIBIDO, or sexual energy, in the psyche. In the **erotic type** the libido remains largely in the ID and the main interest is in loving and being loved. In the **obsessional type** the libido is largely invested in the SUPEREGO and the individual is dominated by conscience. In the **narcissistic type** the libido is primarily invested in the EGO and the main interest is in self-preservation, with little concern for others or for the dictates of the superego. [devised by Sigmund FREUD]

libidinization *n.* see EROTIZATION.

libido *n.* **1.** in psychoanalytic theory, either the PSYCHIC ENERGY of the LIFE INSTINCT in general, or the energy of the SEXUAL INSTINCT in particular. In his first formulation, Sigmund FREUD conceived of this energy as narrowly sexual, but subsequently he broadened the concept to include all expressions of love, pleasure, and self-preservation. See also EROS. **2.** in the ANALYTIC PSYCHOLOGY of Carl JUNG, the general life force that provides energy for all types of activities: biological, sexual, social, cultural, and creative. **3.** more generally, sexual energy or desire. **—libidinal** *adj.* **—libidinize** *vb.* **—libidinous** *adj.*

libido-binding activity an activity in which members of a therapy group concentrate libidinal energies on a specific interest or occupation, rather than on activities that stimulate the libido. Also called **immobilizing activity**. [introduced by Russian-born U.S. psychotherapist Samuel Richard Slavson (1890–1981)]

Librium *n.* a trade name for CHLORDIAZEPOXIDE.

license *n.* permission granted by a government agency for an individual or organization to engage in a given occupation or business on the basis of examination, proof of education, or both rather than on measures of performance. See PROFESSIONAL LICENSING. **—licensed** *adj.* **—licensure** *n.*

lie scale a group of items on a test (e.g., the MINNESOTA MULTIPHASIC PERSONALITY INVENTORY) used to help evaluate the general truthfulness of a person's responses on the test.

life-change unit (**LCU**) a unit of measurement on the LIFE EVENTS RATING SCALE, on which diverse life experiences are assigned numerical values in accordance with their stress-generating potential. For example, divorce and death of a spouse or significant other are ranked as high stress generators on the scale, retirement falls at about midscale, and moving to a new house and change in sleeping habits are ranked progressively lower. Some research indicates that individuals with a high cumulative LCU score (i.e., a high **potential-stress score**) show more health changes than other participants. See also LIFE CRISIS.

life coaching a form of teaching and encouragement (one-to-one or coach-to-group) based on counseling principles of sensitivity to needs and personality differences.

life crisis a period of distress and major adjustment associated with a significant life experience, such as divorce or death of a family member. In studies relating health to life crises, individuals experiencing recent major stress-producing experiences are more likely than others to show significant alterations in mental and physical health status.

life events important occasions throughout the life span that are either age-related and thus expected (e.g., marriage, retirement) or unrelated to age and unexpected (e.g., accidents, relocation). Contextual theories of personality often assume that personality is shaped by reactions to stress produced by CRITICAL LIFE EVENTS.

Life Events Rating Scale an instrument used to measure the relative impact of diverse stress-producing life experiences, changes, and crises. The derived score is expressed in LIFE-CHANGE UNITS.

life goal in the individual psychology of Alfred ADLER, the individual's concept of what he or she could attain in life, seen as a means of compensating for real or imagined inferiority. See also LIFE PLAN.

life history in therapy and counseling, a systematic account of the client's development from birth to the present, including the meaningful aspects of the client's emotional, social, and intellectual development. The account is taken by the therapist or counselor directly from the client and may additionally be derived from autobiographical material.

life-history method a STRUCTURED INTERVIEW that attempts to summarize historical data about events that are relevant to evaluating the person's current functioning.

life instinct in psychoanalytic theory, the drive comprising the SELF-PRESERVATION INSTINCT, which is aimed at individual survival, and the SEXUAL INSTINCT, which is aimed at the survival of the species. In the DUAL INSTINCT THEORY of Sigmund FREUD, the life instinct, or EROS, stands opposed to the DEATH INSTINCT, or THANATOS. Also called **erotic instinct**.

life lie 1. the false conviction held by some individuals that their life plan is bound to fail due to other people or to circumstances beyond their control. This was postulated as a method of freeing oneself from personal responsibility. [defined by Alfred ADLER] **2.** any false belief around which an individual's life is built.

lifeline *n.* a therapeutic technique used in group or individual therapy in which each individual draws lines representing his or her life, marking past and future expected events with angles indicating even, upward, or downward progression of functioning, as well as specific dates and the affect surrounding these events. Discussion of this diagram with the therapist can enhance awareness and understanding of the individual's life patterns.

life plan in the individual psychology of Alfred ADLER, an individual's style of life and GUIDING FICTION as he or she strives to reach his or her LIFE GOAL.

life review the tendency of individuals, especially older adults, to reflect upon and analyze past life experiences. Life review, or analytical REMINISCENCE, is often made use of in counseling older adults showing symptoms of mild depression or people with terminal illness, sometimes as an adjunct to psychotherapy. [defined in 1961 by U.S. psychiatrist Robert N. Butler (1927–2010)]

life satisfaction the extent to which a person finds life rich, meaningful, full, or of high quality. Numerous standardized measures have been developed to provide an index of a person's life satisfaction in comparison to various normative groups. Improved life satisfaction is often a goal of treatment, especially with older people. See also QUALITY OF LIFE.

life space in the FIELD THEORY of Kurt LEWIN, the "totality of possible events" for one person at a particular time, that is, a person's possible options together with the environment that contains them. The life space is a representation of the environmental, biological, social, and psychological influences that define one person's unique reality at a given moment in time. Contained within the life space are positive and negative valences, that is, forces or pressures on the individual to approach a goal or move away from a perceived danger.

life-space interview a form of CRISIS INTERVENTION involving techniques and strategies in which children in day and residential treatment are interviewed by staff members during moments of crisis or stress, for example, immediately after receiving an upsetting letter or after being attacked by another child. Efforts are made to convert these everyday events into therapeutic experiences by such means as restoring the children's belief in themselves and strengthening their ego. [originated by Austrian-born U.S. psychologist Fritz Redl (1902–1988)]

life-span contextualism a perspective on human development that views people as both products and producers of their own development, interacting throughout life with family, peers, and other social groups and institutions.

life-span developmental psychology the study of psychological and behavioral change across and within individuals from birth through death using a LIFE-SPAN PERSPECTIVE. Such an approach assumes that human developmental processes are complex, interactive, and fully understood only in the context of influencing events. It also assumes that there is no end state of maturity, that no specific period of the life course is more important or influential than another in subsequent development, and that not all developmental change is related to chronological age.

life-span perspective a general perspective emphasizing (a) that human development is a lifelong process of change; (b) that developmental change is multidimensional and multidirectional, involving both growth and decline in one's performance (e.g., of cognitive tasks); and (c) that there is plasticity in human behavior throughout the entire life span.

life stress severe strain produced by CRITICAL LIFE EVENTS or similar experiences, such as failure at work, marital separation, or loss of a loved one.

lifestyle *n.* **1.** the typical way of life or manner of living that is characteristic of an individual or group, as expressed by behaviors, attitudes, interests, and other factors. **2.** in the INDIVIDUAL PSYCHOLOGY of Alfred ADLER, an individual's characteristic way of overcoming or compensating for feelings of inadequacy. According to Adler, a lifestyle is first adopted in childhood, when the key factors informing it will be genetic endowment, upbringing, and interpersonal relations within the family.

lifetime personality the pattern of behavior that dominates a person's lifestyle between birth and death. [from the personality theory of U.S. psychologist Henry Alexander Murray (1893–1988)]

lifetime risk the odds of a person being diagnosed with a disease or condition during his or

L

her lifetime (usually stated in terms of 70 to 85 years). It is often important for individuals undergoing GENETIC COUNSELING to differentiate lifetime risk from the risk of being diagnosed with the disease in the next 5 or 10 years.

light therapy see PHOTOTHERAPY.

likelihood ratio the ratio of two probabilities, *a*/*b*, where *a* is the probability of obtaining the data observed if a particular research hypothesis (A) is true and *b* is the probability of obtaining the data observed when a different hypothesis (B) is true.

Likert scale a type of direct attitude measure that consists of statements reflecting strong positive or negative evaluations of an attitude object. Respondents indicate their reaction to each statement on a response scale ranging from "strongly agree" to "strongly disagree," and these ratings are summed to provide a total attitude score. Also called **Likert summated rating procedure**. [Rensis **Likert** (1903–1981), U.S. psychologist]

Lilliputian hallucination a VISUAL HALLUCINATION of objects, animals, or people greatly reduced in size, which may result from a number of conditions, such as DELIRIUM TREMENS, typhoid, or brain tumors in the temporal lobe. The name is derived from Jonathan Swift's *Gulliver's Travels* (1726), in which Gulliver journeys to the imaginary land of Lilliput, populated by tiny people. Also called **diminutive visual hallucination**; **microptic hallucination**.

limbic system a loosely defined, widespread group of brain nuclei that innervate each other to form a network that is involved in autonomic and visceral processes and mechanisms of emotion, memory, and learning. It includes portions of the cerebral cortex, THALAMUS, and certain subcortical structures, such as the AMYGDALA, HIPPOCAMPUS, and SEPTAL AREA.

Limbitrol *n.* a trade name for a combination of the tricyclic antidepressant AMITRIPTYLINE and the benzodiazepine CHLORDIAZEPOXIDE, appropriate for the treatment of concurrent anxiety and depression but not now commonly used.

limited competency a determination by a court that a person has the capacity to manage some but not all of his or her activities. A limited guardian is appointed to assist the individual in exercising certain legal rights, such as the right to enter into contracts, get married, provide consent (e.g., for medical treatment), or vote.

limited guardianship a form of legal guardianship of a child or adult with a disability (e.g., mental retardation) in which a guardian has authority with respect to some areas of activity (e.g., legal, financial, health-related) in which the ward is not capable.

limited symptom attack in *DSM–IV–TR*, a discrete episode of intense fear or discomfort in the absence of real danger that meets all the criteria for a PANIC ATTACK but features fewer than four somatic or cognitive symptoms.

limited-term psychotherapy see TIME-LIMITED PSYCHOTHERAPY.

linear *adj.* describing any relationship between two variables (*X* and *Y*) that can be expressed in the form $Y = a + bX$, where *a* and *b* are numerical constants. No COEFFICIENT can be raised to a power greater than 1 or be the denominator of a fraction. When depicted graphically, the relationship is a straight line.

linearity *n.* a relationship in which one variable is expressed as a linear function of another variable, that is, all COEFFICIENTS are to the first power. Linear relationships are often, but not necessarily, straight-line relationships.

linear model any model for empirical data that attempts to relate the values of the dependent variable to linear functions of the independent variables. Most commonly used statistical techniques (analysis of variance, regression analysis, etc.) can be represented as linear models.

linear regression a REGRESSION ANALYSIS that assumes that the predictor (independent) variable is related to the criterion (dependent) variable through a linear function.

linear system a system in which the response to a complex input is the sum of the separate responses to the separate components of the input (this is the principle of **superposition**). In addition, another condition (**homogeneity**) is necessary: If an input is increased by a certain factor, the output must increase by the same factor.

linear transformation a transformation of *X* to *Y* by means of the equation $Y = a + bX$, where *a* and *b* are numerical constants.

linguistic–kinesic method the objective study of disordered behavior in terms of language and movement involved in interactions between individuals.

Lioresal *n.* a trade name for BACLOFEN.

liothyronine *n.* a pharmaceutical preparation of L-TRIIODOTHYRONINE, a naturally occurring thyroid hormone, used to treat conditions associated with thyroid deficiency. Occasionally it is used as an adjunct to standard antidepressant therapy in the management of depression that has not responded to standard therapy alone. U.S. trade name (among others): **Cytomel**.

lip biting habitual biting of the lips, which may be a nervous habit, a stereotyped behavior (see STEREOTYPY), or associated with a disorder, such as LESCH–NYHAN SYNDROME. Also called **morsicatio labiorum**.

lipid-metabolism disorders a group of metabolic anomalies characterized by abnormal levels of fatty substances in the blood or other tissues, resulting from genetic, endocrine, or external factors or organ failure. Lipid-metabolism disorders include Niemann–Pick disease and Tay–Sachs disease.

lipodystrophy *n.* any disorder of lipid metabolism. Kinds of lipodystrophy include **intestinal lipodystrophy**, in which a malabsorption of fats from the digestive tract may be associated with lesions in the central nervous system (as in **Whipple's disease**); and **progressive lipodystrophy**, marked by a symmetrical loss of subcutaneous fat deposits and abnormal deposits of fat around the kidney, heart, and abdominal cavity. No consistent neurological abnormalities are associated with the latter form of lipodystrophy, but nearly 20% of the patients in one study showed signs of mental retardation. The cause of progressive lipodystrophy is unknown. Lipodystrophy is also associated with diabetes mellitus in a form marked by loss of subcutaneous fat in areas injected with insulin; this is known as **lipotrophic diabetes mellitus** or **insulin lipodystrophy**. Manifestations of lipodystrophy are also often found in people living with HIV.

lip pursing a facial contortion in which the lips protrude in a manner that resembles pouting or a snout. First described (as **Schnauzkrampf**) by German psychiatrist Karl Ludwig Kahlbaum (1828–1899), it is most commonly associated with CATATONIC SCHIZOPHRENIA.

liquidation of attachment the process of freeing a patient from a painful situation by unraveling the ATTACHMENTS in which he or she is bound. [defined by French psychologist Pierre Janet (1859–1947)]

listening *n.* an essential activity in therapy and counseling that involves attending to the words and actions of the client as well as to the intentions conveyed by the words. See also ACTIVE LISTENING.

listening attitude 1. in a therapeutic setting, a therapist's openness to a client's personal experience, or a client's openness to his or her own personal experience. **2.** a behavior set in which a person expects and prepares to receive a message. Italian-born U.S. psychiatrist Silvano Arieti (1914–1982) claimed that a person with schizophrenia who is habitually prepared to experience a hallucination may learn to avoid it when made aware of this attitude.

literary psychoanalysis the application of psychoanalysis and psychoanalytic theory to literary interpretation.

lithium *n.* an element of the alkali metal group whose salts are used in psychopharmacotherapy as MOOD STABILIZERS. Lithium salts were first used for the treatment of mania in the 1940s, but widespread use was limited by their toxicity. However, after further investigations into their role in treating bipolar depression, and better appreciation of the appropriate dosage, lithium salts entered broader clinical practice in the 1970s. Although its primary indication (appropriate use) is in managing bipolar disorder, lithium has some efficacy in managing acute manic phases and in reducing relapse. Its mechanism of action remains unclear; it most likely works via inhibition of the recycling of inositol from the INOSITOL PHOSPHATES, which are second messengers in cellular signaling. Toxic doses are no more than two to three times the therapeutic dose, and serum monitoring is required. Symptoms of acute toxicity include tremor, diarrhea, vomiting, and incoordination; at higher doses, disturbances of heart rhythm and neurological function leading to coma and death may occur. Long-term lithium use can cause thyroid and renal dysfunction in a small percentage of patients. Lithium has been associated with fetal cardiac malformation (Ebstein's malformation), and its use in pregnancy is not recommended. U.S. trade names (among others): **Eskalith**; **Lithobid**.

litigious paranoia a type of paranoid disorder characterized by constant quarreling, claims of persecution, and insistence that one's rights have been breached. The individual usually threatens to go to court—and frequently does so—to seek redress for exaggerated or fancied wrongs. Also called **paranoia querulans**; **paranoid litigious state**.

Little Hans a landmark case of Sigmund FREUD's, illustrating the OEDIPUS COMPLEX. Freud traced a child's phobia for horses to CASTRATION ANXIETY stemming from masturbation, to repressed death wishes toward the father, and to fear of retaliation owing to rivalry with the mother, with DISPLACEMENT of these emotions onto horses. Freud never actually met the boy but analyzed him through written communication with the father. The case was reported in "Analysis of a Phobia in a Five-Year-Old Boy" (1909).

living will see ADVANCE DIRECTIVE.

LNNB abbreviation for LURIA–NEBRASKA NEUROPSYCHOLOGICAL BATTERY.

lobe *n.* a subdivision of an organ, such as the brain or the lungs, particularly when rounded and surrounded by distinct structural boundaries, such as fissures. The four main lobes of each cerebral hemisphere of the brain are the FRONTAL LOBE, PARIETAL LOBE, TEMPORAL LOBE, and OCCIPITAL LOBE. There are also subdivisions of each of these lobes; for example, the temporal lobe comprises the inferior, middle, and superior temporal lobes. **—lobar** *adj.* **—lobate** *adj.*

lobectomy *n.* complete or partial surgical removal of a lobe, particularly in the brain. The most frequently performed lobectomy is done for seizure control and involves the anterior temporal lobe (see TEMPORAL LOBECTOMY).

lobotomy *n.* incision into various nerve tracts in the FRONTAL LOBE of the brain. The original surgical procedure, called **prefrontal** (or **frontal**) **lobotomy**, was introduced in 1936 by Portuguese neurologist Antonio Egas Moniz (1874–1955): Connections between the frontal lobe and other brain structures—notably the thalamus—were severed by manipulating a narrow blade known as a leukotome inserted into brain tissue through several small holes drilled in the skull. A second

L

procedure, called **transorbital lobotomy**, was devised in 1945 and involved the manipulation of a pointed instrument resembling an ice pick driven with a mallet through the thin bony wall of the eye socket and into the prefrontal brain. Both procedures were widely used to relieve the symtoms of severe mental disorder (including depression and schizophrenia) until the advent of ANTIPSYCHOTIC drugs in the 1950s. These operations have been replaced by more sophisticated, stereotactic forms of neurosurgery that are less invasive and whose effects are more certain and less damaging. Also called **leukotomy**.

LOC abbreviation for LOSS OF CONSCIOUSNESS.

localization of function the concept that specific parts of the cerebral cortex are relatively specialized for particular types of cognitive and behavioral processes. Also called **cortical localization**; **localization**.

localized amnesia a memory loss restricted to specific or isolated experiences. Also called **circumscribed anmesia**; **lacunar amnesia**.

locked-in syndrome a neurological condition, due to an injury to the brain, in which the individual is conscious but completely paralyzed, unable to speak or move. Cognition is intact, and electroencephalograms (see ELECTROENCEPHALOGRAPHY) are normal.

locked ward a secured hospital unit in which patients with severe mental disorders reside. The present trend is toward elimination of locked wards, since patients may feel they are being incarcerated and punished for being ill. Other factors leading to less frequent use of such wards are improvements in psychological interventions, the use of psychoactive drugs, an increase in the staff–patient ratio, and the concepts of the OPEN HOSPITAL and THERAPEUTIC COMMUNITY.

loco plant any of certain plants belonging to the genera *Astragalus* or *Oxytropis* that grow wild in western North America, particularly in the Rocky Mountains, and damage the nerve tissue of humans and animals that ingest them (*loco* is the Spanish word for "crazy"). The substances responsible include miserotoxin, swainsonine, and selenium. Symptoms of poisoning include muscular trembling or incoordination, staggering gait, and impairment of depth and other sensory perception. In sufficient doses, these toxins produce irreversible changes in the central nervous system, including brain lesions and eventual paralysis, and may cause coma or death. Also called **loco weed**.

locura *n.* a CULTURE-BOUND SYNDROME found among Latino groups in the United States and Latin America and attributed to hereditary vulnerability, the consequences of stressful and difficult life events, or a combination of the two. Symptoms include incoherence, agitation, auditory and visual hallucinations, social dysfunction, erratic behavior, and possibly violence.

locus *n.* (*pl.* **loci**) **1.** the place or position of an anatomical or pathological entity (e.g., a hemorrhage in the brain, a butterfly rash on the skin). **2.** the position of a gene on a chromosome.

locus of control a construct that is used to categorize people's basic motivational orientations and perceptions of how much control they have over the conditions of their lives. People with an **external locus of control** tend to behave in response to external circumstances and to perceive their life outcomes as arising from factors out of their control. People with an **internal locus of control** tend to behave in response to internal states and intentions and to perceive their life outcomes as arising from the exercise of their own agency and abilities. [introduced into psychology by U.S. psychologist Julian Rotter (1916–)]

logical positivism a philosophical perspective that is committed to the principle of VERIFICATION, which holds that the meaning and truth of all nontautological statements is dependent on empirical observation. In the early 20th century, the positivists of the so-called Vienna Circle sought to establish the essential unity of logic, philosophy, and science and to distinguish these disciplines from such others as metaphysics, ethics, and religion, which were dismissed for their speculative character. The positivist view of science was influential during the period in which psychology emerged as a science and has had a recognizable influence on the discipline. This is most pronounced in BEHAVIORISM and in psychology's commitment to empirical scientific methods. Logical positivism had waned by the middle of the century. See POSITIVISM. See also PHYSICALISM REDUCTIONISM.

logistic regression a statistical technique for the prediction of a binary DEPENDENT VARIABLE from one or more continuous variables.

logopathy *n.* a speech disorder of any kind.

logorrhea *n.* rapid, uncontrollable, and incoherent speech, sometimes occurring as part of a MANIC EPISODE. It was formerly known as **hyperlogia** or **hyperphrasia**. Also called **verbomania**.

logotherapy *n.* an approach to psychotherapy that focuses on the "human predicament," helping the client to overcome crises in meaning. The therapeutic process typically consists of examining three types of values: (a) creative (e.g., work, achievement); (b) experiential (e.g., art, science, philosophy, understanding, loving); and (c) attitudinal (e.g., facing pain and suffering). Each client is encouraged to arrive at his or her own solution, which should incorporate social responsibility and constructive relationships. Also called **meaning-centered therapy**. See also EXISTENTIAL PSYCHOTHERAPY; EXISTENTIALISM. [developed in the 1950s and 1960s by Austrian psychiatrist Viktor E. Frankl (1905–1997)]

Lokian personality a personality pattern characterized by the desire to cause distress to others, manipulative behavior, and deceit. The name is derived from Loki, the Norse god of mischief.

Lolita complex see NYMPHOLEPSY.

London syndrome explicit and constant resistance and refusal by hostages to do what captors expect during a hostage situation, first identified in 1981 after a hostage-taking incident in London. It may result in serious injury and death to the resistors.

loneliness *n.* affective and cognitive discomfort or uneasiness from being or perceiving oneself to be alone or otherwise solitary. Psychological theory and research offer multiple perspectives: Social psychology emphasizes the emotional distress that results when inherent needs for intimacy and companionship are not met; cognitive psychology emphasizes the unpleasant and unsettling experience that results from a perceived discrepancy (i.e., deficiency in quantity or quality) between an individual's desired and actual social relationships. Psychologists from the existential or humanistic perspectives may see loneliness as an inevitable, painful aspect of the human condition that, nevertheless, may contribute to increased self-awareness and renewal.

longitudinal *adj.* **1.** in anatomy, referring to the long AXIS of the body. **2.** in research, referring to the time dimension, that is, running over an extended period.

longitudinal design the study of a variable or group of variables in the same cases or participants over a period of time, sometimes of several years. An example of a longitudinal design is a comparative study of the same group of children in an urban and a suburban school over several years for the purpose of recording their cognitive development in depth. Compare CROSS-SECTIONAL DESIGN.

longitudinal stability the degree to which an individual's possession or expression of a psychological characteristic is consistent over a period.

long-term care facility an EXTENDED CARE institution, such as a NURSING HOME, that provides medical and personal services for patients who are unable to live independently but do not require the inpatient services of a hospital.

long-term depression (**LTD**) a long-lasting decrease in the amplitude of neuronal response due to persistent weak synaptic stimulation (in the case of the hippocampus) or strong synaptic stimulation (in the case of the cerebellum). Compare LONG-TERM POTENTIATION.

long-term memory (**LTM**) a relatively permanent information storage system, enabling one to retain, retrieve, and make use of skills and knowledge hours, weeks, or even years after they were originally learned. Various theories have been proposed to explain the biological processes by which this occurs and a major distinction is made between LTM and SHORT-TERM MEMORY. Additionally, LTM is divided into several categories, including DECLARATIVE MEMORY and PROCEDURAL MEMORY. See also SECONDARY MEMORY.

long-term potentiation (**LTP**) enhancement of synaptic transmission (see SYNAPSE), which can last for weeks, caused by repeated brief stimulations of one nerve cell that trigger stimulation of a succeeding cell. The capacity for potentiation has been best shown in hippocampal tissue. LTP is studied as a model of the neural changes that underlie memory formation and it may be a mechanism involved in some kinds of learning. Compare LONG-TERM DEPRESSION.

long-term therapy psychotherapy over a period of many months or years. Classic PSYCHOANALYSIS, which may last 2–5 years or longer, is a primary example.

loosening of associations a thought disturbance demonstrated by speech that is disconnected and fragmented, with the individual jumping from one idea to another unrelated or indirectly related idea. It is essentially equivalent to DERAILMENT.

loperamide *n.* an OPIOID that slows gastrointestinal motility and is used for the treatment of diarrhea. Because it is not effectively transported across the BLOOD–BRAIN BARRIER, it has few (if any) psychotropic effects and its abuse potential is low. U.S. trade name: **Imodium**.

lorazepam *n.* a highly potent BENZODIAZEPINE approved for the treatment of anxiety and as premedication in surgical anesthesia. Unlike many other benzodiazepines, it has no active metabolic products and therefore requires minimal processing in the liver. This, together with its predictable duration of action, make it a favored drug in the management of alcohol withdrawal in patients with liver impairment. U.S. trade name (among others): **Ativan**.

LOS abbreviation for LENGTH OF STAY.

loss of affect loss of the ability to respond emotionally, which results in FLAT AFFECT.

loss of consciousness (**LOC**) a state in which an organism capable of consciousness can no longer experience events or exert voluntary control. Examples of conditions associated with loss of consciousness include fainting (syncope), deep sleep, traumatic brain injury, coma, general anesthesia, narcolepsy, and epileptic absence.

love *n.* a complex yet basically integrated emotion involving strong feelings of affection and tenderness for the love object, pleasurable sensations in his or her presence, devotion to his or her well-being, and sensitivity to his or her reactions to oneself. Although love takes many forms, including concern for one's fellow humans (brotherly love), parental love, erotic love, SELF-LOVE, and identification with the totality of being (e.g., love of God), the TRIANGULAR THEORY OF LOVE proposes three essential components: passion, intimacy, and commitment.

Social psychological research in this area has focused largely on PASSIONATE LOVE, in which passion (sexual desire and excitement) is predominant, and COMPANIONATE LOVE, in which passion is relatively weak and commitment is strong.

lovemap *n.* a person's mental image of the ideal lover, the ideal love relationship, and ideal sexual activity with that partner, expressed in fantasy and in actual sexual behavior. It incorporates issues of SEXUAL ORIENTATION and also of desire for deviant behaviors (see PARAPHILIA), which are called **altered lovemaps.** [developed by New Zealand-born psychologist John Money (1921–2006)]

love need in MASLOW'S MOTIVATIONAL HIERARCHY, the third level of the hierarchy of needs, characterized by the striving for affiliation and acceptance. Also called **belongingness and love needs**; **social need**.

love object 1. the person in whom an individual invests the emotions of affection, devotion, and, usually, sexual interest. **2.** in psychoanalytic theory, the person who is loved by the individual's EGO, as opposed to the OBJECT that satisfies an INSTINCT.

L

love withdrawal a form of discipline in which parents threaten to withdraw their love and affection from children if they misbehave.

Lowe's syndrome see OCULOCEREBRORENAL SYNDROME.

low normal see BELOW AVERAGE.

low vision reduction of visual capacity (especially visual acuity and visual field), regardless of the underlying cause, that cannot be corrected to the normal range with glasses, contact lenses, or medical or surgical treatment. Low vision causes problems with various aspects of visual performance (e.g., mobility, reading) and is often associated with a decline in quality of life, an increased risk of depression, and decreased functional status. **Low vision services** provided to those with this condition include assessment of an individual's residual vision and instruction in the use of high-powered optical devices (see VISION REHABILITATION). Also called **partial sight**. See also BLINDNESS; VISUAL IMPAIRMENT.

loxapine *n.* an ANTIPSYCHOTIC introduced into the U.S. market in the early 1970s. Loxapine differs from the traditional antipsychotics in that it binds strongly to serotonergic as well as dopaminergic receptors. Although its chemical structure (see DIBENZOXAZEPINE) is similar to that of the atypical antipsychotic CLOZAPINE, loxapine has the same antipsychotic, antiemetic, sedative, and extrapyramidal properties as the traditional antipsychotic agents. U.S. trade name: **Loxitane**.

LPAD abbreviation for LEARNING POTENTIAL ASSESSMENT DEVICE.

LRE abbreviation for LEAST RESTRICTIVE ENVIRONMENT.

LRP abbreviation for LATERALIZED READINESS POTENTIAL.

LSD *ly*sergic acid *d*iethylamide: a highly potent HALLUCINOGEN that structurally resembles the neurotransmitter SEROTONIN and presumably exerts its psychoactive effects by acting as a PARTIAL AGONIST at the 5-HT_{2A} serotonin receptor. It was originally synthesized from the ERGOT ALKALOID lysergic acid in 1938 by Swiss chemist Albert Hoffman, who then discovered its hallucinogenic effects on accidental ingestion in 1943. At very low doses it is capable of producing visual distortions (sharpened sense of color) or frank hallucinations, together with feelings of euphoria or arousal; it became a widely used and controversial recreational drug during the mid-1960s and early 1970s. The effects of LSD were the subject of research during the 1950s as a possible model for psychosis, and various attempts were made to use LSD as an aid to psychotherapy (see PSYCHEDELIC THERAPY), although they did not prove effective. Although the drug is usually taken orally, it has been known to be injected subcutaneously or intravenously. It can also be smoked, in which case intoxication is quite mild.

LSD psychotherapy an experimental technique, used in the 1960s, in which the drug LSD (lysergic acid diethylamide) was administered to patients with chronic alcoholism and serious mental disorders (e.g., schizophrenia) as a means of facilitating the process of uncovering and reliving memories and increasing the patients' ability to communicate their thoughts and feelings. Subsequent research not only failed to confirm therapeutic value but also revealed significant physiological, behavioral, and mental health risks in the therapeutic use of LSD, resulting in the abandonment of the technique. See HALLUCINOGEN; PSYCHEDELIC THERAPY.

LTM abbreviation for LONG-TERM MEMORY.

LTP abbreviation for LONG-TERM POTENTIATION.

lucid dream a dream in which the sleeper is aware that he or she is dreaming and may be able to influence the progress of the dream narrative. Voluntary signaling of prespecified dream features is also possible.

lucid interval a period of mental clarity following a period of delirium, disorganization, or confusion brought on by a mental condition, such as a psychotic state.

lucidity *n.* a mental state in which a person may not have complete ability to reason or comprehend complex matters but has adequate mental powers to be legally responsible for his or her actions. **—lucid** *adj.*

ludes *n.* slang for METHAQUALONE.

Ludiomil *n.* a trade name for MAPROTILINE.

Luminal *n.* a trade name for PHENOBARBITAL.

lunacy *n.* **1.** an obsolete name for any mental illness. **2.** in legal use, an obsolete name for mental incompetence or legal INSANITY. **3.** the theory that some forms of mental illness correspond with the phases of the moon. See also MOON-PHASE STUDIES. —**lunatic** *adj., n.*

lunatic asylum an obsolete name for a psychiatric hospital or a mental institution.

Lunesta *n.* a trade name for ESZOPICLONE.

Lupron *n.* a trade name for LEUPROLIDE.

lupus erythematosus (**LE**) an autoimmune disorder causing chronic inflammation of connective tissue and characterized by joint pains, a butterfly-shaped rash on the nose and cheeks, and scaly red patches on the skin. The condition may be limited to the skin (**discoid lupus erythematosus**; **DLE**) or it may also affect internal organs, such as the heart, lungs, and central nervous system (**systemic lupus erythematosus**; **SLE**) and involve neurological abnormalities, such as seizures and psychosis.

Luria, Alexander R. (1902–1977) Russian neuropsychologist. Luria earned a degree in medicine in 1937 from the Moscow Medical School, having already worked in the field of psychology for over a decade. In the 1920s, before his medical training, Luria collaborated with Lev VYGOTSKY on the sociocultural theory of language. During World War II, Luria headed psychological services in a brain trauma hospital; following the war he became a faculty member in neuropsychology at Moscow University and head of the neuropsychological laboratory at the Burdenko Institute of Neurosurgery, from which he was forced to resign for political reasons. It is for his research and theories on brain trauma and brain function that Luria is perhaps best known. He developed a system of NEUROPSYCHOLOGICAL ASSESSMENT that aided in diagnosis, treatment, and rehabilitation of brain trauma patients. His assessment techniques also proved valuable in the cognitive assessment of children. Luria's work became influential outside Russia in the 1960s and 1970s. Some of his best known books include *The Working Brain* (1973), *Cognitive Development: Cultural and Social Foundations* (1976), *The Making of Mind* (1979), and *Language and Cognition* (1982).

Luria–Nebraska Neuropsychological Battery (**LNNB**) a set of tests to assess the cognitive functioning of individuals aged 15 years and older that is intended to represent a standardized, quantitative version of Alexander LURIA's neuropsychological testing procedures. The battery is available in two versions (Form I comprising 269 items and Form II comprising 279 items) and is used to diagnose general and specific cerebral dysfunction and to localize impaired brain areas. It includes 11 clinical scales, each representing different aspects of relevant skills: motor functions, tactile functions, visual functions, rhythm, receptive speech, expressive speech, writing, reading, arithmetic, memory, and intellectual processes; Form II also includes an intermediate-term memory scale. [originally developed in 1978 by U.S. clinical psychologists Charles J. Golden (1949–), Thomas A. Hammeke (1950–), and Arnold D. Purisch (1951–)]

lust *n.* a very intense desire, usually associated with erotic excitement or arousal.

lust murder an extreme form of SEXUAL SADISM in which an individual experiences sexual arousal from the murder of a partner during the sexual act, often including elaborate staging of the act and mutilation of the victim's body. Also called **erotophonophilia**. See also HOMICIDOPHILIA.

Luvox *n.* a trade name for FLUVOXAMINE.

lygophilia *n.* an abnormal desire to be in dark or gloomy places.

L

Lyme disease a multisystemic illness caused by spirochete bacteria transmitted through the bite of an infected deer tick. Initial effects are a red rash around the site of the bite as well as flulike symptoms of fever, fatigue, headache, and body ache. If left untreated, the disease can result in ARTHRITIS, neurological symptoms (e.g., severe headache and temporary paralysis), and problems with memory loss, concentration, sleep, and mood changes. Its manifestation of physical, cognitive, and psychiatric symptoms makes it difficult to diagnose. The disease was first recognized in 1975 after a large number of children in Lyme, Connecticut, and nearby towns were initially diagnosed with rheumatoid arthritis.

lysergic acid diethylamide see LSD.

lysinuria *n.* the presence of the amino acid lysine in the urine, due to deficiency of an enzyme involved in its metabolism. It is an inherited condition associated with muscle weakness and mental retardation.

Mm

M 1. abbreviation for memory. **2.** symbol for MEAN.

mace *n.* an aromatic spice made from the fibrous seed coat of the NUTMEG. Mace has been associated with the euphoric effects produced by nutmeg intoxication, although the active ingredients of nutmeg are concentrated primarily in the oil of the nut.

Machover Draw-a-Person Test (**DAP Test**) a projective technique based on the interpretation of drawings of human figures. The participant is given a sheet of blank paper and asked first to draw an entire person, without specification of details of age, sex, clothing, and so forth, and then to draw another person, without any specification other than that it must be of opposite sex from the first. The examiner, relying on his or her individual clinical experience, then interprets the drawings and any verbalizations the participant made while creating them in order to formulate a description of the participant's personality and identify signs of pathology. Various features of the drawings that are assessed include sequence of sex (whether a male or female is drawn first), the order in which body parts are drawn, distortions, omissions, size, and clothing, as well as more structural elements, such as direction of pencil strokes, shadings, and erasures. Analogous to this test is the **Machover Draw-a-House Test** (**DAH Test**). [developed in 1949 by Karen **Machover** (1902–1996), U.S. psychologist]

macrobiotics *n.* a theory of nutrition that is based on achieving balance and harmony between foods that are classified, according to the Chinese concept, as either yin or yang (the two opposite but contrary principles governing the universe in Chinese philosophy). **Macrobiotic diets** consist mainly of whole grains and vegetables, with fruit and occasional fish; animal products are avoided. Food is prepared and cooked in particular ways to preserve the yin and yang characteristics. [introduced to the West by Japanese educator George Ohsawa (1893–1966)]

macrocephaly *n.* a condition in which the head is abnormally large in relation to the rest of the body. It can result in moderate to severe mental retardation with impaired vision and seizures. Also called **megalocephaly**. Compare MICROCEPHALY. —**macrocephalic** *adj.*

MADD abbreviation for MOTHERS AGAINST DRUNK DRIVING.

Mad Hatter's disease a condition caused by chronic mercury poisoning and characterized by changes in mental status, emotional disturbance, gastrointestinal disturbances, and weakness or partial paralysis of the legs. The condition may also cause psychosis, behavioral changes, ERETHISM, and several other symptoms. Also called **Mad Hatter's syndrome**.

madness *n.* an obsolete name for mental illness or for legal INSANITY.

MAE abbreviation for MULTILINGUAL APHASIA EXAMINATION.

magic *n.* **1.** a system of practices in which humans attempt to manipulate natural or supernatural forces through such means as rituals, incantations, and spells. Magic had an important social role in many prescientific societies, where its practitioners often held great power and authority. In the modern world, magical belief has survived most obviously as an underground esoteric tradition but also in many popular superstitions and "New Age" practices. Magical rituals can be said to differ from religious rituals in that they involve a direct attempt to control certain physical facts (e.g., the weather), as opposed to a supplication to a higher power or powers. **2.** in some individuals with OBSESSIVE-COMPULSIVE DISORDER, attempts to allay anxiety by invoking certain numbers or performing certain rituals. See also MAGICAL THINKING. —**magical** *adj.*

magical thinking the belief that events or the behavior of others can be influenced by one's thoughts, wishes, or rituals. Magical thinking is typical of children up to 4 or 5 years of age, after which reality thinking begins to predominate.

magic bone see VOODOO DEATH.

magic circle a group technique, usually used with children, who gather in a circle and discuss personal issues and concerns. A variation for use in school was developed by U.S. psychiatrist William Glasser (1925–) to increase motivation for learning.

magic mushroom see PSILOCIN.

magic omnipotence see COSMIC IDENTIFICATION.

Magna Mater Carl JUNG'S ARCHETYPE of the primordial mother image, based on the Great Mother of the Roman gods, Cybele. She represents that which is loving, sustaining, and fostering of growth and creativity. See also MOTHER ARCHETYPE. [Latin: "great mother"]

magnetic resonance imaging (**MRI**) a noninvasive diagnostic technique that uses the responses of hydrogen in tissue molecules to strong magnetic impulses to form a three-dimensional picture of body organs and tissues (e.g., the brain) with more accuracy than COMPUTED TOMOGRAPHY. See also FUNCTIONAL MAGNETIC RESONANCE IMAGING.

magnetoencephalography (**MEG**) *n.* the measurement of the magnetic fields arising from the electrical activity of the brain, using a device called a **magnetoencephalograph** (MEG). See also SUPERCONDUCTING QUANTUM INTERFERENCE DEVICE.

magnitude of effect see EFFECT SIZE.

maieutic technique in psychotherapy, a commonly used form of SOCRATIC DIALOGUE in which pertinent questions are asked to achieve understanding on the part of the person being questioned. The questioner often already knows the answers. [from Greek *maieutikos*, literally: relating to midwifery or acting as a midwife]

main effect the consistent total effect of a particular independent variable on a dependent variable over all other independent variables in an experimental design. It is separate from, but may be obscured by, an INTERACTION EFFECT.

mainlining *n.* slang for taking illicit drugs by intravenous injection. See INTRAVENOUS DRUG USAGE. **—mainliner** *n.*

mainstreaming *n.* **1.** the placement of children with disabilities into regular classroom environments on a part-time basis, such that they attend only some regular education classes during the school day and spend the remaining time in special education classes. The aim is to offer each child the opportunity to learn in an environment that has the highest probability of facilitating rehabilitation efforts and supporting academic growth, although some critics have denounced the practice as requiring that children with disabilities "earn" their opportunity to participate in a regular classroom. See also FULL INCLUSION; LEAST RESTRICTIVE ENVIRONMENT. **2.** the return of recovered or deinstitutionalized patients to the community, where they receive rehabilitative assistance directed toward helping them achieve as full and normal a life as possible.

maintaining cause an influence in a person's environment that tends to maintain and reinforce maladaptive behavior. An example is the required participation at cocktail parties of a professional person with alcoholism.

maintenance therapy treatment or therapy designed to maintain patients in a stable condition and to promote gradual healing or prevent relapse. It usually (but not always) refers to **maintenance drug therapy** (**maintenance pharmacotherapy** or **prophylactic maintenance**). Drug therapy is generally divided into three phases—acute, continuation, and maintenance—roughly corresponding to intervals of 1 month, 6 months, and a year or longer. Patients who respond in the acute and continuation phases may be placed on maintenance pharmacotherapy in the hopes of preventing relapse. Drugs that may be used for maintenance include methadone (see METHADONE MAINTENANCE THERAPY), antipsychotics, lithium, and antidepressants. Prophylactic maintenance alone, however, does not eliminate relapse; for several conditions, evidence suggests that psychotherapy must also be included to minimize relapse. Although maintenance therapy is often continued indefinitely, patients should be periodically reassessed to determine if such treatment is still necessary.

major depressive disorder a DEPRESSIVE DISORDER in which the individual has experienced at least one MAJOR DEPRESSIVE EPISODE but has never experienced a MANIC EPISODE, MIXED EPISODE, or HYPOMANIC EPISODE. Also called **major depression**.

major depressive episode an episode of a MOOD DISORDER in which, for at least 2 weeks, the individual has either persistent depressed mood or ANHEDONIA as well as at least four other symptoms. These other symptoms include: poor or increased appetite with significant weight loss or gain; insomnia or excessive sleep; PSYCHOMOTOR AGITATION or PSYCHOMOTOR RETARDATION; loss of energy with fatigue; feelings of worthlessness or inappropriate guilt; reduced ability to concentrate or make decisions; and recurrent thoughts of death, SUICIDAL IDEATION, or ATTEMPTED SUICIDE. All of these symptoms cause significant distress or impair normal functioning (social, occupational, etc.). One or more major depressive episodes are a characteristic feature of MAJOR DEPRESSIVE DISORDER and bipolar II disorder and often occur in bipolar I disorder (see BIPOLAR DISORDER).

major tranquilizer see ANTIPSYCHOTIC.

maladaptation *n.* a condition in which biological traits or behavior patterns are detrimental, counterproductive, or otherwise interfere with optimal functioning in various domains, such as successful interaction with the environment and effectual coping with the challenges and stresses of daily life. Compare ADAPTATION. **—maladaptive** *adj.*

maladjustment *n.* **1.** inability to maintain effective relationships, function successfully in various domains, or cope with difficulties and stresses. **2.** any emotional disturbance of a relatively minor nature. **—maladjusted** *adj.*

malaise *n.* a vague feeling of general illness, discomfort, or uneasiness.

mal de ojo a CULTURE-BOUND SYNDROME, reported in many Mediterranean regions, that is characterized by fever, sleep disturbances, and gastrointestinal problems. It most commonly affects children; the Spanish name translates to *evil eye*.

mal de pelea a CULTURE-BOUND SYNDROME found in Puerto Rico that is similar to AMOK. Individuals experience a period of brooding and then suddenly become violent and attack others around them (the Spanish name literally means "fighting sickness"). Also called **Puerto Rican syndrome**.

maldevelopment *n.* the abnormal development of an individual because of genetic, dietary, or external factors that interfere with growth of tissues and bodily functions.

male climacteric a hypothetical period in some men's lives that has been compared to female menopause (see CLIMACTERIC). Popularly known as **male menopause**, it occurs some 10 years later than in women and appears to be associated with declines in the levels of various hormones, such as testosterone. Symptoms, when they occur, include fatigue, problems with memory and concentration, decreased sexual desire, erectile dysfunction, and (in some cases) depression. Also called **andropause**; **male climacterium**.

male continence see EJACULATIO RETARDATA; COITUS RESERVATUS.

male erectile disorder in *DSM–IV–TR*, persistent or recurrent inability in a man to achieve or maintain an erection adequate to complete the sex act. It causes marked distress and impairment of interpersonal relations and is not due to the physiological effects of a physical disorder, medication, or a substance of abuse. The disorder may be lifelong or acquired and either situational (occurring only in certain situations or with certain partners) or generalized (occurring in all situations). See also ERECTILE DYSFUNCTION; IMPOTENCE.

M

male homosexual prostitution sexual contact between males for the financial or other gain of one of the participants. Studies indicate that a social hierarchy exists among male prostitutes, as in female prostitution. Lowest in status are the **street hustlers**, who are usually teenage boys and not necessarily gay themselves; next are the **bar hustlers**; and highest in prestige are the **call boys**, who do not solicit in public.

maleness *n.* the quality of being male in the anatomical and physiological sense by virtue of possessing the XY combination of SEX CHROMOSOMES. Compare MASCULINITY.

male orgasmic disorder in *DSM–IV–TR*, persistent or recurrent delay in, or absence of, male orgasm during sexual stimulation that produces arousal. The man's age and the quality and duration of stimulation are considered in making this diagnosis, which does not apply if the condition is due only to the effects of drugs, medications, or medical conditions.

male sexual disorder any problem in sexual function experienced by males. See HYPOACTIVE SEXUAL DESIRE DISORDER; MALE ORGASMIC DISORDER; PREMATURE EJACULATION; PRIMARY ERECTILE DYSFUNCTION; SECONDARY ERECTILE DYSFUNCTION.

malevolent transformation the feeling that one lives among enemies and can trust no one. This attitude, purported to be the result of harsh or unfair treatment during childhood, has been posited to be the basis for social withdrawal, hostility, and, in some cases, mental disorder of a persecutory nature. [first described by U.S. psychiatrist Harry Stack Sullivan (1892–1949)]

malformation *n.* any abnormality of structure: a deformity.

malice aforethought the mental elements of PREMEDITATION and deliberation or extreme disregard for human life that are required for a person to be convicted of first-degree murder.

malignant *adj.* **1.** describing a disorder that gets progressively worse or is resistant to treatment, eventually causing death. **2.** describing a tumor that invades and destroys tissues and may also spread to other sites (i.e., undergo metastasis). See CANCER; NEOPLASM. Compare BENIGN.

mali-mali *n.* a CULTURE-BOUND SYNDROME found in the Philippines, with symptoms similar to those of LATAH.

malingering *n.* the deliberate feigning of an illness or disability to achieve a particular desired outcome (e.g., financial gain or escaping responsibility, punishment, imprisonment, or military duty). For example, it may take the form of faking mental illness as a defense in a trial, faking physical illness to win compensation, and, in sport, faking an injury or misinforming people of one's state of rehabilitation in order to avoid practicing or playing. Malingering is distinguished from FACTITIOUS DISORDER in that it involves a specific external factor as the motivating force. **—malingerer** *n.*

malnutrition *n.* a state of health characterized by an improper balance of carbohydrates, fats, proteins, vitamins, and minerals in the diet with respect to energy needs as reflected in physical activity. Malnutrition may be due to excessive intakes of food categories, as in OBESITY and hypervitaminosis (see VITAMIN A TOXICITY; VITAMIN D TOXICITY), as well as inadequate levels. Dietary deficiencies are associated with many physical and psychological disorders. For example, nicotinic acid deficiency is marked by depression and other mental disturbances (see PELLAGRA). See also KWASHIORKOR; MARASMUS; VITAMIN DEFICIENCY.

malpractice *n.* professional misconduct or negligent behavior on the part of a practitioner (e.g., a psychotherapist, psychiatrist, doctor, lawyer, or financial adviser) that may lead to legal action.

mal puesto see ROOTWORK.

maltreatment *n.* ABUSE or NEGLECT of another person, which may involve emotional, sexual, or physical action or inaction, the severity or chronicity of which can result in significant harm or injury. Maltreatment also includes such actions as exploitation and denial of basic needs (e.g., food, shelter, medical attention).

mammalingus *n.* the act of suckling the breast during sexual intercourse, particularly in terms of the concept, proposed by British psychoanalyst Ernest Jones (1879–1958), that the act represents a type of fellatio. Mammalingus is distinguished from the normal interest and pleasure derived from caressing or orally stimulating the breasts as a part of sexual activity.

mammillary body either of a pair of small, spherical nuclei at the base of the brain, slightly posterior to the infundibulum (pituitary stalk), that are components of the LIMBIC SYSTEM. Also called **corpus mammillare**.

managed behavioral health organization (**MBHO**) a health maintenance organization (see HMO) that specializes in the management, administration, and provision of health care benefits with an emphasis on BEHAVIORAL HEALTH.

managed care any system of health care delivery that regulates the use of member benefits to contain expenses. The term originally referred to prepaid health plans (e.g., HMOs) but is now applied to many different kinds of reimbursement and UTILIZATION REVIEW mechanisms. It is also used to denote the organization of health care services and facilities into groups to increase cost-effectiveness. **Managed care organizations** (**MCOs**) include HMOs, PPOs (preferred provider organizations), point of service plans (POSs), exclusive provider organizations (EPOs), PHYSICIAN–HOSPITAL ORGANIZATIONS (PHOs), INTEGRATED DELIVERY SYSTEMS (IDSs), and INDEPENDENT PRACTICE ASSOCIATIONS (IPAs).

mandated reporting the legal requirement in the United States that psychologists and other human services personnel (e.g., social workers and nurses) report any suspected or known cases of child abuse or neglect. Those who fail to report such cases may be subject to legal and professional sanctions.

mandibulofacial dysostosis see TREACHER COLLINS SYNDROME.

mandrake *n.* the root or other parts of the plant *Mandragora officinarum*, traditionally used as an anesthetic, aphrodisiac, hallucinogen, and folk remedy for asthma, whooping cough, stomach ulcers, and other conditions. The name derives from the supposed resemblance of the root to the human form; *-drake* (from the Old English word for dragon) alludes to the alleged magical powers of the plant. A member of the nightshade family, it contains the anticholinergic alkaloids SCOPOLAMINE, mandragorine, and hyoscyamine, which are poisonous and potentially fatal. Symptoms of poisoning include flushing, pupillary dilation, dry mucous membranes, and dry mouth, progressing to visual disturbances, hallucinations, restlessness, agitation, delirium, and possibly death from respiratory failure.

mania *n.* **1.** a MANIC EPISODE or, sometimes, a HYPOMANIC EPISODE. **2.** excitement, overactivity, and PSYCHOMOTOR AGITATION, often accompanied by impaired judgment. **3.** excessive preoccupation with a particular activity or idea.

mania a potu see IDIOSYNCRATIC INTOXICATION.

maniac *n.* **1.** a lay term for a mentally or emotionally disturbed person, particularly one who is considered dangerous to others. **2.** an obsolete name for a person who experiences MANIA. See also MANIC.

manic 1. *adj.* relating to MANIA. **2.** *n.* an obsolete name for a person experiencing a MANIC EPISODE.

manic-depressive illness see BIPOLAR DISORDER.

manic episode a period lasting at least 1 week characterized by elevated, expansive, or irritable mood with three or more of the following symptoms: an increase in activity or PSYCHOMOTOR AGITATION; talkativeness or PRESSURED SPEECH; FLIGHT OF IDEAS or racing thoughts; inflated self-esteem or grandiosity; a decreased need for sleep; extreme distractibility; and involvement in pleasurable activities that are likely to have unfortunate consequences, such as buying sprees, foolish investments, sexual indiscretions, or reckless driving. All of these symptoms impair normal functioning and relationships with others. One or more manic episodes are characteristic of bipolar I disorder (see BIPOLAR DISORDER). See also MIXED EPISODE.

manic state a condition that meets all the criteria for a MANIC EPISODE or a HYPOMANIC EPISODE with regard to symptoms but not necessarily the duration required.

manifest anxiety in psychoanalysis, anxiety with overt symptoms that indicate underlying emotional conflict or repression.

Manifest Anxiety Scale see CHILDREN'S MANIFEST ANXIETY SCALE; TAYLOR MANIFEST ANXIETY SCALE.

manifestation *n.* an observable expression, indication, or sign of a physical or psychological condition.

manifest content 1. the matter that is overtly expressed and consciously intended in any utterance or other form of communication. **2.** in psychoanalytic theory, the images and events of a DREAM or FANTASY as experienced and recalled by the dreamer or fantasist, as opposed to the LATENT CONTENT, which is posited to contain the hidden meaning. See also DREAM ANALYSIS; DREAM CENSORSHIP; DREAM-WORK.

manifest goal in evaluation research, an openly stated, objectively defined goal or objective of an organization or program. Manifest goals are specified by indicators of success and assessed in an evaluation program.

manifest variable a variable that is directly observed or measured, as opposed to one whose value is inferred (see LATENT VARIABLE).

manipulation *n.* conscious behavior designed to exploit, control, or otherwise influence others to one's advantage.

manipulation check any means by which an

experimenter evaluates the efficacy of the experimental manipulation, that is, verifies that the manipulation affected the participants as intended.

manipulative behavior see MANIPULATION.

mannosidosis *n.* a rare and progressive disorder involving deficient activity of an enzyme (α-mannosidase) needed to metabolize the sugar mannose. Affected individuals have slow motor development, mental retardation, and hypotonic (flaccid) muscles, although these effects vary in magnitude. Laboratory tests may reveal brain and liver levels of mannose 8 to 10 times normal. It is thought to be an autosomal recessive trait.

MANOVA acronym for MULTIVARIATE ANALYSIS OF VARIANCE.

mantra *n.* **1.** in Hinduism and Buddhism, a sacred utterance, such as a syllable, phrase, or hymn (often in Sanskrit). **2.** any verbal formula used for spiritual, religious, or meditative purposes to help block out extraneous thoughts and induce a state of relaxation that enables the individual to reach a deeper level of consciousness. See also CONCENTRATIVE MEDITATION; TRANSCENDENTAL MEDITATION. Compare YANTRA.

manual arts therapy training in industrial arts, such as woodworking and metalworking, for therapeutic purposes as part of the rehabilitation process. See also OCCUPATIONAL THERAPY.

M

manual-assisted therapy see MANUALIZED THERAPY.

manual-based therapy see MANUALIZED THERAPY.

manualized therapy interventions that are performed according to specific guidelines for administration, maximizing the probability of therapy being conducted consistently across settings, therapists, and clients. Also called **manual-assisted therapy**; **manual-based therapy**.

MAO abbreviation for MONOAMINE OXIDASE.

MAOI (**MAO inhibitor**) abbreviation for MONOAMINE OXIDASE INHIBITOR.

maple-sugar urine disease (**MSUD**) a disorder of amino acid metabolism involving a deficiency of enzymes required for processing the amino acids leucine, isoleucine, valine, and alloisoleucine. The urine and sweat of affected individuals have a distinctive maple-syrup odor. Other characteristics include mental retardation, increased muscle tension, altered reflexes, and convulsions. Special diets, dialysis, and transfusions are among the therapeutic measures needed. Also called **maple-syrup urine disease**.

maprotiline *n.* a tetracyclic antidepressant closely related to the TRICYCLIC ANTIDEPRESSANTS. Like the tricyclic agents, it can cause adverse ANTICHOLINERGIC EFFECTS and serious disturbances in heart rhythm; its use has therefore declined, and it is rarely encountered in modern clinical practice. U.S. trade name: **Ludiomil**.

marasmus *n.* a condition, usually occurring in infancy, that is characterized by apathy, withdrawal, and emaciation (from Greek *marasmos*, "consumption") resulting from severe protein–energy malnutrition. If left untreated, it can result in delayed physical and cognitive development and, in some cases, death. Marasmus tends to occur mostly in developing countries, often as a result of premature or abrupt weaning, famine, or vitamin insufficiency due to limitations in food variety. It can, however, occur in developed nations as well—for example, in children living in poor rural and urban areas, children with chronic disease, and children who are institutionalized. Also called **infantile atrophy**. See also KWASHIORKOR.

marathon group an ENCOUNTER GROUP that meets in seclusion for a long period, usually varying from 6 hours to several days. Marathon groups are based on the theory that a single, extended session will elicit more intense interactions, foster a greater sense of intimacy and sharing, and encourage a freer expression of feelings as the time elapses than a series of shorter, interrupted sessions. They are often organized around addressing a single issue or related set of issues. See also TIME-EXTENDED THERAPY.

marginal consciousness the background contents of CONSCIOUSNESS that, although above the threshold of awareness, are not the center of attention. Marginal stimuli are not equivalent to subliminal stimuli (see SUBLIMINAL PERCEPTION).

marginal frequency the sum of any one of the rows or columns in a data matrix, such as a table of students classified by sex and area of study. In this example, the number of female students, regardless of area of study, would be one marginal frequency, and the number of students enrolled in a specific area of study, regardless of sex, would be another. Also called **marginal**.

margin of error a statistic expressing the CONFIDENCE INTERVAL associated with a given measurement; it is an allowance for a slight miscalculation or an acceptable deviation. The larger the margin of error for the sample data, the less confidence one has that the results obtained are accurate for the entire population of interest.

marijuana (**marihuana**) *n.* see CANNABIS.

Marinesco–Sjögren syndrome an autosomal recessive hereditary disorder marked by cataracts, short stature, CEREBELLAR ATAXIA (incoordination of voluntary movements), and mental retardation. Affected individuals have cataracts in both eyes; some have very small heads (see MICROCEPHALY). Cerebellar ataxia is present at infancy, and mild to moderate mental retardation becomes evident. Affected individuals may live well past middle age but often lose their ability to walk because of progressive muscle weakness. [reported in the 1930s by Georges **Marinesco** (1864–1938), Romanian neurologist, and Torsten **Sjögren** (1896–1974), Swedish physician]

Marinol *n.* a trade name for dronabinol. See TETRAHYDROCANNABINOL.

marital adjustment the process by which married couples attain mutual gratification and achieve common goals while simultaneously maintaining an appropriate degree of individuality. Especially important to marital adjustment are (a) the sharing of experiences, interests, and values; (b) respect for the partner's individual needs, aims, and temperament; (c) maintenance of open lines of communication and expression of feeling; (d) clarifying roles and responsibilities; (e) cooperation in decision making, problem solving, and rearing of children; and (f) attainment of mutual sexual gratification.

marital conflict open or latent antagonism between marriage partners. The nature and intensity of conflicts varies greatly, but studies indicate that the prime sources are often sexual disagreement, child-rearing differences, temperamental differences (particularly the tendency of one partner to dominate), and, to a lesser extent, religious differences, differences in values and interests, and disagreements over money management.

marital counseling see MARRIAGE COUNSELING.

marital schism a condition of open discord between marital partners, which puts a strain on the marriage and may lead to separation or divorce.

marital skew a defective family pattern in which the pathological behavior of the dominant partner is accepted by the other partner. See also COLLUSIONAL MARRIAGE.

marital subsystem the relationship between two spouses or partners in a family and their particular interactional rules for cooperation, conflict, and conflict resolution over marital issues (e.g., child rearing).

marital therapy see COUPLES THERAPY.

marketing orientation in the existential psychoanalysis of Erich FROMM, a character pattern in which the individual regards people as commodities and evaluates personal worth in terms of salability. Attributes perceived as leading to business or social success are valued more than knowledge, creativity, integrity, or dedication. According to Fromm, the marketing orientation contributes to shallow relationships and alienation from self and society. Also called **marketing character**. See also EXPLOITATIVE ORIENTATION; HOARDING ORIENTATION.

Marlowe–Crowne Social Desirability Scale (**M–C SDS**) a widely used research scale that attempts to assess the degree to which participants answer questions in such a manner as to present themselves in a favorable light. Test scores are often used in research where people might be inclined to bias their behavior in a socially desirable direction, rather than being perfectly frank. Although currently available in a variety of forms, the Marlowe–Crowne scale as it was originally developed in 1960 consisted of 33 self-descriptive statements (e.g., "I am sometimes irritated by people who ask favors of me") to which participants responded "true" or "false." [David **Marlowe** (1931–1990) and Douglas P. **Crowne** (1928–), U.S. psychologists]

Maroteaux–Lamy syndrome an inherited disorder of connective tissue and skeletal development. It is marked by dwarfism of the trunk and extremities and in some cases delayed closure of the cranial sutures and maldevelopment of the facial bones. Mental retardation and deafness often accompany the condition. Also called **mucopolysaccharidosis VI**; **systemic mucopolysaccharidosis**. [Pierre **Maroteaux** (1926–), French geneticist; Maurice **Lamy** (1895–1975), French physician]

Marplan *n.* a trade name for ISOCARBOXAZID.

marriage *n.* the social institution in which two (or, less frequently, more) people commit themselves to a socially sanctioned relationship in which sexual intercourse is legitimated and there is legally recognized responsibility for any offspring as well as for each other. Although there are exceptions, the marital partners typically live together in the same residence. See also CLOSED MARRIAGE; COLLUSIONAL MARRIAGE; COMMON-LAW MARRIAGE; DOMESTIC PARTNERSHIP; GROUP MARRIAGE; NONTRADITIONAL MARRIAGE; OPEN MARRIAGE; SAME-SEX MARRIAGE; SYMBIOTIC MARRIAGE; SYNERGIC MARRIAGE; TRADITIONAL MARRIAGE. **—marital** *adj.*

marriage counseling COUPLES COUNSELING when the couples are married. Also called **marital counseling**.

marriage-enrichment group a support or therapy group in which married couples meet under the guidance of a professional or nonprofessional leader to discuss marriage-related problems and issues. See also COUPLES THERAPY.

marriage therapy see COUPLES THERAPY.

masculinity *n.* possession of social role behaviors that are presumed to be characteristic of a man, as contrasted with MALENESS, which is genetically determined. **—masculine** *adj.*

masculinity–femininity test any test designed to measure the degree of masculinity or femininity in participants. The earliest was the Terman–Miles Attitude–Interest Analysis Test (1938); others, usually in inventory form, are the MINNESOTA MULTIPHASIC PERSONALITY INVENTORY, the GUILFORD–ZIMMERMAN TEMPERAMENT SURVEY, and the Gough Femininity Scale. The BEM SEX ROLE INVENTORY is one of the few masculinity–femininity tests to include androgyny.

M

masked depression 1. a condition in which an individual experiencing a MAJOR DEPRESSIVE EPISODE complains of physical symptoms (e.g., headache, backache) rather than mood disturbance, and no organic cause of the physical symptoms can be found. **2.** a hypothesized state in which symptoms other than those normally associated with depression are held to be a result of underlying depression. This view has been difficult to test or verify and is no longer popular.

masked homosexuality theoretically, an unconscious form of same-sex sexual orientation in which a person seeks in heterosexual activities the pleasures presumed to be obtained only in same-sex acts, such as oral or anal intercourse. This hypothesized transposition, however, is essentially rendered meaningless because heterosexual couples may engage routinely in (for example) oral sex with no indication that such activities are exclusively related to gay or lesbian tendencies.

Maslach Burnout Inventory (**MBI** a method for the evaluation of BURNOUT on three dimensions: emotional exhaustion, DEPERSONALIZATION, and reduced personal accomplishment. It consists of 22 statements about feelings and attitudes to which participants respond in terms of frequency on a 7-point scale ranging from "never" to "every day." [Christina **Maslach** (1946–), U.S. psychologist]

M

Maslow, Abraham Harold (1908–1970) U.S. psychologist. Maslow earned his PhD in 1934 from the University of Wisconsin, where he studied with the primatologist Harry Harlow (1905–1981). Initially a behaviorist but frustrated by what he perceived as its limitations, Maslow broadened his orientation to include the subjective in human experience, so becoming a founder of HUMANISTIC PSYCHOLOGY. Maslow originated the concept of a hierarchy of needs that motivate all individuals (see MASLOW'S MOTIVATIONAL HIERARCHY): According to this concept, the ultimate goal of being human is SELF-ACTUALIZATION; only when a person's basic needs are met can self-actualization occur. His emphasis on self-fulfillment made him a leader in the HUMAN-POTENTIAL MOVEMENT of the 1960s and 1970s. Maslow's most influential works include his *Theory of Human Motivation* (1943), *Toward a Psychology of Being* (1968), and *The Farther Reaches of Human Nature* (1971). A founder of the American Association for Humanistic Psychology in 1962, and cofounder of the *Journal of Humanistic Psychology*, Maslow was elected president of the American Psychological Association in 1967. See also MASLOW'S THEORY OF HUMAN MOTIVATION; DEFICIENCY MOTIVATION; HUMANISTIC PERSPECTIVE; METAMOTIVATION; PERSONALITY STRUCTURE.

Maslow's being psychology see BEING PSYCHOLOGY.

Maslow's motivational hierarchy the hierarchy of human motives, or needs, as described by Abraham MASLOW, which he developed as a reaction against the determinism of the theories of Sigmund FREUD and B. F. SKINNER. PHYSIOLOGICAL NEEDS (air, water, food, sleep, sex, etc.) are at the base; followed by safety and security (the SAFETY NEEDS); then love, affection, and gregariousness (the LOVE NEEDS); then prestige, competence, and power (the ESTEEM NEEDS); and, at the highest level, aesthetic needs, the need for knowing, and SELF-ACTUALIZATION (the METANEEDS).

Maslow's theory of human motivation the humanistic view of motivation proposed by Abraham MASLOW, in which the higher human needs for understanding, aesthetic values, self-realization, and PEAK EXPERIENCES are emphasized. Maslow contrasted the METAMOTIVATION arising from such METANEEDS with the DEFICIENCY MOTIVATION arising from physical needs, insecurity, and alienation.

masochism *n.* the derivation of pleasure from experiencing pain and humiliation. The term generally denotes SEXUAL MASOCHISM but is also applied to other experiences not involving sex, such as martyrdom, religious flagellation, or asceticism. In psychoanalytic theory, masochism is interpreted as resulting from the DEATH INSTINCT or from aggression turned inward because of excessive guilt feelings. [Leopold Sacher **Masoch** (1835–1895), Austrian writer] **—masochist** *n.* **—masochistic** *adj.*

masochistic fantasies fantasies of being whipped, choked, or otherwise hurt or abused as an expression of masochistic tendencies, particularly as a means of achieving sexual excitement. See SEXUAL MASOCHISM.

masochistic personality disorder a personality disorder in which individuals persistently and characteristically obtain gratification or freedom from guilt feelings as a consequence of humiliation, self-derogation, self-sacrifice, wallowing in misery, and, in some instances, submitting to physically sadistic acts. This disorder was listed in *DSM–III–TR* as SELF-DEFEATING PERSONALITY DISORDER.

mass action the generalization of U.S. psychologist Karl S. Lashley (1890–1958) that the size of a cortical lesion, rather than its specific location, determines the extent of any resulting performance decrement. Proposed in 1929 following experimental observations of the effects of different brain lesions on rats' ability to learn a complex maze, the concept reflects Lashley's belief that large areas of the cortex function together in learning and other complex processes. See also EQUIPOTENTIALITY.

massage *n.* the structured stroking or kneading of a body area or of the entire body by hand or by a mechanical or electrical device. Manual massage is usually administered for therapeutic and rehabilitative purposes because the hands can detect abnormalities, such as swellings or muscle spasms. Among the benefits of massage are improved circulation, the promotion of relaxation and healing from injury, and release from tension and psychological stress. Massage may also be performed in a fluid environment, as in a whirlpool bath.

mass contagion a form of CONTAGION in which behaviors, attitudes, or affect rapidly spread throughout large groups or populations, including those who are widely dispersed across a large area.

mass hysteria see COLLECTIVE HYSTERIA.

mass reflex **1.** an indiscriminate response of many body effectors to a single stimulus, as in "freezing" with fear. **2.** a life-threatening condition associated with spinal cord injury in which uncontrolled activation of both autonomic and somatic motor systems occurs.

mass suicide the deliberate ending of the lives of all or most of the members of an intact social group or aggregate by the members themselves, either directly through self-injurious behavior or indirectly by choosing a course of action that will very likely be fatal. Examples include extremely hazardous missions undertaken by combat units (see ALTRUISTIC SUICIDE) and the suicides of nearly all the members of the People's Temple (Jonestown mass suicide), the 70 members of the Order of the Solar Temple in Europe and Canada between 1994 and 1997, and the 39 Heaven's Gate followers of Marshall Appelwhite in San Diego in 1997. Mass suicide often occurs at the command of a charismatic leader and may be provoked not by despair but by the desire to seek a "higher state of existence" promised by the leader. Also called **collective suicide**. Compare CLUSTER SUICIDES.

MAST acronym for MICHIGAN ALCOHOLISM SCREENING TEST.

mastery goal see LEARNING GOAL.

masturbation *n.* manipulation of one's own genital organs, typically the penis and clitoris, for purposes of sexual gratification. The act is usually accompanied by sexual fantasies or erotic literature, pictures, or videos. Masturbation may also include the use of mechanical devices (e.g., vibrators) or self-stimulation of other organs, such as the anus or nipples. **—masturbate** *vb.*

mata elap see AMOK.

matched samples two or more SAMPLES that are equivalent to one another with respect to certain relevant variables.

matching patients the process of prescribing specific interventions or choosing specific therapists for particular patients or diagnostic groups of patients to improve compliance with or effectiveness of treatment. The process is based on the diagnoses, needs, problems, and characteristics of particular patients; on therapist variables, such as race, ethnicity, and experience levels; and on setting variables, such as inpatient or outpatient clinics. Also called **psychotherapy matching**.

materialism *n.* **1.** the philosophical position that everything, including mental events, is composed of physical matter and is thus subject to the laws of physics. From this perspective, the mind is considered to exist solely as a set of brain processes (see MIND–BODY PROBLEM). Such philosophies can be traced back to ancient times but gained a new impetus from advances in the physical sciences beginning in the 17th century. **2.** a value system that emphasizes the pursuit and acquisition of material goods and luxuries, typically perceived by the individual as a measure of personal worth and achievement, often at the expense of moral, psychological, and social considerations. **3.** the position that the causes of behavior are to be found in the material of the body, particularly the nervous system. See also IDENTITY THEORY; PHYSICALISM. Compare IDEALISM. **—materialist** *adj., n.* **—materialistic** *adj.*

maternal attitudes attitudes of the mother toward her children, particularly those attitudes that play an important role in her children's health, character formation, emotional adjustment, and self-image, as well as in her own self-perception as a mother.

maternal behavior the actions of female animals associated with caring for their young. These can range from nursing in mammals and feeding in other species to protection, thermoregulation, and teaching skills to the young.

maternal deprivation lack of adequate nurturing for a young animal or child due to the absence or premature loss of, or neglect by, its mother or primary caregiver, postulated to negatively impact a child's emotional development by disrupting ATTACHMENT formation. See also FAILURE TO THRIVE; MARASMUS.

maternal drive the motivation of female animals to care for offspring.

maternal PKU a condition in women that is secondary to successful treatment of PHENYLKETONURIA through dietary intervention beginning at birth. Expectant mothers with high levels of blood phenylalanine are at risk of giving birth to offspring with high rates of congenital heart defects, intrauterine growth retardation, mental retardation, and microcephaly (a small head). Treatment entails dietary management for the expectant mother before and during pregnancy to reduce blood levels of phenylalanine.

maternity blues see BABY BLUES.

mathematics disorder in *DSM–IV–TR*, a LEARNING DISORDER in which mathematical ability is substantially below what is expected given the person's chronological age, formal education experience, and measured intelligence. It may involve (among other problems) difficulties in counting, learning multiplication tables, understanding mathematical problems and performing mathematical operations, reading numerical symbols, and copying numbers.

matricide *n.* **1.** the killing of one's own mother. **2.** a person who kills his or her own mother. Compare PATRICIDE. **—matricidal** *adj.*

matrix *n.* **1.** a context or environment within which something else is enclosed, embedded, originates, or develops. **2.** a rectangular ordered arrangement (ARRAY) of numbers in rows and columns.

maturational crisis a life-changing event, such as marriage or retirement, that often is encountered during the typical course of development and that requires significant psychological, behavioral, or other adjustments. Also called **developmental crisis**; **normative crisis**.

maturational lag slowness or delay in some aspects of neurological development that may affect cognition, perception, and behavior.

maturation hypothesis a generalization that some behaviors and processes, such as language acquisition, are innate but do not appear until appropriate organs and neural systems have matured.

maturity rating an evaluation of behavior on a particular trait in comparison with a relevant peer-group norm.

M

matutinal insomnia a less common name for TERMINAL INSOMNIA.

Maudsley Personality Inventory see EYSENCK PERSONALITY INVENTORY.

maximum-security unit a section of a mental institution reserved for patients who are likely to harm themselves or others.

May, Rollo (1909–1994) U.S. psychologist, psychoanalyst, and existentialist. May earned his PhD in clinical psychology at Columbia University in 1949 and spent the bulk of his career at the William Alanson White Institute in New York City, where he served as training analyst and president of the institute for many years. A broad-ranging thinker who incorporated classical, religious, and philosophical studies into his views on psychology and psychotherapy, May is best known as a proponent of HUMANISTIC PSYCHOLOGY and a spokesperson for the EXISTENTIAL PSYCHOLOGY movement. He was particularly concerned with combating feelings of emptiness, cynicism, and despair by emphasizing basic human values, such as love, free will, and self-awareness. Among his most influential writings are *Existence: A New Dimension in Psychiatry and Psychology* (1958, coauthored by Ernest Angel and Henri Ellenberger), *The Meaning of Anxiety* (1950), and *Love and Will* (1969).

MBD 1. abbreviation for MINIMAL BRAIN DAMAGE. **2.** abbreviation for MINIMAL BRAIN DYSFUNCTION.

MBHO abbreviation for MANAGED BEHAVIORAL HEALTH ORGANIZATION.

MBI abbreviation for MASLACH BURNOUT INVENTORY.

MBTI abbreviation for MYERS–BRIGGS TYPE INDICATOR.

McClelland, David (1917–1998) U.S. psychologist. McClelland was awarded his doctorate at Yale University in 1941. He taught at Connecticut College and Wesleyan University before joining the faculty at Harvard University, where he remained from 1956 until 1987. He then taught at Boston University until his death. McClelland is best known for his empirical and theoretical contributions to the study of personality and motivation. With John W. Atkinson (1923–2003) he developed a method of quantitatively scoring the THEMATIC APPERCEPTION TEST (TAT), using it to assess individual ACHIEVEMENT MOTIVATION. In later years he conducted research on power motivation. Representative writings include his classic *The Achieving Society* (1961), *Human Motivation* (1985), and *Power: The Inner Experience* (1975). McClelland received the American Psychological Association's Award for Distinguished Scientific Contributions in 1987 and was elected a fellow of the American Academy of Arts and Sciences. See also NEED FOR ACHIEVEMENT.

MCE abbreviation for MEDICAL CARE EVALUATION.

MCI abbreviation for MILD COGNITIVE IMPAIRMENT.

MCMI abbreviation for MILLON CLINICAL MULTIAXIAL INVENTORY.

McNaughten rule (**McNaughton rule**; **M'Naghten rule**) a rule for defining INSANITY that focuses on the cognitive state of the defendant at the time of committing the act with which he or she is charged. It states that to plead insanity, the accused must be "laboring under such a defect of reason, from disease of the mind, as not to know the nature and quality of the act he was doing, or if he did know it, he did not know that what he was doing was wrong." The rule was established in 1843 by judges in England after the trial of Daniel McNaughten, who believed the government was persecuting him and killed prime minister Sir Robert Peel's secretary in mistake for the prime minister. Also called **right-and-wrong test**; **right-or-wrong test**. See also AMERICAN LAW INSTITUTE MODEL PENAL CODE INSANITY TEST; CRIMINAL RESPONSIBILITY; IRRESISTIBLE IMPULSE RULE; PARTIAL INSANITY.

MCO abbreviation for managed care organization (see MANAGED CARE).

M–C SDS abbreviation for MARLOWE–CROWNE SOCIAL DESIRABILITY SCALE.

MDA *n.* 3,4-*m*ethylene*d*ioxy*a*mphetamine: a synthetic HALLUCINOGEN of the phenylisopropylamine family (see PHENYLETHYLAMINES). Because at low doses it acts as a CNS STIMULANT and euphoriant, MDA was once proposed as an aid to psychotherapy, but this use has not been supported. It is thought that MDA's psychostimulant properties occur through enhanced neurotransmission of norepinephrine and its hallucinogenic action through augmentation of serotonin transmission. MDA is a metabolite of MDMA and may be responsible for much of MDMA's action; there is some concern that these drugs and other synthetic amphetamine derivatives cause neuronal degeneration.

MDMA *n.* 3,4-*m*ethylene*d*ioxy*m*eth*a*mphetamine: a substituted PHENYLETHYLAMINE that, like its analog MDA, is a catecholamine-like HALLUCINOGEN with amphetamine-like stimulant properties that may produce visual disturbances and hallucinations at high doses. It is among the most commonly used illicit drugs, generally sold under the name **Ecstasy**. Taken orally, onset of effects is rapid; the high lasts several hours, and residual effects can be experienced for several days. Intoxication is characterized by euphoria, feelings of closeness and spirituality, and diverse symptoms of autonomic arousal. Widespread illicit use of MDMA as a "club drug" has caused increasing concern as nerve damage and serotonin dysfunction have been established as resulting from prolonged use. Persistent memory dysfunction and impaired decision making and self-control as well as depressed mood have been well documented. When used during periods of intense activity (as often occurs during rave parties), it may be toxic or fatal.

mean (symbol: $\bar{X}$; *M*) *n.* the numerical average of a batch of scores (X_i): the most widely used statistic for describing CENTRAL TENDENCY. It is computed as:

$$\bar{X} = (\sum_i X_i)/n,$$

where n is the number of scores; that is, the scores are added up, and the total is divided by the number of scores. Also called **arithmetic mean**; **arithmetic average**.

mean deviation for a set of numbers, a measure of dispersion or spread equal to the average of the differences between each number and the mean value. It is given by $(\Sigma|x_i - \mu|)/n$, where μ is the mean value and n the number of values.

meaning *n.* the cognitive or emotional significance of a word or sequence of words, or of a concept, sign, or symbolic act. This may include a range of implied or associated ideas (connotative meaning) as well as a literal significance (denotative meaning). The study of meaning in language is semantics, and that of meaning in symbolic systems generally is semiotics. **—mean** *vb.* **—meaningful** *adj.*

meaning-centered therapy see LOGOTHERAPY.

meaninglessness *n.* a pervasive sense of the absence of significance, direction, or purpose. A sense of meaninglessness regarding one's life or life in general is sometimes a focal issue in psychotherapy. The perception of meaninglessness poses the central problem that the existential approach attempts to solve or accommodate. See also EXISTENTIALISM; LOGOTHERAPY; WILL TO MEANING.

mean square a SUM OF SQUARES divided by its DEGREES OF FREEDOM. The mean square is a variance ESTIMATOR.

measurement error a difference between an observed measurement and the true value of the parameter being measured that is attributable to flaws or biases in the measurement process.

measure of association any of various indices of the degree to which two or more variables are related.

mecamylamine *n.* a GANGLIONIC BLOCKING AGENT formerly widely used in the treatment of hypertension. Because of the severity of its side effects, which include tremor, sedation, and movement disorders, this use is now rare. However, because mecamylamine has preferential antagonistic action at NICOTINIC RECEPTORS, it has been investigated as a possible antismoking agent. It has also been used in the treatment of TOURETTE'S DISORDER. U.S. trade name: **Inversine**.

mechanical-aptitude test any of various tests designed to measure abilities related to mechanical work, such as mechanical information, mechanical reasoning, spatial relations, perceptual skills, understanding of mechanical principles, mechanical assembly, and manual dexterity.

mechanistic interactionism a theory that considers both individual (dispositional) and situational variables in the determination of behavior. The relative weight assigned to dispositional and situational factors may be affected by certain moderating variables, for example, the nature of a situation: A highly structured situation may influence behavior more than will dispositional factors, and a highly ambiguous situation may allow dispositional factors to play a larger role in determining behavior.

Medea complex a mother's wish to kill her children as a means of revenge against the father. The term is derived from Greek mythology, in which Medea killed her children fathered by Jason after he deserted her for a younger woman. See also FILICIDE.

medial prefrontal cortex a region of the PREFRONTAL CORTEX of the brain that has a prominent role in the control of mood, having extensive connections throughout the LIMBIC SYSTEM.

medial temporal amnesia memory loss (amnesia) caused by damage to the MEDIAL TEMPORAL LOBE. Causes include infarction of the posterior cerebral artery, anoxia, encephalitis, temporal lobectomy, and trauma. See AMNESTIC DISORDER.

medial temporal lobe the region toward the middle of the temporal lobe of each cerebral hemisphere. It contains the pyriform area, the amygdala, and the hippocampus.

median *n.* the score that divides a DISTRIBUTION into two equal-sized halves.

median-cleft-face syndrome a congenital disorder characterized by defective fusion of structures in the midline of the face. The cleft may involve the eyes, the tip of the nose, the palate, and the premaxilla. About 20% of affected individuals have some degree of mental retardation.

median effective dose see EFFECTIVE DOSE.

mediated response a response that is elicited by a stimulus and is subsequently responsible for the initiation of a behavior.

mediate experience conscious awareness and interpretation of external events and stimuli. Mediate experience provides meaning and additional information not contained in the event or stimulus itself. It is contrasted with **immediate experience**: the elements or characteristics of the event or stimuli as perceived directly and without interpretation. INTROSPECTION makes use of immediate experience in analyzing the contents of mediate experience. [defined by Wilhelm WUNDT]

mediation *n.* in dispute resolution, use of a neutral outside person—the MEDIATOR—to help the contending parties communicate and reach a compromise. The process of mediation has gained popularity, for example for couples involved in separation or divorce proceedings (see DIVORCE MEDIATION).

mediation theory the hypothesis that stimuli affect behavior indirectly through an intervening process, as opposed to a simpler stimulus–response model. For example, cognitive therapists maintain that the effect an external event has on an individual is influenced by the individual's thoughts and perceptions of that event.

mediator *n.* **1.** a process or system that exists between a stimulus and a response, between the source and destination of a neural impulse, or between the transmitter and receiver of communications. **2.** a person—for example, a lawyer or psychologist—who helps contending parties communicate and reach a compromise. See also DIVORCE MEDIATION; MEDIATION. **3.** in statistical analyses of the interrelations among variables, a variable that accounts for an observed relation between two other variables.

mediator variable see INTERVENING VARIABLE.

Medicaid *n.* a joint federal and state program, instituted by law in 1965 (Title XIX of the Social Security Act), that provides medical benefits for people with low incomes and limited resources. Medicaid programs follow broad federal guidelines but each state determines specific benefits and amounts of payments.

Medicaid Waiver see HOME AND COMMUNITY-BASED SERVICES.

medical audit a systematic evaluation of the effectiveness of diagnostic and treatment procedures. A **retrospective medical audit** is based on a review of a patient's charts after he or she has been discharged; a **concurrent medical audit** is conducted while the patient is still under treatment.

medical care evaluation (**MCE**) a health care review in which an assessment of the quality of care and its utilization is made. It will include an investigation of any suspected problems, analysis of the problems identified, and a plan for corrective action.

medical family therapy a form of psychotherapy that combines a BIOPSYCHOSOCIAL systems approach with FAMILY SYSTEMS THEORY to help individuals and their families deal with the health problems of the individual. This therapy emphasizes collaboration with others—physicians, nurses, occupational therapists, nutritionists, and the like—in the individual's health care team.

medical history in psychology, the portion of the developmental history, or ANAMNESIS, that focuses on the patient's health throughout life, including congenital or acquired illnesses and disorders. The object is to uncover, where possible, clues to the cause of the patient's current psychological condition.

medical model 1. the concept that mental and emotional problems are analogous to biological problems, that is, they have detectable, specific, physiological causes (e.g., an abnormal gene or damaged cell) and are amenable to cure or improvement by specific treatment. **2.** in evaluation research, a systems-analysis approach to evaluation that considers the interrelatedness of all the factors that may affect performance and monitors possible side effects of treatment. The medical model is in contrast to the **engineering model**, which is a simple comparison of gains for different groups, some of which have been exposed to the program of interest.

medical psychology 1. an area of applied psychology devoted to psychological questions arising in the practice of medicine, including emotional reactions to illness; treatment compliance; attitudes toward terminal illness and impending death; psychological means of relieving pain (e.g., hypnotic suggestion); and reactions to disability. **2.** see PRESCRIBING PSYCHOLOGY.

medical psychotherapy psychotherapy that makes use of medication and other medical techniques in the treatment of mental illness.

medical rehabilitation the process of restoring to the fullest possible degree the physical functioning of an individual who has a physiological or anatomical impairment. See also REHABILITATION.

medical social worker a licensed social worker, usually with a master's degree in social work, who assists patients and their families with health-related problems in such areas as employment, finances, living arrangements, marriage, child care, social life, and emotional adjustment.

Medicare *n.* a federal program of HEALTH INSURANCE operated by the Health Care Financing Administration of the U.S. Department of Health and Human Services for those over 65, certain younger people with disabilities, and people with end-stage renal disease. Monies from payroll taxes and premiums from subscribers are deposited in trust funds to meet the expenses of the insured. Medicare consists of two programs: Part A includes inpatient costs and Part B provides supplementary medical insurance.

medication *n.* PSYCHOACTIVE DRUGS that aid in the treatment of affective and behavioral disorders. Until recently, in the United States only medical physicians could legally prescribe psychoactive drugs, but prescription privileges have now been extended to psychologists in the military and to those in New Mexico and Louisiana. **Overmedication**—the taking of more than the prescribed dose of a drug or drugs—may occur when medication is not properly monitored. **Self-medication** is usually associated with individuals who use drugs or alcohol inappropriately to alleviate emotional problems.

medication-induced movement disorder any movement disorder that occurs as an adverse effect of medication. It may involve rigidity, tremor, hypertonia (increased muscle tone), and other motor symptoms and is commonly seen after treatment with antipsychotic drugs. See TARDIVE DYSKINESIA.

meditation *n.* profound and extended contemplation or reflection, sometimes in order to attain an ALTERED STATE OF CONSCIOUSNESS. Traditionally associated with spiritual and religious exercises, it is now increasingly also used to provide relaxation and relief from stress. See also CONCENTRATIVE MEDITATION; MINDFULNESS MEDITATION; TRANSCENDENTAL MEDITATION.

medulla *n.* **1.** the central or innermost region of an organ, such as the adrenal medulla, the central portion of the adrenal gland. Compare CORTEX. **2.** see MEDULLA OBLONGATA. **—medullary** *adj.*

medulla oblongata the most inferior (lowest), or caudal (tailward), part of the HINDBRAIN. It contains many nerve tracts that conduct impulses between the spinal cord and higher brain centers, as well as autonomic nuclei involved in the control of breathing, heartbeat, and blood pressure. Also called **myelencephalon**.

Meehl, Paul Everett (1920–2003) U.S. psychologist. Meehl received his PhD in psychology from the University of Minnesota and served on the faculty there for the remainder of his career. Both a practicing psychotherapist and an academic psychologist, Meehl made important contributions to research in the fields of clinical psychology and cliometrics, the use of mathematics and statistics to analyze historical data. In clinical psychology, his research focused on diagnosis and classification of mental disorders using quantitative methods that revolutionized the field by developing computerized scoring techniques for psychological tests. Meehl also applied his statistical expertise to problems in the history and philosophy of science, publishing many articles in those fields. Representative works include *Clinical Versus Statistical Prediction: A Theoretical Analysis and a Review of the Evidence* (1954; reprinted 1996) and *Selected Philosophical and Methodological Papers* (1991). Among his many honors were the American Psychological Association's awards for Distinguished Scientific Contributions and for Outstanding Lifetime Contribution to Psychology, and membership of the National Academy of Sciences and the American Academy of Arts and Sciences.

mefloquine *n.* a chemical analog of quinine used in the treatment of malarial infections and prevention of malaria. It has been associated with seizures or psychological disturbances, including sleep disturbance, depression, panic attacks, and psychotic symptoms. Although such reactions are rare, mefloquine should not be taken by individuals with histories of depression, generalized anxiety disorder, psychosis, or seizure disorders. U.S. trade name: **Lariam**.

MEG abbreviation for MAGNETOENCEPHALOGRAPHY or magnetoencephalograph.

megadose pharmacotherapy a dosing strategy popular in the 1970s and 1980s in the United States and other countries, generally involving the rapid administration of very high doses of an antipsychotic drug in the hopes that this would hasten an antipsychotic response. It was based on the presumption that rapid blockade of postsynaptic dopamine D2 receptors would lead to faster resolution of psychotic symptoms. This strategy was largely ineffective in producing a more rapid response and had numerous adverse effects, such as severe movement disorders and death due to NEUROLEPTIC MALIGNANT SYNDROME. Research published in the late 1980s showed that lower doses were as effective as higher doses and had fewer adverse consequences. Because of the lack of clinical benefit and the high incidence of adverse side effects associated with megadose pharmacotherapy, it has fallen into disuse. Also called **rapid neuroleptization**.

megalocephaly *n.* see MACROCEPHALY. **—megalocephalic** *adj.*

megalomania *n.* a highly inflated conception of one's importance, power, or capabilities, as can be observed in many individuals with mania and paranoid schizophrenia. In the latter, megalomania is often accompanied or preceded by delusions of persecution. See DELUSION OF GRANDEUR.

Megan's law U.S. legislation requiring that convicted but released sex offenders register with the authorities so that communities will be notified of their presence in a particular neighborhood. More formally known as the **Community Notification Act**, it was initially passed in New Jersey in 1994 after a repeat sex offender murdered a 7-year-old girl named Megan Nicole Kanka; it became a federal law in 1996.

megavitamin therapy the use of very high doses of vitamins and mineral supplements, particularly vitamin C (ascorbic acid), nicotinic acid (niacin), vitamin B_6(pyridoxine), and magnesium, to treat certain mental disorders. Such an approach is not widely adopted, and effectiveness is uncertain.

melancholia *n.* an archaic name for depression, which still has some popular currency. **—melancholic** *adj.*

melancholia agitata a 19th-century term for CATATONIC EXCITEMENT. It is occasionally still used for AGITATED DEPRESSION.

melancholic features features that may be associated with a MAJOR DEPRESSIVE EPISODE. These include loss of pleasure in most or all activities or inability to take pleasure in anything that normally elicits this feeling, together with three or more of the following: The depressed mood is experienced as quite distinct from normal sadness; it is worse in the morning; and there is early morning awakening, psychomotor agitation or retardation, loss of appetite or weight, or excessive guilt feelings.

melatonin *n.* a hormone, produced mainly by the PINEAL GLAND as a metabolic product of the neurotransmitter SEROTONIN, that helps to regulate seasonal changes in physiology and may also influence puberty. It is implicated in the initiation of sleep and in the regulation of the sleep–wake cycle. Melatonin has been investigated in clinical studies as a hypnotic and for the management of CIRCADIAN RHYTHM SLEEP DISORDERS. Although these studies are as yet inconclusive, melatonin is widely available as an over-the-counter medication.

Mellaril *n.* a trade name for THIORIDAZINE.

melodic intonation therapy (**MIT**) speech therapy that uses melody to regain or improve speech in individuals with certain kinds of APHASIA, MOTOR SPEECH DISORDER, or EXPRESSIVE LANGUAGE DISORDER. Based on the theory of right-hemisphere dominance for music, MIT trains the speaker to intone, or "sing," text in pitches and rhythms that parallel natural spoken prosody. MIT is primarily an auxiliary to other forms of speech therapy.

memorandum as a whole see OBJECTIVE PSYCHOTHERAPY.

memory *n.* **1.** the ability to retain information or a representation of past experience, based on the mental processes of learning or ENCODING, RETENTION across some interval of time, and RETRIEVAL or reactivation of the memory. **2.** specific information or a specific past experience that is recalled. **3.** the hypothesized part of the brain where traces of information and past experiences are stored (see MEMORY SYSTEM). See also ASSOCIATIVE MEMORY; CONSTRUCTIVE MEMORY; EXPLICIT MEMORY; IMMEDIATE MEMORY; IMPLICIT MEMORY; LONG-TERM MEMORY; SHORT-TERM MEMORY.

memory disorder any impairment in the ability to encode, retain, or retrieve information or representations of experiences. A notable example is AMNESIA. Memory disorders may be partial or global, mild or severe, permanent or transitory, anterograde (pertaining to difficulty with new information) or retrograde (pertaining to difficulty with previously known information). The cause may be medical conditions leading to structural lesions of the brain or metabolic disruption of brain function, aging, psychological trauma, fugue states, or intrapsychic conflicts.

memory distortion any inaccurate or illusory recall or recognition, such as DÉJÀ VU, a FALSE MEMORY, or a memory illusion.

memory-enhancing drugs see NOOTROPIC.

memory hardening an increased conviction, with the passage of time, that FALSE MEMORIES or PSEUDOMEMORIES are accurate. The phenomenon is of particular concern in the context of eyewitness testimony and hypnosis.

memory impairment the loss of memory associated with MEMORY DISORDERS.

memory loss see MEMORY IMPAIRMENT.

memory retraining strategies to help individuals with neurological deficits improve their ability to process information in WORKING MEMORY. These strategies are typically applied with patients with brain injury or Alzheimer's disease and those with HIV/AIDS who are experiencing memory problems.

memory span the number of items that can be recalled immediately after one presentation. Usually, the items consist of letters, words, numbers, or syllables that the participant must reproduce in order. A distinction may be drawn between visual memory span and auditory memory span, depending on the nature of the presentation. See also DIGIT SPAN.

memory system any of several different kinds of memory that are hypothesized to be located in separate brain areas and primarily employed in different sorts of memory tasks. Examples of hypothesized systems include WORKING MEMORY (a temporary store used in manipulating information), SEMANTIC MEMORY (general knowledge), EPISODIC MEMORY (memories of one's personal past), and PROCEDURAL MEMORY (habits and skills).

memory trace a hypothetical modification of the nervous system that encodes a representation of information or experience.

ménage à trois **1.** a sexual relationship involving three people who are members of the same household, for example, a married couple and the husband's mistress sharing an apartment. **2.** three people having sex together (see TROILISM).

menarche *n.* the first incidence of MENSTRUATION in a female, marking the onset of puberty. The age at which menarche occurs varies among individuals and cultures: It tends to occur earlier in Western countries, possibly associated with better nutrition. **—menarcheal** *adj.*

meningitis *n.* inflammation of the meninges, the three membranous layers that cover the brain and spinal cord, usually due to infection by bacteria, viruses, or fungi. Symptoms include high fever, nausea, vomiting, stiff neck, and headache. **Bacterial meningitis** includes meningococcal meningitis and tuberculous meningitis. **Viral** (or **aseptic**) **meningitis** is a milder nonbacterial disease; causes include the mumps, poliomyelitis, herpes viruses, and the echoviruses (which mainly affect young children during the summer). If untreated or not treated promptly, many types of meningitis can result in confusion, lethargy, coma, and eventually death.

meningomyelocele *n.* protrusion of the spinal cord and its covering meninges through a defect in the spinal column. This results in an external sac containing cerebrospinal fluid, poorly formed meninges, and a malformed spinal cord. Also called **myelomeningocele**. See SPINA BIFIDA.

menkeiti *n.* see MYRIACHIT.

menopausal depression severe DYSPHORIA occurring during the female CLIMACTERIC (menopause), particularly among women who have had a prior tendency to depression.

menopause *n.* the period during which menstruation ceases at the end of the reproductive cycle in women. See CLIMACTERIC. **—menopausal** *adj.*

menorrhagia *n.* excessive bleeding during menstruation. Also called **epimenorrhagia**.

mens rea the malicious or blameworthy state of mind (Latin, "guilty mind") that must be proved in addition to the actus reus (the illegal act) in order to establish CRIMINAL RESPONSIBILITY and secure a conviction. It involves a conscious disregard for the law, which is presumed to be known by the defendant. For some crimes the mens rea may be recklessness or negligence rather than a deliberate intention to bring about certain consequences. Also called **criminal intent**.

menstrual cycle a modified estrous cycle that occurs in most primates, including humans (in which it averages about 28 days). The events of the cycle are dependent on cyclical changes in the concentrations of GONADOTROPINS secreted by the anterior pituitary gland, under the control of GONADOTROPIN-RELEASING HORMONE, and can be divided into two phases. In the follicular phase, follicle-stimulating hormone (FSH) and luteinizing hormone (LH) stimulate development of an ovum and secretion of estrogen within the ovary, in a graafian follicle, culminating in ovulation, which occurs half way through the cycle. The estrogen stimulates thickening of the endometrium of the uterus in preparation to receive a fertilized ovum. The luteal phase begins immediately after ovulation, when the ruptured follicle becomes the corpus luteum and secretes progesterone, which inhibits further secretion of releasing hormone (and hence of FSH and LH). If fertilization does not occur, this phase ends with menstruation and a repeat of the follicular phase.

menstrual taboo any culture-bound tradition associated with menstruating women, typically involving physical separation from men, abstention from sexual intercourse, or the exclusion of women from certain daily activities (e.g., the preparation of food).

menstruation *n.* a periodic discharge of blood and endometrial tissue from the uterus through the vagina that occurs in fertile women as part of the MENSTRUAL CYCLE. Also called **menses**; **menstrual** (or **monthly**) **period**.

mental *adj.* **1.** of or referring to the MIND or to processes of the mind, such as thinking, feeling, sensing, and the like. **2.** phenomenal or consciously experienced. In contrast to physiological or physical, which refer to objective events or processes, mental denotes events known only privately and subjectively; it may refer to the COGNITIVE PROCESSES involved in these events, to differentiate them from physiological processes.

M

mental aberration a pathological deviation from normal thinking, particularly as a symptom of a mental or emotional disorder.

mental age (**MA**) a numerical scale unit derived by dividing an individual's results in an intelligence test by the average score for other people of the same age. Thus, a 4-year-old child who scored 150 on an IQ test would have a mental age of 6 (the age-appropriate average score is 100; therefore, MA = (150/100) × 4 = 6). The MA measure of performance is not effective beyond the age of 14.

mental apparatus see PSYCHIC APPARATUS.

mental asthenia subjective loss of mental strength characterized by lack of energy or motivation for mental tasks, often expressed as **concentration difficulty**.

mental asymmetry an unbalanced relationship between mental processes, as in individuals with HYPERCALCEMIA syndrome (Williams syndrome), who may exhibit severe impairment in visuospatial abilities while possessing good to exceptional language abilities.

mental ataxia see INTRAPSYCHIC ATAXIA.

mental balance INTEGRATION of mental processes.

mental confusion see CONFUSION.

mental defective an obsolete name for a person with mental retardation, intellectual disability, or learning disability.

mental deficiency another (and now seldom used) name for mental retardation, sometimes referring to severe or profound mental retardation with known organic causes.

mental development the progressive changes in mental processes due to maturation, learning, and experience. See COGNITIVE DEVELOPMENT.

mental diplopia the experience of illusions, hallucinations, or false memories with concurrent awareness that these experiences are not real and are an abnormal occurrence.

mental disease an obsolete name for a MENTAL DISORDER.

mental disorder any condition characterized by cognitive and emotional disturbances, abnormal behaviors, impaired functioning, or any combination of these. Such disorders cannot be accounted for solely by environmental circumstances and may involve physiological, genetic, chemical, social, and other factors. Specific classifications of mental disorders are elaborated in the American Psychiatric Association's *Diagnostic and Statistical Manual of Mental Disorders* (see DSM–IV–TR) and the World Health Organization's INTERNATIONAL CLASSIFICATION OF DISEASES. Also called **mental illness**; **psychiatric disorder**; **psychiatric illness**.

M

mental energy see PSYCHIC ENERGY.

mental examination a comprehensive evaluation of an individual's behavior, attitudes, and intellectual abilities for the purpose of establishing or ruling out pathology.

mental fog see CLOUDING OF CONSCIOUSNESS.

mental function any cognitive process or activity, such as thinking, sensing, or reasoning.

mental handicap the condition of being unable to function independently in the community because of arrested or delayed cognitive development or any severe and disabling mental disorder. Its use is generally discouraged nowadays in preference to MENTAL RETARDATION and other terms considered more objective and less offensive. Also called **mental disability**.

mental healing the process of alleviating or attempting to alleviate mental or physical illness through the power of the mind, typically utilizing such methods as visualization, suggestion, and the conscious manipulation of energy flow. See also FAITH HEALING; PSYCHIC HEALING.

mental health a state of mind characterized by emotional well-being, good behavioral adjustment, relative freedom from anxiety and disabling symptoms, and a capacity to establish constructive relationships and cope with the ordinary demands and stresses of life. See also FLOURISHING; NORMALITY.

mental health care a category of health care service and delivery involving scientific and professional disciplines across several fields of knowledge and technology involved in psychological assessment and intervention (psychology, psychiatry, neurology, social work, etc.). This type of care includes but is not limited to psychological screening and testing, psychotherapy and family therapy, and neuropsychological rehabilitation. See also MENTAL HEALTH SERVICES.

mental health clinic an outpatient facility for the diagnosis and treatment of psychological and behavioral problems.

mental health counselor a certified mental health professional who provides counseling services either independently or as part of a treatment team.

mental health nursing see PSYCHIATRIC NURSING.

mental health program a treatment, prevention, rehabilitation, or educational service offered by a community mental health center or other entity, for the purpose of maintaining or improving the mental health of an individual or community.

mental health services any interventions—assessment, diagnosis, treatment, or counseling—offered in private, public, inpatient, or outpatient settings that are aimed at the maintenance or enhancement of mental health or the treatment of mental or behavioral disorders in individual and group contexts.

mental health worker a member of a mental health treatment team who assists professional staff in a wide range of services.

mental history a record of information relating to a person's mental health (see CASE HISTORY). A mental history, which may be compiled by means of structured or unstructured INTERVIEWS, usually covers the history of both the client and family members.

mental hospital see PSYCHIATRIC HOSPITAL. See also MENTAL INSTITUTION; PRIVATE MENTAL HOSPITAL; PUBLIC MENTAL HOSPITAL.

mental hygiene a general approach aimed at maintaining mental health and preventing mental disorder through such means as educational programs, promotion of a stable emotional and family life, prophylactic and early treatment services (see PRIMARY PREVENTION), and public health measures. The term itself is now less widely used than formerly.

mental hygiene clinic a former name for a MENTAL HEALTH CLINIC or a COMMUNITY MENTAL HEALTH CENTER.

mental illness see MENTAL DISORDER.

mental institution a treatment-oriented facility in which patients with mental retardation or severe psychological disorder are provided with supervised general care and therapy by trained psychologists and psychiatrists as well as auxiliary staff. The patients of a mental institution will generally be those who are unable to function independently as outpatients when supported by psychoactive drugs. See also PSYCHIATRIC HOSPITAL.

mentally defective an obsolete and pejorative descriptor for a person with mental retardation.

mental map 1. a mental representation of the world or some part of it based on subjective perceptions rather than objective geographical knowledge. Such a map will normally prioritize the individual's neighborhood, city, and nation and give prominence to more distant places according to personal experience (e.g., vacations), cultural connections (e.g., family history or language links), and the level of coverage in the mass media. The map will also incorporate the individual's negative or positive feelings about these places, which will often reflect conventional ideas or stereotypes. Research suggests that mental maps vary widely with nationality, region, ethnicity, gender, education, and socioeconomic class. **2.** any internal representation of two-dimensional or three-dimensional space. See COGNITIVE MAP.

mental mechanism in PSYCHODYNAMICS, the psychological functions, collectively, that help individuals meet environmental demands, protect the ego, satisfy inner needs, and alleviate internal and external conflicts and tensions. Among them are (a) language, which enables expression of thoughts; (b) memory, which stores information needed in solving problems; and (c) perception, which involves recognition and interpretation of phenomena. In addition, in psychoanalytic and psychodynamic theory, various defense mechanisms, such as RATIONALIZATION and COMPENSATION, help to prevent anxiety and protect self-esteem.

mental model any internal representation of the relations between a set of elements, as, for example, between workers in an office or department, the elements of a mathematics or physics problem, the terms of a syllogism, or the configuration of objects in a space. Such models may contain perceptual qualities and may be abstract in nature. They can be manipulated to provide dynamic simulations of possible scenarios and are thought to be key components in decision making. In the context of ergonomics, for example, a mental model of a system or product would include its various attributes, rules for operation and handling, and expectations regarding use and consequences and would be used to guide the individual's interactions with the system or product in question.

mental patient organization a club or other organization established to provide social and recreational activities to former mental patients and to help them maintain their morale and readjust to community life. Many mental patient organizations are independent, but others are affiliated with clinics, hospitals, and mental health associations or centers. See EX-PATIENT CLUB.

mental process any process that takes place in the mind. This term is often used synonymously with COGNITIVE PROCESS. See also HIGHER MENTAL PROCESS.

mental representation a hypothetical entity that is presumed to stand for a perception, thought, memory, or the like in the mind during cognitive operations. For example, when doing mental arithmetic, one presumably operates on mental representations that correspond to the digits and numerical operators; when one imagines looking at the reverse side of an object, one presumably operates on a mental representation of that object; when one repeats a phone number aloud while dialing, one presumably operates on mental representations of the names of the digits. However, there is no consensus yet as to what mental representations might be. See THINKING.

mental retardation (**MR**) in *DSM–IV–TR*, a disorder characterized by intellectual function that is significantly below average: specifically that of an individual with a measured IQ of 70 or below on tests with a standard deviation of 15, whose ADAPTIVE BEHAVIOR is impaired, and in whom the condition is manifested during the developmental period, defined variously as below the ages of 18 or 22. In infants, diagnosis is based on clinical judgment. Mental retardation may be the result of brain injury, disease, or genetic causes and is typically characterized by an impairment of educational, social, and vocational abilities. See MILD MENTAL RETARDATION; MODERATE MENTAL RETARDATION; PROFOUND MENTAL RETARDATION; SEVERE MENTAL RETARDATION; UNSPECIFIED MENTAL RETARDATION. Also called **intellectual disability**, which is increasingly the preferred term.

Mental scale see BAYLEY SCALES OF INFANT AND TODDLER DEVELOPMENT.

mental set a temporary readiness to perform certain psychological functions that influences response to a situation or stimulus, such as the tendency to apply a previously successful technique in solving a new problem. It is often determined by instructions but need not be.

mental status the global assessment of an individual's cognitive, affective, and behavioral state as revealed by MENTAL EXAMINATION that covers such factors as general health, appearance, mood, speech, sociability, cooperativeness, facial expression, motor activity, mental activity, emotional state, trend of thought, sensory awareness, orientation, memory, information level, general intelligence level, abstraction and interpretation ability, and judgment.

mental status examination (**MSE**) a comprehensive WORK-UP of a patient, based on interviews, tests, and other sources of information and including details of mental status, personality characteristics, diagnosis, prognosis, and treatment options.

mental subnormality an obsolete name for MENTAL RETARDATION.

mental tension mental activity, usually involving unpleasant emotions.

mental topography see TOPOGRAPHICAL PSYCHOLOGY.

mentoring *n.* the provision of instruction, encouragement, and other support to an individual (e.g., a student, youth, or colleague) to aid his or her overall growth and development or the pursuit of greater learning skills, a career, or other educational or work-related goals. Numerous **mentoring programs** exist today within occupational, educational, and other settings; they use frequent communication and contact between mentors and their respective protégés as well as a variety of other techniques and procedures to develop positive productive relationships.

meperidine *n.* a synthetic OPIOID used in the acute management of moderate to severe pain (see OPIOID ANALGESIC). It is an agonist at the mu OPIOID RECEPTOR and has the side effects of other opioid analgesics. Fatal reactions have resulted when meperidine is administered to patients taking monoamine oxidase inhibitors (MAOIs), and it should therefore not be used in patients who have taken MAOIs within 14 days. Patients taking phenothiazine antipsychotics or tricyclic antidepressants concurrently with meperidine may experience severe respiratory depression. Also called **pethidine**. U.S. trade name (among others): **Demerol**.

M

mephenytoin *n.* see HYDANTOIN.

meprobamate *n.* one of the drugs introduced into the U.S. market in the early 1950s as an alternative to the BARBITURATES. It was commonly and widely prescribed in the 1950s and 1960s for daytime sedation and the treatment of anxiety. Meprobamate is a less potent respiratory depressant than the barbiturates unless taken in combination with other CNS depressants, such as alcohol and OPIOIDS. Like the barbiturates, use of meprobamate has been almost completely supplanted by the benzodiazepines. U.S. trade name: **Miltown**. See also SEDATIVE, HYPNOTIC, AND ANXIOLYTIC DRUGS.

mercy *n.* kindness, compassion, or leniency toward a transgressor, toward someone over whom one has power or authority, or toward someone in distress.

mercy killing a direct action intended to end what would otherwise be the prolonged agony of a dying person or animal. The concept has been known since ancient times: Warriors often were expected to kill a desperately wounded comrade or enemy. Severely injured animals are also put out of their misery by mercy killing. See also ASSISTED DEATH; EUTHANASIA.

Meridia *n.* a trade name for SIBUTRAMINE.

Merital *n.* a trade name for NOMIFENSINE.

Meritor Savings Bank v. Vinson a case resulting in an influential 1986 U.S. Supreme Court ruling that a HOSTILE WORK ENVIRONMENT constitutes SEXUAL HARASSMENT and that victims do not bear the burden of demonstrating they were harmed by the harassment.

merycism *n.* see RUMINATION.

mescal buttons see PEYOTE.

mescaline *n.* a HALLUCINOGEN derived from the PEYOTE cactus and long used by indigenous peoples of the southwestern United States and central America. Its effects often include nausea and vomiting as well as visual hallucinations involving lights and colors; they have a slower onset than those of LSD and usually last 1–2 hours. Mescaline is the oldest classic hallucinogen known to Western science; its pharmacology was defined in 1896, and its structure was verified by synthesis in 1919. It is a substituted PHENYLETHYLAMINE, and its likely mechanism of action is via the 5-HT_2 SEROTONIN RECEPTOR. Mescaline is classified by the U.S. Drug Enforcement Administration as a Schedule I controlled substance (see SCHEDULED DRUG).

mesmerism *n.* an old name, used in the mid-18th through the mid-19th centuries, for HYPNOSIS. See ANIMAL MAGNETISM. [Franz Anton **Mesmer** (1733–1815), Austrian physician and an early proponent of hypnosis] **—mesmerist** *n.* **—mesmeric** *adj.*

mesmerize *vb.* an archaic word for hypnotize.

mesocortical system a network of DOPAMINERGIC neurons in the brain that consists of the medial PREFRONTAL CORTEX and the anterior CINGULATE GYRUS. It has connections to other parts of the limbic system, and its activity is related to emotion, reward, and substance abuse.

mesolimbic system a network of DOPAMINERGIC neurons in the brain consisting of the nucleus accumbens, amygdala, and olfactory tubercle. Its activity is related to emotion, reward, and substance abuse.

mesomorph *n.* a constitutional type (SOMATOTYPE) in SHELDON'S CONSTITUTIONAL THEORY OF PERSONALITY characterized by a muscular, athletic physique, which—according to this theory—is highly correlated with SOMATOTONIA. Also called **mesomorphic body type**. See also BODY-BUILD INDEX. **—mesomorphic** *adj.* **—mesomorphy** *n.*

mesoridazine *n.* a first-generation (typical or conventional) ANTIPSYCHOTIC of the piperidine PHENOTHIAZINE class. Mesoridazine is a low-potency agent that is a metabolic product of THIORIDAZINE. Like the latter drug, its use is associated with life-threatening disturbances in heart rhythm (prolongation of the Q-T interval potentially leading to torsades de pointes syndrome; see ELECTROCARDIOGRAPHIC EFFECT). It should not be administered to individuals taking other drugs that prolong the Q-T interval or who have a history of heart rhythm disturbances, and it is appropriate for the treatment of schizophrenia only in individuals who have not responded to other antipsychotic agents. U.S. trade name: **Serentil**.

messenger RNA (**mRNA**) a type of RNA that carries instructions from a cell's genetic material (usually DNA) to the protein-manufacturing apparatus elsewhere in the cell and directs the assembly of protein components in precise accord with those instructions. The instructions are embodied in the sequence of bases in the mRNA, according to the GENETIC CODE.

Messiah complex the desire and compulsion to redeem or save others or the world. The individual may harbor the delusion of being divine. See also JEHOVAH COMPLEX.

Mestinon *n.* a trade name for PYRIDOSTIGMINE.

meta-analysis *n.* a quantitative technique for synthesizing the results of multiple studies of a phenomenon into a single result by combining the EFFECT SIZE estimates from each study into a single estimate of the combined effect size or into a distribution of effect sizes.

metabolic defect any deficiency in the structure or enzymatic function of protein molecules or in the transport of substances across cell membranes due to INBORN ERRORS OF METABOLISM or disturbances caused by toxic agents or dietary excesses (e.g., alcoholism or cholesterol-rich foods).

metabolic–nutritional model a system of studying mental disorders in which the emphasis is on long-term assessments of the influence of such factors as toxins and deprivations in populations.

metabolic screening examination procedures used in predicting or diagnosing possible INBORN ERRORS OF METABOLISM (e.g., phenylketonuria). The procedures include routine blood tests for newborns, GENETIC COUNSELING of parents with known familial metabolic deficiencies, and AMNIOCENTESIS.

metabolic tolerance see PHARMACODYNAMIC TOLERANCE.

metabolism *n.* the physical and chemical processes within a living cell or organism that are necessary to maintain life. It includes **catabolism**, the breaking down of complex molecules into simpler ones, often with the release of energy; and **anabolism**, the synthesis of complex molecules from simple ones. [term coined by German physiologist Theodor Schwann (1810–1882)] **—metabolic** *adj.*

metacognition *n.* awareness of one's own cognitive processes, often involving a conscious attempt to control them. The so-called TIP-OF-THE-TONGUE PHENOMENON, in which one struggles to "know" something that one knows one knows, provides an interesting example of metacognition. **—metacognitional** *adj.*

Metadate *n.* a trade name for METHYLPHENIDATE.

metaemotion *n.* one's awareness of and attitude toward one's own and others' emotions. For example, some people have negative attitudes toward anger in themselves or anyone else; others like to encourage anger. Some are ashamed of being too happy; others strive for such a state.

metamemory *n.* awareness of one's own memory processes, often involving a conscious attempt to direct or control them. It is an aspect of METACOGNITION.

metamorphosis *n.* a change in form or structure, typically from one developmental stage to another. See also SEXUAL METAMORPHOSIS. **—metamorphose** *vb.*

metamotivation *n.* in the HUMANISTIC PSYCHOLOGY of Abraham MASLOW, those motives that impel an individual to "character growth, character expression, maturation, and development," that is, the motivation that operates on the level of SELF-ACTUALIZATION and transcendence in the hierarchy of needs (see MASLOW'S MOTIVATIONAL HIERARCHY). In Maslow's view, metamotivation is distinct from the motivation operating in the lower level needs, which he calls DEFICIENCY MOTIVATION, and it emerges after the lower needs are satisfied. Also called **being motivation**; **B-motivation**; **growth motivation**. See METANEEDS. See also MASLOW'S THEORY OF HUMAN MOTIVATION.

metaneeds *pl. n.* in the HUMANISTIC PSYCHOLOGY of Abraham MASLOW, the highest level of needs that come into play primarily after the lower level needs have been met. Metaneeds constitute the goals of self-actualizers and include the needs for knowledge, beauty, and creativity. In Maslow's view, the inability to fulfill them results in METAPATHOLOGY. Also called **being values**; **B-values**. See METAMOTIVATION. See also MASLOW'S THEORY OF HUMAN MOTIVATION.

metapathology *n.* in the HUMANISTIC PSYCHOLOGY of Abraham MASLOW, the state of vague frustration or discontent experienced by individuals who are unable to satisfy their METANEEDS (e.g., specific creative, intellectual, or aesthetic needs). See also METAMOTIVATION; MASLOW'S THEORY OF HUMAN MOTIVATION.

metaphor therapy a system that focuses on the symbolic meaning of language and the use of metaphors in therapy. It is theorized that metaphors may provide means for restructuring thinking and approaches to problem solving in treatment. [developed by U.S. psychotherapist Richard R. Kopp (1942–)]

metapsychological profile in psychoanalysis, a systematic profile of a patient's intrapsychic functioning, in contrast to a mere list of symptoms; such a profile offers a picture of his or her entire personality. The technique was developed by Anna FREUD in 1965.

metapsychology *n.* the study of, or a concern for, the fundamental underlying principles of any psychology. The term was used by Sigmund FREUD to denote his own psychological theory, emphasizing its ability to offer comprehensive explanations of psychological phenomena on a fundamental level. Freud's criteria for a metapsychology were that it should explain a psychical phenomenon in terms of (a) its dynamics, (b) its topology, and (c) its economic aspects. Although these specific criteria apply most clearly to Freud's own theory, the notion of metapsychology as explanation at a fundamental and comprehensive level continues to be a useful construct. —**metapsychological** *adj.*

metastasis *n.* see CANCER.

meth *n.* slang for METHAMPHETAMINE.

methadone *n.* a synthetic OPIOID ANALGESIC that is used for pain relief and as a substitute for heroin in METHADONE MAINTENANCE THERAPY. It is quite effective when orally ingested and has a long duration of action, both preventing withdrawal symptoms and blocking the reinforcing effects of heroin. U.S. trade name (among others): **Dolophine**.

methadone maintenance therapy a drug-rehabilitation therapy in which those with HEROIN DEPENDENCE are prescribed a daily oral dose of METHADONE to blunt craving for opioid drugs. A controversial treatment, it is nonetheless widely considered the most effective approach to heroin addiction.

Methadrine *n.* a trade name for METHAMPHETAMINE hydrochloride.

M

methamphetamine *n.* a CNS STIMULANT whose chemical structure is similar to that of amphetamine but that has a more pronounced effect on the central nervous system. It is used for treating attention-deficit/hyperactivity disorder in children and as a short-term aid to obesity treatment in adults. Like all AMPHETAMINES, methamphetamine is prone to abuse and dependence. It can be smoked, snorted, ingested orally, or injected. After the initial rush—it increases activity levels and induces a general sense of well-being—a state of high agitation that can lead to violence is experienced by some users. Long-term abuse is associated with nerve damage and behavioral and mental status changes, including psychosis. U.S. trade name: **Desoxyn**.

methaqualone *n.* a synthetic drug with sedative and hypnotic effects, unrelated chemically to other sedatives, and having a potency roughly equal to that of PENTOBARBITAL. It is used to treat patients who are unable to tolerate barbiturate drugs. In small doses, the drug depresses the sensory cortex; in larger doses, it affects the spinal reflexes. It has caused more deaths from overdose than such drugs as PCP and heroin. Trade name: **Quaalude**. See SEDATIVE, HYPNOTIC, AND ANXIOLYTIC DRUGS.

methocarbamol *n.* a member of a group of centrally acting MUSCLE RELAXANTS used as an adjunctive agent in the management of musculoskeletal pain. Because methocarbamol does not directly reduce skeletal muscle tension, its therapeutic action is thought to be due to its sedative or CNS DEPRESSANT properties. It is available in tablet and injectable forms. U.S. trade name: **Robaxin**.

methodological behaviorism a form of BEHAVIORISM that concedes the existence and reality of conscious events but contends that the only suitable means of studying them scientifically is via their expression in behavior. Compare RADICAL BEHAVIORISM. See NEOBEHAVIORISM.

methotrimeprazine *n.* a low-potency antipsychotic of the aliphatic PHENOTHIAZINE class. In the United States, it is currently used only for the treatment of pain. Also called **levomepromazine**. U.S. trade name: **Levoprome**.

methyldopa *n.* a drug used for treating hypertension. It acts as an agonist at ALPHA-ADRENERGIC RECEPTORS in brainstem centers that control the vascular system. When stimulated by methyldopa, these receptors, which act via an inhibitory feedback mechanism, slow the release of catecholamines from central neurons involved in the regulation of blood pressure. U.S. trade name: **Aldomet**.

3,4-methylenedioxyamphetamine *n.* see MDA.

3,4-methylenedioxymethamphetamine *n.* see MDMA.

methylphenidate *n.* a stimulant related to the AMPHETAMINES and with a similar mechanism of action. It is an INDIRECT AGONIST of catecholamine neurotransmission, blocking the reuptake of catecholamines from the synaptic cleft and stimulating presynaptic release of catecholamines. Unlike amphetamine, methylphenidate is more potent as a reuptake blocker than as a releasing agent. Methylphenidate is used as an adjunct to antidepressant therapy and to increase concentration and alertness in patients with brain injuries, brain cancer, or dementia. It is officially approved by the U.S. Food and Drug Administration for the treatment of attention-deficit/hyperactivity disorder (ADHD) and narcolepsy in both children and adults. In children with ADHD, methylphenidate increases attention and decreases impulsivity and physical overactivity, leading to improvement in academic and social functioning, at least while the drug is being administered. Potential long-term side effects in children include growth suppression, which may occur at least transiently in some children taking these drugs. It is not recommended to use methylphenidate or other stimulants in children without concurrent behavioral therapy or counseling. Methylphenidate is a drug of potential abuse; it is classified by the U.S. Drug Enforcement Administration as a Schedule II controlled substance (see SCHEDULED DRUG). U.S. trade names (among others): **Concerta**; **Metadate**; **Ritalin**.

methylphenyltetrahydropyridine *n.* see MPTP.

methylxanthines *pl. n.* methylated derivatives

of **xanthines** (stimulant plant alkaloids) with similar pharmacological actions. The most common are CAFFEINE (1,3,7-trimethylxanthine), the active ingredient in coffee; THEOBROMINE (3,7-dimethylxanthine), the active ingredient in cocoa; and **theophylline** (1,3-dimethylxanthine), the active ingredient in tea. At low doses methylxanthines cause CNS stimulation and arousal; at high doses, anxiety, agitation, and coma may result. Methylxanthines also relax bronchial muscles: Some (e.g., theophylline) have been used in the medical management of reactive airway disease, although they have now largely been supplanted by newer agents.

methysergide *n.* an ERGOT DERIVATIVE used in the treatment of migraine headaches. It reduces the frequency and intensity of migraine attacks in most individuals and is thought to act by opposing the action of serotonin (see SEROTONIN ANTAGONISTS). Methysergide is closely related to LSD and has similar effects at some tissue sites. Side effects of methysergide include lightheadedness or dizziness, nausea or vomiting, euphoria, insomnia, and unsteadiness. U.S. trade name: **Sansert**.

metonymic distortion a cognitive disturbance, observed in schizophrenia, in which related but inappropriate verbal expressions are used in place of the proper expression. For example, a person may say that he or she had three menus (instead of three meals) a day.

metonymy *n.* in speech pathology, a disturbance in which imprecise or inappropriate words and expressions are used. See METONYMIC DISTORTION. **—metonymic** *adj.*

Metrazol shock treatment a form of SHOCK THERAPY involving the intravenous injection of Metrazol, a trade name for pentylenetetrazol, a powerful CNS STIMULANT that induces convulsions and coma. Because the procedure produced intense feelings of dread, and the incidence of fatality was high, it is now rarely used. Also called **Metrazol therapy**; **Metrazol treatment**. [introduced in 1934 by Hungarian psychiatrist Ladislas von Meduna (1896–1964)]

Meyer's theory the theory of mental illness proposed by Swiss-born U.S. psychiatrist Adolf Meyer (1866–1950), who believed that mental disorders resulted from behavior patterns that developed as faulty responses to specific situations. He advocated a holistic approach (see PSYCHOBIOLOGY) to diagnosis and treatment of mental disorders.

mianserin *n.* an antidepressant with a mechanism of action similar to that of the related compound MIRTAZAPINE. Mianserin is marketed in several countries (e.g., under the trade name **Tolvon**) but not in the United States.

Michigan Alcoholism Screening Test (**MAST**) a widely used measure designed to provide a rapid screening for problematic alcohol consumption, alcohol abuse, and alcoholism. It comprises 25 yes–no questions, such as "Do you ever feel guilty about your drinking?" or "Are you able to stop drinking when you want to?". Various other forms of the instrument are available, including the 10-question **Brief MAST** (BMAST) and the 13-question **Short MAST** (SMAST). [developed in 1971 by U.S. psychiatrist Melvin L. Selzer at the University of Michigan, Ann Arbor]

Mickey Finn see KNOCKOUT DROPS.

microcephaly *n.* a condition in which the head is abnormally small in relation to the rest of the body. There are numerous causes and manifestations. Mental retardation ranging from moderate to profound often accompanies microcephaly. See also PRIMARY MICROCEPHALY; PURE MICROCEPHALY. Compare MACROCEPHALY. **—microcephalic** *adj.*

microgeny *n.* the series of small steps that lead up to a patient's symptoms or to an individual's specific behavior or mental processes. The term is used in the PSYCHODYNAMIC APPROACH.

micromelia *n.* a developmental defect marked by abnormal shortness or smallness of the limbs, sometimes associated with mental retardation.

microphthalmos–corneal opacity–spasticity syndrome a presumably hereditary disorder of children born with MICROCEPHALY, small eyes with opaque corneas, spastic diplegia (spasticity in both legs or both arms), and mental retardation. Scissoring (crossing) of the legs is a common sign in such patients.

micropsychosis *n.* psychotic episodes of very brief duration (minutes to hours) that occur during times of stress. Micropyschoses have been observed primarily in BORDERLINE PERSONALITY DISORDER and PSEUDONEUROTIC SCHIZOPHRENIA, although the latter is no longer a valid diagnostic entity.

microptic hallucination see LILLIPUTIAN HALLUCINATION.

microsleep *n.* a brief interval of dozing or loss of awareness that occurs during periods when a person is fatigued and trying to stay awake while doing monotonous tasks, such as driving a car, looking at a computer screen, or monitoring controls. Such periods of "nodding off" typically last for 2–30 s and are more likely to occur in the predawn and mid-afternoon hours. They increase the risk of accidents.

microsocial engineering a technique of conflict resolution among family members in which a BEHAVIORAL CONTRACT is established through a specific schedule of responsibilities, privileges, sanctions for violations, and bonuses for compliance.

midazolam *n.* a highly potent, short-acting BENZODIAZEPINE used chiefly for the induction of anesthesia or conscious sedation for operative procedures. It is available in a form for intravenous or intramuscular administration and as a syrup for oral administration. Because of its

M

potential to induce respiratory depression (particularly when used as a sedating agent in nonsurgical situations), its short HALF-LIFE, and the need for continuous monitoring of respiratory and cardiac function, midazolam has little, if any, application in mental health settings. It has reportedly been used as a DATE-RAPE DRUG. U.S. trade name: **Versed**.

midbrain *n.* a relatively small region of the upper brainstem that connects the FOREBRAIN and HINDBRAIN. Also called **mesencephalon**.

middle-child syndrome a hypothetical condition purported to be shared by all middle-born children, based on the assumption that middle children in a family develop personality characteristics that are different from first-born and later born children. Current research indicates that a child's birth order in a particular family may have small, subtle influences on personality and intelligence but not strong and consistent effects on psychological outcomes. See also BIRTH ORDER.

middle insomnia a period of sleeplessness that occurs after falling asleep normally, with difficulty in falling asleep again. It is a common symptom of a MAJOR DEPRESSIVE DISORDER. Compare INITIAL INSOMNIA; TERMINAL INSOMNIA.

M

midlife crisis a period of psychological distress occurring in some individuals during the middle years of adulthood, roughly from ages 35 to 65. Causes may include significant life events and health or occupational problems and concerns. See also AGE CRISIS. [term coined in 1965 by Canadian consulting organizational psychologist Elliot Jaques (1917–2003)]

midpoint *n.* the point or value halfway between the highest and lowest values in a FREQUENCY DISTRIBUTION.

Mignon delusion a variation of the family-romance fantasy in which children believe that their parents are actually foster parents and their real families are of distinguished lineage. The name is derived from the child character in Goethe's novel *Wilhelm Meister's Apprenticeship* (1796).

Migranal *n.* a trade name for DIHYDROERGOTAMINE.

migration adaptation adjustment to a new community or area, which involves withstanding the stresses of geographic mobility (e.g., leaving familiar surroundings, adapting to unfamiliar surroundings and customs). Though stressful, such factors have not been proved to be a common source of mental illness.

mild cognitive impairment (**MCI**) a transitional condition between normal healthy aging and early DEMENTIA, characterized by a memory impairment greater than would be expected for age and education. Other cognitive functions are intact, and activities of daily living are normal. Individuals with MCI are at increased risk for developing ALZHEIMER'S DISEASE.

mild depression a mild form of depression, typically MINOR DEPRESSIVE DISORDER or a MAJOR DEPRESSIVE EPISODE with mild or few symptoms.

mild mental retardation a diagnostic and classification category applying to those with IQs of 50 to 69, comprising 80% of people with MENTAL RETARDATION. These individuals usually develop good communication skills and reach a sixth-grade level of academic performance in their late teens, but may not develop beyond the social skill levels typical of adolescents. Usually they are able to learn life and vocational skills adequate for basic self-support and independent living.

milieu *n.* (*pl.* **milieux**) in psychology and psychiatry, the social environment, especially the atmosphere and character of the home, neighborhood, school, workplace, and so on as they affect the personality and adjustment of the individual.

milieu therapy psychotherapeutic treatment based on modification or manipulation of the client's life circumstances or immediate environment. Milieu therapy attempts to organize the social and physical setting in which the client lives or is being treated in such a way as to promote healthier, more adaptive cognitions, emotions, and behavior. See also ENVIRONMENTAL THERAPY; THERAPEUTIC COMMUNITY.

military psychology the application of psychological principles, theories, and methods to the evaluation, selection, assignment, and training of military personnel, as well as to the design of military equipment. This field of applied psychology also includes the application of clinical and counseling techniques to the maintenance of morale and mental health in military settings and covers human functioning in a variety of environments during times of peace and war.

military stress models models for assessing stress in military operations and strategies for coping with it. Factors affecting the number of military personnel that become STRESS CASUALTIES include the nature of the operation in which they are involved, the intensity of the conflict, the number of battle casualties occurring, and the size, cohesion, and leadership of the unit in which they are serving.

Miller, Neal Elgar (1909–2002) U.S. psychologist. Miller received his doctorate in psychology from Yale University in 1935, working with Walter Miles (1885–1978) and Clark HULL. After a postdoctoral year studying psychoanalysis in Vienna, he taught at Yale for 30 years before moving in 1966 to Rockefeller University, where he remained for the remainder of his career. Miller's abiding interest was in the motivational aspects of reward and drive reduction and in the applications of experimental work to clinical psychology. Much of his early research attempted to reconcile Sigmund FREUD's theories of psychopathology with Ivan PAVLOV's learning theory, through the laboratory study of experimentally induced pathological behavior. His work was fundamental to the fields of learning and motivation, clinical psychology, and especially the newer field of BEHAVIORAL MEDICINE, of which he is regarded as a founder. Among his books that are considered to be classics are *Social Learning and Imitation* (1941) and *Personality and Psychotherapy* (1950), both coauthored with John Dollard (1900–1980). His many honors included the National Medal of Science, the American Psychological Association's Distinguished Scientific Contributions Award, and election to the National Academy of Sciences.

Milligan annihilation method a type of ELECTROCONVULSIVE THERAPY in which three treatments are administered the first day, followed by two treatments daily until the desired level of regression is achieved.

milling around the initial stage in an ENCOUNTER GROUP, during which participants discuss trivial topics in order to avoid exposing themselves to new people and new interpersonal processes.

Millon Clinical Multiaxial Inventory (**MCMI**) a true–false questionnaire, consisting of 175 items, that is widely used to assess clinical conditions and personality disorders in psychiatric patients in the United States. First published in 1977, it has been revised twice; the most recent version, **MCMI–III**, includes 24 scales arranged into four groups: clinical personality patterns, severe personality pathology, clinical syndromes, and severe clinical syndromes. Additionally, there are four corrections scales to help detect random or dishonest responding. BASE RATE scores are used in interpreting results. [Theodore **Millon** (1929–), U.S. psychologist]

Miltown *n.* a trade name for MEPROBAMATE.

mind *n.* **1.** most broadly, all intellectual and psychological phenomena of an organism, encompassing motivational, affective, behavioral, perceptual, and cognitive systems; in other words, the organized totality of the MENTAL and PSYCHIC processes of an organism and the structural and functional cognitive components on which they depend. The term, however, is often used more narrowly to denote only cognitive activities and functions, such as perceiving, attending, thinking, problem solving, language, learning, and memory. The nature of the relationship between the mind and the body, including the brain and its mechanisms or activities, has been, and continues to be, the subject of much debate. See MIND–BODY PROBLEM. **2.** the substantive content of such mental and psychic processes. **3.** consciousness or awareness, particularly as specific to an individual. **4.** a set of EMERGENT PROPERTIES automatically derived from a brain that has achieved sufficient biological sophistication. In this sense, the mind is considered more the province of humans and of human consciousness than of organisms in general. **5.** human consciousness regarded as an immaterial entity distinct from the brain. See CARTESIAN DUALISM. **6.** the brain itself and its activities: in this view, the mind essentially is both the anatomical organ and what it does. **7.** concentration or focused attention. **8.** intention or volition. **9.** opinion or point of view. **10.** the characteristic mode of thinking of a group, such as the criminal mind or the military mind.

mindblindness *n.* a deficit in THEORY OF MIND that is characteristic of people with autism. A person with mindblindness cannot "read the minds" of others, that is, understand their behavior in terms of BELIEF–DESIRE REASONING. [first described by British psychologist Simon Baron-Cohen (1958–)]

mind–body intervention therapeutic approaches that focus on harnessing the power of the mind to bring about change in the body or achieve reduction of symptoms of disease or disorder. The various techniques used include relaxation training (e.g., AUTOGENIC TRAINING, PROGRESSIVE RELAXATION), MEDITATION, prayer, and CREATIVE ARTS THERAPY. See also COMPLEMENTARY AND ALTERNATIVE MEDICINE.

mind–body problem the problem of accounting for and describing the relationship between mental and physical processes (psyche and soma). Solutions to this problem fall into six broad categories: (a) **interactionism**, in which mind and body are separate processes that nevertheless exert mutual influence (see CARTESIAN DUALISM); (b) parallelism, in which mind and body are separate processes with a point-to-point correspondence but no causal connection; (c) IDEALISM, in which only mind exists and the soma is a function of the psyche; (d) double-aspect theory, in which body and mind are both functions of a common entity; (e) EPIPHENOMENALISM, in which mind is a by-product of bodily processes; and (f) MATERIALISM, in which body is the only reality and the psyche is nonexistent. Categories (a) and (b) are varieties of DUALISM; the remainder are varieties of MONISM. In the context of psychopathology, two central questions arising from the mind–body problem are which sphere takes precedence in the genesis and development of illness and how does each sphere affect the other. Also called **body–mind problem**.

mind control 1. an extreme form of social influence used to indoctrinate an individual in the attitudes and beliefs of a group, usually one that is religious or political in nature. See BRAINWASHING. **2.** the control of physical activities of the body, particularly autonomic functions, by mental processes. See AUTOGENIC TRAINING; BIOFEEDBACK; TRANSCENDENTAL MEDITATION; YOGA. See also MIND–BODY INTERVENTION.

mind-cure movement a self-help movement in the 19th century that assumed that physical

M

health was the product of "right" thinking, usually regarded as optimism, self-affirmation, and self-regulation of moods.

mindfulness *n.* full awareness of one's internal states and surroundings: the opposite of ABSENT-MINDEDNESS. The concept has been applied to various therapeutic interventions—for example, mindfulness-based COGNITIVE BEHAVIOR THERAPY, mindfulness-based stress reduction, mindfulness for addictions, and MINDFULNESS MEDITATION—to help people avoid destructive or automatic habits and responses by learning to observe their thoughts, emotions, and other present-moment experiences without judging or reacting to them. **—mindful** *adj.*

mindfulness meditation a type of MEDITATION in which thoughts, feelings, and sensations are experienced freely as they arise. Mindfulness meditation is intended to enable individuals to become highly attentive to sensory information and to focus on each moment as it occurs. See also MINDFULNESS; TRANSCENDENTAL MEDITATION. Compare CONCENTRATIVE MEDITATION.

mindsight *n.* a proposed mode of visual perception, hypothesized to work in parallel with everyday vision, in which a person registers a nonvisual sense of change in visual information before conscious awareness of the change through actually "seeing" it. [proposed by 21st-century Canadian psychologist and computer scientist Ronald A. Rensink]

M

mineralocorticoid *n.* any CORTICOSTEROID hormone that affects ion concentrations in body tissues and helps to regulate the excretion of salt and water. In humans the principal mineralocorticoid is aldosterone.

minimal brain damage (**MBD**) **1.** a mild degree of brain damage that is presumed to exist because of the presence of a constellation of SOFT SIGNS, which may include short attention span, distractibility, impulsivity, hyperactivity, emotional lability, poor motor coordination, visual-perceptual disturbance, language difficulties, and learning problems. These symptoms occur among a number of conditions involving neurologically based disturbance, including ATTENTION-DEFICIT/HYPERACTIVITY DISORDER, LEARNING DISORDERS, COMMUNICATION DISORDERS, and DEVELOPMENTAL COORDINATION DISORDER. **2.** an old name for ATTENTION-DEFICIT/HYPERACTIVITY DISORDER.

minimal brain dysfunction (**MBD**) **1.** a relatively mild impairment of brain function that is presumed to account for a variety of SOFT SIGNS seen in certain learning or behavioral disabilities. These signs include hyperactivity, impulsivity, emotional lability, and distractibility. Also called **minimal cerebral dysfunction**. **2.** an old name for ATTENTION-DEFICIT/HYPERACTIVITY DISORDER.

Mini-Mental State Examination (**MMSE**) an instrument used extensively to provide a quick assessment of cognitive status as a tool for the diagnosis of dementia. The patient is asked simple questions relating to orientation (e.g., "What day is today?") and required to perform simple tasks (e.g., remember the names of three common objects, fold a piece of paper in half, write an intelligible sentence) assessing memory, attention and calculation, and language. Also called **Folstein Mini-Mental State Examination**. [devised in 1975 by U.S. psychiatrists Marshal F. Folstein (1941–), Susan E. Folstein (1944–), and Paul R. McHugh]

minimization *n.* COGNITIVE DISTORTION consisting of a tendency to present events to oneself or others as insignificant or unimportant. Minimization often involves being unclear or nonspecific, so the listener does not have a complete picture of all the details and may be led to draw inaccurate or incomplete conclusions. See also DENIAL.

Minnesota Multiphasic Personality Inventory (**MMPI**) a PERSONALITY INVENTORY first published in 1940 and now one of the most widely used SELF-REPORT tools for assessing personality. It has broad applications across a range of mental health, medical, substance abuse, forensic, and personnel screening settings as a measure of psychological maladjustment. The original inventory consisted of 550 true–false items grouped into nine scales reflecting common clinical problems: hypochondria, depression, hysteria, psychopathic deviate, masculine–feminine interest, paranoia, psychasthenia (i.e., anxiety), schizophrenia, and hypomania. The results were scored by the examiner or by computer to determine the participant's personality profile as well as any tendency to lie or to fake good or bad. The version currently in use, the **MMPI–2** (1989), features 567 true–false questions that assess symptoms, attitudes, and beliefs that relate to emotional and behavioral problems, including substantial revisions of the original items and the addition of new scales. The early 1990s saw the publication of a version of the instrument, the **MMPI–A**, with content items specifically relevant to adolescents aged 14–18. The instrument's 478 items help identify personal, social, and behavioral problems (e.g., family issues, eating disorders, chemical dependency). [originally developed by U.S. psychologist Starke Rosecrans Hathaway (1903–1984) and U.S. psychiatrist John Charnley McKinley (1891–1950) at the University of Minnesota]

minor *n.* a person who is not legally an ADULT.

minor depressive disorder a mood disorder in which, for at least 2 weeks, the individual has either persistent depressed mood or ANHEDONIA as well as at least two of a range of other symptoms. These other symptoms include: poor or increased appetite with significant weight loss or gain; insomnia or excessive sleep; PSYCHOMOTOR AGITATION or PSYCHOMOTOR RETARDATION; loss of energy with fatigue; feelings of worthlessness or inappropriate guilt; reduced ability to concentrate or make decisions; and recurrent thoughts of death, SUICIDAL IDEATION, or ATTEMPTED SUICIDE. These symptoms do not meet the criteria for DYSTHYMIC DISORDER and, according to proposed formal diagnostic criteria, they must occur in an individual who has never had a MAJOR DEPRESSIVE EPISODE. However, in clinical practice, a diagnosis of minor depressive disorder is widely applied to people who have significant symptoms of, but fail to meet the full criteria for, MAJOR DEPRESSIVE DISORDER, regardless of their history of depression. See also DEPRESSIVE DISORDER NOT OTHERWISE SPECIFIED.

minority stress the physiological and psychological effects associated with the adverse social conditions experienced by ethnic and racial minorities, lesbians, gay men, bisexual and transgender individuals, and others who are members of stigmatized social groups. Common sources of minority stress include experiencing prejudice, discrimination, harassment, or verbal or physical violence; expecting or experiencing rejection by others; concealing one's minority identity; and internalizing negative societal attitudes about one's social group that results in a negative self-view. The concept frequently is invoked by researchers to explain the increased rates of depression, suicide, anxiety, substance abuse, workplace problems, body image problems, eating disorders, high blood pressure, cardiovascular disease, and other mental and physical conditions among members of minority or marginalized groups. Conversely, researchers have hypothesized certain protective factors that help ameliorate the adverse health outcomes of minority stress. These include personal characteristics, such as RESILIENCE and an effective COPING STRATEGY, and SOCIAL SUPPORT mechanisms, such as COHESION. [coined in 1995 by Israeli-born U.S. social psychologist Ilan H. Meyer]

minor tranquilizer see ANXIOLYTIC.

mirroring *n.* **1.** reflecting or emulating speech, affect, behavior, or other qualities in psychotherapeutic contexts. A therapist may adopt the movements, speech style, or locutions of a client, and vice versa, to indicate comprehension of what is being said or to reflect bonding, either unconsciously or with the intent of empathizing. **2.** the positive responses of parents to a child that are intended to instill internal self-respect. **3.** see MIRROR TECHNIQUE.

mirror phase the stage in development occurring around 6–18 months of age when the infant becomes able to imagine himself or herself as an autonomous ego in the image of the parent and also starts to recognize his or her reflection in a mirror. In sum, the child begins to acquire a self-image. French psychoanalyst Jacques Lacan (1901–1981), who introduced the phrase, saw this as marking the start of the infant's transition from the realm of the IMAGINARY to that of the SYMBOLIC. See also NAME-OF-THE-FATHER.

mirror reading **1.** reading in a pattern that is the reverse of that generally followed. **2.** a task in which a person must read words that are presented one at a time in mirror image. **3.** a preference for reading mirror-reversed rather than normally written words.

mirror sign **1.** the inability to recognize the reflection of oneself in a mirror. **2.** the tendency to look at oneself in a reflecting surface (window, mirror, etc.) frequently and for an extended period of time. [first described in 1927 by Paul Abely as an early symptom of schizophrenia]

mirror technique **1.** the conscious use of ACTIVE LISTENING by the therapist in psychotherapy, accompanied by reflection of the client's affect and body language in order to stimulate a sense of empathy and to further the development of the THERAPEUTIC ALLIANCE. **2.** in PSYCHODRAMA, a technique in which an AUXILIARY EGO imitates a client's behavior patterns to show that person how others perceive and react to him or her. Also called **mirroring**.

mirror transference in psychoanalysis, a TRANSFERENCE technique used in the treatment of NARCISSISTIC PERSONALITY DISORDERS in which the patients' grandiose selves are reactivated as a replica of the early phase of their lives when their mothers established their sense of perfection by admiring their exhibitionistic behavior. This "reactivation process" helps to restore the patient's self-esteem.

mirror writing the production of individual letters and whole word strings in reverse direction. Mirror writing is characterized by an inversion of letters and words such that they appear reversed unless viewed in a mirror. It is related to STREPHOSYMBOLIA. Also called **palingraphia**; **retrography**.

mirtazapine *n.* an antidepressant whose mechanism of action differs from that of most other antidepressants. It is considered to be a MIXED-FUNCTION ANTIDEPRESSANT in that two separate actions result in increased neurotransmission of norepinephrine and serotonin. By binding to presynaptic α_2-adrenoreceptors (see ADRENERGIC RECEPTOR; AUTORECEPTOR), it enables continued release of norepinephrine from presynaptic neurons. It also acts as a SEROTONIN-RECEPTOR AGONIST at postsynaptic 5-HT_1 receptors. Other actions of mirtazapine include potent antagonism of other serotonin receptors and histamine receptors, but it does not inhibit the reuptake of serotonin or norepinephrine. Sedation and weight gain are common adverse effects of mirtazapine, probably due to its potent ability to block the HISTAMINE H_1 receptor. Unlike many other antidepressants, in most patients mirtazapine does not cause sexual dysfunction. Rarely, AGRANULOCYTOSIS has been associated with its use. U.S. trade name: **Remeron**.

misandry *n.* hatred or contempt for men. Compare MISOGYNY. **—misandrist** *n., adj.*

misanthropy *n.* a hatred, aversion, or distrust

of human beings and human nature. **—misanthrope** *n.* **—misanthropic** *adj.*

misattribution *n.* an incorrect inference as to the cause of an individual's or group's behavior or of an interpersonal event. For example, **misattribution of arousal** is an effect in which the physiological stimulation generated by one stimulus is mistakenly ascribed to another source. See also ATTRIBUTION THEORY.

miscarriage *n.* see ABORTION.

misidentification *n.* **1.** failure to identify individuals correctly due to impaired memory or a confused state, as in dementia or alcoholic intoxication or sometimes in mania. **2.** failure to recognize people or objects due to a delusion that they have been transformed (**delusional misidentification**). See MISIDENTIFICATION SYNDROME.

misidentification syndrome a disorder characterized by the delusional MISIDENTIFICATION of oneself, other people, places, or objects. The misidentification may be expressed as the mistaken belief that a person has altered his or her identity in some way, either physically or psychologically, or that some place or object has undergone some aspect of transformation. Also called **delusional misidentification syndrome**. See also CAPGRAS SYNDROME; FREGOLI'S PHENOMENON; INTERMETAMORPHOSIS SYNDROME.

M

misinformation effect a phenomenon in which a person mistakenly recalls misleading information that an experimenter has provided, instead of accurately recalling the correct information that had been presented earlier. The misinformation effect is studied in the context of EYEWITNESS MEMORY.

misocainia (**misocainea**) *n.* see MISONEISM.

misogamy *n.* hatred of or aversion to marriage. **—misogamist** *n.*

misogyny *n.* hatred or contempt for women. Compare MISANDRY. **—misogynist** *n.* **—misogynistic** *adj.*

misologia *n.* an aversion to speaking or arguing. Also called **misology**.

misoneism *n.* an extreme resistance to change and intolerance of anything new, sometimes expressed as an obsessive desire to maintain routines and preserve the status quo. It is often associated with AUTISTIC DISORDER. Also called **misocainia**. **—misoneist** *n.*

misopedia *n.* a hatred of children. Also called **misopedy**.

mistress *n.* a woman with whom a married man has a continuing sexual relationship, usually without the knowledge of his wife. The man may provide for the woman, but the relationship is not one of prostitution.

MIT abbreviation for MELODIC INTONATION THERAPY.

mitigating factor a fact relating to a crime or to a convicted defendant that supports the argument for a more lenient sentence. Examples of mitigating factors are the defendant's youth, personal or family circumstances, or DIMINISHED RESPONSIBILITY. Also called **mitigating circumstance**. Compare AGGRAVATING FACTOR.

mixed-effects model a statistical procedure for analyzing data from experimental designs that use one or more independent variables whose levels are specifically selected by the researcher (fixed factors; e.g., male and female) and one or more additional independent variables whose levels are chosen randomly from a wide range of possible values (random factors; e.g., age). See also FIXED-EFFECTS MODEL.

mixed emotions two or more emotions, differing in feeling quality and ACTION TENDENCY, elicited by the same event. For example, a father may be happy that his son is getting married but sorrowful if the marriage takes the son away from home; a person may become angry at an insult from a superior and also frightened by the implications for his or her employment. Also called **mixed feelings**. See AMBIVALENCE.

mixed episode an episode of a MOOD DISORDER lasting at least 1 week in which symptoms meeting criteria for both a MAJOR DEPRESSIVE EPISODE and a MANIC EPISODE are prominent over the course of the disturbance. One or more mixed episodes may be a feature of bipolar I disorder (see BIPOLAR DISORDER).

mixed feelings see MIXED EMOTIONS.

mixed-function antidepressants antidepressants that act primarily via more than one major neurotransmitter system. The term is often applied to the SNRIS (e.g., VENLAFAXINE), which inhibit the reuptake of both norepinephrine and serotonin, to distinguish them from the SSRIS (selective serotonin reuptake inhibitors). Also called **dual-action antidepressants**.

mixed model see MIXED-EFFECTS MODEL.

mixed neurosis in psychoanalysis, a condition in which a patient shows symptoms of two or more neuroses. The term is rarely used now.

mixed receptive-expressive language disorder in *DSM–IV–TR*, a communication disorder characterized by levels of language comprehension and expressive language development substantially below the expected level of verbal or nonverbal intellectual ability, as demonstrated by scores on standardized, individually administered measures of both receptive and expressive language development or functional assessment. The deficit interferes substantially with scholastic, academic, or occupational achievement or social interactions and is not due solely to mental retardation, motor speech disorders, sensory deficit, environmental deprivation, or a pervasive developmental disorder.

mixed schizophrenia 1. a form of schizophrenia in which either both negative and positive symptoms are prominent or neither is prominent. [defined in 1982 by U.S. psychiatrist Nancy C. Andreasen and Scott A. Olsen] **2.** historically, a form of schizophrenia that is manifested by symptoms of two or more of the four major types of schizophrenia described by German psychiatrist Emil Kraepelin (1856–1926) and Swiss psychiatrist Eugen Bleuler (1857–1939): simple, paranoid, catatonic, and hebephrenic (disorganized).

mixoscopia *n.* a form of VOYEURISM in which an orgasm is achieved by observing sexual intercourse between the person one loves and another person.

mixoscopia bestialis a type of sexual deviancy in which a person is excited or aroused by watching another individual have coitus with an animal.

MMECT abbreviation for MULTIPLE MONITORED ELECTROCONVULSIVE TREATMENT.

MMPI abbreviation for MINNESOTA MULTIPHASIC PERSONALITY INVENTORY.

MMPI–2 abbreviation for the revised version of the MINNESOTA MULTIPHASIC PERSONALITY INVENTORY.

MMPI–A abbreviation for the version of the MINNESOTA MULTIPHASIC PERSONALITY INVENTORY designed for use with adolescents.

MMSE abbreviation for MINI-MENTAL STATE EXAMINATION.

MMT abbreviation for MULTIMODAL THERAPY.

mnemonic *n.* any device or technique used to assist memory, usually by forging a link or association between the new information to be remembered and information previously encoded. For instance, one might remember the numbers in a password by associating them with familiar birth dates, addresses, or room numbers.

Moban *n.* a trade name for MOLINDONE.

moclobemide *n.* an antidepressant drug that is a reversible MONOAMINE OXIDASE INHIBITOR (RIMA) and relatively selective for MONOAMINE OXIDASE A. It therefore lacks many of the food interactions that limit the use of irreversible, nonselective MAO inhibitors. Moclobemide has not yet been approved for use in the United States.

modafinil *n.* a CNS STIMULANT used for the treatment of narcolepsy. Its exact mechanism of action is unclear, but modafinil may exert its stimulant effects by decreasing GABA-mediated neurotransmission (see GAMMA-AMINOBUTYRIC ACID) and potentiating GLUTAMATE transmission. Modafinil may therefore serve as an alternative agent for patients who are intolerant of amphetamines and related stimulants, which have a different mechanism of action. Because it inhibits the CYTOCHROME P450 2C19 enzyme and induces the cytochrome P450 3A4 enzyme, it may have clinically significant interactions with drugs metabolized via those enzymes. U.S. trade name: **Provigil**.

modality *n.* **1.** a particular therapeutic technique or process. **2.** a medium of sensation, such as vision or hearing. See SENSE.

modality profile in MULTIMODAL THERAPY, a list of problems and proposed treatments across the seven parameters (modalities) explored in the approach. The parameters, or dimensions (e.g., affect, sensation), are considered to be distinct yet interactive. The profiles are created specifically with clients for descriptive and therapeutic purposes.

mode *n.* **1.** a characteristic manner of behavior or way of doing things, as in a technique. **2.** the most frequently occurring score in a batch of data, which is sometimes used as a measure of CENTRAL TENDENCY.

model *n.* **1.** a graphic, theoretical, or other type of representation of a concept (e.g., a disorder) or of basic behavioral or bodily processes that can be used for various investigative and demonstrative purposes, such as enhancing understanding of the concept, proposing hypotheses, showing relationships, or identifying epidemiological patterns. **2.** see MODELING.

modeling *n.* **1.** a technique used in COGNITIVE BEHAVIOR THERAPY and BEHAVIOR THERAPY in which learning occurs through observation and imitation alone, without comment or reinforcement by the therapist. **2.** in developmental psychology, the process in which one or more individuals or other entities serve as examples (**models**) that a child will emulate. Models are often parents, other adults, or other children, but may also be symbolic, for example, a book or television character. See also SOCIAL LEARNING THEORY.

modeling effect a type of experimenter effect in which a participant is unwittingly influenced to give responses similar to the responses the experimenter would give if the experimenter were a participant.

modeling theory the idea that changes in behavior, cognition, or emotional state result from observing someone else's behavior or the consequences of that behavior. See OBSERVATIONAL LEARNING; SOCIAL LEARNING THEORY.

model psychosis psychotic symptoms (e.g., delusions, hallucinations, disorientation, disorganized speech) deliberately produced by a PSYCHOTOMIMETIC drug, such as LSD, for purposes of research. This technique was particularly popular during the 1950s and 1960s.

moderate depression a MAJOR DEPRESSIVE EPISODE whose severity and number of symptoms do not meet the criteria for ACUTE DEPRESSION but exceed the criteria for MILD DEPRESSION.

moderate mental retardation a diagnostic and classification category applying to those with IQs of 35 to 49, comprising about 12% of people with MENTAL RETARDATION. These individuals rarely progress beyond the second grade in academic subjects. Although often poorly coordinated, they can learn to take care of themselves and to develop sufficient social and occupational skills to be able to perform unskilled or semiskilled work under supervision in sheltered and supportive environments, as well as in regular workplaces where accommodations are made.

moderator variable in statistics, a variable that alters the relationship between other variables. In REGRESSION ANALYSIS, for example, it is a variable that is unrelated to a criterion variable but is retained in the REGRESSION EQUATION because of its significant relationship to other predictor variables.

modesty *n.* **1.** absence of self-importance or conceit. **2.** propriety in appearance, dress, demeanor, and social behavior. **—modest** *adj.*

module *n.* **1.** in cognitive theory, a hypothetical center of information processing that is presumed to be relatively independent and highly specialized in its operations, such as a language module or face-processing module. **2.** in neuroscience, a unit of a region of the central nervous system. For example, regions of the NEOCORTEX in the brain are divided into cortical columns of basically similar structure. **—modular** *adj.*

mogilalia *n.* difficulty or hesitancy in speaking (e.g., STUTTERING). Also called **molilalia**.

M

molar approach any theory or method that stresses comprehensive concepts or overall frameworks or structures.

molar behavior a large but unified segment, or holistic unit, of behavior, such as kicking a ball. Compare MOLECULAR BEHAVIOR.

molecular behavior behavior that can be analyzed into smaller, more specific units, such as reflexes. Compare MOLAR BEHAVIOR.

molecular genetics the branch of biology that is concerned with the structure and processes of genetic material at the molecular level.

molestation *n.* the act of making sexual advances toward a person who does not want them. Molestation generally implies sexual fondling or touching an individual "without lawful consent." When the victim of molestation is a child or a person who is mentally challenged, it may be assumed that he or she does not have the capacity to give lawful consent. See also SEX OFFENSE. **—molest** *vb.*

molilalia *n.* see MOGILALIA.

molindone *n.* a conventional (typical or first-generation) antipsychotic of the DIHYDROINDOLONE class. It is of intermediate potency and has few anticholinergic side effects. Until the advent of the atypical, or second-generation, antipsychotics, it was frequently used, usually in low doses, for the management of psychoses accompanying medical conditions (e.g., HIV-related dementia). U.S. trade name: **Moban**.

mongolism *n.* an obsolete name for DOWN SYNDROME.

monism *n.* the position that reality consists of a single substance, whether this is identified as mind, matter, or God. In the context of the MIND–BODY PROBLEM, monism is any position that avoids DUALISM. **—monist** *adj., n.* **—monistic** *adj.*

monoamine hypothesis the theory that depression is caused by a deficit in the production or uptake of monoamines (serotonin, norepinephrine, and dopamine). This theory has been used to explain the effects of MONOAMINE OXIDASE INHIBITORS, but is now regarded as too simplistic.

monoamine oxidase (**MAO**) an enzyme that breaks down and inactivates monoamines, including the neurotransmitters serotonin, norepinephrine, and dopamine. It is found in most tissues and, in humans, exists in two forms, MAO-A and MAO-B. MAO-B is the predominant enzyme in the brain, whereas MAO-A is found primarily in the gastrointestinal tract (it accounts for only 20% of brain monoamine oxidase). Drugs that inhibit MAO (see MONOAMINE OXIDASE INHIBITOR) are used to treat depression. There is some evidence that inhibition of MAO-A, which primarily degrades serotonin and norepinephrine, may lead to greater antidepressant effects than inhibition of MAO-B, which primarily degrades dopamine.

monoamine oxidase inhibitor (**MAOI**; **MAO inhibitor**) a group of antidepressant drugs that function by inhibiting the activity of the enzyme MONOAMINE OXIDASE in presynaptic neurons, thereby increasing the amounts of monoamine neurotransmitters (serotonin, norepinephrine, and dopamine) available for release at the presynaptic terminal. There are two categories of MAOIs: irreversible and reversible inhibitors. **Irreversible MAOIs** bind tightly to the enzyme and permanently inhibit its ability to metabolize any monoamine. This may lead to dangerous interactions with foods and beverages containing the amino acid tryptophan or TYRAMINE, which are present in many foods, particularly those produced by enzymatic action or by aging (e.g., cheeses, preserved meats and fish). A hypertensive crisis (a potentially fatal rise in blood pressure) may result from these interactions, a phenomenon that is sometimes known as the "cheese effect." Irreversible MAOIs are of two classes: hydrazines related to isoniazid (see ISOCARBOXAZID; PHENELZINE), and nonhydrazines, of which **tranylcypromine** (U.S. trade name: Parnate) is the only agent used for mental disorders in the United States. **Reversible inhibitors of monoamine oxidase** (RIMAs) do not bind irreversibly to the enzyme, thereby freeing it to take part in the metabolism of amino acids and other amines. RIMAs may be less prone to producing a hypertensive crisis, which would obviate the need for dietary restrictions on tyramine-containing foods. Examples of RIMAs are MOCLOBEMIDE and BROFAROMINE, which are available in Europe but have not yet been approved for use in the United States. The availability of other effective antidepressants lacking the drug–food interactions of the MAOIs has led to a precipitous decline in their use, particularly of the irreversible agents.

monodrama *n.* in GROUP THERAPY, a role-playing technique in which a member of the group acts out a scene alone. The member's behavior is then evaluated by the group.

monogamy *n.* **1.** a mating system in which two individuals mate exclusively with each other. Recent genetic studies of paternity indicate that some offspring of male–female pairs exhibiting monogamy are not related to the father, leading to a distinction between **social monogamy**, in which there is an appearance of a close PAIR BOND, and **genetic monogamy**, in which there is exclusive mating. Many species, including human beings, display **serial monogamy**, in which there is an exclusive social bond with each of a series of sexual partners at different times during the individual's life. **2.** traditionally, marriage to only one spouse at a time. Compare POLYGAMY. **—monogamous** *adj.*

monoideism *n.* obsessive preoccupation with a single idea to the exclusion of anything else.

monomania *n.* **1.** extreme enthusiasm or zeal for a single subject or idea, often manifested as a rigid, irrational idea. See also IDÉE FIXE. **2.** an obsolete name for a pattern of abnormal behavior with reference to a single subject in an otherwise apparently normally functioning individual. **—monomaniac** *n.*

monopediomania *n.* sexual interest in and arousal by people who have only one leg.

monophagism *n.* a pathological eating behavior in which the individual habitually eats only one type of food or only one meal a day.

monophasic sleep a sleep pattern in which sleeping occurs in one long period once a day, typically at night. Both it and biphasic sleep (see POLYPHASIC SLEEP) contribute to physical and emotional health and greater alertness. See also SLEEP–WAKE CYCLE.

monosomy *n.* see AUTOSOME. **—monosomic** *adj.*

monosomy 5p see CRI DU CHAT SYNDROME.

monosymptomatic circumscription a mental disorder characterized by a single symptom.

monotherapy *n.* the use of a single method or approach to treat a particular disorder or PRESENTING SYMPTOM, as opposed to the use of a combination of methods. An example is the use of only PHARMACOTHERAPY, instead of pharmacotherapy and psychotherapy in combination, to treat depression.

monozygotic twins (**MZ twins**) twins, always of the same sex, that develop from a single fertilized ovum (zygote) that splits to produce two individuals who carry exactly the same complement of genes; that is, they are clones, with identical DNA. For every 1,000 pregnancies there are, on average, 3–4 MZ twins. Also called **identical twins**. Compare DIZYGOTIC TWINS. See also TWIN STUDY.

mood *n.* **1.** any short-lived emotional state, usually of low intensity (e.g., a cheerful mood, an irritable mood). **2.** a disposition to respond emotionally in a particular way that may last for hours, days, or even weeks, perhaps at a low level and without the person knowing what prompted the state. Moods differ from EMOTIONS in lacking an object; for example, the emotion of anger can be aroused by an insult, but an angry mood may arise when one does not know what one is angry about or what elicited the anger. Disturbances in mood are characteristic of MOOD DISORDERS.

mood-altering drugs substances that change the affective state of the individual through pharmacological action, usually without clouding of consciousness. They include certain tranquilizing, sedating, and antidepressant agents.

mood congruent relating to a consistency or agreement between a particular expressed feeling and the general emotional context within which it occurs. Thus, crying at a time of sadness or personal distress is viewed as mood congruent. Similarly, in psychiatric diagnosis, the term relates to a consistency between the expression of a particular symptom or behavior with those characteristics or patterns of ideation or action used to classify a particular mental disorder. In both instances, inconsistencies are described as **mood incongruent**.

mood-congruent psychotic features delusions or hallucinations that are thematically consistent with either depressed or manic mood and may occur in severe MAJOR DEPRESSIVE EPISODES, MANIC EPISODES, or MIXED EPISODES.

mood-dependent memory a condition in which memory for some event can be recalled more readily when one is in the same emotional mood (e.g., happy or sad) as when the memory was initially formed. See also CONTEXT-SPECIFIC LEARNING; STATE-DEPENDENT MEMORY.

mood disorder in *DSM–IV–TR*, a psychiatric disorder in which the principal feature is a prolonged, pervasive mood disturbance, such as a DEPRESSIVE DISORDER (e.g., MAJOR DEPRESSIVE DISORDER, DYSTHYMIC DISORDER) or BIPOLAR DISORDER, MOOD DISORDERS DUE TO A GENERAL MEDICAL CONDITION, SUBSTANCE-INDUCED MOOD DISORDER, and **mood disorder not otherwise specified**, which does not meet the diagnostic criteria for any of the specific mood disorders. A mood disorder is also called an **affective disorder**.

mood disorder due to a general medical condition in *DSM–IV–TR*, significant and persistent mood disturbance (with depressive symptoms, manic symptoms, or both) associated with a medical condition and believed to be caused directly by the physiological effects of that con-

M

dition. A variety of medical conditions may cause mood disturbance, including Parkinson's disease, Huntington's disease, stroke, hyper- or hypothyroidism, some infections (e.g., hepatitis, AIDS), and certain cancers (e.g., pancreatic).

mood incongruent see MOOD CONGRUENT.

mood-incongruent psychotic features delusions or hallucinations whose content does not include manic or depressed themes. They may occur in severe MAJOR DEPRESSIVE EPISODES, MANIC EPISODES, or MIXED EPISODES.

mood induction any method for producing a negative or positive change in mood, often by selectively reminding individuals of pleasant or unpleasant aspects of their lives.

moodiness *n.* an AFFECTIVE STATE characterized by irritability or DYSPHORIA combined with sensitivity to negative interpersonal cues. **—moody** *adj.*

mood stabilizer any of various drugs used in the treatment of cyclic mood disorders (BIPOLAR DISORDERS and CYCLOTHYMIC DISORDER). Because they reduce the symptoms of mania or manic episodes, mood stabilizers are sometimes known as **antimanics**. LITHIUM is usually the FIRST-LINE MEDICATION for bipolar I disorder, but ANTICONVULSANTS, such as VALPROIC ACID, CARBAMAZEPINE, and oxcarbazine, are becoming more commonly used for this condition and are now preferred for other cyclic disorders. The CALCIUM-CHANNEL BLOCKER verapamil is also being investigated as a mood stabilizer. Mood stabilizers are occasionally used in the management of severe affective lability found in some personality disorders (e.g., borderline personality disorder). Because of the potential for self-injurious behavior in bipolar disorders and personality disorders, great caution must be taken when prescribing medications that are potentially lethal in overdose.

mood swings oscillations in mood, particularly between feelings of happiness and sadness, ranging in intensity from normal fluctuations to cyclothymia (see CYCLOTHYMIC DISORDER) or a BIPOLAR DISORDER.

moon-phase studies research into the possible relationship between the phases of the moon and episodes of violence or mental disorder. The relationship has long been expressed in folklore, folk medicine, and language itself (e.g., the words *lunacy* and *lunatic*). Methodologically sound studies of the effects of moon phase on behavior are infrequent.

moral development the gradual formation of an individual's concepts of right and wrong, conscience, ethical and religious values, social attitudes, and behavior. Some of the major theorists in the area of moral development are Sigmund FREUD, Jean PIAGET, and Erik ERIKSON.

moral masochism in psychoanalytic theory, the unconscious need for punishment by authority figures caused by unconscious guilt arising from the repressed OEDIPUS COMPLEX. It is a nonsexual form of MASOCHISM.

moral therapy a form of psychotherapy from the 19th century based on the belief that a person with a mental disorder could be helped by being treated with compassion, kindness, and dignity in a clean, comfortable environment that provided freedom of movement, opportunities for occupational and social activity, and reassuring talks with physicians and attendants. This approach advocating humane and ethical treatment was a radical departure from the prevailing practice at that time of viewing the "insane" with suspicion and hostility, confining them in unsanitary conditions, and routinely abusing them through the use of such practices as mechanical restraint, physical punishment, and bloodletting. Moral therapy originated in the family-care program established in the Gheel colony, Belgium, during the 13th century, but came to fruition in the 19th century through the efforts of Philippe Pinel and Jean Esquirol (1772–1840) in France, William Tuke (1732–1822) in England, and Benjamin Rush (1745–1813), Isaac Ray (1807–1881), and Thomas Kirkbride (1809–1883) in the United States. The THERAPEUTIC COMMUNITY of today has its roots in this movement. Also called **moral treatment**.

moratorium *n.* in Erik ERIKSON's theory of psychosexual development, the experimental period of adolescence in which, during the task of discovering who one is as an individual separate from family of origin and as part of the broader social context, young people try out alternative roles before making permanent commitments to an IDENTITY. Adolescents who are unsuccessful at negotiating this stage risk confusion over their role in life. See ERIKSON'S EIGHT STAGES OF DEVELOPMENT; IDENTITY VERSUS IDENTITY CONFUSION.

morbid *adj.* unhealthy, diseased, or otherwise abnormal.

morbid dependency excessive reliance on or need for another person or situation such that the dependent person has difficulty functioning independently. See DEPENDENCY NEED.

morbidity *n.* a pathological (diseased) condition or state, either organic or functional.

morbidity rate the incidence of disease, expressed as a ratio denoting the number of people in a population who are ill or have a specific disease compared with the number who are well.

morbidity risk in EPIDEMIOLOGY, the statistical chance that an individual will develop a certain disease or disorder. The probability is often expressed in terms of risk factors, using 1.0 as a base: The larger the number, the greater the morbidity risk.

morbid jealousy see DELUSIONAL JEALOUSY.

morbid obesity OBESITY that causes disease. The excess body weight begins first to interfere with agility and then day-to-day movement. As the obesity increases, the massive weight of tissue on the chest interferes with breathing. Affected people gradually develop HYPOXEMIA (decreased blood oxygen) and SLEEP APNEA (periodic cessation of breathing while asleep), which may result in chronic fatigue and SOMNOLENCE and, eventually, high blood pressure, pulmonary hypertension, myocarditis, right-sided heart failure, and ultimately death. See also BODY MASS INDEX.

moria *n.* an obsessive or morbid desire to joke, as in some cases of DEMENTIA, particularly when the humor is inappropriate.

Morita therapy a therapy for SHINKEISHITSU consisting of an initial 7-day period of strict and isolated bed rest followed by step-by-step OCCUPATIONAL THERAPY and final reintegration into job and family. A central concept is the attainment of **arugamama**, an attitude of acceptance toward one's self and one's feelings. [Shoma **Morita** (1874–1938), Japanese psychiatrist]

morning-after pill a popular name for postcoital, or emergency, oral contraception. It consists of two doses of a progestin, or a combined formulation of a progestin and an estrogen, taken at spaced intervals no later than 72 hours after intercourse.

morning-glory seeds seeds of the plant *Rivea corymbosa*, which contain psychoactive agents and have been used as HALLUCINOGENS, notably in 16th-century Mexico.

morphine *n.* the primary active ingredient in OPIUM, first synthesized in 1806 and widely used as an analgesic and sedative, especially in terminally ill cancer patients (see OPIATE; OPIOID ANALGESIC). Prolonged administration or abuse can lead to dependence and to withdrawal symptoms on cessation. The substance is 10 times as potent as opium. See OPIOID ABUSE; OPIOID DEPENDENCE; OPIOID INTOXICATION; OPIOID WITHDRAWAL.

morphophilia *n.* interest in sexual partners whose body characteristics (e.g., height, weight, or skin and hair color) are very different from one's own.

morsicatio buccarum habitual biting of the inside of the cheeks (buccal mucosa), sometimes causing lesions or the formation of white excess tissue.

morsicatio labiorum see LIP BITING.

mortality *n.* the death rate in a population.

mortality salience the cognitive accessibility of thoughts about the inevitability of one's death. Such thoughts are believed by some theorists to be a motivating force behind a diverse set of actions designed to defend oneself or one's social group.

mort douce primarily in literary contexts, a peaceful death (French, literally "sweet death") in which all tensions are released in a manner reminiscent of the fulfillment of sexual intercourse. **Petit mort** (little or quiet death) makes use of the same analogy, but with a less dramatic conclusion. By contrast, **le grand mort** (the great death) of Elizabethan poets visualizes death as the ultimate tumultuous orgasm.

mortido *n.* in psychoanalytic theory, the energy of the DEATH INSTINCT and counterpart to the LIBIDO. See also DESTRUDO. [defined in 1936 by Austrian psychoanalyst Paul Federn (1872–1950)]

mother archetype in Carl JUNG'S ANALYTIC PSYCHOLOGY, the primordial image of the generative and sustaining mother figure that has occurred repeatedly in various cultural concepts and myths since ancient times and is located within the COLLECTIVE UNCONSCIOUS. See also ARCHETYPE; MAGNA MATER.

mother figure 1. a person who occupies the mothering role in relation to a child: a MOTHER SURROGATE. **2.** in psychoanalytic theory, a person onto whom the patient transfers feelings and attitudes that he or she had toward the real mother. Also called **mother substitute**.

mothering *n.* the process of nurturing, caring for, and protecting a child by a mother or maternal figure.

Mothers Against Drunk Driving (MADD) an organization whose mission is to stop drunk driving and to support its victims. It was known as **Mothers Against Drunk Drivers** until 1984. See SELF-HELP GROUP.

M

mother–son incest sexual activity between mother and son, which is rarer than FATHER–DAUGHTER INCEST. See also PHAEDRA COMPLEX.

mother substitute 1. see MOTHER FIGURE. **2.** see MOTHER SURROGATE.

mother surrogate a substitute for an individual's biological mother (e.g., a sister, grandmother, stepmother, or adoptive mother), who assumes the responsibilities of that person and may function as a role model and significant attachment figure. U. S. psychologist Harry Harlow's (1905–1981) classic research with young monkeys demonstrated that monkeys preferred a mother surrogate covered in cloth to one that was simply a wire frame, even though the latter was the source of food. Also called **mother figure**; **surrogate mother**.

motility psychosis an obsolescent name for a BIPOLAR DISORDER that has as a prominent feature extreme PSYCHOMOTOR AGITATION or PSYCHOMOTOR RETARDATION.

motivated forgetting a memory lapse motivated by a desire to avoid a disagreeable recollection. It is one of the cognitive mechanisms that has been suggested as a cause of delayed memories of childhood trauma.

motivation *n.* **1.** the impetus that gives purpose or direction to human or animal behavior and operates at a conscious or unconscious level (see UNCONSCIOUS MOTIVATION). Motives are frequently divided into (a) physiological, primary, or organic motives, such as hunger, thirst, and need for sleep, and (b) personal, social, or secondary motives, such as affiliation, competition, and individual interests and goals. An important distinction must also be drawn between internal motivating forces and external factors, such as rewards or punishments, that can encourage or discourage certain behaviors. See EXTRINSIC MOTIVATION; INTRINSIC MOTIVATION. **2.** in CONDITIONING, the variables, collectively, that alter the effectiveness of REINFORCERS. **3.** a person's willingness to exert physical or mental effort in pursuit of a goal or outcome. **4.** the act or process of encouraging others to exert themselves in pursuit of a group or organizational goal. The ability to motivate followers is an important function of leadership. **—motivate** *vb.* **—motivated** *adj.* **—motivational** *adj.*

motivational enhancement therapy a transtheoretical treatment, based on the STAGES OF CHANGE, that matches clients to interventions on the basis of individual differences in readiness to change. This treatment was initially applied to substance abuse but has now generalized to other problem behaviors.

motivational factor any physiological or psychological factor that stimulates, maintains, and directs behavior. Examples are basic PHYSIOLOGICAL NEEDS, interests, and EXTRINSIC REWARDS.

motivational hierarchy see MASLOW'S MOTIVATIONAL HIERARCHY.

M

motivational styles a way of classifying people with regard to their learning and performance, in which categories are based on individual differences in motivation, including but not limited to intrinsic–extrinsic motivation, mastery orientation, and competitiveness. The notion of motivational styles is particularly used in education, business, and sport to help people recognize both strengths and weaknesses and develop strategies to improve learning and performance.

motive *n.* **1.** a specific physiological or psychological state of arousal that directs an organism's energies toward a goal. See MOTIVATION. **2.** a reason offered as an explanation for or cause of an individual's behavior.

motor area an area of the MOTOR CORTEX that, when stimulated, produces movements of skeletal muscles in various parts of the body. It has somatotopic organization, with individual neurons controlling a specific movement direction of an associated body part that might involve coordinated action of several muscles. Also called **Brodmann's area 4**; **primary motor cortex**.

motor conversion symptoms one of two types of symptoms of CONVERSION DISORDER, the other being SENSORY CONVERSION SYMPTOMS. Examples of motor conversion symptoms include impaired coordination and balance, paralysis or weakness confined to a specific area of the body, difficulty in swallowing, aphonia (loss of voice), and urinary retention.

motor cortex the region of the frontal lobe of the brain responsible for the control of voluntary movement. It is divided into two parts. The **primary motor cortex**, or MOTOR AREA, is the main source of neurons in the corticospinal tract. The **secondary** (or **nonprimary**) **motor cortex**, made up of the PREMOTOR AREA and the SUPPLEMENTARY MOTOR AREA, is specialized for planning upcoming movements and learning new movements. Lesions in the primary motor cortex due to stroke or traumatic injury usually cause initial paralysis that may improve to a condition involving weakness and poor muscle tone. Lesions in the secondary motor cortex usually cause complex disruptions in motor planning for complex movements (see APRAXIA). Also called **motor strip**.

motor disorder loss of the ability to perform simple or complex acts or skills because of temporary or permanent damage to tissues in the premotor or MOTOR AREAS of the central nervous system. The cause of the damage may be a congenital or inherited defect, injury, surgical excision, or a psychochemical factor.

motor disturbance any disturbance of motor behavior, such as hyperactivity, retarded activity, automatism, repetitive movements, rigid posture, grimacing, or tics.

motor neuron a neuron whose axon connects directly to muscle fibers. Because motor neurons are the final stage of output from the nervous system and are the only means of stimulating muscle fibers, they are known as the **final common path**. There are two types: **lower motor neurons** (or **alpha motor neurons**), found in the cranial nerves and the anterior horn of the spinal cord and which are responsible for muscle contraction; and **upper motor neurons** (or **gamma motor neurons**), found in the corticospinal tract and which modulate the sensitivity of MUSCLE SPINDLES, thus influencing activity of the lower motor neurons. Also called **motoneuron**.

motor speech disorder any of several communication disorders arising from inaccurate production of speech sounds because of lack of strength or coordination of the muscles involved in speaking, as occurs in CEREBELLAR ATAXIA or PARKINSON'S DISEASE.

motor system the complex of skeletal muscles, neural connections with muscle tissues, and structures of the central nervous system associated with motor functions. Also called **neuromuscular system**.

motor tension a state of muscle tension in which the individual is restless and tires easily. This symptom is associated with GENERALIZED ANXIETY DISORDER.

motor test any test designed to measure motor skills, ranging from GROSS MOTOR to FINE MOTOR manipulation.

mourning *n.* the process of feeling or expressing grief following the death of a loved one, or the period during which this occurs. It typically involves feelings of apathy and dejection, loss of interest in the outside world, and diminution in activity and initiative. These reactions are similar to depression, but are less persistent and are not considered pathological. See also BEREAVEMENT.

movement disorder any abnormality in motor processes, relating primarily to posture, coordination, or locomotion. **Medication-induced movement disorders**, such as TARDIVE DYSKINESIA, occur as an adverse effect of medication and are particularly common with antipsychotic drugs.

movement therapy a therapeutic technique in which individuals use rhythmic exercises and bodily movements to achieve greater body awareness and social interaction and enhance their psychological and physical functioning. See also DANCE THERAPY.

MPI abbreviation for Maudsley Personality Inventory. See EYSENCK PERSONALITY INVENTORY.

MPS 1. abbreviation for MUCOPOLYSACCHARIDOSIS. **2.** abbreviation for myofascial pain syndrome (see CHRONIC MYOFASCIAL PAIN).

MPTP *n.* 1-*m*ethyl-4-*p*henyl-1,2,3,6-*t*etrahydro*p*yridine: a by-product of heroin synthesis that is used experimentally to induce symptoms of Parkinson's disease in laboratory animals. It was discovered accidentally in 1976 when it was synthesized and injected by a recreational drug user who was attempting to produce an analog of meperidine (Demerol). This individual developed acute symptoms of Parkinson's disease, as did other users of the drug. Autopsy revealed massive degeneration of dopamine-containing neurons in the NIGROSTRIATAL TRACT. MPTP is not in itself neurotoxic (damaging to nerve tissue), but it is converted to the methylphenylpyridinium ion (MPP^+), a potent neurotoxin at dopaminergic neurons, by the enzyme MONOAMINE OXIDASE B.

MR abbreviation for MENTAL RETARDATION.

MRI abbreviation for MAGNETIC RESONANCE IMAGING.

mRNA abbreviation for MESSENGER RNA.

MS abbreviation for MULTIPLE SCLEROSIS.

MSE abbreviation for MENTAL STATUS EXAMINATION.

MSIS abbreviation for MULTISTATE INFORMATION SYSTEM.

MSLT abbreviation for MULTIPLE SLEEP LATENCY TEST.

MSP abbreviation for MUNCHAUSEN SYNDROME BY PROXY.

MSUD abbreviation for MAPLE-SUGAR URINE DISEASE.

mucopolysaccharidosis (MPS) *n.* (*pl.* **mucopolysaccharidoses**) any of various metabolic disorders, classified into six groups (I–VI), that are marked by excess mucopolysaccharide—glyccosaminoglycan (GAG), a complex carbohydrate—in the tissues. Certain forms of the disease are associated with mental retardation. See HUNTER'S SYNDROME; HURLER'S SYNDROME; MAROTEAUX–LAMY SYNDROME; SANFILIPPO'S SYNDROME.

mucous colitis see IRRITABLE BOWEL SYNDROME.

muina *n.* see BILIS.

muliebrity *n.* the state or condition of being a woman (from Latin *mulier*, "woman") or the qualities considered to be characteristic of women.

multa loca tenens principle a rule stating that if a drug can substitute for or mimic one action of a natural physiological agent, it may be able to simulate other natural functions as well. Because of such multiple effects, the administered drug may compete for receptors, enzymes, and other physiological targets.

multiattribute-utility analysis a method of using the ratings of judges to quantify the social utility or value of a given program. Dimensions relevant to program outcomes are ranked and then weighted in terms of their comparative social importance; each program is scored on all social-value dimensions. This form of analysis enables comparisons of different social programs to be made.

multiaxial classification a system of classifying mental disorders according to several categories of factors, for example, social and cultural influences, as well as clinical symptoms. DSM–IV–TR uses multiaxial classification, which takes account of the many factors involved in the etiology of these disorders and enables a more comprehensive clinical assessment to be made. See AXIS.

multicultural therapy 1. any form of psychotherapy that takes into account not only the increasing racial and ethnic diversity of clients in many countries but also diversity in spirituality, sexual orientation, ability and disability, and social class and economics; the potential cultural bias (e.g., racism, sexism) of the practitioner; the history of oppressed and marginalized groups; diversity within diversity; acculturation and issues involving living in two worlds; and the politics of power as they affect clients. **2.** any form of therapy that assesses, understands, and evaluates a client's behavior in the multiplicity of cultural contexts (e.g., ethnic, national, demographic, social, and economic) in which that behavior was learned and is displayed.

multidetermination *n.* the interaction of several different factors in the etiology of a disorder (e.g., biological, psychological, environmental). **—multidetermined** *adj.*

multidetermined behavior the concept that human behavior is influenced by the interaction of multiple factors, past and present. In general, the major influences are genetic, environmental, physiological, and psychological.

multidimensional *adj.* **1.** describing any form of analysis in which factors or variables are represented on more than one dimension. **2.** of scales or measures, having a number of different dimensions. Compare UNIDIMENSIONAL.

Multidimensional Scale for Rating Psychiatric Patients see INPATIENT MULTIDIMENSIONAL PSYCHIATRIC SCALE.

multidimensional scaling (MDS) a scaling method that represents perceived similarities among stimuli by arranging similar stimuli in spatial proximity to one another, while disparate stimuli are represented far apart from one another. Multidimensional scaling is an alternative to FACTOR ANALYSIS for dealing with large multidimensional matrices of data or stimuli.

multifactorial *adj.* consisting or arising out of several factors, variables, or causes.

multifactorial inheritance inheritance of a trait, such as height or predisposition to a certain disease, that is determined not by a single gene but by many different genes acting cumulatively. Such traits show continuous, rather than discrete, variation among the members of a given population and are often significantly influenced by environmental factors, such as nutritional status. Also called **polygenic inheritance**.

M

multigenerational transmission process the passing on of psychological problems, primarily anxiety, over several generations through family relationships. A central concept in FAMILY SYSTEMS THEORY, the principal process involves the unconscious passing on of a higher level of anxiety, which overrides adaptive thinking and behavior, to members in each succeeding generation. Interventions to change this transmission involve charting family relationships and coaching individuals on how to interact with targeted relatives, usually those who are lowest in anxiety and who function at the most adaptive level. [developed by U.S. psychiatrist Murray Bowen (1913–1990)]

Multilingual Aphasia Examination (MAE) a neuropsychological test battery used to determine the presence, type, and severity of APHASIA. The 11 subtests, assessing various aspects of expressive and receptive language function, include Visual Naming, Sentence Repetition, CONTROLLED ORAL WORD ASSOCIATION, Oral Spelling, Written Spelling, Block Spelling, a TOKEN TEST, Aural Comprehension of Words and Phrases, Reading Comprehension of Words and Phrases, Rating of Articulation, and Rating of Praxic Features of Writing. The MAE was originally developed in 1978 and is now in its third edition (published in 2001). Despite the implications of its name, the MAE currently is available only in English and Spanish versions. [developed by U.S. psychologists Arthur Lester Benton (1909–2006), Kerry deS. Hamsher (1946–), and Abigail B. Sivan (1943–)]

multimodal therapy (MMT) a form of psychotherapy in which the therapist assesses the client's significant *B*ehaviors, *A*ffective responses, *S*ensations, *I*magery, *C*ognitions, *I*nterpersonal relationships, and the need for *D*rugs and other biological interventions. The first letters yield the acronym **BASIC ID**, which summarizes the seven basic interactive modalities of the approach. MMT posits that these modalities exist in a state of reciprocal transaction and flux, connected by complex chains of behavior and other psychophysiological processes. The therapist, usually in concert with the client, determines which specific problems across the BASIC ID are most salient. MMT uses an eclectic approach drawing mainly from a broad-based social and cognitive learning theory. Also called **multimodal behavior therapy**. [developed by South African-born U.S. clinical psychologist Arnold Allan Lazarus (1932–)]

multimodal treatment a manner of treating a disease, disorder, or syndrome by simultaneously applying several different methods, often from different disciplines or traditions.

multinomial distribution a theoretical probability distribution that describes the distribution of *n* objects sampled at random from a population of *k* kinds of things with regard to the number of each of the kinds that appears in the sample.

multipayer system see ALL-PAYER SYSTEM.

multiphilia *n.* interest in multiple, short-term sexual relationships only, with no desire for any long-term relationship or commitment.

multiple delusions concurrent DELUSIONS, not necessarily interconnected.

multiple family therapy a form of GROUP THERAPY in which a group of two or more family members meets with two or more therapists at once. See also FAMILY THERAPY; COTHERAPY.

multiple-impact therapy a treatment method in which a group of mental health professionals works with a client family during an intensive, limited period.

multiple marital therapy a form of therapy in which each marital partner is treated independently by individual therapists. The two therapists may meet privately to discuss their clients, and sessions involving all four parties or a combination of the parties may be held. See also CONJOINT THERAPY.

multiple monitored electroconvulsive treatment (MMECT) a form of ELECTROCONVULSIVE THERAPY in which an attempt is made to shorten the overall period of treatment by inducing several seizures in a single session. Also called **multimonitored electroconvulsive treatment**.

multiple orgasm in women, the occurrence of more than one orgasm, without a resolution phase (see SEXUAL-RESPONSE CYCLE) separating the orgasms. Studies have found that as many as 30% of women experience this. Male multiple orgasm does not occur, because further arousal and response are not possible during the REFRACTORY PHASE following male orgasm. However, some men do carefully monitor and control their arousal and may experience the first elements of an orgasm, without ejaculation, more than once before having a complete orgasm, with ejaculation.

multiple personality disorder see DISSOCIATIVE IDENTITY DISORDER.

multiple regression a statistical technique for examining the linear relationship between a continuous DEPENDENT VARIABLE and a set of two or more INDEPENDENT VARIABLES. It is often used to predict the score of individuals on a criterion variable from multiple predictor variables.

multiple relationship in a therapeutic context, a situation in which a psychologist has more than one type of relationship with a client. A multiple relationship occurs when a psychologist is in a professional role with a person and (a) concurrently is in another role with the same person, (b) concurrently is in a relationship with a person closely associated with or related to the client, or (c) promises to enter into another relationship in the future with the client or a person closely associated with or related to the client. Psychologists are ethically expected to refrain from entering into a multiple relationship because it might impair their objectivity, competence, or effectiveness in performing their functions as a psychologist or exploit or harm the client with whom the professional relationship exists. Also called **dual relationship**.

multiple sclerosis (**MS**) a demyelinating disease of the central nervous system (brain and spinal cord) characterized by inflammation and multifocal scarring of the protective MYELIN SHEATH of nerves, which damages and destroys the sheath and the underlying nerve, disrupting neural transmission. The initial symptom of MS is often a visual disturbance, such as blurred or double vision, red–green color distortion, or blindness in one eye. Later symptoms include fatigue, weakness in the hands and feet, numbness, stiffness or muscular spasms, muscle and back pain, difficulties with coordination and balance, loss of bladder or bowel control, and depression. Some individuals also experience cognitive impairments, such as difficulties with concentration, attention, memory, and judgment. The onset is usually between the ages of 20 and 40, and, with periods of remission, the disease may continue for 25 years or more. Rapid progression to death is rare. The cause of MS, which occurs twice as frequently in females as in males, is unknown. However, the destruction of myelin may be due to an autoimmune response (see AUTOIMMUNITY).

Multiple Sleep Latency Test (**MSLT**) an inpatient test performed in a SLEEP LABORATORY in which the individual is monitored during a series of five 20-minute nap periods scheduled 2 hours apart. The object is to assess daytime sleep tendency by measuring the number of minutes it takes the individual to fall asleep. The individual is monitored by means of electrodes that measure brain waves, eye movements, heartbeat, and muscle tone. The test is used in the diagnosis of PRIMARY HYPERSOMNIA and NARCOLEPSY.

multiple suicides see CLUSTER SUICIDES; MASS SUICIDE.

multistage sampling a sampling technique in which samples are drawn first from higher order groupings (e.g., states) and in later stages of the process from successively lower level groupings (e.g., counties within states, towns within counties) in order to avoid the necessity of having a SAMPLING FRAME for the entire population.

multistate information system (**MSIS**) an automated record-keeping system designed to provide comparative statistics for evaluation of programs and treatment procedures in U.S. mental hospitals and community mental health facilities.

multivariate *adj.* consisting of or otherwise involving two or more variables. Compare UNIVARIATE. See also BIVARIATE.

multivariate analysis any of several types of statistical analysis that simultaneously model multiple DEPENDENT VARIABLES.

multivariate analysis of variance (**MANOVA**) an extension of the ANALYSIS OF VARIANCE (ANOVA) model that identifies the simultaneous effects of the independent variables upon a set of dependent variables.

Munchausen syndrome a severe and chronic form of FACTITIOUS DISORDER characterized by repeated and elaborate fabrication of clinically convincing physical symptoms and a false medical and social history (see PSEUDOLOGIA FANTASTICA). Other features are recurrent hospitalization and PEREGRINATION, and there may be multiple scars from previous (unnecessary) investigative surgery. The patient's motivation is a psychological need to assume the SICK ROLE. See also PATHOMIMICRY. [Baron Karl Friedrich Hieronymus von **Münchhausen** (1720–1797), German soldier-adventurer famous for his tall tales]

Munchausen syndrome by proxy (**MSP**) a psychological disorder in which caregivers fabricate or intentionally cause symptoms in those they are caring for in order to seek and obtain medical investigation or treatment. Typically, the caregiver is the mother, who behaves as if distressed about her child's illness and denies knowing what caused it: She is believed to be motivated by the hope that she will be seen as an exceptionally attentive parent, and her behavior may be an attempt to arouse sympathy. In *DSM–IV–TR* this condition is called **factitious disorder by proxy** (see FACTITIOUS DISORDER NOT OTHERWISE SPECIFIED).

murder–suicide the intentional killing of an-

M

other person followed by the suicide of the killer. See also EXTENDED SUICIDE.

mu receptor see OPIOID RECEPTOR.

muscarine *n.* a toxic alkaloid, isolated from FLY AGARIC (*Amanita muscaria*) and some other fungi, that stimulates certain types of acetylcholine receptors (the MUSCARINIC RECEPTORS) in smooth muscle, cardiac muscle, endocrine glands, and the central nervous system. See also NICOTINE.

muscarinic receptor (**mAChR**) a type of ACETYLCHOLINE RECEPTOR that responds to MUSCARINE as well as to acetylcholine. Muscarinic receptors mediate chiefly the inhibitory activities of acetylcholine. Compare NICOTINIC RECEPTOR.

muscimol *n.* see FLY AGARIC; GABA AGONISTS; IBOTENIC ACID.

muscle dysmorphia a form of BODY DYSMORPHIA characterized by chronic dissatisfaction with one's muscularity and the perception that one's body is inadequate and undesirable, although objective observers would disagree with such an assessment. This condition often leads to excessive exercising, steroid abuse, and eating disorders. It is typically found in males, especially bodybuilders. Also called **bigorexia**. See also REVERSE ANOREXIA.

muscle relaxant any of various drugs used in the management of spasms of skeletal muscle generally resulting from mechanical injury, stroke, cerebral palsy, or multiple sclerosis. Most act on the central nervous system or its associated structures to reduce muscle tone and spontaneous activity. Although the precise mode of action varies with the drug, muscle relaxants generally act by depressing spinal reflexes without loss of consciousness. Common muscle relaxants include BENZODIAZEPINES, BACLOFEN, DANTROLENE, and botulinum toxin. Others used for localized muscle spasms include CARISOPRODOL, CYCLOBENZAPRINE, METHOCARBAMOL, and ORPHENADRINE.

muscle spindle a receptor that lies within skeletal muscle and sends impulses to the central nervous system when the muscle is stretched.

musculoskeletal disorder any disease, injury, or significant impairment to tendons, muscles, bones, joints, and supporting connective (soft) tissues.

musician's cramp a type of OCCUPATIONAL CRAMP experienced by musicians, usually in the arm or hand, that prevents them from performing. The condition may be due to electrolyte imbalance. See also REPETITIVE STRAIN INJURY.

music therapy the use of music as an adjunct to the treatment or rehabilitation of individuals to enhance their psychological, physical, cognitive, or social functioning.

musturbation *n.* the behavior of individuals who believe that they must absolutely meet often perfectionist goals in order to achieve success, approval, or comfort. Cognitive and behavioral therapies may be useful in bringing awareness and perspective to such maladaptive cognitions. See also RATIONAL EMOTIVE BEHAVIOR THERAPY. [defined by U.S. psychotherapist Albert Ellis (1913–2007)]

mutation *n.* a permanent change in the genetic material of an organism. It may consist of an alteration to the number or arrangement of chromosomes (a **chromosomal mutation**) or a change in the composition of DNA, generally affecting only one or a few bases in a particular gene (a **point mutation**). Mutations can occur spontaneously, but many are due to exposure to agents (**mutagens**) that significantly increase the rate of mutation; these include X-rays and other forms of radiation and certain chemicals. A mutation occurring in a body cell (i.e., a **somatic mutation**) cannot be inherited, whereas a mutation in a reproductive cell producing ova or spermatozoa (i.e., a **germ-line mutation**) can be transmitted to that individual's offspring. Most mutations either have no discernible effect or have a deleterious effect; however, a tiny majority are beneficial and thus give that individual and his or her descendants a selective advantage. Mutations responsible for SINGLE-GENE DISORDERS are sought in genetic testing of high-risk families or groups.

mutilation *n.* **1.** the destruction or removal of a limb or an essential part of the body. **2.** a destructive act causing a disfiguring injury to the body. See also SELF-MUTILATION.

mutism *n.* lack or absence of speaking due to physical or PSYCHOGENIC factors. The condition may result from neurological damage or disorder, a structural defect in the organs necessary for speech, congenital or early deafness in which an individual's failure to hear spoken words inhibits the development of speech, psychological disorders (e.g., CONVERSION DISORDER, CATATONIC SCHIZOPHRENIA), or severe emotional disturbance (e.g., extreme anger). The condition may also be voluntary, as in monastic vows of silence or the decision to speak only to selected individuals. See also AKINETIC MUTISM; ALALIA; SELECTIVE MUTISM; STUPOR.

muttering delirium a type of DELIRIUM in which an individual's speech is marked by low utterances, slurring, iteration, DYSARTHRIA, PERSEVERATION, or any combination of these. Typically, the individual's movements are dominated by restlessness and trembling.

mutual help a form of SELF-HELP that is not professionally guided and that involves joining with others similar to oneself to explore ways to cope with life situations and problems. Mutual help can occur in person, by telephone, or through the Internet.

mutual masturbation 1. sexual activity in which two individuals stimulate each other's genitals at the same time for the purpose of sexual gratification. This is more properly considered a type of PETTING BEHAVIOR, as masturbation is defined as self-stimulation. **2.** sexual activity in which two or more individuals stimulate their own genitals while jointly viewing erotic materials. Such activity, especially when involving adolescent males, is popularly known as "a circle jerk."

mutual pretense an interaction pattern in which all participants try to act as if they are unaware of the most crucial facts in a situation (e.g., a situation in which one of the participants is terminally ill). This pattern is often regarded by therapists and researchers as an anxiety-driven strategy that inhibits communication, increases tension, and leads to missed opportunities for meaningful mutual support.

mutual support group a group composed of individuals who meet on a regular basis to help one another cope with a shared life problem. This term is sometimes used by researchers and practitioners instead of the traditional term SELF-HELP GROUP, as it emphasizes the mutual, interdependent nature of SELF-HELP GROUP PROCESSES.

myasthenia gravis an autoimmune disorder (see AUTOIMMUNITY) in which the body produces antibodies against ACETYLCHOLINE RECEPTORS, causing faulty transmission of nerve impulses at neuromuscular junctions. Affected muscles—initially those of the face and neck—are easily fatigued and may become paralyzed temporarily (e.g., muscles involved in eating may fail to function normally toward the end of a meal, or speech may become slurred after a period of talking). The disease is progressive, eventually affecting muscles throughout the body.

mydriasis *n.* excessive dilation (widening) of the pupil of the eye caused by anticholinergic drugs (e.g., atropine and scopolamine) acting on MUSCARINIC RECEPTORS. —**mydriatic** *adj., n.*

myelination *n.* the formation and development of a MYELIN SHEATH around the AXON of a neuron, which is effected by neuroglia, such as SCHWANN CELLS. Researchers look to anomalies in this process to explain some forms of severe mental illness (e.g., schizophrenia). Also called **axonal myelination**; **medullation**; **myelinization**.

myelin sheath the insulating layer around many axons that increases the speed of conduction of nerve impulses. It is laid down by GLIA, which wrap themselves around adjacent axons. The myelin sheath is interrupted by small gaps (nodes of Ranvier) which are spaced about every millimeter along the axon. Also called **medullary sheath**.

Myers–Briggs Type Indicator (**MBTI**) a personality test designed to classify individuals according to their expressed choices between contrasting alternatives in certain categories of traits. The categories, based on JUNGIAN TYPOLOGY, are (a) Extraversion–Introversion, (b) Sensing–Intuition, (c) Thinking–Feeling, and (d) Judging–Perceiving. The participant is assigned a type (e.g., INTJ or ESFP) according to the pattern of choices made. The test has little credibility among research psychologists but is widely used in educational counseling and human resource management to help improve work and personal relationships, increase productivity, and identify interpersonal communication preferences and skills. [Isabel Briggs **Myers** (1897–1980), U.S. personologist, and her mother Katharine Cook **Briggs** (1875–1968)]

myocardial infarction see INFARCTION.

myoclonus *n.* rapid, involuntary contraction of a muscle or group of muscles. This may occur normally, as when a limb or other part of the body suddenly jerks while falling asleep (see NOCTURNAL MYOCLONUS), or abnormally, as in CREUTZFELDT–JAKOB DISEASE and other neurological disorders.

myofascial pain syndrome (**MPS**) see CHRONIC MYOFASCIAL PAIN.

myriachit *n.* a CULTURE-BOUND SYNDROME found in Siberian populations. Similar to LATAH, it is characterized by indiscriminate, apparently uncontrolled imitations of the actions of other people encountered by the individual. Also called **ikota**; **irkunii**; **menkeiti**; **olan**. See also IMU; JUMPING FRENCHMEN OF MAINE SYNDROME.

Mysoline *n.* a trade name for PRIMIDONE.

mysophilia *n.* a pathological interest in dirt or filth, often with a desire to be unclean or in contact with dirty objects. Mysophilia may be expressed as a PARAPHILIA in which the person is sexually aroused by a dirty partner.

mystic union the feeling of spiritual identification with God, nature, or the universe as a whole. See COSMIC IDENTIFICATION; OCEANIC FEELING; TRANSCENDENTAL MEDITATION; YOGA; ZEN THERAPY.

Mytelase *n.* a trade name for AMBENOMIUM.

mythology *n.* **1.** a body of traditional stories (myths) associated with the early history of a particular culture. Such stories generally involve supernatural beings and events and often seek to explain particular natural or cultural phenomena (e.g., the cycle of the seasons or a specific custom) in terms of their supposed origins. Myths are often distinguished from legends as having little or no basis in historical events. **2.** the study of myths. Sigmund FREUD compared myths to DREAMS, which contain hidden meanings, and believed they throw unique light on the cultures from which they stem, and in some instances, as in the myth of Oedipus, on human nature in general. **3.** in Carl JUNG'S ANALYTIC PSYCHOLOGY, primordial images, or ARCHETYPES, that are stored in the COLLECTIVE UNCONSCIOUS. —**mythological** *adj.*

mythomania *n.* **1.** a tendency to elaborate, exaggerate, and tell lies, including reports of imagined experiences, often involving SELF-DECEPTION. See also FACTITIOUS DISORDER; PATHOLOGICAL LYING. **2.** an abnormal interest in myths, in which the individual may believe fantasy to be reality, and a tendency to fabricate incredible stories. Also called **pseudologia fantastica**. See also FABULATION.

myxedema *n.* a metabolic disorder that develops in adulthood due to a deficiency of thyroid hormone (see HYPOTHYROIDISM). The condition is characterized by subnormal heart rate, circulation, and body temperature and a decrease in most other metabolic activities. Affected individuals tend to be fatigued, listless, and overweight, but usually respond to administration of thyroxine. **—myxedemic** *adj.*

MZ twins abbreviation for MONOZYGOTIC TWINS.

Nn

n symbol for the number of scores or observations obtained from a particular experimental condition or subgroup.

NA abbreviation for NARCOTICS ANONYMOUS.

nabilone *n.* a synthetic cannabinoid, closely related to TETRAHYDROCANNABINOL, that is used clinically to manage nausea and vomiting in patients recovering from surgical anesthesia or undergoing chemotherapy. U.S. and Canadian trade name: **Cesamet**.

n-Ach abbreviation for NEED FOR ACHIEVEMENT.

n-Aff abbreviation for NEED FOR AFFILIATION.

naikan *n.* a Japanese therapy that emphasizes character building through rigorous self-reflection upon (a) what the client has received from others, (b) what the client has returned to others, and (c) how the client's actions may have hurt others. Through this process of self-reflection, guided by the therapist, the client acquires a sense of responsibility for his or her actions and an appreciation of the positive influences in his or her life. [introduced by Japanese Buddhist of the Jodo Shinshu sect Yoshimoto Ishin (1916–1988)]

nail biting the compulsive habit of chewing on one's fingernails, usually thought to be a means of releasing tension. Also called **onychophagia**; **onychophagy**.

naive participant a participant who has not previously participated in a particular research study and has not been made aware of the experimenter's hypothesis. Compare CONFEDERATE.

Nalline test a test to determine abstinence from opiates, in which the subject is given an injection of the OPIOID ANTAGONIST nalorphine (Nalline). This precipitates withdrawal symptoms if opiates have been used recently.

nalmefene *n.* see OPIOID ANTAGONIST.

nalorphine *n.* see OPIOID ANTAGONIST.

naloxone *n.* a morphine-derived OPIOID ANTAGONIST that prevents the binding of opioids to OPIOID RECEPTORS, having primary activity at the mu receptor. Like other opioid antagonists, it can quickly reverse the effects of opioid overdose and is useful in emergency settings to reverse respiratory depression. U.S. trade name: **Narcan**.

naltrexone *n.* an OPIOID ANTAGONIST that, like the shorter acting NALOXONE, prevents the binding of opioid agonists to opioid receptors. Accordingly, both drugs may precipitate a rapid withdrawal syndrome. If naltrexone is taken prior to use of opiate drugs, it will prevent their reinforcing effects and can therefore be used for the management of opioid dependence in individuals desiring abstinence. Naltrexone is also appropriate as an adjunctive treatment in the management of alcoholism. U.S. trade name: **ReVia**.

name-of-the-father *adj.* in the theory of French psychoanalyst Jacques Lacan (1901–1981), denoting the stage at which the infant first enters the realm of the SYMBOLIC. The child's ability to "name the father" as a symbol for the absence of the mother represents his or her first use of symbolization and the first recognition that the father is a rival at the beginning of the OEDIPUS COMPLEX. See also MIRROR PHASE.

NAMI abbreviation for NATIONAL ALLIANCE ON MENTAL ILLNESS.

naming *n.* an association disturbance observed in schizophrenia, in which the individual relates to the external world solely by naming objects and actions (e.g., naming furniture or other objects in an examining room).

Narcan *n.* a trade name for NALOXONE.

narcissism *n.* **1.** excessive self-love or egocentrism. See NARCISSISTIC PERSONALITY DISORDER. **2.** in psychoanalytic theory, the taking of one's own EGO or body as a sexual object or focus of the LIBIDO or the seeking or choice of another for relational purposes on the basis of his or her similarity to the self. See BODY NARCISSISM; PRIMARY NARCISSISM. **—narcissist** *n.* **—narcissistic** *adj.*

narcissistic character see NARCISSISTIC PERSONALITY.

narcissistic object choice in psychoanalytic theory, selection of a mate or other LOVE OBJECT similar to oneself. Compare ANACLITIC OBJECT CHOICE.

narcissistic personality a pattern of traits and behaviors characterized by excessive self-concern and overvaluation of the self. Also called **narcissistic character**.

narcissistic personality disorder in *DSM–IV–TR*, a personality disorder with the following characteristics: (a) a long-standing pattern of grandiose self-importance and exaggerated sense of talent and achievements; (b) fantasies of unlimited sex, power, brilliance, or beauty; (c) an exhibitionistic need for attention and admiration; (d) either cool indifference or feelings of rage, humiliation, or emptiness as a response to criticism, indifference, or defeat; and (e) various interpersonal disturbances, such as feeling entitled to special favors, taking advantage of others, and inability to empathize with the feelings of others. [originally formulated by U.S. psychiatrists Wilhelm Reich (1897–1957), Otto Kernberg, and Heinz Kohut (1913–1981), and U.S. psychologist Theodore Millon (1929–)]

narcissistic type see LIBIDINAL TYPES.

narcoanalysis *n.* a form of psychoanalysis in which injections of drugs (often opioids) are used to induce a semihypnotic state in order to facilitate exploration and ventilation of feelings, uncover repressed traumatic memories, and, through the analyst's review and interpretation with the patient afterward, promote the patient's insight into the unconscious forces that underlie his or her symptoms. The technique was developed initially to treat COMBAT STRESS REACTIONS in the 1940s and is rarely if ever used now.

narcolepsy *n.* a disorder consisting of excessive daytime sleepiness accompanied by brief "attacks" of sleep during waking hours. These sleep attacks may occur at any time or during any activity, including in potentially dangerous situations, such as driving an automobile. The attacks are often associated with hypnagogic hallucinations (hallucinations occurring just before falling asleep), SLEEP PARALYSIS, and CATAPLEXY and are marked by immediate entry into REM sleep without going through the usual initial stages of sleep. Also called **paroxysmal sleep**. **—narcoleptic** *adj.*

N

narcomania *n.* **1.** a pathological desire for narcotic drugs to relieve pain or discomfort. **2.** an obsolete name for psychosis resulting from long-term abuse of narcotic drugs.

narcosynthesis *n.* a treatment technique that involves the administration of narcotic drugs to stimulate recall of emotional traumas, followed by "synthesis" of these experiences with the patient's emotional life through therapeutic discussions in the waking state. [developed during World War II by U.S. psychiatrists Roy Richard Grinker and John P. Spiegel]

narcotherapy *n.* psychotherapy conducted while the patient is in a semiconscious state induced by injection of narcotic drugs, such as amobarbital (Amytal) or thiopental. Narcotherapy was used, for example, with individuals experiencing COMBAT STRESS REACTIONS during and after World War II. See also NARCOANALYSIS; NARCOSYNTHESIS.

narcotic 1. *n.* originally, any drug that induces a state of stupor or insensibility (narcosis). More recently, the term referred to strong OPIOIDS used clinically for pain relief but this usage is now considered imprecise and pejorative; the term is still sometimes used in legal contexts to refer to a wide variety of abused substances. **2.** *adj.* of or relating to narcotics or narcosis.

narcotic addiction see OPIOID DEPENDENCE.

narcotic agonist see OPIOID AGONIST.

narcotic analgesic see OPIOID ANALGESIC.

narcotic antagonist see OPIOID ANTAGONIST.

narcotic dependence see OPIOID DEPENDENCE.

Narcotics Anonymous (NA) a self-help organization for those who seek help with a drug addiction, based on a TWELVE-STEP PROGRAM and modeled after ALCOHOLICS ANONYMOUS. The only requirement for membership is the desire to stop using drugs.

narcotic stupor a state of lethargy or limited mobility and decreased responsiveness to stimulation due to the effects of an opioid drug. This state may border on loss of consciousness and be followed by coma.

NARHC abbreviation for NATIONAL ASSOCIATION OF RURAL HEALTH CLINICS.

narrative theory any theory of consciousness stating that beliefs arise as part of an explanatory narrative about oneself and society.

narrative therapy treatment for individuals, couples, or families that helps clients reinterpret and rewrite their life events into true but more life-enhancing narratives or stories. Narrative therapy posits that individuals are primarily meaning-making beings who are the linguistic authors of their lives and who can reauthor these stories by learning to deconstruct them, by seeing patterns in their ways of interpreting life events or problems, and by reconstruing problems or events in a more helpful light. See also CONSTRUCTIVISM; CONSTRUCTIVIST PSYCHOTHERAPY.

narrotophilia *n.* sexual interest and arousal obtained from speaking or hearing sexually explicit words during sexual activity. It most commonly occurs in telephone sex or online computer sex, in which partners talk while masturbating. There are commercial services that employ people to engage in narratophilia with clients for a fee. In some cases of narratophilia, however, people prefer to make obscene phone calls to strangers or randomly selected numbers, as the involvement of a noncooperating person adds to their pleasure. **—narratophile** *n.*

National Alliance on Mental Illness (NAMI) a network of SELF-HELP GROUPS that provides emotional and educational support for relatives and individuals affected by mental illness. Formerly called **National Alliance for the Mentally Ill.**

National Association of Rural Health Clinics (NARHC) an organization that seeks to promote, expand, improve, and protect the delivery of quality, cost-effective health care services in underserved rural areas. NARHC actively engages in the legislative and regulatory process with the U.S. Congress, federal agencies, and rural health organizations.

National Committee for Quality Assurance (NCQA) a national organization, founded in 1979, that reviews and accredits MANAGED

CARE plans and measures the quality of care offered by them.

National Health Interview Survey (NHIS) a questionnaire that provides the principal source of information on the health of the civilian noninstitutionalized population of the United States and is one of the major data-collection programs of the National Center for Health Statistics (NCHS). The survey includes core questions and sometimes questions relating to specific initiatives (e.g., aging, healthy people, AIDS).

National Institute of Mental Health (NIMH) an agency of the federal government established in 1949 to understand the mind, the brain, and behavior and thereby reduce the burden of mental illness through research. It is committed to scientific programs to educate and train future mental health researchers, including scientists trained in molecular science, cognitive and affective neuroscience, and other disciplines required for the study of mental illness and the brain.

National Mental Health Association (NMHA) the largest nonprofit organization in the United States that addresses all aspects of mental health and illness. Established in 1909, it is dedicated to promoting mental health, preventing mental disorders, and achieving victory over mental illness through advocacy, education, research, and service.

National Practitioner Data Bank a computerized database, established through Title IV of Public Law 99-660 (the Health Care Quality Improvement Act of 1986) and maintained and operated by the U.S. Department of Health and Human Services, that contains information on physicians and other health care professionals against whom MALPRACTICE claims have been paid or certain disciplinary actions taken. The database is primarily an alert or flagging system intended to facilitate a comprehensive review of health care practitioners' professional credentials.

National Register of Health Service Providers in Psychology a national, nonprofit CREDENTIALING organization for professional psychologists, founded in 1974 to advance psychology as a profession and improve the delivery of health services to the public.

natural child 1. one of the child ego states in TRANSACTIONAL ANALYSIS, characterized as carefree, fun-loving, creative, impulsive, and impatient. Compare ADAPTED CHILD. **2.** a biological offspring of a parent, in contrast to an adopted child.

natural family planning controlling the number of children in a family by the use of natural techniques of birth control, such as the RHYTHM METHOD, as opposed to the use of oral contraceptives, intrauterine devices, diaphragms, and similar methods.

natural high a state of well-being and happiness that is often associated with physical or mental exertion, in contrast to similar mood states induced by drugs. A natural high is produced by activities that are part of everyday life as opposed to methods that have a direct effect on brain chemistry.

naturalistic observation data collection in a field setting, usually without laboratory controls or manipulation of variables. These procedures are usually carried out by a trained observer, who watches and records the everyday behavior of participants in their natural environments. Examples of naturalistic observation include an ethologist's study of the behavior of chimpanzees and an anthropologist's observation of playing children.

nature–nurture the dispute over the relative contributions of hereditary and constitutional factors (nature) and environmental factors (nurture) to the development of the individual. Nativists emphasize the role of heredity, whereas environmentalists emphasize sociocultural and ecological factors, including family attitudes, child-rearing practices, and economic status. Most scientists now accept that there is a close interaction between hereditary and environmental factors in the ontogeny of behavior (see EPIGENESIS). Also called **heredity–environment controversy**; **nature–nurture issue**; **nature–nurture problem**.

naturopathy *n.* an alternative health care system that aims to prevent disease and promote physical and mental health by using natural and physiologically based therapies (e.g., dietary measures, acupuncture, and massage) to address underlying disease processes. See also COMPLEMENTARY AND ALTERNATIVE MEDICINE.

nay-saying *n.* answering questions negatively regardless of their content, which can distort the results of surveys, questionnaires, and similar instruments. Compare YEA-SAYING.

NBAS abbreviation for Neonatal Behavioral Assessment Scale (see BRAZELTON NEONATAL BEHAVIORAL ASSESSMENT SCALE).

NCQA abbreviation for NATIONAL COMMITTEE FOR QUALITY ASSURANCE.

NE abbreviation for NOREPINEPHRINE.

near-death experience (NDE) an image, perception, event, interaction, or feeling (or a combination of any of these) reported by some people after a life-threatening episode. Typical features include a sense of separation from the body, often accompanied by the ability to look down on the situation; a peaceful and pleasant state of mind; and an entering into the light, sometimes following an interaction with a spiritual being. There is continuing controversy regarding the existence, cause, and nature of NDEs. Spiritual, biomedical, and contextual lines of explanation are still in play, and there is no solid evidence to support the proposition that NDEs prove survival of death. [term coined in 1975 by U.S. parapsychologist Ray-

N

mond A. Moody (1944–) in his book *Life After Life*]

necromania *n.* a morbid preoccupation with corpses, usually including sexual desire for dead bodies, and a morbid interest in funerals, morgues, autopsies, and cemeteries. See NECROPHILIA.

necrophilia *n.* **1.** sexual interest in or sexual contact with dead bodies. It is a rare PARAPHILIA seen almost exclusively in men. In some cases they kill the victim themselves, but most frequently they gain access to corpses from funeral parlors, mortuaries, morgues, or graves. Numerous explanations have been offered for the behavior since it was first described by German psychiatrist Richard von Krafft-Ebing (1840–1902) in his 1886 book *Psychopathia Sexualis*, many of which were psychoanalytically oriented and have now generally been abandoned. More recent explanations of necrophilia, however, have received some empirical support and include desire for a partner who is incapable of resistance or rejection, desire to exercise power over others as a means of enhancing self-esteem, and desire to counteract feelings of isolation. See KATASEXUALITY. **2.** as described in 1964 by Erich FROMM, an attraction to death, decay, and sickness. He considered this passion for the lifeless to be a fundamental yet pathological orientation within certain individuals' characters that revealed itself through increasing tendencies toward greed, narcissism, destruction, cruelty, and murder and a growing attachment to mechanical (i.e., nonliving) artifacts at the expense of interest in living beings and the natural world. According to Fromm, necrophilia stems from a person's desire to compensate for a lack of authenticity and self-identity. **—necrophile** *n.* **—necrophilic** *adj.*

necrophilic fantasies male (and, occasionally, female) fantasies about viewing or having heterosexual or same-sex intercourse with a corpse as a means of achieving sexual excitement. Such fantasies are sometimes acted out with the aid of prostitutes who satisfy necrophilic clients by simulating a lifeless appearance.

necrophobia *n.* a persistent and irrational fear of corpses. See also THANATOPHOBIA.

necrosis *n.* the death of cells (e.g., neurons, muscle cells) from any of a variety of causes, including obstruction of blood supply to the affected part, disease, injury, or toxins. **—necrotic** *adj.*

need *n.* **1.** a condition of tension in an organism resulting from deprivation of something required for survival, well-being, or personal fulfillment. **2.** a substance, state, or any other thing (e.g., food, water, security) whose absence generates this condition.

need–fear dilemma **1.** a simultaneous need for and fear of close relationships with others. **2.** a conflicting set of conditions facing those who need structured control but have an aversion to external control or influence. In marked form, it is a characteristic condition in schizophrenia, particularly in terms of both greatly needing and greatly fearing other people.

need for achievement (**n-Ach**) a strong desire to accomplish goals and attain a high standard of performance and personal fulfillment. People with a high need for achievement often undertake tasks in which there is a reasonable probability of success and avoid tasks that are either too easy (because of lack of challenge) or too difficult (because of fear of failure). The need for achievement was proposed by U.S. psychologist Henry Alexander Murray (1893–1988) and investigated extensively by David MCCLELLAND.

need for affection the degree to which a person wants to be close or distant in a relationship with another. In intimate relationships, need for affection is often expressed concretely as a desire to be touched or held or to be commended verbally. An exaggerated need for affection and approval is considered by many to be a NEUROSIS and is often seen as resulting from early deprivation, especially of physical affection.

need for affiliation (**n-Aff**) a strong desire to socialize and be part of a group. People with a high need for affiliation often seek the approval and acceptance of others. See AFFILIATION. [proposed by David MCCLELLAND]

need for closure **1.** the motivation to achieve finality and absoluteness in decisions, judgments, and choices. A person with a high need for closure will often have a low tolerance of ambiguity and uncertainty and may be attracted to dogmatic political or religious views. **2.** the need to achieve a sense of finality at the close of a painful or difficult episode in one's life. Some estranged couples, for example, feel a need to obtain a formal divorce for emotional as well as practical reasons. See CLOSURE.

need for cognition a personality trait reflecting a person's tendency to enjoy engaging in extensive cognitive activity. This trait primarily reflects a person's motivation to engage in cognitive activity rather than his or her actual ability to do so. Individuals high in need for cognition tend to develop attitudes or take action based on thoughtful evaluation of information. [originally investigated in 1994 by U.S. psychologists John T. Cacioppo (1951–) and Richard E. Petty (1951–)]

need for power the dispositional tendency to seek control over other people and over one's environment. See POWER.

need-hierarchy theory see MASLOW'S MOTIVATIONAL HIERARCHY.

need–press method in the THEMATIC APPERCEPTION TEST, a system of analyzing and scoring each sentence of the stories told by a participant as a means of evaluating his or her needs and the PRESS of environmental factors to which he or she is exposed.

N

need–press theory in the PERSONOLOGY of U.S. psychologist Henry Alexander Murray (1893–1988), an explanation of behavior in terms of the influence, or PRESS, of both the present environment and past experiences upon the expression and activation of a need.

needs assessment 1. the identification of currently unmet service needs in a community or other group, done prior to implementing a new service program or modifying an existing service program. The perceived needs are generally assessed from multiple perspectives, including those of community or group leaders and those of each individual in the community or group. **2.** the identification of those areas that should be the focus of a personnel training program. Needs assessment involves analyses in three key areas: (a) the knowledge, skills, abilities, and other characteristics of employees; (b) the requirements of the tasks performed by employees; and (c) the requirements of the organization.

need to belong the motivation to be a part of relationships, belong to groups, and be viewed positively by others. See AFFILIATION.

need to evaluate a personality trait reflecting a person's tendency to engage in extensive evaluative thinking when encountering people, issues, or objects. People who are high in need to evaluate tend to form attitudes and categorize objects spontaneously along a positive–negative scale. People who are low in need to evaluate tend to think of objects in evaluative terms only when the context encourages such categorization. [originally investigated in 1996 by U.S. psychologists William Blair Gage Jarvis and Richard E. Petty (1951–)]

nefazodone *n.* a MIXED-FUNCTION ANTIDEPRESSANT chemically related to TRAZODONE but with some important pharmacological distinctions. It is an antagonist at 5-HT_2 SEROTONIN RECEPTORS and an inhibitor of both serotonin and norepinephrine reuptake. This combination of actions is thought to be related to the lack of SSRI-like side effects associated with its antidepressant properties. Its sedative effects may be useful in the treatment of depression-related anxiety and insomnia.

negative adaptation a gradual loss of sensitivity or weakening of response due to prolonged stimulation.

negative affect the internal feeling state (AFFECT) that occurs when one has failed to achieve a goal or to avoid a threat or when one is not satisfied with the current state of affairs. The tendency to experience such states is known as **negative affectivity**.

negative attitude in psychotherapy and counseling, the client's feeling of rejection or disapproval of the therapist or counselor or of the therapeutic or counseling process, of another person, or of himself or herself. Compare POSITIVE ATTITUDE.

negative correlation a relationship between two variables in which the value of one variable increases while the value of the other variable decreases. For example, in a study about babies crying and being held, the discovery that those who are held more tend to cry less is a negative correlation. See also CORRELATION COEFFICIENT.

negative emotion an unpleasant, often disruptive, emotional reaction designed to express a NEGATIVE AFFECT. Negative emotion is not conducive to progress toward obtaining one's goals. Examples are anger, envy, sadness, and fear. Compare POSITIVE EMOTION.

negative exercise addiction an inordinate attraction to habitual participation in physical exercise activities that has a negative effect on physical, psychological, or social well-being. Also called **exercise compulsion**; **exercise obsession**. Compare POSITIVE EXERCISE ADDICTION.

negative feedback in social psychology, nonconstructive criticism, disapproval, and other negative information received by a person in response to his or her performance.

negative hallucination a false perceptual experience characterized by failure to see a person or object while looking directly at it, as in failing to perceive a certain person in a group in response to hypnotic suggestion. Compare POSITIVE HALLUCINATION.

negative imagery mental images that incorporate sensations of performance errors, unwanted outcomes, DEMOTIVATION, or self-degradation.

N

negative incentive an object or condition that constitutes an AVERSIVE STIMULUS and therefore facilitates avoidance behavior. Compare POSITIVE INCENTIVE.

negative Oedipus complex in psychoanalytic theory, the opposite or reverse aspect of the OEDIPUS COMPLEX, in which the son desires the father and regards the mother as rival, or the daughter is attached to the mother and regards the father as rival. The more familiar attachment is the heterosexual form (the positive Oedipus complex). Sigmund FREUD held that both aspects are part of the normal Oedipus complex in boys and girls. Also called **inverted Oedipus complex**.

negative punishment punishment that results because some stimulus or circumstance is removed as a consequence of a response. For example, if a response results in a subtraction of money from an accumulating account, and the response becomes less likely as a result of this experience, then negative punishment has occurred. Compare POSITIVE PUNISHMENT.

negative reinforcement the removal, prevention, or postponement of an AVERSIVE STIMULUS as a consequence of a response, which, in turn, increases the probability of that response. Compare POSITIVE REINFORCEMENT.

negative response a response that results in avoidance of or withdrawal from a stimulus.

negative schizophrenia a form of schizophrenia characterized by a predomination of NEGATIVE SYMPTOMS, suggesting deficiency or absence of behavior normally present in a person's repertoire, as shown in apathy, blunted affect, emotional withdrawal, poor rapport, and lack of spontaneity. Compare POSITIVE SCHIZOPHRENIA. [defined in 1982 by U.S. psychiatrist Nancy C. Andreasen and Scott A. Olsen]

negative self-verification theory the theory that a depressed mood is exacerbated or maintained because depressed individuals solicit or inspire feedback or treatment from others that confirms or reinforces their negative beliefs about themselves.

negative-state-relief model the hypothesis that HELPING behavior is used by some people in stress situations and periods of boredom and inactivity to avoid or escape negative moods.

negative suggestion a statement intended to deter or suppress a feeling, thought, or action on the part of another person.

negative symptom a deficit in the ability to perform the normal functions of living—logical thinking; self-care; social interaction; planning; initiating; and carrying through constructive actions; and so forth—as shown in apathy, blunted affect, emotional withdrawal, poor rapport, and lack of spontaneity. In schizophrenia, a predominance of negative symptoms is often associated with a poor prognosis. Compare POSITIVE SYMPTOM. See NEGATIVE SCHIZOPHRENIA.

negative transference in psychoanalysis, transfer of anger or hostility felt toward the parents, or other individuals significant during childhood, onto the therapist. Compare POSITIVE TRANSFERENCE.

negative triad see COGNITIVE TRIAD.

negativism *n.* **1.** an attitude characterized by persistent resistance to the suggestions of others (**passive negativism**) or the tendency to act in ways that are contrary to the expectations, requests, or commands of others (**active negativism**), typically without any identifiable reason for opposition. In young children and adolescents, such reactions may be considered a healthy expression of self-assertion. Negativism may also be associated with a number of disorders (extreme negativism is a feature of CATATONIC SCHIZOPHRENIA) and it can be an expression of opposition, withdrawal, or anger or a method of gaining attention. Also called **negativistic response**. See also OPPOSITIONAL DEFIANT DISORDER; PASSIVE-AGGRESSIVE PERSONALITY DISORDER. **2.** any philosophy or doctrine based on negation, such as nihilism or skepticism. **—negativistic** *adj.*

negativistic personality disorder see PASSIVE-AGGRESSIVE PERSONALITY DISORDER.

negativistic response see NEGATIVISM.

neglect *n.* **1.** failure to provide for the basic needs of a person in one's care. The neglect may be emotional (e.g., rejection or apathy), material (e.g., withholding food or clothing), or service-oriented (e.g., depriving of education or medical attention). See CHILD NEGLECT; ELDER NEGLECT. See also MALTREATMENT. **2.** a syndrome characterized by lack of awareness of a specific area or side of the body caused by a brain injury. It may involve failure to recognize the area as belonging to oneself or ignoring the existence of one side of the body or one side of the visual field (see UNILATERAL NEGLECT; VISUAL NEGLECT). This is most often associated with an injury to the right cerebral hemisphere with corresponding left-sided neglect. Neglect has also been found in auditory, tactile, and proprioceptive tasks. Also called **perceptual neglect**. See also SENSORY NEGLECT; SPATIAL NEGLECT.

neglect dyslexia a form of acquired dyslexia (see ALEXIA) associated with VISUAL NEGLECT, a condition in which a person is unaware of half of the visual field as a result of neurological damage. Either the initial parts of words are misread (left neglect) or the terminal parts of words are misread (right neglect), and the errors are not simple deletions but typically guesses of real though incorrect words with approximately the right number of letters.

negligence *n.* failure to fulfill a duty or to provide some response, action, or level of care that is appropriate or reasonable to expect. In ergonomics, for example, negligence involves failure to take reasonable care to protect human safety or equipment in the design, development, or evaluation of a system. A variety of different types of negligence exist in law. See also MALPRACTICE. **—negligent** *adj.*

Nembutal *n.* a trade name for PENTOBARBITAL.

neobehaviorism *n.* an approach to psychology, influenced by LOGICAL POSITIVISM, that emphasized the development of comprehensive theories and frameworks of behavior, such as those of Clark Leonard HULL and Edward C. TOLMAN, through empirical observation of behavior and the use of consciousness and mental events as explanatory devices. It thus contrasts with classical BEHAVIORISM, which was concerned with freeing psychology of mentalistic concepts and explanations. According to U.S. psychologist and philosopher Sigmund Koch (1917–1996), neobehaviorism replaced classical behaviorism as the dominant 20th-century program for experimental psychology around 1930; its influence began to wane in the 1950s. See also RADICAL BEHAVIORISM. **—neobehaviorist** *adj., n.*

neocortex *n.* regions of the CEREBRAL CORTEX that are the most recently evolved and contain six main layers of cells. Neocortex, which comprises the majority of human cerebral cortex, includes the primary sensory and motor cortex and association cortex. Also called **neopal-**

lium. Compare ALLOCORTEX. **—neocortical** *adj.*

neodissociative theory a theory that explains the paradoxical phenomena of hypnosis as a result of DIVIDED CONSCIOUSNESS. For example, hypnotic analgesia can produce subjectively reported relief from pain while physiological measures indicate that pain is still being registered.

neo-Freudian 1. *adj.* denoting an approach that derives from the CLASSICAL PSYCHOANALYSIS of Sigmund FREUD but with modifications and revisions that typically emphasize social and interpersonal elements over biological instincts. The term is not usually applied to the approaches of Freud's contemporaries, such as Alfred ADLER and Carl JUNG, who broke away from his school quite early. Erik ERIKSON, Erich FROMM, German-born U.S. psychoanalyst Karen Horney (1885–1952), and U.S. psychiatrist Harry Stack Sullivan (1892–1949) are considered to be among the most influential neo-Freudian theorists and practitioners. **2.** *n.* an analyst or theoretician who adopts such an approach.

neolalia *n.* the abnormal tendency to use NEOLOGISMS when speaking. Also called **neolallism**.

neologism *n.* a recently coined word or expression. In a neurological or psychopathological context neologisms, whose origins and meanings are usually nonsensical and unrecognizable (e.g., "klipno" for watch), are typically associated with APHASIA or SCHIZOPHRENIA. **—neologistic** *adj.*

neologistic jargon unintelligible speech containing a mixture of inappropriately combined words and bizarre expressions coined by the speaker. Also called **neologistic paraphasia**. See WORD SALAD.

neonatal drug dependency syndrome a syndrome in which a baby is born with drug dependence due to the mother's drug abuse (most often opioid abuse) during the latter part of pregnancy. Such babies are often of low birth weight. Other severe problems that accompany drug abuse by pregnant women include increased risk of intrauterine death, premature delivery, and increased neonatal mortality.

neonatal period in human development, the period from birth to approximately 1 month of age for infants born after a full-term pregnancy (for infants born prematurely, the period is longer). See also DEVELOPMENTAL LEVELS.

neonaticide *n.* the killing of an infant who is less than 24 hours old.

NEO Personality Inventory (**NEO-PI**) a personality questionnaire designed to assess the factors of the FIVE-FACTOR PERSONALITY MODEL. First published in 1985 and revised in 1992 (**NEO-PI-R**), the inventory takes its name from three factors of the model: *n*euroticism, *e*xtraversion, and *o*penness to experience. It is available in two versions (Form S for self-reports and Form R for observer ratings), each comprising 240 statements to which participants respond using a 5-point LIKERT SCALE format, ranging from "strongly disagree" to "strongly agree." [developed by U.S. psychologists Paul T. Costa, Jr. (1942–) and Robert R. McCrae (1949–)]

neophasia *n.* a complex language system created by and idiosyncratic to a person, with its own vocabulary and rules of grammar.

neophilia *n.* a strong desire for anything new or different, such as new foods.

neophobia *n.* **1.** a persistent and irrational fear of change or of anything new, unfamiliar, or strange. **2.** the avoidance of new stimuli, especially foods. **—neophobic** *adj.*

neoplasm *n.* a new, abnormal growth, that is, a benign or malignant tumor. The term is generally used to specify a malignant tumor (see CANCER). A neoplasm usually grows rapidly by cellular proliferation but generally lacks structural organization. A malignant neoplasm is usually invasive, destroying or damaging neighboring normal tissues, and can spread to distant sites by the process of metastasis; benign neoplasms are usually encapsulated and do not spread, but they may damage neighboring tissues by compression. **—neoplastic** *adj.*

neostigmine *n.* an anticholinesterase (see CHOLINERGIC DRUG) used in the diagnosis and treatment of myasthenia gravis and glaucoma. U.S. trade name: **Prostigmin**.

nephrogenic diabetes insipidus a form of diabetes in which the kidneys are unable to produce a normal concentration of urine because the kidney tubules do not respond to VASOPRESSIN produced by the pituitary gland. The patient drinks enormous amounts of water and excretes large volumes of dilute urine. The disorder can be critical for infants, who cannot communicate their thirst and therefore suffer water depletion, which may lead to brain damage and mental retardation before the cause can be diagnosed.

nepiophilia *n.* sexual interest in and arousal by infants: a type of PEDOPHILIA. The person generally does not find adults, or sometimes even older children, sexually arousing. Nepiophilia is rarely seen in females.

nerve *n.* a bundle of AXONS outside the central nervous system (CNS), enclosed in a sheath of connective tissue to form a cordlike structure. Nerves serve to connect the CNS with the tissues and organs of the body. They may be motor, sensory, or mixed (containing axons of both motor and sensory neurons). See CRANIAL NERVE; SPINAL NERVE. Compare TRACT.

nerve block the blocking of nerve impulses by drugs (e.g., anesthetics) or by mechanical means.

nerve impulse a wave of depolarization, in the form of an ACTION POTENTIAL, that is propagated along a neuron or chain of neurons as the means of transmitting signals in the nervous system. Also called **nervous impulse**; **neural impulse**. See also SYNAPSE.

nervios *n.* a wide range of symptoms affecting Latino groups in the United States and Latin America (the word literally means "nerves") and attributed to stressful and difficult life experiences and circumstances. Symptoms include headache, dizziness, concentration difficulties, sleep disturbance, stomach upsets, and tingling sensations; mental disorder may or may not be present. See also ATAQUE DE NERVIOS.

nervous *adj.* **1.** in a transient emotional state of anxious apprehension. **2.** of an excitable, highly strung, or easily agitated disposition. **3.** referring to the structures or functions of the nervous system.

nervous breakdown a lay term for an emotional illness or other mental disorder that has a sudden onset, produces acute distress, and significantly interferes with one's functioning. Also called **nervous prostration**.

nervous exhaustion a lay term for a state of severe fatigue due to emotional strain. See also NEURASTHENIA.

nervous habit stereotyped behavior, such as nail biting or tics, presumed to be based on anxiety and performed to reduce tension.

nervousness *n.* a state of restless tension and emotionality in which people tend to tremble, feel apprehensive, or show other signs of anxiety or fear.

N

nervous prostration see NERVOUS BREAKDOWN.

nervous system the system of NEURONS, NERVES, TRACTS, and associated tissues that, together with the ENDOCRINE SYSTEM, coordinates activities of the organism in response to signals received from the internal and external environments. The nervous system of higher vertebrates is often considered in terms of its divisions, principally the CENTRAL NERVOUS SYSTEM, the PERIPHERAL NERVOUS SYSTEM, and the AUTONOMIC NERVOUS SYSTEM.

NES 1. abbreviation for NEUROLOGICAL EVALUATION SCALE. **2.** abbreviation for NONEPILEPTIC SEIZURE.

nesting *n.* in an experimental design, the appearance of the levels of one factor (the **nested factor**) only within a single level of another factor. For example, classrooms are nested within a school because each specific classroom is found only within a single school; similarly, schools are nested within school districts.

network *n.* **1.** the system of interpersonal interactions and relationships in an individual's environment that play an important part in the production of mental health or psychological disorder. The specific impact that these interactions and relationships have on the development of psychopathology is called the **network effect**. **2.** in SOCIOMETRY, a complex chain of interrelations that shape social tradition and public opinion, either spontaneously or through propaganda.

network effect see NETWORK.

network therapy individual PSYCHOTHERAPY or FAMILY THERAPY in which an attempt is made to involve not only family members but also other relatives, friends, and neighbors as sources of emotional support and possible vocational opportunity. See also SOCIAL-NETWORK THERAPY.

neural circuit an arrangement of NEURONS and their interconnections. Neural circuits often perform particular limited functions, such as negative feedback circuits, positive feedback circuits, or oscillator circuits. In a **local circuit** the neurons are all contained within a level of brain organization of a particular region.

neural pathway any route followed by a nerve impulse through central or peripheral nerve fibers of the nervous system. A neural pathway may consist of a simple reflex arc or a complex but specific routing, such as that followed by impulses transmitting a specific wavelength of sound from the cochlea to the auditory cortex. Also called **nerve pathway**.

neural plasticity the ability of the nervous system to change in response to experience or environmental stimulation. For example, following an injury remaining neurons may adopt certain functions previously performed by those that were damaged, or a change in reactivity of the nervous system and its components may result from constant, successive activations. Also called **neuroplasticity**.

neural tube a structure formed during early development of an embryo, when folds of the neural plate curl over and fuse. Cells of the neural tube differentiate along its length on the anterior–posterior axis to form swellings that correspond to the future FOREBRAIN, MIDBRAIN, and HINDBRAIN; the posterior part of the tube develops into the spinal cord. The cavity of the tube ultimately becomes the interconnected cerebral VENTRICLES and the central canal of the spinal cord. Many congenital defects of the nervous system originate at this stage of development (see NEURAL TUBE DEFECT).

neural tube defect any of a group of congenital defects caused by faulty development of the NEURAL TUBE. As a result, portions of the brain or spinal cord or their covering membranes (the meninges) protrude through a gap in the skull or spinal column, giving rise to neurological disorders, mental retardation, or physical disability of varying severity. Anencephaly and spina bifida are examples of such defects.

neurasthenia *n.* a condition marked by fatigue, weakness, insomnia, aches, and pains. The name (from Greek *neurastheneia*, "nerve weakness") originated in the 19th century, when the symptoms were believed to be due to exhaustion, primarily from overwork, and is rarely used today. The condition is now attributed primarily to emotional conflicts, tensions, frustrations, and other psychological factors, and in *DSM–IV–TR* it is classified as UNDIFFERENTIATED SOMATOFORM DISORDER. [coined in 1869 by U.S. neurologist George Miller Beard (1839–1883)] **—neurasthenic** *adj.*

neuritic plaque see SENILE PLAQUE.

neurobiofeedback *n.* see NEUROFEEDBACK.

neurobiotaxis *n.* the growth of a nerve fiber toward the tissue it will innervate, which occurs during embryological development. Those factors that influence neurobiotaxis are currently the subject of research on nerve growth in adult organisms, suggesting the possibility of nerve regeneration or replacement after injury or disease.

neurodermatitis *n.* an eczematous skin lesion that may be associated with psychological stress and is exacerbated by rubbing or scratching the skin.

neurodevelopmental hypothesis a prominent theory stating schizophrenia results from an early brain lesion, either fetal or neonatal, that disrupts normal neurological development and leads to abnormalities and later psychotic symptoms. Consequences of this early disruption appear in childhood and adolescence, prior to the actual onset of schizophrenic symptoms, as subtle differences in motor coordination, cognitive and social functioning, and temperament. Much evidence supports this hypothesis and risk factors operating in early life (e.g., obstetric complications) have been shown to be associated with the later development of schizophrenia.

neuroendocrinology *n.* the study of the relationships between the nervous system, especially the brain, and the endocrine system. Some cells within the nervous system release hormones into the local or systemic circulation; these are called **neuroendocrine** (or **neurosecretory**) **cells**. The HYPOTHALAMUS, for example, produces RELEASING HORMONES that regulate secretion of pituitary hormones. Certain substances, such as NOREPINEPHRINE, act both as hormones and as neurotransmitters. **—neuroendocrinological** *adj.* **—neuroendocrinologist** *n.*

neurofeedback *n.* a learning strategy that enables people to alter their own brain waves using information about their brain-wave characteristics that is made available through electroencephalograph recordings that may be presented to them as a video display or an auditory signal. Also called **neurobiofeedback**. See BIOFEEDBACK.

neurofibrillary tangles twisted strands of abnormal filaments within neurons that are associated with Alzheimer's disease. The filaments form microscopically visible knots or tangles consisting of tau protein, which normally is associated with microtubules. If the structure of tau is rendered abnormal, the microtubule structure collapses, and the tau protein collects in neurofibrillary tangles.

neurofibroma *n.* a tumor of peripheral nerves caused by abnormal proliferation of SCHWANN CELLS. A neurofibroma is very similar to a SCHWANNOMA but is distinguished by its lack of a capsule.

neurofibromatosis *n.* see VON RECKLINGHAUSEN'S DISEASE.

neurogenic *adj.* pertaining to a condition or event caused or produced by a component of the nervous system.

neurogenic communication disorder any speech or language problem due to nervous system impairment that causes some level of difficulty or inability in exchanging information with others.

neurohormone *n.* a hormone produced by neural tissue and released into the general circulation. See NEUROENDOCRINOLOGY.

neuroleptic *n.* see ANTIPSYCHOTIC.

neuroleptic malignant syndrome a rare complication of therapy with conventional (typical or first-generation) ANTIPSYCHOTICS, characterized by fever, inability to regulate blood pressure, difficulty in breathing, and changes in consciousness (including coma); mortality rates approaching 25% have been observed. It occurs primarily at the start of treatment or with a sudden increase in dose. The incidence of the syndrome, never high, has declined further with the abandonment of MEGADOSE PHARMACOTHERAPY with conventional antipsychotics and the advent of second-generation ATYPICAL ANTIPSYCHOTICS.

neuroleptic syndrome the series of effects observed in individuals who have taken ANTIPSYCHOTICS. It is characterized by reduced motor activity and emotionality, an indifference to external stimuli, and a decreased ability to perform tasks that require good motor coordination. With high doses, patients may become cataleptic.

neurolinguistic programming (**NLP**) a set of techniques and strategies designed to improve interpersonal communications and relations by modifying the "mental programs," or MENTAL MODELS of the world, that individuals develop and use to respond to and interact with the environment and other people. This approach presumes that these programs, as well as the behaviors they influence, result from the interaction among the brain, language, and the body. In order to achieve desired change, one must first understand subjective experience and the structures of thought (i.e., mental programs) underlying that experience, and then learn to modify these programs as needed, for example, to enhance adaptive behavior across a variety of situations or to attain excellence in personal performance. Although originally applied to psychotherapy and counseling, neurolinguistic programming has developed applications in other fields, such as business management, artificial intelligence, and education. [developed in the United States in 1976 by U.S. mathematician and therapist Richard Bandler (1950–) and U.S. linguist John Grinder (1940–)]

neurological amnesia a loss or impairment of memory due to disease or injury that affects the nervous system.

neurological evaluation analysis of the data gathered by an examining physician of an individual's mental status and sensory and motor functioning. The examination typically includes assessment of cognition, speech and behavior, orientation and level of alertness, muscular strength and tone, muscle coordination and movement, tendon reflexes, cranial nerves, pain and temperature sensitivity, and discriminative senses.

Neurological Evaluation Scale (**NES**) an assessment instrument originally developed in 1989 to provide a standardized tool for the evaluation of neurological abnormalities and impairments associated with schizophrenia. Currently, it is often used in researching other severe mental illnesses, such as bipolar disorders, as well. [developed by U.S. psychiatrists Robert W. Buchanan and Douglas W. Heinrichs]

neurological examination see NEUROLOGICAL EVALUATION.

neurology *n.* a branch of medicine that deals with the nervous system in both healthy and diseased states. The diagnosis and treatment of diseases of the nervous system is called **clinical neurology; neurologists** diagnose and treat patients with stroke, dementia, headaches, and back pain, among other disorders. **—neurological** *adj.*

N

neuron (**neurone**) *n.* the basic cellular unit of the nervous system. Each neuron is composed of a CELL BODY; fine, branching extensions (DENDRITES) that receive incoming nerve signals; and a single, long extension (AXON) that conducts nerve impulses to its branching terminal. The axon terminal transmits impulses to other neurons, or to effector organs (e.g., muscles and glands), via junctions called SYNAPSES or neuromuscular junctions. Neurons can be classified according to their function as MOTOR NEURONS, SENSORY NEURONS, or INTERNEURONS. There are various structural types, including unipolar neurons, bipolar neurons, and multipolar neurons. The axons of vertebrate neurons are often surrounded by a MYELIN SHEATH. Also called **nerve cell**. [term coined by German physician Heinrich Wilhelm von Waldeyer-Hartz (1836–1921)] **—neuronal** *adj.*

Neurontin *n.* a trade name for GABAPENTIN.

neuropathic pain pain caused by damage to peripheral nerves. It is often difficult to treat.

neuropathology *n.* the study of diseases of the nervous system. **—neuropathological** *adj.* **—neuropathologist** *n.*

neuropeptide *n.* any of several peptides that are released by neurons as NEUROTRANSMITTERS or NEUROHORMONES. They include the ENDOGENOUS OPIOIDS (e.g., enkephalin and endorphin); peptides found in both the brain and the peripheral nervous system (e.g., SUBSTANCE P); hypothalamic RELEASING HORMONES (e.g., thyrotropin-releasing hormone); pituitary hormones (e.g., PROLACTIN); and other circulating peptides (e.g., atrial natriuretic peptide and bradykinin).

neuropharmacology *n.* the scientific study of the effects of drugs on the nervous system. **—neuropharmacological** *adj.* **—neuropharmacologist** *n.*

neuroplasticity *n.* see NEURAL PLASTICITY.

neuropsychological assessment an evaluation of the presence, nature, and extent of brain damage or dysfunction derived from the results of various NEUROPSYCHOLOGICAL TESTS.

neuropsychological rehabilitation the use of psychological techniques to treat and manage cognitive, emotional, and behavioral problems that arise from brain damage or dysfunction.

neuropsychological test any of various clinical instruments for assessing cognitive impairment, including those measuring memory, language, learning, attention, and visuospatial and visuoconstructive functioning. Examples of batteries of such tests are the HALSTEAD–REITAN NEUROPSYCHOLOGICAL BATTERY and the LURIA–NEBRASKA NEUROPSYCHOLOGICAL BATTERY.

neuropsychology *n.* the branch of science that studies the physiological processes of the nervous system and relates them to behavior and cognition. See also CLINICAL NEUROPSYCHOLOGY. **—neuropsychological** *adj.* **—neuropsychologist** *n.*

neuroreceptor *n.* a RECEPTOR molecule located in a neuron cell membrane that binds molecules of a particular neurotransmitter, hormone, drug, or the like and initiates a particular response within the neuron. Also called **neurotransmitter receptor**.

neuroscience *n.* the scientific study of the nervous system, including neuroanatomy, neurochemistry, NEUROLOGY, neurophysiology, and NEUROPHARMACOLOGY, and its applications in psychology and psychiatry. See also BEHAVIORAL NEUROSCIENCE; COGNITIVE NEUROSCIENCE.

neurosis *n.* any one of a variety of mental disorders characterized by significant anxiety or other distressing emotional symptoms, such as persistent and irrational fears, obsessive thoughts, compulsive acts, dissociative states, and somatic and depressive reactions. The symptoms do not involve gross personality disorganization, total lack of insight, or loss of contact with reality (compare PSYCHOSIS). In psychoanalysis, neuroses are generally viewed as exaggerated, unconscious methods of coping with internal conflicts and the anxiety they produce. In DSM–IV–TR, most of what used to be called neuroses are now classified as ANXIETY DISORDERS. Also called **psychoneurosis**. **—neurotic** *adj.*, *n.*

neurosurgery *n.* surgical procedures performed on the brain, spinal cord, or peripheral nerves for the purpose of restoring functioning or preventing further impairment. See also PSYCHOSURGERY. **—neurosurgeon** *n.* **—neurosurgical** *adj.*

neurotic anxiety in psychoanalytic theory, anxiety that originates in unconscious conflict and is maladaptive in nature: It has a disturbing effect on emotion and behavior and also intensifies resistance to treatment. Neurotic anxiety contrasts with REALISTIC ANXIETY, about an external danger or threat, and with moral anxiety, which is guilt posited to originate in the superego.

neurotic character see CHARACTER NEUROSIS.

neurotic conflict 1. in psychoanalytic theory, an INTRAPSYCHIC CONFLICT that leads to persistent maladjustment and emotional disturbance. **2.** in the approach of German-born U.S. psychoanalyst Karen D. Horney (1885–1952), the clash that occurs between opposing NEUROTIC NEEDS, such as an excessive need for power and independence and the need for love and dependence. See also NEUROTIC TREND.

neurotic depression 1. see REACTIVE DEPRESSION. **2.** any MAJOR DEPRESSIVE EPISODE that does not include psychotic features.

neurotic disorder any mental disorder characterized by distressing symptoms that are recognized by the individual as being unacceptable and alien. REALITY TESTING is largely intact, and behavior does not actively violate social norms (although functioning may be markedly impaired). The disturbance is relatively enduring or recurrent without treatment, is not limited to a transitory reaction to stressors, and has no demonstrable organic cause. In *DSM–IV–TR*, neurotic disorders are not recognized as a valid diagnostic entity, and the individual disorders that were included under that heading in earlier editions of the *DSM* have been subsumed under various other categories.

neurotic inventory a questionnaire designed to reveal an individual's tendency toward NEUROTICISM. Statements are taken from case histories and related material, and the participant indicates agreement or disagreement with each statement. Theoretically, the more statements with which participants agree, the greater their tendency toward neuroticism.

neuroticism *n.* **1.** the state of being neurotic or a proneness to NEUROSIS. **2.** a mild condition of neurosis. **3.** one of the dimensions of the FIVE-FACTOR PERSONALITY MODEL and the BIG FIVE PERSONALITY MODEL, characterized by a chronic level of emotional instability and proneness to psychological distress. **4.** in EYSENCK'S TYPOLOGY, one of three major dimensions whose polar opposite is emotional stability, the others being introversion versus EXTRAVERSION and PSYCHOTICISM versus impulse control. See also FACTOR THEORY OF PERSONALITY.

neurotic need in psychoanalytic theory, an excessive drive or demand that may arise out of the strategies individuals use to defend themselves against BASIC ANXIETY. German-born U.S. psychoanalyst Karen D. Horney (1885–1952) enumerated ten neurotic needs: for affection and approval, for a partner to take over one's life, for restriction of one's life, for power, for exploitation of others, for prestige, for admiration, for achievement, for self-sufficiency and independence, and for perfection. When an individual's personality is dominated by a few neurotic needs he or she may exhibit a NEUROTIC TREND.

neurotic resignation the avoidance of any aspect of reality that may bring inner conflicts into one's awareness, involving withdrawal that may take the form of total inactivity or overactivity in other areas. Neurotic resignation is distinguished from **dynamic resignation**, which is viewed as a temporary decision to postpone action until more favorable circumstances emerge. See also ESCAPE FROM REALITY; FLIGHT FROM REALITY; FLIGHT INTO REALITY. [first described by German-born U.S. psychoanalyst Karen D. Horney (1885–1952)]

neurotic solution a method of resolving a NEUROTIC CONFLICT by removing it from awareness.

neurotic trend in the theory of German-born U.S. psychoanalyst Karen D. Horney (1885–1952), one of three basic tendencies stemming from an individual's choice of strategies to counteract BASIC ANXIETY. These strategies generate insatiable NEUROTIC NEEDS, which group themselves into three trends: (a) moving toward people, or clinging to others (see COMPLIANT CHARACTER); (b) moving away from people, or insisting on independence and self-dependence (see DETACHED CHARACTER); and (c) moving against people, or seeking power, prestige, and possessions (see AGGRESSIVE CHARACTER).

neurotransmission *n.* the process by which a signal or other activity in a neuron is transferred to an adjacent neuron or other cell. Synaptic transmission, which occurs between two neurons via a SYNAPSE, is largely chemical, by the release and binding of NEUROTRANSMITTER, but it may also be electrical. Neurotransmission also occurs between a neuron and an effector organ or gland and between a neuron and a skeletal muscle cell. Also called **neural transmission**; **neuronal transmission**.

neurotransmitter *n.* any of a large number of chemicals that can be released by neurons to mediate transmission or inhibition of nerve signals across the junctions (SYNAPSES) between neurons. When triggered by a nerve impulse, the neurotransmitter is released from the terminal button (see AXON), travels across the SYNAPTIC CLEFT, and binds to and reacts with RECEPTOR molecules in the postsynaptic membrane. Neurotransmitters include amines, such as ACETYLCHOLINE, NOREPINEPHRINE, DOPAMINE, and SEROTONIN; and amino acids, such as GAMMA-AMINOBUTYRIC ACID, GLUTAMATE, and GLYCINE. Also called **chemical transmitter**; **synaptic transmitter**.

neurotrophin *n.* any of various proteins that promote the development and survival of specific populations of neurons. Neurotrophins include nerve growth factor, deficits in the axonal transport of which have been linked to Alzheimer's disease, and brain-derived neurotrophic factor, which plays a crucial role in cognition, learning, and memory formation by modulating synaptic PLASTICITY. Also called **neurotrophic factor**.

neutrality *n.* a role or a manner of behavior adopted by the therapist, who not only remains passive and permissive but also does not express judgments of right and wrong or suggest what is proper behavior on the part of the client.

neutralization *n.* in psychoanalytic theory, the use of sexual or aggressive energy in the service of the EGO rather than for gratification of the INSTINCTS, that is, in functions such as problem solving, creative imagination, scientific inquiry, and decision making. SUBLIMATION uses neutralized energy. Also called **taming of the instinct**. See also DESEXUALIZATION. **—neutralize** *vb.*

N

neutralizer *n.* a member of a therapy group who plays a role of modifying and controlling impulsive, aggressive, or destructive behaviors of other members of the group. [first described by Russian-born U.S. psychotherapist Samuel Richard Slavson (1890–1981)]

Nevo syndrome see SOTOS SYNDROME.

new-age therapy any of a number of popular treatments that lack a sound scientific basis and are generally not accepted by mental health professionals as valid, effective therapeutic practice. Support for such therapies does not come from independent scientific studies but rather is derived primarily from the "insights" and observations of their founders or the analysis and evaluation of participant feedback. An example of a new-age therapy is REBIRTHING.

NHIS abbreviation for NATIONAL HEALTH INTERVIEW SURVEY.

NHST abbreviation for NULL HYPOTHESIS SIGNIFICANCE TESTING.

nicotine *n.* an alkaloid obtained primarily from the TOBACCO plant (*Nicotiana tabacum*). Today nicotine is one of the most widely used psychoactive drugs; it is the primary active ingredient in tobacco and accounts for both the acute pharmacological effects of smoking or chewing tobacco (e.g., a discharge of EPINEPHRINE; a sudden release of glucose; an increase in blood pressure, respiration, heart rate, and cutaneous vasoconstriction) and the dependence that develops (see NICOTINE DEPENDENCE; NICOTINE WITHDRAWAL). The behavioral effects of the drug include enhanced alertness and feelings of calm. Nicotine produces multiple pharmacological effects on the central nervous system by activating NICOTINIC RECEPTORS, facilitating the release of several neurotransmitters, particularly dopamine (a reaction similar to that seen with such drugs as cocaine and heroin), along with other actions in the periphery. In large doses it is highly poisonous, producing such symptoms as dizziness, diarrhea, vomiting, tremors, spasms, unconsciousness, heart attack, and potentially death via paralysis of the muscles of respiration. Nicotine was isolated from the tobacco plant in 1828 and was named for the French diplomat Jean Nicot, who introduced tobacco into France in 1560. **—nicotinic** *adj.*

nicotine dependence in *DSM–IV–TR*, a cluster of cognitive, behavioral, and physiological symptoms indicating continued use of nicotine despite significant nicotine-related problems. There is a pattern of repeated nicotine ingestion resulting in tolerance, characteristic withdrawal symptoms if use is suspended (see NICOTINE WITHDRAWAL), and an uncontrollable drive to continue use. There is no *DSM–IV–TR* diagnosis of nicotine abuse. See also SUBSTANCE DEPENDENCE.

nicotine withdrawal a characteristic withdrawal syndrome that develops after cessation of (or reduction in) prolonged, heavy nicotine consumption. Two or more of the following are required for a *DSM–IV–TR* diagnosis of nicotine withdrawal: DYSPHORIA or depressed mood; insomnia; irritability, frustration, or anger; anxiety; difficulty in concentrating; restlessness; decreased heart rate; and increased appetite or weight gain.

nicotinic receptor (**nAchR**) a type of ACETYLCHOLINE RECEPTOR that responds to NICOTINE as well as to acetylcholine. Nicotinic receptors mediate chiefly the excitatory activities of acetylcholine, including those at neuromuscular junctions. Compare MUSCARINIC RECEPTOR.

Niemann–Pick disease an inherited lipid-storage disorder generally marked by a deficiency of the enzyme sphingomyelinase and accumulation of lipids in brain tissue and visceral organs. Massive liver and spleen enlargement (hepatomegaly and splenomegaly) may occur. Mental retardation, blindness, and death before adulthood are common. About 95% of individuals with this disorder have a defective *NPC1* gene (chromosomal locus 18q11–12). Also called **sphingomyelin lipidosis**. See also LIPID-METABOLISM DISORDERS. [Albert **Niemann** (1880–1921) and Ludwig **Pick** (1868–1944), German physicians]

night-eating syndrome an eating disorder characterized by INSOMNIA, nocturnal HYPERPHAGIA, and morning ANOREXIA that persist for at least 3 months. Recent research suggests night-eating syndrome is related to hormonal irregularities and a disturbed CIRCADIAN RHYTHM of food intake, although chronic stress may also be a contributing factor. This type of eating disorder is estimated to affect 1.5% of the global population and is thought to occur in 10–25% of obese individuals. [first described in 1955 by U.S. psychiatrist Albert J. Stunkard]

night hospital a unit within a hospital in which patients receive psychiatric care at night, having spent the day in the community. See also PARTIAL HOSPITALIZATION.

nightmare *n.* a frightening or otherwise disturbing dream, in which fear, sadness, despair, disgust, or some combination of these forms the emotional content. Nightmares contain visual imagery and some degree of narrative structure and typically occur during REM SLEEP. The dreamer tends to waken suddenly from a nightmare and is immediately alert and aware of his or her surroundings. In *DSM–IV–TR*, the occurrence of frequent nightmares is classified as NIGHTMARE DISORDER. Nightmares are also a symptom of POSTTRAUMATIC STRESS DISORDER. **—nightmarish** *adj.*

nightmare-death syndrome the unexpected and mysterious nocturnal death of a healthy individual that occurs among southeast Asian refugees, especially Hmong, arriving in the United States. It is attributed by Hmong informants to a nocturnal spirit encounter and is similar to the Filipino concept of BANGUNGUT. Also called **sudden unexpected nocturnal-death syndrome**.

nightmare disorder in *DSM–IV–TR*, a SLEEP DISORDER characterized by the repeated occurrence of frightening dreams that lead to awakenings from sleep. It was formerly known as **dream anxiety disorder**. See PARASOMNIA.

night terror see SLEEP TERROR DISORDER.

nigrostriatal tract the neural pathway that extends from the SUBSTANTIA NIGRA to the striatum of the BASAL GANGLIA. It contains DOPAMINERGIC neurons and is associated with the production of voluntary movement.

nihilism *n.* **1.** the delusion of nonexistence: a fixed belief that the mind, body, or the world at large—or parts thereof—no longer exists. Also called **delusion of negation**; **nihilistic delusion**. **2.** the belief that existence is without meaning. **—nihilistic** *adj.*

nilutamide *n.* see ANTIANDROGEN.

NIMH abbreviation for NATIONAL INSTITUTE OF MENTAL HEALTH.

nirvana principle in psychoanalytic theory, the tendency of all INSTINCTS and life processes to remove tension and seek the stability and equilibrium of the inorganic state, that is, death. This is the trend of the DEATH INSTINCT, which Sigmund FREUD believed to be universal. See also PRINCIPLE OF INERTIA.

Nitoman *n.* a Canadian trade name for TETRABENAZINE.

nitrazepam *n.* a long-acting BENZODIAZEPINE with a HALF-LIFE of more than 24 hours, used as a hypnotic. Though nitrazepam has no active metabolic products, its lengthy half-life may cause unwanted accumulation with daily dosing. It is not currently marketed in the United States. Canadian trade name: **Mogadon**.

nitric oxide a compound present in numerous body tissues, where it has a variety of functions. In the body it is synthesized by the enzyme nitric oxide synthase from arginine, NADPH, and oxygen. Nitric oxide functions as a neurotransmitter, or an agent that influences neurotransmitters, in the brain and other parts of the central nervous system. In peripheral tissues it is involved in the relaxation of smooth muscle, and thus acts as a vasodilator, a bronchodilator, and a relaxant of smooth muscle in the penis and clitoris, being involved in erection and other components of the sexual response.

nitrous oxide an analgesic gas that is commonly used in outpatient dental procedures and as an adjunct in surgical anesthesia. It is also used as a propellant in aerosolized foods (e.g., whipping cream). In low doses nitrous oxide produces sensations of giddiness, elation, and euphoria. This property was apparent when it was initially synthesized in 1772 by British chemist Joseph Priestley (1733–1804), and nitrous oxide has long been known colloquially as **laughing gas**. Its euphoriant effects make nitrous oxide a popular inhalant in social settings. Also called **dinitrogen monoxide**.

N

Nizoral *n.* a trade name for KETOCONAZOLE.

NLD abbreviation for NONVERBAL LEARNING DISORDER.

NLP abbreviation for NEUROLINGUISTIC PROGRAMMING.

NMDA *N*-methyl-D-aspartate: an AGONIST that binds to a class of GLUTAMATE RECEPTORS that are both ligand-gated and voltage-sensitive (see NMDA RECEPTOR).

NMDA receptor a type of GLUTAMATE RECEPTOR that binds NMDA as well as GLUTAMATE. NMDA receptors are ligand-gated and voltage-sensitive, which enables them to participate in a variety of information-processing operations at synapses where glutamate is the neurotransmitter. The drugs of abuse KETAMINE and PCP are antagonists at NMDA receptors, preventing the influx of calcium ions, which may cause the hallucinogenic effects of these drugs. Excessive flow of calcium ions into the presynaptic neuron via the NMDA receptor is thought to contribute to glutamate toxicity. A recently emerging hypothesis on the etiology of schizophrenia involves dysfunction of the NMDA glutamate receptor (see GLUTAMATE HYPOTHESIS). Compare AMPA RECEPTOR.

N-methyl-D-aspartate *n.* see NMDA.

NMHA abbreviation for NATIONAL MENTAL HEALTH ASSOCIATION.

nocebo *n.* an adverse or otherwise unwanted physical or emotional symptom caused by the administration of a PLACEBO.

noctambulation *n.* see SLEEPWALKING DISORDER.

noctiphilia (**noctophilia**) *n.* see NYCTOPHILIA.

nocturnal emission an involuntary ejaculation that occurs during a nocturnal dream, known popularly as a **wet dream**. Studies show that the majority of males experience a nocturnal emission before the age of 21. A small percentage of total sexual release in a young adult male is through nocturnal emissions. Orgasm as part of nocturnal dreams is rare among adolescent females but increases among mature females.

nocturnal enuresis see ENURESIS.

nodal behavior in group psychotherapy, a period of increased activity, which may be interpersonally challenging, aggressive, or disorderly, followed by a relatively quiet period of **antinodal behavior**.

noetic *adj.* describing a level of knowledge or memory in which there is awareness of the known or remembered thing but not of one's personal experience in relation to that thing. **Noetic consciousness** is a state of consciousness in which one is aware of facts, concepts, words, and meanings but not of any connection to one's own experience. Compare ANOETIC; AUTONOETIC. [defined by Estonian-born Canadian psychologist Endel Tulving (1927–)]

N

no excuse in REALITY THERAPY, the concept that there are no acceptable reasons to condone irresponsible behavior or attribute it to another source. According to this concept, all behavior stems directly from the client and the client is therefore completely and solely responsible for his or her behavior. [devised by U.S. psychiatrist William Glasser (1925–)]

N-of-1 experimental design see SINGLE-CASE EXPERIMENTAL DESIGN.

noise *n.* **1.** a random or aperiodic waveform whose properties are described statistically. There are many types of noise, which are distinguished by their spectral or statistical properties. **White noise** (or **background noise**) has equal energy at all frequencies; **broadband noise** has energy over a relatively wide frequency range (e.g., 50 Hz to 10 kHz for audition); **pink noise** has energy that is inversely proportional to frequency; and **Gaussian noise** has instantaneous values that are determined according to a normal probability density function. **2.** anything that interferes with, obscures, reduces, or otherwise adversely affects the clarity or precision of an ongoing process, such as the communication of a message or signal.

nomadism *n.* **1.** a pathological tendency to wander from place to place and repeatedly change one's residence and occupation, often giving rise to instability and social MALADJUSTMENT. In milder form this tendency may be an attempt to escape from a distressing situation or from responsibility, but in extreme form it may be associated with brain damage, epilepsy, mental retardation, or psychosis. See also DROMOMANIA; PORIOMANIA. **2.** the lifestyle of a group of people with no fixed residence, characterized by frequent movement from place to place, often in search of resources or in accordance with seasonal changes.

nomifensine *n.* an antidepressant that is structurally different from any in current use. It blocks the synaptic reuptake of norepinephine and dopamine but not of serotonin. Due to severe, sometimes fatal, drug reactions, including acute hemolytic anemia, it was withdrawn worldwide in 1986. Former U.S. trade name: **Merital**.

nominal data numerical values that represent membership in specific categories. For example, the category male could be labeled 0 and the category female labeled 1, and each person within the population of interest (e.g., a particular town) assigned the number corresponding to their sex. Nominal data are similar to CATEGORICAL DATA, and the two terms are often used interchangeably.

nominal fallacy the false belief that a phenomenon is understood if it is merely named or labeled.

nominal scale a sequence of numbers that do not indicate order, magnitude, or a true zero point but rather identify items as belonging to mutually exclusive categories. For example, a nominal scale for the performance of a specific group of people on a particular test might use the number 1 to denote pass and the number 2 to denote fail. Also called **categorical scale**.

nomothetic *adj.* relating to the formulation of general laws as opposed to the study of the individual case. A **nomothetic approach** involves the study of groups of people or cases for the purpose of discovering those general and universally valid laws or principles that characterize the average person or case. Compare IDIOGRAPHIC.

nonadherence *n.* failure of an individual to follow a prescribed therapeutic regimen. Although nonadherence has traditionally been ascribed to oppositional behavior, it is more likely due to inadequate communication between the practitioner and the individual, physical or cognitive limitations that prevent the patient from following therapeutic recommendations (e.g., language differences between patient and practitioner, physical disabilities), or adverse effects that are not being adequately addressed. A primary aspect of HEALTH PSYCHOLOGY involves methods of reducing nonadherence and increasing adherence. Also called **noncompliance**.

nonaffective hallucination a hallucination whose content is not thematically related to depressed or manic affect. See MOOD-INCONGRUENT PSYCHOTIC FEATURES.

nonaggressive erotica sexually explicit literature, pictures, or other artistic material that does not contain any violence, coercion, or exploitation but instead presents a caring, consensual, mutually gratifying view of sexuality.

noncardiac chest pain recurrent chest pain that cannot be attributed to heart disease. It is commonly caused by problems with the esophagus (gullet), such as gastroesophageal reflux disease or esophageal spasm, or by musculoskeletal disorders, especially fibromyositis (muscle inflammation). Anxiety and panic attacks can also produce pain that resembles cardiac chest pain. See also PSEUDOANGINA.

noncompliance *n.* see NONADHERENCE.

non compos mentis in law, mentally deficient or legally insane and therefore not responsible for one's conduct. See INCOMPETENCE; INSANITY. Compare COMPOS MENTIS.

nonconscious *adj.* describing anything that is not available to conscious report. See UNCONSCIOUS.

nonconscious processes processes that do not themselves reach consciousness, although their eventual outcomes or consequences may have conscious impact.

nondeclarative memory a collection of various forms of memory that operate automatically and accumulate information that is not accessible to conscious recollection. For instance, one can do something faster if one has done it before, even if one cannot recall the earlier performance. Nondeclarative memory includes PRIMING. Nondeclarative memory does not depend on the MEDIAL TEMPORAL LOBES and is preserved in individuals with AMNESTIC DISORDER. Compare DECLARATIVE MEMORY.

nondemand pleasuring caressing of a partner's body for the sensual pleasure involved, with no expectation of sexual arousal. In sex therapy this practice, which excludes any touching of breasts or genitals, is often prescribed to eliminate performance anxiety: It allows a couple with a sexual dysfunction to begin to enjoy physical relations with each other without the risk of experiencing another failure. Also called **nondemanding pleasuring**.

nondirectional test see TWO-TAILED TEST.

nondirective approach an approach to psychotherapy and counseling in which the client leads the way by expressing his or her own feelings, defining his or her own problems, and interpreting his or her own behavior, while the therapist or counselor establishes an encouraging atmosphere and clarifies the client's ideas rather than directing the process. This approach is a cornerstone of CLIENT-CENTERED THERAPY. [originally advocated by Carl ROGERS]

nondirective counseling see CLIENT-CENTERED THERAPY.

nondirective play therapy a form of PLAY THERAPY based on the principle that a child has the capacity to revise his or her own attitudes and behavior. The therapist provides a variety of play materials and either assumes a friendly, interested role without giving direct suggestions or interpretations or engages the child in conversation that focuses on the child's present feelings and present life situations. The therapist's accepting attitude encourages the child to try new and more appropriate ways of dealing with problems.

nondirective therapy see CLIENT-CENTERED THERAPY.

nondisjunction *n.* the failure of pairs of chromosomes to separate during cell division with the result that both chromosomes move to the nucleus of one daughter cell, while the other daughter cell fails to receive its normal complement.

nonepileptic seizure (**NES**) an episode that resembles an epileptic seizure but is not produced by an abnormal electrical discharge in the brain. According to the Epilepsy Foundation, such seizures may be classified as **physiologic nonepileptic seizures**, which are associated with metabolic disturbances (e.g., changes in heart rhythm or sudden drops in blood pressure) and include SYNCOPE and TRANSIENT ISCHEMIC ATTACKS, or as PSYCHOGENIC NONEPILEPTIC SEIZURES. Nonepileptic seizures are also called **nonepileptic events** (or **attacks**), **pseudoseizures**, or **pseudoepilepsy**, although use of the latter two terms is now discouraged.

nonjudgmental approach in psychotherapy, the presentation or display of a neutral, noncritical attitude on the part of the therapist in order to encourage the client to give free expression to ideas and feelings. See also NEUTRALITY.

nonnormative influences influences on lifespan development that are irregular, in that they happen to just one or a few individuals and do not follow a predictable timetable.

nonorganic hearing loss hearing loss that cannot be accounted for by a known biological cause.

nonparametric statistics statistical tests that do not make assumptions about the distribution of the attribute (or attributes) in the population being tested, such as normality and homogeneity of variance. Compare PARAMETRIC STATISTICS.

nonperson *n.* see PERSONALITY DETERIORATION.

nonprescription drugs see OVER-THE-COUNTER.

nonrapid-eye-movement sleep see NREM SLEEP.

nonregulatory drive a DRIVE that serves functions that are unrelated to preserving physiological HOMEOSTASIS and thus not necessary for the physical survival of the individual organism, for

N

example, sex or achievement. Also called **general drive**. Compare REGULATORY DRIVE.

non-REM sleep see NREM SLEEP.

nonsedating antihistamines see ANTIHISTAMINE.

nonshared environment in behavior genetic analyses, those aspects of an environment that individuals living together (e.g., in a family household) do not share and that therefore cause them to become dissimilar to each other. Examples of nonshared environmental factors include the different friends or teachers that siblings in the same household might have outside of the home. Also called **unshared environment**. Compare SHARED ENVIRONMENT.

nonsteroidal anti-inflammatory drugs see NSAIDS.

nontraditional marriage a marriage that deviates from the traditional patterns of marriage in a society. In the United States and western Europe, such marriages may include marriages without the intent of having children or that permit the partners to have sexual relations with other people. Compare TRADITIONAL MARRIAGE.

nonulcer dyspepsia see DYSPEPSIA.

nonverbal behavior actions that can indicate an individual's attitudes or feelings without the need for speech. Nonverbal behavior can be apparent in FACIAL EXPRESSION, gaze direction, INTERPERSONAL DISTANCE, posture and postural changes, and gestures. It serves a number of functions, including providing information to other people (if they can detect and understand the signals), regulating interactions among people, and revealing the degree of intimacy between those present. Nonverbal behavior is often used synonymously with NONVERBAL COMMUNICATION, despite the fact that nonverbal actions are not always intended for, or understood by, other people.

nonverbal communication (**NVC**) the act of conveying information without the use of words. Nonverbal communication occurs through facial expressions, gestures, body language, tone of voice, and other physical indications of mood, attitude, approbation, and so forth, some of which may require knowledge of the culture or subculture to understand. In psychotherapy, clients' nonverbal communication can be as important to note as their verbal communication. See also NONVERBAL BEHAVIOR.

nonverbal intelligence an expression of intelligence that does not require language. Nonverbal intelligence can be measured with PERFORMANCE TESTS.

nonverbal language see NONVERBAL BEHAVIOR; NONVERBAL COMMUNICATION.

nonverbal leakage see VERBAL LEAKAGE.

nonverbal learning disorder (**NLD**) a LEARNING DISORDER that is characterized by limited skills in critical thinking and deficits in processing nonverbal information. This affects a child's academic progress as well as other areas of functioning, which may include social competencies, visual-spatial abilities, motor coordination, and emotional functioning.

nonverbal reinforcement any form of NONVERBAL COMMUNICATION, such as a gesture, facial expression, or body movement, that increases the frequency of the behavior that immediately precedes it. For example, a parent's smile following a desired response from a child, such as saying "thank you," reinforces the child's behavior. See also REINFORCEMENT; SOCIAL REINFORCEMENT.

non-Western therapies alternatives or complements to traditional Western forms of and approaches to psychotherapy and counseling that emphasize the body (e.g., acupuncture, yoga) and the interdependency of all beings and deemphasize individualism and rigid autonomy. These therapies have typically developed outside of Europe and North America. See also COMPLEMENTARY AND ALTERNATIVE MEDICINE.

Noonan's syndrome a genetic disorder that involves the skin, heart, gonads, and skeleton and is transmitted as an autosomal dominant trait. Affected individuals often have short stature, cardiovascular defects, and deafness. Intellectual development varies: Some have above average intelligence, most have mild to moderate mental retardation, and a few have profound retardation. Male patients are seldom fertile. Also called **familial Turner syndrome**; **Ullrich–Noonan syndrome**. [reported in 1963 by Jacqueline **Noonan** (1921–), U.S. pediatrician]

nootropic *n.* any of various drugs that are used to enhance cognitive function, usually in the treatment of progressive dementias, such as Alzheimer's disease, but also of cognitive dysfunction due to traumatic brain injury. They do not reverse the course of the dementia, but are reported to slow its progress in mild to moderate forms of the disease. Many of these drugs work by inhibiting the activity of acetylcholinesterase in the central nervous system, thereby counteracting the disruption of cholinergic neurotransmission observed in patients with Alzheimer's disease. Other drugs use different mechanisms for improving cognitive performance in patients with Alzheimer's disease, including NMDA RECEPTOR antagonism and potentially the prevention of BETA-AMYLOID plaque formation in the brain. Current nootropics include TACRINE, DONEPEZIL, RIVASTIGMINE, and GALANTAMINE. Also called **cognitive enhancer**; **memory-enhancing drug**.

norepinephrine (**NE**) *n.* a catecholamine NEUROTRANSMITTER and hormone produced mainly by brainstem nuclei and in the adrenal medulla (the central portion of the adrenal gland). Also called **noradrenaline**.

Norflex *n.* a trade name for ORPHENADRINE.

norm *n.* **1.** a standard or range of values that represents the typical performance of a group or of an individual (of a certain age, for example) against which comparisons can be made. **2.** a conversion of a raw score into a scaled score that is more easily interpretable, such as percentiles or IQ scores. **—normative** *adj.*

normal *adj.* relating to what is considered standard, average, typical, or healthy. This general meaning is applied in a variety of different contexts, including statistics (referring to scores that are within the usual or expected range), biology (referring to the absence of malformation or other pathology), and development (referring to progression and growth that is comparable to those of similar age). The term, however, is most often applied to behavior that conforms to a culturally accepted norm, especially as an indication that a person is mentally healthy and does not have a psychological disorder.

normal distribution a theoretical continuous PROBABILITY DISTRIBUTION that is a function of two parameters: the EXPECTED VALUE, μ, and the VARIANCE, σ^2. It is given by

$$P(x) = [\exp(-(x - \mu)^2/2\sigma^2)]/\sigma\sqrt{(2\pi)}$$

The normal distribution is the type of distribution expected when the same measurement is taken several times and the variation about the mean value is random. It has certain convenient properties in statistics, and unknown distributions are often assumed to be normal distributions. Also called **Gaussian distribution**.

normality *n.* a broad concept that is roughly the equivalent of MENTAL HEALTH. Although there are no absolutes and there is considerable cultural variation, some flexible psychological and behavioral criteria can be suggested: (a) freedom from incapacitating internal conflicts; (b) the capacity to think and act in an organized and reasonably effective manner; (c) the ability to cope with the ordinary demands and problems of life; (d) freedom from extreme emotional distress, such as anxiety, despondency, and persistent upset; and (e) the absence of clear-cut symptoms of mental disorder, such as obsessions, phobias, confusion, and disorientation.

normalization principle the concept that people with mental or physical disability should not be denied social and sexual relationships and participation in community life merely because of their disability. Social and sexual relationships can include a wide range of emotional and physical contacts, from simple friendship to sexual stimulation and satisfaction. Participation in community life includes engaging in typical life activities, such as work and recreation. See also SOCIAL ROLE VALORIZATION. [introduced in 1969 by Swedish psychologist Bengt Nirje]

normalize *vb.* to apply a TRANSFORMATION to a batch of data that produces a new set of scores that approximately follow the NORMAL DISTRIBUTION.

norm group a group whose performance serves as the basis for establishing NORMS.

norm-referenced testing an approach to testing based on a comparison of one person's performance with that of a NORM GROUP on the same test. Norm-referenced testing differentiates among individuals and ranks them on the basis of their performance. For example, a nationally standardized norm-referenced test will indicate how a given person performs compared to the performance of a national sample. See CRITERION-REFERENCED TESTING.

Norpramin *n.* a trade name for DESIPRAMINE.

Norrie's disease a type of congenital blindness that is transmitted as an X-linked genetic defect affecting only males. Progressive loss of hearing often accompanies the blindness. About two thirds of affected individuals show mental retardation, and some experience hallucinations or other psychological difficulties. [reported in 1927 by Gordon **Norrie** (1855–1941), Danish ophthalmologist]

nortriptyline *n.* a TRICYCLIC ANTIDEPRESSANT, a so-called secondary tricyclic, that is the principal metabolic product of AMITRIPTYLINE. Although its clinical efficacy is the same as other tricyclics, nortriptyline and the other secondary tricyclic agent, DESIPRAMINE, were often preferred because they were less sedating and had fewer ANTICHOLINERGIC EFFECTS. A THERAPEUTIC WINDOW is thought to exist for nortriptyline: Although plasma levels do not always correlate with clinical effectiveness, optimum responses are thought to occur when serum levels of the drug are between 50 and 150 ng/ml. Plasma levels over 500 ng/ml are toxic. The availability of newer antidepressants that do not require therapeutic monitoring has led to a decline in its use. U.S. trade names: **Aventyl**; **Pamelor**.

NOS abbreviation for NOT OTHERWISE SPECIFIED.

nosocomial *adj.* denoting or relating to a hospital-acquired infection that is unrelated to the patient's primary illness.

nosogenesis *n.* see PATHOGENESIS.

nosological approach a method or procedure that focuses on the naming and classifying of disorders together with the identification of PATHOGNOMONIC signs and symptoms and their grouping into syndromes for diagnostic purposes. The nosological approach contrasts with the PSYCHODYNAMIC APPROACH, which emphasizes causal factors.

nosology *n.* the scientific study and classification of diseases and disorders, both mental and physical. See also PSYCHIATRIC CLASSIFICATION. **—nosological** *adj.*

nosomania *n.* a rarely used term for an unfounded, abnormal belief that one is suffering from a particular disease. See HYPOCHONDRIASIS.

nostalgia *n.* **1.** a longing to return to an earlier period or condition of life recalled as being better than the present in some way. **2.** a longing to return to a place to which one feels emotionally bound (e.g., home or a native land). **—nostalgic** *adj.*

no-suicide contract a specific agreement, used when the potential for suicide is at issue, made between the client and the therapist that the client will not take his or her own life. It is often used as an intermediary measure for an agreed-upon period of time (e.g., until the next therapy session). See also CONTRACT.

not guilty by reason of insanity (**NGRI**) a final judgment made in a court of law if the defendant has been found to lack the mental capacity to be held criminally responsible for his or her actions. See CRIMINAL RESPONSIBILITY; INSANITY.

nothingness *n.* in EXISTENTIALISM, the belief that nothing is seen to structure existence. The nothingness or meaninglessness of human existence is thought to be the primary cause of anxiety or anguish.

not me in the SELF-SYSTEM theory of U.S. psychoanalyst Harry Stack Sullivan (1892–1949), the part of the personified self that is based on interpersonal experiences that have evoked overwhelming anxiety, dread, and horror, and which may lead to nightmares, emotional crises, and schizophrenic reactions. Compare BAD ME; GOOD ME.

not otherwise specified (**NOS**) in DSM–IV–TR, denoting a broad-based diagnostic category, for example, DEPRESSIVE DISORDER NOT OTHERWISE SPECIFIED. The NOS diagnosis is chosen when the patient's problems seem to fall into a particular family of disorders (e.g., depressive disorders, anxiety disorders), but the syndrome is not typical or there is not enough information available at the time of diagnosis to specify more accurately the type of disorder that is present.

novel antipsychotics see ATYPICAL ANTIPSYCHOTIC.

novelty fear see NEOPHOBIA.

novelty hypothesis the claim that the contents of CONSCIOUSNESS can be predicted by their novelty, based on the observation that novel or unexpected events frequently intrude in ongoing conscious functioning.

noxious stimulus an aversive stimulus that can serve as a negative reinforcer of behavior, in severe cases because it causes pain or damage to the experiencing organism and in lesser cases because it is unpleasant.

NREM sleep *n*on*r*apid-*e*ye-*m*ovement sleep: periods of sleep in which dreaming, as indicated by RAPID EYE MOVEMENTS (REM), usually does not occur. During these periods, which occur most frequently in the first hours of sleep, the electroencephalogram shows only minimal activity, and there is little or no change in pulse, respiration, and blood pressure. Also called **non-REM sleep**. Compare REM SLEEP.

n=1 research see SINGLE-CASE EXPERIMENTAL DESIGN.

NSAIDs *n*on*s*teroidal *a*nti-*i*nflammatory *d*rugs: a large class of analgesic and anti-inflammatory agents that includes ASPIRIN, ibuprofen, naproxen, and many others. They achieve their effects by blocking the synthesis of PROSTAGLANDINS involved in inflammation and the pain response. Concurrent administration of NSAIDs and LITHIUM may cause increased serum levels of lithium.

nubile *adj.* **1.** describing a girl or young woman who is of marriageable age, ready for marriage, or going through puberty. **2.** describing a sexually attractive young woman. **—nubility** *n.*

nuclear complex a central conflict or problem that is rooted in infancy, for example, feelings of inferiority (according to Alfred ADLER) or the OEDIPUS COMPLEX (according to Sigmund FREUD).

nuclear family a family unit consisting of two parents and their dependent children (whether biological or adopted). With various modifications, the nuclear family has been and remains the norm in developed Western societies. Compare EXTENDED FAMILY; PERMEABLE FAMILY.

nuclear imaging imaging that involves scanning for emissions from radioactive isotopes injected into the body. Techniques include POSITRON EMISSION TOMOGRAPHY (PET) and SINGLE PHOTON EMISSION COMPUTED TOMOGRAPHY (SPECT). These forms of scanning yield information not only about the anatomy of an organ but also about its functions; they are therefore valuable for medical diagnosis and research. See also BRAIN IMAGING.

nuclear schizophrenia a type of schizophrenia whose defining features, which include social inadequacy and withdrawal, blunted affect, and feelings of DEPERSONALIZATION and DEREALIZATION, are highly similar to those described by German psychiatrist Emil Kraepelin (1856–1926) for DEMENTIA PRAECOX. It is of early, insidious onset and is associated with a degenerative, irreversible course and poor prognosis. This term is often used interchangeably with PROCESS SCHIZOPHRENIA. Also called **authentic schizophrenia**; **true schizophrenia**; **typical schizophrenia**. Compare SCHIZOPHRENIFORM PSYCHOSIS. [proposed in the late 1930s by Norwegian psychiatrist Gabriel Langfeldt (1895–1983)]

null finding the result of an experiment indicating that there is no relationship, or no significant relationship, between variables. Also called **null result**.

null hypothesis (symbol: H_0) the statement that an experiment will find no difference be-

N

tween the experimental and control conditions, that is, no relationship between variables. Statistical tests are applied to experimental results in an attempt to disprove or reject the null hypothesis at a predetermined SIGNIFICANCE LEVEL. See also ALTERNATIVE HYPOTHESIS.

null hypothesis significance testing (**NHST**) computation of a test of significance to evaluate the tenability of the NULL HYPOTHESIS. See SIGNIFICANCE TESTING.

null result see NULL FINDING.

number-completion test an intelligence test, or a component of one, in which the subject is required to supply a missing item in a series of numbers or to continue the series. A component of such a test might be: 6, 9, 13, 18,—(the next number is 24).

numerical scale any scale or measurement instrument that yields a quantitative (numerical) representation of an attribute.

nurse practitioner a REGISTERED NURSE who has undergone extensive postgraduate training (often in a specialty area, such as internal medicine or pediatrics) and is licensed to perform some of the activities of a physician, including the prescription of medicine. Nurse practitioners generally function under the supervision of physicians, but not in their presence.

nurse's aide a person who works in a hospital or nursing home, has completed at least a brief course of health care training, and assists nursing staff in providing care for patients. Also called **nurse's assistant**.

nursing *n.* **1.** the health care profession that focuses on the protection and promotion of health through the alleviation and treatment of illness, injury, disease, and physical suffering. **Nurses** practice in a variety of contexts, including hospitals, nursing and independent-living homes, schools, workplaces, and community centers, among others. In the United States, nurses must graduate from a state-approved school of nursing (either a four-year university program, a two-year associate degree program, or a three-year diploma program) and pass a state licensing examination. **2.** the provision by a female of nourishment for her young offspring until they are capable of obtaining their own food. Nursing in mammals (including humans, in whom it typically is called **breast-feeding**) primarily involves the secretion of milk from the mammary glands, as stimulated by the hormones PROLACTIN and OXYTOCIN. Other vertebrates exhibit different forms of nursing behavior. For example, some birds produce a milklike substance within their digestive system called crop milk that is regurgitated to feed young chicks. The length of the nursing period varies across animals, ranging from mere days (e.g., Sprague–Dawley rats) to several years (e.g., bottlenose dolphins). Regardless of its form or duration, however, successful nursing is critical to survival and often depends upon maternally emitted odorants known as **mammary pheromones** that enable the young to locate the nipple and initiate suckling.

nursing home a LONG-TERM CARE FACILITY that provides 24-hour nursing care in addition to supportive services for people with chronic disability or illness, particularly older people who have mobility, eating, and other self-care problems.

nurturance *n.* **1.** the provision of affectionate attention, protection, and encouragement to others. **2.** the need or tendency to provide such nurturance.

nutmeg *n.* the seed of the trees *Myristica acuminata* and *M. fragrans*, which are indigenous to the Moluccas (Indonesia) and cultivated in South America, the Philippines, and the West Indies. It has a history of folk use as a remedy for stomach and gastrointestinal complaints. Nutmeg has volatile oils containing elemecin, myristicin, and other active ingredients that in sufficient doses produce intoxicating effects, some of which have been compared to those produced by CANNABIS. In larger doses, however, nutmeg is poisonous; signs of toxicity include abnormally dilated or contracted pupils, hallucinations, severe nausea and vomiting, and rapid heartbeat. See also MACE.

nutrient *n.* any substance required as part of the diet for growth, maintenance, and repair of the body's tissues or as a source of energy. Nutrients include carbohydrates, fats, proteins (see also AMINO ACID), VITAMINS, and some minerals (e.g., calcium, sodium, potassium).

nutritional disorder any medical or psychological condition that results from MALNUTRITION. Such disorders include obesity and vitamin deficiency disorders. See also EATING DISORDER.

nux vomica the seed of a plant, *Strychnos nux vomica*, that grows in tropical Asia and has been used as an emetic (the name means literally "a nut that causes vomiting"). Nux vomica contains two substances, STRYCHNINE and BRUCINE, which are CNS STIMULANTS and highly poisonous, causing powerful, painful convulsions and eventually death from paralysis of respiratory muscles. In low doses, nux vomica increases glandular secretion in the gastrointestinal tract and has been used as a homeopathic remedy to stimulate digestion and treat a variety of gastrointestinal conditions.

NVC abbreviation for NONVERBAL COMMUNICATION.

nyakwana *n.* see EPENA.

nyctophilia *n.* a strong preference for darkness or night. Also called **noctiphilia**; **noctophilia**; **scotophilia**.

nympholepsy *n.* **1.** a type of PEDOPHILIA in which the individual has a strong preference or obsessive desire for young girls who are sexually precocious (nymphets: a word coined by Vladimir Nabokov in his 1955 novel *Lolita*). Also called **Lolita complex**. **2.** a mania or frenzy, especially of an erotic nature, characterized by a desire for some unattainable ideal. The name is derived from myths in which an individual glimpses a nymph and becomes possessed by a demonic frenzy in pursuit of her.

nymphomania *n.* excessive or uncontrollable desire for sexual stimulation and gratification in a woman. The word is often used loosely to denote a high degree of sexuality in a woman, reflecting negative cultural attitudes toward female sexuality and male fears of being unable to meet the sexual needs of women. **—nymphomaniac** *n., adj.*

nystagmus *n.* involuntary, rapid movement of the eyeballs. The eyeball motion may be rotatory, horizontal, vertical, or a mixture. See also PHYSIOLOGICAL NYSTAGMUS; VESTIBULAR NYSTAGMUS.

N

Oo

OA abbreviation for OVEREATERS ANONYMOUS.

obesity *n.* the condition of having excess body fat resulting in overweight, variously defined in terms of absolute weight, weight–height ratio (see BODY MASS INDEX), distribution of subcutaneous fat, and societal and aesthetic norms. The basic causes are genetic, environmental, behavioral, or some interaction of these. Overeating may have a psychological cause (see BINGE-EATING DISORDER; FOOD ADDICTION; NIGHT-EATING SYNDROME) but in some cases it may be due to an organic disorder (see HYPERPHAGIA). The consequences of obesity are a matter for concern: It predisposes to heart disease, diabetes, and other serious medical conditions (see MORBID OBESITY), and obese individuals may develop emotional and psychological problems relating to BODY IMAGE. **—obese** *adj.*

obesity treatments therapeutic efforts used to produce substantial weight reduction in an individual. Treatments include long-term diets, crash diets, group support, HYPNOTHERAPY, exercise programs, nutritional education, drug therapy, BEHAVIOR MODIFICATION of eating patterns, hormonal treatment when indicated, and PSYCHODYNAMIC PSYCHOTHERAPY focused on insight into the unconscious purposes served by the individual's excessive food intake.

object *n.* **1.** the "other," that is, any person or symbolic representation of a person that is not the self and toward whom behavior, cognitions, or affects are directed. The term is sometimes used to refer to nonpersonal phenomena (e.g., an interest might be considered to be an "object") but the other-person connotation is far more typical and central. **2.** in psychoanalytic theory, the person, thing, or part of the body through which an INSTINCT can achieve its AIM of gratification. See OBJECT CATHEXIS; OBJECT RELATIONS. **3.** the person who is loved by an individual's EGO: his or her LOVE OBJECT.

object cathexis in psychoanalytic theory, the investment of LIBIDO or PSYCHIC ENERGY in objects outside the self, such as a person, goal, idea, or activity. Also called **object libido**. Compare EGO CATHEXIS. See CATHEXIS.

object choice in psychoanalytic theory, the selection of a person toward whom LIBIDO or PSYCHIC ENERGY is directed. See ANACLITIC OBJECT CHOICE; NARCISSISTIC OBJECT CHOICE.

object constancy in OBJECT RELATIONS THEORY, the ability of an infant to maintain an attachment that is relatively independent of gratification or frustration, based on a cognitive capacity to conceive of a mother who exists when she is out of sight and who has positive attributes when she is unsatisfying. Thus an infant becomes attached to the mother herself rather than to her tension-reducing ministrations; she comes to exist continuously for the infant and not only during instances of need satisfaction. This investment by an infant in a specific libidinal object indicates that he or she no longer finds people to be interchangeable.

object fetish sexual interest and arousal focused on a particular item. Common targets of such interest are feet, shoes, and undergarments, but almost anything can be the focus of an object fetish. See also RETIFISM.

objectification *n.* see REIFICATION.

objectifying attitude a tendency to react to an object, person, or event while disregarding personal feelings about it.

objective 1. *adj.* having actual existence in reality, based on observable phenomena. **2.** *adj.* impartial or uninfluenced by personal feelings, interpretations, or prejudices. Compare SUBJECTIVE. **3.** *n.* something that is to be obtained or worked toward. See AIM.

objective anxiety see REALISTIC ANXIETY.

objective indicator a marker or other measure of an entity, condition, emotion, or behavior that is free of subjective bias, that is, it is not an opinion or rating but an independent measure of the condition. An objective indicator is generally viewed as more reliable than a subjective assessment.

objective psychotherapy a treatment procedure developed primarily for use with institutionalized patients and patients with mild-to-moderate emotional disturbances. To reduce the subjectivity resulting from a personal relationship with the therapist, all therapeutic communication is carried out in writing. The patient answers written autobiographical questions, relates and comments on dreams, and reacts to assigned readings. In return, the therapist gives interpretations and points out underlying motivations in written memoranda, including a **memorandum as a whole**, which summarizes all the insights reached in the process. [developed by U.S. psychoanalyist Benjamin Karpman (1886–1962)]

objective self-awareness a reflective state of self-focused attention in which a person evaluates him- or herself and attempts to attain correctness and consistency in beliefs and behaviors. This involves the viewing of oneself as a separate object, acknowledging limitations and the existing disparity between the ideal self and the actual self. Objective self-awareness is often a necessary part of SELF-REGULATION.

objective sociogram see SOCIOGRAM.

object libido see OBJECT CATHEXIS.

object loss in psychoanalytic theory, the actual loss of a person who has served as a GOOD OBJECT, which precedes INTROJECTION and is involved in SEPARATION ANXIETY. Anxiety about the possible loss of a good object begins with the infant's panic when separated from its mother. In this perspective, adult GRIEF and MOURNING are related to object loss and separation anxiety in infancy and childhood, which often intensifies and complicates the grief reaction.

object love in psychoanalytic theory, love of a person other than the self. It is a function of the EGO and not the instincts as in OBJECT CATHEXIS. See LOVE OBJECT.

object of consciousness in conscious perception, the perceived object as distinct from the perceiver. In Buddhism and Hinduism, there is a related notion that the real self is "overshadowed" by the object of perception. The separation of observer and observed is criticized as artificial in phenomenological philosophies (see PHENOMENOLOGY). Compare SUBJECT OF CONSCIOUSNESS.

object of instinct in psychoanalytic theory, that which is sought (the **external aim**, e.g., a person, object, or behavior) in order to achieve satisfaction (the **internal aim**). See AIM OF THE INSTINCT.

O

object relations 1. an individual's relationship to his or her entire external world. **2.** in psychoanalysis, an individual's relationships to his or her OBJECTS (real and imagined), that is, the persons, activities, or things that function as sources of libidinal or aggressive gratification.

object relations theory any psychoanalytically based theory that views the need to relate to OBJECTS as more central to personality organization and motivation than the vicissitudes of the INSTINCTS. These theories developed from and in reaction to classic Freudian theories of psychodynamics. Some theories view the personality as organized in terms of a complex world of internal object representations and their relationships with each other, for example, FAIRBAIRNIAN THEORY and the approach of Melanie KLEIN.

obnubilation *n.* CLOUDING OF CONSCIOUSNESS or STUPOR.

obscenity *n.* verbal expressions, drawings, gestures, and written material that grossly violate the norms of good taste and decency in a given society. See PORNOGRAPHY. **—obscene** *adj.*

observational learning 1. the acquisition of information, skills, or behavior through watching the performance of others, either directly or via such media as films and videotapes. Also called **vicarious learning**. **2.** the conditioning of an animal to perform an act observed in a member of the same or a different species. For example, the mockingbird can learn to imitate the song patterns of other kinds of birds. Also called **vicarious conditioning**. See also MODELING THEORY.

observation commitment the confinement of a person in a hospital by a court order for a limited period of observation, usually to determine COMPETENCY TO STAND TRIAL or overall legal COMPETENCE.

observation delusion see DELUSION OF OBSERVATION.

observer's sociogram see SOCIOGRAM.

obsession *n.* a persistent thought, idea, image, or impulse that is experienced as intrusive and inappropriate and results in marked anxiety, distress, or discomfort. Obsessions are often described as EGO-DYSTONIC in that they are experienced as alien or inconsistent with one's self and outside one's control. Common obsessions include repeated thoughts about contamination, a need to have things in a particular order or sequence, repeated doubts, aggressive or horrific impulses, and sexual imagery. Obsessions can be distinguished from excessive worries about everyday occurrences in that they are not concerned with real-life problems. The response to an obsession is often an effort to ignore or suppress the thought or impulse or to neutralize it by a COMPULSION. See OBSESSIVE-COMPULSIVE DISORDER. **—obsessional** *adj.* **—obsessive** *adj.*

obsessional type see LIBIDINAL TYPES.

obsessive behavior behavior characteristic of obsessive-compulsive personality disorder or obsessive-compulsive disorder, such as persistent brooding, doubting, ruminating, worrying over trifles, cleaning up and keeping things in perfect order, or performing rituals.

obsessive-compulsive disorder (OCD) an ANXIETY DISORDER characterized by recurrent intrusive thoughts (OBSESSIONS) that prompt the performance of neutralizing rituals (COMPULSIONS). Typical obsessions involve themes of contamination, dirt, or illness (fearing that one will contract or transmit a disease) and doubts about the performance of certain actions (e.g., an excessive preoccupation that one has neglected to turn off a home appliance). Common compulsive behaviors include repetitive cleaning or washing, checking, ordering, repeating, and hoarding. The obsessions and compulsions—which are recognized by the individual as excessive or unreasonable—are time consuming (more than one hour per day), cause significant distress, or interfere with the individual's functioning.

obsessive-compulsive personality disorder in *DSM–IV–TR*, a personality disorder characterized by an extreme need for perfection, an excessive orderliness, an inability to compromise, and an exaggerated sense of responsibility.

Also called **compulsive personality disorder**.

obsessive personality an obsolete *DSM–I* personality trait disturbance characterized by excessive orderliness, perfectionism, indecisiveness, constant worry over trivia, and the imposition of rigid standards on others. See COMPULSIVE CHARACTER.

obtrusive idea an obsessive, unwanted, and alien idea that intrudes on a person's normal flow of thought. See also OBSESSION.

obtrusive measure any method of obtaining measurements or observations in which the participants are aware that a measurement is being made. Compare UNOBTRUSIVE MEASURE.

occasional inversion a form of same-gender sexual behavior that may occur when a person is deprived of the presence of individuals of the opposite sex, for example, in prison or in military service. See also SITUATIONAL HOMOSEXUALITY.

occipital lobe the most posterior (rearward) subdivision of each cerebral hemisphere, roughly shaped like a pyramid and lying under the skull's occipital bone. It is associated with vision, containing the several visual areas that receive and process information regarding visual stimuli, being involved in the basic functions (e.g., visual acuity, contrast sensitivity, and perception of color, form, and motion) as well as the higher level ones (e.g., figure-ground segregation based on textural cues).

occupational counseling an early 20th-century approach to vocational guidance. Three steps were identified in the process: (a) relevant knowledge of self, (b) realistic knowledge of occupations, and (c) true reasoning in making sensible choices. [proposed by U.S. educator Frank Parsons (1854–1908)]

occupational cramp painful spasm of the muscles, usually in the hand or arm, that prevents the individual from engaging in his or her occupation, such as writing, driving, sewing, playing a musical instrument, or firing a gun. See MUSICIAN'S CRAMP; WRITER'S CRAMP. See also REPETITIVE STRAIN INJURY.

occupational health psychology a specialty within psychology devoted to understanding workplace sources of health, illness, and injury and the application of this knowledge to improve the physical and mental well-being of employees.

occupational neurosis a PSYCHOGENIC inhibition associated with employment in which the individual experiences distress and increasing aversion to work, which may be expressed as poor work performance or reactive symptoms of illness (e.g., fatigue, vertigo) that increase in severity as the individual continues to work. In some cases, there is a specific inhibition that interferes with the ability to work, often affecting an essential function necessary for that work, such as WRITER'S CRAMP. These inhibitions were originally believed to be CONVERSION symptoms reflecting inner conflicts but have increasingly been found to have a medical explanation. Also called **occupational inhibition**.

occupational stress a state of physiological and psychological response to events or conditions in the workplace that is detrimental to health and well-being. It is influenced by such factors as autonomy and independence, decision latitude, workload, level of responsibility, job security, physical environment and safety, the nature and pace of work, and relationships with coworkers and supervisors.

occupational therapy (**OT**) a therapeutic, rehabilitative process that uses purposeful tasks and activities to improve health; prevent injury or disability; enhance quality of life; and develop, sustain, or restore the highest possible level of independence of individuals who have been injured or who have an illness, impairment, or other mental or physical disability or disorder. It typically includes assessment of an individual's FUNCTIONAL STATUS, the development and implementation of a customized treatment program, and recommendations for adaptive modifications in home and work environments as well as training in the use of appropriate ASSISTIVE TECHNOLOGY devices. The term **occupation** is used by practitioners of the therapy to denote three broad categories of human activity: (a) ACTIVITIES OF DAILY LIVING, (b) work and productive activities, and (c) play or leisure activities.

OCD abbreviation for OBSESSIVE-COMPULSIVE DISORDER.

oceanic feeling an expansion of consciousness beyond one's body (limitless extension) and a sense of unlimited power associated with identification with the universe as a whole (see COSMIC IDENTIFICATION). According to psychoanalytic theory, this feeling originates in the earliest period of life, before the infant is aware of the outside world or the distinction between the ego and nonego. Oceanic feelings may be revived later in life as a delusion or as part of a religious or spiritual experience.

oceanic state a condition of perceived boundlessness of the self, sometimes involving the perception of omnipotence. It may be an ecstatic state, a state of altered awareness, a state of interpersonal connection or union or of spiritual union, or a dissociative experience. See also ALTERED STATE OF CONSCIOUSNESS.

O'Connor v. Donaldson a 1975 lawsuit in the U.S. Supreme Court in which it was determined that people cannot be involuntarily committed to a facility on the basis of mental illness alone if they are not dangerous to themselves or others and are able to survive safely outside the facility. A lower court ruling in this case assisted the court in its final ruling in *Wyatt v. Stickney* (1972) regarding right to treatment with involuntary commitment (see FORCED TREATMENT; WYATT V. STICKNEY DECISION).

ocular hypertelorism see HYPERTELORISM.

oculocerebral-hypopigmentation syndrome a hereditary disorder marked by eye anomalies, absence of hair and skin pigmentation, mental retardation, and spasticity. The cases studied have involved children of Old Order Amish families. The syndrome is believed to be due to an autosomal recessive trait that becomes manifested through consanguinity (relationship by blood).

oculocerebrorenal syndrome an X-linked recessive genetic disorder affecting male children and marked by renal-tubule dysfunction, mental retardation, and eye disorders, including congenital glaucoma, cataracts, and distension of the eyeball because of fluid accumulation. The renal disorders include acidosis, hypophosphatemia, and excess amino acids in the urine. Neurological deficits vary from absence of brain abnormalities to hydrocephalus and cerebral atrophy. Also called **Lowe's disease**; **Lowe's syndrome**; **oculocerebrorenal syndrome of Lowe**.

oculogyric crisis prolonged fixation of the eyeballs in a single position for minutes to hours. It may result from encephalitis or be produced by certain antipsychotic drugs. Also called **oculogyric spasm**.

OD 1. *n.* a colloquial name (an abbreviation) for an OVERDOSE, most often of an opioid or a sedative. **2.** *vb.* to take an overdose.

O data *o*ther data: information about an individual gathered from the observations, judgments, and evaluations of third parties who know him or her personally, such as family and friends. See also L DATA; Q DATA; T DATA.

odd–even reliability a method of assessing the reliability of a test by correlating scores on the odd-numbered items with scores on the even-numbered items. It is a special case of SPLIT-HALF RELIABILITY.

odds *n.* the ratio of the probability of an event occurring to the probability of the event not occurring, usually expressed as the ratio of integers (e.g., 3:2).

odds ratio the ratio of two ODDS. For example, in a study on a drug, the odds ratio is calculated as the odds of an effect in a treated group divided by the odds of the same effect in a control group.

oedipal conflict see OEDIPUS COMPLEX.

oedipal phase in psychoanalytic theory, the later portion of the PHALLIC STAGE of psychosexual development, usually between ages 3 and 5, during which the OEDIPUS COMPLEX manifests itself. Also called **oedipal stage**.

Oedipus complex in psychoanalytic theory, the erotic feelings of the son toward the mother, accompanied by rivalry and hostility toward the father, during the PHALLIC STAGE of development. The corresponding relationship between the daughter and father is referred to as the **female Oedipus complex**. The complete Oedipus complex includes both this heterosexual form, called the **positive Oedipus complex**, and its homosexual counterpart, the NEGATIVE OEDIPUS COMPLEX. Sigmund FREUD derived the name from the Greek myth in which Oedipus unknowingly killed his father and married his mother. Although Freud held the complex to be universal, most anthropologists question this universality because there are many cultures in which it does not appear. Freud saw the Oedipus complex as the basis for NEUROSIS when it is not adequately resolved by the boy's fear of castration and gradual IDENTIFICATION with the father. The female Oedipus complex is posited to be resolved by the threat of losing the mother's love and by finding fulfillment in the feminine role. Contemporary psychoanalytic thought has decentralized the importance of the Oedipus complex and has largely modified the classical theory by emphasizing the earlier, primal relationship between child and mother. Also called **oedipal conflict**; **oedipal situation**. See also CASTRATION COMPLEX; NUCLEAR COMPLEX.

off-label *adj.* denoting or relating to the clinical use of a drug for a purpose that has not been approved by the U.S. Food and Drug Administration. Manufacturers generally do not promote drugs for off-label uses, although medical literature may support such uses.

'ohana *n.* the family unit in the Hawaiian culture, characterized by a value system that emphasizes multigenerational kinship, including the prescription of age-appropriate roles, connection to one's ancestors, respect for the wisdom of elders, promotion of the welfare of children, and the overall sustenance of the family system. Similar ways of conceptualizing family are found in other Polynesian cultures.

6-OHDA abbreviation for 6-HYDROXYDOPAMINE.

oikofugic *adj.* having or relating to an urge to travel or wander from home. See DROMOMANIA; NOMADISM.

oikomania *n.* see ECOMANIA.

oikotropic *adj.* affected with homesickness or nostalgia for home.

olan *n.* see MYRIACHIT.

olanzapine *n.* an ATYPICAL ANTIPSYCHOTIC used for the treatment of acute mania, schizophrenia, and other psychotic disorders in adults. It is closely related to CLOZAPINE, but lacks the latter drug's association with agranulocytosis. Common side effects are sedation, lethargy, weight gain, and ORTHOSTATIC HYPOTENSION. Rarely, like all antipsychotics, it may be associated with TARDIVE DYSKINESIA or NEUROLEPTIC MALIGNANT SYNDROME. U.S. trade names: **Zydis**; **Zyprexa**.

Older Adult Resources and Services a questionnaire used as a community assessment tool to determine the level of functioning of older adults in five areas: mental health, physical health, social resources, economic resources, and ACTIVITIES OF DAILY LIVING. It must be administered by a trained individual and can be administered in separate segments if assessment of only one area is desired. The responses to the questionnaire can be used to determine choices of supportive services for the geriatric population.

olfactophilia *n.* sexual interest in and arousal by body odors, especially those from the genital areas.

olfactory eroticism pleasurable sensations, particularly of an erotic nature, associated with the sense of smell.

olfactory hallucination a false perception of odors, which are usually unpleasant or repulsive, such as poison gas or decaying flesh.

oligocephaly *n.* see OLIGOENCEPHALY.

oligoencephaly *n.* a form of mental retardation associated with asymmetrical physical development and often marked by an abnormally small brain, nervous-system irregularities, and low resistance to disease. Also called **oligocephaly**.

olisbos *n.* see DILDO.

olivopontocerebellar atrophy a slowly progressive neurological disorder characterized by degeneration of neurons in the pons, cerebellum, and olivary nucleus, an olive-shaped mass of gray matter in the medulla oblongata. Symptoms are highly variable across individuals but typically include ATAXIA, difficulties with balance and walking, tremors, and DYSARTHRIA. In many cases onset is in middle adulthood and death occurs within 10–20 years.

ololiuqui *n.* the seed of a Latin American vine, *Rivea corymbosa*, which contains substances chemically related to LSD but less potent. Ololiuqui was first described in the reports of the 16th-century Spanish physician Francisco Hernández while studying the indigenous peoples of Mexico, who used it for both medicinal and religious purposes.

ombudsman *n.* a person or program responsible for investigating consumer complaints and grievances and acting as a consumer advocate in resolving problems, for example in a health-care facility.

omission training see DIFFERENTIAL REINFORCEMENT OF OTHER BEHAVIOR.

omnipotence *n.* in psychology, the delusion that one can personally direct, or control, reality outside of the self by thought or wish alone. In psychoanalytic theory, the main emphasis is on the infant's feeling that he or she is all-powerful, which is thought to arise (a) out of the fact that the child's slightest gesture leads to satisfaction of the need for food; (b) out of increasing abilities; and (c) as a REACTION FORMATION to feelings of helplessness and anxiety. Psychology generally considers feelings of omnipotence to fall anywhere between neurosis, in its milder forms, and psychosis, when the delusion is expressed as alienation from or outright denial of reality. See also MEGALOMANIA. —**omnipotent** *adj.*

omnipotent therapist see PRESTIGE SUGGESTION.

onanism *n.* COITUS INTERRUPTUS or MASTURBATION. Onanism is named for the biblical character Onan, who "went to his brother's wife and spilled it [his seed] on the ground" (Genesis 38:9).

ondansetron *n.* a SEROTONIN ANTAGONIST at the 5-HT_3 SEROTONIN RECEPTOR that is used for the prevention and treatment of nausea resulting from chemotherapy or anesthesia. Recent studies have also demonstrated that, when combined with appropriate behavior therapy, it may be an effective adjunctive agent in managing certain types of alcoholism, although it is not officially approved by the U.S. Food and Drug Administration for such treatment. U.S. trade name: **Zofran**.

oneirism *n.* a dreamlike state in a condition of wakefulness. —**oneiric** *adj.*

oneirodynia *n.* a form of dreaming characterized by NIGHTMARES or unpleasant dreams.

oneirophrenia *n.* a dreamlike, hallucinatory state resembling schizophrenia in certain symptoms, such as disturbances of emotion and associations, but distinguished from schizophrenia by disturbances of the senses and clouding of consciousness. It is associated with prolonged sleep deprivation, sensory deprivation, or drug use, but currently is not widely considered a distinct clinical entity. [first described in the 1950s by Hungarian-born U.S. psychiatrist Ladislas von Meduna (1896–1964)]

one-tailed test a statistical test of an experimental hypothesis in which the expected direction of an effect or relationship is specified. Also called **directional test**. Compare TWO-TAILED TEST.

one-way analysis of variance a statistical test of the probability that the means of three or more samples have been drawn from the same population; that is, an ANALYSIS OF VARIANCE with a single independent variable.

oniomania *n.* compulsive shopping, or an uncontrollable impulse to spend money and to buy without regard to need or use.

online self-help group a self-help group composed of individuals who communicate via personal computer over the Internet on a regular basis to help one another cope with a shared life problem. Online groups overcome some of the traditional barriers to self-help participation, including lack of local group availability, rarity of problem, and time or transportation constraints.

online therapy see E-THERAPY.

onset insomnia see SLEEP-ONSET INSOMNIA.

onset of action the point at which the activity of a drug is apparent, generally measured in terms of the time elapsed between administration and the appearance of its pharmacological effects.

ontoanalysis *n.* a form of EXISTENTIAL ANALYSIS that probes the ultimate nature of being.

ontogeny *n.* the biological origin and development of an individual organism from fertilization of the egg cell until death. Also called **ontogenesis**. Compare PHYLOGENY. **—ontogenetic** *adj.*

ontogeny of conscious experience the developmental origins of conscious sensory experience in an organism. In humans, conscious experience can be demonstrated from the 5th or 6th month of gestation.

OPD syndrome *o*to*p*alato*d*igital syndrome: a congenital disorder affecting males or females, believed to be X-linked, and marked by short stature, MILD MENTAL RETARDATION, bone anomalies, and a variety of other possible defects, including hearing impairment, cleft palate, and abnormalities of the digits.

open-door hospital see OPEN HOSPITAL.

open-door policy the policy of maintaining an OPEN HOSPITAL or OPEN WARD (without locked doors or physical restraints). Such a policy is associated with the concept of a THERAPEUTIC COMMUNITY.

open-ended question a question that respondents answer in their own words (e.g., an essay question). Compare CLOSED-ENDED QUESTION.

open group a psychotherapy or counseling group to which new members may be admitted during the course of therapy. Also called **continuous group**. Compare CLOSED GROUP.

open head injury a HEAD INJURY, such as a gunshot wound, in which the skull is penetrated or broken open. Compare CLOSED HEAD INJURY.

open hospital a psychiatric hospital without locked doors or physical restraints. Also called **open-door hospital**.

opening moves see OPENING TECHNIQUE.

opening technique the means by which a therapist establishes initial rapport and trust at the beginning of a professional relationship with a client in therapy or at the beginning of each session in individual or family therapy. Also called **opening moves**.

open marriage 1. a MARRIAGE in which both partners allow and encourage each other to grow and change over the years. Compare CLOSED MARRIAGE. **2.** a marital arrangement (formal or common-law) in which the partners permit each other to have sexual relations with other people. See also NONTRADITIONAL MARRIAGE.

openmindedness *n.* a personality trait reflecting a relative lack of DOGMATISM. **—openminded** *adj.*

openness to experience a dimension of the BIG FIVE PERSONALITY MODEL and the FIVE-FACTOR PERSONALITY MODEL that refers to individual differences in the tendency to be open to new aesthetic, cultural, or intellectual experiences.

open ward a hospital ward or unit in which the doors are not locked.

operant behavior behavior that produces an effect on the environment and whose likelihood of recurrence is influenced by consequences. Operant behavior is nearly synonymous with VOLUNTARY BEHAVIOR.

operant conditioning the process in which behavioral change (i.e., learning) occurs as a function of the consequences of behavior. Examples are teaching a dog to do tricks and rewarding behavioral change in a misbehaving child (see BEHAVIOR THERAPY). The term is essentially equivalent to INSTRUMENTAL CONDITIONING. Also called **operant learning**. See BEHAVIOR MODIFICATION; SHAPING. [first described by B. F. SKINNER]

operant conditioning therapy a therapeutic approach that relies on the use of antecedents, behaviors, and consequences. For example, REINFORCEMENT through rewards may be used to improve behaviors in everyday situations.

operationalism *n.* the position that the meaning of a scientific concept depends upon the procedures used to establish it, so that each concept can be defined by a single observable and measurable operation. An example is defining an emotional disorder as a particular score on a diagnostic test. This approach was mainly associated with radical BEHAVIORISM. Also called **operationism**.

ophidiophilia *n.* an abnormal fascination with snakes.

opiate *n.* any of a variety of natural and semisynthetic compounds derived from OPIUM. They include the alkaloids MORPHINE and CODEINE and their derivatives (e.g., HEROIN [diacetylmorphine]). Opiates, together with synthetic compounds having the pharmacological properties of opiates, are known as OPIOIDS.

opioid *n.* any of a group of compounds that include the naturally occurring OPIATES (e.g., morphine, codeine) and their semisynthetic derivatives (e.g., heroin); synthetic compounds with morphinelike effects (OPIOID AGONISTS, e.g., meperidine, methadone); OPIOID ANTAGONISTS (e.g., naloxone, naltrexone) and mixed agonist–antagonists (e.g., BUPRENORPHINE); and ENDOGENOUS OPIOIDS. The effects of opioids include analgesia, drowsiness, euphoria or other mood changes, RESPIRATORY DEPRESSION, and reduced gastrointestinal motility. Many natural opioids are subject to abuse and dependence (see OPIOID ABUSE; OPIOID DEPENDENCE; OPIOID INTOXICATION; OPIOID WITHDRAWAL). Opioids are used clinically as pain relievers (see OPIOID ANALGESIC), anesthetics (e.g., FENTANYL), cough suppressants (e.g., DEXTROMETHORPHAN), and antidiarrheal drugs (e.g., LOPERAMIDE). Opioid agonists are used for (among other things) the management of opioid addiction.

opioid abuse in *DSM–IV–TR*, a pattern of opioid use manifested by recurrent significant adverse consequences related to the repeated ingestion of an opioid. This diagnosis is preempted by the diagnosis of OPIOID DEPENDENCE: If the criteria for opioid abuse and opioid dependence are both met, only the latter diagnosis is given. See also SUBSTANCE ABUSE; SUBSTANCE DEPENDENCE.

opioid agonist any drug with enhancing effects at OPIOID RECEPTORS in the central nervous system. Opioid agonists may be complete (pure) or partial agonists. MORPHINE is a pure opioid agonist; other examples include CODEINE, HEROIN, METHADONE, MEPERIDINE, and LAAM. Partial opioid agonists (e.g., BUPRENORPHINE, tramadol) have lower levels of activity than complete opioid agonists at the same receptors and consequently have less analgesic activity. Also called **narcotic agonist**.

opioid analgesic any OPIOID used clinically to reduce both the sensation of pain and the emotional response to pain. This analgesia results from agonist activity at the mu OPIOID RECEPTOR. CODEINE, **dihydrocodeine**, PROPOXYPHENE, and HYDROCODONE are among opioids used for the relief of mild to moderate pain; severe pain is managed with more potent agents, such as MORPHINE, MEPERIDINE, **oxycodone** (U.S. trade name: OxyContin), and LEVORPHANOL. METHADONE, FENTANYL, and BUPRENORPHINE are potent analgesics that have additional uses. Side effects associated with opioid analgesics include nausea and vomiting, constipation, sedation, and respiratory depression; many also have the potential for abuse and physical dependence. Also called **narcotic analgesic**. See also OPIOID ANTAGONIST.

opioid analgesic addiction psychological and physical dependence on an opioid drug, such as morphine, that is administered to relieve pain. A sign is the need to increase the dosage in order to obtain the same degree of relief. See OPIOID DEPENDENCE; OPIOID WITHDRAWAL.

opioid antagonist an agent that acts as an antagonist at OPIOID RECEPTORS. Generally, opioid antagonists are synthetic derivatives of morphine that, as a result of structural changes in the molecule, bind to opioid receptors but do not produce the effects of euphoria, respiratory depression, or analgesia that are observed with opioid agonists. Opioid antagonists may be complete (pure) or mixed. Complete antagonists, such as NALOXONE, NALTREXONE, **nalmefene** (U.S. trade name: Revex), and **nalorphine**, are generally used to reverse the effects of opiate overdose (notably respiratory depression). Mixed AGONIST–ANTAGONIST opioids, such as BUTORPHANOL and **pentazocine** (U.S. trade name: Talwin), were developed in attempts to produce opioid analgesics that did not possess the abuse potential of opioid agonists. Also called **narcotic antagonist**.

opioid blockade the inhibition of the euphoric effects of such opioids as heroin by administration of a blocking agent, especially METHADONE, as maintenance treatment for drug abuse. See METHADONE MAINTENANCE THERAPY; OPIOID ANTAGONIST.

opioid dependence in *DSM–IV–TR*, a cluster of cognitive, behavioral, and physiological symptoms indicating continued use of opioids despite significant opioid-related problems. There is a pattern of repeated opioid ingestion resulting in tolerance, characteristic withdrawal symptoms if use is suspended (see OPIOID WITHDRAWAL), and an uncontrollable drive to continue use. Also called **narcotic addiction; narcotic dependence**. See also OPIOID ABUSE.

opioid intoxication a reversible syndrome due to the recent ingestion of an opioid. It includes clinically significant behavioral or psychological changes (e.g., initial euphoria followed by apathy, DYSPHORIA, PSYCHOMOTOR AGITATION or PSYCHOMOTOR RETARDATION, impaired judgment, and impaired social or occupational functioning), as well as one or more signs of physiological involvement (e.g., pupillary constriction, drowsiness or unconsciousness, slurred speech, RESPIRATORY DEPRESSION).

opioid neurotransmitter see ENDOGENOUS OPIOID.

opioid receptor a RECEPTOR that binds OPIOIDS (including ENDOGENOUS OPIOIDS) and mediates their effects via G PROTEINS. It is generally agreed that there are at least three classes: delta (δ), kappa (κ), and mu (μ) receptors. Opioid receptors are widely distributed in the brain, spinal cord, and periphery and each type of receptor is differentially distributed. **Mu receptors** are largely responsible for the analgesic and euphoric effects associated with opioid use. Most exogenously administered opioids bind to mu receptors, which also mediate the respiratory depression, sedation, and reduced gastrointestinal motility associated with opioids. **Kappa receptors** are localized primarily in the dorsal root ganglia of the spinal cord. Stimulation of these receptors produces more modest analgesia and dysphoric responses and may also be responsible for some of the perceptual and cognitive effects of opioids. **Delta receptors** may potentiate activity of opioids at the mu receptor site and have a less direct involvement in the production of analgesia. The more recently discovered **N/OFQ receptor** has not been completely characterized.

opioid withdrawal a characteristic withdrawal syndrome that develops after cessation of (or reduction in) prolonged, heavy opioid consumption. Features may include DYSPHORIA or anxiety, nausea or vomiting, muscle aches, dilation of the pupils, piloerection (goose flesh) or sweating, diarrhea, fever, and insomnia. See also SUBSTANCE WITHDRAWAL.

Opitz–Frias syndrome see TELECANTHUS-HYPOSPADIAS SYNDROME. [reported in 1969 by John M. **Opitz** (1935–) and Jaime L. **Frias**, U.S. geneticists]

opium *n.* the dried resin of the unripe seed pods of the opium poppy, *Papaver somniferum*. Opium contains more than 20 alkaloids (see OPIUM ALKALOIDS), the principal one being MORPHINE, which accounts for most of its pharmacological (including addictive) properties. Natural and synthetic derivatives (see OPIATE; OPIOID) are eaten, smoked, injected, sniffed, and drunk. Their action, due mainly to their morphine content, is to induce analgesia and euphoria and produce a deep, dreamless sleep from which the user can be easily aroused.

opium alkaloids alkaloids derived from opium, of which there are more than 20. The principal alkaloid is MORPHINE; others include codeine, THEBAINE, and PAPAVERINE. See also OPIATE.

opponent process theory of acquired motivation a theory that a stimulus or event simultaneously arouses a primary affective state, which may be pleasurable or aversive, and an opponent (opposite) affective state, which serves to reduce the intensity of the primary state: These two states together constitute emotional experience. According to this theory, the opponent state has a long latency, a sluggish course of increase, and a sluggish course of decay after the initiating stimulus is removed, all of which lead to its domination for a period following removal of the stimulus. In contrast to the primary state, it is also strengthened through use and weakened through disuse. This theory sought to account for such diverse acquired motives as drug addiction, love, affection and social attachment, and cravings for sensory and aesthetic experiences. Also called **opponent process theory of emotion; opponent process theory of motivation**. [originated by U.S. psychologist Richard Lester Solomon (1918–1995)]

opportunistic sampling the selection of participants or other sampling units for an experiment or survey simply because they are readily available.

opposites test see ANTONYM TEST.

oppositional defiant disorder in *DSM–IV–TR*, a behavior disorder of childhood characterized by recurrent disobedient, negativistic, or hostile behavior toward authority figures that is more pronounced than usually seen in children of similar age and lasts for at least 6 months. It is manifest as temper tantrums, active defiance of rules, dawdling, argumentativeness, stubbornness, or being easily annoyed. The defiant behaviors typically do not involve aggression, destruction, theft, or deceit, which distinguishes this disorder from CONDUCT DISORDER. Oppositional defiant disorder should be distinguished from ATTENTION-DEFICIT/HYPERACTIVITY DISORDER, with which it often co-occurs.

optimal adjustment the ideal degree and quality of coping with life or with a specific stressful event.

optimal functioning the highest possible level of functioning, especially in the areas of meaningful relationships, work life, education, and subjective well-being.

optimism *n.* hopefulness: the attitude that good things will happen and that people's wishes or aims will ultimately be fulfilled. **Optimists** are people who anticipate positive outcomes, whether serendipitously or through perseverance and effort, and who are confident of attaining desired goals (compare PESSIMISM). Most individuals lie somewhere on the spectrum between the two polar opposites of pure optimism and pure pessimism but tend to demonstrate sometimes strong, relatively stable or situational tendencies in one direction or the other. **—optimistic** *adj.*

oral administration see ADMINISTRATION.

oral-aggressive personality in psychoanalytic theory, a personality type resulting from fixation at the ORAL-BITING PHASE of the ORAL STAGE and marked by aggressiveness, envy, and exploitation. Compare ORAL-RECEPTIVE PERSONALITY. See ORAL PERSONALITY.

oral behavior activities involving the mouth, such as thumb sucking, smoking, eating, kissing, nail biting, talking, and oral sex.

oral-biting phase in psychoanalytic theory, the second phase of the ORAL STAGE of PSYCHOSEXUAL DEVELOPMENT, from about the 8th to the 18th month of life. During this phase the child begins to feel that he or she is an independent person, develops ambivalent attitudes toward the mother, and expresses hostility by biting her breast or the nipple of the bottle. In later life the urge to bite may take the form of nail-biting, spitting, sticking out the tongue, or chewing on a pencil or gum. Also called **oral-sadistic phase**. Compare ORAL-SUCKING PHASE. See ORAL-AGGRESSIVE PERSONALITY; ORAL SADISM. [identified by German psychoanalyst Karl Abraham (1877–1925)]

oral character see ORAL PERSONALITY.

oral coitus see FELLATIO.

oral contraceptives tablets ("pills") taken regularly by women to prevent pregnancy. Most are combined formulations of a synthetic estrogen and a progestin; some are progestin-only formulations. The synthetic hormones in these pills alter the normal menstrual activities so that ovulation and related functions are prevented. Introduced in 1960, this type of contraceptive became known popularly as simply "the Pill."

oral eroticism in psychoanalytic theory, the pleasure derived from oral activities such as smoking, chewing, biting, talking, kissing, and oral-genital contact. Also called **oral erotism**; **oral gratification**. See also ORALITY; ORAL-SUCKING PHASE.

oral-eroticism phase see ORAL-SUCKING PHASE.

Oralet *n.* a trade name for FENTANYL.

oral–genital contact see OROGENITAL ACTIVITY.

oral gratification see ORAL EROTICISM.

orality *n.* in psychoanalytic theory, the oral factor in EROTICISM or neurosis, ranging from pleasure in biting, sucking, smoking, or oral sex to such habits as speech-making, overeating, alcoholism, and excessive generosity. See ORAL PERSONALITY.

oral–lingual dyskinesia see BUCCOLINGUAL MASTICATORY SYNDROME.

oral-passive type see ORAL-RECEPTIVE PERSONALITY.

oral personality in psychoanalytic theory, a pattern of personality traits derived from fixation at the ORAL STAGE of PSYCHOSEXUAL DEVELOPMENT. If the individual has experienced sufficient sucking satisfaction and adequate attention from the mother during the oral-sucking phase, he or she is posited to develop an oral-receptive personality marked by friendliness, OPTIMISM, generosity, and dependence on others. If the individual does not get enough satisfaction during the sucking and biting phases, he or she is posited to develop an ORAL-AGGRESSIVE PERSONALITY marked by tendencies to be hostile, critical, envious, exploitative, and overcompetitive. Also called **oral character**.

oral phase see ORAL STAGE.

oral-receptive personality in psychoanalytic theory, a personality pattern characterized by dependence, OPTIMISM, and expectation of nourishment and care from external sources (just as the mother provided these satisfactions in infancy), which is believed to be caused by fixation at the oral-sucking phase. Also called **oral-passive type**. Compare ORAL-AGGRESSIVE PERSONALITY. See also ORAL PERSONALITY; RECEPTIVE CHARACTER.

oral sadism in psychoanalytic theory, the primitive urge to use the mouth, lips, and teeth as instruments of aggression, mastery, or sadistic sexual gratification. This impulse is believed to originate in the ORAL-BITING PHASE of infancy. See also ORAL-AGGRESSIVE PERSONALITY.

oral-sadistic phase see ORAL-BITING PHASE.

oral sex stimulation of the external genitals by the partner's mouth (see OROGENITAL ACTIVITY). Oral sex may be carried to the point of orgasm or done as part of FOREPLAY. Research has shown that some adolescents who wish to remain virgins will have oral sex to orgasm, as this is not considered to constitute a loss of virginity.

oral stage in psychoanalytic theory, the first stage of PSYCHOSEXUAL DEVELOPMENT, occupying the first year of life, in which the LIBIDO is concentrated on the mouth, which is the principal erotic zone. The stage is divided into the early ORAL-SUCKING PHASE, during which gratification is achieved by sucking the nipple during feeding, and the later ORAL-BITING PHASE, when gratification is also achieved by biting. FIXATION during the oral stage is posited to cause an oral personality. Also called **oral phase**. See also ORAL-AGGRESSIVE PERSONALITY; ORAL EROTICISM.

oral-sucking phase in psychoanalytic theory, the earliest part of the ORAL STAGE of PSYCHOSEXUAL DEVELOPMENT, in which the infant is posited to feel that he or she is ingesting the mother's being along with the milk swallowed (see INCORPORATION). This phase is believed to lay the foundation for feelings of closeness and dependence, as well as for possessiveness, greed, and voraciousness. Also called **oral-eroticism phase**. Compare ORAL-BITING PHASE. See ORAL-RECEPTIVE PERSONALITY. [identified by German psychoanalyst Karl Abraham (1877–1925)]

Orap *n.* a trade name for PIMOZIDE.

orchidectomy *n.* the surgical removal of a testis. An orchidectomy may be performed when a testis is injured or diseased, as when the male reproductive system has been affected by cancer. It does not necessarily cause impotence but may reduce the desire for coitus. Orchidectomy performed before puberty can affect the development of secondary male sex characteristics. Also called **orchiectomy**. See also CASTRATION.

order effect in WITHIN-SUBJECTS DESIGNS, the effect of the order in which treatments are administered, that is, the effect of being the first administered treatment (rather than the second, third, and so forth). This is often confused with the SEQUENCE EFFECT.

orderliness *n.* the tendency to be neat and tidy and to keep everything in place. Excessive orderliness may be a symptom of OBSESSIVE-COMPULSIVE DISORDER or OBSESSIVE-COMPULSIVE PERSONALITY DISORDER.

order of magnitude the approximate magnitude of a number or value within a range, usually to the nearest power of 10. For example, 2,500 (2.5×10^3) and 4,300 (4.3×10^3) are of the same order of magnitude, but both are one order of magnitude greater than 240 (2.4×10^2).

ordinal data numerical values that represent rankings along a continuum of lowest and highest, as in a judge's assignment of a 1 to denote that a particular athlete's performance was fair and a 2 to denote that a subsequent athlete's performance was better. Ordinal data may be counted (i.e., how many athletes obtained a 1, how many a 2, etc.) and arranged in descending or ascending sequence but may not be manipulated; it is meaningless to add, subtract, divide, or multiply any rank by any other because the actual differential in performance between adjacent values is unspecified and may vary. In other words, one does not know how much better a 2 is than a 1, and the difference between a 1 and a 2 may not be the same as the difference between a 2 and a 3.

ordinal position a place or rank, such as a child's position or birth order in a family, indicated by an ordinal number (e.g., first, second, etc.).

ordinal scale a sequence of numbers that do not indicate magnitude or a true zero point but rather reflect a rank ordering of the attribute being measured. For example, an ordinal scale for the performance of a specific group of people on a particular test might use the number 1 to indicate the person who obtained the highest score, the number 2 to indicate the person who obtained the next highest score, and so on. It is important to note, however, that an ordinal scale does not provide any information about the degree of difference between adjacent ranks (e.g., it is not clear what the actual point difference is between the rank 1 and 2 scores).

Orestes complex in classical Freudian psychoanalysis, a son's repressed impulse to kill his mother. The name is derived from the ancient Greek story of Orestes, who killed his mother, Clytemnestra, and her lover, Agamemnon.

orexis *n.* the affective, appetitive character of an activity or behavior, as opposed to the cognitive aspects. Also called **orexia**. **—orectic** *adj.*

organ eroticism sexual arousal or sexual attachment associated with a particular organ of the body.

organic *adj.* denoting a condition or disorder that results from structural alterations of an organ or tissue. In psychology and psychiatry, the term is equivalent to somatic or physical, as contrasted with FUNCTIONAL or PSYCHOGENIC.

organic-affective syndrome in *DSM–III–R*, any disturbance of mood with symptoms that meet the criteria for a mood disorder but that result from a specific identifiable organic disorder. This diagnostic category was removed from *DSM–IV–TR*. Also called **organic mood syndrome**.

organic amnesia see AMNESTIC DISORDER.

organic approach the theory that all mental disorders have a physiological basis, resulting from structural brain changes or alterations in other bodily organs. Also called **organicism**.

organic brain syndromes in *DSM–III*, a group of disorders, including delirium, dementia, AMNESTIC DISORDER, ORGANIC DELUSIONAL SYNDROME, and ORGANIC PERSONALITY SYNDROME, each characterized by a pattern of psychological and behavioral symptoms (e.g., memory loss, impaired intellectual functioning, disorientation, poor judgment) associated with transient or permanent brain dysfunction, but without reference to cause. This diagnostic category was removed from *DSM–IV–TR*. Also called **organic mental syndromes**. See also ORGANIC MENTAL DISORDERS.

organic defect a congenital disorder that is not the result of a genetic anomaly. For example, a mental or physical disability in an individual can result from maternal disorders or other conditions in pregnancy, including preeclampsia, viral infections (e.g., rubella), sexually transmitted infections, protozoan infections (e.g., toxoplasmosis), dietary deficiencies, or drug abuse (e.g., alcoholism).

organic delusional syndrome in *DSM–III*, a condition characterized by the occurrence of prominent delusions, usually persecutory in nature, that are produced most often by such substances as amphetamines, cannabis (marijuana), and hallucinogens but may also be associated with brain damage or dysfunction. This diagnostic category was removed from *DSM–IV–TR*.

organic dementia in *DSM–III*, DEMENTIA due to any condition that causes injury to the brain.

organic hallucinations hallucinations associated with a specific brain-based factor. Stimulation or irritation of part of the brain or a sensory pathway may be a factor, and precipitating causes include aneurysm, tumor, epilepsy, drug use (including some prescribed drugs), and abuse of alcohol, cocaine, amphetamines, or similar substances.

organic hallucinosis in *DSM–III*, a condition characterized by persistent or recurrent hallucinations produced by hallucinogens (which usually cause visual hallucinations), alcohol (which usually causes auditory hallucinations), brain damage or dysfunction, or, in some cases, sensory deprivation (blindness, deafness). This diagnostic category was removed from *DSM–IV–TR*.

organicism *n.* see ORGANIC APPROACH.

organic mental disorders in *DSM–III*, a heterogeneous group of mental disturbances resulting from transient or permanent brain dysfunction due to specific organic factors. Specification of cause is what distinguished these disturbances from ORGANIC BRAIN SYNDROMES. This diagnostic category was removed from *DSM–IV–TR*.

organic mood syndrome see ORGANIC-AFFECTIVE SYNDROME.

organic personality syndrome in *DSM–III*, a disorder characterized by a marked change in personality or behavior due to a factor that damages the brain, for example, a tumor, head injury, or vascular disease. The personality change involves at least one of the following: emotional lability (temper outbursts, unprovoked crying), impulse dyscontrol (shoplifting, sexual indiscretions), marked apathy and lack of interest, and suspiciousness or paranoid ideation. This diagnostic category was removed from *DSM–IV–TR*.

organic repression a retroactive form of amnesia in which the patient may be unable to recall events prior to the injury although examiners are unable to find a personal motive for the amnesia, such as the kind of repression observed in dissociative amnesia.

organic retardation failure of an organ or organ system to develop normally because of a genetic defect, dietary deficiency, or hormonal disorder. A failure of one or more parts of the skeletal system to grow normally could be caused by pituitary, hereditary, or dietary factors, or a combination of these.

organic therapies somatic treatments for serious or recalcitrant mental disorder and disease, among which are ELECTROCONVULSIVE THERAPY, PSYCHOPHARMACOLOGY, and PSYCHOSURGERY.

organic variable a process or state within an organism that combines with a stimulus to produce a particular response. For example, a headache may be an organic variable, and the response may be an irritable reaction to a stimulus (e.g., noise in the neighborhood). Also called **O variable**.

organ inferiority the sense of being deficient or somehow less than others as a result of negative feelings about any type of real or imagined abnormal organ function or structure. [defined by Alfred ADLER]

organismic personality theory an approach to personality theory in which personal functioning is understood in terms of the action of the whole, coherent, integrated organism, rather than in terms of psychological variables representing one versus another isolated aspect of body or mind. [developed by German-born U.S. physician and psychiatrist Kurt Goldstein (1878–1965) and Hungarian psychologist Andras Angyal (1902–1960)]

organismic psychology an approach to psychology that emphasizes the total organism, rejecting distinctions between mind and body. It embraces a MOLAR APPROACH that takes account of the interaction between the organism and its environment. See HOLISTIC PSYCHOLOGY.

organismic valuing process in client-centered theory, the presumed healthy and innate internal guidance system that a person can use to "stay on the track" toward self-actualization. One goal of treatment within the client-centered framework is to help the client listen to this inner guide. See CLIENT-CENTERED THERAPY.

organismic variable one of the four factors considered in behavioral assessment using the SORC system, referring to the physiological and psychological features of the organism that influence behavior.

organizational approach in the study of emotion, a conceptual framework, based on GENERAL SYSTEMS THEORY, emphasizing the role of emotions as regulators and determinants of both intrapersonal and interpersonal behaviors, as well as stressing the adaptive role of emotions. The organizational approach also emphasizes how perception, motivation, cognition, and action come together to produce important emotional changes.

organizational assessment activities involved in evaluating the structure, process, climate, and environmental factors that influence the effectiveness of an organization and the morale and productivity of employees. General or specific evaluations (e.g., readiness to change, job satisfaction, turnover) may be performed by practitioners from a variety of disciplines, including CONSULTING PSYCHOLOGY and INDUSTRIAL AND ORGANIZATIONAL PSYCHOLOGY.

organizational behavior modification the application of the principles of learning theory to effect changes within an organization.

organ language in the context of classical psychoanalytic explanations of PSYCHOSOMATIC illness, the bodily expression of emotional conflict or disturbance. Some believe that knowledge of the significance to the patient of the organ affected by the illness is essential for accurate diagnosis and treatment. For example, chronic lumbago (lower backache) with no identifiable organic cause may mean that the patient is feeling put upon, is being a martyr, or is aiming too low in life. Also called **organ speech**.

organ speech see ORGAN LANGUAGE.

orgasm *n.* the climax of sexual stimulation or activity, when the peak of pleasure is achieved, marked by the release of tension and rhythmic contractions of the perineal muscles, anal sphincter, and pelvic reproductive organs. In men, orgasm is also accompanied by the emission of semen (**ejaculation**); in women, it is accompanied by contractions of the wall of the outer third of the vagina. See also SEXUAL-RESPONSE CYCLE. **—orgasmic** or **orgastic** *adj.*

O

orgasmic dysfunction inability of a woman to reach orgasm in general or with certain forms of sexual stimulation. It may be primary, in which the woman has never been able to achieve an orgasm with any type of stimulation, with or without a partner; secondary, in which the woman had previously been but is currently unable to attain orgasm through physical contact; or situational, in which the woman is unable to experience orgasm with a particular partner or in a particular situation. Orgasmic dysfunction is a gender-specific term, whereas **orgasmic disorder** is gender neutral and includes FEMALE ORGASMIC DISORDER, MALE ORGASMIC DISORDER, and PREMATURE EJACULATION.

orgasmic phase see SEXUAL-RESPONSE CYCLE.

orgastic impotence inability of a male to achieve orgasm in spite of normal erection and ejaculation. See MALE ORGASMIC DISORDER.

orgastic potency the ability of a man or woman to achieve full orgasm during the sex act. See POTENCY.

orgiastic *adj.* relating to a situation characterized by indulgence, revelry, frenzy, and indiscriminate sexual behavior.

orgone *n.* the "life energy" and creative force in nature that was believed by Austrian psychoanalyst Wilhelm Reich (1897–1957) to pervade the universe. According to Reich, orgone was emitted by energy vesicles called BIONS, which he claimed to find in organic material. He also posited that it related to cosmic radiation and speculated that it might be responsible for the origin of life from earth and water (biogenesis), as well as the formation of weather patterns and the sexual potency of human beings. See also ORGONE THERAPY.

orgone accumulator in the ORGONE THERAPY of Austrian psychoanalyst Wilhelm Reich (1897–1957), an enclosure in which the patient sat for the purpose of capturing vital ORGONE energy, which Reich supposed to have the effect of improving the flow of life energy and releasing energy blocks. Also called **orgone box**.

orgone therapy the therapeutic approach of Austrian psychoanalyst Wilhelm Reich (1897–1957), based on the concept that the achievement of "full orgastic potency" is the key to psychological well-being. Reich believed the orgasm to be the emotional-energy regulator of the body, the purpose of which is to dissipate sexual tensions that would otherwise be transformed into neuroses. He further held that the orgasm derives its power from a hypothetical cosmic force, ORGONE energy, which accounts not only for sexual capacity but also for all functions of life and for the prevention of disease. The psychoanalytic community largely rejected and disapproved of Reich's highly unorthodox theories and approaches. Also called **vegetotherapy**.

orgy *n.* a type of social gathering at which a number of people engage in unrestrained sexual activity, often with other forms of revelry, including singing, dancing, and drinking.

O

oriental nightmare-death syndrome see BANGUNGUT.

orientation *n.* **1.** awareness of the self and of outer reality, that is, the ability to identify one's self and to know the time, the place, and the person one is talking to. See also REALITY ORIENTATION. **2.** the process of familiarizing oneself with a new setting (e.g., a new home, neighborhood, or city) so that movement and use do not depend upon memory cues, such as maps, and eventually become habitual. **—orient** *vb.*

orientation illusion see ILLUSION OF ORIENTATION.

orienting response 1. a behavioral response to an altered, novel, or sudden stimulus, for example, turning one's head toward an unexpected noise. Various physiological components of the orienting response have subsequently been identified as well, including dilation of pupils and blood vessels and changes in heart rate and electrical resistance of the skin. [described in 1927 by Ivan PAVLOV] **2.** any response of an organism in relation to the direction of a specific stimulus. Also called **orienting reflex**.

originality *n.* see CREATIVITY.

ornithinemia *n.* excessive ornithine in the blood, possibly due to an inborn error of amino acid metabolism or to liver disease. The condition sometimes occurs in siblings, who manifest mental retardation and severe speech disturbance.

orofacial dyskinesia behavior characterized by abnormal chewing, mouthing, and tongue movements that resemble symptoms of TARDIVE DYSKINESIA.

orogenital activity the application of the mouth to the genitalia. The activity may be performed by couples of opposite sexes or the same sex, either as a precoital form of stimulation or carried to orgasm. Application of the mouth to the male genitalia is called FELLATIO; application of the mouth to the female genitalia is known as CUNNILINGUS. Also called **buccal intercourse**; **oral–genital contact**. See also ORAL SEX.

orphenadrine *n.* an ANTICHOLINERGIC DRUG used in the treatment of drug-induced parkinsonian symptoms, such as those produced by conventional antipsychotics. It is also used for the relief of localized muscle spasms (see MUSCLE RELAXANT). Orphenadrine is also sold in combination with ANALGESICS (e.g., with aspirin and caffeine as **Norgesic** in the United States). U.S. trade name: **Norflex**.

orthergasia *n.* see EUERGASIA.

orthodox psychoanalysis see CLASSICAL PSYCHOANALYSIS.

orthodox sleep a less common name for NREM SLEEP.

orthonasia *n.* a program in which children are taught about death as a part of life, to enable them to incorporate healthy attitudes toward death in their coping repertoire. [introduced by Austrian-born U.S. psychologist Kurt R. Eissler (1908–1999)]

orthopsychiatry *n.* an interdisciplinary approach to mental health in which psychiatrists, psychologists, social workers, pediatricians, sociologists, nurses, and educators collaborate on the early treatment of mental disorders, with an emphasis on their prevention. **—orthopsychiatric** *adj.* **—orthopsychiatrist** *n.*

orthostatic hypotension a drop in blood pressure when moving from a lying or sitting position to a standing position. Blood pressure is normally maintained in the face of changes in position by activation of baroreceptors in the walls of the heart and the major arteries. Activation of these receptors in turn activates ALPHA-ADRENERGIC RECEPTORS in peripheral blood vessels, leading to arterial constriction and maintenance of blood pressure. Numerous psychotropic drugs (e.g., antidepressants, antipsychotics) block the activity of peripheral alpha adrenoreceptors, leading to orthostatic hypotension and an increased risk of falls, particularly in older adults. Orthostatic hypotension can also be caused by such disorders as diabetes mellitus, amyloidosis, and Parkinson's disease. Also called **postural hypotension**.

Osgood, Charles Egerton (1916–1991) U.S. psychologist. Osgood received his PhD in psychology at Yale University in 1946. He joined the faculty at the University of Illinois in 1950, remaining there throughout his career. His most important general contribution is the text *Method and Theory in Experimental Psychology* (1953). Osgood's research has been particularly relevant to the fields of psycholinguistics and cross-cultural psychology. Influenced by Clark HULL'S NEOBEHAVIORISM, Osgood developed a theory that explicitly named mental representations as INTERVENING VARIABLES between stimulus and response in the behaviorist's model. Along with colleagues, he developed the SEMANTIC DIFFERENTIAL method of determining the meaning of words. Although this method was criticized by other linguists, such as Noam Chomsky (1928–) and Roger BROWN, it was nonetheless very influential, inspiring a great deal of research. Osgood's views are summarized in *The Measurement of Meaning* (1957), coauthored with George J. Suci and Percy H. Tannenbaum. His later research focused on cross-cultural studies of meaning as well as language pathology. Among other honors, Osgood received the American Psychological Association's Distinguished Contributions Award and was elected to fellowships of the American Academy of Arts and Sciences and the National Academy of Sciences.

osmolagnia *n.* sexual interest in and pleasure derived from smells emanating from the body, especially from the genitals.

osphresiolagnia *n.* sexual arousal or erotic experience produced by odors.

osphresiophilia *n.* an abnormal attraction to odors.

osteoarthritis *n.* see ARTHRITIS.

osteoporosis *n.* see CALCIUM-DEFICIENCY DISORDERS.

OT abbreviation for OCCUPATIONAL THERAPY.

OTC abbreviation for OVER-THE-COUNTER.

Othello syndrome see DELUSIONAL JEALOUSY. [derived from the name of the protagonist of William Shakespeare's tragedy *Othello*]

other conditions that may be a focus of clinical attention in *DSM–IV–TR*, a category that includes various conditions or problems that warrant psychiatric attention or treatment even though they do not meet the criteria of MENTAL DISORDER.

other-conscious emotion see SELF-CONSCIOUS EMOTION.

other-directed *adj.* describing or relating to people whose values, goals, and behavior stem primarily from identification with group or collective standards rather than with individually defined standards. Also called **outer-directed**. Compare INNER-DIRECTED; TRADITION-DIRECTED. [introduced by U.S. sociologist David Riesman (1909–2002)]

other psychosexual disorders the *DSM–III* designation for what *DSM–IV–TR* terms SEXUAL DISORDER NOT OTHERWISE SPECIFIED.

otopalatodigital syndrome see OPD SYNDROME.

ought self in analyses of self-concept, a mental representation of a set of attributes that one is obligated to possess according to social norms or one's personal responsibilities.

outcome *n.* the result of an experiment, treatment, interaction, or any other event, for example, a client's condition after psychotherapy.

outcome evaluation a process used to decide whether a program has achieved its stated goals and had the desired impact on the participants. Also called **payoff evaluation**. See also IMPACT ANALYSIS; SUMMATIVE EVALUATION.

outcome expectancies cognitive, emotional, and behavioral outcomes that individuals believe are associated with future, or intended, behaviors (e.g., alcohol consumption, exercise) and that are believed to either promote or inhibit these behaviors.

outcome measures assessments of the effectiveness of an intervention on the basis of measurements taken before, during, and after the intervention.

outcome research a systematic investigation of the effectiveness of a single type or technique of psychotherapy, or of the comparative effectiveness of different types or techniques, when applied to one or more disorders. See also PSYCHOTHERAPY RESEARCH.

outercourse *n.* noncoital sexual activity, which may include achieving orgasm by manual stimulation of the genitals or by ORAL SEX.

outer-directed *adj.* see OTHER-DIRECTED.

outing *n.* revealing one's own or another person's same-sex sexual orientation to others. The term refers to COMING OUT of the closet (see CLOSET HOMOSEXUAL). **—out** *vb.*

outlier *n.* an extreme observation or measurement, that is, one that significantly differs from all others obtained. Outliers can have a high degree of influence on summary statistics and estimates of parametric values and their precision and may distort research findings if they are the result of error.

out-of-body experience a dissociative experience in which the individual imagines that his or her mind, soul, or spirit has left the body and is acting or perceiving independently. Such experiences are sometimes reported by those who have recovered from the point of death (see NEAR-DEATH EXPERIENCE); they have also been reported by those using hallucinogens or under hypnosis. Certain occult or spiritualistic practices may also attempt to induce such experiences.

outpatient *n.* a person who obtains diagnosis, treatment, or other service at a hospital, clinic, physician's office, or other health care facility without overnight admission. See also AMBULATORY CARE. Compare INPATIENT.

outpatient commitment a form of court-ordered psychiatric or psychological treatment in which individuals are allowed to remain in the community so long as they are closely monitored and continue to receive treatment.

outpatient services health care services performed for registered ambulatory patients in hospital units, clinics, doctors' offices, and mental health centers.

O variable see ORGANIC VARIABLE.

ovariectomy *n.* the surgical removal of an ovary. This procedure may be performed when the ovaries are diseased or injured. Under some circumstances, as when a woman is at very high risk for ovarian cancer, it may be carried out for prevention or prophylaxis (see PROPHYLACTIC SURGERY). Removal of ovaries in premenopausal women will induce menopause. Also called **oophorectomy**.

overactivity *n.* excessive, restless activity that is usually less extreme than HYPERACTIVITY.

overanxious disorder disproportionate and persistent anxiety or worry occurring in childhood or adolescence across a variety of different situations and objects. In some current diagnostic classifications, notably the DSM–IV–TR, overanxious disorder has been subsumed under GENERALIZED ANXIETY DISORDER.

O

overcompensation *n.* see COMPENSATION. **—overcompensate** *vb.*

overconfidence *n.* an unsupported belief or unrealistically positive expectation that a desired outcome will occur. In a sports setting, for example, overconfidence might involve overestimating one's ability to perform or underestimating the ability of a competitor to perform. **—overconfident** *adj.*

overcontrolled *adj.* denoting behavior that is inhibited and often driven by shyness or fear of rejection. The word is typically used to describe the behavior of children thought to be at risk for depression, but may also refer to similar behavior in adults.

overcorrection *n.* in therapy, a technique used when a client exhibits inappropriate behavior, in which the therapist asks the client to repeat the behavior in an appropriate but exaggerated way.

overdetermination *n.* in psychoanalytic theory, the concept that several unconscious factors may combine to produce one symptom, dream, disorder, or aspect of behavior. Because drives and defenses operate simultaneously and derive from different layers of the personality, a dream may express more than one meaning, and a single symptom may serve more than one purpose or fulfill more than one unconscious wish. **—overdetermined** *adj.*

overdose 1. *n.* the ingestion of an excessive amount of a drug, with resulting adverse and potentially lethal effects. The precise toxic effects differ according to many factors, including the properties and dosage of the drug, the body weight and health of the individual, and the individual's tolerance for the drug. **2.** *vb.* to take an excessive amount of a drug.

Overeaters Anonymous (**OA**) a voluntary organization of men and women who seek to help each other understand and overcome compulsive eating disorders through a TWELVE-STEP PROGRAM. See also SELF-HELP GROUP.

overgeneralization *n.* a cognitive distortion in which an individual views a single event as an invariable rule, so that, for example, failure at accomplishing one task will predict an endless pattern of defeat in all tasks.

overinclusion *n.* failure of an individual to eliminate ineffective or inappropriate responses associated with a particular stimulus.

overload *n.* a psychological condition in which situations and experiences are so cognitively, perceptually, and emotionally stimulating that they tax or even exceed the individual's capacity to process incoming information. See COGNITIVE OVERLOAD; INFORMATION OVERLOAD; SENSORY OVERLOAD; STIMULUS OVERLOAD.

overmedication *n.* see MEDICATION.

overproductive ideas racing thoughts or FLIGHT OF IDEAS often present in a MANIC EPISODE.

overprotection *n.* the process of sheltering a child to such an extent that he or she fails to become independent and may experience later adjustment and other difficulties, including development of a DEPENDENT PERSONALITY DISORDER.

overreaction *n.* a reaction, particularly an emotional response, that exceeds an appropriate level.

overt behavior behavior that is explicit, that is, observable without instruments or expertise.

over-the-counter (**OTC**) *adj.* able to be purchased without a doctor's prescription. A variety of OTC drugs, including acetaminophen and aspirin, are available.

overt homosexuality gay or lesbian tendencies that are consciously recognized and expressed in sexual contact, in contrast to LATENT HOMOSEXUALITY.

overtraining syndrome the unwanted physical and mental effects, collectively, of training beyond the individual's capacities. Characteristic symptoms include decreased performance, easily tiring, loss of motivation, emotional instability, inability to concentrate, and increased susceptibility to injury and infection. See BURNOUT.

overt response any observable or external reaction, such as pointing to indicate one's preference from among a set of objects or verbally answering "yes" to a question. Compare COVERT RESPONSE.

overvalued idea a false or exaggerated belief that is maintained by an individual, but less rigidly and persistently than a delusion (e.g., the idea that one is indispensable in an organization). The presence of an overvalued idea implies an unconscious motivation that, if made conscious, would reduce its importance and corresponding dysfunctions.

oxazepam *n.* a short-acting BENZODIAZEPINE that is the final active product of the metabolism of DIAZEPAM. Oxazepam possesses the advantage of having no metabolic products; it therefore has a predictable HALF-LIFE and elimination time and requires minimal processing in the liver. Because of this, some consider it to be the preferred agent in the management of alcohol withdrawal. However, the need for close monitoring of dosing schedules leads others to prefer longer-acting agents for this condition. U.S. trade name: **Serax**.

oxidation *n.* a chemical reaction in which a substance combines with oxygen or in which electrons are lost. In DRUG METABOLISM, oxidation is a common mechanism of Phase I metabolism, in which drugs are made more polar (i.e., more water soluble) by the addition of an oxygen atom, often via the action of CYTOCHROME P450 enzymes.

oxycodone *n.* see OPIOID ANALGESIC.

oxytocics *pl. n.* drugs that are capable of stimulating contractions of the uterine muscles and are used clinically to induce labor and elective or therapeutic abortion and to control postpartum bleeding. They include ERGOT DERIVATIVES (e.g., ergonovine) and some PROSTAGLANDINS. See also OXYTOCIN.

oxytocin *n.* a PEPTIDE produced in the hypothalamus and released by the posterior PITUITARY GLAND into the blood, where it acts as a hormone, or into the central nervous system, where it acts as a neurotransmitter and binds to oxytocin receptors to influence behavior and physiology. Although perhaps best known for its role in stimulating contractions of smooth muscle in the wall of the uterus to facilitate labor and in the mammary glands to facilitate expression of milk—the so-called milk letdown reflex—oxytocin is present and serves important functions in both sexes. Indeed, it has earned a reputation as a facilitator of social affiliation and the TEND-AND-BEFRIEND RESPONSE in particular, and also has been shown to be involved in stressful experiences (e.g., social isolation, unhappy relationships) and to influence sexual pleasure, reproductive functions, parental behavior (especially maternal behavior), and emotional behavior such as anxiety and depression. Additionally, research with nonhuman animals suggests oxytocin—and the structurally similar compound VASOPRESSIN—is important for a variety of other activities, including PAIR-BOND formation, mate guarding, and recognition of social stimuli. A possible reason for the varied roles that oxytocin appears to play is that it has dual pathways and purposes. It has been theorized that when operating during times of low stress, oxytocin physiologically rewards those who maintain good social bonds with feelings of well-being. When operating during times of high social stress or pain, however, it may produce physiological changes that then encourage people to seek contact with others.

Pp

PA abbreviation for PHYSICIAN ASSISTANT.

padded cell a room in a psychiatric hospital or ward that is lined with mattresses or other heavy padding on the floor and walls to protect a violent or self-destructive patient from self-injury or from injuring others. In most institutions padded cells have been replaced by some combination of physical restraints, psychological interventions, and tranquilizing medications.

pain *n.* an unpleasant sensation due to damage to nerve tissue, stimulation of free nerve endings, or excessive stimulation (e.g., extremely loud sounds). Physical pain is elicited by stimulation of pain receptors, which occur in groups of myelinated or unmyelinated fibers throughout the body, but particularly in surface tissues. Pain that is initiated in surface receptors generally is perceived as sharp, sudden, and localized; pain experienced in internal organs tends to be dull, longer lasting, and less localized. Because of psychological factors, as well as previous experience and training in pain response, individual reactions vary widely. Although pain is generally considered a physical phenomenon, it involves various cognitive, affective, and behavioral factors: It is an unpleasant emotional as well as sensory experience. Pain may also be a feeling of severe distress and suffering resulting from acute anxiety, loss of a loved one, or other psychological factors (see PSYCHIC PAIN). Psychologists have made important contributions to understanding pain by demonstrating the psychosocial and behavioral factors in the etiology, severity, exacerbation, maintenance, and treatment of both physical and mental pain. See also CHRONIC PAIN; GATE-CONTROL THEORY.

pain disorder in *DSM–IV–TR*, a SOMATOFORM DISORDER characterized by severe, prolonged pain that significantly interferes with a person's ability to function. The pain cannot be accounted for solely by a medical condition, and there is evidence of psychological involvement in its onset, severity, exacerbation, or maintenance. Although not feigned or produced intentionally (compare FACTITIOUS DISORDER; MALINGERING), the pain may serve such psychological ends as avoidance of distasteful activity or gaining extra attention or support from others. Pain disorder was formerly referred to as **psychogenic pain disorder** or **somatoform pain disorder**.

painful bruising syndrome see GARDNER–DIAMOND SYNDROME.

pain management the prevention, reduction, or elimination of physical or mental suffering or discomfort, which may be achieved by pharmacotherapy (e.g., administration of opioids or other analgesics), behavioral therapies, neurological and anesthesiologic methods (e.g., nerve blocks, self-administered pumps), complementary or alternative methods (e.g., ACUPUNCTURE or ACUPRESSURE), or a combination of these. A wide range of psychological interventions have been used successfully in treatment to help people deal with or control their pain. For example, BIOFEEDBACK and relaxation have been used alone and in conjunction with other cognitive techniques to treat chronic headaches and facial pain. HYPNOTHERAPY has also been used successfully to treat acute pain and pain associated with burns and metastatic disease. Cognitive and behavioral COPING-SKILLS TRAINING, along with external attentional focus, neutral or positive IMAGERY, problem solving, communication skills, and psychotherapeutic approaches, have been combined with physical modalities in the treatment of CHRONIC PAIN syndromes.

pain mechanisms neural mechanisms that mediate pain. These extend from peripheral nerve endings to the cerebral cortex, especially the CINGULATE GYRUS. Some investigators propose that sharp pain sensations are transmitted by rapidly conducting A fibers (myelinated nerve fibers or axons of the somatosensory system) and dull pain sensations are transmitted by slowly conducting C fibers (unmyelinated peripheral nerve fibers or axons). See also GATE-CONTROL THEORY.

pain pathway any neural pathway that mediates sensations of pain. Afferent pain pathways include rapidly conducting myelinated A fibers and slowly conducting unmyelinated C fibers, ascending tracts in the anterolateral system, the PERIAQUEDUCTAL GRAY matter, the RETICULAR FORMATION, and many thalamic and cerebral cortical areas, especially the CINGULATE GYRUS. There are also efferent pathways that inhibit pain signals at various levels down to spinal synapses, including release of ENDOGENOUS OPIOIDS that inhibit pain.

pain perception the perception of physiological pain, usually evoked by stimuli that cause or threaten to cause tissue damage. In some cases, such as PHANTOM LIMB pain, the persistence of pain cannot be explained by stimulation of neural pathways. Pain perception can be measured in terms of its intensity and can be classified according to several categories: These include sharp or dull; focal or general; and chronic or intermittent or transitory. Also called **nociception**.

pain scale a standardized rating scale for judging the experience of pain. It may take the form of verbal self-description, numerical rating, or graphical depictions of faces.

paint sniffing a type of substance abuse involving the inhalation of the fumes of paint thinners and other volatile solvents. See INHALANT ABUSE.

pair bond a relationship between two individuals characterized by close affiliative behavior between partners, emotional reaction to separation or loss, and increased social responsiveness on reunion.

paired comparison a systematic procedure for comparing a set of stimuli or other items. A pair of stimuli is presented to the participant, who is asked to compare them on a particular dimension, such as size, loudness, or brightness; the process is continued until every item in the set has been compared with every other item. The method is mainly associated with research into psychophysical judgments but has also been used to study preferences between works of art or different personality characteristics.

paleologic thinking PRELOGICAL THINKING characterized by concrete, dreamlike thought processes, as occurs in children. Mental activity is limited to feeling and perception and excludes logic and reasoning. [defined by Italian-born U.S. psychiatrist Silvano Arieti (1914–1982)]

paleopsychology (**palaeopsychology**) *n.* **1.** the study of certain psychological processes in contemporary humans that are believed to have originated in earlier stages of human and, perhaps, nonhuman animal evolution. These include unconscious processes, such as the COLLECTIVE UNCONSCIOUS. The term was introduced in this sense by Carl JUNG. **2.** the present-day reconstruction of the psychological reactions of prehistoric human beings. **—paleopsychological** *adj.*

palinopsia *n.* the persistence or reappearance of a visual image after the stimulus has been removed. Palinopsia is associated with posterior brain injury, drug effects, and seizures. Also called **palinopia**; **paliopsy**; **visual perseveration**. See also VISUAL ILLUSION.

palinphrasia *n.* involuntary repetition of words or phrases in speaking. Also called **paliphrasia**.

paliphrasia *n.* see PALINPHRASIA.

palliative care terminal care that focuses on symptom control and comfort instead of aggressive, cure-oriented intervention. This is the basis of the HOSPICE approach. Emphasis is on careful assessment of the patient's condition throughout the end phase of life in order to provide the most effective medications and other procedures to relieve pain.

pallidotomy *n.* a neurosurgical technique in which electrodes are used to selectively lesion the GLOBUS PALLIDUS. Pallidotomy is used for the management of disorders involving damage to the EXTRAPYRAMIDAL TRACT, such as Parkinson's disease.

palpitation *n.* a rapid heartbeat associated with an anxiety attack, excessive tension, or physical exertion.

Pamelor *n.* a trade name for NORTRIPTYLINE.

panarteritis *n.* a diffuse inflammation of the walls of the small and medium arteries. Arteries of the skeletal muscles, kidneys, heart, and gastrointestinal tract may be involved.

pancreatitis *n.* an inflammation of the pancreas, marked by severe abdominal pain and caused by biliary tract disorders (e.g., gallstones), alcoholism, viral infection, or reactions to certain drugs (e.g., some antipsychotic agents).

pandemic *adj.* widespread or universal: affecting significant proportions of many populations over a large area (e.g., several countries), particularly with reference to a disease or disorder. Compare ENDEMIC; EPIDEMIC.

panel study a longitudinal study (see LONGITUDINAL DESIGN) in which one or more groups (panels) are followed over time.

panic *n.* a sudden, uncontrollable fear reaction that may involve terror, confusion, and irrational behavior, precipitated by a perceived threat (e.g., earthquake, fire, or being stuck in an elevator).

panic attack a sudden onset of intense apprehension and fearfulness in the absence of actual danger, accompanied by the presence of such physical symptoms as palpitations, difficulty in breathing, chest pain or discomfort, choking or smothering sensations, excessive perspiration, and dizziness. The attack occurs in a discrete period of time and often involves fears of going crazy, losing control, or dying. In *DSM–IV–TR* the diagnosis of a panic attack requires the presence of at least 4 of 13 somatic or cognitive symptoms. Attacks may occur in the context of any of the ANXIETY DISORDERS as well as in other mental disorders (e.g., mood disorders, substance-related disorders) and in some general medical conditions (e.g., hyperthyroidism). See also CUED PANIC ATTACK; SITUATIONALLY PREDISPOSED PANIC ATTACK; UNCUED PANIC ATTACK.

panic control treatment a COGNITIVE BEHAVIOR THERAPY for panic disorder focusing on education about panic, training in slow breathing, and graded IN VIVO exposures to cues associated with panic. [developed by U.S. clinical psychologists Michelle G. Craske and David H. Barlow (1942–)]

panic disorder in *DSM–IV–TR*, an ANXIETY DISORDER characterized by recurrent, unexpected PANIC ATTACKS that are associated with (a) persistent concern about having another attack, (b) worry about the possible consequences of the attacks, (c) significant change in behavior re-

P

lated to the attacks (e.g., avoiding situations, engaging in SAFETY BEHAVIOR, not going out alone), or (d) a combination of any or all of these. Panic disorder associated with significant avoidance is classified as **panic disorder with agoraphobia** (see AGORAPHOBIA).

pansexualism *n.* the view that all human behavior is motivated by the sexual drive. Sigmund FREUD has been popularly associated with such a view; however, although he emphasized the power of the sexual instinct, Freud also recognized nonsexual interests, such as the self-preservative drives (e.g., hunger and thirst) and the aggressive drive associated with the DEATH INSTINCT. **—pansexual** *adj.*

pantomime *n.* a nonverbal therapeutic technique sometimes employed when verbal expression is blocked.

papaverine *n.* an OPIUM ALKALOID first isolated in the 1840s. It has no psychopharmacological activity but is a potent vasodilator, being occasionally used in the treatment of angina pectoris, to increase blood flow in the cerebral arteries, or—when injected into the corpora cavernosa of the penis—to produce erection in the management of impotence. U.S. trade name: **Para-Time S.R.**

Papez circuit a circular network of nerve centers and fibers in the brain that is associated with emotion and memory. It includes the hippocampus, FORNIX, MAMMILLARY BODY, anterior thalamus, CINGULATE GYRUS, and PARAHIPPOCAMPAL GYRUS. Damage to any component of this system leads to amnesia. Also called **Papez circle**. [first described in 1937 by James W. **Papez** (1883–1958), U.S. neuroanatomist]

P

paracetamol *n.* see ACETAMINOPHEN.

parachlorophenylalanine *n.* a substance that blocks the synthesis of SEROTONIN from tryptophan, resulting in depletion of serotonin from brain cells.

paradoxical directive an instruction by a therapist to the client to do precisely the opposite of what common sense would dictate in order to show the absurdity or self-defeating nature of the client's original intention. See also PARADOXICAL TECHNIQUE.

paradoxical intention a psychotherapeutic technique in which the client is asked to magnify a distressing, unwanted symptom. For example, an individual who is afraid of shaking in a social situation would be instructed to imagine the feared situation and purposely exaggerate the shakiness. The aim is to help clients distance themselves from their symptoms, often by appreciating the humorous aspects of their exaggerated responses. In this way clients can learn that the predicted catastrophic consequences attributed to their symptoms are very unlikely to occur. Paradoxical intention may be used to treat anxiety disorders but is not appropriate for suicidal behavior or schizophrenia. [originally developed by Austrian psychiatrist Viktor E. Frankl (1905–1997) for the treatment of phobias]

paradoxical reaction in pharmacology, a drug reaction that is contrary to the expected effect, for example, worsening of anxiety after the administration of an anxiolytic agent.

paradoxical sleep see REM SLEEP.

paradoxical technique a therapeutic technique in which a client is directed by the therapist to continue undesired symptomatic behavior, and even increase it, to show that the client has voluntary control over the symptoms. Also called **paradoxical intervention**. See also PARADOXICAL DIRECTIVE.

paradoxical thinking cognition marked by contradiction of typical logical processes. Although this type of thinking can be associated with distorted thought processes, such as those present in SCHIZOID PERSONALITY DISORDER or some forms of schizophrenia, it can also be used as a way of reframing problems or negative beliefs in a positive manner. This approach is often embraced to promote creativity and used as a vehicle for personal, familial, and organizational change.

parahippocampal gyrus a ridge (gyrus) on the medial (inner) surface of the TEMPORAL LOBE of cerebral cortex, lying over the HIPPOCAMPUS. It is a component of the LIMBIC SYSTEM thought to be involved in spatial or topographic memory. Also called **parahippocampal cortex**.

paralalia *n.* **1.** a speech disorder or disturbance that involves the substitution of one speech sound for another (e.g., saying "wabbit" for *rabbit* or "lellow" for *yellow*). See also LALLING. **2.** a rarely used term for speech disorders generally.

paraldehyde *n.* a sedative and hypnotic drug formerly used in the treatment of agitation or delirium tremens. It was relatively toxic, with a noted side effect of producing a characteristic breath odor, and has been abandoned in favor of safer alternatives. U.S. trade name: **Paral**.

paralexia *n.* the substitution or transposition of letters, syllables, or words during reading. See also VISUAL DYSLEXIA.

parallel processing INFORMATION PROCESSING in which two or more sequences of operations are carried out simultaneously by independent processors. A capacity for parallel processing in the human mind would account for people's apparent ability to carry on different cognitive functions at the same time, as, for example, when driving a car while also listening to music and having a conversation. However, those who believe that there is no truly parallel processing in the brain explain this ability in terms of very rapid shifts between functions and information sources. The term parallel processing is usually reserved for processing at a higher, symbolic level. Also called **simultaneous processing**. Compare SERIAL PROCESSING.

paralogia *n.* insistently illogical or delusional

thinking and verbal expression, sometimes observed in schizophrenia. Swiss psychiatrist Eugen Bleuler (1857–1939) cited the example of a patient who justified his insistence that he was Switzerland by saying "Switzerland loves freedom. I love freedom. I am Switzerland." Also called **paralogical thinking**; **perverted logic**; **perverted thinking**. See also EVASION.

paralysis *n.* loss of function of voluntary muscles. A common cause is a lesion of the nervous or muscular system due to injury, disease, or congenital factors. The lesion may involve the central nervous system, as in a stroke, or the peripheral nervous system. **—paralytic** *adj.*

paramedic *n.* a health care professional who is specially trained and certified to assist medical professionals and, especially, to provide a wide range of emergency services prior to and during transportation to a hospital.

parameter *n.* a numerical constant that characterizes a population with respect to some attribute, for example, the location of its central point. **—parametric** *adj.*

parametric statistics statistical procedures that are based on assumptions about the distribution of the attribute (or attributes) in the population being tested. Compare NONPARAMETRIC STATISTICS.

paramimia *n.* the use of gestures inappropriate to or not congruent with one's underlying feelings.

paramimism *n.* a gesture or other movement that has a meaning to the patient although others may not understand its significance.

paramnesia *n.* see FALSE MEMORY.

paranoia *n.* **1.** a PARANOID STATE. **2.** in *DSM–III*, a relatively rare disorder, distinct from paranoid schizophrenia, in which the person reasons rightly from a wrong premise and develops a persistent, well-systematized, and logically constructed set of persecutory delusions, such as being conspired against or poisoned or maligned. The equivalent *DSM–IV–TR* diagnostic category is persecutory-type DELUSIONAL DISORDER. **3.** historically, any psychiatric disorder characterized by persistent delusions. See also CLASSICAL PARANOIA. **—paranoiac** *n., adj.*

paranoiac character a personality type whose primary characteristic is a tendency to blame the environment for his or her difficulties.

paranoia querulans see LITIGIOUS PARANOIA.

paranoid *adj.* **1.** relating to or exhibiting extreme distrust or suspiciousness. See also PARANOID PERSONALITY DISORDER; PARANOID TENDENCY. **2.** relating to or characterized by DELUSIONS. See also DELUSIONAL DISORDER; PARANOID SCHIZOPHRENIA.

paranoid condition see PARANOID STATE.

paranoid delusion loosely, any of a variety of false personal beliefs tenaciously sustained even in the face of incontrovertible evidence to the contrary: DELUSIONS OF GRANDEUR, DELUSIONAL JEALOUSY, or, most frequently, DELUSIONS OF PERSECUTION.

paranoid disorder see DELUSIONAL DISORDER.

paranoid hostility anger and desire to harm others arising out of the delusion that they are persecuting or plotting against one.

paranoid ideation thought processes involving persistent suspiciousness and nondelusional beliefs of being persecuted, harassed, or treated unfairly by others.

paranoid litigious state see LITIGIOUS PARANOIA.

paranoid personality disorder in *DSM–IV–TR*, a personality disorder characterized by (a) pervasive, unwarranted suspiciousness and mistrust (such as expectation of trickery or harm, guardedness and secretiveness, avoidance of accepting blame, overconcern with hidden motives and meanings, and pathological jealousy); (b) hypersensitivity (such as being easily slighted and quick to take offense, exaggerated concerns over significant behaviors or events, and readiness to counterattack); and (c) restricted affectivity (such as emotional coldness, no true sense of humor, or absence of tender feelings).

paranoid pseudocommunity see PSEUDOCOMMUNITY.

paranoid psychosis a psychotic condition characterized by persecutory delusions without personality disorganization or deterioration. See DELUSIONAL DISORDER; PARANOID STATE.

paranoid-schizoid position in the OBJECT RELATIONS THEORY of Melanie KLEIN, the period from birth up to the 6th month of life during which infants perceive the world in terms of PART-OBJECTS and develop a fear of annihilation and persecutory anxiety due to the power of their DEATH INSTINCT. Infants use various primitive DEFENSE MECHANISMS against these fears, including (a) PROJECTION of aggression onto an external object; (b) directing their own aggression against the imagined persecutory object; and (c) INTROJECTION and SPLITTING of the breast into a good object and a bad object (see BAD BREAST; GOOD BREAST). Compare DEPRESSIVE POSITION.

paranoid schizophrenia in *DSM–IV–TR*, a subtype of SCHIZOPHRENIA, often with a later onset than other types, characterized by prominent delusions or auditory hallucinations. Delusions are typically persecutory, grandiose, or both; hallucinations are typically related to the content of the delusional theme. Cognitive functioning and mood are affected to a much lesser degree than in other types of schizophrenia. The *DSM–III* designation was **paranoid type schizophrenic disorder**.

paranoid state a condition characterized by delusions of persecution or grandiosity that are not as systematized and elaborate as in a DELUSIONAL DISORDER or as disorganized and bizarre as in paranoid schizophrenia. Paranoid states are

P

described in the *International Classification of Diseases* (9th edition) but not in *DSM–IV–TR*. Also called **paranoid condition**.

paranoid system of beliefs delusional beliefs of persecution, reference to the self, grandiosity, and the like. See also CIRCUMSCRIBED BELIEF.

paranoid tendency a propensity toward feelings of mistrust, persecutory beliefs, and negative perceptions of oneself and others. See also PARANOID PERSONALITY DISORDER; PARANOID STATE.

paranosic gain see PRIMARY GAIN.

paraphasia *n.* a speech disturbance characterized by the use of incorrect, distorted, or inappropriate words, which in some cases resemble the correct word in sound or meaning and in other cases are irrelevant or nonsensical. For example, a wheelchair may be called a "spinning wheel," and a hypodermic needle might be called a "tie pin." The disorder occurs in a variety of forms (e.g., literal paraphasia, semantic paraphasia) and is seen most commonly in organic brain disorders and PICK'S DISEASE. **—paraphasic** *adj.*

paraphemia *n.* a speech disorder marked by the habitual introduction of inappropriate words or by the meaningless combination of words.

paraphilia *n.* in *DSM–IV–TR*, a sexual disorder in which unusual or bizarre fantasies or behavior are necessary for sexual excitement. The fantasies or acts persist over a period of at least 6 months and may take several forms: preference for a nonhuman object, such as animals or clothes of the opposite sex; repetitive sexual activity involving real or simulated suffering or humiliation, as in whipping or bondage; or repetitive sexual activity with nonconsenting partners. Paraphilias include such specific types as FETISHISM, FROTTEURISM, PEDOPHILIA, EXHIBITIONISM, VOYEURISM, SEXUAL MASOCHISM, and SEXUAL SADISM. **—paraphiliac** *adj.*

P

paraphilia not otherwise specified in *DSM–IV–TR*, a residual category comprising PARAPHILIAS, such as COPROPHILIA, NECROPHILIA, and UROPHILIA, that do not meet the diagnostic criteria for any specific type.

paraphonia *n.* an abnormal change in voice quality.

paraphrenia *n.* **1.** a late-onset psychotic condition that is marked by delusions and hallucinations but is distinct from schizophrenia by virtue of the absence of generalized intellectual impairment and distinct from degenerative dementias by virtue of the absence of a progressively deteriorating course. Although paraphrenia is not listed in *DSM–IV–TR* or *ICD–10*, it is still used as a diagnostic entity in some parts of the world. See also LATE PARAPHRENIA. [first described by German psychiatrist Emil Kraepelin (1856–1926)] **2.** any of various mental disorders that are associated with transitional periods of life (i.e., adolescence or old age). [defined in 1863 by German physician Karl Ludwig Kahlbaum (1828–1899)] **3.** loosely, any of a variety of psychotic conditions, such as LATE-ONSET SCHIZOPHRENIA, PARANOID SCHIZOPHRENIA, or certain PARANOID STATES.

parapraxis *n.* an error that is believed to express unconscious wishes, attitudes, or impulses. Examples of such errors include slips of the pen, SLIPS OF THE TONGUE and other forms of VERBAL LEAKAGE, forgetting significant events, mislaying objects with unpleasant associations, unintentional puns, and motivated accidents. Also called **parapraxia**. See also FREUDIAN SLIP; SYMPTOMATIC ACT.

paraprofessional *n.* a trained but not professionally credentialed worker who assists in the treatment of patients in both hospital and community settings.

parareaction *n.* an abnormal or exaggerated reaction to a relatively minor incident (e.g., tripping), which may become the basis for a delusion.

parasomnia *n.* a SLEEP DISORDER characterized by abnormal behavior or physiological events occurring during sleep or the transitional state between sleep and waking. In *DSM–IV–TR* parasomnias comprise NIGHTMARE DISORDER, SLEEP TERROR DISORDER, SLEEPWALKING DISORDER, and PARASOMNIA NOT OTHERWISE SPECIFIED and form one of two broad groups of primary sleep disorders, the other being DYSSOMNIAS. See also DYSFUNCTIONS ASSOCIATED WITH SLEEP, SLEEP STAGES, OR PARTIAL AROUSALS.

parasomnia not otherwise specified in *DSM–IV–TR*, a diagnostic category reserved for sleep disturbances that are characterized by abnormal behavior or physiological events during sleep but do not meet criteria for a more specific PARASOMNIA. Examples include REM BEHAVIOR DISORDER and SLEEP PARALYSIS.

parasuicide *n.* a range of behaviors involving deliberate self-harm that falls short of suicide and may or may not be intended to result in death. It includes ATTEMPTED SUICIDE and PASSIVE SUICIDE.

parasympathetic drug see CHOLINERGIC DRUG.

parasympathetic nervous system one of two branches of the AUTONOMIC NERVOUS SYSTEM (ANS, which controls smooth muscle and gland functions), the other being the SYMPATHETIC NERVOUS SYSTEM. Anatomically it comprises the portion of the ANS whose preganglionic fibers leave the central nervous system from the brainstem via the oculomotor, facial, glossopharyngeal, and vagus nerves and the spinal cord via three sacral nerves (see SPINAL NERVE). It is defined functionally as the system controlling rest, repair, enjoyment, eating, sleeping, sexual activity, and social dominance, among other functions. The parasympathetic nervous system stimulates salivary secretions and digestive secretions in the stomach and produces pupillary constriction, decreases in heart rate, and increased blood flow to the genitalia during sexual excitement. Also called **parasympathetic division**.

parasympatholytic drug see ANTICHOLINERGIC DRUG.

parasympathomimetic drug see CHOLINERGIC DRUG.

parataxic distortion in psychoanalytic theory, a distorted perception or judgment of others on the basis of past experiences or of the unconscious. Also called **transference distortion**. [introduced by U.S. psychoanalyst Harry Stack Sullivan (1892–1949)]

parataxis *n.* broadly, a lack of integration among components of personality, cognitive style, or emotions. The term is now infrequently used.

Para-Time S.R. a trade name for PAPAVERINE.

paraverbal therapy a method of psychotherapy, introduced in the 1970s, for children who have difficulty communicating verbally and are also affected by such conditions and disorders as hyperactivity, autism, withdrawal, or language disturbances. Assuming that these children would feel more intrigued and less threatened by a nonverbal approach, the therapy uses various expressive media, including the components of music (tempo and pitch), mime, movement, and art to help the children express themselves. The therapist participates on the children's level, and eventually the children feel safe enough to verbalize their real feelings, enabling them to participate in more conventional therapy. [developed by Evelyn P. Heimlich]

paregoric *n.* a medication containing a tincture of opium that is administered to control severe cases of diarrhea. It relieves pain and discomfort and reduces intestinal motility. It is also used to treat opioid withdrawal in neonates and may be used as well with children and adults. Besides opium, paregoric contains camphor, benzoic acid, glycerin, anise oil, and alcohol. It was developed in the early 18th century. Also called **camphorated tincture of opium**.

parens patriae a doctrine promoting the power and interest of the government (Latin, "parent of the country") in caring for and protecting minors and individuals who are unable to care for themselves or to provide for their own basic needs, even if this necessitates restricting their rights. In the United States, this power and interest is vested with the individual states.

parental imperative a hypothesis stating that while raising children both men and women adopt distinct, stereotypical gender roles as a means of successfully fulfilling the demands of parenthood. Once this parental imperative lessens, however, these gender role orientations change in favor of more androgynous identities; for example, women become more assertive and competitive, while men become more contemplative and expressive. [proposed by U.S. psychologist David L. Gutmann (1925–)]

parental perplexity a parent–child relationship marked by a lack of parental spontaneity, extreme indecisiveness, and an inability to sense and satisfy the child's needs. Such primary relationships may result in psychological problems (e.g., overdependency) during childhood and have further consequences throughout development.

parental rejection persistent denial of approval, affection, or care by one or both parents, sometimes concealed beneath a cover of overindulgence or overprotection. The frequent result is corrosion of the child's self-esteem and self-confidence, a poor self-image, inability to form attachments to others, tantrums, generalized hostility, and development of psychophysical and emotional disturbances. See CHILD NEGLECT.

parent–child psychotherapy a psychodynamically informed, attachment-based intervention for infants, toddlers, and preschoolers (i.e., children age 0–5 years) whose behavior and emotions have been adversely affected by negative relationships with their mothers or other primary caregivers. Common difficulties in these young children include oppositionality or aggression, frequent tantrums, eating problems, and sleeping disturbances. In this approach, the therapist offers guidance that helps the parent to recognize recurring perceptions, attributions, affects, and behavioral responses in himself or herself and to understand how these influence the child and contribute to current relationship difficulties. In a typical therapeutic session, the mother and child play together while the therapist comments upon the child's actions and emotions and links these to the parent's past experiences, current stresses, and current attitudes. In thus reflecting upon themselves and becoming aware of their own emotional patterns and behavioral tendencies, parents theoretically become better able to understand what the young child is experiencing and to respond more sensitively to his or her physiological and psychological needs. This in turn theoretically creates a healthier, more loving relationship between the parents and child and consequently improves the child's socioemotional functioning. Parent–child psychotherapy is an extension of the earlier **parent–infant psychotherapy**, developed in the 1970s by U.S. clinical social worker Selma H. Fraiberg (1918–1981). [created by Paraguayan-born U.S. developmental psychologist Alicia F. Lieberman (1947–)]

parent counseling professional guidance of parents on problems related to raising their children, including their own roles in this process.

parent effectiveness training (**PET**) a set of principles providing guidance for prosocial interactions between children and parents related to discipline, communication, and responsible relationships. Guidelines are also provided for client-centered discussions of principles, practices, and problems of child rearing conducted by a mental health professional on a group basis. A balance is maintained between the child's feelings and needs and those of the parents. One of the most notable concepts is to determine who is responsible for (i.e., owns) the problem and who owns the solution for resolving a conflict. [introduced in 1962 by U.S. psychologist Thomas Gordon (1918–2002)]

parenteral drug administration any route of administration of a drug other than via the digestive tract (parenteral literally means not enteric, or not through the gut). Such routes include subcutaneous, intramuscular, and intravenous injection; rectal and vaginal suppositories; inhalation; and absorption through the skin or mucous membranes.

parent image a representation of the parent that exists in the mind of the individual but not necessarily as an accurate image: for example, it may be an idealized version of the real parent.

parenting *n.* all actions related to the raising of offspring. Researchers have described different human **parenting styles**—ways in which parents interact with their children—with most classifications varying on the dimensions of emotional warmth (warm versus cold) and control (high in control versus low in control). One of the most influential of these classifications is that of U.S. developmental psychologist Diana Baumrind (1927–), involving four types of styles: **authoritarian parenting**, in which the parent or caregiver stresses obedience, deemphasizes collaboration and dialogue, and employs strong forms of punishment; **authoritative parenting**, in which the parent or caregiver encourages a child's autonomy yet still places certain limitations on behavior; **permissive parenting**, in which the parent or caregiver is accepting and affirmative, makes few demands, and avoids exercising control; and **rejecting–neglecting parenting**, in which the parent or caregiver is unsupportive, fails to monitor or limit behavior, and is more attentive to his or her needs than those of the child.

Parenting Stress Index (**PSI**) an instrument used to assess stress in parent–child interactions and to identify potentially dysfunctional parenting behaviors or potential behavior problems in the child. It currently consists of 120 questionnaire items to which parents respond using a 5-point LIKERT SCALE format, ranging from "strongly agree" to "strongly disagree." Originally published in 1983, the PSI is now in its third edition (published in 1995). [developed by U.S. educational psychologist Richard R. Abidin (1938–)]

parenting training any program that instructs parents and other caregivers in techniques for effectively dealing with problem behavior in their children. Also called **parent training**.

parent management training a treatment approach based on the principles of OPERANT CONDITIONING. Parents use antecedents, behaviors, and consequences to change child and adolescent behavior at home, at school, and in other settings. The goals are to help children develop prosocial behaviors and decrease oppositional, aggressive, and antisocial behaviors.

Parents Anonymous a peer-led, professionally facilitated group for parents who would like to learn more effective methods of childrearing, thus strengthening families and providing a means of preventing child abuse.

Parents Without Partners an international organization providing mutual social support, educational programs, and activities for single parents and their children.

parergasia *n.* **1.** a symptom of SCHIZOPHRENIA in which the individual performs an action that is not intended, such as opening the mouth when asked to close the eyes. [defined by German psychiatrist Emil Kraepelin (1856–1926)] **2.** a former name for schizophrenia, introduced by Swiss-born U.S. psychiatrist Adolf Meyer (1866–1950) to replace DEMENTIA PRAECOX, since he believed this disorder is best described in terms of disorganized behavior and distorted thought processes.

paresthesia *n.* an abnormal skin sensation, such as tingling, tickling, burning, itching, or pricking, in the absence of external stimulation. Paresthesia may be temporary, as in the "pins and needles" feeling that many people experience (e.g., after having sat with legs crossed too long), or chronic and due to such factors as neurological disorder or drug side effects. **—paresthetic** *adj.*

parica *n.* see EPENA.

parietal lobe one of the four main subdivisions of each cerebral hemisphere. It occupies the upper central area of each hemisphere, behind the FRONTAL LOBE, ahead of the OCCIPITAL LOBE, and above the TEMPORAL LOBE. Parts of the parietal lobe participate in somatosensory activities, such as discrimination of size, shape, and texture of objects; visual activities, such as visually guided actions; and auditory activities, such as speech perception.

parietal neglect see UNILATERAL NEGLECT.

Paris Medical School a group of doctors and students at the Salpêtrière hospital in Paris who advanced the hypotheses and research of French neurologist Jean-Martin Charcot (1825–1893), particularly with regard to his neurological studies of a posited relation between hysteria and hypnotism. Sigmund FREUD, who studied through a fellowship under Charcot, was greatly influenced by the Paris Medical School in his early studies and in the direction of his future work.

Parkes–Weber syndrome see STURGE–WEBER SYNDROME.

parkinsonism *n.* any disorder whose symptoms resemble those of PARKINSON'S DISEASE without the actual presence of the disease entity. Antipsychotic agents with strong dopamine-blocking activity, particularly the HIGH-POTENCY ANTIPSYCHOTICS (e.g., haloperidol), may cause the reversible syndrome known as **drug-induced parkinsonism** (**pseudoparkinsonism**).

Parkinson's disease a progressive neurodegenerative disease caused by the death of dopamine-producing neurons in the SUBSTANTIA NIGRA of the brain, which controls balance and coordinates muscle movement. Symptoms typically begin late in life with mild tremors (see RESTING TREMOR), increasing rigidity of the limbs, and slowness of voluntary movements. Later symptoms include postural instability, impaired balance, and difficulty walking. DEMENTIA occurs in some 20–60% of patients, usually in older patients in whom the disease is far advanced. [first described in 1817 by James **Parkinson** (1755–1824), British physician]

Parlodel *n.* a trade name for BROMOCRIPTINE.

parole *n.* **1.** in psychology and psychiatry, a method of maintaining supervision of a patient whose treatment is mandated by the court and who has not been discharged, but who is away from the confines of a restrictive setting, such as a mental institution or halfway house. A patient on parole may be returned to the hospital at any time without formal action by a court. **2.** supervised release from confinement in a correctional facility.

parorexia *n.* a pathological compulsion to consume unusual foods or nonnutritive substances. See also CISSA; PICA.

paroxetine *n.* an antidepressant of the SSRI class. It is currently one of the most commonly prescribed antidepressants. Like other SSRIs, it is used to treat depression and anxiety disorders, such as panic disorder, social phobia, and obsessive-compulsive disorder. It differs from other SSRIs in that most patients find it to be sedating rather than activating; paroxetine should therefore be taken in the evening rather than on rising. It should not be taken by patients who are already taking MONOAMINE OXIDASE INHIBITORS. Paroxetine is available in immediate- and controlled-release preparations. U.S. trade name: **Paxil**.

paroxysm *n.* **1.** the sudden intensification or recurrence of a disease or an emotional state. **2.** a convulsion, spasm, or seizure. **—paroxysmal** *adj.*

partial agonist a substance that binds to a receptor but fails to produce the same degree of response as a full AGONIST at the same receptor site or exerts only part of the action exerted by the endogenous neurotransmitter that it mimics. Partial agonists may exhibit the same affinity for the receptor site as do full agonists and may act as competitive inhibitors of full agonists. Minor variations in the chemical structure of either the receptor or the binding substance may dictate whether the substance acts as a full or partial agonist at any particular receptor site.

partial correlation the correlation between two variables with the influence of one or more other variables on their intercorrelation statistically removed or held constant.

partial hospitalization hospital treatment of patients on a part-time basis (i.e., less than 24 hours per day). See DAY HOSPITAL; NIGHT HOSPITAL; WEEKEND HOSPITALIZATION.

partial insanity a borderline condition in which mental impairment is present but is not sufficiently severe to render the individual completely irresponsible for his or her criminal acts. In legal proceedings, a conclusion of partial insanity may arise when there is evidence that a mental disorder was probably a contributing cause to a defendant's actions, or that the disorder rendered the individual incapable of deliberation, premeditation, malice, or another mental state usually requisite for first-degree offenses; in such circumstances it may lead to conviction for a lesser offense. See also DIMINISHED RESPONSIBILITY; INSANITY; MCNAUGHTEN RULE.

partial instinct see COMPONENT INSTINCT.

partialism *n.* a type of PARAPHILIA in which a person obtains sexual satisfaction from contact with a body part of the sexual partner other than the usual erotic areas such as lips, breasts, and genitals (e.g., a leg). Partialism is distinguished from FETISHISM in which an object, such as a shoe, replaces the sexual partner.

partial seizure a seizure that begins in a localized area of the brain, although it may subsequently progress to a GENERALIZED SEIZURE. **Simple partial seizures** produce no alteration of consciousness despite clinical manifestations, which may include sensory, motor, or autonomic activity. COMPLEX PARTIAL SEIZURES may produce similar sensory, motor, or autonomic symptoms but are also characterized by some impairment or alteration of consciousness during the event. Partial seizures of both types are most commonly focused in the temporal lobe. Also called **focal seizure**.

participant *n.* a person who takes part in an investigation, study, or experiment, for example by performing tasks set by the experimenter or by answering questions set by a researcher. The participant may be further identified as an **experimental participant** (see EXPERIMENTAL GROUP) or a **control participant** (see CONTROL GROUP). Participants are also called SUBJECTS, although the former term is now often preferred when referring to humans.

participant modeling a procedure for changing behavior in which effective styles of behavior are modeled (i.e., broken down, demonstrated step-by-step, and analyzed) by a therapist for an

P

individual. Various aids are introduced to help the individual master the tasks, such as the viewing of videotaped enactments of effective and ineffective behavioral responses to prototypical situations in a variety of social contexts (e.g., at school or work). [developed by Albert BANDURA]

partner abuse see DOMESTIC VIOLENCE.

part-object *n.* **1.** in psychoanalytic theory, an OBJECT toward which a COMPONENT INSTINCT is directed. Such an object is usually a part of the body rather than a whole person. **2.** in the OBJECT RELATIONS THEORY of Melanie KLEIN, an early object representation that derives from SPLITTING the object into parts containing negative and positive qualities. It is held that such objects constitute the infant's first experience of the world, being perceived as a GOOD OBJECT or a BAD OBJECT according to whether they are gratifying or frustrating. INTERNALIZATION of part-objects is further posited to represent the beginning of the inner world of objects whose relationships create the infant's personality. See also DEPRESSIVE POSITION; PARANOID-SCHIZOID POSITION.

pasmo *n.* see SUSTO.

passionate love a type of love in which sexual passion and a high level of emotional arousal are prominent features; along with COMPANIONATE LOVE, it is one of the two main types of love identified by social psychologists. Passionate lovers typically are greatly preoccupied with the loved person, want their feelings to be reciprocated, and are usually greatly distressed when the relationship seems awry. See also LIMERENCE; ROMANTIC LOVE; TRIANGULAR THEORY OF LOVE.

P

passionflower *n.* a climbing herb, *Passiflora incarnata*, indigenous to the southeastern United States and other subtropical areas but also cultivated as an ornamental plant. Parts of the plant have been used both externally and internally for a variety of medicinal purposes, ranging from treatment of burns and hemorrhoids to the alleviation of neuralgia and spasms or seizures. **Passionflower tea** has long been a folk remedy for the relief of nervous tension. Although some studies suggest passionflower has sedative properties and it has been approved by Commission E, a committee of 24 interdisciplinary health care professionals formed in 1978 by the German Federal Institute for Drugs and Medical Devices, for treatment of insomnia and anxiety, definitive clinical evidence of this effect has not been established. Adverse reactions are rare, but may include nausea, vomiting, and rapid heart rate.

passive *adj.* **1.** acted upon rather than acting. **2.** describing a personality pattern that is submissive, compliant, easily influenced by external forces, and dependent on others. See also DEPENDENT PERSONALITY DISORDER.

passive-aggressive *adj.* characteristic of behavior that is seemingly innocuous, accidental, or neutral but that indirectly displays an unconscious aggressive motive. For example, a child who appears to be compliant but is routinely late for school, misses the bus, or forgets his or her homework may be expressing unconscious resentment at having to attend school.

passive-aggressive personality disorder a personality disorder of long standing in which AMBIVALENCE toward the self and others is expressed by such means as procrastination, dawdling, stubbornness, intentional inefficiency, "forgetting" appointments, or misplacing important materials. These maneuvers are interpreted as passive expressions of underlying ambivalence and NEGATIVISM. The pattern persists even where more adaptive behavior is clearly possible; it frequently interferes with occupational, domestic, and academic success. This disorder is classified in the appendix of *DSM–IV–TR* and given an alternative name, **negativistic personality disorder**, in accordance with the theoretical proposals of U.S. psychologist Theodore Millon (1929–).

passive algolagnia interest and pleasure derived from experiencing pain during sexual activity, that is, from being the masochist in a relationship involving SADOMASOCHISM.

passive avoidance a type of OPERANT CONDITIONING in which the individual must refrain from an explicit act or response that will produce an aversive stimulus. Compare ACTIVE AVOIDANCE.

passive coping a stress-management strategy in which a person absolves himself or herself of responsibility for managing a stressor and instead relinquishes control over its resolution to external resources, such as other people and environmental factors. Individuals who cope passively often withdraw from interpersonal relationships and instead engage in such activities as hoping, praying, or avoiding the stressor. This type of COPING STRATEGY generally is considered maladaptive, having been associated with increased depression, poorer psychological adjustment, and other adverse consequences. It is similar to the earlier conceptualization of EMOTION-FOCUSED COPING but distinguished by its focus upon external factors and abdication of personal responsibility. Compare ACTIVE COPING. [identified in 1987 by Gregory K. Brown and Perry M. Nicassio (1947–), U.S. clinical psychologists]

passive deception the withholding of certain information from research participants, such as not informing them of the full details of the study. Also called **deception by omission**. Compare ACTIVE DECEPTION.

passive-dependent personality see DEPENDENT PERSONALITY DISORDER.

passive euthanasia the intentional withholding of treatment that might prolong the life of a person who is approaching death. It is distinguished from ACTIVE EUTHANASIA, in which direct action (e.g., a lethal injection) is taken to end the life. Courts have ruled that physicians do not have to try every possible intervention to prolong life, but opinions differ on where the line should be drawn. There is also controversy regarding the significance of the passive–active distinction, since both approaches result in shortening the life. See also EUTHANASIA.

passive listening in psychotherapy and counseling, attentive listening by the therapist or counselor without intruding upon or interrupting the client in any way. See also ACTIVE LISTENING.

passive negativism see NEGATIVISM.

passive scopophilia sexual interest in and arousal by having others view one's genitals. Passive scopophilia differs from EXHIBITIONISM in that it usually involves the participation of a consenting partner rather than a stranger.

passive suicide ambiguous behavior that tends to be self-destructive, but not actively so, and is sometimes thought to reflect suicidal intentions. Examples of this behavior include failing to feed oneself or to engage in rudimentary self-care.

passivity *n.* a form of adaptation, or maladaptation, in which the individual adopts a pattern of submissiveness, dependence, and retreat into inaction.

passivity phenomena phenomena in which individuals feel that some aspect of themselves is under the control of others. These aspects can include acts, impulses, movements, emotions, or thoughts; patients typically report feeling that they are being made to do or think things by someone else or that they are experiencing the behaviors or emotions of someone else.

pastoral counseling a form of counseling or psychotherapy in which insights and principles derived from the disciplines of theology and the behavioral sciences are used in working with individuals, couples, families, groups, and social systems to achieve healing and growth. Pastoral counseling is centered in theory and research concerning the interaction of religion and science, spirituality and health, and spiritual direction and psychotherapy. A **pastoral counselor** receives advanced training in one or several of the behavioral sciences (often psychology specifically) in addition to religious training, theological training, or both. Also called **pastoral psychotherapy**.

Patau's syndrome see CHROMOSOME-13 TRISOMY. [Klaus **Patau**, 20th-century U.S. geneticist]

paternal behavior actions by males directed toward care and protection of their young. **Direct paternal behavior** consists of such actions as feeding, carrying, or otherwise nurturing the offspring; **indirect paternal behavior** consists of acquiring resources or defending the group from harm, which indirectly leads to increased survival of the young. Males of species with biparental care undergo some hormonal changes similar to those in females: increased secretion of PROLACTIN and ESTROGENS. Early experience with young offspring is important for competent paternal behavior in many species.

path analysis a set of quantitative procedures used to verify the existence of causal relationships among several variables, the results of which are displayed graphically to show the various hypothesized routes of causal influence. The causal relationships are theoretically determined, and the path analysis determines both the accuracy and the strength of the hypothesized relationships.

pathogen *n.* any agent (e.g., a bacterium or virus) that contributes to disease or otherwise induces unhealthy structural or functional changes. **—pathogenicity** *n.*

pathogenesis *n.* the origination and development of a mental or physical disease or disorder. Also called **nosogenesis**; **pathogeny**. **—pathogenetic** *adj.*

pathogenic family pattern negative or harmful family attitudes, standards, and behavior that lay the groundwork for mental and behavioral disorder. Examples are parental rejection; TRIANGULATION of the child into the marital relationship between the parents; and excessively harsh, excessively lenient, or inconsistent discipline.

pathogeny *n.* see PATHOGENESIS.

pathognomonic *adj.* describing a sign, symptom, or a group of signs or symptoms that is indicative of a specific physical or mental disorder and not associated with other disorders.

pathognomy *n.* the recognition of feelings, emotions, and character traits, particularly when they are signs or symptoms of disease.

pathological aging changes that occur because of age-related disease, as distinct from changes associated with normal healthy aging.

pathological doubt **1.** abnormal concern about having failed to perform a particular action, such as locking the door upon leaving the house. Pathological doubt is a common feature of OBSESSIVE-COMPULSIVE DISORDER. **2.** a negative belief about one's ability or future that often results in the inhibition of behavior and is commonly associated with a MAJOR DEPRESSIVE EPISODE.

pathological fallacy an error of overgeneralization in which pathological characteristics observed in one individual or in a limited group of individuals are extrapolated and attributed to the general population. For example, most non-Freudians contend that Sigmund FREUD's theories are tenuous because they are based on a handful of clinical cases.

pathological gambling an impulse-control disorder characterized by chronic, maladaptive wagering, leading to significant interpersonal, professional, or financial difficulties. In *DSM–*

IV–TR it is included in the category IMPULSE-CONTROL DISORDERS NOT ELSEWHERE CLASSIFIED.

pathological inertia 1. the inability to switch SETS or show flexibility due to a brain injury or psychological condition. **2.** severely impaired initiative, drive, or motivation sometimes associated with brain damage, particularly to the frontal lobes. See ABULIA.

pathological intoxication see IDIOSYNCRATIC INTOXICATION.

pathological jealousy see DELUSIONAL JEALOUSY.

pathological lying a persistent, compulsive tendency to tell lies out of proportion to any apparent advantage that can be achieved. This often occurs among people with alcohol dependence or brain damage, but it is most common among individuals with ANTISOCIAL PERSONALITY DISORDER, who in some cases do not seem to understand the nature of a falsehood. See also PSEUDOLOGIA FANTASTICA.

pathology *n.* **1.** the scientific study of functional and structural changes involved in physical and mental disorders and diseases. **2.** more broadly, any departure from what is considered healthy or adaptive. **—pathological** *adj.* **—pathologist** *n.*

pathomimicry *n.* conscious or unconscious mimicking, production, or feigning of symptoms of disease or disorder. Also called **pathomimesis**. See FACTITIOUS DISORDER; LASTHENIE DE FERJOL SYNDROME; MALINGERING.

pathomiosis *n.* a patient's minimization or denial of his or her illness.

pathophysiology *n.* the functional alterations that appear in an individual or organ as a result of disease or disorder, as distinguished from structural alterations. **—pathophysiological** *adj.*

patient *n.* a person receiving health care from a licensed health professional (including the services of most psychologists and psychiatrists). See INPATIENT; OUTPATIENT. See also PATIENT–CLIENT ISSUE.

patient–client issue the dilemma of how to identify the recipient of psychological services or intervention (i.e., the nomenclature used for the recipient). Psychiatrists, many clinical psychologists, and some other mental health providers tend to follow the traditional language of the medical model and refer to the people seeking their services as patients. Counseling psychologists, some clinical psychologists, social workers, and counselors tend to avoid the word "patient," which is associated with illness and dysfunction, using instead the word client to refer to the person seeking their services.

patients' rights any statement, listing, summary, or the like, that articulates the rights that health care providers (e.g., physicians, medical facilities) ethically ought to provide to those receiving their services in such basic categories as (a) the provision of adequate information regarding benefits, risks, costs, and alternatives; (b) fair treatment (e.g., respect, responsiveness, timely attention to health issues); (c) autonomy over medical decisions (e.g., obtaining full consent for medical interventions); and (d) CONFIDENTIALITY.

patricide *n.* **1.** the murder of one's own father. **2.** a person who murders his or her own father. Compare MATRICIDE. **—patricidal** *adj.*

Pavlov, Ivan Petrovich (1849–1936) Russian physiologist. Pavlov earned a medical degree in 1883 at the Military-Medical Academy of Saint Petersburg and subsequently worked in the laboratories of the German physiologists Rudolph Heidenhain (1834–1897) and Carl Ludwig (1816–1895). He then returned to the Military-Medical Academy, where he remained for the rest of his career. Pavlov's major interest was in the physiology of digestion and the manner in which it is controlled by the nervous system. Although he was awarded the 1904 Nobel Prize in physiology or medicine for his research on the digestive processes, it is for his subsequent research on the conditioned response that he is best known in psychology (see PAVLOVIAN CONDITIONING). His observations led to further experiments that yielded the concepts of the UNCONDITIONED RESPONSE (or reflex), the CONDITIONED STIMULUS, discrimination of stimuli, EXTINCTION of response, and the production and elimination of experimental neuroses in animals. He later focused on human neuroses, developing the theory that they are due to an imbalance between the excitatory and inhibitory functions of the cortex; for this condition he advocated treatment by prolonged sleep, sedatives, and verbal and environmental therapy. **—Pavlovian** *adj.*

Pavlovian conditioning a type of learning in which an initially neutral stimulus—the CONDITIONED STIMULUS (CS)—when paired with a stimulus that elicits a reflex response—the UNCONDITIONED STIMULUS (US)—results in a learned, or conditioned, response (CR) when the CS is presented. For example, the sound of a tone may be used as a CS, and food in a dog's mouth as a US. After repeated pairings, namely, the tone followed immediately by food, the tone, which initially had no effect on salivation (i.e., was neutral with respect to it), will elicit salivation even if the food is not presented. Also called **classical conditioning**; **respondent conditioning**; **Type I conditioning**; **Type S conditioning**. See CONDITIONING. [discovered in the early 20th century by Ivan PAVLOV]

pavor *n.* a frightening dream characterized by its realism and residual feelings of terror on waking. **Pavor nocturnus** occurs during the night (see SLEEP TERROR DISORDER); **pavor diurnus** may occur in young children during a daytime nap. See also NIGHTMARE.

Paxil *n.* a trade name for PAROXETINE.

PCP 1. *n.* 1-(1-*p*henyl*c*yclohexyl)*p*iperidine (phencyclidine): a hallucinogenic drug sometimes referred to as a "psychedelic anesthetic" because it was originally developed as an amnestic analgesic for use in surgical anesthesia and was later found to produce a psychedelic or dissociative reaction. Its medical use was discontinued because of adverse reactions, including agitation, delirium, disorientation, and hallucinations. PCP has a complex mechanism of action. It binds as an ANTAGONIST to the NMDA RECEPTOR; it also acts as a DOPAMINE-RECEPTOR AGONIST and blocks the reuptake of dopamine, norepinephrine, and serotonin, among other actions. Because intoxication with PCP can produce symptoms resembling both the positive and negative symptoms of schizophrenia, some consider it to be a useful drug model of schizophrenia. High doses of PCP may induce stupor or coma. PCP became common as an illicit drug in the 1970s. It can be smoked (often in combination with marijuana or tobacco), insufflated (inhaled nasally), or taken orally or intravenously (see ANGEL DUST). Despite speculation about its potential neurotoxicity (ability to damage nerve tissue), it remains a popular illicit drug. PCP is still used in veterinary medicine, primarily as an immobilizing anesthetic during surgical procedures. See also HALLUCINOGEN. **2.** abbreviation for PRIMARY CARE PROVIDER.

PCP intoxication a reversible syndrome due to the recent ingestion of PCP. It includes clinically significant behavioral or psychological changes (e.g., belligerence, assaultiveness, impulsiveness, unpredictability, PSYCHOMOTOR AGITATION, impaired judgment, and impaired social or occupational functioning), as well as one or more signs of physiological involvement (e.g., vertical or horizontal NYSTAGMUS, hypertension or tachycardia, numbness or diminished responsiveness to pain, unsteady gait, unclear speech, muscle rigidity, seizures, and coma). See also SUBSTANCE INTOXICATION.

PCP intoxication delirium a reversible syndrome that develops over a short period of time (usually hours to days) following heavy PCP consumption. It includes disturbance of consciousness (e.g., reduced ability to focus, sustain, or shift attention), accompanied by changes in cognition (e.g., memory deficit, disorientation, or language disturbance) in excess of those usually associated with PCP INTOXICATION. See also SUBSTANCE INTOXICATION DELIRIUM.

Pcs abbreviation for PRECONSCIOUS.

PD abbreviation for PERSONAL DISPOSITION.

PDAT abbreviation for PRESENILE DEMENTIA OF THE ALZHEIMER'S TYPE.

PDDNOS abbreviation for PERVASIVE DEVELOPMENTAL DISORDER NOT OTHERWISE SPECIFIED.

PDM abbreviation for PSYCHODYNAMIC DIAGNOSTIC MANUAL.

Peabody Picture Vocabulary Test (PPVT) a norm-referenced screening, diagnostic, and progress-monitoring test in which sets of four full-color drawings are presented to the participant, who selects the one that corresponds to a word uttered by the examiner. There are 228 stimulus words each in two parallel forms (A and B) that are administered individually. The test, now in its fourth edition (**PPVT–4**, 2006), may be used with individuals aged 2 years 6 months to over 90 years to assess receptive vocabulary and verbal ability. [originally developed in 1959 by psychologists Lloyd M. Dunn (1917–2006) and Leota M. Dunn (1917–2001) at Peabody College of Vanderbilt University, Nashville]

peak experience in the HUMANISTIC PSYCHOLOGY of U.S. psychologist Abraham Maslow (1908–1970), a moment of awe, ecstasy, or sudden insight into life as a powerful unity transcending space, time, and the self that may at times be experienced by individuals in their pursuit of SELF-ACTUALIZATION. See also BEING COGNITION; TIMELESS MOMENT; TRANSPERSONAL PSYCHOLOGY.

pederasty *n.* anal sexual intercourse, especially between an adult male (**pederast**) and a boy or young man (see CATAMITE). Also called **pedication**.

pediatric *adj.* pertaining to the health and medical care of children or to child development.

pediatric psychology an interdisciplinary field of research and practice that addresses the interaction of physical, behavioral, and emotional development with health and illness issues affecting children, adolescents, and families. Related to the larger field of HEALTH PSYCHOLOGY, pediatric psychology differs not only in its specific focus but also in its emphasis on the child in the contexts of the family, school, and health care settings. The field tends to take a normative developmental view of adaptation based on physical conditions, medical treatment, and psychosocial interactions with family and peers, rather than a psychopathological view of adjustment to disease and disorders.

pediatric psychopharmacology the branch of pharmacology that is involved in the understanding and administration of drugs used in the treatment of mental and behavioral disorders of childhood and adolescence. It helps determine the choice of drug according to the age of the child, the diagnosis, the duration of the disorder, the severity of the illness, and the availability of the patient for behavioral and laboratory monitoring of the drug effects.

pedication *n.* see PEDERASTY.

pedigree *n.* **1.** in medical genetics, a pictoral representation of the history of an illness in a family. It depicts the relationship of family members and—for each member—current status (alive or not), the date of diagnosis, kind of relevant illness, and age at diagnosis. Geneticists can often estimate a family member's likelihood of developing the disease from reviewing such a pedi-

P

gree. **2.** family lineage or ancestry, especially when this is regarded as distinguished or notable.

pedomorphism *n.* the attribution of childish behavior characteristics to adults. Compare ADULTOMORPHISM. **—pedomorphic** *adj.*

pedomorphosis *n.* the retention of juvenile characteristics in adult organisms.

pedophilia *n.* a PARAPHILIA in which sexual acts or fantasies with prepubertal children are the persistently preferred or exclusive method of achieving sexual excitement. The children are usually many years younger than the **pedophile** (or **pedophiliac**). Sexual activity may consist of looking and touching but sometimes includes intercourse, even with very young children. Pedophilia is rarely seen in women. **—pedophilic** *adj.*

peduncular hallucinosis recurrent visual hallucinations caused by pathological processes in the upper brainstem, which indirectly affect the central visual system. The hallucinations, which may be long-lasting, vivid, and scenic, are often accompanied by agitation and sleep disturbances. The hallucinations are usually recognized as such by the patient, who may see a panorama of people and events from his or her past life. Peduncular hallucinosis may be mixed with nonhallucinatory perceptions.

peer counseling counseling by an individual who has a status equal to that of the client, such as a college student trained to counsel other students or an employee trained to counsel his or her coworkers.

peer pressure the influence exerted by a peer group on its individual members to fit in with or adapt to group expectations by thinking, feeling, and (most importantly) behaving in a similar or acceptable manner (see CONFORMITY). Peer pressure may have positive SOCIALIZATION value but may also have negative consequences for mental or physical health. Also called **peer-group pressure**.

P

pegboard test a test of manual dexterity and fine motor speed in which the participant—first with his or her dominant hand, then with the nondominant hand, and finally with both hands—inserts pegs in a series of holes as rapidly as possible. One of the best known examples is the **Purdue Pegboard Test** (developed at Purdue University, West Lafayette, Indiana).

pejorism *n.* severe PESSIMISM.

pellagra *n.* deficiency of the B vitamin nicotinic acid (niacin), marked by weakness, gastrointestinal disturbances, skin disorders, and neurological symptoms, for example, apathy, confusion, disorientation, and neuritis. Also called **nicotinic acid deficiency**.

pemoline *n.* a nonamphetamine CNS STIMULANT used for the management of attention-deficit/hyperactivity disorder (ADHD). Its effects resemble those of the AMPHETAMINES and METHYLPHENIDATE, and its mechanism of action includes blockade of dopamine reuptake. Pemoline has been associated with rare but occasionally fatal liver failure and with the development of TOURETTE'S DISORDER. Safety concerns led to its withdrawal from the Canadian market in 1999 and the U.S. market in 2005. U.S. trade name (among others): **Cylert**.

PEN acronym for psychoticism, extraversion, neuroticism. See EYSENCK'S TYPOLOGY.

penetration *n.* the entry of the penis into the vagina. In the United States, legal definitions in cases of rape or illicit intercourse vary from state to state, but penetration is generally considered to have occurred if the glans penis passes beyond the labia majora. In some states, if penetration has not occurred during sexual assault, there cannot be a charge of rape. In such cases, the crime is some variety of felonious sexual assault, which usually has lower penalties than rape.

penetration response a response in a projective test that can be interpreted to contain a suggestion of weakness or penetrability (e.g., "a hole in the wall"). Such interpretation ultimately derives from an imprecise use of the psychoanalytic concept of PROJECTION and is of limited validity.

penile prosthesis an implanted device that is used to restore male sexual potency. Such devices are typically either made of malleable material or are inflatable, and their insertion requires surgery.

penilingus *n.* see FELLATIO.

penis envy in the classic psychoanalytic theory of Sigmund FREUD, the hypothesized desire of girls and women to possess a male genital organ. Freud held it to originate in the PHALLIC STAGE, between ages 3 and 6, when the girl discovers that she lacks this organ, and further posited that the girl feels "handicapped and ill-treated," blames her mother for the loss, and wants to have her penis back. German-born U.S. psychoanalyst Karen D. Horney (1885–1952), among others, later argued that penis envy is not an envy of the biological organ itself but represents women's envy of men's superior social status. In any sense, the concept has been actively disputed from the beginning and is rarely considered seriously in current psychology. See also CASTRATION COMPLEX.

Pennhurst Consent Decree a judicial decree ordering the closure of the Pennhurst State School and Hospital in Philadelphia, Pennsylvania, and the movement of its residents with mental retardation to least restrictive environments within the community. The decree further ordered team planning for individual movement to the community, provision of case management, and establishment of individual habilitation plans. The decree was based on the court's determination that conditions at the facility were dangerous to the well-being of residents and violated the due process and equal protection clauses of the U.S. Constitution and other federal and state legislation. The Pennhurst facility closed in 1980. See also YOUNGBERG V. ROMEO.

pentazocine *n.* see OPIOID ANTAGONIST.

pentobarbital *n.* a short- to intermediate-acting BARBITURATE formerly in common use as a sedative and hypnotic drug. Like all barbiturates, it has been supplanted by safer agents, such as the benzodiazepines. It is still used in the induction of anesthesia and very rarely in the treatment of a specific epileptic condition; otherwise it has no mental health applications. It was formerly used in psychotherapy to make clients less inhibited and therefore able to express themselves more effectively, but this use has been discredited. U.S. trade name: **Nembutal**.

Pentothal *n.* a trade name for THIOPENTAL.

people-first language language that places a person before his or her disability by describing what a person has rather than equating the person with the disability. Examples of the use of such language include "a child with a learning disability" (rather than "a learning-disabled child"), "a child with Down syndrome" (rather than "a Down child"), and "a person who uses a wheelchair" (rather than "a wheelchair-bound person").

peptide *n.* a short chain of AMINO ACIDS linked by **peptide bonds**. Peptides are usually identified by the number of amino acids in the chain, for example, dipeptides have two, tripeptides three, tetrapeptides four, and so on. See also PROTEIN.

perceived reality a person's subjective experience of reality, in contrast to objective, external reality. Client-centered, humanistic-existential, and related phenomenological theories propose that individuals behave in accordance with perceived, rather than objective, reality.

perceived risk the extent to which individuals feel they are subject to a health threat. Risk is a joint function of the probability of occurrence of a negative event and the magnitude of its consequence.

perceived self the subjective appraisal of personal qualities that one ascribes to oneself.

perceived self-efficacy an individual's subjective perception of his or her capability for performance in a given setting or ability to attain desired results, proposed by Albert BANDURA as a primary determinant of emotional and motivational states and behavioral change.

perceived susceptibility a subjective estimate of the likelihood of personally contracting a disease, without any consideration of severity. Also called **perceived vulnerability**.

percentile *n.* the location of a score in a distribution coded to reflect the percentage of cases in the set that have scores equal to or below the score in question. Thus, if a score is said to be at the 90th percentile, the implication is that 90% of the scores in the set are equal to or lower than that score.

percept *n.* the product of PERCEPTION: the stimulus object or event as experienced by the individual.

perception *n.* the process or result of becoming aware of objects, relationships, and events by means of the senses, which includes such activities as recognizing, observing, and discriminating. These activities enable organisms to organize and interpret the stimuli received into meaningful knowledge.

perceptual defense in psychoanalytic theory, a misperception that occurs when anxiety-arousing stimuli are unconsciously distorted. If taboo words are rapidly presented, they may be misinterpreted; for example, if the stimulus word *anal* is presented, participants may report seeing the innocuous *canal*.

perceptual distortion an inaccurate interpretation of perceptual experience. Examples include the distorted images produced by dreams or hallucinogenic drugs, geometric illusions, visions occurring in states of sensory deprivation or dehydration, and distortions produced by modifying auditory stimuli. Perceptual distortion may also occur as a consequence of acquired brain injury.

perceptual expansion 1. the development of the ability to recognize, interpret, and organize intellectual, emotional, and sensory data in a meaningful way. **2.** the enriched understanding of experience that takes place in psychotherapy when greater INSIGHT is achieved through the therapeutic dynamic and process.

P

perceptualization *n.* **1.** see PERCEPTUAL ORGANIZATION. **2.** in schizophrenia, the transformation of abstract concepts into specific perceptions. For example, an individual who thinks poorly of him- or herself may later experience hallucinations that bad odors are emanating from his or her body; the rotten personality becomes the rotten body that smells. Perceptualization is the most advanced level of ACTIVE CONCRETIZATION. [defined by Italian-born U.S. psychiatrist Silvano Arieti (1914–1982)]

perceptual neglect see NEGLECT.

perceptual organization the process enabling such properties as structure, pattern, and form to be imposed on the senses to provide conceptual organization. Each of the senses establishes (or learns) such organizational schemata. According to traditional GESTALT PSYCHOLOGY, the parts of a group are organized to form whole figures that constitute more than the parts separately (see GESTALT PRINCIPLES OF ORGANIZATION). Recent research has more precisely defined the properties that enable such organized tasks. Artists have traditionally used the principles of perceptual organization to create desired moods or feelings and to challenge viewers' expectations. Also called **perceptualization**.

perceptual schema a mental model that provides a FRAME OF REFERENCE for interpreting information entering the mind through the senses or for activating an expectation of how a particular perceptual scene may look. See SCHEMA.

perceptual sensitization the lowering of an individual's sensory thresholds for events that are emotionally sensitive or threatening.

perceptual set 1. a temporary readiness to perceive certain objects or events rather than others. For example, a person driving a car has a perceptual set to identify anything that might impact his or her safety. See SET. **2.** a SCHEMA or FRAME OF REFERENCE that influences the way in which a person perceives objects, events, or people. For example, an on-duty police officer and a painter might regard a crowded street scene with very different perceptual sets.

perceptual sociogram see SOCIOGRAM.

perceptual style the characteristic way in which an individual attends to, selects, alters, and interprets sensory stimuli. Some believe perceptual functions are distorted among individuals manifesting various forms of psychological dysfunction.

perceptual transformation 1. any modification in a PERCEPT produced by (a) an addition to, deletion from, or alteration in a physical stimulus or (b) a novel interpretation of the stimulus, a change in a SET or attitude, or a sudden insight concerning the material. **2.** a change in the way a problem, event, or person is perceived by the inclusion of new information or a different perspective.

perdida del alma see SUSTO.

peregrination *n.* widespread or excessive traveling from place to place. Peregrination is one of the essential features of MUNCHAUSEN SYNDROME: The individual feels impelled to travel from town to town or from hospital to hospital in order to find a new audience every time the false nature of the illness is discovered. Also called **itinerancy**.

perfectionism *n.* the tendency to demand of others or of oneself an extremely high or even flawless level of performance, particularly when this is not required by the situation. It is thought by some to be a risk factor for depression and other disorders. **—perfectionist** *adj., n.*

performance anxiety anxiety associated with the apprehension and fear of the consequences of being unable to perform a task or of performing the task at a level that will lead to expectations of higher levels of performance achievement. TEST ANXIETY is a common example of performance anxiety. Other examples include fear of public speaking, participating in classes or meetings, playing a musical instrument in public, or even eating in public. If the fear associated with performance anxiety is focused on negative evaluation by others, embarrassment, or humiliation, the anxiety may be classified as a SOCIAL PHOBIA.

performance assessment an appraisal of growth or deterioration in learning, memory, or both through performance on ability and achievement tests.

performance goal 1. in the motivational theory of U.S. personality psychologist Carol Dweck (1946–), the goal of demonstrating to others who may be evaluating one's performance that one possesses a particular ability or other attribute. This is in contrast to a LEARNING GOAL, in which one aims to develop an ability or attribute. **2.** a goal that is set in terms of a specific level of achievement, such as running a mile in 5 min 30 s.

performance test any test of ability requiring primarily motor, rather than verbal, responses, such as a test requiring manipulation of a variety of different kinds of objects.

periaqueductal gray (**PAG**) a region of the brainstem, rich in nerve cell bodies (i.e., gray matter), that surrounds the cerebral aqueduct. A component of the LIMBIC SYSTEM, it plays an important role in organizing defensive behaviors (e.g., freezing). Also called **central gray**.

perinatal herpes-virus infection a complication of infection with herpes simplex Type 2 in which the virus in a pregnant woman may be transmitted to the fetus. The fetal infection may develop into a severe blood disorder and can also result in a fatal form of encephalitis. The complication is most likely to develop in late pregnancy. See HERPES INFECTION.

periodicity *n.* the state of recurring more or less regularly, that is, at intervals.

peripheral anticholinergic syndrome see ANTICHOLINERGIC SYNDROME.

peripheral dyslexia a form of acquired dyslexia (see ALEXIA) that is characterized by difficulties in processing the visual aspects of words (e.g., difficulties identifying letter forms) and results from damage to the visual analysis system. Compare CENTRAL DYSLEXIA.

peripheral dysostosis with nasal hypoplasia a congenital abnormality characterized by short, wide hands and feet and a short, flat nose with nostrils bent forward. Most affected individuals show some degree of mental retardation. Because of foot anomalies, learning to walk may be slow.

peripheralism *n.* the view of some behaviorists that emphasizes events at the periphery of an organism, such as the skeletal and laryngeal muscles and sex organs, rather than the functions of the central nervous system. For example, John B. WATSON believed (falsely) that thinking was not a function taking place in the brain but involved minute movements of the vocal apparatus (subvocal speech) and thus was an objective behavior. Also called **peripheralistic psychology**. Compare CENTRALISM.

peripheral nervous system (**PNS**) the portion of the nervous system that lies outside the brain and spinal cord, that is, all parts outside the CENTRAL NERVOUS SYSTEM. Afferent fibers of the PNS bring messages from the sense organs to the central nervous system; efferent fibers transmit messages from the central nervous system to the muscles and glands. It includes the CRANIAL NERVES, SPINAL NERVES, and parts of the AUTONOMIC NERVOUS SYSTEM.

peripheral neuropathy a neuromuscular disorder of the extremities caused by damage to the peripheral nervous system and usually characterized by weakness, numbness, clumsiness, and sensory loss. Causes are numerous and include diabetes, nutritional deficiencies, injury or trauma, and exposure to toxic substances. It is seen in 5–15% of chronic alcoholics (see ALCOHOLIC NEUROPATHY).

peritraumatic dissociation a transient dissociative experience (see DISSOCIATION) that occurs at or around the time of a traumatic event. Affected individuals may feel as if they are watching the trauma occur to someone else, as if in a movie, or they may feel "spaced out" and disoriented after the trauma. The occurrence of peritraumatic dissociation is a predictor for the later development of POSTTRAUMATIC STRESS DISORDER.

permeable family a more fluid and flexible version of the NUCLEAR FAMILY that some sociologists regard as an emerging norm in contemporary Western society. The permeable family differs from the stereotypical nuclear family in five main areas: (a) the greater variety of family structures produced by divorce, remarriage, and the acceptance of COHABITATION and single-parent families; (b) a looser sense of family boundaries, so that the offspring of former relationships may be regarded as part of the family unit for some purposes but not for others (see BOUNDARY AMBIGUITY); (c) the erosion of traditional sex roles within the family and the greater role played by women in the workforce; (d) the erosion of a sense of hierarchy and deference within the family, so that children and teenagers expect greater freedom and respect for their views and preferences; and (e) the tendency for all members of the family to expect greater autonomy, so that individual activities sometimes take precedence over shared pursuits and rituals (e.g., family meals). See also STEPFAMILY.

perphenazine *n.* a conventional (typical or first-generation) ANTIPSYCHOTIC agent of the piperazine PHENOTHIAZINE class. It is used for the treatment of schizophrenia, and its efficacy and side effects are similar to those of other phenothiazines. As with all phenothiazines, long-term use may be associated with the production of TARDIVE DYSKINESIA or other neuromuscular deficits. U.S. trade name: **Trilafon**.

persecution delusional disorder a type of DELUSIONAL DISORDER in which the central delusion is persecutory (e.g., that one is being plotted against).

persecutory delusion see DELUSION OF PERSECUTION.

perseverance *n.* see PERSISTENCE.

perseverance effect the phenomenon in which people's beliefs about themselves and others persist despite a lack of supporting evidence or even a contradiction of supporting evidence.

perseveration *n.* **1.** in neuropsychology, the inappropriate repetition of behavior that is often associated with damage to the FRONTAL LOBE of the brain. **2.** an inability to interrupt a task or to shift from one strategy or procedure to another. Perseveration may be observed, for example, in workers under extreme task demands or environmental conditions. **3.** the repetition, after a learning experience, of neural processes that are responsible for memory formation, which is necessary for the consolidation of LONG-TERM MEMORY. **4.** in speech and language, the persistence of abnormal or inappropriate repetition of a sound, word, or phrase, as occurs in stuttering. **—perseverate** *vb.*

persistence *n.* **1.** continuance or repetition of a particular behavior, process, or activity despite cessation of the initiating stimulus. **2.** the quality or state of maintaining a course of action or keeping at a task and finishing it despite the obstacles (such as opposition or discouragement) or the effort involved. Also called **industriousness**; **perseverance**. **—persistent** *adj.*

persistent puberism a condition in which secondary sexual characteristics become arrested in development and individuals remain in effect pubescent for the rest of their lives.

persistent vegetative state (**PVS**) a prolonged biomedical condition in which rudimentary brain function and, usually, spontaneous respiration continue but there is no awareness of self or environment, no communication, and no voluntary response to stimuli. The condition should be distinguished from BRAIN DEATH. Young trauma victims have sometimes recovered from PVS, but adults rarely recover after 3 months in this state. The term **permanent vegetative state** is sometimes used for people who have been in PVS for an extended period.

persona *n.* in the ANALYTIC PSYCHOLOGY of Carl JUNG, the public face an individual presents to the outside world, in contrast to more deeply rooted and authentic personality characteristics. This sense has now passed into popular usage. The term is taken from the mask worn by actors in Roman antiquity.

personal adjustment **1.** adaptation by an individual to living and working conditions in his or her family and community, especially in respect of social interactions with those with whom regular personal contacts are necessary.

2. the degree to which a person is able to cope with the demands of life.

personal audit an oral or written interview or questionnaire designed to encourage individuals to assess their own personal strengths and weaknesses.

personal construct one of the concepts by which an individual perceives, understands, predicts, and attempts to control the world. Understanding a client's personal constructs is a central way of beginning to help that person change rigid or negative beliefs. See REPERTORY GRID. [formulated by U.S. psychologist George A. Kelly (1905–1967)]

personal construct therapy a therapy based on the concept of the PERSONAL CONSTRUCT. The essence of the approach is to help individuals test the usefulness and validity of their constructs and to revise and elaborate them as necessary to enhance their understanding and positive interpretations of and interactions with the world. [developed in the 1950s by U.S. psychologist George A. Kelly (1905–1967)]

personal disjunction an individual's feeling or perception of dissimilarity or discrepancy between what is or might be and the objective reality or likelihood.

personal disposition (**PD**) in the personality theory of Gordon W. ALLPORT, any of a number of enduring characteristics that describe or determine an individual's behavior across a variety of situations and that are peculiar to and uniquely expressed by that individual. Personal dispositions are divided into three categories according to their degree of influence on the behavior of the person possessing them. **Cardinal dispositions**, such as a thirst for power, are so pervasive as to influence virtually every behavior of that person; **central dispositions**, such as friendliness, are less pervasive but nonetheless generally influential and easy to identify; and **secondary dispositions**, such as a tendency to keep a neat desk, are much more narrowly expressed and situation specific.

personal documents writings (diaries, letters, essays, etc.), recordings, and similar material produced by a person that, when examined in **personal-document analysis**, may provide insights into that person's personality, values, attitudes, beliefs, fears, and so forth.

personal fable a belief in one's uniqueness and invulnerability, which is an expression of adolescent egocentrism and may extend further into the lifespan.

personal-growth group a small group of individuals that uses "encounter" methods, such as games, confrontation, and reenactment, for self-discovery and the development of the members' potential. See also ENCOUNTER GROUP; HUMAN-POTENTIAL MOVEMENT.

personal-growth laboratory a sensitivity-training course or group (see SENSITIVITY TRAINING) that seeks to develop the participants' capabilities for constructive relationships, creative effort, leadership, and understanding of others. This is achieved by various methods, such as art activities, intellectual discussions, sensory stimulation, and emotional interactions.

personal identity see IDENTITY.

personalism *n.* **1.** the philosophical position that human personality is the sole means through which reality can be understood or interpreted. At the core of this approach is the concept of the person as a unique living whole irreducible in value or worth, who is striving toward goals and is simultaneously self-contained yet open to the world around him or her. Personalism thus reorients the material of psychology around an experiencing individual as a systematic focal point. In other words, the findings of psychology can be organized only by reference to such a unique, living individual as the originator, carrier, and regulator of all psychological states and processes. This school of psychology stressing individual personality is more properly termed personalistic psychology. **2.** a tendency to believe that another person's actions are directed at oneself rather than being an expression of that individual's characteristics.

personalistic psychology a school of psychology in which the primary emphasis is on personality as the core of psychology (see PERSONALISM), the uniqueness of every human being, and the study of an individual's traits (and organization of traits) as the key to personality and adjustment to the environment. Personalistic psychology originated with German psychologists Eduard Spranger (1882–1963), Louis William Stern (1871–1938), and other Europeans and was developed in the United States by Gordon ALLPORT.

personality *n.* the configuration of characteristics and behavior that comprises an individual's unique adjustment to life, including major traits, interests, drives, values, self-concept, abilities, and emotional patterns. Personality is generally viewed as a complex, dynamic integration or totality, shaped by many forces, including: hereditary and constitutional tendencies; physical maturation; early training; identification with significant individuals and groups; culturally conditioned values and roles; and critical experiences and relationships. Various theories explain the structure and development of personality in different ways but all agree that personality helps determine behavior. See also PERSONALITY DEVELOPMENT; PERSONALITY PSYCHOLOGY; PERSONALITY STRUCTURE.

personality assessment the evaluation of such factors as intelligence, skills, interests, aptitudes, creative abilities, attitudes, and facets of psychological development by a variety of techniques. These include (a) observational methods that use behavior sampling, interviews, and rating scales; (b) personality inventories, such as

P

the MINNESOTA MULTIPHASIC PERSONALITY INVENTORY; and (c) projective techniques, such as the RORSCHACH INKBLOT TEST and THEMATIC APPERCEPTION TEST. The uses of personality assessment are manifold, for example, in clinical evaluation of children and adults; in educational and vocational counseling; in industry and other organizational settings; and in rehabilitation.

personality breakdown a disintegration of personality structure and defenses that results in maladaptive and regressive behavior.

personality change a modification of psychological functioning in relation to personality that could be manifested in many ways. For example, there may be a change in the degree to which one is shy versus socially open or a shift in how internally controlled versus externally determined one views events and behavior.

personality correlates 1. personality traits that are associated with a particular illness or disorder. For example, personality correlates of stress sensitivity may include introversion, obsession, and dependency. **2.** variables that correlate with measures of personality. Correlations between personality traits and observed behaviors, for example, provide evidence for the validity of measures of such traits.

personality deterioration a progressive decline in an individual's sense of personal identity, self-worth, motivational forces, and emotional life to the point at which he or she appears to be a "changed person" or even a "nonperson." See DETERIORATION.

personality development the gradual development of personality in terms of characteristic emotional responses or temperament, a recognizable style of life, personal roles and role behaviors, a set of values and goals, typical patterns of adjustment, characteristic interpersonal relations and sexual relationships, characteristic traits, and a relatively fixed self-image. See also PERSONALITY PSYCHOLOGY; PERSONALITY STRUCTURE.

personality disintegration a rapid breakdown in personality, cohesion, and functioning, usually owing to particularly stressful life circumstances.

personality disorder a group of disorders involving pervasive patterns of perceiving, relating to, and thinking about the environment and the self that interfere with long-term functioning of the individual and are not limited to isolated episodes. *DSM–IV–TR* recognizes 10 specific personality disorders—paranoid, schizoid, schizotypal, histrionic, narcissistic, antisocial, borderline, avoidant, dependent, and obsessive-compulsive—each of which has its own entry in the dictionary.

personality-guided therapy a therapeutic framework that considers an understanding of each individual's unique cognitive, affective, and behavioral traits to be essential for effective clinical treatment. According to this approach, psychopathology emerges from poorly functioning personality systems. Thus, to best facilitate a client's long-term recovery and return to healthy functioning, the approach does not address symptoms per se but rather focuses on changing the underlying ways of thinking, feeling, perceiving, and relating that are associated with the pathology. Once a practitioner becomes familiar with the whole person, he or she may then selectively apply various therapeutic techniques and perspectives (cognitive–behavioral, humanistic, psychodynamic, etc.) if and when appropriate to a given personality system. For example, a nurturing, supportive approach to treating depression would be appropriate for clients with dependent personalities (who feel helpless and fear abandonment) but not for those with antisocial personalities (who are exploitative and impulsive). [introduced in 1999 by U.S. psychologist Theodore Millon (1929–)]

personality inventory a personality assessment device that usually consists of a series of statements covering various characteristics and behavioral patterns to which the participant responds by fixed answers, such as True, False, Always, Often, Seldom, or Never, as applied to himself or herself. The scoring of such tests is objective, and the results are interpreted according to standardized norms. An example is the MINNESOTA MULTIPHASIC PERSONALITY INVENTORY.

personality processes the dynamics of personality functioning, that is, personality systems that change over time and across situations as the individual interacts with different people and events in the environment. Personality processes are usually contrasted with PERSONALITY STRUCTURE, that is, the stable, enduring elements of an individual's personality.

personality profile a presentation of the results of psychological testing in graphic form so as to provide a summary of a person's TRAITS or other unique attributes and tendencies. Personality profiles are used to summarize the characteristics of groups of individuals as well (e.g., people with a particular disorder, people employed in a particular profession).

personality psychology the systematic study of the human personality, including (a) the nature and definition of personality; (b) its maturation and development; (c) the structure of the self; (d) key theories (e.g., trait theories, psychoanalytic theories, role theories, learning theories, type theories); (e) personality disorders; (f) individual differences; and (g) personality tests and measurements. Personality psychologists tend to study more-or-less enduring and stable individual differences in adults and have traditionally assigned a central role to human motivation and the internal dynamics of human behavior, including both conscious and unconscious motivational forces, factors, and conflicts. Personality theories aim to synthesize cognitive, emotional, motivational, developmental, and social aspects of human individuality into integrative frameworks for making sense of the individual human life. The major families of personality theories include the psychodynamic, behavioral, and humanistic families.

personality structure the organization of the personality in terms of its basic components and their relationship to each other. Structural theories vary widely according to their key concepts, for example, clusters of PERSONALITY TRAITS in Gordon ALLPORT's approach; the surface traits and source traits in CATTELL'S PERSONALITY TRAIT THEORY; the ID, EGO, and SUPEREGO of Sigmund FREUD; the individual style of life of Alfred ADLER's approach; and needs and motivations in MASLOW'S MOTIVATIONAL HIERARCHY.

personality test any instrument used to help evaluate personality or measure PERSONALITY TRAITS. Personality tests may be self-reports, in which participants answer questions about their personality or select items that describe themselves, or they may take the form of projective tests (see PROJECTIVE TECHNIQUE), which claim to measure unconscious aspects of a participant's personality.

personality trait a relatively stable, consistent, and enduring internal characteristic that is inferred from a pattern of behaviors, attitudes, feelings, and habits in the individual. Personality traits can be useful in summarizing, predicting, and explaining an individual's conduct, and a variety of **personality trait theories** exist, among them ALLPORT'S PERSONALITY TRAIT THEORY and CATTELL'S PERSONALITY TRAIT THEORY. However, because they do not explain the proximal causes of behavior nor provide a developmental account, they must be supplemented by dynamic and processing concepts, such as motives, schemas, plans, projects, and life stories.

personality type any of the specific categories into which human beings may be classified on the basis of personality traits, attitudes, behavior patterns, physique (see CONSTITUTIONAL TYPE), or other outstanding characteristics. Examples are the INTROVERSION–EXTRAVERSION distinction and FUNCTIONAL TYPES of Carl JUNG and Erich FROMM's character types, such as the EXPLOITATIVE ORIENTATION and MARKETING ORIENTATION.

Personal Orientation Inventory (**POI**) an inventory intended to measure SELF-ACTUALIZATION. Originally developed in 1966, it consists of 150 items that each contain two statements descriptive of values or behavior. For each item, the participant selects the statement most descriptive of him- or herself. The POI is scored for 2 major scales (time ratio, support ratio) plus 10 subscales: self-actualizing value, existentiality, feeling reactivity, spontaneity, self-regard, self-acceptance, nature of man, synergy, acceptance of aggression, and capacity for intimate contact. [developed by U.S. psychologist Everett L. Shostrom (1921–1992)]

personal plan 1. a conception of one's future that includes goals to be achieved. **2.** in psychotherapy, a written plan of intervention and action developed for a client with the participation of all parties concerned. Usually compiled with reference to diagnostic and other data relevant to the client's situation, it identifies a continuum of development outlining progressive steps to be achieved by the client.

personal projects the aims of an individual that involve an organized set of activities of personal relevance over an extended period. [analyzed by Canadian personality psychologist Brian R. Little]

personal strivings personal goal systems that involve multiple interrelated aims, some of which may support one another while others may be in conflict. [analyzed by U.S. personality psychologist Robert A. Emmons (1958–)]

personal therapy see INDIVIDUAL THERAPY.

personal unconscious in the ANALYTIC PSYCHOLOGY of Carl JUNG, the portion of each individual's unconscious that contains the elements of his or her own experience as opposed to the COLLECTIVE UNCONSCIOUS, which contains the ARCHETYPES universal to humankind. The personal unconscious consists of everything subliminal, forgotten, and repressed in an individual's life. Some of these contents may be recalled to consciousness, as in Sigmund FREUD's notion of the PRECONSCIOUS, but others cannot and are truly unconscious. The personal unconscious also contains COMPLEXES based on the individual's personal experience. In Jung's view the personal unconscious must be integrated into the conscious EGO for INDIVIDUATION to occur.

person-centered planning an individual planning process that focuses on people's gifts, strengths, preferences, and achievements. In the case of a person with a developmental disability, emphasis is placed on the person, his or her family members, and the supports needed to enable the person to make choices, participate in the community, and achieve dignity. The process requires an extended commitment from participants and the development of an action-oriented plan. Methods of person-centered planning include Essential Lifestyles Planning, Making Action Plans (MAPS), Personal Future Planning, Planning Alternative Tomorrows With Hope (PATH), and Whole Life Planning. See also PERSON-CENTERED TEAM.

person-centered team a group of people who meet periodically in order to develop plans for supports and services to enhance the lifestyle and self-determination of someone with mental retardation or a related condition. The team uses methods based on principles of PERSON-CENTERED PLANNING. Team participants are invited by the person with mental retardation or his or her advocate, rather than by a service organization or agency, and they need not be trained professionals in human services.

person-centered therapy see CLIENT-CENTERED THERAPY.

person–environment interaction the relationship between a person's psychological and physical capacities and the demands placed on those capacities by the person's social and physical environment in which an "environmental press," or a stimulus or situation, arouses a need, especially for adaptation. Quality of life is strongly influenced by **person–environment congruence**: Too little or too much environmental press can lead to poor quality of life.

personification *n.* **1.** in the approach of U.S. psychoanalyst Harry Stack Sullivan (1892–1949), the pattern of feelings and attitudes toward another person arising out of interpersonal relations with him or her. **2.** a person viewed as representing or embodying some quality, thing, or idea. **—personify** *vb.*

person in the patient in the psychosomatic approach to therapy, the role of the patient's personality, character, and emotional factors as causative agents.

personology *n.* **1.** the study of personality from the holistic point of view, based on the theory that an individual's actions and reactions, thoughts and feelings, and personal and social functioning can be understood only in terms of the whole person. **2.** the theory of personality as a set of enduring tendencies that enable individuals to adapt to life, proposed by U.S. psychologist Henry Alexander Murray (1893–1988). According to Murray, personality is also a mediator between the individual's fundamental needs, both viscerogenic (see VISCEROGENIC NEED) and psychogenic (see PSYCHOGENIC NEED), and the demands of the environment.

person-years *pl. n.* the sum of the number of years that each individual in a population of interest has been affected by an event, occurrence, or condition of interest (e.g., by a particular disorder or disease or by a certain treatment protocol).

perspective *n.* **1.** the ability to view objects, events, and ideas in realistic proportions and relationships. **2.** the capacity of an individual to take into account and potentially understand the perceptions, attitudes, or behaviors of him- or herself and of other individuals.

perspective taking looking at a situation from a viewpoint that is different from one's usual viewpoint. This may involve adopting the perspective of another person or that associated with a particular social role, as in role play exercises.

perspectivism *n.* a philosophical position applied to psychotherapy in which it is assumed that there is no objective, context-independent truth. [derived from the work of German philosopher Friedrich Nietzsche (1844–1900)]

persuasion therapy a type of SUPPORTIVE PSYCHOTHERAPY in which the therapist attempts to induce the client to modify faulty attitudes and behavior patterns by appealing to the client's powers of reasoning, will, and self-criticism. The technique was advocated by Alfred ADLER and others, notably Swiss-born French physicians Paul-Charles Dubois (1848–1918) and Joseph Jules Déjerine (1849–1917), as a briefer alternative to reconstructive methods (see RECONSTRUCTIVE PSYCHOTHERAPY) in some therapies.

perturbation *n.* **1.** an anxious or distressed mental state. In the context of a completed or attempted suicide, it is a measure of the extent to which a person is (or was) upset or disturbed. **2.** an influence or activity that causes an interruption or interference in a mental or physical phenomenon or system.

pervasive developmental disorder any one of a class of disorders characterized by severe and widespread impairment in social interaction and verbal or nonverbal communication or the presence of stereotyped behavior, interests, and activities. These disorders are frequently apparent from an early age; they include ASPERGER'S DISORDER, AUTISTIC DISORDER, CHILDHOOD DISINTEGRATIVE DISORDER, and RETT SYNDROME. This term is synonymous with AUTISTIC SPECTRUM DISORDER.

pervasive developmental disorder not otherwise specified (**PDDNOS**) in *DSM–IV–TR*, a residual category comprising PERVASIVE DEVELOPMENTAL DISORDERS characterized by impaired development of social interaction skills associated with communication difficulties or stereotyped behavior that do not conform to the diagnostic criteria of other pervasive developmental disorders, such as AUTISTIC DISORDER, ASPERGER'S DISORDER, RETT SYNDROME, or CHILDHOOD DISINTEGRATIVE DISORDER. This category includes **atypical autism**, a disorder in which children have notable difficulties in play, nonverbal communication, social interaction, and speech but are more social than peers diagnosed with autistic disorder. Also, unlike this disorder, which must occur by the age of 3 years, onset of atypical autism may not be noted until the age of 5 to 6 years. Recent research has suggested that about half of the children with atypical autism also manifest varying degrees of mental retardation. See also AUTISTIC SPECTRUM DISORDER.

perversion *n.* a culturally unacceptable or prohibited form of behavior, particularly sexual behavior. See SEXUAL PERVERSION.

perverted logic (**perverted thinking**) see PARALOGIA.

pessimism *n.* the attitude that things will go wrong and that people's wishes or aims are unlikely to be fulfilled. **Pessimists** are people who expect unpleasant or bad things to happen to them and to others or who are otherwise doubtful or hesitant about positive outcomes of behavior. Pessimism can be defined in terms of expectancy: lack of confidence of attaining desired goals (compare OPTIMISM). Most individuals lie somewhere on the spectrum between the two polar opposites of pure optimism and pure pessimism but tend to demonstrate sometimes strong, relatively stable or situational tendencies in one direction or the other. —**pessimistic** *adj.*

PET **1.** abbreviation for PARENT EFFECTIVENESS TRAINING. **2.** acronym for POSITRON EMISSION TOMOGRAPHY.

pet-assisted therapy see ANIMAL-ASSISTED THERAPY.

pethidine *n.* see MEPERIDINE.

petit mal see ABSENCE SEIZURE.

pet therapy see ANIMAL-ASSISTED THERAPY.

petting behavior sexual activity that may not continue to orgasm or may be foreplay engaged in prior to orgasm. Petting behavior may include kissing, caressing the breasts and genitals, oral sex, and placing the genitals in apposition.

peyote *n.* a small, spineless cactus, *Lophophora williamsii*, that grows wild in Mexico and southern Texas. The name is derived from the Aztec word *peyotl*, which describes the plant as resembling a caterpillar's cocoon. The principal active ingredient is the hallucinogen MESCALINE, found in discoid protuberances on the crown of the plant that are called **mescal buttons**. These buttons are cut from the roots and dried, and then generally chewed or soaked in water to produce an intoxicating liquid. From earliest recorded time, peyote has been used by indigenous peoples of northern Mexico and the southwestern United States as a part of their religious ceremonies; it is still incorporated into the rituals of the Native American Church. Both peyote and mescaline are classified by the U.S. Drug Enforcement Administration as Schedule I controlled substances (see SCHEDULED DRUG).

P factor analysis FACTOR ANALYSIS that involves statistically analyzing multiple responses provided by a single individual across multiple occasions, rather than studying multiple responses of a large number of individuals, each of whom is studied on only one occasion.

Pfaundler–Hurler syndrome see HURLER'S SYNDROME.

Pfeiffer's syndrome an inherited disorder marked by premature fusion of the cranial bones, causing a skull deformity. The patients also have facial deformities with protruding, widely spaced eyes (which often show signs of strabismus), large thumbs, and large toes. Some affected individuals have below average intelligence. The syndrome is inherited as a dominant trait (see ACROCEPHALOSYNDACTYLY). Also called **acrocephalosyndactyly Type V**. [Emil **Pfeiffer** (1846–1921), German physician]

PGO spikes *p*ontine–*g*eniculo–*o*ccipital spikes: peaks, recorded on an electroencephalogram, that occur during sleep and indicate neural activity in the pons, lateral geniculate nucleus, and occipital cortex. They are associated with dreaming. See DREAM STATE.

Phaedra complex the incestuous love of a mother for her son. The name derives from the Greek myth of Phaedra, wife of Theseus. When her stepson, Hippolytus, rejected her love, Phaedra accused him of violating her and hanged herself. See also MOTHER–SON INCEST.

phagomania *n.* an insatiable hunger or morbid desire to consume food.

phallic *adj.* of, relating to, or resembling the penis.

phallic character see PHALLIC PERSONALITY.

phallic mother in psychoanalytic theory, the fantasy that the mother has a penis.

phallic personality in psychoanalytic theory, a pattern of narcissistic behavior exemplified by boastfulness, excessive self-assurance, vanity, compulsive sexual behavior, and in some cases aggressive or exhibitionistic behavior. Also called **phallic character**; **phallic-narcissistic character**; **phallic-narcissistic personality**.

phallic phase see PHALLIC STAGE.

phallic pride in psychoanalytic theory, the sense of superiority and feelings of power experienced by boys when they discover that they have a penis and girls do not. These feelings are believed to help master intense CASTRATION ANXIETY. See also PHALLIC STAGE.

phallic sadism in psychoanalytic theory, aggression that is associated with the child's PHALLIC STAGE of PSYCHOSEXUAL DEVELOPMENT. The child interprets sexual intercourse as a violent, aggressive activity on the part of the man, and particularly on the part of the penis. See also PRIMAL SCENE; SADISM.

phallic stage in the classic psychoanalytic theory of Sigmund FREUD, the third stage of PSYCHOSEXUAL DEVELOPMENT beginning around age 3, when the LIBIDO is focused on the genital area (penis or clitoris) and discovery and manipulation of the body become a major source of pleasure. During this period boys are posited to experience CASTRATION ANXIETY, girls to experience PENIS ENVY, and both to experience the OEDIPUS COMPLEX. Also called **phallic phase**.

phallic symbol any object that resembles or might be taken as a representation of the penis, such as a cigar, pencil, tree, skyscraper, snake, or hammer.

phallus *n.* (*pl.* **phalli**) the penis or an object that resembles the form of the penis. As a symbolic object, it often represents fertility or potency.

phantasm *n.* an illusion or apparition, often of an absent person appearing in the form of a spirit or ghost. The observer may recognize it as being imaginary or illusory, unlike a true hallucination, which is associated with lack of insight on the part of the observer.

phantasticum *n.* (*pl.* **phantastica**) a category of drugs identified in the 1920s as capable of producing hallucinatory experiences. These drugs are now known as HALLUCINOGENS. [named by German toxicologist Louis Lewin (1850–1929)]

phantasy *n.* in the OBJECT RELATIONS THEORY of Melanie KLEIN, one of the unconscious constructions, wishes, or impulses that are presumed to underlie all thought and feeling. The *ph* spelling is used to distinguish this from the everyday form of FANTASY, which can include conscious daydreaming.

phantom limb the feeling that an amputated limb is still present, often manifested as a tingling or, occasionally, painful sensation in the area of the missing limb (**phantom limb pain**). In some cases the individual may even deny that the limb has been removed. It is thought that the brain's representation of the limb remains intact and becomes active spontaneously or as a result of stimulation from other brain tissue.

phantom-lover syndrome a type of EROTIC DELUSION elaborated around a person who in fact does not exist. [defined in 1978 by Canadian psychiatrist Mary V. Seeman]

phantosmia *n.* perception of an odor when no smell stimulus is present (i.e., an olfactory hallucination).

pharmacodynamics *n.* the study of the effects of drugs on the body and their mechanism of action. Basic studies involve the activity of drugs at the receptor sites to which the drugs attach as well as the changes in cell function and behavior that result. —**pharmacodynamic** *adj.*

pharmacodynamic tolerance a form of drug TOLERANCE in which the chemistry of the brain becomes adjusted to the presence of the drug, which in turn then loses its capacity for modifying brain activity. Neurons adapt to continued drug presence by reducing the number or sensitivity of receptors available to the drug (i.e., down-regulation). This cellular-adaptive tolerance is associated with the use of many drugs, including sedative-hypnotics and psychostimulants, and may be followed by withdrawal symptoms when regular doses of the drug are interrupted. This may be contrasted with **metabolic tolerance,** in which the body reacts to continued presence of the drug by metabolizing it at an increased rate. Both forms of tolerance lead to higher doses of the drug being needed to produce the same effects.

pharmacogenetics *n.* the study of genetic factors that influence the response of individuals to different drugs and to different dosages of drugs. Inherited variations in enzymes or other metabolic components can affect the efficacy of a drug or cause adverse reactions to normal doses. For example, some 40–70% of Caucasians have an enzyme variant that causes them to metabolize the antituberculosis drug, isoniazid, very slowly. They require only a fraction of the standard dose.

pharmacogenomics *n.* the study of the ways in which genetic knowledge can be utilized for the accurate and effective administration of medications and other drugs.

pharmacokinetics *n.* the study of how pharmacological agents are processed within a biological system, in vivo or in vitro, including factors that influence the absorption, distribution, metabolism, and elimination of the substance or its metabolic products.

pharmacological antagonism see ANTAGONIST.

pharmacology *n.* the branch of science that involves the study of substances that interact with living organisms to alter some biological process affecting the HOMEOSTASIS of the organism. **Therapeutic** (or **medical**) **pharmacology** deals with the administration of substances to correct a state of disease or to enhance well-being. —**pharmacological** or **pharmacologic** *adj.*

pharmacopeia (**pharmacopoeia**) *n.* a book, usually issued by a recognized authority, that lists drugs and their chemical properties, preparation, recommended dosages, method of administration, side effects, dangers, and other information.

pharmacotherapeutic regimen a plan for the treatment of a condition through the use of medication, outlining, for example, the type of drug or drugs to be used, dosage requirements, schedule of administration, and expected duration of use.

pharmacotherapy *n.* the treatment of a disorder by the administration of drugs, as opposed to such means as surgery, psychotherapy, or complementary and alternative methods. Also called **drug therapy**. See PSYCHOPHARMACOTHERAPY.

phase shift 1. a disruption of the normal sleep–wake cycle, with the result that the individual is alert during a usual sleeping period and sleepy when he or she should be alert. See CIRCADIAN RHYTHM SLEEP DISORDER; DISORDERS OF THE SLEEP–WAKE CYCLE SCHEDULE. **2.** a change in the diurnal or CIRCADIAN RHYTHM brought about by such things as changes in daylight exposure or changing time zones.

phencyclidine *n.* see PCP.

phenelzine *n.* a MONOAMINE OXIDASE INHIBITOR that exerts its antidepressant effects by irreversibly binding to monoamine oxidase, thus preventing the breakdown of monoamine neurotransmitters. As with other drugs in its class, phenelzine has been supplanted by safer drugs without the associated toxicities, dietary restrictions, and potentially fatal drug interactions. U.S. trade name: **Nardil**.

Phenergan *n.* a trade name for PROMETHAZINE.

phenobarbital *n.* an anticonvulsant BARBITU-

RATE used for treatment of generalized tonic–clonic or partial seizures. Formerly widely used as a sedative and hypnotic, it has been largely supplanted for these purposes by safer medications lacking the toxicity and adverse effects associated with barbiturates. Phenobarbital is also sometimes used in the management of SEDATIVE, HYPNOTIC, OR ANXIOLYTIC WITHDRAWAL. U.S. trade name: **Luminal**.

phenocopy *n.* an imitation of a PHENOTYPE resulting from the interaction of an environmental factor and a GENOTYPE. An example is the effect of sunlight on skin or hair, resulting in variations that mimic the natural coloring or texture of other phenotypes.

phenomenal field see PHENOMENAL SPACE.

phenomenal self the SELF as experienced by the individual at a given time. Only a small portion of self-knowledge is active in working memory or consciousness at any time, with the remainder lying dormant or inactive. The same person might have a very different phenomenal self at different times, without any change in actual self-knowledge, simply because different views are brought into awareness by events. Also called **working self-concept**.

phenomenal space the environment as experienced by a given individual at a given time. The term refers not to objective reality but to personal and subjective reality, including everything within one's field of awareness. In the phenomenological personality theory of Carl ROGERS, it is also known as the **phenomenological field**. Also called **phenomenal field**.

phenomenological analysis an approach to psychology in which mental experiences are described and studied without theoretical presuppositions or speculation as to their causes or consequences. In general, such an approach will favor observation and description over analysis and interpretation; it will also attempt to understand a person's experience from the point of view of that person, rather than from some more abstract theoretical perspective. See also PHENOMENOLOGY.

phenomenological death the subjective sense that one has become inert, insensitive, and unresponsive. Phenomenological death occurs in some psychotic conditions. Patients may speak of themselves as dead and behave (although inconsistently) in accord with that belief. Phenomenological death is conceived as the extreme point on a continuum of self-assessment; it is not necessarily a condition that is permanent.

phenomenological field see PHENOMENAL SPACE.

phenomenological theory an approach to personality theory that places questions of individuals' current experiences of themselves and their world at the center of analyses of personality functioning and change. See also PERSONAL CONSTRUCT. [proposed by U.S. psychologist George A. Kelly (1905–1967)]

phenomenological therapy any form of therapy, perhaps best exemplified by CLIENT-CENTERED THERAPY, in which the emphasis is on the client's process of self-discovery as opposed to an interpretive focus, such as that found in psychoanalysis.

phenomenology *n.* a movement in modern European philosophy initiated by German philosopher Edmund Husserl (1859–1938). In his writings of the 1910s and 1920s, Husserl argued for a new approach to human knowledge in which both the traditional concerns of philosophy (such as metaphysics and epistemology) and the modern concern with scientific causation would be set aside in favor of a careful attention to the nature of immediate conscious experience. Mental events should be studied and described in their own terms, rather than in terms of their relationship to events in the body or in the external world. However, phenomenology should be distinguished from introspection as it is concerned with the relationship between acts of consciousness and the objects of such acts (see INTENTIONALITY). Husserl's approach proved widely influential in psychology (especially GESTALT PSYCHOLOGY) and the social sciences; it also inspired the work of German philosopher Martin Heidegger (1889–1976), whose existential phenomenology provided the basis for EXISTENTIALISM and EXISTENTIAL PSYCHOLOGY. **—phenomenological** *adj.* **—phenomenologist** *n.*

phenothiazine *n.* any of a group of chemically related compounds most of which are used as ANTIPSYCHOTIC drugs, originally developed as such in the 1950s. The drugs in this class of traditional (or first-generation) antipsychotics were formerly the most widely used agents for the treatment of schizophrenia. The phenothiazines were the first effective antipsychotic medications and largely responsible for the deinstitutionalization of tens of thousands of people with schizophrenia. It is commonly assumed that their therapeutic effects are produced by blockade of dopamine D2 receptors (see DOPAMINE-RECEPTOR ANTAGONISTS); they also block acetylcholine, histamine, and norepinephrine receptors, actions that are associated with many of their adverse effects. Phenothiazines are used for the treatment of acute mania, psychotic agitation, and schizophrenia as well as nausea and vomiting and for preanesthesia sedation. They can be divided into three subgroups: aliphatic, piperazine, and piperidine. A variety of adverse side effects is associated with their use, including EXTRAPYRAMIDAL SYMPTOMS, TARDIVE DYSKINESIA, sedation, and ANTICHOLINERGIC EFFECTS.

phenotype *n.* the observable characteristics of an individual, such as morphological or biochemical features and the presence or absence of a particular disease or condition. Phenotype is determined by the expression of the individual's GENOTYPE coupled with the effects of environmental factors (e.g., nutritional status or climate). **—phenotypic** *adj.*

phensuximide *n.* see SUCCINIMIDE.

phentermine *n.* an APPETITE SUPPRESSANT with a mechanism of action similar to the AMPHETAMINES. Like other appetite suppressants, it is effective only for short-term weight loss: Long-term results require concurrent adherence to effective behavioral weight-loss strategies. Phentermine was previously marketed in combination with fenfluramine or dexfenfluramine—a combination known as "phen-fen"—which was taken off the market after cases of pulmonary hypertension and heart-valve disease were reported in users. These serious side effects cannot be ruled out with the use of phentermine alone. Phentermine should not be given in combination with monoamine oxidase inhibitors, and should be used with caution in individuals taking SSRI antidepressants. U.S. trade names: **Adipex**; **Ionamin**.

phentolamine *n.* an alpha-ADRENERGIC BLOCKING AGENT with direct action on heart and smooth muscle. It is a potent vasodilator used in the management of severe hypertension associated with catecholamine excess. It is in infrequent clinical use. U.S. trade name: **Regitine**.

phenylalkylamines *pl. n.* a group of natural and synthetic drugs that can produce hallucinogenic effects. They include the PHENYLETHYLAMINES, such as MESCALINE, and the phenylisopropylamines (substituted phenylethylamines), such as MDMA.

phenylcyclohexyl derivatives a category of drugs introduced in 1960 as potential general anesthetics but discontinued because they caused serious psychological disturbances in patients. The prototype drug, PCP, produces sensory deprivation effects similar to those observed in some cases of schizophrenia. Drugs of this series are considered to be HALLUCINOGENS but may be used as anesthetics and analgesics in veterinary medicine.

phenylethylamines *pl. n.* a group of drugs with hallucinogenic effects and a common basic chemical structure. The prototype is MESCALINE, an alkaloid first isolated from the PEYOTE cactus in 1896. Mescaline is one of the least potent of the hallucinogens, but potency is increased by adding methyl groups to the basic molecule, thereby creating **substituted phenylethylamines**. The latter include the amphetamine derivatives DOM, MDA, and MDMA. See also PHENYLALKYLAMINES.

phenylketonuria **(PKU)** *n.* an inherited metabolic disease transmitted as an autosomal recessive trait and marked by a deficiency of an enzyme (phenylalanine hydroxylase) needed to utilize the amino acid phenylalanine. Unless it is diagnosed in early infancy and treated by a restricted dietary intake of phenylalanine, phenylketonuria leads to severe mental retardation and other nervous-system disorders. Most untreated patients have IQs below 20. Women who have been treated for the disease must adopt a restricted diet during pregnancy to prevent neurological damage to their children (see MATERNAL PKU).

phenylpyruvic oligophrenia a severe form of mental retardation that is associated with or due to an inborn error of metabolism of phenylalanine, as in cases of PHENYLKETONURIA. Early dietary restriction of phenylalanine may bring intelligence up to average or near-average range.

phenytoin *n.* an ANTICONVULSANT drug: the prototype of the HYDANTOINS. Phenytoin is prescribed mainly for the management of partial and tonic–clonic seizures but is also used in the treatment of some cases of migraine and neuralgia. It is occasionally used to manage behavioral disturbances in children. U.S. trade name (among others): **Dilantin**.

pheromone *n.* a chemical signal that is released outside the body by members of a species and that influences the behavior of other members of the same species. For example, it may serve to attract the opposite sex or to act as an alarm. In nonhuman animals, sensitivity to pheromones occurs via specialized receptor cells called the vomeronasal system. The existence of true pheromones in humans is controversial, although scents (e.g., perfumes, body odors) may play a role in sexual attraction and arousal. Pheromones have also been suggested as a cause of menstrual synchrony. Also called **ectohormone**.

Phillips Rating Scale of Premorbid Adjustment in Schizophrenia a method of analyzing the PREMORBID ADJUSTMENT of patients with schizophrenia as part of a determination of their prognosis. It is based on questions derived by a researcher from case-history information. Also called **Phillips scale**; **Phillips scale of premorbid adjustment**. [developed in 1953 by psychopharmacologist Leslie **Phillips**]

philosophical psychotherapy psychotherapy based on philosophical principles of belief and attitude generally, as they relate to cognition, emotion, and behavior, or based on the principles of some particular philosophical perspective (e.g., EXISTENTIAL PSYCHOTHERAPY). Training in philosophy without appropriate training in the mental health field, however, is deemed inadequate for offering psychotherapy or counseling services.

PHO abbreviation for PHYSICIAN–HOSPITAL ORGANIZATION.

phobia *n.* a persistent and irrational fear of a specific situation, object, or activity (e.g., heights, dogs, water, blood, driving, flying), which is consequently either strenuously avoided or endured with marked distress. In *DSM–IV–TR* the many types of individual phobia are classified under the heading SPECIFIC PHOBIA. See also SOCIAL PHOBIA. —**phobic** *adj.*

phobic anxiety anxiety that focuses on or is directed toward objects or situations (e.g., insects, telephone booths, open areas) that represent the real fear but pose little if any actual danger themselves.

phobic attitude a behavior pattern apparently characterized by disruptions in the awareness of and attention to experience in the present. An example is engaging in a fantasy of the future to escape a painful present reality. [defined by German-born U.S. psychotherapist Frederick (Fritz) S. Perls (1893–1970)]

phobic avoidance the active evasion of feared objects or situations by individuals with phobias.

phobic character in psychoanalytic theory, an individual who tends to deal with anxiety by extreme or fearful avoidance. [first used in 1945 by Austrian psychoanalyst Otto Fenichel (1897–1946)]

phobic disorders in *DSM–III*, a group of disorders in which the essential feature is a persistent, irrational fear and consequent avoidance of specific objects, activities, or situations (see PHOBIA). The fear is recognized as unreasonable, but is nevertheless so intense that it interferes with everyday functioning and is often a significant source of distress. Phobic disorders included SPECIFIC PHOBIAS, SOCIAL PHOBIA, and AGORAPHOBIA.

Phoenix House an organization devoted to the treatment and prevention of substance abuse in adolescents and adults. Phoenix House offers both residential and outpatient programs, as well as other services related to or in support of the treatment process. See also THERAPEUTIC COMMUNITY.

phonological disorder in *DSM–IV–TR*, a communication disorder characterized by failure to develop and consistently use speech sounds that are appropriate for the child's age. It most commonly involves misarticulation of the later acquired speech sounds, such as [l], [r], [s], [z], [ch], [sh], or [th] (as in LALLING or lisps), but may also include substitution of sounds (e.g., [t] for [k]) or omission of sounds (e.g., final consonants). These problems are not due to, or are in excess of those normally associated with, hearing loss, structural deficits in the mechanism of speech production (e.g., cleft palate), or a neurological disorder. In *DSM–III* this disorder was categorized as **developmental articulation disorder**.

phonological dyslexia a form of acquired dyslexia (see ALEXIA) characterized primarily by difficulties in reading pronounceable nonwords. Semantic errors are not seen in this type of dyslexia, a feature that distinguishes it from DEEP DYSLEXIA. Phonological dyslexia manifested as a form of DEVELOPMENTAL DYSLEXIA has also been described. See also SURFACE DYSLEXIA. [first described in 1979 by Marie-France Beauvois and Jacqueline Derouesné]

phonological loop see WORKING MEMORY.

photism *n.* **1.** a false perception or hallucination of light. See PHOTOPSIA. **2.** a form of SYNESTHESIA in which light or color sensations occur in response to stimulation of other senses (e.g., hearing).

photocounseling *n.* the use of photographs or videotapes depicting aspects of a client's life to obtain insight into his or her behavior and needs and also to increase the rapport between the client and the therapist.

photoma *n.* a visual hallucination in which sparks or light flashes are seen in the absence of external stimuli. See also PHOTOPSIA.

photomania *n.* **1.** an abnormal craving for light, particularly sunlight. See also SEASONAL AFFECTIVE DISORDER. **2.** the practice of sun worship.

photophobia *n.* an extreme and often painful sensitivity to light. It may be associated with migraine headaches or with certain types of brain trauma. —**photophobic** *adj.*

photopsia *n.* visual sensations in the absence of external visual stimuli, which can be unstructured or structured. Structured photopsia consists of regular achromatic or chromatic visual patterns (e.g., circles, squares, diamonds) and is caused by pathological activation of prestriate cortical neurons. Also called **photopsy**. See also VISUAL HALLUCINATION.

photosensitivity *n.* sensitivity to light, especially sunlight, as occurs in albinism. Conditions marked by increased sensitivity to the effects of sunlight on the skin include systemic LUPUS ERYTHEMATOSUS and XERODERMA PIGMENTOSUM. Photosensitivity may occur as an adverse reaction to certain drugs, such as the phenothiazines (e.g., chlorpromazine), carbamazepine, St. John's wort, thiazides, sulfonamides, and tetracyclines. In such cases it often takes the form of a rash or other skin reaction. Photosensitivity may also represent an immune reaction in some individuals who manifest allergy symptoms after exposure to intense light. —**photosensitive** *adj.*

phototherapy *n.* therapy involving exposure to ultraviolet or infrared light, which is used for treating not only certain skin conditions or disorders (e.g., jaundice, psoriasis) but also depression, particularly for patients with SEASONAL AFFECTIVE DISORDER (SAD). Typically, in phototherapy for SAD, a specially designed lamp that delivers 5,000 to 10,000 lx of light is shone on the retina, and a signal is transmitted via the optic nerve to the pineal gland, which secretes MELATONIN in response to darkness. Inhibition of melatonin release by bright light relieves the symptoms of SAD. Also called **bright light therapy**.

phrenology *n.* a theory of personality formulated in the 18th and 19th centuries by German physician Franz Josef Gall (1757–1828) and Austrian philosopher and anatomist Johann Kaspar Spurzheim (1776–1832). It stated that specific abilities or personality traits are represented by specific areas of the brain: The size of these brain areas determines the degree of the corresponding skill or trait. Proponents of the theory argued that the size of such locations could be indicated by bumps and hollows on the skull surface, based on the observation that the contours of the brain follow the skull contours. Although wrong in most respects, the theory suggested the idea of LOCALIZATION OF FUNCTION. See also PHYSIOGNOMY. —**phrenological** *adj.* —**phrenologist** *n.*

phylogenetic principle the theory that ONTOGENY recapitulates PHYLOGENY in the development of an organism: In humans, this supposes that human life, across development from embryo to adult, repeats the stages of organic and social evolution.

phylogeny *n.* **1.** the evolutionary origin and development of a particular group of organisms. Also called **phylogenesis**. Compare ONTOGENY. **2.** a diagram that shows genetic linkages between ancestors and descendants. Also called **phylogenetic tree**. —**phylogenetic** *adj.*

physical abuse deliberately aggressive or violent behavior by one person toward another that results in bodily injury. Physical abuse may involve such actions as punching, kicking, biting, choking, burning, shaking, and beating, which may at times be severe enough to result in permanent damage (e.g., TRAUMATIC BRAIN INJURY) or death. It is most frequently observed in relationships of trust, particularly between parents and children or between intimate partners (e.g., in a marriage); indeed, violence against women and children is recognized as a major public health problem. Individuals who experience physical abuse often feel helpless and isolated, and are prone to the subsequent development of numerous pathological conditions, including depression, eating disorders, posttraumatic stress disorder, anxiety disorders, and substance use problems. See also BATTERED-CHILD SYNDROME; BATTERED-WOMAN SYNDROME.

physical activity any bodily movement produced by the contraction of skeletal muscle that increases energy expenditure above the basal level.

physical dependence the state of an individual who has repeatedly taken a drug and will experience unpleasant physiological symptoms (see SUBSTANCE WITHDRAWAL) if he or she stops taking the drug. In *DSM–IV–TR*, SUBSTANCE DEPENDENCE with physical (or physiological) dependence is diagnosed if there is evidence of withdrawal or TOLERANCE. Compare PSYCHOLOGICAL DEPENDENCE.

physical disorder see GENERAL MEDICAL CONDITION.

physical examination an assessment of the body and its specific functions, generally by a physician or other health care professional, using inspection, palpation, percussion, and auscultation. It also frequently includes laboratory tests and other forms of screening for various physiological abnormalities, malfunctions, and diseases.

physicalism *n.* **1.** the doctrine that reality is composed of matter and that mind is therefore reducible to matter. See IDENTITY THEORY; MATERIALISM; MIND–BODY PROBLEM. **2.** the view that all meaningful propositions can be stated in the language of the physical sciences and in operational definitions. See LOGICAL POSITIVISM; POSITIVISM. —**physicalist** *adj.*

physically correct doll see ANATOMICALLY DETAILED DOLL.

physical medicine the branch of medicine that specializes in the diagnosis and treatment of illness and disorders through physical means (e.g., exercise and massage) and mechanical devices. Physical medicine is also concerned with the REHABILITATION of patients with physical disabilities. Also called **physiatrics**; **physiatry**.

physical modality a therapeutic intervention that involves the use of a physical agent, such as heat or ice.

physical therapy (**PT**) **1.** the treatment of pain, injury, or disease using physical or mechanical methods, such as exercise, heat, water, massage, or electric current (diathermy). The treatment is administered by a trained **physical therapist**. Also called **physiotherapy**. **2.** a branch of medicine and health care that identifies, corrects, alleviates, and prevents temporary, prolonged, or permanent movement dysfunction or physical disability.

physician assistant (**PA**) a licensed health care professional who provides services under the direction of a supervising physician.

physician-assisted suicide see ASSISTED DEATH.

physician–hospital organization (**PHO**) an organization formed, owned, and governed by one or more hospitals and physician groups to obtain payer contracts and to further mutual interests.

physiogenic *adj.* pertaining to a disorder that is organic in origin.

physiognomy *n.* **1.** the form of a person's physical features, especially the face. **2.** the attempt to read personality from facial features and expressions, assuming, for example, that a person with a receding chin is weak or one with a high forehead is bright. The idea dates back to Greek philosopher Aristotle (383–322 BCE) and was later developed into a pseudoscientific system by Swiss pastor Johann Lavater (1741–1801) and Italian psychiatrist Cesare Lombroso (1835–1909). Also called **physiognomics**. See also CHARACTEROLOGY; PHRENOLOGY.

physiological antagonism see ANTAGONIST.

physiological assessment evaluation of the functioning state of the body, a tissue, or an organ, including physical and chemical factors and processes.

physiological factors factors pertaining to the functions of a living organism and its parts as well as to the chemical and physical processes involved in this functioning.

physiological need any of the requirements for survival, such as food, water, oxygen, and sleep. Physiological needs make up the lowest level of MASLOW'S MOTIVATIONAL HIERARCHY. Also called **basic need**; **fundamental need**. See also PRIMARY NEED; VISCEROGENIC NEED.

physiological paradigm the concept that mental disorders are caused by abnormalities in neurological structures and processes. This perspective, which underlies the field and practice of psychiatry, holds that mental disorders can be treated with drugs, surgery, or other techniques ordinarily used to correct malfunctioning of the body.

physiological psychology a term used interchangeably with PSYCHOPHYSIOLOGY or, less commonly, BIOLOGICAL PSYCHOLOGY.

physostigmine *n.* a CHOLINERGIC DRUG—an alkaloid derived from the dried seed of an African vine—used in the treatment of glaucoma and to cause the pupil of the eye to contract. It is also employed as a cholinesterase inhibitor to reverse the toxic effects on the central nervous system of overdoses of ANTICHOLINERGIC DRUGS. U.S. trade names: **Antilirium**; **Isopto Eserine**.

phytoestrogens *pl. n.* see ESTROGEN.

P

Piaget, Jean (1896–1980) Swiss child psychologist and epistemologist. Piaget earned his doctorate from the University of Neuchâtel in 1918, with a dissertation on the classification of mollusks. He then studied psychology and philosophy at the universities of Zürich and Paris before taking a position at the Jean-Jacques Rousseau Institute of Geneva, a center for research on child development. Piaget is best known for his research and theoretical work on cognitive development. He proposed that all children develop through a prescribed series of cognitive stages: sensorimotor, preoperational, concrete operational, and formal operational. He held that although the age of onset for each stage might vary due to cultural and historical factors, the order of the stages is the same for all cultures. In the **sensorimotor stage**, the child's ability to recognize object permanence develops; the older infant becomes aware that an object exists even when it is out of sight. During the **preoperational stage**, the child is egocentric, showing little awareness of the perspective of others; language develops, as well as a rudimentary number system. The **concrete operational stage** is characterized by the development of conceptually based thinking rather than the earlier perceptually based thinking. Finally, in the **formal operational stage**, abstract thinking, deductive reasoning, and moral reasoning develop. Among Piaget's most influential works are *The Origins of Intelligence* (1936), *The Construction of Reality* (1937), and (with Barbel Inhelder) *The Growth of Logical Thinking from Childhood to Adolescence* (1953) and *The Early Growth of Logic in the Child* (1959). In 1969 Piaget was awarded the Distinguished Scientific Contribution Award of the American Psychological Association. See also CONSTRUCTIVISM. **—Piagetian** *adj.*

piblokto *n.* a CULTURE-BOUND SYNDROME observed primarily in female Inuit and other arctic populations. Individuals experience a sudden dissociative period of extreme excitement in which they often tear off clothes, run naked through the snow, scream, throw things, and perform other wild behaviors. This typically ends with convulsive seizures, followed by an acute coma and amnesia for the event. Also called **arctic hysteria**; **pibloktoq**.

pica *n.* a rare eating disorder found primarily in young children and marked by a persistent craving for unnatural, nonnutritive substances, such as plaster, paint, hair, starch, or dirt. In *DSM–IV–TR* it is classified with the FEEDING AND EATING DISORDERS OF INFANCY OR EARLY CHILDHOOD. **Lead pica** is often found in children living in older housing with lead paint and can lead to irreversible mental impairment. Studies on rats and monkeys demonstrated that lead pica can be induced by calcium deficiency. Animals with normal nutrition learn that lead ingestion is aversive, but calcium-deficient animals do not learn aversions to lead.

Pick's disease a form of DEMENTIA characterized by progressive degeneration of the frontal and temporal areas of the brain with the presence of particles called **Pick bodies** in the cytoplasm of the neurons. The disease is characterized by personality changes and deterioration of social skills and complex thinking; symptoms include problems with new situations and abstractions, difficulty in thinking or concentrating, loss of memory, lack of spontaneity, gradual emotional dullness, loss of moral judgment, and disturbances of speech. [described in 1892 by Arnold **Pick** (1851–1924), Czech psychiatrist and neuroanatomist]

picrotoxin *n.* a CNS STIMULANT derived from the berries of a southeast Asian shrub, *Anamirta cocculus*. Originally used as a fish poison, picrotoxin was introduced in the 1930s as therapy for barbiturate overdose. It is a convulsant agent and acts as a GABA ANTAGONIST by binding to a specific site on the $GABA_A$ receptor complex, blocking the effects of GABA agonists (e.g., the benzodiazepines). Picrotoxin has no modern clinical applications but may be used to induce seizures in nonhuman animals for research purposes.

pictophilia *n.* sexual interest in and arousal by

viewing erotic pictures or films, alone or with a partner.

picture-anomalies test a type of nonverbal test of social intelligence that depends on the ability of the participant to detect absurdities in cartoon pictures.

picture-completion test a type of test consisting of drawings of familiar objects with features missing. The task is to recognize and specify the missing parts.

picture-interpretation test a test in which the participant is asked to interpret a visual image (e.g., a drawing, photograph, or painting). This type of test may aid in the assessment of intelligence or personality traits.

picture-world test a PROJECTIVE TECHNIQUE for children in which the participant composes a story about realistic scenes, adding objects or figures as he or she wishes. The child is instructed to picture either a world that actually exists or one that he or she would like to exist.

Pierre Robin's syndrome a congenital disorder with anomalies that include micrognathia (abnormally small jaw) and cleft palate. Serious eye disorders occur in most affected individuals, along with a small, receding chin and a tongue that falls backward into the pharynx (glossoptosis), interfering with breathing and feeding. The incidence of mental retardation ranges from 5 to 50%. [initially reported in 1923 by **Pierre Robin** (1867–1950), French pediatrician]

Pigem's question a question designed to elicit projective responses by a patient undergoing a MENTAL STATUS EXAMINATION. The question is usually a variation of "What would you like most to change in your life?" [Spanish psychiatrist José M. **Pigem**]

PIL abbreviation for PURPOSE IN LIFE.

pilocarpine *n.* an alkaloid derived from several tropical American plants but mainly from *Pilocarpus jaborandi*. Pilocarpine is a powerful parasympathomimetic agent, affecting postganglionic cholinergic receptors (see CHOLINERGIC DRUG). It is used in the treatment of glaucoma and to contract the pupil of the eye. U.S. trade names (among others): **Isopto Carpine**; **Pilocar**; **Pilostat**.

pimozide *n.* a first-generation (typical or conventional) ANTIPSYCHOTIC of the diphenylbutylpiperidine class. Like other conventional antipsychotics, it is a blocker of postsynaptic dopamine D2 receptors. In the United States it is officially approved by the Food and Drug Administration only for the management of vocal and motor tics associated with Tourette's disorder, although it is widely used as an antipsychotic drug in Europe and South America. Pimozide has been associated with potentially lethal disturbances of heart rhythm, and it should not be used in patients with histories of arrhythmias or in doses exceeding 10 mg/day. Because pimozide has no apparent special advantages over similar antipsychotics that are less damaging to the heart (e.g., haloperidol), it should be used in Tourette's disorder only if other medications have failed to produce the desired response. U.S. trade name: **Orap**.

pineal gland a small, cone-shaped gland attached by a stalk to the posterior wall of the third ventricle of the brain; it is part of the epithalamus. In amphibians and reptiles, the gland appears to function as a part of the visual system. In mammals it secretes the hormone MELATONIN and is an important component of the circadian system regulating BIOLOGICAL RHYTHMS. Because it is an unpaired organ located in the middle of the brain, French philosopher René Descartes (1596–1650) believed it was the seat of the rational soul and the connection between mind and body. Also called **epiphysis cerebri**; **pineal body**.

Pinel's system a classification of mental disorders and symptoms outlined in the 18th century. The four major categories were melancholias, manias with delirium, manias without delirium, and dementia or mental deterioration. [Philippe **Pinel** (1745–1826), French psychiatrist]

piperidinediones *pl. n.* a class of chemically related drugs formerly used for daytime sedation or the management of insomnia but no longer in common clinical use. Their mechanism of action and toxicity are similar to the BARBITURATES. The prototype of the class is GLUTETHIMIDE.

pithiatism *n.* a former name (from Greek *pithanotes*, "persuasiveness") for SOMATIZATION DISORDER, proposed in 1918 by French neurologist Joseph Babinski (1857–1932) as a substitute for HYSTERIA. It was based on the theory that some hysterical symptoms are produced by suggestion and can therefore be eliminated by suggestion and would therefore distinguish hysterical disorders from those on which persuasion has no effect.

pituitarism *n.* disordered functioning of the pituitary gland, which may be overactive (hyperpituitarism) or underactive (hypopituitarism).

pituitary gland a gland, pea-sized in humans, that lies at the base of the brain, connected by a stalk (the infundibulum) to the HYPOTHALAMUS. The pituitary gland is divided into an anterior and a posterior lobe, which differ in function. The anterior lobe (**adenohypophysis**) produces and secretes seven hormones—thyroid-stimulating hormone, follicle-stimulating hormone, adrenocorticotropic hormone, growth hormone, luteinizing hormone, prolactin, and melanocyte-stimulating hormone—in response to RELEASING HORMONES from the hypothalamus. The posterior lobe (**neurohypophysis**) secretes two hormones, vasopressin and oxytocin, which are synthesized in the hypothalamus and transported down axons in the infundibulum to the neurohypophysis in response to direct neural stimulation. The pituitary's role of secreting tropic hormones, which regulate the production of other hormones, has resulted in its designation as the "master gland of the endocrine system." Also called **hypophysis; hypophysis cerebri**.

pituri *n.* an Australian shrub, *Duboisia hopwoodii*, whose leaves have traditionally been used for their stimulant, analgesic, and hallucinogenic effects by members of Aboriginal tribes. The leaves were cured, powdered, and then rolled into a quid to be chewed or smoked. The primary active ingredient is NICOTINE. Although some indigenous peoples still use pituri, it was most popular during the 19th and early 20th centuries.

PKU abbreviation for PHENYLKETONURIA.

placebo *n.* (*pl.* **placebos**) **1.** a pharmacologically inert substance, such as a sugar pill, that is often administered as a control in testing new drugs. Placebos used in double-BLIND trials may be DUMMIES or ACTIVE PLACEBOS. Formerly, placebos were occasionally used as diagnostic or psychotherapeutic agents, for example, in relieving pain or inducing sleep by suggestion, but the ethical implications of deceiving patients in such fashion makes this practice problematic. **2.** any medical or psychological intervention or treatment that is believed to be "inert," thus making it valuable as a control condition against which to compare the intervention or treatment of interest. See PLACEBO EFFECT.

placebo control group a group of participants in a study who receive an inert substance (placebo) instead of the active drug under investigation, thus functioning as a neutral condition against which to make comparisons regarding the actual pharmacological effects of the active drug.

placebo effect a clinically significant response to a therapeutically inert substance or nonspecific treatment, based on the recipient's expectations or beliefs regarding the intervention. It is now recognized that placebo effects accompany the administration of any drug (active or inert) and contribute to the therapeutic effectiveness of a specific treatment. See PLACEBO.

placement counseling 1. services designed to advise and assist individuals to find suitable or optimal employment. Placement counseling may include coaching or training for job interviews, procedures for filling out applications, and assistance with other activities relevant to obtaining a job. **2.** in education, a service that provides guidance to students in deciding upon an appropriate educational program, class, or level of instruction. **3.** in foster care, services provided to help children and their adoptive parents adjust to adoptive placement. **4.** in VOCATIONAL REHABILITATION, a service that advises and prepares people with disabilities for appropriate job opportunities.

Placidyl *n.* a trade name for ETHCHLORVYNOL.

planned behavior behavior that is under the organism's direct control, as opposed to more reactive behavior or REFLEXIVE BEHAVIOR. In social psychology, the theory of planned behavior suggests that the intent to engage in a specific behavior is determined by attitudes, norms, and perceived control surrounding the behavior in question.

Planned Parenthood Federation of America (PPFA) an organization that promotes comprehensive reproductive and complementary health care services; advocates public policy that guarantees access to such services and the privacy and rights of individuals using such services; and supports research and technology in reproductive health care, as well as education on human sexuality. Formerly known as the American Birth Control League, the organization adopted its current name in 1942.

plaque *n.* a small patch of abnormal tissue on or within a bodily structure, formed as the result of an accumulation of substances or as the result of localized damage. Examples of the former type include the SENILE PLAQUES of Alzheimer's disease, arising from clumps of beta-amyloid protein, and the atheromatous plaques of ATHEROSCLEROSIS, consisting of lipid deposits on the lining of arterial walls. Examples of the latter type include the demyelination plaques on the protective nerve sheaths of individuals with MULTIPLE SCLEROSIS.

plasticity *n.* flexibility and adaptability. Plasticity of the nervous or hormonal systems makes it possible to learn and register new experiences. Early experiences can also modify and shape gene expression to induce long-lasting changes in neurons or endocrine organs. See also FUNCTIONAL PLASTICITY; NEURAL PLASTICITY. Compare RIGIDITY.

plateau phase see SEXUAL-RESPONSE CYCLE.

play *n.* activities that appear to be freely sought and pursued solely for the sake of individual or group enjoyment. Although play is typically regarded as serving no immediate purpose beyond enjoyment, studies indicate that the motivation to play is as natural as the urge to eat or sleep and that it contributes significantly to development. In the research in this area, various types of play have been described, ranging from locomotor play to object play to social play to cognitive play, and numerous theories about play have been proposed. Jean PIAGET, for example, regarded it as advancing children's cognitive development through mastery play, playing games with defined rules (such as hide-and-seek), and symbolic play. Advocates of the **practice theory of play** propose that play prepares children for activities or roles they will encounter as adults, whereas others suggest that it serves a more immediate function, such as exercise, establishing social relations among peers, or—according to the surplus energy theory—using up excess energy. Although the preponderance of research on play focuses on the activities of children, the play behavior of nonhuman animals is also actively studied. Also called **ludic activity**.

playacting *n.* dramatic play in which children, adolescents, or adults (including group-therapy participants) take different roles. In the process, the participants test out relationships; rehearse different ways of dealing with situations; identify with significant figures; and play out any of a broad range of affective states and behaviors within the safe realm of make-believe. See also PSYCHODRAMA.

play-group psychotherapy a technique used in group therapy for preschool and early elementary school children. Materials of many kinds (e.g., clay, toys, blocks, and figurines) are used to foster the expression of conflicts and fantasies and to give the therapist an opportunity to ask questions and help the children in the group understand their feelings, behavior, and relationships within the context of the group. See also GROUP THERAPY. [introduced in the early 1940s by Russian-born U.S. psychotherapist Samuel Richard Slavson (1890–1981)]

play therapy the use of play activities and materials (e.g., clay, water, blocks, dolls, puppets, drawing, and finger paint) in CHILD PSYCHOTHERAPY. Play-therapy techniques are based on the theory that such activities mirror the child's emotional life and fantasies, enabling the child to "play out" his or her feelings and problems and to test out new approaches and understand relationships in action rather than words. This form of psychotherapy, which focuses on a child's internal world and unconscious conflicts in addition to his or her daily life and current relationships, may be nondirective, but may alternatively be conducted on a more directive or a more analytic, interpretive level (see DIRECTIVE PLAY THERAPY; NONDIRECTIVE PLAY THERAPY). See also PROJECTIVE PLAY.

pleasantness *n.* a conscious, hedonic state, typically deemed highly desirable, that is experienced when an event is congruent with one's goals or is associated with pleasure. See also DIMENSIONAL THEORY OF EMOTION. **—pleasant** *adj.*

pleasure center any of various areas of the brain (including areas of the hypothalamus and limbic system) that, upon intracranial stimulation, have been implicated in producing pleasure. The existence of pure pleasure centers has not been definitively established, particularly because the self-stimulation response rate varies according to such factors as the duration and strength of the electrical stimulation. Also called **reward center**. [proposed by U.S. psychologist James Olds (1922–1976)]

pleasure principle the view that human beings are governed by the desire for instinctual gratification, or pleasure, and for the discharge of tension that builds up as pain or "unpleasure" when gratification is lacking. According to psychoanalytic theory, the pleasure principle is the psychic force that motivates people to seek immediate gratification of instinctual, or libidinal, impulses, such as sex, hunger, thirst, and elimination. It dominates the ID and operates most strongly during childhood. Later, in adulthood, it is opposed by the REALITY PRINCIPLE of the EGO. Also called **pleasure–pain principle**.

pleniloquence *n.* a compulsion to talk incessantly. **—pleniloquent** *adj.*

pleonexia *n.* **1.** an abnormal greediness or desire for the acquisition of objects. **2.** an abnormal intake of oxygen.

PLISSIT *n.* acronym for a model, developed in the 1970s, that is used in counseling clients about sexual problems. The model offers successive levels of communication or intervention: (a) *P*ermission, in which the client is told it is acceptable to do things he or she might think are not allowed; (b) *L*imited *I*nformation, in which the client is given information limited to that directly relevant to his or her concerns; (c) *S*pecific *S*uggestion, in which actions are specified; and (d) *I*ntensive *T*herapy, which may be required if the client has a complex problem (usually involving another therapist). The approach enables the counselor or therapist to determine at which point the problem is beyond his or her level of comfort and competence and it is appropriate to refer the client elsewhere.

plutomania *n.* an inordinate striving for money and possessions.

PM abbreviation for PRIMARY MEMORY.

PMS abbreviation for PREMENSTRUAL SYNDROME.

PNES abbreviation for PSYCHOGENIC NONEPILEPTIC SEIZURE.

PNS abbreviation for PERIPHERAL NERVOUS SYSTEM.

poetry therapy a form of BIBLIOTHERAPY that employs the reading or writing of poetry to facilitate emotional expression in an individual and foster healing and personal growth. Also (but less frequently) called **psychopoetry**.

POI abbreviation for PERSONAL ORIENTATION INVENTORY.

point biserial correlation coefficient a numerical index reflecting the degree of relationship between two random variables, one continuous and one dichotomous.

point estimate a single estimated numerical value of a given population parameter. Compare INTERVAL ESTIMATE.

pointing *n.* a test in which the participant, first with the eyes open and then with the eyes closed, extends a forefinger and touches the forefingers of the examiner as they stand facing each other. Knowing the location of the examiner's fingers, participants should be able to touch them with their eyes closed. Failure to do so is called **past-pointing**.

polarized thinking see DICHOTOMOUS THINKING.

Pollitt syndrome see TRICHORRHEXIS NODOSA WITH MENTAL RETARDATION. [reported in 1968 by Rodney J. **Pollitt**, British physician]

polydipsia *n.* excessive thirst, manifest as an extreme amount of drinking. It commonly results from diabetes, and can be an important diagnostic sign of the condition, or—in the case of **psychogenic polydipsia**—may be related to psychological factors. It may also be induced by conditioning procedures (**schedule-induced polydipsia**). Compare ADIPSIA.

polydrug abuse SUBSTANCE ABUSE involving more than one drug.

polydrug dependence dependence (physical, psychological, or both) on more than one drug of abuse. Also called **polysubstance dependence**. See SUBSTANCE DEPENDENCE.

polydystrophic oligophrenia see SANFILIPPO'S SYNDROME.

polygamy *n.* marriage to more than one spouse at the same time, which is an accepted custom in certain cultures. See also BIGAMY; GROUP MARRIAGE. Compare MONOGAMY. **—polygamous** *adj.* **—polygamist** *n.*

polygenic inheritance see MULTIFACTORIAL INHERITANCE.

polygraph *n.* a device that measures and records several physiological indicators of anxiety or emotion, such as heart rate, blood pressure, and skin response to stimuli. The instrument has been widely used in the interrogation of criminal suspects and in employee screening to measure marked physiological reactions to questions about such issues as theft, sexual deviation, or untruthfulness. It has been colloquially referred to as a **lie detector**, although no one has ever documented a close relation between physiological patterns and deceptive behavior. The accuracy of polygraph examinations is controversial, and the results are not accepted as evidence in many U.S. courts of law. The polygraph was invented in 1917 by U.S. experimental psychologist William Marston (1893–1947); an improved version, the **Keeler polygraph**, was designed by U.S. criminologist Leonard Keeler (1903–1949).

P

polyiterophilia *n.* sexual interest and arousal focused on repeating the same sexual actions and behaviors many times, and with many different partners.

polymorphism *n.* **1.** in biology, the condition of having multiple behavioral or physical types within a species or population. In some fish species there are two distinct sizes of males: Larger males defend territory and attract females to mate with them; much smaller males, often with the physical appearance of females, stay close to the large male and inseminate some of the eggs. Peppered moths in England are another example, existing as black morphs (forms) in polluted areas and white morphs in nonpolluted areas. **2.** in genetics, the presence in a population of two or more variants of a gene (i.e., ALLELES) at a given genetic locus. For example, the variety of human blood groups is due to polymorphism of particular genes governing the characteristics of red blood cells. See also SINGLE-NUCLEOTIDE POLYMORPHISM. **—polymorphic** *adj.*

polymorphous perversity in the classic psychoanalytic theory of Sigmund FREUD, the response of the human infant to many kinds of normal, daily activities posited to provide sexual excitation, such as touching, smelling, sucking, viewing, exhibiting, rocking, defecating, urinating, hurting, and being hurt.

polyneuropathy *n.* any disease that affects many or all of the peripheral nerves. See PERIPHERAL NEUROPATHY.

polyopia *n.* the formation of multiple images of one object on the retina due to a refractive error of the eye, brain injury (see PALINOPSIA), fatigue, or PSYCHOGENIC DISORDER. See VISUAL ILLUSION.

polyphagia *n.* an abnormal compulsion to eat excessive quantities of food.

polypharmacy *n.* the simultaneous use of a variety of drugs of the same or different classes with the intent of producing a more robust therapeutic response. Polypharmacy for mental disorders may, for example, involve the administration of two or more antidepressants in the hope that agents with different mechanisms of action will produce greater clinical improvement than that seen with any one drug alone. Polypharmacy is often criticized because of the lack of well-controlled studies supporting its use and the greater likelihood of drug interactions when two or more drugs are used simultaneously. However, for those individuals unsuccessfully treated with several trials of monotherapy, or for whom monotherapy achieves suboptimal results, polypharmacy may be therapeutically indicated and appropriately managed.

polyphasic sleep a sleep pattern in which sleep occurs in relatively short naps throughout a 24-hour period. A human infant may begin life with a polyphasic sleep rhythm that consists of half a dozen sleep periods. The rhythm becomes monophasic, with one long, daily sleep period, by about school age. **Biphasic sleep** patterns, which include one daytime nap period in addition to the long, typically nocturnal, period of sleep, are seen in a variety of cultures (e.g., as the siesta) and in older adults. See also SLEEP–WAKE CYCLE. Compare MONOPHASIC SLEEP.

polysomnography *n.* the recording of various physiological processes (e.g., eye movements, brain waves, heart rate, respiration) throughout the night, for the diagnosis of sleep-related disorders. **—polysomnograph** *n.*

polysubstance dependence see POLYDRUG DEPENDENCE.

polysurgical addiction a condition characterized by a compulsive drive to undergo one surgical procedure after another even when organic pathology cannot be found. The condition may be a manifestation of FACTITIOUS DISORDER with predominantly physical signs and symptoms, HYPOCHONDRIASIS, or SOMATIZATION DISORDER.

POMR abbreviation for problem-oriented medical record. See PROBLEM-ORIENTED RECORD.

POMS acronym for PROFILE OF MOOD STATES.

pons *n.* a part of the brainstem lying between the MIDBRAIN and the MEDULLA OBLONGATA, appearing as a swelling on the ventral surface of the brainstem. It consists of bundles of transverse, ascending, and descending nerve fibers and nuclei, including facial nerve nuclei. It serves primarily as a bridge, or transmission structure, between different areas of the nervous system. It also works with the CEREBELLUM in controlling equilibrium, and with the CEREBRAL CORTEX in smoothing and coordinating voluntary movements. With the cerebellum it forms the region called the metencephalon. **—pontine** *adj.*

pontine sleep dreaming sleep; sleep characterized by the presence of PGO SPIKES. See DREAM STATE.

pooled variance the estimate of a single common variance achieved by combining several independent estimates of that variance. Also called **pooled within-cell variance**; **within-cell variance**.

poor premorbid schizophrenia see PROCESS SCHIZOPHRENIA.

popular psychology 1. psychological knowledge as understood by members of the general public, which may be oversimplified, misinterpreted, and out of date. **2.** psychological knowledge intended specifically for use by the general public, such as self-help books and television and radio advice programs.

population *n.* in statistics, a theoretically defined, complete group of objects (people, animals, institutions) from which a sample is drawn in order to obtain empirical observations and to which results can be generalized. Also called **universe**.

POR abbreviation for PROBLEM-ORIENTED RECORD.

poriomania *n.* an irresistible impulse to run away or wander off, either consciously or in a state of amnesia. The condition may occur in some types of epilepsy and dementia. Also called **poriomanic fugue**. See also FUGUE; NOMADISM.

pornographomania *n.* **1.** a morbid impulse to write obscene letters. **2.** sexual arousal associated with writing obscenities.

pornography *n.* writings or images (e.g., illustrations, films) with sexual content that are likely to cause sexual arousal in some individuals. Legal interpretations vary, but all focus on the violation of community standards and the lack of any redeeming artistic value. See also EROTICA. **—pornographic** *adj.*

pornolagnia *n.* an obscure term for attraction to prostitutes as sexual partners, in preference to partners who choose to have sex out of mutual interest.

porphyria *n.* a metabolic disorder involving the excretion of excessive or abnormal **porphyrins** (breakdown products of hemoglobin) in the urine. The acute intermittent form is characterized by abdominal pain, nausea, weakness or paralysis of the extremities, and psychiatric symptoms, such as irritability, depression, agitation, and delirium.

PORT abbreviation for SCHIZOPHRENIA PATIENT OUTCOMES RESEARCH TEAM.

Portman Clinic a major British clinic set up in 1933 in Portman Square, London, England, by three psychoanalysts to work with criminals and psychopaths. This led to the study and treatment of all mental and behavioral abnormalities and disorders. The clinic joined the TAVISTOCK CLINIC in the Tavistock and Portman National Health Service Trust in 1994. Apart from clinical and mental health services, this trust now provides training in forensic psychotherapy to qualified psychiatrists.

positioning *n.* in psychotherapy, deviation of the therapist from his or her typical method of operation or of conducting a session. For example, the therapist may give information or direction contrary to that anticipated by the client on the basis of the therapist's usual approach.

positive addiction a concept based on the assumption that some life activities in which a person feels a need or urge to participate, such as meditation or exercising, are positive even though they may possibly attain a level or a form of addiction. Positive addictions are considered healthy therapeutic alternatives relative to negative addictions, such as drug abuse, alcohol dependence, or cigarette smoking. [developed by U.S. psychiatrist William Glasser (1925–)]

positive affect the internal feeling state (AFFECT) that occurs when a goal has been attained, a source of threat has been avoided, or the individual is satisfied with the present state of affairs. The tendency to experience such states is called **positive affectivity**.

positive attitude in psychotherapy, the client's feelings of self-approval or of acceptance and approval of the therapist or another person, or object, or event. Compare NEGATIVE ATTITUDE.

positive correlation a relationship between two variables in which as the value of one variable increases or decreases the value of the other variable does as well. For example, people with more years of education tend to have higher incomes. See also CORRELATION COEFFICIENT.

positive emotion an emotional reaction designed to express a POSITIVE AFFECT, such as happiness when one attains a goal, relief when a danger has been avoided, or contentment when one is satisfied with the present state of affairs. Compare NEGATIVE EMOTION.

positive exercise addiction an inordinate attraction to habitual participation in physical exercise activities that brings about a positive sense of physical and psychological well-being. Compare NEGATIVE EXERCISE ADDICTION.

positive feedback 1. an arrangement whereby some of the output of a system, whether mechanical or biological, is fed back to increase the effect of input signals. Positive feedback is rare in biological systems. **2.** in social psychology, acceptance, approval, affirmation, or praise received by a person in response to his or her performance. Compare NEGATIVE FEEDBACK.

positive hallucination a false experience characterized by perceiving that something is there when it is not there. In general, positive hallucination is an exaggeration of normal perception. Although positive hallucinations are a hallmark of psychotic disturbances, such as schizophrenia, these perceptual experiences can also be generated by hypnosis. See HALLUCINATION. Compare NEGATIVE HALLUCINATION.

positive illusion a belief about oneself that is pleasant or positive and that is held regardless of its truth. The most common positive illusions involve exaggerating one's good traits (beneffectance), overestimating one's degree of control over personally important events (see ILLUSION OF CONTROL), and sustaining unrealistic optimism (see REPRESSIVE COPING STYLE).

P

positive incentive an object or condition that constitutes a desired goal and may result in GOAL-DIRECTED BEHAVIOR. Compare NEGATIVE INCENTIVE.

positive motivation the impulse to engage in behaviors that result in desired outcomes, for example, wanting to work hard in order to obtain praise or promotion from an employer.

positive Oedipus complex see OEDIPUS COMPLEX.

positive psychology a field of psychological theory and research that focuses on the psychological states (e.g., contentment, joy), individual traits or CHARACTER STRENGTHS (e.g., intimacy, integrity, altruism, wisdom), and social institutions that enhance SUBJECTIVE WELL-BEING and make life most worth living. A manual, *Character Strengths and Virtues: A Handbook and Classification*, serves this perspective in a manner parallel to the *DSM–IV–TR* for the categorization of mental illness. [term coined by Abraham MASLOW and adapted by U.S. psychologist Martin P. Seligman]

positive punishment punishment that results because some stimulus or circumstance is presented as a consequence of a response. For example, if a response results in presentation of a loud noise and the response becomes less likely as a result of this experience, then positive punishment has occurred. Compare NEGATIVE PUNISHMENT.

positive regard feelings of warmth, caring, acceptance, and importance expressed by someone toward another. Positive regard is considered necessary for psychological health and the development of a consistent sense of self-worth and is also a cornerstone of certain therapeutic approaches, particularly that of U.S. psychologist Carl Rogers (1902–1987). See also CONDITIONAL POSITIVE REGARD; UNCONDITIONAL POSITIVE REGARD.

positive reinforcement 1. an increase in the probability of occurrence of some activity because that activity results in the presentation of a stimulus or of some circumstance. **2.** the procedure of presenting a positive reinforcer after a response. See REINFORCEMENT. Compare NEGATIVE REINFORCEMENT.

positive schizophrenia a form of schizophrenia in which POSITIVE SYMPTOMS predominate, as evidenced in the person's bizarre behavior, illogical speech or writing, or expression of hallucinations and delusions. Although more dramatically evident than NEGATIVE SCHIZOPHRENIA, the positive aspect is usually less challenging to treat. [defined in 1982 by U.S. psychiatrist Nancy C. Andreasen and Scott A. Olsen]

positive self-regard an attitude of self-esteem or self-worth. Positive self-regard is often sought as a goal in treatment and is fostered by the therapist's regard for the client.

positive symptom a symptom of schizophrenia that represents an excess or distortion of normal function, as distinct from a deficiency in or lack of normal function (compare NEGATIVE SYMPTOM). Positive symptoms include delusions or hallucinations, disorganized behavior, and manifest conceptual disorganization. Positive symptoms are more dramatic than negative symptoms and are less distinctive of schizophrenia: Swiss psychiatrist Eugen Bleuler (1857–1939) regarded them as SECONDARY SYMPTOMS. See POSITIVE SCHIZOPHRENIA.

positive transference in psychoanalytic theory, DISPLACEMENT onto the therapist of feelings of attachment, love, idealization, or other positive emotions that were originally experienced toward the parents or other significant individuals. Compare NEGATIVE TRANSFERENCE. See TRANSFERENCE.

positivism *n.* a family of philosophical positions holding that all meaningful propositions must be reducible to sensory experience and observation, and thus that all genuine knowledge is to be built on strict adherence to empirical methods of verification. Positivism first became an explicit position in the work of French thinkers Auguste Comte (1798–1857) and Claude Henri de Rouvroy, Comte de Saint-Simon (1760–1825), although it is implicit to varying degrees in most earlier forms of empiricism. Its effect is to establish science as the model for all forms of valid inquiry and to dismiss the truth claims of religion, metaphysics, and speculative philosophy. Positivism, particularly LOGICAL POSITIVISM, was extremely influential in the early development of psychology and helped to form its commitment to empirical methods. It continues to be a major force in contemporary psychology. See also MACHIAN POSITIVISM. **—positivist** *adj.*

positron emission tomography (**PET**) a technique used to evaluate cerebral metabolism using radiolabeled tracers, such as 2-deoxyglucose labeled with fluorine-18, which emit positrons as they are metabolized. This technique enables documentation of functional changes that occur during the performance of mental activities.

possession trance see DISSOCIATIVE TRANCE DISORDER.

possessiveness *n.* **1.** in general, excessive striving to claim possession or ownership. **2.** an abnormal tendency to control or dominate others, generally involving the restriction of their social relationships. In its most extreme form, this pattern of behavior is often associated with abusive relationships. See also JEALOUSY.

possible self in models of self-concept, a mental representation of what one could become. Possible selves are cognitive manifestations of enduring goals, aspirations, fears, and threats that provide plans and strategies for the future. They may be positive, providing an image of something to strive for, or negative, providing an image of something to be avoided.

postcaptivity health problems health problems that develop after a period of captivity, especially in prisoners of war, which may include injuries, posttraumatic stress reactions, affective reactions, or a combination of these. Many former captives, but not all, may show POSTTRAUMATIC STRESS DISORDER in the years following release, sometimes with a delayed onset.

postconcussion syndrome persistent, pervasive changes in cognitive abilities and emotional functioning that occur as a result of diffuse trauma to the brain during concussion. An individual with this syndrome may appear to be within normal limits neurologically but suffers from persistent depression, fatigue, impulse-control problems, and difficulties with concentration and memory. Postconcussion syndrome is frequently seen in individuals who have been repeatedly beaten on the head and face, such as battered children or women (see BATTERED-CHILD SYNDROME; BATTERED-WOMAN SYNDROME).

postemployment services 1. in VOCATIONAL REHABILITATION, follow-up assistance or programs designed to help recently employed individuals with disabilities adjust to their new job situation. Examples include counseling, financial support, and continuing medical treatment and care. **2.** training and services provided to help individuals who are economically disadvantaged (e.g., those receiving public assistance in the form of welfare) obtain employment, develop various work-related skills essential to sustained long-term employment, and enhance their potential for wage increases and career advancement. Such services may include access to and assistance with child care and transportation; flexible work hours; on-the-job training; continuing education classes; and mentoring programs designed to help newly hired individuals adjust to the workplace.

post hoc comparison a comparison among two or more means in ANALYSIS OF VARIANCE or MULTIPLE REGRESSION analysis that is formulated after the data have been examined. Also called **post hoc contrast**.

posthypnotic amnesia an individual's incapacity to remember what transpired during a period of hypnosis, typically by instruction of the hypnotist. However, highly susceptible individuals may show spontaneous posthypnotic amnesia.

posthypnotic suggestion a suggestion made to a person under hypnosis and acted upon after awakening from the hypnotic trance. Usually, the act is carried out in response to a prearranged cue from the hypnotist, and the participant does not know why he or she is performing the act.

postictal *adj.* following a sudden attack, especially a seizure or a stroke. During the **postictal period** following a seizure, the individual may be confused, disoriented, and unable to form new memories. The length of the postictal period may vary from less than a second to many hours and depends on the type of seizure.

postpartum blues see BABY BLUES.

postpartum depression a MAJOR DEPRESSIVE EPISODE or, less commonly, MINOR DEPRESSIVE DISORDER that affects women within 4 weeks after childbirth. Compare BABY BLUES.

postpartum emotional disturbance 1. any MOOD DISORDER that affects women following childbirth. **2.** fluctuations in mood following childbirth that do not meet the criteria for any mood disorder.

postpartum psychosis psychotic symptoms (e.g., delusions or hallucinations) that occur in women shortly after childbirth, often associated with POSTPARTUM DEPRESSION.

postschizophrenic depression a depressive episode that may follow an ACUTE SCHIZOPHRENIC EPISODE. Postschizophrenic depression is viewed variously as a routine event in recovery from schizophrenic decompensation, as a mood disturbance that existed previously and was masked by the schizophrenic episode, or as a side effect to drug treatment for schizophrenia.

postsynaptic receptor any receptor that is located on the cell membrane or in the interior of a postsynaptic neuron. Interaction with an effector substance (e.g., a neurotransmitter), released either by the presynaptic neuron or from another site, initiates a chain of biochemical events contributing, for example, to excitation or inhibition of the postsynaptic neuron.

posttest 1. *n.* a test administered after completion of the principal test or instruction program. It may be given in conjunction with a PRETEST to assess comprehension of the content and nature of the main test as well as its effectiveness as an assessment instrument. **2.** *n.* a test administered after the application of an intervention or control condition. **3.** *vb.* to administer a posttest.

posttest counseling a type of GENETIC COUNSELING that occurs during and after disclosure of genetic test results. Posttest counseling focuses on the individual's understanding of the meaning of the test result and of the options for SCREENING. Considerable attention is given to the psychological status of the individual and to assessing whether the individual needs further genetic or psychological services.

posttraumatic amnesia (**PTA**) a disturbance of memory following a a physical injury (e.g., a concussion) or a psychologically upsetting experience (e.g., sexual abuse). The traumatic event itself may be forgotten or events following the trauma may be forgotten. The period of forgetting may be continuous, or the person may experience vague, incomplete recollections of the traumatic event.

posttraumatic disorders emotional or other disturbances whose symptoms appear after a patient has endured a traumatic experience. Common posttraumatic disorders include POSTTRAUMATIC STRESS DISORDER, ACUTE STRESS DISORDER, the DISSOCIATIVE DISORDERS, and some types of PHOBIAS and ANXIETY DISORDERS.

posttraumatic personality disorder a personality disorder occasionally observed after a severe head injury. Some patients become indifferent and withdrawn, but most are irritable, impulsive, petulant, extremely selfish, and irresponsible. Older patients and those suffering from frontal-lobe damage may show impaired memory with CONFABULATION. See also POSTCONCUSSION SYNDROME.

posttraumatic stress disorder (**PTSD**) in *DSM–IV–TR*, a disorder that results when an individual lives through or witnesses an event in which he or she believes that there is a threat to life or physical integrity and safety and experiences fear, terror, or helplessness. The symptoms are characterized by (a) reexperiencing the trauma in painful recollections, flashbacks, or recurrent dreams or nightmares; (b) diminished responsiveness (emotional anesthesia or numbing), with disinterest in significant activities and with feelings of detachment and estrangement from others; and (c) chronic physiological arousal, leading to such symptoms as exaggerated startle response, disturbed sleep, difficulty in concentrating or remembering, guilt about surviving when others did not (see SURVIVOR GUILT), and avoidance of activities that call the traumatic event to mind. Subtypes are CHRONIC POSTTRAUMATIC STRESS DISORDER and DELAYED POSTTRAUMATIC STRESS DISORDER. When the symptoms do not last longer than 4 weeks a diagnosis of ACUTE STRESS DISORDER is given instead.

posttreatment follow-up a periodic check on the progress of people who have received some form of psychotherapeutic or medical treatment. In research studies, posttreatment follow-up is used to see if the effects of treatment are maintained or if relapse occurs. If the effects of treatment are maintained, it is inferred that the treatment has lasting rather than temporary effects.

postural hypotension see ORTHOSTATIC HYPOTENSION.

posturing *n.* the assumption of a bizarre or inappropriate body position or attitude for an extended period of time. It is commonly observed in CATATONIA.

postvention *n.* the emotional release needed by helpers and others who work with those who have survived a traumatic event or who have directly experienced personal trauma or natural catastrophe. It is similar to debriefing following experience in working with victims of disasters (see CRITICAL-INCIDENT STRESS DEBRIEFING). [defined by 20th-century U.S. psychologist Edwin S. Schneidman]

pot *n.* slang for marijuana. See CANNABIS.

potassium channel see ION CHANNEL.

potency *n.* **1.** the ability of a male to perform sexual intercourse, that is, to maintain an erection and achieve ejaculation. Compare IMPOTENCE. **2.** in pharmacology, see DOSE–RESPONSE RELATIONSHIP. **—potent** *adj.*

potential-stress score see LIFE-CHANGE UNIT.

potentiation *n.* a form of DRUG INTERACTION in which the addition of a second drug intensifies certain properties of the first drug administered. It often refers to the ability of a nontoxic drug to render the effects of a toxic drug more severe than when the toxic agent is administered singly.

potlatch *n.* a ceremony among some Native American peoples of the northwestern United States that involves a ceremonial feast and the distribution of impressive gifts, typically to establish prestige or to affirm social status.

Pötzl phenomenon (**Poetzl phenomenon**) the phenomenon whereby words or pictures that are presented subliminally may appear in imagery or dreams a short time later. It is taken as an example of SUBLIMINAL PERCEPTION. [Otto **Pötzl** (1877–1962), Austrian neurologist and psychiatrist]

Pötzl's syndrome a form of pure ALEXIA associated with visual field defects and disturbances of the color sense. The syndrome is believed to be the result of a lesion in the medullary layer of the lingual gyrus of the dominant hemisphere of the brain, with damage to the CORPUS CALLOSUM. [Otto **Pötzl**]

poverty of content of speech speech that is adequate in quantity but too vague, repetitious, and lacking in content to be qualitatively adequate. It is frequently observed in schizophrenia and is distinct from POVERTY OF SPEECH, in which the quantity of speech is diminished.

poverty of ideas a thought disturbance, often associated with schizophrenia, dementia, and severe depression, in which there is reduced spontaneity and productivity of thought as evidenced by speech that is vague or full of simple or meaningless repetitions or stereotyped phrases. The term is sometimes used interchangeably with INTELLECTUAL IMPOVERISHMENT. See also POVERTY OF SPEECH.

poverty of speech excessively brief speech with few elaborations that occurs in schizophrenia or occasionally in the context of a major depressive episode. It is distinct from POVERTY OF CONTENT OF SPEECH, in which the quality of speech is diminished. Also called **laconic speech**.

power *n.* **1.** the capacity to influence others, even when they try to resist this influence. Social power derives from a number of sources: control over rewards (reward power) and punishments (coercive power); a right to require and demand obedience (legitimate power); others' identification with, attraction to, or respect for the powerholder (referent power); others' belief that the powerholder possesses superior skills and abilities (expert power); and the powerholder's access to and use of informational resources (**informational power**). **2.** in hypothesis testing, the probability that the NULL HYPOTHESIS will be rejected when the ALTERNATIVE HYPOTHESIS is true. In this case, it is likely that the experiment will be able to yield the results that the researcher expects because the alternative hypothesis typically expresses the belief of the researcher.

power function 1. a relationship in which the values for one variable vary as a function of another variable raised to a power. In mathematics, it is expressed by the equation $Y = aX^b$, where X and Y are the variables and a and b are numerical constants. When plotted on paper, a power function is linear. Power functions have been used to characterize the scales relating perceived and physical intensity, as well as to characterize the relationship between response speed and practice. **2.** in HYPOTHESIS TESTING, a functional relationship between the power of a statistical test and one of the variables that affect power, such as sample size.

powerlessness *n.* a state of mind in which individuals feel they lack control or influence over factors or events that affect their health (mental or physical), personal lives, or the society in which they live.

P-O-X triads see BALANCE THEORY.

PPA abbreviation for PREFERRED PROVIDER ARRANGEMENT.

PPFA abbreviation for PLANNED PARENTHOOD FEDERATION OF AMERICA.

PPO *p*referred *p*rovider *o*rganization: a formally organized entity created by contractual arrangements among hospitals, physicians, employers, insurance companies, or third-party administrators to provide health care services to subscribers at a negotiated, often discounted, price.

PPVT abbreviation for PEABODY PICTURE VOCABULARY TEST.

practical intelligence the ability to apply one's intelligence in practical, everyday situations. In the TRIARCHIC THEORY OF INTELLIGENCE it is the aspect of intelligence that requires adaptation to, shaping of, and selection of new environments. Compare ANALYTICAL INTELLIGENCE; CREATIVE INTELLIGENCE.

practice guidelines criteria and strategies designed to assist mental health clinicians and practitioners and physicians in the recognition and treatment of specific disorders and diseases, as well as for ethical practice. Such guidelines are often based on the latest and best available scientific research or the considered judgment of expert panel committees representing specific professions or subdisciplines. See also CLINICAL PRACTICE GUIDELINES.

practice trial the first of a series of opportunities to respond to a test, which is given to participants to acquaint them with the procedure of the test and is therefore not scored.

Prader–Willi syndrome (**PWS**) a congenital disorder marked by mental retardation, short stature, hypotonia (flaccid muscles), hypogonadism (underdeveloped sex organs), obesity, insensitivity to pain, and short hands and feet. Caused by an abnormality of chromosome 15 (lack of the paternal segment 15q11.2–12), it is observed most frequently in males, perhaps because the gonadal abnormality is more easily detected in males. Affected individuals have an excessive appetite and are constantly foraging for food. When diabetes mellitus is associated with the condition, it is called **Royer's syndrome**. Also called **Prader–Labhart–Willi syndrome**; **Prader–Labhart–Willi–Fanconi syndrome**. [reported in 1956 by Andrea **Prader** (1919–2001) and Heinrich **Willi** (1900–1971), with Alexis **Labhart** (1916–), Swiss pediatricians]

pragmatism *n.* a philosophical position holding that the truth value of a proposition or a theory is to be found in its practical consequences:

If, for example, the hypothesis of God makes people virtuous and happy, then it may be considered true. Although some forms of pragmatism emphasize only the material consequences of an idea, more sophisticated positions, including that of William JAMES, recognize conceptual and moral consequences. Arguably, all forms of pragmatism tend toward relativism, because they can provide no absolute grounds—only empirical grounds—for determining truth, and no basis for judging whether the consequences in question are to be considered good or bad. [coined by U.S. physicist and philosopher Charles Sanders Peirce (1839–1914)] —**pragmatist** *adj., n.*

Prägnanz *n.* one of the GESTALT PRINCIPLES OF ORGANIZATION. It states that people tend to perceive forms as the simplest and most meaningful, stable, and complete structures that conditions permit. Also called **law of Prägnanz**; **principle of Prägnanz**. [German: "terseness"]

prana *n.* see CHI.

prayer *n.* communication (voiced or contemplative) with a deity or other such entity, generally for the purposes of praise, thanksgiving, supplication, or self-examination or to seek forgiveness, guidance, or serenity. The behavior has been studied periodically, at least since William JAMES, and with varied results, often supporting contradictory theoretical stances and goals. For instance, researchers and practitioners have noted, variously, that prayer can be used, on the one hand, as a defense or escape from the exploration of painful issues and as a form of magical thinking, and, on the other hand, that it can be both cognitively meaningful and therapeutically beneficial in some conditions for those with specific religous beliefs or SPIRITUALITY. Much work has been done, since the last quarter of the 20th century, by a growing body of researchers to integrate religion or religious values and intervention with psychotherapy. In appropriate circumstances, prayer may be explicitly used by some therapists as a component of intervention and treatment. The therapist and client may pray individually or together for such goals as personal or interpersonal healing, forgiveness and the ability to forgive, and the ability to examine problems and issues freely and with discernment.

preadolescence *n.* the period of CHILDHOOD preceding adolescence, comprising approximately the 2 years preceding the onset of puberty. Also called **prepubertal stage**; **prepuberty**; **prepubescence**. —**preadolescent** *adj., n.*

preattentive processing unconscious mental processing of a stimulus that occurs before attention has focused on this particular stimulus from among the array of those present in a given environment. An example of this is the disambiguation of the meaning of a particular word from among an array of words present in a given visual stimulus before conscious perception of the word. Preattentive processing is thought to identify basic stimulus features in parallel, with no limit on capacity. Also called **preattentive analysis**; **preperceptual processing**; **unconscious processing**. See also PARALLEL PROCESSING.

precipitating cause the particular factor, sometimes a traumatic or stressful experience, that is the immediate cause of a mental or physical disorder. A single precipitating event may turn a latent condition into the manifest form of the disorder. Compare PREDISPOSING CAUSE.

preclinical psychopharmacology the area of psychopharmacology that precedes the actual clinical application of a new drug on an individual patient or patient population. It usually includes laboratory studies of the pharmacological mechanisms of the drug, extrapolation of research data into human-use terms, and evaluation of possible interactions with current drugs or in patients with various medical conditions.

precocious puberty abnormally early development of sexual maturity, usually before the age of 8 in a female and 10 in a male. True precocious puberty is marked by mature gonads capable of ovulation or spermatogenesis, adult levels of female or male sex hormones, and secondary sexual characteristics. **Pseudoprecocious puberty** is a condition usually caused by an endocrine tumor that results only in premature development of secondary sex characteristics. Also called **pubertas praecox**.

precocity *n.* very early, often premature, development in a child of physical or mental functions and characteristics. —**precocious** *adj.*

preconscious (Pcs) 1. *n.* in the classical psychoanalytic theory of Sigmund FREUD, the level of the psyche that contains thoughts, feelings, and impulses not presently in awareness, but which can be more or less readily called into consciousness. Examples are the face of a friend, a verbal cliché, or the memory of a recent event. Compare CONSCIOUS; UNCONSCIOUS. **2.** *adj.* denoting or relating to thoughts, feelings, and impulses at this level of the psyche. Also called **foreconscious**.

preconscious thinking 1. the pictorial, magical, fantasy thinking of children that precedes the development of logical thinking. [introduced in 1938 by Austrian psychoanalyst Otto Fenichel (1897–1946)] **2.** in psychoanalytic theory, thinking that takes place at the level of the PRECONSCIOUS. Preconscious thinking has sometimes been cited to explain apparently unconscious, intuitive thought processes, as well as certain kinds of creative leaps and insights.

predatory paraphilia sexual interest and arousal focused on an activity that involves an unwilling participant rather than a consenting partner (see PARAPHILIA). Examples include EXHIBITIONISM and FROTTEURISM.

predicate thinking a thought process in

which objects are considered similar or even identical because they share a particular attribute. Jean PIAGET considered such thinking to be typical of early cognitive development. Likewise, psychoanalysis associates it with the PRIMARY PROCESS thinking typical of the ID, which manifests itself in dreams and fantasies.

prediction *n.* an attempt to foretell what will happen in a particular case, generally on the basis of past instances or accepted principles. A **theoretical prediction** gives the expected results of an experiment or controlled observation in accordance with the logic of a particular theory. In science, the use of prediction and observation to test hypotheses is a cornerstone of the empirical method. However, by their very nature, the theories, constructs, and explanatory models current in psychology are not always open to direct validation or falsification in this way. In psychological assessment, personality tests and other psychometric instruments can often predict participants' behaviors or other characteristics with an impressive level of accuracy. In psychiatry, it may be possible to predict the general behavior or prognosis of patients whose personality pattern is known but not their specific behavior, since so many factors are involved. See also PSEUDOSCIENCE. **—predict** *vb.* **—predictable** *adj.* **—predictive** *adj.*

predictive testing see PREDISPOSITION.

predictive validity an index of how well a test correlates with a variable that is measured in the future, at some point after the test has been administered. For example, the predictive validity of a test designed to predict the onset of a disease would be calculated by the extent to which it was successful at identifying those individuals who did, in fact, later develop that disease.

predictor variable in REGRESSION ANALYSIS, a variable that may be used to predict the value of another variable; that is, an INDEPENDENT VARIABLE.

predisposing cause a factor that increases the probability that a mental or physical disorder or hereditary characteristic will develop but is not the immediate cause of it. Compare PRECIPITATING CAUSE.

predisposition *n.* **1.** a susceptibility to developing a disorder or disease, the actual development of which is initiated by the interaction of certain biological, psychological, or environmental factors. **2.** in genetics, any hereditary factor that, given the necessary conditions, will lead to the development of a certain trait or disease. **Predisposition testing** is genetic testing for mutations that are less than 100% penetrant. Thus, a positive test result indicates that the individual has an increased predisposition to develop the disease but might not necessarily do so. If a mutation is fully penetrant, the testing is referred to as **predictive testing**, since all those who carry the mutated gene will develop the disease.

preeclampsia *n.* an increase in blood pressure (see HYPERTENSION), associated with edema or proteinuria (the presence of protein in the urine), or both, occurring in a pregnant woman. There may also be signs of headaches, dizziness, and nervous irritability. Preeclampsia may progress to the serious condition of eclampsia, or convulsions usually followed by coma.

preference for consistency a personality trait reflecting the extent to which a person desires to maintain consistency among elements in his or her cognitive system. See also COGNITIVE DISSONANCE; COGNITIVE DISSONANCE THEORY. [originally proposed by U.S. psychologists Robert B. Cialdini (1945–), Melanie R. Trost, and Jason T. Newsom (1965–)]

preferred provider arrangement (**PPA**) a contractual arrangement between a health care insurer and a health care provider or group of providers who agree to provide services at reduced or prenegotiated rates.

preferred provider organization see PPO.

prefrontal cortex the most anterior (forward) part of the cerebral cortex of each FRONTAL LOBE in the brain. It functions in attention, planning, working memory, and the expression of emotions and appropriate social behaviors and is divided into a dorsolateral region and an orbitofrontal region. Damage to the prefrontal cortex in humans leads to emotional, motor, and cognitive impairments. Also called **frontal association area**.

prefrontal lobe the furthest forward area of each CEREBRAL HEMISPHERE of the brain, which is concerned with such functions as memory and learning, emotion, and social behavior. See also FRONTAL LOBE.

prefrontal lobotomy see LOBOTOMY.

pregenital organization in psychoanalytic theory, organization of LIBIDO functions in the early stages of PSYCHOSEXUAL DEVELOPMENT preceding the GENITAL STAGE.

pregenital phase in psychoanalytic theory, the early stages of PSYCHOSEXUAL DEVELOPMENT that precede the organization of the LIBIDO around the genital zone (i.e., the ORAL STAGE and the ANAL STAGE). Some theorists also include the PHALLIC STAGE in the pregenital phase, whereas others use the term synonymously with the PREOEDIPAL phase.

prejudice *n.* a negative attitude toward another person or group formed in advance of any experience with that person or group. Prejudices include an affective component (emotions that range from mild nervousness to hatred), a cognitive component (assumptions and beliefs about groups, including STEREOTYPES), and a behavioral component (negative behaviors, including discrimination and violence). They tend to be resistant to change because they distort the prejudiced individual's perception of information pertaining to the group. Prejudice based on racial grouping is racism; prejudice based on sex is sexism.

prelogical thinking in psychoanalytic theory, primitive thought processes that are characteristic of early childhood, when thought is under the control of the PLEASURE PRINCIPLE rather than the REALITY PRINCIPLE. Such thinking may also occur later in life, as in daydreaming, in which WISH-FULFILLMENT is dominant. See also PRIMARY PROCESS.

premarital counseling educational and supportive guidance provided to individuals planning marriage by a member of the clergy trained in counseling, a therapist, or some other appropriately qualified person. Premarital counseling may take the form of advice and answers to questions covering a wide range of matters, such as the timing of marriage, rights and responsibilities of spouses in marriage, birth-control methods, and sexual intimacy. Assessment instruments to identify potential conflicts in the marriage can help the premarital counselor to focus sessions appropriately.

premarital sex sexual relations before marriage. See also FORNICATION.

premature ejaculation a sexual dysfunction in which EJACULATION occurs with minimal sexual stimulation, before, on, or shortly after PENETRATION or simply earlier than desired. The diagnosis takes into account such factors as age, novelty of the sexual partner, and the frequency and duration of intercourse. The diagnosis does not apply if the disturbance is due to the direct effect of a substance (e.g., withdrawal from opioids). See also SQUEEZE TECHNIQUE.

premature termination see TERMINATION.

premeditation *n.* a deliberate resolve to commit a crime, especially a violent crime, as revealed by evidence of planning or other forethought. A premeditated crime is often considered more serious than the same offense committed intentionally but without prior resolve. See MALICE AFORETHOUGHT. **—premeditated** *adj.*

premenstrual dysphoric disorder a MOOD DISORDER in women that begins in the week prior to the onset of menstruation and subsides within the first few days of menstruation. Women experience emotional mood swings, including markedly depressed mood, anxiety, feelings of helplessness, and decreased interest in activities. In contrast to PREMENSTRUAL SYNDROME, the symptoms must be severe enough to impair functioning in social activities, work, and relationships. The symptoms of premenstrual dysphoric disorder are of comparable severity to those experienced in MINOR DEPRESSIVE DISORDER. Also called **late luteal phase dysphoric disorder**; **premenstrual stress syndrome**. See also DEPRESSIVE DISORDER NOT OTHERWISE SPECIFIED.

premenstrual syndrome (**PMS**) a collection of psychological and physical symptoms experienced by women during the week prior to the onset of menstruation and subsiding within the first few days of menstruation. Symptoms can include mood swings, irritability, fatigue, headache, bloating, abdominal discomfort, and breast tenderness. In contrast to the more severe PREMENSTRUAL DYSPHORIC DISORDER, premenstrual syndrome has a less distinctive pattern of symptoms and does not involve major impairment in social and occupational functioning. Also called **premenstrual stress syndrome**; **premenstrual tension**.

premorbid *adj.* characterizing an individual's condition before the onset of a disease or disorder. **—premorbidity** *n.*

premorbid abilities an estimate of an individual's psychological abilities prior to a neurological trauma or disease that is used to determine the degree of loss caused by the damage. This estimate is based on testing and assessments conducted after the damage has occurred; it may include consideration of such factors as educational level, occupational history, and client and family reports.

premorbid adjustment a measure of the level of a person's functioning before the onset of an acute psychological disorder. The measure, as used in the PHILLIPS RATING SCALE OF PREMORBID ADJUSTMENT IN SCHIZOPHRENIA, has been found to be of value in predicting the course of schizophrenia.

premorbid personality 1. personality traits that existed before a physical injury or other traumatic event or before the development of a disease or disorder. **2.** personality strengths and weaknesses that predispose the individual toward mental health and well-being or to a particular mental disorder (e.g., depression or schizophrenia) or that affect the speed or likelihood of recovery from a disorder. Also called **primary personality**.

premorbid schizophrenia the quality of physical, psychological, and emotional functioning in an individual prior to the emergence of schizophrenia.

premotor area an area of the MOTOR CORTEX concerned with motor planning. In contrast to the SUPPLEMENTARY MOTOR AREA, input to the premotor area is primarily visual, and its activity is usually triggered by external events. Also called **Brodmann's area 6**; **intermediate precentral area**; **premotor cortex**.

prenatal *adj.* prior to birth: pertaining to that which exists or occurs between conception and birth.

prenatal care medical, health, and educational services provided to or obtained by a woman during pregnancy. Such services are intended to prevent complications and decrease the risk of maternal or prenatal mortality.

prenatal counseling counseling given to couples or to single women who are expecting a baby or planning a pregnancy. It sometimes also covers advice on terminating the pregnancy (see ABORTION). For those who are considering adoption, prenatal counseling includes advice on the child's arrival and future, dealing with friends and relatives, and coping with any impact on the biological mother and father.

prenatal developmental anomaly a congenital abnormality that originates in the course of development before birth. Examples include cleft palate and spina bifida.

prenatal diagnosis determination of a pathological condition or the presence of disease or genetic abnormalities in a fetus. See AMNIOCENTESIS; CHORIONIC VILLUS SAMPLING; ULTRASOUND.

prenatal influence any influence on the developing organism between conception and birth. Prenatal influences include radiation effects, maternal diseases (e.g., rubella, toxoplasmosis), alcohol or drug abuse, excessive smoking, blood incompatibility, nutritional deficiency, and emotional stress.

prenatal stress stress in a pregnant woman, which is marked by elevation of stress hormones and other biological changes, with an increased likelihood of intrauterine infection. Preterm births and low birth weight are among the most widely recognized effects of maternal stress during pregnancy. Women who experience high levels of psychological stress are significantly more likely to deliver preterm. Preterm babies are susceptible to a range of complications, including chronic lung disease. Some recent studies suggest that stress in the womb can also affect a baby's temperament and neurobehavioral development: Infants whose mothers experienced high levels of stress while pregnant, particularly in the first trimester, show signs of increased depression and irritability.

preoccupation *n.* a state of being self-absorbed and "lost in thought," which ranges from transient absent-mindedness to a symptom of schizophrenia in which the individual withdraws from external reality and turns inward upon the self.

preoccupied attachment an adult attachment style that combines a negative INTERNAL WORKING MODEL OF ATTACHMENT of oneself, characterized by doubt in one's own competence and efficacy, and a positive internal working model of attachment of others, characterized by one's trust in the ability and dependability of others. Individuals with preoccupied attachment are presumed to seek others' help when distressed. Compare DISMISSIVE ATTACHMENT; FEARFUL ATTACHMENT; SECURE ATTACHMENT.

preoedipal *adj.* **1.** in psychoanalytic theory, pertaining to the first stages of PSYCHOSEXUAL DEVELOPMENT, before the development of the OEDIPUS COMPLEX during the PHALLIC STAGE. During this phase the mother is the exclusive love object of both sexes and the father is not yet considered either a rival or a love object. **2.** more generally, denoting organization or functions before the onset of the Oedipus complex. See also PREPHALLIC.

preorgasmic *adj.* **1.** relating to the state immediately before ORGASM. It is characterized by increased breathing, heart rate, and blood pressure; semispastic muscle contractions; and maximum increase in the size of the glans penis, testes, and upper vaginal walls. **2.** denoting the status of a person who has never experienced orgasm. See PRIMARY ORGASMIC DYSFUNCTION.

preparation *n.* in cognitive psychology, the process of increasing readiness for an activity, for example, by planning or imagining a movement before it is executed. **—prepare** *vb.*

preparatory response any response (except the final one) in a series of behaviors that leads to a goal or reinforcement. Preparatory responses themselves are not immediately goal-directed.

prepared learning a species-specific and innate tendency to quickly learn a certain type of knowledge. Some associations between stimuli, responses, and reinforcers may be more easily formed due to biological preparedness. For example, animals may be prepared to associate new foods with illness, and it has been suggested that humans learn certain phobias more readily due to preparedness.

prephallic *adj.* in psychoanalytic theory, referring to the stages of PSYCHOSEXUAL DEVELOPMENT preceding the PHALLIC STAGE (i.e., the ORAL STAGE and the ANAL STAGE). See also PREGENITAL PHASE; PREOEDIPAL.

pre–post design see BEFORE–AFTER DESIGN.

prepsychotic panic a stage in the development of schizophrenia in which self-image is disordered: Individuals feel guilty, unlovable, humiliated, or otherwise different but have not yet acquired symptoms of delusions and hallucinations. [defined by Italian-born U.S. psychiatrist Silvano Arieti (1914–1982)]

prepsychotic personality characteristics and behavior of a person, such as eccentricities, withdrawal, litigiousness, apathy, or hypersensitivity, that may be indicative of later development of a psychotic disorder.

prepuberty *n.* see PREADOLESCENCE.

prerelease anxiety state anxiety experienced by an individual about to leave an institutional setting and reenter the everyday world. For example, prison inmates may fear having to compete in the real world again.

preschool program an educational curriculum for children who are below the required minimum age for participation in regular classroom work. Preschool programs for intellectually or emotionally challenged children are designed to develop social skills and provide stimulation at levels appropriate for each child.

prescribing *n.* **1.** in psychotherapy and medicine, advising or telling a patient what to do in specific situations. **2.** ordering the use of a MEDICATION.

prescribing psychology an emerging area of CLINICAL PSYCHOLOGY in which licensed, appropriately trained practitioners are legally authorized to prescribe medications for the treatment of emotional and mental disorders (see PSYCHOACTIVE DRUG). This integration of medication management with psychological practice is controversial—within the United States, only New Mexico and Louisiana have enacted laws permitting it, the former in 2002 and the latter in 2004. In addition to fulfilling all other requirements required for professional licensure as a practicing clinician, prescribing psychologists in these states must complete a postdoctoral psychopharmacology training program and pass a national certification exam. New Mexico also requires a supervised 400-hour, 100-patient practicum. Also called **medical psychology**. See PRESCRIPTIVE AUTHORITY.

prescription privilege the legal right to prescribe drugs and other medications necessary for the treatment of medical or mental health disorders.

prescriptive authority (**RxP**) the legally recognized right of specially trained psychologists to dispense PSYCHOACTIVE DRUGS to their clients. The practice is highly controversial, both within the United States and abroad. Indeed, of the several states that have introduced RxP legislation, only New Mexico and Louisiana have passed it. Those who oppose RxP cite concerns that psychologists, not having attended medical school, do not have the requisite knowledge and training to be able to prescribe safely. For example, they worry that psychologists with RxP may not screen clients carefully for health concerns or may mistakenly attribute symptoms of medical conditions to mental disorders and thus inadvertently prescribe an inappropriate medicine. Opponents also fear that psychologists trained in psychopharmacology will abandon emotional, interpersonal, and behavioral interventions in favor of medication management, rather than incorporating the one with the other. Those in favor of RxP, however, say not only that it can be done safely, but also that it will enable psychologists to provide improved care at a reduced cost because they can combine their communication skills and understanding of behavior with advanced training in the biological bases and treatments of mental illness. Supporters also cite such benefits as enhancing the quality and accessibility of health care for those in rural and other underserved communities; facilitating more frequent and thorough communication between psychologists and PRIMARY CARE PROVIDERS; reducing multiple medications and better utilizing those that are necessary through knowledge of alternative psychological treatments; and improving management of the psychological concomitants of health care issues. Despite the heated debate surrounding RxP, many universities and independent training facilities are seeking to establish appropriate postdoctoral training programs that meet the criteria contained within the American Psychological Association's Recommended Postdoctoral Training in Psychopharmacology for Prescription Privilege. Additionally, the affiliated College of Professional Psychology has developed the Psychopharmacology Examination for Psychologists for use by U.S. and Canadian licensing boards. See also PRESCRIBING PSYCHOLOGY.

prescriptive eclectic psychotherapy see ECLECTIC PSYCHOTHERAPY.

presenile dementia DEMENTIA with an onset before the age of 65.

presenile dementia of the Alzheimer's type (**PDAT**) an older name for DEMENTIA of the Alzheimer's type with onset before age 65. See also ALZHEIMER'S DISEASE.

presenility *n.* **1.** DEMENTIA that occurs prior to old age (typically, prior to age 65). **2.** the period of life immediately preceding dementia in old age.

presentation *n.* **1.** in interpersonal relations and social interaction, the way in which an individual behaves or expresses himself or herself. **2.** in psychoanalytic theory, the means or vehicle through which an INSTINCT is expressed. Also called **instinct representation**. **—present** *vb.*

presenting symptom a symptom or problem that is offered by a client or a patient as the reason for seeking treatment. In psychotherapy, a client may present with depression, anxiety, panic, anger, chronic pain, or family or marital problems, for example; such symptoms may become the focus of treatment or may represent a different, underlying problem that is not recognized or regarded by the client as requiring help. Also called **presenting problem**.

Present State Examination (**PSE**) a structured interview comprising about 400 items, including a wide range of symptoms likely to be manifested during an acute episode of one of the functional psychoses. The PSE was developed for the WHO-sponsored INTERNATIONAL PILOT STUDY OF SCHIZOPHRENIA.

presolution variability the variability observed in behavior prior to arriving at a successful solution to a difficult problem.

press *n.* in the PERSONOLOGY of U.S. psychologist Henry Alexander Murray (1893–1988), an environmental stimulus, such as a person or situation, that arouses a need. Examples are the birth of a sibling, parental discord, feelings of social inferiority, or the sight of food when hungry. See NEED–PRESS THEORY.

pressure *n.* in psychology, excessive or stressful demands, imagined or real, made on an individual by another individual or group to think, feel, or act in particular ways. The experience of pressure is often the source of cognitive and affective discomfort or disorder, as well as of maladaptive coping strategies, the correction of which may be a mediate or end goal in psychotherapy.

pressured speech accelerated and sometimes uncontrolled speech that often occurs in the context of a HYPOMANIC EPISODE or a MANIC EPISODE. Also called **pressure of speech**.

pressure of activity compulsive and occasionally uncontrolled activity and PSYCHOMOTOR AGITATION, usually occurring in the context of a MANIC EPISODE.

pressure of ideas a characteristic symptom of MANIA in which there is increased spontaneity and productivity of thought: Numerous, widely varied ideas arise quickly and pass through the mind rapidly. It is usually manifested as PRESSURED SPEECH or PRESSURE OF ACTIVITY. Also called **thought pressure**.

pressure of speech see PRESSURED SPEECH.

prestige suggestion a method of supportive, SYMPTOMATIC TREATMENT that relies on the prestige of the therapist in the eyes of the patient. The so-called **omnipotent therapist** may be able to abolish undesirable symptoms, at least temporarily, by suggestion.

pretest 1. *n.* a preliminary test or trial run to familiarize the person or group tested with the content and nature of a particular test. It may be given in conjunction with a POSTTEST. **2.** *n.* a trial run administered before the application of an intervention or control condition. **3.** *vb.* to administer a pretest.

pretest counseling a type of GENETIC COUNSELING undertaken before deciding whether to undergo genetic testing. Pretest counseling includes educating individuals about the contribution of genetics to the etiology of disease, taking a family history and creating a PEDIGREE, estimating risk, and discussing the risks, benefits, and limitations of genetic testing.

pretest–posttest design see BEFORE–AFTER DESIGN.

prevalence *n.* the total number of cases (e.g., of a disease or disorder) existing in a given population at a given time (**point prevalence**) or during a specified period (**period prevalence**). See also INCIDENCE.

prevention *n.* behavioral, biological, or social interventions intended to reduce the risk of disorders, diseases, or social problems for both individuals and entire populations. See PRIMARY PREVENTION; SECONDARY PREVENTION; TERTIARY PREVENTION.

prevention research research directed toward finding interventions to reduce the likelihood of future pathology. Such research is often concentrated on individuals or populations considered to be particularly at risk of developing a condition, disease, or disorder.

preventive care care that aims to prevent disease or its consequences, emphasizing early detection and early treatment of conditions and generally including routine physical examination, immunizations, and well-person care. See also PREVENTION; PRIMARY PREVENTION.

preventive counseling counseling that aims to prevent anticipated problems or conflicts. It is most useful when individuals may be exposed to increased stress (e.g., during adolescence or prior to an important exam or commitment) or are at risk from high levels of stress.

preventive stress management an intervention involving a session or series of sessions prior to the occurrence of anticipated stressful situations during which information on stressors, coping strategies, and opportunities to practice these strategies are provided. See also PRIMARY PREVENTION; STRESS MANAGEMENT.

preverbal *adj.* before the acquisition of language. Preverbal children communicate using nonword sounds and gestures.

prevocational training programs designed to help individuals prepare to enter a competitive work situation and workplace environment. Training is not career- or position-specific but rather focuses on helping individuals develop good work habits and gain the basic skills and abilities essential for employment in any field, such as following directions and being punctual. Prevocational training may be provided to any individual who has not had actual work experience in a competitive job market, such as a college student nearing graduation or an adult entering the workforce late in life, but is typically offered to adolescents and adults with disabilities.

priapism *n.* **1.** persistent penile erection that occurs independently of sexual arousal or that continues long after orgasm has occurred and sexual activity ceased. The condition is associated with leukemia and sickle-cell anemia and is usually painful. Immediate causes may be thrombosis, cancer, hemorrhage, inflammation, lesions involving nerve tracts between the brain and the urethra, or overdose of drugs injected into the penis to treat ERECTILE DYSFUNCTION. **2.** another name for SATYRIASIS. Priapism is named for Priapus, the Greco-Roman god of procreation and of the generative force in nature, who was the basis of a cult that worshiped the phallus.

pride *n.* a SELF-CONSCIOUS EMOTION that occurs when a goal has been attained and one's achievement has been recognized and approved by others. It differs from JOY and HAPPINESS in that these emotions do not require the approval of others for their existence. Pride also has expressive reactions that differ from joy, such as puffing up of the chest and directing attention to others or an audience. Pride can become antisocial if the sense of accomplishment is not deserved or the reaction is excessive. See also HUBRIS. **—proud** *adj.*

primacy effect the tendency for facts, impressions, or items that are presented first to be better learned or remembered than material presented later in the sequence. This can occur in both formal learning situations and social contexts. For example, it can result in a **first-impression bias**, in which the first information gained about a person has an inordinate influence on later impressions and evaluations of that person. Also called **law of primacy**; **principle of primacy**. Compare RECENCY EFFECT.

primal anxiety in psychoanalytic theory, the most basic form of anxiety, first experienced when the infant is separated from the mother at birth and suddenly has to cope with the flood of new stimuli. See also BIRTH TRAUMA; PRIMAL TRAUMA.

primal depression an obsolescent name for depression that occurs in early childhood and is theoretically attributed to absent or distant parents.

primal fantasy in psychoanalytic theory, any of a range of fantasies employed by children to fill gaps in their knowledge of sexual experience, especially one about conception and birth (see CLOACAL THEORY), parental intercourse, or castration.

primal father the head of a hypothetical primitive tribe who is slain and devoured by his sons (or other younger men) and later revered as a god, as described by Sigmund FREUD in 1913 in *Totem and Taboo*. The crime has a tragic effect on the son or sons who kill the dominant male and becomes enshrined in the culture of the tribe as a TOTEM. See also PRIMAL-HORDE THEORY.

primal-horde theory Sigmund FREUD's speculative reconstruction in *Totem and Taboo* (1913) of the original human family, which comprised a dominant male (the PRIMAL FATHER) holding sway over a subordinate group of females and younger men or sons. Freud used the theory to account for the origin of the INCEST TABOO, guilt, and totemism (see TOTEM).

primal repression see PRIMARY REPRESSION.

primal sadism in psychoanalytic theory, an aspect of the DEATH INSTINCT that is identical with MASOCHISM and remains within the person, partly as a component of the LIBIDO and partly with the self as an OBJECT.

primal scene in psychoanalytic theory, the child's first observation, in reality or fantasy, of parental intercourse or seduction, which is interpreted by the child as an act of violence (see PHALLIC SADISM). See also PRIMAL FANTASY.

primal therapy a therapeutic technique used to release deep-seated feelings and emotional frustration by crying, screaming, and hitting objects. The client is encouraged to reexperience traumatic early childhood (even peri- and prenatal) experiences and react vocally and physically to release the psychic pain associated with them. The technique, sometimes popularly and erroneously known as **primal scream therapy**, has received little scientific validation and is not advocated by most psychotherapists or counselors. [developed in the 1960s and 1970s by U.S. psychologist Arthur Janov (1924–)]

primal trauma in psychoanalytic theory, a painful situation to which an individual was subjected in early life that is presumed to be the basis of a neurosis in later life. The primal trauma is considered by some in psychoanalysis to be the BIRTH TRAUMA. See also PRIMAL ANXIETY.

primary ability any of the seven unitary factors revealed by factor analysis to be essential components of intelligence. There are seven primary abilities: verbal ability (V), word fluency (WF), numerical ability (N), spatial intelligence (S), memory (M), perceptual speed (P), and reasoning (R). These factors are measured by the **Primary Mental Abilities Test**. Also called **primary mental ability**. [proposed around 1936 by Louis L. THURSTONE]

primary aging changes associated with normal aging that are inevitable and caused by intrinsic biological or genetic factors. Examples include the appearance of gray hair and skin wrinkles. However, some age-related diseases have genetic influences, making the distinction between primary aging and SECONDARY AGING imprecise.

primary amenorrhea see AMENORRHEA.

primary anxiety in psychoanalytic theory, anxiety experienced as a spontaneous response to trauma or in response to dissolution of the EGO. Also called **automatic anxiety**. Compare SIGNAL ANXIETY.

primary appraisal in the COGNITIVE APPRAISAL THEORY of emotions, evaluation of the relevance of an event to one's goals, one's moral norms, and one's personal preferences. It is followed by SECONDARY APPRAISAL. See also CORE RELATIONAL THEMES. [proposed by U.S. psychologist Richard S. Lazarus (1922–2002)]

primary behavior disorder any of various behavior problems in children and adolescents, including habit disturbances (e.g., nail biting, temper tantrums), bed-wetting, conduct disorders (e.g., vandalism, fire setting, alcohol or drug use, sex offenses, stealing), and school-centered difficulties (e.g., truancy, school phobia, disruptive behavior).

primary care the basic or general health care a patient receives when he or she first seeks assistance from a health care system. General practitioners, family practitioners, internists, obstetricians, and pediatricians are known as PRIMARY CARE PROVIDERS (PCPs). Also called **primary health care**. Compare SECONDARY CARE; TERTIARY CARE.

primary care provider (**PCP**) a physician who provides PRIMARY CARE services and may act as the GATEKEEPER controlling patients' access to the rest of the health care system through referrals. PCPs are usually generalist physicians (e.g., internists, pediatricians, family physicians, and general practitioners) and occasionally obstetricians and gynecologists. Also called **primary physician**.

primary care psychology a specialty discipline within health, clinical, and counseling psychology that involves providing psychological preventive and treatment services under the auspices of medical professionals in such settings as clinics, hospitals, and private practices, either on site or on a consultation basis.

primary caretaker standard a standard of evaluation used in CHILD CUSTODY disputes that awards custody of the child to the parent who has previously assumed the most responsibility for and spent the most time with the child.

primary cause a condition or event that predisposes an individual to a particular disorder, which probably would not have occurred in the absence of that condition or event. Sexual contact, for example, is a common primary cause of a sexually transmitted disease.

primary consciousness sensory experience. The descriptor implies that sensory experience is an early stage in the evolution of consciousness.

primary control behavior that is aimed at producing a sense of control through an individual's direct alteration of the environment. Compare SECONDARY CONTROL. See LOCUS OF CONTROL.

primary coping a stress-management strategy in which a person actively seeks to alter objective conditions, including environmental events and other people's behavior, to bring them into line with his or her wishes. Primary coping encompasses a variety of different actions, such as seeking support, obtaining information, expressing one's emotions, or regulating one's emotions. It is a dynamic, approach-oriented COPING STRATEGY that provides an important sense of control over environmental circumstances. Also called **primary control coping**. Compare SECONDARY COPING. [identified in 1982 by Fred M. Rothbaum (1949–2011) and John R. Weisz (1945–), U.S. clinical and developmental psychologists, and Samuel S. Snyder, U.S. developmental psychologist]

primary degenerative dementia in *DSM–III*, dementia of subtle onset with a gradually progressive course but no specific cause, usually starting after the age of 65 (senile onset) but in some cases before this age (presenile onset). Subtypes with delirium, delusions, or depression were also specified. This diagnostic category has been removed from *DSM–IV–TR*, since the current definition of dementia is based on symptom pattern and does not carry the historical implication of progressively worsening or irreversible course.

primary deviance in theories of deviance and identity, an initial rule-breaking act (such as nonconformity or disobedience) performed by an otherwise socially compliant individual. In most cases individuals amend their behaviors in response to social pressure, but if they continue to violate social norms (**secondary deviance**) other people may label them as deviant. See also LABELING THEORY.

primary drive an innate DRIVE, which may be universal or species-specific, that is created by deprivation of a needed substance (e.g., food) or by the need to engage in a specific activity (e.g., nest building in birds). Compare SECONDARY DRIVE.

primary dysmenorrhea see DYSMENORRHEA.

primary emotion any one of a limited set of emotions that typically are manifested and recognized universally across cultures. They include FEAR, ANGER, JOY, SADNESS, DISGUST, CONTEMPT, and SURPRISE; some theorists also include SHAME, SHYNESS, and GUILT. Also called **basic emotion**. Compare SECONDARY EMOTION.

primary empathy an approach to CLIENT-CENTERED THERAPY in which the therapist actively tries to experience the client's situation as the client has and then tries to restate the client's thoughts, feelings, and experiences from the client's point of view.

primary environment an environment that is central in a person's life and in which personal or family interactions can be sustained, for example, a workplace or home. Compare SECONDARY ENVIRONMENT.

primary erectile dysfunction a male sexual dysfunction in which the man has never been able to achieve penile erection sufficient for sexual intercourse. Also called **primary impotence**. See ERECTILE DYSFUNCTION; IMPOTENCE; MALE ERECTILE DISORDER. Compare SECONDARY ERECTILE DYSFUNCTION.

primary gain in psychoanalytic theory, any of the basic psychological benefits derived from possessing neurotic symptoms, essentially relief from anxiety generated by conflicting impulses or threatening experiences. Also called **paranosic gain**. Compare SECONDARY GAIN.

primary group any of the small, long-term groups characterized by face-to-face interaction and high levels of COHESION, solidarity, and GROUP IDENTIFICATION. These groups are primary in the sense that they are the initial socializers of the individual members, providing them with the foundation for attitudes, values, and a social orientation. Families, partnerships, and long-term psychotherapy groups are examples of such groups. Compare SECONDARY GROUP.

primary health care see PRIMARY CARE.

primary homosexuality same-sex sexual orientation in which the individual has never experienced sexual arousal or activity with a person of the opposite sex.

primary hypersomnia in *DSM–IV–TR*, a sleep disorder characterized by excessive sleepiness (evidenced by prolonged episodes of sleep, daytime episodes of sleep on an almost daily basis,

P

or both), the severity and persistence of which cause clinically significant distress or impairment in functioning. The disorder is not caused by a general medical condition and is not an aspect of another sleep disorder or mental disorder. See DYSSOMNIA. See also DISORDERS OF EXCESSIVE SOMNOLENCE. Compare PRIMARY INSOMNIA.

primary identification in psychoanalytic theory, the first and most basic form of IDENTIFICATION, which occurs during the ORAL STAGE of development when the infant experiences the mother as part of himself or herself. After weaning, the infant begins to differentiate between the self and external reality and then becomes capable of SECONDARY IDENTIFICATION. Primary identification is closely tied to oral INCORPORATION. Also called **primary narcissistic identification**.

primary impotence see PRIMARY ERECTILE DYSFUNCTION.

primary insomnia in *DSM–IV–TR*, a sleep disorder characterized by difficulty in initiating or maintaining a restorative sleep to a degree in which the severity and persistence of the sleep disturbance causes clinically significant distress, impairment in a significant area of functioning, or both. The disorder is not caused by a general medical condition or the effects of a substance and is not exclusively an aspect of another sleep disorder or mental disorder. See DYSSOMNIA. See also INSOMNIA. Compare PRIMARY HYPERSOMNIA.

primary masochism in psychoanalytic theory, the portion of the DEATH INSTINCT or AGGRESSIVE INSTINCT that is directed toward the self after the LIBIDO has absorbed it emotionally and directed a large portion of it toward the external world. Also called **erotogenic masochism**.

primary maternal preoccupation in the OBJECT RELATIONS THEORY of British psychoanalyst Donald Winnicott (1896–1971), a state immediately following childbirth in which a mother becomes preoccupied with her infant to the exclusion of everything else, which permits a heightened sensitivity to the child's needs.

primary memory (PM) memory that retains a few items for only several seconds, in contrast to SECONDARY MEMORY. The term was used in DUAL-STORE MODELS OF MEMORY before being replaced by SHORT-TERM MEMORY. [introduced by William JAMES]

Primary Mental Abilities Test see PRIMARY ABILITY.

primary mental deficiency below average intelligence due to genetic factors.

primary microcephaly a congenital disorder in which MICROCEPHALY is the primary, and usually the only, evidence of anomalous fetal development. The most common characteristic is a normal-size face combined with a small cranium. The forehead is low and narrow but recedes sharply. The back of the head is flat, and the vertex often is pointed. Mental retardation and spasticity of limbs occur as neurological deficits. Compare PURE MICROCEPHALY.

primary mood disorder a MOOD DISORDER that does not occur in the context of another disorder.

primary motivation MOTIVATION created by the presence of a PRIMARY NEED. Compare SECONDARY MOTIVATION.

primary narcissism in psychoanalytic theory, the earliest type of NARCISSISM, in which the infant's LIBIDO is directed toward his or her own body and its satisfaction rather than toward the environment or OBJECTS. At this stage the child forms a narcissistic EGO-IDEAL stemming from his or her sense of OMNIPOTENCE. See also BODY NARCISSISM.

primary narcissistic identification see PRIMARY IDENTIFICATION.

primary need an innate need that arises out of biological processes and leads to physical satisfaction, for example, the need for water and sleep. See also PHYSIOLOGICAL NEED; VISCEROGENIC NEED.

primary orgasmic dysfunction a female sexual dysfunction in which the woman has never been able to achieve an orgasm with any type of stimulation, with or without a partner. Studies have found that 10–15% of sexually active women in the United States fall into this category. Rates in other cultures are related to how positive or negative the culture is toward female sexuality.

primary personality 1. the original personality, as opposed to a SECONDARY PERSONALITY or secondary personalities, of an individual with DISSOCIATIVE IDENTITY DISORDER. **2.** see PREMORBID PERSONALITY.

primary physician see PRIMARY CARE PROVIDER.

primary prevention research and programs, designed for and directed to nonclinical populations or populations at risk, that seek to promote and lay a firm foundation for mental, behavioral, or physical health so that psychological disorders, illness, or disease will not develop. Compare SECONDARY PREVENTION; TERTIARY PREVENTION.

primary process in psychoanalytic theory, unconscious mental activity in which there is free, uninhibited flow of PSYCHIC ENERGY from one idea to another. Such thinking operates without regard for logic or reality, is dominated by the PLEASURE PRINCIPLE, and provides hallucinatory fulfillment of wishes. Examples are the dreams, fantasies, and magical thinking of young children. These processes are posited to predominate in the ID. Also called **primary-process thinking**. See also PRELOGICAL THINKING.

primary reinforcement 1. in OPERANT CONDITIONING, the process in which presentation of a stimulus or circumstance following a response increases the future probability of that response, without the need for special experience with the stimulus or circumstance. That is, the stimulus or circumstance, known as an **unconditioned primary reinforcer**, functions as effective REINFORCEMENT without any special experience or training. **2.** the contingent occurrence of such a stimulus or circumstance after a response. Also called **unconditioned reinforcement**.

primary relationship a person's closest relationship, in terms of the time, energy, and priority given to it. A primary relationship will typically include high degrees of intimacy, attraction, and commitment.

primary repression in psychoanalytic theory, the first phase of REPRESSION, in which ideas associated with instinctual wishes are screened out and prevented from becoming conscious. Primary repression contrasts with REPRESSION PROPER, in which the repressed material has already been in the realm of consciousness. Also called **primal repression**.

primary sexual dysfunction any failure in sexual functioning that has always been present in the person and happens in all sexual situations. See SEXUAL DYSFUNCTION. Compare SECONDARY SEXUAL DYSFUNCTION.

primary sleep disorder see SLEEP DISORDER.

primary stuttering dysfluency in the speech of young children without accompanying signs of awareness, stress, or emotion. This simple, nonanxiety-producing stage is not accepted as true stuttering by some speech and language pathologists. Compare SECONDARY STUTTERING.

primary symptoms **1.** see FUNDAMENTAL SYMPTOMS. **2.** symptoms that are a direct result of a disorder and essential for its diagnosis. **3.** symptoms that appear in the initial stage of a disorder. Compare SECONDARY SYMPTOMS.

primary thought disorder a disturbance of cognition, observed primarily in schizophrenia, characterized by incoherent and irrelevant intellectual functions and peculiar language patterns (including bizarre syntax, NEOLOGISMS, and WORD SALAD). See SCHIZOPHRENIC THINKING.

primidone *n.* a barbiturate ANTICONVULSANT drug whose primary metabolic product is PHENOBARBITAL. It is appropriate for the treatment of partial and tonic–clonic seizures but has been largely supplanted by newer, safer agents. U.S. trade name: **Mysoline**.

priming *n.* in cognitive psychology, the effect in which recent experience of a stimulus facilitates or inhibits later processing of the same or a similar stimulus. In repetition priming, presentation of a particular sensory stimulus increases the likelihood that participants will identify the same or a similar stimulus later in the test. In semantic priming, presentation of a word or sign influences the way in which participants interpret a subsequent word or sign. **—prime** *vb.*

priming-the-pump technique see DOUBLE TECHNIQUE.

primitive defense mechanism in psychoanalytic theory, any DEFENSE MECHANISM that protects against anxiety associated with the DEATH INSTINCT. Primitive defense mechanisms include DENIAL, SPLITTING, PROJECTION, and IDEALIZATION.

primitive superego in OBJECT RELATIONS THEORY, an early SUPEREGO that is formed in the PREGENITAL PHASE by the INTROJECTION of especially harsh and terrifying BAD OBJECTS. [first used in 1934 by British psychoanalyst James Strachey (1887–1967)]

primitivization *n.* in psychoanalytic theory, the REGRESSION of higher EGO functions, such as objective thinking, reality testing, and purposeful behavior, with a return to primitive stages of development characterized by magical thinking (e.g., wish-fulfilling fantasies and hallucinations), helplessness, and emotional dependence. Primitivization occurs primarily in traumatic neuroses, in which higher functions are blocked by the overwhelming task of meeting the emergency, and in advanced schizophrenia, in which the ego breaks down and PSYCHIC ENERGY is withdrawn from external reality and concentrated on a narcissistic fantasy life. [first used in 1950 by Austrian psychoanalyst Ernst Kris (1900–1957)]

primordial image see ARCHETYPE.

principle of constancy in psychoanalytic theory, the idea that all mental processes tend toward a state of equilibrium and the stability of the inorganic state. Also called **constancy law**; **law of constancy**. See also DEATH INSTINCT; NIRVANA PRINCIPLE; PRINCIPLE OF INERTIA.

principle of inertia in psychoanalytic theory, the tendency of the organism to expend minimum energy by preferring unconscious automatic actions to conscious ones. This principle is posited to be the mechanism that underlies the REPETITION COMPULSION and is one type of ID RESISTANCE. Also called **inertia principle**. See also DEATH INSTINCT; NIRVANA PRINCIPLE.

prison psychosis a severe emotional disturbance precipitated by actual or anticipated incarceration. The types of disturbance vary; in many cases they result from long-standing tendencies toward schizophrenia or are paranoid reactions released by the stress of imprisonment. Symptoms include delusions of innocence, pardon, ill treatment, or persecution; periods of excitement; or rage and destructiveness. See GANSER SYNDROME.

privacy *n.* **1.** the state in which an individual's or a group's desired level of social interaction is not exceeded. **2.** the right to control (psychologically and physically) others' access to one's personal world, for example by regulating others' input through use of physical or other barriers (e.g., doors, partitions) and by regulating one's own output in the form of communication with others. **3.** the right of patients and others (e.g., consumers) to control the amount and disposition of the information they divulge about themselves. See PRIVILEGED COMMUNICATION. **—private** *adj.*

private mental hospital a hospital for patients with mental disorders that is organized and run by a group of health care professionals (e.g., psychiatrists, psychologists). A private mental hospital is typically considerably smaller than a PUBLIC MENTAL HOSPITAL, usually has a higher doctor–patient ratio, and generally offers specialized, intensive treatment rather than chronic care.

private practice 1. the practice of a medical or mental health care professional who operates as a self-employed individual. **2.** in the United Kingdom, any medical practice outside the National Health Service.

private self the part of the SELF that is known mainly to oneself, such as one's inner feelings and SELF-CONCEPT. The private self is distinguished from the PUBLIC SELF and the COLLECTIVE SELF.

private self-consciousness see SELF-CONSCIOUSNESS.

private speech spontaneous self-directed talk in which a person "thinks aloud," particularly as a means of regulating cognitive processes and guiding behavior. In the theorizing of Russian psychologist Lev Semenovich Vygotsky (1896–1934), private speech is considered equivalent to EGOCENTRIC SPEECH.

privilege *n.* the legal right of an individual to confidentiality of personal information obtained by a professional in the course of their relationship, as between a patient and a health care professional during the course of treatment or diagnosis. See PRIVILEGED COMMUNICATION.

privileged communication confidential information, especially as provided by an individual to a professional in the course of their relationship, that may not be divulged to a third party without the knowledge and consent of that individual. This protection applies to communications not only between patients and physicians, clinical psychologists, psychiatrists, or other health care professionals, but also between clients and attorneys, confessors and priests, and spouses.

probability (symbol: *p*) *n.* the degree to which an event is likely to occur. **—probabilistic** *adj.*

probability curve a graphic representation of the expected frequency of occurrence of a variable.

probability distribution a curve that specifies, by the areas below it, the probability that a random variable occurs at a particular point. The best known example is the bell-shaped NORMAL DISTRIBUTION; others include the CHI-SQUARE DISTRIBUTION, Student's T DISTRIBUTION, and the F DISTRIBUTION.

probability sample a sample chosen from a population in such a way that the likelihood of each unit in the population being selected is known in advance of the sampling. See RANDOM SAMPLING.

probability theory a branch of mathematics concerned with the study of probabilistic phenomena.

proband *n.* the family member whose possible genetic disease or disorder forms the center of the investigation into the extent of the illness in the family. He or she is the person around whom a PEDIGREE is drawn and from whom the information about other family members is obtained. Also called **index case**.

probing *n.* in psychotherapy, the use of direct questions intended to stimulate additional discussion, in the hope of uncovering relevant information or helping the client come to a particular realization or achieve a particular insight.

problem behavior any conduct that is maladaptive, destructive, or antisocial.

problem checklist a type of self-report scale listing various personal, social, educational, or vocational problems. The participant indicates the items that apply to his or her situation.

problem drinking see ALCOHOL ABUSE; ALPHA ALCOHOLISM.

problem-focused coping a stress-management strategy in which a person directly confronts a stressor in an attempt to decrease or eliminate it. This may involve seeking information, generating possible solutions to a problem, confronting others who are responsible for or otherwise associated with the stressor, and other forms of instrumental action. For example, a student who is anxious about an upcoming examination might cope by studying more, attending every class, and attending special review sessions to ensure he or she fully understands the course material. It has been proposed that problem-focused coping is used primarily when a person appraises a stressor as within his or her capacity to change. Compare EMOTION-FOCUSED COPING. [identified in 1984 by Richard S. Lazarus (1922–2002) and Susan Folkman (1938–), U.S. psychologists]

problem-oriented record (**POR**) a form of patient-care record that has four components: (a) a database (standardized information on history, physical examination, mental status, etc.); (b) a problem list, based on the database; (c) a treatment plan for each problem; and (d) progress notes as related to the problems and to the patient's response to each treatment. Also called **problem-oriented medical record** (**POMR**).

problem representation a scheme, often a drawing, that represents the relations among elements of a problem. For example, a table might be used to express the relations among two sets of items or a flow chart might be used to express the series of steps to be followed in solving a problem.

problems in living concrete problems with which patients with chronic mental illness (e.g., schizophrenia) frequently struggle (e.g., inability to keep a job or a place of residence), which are believed to be the most useful next focus of treatment after symptoms stabilize with medication. Problems in living are often addressed in day treatment or in aftercare following hospitalization. [proposed by Hungarian-born U.S. psychiatrist Thomas S. Szasz (1920–)]

problem solving the process by which individuals attempt to overcome difficulties, achieve plans that move them from a starting situation to a desired goal, or reach conclusions through the use of higher mental functions, such as reasoning and CREATIVE THINKING. Problem solving is seen in animals in laboratory studies involving mazes and other tests as well as in natural settings to obtain hidden foods. Many animals display problem-solving strategies, which allow an animal to solve a new problem quickly, based on whether the first response was successful or unsuccessful. In terms of CONDITIONING, problem solving involves engaging in behavior that results in the production of discriminative stimuli in situations involving new CONTINGENCIES.

problem space the set of all possible paths to the solution of a given problem.

procedural memory long-term memory for the skills involved in particular tasks. Procedural memory is demonstrated by skilled performance and is often separate from the ability to verbalize this knowledge (see DECLARATIVE MEMORY). Knowing how to type or skate, for example, requires procedural memory. Also called **sensorimotor memory**.

process analysis in psychotherapy, the examination of the interaction between the therapist and the client and of their evolving relationship, as opposed to the content of their discussions.

process evaluation in evaluation research, an in-house function in which the evaluator quickly moves into the situation to be evaluated, conducts the evaluation, feeds back findings to the program administrator for immediate program modification (if necessary), then repeats the process. See also FORMATIVE EVALUATION.

process experiential psychotherapy an approach to psychotherapy that focuses on the client's moment-to-moment experience and guides the client's cognitive and affective processing in the direction of client-defined goals. The THERAPEUTIC ALLIANCE, internal patterns of viewing the self and others, and an emphasis on therapeutic process over content are core elements of this therapy. See also CLIENT-CENTERED THERAPY; GESTALT THERAPY; HUMANISTIC THERAPY. [proposed by South African-born Canadian psychologist Leslie Greenberg (1945–)]

processing-efficiency theory a theory that attempts to explain the relationship between anxiety and performance (see AROUSAL–PERFORMANCE RELATIONSHIP). It suggests that anxiety serves two functions: (a) It increases worry and takes part of the attentional resources, and (b) the worry created serves a monitoring function by identifying the task as important, so that the individual increases the effort, which overcomes the depleted attentional capacity.

Processing Speed Index an index from the WECHSLER ADULT INTELLIGENCE SCALE and other Wechsler tests that measures the speed of nonverbal processing.

process–reactive *adj.* relating to a disease model of schizophrenia based on the distinction between gradual and acute onset of symptoms. PROCESS SCHIZOPHRENIA is marked by a long-term gradual deterioration before the disease is manifest, whereas REACTIVE SCHIZOPHRENIA is associated with a rapid onset of symptoms after a relatively normal premorbid period.

process research the study of various psychological mechanisms or processes of psychotherapy as they influence the outcome of treatment or the reactions that the therapist or client may have. A basic goal of such research is to identify therapeutic methods and processes that are most effective in bringing about positive change, as well as inadequacies and other limitations. See also PSYCHOTHERAPY RESEARCH.

process schizophrenia a form of schizophrenia that begins early in life, develops gradually, is believed to be due to endogenous (biological or physiological) rather than environmental factors, and has a poor prognosis. Psychosocial development before the onset of the disorder is poor; individuals are withdrawn, are socially inadequate, and indulge in excessive fantasies. This term is often used interchangeably with NUCLEAR SCHIZOPHRENIA. Also called **poor premorbid schizophrenia**. Compare REACTIVE SCHIZOPHRENIA. [proposed in 1959 by U.S. psychologists Norman Garmezy (1918–2009) and Eliot H. Rodnick (1911–1999)]

process study any investigation undertaken to assess the mechanisms and variables that contribute to and influence the outcome of a particular activity. For example, a process study of GROUP THERAPY sessions may seek to determine characteristics of the therapeutic interaction that are associated with positive, neutral, or negative changes individually and across the group. See also PROCESS RESEARCH.

process variable 1. an interpersonal, affective, cognitive, or behavioral factor that is operative during the course of psychotherapy or counseling and influences the progress or the course of behavior. **2.** any set of PSYCHOLOGICAL FACTORS that has an effect on the development or modification of a process over time.

prochlorperazine *n.* a low-potency PHENOTHIAZINE used for the treatment of nausea and vomiting and, occasionally, for the control of anxiety. It was formerly used as an antipsychotic agent. U.S. trade name (among others): **Compazine**.

procreative sex sexual activity that can result in pregnancy. In some cultures and religions this is regarded as the basis for what is considered to be normal sex, as opposed to deviant or sinful sexual activity.

procyclidine *n.* an ANTICHOLINERGIC DRUG that is used in the treatment of Parkinson's disease and drug-induced EXTRAPYRAMIDAL SYMPTOMS. U.S. trade name: **Kemadrin**.

prodromal syndrome a set of traits, symptoms, or neurological deficits that may predispose an individual to developing a psychological or neurological disorder.

prodrome *n.* an early symptom or symptoms of a mental or physical disorder. A prodrome frequently serves as a warning or premonitory sign that may, in some cases, enable preventive measures to be taken. Examples are the AURAS that often precede epileptic seizures or migraine headaches and the headache, fatigue, dizziness, and insidious impairment of ability that often precede a stroke. Also called **prodromic phase**. **—prodromic** *adj.* **—prodromal** *adj.*

prodrug *n.* a drug that is either biologically inert or of limited activity until metabolized to a more active derivative.

productive love in psychoanalytic theory, the capacity of healthy individuals to establish close, interdependent relationships without abridging their individuality. Respect, care, responsibility, and knowledge of the other are essential components. According to Erich FROMM, productive love is accomplished through active effort and is an aspect of the productive orientation.

productive orientation in psychoanalytic theory, a personality pattern in which the individual is able to develop and apply his or her potentialities without being unduly dependent on outside control. Such an individual is highly active in feeling, thinking, and relating to others, and at the same time retains the separateness and integrity of his or her own self. [introduced by Erich FROMM]

productive thinking in the theory of Erich FROMM, thinking in which a given question or issue is considered with objectivity as well as respect and concern for the problem as a whole. It is a feature of the PRODUCTIVE ORIENTATION.

product–moment correlation (symbol: r) a statistic that indexes the degree of linear relationship between two variables. Invented by British statistician Karl Pearson (1857–1936), it is often known as the **Pearson product–moment correlation** (**Pearson's r**).

professional–client sexual relations a boundary violation (see BOUNDARY ISSUES) in which a health care professional engages in sexual relations with a patient under his or her care. See also PROFESSIONAL ETHICS.

professional ethics rules of acceptable conduct that members of a given profession are expected to follow. See BOUNDARY ISSUES; CODE OF ETHICS; ETHICS; PROFESSIONAL STANDARDS; STANDARDS OF PRACTICE.

professional licensing the imposition of state-regulated minimal standards for legal employment as a member of a given profession. Professional licensing usually consists of three parts: provisional certification, full certification, and recertification. See LICENSE.

professional standards the levels of performance and conduct required or expected in a particular profession. See also CODE OF ETHICS; PROFESSIONAL ETHICS; STANDARDS OF PRACTICE.

profile of a disorder a drawn or mechanically generated outline, often a graph, representing the symptoms and characteristics of a disorder.

Profile of Mood States (**POMS**) a brief self-report instrument measuring six dimensions of transient and fluctuating mood states over time: tension or anxiety, depression or dejection, anger or hostility, vigor or activity, fatigue or inertia, and confusion or bewilderment. Participants indicate on a 5-point scale ranging from "not at all" to "extremely" whether each of the 65 adjectives (e.g., confused, spiteful, energetic, good-natured) listed is descriptive of themselves within the specified time frame. A mentally healthy profile on the POMS is known as the iceberg profile. [originally developed in 1971 by U.S. psychologist Douglas M. McNair (1927–2008), U.S. psychometrician Maurice Lorr (1910–1998), and U.S. psychologist Leo F. Droppleman (1936–2009)]

profound mental retardation a diagnostic category for those with IQs below 20, comprising about 1% of people with MENTAL RETARDATION. It is due to sensorimotor abnormalities as well as intellectual factors; typical developmental attainments include rudimentary speech and limited self-care, and affected individuals require lifelong, highly structured environments with constant aid and supervision.

progesterone *n.* a hormone, secreted mainly by the corpus luteum in the ovary, that stimulates proliferation of the endometrium (lining) of the uterus required for implantation of an embryo. If implantation occurs, progesterone continues to be secreted—first by the corpus luteum and then by the placenta—maintaining the pregnant uterus and preventing further release of egg cells from the ovary. It also stimulates development of milk-secreting cells in the breasts.

progestin *n.* see PROGESTOGENS.

progestogens *pl. n.* steroids that include the natural hormone PROGESTERONE and synthetic steroids (known as **progestins**) with physiological effects similar to those of progesterone. Progestins may be derived from progesterone or testosterone. While progesterone has an antiestrogenic action, progestins may have different effects, such as proestrogenic activity. They are used in oral contraceptives, HORMONE REPLACEMENT THERAPY, and medications for menstrual disorders.

prognosis *n.* in general medicine and mental health science, a prediction of the future course, duration, severity, and outcome of a condition, disease, or disorder. Prognosis may be given whether or not treatment is undertaken, in order to give the client an opportunity to weigh the benefits of different treatment options. **—prognostic** *adj.*

program efficacy conclusions drawn about PROGRAM OUTCOMES from testing an intervention under closely controlled scientific conditions, which may narrowly define the type of patients treated, nature of services offered, and so forth. Because this method involves the provision of services under conditions that are very different from everyday real-world service delivery, there are dangers that it may not achieve a high degree of EXTERNAL VALIDITY.

program integrity the extent to which an intended program is actually delivered. Also called **treatment integrity**; **treatment validity**.

program outcome any or all of the effects that arise from the implementation of a program. Also called **program output**.

progressive relaxation a technique in which the individual is trained to relax the entire body by becoming aware of tensions in various muscle groups and then relaxing one muscle group at a time. In some cases, the individual consciously tenses specific muscles or muscle groups and then releases tension to achieve relaxation throughout the body. Also called **Jacobson relaxation method**. [developed by U.S. physician Edmund Jacobson (1888–1983)]

progressive teleologic regression the purposive return of a person with schizophrenia to the PRIMARY PROCESS level, in an attempt to avoid tension, stress and anxiety, and a self-image that has become bizarre, threatening, and frightening. The regression is progressive because it fails to accomplish its purpose and becomes more extreme. [first described by Italian-born U.S. psychiatrist Silvano Arieti (1914–1982)]

projected jealousy a type of behavior in which individuals who are unfaithful, or who repress impulses to be unfaithful, accuse their partners of being unfaithful, thereby projecting their own impulses. See PROJECTION.

projection *n.* in psychoanalytic and psychodynamic theories, the process by which one attributes one's own individual positive or negative characteristics, affects, and impulses to another person or group. This is often a DEFENSE MECHANISM in which unpleasant or unacceptable impulses, stressors, ideas, affects, or responsibilities are attributed to others. For example, the defense mechanism of projection enables a person conflicted over expressing anger to change "I hate him" to "He hates me." Such defensive patterns are often used to justify prejudice or evade responsibility; in more severe cases, they may develop into paranoid delusions in which, for example, an individual who blames others for his or her problems may come to believe that those others are plotting against him or her. In classical psychoanalytic theory, projection permits the individual to avoid seeing his or her own faults, but modern usage has largely abandoned the requirement that the projected trait remain unknown in the self. **—project** *vb.*

projective identification 1. in psychoanalysis, a DEFENSE MECHANISM in which the individual projects qualities that are unacceptable to the self onto another individual and that person—through unconscious or conscious interpersonal pressure—internalizes the projected qualities and believes himself or herself to be characterized by them appropriately and justifiably. See PROJECTION. **2.** in the object relations theory of Melanie KLEIN, a defense mechanism in which a person fantasizes that part of his or her EGO is split off and projected into the OBJECT in order to control or harm it, thus allowing the individual to maintain a belief in his or her omnipotent control. Projective identification is a key feature of Klein's PARANOID-SCHIZOID POSITION.

projective method see PROJECTIVE TECHNIQUE.

projective play a variation of PLAY THERAPY in which dolls and other toys are used by children to express their feelings, which can be helpful in diagnosing mental disturbances.

projective psychotherapy a treatment procedure in psychotherapy in which selected responses on various projective tests are fed back to the client, who associates with them in much the same way that psychoanalytic patients make FREE ASSOCIATIONS to dreams. [developed by U.S. psychologist Molly Harrower (1906–1999)]

projective technique any personality assessment procedure that consists of a fixed series of relatively ambiguous stimuli designed to elicit unique, sometimes highly idiosyncratic, responses. Examples of this type of procedure are the RORSCHACH INKBLOT TEST, the THEMATIC APPERCEPTION TEST, and various sentence completion and word association tests. Projective techniques are quite controversial, with opinions ranging from the belief that personality assessment is incomplete without data from at least one or more of these procedures to the view that such techniques lack reliability and validity and that interpretations of personality organization and functioning derived from them are completely hypothetical and unscientific. Also called **projective method**.

prolactin *n.* a PEPTIDE hormone both synthesized and released into the bloodstream by specialized cells in the anterior PITUITARY GLAND called **lactotrophs**. Although generally known

P

for its originally described role in initiating and maintaining lactation—prolactin levels rise significantly in women during pregnancy, stimulating the mammary glands to grow and subsequently produce milk—prolactin also performs hundreds of other essential reproductive, homeostatic, and behavioral functions in both sexes. These include such activities as preserving the corpus luteum and enhancing its secretion of PROGESTERONE, modulating sexual arousal and the orgasmic REFRACTORY PHASE, influencing spermatogenesis, regulating prostate gland development, regulating the response of the IMMUNE SYSTEM, regulating water and electrolyte concentrations (osmoregulation), and inhibiting fat metabolism. Prolactin also is associated with mammalian and avian parental behavior, with prolactin variation possibly explaining individual differences in parental decision making and the initiation of parental interactions. Given such versatility of action, it is not surprising that prolactin receptors are found throughout the body, including within the HYPOTHALAMUS, HIPPOCAMPUS, AMYGDALA, and other areas of the central nervous system; the THYMUS and lymphocytes of the immune system; and the liver, kidney, prostate, testis, ovary, uterus, mammary glands, and numerous other organs. Also called **lactogenic hormone**; **lactotropic hormone**; **lactotropin**; **luteotropic hormone** (**LTH**); **luteotropin**.

Prolixin *n.* a trade name for FLUPHENAZINE.

prolonged exposure therapy a form of COGNITIVE-BEHAVIOR THERAPY for posttraumatic stress disorder in adults. Based on EMOTIONAL PROCESSING THEORY, it is a brief treatment, involving 9–12 sessions of 60–90 minutes each conducted once or twice weekly. The first two sessions are devoted to information gathering, explanation of treatment rationale, treatment planning, and BREATHING RETRAINING. During the remaining sessions, clients relive their traumatic experiences by imagining them as vividly as possible and describing them aloud in the present tense (i.e., IMAGINAL EXPOSURE), including their thoughts, feelings, and physical sensations at the time. These narratives are recorded, and clients are instructed to listen to the recordings as homework. They are also instructed to confront, as homework, situations and stimuli that trigger distressing memories and thoughts and thus have been avoided (i.e., IN VIVO EXPOSURE). The homework assignments and imaginal exposure are reviewed in session: Clients discuss their emotions, cognitions, and other responses to the activity, while the therapist uses nondirective statements to validate and normalize the clients' experiences and reactions. The exposure exercises are intended to teach clients that trauma memories are in fact not harmful and that they can cope with them; the in-session discussion seeks to help clients change their erroneous beliefs about the trauma and reevaluate their feelings about it. Ultimately, this method aims to habituate clients to the traumatic event so that it no longer evokes the excessive anxiety, fear, and other distressing emotions that it previously did. [developed in the 1980s by U.S. psychologist Edna B. Foa (1937–) and colleagues]

promethazine *n.* a PHENOTHIAZINE used for the treatment of nausea, motion sickness, and allergies and as a sedative. Its mechanism of action includes blockade of H_1 HISTAMINE receptors and of dopamine receptors in the MESOLIMBIC SYSTEM. U.S. trade name: **Phenergan**.

promiscuity *n.* transient, casual sexual relations with a variety of partners. In humans, this type of behavior is generally regarded unfavorably; however, it has been argued that there can be healthy promiscuity in the simple enjoyment of casual, consensual, nonexploitative relationships. In bonobos (pygmy chimpanzees) sexual activity occurs frequently both between and within sexes in exchange for resources (e.g., food) or to calm tensions. In many species females appear to display promiscuity to prevent certainty of paternity but often mate with the most dominant or successful male at the time when conception is most likely. —**promiscuous** *adj.*

prompting *n.* in psychotherapy, suggesting or hinting at topics by the therapist to encourage the client to discuss certain issues. Prompting may include reminding the client of previously discussed material, tying previously discussed topics together, or finishing a sentence or thought for the client to aid in his or her understanding of an issue.

pronoun reversal a speech phenomenon observed in children with AUTISTIC DISORDER, in which the child refers to him- or herself in the second or third person (e.g., *you, him, she*) while identifying others by first-person pronouns (e.g., *me*). Also called **pronominal reversal**.

propanediols *pl. n.* a group of chemically related compounds derived from propyl alcohol and originally developed as antianxiety drugs. Their pharmacological actions include muscle relaxation, depression of the central nervous system, and a calming effect through interference with autonomic reactions. The prototype of the group is MEPROBAMATE. Due to their toxicity in overdose, propanediols have largely been supplanted as anxiolytics by benzodiazepines and other sedative-hypnotics; CARISOPRODOL, a precursor of meprobamate, is currently used as a muscle relaxant.

prophylactic maintenance see MAINTENANCE THERAPY.

prophylactic surgery the removal of an organ prior to the expected onset of cancer in that organ, usually because the individual has a positive family history of the disease or is a carrier of a predisposing genetic mutation (e.g., women who carry mutations in genes BRCA1 and BRCA2 are at a greatly increased risk of breast cancer).

prophylaxis *n.* the use of methods or procedures designed to avoid or prevent mental or physical disease or disorder. **—prophylactic** *adj., n.*

propoxyphene *n.* a synthetic OPIOID ANALGESIC that has approximately half the pain-control efficacy of codeine. It is generally marketed in combination with a nonsteroidal anti-inflammatory agent, such as aspirin, for the management of moderate pain. In 2010, propoxyphene was withdrawn from the U.S. market. Former U.S. trade names: **Darvon**; **Darvocet** (in combination with ACETAMINOPHEN).

propranolol *n.* a beta blocker used primarily to treat hypertension. In low doses it is used as an adjunctive agent in the treatment of certain forms of social phobia, such as fear of public speaking or performance, predominantly due to its ability to control certain peripheral symptoms of anxiety, such as tremor and vocal quavering. Because it produces a nonspecific blockade of BETA-ADRENERGIC RECEPTORS, it should not be taken by individuals with asthma or reactive airway disease, due to its ability to constrict bronchial smooth musculature and thereby induce breathing difficulties. U.S. trade name: **Inderal**.

propriate striving the final stage in the development of the PROPRIUM. According to Gordon W. ALLPORT, who originated the concept, propriate striving emerges in adolescence with the search for identity and includes the experimentation common to adolescents before making long-range commitments. Because Allport believed in the independence of adult motivation, in contrast to childhood motivation, adolescence is considered especially significant as the time when conscious intentions and future-oriented planning begin to motivate the personality. See FUNCTIONAL AUTONOMY.

proprietary drug any chemical used for medicinal purposes that is formulated or manufactured under a name that is protected from competition by TRADEMARK or patent. The ingredients, however, may be components of generic drugs that have the same or similar effects.

propriety standards the legal and ethical requirements of an evaluation research study. These standards include having formal or written agreements between parties in the study, protecting the rights of participants, avoiding conflicts of interest by both program evaluators and participants, conducting complete and fair program assessments, fully reporting all findings, and maintaining fiscal soundness. See also ACCURACY STANDARDS; FEASIBILITY STANDARDS; UTILITY STANDARDS.

proprium *n.* a concept of the self, or that which is consistent, unique, and central in the individual, that was developed by Gordon W. ALLPORT. According to Allport, the proprium incorporates body sense, self-identity, self-esteem, self-extension, rational thinking, self-image, PROPRIATE STRIVING, and knowing.

prosocial *adj.* denoting or exhibiting behavior that benefits one or more other people, such as providing assistance to an older adult crossing the street. Compare ANTISOCIAL.

prosocial behavior any act that is socially constructive or in some way beneficial to another person or group. A broad range of behavior can be described as prosocial, including simple everyday acts, such as providing assistance to an elderly person crossing the street. Compare ANTISOCIAL BEHAVIOR. See ALTRUISTIC BEHAVIOR; HELPING.

ProSom *n.* a trade name for ESTAZOLAM.

prospective research research that is planned before the data have been collected; that is, research that starts with the present and follows subjects forward in time, as in randomized experiments and in longitudinal research. Compare RETROSPECTIVE RESEARCH.

prospect theory a theory of decision making that attempts to explain how people's decisions are influenced by their attitudes toward risk, uncertainty, loss, and gain. In general, it finds that people are motivated more strongly by the fear of loss than the prospect of making the equivalent gain. See ANTICIPATORY REGRET. [formulated by Israeli-born U.S. psychologists Daniel Kahneman (1934–) and Amos Tversky (1937–1996)]

prostaglandin (**PG**) *n.* any of a group of chemically related substances that act as local hormones in animal tissue and cause a variety of physiological effects. There are several basic types, designated by capital letters with subscript numbers indicating the degree of saturation of fatty acid side chains (e.g., PGE_2, PGH_2). Among their many activities, they influence blood pressure, cause stimulation of smooth muscle, and promote inflammation.

prosthesis *n.* (*pl.* **prostheses**) an artificial replacement for a missing or dysfunctional body part that is attached to or implanted in the body. Prostheses include artificial limbs, artificial joints, and plastic heart valves. Also called **prosthetic device**. **—prosthetic** *adj.*

Prostigmin *n.* a trade name for NEOSTIGMINE.

prostitution *n.* a sex service that is based on the payment of money or the exchange of other property or valuables. Prostitution may involve heterosexual or same-sex services provided by male or female **prostitutes**. The sex service may be simple coitus, other common sexual acts (e.g., fellatio, cunnilingus, masturbation), or acts leading to gratification of PARAPHILIAS.

protagonist *n.* in PSYCHODRAMA, the person selected as the central character in the drama or ROLE PLAY.

protected relationships professional provider–client contacts that are subject to ethical standards regarding confidentiality of records

P

and other information provided by the client, information about sessions, and the existence of the professional relationship itself.

protective factor a variable or clearly defined behavior that promotes relative healthiness and well-being because it is associated with a decreased probability that a particular disease or disorder will develop or because it reduces the severity of an existing pathological condition. For example, exercising regularly can serve as a protective factor by decreasing the likelihood or severity of coronary heart disease, hypertension, and depression. Likewise, supportive social networks and positive coping skills are examples of protective factors that help alleviate depression and anxiety and enhance mental health generally.

protective reflex the reflex withdrawal of the body or a body part away from painful or annoying stimulation. Also called **protective response**.

protein *n.* a molecule that consists of a long-chain polymer of AMINO ACIDS. Proteins are involved in virtually every function performed by a cell; they are the principal building blocks of living organisms and, in the form of ENZYMES, the basic tools for construction, repair, and maintenance. Proteins play an essential role in human nutrition, including the provision of all of the essential amino acids that humans cannot produce themselves. PROTEIN DEFICIENCY leads to a variety of symptoms and conditions. Excess protein can cause overreaction of the immune system and liver dysfunction and is implicated in obesity. See also PEPTIDE.

P

protein deficiency lack of a normal quantity of proteins, particularly complete proteins, in the diet or body tissues. Complete proteins contain the essential AMINO ACIDS, which must be acquired from the external environment in meals since they cannot be synthesized by the body's own chemistry. In addition to being required for basic structural and functional processes, several amino acids, including glutamic acid, lysine, and cystine, are needed for learning and other mental activities. Protein deficiency may lead to fatigue, retarded growth, loss of muscle mass, hair loss, insulin resistance, and hormonal irregularities. It may occur as a result of a lack of carbohydrates or fats in the diet, a condition that causes the body to consume its own proteins as a source of energy. If this self-digestion process is not controlled, irreversible damage to vital organs results. See also KWASHIORKOR; MARASMUS.

protensity *n.* the temporal attribute (i.e., duration spread) of a mental process or of consciousness.

protocol *n.* **1.** the original notes of a study or experiment recorded during or immediately after a particular session or trial, particularly as recorded from participant's verbalizations during the process. **2.** a case history and WORK-UP. **3.** a treatment plan.

prototypal approach to classification the process of classifying abnormal behavior on the assumption that there are combinations of characteristics (prototypes of behavior disorders) that tend to occur together regularly. The prototypal approach recognizes that the ideal combination of traits does not exist in reality and that prototypes with similar characteristics can blend into one another.

prototype *n.* **1.** in CONCEPT FORMATION, the best or average exemplar of a category. For example, the prototypical bird is some kind of mental average of all the different kinds of birds of which a person has knowledge or with which a person has had experience. Also called **cognitive prototype**. **2.** more generally, an object, event, or person that is held to be typical of a category and comes to represent or stand for that category. **3.** an early model of something that represents or demonstrates its final form. —**prototypal**, **prototypical**, or **prototypic** *adj.*

protriptyline *n.* see TRICYCLIC ANTIDEPRESSANT.

provider *n.* a health care professional or facility, such as a psychologist, psychiatrist, physician, hospital, or skilled nursing or intensive care facility, that provides health care services to patients. See PRIMARY CARE PROVIDER. See also PPO; PREFERRED PROVIDER ARRANGEMENT.

Provigil *n.* a trade name for MODAFINIL.

provocative testing any type of testing in which symptoms of a condition are intentionally caused or reproduced in a patient or other person presenting for evaluation. This can be done in order to test the effectiveness of treatments for the condition, to rule in or rule out the possibility of a similar diagnosis, or, in the case of PSYCHOGENIC DISORDERS, to test the veracity of the condition. For example, provocative testing has been used somewhat controversially in distinguishing NONEPILEPTIC SEIZURES from neurologically based epileptic seizures.

proximate cause the most direct or immediate cause of an event. In a causal chain, it is the one that directly produces the effect. For example the proximate cause of Smith's aggression may be an insult, but the REMOTE CAUSE may be Smith's early childhood experiences. In law, proximate cause is important in liability cases where it must be determined whether the actions of the defendant are sufficiently related to the outcome to be considered causal, or if the action set in motion a chain of events that led to an outcome that could have been reasonably foreseen.

Prozac *n.* a trade name for FLUOXETINE.

prudence *n.* farsighted and deliberate concern for the consequences of one's actions and decisions. It is a form of practical reasoning and self-management that resists the impulse to satisfy short-term pleasures at the expense of long-term goals. **—prudent** *adj.*

prudery *n.* the quality of being excessively modest or priggish, particularly in having a negative view of sexual matters. **—prude** *n.* **—prudish** *adj.*

pruritus *n.* itching that may result from physiological or psychological conditions. See also PSYCHOGENIC PRURITUS. **—pruritic** *adj.*

PSE abbreviation for PRESENT STATE EXAMINATION.

pseudoephedrine (**pseudephedrine**) *n.* see EPHEDRA.

pseudoangina *n.* **1.** chest pain that resembles the pain (angina pectoris) of a HEART ATTACK but for which there is no clinical evidence of heart disease. **2.** chest pain that resembles angina pectoris but originates from damage to the spinal roots in the neck (cervical) region. Compression of the root of the seventh cervical nerve by a prolapsed intervertebral disk (slipped disk) is commonly identified as the cause. Also called **cervical angina**. See NONCARDIAC CHEST PAIN.

pseudoasthma *n.* a physical condition with symptoms and findings that suggest asthma, although no organic basis can be found. Differences between pseudoasthma and true asthma are detected during physical examination. For example, the patient generally has difficulty breathing in rather than breathing out, the respiratory attack is resolved quickly rather than gradually, and the severity of the attack decreases in the presence of distraction rather than remaining constant. Also called **nonorganic acute upper airway obstruction**; **vocal cord dysfunction**.

pseudocommunication *n.* distorted attempts at communication or vestiges of communication in the form of fragments of words, apparently meaningless sounds, and unfathomable gestures. The condition is sometimes observed in individuals with different types of schizophrenia.

pseudocommunity *n.* a group of real or imagined persons believed, in a persecutory delusion, to be organized for the purpose of conspiring against, threatening, harassing, or otherwise negatively focusing upon one. Also called **paranoid pseudocommunity**. [first described by 20th-century U.S. psychiatrist and clinical psychologist Norman A. Cameron]

pseudoconvulsion *n.* an older name for a type of NONEPILEPTIC SEIZURE in which the person collapses and experiences muscular contractions, although other signs (e.g., pupillary signs, loss of consciousness, and amnesia) are not observed.

pseudocopulation *n.* **1.** bodily contact between a man and a woman with EJACULATION but without actual PENETRATION. **2.** sexual activity in which a couple rub their genitals together, without penetration and sometimes while clothed, with or without orgasm occurring.

pseudocyesis *n.* a condition in which a woman shows many or all of the usual signs of pregnancy when conception has not taken place. In some cases the condition is psychogenic, whereas in others it is due to a medical condition (e.g., a tumor or an endocrine disorder). Also called **false pregnancy**; **pseudopregnancy**.

pseudodementia *n.* **1.** deterioration or impairment of cognitive functions in the absence of neurological disorder or disease (compare DEMENTIA). The condition may occur, reversibly, in a MAJOR DEPRESSIVE EPISODE—particularly among older adults, in which case the preferred term is **dementia syndrome of depression**—or as a psychological symptom of FACTITIOUS DISORDER. **2.** see GANSER SYNDROME.

pseudoepilepsy *n.* see NONEPILEPTIC SEIZURE.

pseudohallucination *n.* a vivid hallucination, usually visual, that the individual recognizes as hallucinatory.

pseudohermaphroditism *n.* a congenital abnormality in which the gonads (ovaries or testicles) are of one sex, but one or more contradictions exist in the morphological criteria of sex. In female pseudohermaphroditism, the individual is a genetic and gonadal female with partial masculinization, such as an enlarged clitoris resembling a penis and labia majora resembling a scrotum. In male pseudohermaphroditism, the individual is a genetic and gonadal male with incomplete masculinization, including a small penis, perineal HYPOSPADIAS, and a scrotum that lacks testes. **—pseudohermaphrodite** *n.*

P

pseudohypoparathyroidism *n.* a condition that resembles hypoparathyroidism (deficiency of parathyroid hormone) but fails to respond to parathyroid hormone treatment. Patients have a round face and thick-set figure and seem to have impaired senses of smell and taste. In most cases they have mild to moderate mental retardation. The disease is believed to be due to a genetic defect that blocks normal response to parathyroid hormone by receptor tissues.

pseudoidentification *n.* a DEFENSE MECHANISM in which individuals adopt or identify with the opinions, values, or orientations of others in order to protect themselves against attack or criticism.

pseudoinsomnia *n.* INSOMNIA reported by an individual who actually sleeps an adequate number of hours. The reason for reporting the complaint is often obscure and may involve a subtle misperception of sleep, dreaming of a sleepless night, or the use of the complaint as a symptom when the individual is anxious or depressed.

pseudologia fantastica a clinical syndrome characterized by elaborate fabrications, which are usually concocted to impress others, to get out of an awkward situation, or to give the individual an ego boost. Unlike the fictions of CONFABULATION, these fantasies are believed only momentarily and are dropped as soon as they are contradicted by evidence. Typical examples are the "tall tales" told by people with antisocial personality disorder, although the syndrome is also found among malingerers and individuals with factitious disorders, neuroses, and psychoses. See also PATHOLOGICAL LYING.

pseudomemory *n.* a fake memory, such as a spurious recollection of events that never took place, as opposed to a memory that is merely inaccurate (see FALSE MEMORY). Pseudomemory is a cause of particular concern when using hypnosis to help eyewitnesses retrieve memories (see HYPERMNESIA). It was formerly called **pseudomnesia**. See also CONFABULATION; RECOVERED MEMORY.

pseudomotivation *n.* a reason created by a person, particularly one with schizophrenia, to justify earlier behavior. The individual may or may not be aware of the inconsistencies in the excuse or may be indifferent to them. [first described by Swiss psychiatrist Eugen Bleuler (1857–1939)]

pseudomutuality *n.* a family relationship that has a superficial appearance of mutuality, openness, and understanding although in fact the relationship is rigid and depersonalizing. Family theories of schizophrenia and other forms of major psychopathology have identified pseudomutuality as a critical etiological factor.

pseudoneurological *adj.* suggesting a neurological condition. The term is generally used in reference to SOMATIZATION DISORDER: According to DSM–IV–TR, at least one pseudoneurological symptom must be present in order to diagnose this disorder.

pseudoneurotic schizophrenia a disorder characterized by all-pervasive anxiety and a wide variety of neurotic symptoms (persistent and irrational fears, obsessive thoughts, compulsive acts, dissociative states), with underlying psychotic tendencies (delusions, hallucinations, disorganized speech, thought, or behavior) that at times emerge very briefly, typically in response to stress (see MICROPSYCHOSIS). Pseudoneurotic schizophrenia is primarily considered to be a personality disorder rather than a type of schizophrenia; in *DSM–IV–TR*, such individuals are diagnosed with SCHIZOTYPAL PERSONALITY DISORDER or BORDERLINE PERSONALITY DISORDER. [described in 1949 by German-born U.S. psychiatrist Paul H. Hoch (1902–1964) and psychiatrist Phillip Polatin (1905–1980) and used in clinical practice and research for the next 25 years]

pseudonomania *n.* an abnormal urge to lie or to falsify information.

pseudoparalysis *n.* loss of limb movement or limb power due to pain, with no identifiable structural or functional etiology within the nervous system.

pseudoparkinsonism *n.* see PARKINSONISM.

pseudopersonality *n.* a fictitious characterization contrived by an individual in an effort to conceal facts about his or her true self from others.

pseudopregnancy *n.* see PSEUDOCYESIS.

pseudopsychology *n.* an approach to understanding or analyzing the mind or behavior that utilizes unscientific or fraudulent methods. Examples include PHRENOLOGY and PHYSIOGNOMY. See PSEUDOSCIENCE. **—pseudopsychological** *adj.*

pseudopsychopathic schizophrenia a disorder in which psychotic tendencies characteristic of SCHIZOPHRENIA are masked or overlaid by antisocial tendencies, such as pathological lying, sexual deviations, and violent or other uninhibited behavior. Pseudopsychopathic schizophrenia is primarily considered to be a personality disorder rather than a type of schizophrenia; in *DSM–IV–TR*, such individuals are diagnosed with SCHIZOTYPAL PERSONALITY DISORDER or BORDERLINE PERSONALITY DISORDER.

pseudoretardation *n.* retarded intellectual development, usually consistent with MILD MENTAL RETARDATION, due to adverse cultural or psychological conditions rather than congenital factors. Among these conditions are maternal deprivation, intellectual impoverishment, severe emotional disturbance, and perceptual deficits. The term may be a misnomer as it can be applied to individuals whose performance is consistent with mental retardation that may not be alleviated by educational intervention. Also called **psychosocial mental retardation**; **psychosocial mental developmental delay**.

pseudoscience *n.* a system of theories and methods that has some resemblance to a genuine science but that cannot be considered such. Examples range from astrology, numerology, and esoteric MAGIC to such modern phenomena as Scientology. Various criteria for distinguishing pseudosciences from true sciences have been proposed, one of the most influential being that of falsifiability. On this basis, certain approaches to psychology and psychoanalysis have sometimes been criticized as pseudoscientific, as they involve theories or other constructs that cannot be directly or definitively tested by observation. **—pseudoscientific** *adj.*

pseudoseizure *n.* see NONEPILEPTIC SEIZURE.

pseudosenility *n.* an acute, reversible confusional state or severe cognitive impairment in an older adult resulting from such factors as drug effects, malnutrition, depression, diminished cardiac output, fever, alcoholism, intracranial tumor, a fall, or a metabolic disturbance. This state is often confused with the irreversible state of DEMENTIA.

pseudotrisomy 18 a congenital disorder, believed to be due to an autosomal recessive trait, marked by the same general anomalies found in patients with chromosome-18 trisomy (e.g., a short neck with webbing, congenital heart disease). However, studies have failed to show signs of chromosome-18 trisomy, chromosomal translocation, or other abnormalities. All affected individuals observed have evidenced mental retardation.

PSI abbreviation for PARENTING STRESS INDEX.

psilocin *n.* an indolealkylamine HALLUCINOGEN that is the principal psychoactive compound in "magic mushrooms" of the genus *Psilocybe*, which were used by the Aztecs for religious and ceremonial purposes. **Psilocybin**, first isolated in 1958, differs from psilocin only in having an additional phosphate group; it is rapidly metabolized in the body and converted to psilocin. Like other indolealkylamine hallucinogens (e.g., LSD, DMT), psilocin is active at various SEROTONIN RECEPTORS: Agonism at 5-HT_{1A} and 5-HT_{2A} receptors in the cerebral cortex of the brain appears to be responsible for the psychoactive effects of these drugs.

psilocybin *n.* see PSILOCIN.

psychache *n.* intense psychological pain that is sometimes thought to be a risk factor for suicide.

psychagogy *n.* a method of reeducation that emphasizes the relationship of the client to the environment, particularly the social environment.

psychasthenia *n.* an archaic name for any of the ANXIETY DISORDERS. It is primarily still in use as an axis on the MINNESOTA MULTIPHASIC PERSONALITY INVENTORY.

psyche *n.* in psychology, the mind in its totality, as distinguished from the physical organism. The term, which earlier had come to refer to the soul or the very essence of life, derives from the character of Psyche in Greek mythology, a beautiful princess who, at the behest of her divine lover, Eros, son of Aphrodite, is made immortal by Zeus.

psychedelic drug a name for any of the HALLUCINOGENS (from Greek, literally: "mind-manifesting"), proposed in 1956 by Humphry Osmond (1917–2004). Also called **psychedelic**.

psychedelic experience see HALLUCINOGEN; HALLUCINOGEN INTOXICATION.

psychedelic therapy the use of HALLUCINOGENS (or psychedelics; so-called mind-expanding or mind-enhancing drugs) in the treatment of some types of mental or physical illness. LSD was used in the 1950s and 1960s in combination with psychotherapy to assist patients in enhancing their awareness of cognitive and psychological processes; it was also used in the management of a number of significant conditions, such as schizophrenia and alcoholism. MDMA was similarly used in the 1980s. However, various studies revealed no lasting benefit; indeed, some patients claimed to have been harmed by such treatments. These findings, coupled with reclassification of these drugs as illegal, ended for a time the use of such agents in psychotherapy. More recently, MDMA has been studied for a potential role in the treatment of POSTTRAUMATIC STRESS DISORDER and IBOGAINE for the treatment of substance dependence and withdrawal symptoms.

psychiatric classification the grouping of mental disorders and other psychological problems into diagnostic categories, as in the *Diagnostic and Statistical Manual of Mental Disorders* (see DSM–IV–TR). Classification serves the purpose of organizing symptomatic states and abnormal functioning to enhance the treatment of disorders and research aimed at understanding causes. Also called **psychiatric nosology**.

psychiatric diagnosis the diagnosis of mental disorders as currently based on the DSM–IV–TR. See CLINICAL DIAGNOSIS.

psychiatric disability chronic loss or impairment of function due to a mental disorder, resulting in severe difficulties in meeting the demands of life.

psychiatric disorder see MENTAL DISORDER.

psychiatric hospital a public or private institution providing a wide range of diagnostic techniques and treatment to individuals with mental disorders on an inpatient basis. Also called **mental hospital**. See also PRIVATE MENTAL HOSPITAL; PSYCHIATRIC UNIT; PUBLIC MENTAL HOSPITAL.

psychiatric illness see MENTAL DISORDER.

psychiatric nosology see PSYCHIATRIC CLASSIFICATION.

psychiatric nursing a specialty within the field of NURSING that provides holistic care to individuals with mental disorders or behavioral problems so as to promote their physical and psychosocial well-being. It emphasizes the use of interpersonal relationships as a therapeutic agent and considers the environmental factors that influence mental health. Thus, **psychiatric nurses** not only provide physical care but also socialize and communicate with their patients to create a safe, comfortable environment that promotes positive change and responsible decision making. Their specific responsibilities often include assisting patients with ACTIVITIES OF DAILY LIVING, administering psychotropic medication and managing side effects, assisting with crisis management, observing patients to evaluate their progress, offering guidance and other forms of interpersonal support to patients, participating in recreational activities with patients, educating patients and their families about mental health issues and lifestyle choices, and conducting group therapy. Registered nurses wishing to become psychiatric nurses complete additional training in pharmacology and the behavioral and social sciences. They practice in a variety of settings—including general and psychiatric hospitals, nursing homes, assisted-living facilities, physicians' offices, correctional facilities, long-term care centers, community mental health centers, rehabilitation centers, and private homes (see HOME CARE)—in conjunction with psychiatrists, psychologists, social workers, and other mental health professionals. Psychiatric nurses are distinct from **psychiatric nurse practitioners**, who have obtained master's or doctoral degrees and more advanced training to practice privately and perform additional assessment, diagnostic, and therapeutic functions, including conducting individual psychotherapy and prescribing medication. Also called **mental health nursing**.

psychiatric unit a unit of a general hospital organized for treatment of acutely disturbed psychiatric patients on an inpatient basis. Such units usually include provision for emergency coverage and admission; treatment with psychotropic drugs or electroconvulsive therapy; group therapy; psychological examinations; and adjunctive modalities, such as social work services, occupational therapy, art therapy, movement therapy, music therapy, and discussion groups.

psychiatrist *n.* a physician who specializes in the diagnosis, treatment, prevention, and study of mental and emotional disorders. In the United States, education for this profession consists of 4 years of premedical training in college; a 4-year course in medical school, the final 2 years of which are spent in clerkships studying with physicians in at least five specialty areas; and a 4-year residency in a hospital or agency approved by the American Medical Association. One year of the residency is spent as a hospital intern, and the final 3 in psychiatric residency, learning diagnosis and treatment as well as the use of psychiatric medicines and other treatment modes. After completing residency, most psychiatrists take a voluntary examination for certification by the American Board of Psychiatry and Neurology.

psychiatry *n.* the medical specialty concerned with the study, diagnosis, treatment, and prevention of personality, behavioral, and mental disorders. As a medical specialty, psychiatry is based on the premise that biological causes are at the root of mental and emotional problems, although some psychiatrists do not adhere exclusively to the biological model and additionally treat problems as social and behavioral ills. Training for psychiatry includes the study of psychopathology, biochemistry, psychopharmacology, neurology, neuropathology, psychology, psychoanalysis, genetics, social science, and community mental health, as well as the many theories and approaches advanced in the field itself. **—psychiatric** *adj.*

psychic 1. *adj.* denoting phenomena associated with the mind. Ivan PAVLOV referred to conditioned responses as "psychic reflexes" because the idea of the physical stimulus evoked the reflexive response. **2.** *adj.* denoting a class of phenomena, such as telepathy and clairvoyance, that appear to defy scientific explanation. The term is also applied to any putative powers, forces, or faculties associated with such phenomena. **3.** *n.* a person with alleged paranormal abilities.

psychic apparatus in psychoanalytic theory, mental structures and mechanisms. Sigmund FREUD initially (1900) divided these into unconscious, preconscious, and conscious areas or systems and later (1923) into the ID, EGO, and SUPEREGO: The id is described as unconscious, and the ego and superego as partly conscious, partly preconscious, and partly unconscious. Also called **mental apparatus**. See also STRUCTURAL MODEL; TOPOGRAPHIC MODEL.

psychic blindness see FUNCTIONAL BLINDNESS.

psychic conflict see INTRAPSYCHIC CONFLICT.

psychic energizer a drug that has an antidepressant effect. The name, now rarely used, was introduced in the late 1950s by U.S. psychiatrist Nathan S. Kline (1916–1983) to identify MONOAMINE OXIDASE INHIBITORS derived from iproniazid, which had been developed for control of tuberculosis. Iproniazid was discontinued as a tuberculosis drug because of its powerful effects on the central nervous system.

psychic energy in psychoanalytic theory, the dynamic force behind all mental processes. According to Sigmund FREUD, the basic sources of this energy are the INSTINCTS or drives that are located in the ID and seek immediate gratification according to the PLEASURE PRINCIPLE. Carl JUNG also believed that there is a reservoir of psychic energy, but he objected to Freud's emphasis on the pleasurable gratification of biological instincts and emphasized the means by which this energy is channeled into the development of the personality and the expression of cultural and spiritual values. Also called **mental energy**. See also LIBIDO.

psychic healing the treatment of physical or mental illness by parapsychological or spiritualistic means. See also CRYSTAL HEALING; FAITH HEALING.

psychic numbing a posttraumatic symptom pattern in which the individual feels incapable of emotional expression, love, or closeness to others. See ALEXITHYMIA.

psychic pain intolerable pain caused by intense psychological suffering (rather than organic dysfunction). At its extreme, prolonged psychic pain can lead to suicide attempts. See also ALGOPSYCHALIA.

psychic reality the internal reality of fantasies, wishes, fears, dreams, memories, and anticipations, as distinguished from the external reality of actual events and experiences.

psychic resilience see RESILIENCE.

psychic seizure a type of COMPLEX PARTIAL SEIZURE marked by psychological disturbances, such as illusions, hallucinations, affective experiences, or cognitive alterations (e.g., déjà vu).

psychic suicide a purported form of self-destruction in which the individual decides to die and actually does so without resorting to a physical agency. See also VOODOO DEATH.

psychic tension a sense of emotional strain experienced in emergencies or other situations that generate inner conflict or anxiety. See STRESS; TENSION.

psychic trauma an experience that inflicts damage on the psyche, often of a lasting nature. Examples are sexual assault and child abuse. See TRAUMA.

psychic vaginismus a painful vaginal spasm that makes intercourse painful and in some cases impossible. The corresponding *DSM–IV–TR* designation is FUNCTIONAL VAGINISMUS.

psychoactive drug a group of drugs that have significant effects on psychological processes, such as thinking, perception, and emotion. Psychoactive drugs include those deliberately taken to produce an altered state of consciousness (e.g., HALLUCINOGENS, OPIOIDS, INHALANTS, CANNABIS) and therapeutic agents designed to ameliorate a mental condition; these include ANTIDEPRESSANTS, MOOD STABILIZERS, SEDATIVES, HYPNOTICS, and ANXIOLYTICS (which are CNS depressants), and ANTIPSYCHOTICS. Psychoactive drugs are often referred to as **psychotropic drugs** (or **psychotropics**) in clinical contexts.

psychoanalysis *n.* an approach to the mind, psychological disorders, and psychological treatment originally developed by Sigmund FREUD at the beginning of the 20th century. The hallmark of psychoanalysis is the assumption that much of mental activity is unconscious and, consequently, that understanding people requires interpreting the unconscious meaning underlying their overt, or manifest, behavior. Psychoanalysis (often shortened to **analysis**) focuses primarily, then, on the influence of such unconscious forces as repressed impulses, internal conflicts, and childhood traumas on the mental life and adjustment of the individual. The foundations on which classic psychoanalysis rests are: (a) the concept of INFANTILE SEXUALITY; (b) the OEDIPUS COMPLEX; (c) the theory of INSTINCTS; (d) the PLEASURE PRINCIPLE and the REALITY PRINCIPLE; (e) the threefold division of the psyche into ID, EGO, and SUPEREGO; and (f) the central importance of anxiety and DEFENSE MECHANISMS in neurotic reactions. Psychoanalysis as a form of therapy is directed primarily to psychoneuroses, which it seeks to eliminate by bringing about basic modifications in the personality. This is done by establishing a constructive therapeutic relationship, or TRANSFERENCE, with the analyst, which enables him or her to elicit and interpret the unconscious conflicts that have produced the neurosis. The specific methods used to achieve this goal are FREE ASSOCIATION, DREAM ANALYSIS, analysis of RESISTANCES and defenses, and WORKING THROUGH the feelings revealed in the transference process. Also called **Freudian approach**; **Freudianism**. **—psychoanalytic** *adj.*

psychoanalyst *n.* a therapist who has undergone special training in psychoanalytic theory and practice and who applies the techniques developed by Sigmund FREUD to the treatment of mental disorders. In the United States, psychoanalysts are usually trained first as psychiatrists or clinical psychologists and then undergo extensive training at a psychoanalytic institute; European institutes permit so-called LAY ANALYSIS and accept other interested and qualified professionals for psychoanalytic training. All recognized training centers, however, require a thorough study of the works of Freud and others in the field, supervised clinical training, a TRAINING ANALYSIS, and a personal program of psychoanalysis. See also ANALYST.

psychoanalytic group psychotherapy GROUP THERAPY in which basic psychoanalytic concepts and methods, such as FREE ASSOCIATION, analysis of RESISTANCES and defenses, and DREAM ANALYSIS, are used in modified form. The most prominent exponent of such therapy was British psychoanalyst Wilfred Bion (1897–1979).

psychoanalytic play technique a method of CHILD ANALYSIS developed by Melanie KLEIN during the 1920s, in which play activity is interpreted as symbolic of underlying fantasies and conflicts and substitutes for FREE ASSOCIATION. The therapist provides toys for the child and encourages free, imaginative play in order to reveal the child's unconscious wishes and conflicts.

psychoanalytic psychotherapy therapy conducted in the form of classical PSYCHOANALYSIS or in one of the generally shorter forms of treatment that evolved from the classical form, such as PSYCHODYNAMIC PSYCHOTHERAPY. Generally, it involves a systematic one-on-one interaction between a therapist and a client that emphasizes the importance of unconscious motives and conflicts as determinants of human behavior while helping the client overcome abnormal behavior or adjust to the problems of life. The use of FREE ASSOCIATION and therapist interpretation, as well as the development of a THERAPEUTIC ALLIANCE, are common techniques.

psychoanalytic theory the diverse complex of assumptions and constructs underlying the approach known as PSYCHOANALYSIS. Classically—and properly—the term focuses specifically on the formulations of Austrian psychiatrist Sigmund Freud (1856–1939), but it may also be taken to include such subsequent offshoots and counterapproaches as ANALYTIC PSYCHOLOGY, INDIVIDUAL PSYCHOLOGY, OBJECT RELATIONS THEORY, and others that are based on PSYCHODYNAMIC THEORY.

psychobiography *n.* a form of biographical literature that offers a psychological profile or analysis of an individual's personality in addition to the usual account of his or her life and experiences. —**psychobiographical** *adj.*

psychobiological factors the multiple determinants of personality and behavior—biological, psychological, and sociological—that are cited in the holistic, multidisciplinary approach of PSYCHOBIOLOGY.

psychobiology *n.* **1.** a school of thought in the mental health professions in which the individual is viewed as a holistic unit and both normal and abnormal behavior are explained in terms of the interaction of biological, sociological, and psychological determinants. Also called **ergasiology**. [developed by Swiss-born U.S. psychiatrist Adolf Meyer (1866–1950)] **2.** a rare synonym for BIOLOGICAL PSYCHOLOGY. —**psychobiological** *adj.*

psychochemistry *n.* the study of the relationships between chemicals, behavior (including the genetic or metabolic aspects of behavior), and psychological processes.

psychocultural stress psychological tension or anxiety and, in many cases, mental illness generated by cultural and SOCIOCULTURAL FACTORS (e.g., racial discrimination, rapid technological advance).

psychocutaneous disorder any skin (dermatological) disorder in which psychological factors are believed to play an important role (see PSYCHOSOMATIC DISORDER). In some cases (e.g., hives, PSYCHOGENIC PRURITUS) the disorder appears to be caused or exacerbated by psychological factors; in others (e.g., acne, psoriasis, eczema, dermatitis) there is a predisposition to the condition, which is precipitated by stress factors (see DIATHESIS–STRESS MODEL).

P

psychodiagnosis *n.* **1.** any procedure designed to discover the underlying factors that account for behavior, especially disordered behavior. **2.** diagnosis of mental disorders through psychological methods and tests.

psychodrama *n.* a method of psychotherapy in which clients enact their concerns to achieve new insight about themselves and others. Its central premise is that spontaneity and creativity are crucial for the balanced, integrated personality and that humans are all improvising actors on the stage of life. Clients may ROLE PLAY in a variety of scenes either lived or imagined. The process involves: (a) a PROTAGONIST, the client or central figure in the drama; (b) a DIRECTOR, or therapist, who guides this process and assists the client to alternative enactment and interpretation; and (c) AUXILIARY EGOS, therapeutic actors or stand-ins for absentees, who assist the protagonist in completing his or her interaction with significant others. When psychodrama is used in a group, the members become THERAPEUTIC AGENTS by sharing common themes or experiences touched on in the drama. It can also be employed as individual treatment, with the protagonist taking the needed roles, though some therapists become involved in the action. Various special techniques are used to advance the therapy, among them ROLE REVERSAL, soliloquy, doubling (see DOUBLE), and future exploration. See also HYPNODRAMA; SOCIODRAMA; THEATER OF SPONTANEITY. [developed in the 1920s by Romanian-born U.S. psychiatrist Jacob Levi Moreno (1889–1974)]

psychodynamic approach the psychological and psychiatric approach that views human behavior from the standpoint of unconscious motives that mold the personality, influence attitudes, and produce emotional disorder. The psychodynamic approach is interested in affect rather than cognition and rejects introspective methods in favor of clinical material as a basis for inference. The emphasis is on tracing behavior to its origins, as contrasted with the systematic approach (see TOPOGRAPHIC MODEL) and the NOSOLOGICAL APPROACH, which concentrate on overt events, personality characteristics, and symptoms. See PSYCHODYNAMIC PSYCHOTHERAPY.

Psychodynamic Diagnostic Manual (PDM) a handbook for the diagnosis and treatment of mental health disorders that attempts to characterize an individual's personality and the full range of his or her emotional, social, and interpersonal functioning. Published in 2006, by a task force of the American Psychoanalytic Association, the International Psychoanalytic Association, Division 39 (Psychoanalysis) of the American Psychological Association, the American Academy of Psychoanalysts and the Dynamic Psychiatry, and the National Membership Committee on Psychoanalysis in Clinical Social Work, the *PDM* is meant to serve as a complement to the *Diagnostic and Statistical Manual of Mental Disorders* (see DSM–IV–TR) and the *ICD* (see INTERNATIONAL CLASSIFICATION OF DISEASES). Although based on current neuroscience and treatment OUTCOME RESEARCH the classification adapts many concepts from classical PSYCHOANALYTIC PSYCHOTHERAPY. The diagnostic framework describes (a) healthy and disordered personality functioning; (b) individual profiles of mental functioning, including patterns of relating, comprehending, and expressing emotions, coping with stress and anxiety, self-observation of emotions and behaviors, and forming moral judgments; and (c) symptom patterns, including differences in each individual's experience of his or her symptoms.

psychodynamic group psychotherapy PSYCHODYNAMIC PSYCHOTHERAPY conducted in a group that focuses on insight, with group members providing support and modeling for gaining awareness of previously disregarded aspects of their personality and behavior.

psychodynamic psychotherapy those forms of psychotherapy, falling within or deriving from the psychoanalytic tradition, that view individuals as reacting to unconscious forces (e.g., motivation, drive), that focus on processes of change and development, and that place a premium on self-understanding and making meaning of what is unconscious. Most psychodynamic approaches have certain shared features, such as emphasis on dealing with the unconscious in treatment, emphasis on the role of analyzing TRANSFERENCE, and the use of dream analysis and INTERPRETATION. Also called **dynamic psychotherapy**.

psychodynamics *n.* **1.** any system or perspective emphasizing the development, changes, and interaction of mental and emotional processes, motivation, and drives. **2.** the pattern of motivational forces, conscious or unconscious, that gives rise to a particular psychological event or state, such as an attitude, action, symptom, or mental disorder. These forces include drives, wishes, emotions, and defense mechanisms, as well as biological needs (e.g., hunger and sex). **—psychodynamic** *adj.*

psychodynamic theory a constellation of theories of human functioning that are based on the interplay of drives and other forces within the person, especially (and originating in) the psychoanalytic theories developed by Sigmund FREUD and his colleagues and successors, such as Anna FREUD, Carl JUNG, and Melanie KLEIN. Later psychodynamic theories, while retaining concepts of the interworking of drives and motives to varying degrees, moved toward the contemporary approach, which emphasizes the process of change and incorporates interpersonal and transactional perspectives of personality development. See PSYCHODYNAMIC APPROACH; PSYCHODYNAMICS.

psychoeducational diagnostician a specialist trained in the diagnosis and assessment of children with learning disabilities.

psychoendocrinology *n.* the study of the hormonal system in order to discover sites and processes that underlie and influence biological, behavioral, and psychological processes. It is often concerned with identifying biochemical abnormalities that may play a significant role in the production of mental disorders.

psychogender *n.* a less common name for GENDER IDENTITY or gender self-identity, used to distinguish between psychological sex identification and biological sex in the treatment of INTERSEXUALITY and GENDER IDENTITY DISORDER.

psychogenesis *n.* **1.** the origin and development of personality, behavior, and mental and psychic processes. **2.** the origin of a particular psychic event in an individual. See PSYCHOGENIC. **—psychogenetic** *adj.*

psychogenetics *n.* the study of the inheritance of psychological attributes. **—psychogenetic** *adj.*

psychogenic *adj.* resulting from mental factors. The term is used particularly to denote or refer to a disorder that cannot be accounted for by any identifiable organic dysfunction and is believed to be due to psychological factors (e.g., a conversion disorder). In psychology and psychiatry, psychogenic disorders are improperly considered equivalent to FUNCTIONAL disorders.

psychogenic amnesia see DISSOCIATIVE AMNESIA.

psychogenic cardiovascular disorder any disorder of the heart or circulation that cannot be accounted for by any identifiable organic dysfunction or a general medical condition and is thought to be related to psychological factors. It can include chest pain, racing heart, and tightness in the chest.

psychogenic disorder any disorder that cannot be accounted for by any identifiable organic dysfunction and is believed to be due to psychological factors, such as emotional conflict or stress. Psychogenic disorders include anxiety disorders, somatoform disorders, personality disorders, and functional psychoses. In psychology and psychiatry, psychogenic disorders are improperly considered equivalent to FUNCTIONAL DISORDERS.

psychogenic fugue see DISSOCIATIVE FUGUE.

psychogenic hallucination a HALLUCINATION arising from psychological factors, such as a need to enhance self-esteem or obtain relief from a sense of guilt, as opposed to hallucinations produced primarily by physiological conditions, such as intoxication.

psychogenic hypersomnia episodes of sleep or sleep of excessive duration precipitated by psychological factors, such as a wish to escape from a threatening or other anxiety-provoking situation. Also called **somnolent detachment**. See also HYPERSOMNIA.

psychogenic mutism loss of speech due to psychological rather than physical factors. See also MUTISM.

psychogenic need in the PERSONOLOGY of U.S. psychologist Henry Alexander Murray (1893–1988), a need that is concerned with emotional satisfaction as opposed to biological satisfaction. The psychogenic needs defined by Murray include the affiliative need (see AFFILIATION), the DOMINANCE NEED, and the seclusion need. Compare VISCEROGENIC NEED.

psychogenic nocturnal polydipsia excessive nighttime thirst with a psychological rather than organic or physical basis. It is most often seen in patients with schizophrenia and is recognized as a dangerous and potentially life-threatening disorder, because chronic overconsumption of substantial amounts of water can fatally damage the body's fluid balance.

psychogenic nonepileptic seizure (PNES) a behavioral or emotional manifestation of psychological distress, conflict, or trauma that resembles an epileptic SEIZURE but is not produced by abnormal electrical activity in the brain. Most PNESs are CONVERSION NONEPILEPTIC SEIZURES, but they may also be associated with FACTITIOUS

DISORDER or MALINGERING. Also called **psychogenic seizure**.

psychogenic pain disorder see PAIN DISORDER.

psychogenic pruritus a psychosomatic skin disorder characterized by a functional itching that resists treatment. Psychogenic pruritus often occurs in individuals with anxiety, depression, or obsessive-compulsive disorder.

psychogenic purpura see GARDNER–DIAMOND SYNDROME.

psychogenic seizure see PSYCHOGENIC NONEPILEPTIC SEIZURE.

psychogenic torticollis see TORTICOLLIS.

psychogenic vertigo an unpleasant, illusory sensation of movement of oneself or the environment that cannot be accounted for fully by any identifiable neurological or other organic dysfunction and is thought to be related to psychological factors. Psychogenic vertigo is common in a number of psychological disorders, including panic disorder, agoraphobia, schizophrenia, and somatoform disorder.

psychography *n.* **1.** the natural history and description of mental phenomena, as in psychoanalysis. **2.** the art of literary characterization of an individual—real or fictional—making free use of psychological categories and theories. **3.** a psychological biography or character description. See also PSYCHOBIOGRAPHY; PSYCHOHISTORY.

psychohistory *n.* the application of psychoanalytic theory to the study of historical figures, events, and movements. Also called **historical psychoanalysis**.

P

psycholepsy *n.* the sudden onset of a MAJOR DEPRESSIVE EPISODE, often occurring in the context of a BIPOLAR DISORDER.

psychological abuse see EMOTIONAL ABUSE.

psychological anaphylaxis a psychological hypersensitivity resulting from a previous disturbing or traumatic event. Exposure to circumstances or events that are similar to the one that produced the original sensitivity may result in a reappearance of the earlier psychological symptoms.

psychological assessment the gathering and integration of data in order to evaluate a person's behavior, abilities, and other characteristics, particularly for the purposes of making a diagnosis or treatment recommendation. Psychologists assess diverse psychiatric problems (e.g., anxiety, substance abuse) and nonpsychiatric concerns (e.g., intelligence, career interests) across a range of areas, including clinical, educational, organizational, health, and forensic settings. Assessment data may be gathered through various methods, such as interviews, observation, PROJECTIVE TECHNIQUES, standardized tests, physiological or psychophysiological measurement devices, or other specialized procedures and apparatuses.

psychological autopsy an analysis that is conducted following a person's death in order to determine his or her mental state prior to death. Psychological autopsies are often performed when a death occurs in a complex or ambiguous manner and are frequently used to determine if a death was the result of natural causes, accident, homicide, or suicide. Attention is given to the total course of the individual's life in order to reconstruct the facts, motivations, and meanings associated with the death. [pioneered in the 1970s by psychologists Edwin S. Shneidman and Norman L. Farberow and medical examiner Theodore J. Murphy at the Los Angeles Suicide Prevention Center]

psychological counseling interaction with a client for the purpose of exploring and, particularly, offering direct advice about affective, cognitive, or behavioral problems and reaching solutions. See also COUNSELING PSYCHOLOGY.

psychological deficit cognitive, behavioral, or emotional performance of any individual at a level that is significantly below, or less adept than, that of a typical person.

psychological dependence dependence on a psychoactive substance for the reinforcement it provides. It is signaled by a high rate of drug use, drug craving, and the tendency to relapse after cessation of use. Many believe reinforcement is the driving force behind drug addiction, and that TOLERANCE and PHYSICAL DEPENDENCE are related phenomena that sometimes occur but are probably not central to the development of dependency-inducing patterns of drug use.

psychological disorder see MENTAL DISORDER; PSYCHOPATHOLOGY.

psychological distress a set of psychological and physical symptoms of both anxiety and depression that occur in individuals who do not meet the criteria for any particular psychological disorder. It is thought to be what is assessed by many putative self-report measures of depression. Psychological distress likely reflects normal fluctuations of mood in most people but may indicate the beginning of a MAJOR DEPRESSIVE EPISODE in individuals with a history of MAJOR DEPRESSIVE DISORDER.

psychological dysfunction impaired or abnormal mental functioning and patterns of behavior.

psychological examination examination of a patient by means of interviews, observations of behavior, and administration of psychological tests in order to evaluate personality, adjustment, abilities, interests, and functioning in important areas of life. The purpose of the examination may be to assess the patient's needs, difficulties, and problems and contribute to the diagnosis of mental disorder and determination of the type of treatment required.

psychological factors functional factors—as opposed to organic (constitutional, hereditary) factors—that contribute to the development of personality, the maintenance of health and well-being, and the etiology of mental and behavioral disorder. A few examples of psychological factors are the nature of significant childhood and adult relationships, the experience of ease or stress in social environments (e.g., school, work), and the experience of trauma.

psychological factors affecting medical condition in *DSM–IV–TR,* a clinical category, classified under "Other Conditions," comprising psychological and behavioral factors that adversely affect the course, treatment, or outcome of a GENERAL MEDICAL CONDITION (e.g., by exacerbating symptoms or delaying recovery). The factors include mental disorders and psychological symptoms (e.g., major depressive disorder, anxiety), personality traits (e.g., hostile, denying), physiological response to stress, and behavior patterns detrimental to health (e.g., overeating, excessive alcohol consumption). A wide range of medical conditions can be affected by psychological factors: cardiovascular, gastrointestinal, neurological, and rheumatological disorders; cancers and many others.

psychological field in the social psychology of Kurt LEWIN, the individual's LIFE SPACE or environment as he or she perceives it at any given moment. See also FIELD THEORY.

psychological intervention see INTERVENTION.

psychological kidnapping depriving a person of the free functioning of his or her personality. The term is commonly used to describe the psychological mind control attributed to cults. Compare BRAINWASHING.

psychological masquerade a medical condition that can present as a psychological disorder. Examples include epilepsy, multiple sclerosis, Alzheimer's disease, and brain tumors.

psychological moment **1.** the best possible moment for producing a particular effect on another person or other people, as in *He put in his counteroffer at the psychological moment.* **2.** the lived present as it is experienced. See TIMELESS MOMENT.

psychological need any need that is essential to mental health or that is otherwise not a biological necessity. It may be generated entirely internally, as in the need for pleasure, or it may be generated by interactions between the individual and the environment, as in the need for social approval, justice, or job satisfaction. Psychological needs comprise the four higher levels of MASLOW'S MOTIVATIONAL HIERARCHY. Compare PHYSIOLOGICAL NEED.

psychological rapport **1.** Carl JUNG's term for TRANSFERENCE, which he defined as an intensified tie to the analyst that acts as a compensation for the patient's defective relationship to his or her present reality. Jung saw this as an inevitable feature of every analysis. **2.** more generally, a kind of agreement or affinity between individuals in their typical ways of thinking, affective responses, and behaviors.

psychological rehabilitation the development or restoration of an effective, adaptive identity in an individual with a congenital or acquired physical impairment (e.g., through accident, injury, or surgery) through such psychological approaches as individual or group therapy, counseling, ability assessment, and psychopharmacology. The object is to help the individual to improve or regain his or her self-image, ability to cope with emotional problems, competence, and autonomy.

psychological resilience see RESILIENCE.

psychological time the subjective estimation or experience of time. This is mainly dependent upon the processing and interpretation by the brain of time-related internal or external stimuli but can be influenced by other factors. In general, time is experienced as passing more slowly when one is bored or inactive and more rapidly when one is engaged in an absorbing activity. Certain PEAK EXPERIENCES can produce a sense of time dissolving or being suspended (see TIMELESS MOMENT). Drugs and hypnosis can also be used to alter the perception of time.

psychological treatment various forms of treatment and psychoeducation—including psychotherapy, clinical intervention, and behavior modification, among others—aimed at increasing the client's adaptive and independent functioning. Psychological treatment is the specific purview of trained mental health professionals and incorporates a wide array of diverse theories and techniques for producing healthy and adaptive change in a client's actions, thoughts, and feelings. The term is sometimes used in contrast to treatment through the use of medication, although medication is sometimes used as an adjunct to various forms of psychological treatment (see ADJUNCTIVE THERAPY).

psychological tremor see TREMOR.

psychologist *n.* an individual who is professionally trained in the research, practice, or teaching (or all three) of one or more branches or subfields of PSYCHOLOGY. Training is obtained at a university or a school of professional psychology, leading to a doctoral degree in philosophy (PhD), psychology (PsyD), or education (EdD). Psychologists work in a variety of settings, including laboratories, schools, colleges, universities, social agencies, hospitals, clinics, the military, industry and business, prisons, the government, and private practice. The professional activities of psychologists are also varied but can include psychological counseling, health care services, educational testing and assessment, research, teaching, and business and organizational consulting. Formal CERTIFICATION or PROFESSIONAL LICENSING is required in order to practice independently in many of these settings and activities.

psychology *n.* **1.** the study of the mind and behavior. Historically, psychology was an area of philosophy. It is now a diverse scientific discipline comprising several major branches of research (e.g., experimental psychology, biological psychology, cognitive psychology, developmental psychology, personality, and social psychology), as well as several subareas of research and applied psychology (e.g., clinical psychology, industrial/organizational psychology, school and educational psychology, human factors, health psychology, neuropsychology, cross-cultural psychology). Research in psychology involves observation, experimentation, testing, and analysis to explore the biological, cognitive, emotional, personal, and social processes or stimuli underlying human and animal behavior. The practice of psychology involves the use of psychological knowledge for any of several purposes: to understand and treat mental, emotional, physical, and social dysfunction; to understand and enhance behavior in various settings of human activity (e.g., school, workplace, courtroom, sports arena, battlefield, etc.); and to improve machine and building design for human use. **2.** the supposed collection of behaviors, traits, attitudes, and so forth that characterize an individual or a group (e.g., the psychology of women). **—psychological** *adj.*

psychometrician *n.* an individual who is trained to administer psychological tests and interpret their results, working under the supervision of a licensed psychologist. Also called **psychometrist**.

psychometrics *n.* **1.** the psychological theory and technique (e.g., the science and process) of mental measurement. **2.** the branch of psychology dealing with measurable factors. Also called **psychometric psychology**; **psychometry**.

P

Psychometric Society a nonprofit professional organization founded in 1935 to promote the advancement of quantitative measurement practices in psychology, education, and the social sciences. It publishes the journal *Psychometrika*.

psychomimetic *adj., n.* see PSYCHOTOMIMETIC.

psychomimic syndrome a condition in which an individual who lacks organic evidence of an illness develops symptoms of an illness suffered by another person, who may have died of the disorder. The symptoms usually occur around the anniversary of the death of the other person. See also ANNIVERSARY EVENT; ANNIVERSARY REACTION.

psychomotility *n.* a motor action or habit that is influenced or controlled by a mental process (e.g., a tic, handwriting, gait, stammering, or dysarthria), which may be an indicator of psychomotor disturbance.

psychomotor *adj.* relating to movements or motor effects that result from mental activity.

psychomotor agitation restless physical and mental activity that is inappropriate for its context. It includes pacing, hand wringing, and pulling or rubbing clothing and other objects and is a common symptom of both MAJOR DEPRESSIVE EPISODES and MANIC EPISODES. Also called **psychomotor excitement**.

psychomotor disorder 1. a disturbance in the psychological control of movement. **2.** a motor disorder precipitated by psychological factors. Examples include epileptic seizures brought on by stress, PSYCHOMOTOR RETARDATION associated with depression, and hyperactivity exhibited during a MANIC EPISODE.

psychomotor excitement see PSYCHOMOTOR AGITATION.

psychomotor hallucination the sensation that parts of the body are being moved to different areas of the body.

psychomotor retardation a slowing down or inhibition of mental and physical activity, manifest as slow speech with long pauses before answers, slowness in thinking, and slow body movements. Psychomotor retardation is a common symptom of MAJOR DEPRESSIVE EPISODES.

psychomotor skill any ability (e.g., handwriting, drawing, or driving a car) whose performance draws on a combined and coordinated set of cognitive and motor processes.

psychomotor test a test requiring a coordination of cognitive and motor activities, as in the TRAIL MAKING TEST.

psychoneuroendocrinology *n.* the study of the relations among psychological factors, the nervous system, and the endocrine system in determining behavior and health. It includes the effects of psychological stress on neuroendocrine systems (see NEUROENDOCRINOLOGY) and how changes in these systems affect behavior in normal and psychopathological states.

psychoneuroimmunology *n.* the study of how the brain and behavior affect immune responses. [originated by U.S. psychologist Robert Ader (1932–2011)] **—psychoneuroimmunological** *adj.*

psychoneurosis *n.* see NEUROSIS.

psychonosology *n.* the systematic classification of mental disorders. See PSYCHIATRIC CLASSIFICATION.

psychooncology *n.* the study of psychological, behavioral, and psychosocial factors involved in the risk, detection, course, treatment, and outcome (in terms of survival) of cancer. The field examines responses to cancer on the part of patients, families, and caregivers at all stages of the disease. **—psychooncological** *adj.* **—psychooncologist** *n.*

psychopath *n.* a former name for an individual with ANTISOCIAL PERSONALITY DISORDER. **—psychopathic** *adj.*

psychopathia sexualis the name for SEXUAL DEVIANCE coined by German psychiatrist Richard von Krafft-Ebing (1840–1902) and used as the title of his classic work on the subject, first published in 1886.

psychopathic personality a former name for ANTISOCIAL PERSONALITY DISORDER.

psychopathology *n.* **1.** the scientific study of mental disorders, including theory, etiology, progression, symptomatology, diagnosis, and treatment. This broad field of study may involve psychology, biochemistry, pharmacology, psychiatry, neurology, endocrinology, and other related subjects. The term in this sense is sometimes used synonymously with ABNORMAL PSYCHOLOGY. **2.** the behavioral or cognitive manifestations of such disorders. The term in this sense is sometimes considered synonymous with MENTAL DISORDER itself. **—psychopathological** *adj.* **—psychopathologist** *n.*

psychopathy *n.* **1.** a former term for a personality trait marked by egocentricity, impulsivity, and lack of such emotions as guilt and remorse, which is particularly prevalent among repeat offenders diagnosed with ANTISOCIAL PERSONALITY DISORDER. **2.** formerly, any psychological disorder or mental disease. **—psychopathic** *adj.*

psychopharmacological drugs any medications used in the treatment of mental or behavioral disorders.

psychopharmacology *n.* the study of the influence of drugs on mental, emotional, and behavioral processes. Psychopharmacology is concerned primarily with the mode of action of various substances that affect different areas of the brain and nervous system, including drugs of abuse. See also CLINICAL PSYCHOPHARMACOLOGY; GERIATRIC PSYCHOPHARMACOLOGY; PEDIATRIC PSYCHOPHARMACOLOGY; PRECLINICAL PSYCHOPHARMACOLOGY. **—psychopharmacological** *adj.* **—psychopharmacologist** *n.*

psychopharmacotherapy *n.* the use of pharmacological agents in the treatment of mental disorders. For example, acute or chronic schizophrenia is treated by administration of antipsychotic drugs or other agents. Although such drugs do not cure mental disorders, they may—when used appropriately—produce significant relief from symptoms.

psychophysics *n.* a branch of psychology that studies the relationship between the objective physical characteristics of a stimulus (e.g., its measured intensity) and the subjective perception of that stimulus (e.g., its apparent brightness).

psychophysiological assessment the use of physiological measures via electroencephalography, electrocardiography, electromyography, and electrooculography to infer psychological processes and emotion. Also called **psychophysiological monitoring**.

psychophysiological monitoring see PSYCHOPHYSIOLOGICAL ASSESSMENT.

psychophysiology *n.* the study of the relation between the chemical and physical functions of organisms (physiology) and cognitive processes, emotions, and behavior (psychology). Also called **physiological psychology**. **—psychophysiological** *adj.* **—psychophysiologist** *n.*

psychopoetry *n.* see POETRY THERAPY.

psychoscience *n.* any science that deals with the mind and mental behavior, with mental diseases and disorders, and with their treatment and cure. In particular, it refers to PSYCHOLOGY, PSYCHIATRY, and COGNITIVE SCIENCE.

psychosexual *adj.* relating to or denoting any aspects of human sexuality that are based on or influenced by psychological factors, as opposed to genetic, chemical, and other biologically based (organic) aspects.

psychosexual development in the classic psychoanalytic theory of Sigmund FREUD, the step-by-step growth of sexual life as it affects personality development. Freud posited that the impetus for psychosexual development stems from a single energy source, the LIBIDO, which is concentrated in different organs throughout infancy and produces the various **psychosexual stages**: the ORAL STAGE, ANAL STAGE, PHALLIC STAGE, LATENCY STAGE, and GENITAL STAGE. Each stage gives rise to its own characteristic erotic activities (e.g., sucking and biting in the oral stage) and the early expressions may lead to "perverse" activities later in life, such as SADISM, MASOCHISM, VOYEURISM, and EXHIBITIONISM. Moreover, the different stages leave their mark on the individual's character and personality, especially if sexual development is arrested in a FIXATION at one particular stage. Also called **libidinal development**.

psychosexual disorders in *DSM–III*, a group of disorders of sexuality stemming from psychological rather than organic factors. In *DSM–IV–TR* the category of SEXUAL AND GENDER IDENTITY DISORDERS is used for these problems.

psychosexual disorders not elsewhere classified in *DSM–III*, a residual category comprising psychological sexual disturbances not covered by the specific diagnostic categories. In *DSM–IV–TR* this category is termed SEXUAL DISORDERS NOT OTHERWISE SPECIFIED.

psychosexual dysfunction in *DSM–III*, a category of sexual disorders that in *DSM–IV–TR* is termed SEXUAL DYSFUNCTION.

psychosexual stages see PSYCHOSEXUAL DEVELOPMENT.

psychosexual trauma a frightening, degrading, or otherwise traumatic sexual experience in earlier life that is related to current emotional problems. Examples include incest or other forms of child SEXUAL ABUSE, SEXUAL ASSAULT, and DATE RAPE.

psychosis *n.* **1.** an abnormal mental state involving significant problems with REALITY TESTING and characterized by serious impairments or disruptions in the most fundamental higher brain functions—perception, cognition and cognitive processing, and emotions or affect—as manifested in behavioral phenomena, such as delu-

P

sions, hallucinations, and significantly disorganized speech. See PSYCHOTIC DISORDER. **2.** historically, any severe mental disorder that significantly interferes with functioning and ability to perform activities essential to daily living.

psychosis with mental retardation episodes of excitement, depression, hallucinations, or paranoia that occur occasionally in people with mental retardation. Such episodes are usually mild and may recur, either regularly or unpredictably. They must be distinguished from emotional or behavioral characteristics consistent with the intellectual, social, and developmental status of the person.

psychosocial *adj.* describing the intersection and interaction of social and cultural influences on mental health, personality development, and behavior.

psychosocial deprivation lack of adequate opportunity for social and intellectual stimulation. It may be a significant factor in emotional disturbance and delayed mental development or mental retardation in children. Also called **sociocultural deprivation**. See PSEUDORETARDATION.

psychosocial factors social, cultural, and environmental phenomena and influences that affect the mental health and behavior of the individual and of groups. Such influences include social situations, relationships, and pressures, such as competition for and access to education, health care, and other social resources; rapid technological change; work deadlines; and changes in the roles and status of women and minority groups.

psychosocial mental retardation (**psychosocial mental developmental delay**) see PSEUDORETARDATION.

psychosocial rehabilitation the process of restoring normal psychological, behavioral, and social skills to individuals after mental illness, often with assistance from specialized professionals using focused programs and techniques. It aims to help individuals who have been residing in mental institutions or other facilities (e.g., prisons) to reenter the community.

psychosocial stressor a life situation that creates an unusual or intense level of stress that may contribute to the development or aggravation of mental disorder, illness, or maladaptive behavior. Examples of psychosocial stressors include divorce, the death of a child, prolonged illness, unwanted change of residence, a natural catastrophe, or a highly competitive work situation.

psychosocial therapy psychological treatment with a strong emphasis on interpersonal aspects of problem situations, which is designed to help an individual with emotional or behavioral disturbances adjust to situations that require social interaction with other members of the family, work group, community, or any other social unit.

psychosomatic *adj.* characterizing an approach based on the belief that the mind (psyche) plays a role in all the diseases affecting the various bodily systems (soma).

psychosomatic disorder a type of disorder in which psychological factors are believed to play an important role in the origin or course (or both) of the disease. See also PSYCHOLOGICAL FACTORS AFFECTING MEDICAL CONDITION.

psychosomatic medicine a field of study that emphasizes the role of psychological factors in causing and treating disease.

psychostimulant *n.* see CNS STIMULANT.

psychosurgery *n.* the treatment of a mental disorder by surgical removal or destruction of selective brain areas. The most well-known example of psychosurgery is prefrontal LOBOTOMY, historically used particularly for schizophrenia but also a variety of other disorders. Psychosurgery was most popular from 1935 to 1960 and is among the most controversial of all psychiatric treatments ever introduced. Contemporary psychosurgery approaches (e.g., CINGULOTOMY) are far more precisely targeted and confined in extent than the early techniques, employing high-tech imaging and a variety of highly controllable methods of producing minute lesions. Additionally, they are used only as a last resort and only for a handful of specific psychiatric disorders—MAJOR DEPRESSIVE DISORDER, BIPOLAR DISORDER, OBSESSIVE-COMPULSIVE DISORDER, and GENERALIZED ANXIETY DISORDER—that have been resistant to other available therapies.

psychosynthesis *n.* in psychoanalysis, an attempt to unify the various components of the UNCONSCIOUS, such as dreams, fantasies, and instinctual strivings, with the rest of the personality. This "constructive approach" was advocated by Carl JUNG, who contrasted it with what he saw as Sigmund FREUD's "reductive approach." **—psychosynthetic** *adj.*

psychotechnics *n.* **1.** the practical application of psychological principles, as in economics, sociology, and business. **2.** the application of psychological principles to alter or control behavior of an individual.

psychotherapeutic process whatever occurs between and within the client and psychotherapist during the course of psychotherapy. This includes the experiences, attitudes, emotions, and behavior of both client and therapist, as well as the dynamic, or interaction, between them. See also PROCESS RESEARCH.

psychotherapy *n.* any psychological service provided by a trained professional that primarily uses forms of communication and interaction to assess, diagnose, and treat dsyfunctional emotional reactions, ways of thinking, and behavior patterns of an individual, family (see FAMILY THERAPY), or group (see GROUP THERAPY). There are many types of psychotherapy, but generally they fall into four major categories: PSYCHODYNAMIC PSYCHOTHERAPY, COGNITIVE THERAPY

P

or BEHAVIOR THERAPY, HUMANISTIC THERAPY, and INTEGRATIVE PSYCHOTHERAPY. The **psychotherapist** is an individual who has been professionally trained and licensed (in the United States by a state board) to treat mental, emotional, and behavioral disorders by psychological means. He or she may be a clinical psychologist (see CLINICAL PSYCHOLOGY), PSYCHIATRIST, counselor (see COUNSELING PSYCHOLOGY), social worker, or psychiatric nurse. Also called **therapy**; **talk therapy**. **—psychotherapeutic** *adj.*

psychotherapy by reciprocal inhibition a type of BEHAVIOR THERAPY in which emphasis is placed on the weakening of the bond between anxiety responses and anxiety-provoking stimuli by conditioning the anxiety-provoking response to an incompatible response, such as muscle relaxation. See RECIPROCAL INHIBITION; SYSTEMATIC DESENSITIZATION.

psychotherapy integration see INTEGRATIVE PSYCHOTHERAPY.

psychotherapy matching see MATCHING PATIENTS.

psychotherapy research the use of scientific methods to describe, explain, and evaluate psychotherapy techniques, processes, and effectiveness.

psychotic *adj.* of, relating to, or affected by PSYCHOSIS or a PSYCHOTIC DISORDER.

psychotic disorder any one of a number of severe mental disorders, regardless of etiology, characterized by gross impairment in REALITY TESTING. The accuracy of perceptions and thoughts is incorrectly evaluated, and incorrect inferences are made about external reality, even in the face of contrary evidence. Specific symptoms indicative of psychotic disorders are delusions, hallucinations, and markedly disorganized speech, thought, or behavior; individuals may have little or no insight into their symptoms. In *DSM–IV–TR*, the psychotic disorders include SCHIZOPHRENIA, SCHIZOPHRENIFORM DISORDER, SCHIZOAFFECTIVE DISORDER, DELUSIONAL DISORDER, BRIEF PSYCHOTIC DISORDER, SHARED PSYCHOTIC DISORDER, **psychotic disorder due to a general medical condition**, SUBSTANCE-INDUCED PSYCHOTIC DISORDER, and PSYCHOTIC DISORDER NOT OTHERWISE SPECIFIED.

psychotic disorder not otherwise specified in *DSM–IV–TR*, a category that includes disorders with psychotic symptoms (e.g., delusions, hallucinations, disorganized speech or behavior) that do not meet the criteria for any specific psychotic disorder. An example is POSTPARTUM PSYCHOSIS.

psychotic episode a period during which an individual exhibits psychotic symptoms, such as hallucinations, delusions, and disorganized speech. See also ACUTE PSYCHOTIC EPISODE.

psychotic features in mood disorders, delusions or hallucinations that occur during a MAJOR DEPRESSIVE EPISODE, MANIC EPISODE, or MIXED EPISODE. See MOOD-CONGRUENT PSYCHOTIC FEATURES; MOOD-INCONGRUENT PSYCHOTIC FEATURES.

psychoticism *n.* a dimension of personality in EYSENCK'S TYPOLOGY characterized by aggression, impulsivity, aloofness, and antisocial behavior, indicating a susceptibility to psychosis and psychopathic disorders (see ANTISOCIAL PERSONALITY DISORDER). It was originally developed as a factor for distinguishing between normal individuals and those with schizophrenia or bipolar disorders, using tests of judgment of spatial distance, reading speed, level of proficiency in mirror drawing, and adding rows of numbers.

psychotic mannerism a frequently repeated complex movement that appears to be related to or affected by psychosis (e.g., hand wringing, stroking one's hair).

psychotogenic 1. *adj.* describing a drug-induced state resembling PSYCHOSIS, marked, for example, by sensory illusions or distortions, hallucinations, delusions, and behavioral and emotional disturbances. **2.** *n.* an agent, such as a hallucinogen, that induces such a state. Also called **psychotogen**.

psychotomimetic 1. *adj.* tending to induce hallucinations, delusions, or other symptoms of psychosis. **2.** *n.* one of a group of drugs originally used in laboratory experiments to determine if they could induce psychoses, or states mimicking psychoses, on the basis of their effects. The group includes LSD and AMPHETAMINES. Also called **psychomimetic**.

psychotoxic *adj.* denoting or relating to agents that cause brain damage, such as excess alcohol, certain drugs and heavy metals, volatile solvents, and pesticides.

psychotropic drug see PSYCHOACTIVE DRUG.

PT abbreviation for PHYSICAL THERAPY.

PTSD abbreviation for POSTTRAUMATIC STRESS DISORDER.

puberty *n.* the stage of development when the genital organs reach maturity and secondary SEX CHARACTERISTICS begin to appear, signaling the start of ADOLESCENCE. It is marked by ejaculation of sperm in the male, onset of menstruation and development of breasts in the female, and, in both males and females, growth of pubic hair and increasing sexual interest. See also PRECOCIOUS PUBERTY; PERSISTENT PUBERISM. **—pubertal** *adj.*

public health approach a community-based approach to mental and physical health in which agencies and organizations focus on enhancing and maintaining the well-being of individuals by ensuring the existence of the conditions necessary for them to lead healthy lives. The approach involves such activities as monitoring community health status; identifying and investigating health problems and threats to community health; ensuring the competency of health care providers and personnel; disseminating accurate information and educating individuals about health issues; developing, modifying, and enforcing policies and other regulatory measures that support community health and safety; and ensuring the accessibility of quality health services. The approach involves various levels of disease and disorder prevention (primary, secondary, tertiary), the expansion and appropriate use of the scientific knowledge base, and the development and utilization of partnerships within and among communities.

public health nurse a REGISTERED NURSE or NURSE PRACTITIONER who has received additional training in social and public health sciences and services. Public health nurses are usually employed by government health departments and engaged in educational, informational, and preventive activities.

public health services 1. services intended to protect and improve community health. **2.** in some countries, health services provided by the state and financed mainly by general taxation.

public mental hospital a hospital for patients with mental disorders that is organized and run by the state, the county, or the U.S. Department of Veterans Affairs. Compare PRIVATE MENTAL HOSPITAL.

public residential facility any residential setting directly operated by state or local government. Although generally referring to large institutions, such as developmental centers (formerly called TRAINING SCHOOLS or state schools), the number of smaller residential settings, such as COMMUNITY RESIDENCES, that are publicly operated now greatly exceeds the number of remaining large public facilities.

public self information about the self, or an integrated view of the self, that is conveyed to others in actions, self-descriptions, appearance, and social interactions. An individual's public self will vary with the people who constitute the target or audience of such impressions. The public self is often contrasted with the PRIVATE SELF. See also COLLECTIVE SELF; SOCIAL SELF.

public self-consciousness see SELF-CONSCIOUSNESS.

public service psychology an area of psychology defined by the activities of psychologists employed by public sector agencies (e.g., in community mental health centers, state hospitals, correctional facilities, police and public safety agencies) and the psychological condition of people served by these agencies. Particular interests include advocacy, access to services, education and training, public policy formulation, research and program evaluation, and prevention efforts.

public-speaking anxiety fear of giving a speech or presentation in public in the expectation of being negatively evaluated or humiliated by others. This is a common fear, associated with SOCIAL PHOBIA.

puer aeternus the ARCHETYPE of eternal youth. [Latin, "eternal boy"; introduced by Carl JUNG]

puerilism *n.* immature, childish behavior.

puerperal disorder a medical or psychological disorder occurring in a woman during the puerperium, which extends from the termination of labor to the return of the uterus to its normal condition. Puerperal disorders include psychotic and depressive reactions and, occasionally, manic episodes or delirious states precipitated by biological, psychosocial, or environmental factors. See POSTPARTUM DEPRESSION; POSTPARTUM EMOTIONAL DISTURBANCE; POSTPARTUM PSYCHOSIS.

Puerto Rican syndrome see MAL DE PELEA.

pull model a psychological theory emphasizing how positive experience draws a person to establish meaning or to set goals. Compare PUSH MODEL.

puppetry therapy the use of puppets as a projective form of PLAY THERAPY. See also PROJECTIVE PLAY.

pure consciousness awareness without content.

pure microcephaly a condition marked by an abnormally small cranium (see MICROCEPHALY) in the absence of other congenital anomalies. Affected individuals usually have a face of normal size and show mental retardation. They may be smaller than average in height and in many cases are affected by spasticity of the limbs. Compare PRIMARY MICROCEPHALY.

purging *n.* the activity of expelling food that has just been ingested, usually by VOMITING or the use of laxatives. Purging often occurs in conjunction with an eating binge in ANOREXIA NERVOSA or BULIMIA NERVOSA; its purpose is to eliminate or reduce real or imagined weight gain.

purpose *n.* **1.** the reason for which something is done or for which something exists. **2.** a mental goal or aim that directs a person's actions or behavior. **3.** persistence or resolution in pursuing such a goal.

purposeful behavior behavior with a specific goal, as opposed to aimless or random behavior. See GOAL-DIRECTED BEHAVIOR.

purpose in life (**PIL**) the internal, mental sense of a goal or aim in the process of living or in existence itself. This concept is of special significance in EXISTENTIAL PSYCHOTHERAPY, in which it is considered to be central to the development and treatment of anxiety, depression, and related emotional states. Having a clear purpose in life reduces negative states.

purposeless hyperactivity a symptom of certain brain or mental disorders characterized by prolonged periods of excessive activity that has no purpose.

purposive accident an apparent accident that in fact was caused deliberately. It may have been motivated by psychological factors, such as unacknowledged wishes or needs. Also called **intentional accident**. See PARAPRAXIS.

push model a psychological theory emphasizing how negative experience impels a person to establish meaning or to set goals. Compare PULL MODEL.

putamen *n.* a part of the lenticular nucleus in the BASAL GANGLIA of the brain. It receives input from the motor cortex and is involved in control of movements.

p-value *n.* see SIGNIFICANCE LEVEL.

PVS abbreviation for PERSISTENT VEGETATIVE STATE.

PWS abbreviation for PRADER–WILLI SYNDROME.

pycnodysostosis (**pyknodysostosis**) *n.* an autosomal recessive syndrome characterized by dense but defective bones, open skull sutures, and short stature. Affected individuals rarely reach an adult height of 5 ft (1.5 m), and about 20% are likely to show mental retardation.

pygmalionism *n.* the act of falling in love with one's own creation. The term is derived from Greek mythology, in which Pygmalion fell in love with a statue of Aphrodite that he had sculpted.

pyknodysostosis *n.* see PYCNODYSOSTOSIS.

pyridostigmine *n.* an anticholinesterase (see ANTICHOLINERGIC DRUG) used in the treatment of myasthenia gravis. U.S. trade name (among others): **Mestinon**.

pyrolagnia *n.* the arousal of sexual excitement by large fires or conflagrations. Also called **erotic pyromania**.

pyromania *n.* an impulse-control disorder characterized by (a) repeated failure to resist impulses to set fires and watch them burn, without monetary, social, political, or other motivations; (b) an extreme interest in fire and things associated with fire; and (c) a sense of increased tension before starting the fire and intense pleasure, gratification, or release while committing the act. In *DSM–IV–TR* pyromania is included in the category IMPULSE-CONTROL DISORDERS NOT ELSEWHERE CLASSIFIED. An older name is **incendiarism**.

Qq

QALYs acronym for QUALITY ADJUSTED LIFE YEARS.

qat *n.* see KHAT.

Q data *q*uestionnaire data: information about an individual gathered from the observations, judgments, and evaluations of that person as provided via subjective self-report inventories—and therefore also known as **S data** (self data)—or questionnaires. See also L DATA; O DATA; T DATA.

qi *n.* see CHI.

qigong *n.* a Chinese health maintenance and self-healing practice that consists of coordination of specific breathing patterns with a variety of postures and body movements. Various forms are often taught as an auxiliary to Chinese martial arts.

Q sort a data-collection procedure, often used in personality measurement, in which a participant or independent rater sorts a broad set of stimuli into categories using a specific instruction set. The stimuli are often short descriptive statements (e.g., of personal traits) printed on cards. Examples of the instruction set are: "describe yourself"; "describe this child"; "describe your friend." In the classic Q sort, raters are constrained to use a predetermined number of stimuli in each category.

Quaalude *n.* see METHAQUALONE.

quack 1. *n.* an unqualified person who makes false claims about, or misrepresents his or her ability or credentials in, medical diagnosis and treatment. **2.** *adj.* describing a treatment for which false or exaggerated claims are made. **—quackery** *n.*

quadrangular therapy marital therapy involving the married couple and each spouse's individual therapist working together (see COUPLES THERAPY). Each spouse may meet with his or her therapist separately and then come together as a group.

quale *n.* (*pl.* **qualia**) **1.** the characteristic or quality that determines the nature of a mental experience (sensation or perception) and makes it distinguishable from other such experiences, so that (for example) the experiencer differentiates between the sensations of heat and cold. **2.** the phenomenal, conscious state or feeling specific to each emotion. The ineffable phenomenal states of anger, happiness, fear, sadness, and so on are qualia of AFFECT.

qualitative data data that are not expressed numerically, such as descriptions of behavior, thoughts, attitudes, and experiences. If desired, qualitative data can often be expressed quantitatively through a coding process. See QUALITATIVE RESEARCH.

qualitative research a method of research that produces descriptive (nonnumerical) data, such as observations of behavior or personal accounts of experiences. The goal of gathering this QUALITATIVE DATA is to examine how individuals can perceive the world from different vantage points. A variety of techniques are subsumed under qualitative research, including content analyses of narratives, in-depth interviews, FOCUS GROUPS, and CASE STUDIES, often conducted in naturalistic settings. Also called **qualitative design**; **qualitative inquiry**; **qualitative method**; **qualitative study**.

quality adjusted life years (**QALYs**) a measure that combines the quantity of life, expressed in terms of survival or life expectancy, with the quality of life. The value of a year of perfect health is taken as 1; a year of ill health is worth less than 1; death is taken as 0. The measure provides a method to assess the benefits to be gained from medical procedures and interventions.

quality assurance in health administration or other areas of service delivery, a systematic process that is used to monitor and provide continuous improvement in the quality of health care services. It involves not only evaluating the services in terms of effectiveness, appropriateness, and acceptability, but also offering feedback and implementing solutions to correct any identified deficiencies and assessing the results.

quality of care the extent to which health services are consistent with professional standards and increase the likelihood of desired outcomes.

quality of life the extent to which a person obtains satisfaction from life. The following are important for a good quality of life: emotional, material, and physical well-being; engagement in interpersonal relations; opportunities for personal (e.g., skill) development; exercising rights and making self-determining lifestyle choices; and participation in society. Enhancing quality of life is a particular concern for those with chronic disease or developmental and other disabilities and for those undergoing medical or psychological treatment.

quantitative approach Sigmund FREUD's theory that mental processes, such as tensions, obsessions, pleasure, and unpleasure, differ in the quantity as well as quality of PSYCHIC ENERGY associated with them. Even though the amounts cannot be measured as exactly as in the physical sciences, they nevertheless are posited to exist: For example, the amount of tension existing in the psyche at one time can be compared with the amount at another time. See also ECONOMIC MODEL.

quantitative data data expressed numerically, such as test scores or measurements of length or width. These data may or may not have a real zero but they have order and often equal intervals. Compare QUALITATIVE DATA.

quantitative genetics the field of genetics that studies traits that differ in degree rather than in kind.

quantitative research a method of research that relies on measuring variables using a numerical system, analyzing these measurements using any of a variety of statistical models, and reporting relationships and associations among the studied variables. For example, these variables may be test scores or measurements of reaction time. The goal of gathering this QUANTITATIVE DATA is to understand, describe, and predict the nature of a phenomenon, particularly through the development of models and theories. Quantitative research techniques include experiments and surveys. Also called **quantitative design**; **quantitative method**.

quasi-experimental research research in which the investigator cannot randomly assign units or participants to conditions, cannot generally control or manipulate the INDEPENDENT VARIABLE, and cannot limit the influence of extraneous variables. FIELD RESEARCH typically takes the form of quasi-experimental research. Examples of such research are studies that investigate the responses of large groups to natural disasters or widespread changes in social policy. Also called **nonexperimental research**; **nonrandomized research**.

quasineed in the social psychology of Kurt LEWIN, a tension state that initiates goal-directed activity with an origin in intent or purpose rather than a biological deficit.

quaternity *n.* Carl JUNG's fourfold concept of personality, in which there are four functions of the ego: feeling, thinking, intuiting, and sensing (see FUNCTIONAL TYPES). For Jung, the quaternity is an ARCHETYPE exemplified in myriad ways, such as the four points of the compass and the four points of the cross.

quazepam *n.* a BENZODIAZEPINE used as a HYPNOTIC agent. It is of medium potency and is highly lipid soluble, enabling rapid penetration of the BLOOD–BRAIN BARRIER resulting in rapid onset of effects. Because its metabolic products are eliminated slowly, quazepam may accumulate in the body, leading to unwanted daytime sedation. U.S. trade name: **Doral**.

queer *adj., n.* controversial slang, in the main pejorative, referring (in both the adjectival and noun senses) to gays and lesbians or relating to same-sex sexual orientation. The original and still common use of the word, to describe anything that is unusual in an odd or strange way, was extended to refer to gays in the late 19th and throughout much of the 20th century, when it acquired a predominantly negative, derogatory connotation. During the late 1960s and onward (see SEXUAL REVOLUTION), it was appropriated by some members within the gay community as a term of identification that carried no negative connotation and, indeed, took on the role of a label of pride and self-respect. This usage is not embraced, however, by all members of the gay community.

querulent *adj.* quarrelsome, complaining, irritable, and suspicious. These qualities are frequently associated with a paranoid state and a tendency toward litigiousness. See also LITIGIOUS PARANOIA.

quetiapine *n.* an ATYPICAL ANTIPSYCHOTIC used for the management of psychosis and schizophrenia. Like the conventional antipsychotics, its therapeutic effects are in part related to its ability to block D2 dopamine receptors (see DOPAMINE-RECEPTOR ANTAGONISTS); however, it differs from the older agents in its ability to also block 5-HT_2 SEROTONIN RECEPTORS. Sedation is a common adverse effect; thyroid dysfunction, weight gain, and ELECTROCARDIOGRAPHIC EFFECTS are more rarely observed. U.S. trade name: **Seroquel**.

Rr

racial memory thought patterns, feelings, and traces of experiences held to be transmitted from generation to generation and to have a basic influence on individual minds and behavior. Carl JUNG and Sigmund FREUD both embraced the concept of a phylogenetic heritage (see PHYLOGENY), but focused on different examples. Freud cited religious rituals designed to relieve feelings of anxiety and guilt, which he explained in terms of the OEDIPUS COMPLEX and his PRIMAL-HORDE THEORY. Jung cited images, symbols, and personifications that spontaneously appear in different cultures, which he explained in terms of the ARCHETYPES of the COLLECTIVE UNCONSCIOUS. Also called **racial unconscious**.

racial unconscious see RACIAL MEMORY.

radiation *n.* **1.** energy transmitted in the form of waves, such as electromagnetic radiation (e.g., heat, light, microwaves, short radio waves, ultraviolet rays, or X-rays), or in the form of a stream of nuclear particles (e.g., alpha particles, beta particles, gamma rays, electrons, neutrons, or protons). Such waves or particles are used for diagnostic, therapeutic, or experimental purposes (see RADIATION THERAPY). **2.** in neuroscience, the spread of excitation to adjacent neurons.

radiation therapy the use of RADIATION (e.g., X-rays) in the treatment of diseases. Radiotherapy is used mainly in the destruction of cancer cells by implanting radioactive isotopes in the body of the patient or delivering a known dose of radiation to a specific tissue area. Side effects may include fatigue, soreness and redness of the irradiated area, nausea and vomiting, loss of appetite, and a decreased white blood cell count. Also called **radiotherapy**.

radical behaviorism the view that behavior, rather than consciousness and its contents, should be the proper topic for study in psychological science. This term is often used to distinguish classical BEHAVIORISM, as originally formulated in 1913 by John B. WATSON, from more moderate forms of NEOBEHAVIORISM. However, it has evolved to denote as well the form of behaviorism later proposed by B. F. SKINNER, which emphasized the importance of reinforcement and its relationship to behavior (i.e., the environmental determinants of behavior). Skinner conceded the existence of private events, such as thinking, feeling, and imagining, but believed them to be irrelevant, viewing them not as causes of behavior but as more behavior in need of explanation or as private stimuli that function according to the same laws as public stimuli. See BEHAVIOR ANALYSIS; DESCRIPTIVE BEHAVIORISM.

radical psychiatry a variant of RADICAL THERAPY proposing that the psychological problems of individuals are the result of their victimization by the social, economic, and political system in which they live. As such, it is the system, not the individual, that should be the target of intervention and change. This view was most seriously considered during the 1970s and 1980s.

radical therapy any clinical intervention that focuses on the harmful psychological effects of social problems on individuals and that encourages individuals to help themselves by changing society. This approach was actively advanced by some psychologists in the 1970s and 1980s.

rage *n.* intense, typically uncontrolled anger. It is usually differentiated from HOSTILITY in that it is not necessarily accompanied by destructive actions but rather by excessive expressions. In animals, rage appears to be a late stage of AGGRESSION when normal deterrents to physical attack, such as submissive signals, are no longer effective. It generally includes rapid respiration; thrusting and jerking of limbs; and clawing, biting, and snarling.

rage disorder any disturbance characterized by one or more episodes of extreme anger and aggression, such as incidents of ROAD RAGE, or any clinical disorder in which episodes of rage are a primary symptom, such as INTERMITTENT EXPLOSIVE DISORDER.

random *adj.* without order or predictability.

random assignment see RANDOMIZE.

random error an error due to chance alone. Random errors are nonsystematic (occurring arbitrarily) and they are generally assumed to form a NORMAL DISTRIBUTION around a true score. Also called **variable error**. See also ABSOLUTE ERROR; CONSTANT ERROR.

randomize *vb.* to assign participants or other sampling units to the conditions of an experiment at random, that is, in such a way that each participant or sampling unit has an equal chance of being assigned to any particular condition. **—randomization** *n.*

randomized clinical trial an experimental design in which patients are randomly assigned to either a group that will receive an experimental treatment or one that will receive a comparison treatment or PLACEBO. There may be multiple experimental and comparison groups, but each patient is assigned to only a single group.

random observation any observation that is made spontaneously or by chance, is uncontrolled, or is not part of a schedule or pattern of organized observation.

random sampling a process for selecting individuals for a study from a larger potential group of individuals in such a way that each is selected with a fixed probability of inclusion. This selected group of individuals is called a **random sample**.

random selection the procedure used for random sampling.

random variable a variable whose value depends upon the outcome of chance. Also called **stochastic variable**.

range *n.* in statistics, a measure of DISPERSION, obtained by subtracting the lowest score from the highest score in a distribution.

rank 1. *n.* a particular position along an ordered continuum. See RANK ORDER. **2.** *vb.* to arrange items in a graded order, for example, from highest to lowest value.

rank correlation coefficient a numerical index reflecting the degree of relationship between two variables that have each been arranged in ascending or descending order of magnitude (i.e., ranked). It is an assessment not of the association between the actual values of the variables but rather of the association between their rankings. Among the most commonly used is the **Spearman rank correlation coefficient** (**Spearman's rho**, symbolized by ρ), appropriate when the variables being compared do not follow the NORMAL DISTRIBUTION. Also called **rank order correlation coefficient**.

Rankian therapy see WILL THERAPY.

rank order the arrangement of a series of items (e.g., scores or individuals) in order of magnitude.

rape *n.* the nonconsensual oral, anal, or vaginal penetration of an individual by another person with a part of the body or an object, using force or threats of bodily harm, or by taking advantage of someone incapable of giving consent. U.S. laws defining rape vary by state, but in contrast to older definitions the crime of rape is no longer limited to female victims, to vaginal penetration alone, or to forcible situations only, and the exclusion of spouses as possible perpetrators of rape has been dropped.

rape counseling provision of guidance and support for victims of rape and sexual assault. **Rape crisis centers** offer expert counseling for the psychological trauma that individuals typically experience following a sexual attack; both the affected individuals and their families are counseled. Community education and prevention outreach programs are increasingly part of the purview of this area of counseling.

rape-trauma syndrome the symptoms of POSTTRAUMATIC STRESS DISORDER (PTSD) experienced by an individual who has been sexually assaulted (the term was coined prior to the wide acceptance and use of the more inclusive concept of PTSD). The symptoms, which may include fear of being alone, phobic attitudes toward sex, VAGINISMUS, male impotence, or repeated washing of the body, may persist for a year or more after the rape. They may be aggravated by an attitude of others that the victim "invited" rape by dressing in a certain way or other behavior.

rapid cycling mood disturbance that fluctuates over a short period, most commonly between manic and depressive symptoms. A rapid-cycling BIPOLAR DISORDER is characterized by four or more mood episodes over a 12-month period; the episodes must be separated by symptom-free periods of at least 2 months or must be delimited by switching to an episode of opposite polarity (e.g., a major depressive episode switches to a manic, mixed, or hypomanic episode).

rapid eye movement (**REM**) the rapid, jerky, but coordinated movement of the eyes behind closed lids, observed during dreaming sleep. See DREAM STATE; REM SLEEP.

rapid neuroleptization see MEGADOSE PHARMACOTHERAPY.

rapid sequential visual presentation (**RSVP**) in psychophysical testing, a methodology in which a series of visual stimuli, such as shapes or words, are presented in a very short time span, often just a few milliseconds per item.

rapport *n.* a warm, relaxed relationship of mutual understanding, acceptance, and sympathetic compatibility between or among individuals. The establishment of rapport with the client in psychotherapy is frequently a significant mediate goal for the therapist in order to facilitate and deepen the therapeutic experience and promote optimal progress and improvement in the client.

rapprochement *n.* **1.** generally, a state of cordial relations between individuals or groups. **2.** in the theory of SEPARATION–INDIVIDUATION of Austrian child psychoanalyst Margaret Mahler (1897–1985), the phase, after about 18 months of age, in which the child makes active approaches to the mother. This contrasts with the preceding stage in which the child was relatively oblivious to the mother.

ratio data numerical values that indicate magnitude and have a true, meaningful zero point. Ratio data represent exact quantities of the variables under consideration, and when arranged consecutively have equal differences among adjacent values (regardless of the specific values selected) that correspond to genuine differences between the physical quantities being measured. Income provides an example: the difference between an income of $40,000 and $50,000 is the same as the difference between $110,000 and

$120,000, and an income of $0 indicates a complete and genuine absence of earnings. Ratio data are continuous in nature (i.e., able to take on any of an infinite variety of amounts) and of the highest measurement level, surpassing NOMINAL DATA, ORDINAL DATA, and INTERVAL DATA in precision and complexity.

ratio IQ IQ as determined by the ratio of mental age to chronological age, multiplied by 100. Compare DEVIATION IQ.

rational *adj.* **1.** pertaining to REASONING or, more broadly, to higher thought processes. **2.** based on, in accordance with, or justifiable by accepted principles of reasoning or logic. Compare IRRATIONAL. **3.** capable of or exhibiting reason. **4.** influenced by reasoning rather than by emotion. **—rationally** *adv.*

rational emotive behavior therapy (**REBT**) a form of COGNITIVE BEHAVIOR THERAPY based on the concept that an individual's irrational or self-defeating beliefs and feelings influence and cause his or her undesirable behaviors and damaging self-concept. Originally called **rational emotive therapy** (**RET**), it became known as rational emotive behavior therapy during the 1990s. The therapy teaches the individual, through a variety of cognitive, emotive, and behavioral techniques, to modify and replace self-defeating thoughts to achieve new and more effective ways of feeling and behaving. In the process of the therapy, the irrational beliefs and feelings are first unmasked then altered by (a) showing how the beliefs and feelings produce the individual's problems and (b) indicating how they can be changed through behavior therapy. Also called **rational psychotherapy**. See also ABCDE TECHNIQUE; ABC THEORY. [developed in 1955 by U.S. psychotherapist Albert Ellis (1913–2007)]

rationality *n.* **1.** the quality of being reasonable or RATIONAL or of being acceptable to reason. **2.** a rational action, belief, or desire.

rationality of emotions the proposition that emotions show an implacable logic, in that they follow from APPRAISALS made by the individual as inevitably as logical conclusions follow from axioms and premises. This view, which counters the traditional idea that emotions and reason are in opposition to one another, is linked to the work of U.S. psychologist Richard S. Lazarus (1922–2002) and Swiss-born Canadian–British psychologist Ronald B. De Sousa (1940–).

rationalization *n.* in psychotherapy, an explanation, or presentation, in which apparently logical reasons are given to justify unacceptable behavior that is motivated by unconscious instinctual impulses. In psychoanalytic theory, such behavior is considered to be a DEFENSE MECHANISM. Examples are: "Doesn't everybody cheat?" or "You have to spank children to toughen them up." Rationalizations are used to defend against feelings of guilt, to maintain self-respect, and to protect oneself from criticism. In psychotherapy, rationalization is considered counterproductive to deep exploration and confrontation of the client's thoughts and feelings and of how they affect behavior. **—rationalize** *vb.*

rationally suicidal having SUICIDAL IDEATION or intent that could be considered an understandable response to an untenable situation.

rational psychotherapy see RATIONAL EMOTIVE BEHAVIOR THERAPY.

rational type in the ANALYTIC PSYCHOLOGY of Carl JUNG, one of the two major categories of FUNCTIONAL TYPE: It comprises the THINKING TYPE and the FEELING TYPE. Compare IRRATIONAL TYPE.

ratio scale a measurement scale having a true zero (i.e., zero on the scale indicates an absence of the measured attribute) and a constant ratio of values. Thus, on a ratio scale an increase from 3 to 4 (for example) is the same as an increase from 7 to 8. The existence of a true zero point is what distinguishes a ratio scale from an INTERVAL SCALE.

Rat Man a landmark case of Sigmund FREUD's, which he described in "Notes Upon a Case of Obsessional Neurosis" (1909). The name was applied to a patient of Freud's, a 30-year-old lawyer whose obsessional fear of rats was traced to repressed death wishes toward his father generated by oedipal conflicts. One example of the patient's obsession was his belief that a rat that appeared to come out of his father's grave had eaten the corpse; another was a fantasy that a rat had been placed in his father's anus and had eaten through his intestines. Freud's analysis of these reactions laid the groundwork for the psychoanalytic interpretation of obsessional neurosis. See also OEDIPUS COMPLEX.

rauwolfia derivatives alkaloids obtained from plants of the genus *Rauwolfia*, primarily *R. serpentina*, the ancient Hindu snakeroot. They have sedative and antihypertensive actions, and have been used in neuropsychopharmacology since about 1000 BCE by Hindu healers. The genus was named for 16th-century German botanist Leonhard Rauwolf, who reported its tranquilizing effect in 1575 while traveling in India. The prototype drug of the group is **reserpine**, which acts by depleting stores of catecholamine neurotransmitters in both central and peripheral nervous systems. Rauwolfia derivatives were initially used in the management of psychosis, but were erroneously thought to induce depression and therefore abandoned for this use in the 1950s.

RAVLT abbreviation for REY AUDITORY VERBAL LEARNING TEST.

raw score an original score before it is converted to other units or another form through statistical analysis.

Raynaud's disease a disorder characterized by episodes of painful vasoconstriction of the blood vessels in the extremities, especially the fingers and toes. The attacks, usually lasting up to 15 min, are precipitated by cold exposure or, in one third of cases, by emotional stress. **Raynaud's phenomenon** refers to similar symptoms caused by another disease—for example, rheumatic arthritis (see ARTHRITIS)—or by toxic agents, such as vinyl chloride. Drug therapy and behavioral treatment (with thermal biofeedback) have proven effective in relieving the attacks. [identified in 1854 by Maurice **Raynaud** (1834–1881), French physician]

RBD abbreviation for REM BEHAVIOR DISORDER.

RDC abbreviation for RESEARCH DIAGNOSTIC CRITERIA.

reactance theory a model stating that in response to a perceived threat to or loss of a behavioral freedom a person will experience **psychological reactance** (or, more simply, reactance), a motivational state characterized by distress, anxiety, resistance, and the desire to restore that freedom. According to this model, when people feel coerced or forced into a certain behavior, they will react against the coercion, often by demonstrating an increased preference for the behavior that is restrained, and may perform the opposite behavior to that desired. [proposed in 1966 by U.S. psychologist Jack W. Brehm (1928–2009)]

reaction formation in psychoanalytic theory, a DEFENSE MECHANISM in which unacceptable or threatening unconscious impulses are denied and are replaced in consciousness with their opposite. For example, to conceal an unconscious prejudice an individual may preach tolerance; to deny feelings of rejection, a mother may be overindulgent toward her child. Through the symbolic relationship between the unconscious wish and its opposite, the outward behavior provides a disguised outlet for the tendencies it seems to oppose.

reaction time (**RT**) the time that elapses between onset or presentation of a stimulus and occurrence of a response to that stimulus. Also called **cognitive reaction time**; **response time**.

reaction type 1. any of the categories into which a psychiatric syndrome can be classified in terms of its predominant symptoms. For example, Swiss-born U.S. psychiatrist Adolf Meyer (1866–1950) distinguished affective, delirious, deteriorated, disguised-conflict, organic, and paranoid reaction types. **2.** in reaction-time experiments, a particular type of SET, or readiness of the participant or participants: motor (prepared to respond), sensory (prepared to receive a stimulus), or mixed.

reactivation of memory the RETRIEVAL of a memory, which may be triggered by stimuli or environmental conditions that were present when the memory was originally formed. See also PRIMING.

reactive *adj.* associated with or originating in response to a given stimulus or situation. For example, a psychotic episode that is secondary to a traumatic or otherwise stressful event in the life of the individual would be considered reactive and generally associated with a more favorable prognosis than an ENDOGENOUS episode unrelated to a specific happening.

reactive attachment disorder in *DSM–IV–TR*, a disorder of infancy and early childhood characterized by disturbed and developmentally inappropriate patterns of social relating not resulting from mental retardation or pervasive developmental disorder. It is evidenced either by persistent failure to initiate or respond appropriately in social interactions (inhibited type) or by indiscriminate sociability without appropriate selective attachments (disinhibited type). There must also be evidence of inadequate care (e.g., ignoring the child's basic physical or emotional needs, frequent changes of primary caregiver), which is assumed to be responsible for the disturbed social relating. Also called **attachment disorder**.

reactive depression a MAJOR DEPRESSIVE EPISODE that is apparently precipitated by a distressing event or situation, such as a career or relationship setback. Also called **exogenous depression**. Compare ENDOGENOUS DEPRESSION.

reactive disorder an older name for a mental disorder that is apparently precipitated by severe environmental pressure or a traumatic event.

reactive mania a HYPOMANIC EPISODE or MANIC EPISODE that is precipitated by an external event.

reactive psychosis see SITUATIONAL PSYCHOSIS.

reactive schizophrenia an acute form of schizophrenia that clearly develops in response to predisposing or precipitating environmental factors, such as extreme stress. The prognosis is generally more favorable than for PROCESS SCHIZOPHRENIA. [proposed in 1959 by U.S. psychologists Norman Garmezy (1918–2009) and Eliot H. Rodnick (1911–1999)]

reading delay inability to read at the ability level typical for a given age.

reading disability a reading ability that is below that expected for a child of a given age and stage of development. It is associated with neurological damage or impairment, typically in language processing and visual reasoning areas of the brain, that results in difficulty understanding the associations between letters and sounds.

reading disorder in *DSM–IV–TR*, a LEARNING DISORDER that is characterized by a level of reading ability substantially below that expected for a child of a given age, intellectual ability, and educational experience. The reading difficulty, which involves faulty oral reading, slow oral and silent reading, and often reduced comprehension, interferes with achievement or everyday life and is not attributable to neurological impairment, sensory impairment, mental retardation, or environmental deprivation.

reading span **1.** the amount of written or printed material that a person can apprehend during a single FIXATION of the eye during reading. The greater the reading span, the fewer times the eye needs to stop along a line of text. A span of 7–10 characters is considered typical. Also called **eye span**; **recognition span**. **2.** in memory tests, the number of words a person can remember on being asked to recall the last word of each sentence in a passage that he or she has just read.

readmission *n.* the admission to a hospital, clinic, mental hospital, or other institution of a patient who has been admitted previously. Also called **rehospitalization**. See also REVOLVING-DOOR PHENOMENON. **—readmit** *vb.*

Real *n.* the realm of nature or reality: one of three aspects of the psychoanalytic field defined by French psychoanalyst Jacques Lacan (1901–1981). The Real is posited to be unknown and unknowable—in effect, unreal—because all individuals ultimately possess are images and symbols. The other realms are the IMAGINARY and the SYMBOLIC.

real–ideal self congruence the degree to which the characteristics of a person's ideal self match his or her actual characteristics. The discrepancy between the two, when large enough, creates psychological pain; it is theorized to be a motivating force for entering treatment and is the focus of treatment in CLIENT-CENTERED THERAPY. In research studies it is measured by having participants sort cards describing themselves as they would like to be and as they are (see SELF-IDEAL Q SORT).

realistic anxiety anxiety in response to an identifiable threat or danger. This type of anxiety is considered a normal response to danger in the real world and serves to mobilize resources in order to protect the individual from harm. Also called **objective anxiety**.

realistic thinking thinking that is based or focused on the objective qualities and requirements that pertain in different situations. Realistic thinking permits adjustment of thoughts and behavior to the demands of a situation; it depends on the ability to interpret external situations in a fairly consistent, accurate manner. This, in turn, involves the capacity to distinguish fantasy and subjective experience from external reality. See also REALITY TESTING.

reality awareness the perception of external objects as different from the self and from each other. Also called **reality contact**.

reality confrontation an activity in which the therapist raises the possibility that the patient has misconstrued events or the intentions of others. The confrontation is thought to be helpful in reducing maladaptive behaviors that result from distorted thinking.

reality orientation in psychotherapy, a form of REMOTIVATION that aims to reduce a client's confusion about time, place, or person. The therapist continually reminds the client who he or she is, what day it is, where he or she is, and what is happening or is about to take place.

reality principle in psychoanalytic theory, the regulatory mechanism that represents the demands of the external world and requires the individual to forgo or modify instinctual gratification or to postpone it to a more appropriate time. In contrast to the PLEASURE PRINCIPLE, which is posited to dominate the life of the infant and child and govern the ID, or instinctual impulses, the reality principle is posited to govern the EGO, which controls impulses and enables people to deal rationally and effectively with the situations of life.

reality testing any means by which an individual determines and assesses his or her limitations in the face of biological, physiological, social, or environmental actualities or exigencies. It enables the individual to distinguish between self and non-self and between fantasy and real life. Defective reality testing is the major criterion of PSYCHOSIS.

reality therapy treatment that focuses on present ineffective or maladaptive behavior and the development of the client's ability to cope with the stresses of reality and take greater responsibility for the fulfillment of his or her needs (i.e., discover what he or she really wants and the optimal way of achieving it). To these ends, the therapist plays an active role in examining the client's daily activities, suggesting healthier, more adaptive ways for the client to behave. Reality therapy tends to be of shorter duration than many other traditional psychotherapies (see BRIEF PSYCHOTHERAPY). [developed by U.S. psychiatrist William Glasser (1925–)]

real-life test a period during which people seeking sex-reversal surgery (see TRANSSEXUALISM) are required to live as the sex they wish to become, for usually one or two years, before any surgical procedures are performed. As well as a name change, it involves changing clothing, hair, and other aspects of physical appearance to those of the opposite sex. The real-life test is used to give the individual (and the professionals involved) an indication of whether he or she will be able to cope with, and benefit from, a sex-reversal operation.

real self the individual's true wishes and feelings and his or her potential for further growth and development. See SELF. See also ACTUAL SELF; TRUE SELF. [defined by German-born U.S. psychoanalyst Karen D. Horney (1885–1952)]

reason **1.** *n.* consecutive thought, as in deduction or induction. Although at one time reason was considered a mental faculty, this is typically not intended in current usage. See DEDUCTIVE REASONING; INDUCTIVE REASONING. **2.** *n.* in philosophy, the intellect regarded as the source of true knowledge. **3.** *n.* soundness of mind. **4.** *n.* a statement offered to justify an action or decision or to explain the occurrence of an event. **5.** *vb.* see REASONING.

reasonable accommodations adjustments made within an employment or educational setting that allow an individual with a physical, cognitive, or psychiatric disability to perform required tasks and essential functions. This might include installing ramps in an office cafeteria for wheelchair accessibility, altering the format of a test for a person with learning disabilities, or providing a sign language interpreter for a person with hearing loss. Provisions for reasonable accommodations must be made by employers and educators according to the 1990 Americans With Disabilities Act and the 1973 Rehabilitation Act.

reasonable doubt see BEYOND REASONABLE DOUBT.

reasoning *n.* **1.** thinking in which logical processes of an inductive or deductive character are used to draw conclusions from facts or premises. See DEDUCTIVE REASONING; INDUCTIVE REASONING. **2.** the sequence of arguments or proofs used to establish a conclusion in this way. **—reason** *vb.*

reasoning mania a MANIC EPISODE in which judgment is not impaired and there are no PSYCHOTIC FEATURES.

reassociation *n.* in HYPNOANALYSIS, a process of renewing or reviewing a forgotten or inhibited traumatic event so that the experience will be integrated with the individual's personality and consciousness.

reassurance *n.* in psychotherapy and counseling, a supportive approach that encourages clients to believe in themselves and in the possibilities of improvement. The technique is common and has widespread use across many forms of psychotherapy. It is used frequently in SUPPORTIVE PSYCHOTHERAPY and occasionally in RECONSTRUCTIVE PSYCHOTHERAPY to encourage a client in the process of exploring new relationships and feelings. Reassurance is also used to diminish anxiety, for example, by explaining to a client that a period of heightened depression or tension is temporary and not unexpected. Also called **assurance**.

rebirthing *n.* **1.** the therapeutic use of continuous, focused breathing and reflection, initially under the guidance of a rebirthing practitioner (a **rebirther**), to release tension, stress, and intense emotions and attain a state of deep peace and total relaxation that leads to personal growth and positive changes in health, consciousness, and self-esteem (i.e., a personal and spiritual "rebirth"). This type of therapy is increasingly being termed **breathwork** or **rebirthing breathwork**. [developed in the 1970s by California-based New Age guru Leonard Orr] **2.** a highly controversial form of therapy, now largely discredited (both scientifically and ethically), in which an individual attempts to reexperience being born (e.g., through hypnotic age regression) in order to resolve supposed pre- and perinatal conflicts and emotions and to develop new and different outlooks on life.

rebound effect an increase in behavior or the strength of a process following a period of suppression.

rebound insomnia a phenomenon associated with the use of hypnotic agents, particularly short-acting BENZODIAZEPINES, and characterized by a temporary worsening of insomnia following abrupt discontinuation of the drug or an inability to return to sleep after the initial effects of the drug have worn off. Rebound insomnia of the latter type often makes administration of a second dose of the agent ineffective.

rebound phenomenon **1.** an effect in which an activity or occurrence previously suppressed or prevented temporarily increases once the restrictions imposed on it are removed. The term is used particularly to denote the temporary reappearance of symptoms following abrupt discontinuation of a medication used for treatment. An example is **rebound insomnia**, in which the discontinuation of the use of hypnotic agents, particularly short-acting BENZODIAZEPINES, results in a transitory return of insomnia, possibly of increased severity. **2.** a test that demonstrates loss of the ability of the cerebellum to control coordinated movement: If the individual extends the forearm against resistance and the resistance is suddenly removed, the hand or fist will snap back toward the chest. Also called **Holmes's phenomenon**.

reboxetine *n.* a drug that inhibits the reuptake of norepinephrine but has little or no effect on neurotransmission of serotonin, dopamine, acetylcholine, or histamine. It was the first selective norepinephrine reuptake inhibitor developed for clinical use as an antidepressant. It is not available for use in the United States.

REBT abbreviation for RATIONAL EMOTIVE BEHAVIOR THERAPY.

recall **1.** *vb.* to transfer prior learning or past experience to current consciousness: that is, to retrieve and reproduce information. **2.** *n.* the process by which this occurs. See also FREE RECALL.

receiving hospital a health facility that is specially equipped and staffed to handle new patients requiring diagnosis and preliminary treatment, for example, people with suspected mental disorder.

recency effect a memory phenomenon in which the most recently presented facts, impressions, or items are learned or remembered better than material presented earlier. This can occur in both formal learning situations and social contexts. For example, it can result in inaccurate ratings or impressions of a person's abilities or other characteristics due to the inordinate influence of the most recent information received about that person. Also called **law of recency**;

principle of recency; **recency error**. Compare PRIMACY EFFECT.

receptive character in the psychoanalytic theory of Erich FROMM, a passive, dependent, and compliant, or conforming, personality type: roughly equivalent to the ORAL-RECEPTIVE PERSONALITY or the passive-dependent personality (see DEPENDENT PERSONALITY DISORDER) described by others. Such an individual is said to be of a **receptive orientation.**

receptor *n.* **1.** the cell in a sensory system that is responsible for stimulus transduction, the process by which one form of enegy is converted into another. Receptor cells are specialized to detect and respond to specific stimuli in the external or internal environment. **2.** a sense organ, such as the eye or the ear. **3.** a molecule in a cell membrane that specifically binds a particular molecular messenger (e.g., a neurotransmitter, hormone, or drug) and elicits a response in the cell. Also called **receptor molecule**. See also NEURORECEPTOR.

recessive allele the version of a gene (see ALLELE) whose effects are manifest only if it is carried on both members of a HOMOLOGOUS pair of chromosomes. Hence, the trait determined by a recessive allele (the **recessive trait**) is apparent only in the absence of another version of that same gene (the DOMINANT ALLELE). The term **autosomal recessive** is used to describe such patterns of inheritance in which characteristics are conveyed by recessive alleles. Tay–Sachs disease is an example of autosomal recessive disorder.

recessive trait in genetics, a trait that is expressed only if its determining ALLELE is carried on both members of a HOMOLOGOUS pair of chromosomes or on an unmatched sex chromosome. See RECESSIVE ALLELE. Compare DOMINANT TRAIT.

recidivism *n.* relapse. The term typically denotes the repetition of delinquent or criminal behavior, especially in the case of a habitual criminal, or **repeat offender**, who has been convicted several times. **—recidivist** *n., adj.* **—recidivistic** *adj.*

recidivism rate the frequency with which delinquent or criminal behavior recurs or patients relapse. It is sometimes used as a marker of the effects of interventions; for example, the percentage of patients who are rearrested for rape following treatment intended to reduce the likelihood of committing this crime would indicate the effectiveness of the treatment.

reciprocal determinism a concept that opposes the radical or exclusive emphasis on environmental determination of responses and asserts that a reciprocal relation exists among environment, behavior, and the individual. That is, instead of conceptualizing the environment as a one-way determinant of behavior, reciprocal determinism maintains that the environment influences behavior, behavior influences the environment, and both influence the individual, who also influences them. This concept is associated with SOCIAL LEARNING THEORY.

reciprocal inhibition 1. a technique in BEHAVIOR THERAPY that aims to replace an undesired response with one that is desired by COUNTERCONDITIONING. It relies on the gradual substitution of a response that is incompatible with the original one and is potent enough to neutralize the anxiety-evoking power of the stimulus. See also SYSTEMATIC DESENSITIZATION. [devised by South African-born U.S. psychologist Joseph Wolpe (1915–1997)] **2.** in neuroscience, the inhibition of one spinal reflex when another is elicited. [proposed by British neurophysiologist Charles Scott Sherrington (1857–1952)] **3.** a neural mechanism that prevents opposing muscles from contracting at the same time. **4.** the inability to recall two associated ideas or items because of their interference with each other.

reciprocal regulation recurring or mutual adaptation of behavior of a person or people to changed conditions.

reciprocity norm the social standard (NORM) that people who help others will receive equivalent benefits from these others in return.

recoding *n.* the translation of material held in memory from one form into another. For example, a series of random digits (e.g., 239812389712) could be recoded as a series of four-digit prices ($23.98, $12.38, $97.12), thereby making the series much easier to recall. See CHUNKING; ELABORATION. **—recode** *vb.*

Recognition Memory Test (**RMT**) a verbal and nonverbal memory test that is used to detect neuropsychological deficits. In the Recognition Memory for Words subtest of the RMT, participants are presented with 50 stimulus words, one every 3 s, and must respond whether they consider each pleasant or unpleasant. Following the presentation of all 50 stimuli, each word is presented again concurrently with a distractor item, and participants must choose which of the two words had been presented previously. The procedure is the same for the Recognition Memory for Faces subtest, in which the stimuli used are photographs of unfamiliar faces. Also called **Warrington Recognition Memory Test**. [originally developed in 1984 by British neuropsychologist Elizabeth Kerr Warrington]

recombinant DNA a DNA molecule containing a fragment that has been inserted by genetic recombination or some similar process, for example, using the techniques of GENETIC ENGINEERING. Recombinant DNA laboratory techniques involve the creation of novel or modified pieces of genetic material, which can then be inserted in the chromosomes of another species. These techniques allow for the study of the expression of a particular gene or the development of strains of bacteria that can produce natural substances of therapeutic value.

recompensation *n.* an increase in the ability of

an individual to adapt to the environment and alleviate stressful situations. Compare COMPENSATION; DECOMPENSATION.

reconditioning therapy a form of BEHAVIOR THERAPY in which the client is conditioned to replace undesirable responses with desirable responses. See also AVERSION THERAPY.

reconstituted family see STEPFAMILY.

reconstitution *n.* **1.** revision of one's attitudes or goals. **2.** a mental or attitudinal outcome of the grieving process experienced by some patients with catastrophic illnesses resulting in disability.

reconstruction *n.* **1.** in psychoanalysis, the revival and analytic interpretation of past experiences that have been instrumental in producing present emotional disturbance. **2.** the logical recreation of an experience or event that has been only partially stored in memory. **—reconstruct** *vb.*

reconstructive memory a form of remembering marked by the logical recreation of an experience or event that has been only partially stored in memory. It draws on general knowledge and SCHEMAS or on memory for what typically happens in order to reconstruct the experience or event.

reconstructive psychotherapy psychotherapy directed toward basic and extensive modification of an individual's character structure, by enhancing his or her insight into personality development, unconscious conflicts, and adaptive responses. Examples are Freudian PSYCHOANALYSIS, Adlerian INDIVIDUAL PSYCHOLOGY, Jungian ANALYTIC PSYCHOLOGY, and the approaches of German-born U.S. psychoanalyst Karen D. Horney (1885–1952) and U.S. psychiatrist Harry Stack Sullivan (1892–1949).

record keeping an essential aspect of therapy, in which clinical notes are preserved for future reference, training purposes, or both. Clinical notes may be subpoenaed by the courts. The extent of detail in record keeping varies with the situation, but some degree of record keeping is deemed standard procedure for clinicians.

recovered memory the subjective experience of recalling details of a prior traumatic event, such as sexual or physical abuse, that has previously been unavailable to conscious recollection. Before recovering the memory, the person may be unaware that the traumatic event has occurred. The phenomenon is controversial: Because such recoveries often occur while the person is undergoing therapy, there is debate about their veracity vis-à-vis the role that the therapist may have played in suggesting or otherwise arousing them. Also called **repressed memory**. See also DISSOCIATIVE BARRIERS; POSTTRAUMATIC AMNESIA; PSEUDOMEMORY.

recovery *n.* the period during which an individual exhibits consistent progress in terms of measurable return of abilities, skills, and functions following illness or injury.

Recovery, Inc. a SELF-HELP GROUP for individuals with serious mental health problems that focuses on will-training techniques for controlling temperamental behavior and changing members' attitudes toward their problems. Founded in 1937 by U.S. neuropsychiatrist Abraham A. Low (1891–1954), it is one of the oldest self-help organizations in the world.

recovery ratio see DISCHARGE RATE.

recreational drug any substance that is used in a nontherapeutic manner for its effects on motor, sensory, or cognitive activities.

recreational therapy the use of individualized recreational activities (arts and crafts, sports, games, group outings, etc.) as an integral part of the rehabilitation or therapeutic process for individuals with physical or psychological disabilities or illness. Also called **therapeutic recreation**.

rectal administration the administration of a drug by rectal insertion, usually in the form of a SUPPOSITORY, for absorption via the rectal mucosa.

recuperative theory a theory that the function of sleep is to allow the body to recuperate from the rigors of waking, to regather resources, and to reestablish internal HOMEOSTASIS.

recurrent *adj.* occurring repeatedly or reappearing after an interval of time or a period of remission: often applied to disorders marked by chronicity, relapse, or repeated episodes (e.g., depressive symptoms).

recurrent depression MAJOR DEPRESSIVE DISORDER in which there have been two or more MAJOR DEPRESSIVE EPISODES.

recurrent dream a dream that occurs repeatedly. Sigmund FREUD saw recurrent dreams as punishment, rather than WISH-FULFILLMENT, dreams and linked them to a masochistic need for self-criticism arising from fantasies of excessive ambition. Carl JUNG regarded recurrent dreams as more revealing of the UNCONSCIOUS than single dreams, and found that in a dream series the later dreams often throw light on the earlier ones (see SERIAL INTERPRETATION). Other psychologists see them as an attempt to come to terms with disturbing experiences.

recurring-phase theories the view that certain specific issues continually dominate group interactions.

redintegration *n.* **1.** the process of reorganizing, or reintegrating, mental processes after they have been disorganized by psychological disorder, particularly in psychoses. **2.** more generally, restoration to health or to normal condition and functioning. **3.** the process of recovering or recollecting memories from partial cues or reminders, as in recalling an entire song when a few notes are played. **4.** the elicitation of a response by a part of the stimulus complex that was involved in the initial learning. Also called **reintegration**. **—redintegrative** *adj.*

red sage a brushy shrub, *Salvia miltiorrhiza*, whose roots are known to Chinese herbalists as *dan shen* and have traditionally been used (powdered or whole) to treat cardiac and vascular disorders, including heart attacks, stroke, and atherosclerosis. Indeed, red sage has been shown in some studies to decrease the clotting capability of blood; it should not be taken in combination with prescribed blood thinners, as bleeding problems may result. Other studies suggest red sage may interfere with the development of scarlike fibers in the liver (associated primarily with chronic hepatitis and consumption of large quantities of alcohol) and may be effective in preventing the growth of cancer cells and the replication of the HIV virus, but these potential uses have not been confirmed and require further investigation. Side effects of red sage are mild and may include itching, stomach upset, and decreased appetite. The active compounds are miltirone and other diterpene quinones, which act as PARTIAL AGONISTS at the benzodiazepine–GABA receptor complex (see $GABA_A$ RECEPTOR). Because red sage is a partial agonist, it may interact with and enhance the sedative effects of drugs that are full BENZODIAZEPINE AGONISTS—commonly used in the treatment of generalized anxiety and insomnia—leading to extreme drowsiness.

reductionism *n.* the strategy of explaining or accounting for some phenomenon or construct A by claiming that, when properly understood, it can be shown to be some other phenomenon or construct B, where B is seen to be simpler, more basic, or more fundamental. The term is mainly applied to those positions that attempt to understand human culture, society, or psychology in terms of animal behavior or physical laws. In psychology, a common form of reductionism is that in which psychological phenomena are reduced to biological phenomena, so that mental life is shown to be merely a function of biological processes. Compare EMERGENTISM. See also EPIPHENOMENALISM; IDENTITY THEORY; MATERIALISM.

reduplicative paramnesia a disturbance of memory or CONFABULATION characterized by the subjective certainty that a familiar person or place has been duplicated, such as the belief that the hospital where one is treated is duplicated and relocated to another site. It can be caused by a variety of neurological disorders, but brain lesions commonly involve the frontal lobes, the right hemisphere, or both. See also CAPGRAS SYNDROME.

reeducation *n.* **1.** learning or training that focuses on replacing maladaptive cognitions, affects, or behaviors with healthier more adaptive ones or on learning forgotten or otherwise lost skills anew. **2.** a form of psychological treatment in which the client learns effective ways of handling and coping with problems and relationships through a form of nonreconstructive therapy, such as RELATIONSHIP THERAPY, BEHAVIOR THERAPY, hypnotic suggestion (see HYPNOSUGGESTION), COUNSELING, PERSUASION THERAPY, nonanalytic group therapy, or REALITY THERAPY. Also called **reeducative therapy**.

reenactment *n.* in some forms of psychotherapy, the process of reliving traumatic events and past experiences and relationships while reviving the original emotions associated with them. See also ABREACTION.

reentry *n.* **1.** the return of a patient or client to society after experiencing life in an institution (e.g., a psychiatric hospital) or being part of the relatively open and honest environment of an ENCOUNTER GROUP. **2.** the return of a mental health professional from a disaster experience in which he or she dealt with many victims suffering from trauma and other forms of psychological stress. See also POSTVENTION.

reevaluation counseling a therapeutic approach involving COCOUNSELING between individuals. In the process, two people take turns in counseling and being counseled. The process starts with one individual (acting as counselor) asking the other (acting as client) a provocative question and continues with other steps, such as asking the individual acting as client to cite two or three minor upsets that have recently occurred. The client is encouraged to react emotionally in his or her responses, to work through his or her emotions, and then to reverse roles and act as the counselor for the other person. Also called **reevaluation cocounseling**. [developed in the 1950s by U.S. personal counselor Harvey Jackins (1916–1999)]

referenced cognitive test a test of cognitive function that has been standardized and normed so that performances can be compared across individuals.

referential attitude an expectancy attitude sometimes observed in certain individuals with schizophrenia or other forms of psychopathology who are seeking justification, via environmental aspects, for their IDEAS OF REFERENCE or DELUSIONS OF REFERENCE.

referral *n.* **1.** the act of directing a patient to a therapist, physician, agency, or institution for evaluation, consultation, or treatment. **2.** the individual who is so referred. **—refer** *vb.*

reflected appraisals the evaluative feedback that a person receives from others. Some theories of self have treated reflected appraisals as the most important basis for the SELF-CONCEPT, claiming that people learn about themselves chiefly from others. See SYMBOLIC INTERACTIONISM.

reflection of feeling a statement made by a therapist or counselor that is intended to highlight the feelings or attitudes implicitly expressed in a client's communication. The statement reflects and communicates the essence of the client's experience from the client's point of view so that hidden or obscured feelings can be exposed for clarification. Also called **reflection response**.

reflection response **1.** in a RORSCHACH INKBLOT TEST, a response that the inkblot represents a bilateral reflection of one half of the card. That is, the image is perceived not as a single entity across both halves of the card but as two entities in the two halves, one entity being a mirror image of the other. **2.** see REFLECTION OF FEELING.

reflectivity–impulsivity *n.* a dimension of COGNITIVE STYLE based on the observation that some people approach tasks impulsively, preferring to act immediately on their first thoughts or impressions, whereas others are more reflective, preferring to make a careful consideration of a range of alternatives before acting. This aspect of cognitive style—CONCEPTUAL TEMPO—can be assessed by means of the Matching Familiar Figures Test. Also called **reflection–impulsivity**. [first described in 1963 by U.S. developmental psychologist Jerome Kagan (1929–)]

reflex *n.* any of a number of automatic, unlearned, relatively fixed responses to stimuli that do not require conscious effort and that often involve a faster response than might be possible if a conscious evaluation of the input was required. Reflexes are innate in that they do not arise as a result of any special experience.

reflexive affect see AFFECT.

reflexive behavior responses to stimuli that are involuntary or free from conscious control (e.g., the salivation that occurs when food is presented) and therefore serve as the basis for PAVLOVIAN CONDITIONING. Compare PLANNED BEHAVIOR; VOLUNTARY BEHAVIOR.

reflexology *n.* **1.** a school of psychology based on research dealing solely with the outwardly observed and fixed manifestations and reactions of the human being. It is credited to Russian physiologist Vladimir M. Bekhterev (1857–1927), who taught that all behavior could be constructed from the simple reflex as the elementary unit or building block. **2.** the physiological study of involuntary automatic responses to stimuli, particularly as they affect the behavior of humans and other animals. **3.** a form of COMPLEMENTARY AND ALTERNATIVE MEDICINE based on the principle that there are reflex points or zones in the feet and hands that correspond to every part of the body and that manipulating and pressing on these points has beneficial health effects. **—reflexologist** *n.*

reflex strength the potential strength of a response to a reflex stimulus (e.g., the potential for a STARTLE RESPONSE if an organism is touched), often measured by reflex latency.

reformatory paranoia a type of MEGALOMANIA expressed as a personality trait in individuals who concoct plans to reform the world and try to convince others to follow their ideas.

refractory *adj.* **1.** resistant to control, as in a case of a disease or disorder that fails to respond to previously effective therapy. **2.** in neurophysiology, describing a neuron or muscle cell that is unable to respond to a stimulus. **—refractoriness** *n.*

refractory phase the period following orgasm during which further sexual arousal or orgasm is not possible. It occurs only in the male SEXUAL-RESPONSE CYCLE; females can have immediate further arousal and multiple orgasm. The length of the refractory phase increases with advancing age: Older men may not be capable of sexual activity more than once per day.

reframing *n.* a process of reconceptualizing an idea for the purpose of changing an attitude by seeing it from a different perspective. In changing the conceptual or emotional context of a problem, and placing it in a different frame that fits the given facts equally well but changes its entire meaning, perceptions of weakness or difficulty in handling the problem may be changed to strength and opportunity. In psychotherapy, the manner in which a client frames behavior may be part of the problem. Part of the therapist's response might be to reframe thoughts or feelings so as to provide alternative ways to evaluate the situation or respond to others. Compare RESTATEMENT.

regimen *n.* a particular course of action designed to achieve a specific goal. In medicine, it often refers to a detailed treatment program for the regulation of diet, exercise, rest, medication, and other therapeutic measures. Various forms of psychotherapy, such as COGNITIVE BEHAVIOR THERAPY, may also make use of regimens during the course of treatment. Such programs typically include a schedule and specify the components, methods, and duration of the program.

registered nurse (**RN**) a professional nurse who has completed an accredited educational program and passed a required state licensing examination. Registered nurses provide such services as observing and recording patient symptoms and reactions, developing a treatment plan in consultation with the attending physician, administering medication, and educating the patient or family on self-care methods.

Regitine *n.* a trade name for PHENTOLAMINE.

regression *n.* a return to a prior, lower state of cognitive, emotional, or behavioral functioning. This term is associated particularly with psychoanalytic theory, denoting a DEFENSE MECHANISM in which the individual reverts to immature behavior or to an earlier stage of PSYCHOSEXUAL DEVELOPMENT when threatened with anxiety caused by overwhelming external problems or internal conflicts. **—regress** *vb.* **—regressive** *adj.*

regression analysis any of several statistical techniques that are designed to allow the prediction of the score on one variable, the DEPENDENT

VARIABLE, from the scores on one or more other variables, the INDEPENDENT VARIABLES. Regression analysis is a subset of the GENERAL LINEAR MODEL.

regression coefficient the WEIGHT associated with an independent (predictor) variable in a REGRESSION ANALYSIS.

regression effect the tendency for individuals scoring high or low on a test to score closer to the MEAN on a retest.

regression equation the mathematical expression of the relationship between the dependent variable and one or more independent variables that results from conducting a REGRESSION ANALYSIS. It usually takes the form $y = a + bx + e$, in which y is the dependent variable, x is the independent variable, a is the intercept, b is the **regression coefficient** (a specific WEIGHT associated with x), and e is the error term.

regression in the service of the ego the adaptive circumvention of normal ego functioning in order to access primitive material (see PRIMARY PROCESS), often associated with the creative process. [first described by Swiss-born U.S. psychoanalyst Ernst Kris (1900–1957)]

regression therapy see REPARENTING.

regression toward the mean a phenomenon in which earlier measurements that were extremely deviant from a sample mean will tend, on retesting, to result in a value closer to the sample mean than the original value.

regressive electroshock therapy an obsolete form of ELECTROCONVULSIVE THERAPY that was administered several times a day to patients with schizophrenia when other treatment methods failed and the prognosis was poor. The patients typically regressed to a point where they were incontinent, out of contact, and had to be spoon-fed. Recovery from treatment took from a week to a month.

R

regressive reconstructive approach a technique in psychotherapy in which the client is encouraged to reexperience with emotional intensity traumatic situations from an earlier stage of life. Through such concurrent or subsequent mechanisms as TRANSFERENCE and INTERPRETATION, the approach is posited to help bring about personality change and development of greater emotional adaptation and maturity in the client.

regulatory drive any generalized state of arousal or motivation that helps preserve physiological HOMEOSTASIS and thus is necessary for the survival of the individual organism, such as hunger and thirst. Compare NONREGULATORY DRIVE.

rehabilitation *n.* the process of bringing an individual to a condition of health or useful and constructive activity, restoring to the fullest possible degree their independence, well-being, and level of functioning following injury, disability, or disorder. It involves providing appropriate resources, such as treatment or training, to enable such a person (e.g., one who has had a stroke) to redevelop skills and abilities he or she had acquired previously or to compensate for their loss. Compare HABILITATION.

rehabilitation center a facility devoted to restoring individuals with mental or physical disorders or impairments, including those with multiple problems, to an adequate level of functioning. Rehabilitation centers use such techniques as vocational training, work in a sheltered situation, occupational therapy, physical therapy, educational therapy, social therapy, recreational therapy, and psychological therapy and counseling.

rehabilitation counselor a professional worker trained and equipped to evaluate and guide individuals who have a physical, mental, or emotional impairment in all major phases of the rehabilitation process: vocational, educational, personal, psychological, social, and recreational. The rehabilitation counselor typically helps to coordinate the various services offered by the rehabilitation team and to focus them on each individual's needs.

rehabilitation engineering a discipline that integrates multiple areas of research within various fields to develop products, processes, and environments to improve the quality of life for people with disabilities.

rehabilitation medicine the branch of medicine that specializes in the development of individuals to the fullest physical, psychological, cognitive, social, vocational, or educational potential that is consistent with their physiological or anatomical impairment and environmental limitations.

rehabilitation program the overall system of REHABILITATION services provided in support of an individual with an illness, injury, or physical or mental disability, disorder, or impairment. The program is typically customized to meet the specific needs of each individual and may include physical therapy, recreational therapy, and occupational therapy; psychological, social service, educational, and vocational programs; and appropriate specialty services, such as SPEECH THERAPY and audiology.

rehabilitation psychology a specialty branch of psychology devoted to the application of psychological knowledge and understanding to the study, prevention, and treatment of disabling and chronic health conditions. **Rehabilitation psychologists** consider the entire network of factors (biological, psychological, social, environmental, and political) that affect functioning to help individuals attain optimal physical, psychological, and interpersonal functioning.

rehabilitation team a group of health care specialists who coordinate their efforts in the rehabilitation of patients on an individual basis. A rehabilitation team may include plastic surgeons, orthopedic surgeons, neurologists, psychologists, psychiatrists, physical therapists, occupational therapists, and others, depending upon the needs of the patient.

rehearsal *n.* **1.** preparation for a forthcoming event or confrontation that is anticipated to induce some level of discomfort or anxiety. By practicing what is to be said or done in a future encounter, the event itself may be less stressful. Rehearsal may be carried out in psychotherapy with the therapist coaching or role-playing to help the client practice the coming event. See also BEHAVIOR REHEARSAL; ROLE PLAY. **2.** the repetition of information in an attempt to maintain it longer in memory. According to the DUAL-STORE MODEL OF MEMORY, rehearsal occurs in SHORT-TERM MEMORY and may allow a stronger trace to be then stored in LONG-TERM MEMORY. Although rehearsal implies a verbal process, it is hypothesized to occur also in other modalities.

rehospitalization *n.* see READMISSION.

Reichian analysis a highly controversial and largely scientifically discredited system of psychotherapy, developed by Austrian-born U.S. psychoanalyst Wilhelm Reich (1897–1957), in which ORGASTIC POTENCY is emphasized as the criterion of mental health. Notwithstanding the widespread judgment of the approach as alternative (see ALTERNATIVE PSYCHOTHERAPY) and unsupported by research, Reich made early contributions to psychology in his theories concerning emotional catharsis and authoritarianism.

reification *n.* treating an abstraction, concept, or formulation as though it were a real object or static structure.

reiki *n.* a complementary therapy that aims to promote physical, emotional, and spiritual healing through the use of energy and the laying on of hands, which is believed to improve the flow of life energy in the patient. See also COMPLEMENTARY AND ALTERNATIVE MEDICINE. [Japanese, "universal life energy"]

reinforcement *n.* **1.** in OPERANT CONDITIONING, a process in which the frequency or probability of a response is increased by a dependent relationship, or contingency, with a stimulus or circumstance (the REINFORCER). See REINFORCEMENT CONTINGENCY. **2.** the procedure that results in the frequency or probability of a response being increased in such a way. **3.** in PAVLOVIAN CONDITIONING, the presentation of an unconditioned stimulus after a conditioned stimulus. See also NEGATIVE REINFORCEMENT; POSITIVE REINFORCEMENT.

reinforcement contingency the contingency (relationship) between a response and a REINFORCER. The contingency may be positive (if the occurrence of the reinforcer is more probable after the response) or negative (if it is less probable given the response). Reinforcement contingencies can be arranged by establishing dependencies between a particular type of response and a reinforcer (as when an experimenter arranges that a rat's lever presses are followed by presentation of food), or they can occur as natural consequences of a response (as when a door opens when pushed), or they can occur by accident (see ACCIDENTAL REINFORCEMENT). Also called **response–reinforcement contingency**.

reinforcement counseling a behavioral approach to counseling based on the idea that behavior is learned and can be predictably modified by various reinforcement techniques that strengthen or weaken specific types of behavior through schedules of positive or negative reinforcement. See also REINFORCEMENT THERAPY.

Reinforcement Survey Schedule (**RSS**) an assessment form that elicits information about activities, stimuli, or situations that a person finds rewarding or pleasurable. This information is used by behavior therapists to help patients organize contingencies that increase positive behaviors or decrease negative behaviors. [developed in 1967 by U.S. psychologist Joseph R. Cautela (1927–1999) and Robert Kastenbaum]

reinforcement therapy a therapeutic process based on OPERANT CONDITIONING and the use of positive reinforcement to initiate and maintain behavioral change. See also REINFORCEMENT COUNSELING.

reinforcer *n.* a stimulus or circumstance that acts effectively to produce REINFORCEMENT when it occurs in a dependent relationship, or contingency, with a response. Also called **reinforcing stimulus**. See NATURAL REINFORCER.

reinforcing cause a condition that tends to maintain a healthy or maladaptive behavior or behavioral pattern in an individual. An example of the healthy–maladaptive range can be seen when special attention is given to a person who is ill, which can contribute either to a speedy or to a delayed recovery. It is typical, however, to use the term in relation to negative or maladaptive consequences.

reintegration *n.* see REDINTEGRATION.

rejected child in sociometric measures of peer acceptance, a child who is frequently mentioned in negative terms and is actively disliked by his or her peers. Compare ISOLATE.

rejecting–neglecting parenting see PARENTING.

rejection *n.* **1.** denial of love, attention, interest, or approval. **2.** an antagonistic or discriminatory attitude toward a group of people.

relapse *n.* the recurrence of symptoms of a disorder or disease after a period of improvement or apparent cure.

relapse prevention procedures that are used after successful treatment of a condition, disease, or disorder in order to reduce relapse rates. These often include a combination of cognitive and behavioral skills that are taught to clients before therapy is terminated. Such procedures are often used with disorders (e.g., addictions and depression) that have unusually high relapse rates. See also TERTIARY PREVENTION.

relapse rate the incidence of clients or patients who have recovered or improved but who later experience a recurrence of their disorder or disease.

relational aggression behavior that manipulates or damages relationships between individuals or groups, such as bullying, gossiping, and humiliation.

relationship *n.* a continuing and usually binding association between two or more people, as in a family, friendship, marriage, partnership, or other interpersonal link in which the participants have some degree of influence on each other's thoughts, feelings, and even actions. In psychotherapy, the THERAPIST–PATIENT RELATIONSHIP is thought to be an essential aspect of patient improvement. As with other relationships in life, therapeutic relationships characterized by trust, warmth, respect, and understanding are more likely to result in positive outcomes for the patient.

relationship therapy **1.** any form of psychotherapy that emphasizes the nature of the relationship between client and therapist and views it as the primary therapeutic tool and agent of positive change. Relationship therapy is based on the idea of providing emotional support and creating an accepting atmosphere that fosters personality growth and elicits attitudes and past experiences for examination and analysis during sessions. **2.** any form of psychotherapy focused on improving the RELATIONSHIP between individuals, particularly those in a marriage or other committed partnership, by helping them to resolve interpersonal issues and modify maladaptive patterns of interactions, which in turn fosters the healthy psychosocial growth of all parties. It is an umbrella term encompassing COUPLES THERAPY and FAMILY THERAPY. [first described by U.S. social worker Jessie Taft (1882–1960) and child psychiatrist Frederick H. Allen (1890–1964)]

R

relative deprivation the perception by an individual that the amount of a desired resource (e.g., money, social status) he or she has is less than some comparison standard. This standard can be the amount that was expected or the amount possessed by others with whom the person compares him- or herself. The concept was introduced as a result of studies of morale in the U.S. Army during World War II, which indicated that soldiers were dissatisfied if they believed they were not obtaining as many military rewards and benefits as their peers. In 1966 British sociologist Walter Garrison Runciman (1934–) distinguished between **egoistic relative deprivation**, the perceived discrepancy between an individual's own current position and the comparison standard; and **fraternalistic relative deprivation**, the perceived discrepancy between the position that the person's ingroup actually has and the position the person thinks it ought to have. According to some research, social unrest tends to be greatest in areas with high levels of relative deprivation. See also SOCIAL COMPARISON THEORY.

relative risk the ratio of the incidence of a certain disorder or condition in groups exposed to (or possessed of) a specific risk factor and groups not exposed to (or possessed of) that factor.

relaxation technique any therapeutic technique to induce relaxation and reduce stress.

relaxation therapy the use of muscle-relaxation techniques as an aid in the treatment of emotional tension. Also called **therapeutic relaxation**. See also PROGRESSIVE RELAXATION.

relaxation training see PROGRESSIVE RELAXATION.

release *n.* the letting go of physical, mental, or emotional tension or pent-up energy, which tends toward relaxation or arousal reduction.

release therapy **1.** any therapy whose ultimate value is in the release of deep-seated, forgotten, or inhibited emotional and psychic pain through open expression and direct experience of anger, sorrow, or hostility in the therapy context. The technique is used, for example, in PLAY THERAPY. **2.** a form of therapy in which young children reenact anxieties, frightening experiences, and traumatic events with such materials as figurines, toy animals, and water guns. [developed in the 1930s by U.S. psychiatrist David M. Levy (1892–1977)]

releasing hormone any of a class of hypothalamic hormones that travel via the hypothalamic–pituitary portal system to control the release of hormones by the anterior pituitary gland. Examples are CORTICOTROPIN-RELEASING FACTOR and GONADOTROPIN-RELEASING HORMONE.

reliability *n.* the ability of a measurement instrument (e.g., a test) to measure an attribute consistently, yielding the same results across multiple applications to the same sample. The basic index of reliability is the CORRELATION COEFFICIENT. —**reliable** *adj.*

relief *n.* a POSITIVE EMOTION that occurs as a response to a threat that has abated, disappeared, or failed to materialize.

relief–discomfort quotient (**relief–distress quotient**) see DISTRESS–RELIEF QUOTIENT.

religiosity *n.* pious, exaggerated religious zeal.

religious delusions DELUSIONS associated with religious beliefs and grandiose ideas with religious content. Delusional ideation frequently includes beliefs that the individual is the embodiment of a notable religious figure, such as a messiah or prophet, and that he or she possesses special powers, such as being able to cure an illness. Such beliefs may be a feature of grandiose-type DELUSIONAL DISORDER.

religious healing see FAITH HEALING.

religious mania a state of acute hyperactivity, agitation, and restlessness accompanied by hallucinations of a religious nature.

religiousness *n.* a tendency to adhere to religious beliefs and to engage in religious practices.

religious therapy therapeutic intervention through such approaches as PASTORAL COUNSELING, scriptural study, and church-sponsored community activities. Such interventions are sometimes led by a mental health professional but often not. See also SUPPORTIVE PSYCHOTHERAPY.

REM abbreviation for RAPID EYE MOVEMENT.

REM behavior disorder (**RBD**) a SLEEP DISORDER involving motor activity during REM SLEEP, which typically includes an actual physical enactment of dream sequences. Because the dreams that are acted out are generally unpleasant or combative, this behavior is usually disruptive and can result in violence. In *DSM–IV–TR* this disorder is classified as a PARASOMNIA NOT OTHERWISE SPECIFIED.

remedial therapy intervention aimed at assisting a person to achieve a normal or increased level of functioning when functioning is below expectation in a particular area (e.g., reading). Also called **remedial training**.

remembering *n.* the process of consciously reviving or bringing to awareness previous events, experiences, or information. Remembering also involves the process of retaining such material, which is essential to learning, since without it one would not profit from training, practice, or past experience. According to Estonian-born Canadian psychologist Endel Tulving (1927–), remembering is distinct from knowing (see REMEMBER–KNOW PROCEDURE).

remember–know procedure a procedure used to measure two different ways of accessing events from one's past and as an assessment of EPISODIC MEMORY and SEMANTIC MEMORY, respectively. Remembering is the conscious and vivid recollection of a prior event such that a person can mentally travel to the specific time and place of the original event and retrieve the details; he or she is able to bring back to mind a particular association, image, or something more personal from the time of the event. Knowing refers to the experience in which a person is certain that an event has occurred but fails to recollect anything about its actual occurrence or what was experienced at the time of its occurrence; the retrieval of the event is not accompanied by any specific recollection about the time, place, or details. [introduced in 1985 by Estonian-born Canadian psychologist Endel Tulving (1927–)]

Remeron *n.* a trade name for MIRTAZAPINE.

remifentanil *n.* see FENTANYL.

reminiscence *n.* **1.** the recalling of previous experiences, especially those of a pleasant nature. Events that occurred in adolescence and early adulthood (often called the **reminiscence bump**) are most often remembered. See also AUTOBIOGRAPHICAL MEMORY; EPISODIC MEMORY; LIFE REVIEW. **2.** an increase in the amount remembered, or in performance, that occurs after a delay interval following the initial exposure to the information, instead of the more usual forgetting after a delay.

reminiscence therapy the use of LIFE HISTORIES—written, oral, or both—to improve psychological well-being. The therapy is often used with older people.

Razadyne *n.* a trade name for GALANTAMINE.

remission *n.* a reduction or significant abatement in symptoms of a disease or disorder, or the period during which this occurs. Remission of symptoms does not necessarily indicate that a disease or disorder is fully cured. See also SPONTANEOUS REMISSION.

REM latency the time between onset of sleep and the first occurrence of RAPID EYE MOVEMENT (REM).

remorse *n.* a strong sense of guilt and regret for a past action.

remote cause a cause that is removed from its effect in time or space but is nevertheless the ultimate or overriding cause. In a causal chain, it may be considered to be the precipitating event without which the chain would not have begun (the original cause). For example, the PROXIMATE CAUSE of Smith's aggression may be a trivial snub, but the remote cause may be Smith's early childhood experiences. See also CAUSAL LATENCY; DELAYED EFFECT.

remotivation *n.* intervention aimed at increasing the likelihood that a person will cooperate with and benefit from treatments. It includes efforts directed toward stimulating withdrawn patients with chronic disorders in mental hospitals, for example, by involving them in poetry-reading groups or conversation groups in which a **bridge to reality** is established by discussing current topics.

REM sleep *r*apid-*e*ye-*m*ovement sleep: the stage of sleep, formerly called **desynchronized sleep**, in which dreaming occurs and the electroencephalogram shows activity characteristic of wakefulness (hence it is also known as **paradoxical sleep**) except for inhibition of motor expression other than coordinated movements of the eyes. It accounts for one quarter to one fifth of total sleep time. Also called **activated sleep**. See DREAM STATE. Compare NREM SLEEP.

Renard Diagnostic Interview a structured interview developed in 1977 at the Renard Hospital, Washington University (St. Louis), to elicit enough information to establish criteria for the diagnosis of 15 major psychiatric disorders. See RESEARCH DIAGNOSTIC CRITERIA.

renifleur *n.* a person with a morbid interest in

body odors, especially as a means of sexual excitement. See OSPHRESIOLAGNIA.

Renpenning's syndrome a condition that is inherited as an X-linked trait (see SEX-LINKED), marked by eye defects, MICROCEPHALY, psychomotor retardation, short stature, small testes, and mental retardation. [Hans **Renpenning** (1929–), Canadian physician]

renunciation *n.* **1.** in general, the act of giving something up or denying oneself. **2.** in psychoanalytic theory, a refusal of the EGO to follow impulses of the ID. **—renounce** *vb.*

reorganization principle the principle that new learning or perception disrupts old cognitive structures, requiring a reorganized structure. This is in opposition to the associationist principle that new learning is essentially added on to existing structures.

reorientation therapy see CONVERSION THERAPY.

reparation *n.* **1.** amelioration of or expiation for harm previously done. See also RESTITUTION. **2.** in the OBJECT RELATIONS THEORY of Melanie KLEIN, acts that are performed during the DEPRESSIVE POSITION to repair the relationship with the GOOD OBJECT. Klein viewed all creative and positive acts in adulthood as examples of reparation.

reparative therapy 1. therapy given to people who have experienced a sexual assault, including childhood sexual abuse and adult rape. Procedures generally involve working through the emotional trauma that was experienced and cognitive therapy on such issues as self-blame. The aim of reparative therapy is to turn a victim into a survivor, who is able to return to normal functioning emotionally, interpersonally, and sexually. **2.** see CONVERSION THERAPY.

reparenting *n.* **1.** a controversial therapeutic procedure used to provide a client with missed childhood experiences. The client, who typically has severe problems, is treated as a child or infant; for example, he or she may be fed with a spoon or bottle, hugged, sung to, and provided with what the client or therapist feels the client missed in childhood. Reparenting has been unethically used to justify recreation of the birth process by wrapping a client in a blanket and having him or her struggle to get out. **2.** in self-help and some forms of counseling, a therapeutic technique in which individuals are urged to provide for themselves the kind of parenting attitudes or actions that their own parents were unable to provide.

repeated measures design see WITHIN-SUBJECTS DESIGN.

repeat offender see RECIDIVISM.

repertoire *n.* the sum total of potential behavior or responses that a person or nonhuman animal is capable of performing. It usually refers to behavior that has been learned and is generally quantified through the study of past behavior. Also called **behavioral repertoire**.

repertory grid a technique used to analyze an individual's PERSONAL CONSTRUCTS. A number of significant concepts are selected, each of which is rated by the participant on a number of dimensions using a numerical scale. The findings are displayed in matrix form and can be subjected to statistical analysis to reveal correlations. The repertory grid was developed principally as a means of analyzing personal relationships but has also been used to determine the complexity of a person's thinking (COGNITIVE COMPLEXITY) and in various other applications. [introduced by U.S. psychologist George A. Kelly (1905–1967)]

repetition compulsion in psychoanalytic theory, an unconscious need to reenact early traumas in the attempt to overcome or master them. In repetition compulsion the early painful experience is repeated in a new situation symbolic of the repressed prototype. Repetition compulsion acts as a RESISTANCE to therapeutic change, since the goal of therapy is not to repeat but to remember the trauma and to see its relation to present behavior. Also called **compulsion to repeat**.

repetitive strain injury (**RSI**) a group of musculoskeletal disorders involving chronic inflammation of the muscles, tendons, or nerves and caused by overuse or misuse of a specific body part. RSI most commonly affects the hands, wrists, elbows, arms, shoulders, back, or neck and results in pain and fatigue of the affected areas, for example, **tendinitis** (inflammation, irritation, and swelling of a tendon). Repetitive strain injuries are often associated with occupational situations, and their prevention is an important issue in ergonomics and human factors. Also called **cumulative trauma disorder** (**CTD**); **repetitive motion disorder** or **injury** (**RMD**; **RMI**); **repetitive stress injury**.

repetitive transcranial magnetic stimulation (**rTMS**) see TRANSCRANIAL MAGNETIC STIMULATION.

replacement memory see SCREEN MEMORY.

replacement therapy 1. treatment in which a natural or synthetic substance is substituted for one that is deficient or lacking in an individual. See HORMONE REPLACEMENT THERAPY. **2.** the process of replacing abnormal thoughts or behavior with healthier ones through the use of therapy focused on constructive activities and interests.

replication *n.* the repetition of an original experiment to bolster confidence in its results, based on the assumption that correct hypotheses and procedures consistently will be supported. In **exact replication**, procedures are identical to the original experiment or duplicated as closely as possible. In **modified replication**, alternative procedures and additional

R

conditions may be incorporated. In **conceptual replication**, different techniques and manipulations are introduced to gain theoretical information.

reportability *n.* the quality of psychological events that enables them to be described by the experiencing individual. It is the standard behavioral index of conscious experience (see CONSCIOUSNESS). Also called **verbal report**.

representation *n.* that which stands for or signifies something else. For example, in cognitive psychology the term denotes a MENTAL REPRESENTATION whereas in psychoanalytic theory it refers to the use of a SYMBOL to stand for a threatening object or a repressed impulse. **—represent** *vb.* **—representational** *adj.* **—representative** *adj.*

representative design an experimental design in which background variables are intentionally not controlled so that research results will apply more realistically to the real world.

representativeness heuristic a strategy for making categorical judgments about a given person or target based on how closely the exemplar matches the typical or average member of the category. For example, given a choice of the two categories "poet" and "accountant," judges are likely to assign a person in unconventional clothes reading a poetry book to the former category; however, the much greater frequency of accountants in the population means that such a person is more likely to be an accountant. Compare AVAILABILITY HEURISTIC.

representative sampling the selection of individuals for a study from a larger group (population) in such a way that the sample obtained accurately reflects the total population.

repressed memory see RECOVERED MEMORY.

repression *n.* **1.** in classic psychoanalytic theory and other forms of DEPTH PSYCHOLOGY, the basic DEFENSE MECHANISM that consists of excluding painful experiences and unacceptable impulses from consciousness. Repression operates on an unconscious level as a protection against anxiety produced by objectionable sexual wishes, feelings of hostility, and ego-threatening experiences of all kinds. It also comes into play in most other forms of defense, as in denial, in which individuals avoid unpleasant realities by first repressing them and then negating them. See PRIMARY REPRESSION; REPRESSION PROPER. **2.** the suppression or exclusion of individuals or groups within the social context, through limitations on personal rights and liberties. Compare SUPPRESSION. **—repress** *vb.*

repression proper in psychoanalytic theory, a form of REPRESSION that acts upon experiences and wishes that have been conscious to make them unconscious. This is in contrast to PRIMARY REPRESSION, which operates on material that has never been conscious. Sigmund FREUD also called this form of repression "afterexpulsion" because material is expelled from consciousness after it has become conscious. Also called **secondary repression**.

repression-resistance *n.* in psychoanalysis, the RESISTANCE deployed by the patient in order to maintain REPRESSION of unacceptable impulses. This may manifest itself in the patient's forgetting of events, an impeded flow of FREE ASSOCIATIONS, or in the patient's application of interpretations offered by the analyst to others but not to himself or herself. Also called **ego resistance**. Compare ID RESISTANCE.

repression–sensitization defense mechanisms involving approach and avoidance responses to threatening stimuli. The sensitizing process involves intellectualization in approaching or controlling the stimulus, whereas repression involves unconscious denial in avoiding the stimulus.

repressive coping style a pattern of dealing with life characterized by downplaying problems or misfortunes and maintaining an artificially positive view. Repressive coping is diagnosed by a combination of high scores on SOCIAL DESIRABILITY bias and low scores on reported anxiety. See also POSITIVE ILLUSION.

Research Diagnostic Criteria (**RDC**) a modification of criteria developed from the RENARD DIAGNOSTIC INTERVIEW for diagnosis of psychiatric disorders, expanding the number of disorders from the original 15 to 25. It focuses on present or past episodes of illness and gives inclusion and exclusion criteria for diagnosis of the different disorders.

reserpine *n.* see RAUWOLFIA DERIVATIVES.

residential care long-term care for older adults, patients with chronic illness, or individuals undergoing rehabilitation that provides housing and meals and may also provide medical, nursing, and social services.

residential habilitation a HOME AND COMMUNITY-BASED SERVICE provided for a person with mental retardation or a related condition. This service is similar to DAY HABILITATION but is delivered in a supervised or supportive residential setting or in a family home.

residential schools special educational facilities that provide residential services for children with mental retardation. Although historically significant, the use of such facilities greatly diminished during the latter part of the 20th century, and children with mental retardation now receive public education in their home communities.

residential treatment treatment that takes place in a hospital, special center, or other facility that offers a treatment program and residential accommodation. Some programs require residence for a specific time (e.g., a one-month treatment for addictions), and some may include provision for the client to learn or work in the community during the day.

residual 1. *adj.* denoting a condition in which acute symptoms have subsided but chronic or less severe symptoms remain. **2.** *adj.* denoting remaining ability (e.g., residual hearing) or a remaining disability (e.g., residual loss of vision) after a trauma or surgery. **3.** *n.* in statistics, the difference between the value of an empirical observation and the value of that observation predicted by a model.

residual attention-deficit disorder in *DSM–III*, the condition (designated **attention-deficit disorder, residual type**) of a child previously diagnosed as having attention-deficit disorder with hyperactivity in whom the hyperactivity component has ceased. In *DSM–IV–TR* the equivalent diagnosis is ATTENTION-DEFICIT/HYPERACTIVITY DISORDER NOT OTHERWISE SPECIFIED or ATTENTION-DEFICIT/HYPERACTIVITY DISORDER, predominantly inattentive type.

residual schizophrenia a subtype of schizophrenia diagnosed when there has been at least one schizophrenic episode but positive symptoms (e.g., delusions, hallucinations, disorganized speech or behavior) are no longer present and only negative symptoms (e.g., flat affect, poverty of speech, or avolition) or mild behavioral and cognitive disturbances (e.g., eccentricities, odd beliefs) occur.

resignation *n.* an attitude of surrender to or acceptance of one's situation or symptoms.

resilience *n.* the process and outcome of successfully adapting to difficult or challenging life experiences, especially through mental, emotional, and behavioral flexibility and adjustment to external and internal demands. A number of factors contribute to how well people adapt to adversities, predominant among them (a) the ways in which individuals view and engage with the world, (b) the availability and quality of social resources, and (c) specific COPING STRATEGIES. Psychological research demonstrates that resources and skills in each of these domains associated with more positive adaptation (i.e., greater resilience) can be cultivated and practiced. Also called **psychic resilience**; **psychological resilience**. See also COPING BEHAVIOR; COPING-SKILLS TRAINING. **—resilient** *adj.*

R

resistance *n.* **1.** in psychotherapy and analysis, unconscious obstruction, through the client's words or behavior, of the therapist's or analyst's methods of eliciting or interpreting psychic material brought forth in therapy. Psychoanalytic theory classically interprets resistance as a form of defense and distinguishes three types: CONSCIOUS RESISTANCE, ID RESISTANCE, and REPRESSION-RESISTANCE. **2.** the degree to which an organism can defend itself against disease-causing microorganisms. **3.** the degree to which disease-causing microorganisms withstand the action of drugs. **—resist** *vb.* **—resistant** *adj.*

resistance stage see GENERAL ADAPTATION SYNDROME.

resistant attachment see AMBIVALENT ATTACHMENT.

resocialization *n.* the process of enabling individuals with mental disorders to resume appropriate interpersonal activities and behaviors and, generally, to participate in community life through more adaptive attitudes and skills.

resolution phase see SEXUAL-RESPONSE CYCLE.

resource awareness knowledge by a therapist or counselor of community services and agencies that could assist clients in meeting their needs or in bolstering positive strategies, directions, or gains achieved in psychotherapy or counseling.

respect *n.* an attitude of, or behavior demonstrating, esteem, honor, regard, concern, or other such positive qualities on the part of one individual or entity for another individual or entity. Respect can serve an important purpose in interpersonal and intergroup relations by aiding in communication, for example. It is considered to play a crucial role as a bidirectional process in psychotherapy according to many theorists and practitioners.

respiratory depression slow and shallow breathing that can be induced by opioids and other sedatives. These drugs raise the threshold level of respiratory centers in the medulla oblongata of the brain that normally would react to increased carbon dioxide in the tissues by increasing the rate and depth of breathing. Respiratory depression is a primary hazard of the use of morphine and other OPIOID ANALGESICS, but is also observed with CNS DEPRESSANTS, such as barbiturates. Respiratory depression is less common with BENZODIAZEPINES unless they are taken together with another CNS depressant, such as alcohol.

respiratory disorder any disorder involving one or more components of the respiratory system, such as the diaphragm, lungs, trachea, larynx, or nasal cavities. See also ASTHMA; HYPERVENTILATION; PSEUDOASTHMA.

respiratory distress syndrome a disorder of some newborn babies in which the lungs fail to expand due to deficiency of a natural surfactant that prevents the alveoli (air sacs) from collapsing. The alveoli are lined with a membrane of hyaline material. The condition, which is most common in premature infants, may worsen progressively before the lungs begin producing surfactant. Also called **hyaline membrane disease**.

respite care assistance, supervision, and recreational or social activities provided for a person who is unable to care for him- or herself (e.g., because of a disability or chronic illness) for a limited period in order to temporarily relieve family members from caregiving responsibilities or enable them to conduct necessary personal or household affairs. These services may be provided for a child or adult on a scheduled or unscheduled basis, either regularly or occasionally, after school hours, at weekends, or overnight, and either in the home or at another location. Also called **in-home respite**.

respondent *n.* **1.** the organism that responds to a stimulus. **2.** a person who is interviewed or who replies to a survey or questionnaire. **3.** in conditioning, any REFLEX that can be conditioned by PAVLOVIAN CONDITIONING procedures.

response *n.* any glandular, muscular, neural, or other reaction to a stimulus. A response is a clearly defined, measurable unit of behavior discussed in terms of its result (e.g., pressing a lever) or its physical characteristics (e.g., raising an arm.

response acquiescence see YEA-SAYING.

response amplitude the magnitude of a response, especially in conditioning.

response bias a tendency to give one response more than others, regardless of the stimulus condition. In SIGNAL DETECTION THEORY, response bias is the overall willingness to say "yes" (signal present) or "no" (signal not present), regardless of the actual presence or absence of the signal.

response maintenance the extent to which changes are maintained for a period of time after an intervention has been completed.

response prevention a type of behavior therapy used to treat OBSESSIVE-COMPULSIVE DISORDER, involving exposure to situations or cues that trigger OBSESSIONS or provoke COMPULSIONS, followed by the prevention of the compulsive behavior. Also called **exposure and response prevention**.

response set a tendency to answer questions in a systematic manner that is unrelated to their content. [first extensively discussed and studied by Lee J. CRONBACH]

restatement *n.* in psychotherapy and counseling, the verbatim repetition or rephrasing by the therapist or counselor of a client's statement. The purpose is not only to confirm that the client's remarks have been understood, but also to provide a "mirror" in which the client can see his or her feelings and ideas more clearly (see MIRRORING). Compare CLARIFICATION; INTERPRETATION; REFRAMING.

rest-cure technique a treatment approach, developed in the 19th century, for individuals with nervous disorders attributed to the hectic pace of life in the "railroad age." The regimen consisted not only of extended rest, but also physical therapy, massage, environmental change, mild exercise, and a nutritious diet. Although the technique itself is no longer used, the concept it embodies is still applied in such activities as taking time off work for a "mental health day" or spending time at a health spa. [developed by U.S. physician Silas Weir Mitchell (1829–1914)]

rest home a facility for convalescent care or for older adults who do not need continuous medical or nursing care. See ADULT HOME; ASSISTED LIVING.

restitution *n.* the act of restoring or compensating for something lost through prior damaging actions or events. Acts of restitution exist on a behavioral spectrum: They may be a healthy, even necessary, part of acknowledging and dealing with harm committed intentionally or unintentionally, but they may also, more pathologically, take such forms as a compulsive drive to "do for others" or a persistent pattern of martyrdom.

restless-legs syndrome see EKBOM'S SYNDROME.

restoration therapy **1.** treatment that is directed toward the reestablishment of structure and function in a body part or system following disease or injury. For example, vision restoration therapy for individuals following post-geniculate visual system lesions is intended to enlarge the size of the visual field and facilitate recovery of more complex visual function. **2.** a form of COMPLEMENTARY AND ALTERNATIVE MEDICINE that uses techniques and concepts from massage, chiropractic, osteopathy, shiatsu, acupressure, and herbal formulas to treat specific ailments and enhance overall health by balancing the body's life-force energy (see CHI) and breaking down soft tissues, which then rebuild themselves. [created by Japanese professor Henry S. Okazaki (1890–1951)]

restorative environment an environment, often a natural setting, that rejuvenates and can help restore depleted attention resources or reduce emotional and psychophysiological stress. Characteristic features of restorative environments include LEGIBILITY and elements that give rise to contemplation and provide a break from one's normal routine. There is growing interest in the incorporation of restorative elements into health care settings because of evidence that they speed recovery.

Restoril *n.* a trade name for TEMAZEPAM.

restraint *n.* **1.** the ability to control or prevent actions or behaviors that are harmful or otherwise undesirable. See SELF-CONTROL. **2.** the use of control measures to prevent violent patients from injuring themselves or others.

restricted affect emotional expression that is reduced in range and intensity. It is common in depression, inhibited personalities, and schizophrenia. See FLAT AFFECT.

RET abbreviation for rational emotive therapy. See RATIONAL EMOTIVE BEHAVIOR THERAPY.

retardation *n.* **1.** a slowing down of or delay of an activity or process, as in PSYCHOMOTOR RETARDATION or MENTAL RETARDATION. **2.** in conditioning, a delay in the appearance of a conditioned (learned or acquired) response due to prior experience. For example, presentation of a stimulus to be used later as a conditioned stimulus slows the development of conditioning.

retarded depression an obsolescent name for a MAJOR DEPRESSIVE EPISODE that includes PSYCHOMOTOR RETARDATION and appetite loss.

retarded ejaculation see MALE ORGASMIC DISORDER.

retention *n.* **1.** persistence of learned behavior or experience during a period when it is not being performed or practiced, as indicated by the ability to recall, recognize, reproduce, or relearn it. **2.** the storage and maintenance of a memory. Retention is the second stage of memory, after ENCODING and before RETRIEVAL. **3.** the inability or refusal of an individual to defecate or urinate. **—retentive** *adj.*

retest reliability an estimate of the ability of an assessment instrument (e.g., a test) to measure an attribute consistently: It is obtained as the correlation between scores on two administrations of the test to the same individual. Also called **test–retest reliability**.

reticular activating system (**RAS**) a part of the RETICULAR FORMATION thought to be particularly involved in the regulation of arousal, alertness, and sleep–wake cycles.

reticular formation an extensive network of nerve cell bodies and fibers within the brainstem, extending from the medulla oblongata to the upper part of the midbrain, that is widely connected to the spinal cord, cerebellum, thalamus, and cerebral cortex. It is most prominently involved in arousal, alertness, and sleep–wake cycles, but also functions to control some aspects of action and posture. Also called **brainstem reticular formation**. See also RETICULAR ACTIVATING SYSTEM.

retifism *n.* a form of FETISHISM in which sexual excitement is achieved through contact or masturbation with a shoe or foot. Shoes or feet are among the most common varieties of OBJECT FETISH, but there is little understanding of why this occurs. The condition is named for French writer Nicolas-Edme Rétif (1734–1806), also known as Rétif de la Bretonne, who is said to have had a sexual interest in women's footwear.

retinodiencephalic degeneration see LAURENCE–MOON–BIEDL SYNDROME.

retirement counseling individual or group counseling of employees to help them prepare for retirement. Discussions usually include such topics as norms for this transition, mental and physical health, recreational activities, part-time or consultant work, finances, insurance, government programs, and issues related to change of residence.

retreat from reality see FLIGHT FROM REALITY.

retrieval *n.* the process of recovering or locating information stored in memory. Retrieval is the final stage of memory, after ENCODING and RETENTION.

retrieval block a brief RETRIEVAL FAILURE in which the inability to recall a specific piece of information is accompanied by the feeling that there is an impediment or block to its recollection, as in the well-known TIP-OF-THE-TONGUE PHENOMENON.

retrieval cue a prompt or stimulus used to guide memory recall.

retrieval failure the inability to recollect information that is known to be available in memory.

retrograde amnesia see AMNESIA.

retrograde ejaculation the ejaculation of semen in a reverse direction, that is, into the urinary bladder, from which it is excreted later. This may be a result of surgery of the prostate gland, and it also occurs when the penis is squeezed just before ejaculation—a misguided attempt at preventing impregnation. Retrograde ejaculation is occasionally associated with the use of antidepressants, including the TRICYCLIC ANTIDEPRESSANTS and SSRIS, as well as conventional antipsychotic agents (particularly thioridazine). There are also reports of retrograde ejaculation with the use of ATYPICAL ANTIPSYCHOTICS (e.g., risperidone).

retrograde memory the ability to recall events that occurred or information that was acquired prior to a particular point in time, often the onset of illness or physical damage such as brain injury. For example, an individual with deficits of retrograde memory (AMNESIA) might not remember the name of a close childhood friend but would remember the name of a new person just introduced to him or her. Compare ANTEROGRADE MEMORY.

retrogression *n.* the return to a previous inappropriate behavior or to a behavior appropriate to an earlier stage of maturation when more adult techniques fail to solve a conflict. It is approximately equivalent to REGRESSION, but without the full psychoanalytic connotations.

retrospection *n.* the process of reviewing or reflecting upon an experience from the past, either directed (as in learning and memory research) or spontaneous (as in evaluating one's behavior in a given situation).

retrospective audit in health administration, a method of determining medical necessity or appropriate billing practice for services that have already been rendered.

retrospective falsification the addition of false details to memories of past experiences, particularly as done by a person with PARANOID SCHIZOPHRENIA to support a persecutory delusional system.

retrospective information information that is gained by asking people to recall feelings, events, and behaviors from their distant past. This type of information is usually regarded as less accurate and reliable than information gained by recording events and experiences while they are occurring.

retrospective medical audit see MEDICAL AUDIT.

retrospective research observational, nonexperimental research that tries to explain the present in terms of past events; that is, research that starts with the present and follows subjects backward in time. For example, a **retrospective study** may be undertaken in which individuals are selected on the basis of whether they exhibit a particular problematic symptom and are then studied to determine if they had been exposed to a risk factor of interest. Compare PROSPECTIVE RESEARCH.

Rett syndrome a PERVASIVE DEVELOPMENTAL DISORDER that occurs almost exclusively in female children who develop normally early in life but then, between 6 and 18 months, undergo rapid regression in motor, cognitive, and social skills; these skills subsequently stabilize at a level that leaves the child with mental retardation. Symptoms generally include loss of language skills, hand motion abnormalities (e.g., hand wringing and other repetitive, purposeless movements), learning difficulties, gait disturbances, breathing problems, seizures, and pronounced deceleration of head growth. [first described in 1966 by Andreas **Rett** (1924–1997), Austrian pediatrician]

reuptake *n.* the process by which neurotransmitter molecules that have been released at a SYNAPSE are taken up by the presynaptic neuron that released them. Reuptake is performed by TRANSPORTER proteins in the presynaptic membrane.

reversal error a mistake in which a letter or word is read or written backward (e.g. *tip* for *pit* or *b* as *d*). When reversal errors are marked and developmentally inappropriate, they are indicative of DYSLEXIA. See also STREPHOSYMBOLIA.

reversal of affect in psychoanalytic theory, a change in the AIM OF THE INSTINCT into its opposite, as when a masochistic impulse to hurt the self is transformed into a sadistic impulse to hurt others, or vice versa. Also called **affect inversion**; **inversion of affect**.

reversal theory a theory of motivation, emotion, and personality that attempts to explain the relationship between AROUSAL and performance. It suggests that the way an individual interprets the arousal, rather than the amount of arousal, affects performance and that he or she can reverse the positive–negative interpretation from moment to moment.

reverse anorexia a condition characterized by an individual's desire to increase body size, particularly muscularity. As with ANOREXIA NERVOSA, in which the desire is to lose weight or reduce body size, the drive to alter body size is not diminished by achieving extensive body modification. The individual's unhappiness with self-image, despite excessive gains in muscle mass and definition, is still present. See also MUSCLE DYSMORPHIA.

reverse tolerance an effect of certain drugs, usually psychoactive substances (particularly CNS stimulants), in which repeated use alters the body's sensitivity so that repeated administration of a drug will enhance the effects of that drug. Also called **sensitization**. Compare TOLERANCE.

reversible inhibitors of monoamine oxidase (**RIMAs**) see MONOAMINE OXIDASE INHIBITOR.

Reversol *n.* a trade name for EDROPHONIUM.

ReVia *n.* a trade name for NALTREXONE.

revivification *n.* a hypnotic technique in which suggestion is used to induce an individual to revive and relive forgotten or inhibited memories.

revolving-door phenomenon the repeated readmission of patients to hospitals or other institutions, often because they were discharged before they had adequately recovered.

reward system a set of interrelated factors that link a particular stimulus with some form of satisfaction or pleasure.

Rey Auditory Verbal Learning Test (**RAVLT**) a test for evaluating verbal learning and memory, including proactive inhibition, retroactive inhibition, retention, encoding versus retrieval, and organization. Originally developed in the 1940s, the RAVLT now has several variations. The standard format starts with a list of 15 words, and the participant is required to repeat all the words he or she can remember, in any order. This procedure is carried out a total of five times. Next, the examiner presents a second list of 15 words, allowing the participant only one attempt at recall. Immediately following this, the participant is asked to remember as many words as possible from the first list. A delayed recall trial as well as a recognition trial may also be administered. [André **Rey** (1906–1965), Swiss psychologist]

RFT abbreviation for ROD-AND-FRAME TEST.

Rh blood-group incompatibility an antigen-antibody reaction that occurs when blood from an Rh-positive individual is mixed with blood from an Rh-negative individual (see RH FACTOR) during transfusion or pregnancy. In pregnancy, this arises if an Rh-negative mother bears a child that has inherited Rh-positive blood: The fetal Rh antigens pass through the placental membrane, and maternal antibodies react through the placenta to destroy the fetal red blood cells. The damaged blood cells yield bilirubin, which the fetus cannot detoxify, and KERNICTERUS may result. Also called **rhesus incompatibility**. See also RH REACTION.

RHC abbreviation for RURAL HEALTH CLINIC.

rhesus factor see RH FACTOR.

rheumatoid arthritis see ARTHRITIS.

Rh factor (**rhesus factor**) any of at least eight different antigens, each determined genetically, that may be attached to the surface of an individual's red blood cells (the name derives from the rhesus monkey, used in early studies of the factor). A person whose blood cells carry an Rh factor is said to be **Rh-positive**. One whose blood cells lack an Rh factor is **Rh-negative**. Some 99% of African Americans, Native Americans, and Asian Americans and 85% of Caucasians are Rh-positive. See also RH REACTION.

rhizomelic *adj.* relating to or affecting the hip, shoulder, or both. Rhizomelic abnormalities are associated with certain congenital defects that may be accompanied by mental retardation. An affected individual may, for example, have one leg shorter than the other or contractures of the hip and shoulder joints.

Rh reaction an adverse effect that can occur in blood transfusions and pregnancies when an Rh-negative person's blood is mixed with Rh-positive blood from another individual (see RH FACTOR). This reaction is similar to the immune reaction that occurs in response to an invasion of the body tissues by a foreign agent. In pregnancy, an Rh-negative mother may carry an Rh-positive fetus, her body forming anti-Rh antibodies that destroy the red blood cells of the fetus. See also RH BLOOD-GROUP INCOMPATIBILITY.

rhyming delirium compulsive speaking or responding in rhymes, occasionally associated with a MANIC EPISODE.

rhythm *n.* **1.** a regular pattern of changes, fluctuations, or occurrences, for example, a BIOLOGICAL RHYTHM. **2.** the frequency of BRAIN WAVES, identified as alpha waves, beta waves, gamma waves, delta waves, and theta waves. **3.** the cadence or long-term temporal structure of similar sounds. **—rhythmic** or **rhythmical** *adj.*

rhythm method a technique of contraception in which the woman abstains from coitus during the days of her menstrual cycle in which she is most likely to become pregnant, that is, from just before until just after ovulation. The rhythm method is not very effective because of the difficulty in making advance predictions of the precise time of ovulation. The predictions are made by charting rectal or vaginal temperature changes daily or by testing changes in the sugar content of the cervical mucus. See also CALENDAR METHOD OF BIRTH CONTROL.

ribonucleic acid see RNA.

Ribot's law 1. the principle that the most recently acquired memories are the most vulnerable to disruption from brain damage. As a result, a TEMPORAL GRADIENT is observed in retrograde AMNESIA. **2.** a generalization stating that when a multilingual person recovers from APHASIA caused by a stroke or cerebral injury, the language recovered first will be the person's native language. [Théodule **Ribot** (1839–1916), French psychologist]

Rieger's syndrome an autosomal dominant disorder marked by dental and eye abnormalities. The dental anomalies may include missing teeth and hypoplasia (underdevelopment) of the enamel. Visual disorders usually involve anomalies of the iris and cornea. Mental retardation is sometimes present. Also called **hypodontia**. [initially reported in 1935 by Herwigh **Rieger** (1898–1986), German ophthalmologist]

right brain the right cerebral hemisphere. The term is sometimes used to designate functions or COGNITIVE STYLE supposedly mediated by the right (rather than by the left) hemisphere, such as spatial perception. See also HEMISPHERIC LATERALIZATION.

right hemisphere the right half of the CEREBRUM, the part of the brain concerned with sensation and perception, motor control, and higher level cognitive processes. The two CEREBRAL HEMISPHERES differ somewhat in function; for example, in most people the right hemisphere has greater responsibility for spatial attention. See HEMISPHERIC LATERALIZATION. Compare LEFT HEMISPHERE.

right-hemisphere consciousness a hypothesis that the right cerebral hemisphere of the brain is conscious, like the left hemisphere, even though it has no control of spoken communication (compare LEFT-HEMISPHERE CONSCIOUSNESS). The right hemisphere is postulated to function in a holistic, nonlinear manner, specialized for spatial and prosodic perception. [attributed to Roger SPERRY]

rights of patients see PATIENTS' RIGHTS.

rights of people with mental retardation rights enshrined in the United Nations Standard Rules on the Equalization of Opportunities for Persons with Disabilities (1993). People with mental retardation have the same rights as other human beings. These include (a) the right to receive proper medical care, physical therapy, education, training, rehabilitation, assistive technology, and guidance; (b) the right to economic security and to work; (c) the right to live with their families or with foster parents or, if this is not feasible, to live in a residential setting under circumstances as close as possible to family life; and (d) the right to protection from abuse and exploitation.

right to die the right to physician-assisted suicide that some consider should be available for terminally ill patients (see ASSISTED DEATH). This is distinguished from the RIGHT TO REFUSE TREATMENT in cases in which the patient is on life support.

right to effective treatment the policy position or ethical stance that people with a disability or a disorder have the legal, civil, or moral right to receive services to alleviate or cure their condition. With respect to specific therapies, this entails the use of methods that have been empirically and scientifically validated for efficacy and effectiveness.

right to refuse treatment 1. the right of patients with mental illness to refuse treatment that may be potentially hazardous or intrusive (e.g., ELECTROCONVULSIVE THERAPY or PSYCHOACTIVE DRUGS), particularly when such treatment does not appear to be in the best interests of the patient. In the United States, various state laws and court rulings support the rights of patients to receive or reject certain treatments, but there is a lack of uniformity in such regulations. See also FORCED TREATMENT. **2.** the right of terminally ill patients (e.g., those on life-support systems) to refuse treatment intended to prolong their lives. See also RIGHT TO DIE.

right to treatment 1. a statutory right, established at varying governmental levels, stipulating that people with disabilities or disorders, usually persistent or chronic in nature, have the right to receive care and treatment suited to their needs. Such statutory rights may apply nationally or to certain state or provincial areas, or they may be limited to certain conditions and disabilities. **2.** the principle that a facility that has assumed the responsibility of offering treatment for a patient is legally obligated to provide treatment that is adequate and appropriate.

right to withdraw the right of participants in research to remove themselves from the study or procedure at any point. Ethically speaking, this prerogative would follow naturally from voluntary participation and from the guarantee that refusal to continue will not result in penalty or loss of any benefits that a participant might have independent of the study. See also INFORMED CONSENT.

rigid family a family structure in which rules are never questioned and there are no exceptions to rules. Such a structure can be a cause of emotional and behavioral problems for the children of the family.

rigidity *n.* **1.** stiffness or inflexibility, particularly muscular rigidity. **2.** a personality trait characterized by strong resistance to changing one's behavior, opinions, or attitudes or inability to do this. **3.** the tendency, after brain injury, to be inflexible and complete a task in only one manner, despite more effective available alternatives. **—rigid** *adj.*

RIMAs abbreviation for reversible inhibitors of monoamine oxidase. See MONOAMINE OXIDASE INHIBITOR.

ring chromosome 18 a congenital chromosomal disorder characterized by MICROCEPHALY, ear and eye abnormalities, and severe mental retardation. The condition is not hereditary but due to breakage of the arms of chromosome 18, which fuse to form one or more rings of varying sizes.

risk *n.* **1.** the probability or likelihood that an event will occur, such as the risk that a disease or disorder will develop. **2.** the probability of experiencing loss or harm that is associated with an action or behavior. See also AT RISK; MORBIDITY RISK; RISK FACTOR. **—risky** *adj.*

risk assessment the process of determining the threat of dangerousness an individual would be likely to pose if released from the confinement in which he or she is held as a result of mental illness or criminal acts. See ACTUARIAL RISK ASSESSMENT; CLINICAL RISK ASSESSMENT.

risk aversion the tendency, when choosing between alternatives, to avoid options that entail a risk of loss, even if that risk is relatively small.

risk factor a clearly defined behavior or constitutional (e.g., genetic), environmental, or other characteristic that is associated with an increased possibility or likelihood that a disease or disorder will subsequently develop in an individual.

risk metrics numbers, formulas, graphs, or other means of presenting or describing the probability or likelihood of developing a disease or disorder.

risk perception an individual's subjective assessment of the level of risk associated with a particular hazard. Risk perceptions will vary according to such factors as past experiences, age, gender, and culture. For example, women tend to overestimate their risk of developing breast cancer. These exaggerated perceptions of risk often motivate people to seek genetic services, genetic testing, or prophylactic surgery.

risk–rescue rating a formula comparing the inherent risk of a method of attempted suicide with the likelihood of discovery and rescue.

risk taking 1. a pattern of unnecessarily engaging in activities or behaviors that are highly subject to chance or dangerous. This pattern of behavior is often associated with substance abuse, gambling, and high-risk sexual behaviors. **2.** accepting a challenging task that simultaneously involves potential for failure as well as for accomplishment or personal benefit. It is often associated with creativity and taking calculated risks in the workplace or in educational settings.

risk tolerance the level of risk to which an individual is willing to be exposed while performing an action or pursuing a goal. Tolerance of risk is usually based upon an assumption (justified or not) that the risk is slight, the consequences are minor, and that both are outweighed by immediate benefits.

risperidone *n.* an ATYPICAL ANTIPSYCHOTIC of the benzisoxazole class. It was the second atypical antipsychotic introduced into the U.S. market (CLOZAPINE was the first). It has a less frequent incidence of extrapyramidal symptoms than conventional antipsychotics when used at a lower dose range and it acts as a potent inhibitor of both D2 dopamine and 5-HT_2 serotonin receptors. U.S. trade name: **Risperdal**.

Ritalin *n.* a trade name for METHYLPHENIDATE.

ritual *n.* **1.** a form of COMPULSION involving a rigid or stereotyped act that is carried out repeatedly and is based on idiosyncratic rules that do not have a rational basis (e.g., having to perform a task in a certain way). Rituals may be performed in order to reduce distress and anxiety

R

caused by an OBSESSION. **2.** a ceremonial act or rite, usually involving a fixed order of actions or gestures and the saying of certain prescribed words. **3.** more generally, any habit or custom that is performed routinely and with little or no thought. **—ritualism** *n.* **—ritualistic** *adj.*

ritual abuse organized, repetitive, and highly sadistic abuse of a physical, sexual, or emotional nature, perpetrated principally on children. The abuse is reported as using rituals and symbols from religion (e.g., upside-down crosses), the occult, or secret societies. It may also include the creation of pornography or the selling of sexual access to children. Victims may be forced to engage in heinous acts, such as the killing of animals, as a means of coercing their participation and silence.

rivastigmine *n.* a CARBAMATE that is a reversible ACETYLCHOLINESTERASE INHIBITOR, used for the treatment of mild to moderate dementia associated with Alzheimer's disease (see NOOTROPIC). Because it can cause nausea and loss of appetite, low starting doses with a slow upward TITRATION are recommended. U.S. trade name: **Exelon**.

RMD abbreviation for repetitive motion disorder (see REPETITIVE STRAIN INJURY).

RMI abbreviation for repetitive motion injury (see REPETITIVE STRAIN INJURY).

RMT abbreviation for RECOGNITION MEMORY TEST.

RN abbreviation for REGISTERED NURSE.

RNA *r*ibo*n*ucleic *a*cid: a nucleic acid that directs the synthesis of protein molecules in living cells. There are three main types of RNA. MESSENGER RNA carries the GENETIC CODE from the cell nucleus to the cytoplasm. **Ribosomal RNA** is found in ribosomes, small particles where proteins are assembled from amino acids. **Transfer RNA** carries specific amino acids for protein synthesis. Each of the 20 amino acids has a corresponding transfer RNA molecule to place the amino acid in the proper sequence in protein assembly. RNA is similar to DNA in structure except that it consists of a single strand of nucleotides (compared with the double strands of DNA), the base uracil (U) occurs instead of thymine (T), and the sugar unit is ribose, rather than deoxyribose.

road rage aggressive or confrontational behavior while driving, typically triggered by an actual or imagined transgression by another driver. Often associated with traffic congestion, road rage varies in severity and can involve hostile verbal expression, hazardous driving, and interpersonal violence.

Robaxin *n.* a trade name for METHOCARBAMOL.

Roberts syndrome an autosomal recessive disorder in which the child is born with abnormally short arms and legs as well as a cleft lip and palate. Other features include MICROCEPHALY and genital hypertrophy (enlargement). Few affected individuals survive early infancy; of those who do, 50% are likely to have mental retardation. Also called **Appelt–Gerken–Lenz syndrome**. [described in 1919 by John Bingham **Roberts** (1852–1924), U.S. physician, and in 1966 by Hans **Appelt** (1919–1988), H. **Gerken**, and Widukind **Lenz** (1919–1995), German physicians]

Robitussin *n.* see DEXTROMETHORPHAN.

rocking *n.* a stereotyped motor behavior in which the body rocks to and fro, often observed in children or adults with severe or profound mental retardation, AUTISTIC DISORDER, or STEREOTYPIC MOVEMENT DISORDER. Also called **body rocking**.

Rod-and-Frame Test (**RFT**) a test used to study the role of visual and gravitational cues in judging the visual vertical. It is the most widely used measure of FIELD DEPENDENCE and FIELD INDEPENDENCE. The test consists of a movable rod inside a frame; the participant must adjust the rod to a true vertical position as the position of the frame is changed. Degree of error (i.e., the number of degrees away from 90%) is the measure used to score the test. The higher the score, the more field dependent the participant is; the lower the score, the more field independent he or she is. [developed in 1948 by U.S. psychologists Herman A. Witkin (1916–1979) and Solomon ASCH]

Rogerian therapy see CLIENT-CENTERED THERAPY.

Rogers, Carl (1902–1987) U.S. psychologist. Rogers received his doctorate from Columbia University's Teachers College in 1931. He held a number of faculty positions in his career, but it was while teaching at the University of Chicago (1944–1957) that he most fully developed and described his distinctive approach to psychotherapy. Rogers originated CLIENT-CENTERED THERAPY and the NONDIRECTIVE APPROACH, which he conceived as providing the client with a warm, accepting climate that would foster personality growth and the realization of inner potential. Fitting within the loosely associated group of theories and techniques of HUMANISTIC SYCHOLOGY, client-centered therapy offered an important alternative to the Freudian and behaviorist psychotherapies then dominant. Rogers viewed psychological dysfunction as typically resulting from CONDITIONAL POSITIVE REGARD, namely, the conditions put on love and affection by early authority figures, such as parents and teachers. He believed that individuals who suppressed their own needs in order to receive positive regard from others would develop low self-esteem and be unable to achieve self-actualization. Client-centered therapy was designed as a corrective, with the therapist providing an atmosphere of UNCONDITIONAL POSITIVE REGARD, warmth, and UNCRITICALNESS that would theoretically enable the client to thrive and become what Rogers would call a fully functioning person. See also CONDITIONS OF WORTH; GROWTH PRINCIPLE. **—Rogerian** *adj.*

Rokeach Dogmatism Scale a 66-item scale developed in 1960 to measure individual differences in openness or closedness of belief systems (i.e., DOGMATISM) across several continua, such as "isolation and differentiation between belief and nonbelief systems" and "interrelations among primitive, intermediate, and peripheral beliefs." Some studies have found the scale more useful in assessing "general authoritarianism" and "general intolerance." [Milton **Rokeach** (1918–1988), U.S. psychologist]

Rokeach Value Survey (**RVS**) an instrument that assesses participants' values to help them determine what is most important in their lives and make good personal choices (often used as a career development instrument). "Value" is defined as "an enduring belief that a specific mode of conduct or end-state of existence is personally or socially preferable to an opposite or converse mode of conduct or end-state of existence." Two kinds of values are distinguished in the survey: instrumental, that is, modes of conduct and behavioral characteristics that are seen as socially desirable; and terminal, that is, end-states of existence or ultimate modes of living that have been idealized. [Milton **Rokeach**]

rok-joo *n.* see KORO.

role *n.* a coherent set of behaviors expected of an individual in a specific position within a group or social setting. Since the term is derived from the dramaturgical concept of role (the dialogue and actions assigned to each performer in a play), there is a suggestion that individuals' actions are regulated by the part they play in the social setting rather than by their personal predilections or inclinations.

role conflict a state of tension or distress caused by inconsistent or discordant expectations associated with one's social or group ROLE, as when a role's demands are inconsistent with each other (INTRAROLE CONFLICT) or individuals occupy more than one role and the behaviors required by these roles are incompatible with one another (INTERROLE CONFLICT).

role confusion **1.** a state of uncertainty about a given social or group role. **2.** GENDER ROLE behavior in a male or female that is traditionally associated with the opposite sex. See also GENDER IDENTITY DISORDER; TRANSGENDER. **3.** see IDENTITY VERSUS IDENTITY CONFUSION.

role diffusion a state of confusion about one's social role that typically occurs during adolescence. See IDENTITY VERSUS IDENTITY CONFUSION. [described by Erik ERIKSON]

role-divided psychotherapy a form of GROUP THERAPY in which members meet for part of the session without the therapist and part with the therapist. Also called **role-divided therapy**. See also COTHERAPY. [developed by Latvian-born U.S. therapist George R. Bach (1914–1986)]

role-enactment theory a social psychological explanation of hypnosis according to which the person under hypnosis takes on a role assigned by the hypnotist and behaves in accordance with this role while in the hypnotic condition.

role expectations expectations regarding the traits, attitudes, and behaviors appropriate to a particular ROLE. These expectations may be communicated to the occupant of a role by other people or by the occupant himself or herself.

role overload a situation in which one is asked to do more than one is capable of doing in a specific period of time (**quantitative overload**) or in which one is taxed beyond one's knowledge, skills, and abilities (**qualitative overload**).

role play a technique used in HUMAN RELATIONS TRAINING and PSYCHOTHERAPY in which participants act out various social roles in dramatic situations. Originally developed in PSYCHODRAMA, role play is now widely used in industrial, educational, and clinical settings for such purposes as training employees to handle sales problems, testing out different attitudes and relationships in group and family psychotherapy, and rehearsing different ways of coping with stresses and conflicts.

role reversal a technique used for therapeutic, educational, and management development purposes in which an individual exchanges roles with another individual in order to experience alternative cognitive styles (e.g., in problem solving), feelings, and behavioral approaches.

role taking awareness or adoption of the viewpoint of another person, typically for the purpose of understanding his or her thoughts and actions.

role therapy in psychotherapy, a system that uses real-life PSYCHODRAMA. The client selects a role model, works out the aspects of the model with the therapist, and then role-plays the model both in the therapeutic session and in real life. [developed by U.S. psychologist George A. Kelly (1905–1967)]

rolfing *n.* a deep-massage technique developed in the 1930s. It aims to relieve muscular tension, improve posture and balance, and enhance personal functioning through realignment of body structure. The technique is based on a theory that muscle massage will relieve both physical and psychological pain. Also called **structural integration**. [devised by Ida P. **Rolf** (1896–1979), U.S. physical therapist]

Romazicon *n.* a trade name for FLUMAZENIL.

rootedness *n.* in the psychoanalytic theory of Erich FROMM, the need to establish bonds or ties with others that provide emotional security and serve to reduce the isolation and insignificance that Fromm believed to lie at the heart of human existence. It is manifested positively in BROTHERLINESS and negatively in INCESTUOUS TIES.

rootwork *n.* a cultural or folk health belief system, common in some highly localized parts of the southern United States and the Caribbean, that attributes illness to witchcraft, hexing, voodoo, or spells (i.e., "roots"). The individual displays intense fear, symptoms of anxiety, and related somatic complaints and typically remains in this state until a traditional healer, called a **root doctor**, removes the root. Also called **brujeria**; **mal puesto**.

Rorschach, Hermann (1884–1922) Swiss psychiatrist. Rorschach earned his doctorate of medicine at the University of Zürich in 1912. He was the originator of the widely used RORSCHACH INKBLOT TEST of personality. For this, he standardized a set of inkblots, developed criteria for scoring them quantitatively, compared patients of varying diagnoses, and conceived the notion of different experience types that could be differentiated using the inkblot test. He was working on a general theory of personality when he died suddenly of peritonitis. The Rorschach test, developed between 1918 and 1922, did not come into widespread use until the 1950s, when it became, for a time, the test of choice in psychodiagnosis.

Rorschach Inkblot Test a PROJECTIVE TECHNIQUE in which the participant is presented with ten unstructured inkblots (mostly in black and gray but sometimes in color) and is asked "What might this be?" or "What do you see in this?" The examiner classifies the responses according to such structural and thematic (content) factors as color (C), movement (M), detail (D), whole (W), popular or common (P), animal (A), form (F), and human (H). Various scoring systems, either qualitative or quantitative, are used. The object is to interpret the participant's personality structure in terms of such factors as emotionality, cognitive style, creativity, impulse control, and various defensive patterns. Perhaps the best known, and certainly one of the most controversial, assessment instruments in all of psychology—it is almost considered "representative" by the general public—the Rorschach is widely used and has been extensively researched, with results ranging from those that claim strong support for its clinical utility (e.g., for selecting treatment modalities or monitoring patient change or improvement over time) to those that demonstrate little evidence of robust or consistent validity and that criticize the instrument as invalid and useless. [developed in the early 1920s by Hermann RORSCHACH]

rotation system a technique of GROUP THERAPY in which the therapist works with each individual in sequence in the presence of other group members.

rotation treatment see GYRATOR TREATMENT.

Rotter Internal–External Locus of Control Scale (**RIELC**) a scale that is used to provide information regarding a client's feelings for causality of events. Clients who measure high on internal LOCUS OF CONTROL (see INTERNALIZERS) assume causality is primarily under their control; clients who measure high on external locus of control (see EXTERNALIZERS) assume causality is primarily outside their control. Those with high internal measures tend to take more responsibility for and control of their learning, resulting in better performance (e.g., on academic tasks). In contrast, those with high external measures have been shown to take less responsibility, resulting in poorer performance on tasks. [Julian Bernard **Rotter** (1916–), U.S. psychologist]

roughness discrimination test a test of somesthetic sensitivity in which participants are asked to determine by touch which of a choice of surfaces (e.g., grades of sandpaper) has a greater roughness. The ability is sometimes impaired following a lesion in a brain area related to the sense of touch.

round-table technique a GROUP THERAPY technique used in a hospital setting. Three connecting rooms are required. In one, the therapist and others use a one-way window to watch the therapy session in progress. In the second room, selected patients also use a one-way window to watch the same session. The patients in the third room—the therapy room—sit around a table with a microphone in the center. Their task is to recommend a member of their group to go to a staff meeting for possible discharge and, if the member is discharged, to pick a member from the patient group in the adjoining room to join their group. A majority vote prevails. See also MILIEU THERAPY. [pioneered by U.S. psychologist Willis H. McCann (1907–1998)]

Rouse v. Cameron see LEAST RESTRICTIVE ALTERNATIVE.

routes of administration see ADMINISTRATION.

routinized thoughts see AUTOMATIC THOUGHTS.

Royer's syndrome see PRADER–WILLI SYNDROME.

RSH syndrome see SMITH–LEMLI–OPITZ SYNDROME.

RSI abbreviation for REPETITIVE STRAIN INJURY.

RSTS abbreviation for RUBINSTEIN–TAYBI SYNDROME.

RSVP in cognitive psychology, abbreviation for RAPID SEQUENTIAL VISUAL PRESENTATION.

rTMS abbreviation for repetitive TRANSCRANIAL MAGNETIC STIMULATION.

Rubinstein–Taybi syndrome (**RSTS; RTS**) a familial disorder marked by facial abnormalities, including MICROCEPHALY and HYPERTELORISM, broad thumbs and toes, and mental retardation, caused by several different genetic factors. Hypotonia (flaccid muscles) and a stiff gait are common. One study found more than 80% of affected individuals had IQs of less than 50. Also called **Rubinstein syndrome**. [Jack H. **Rubinstein** (1925–2006) and Hooshang **Taybi** (1919–2006), U.S. pediatricians]

rule-governed behavior any behavior that is influenced by verbal antecedents, such as following instructions (as when a child cleans his or her room because told to do so) or reacting to one's own private thinking (as when an adult begins an exercise program after thinking "I need to lose weight"). Also called **verbally governed behavior**.

rule modeling an imitative technique in which people learn to control their behavior by following the same rules that have been followed by a model, even when there are slight situational variations.

rule of abstinence in psychoanalysis, the rule that the patient should abstain from all gratifications that might distract him or her from the analytic process or drain off instinctual energy, anxiety, and frustration that could be used as a driving force in the therapy. Examples of such gratifications are smoking, engaging in idle conversation, or ACTING OUT during the sessions, and unlimited sexual activity, absorbing interests, and other pleasures pursued outside the sessions. Also called **abstinence rule**.

rumination *n.* **1.** obsessional thinking involving excessive, repetitive thoughts or themes that interfere with other forms of mental activity. It is a common feature of OBSESSIVE-COMPULSIVE DISORDER. **2.** the voluntary regurgitation of food from the stomach to the mouth, where it is masticated and tasted a second time. It frequently occurs among people with severe or profound mental retardation, and it is possible that delays in development may be due partly to the disorder. Also called **merycism**. **—ruminate** *vb.*

rumination disorder in *DSM–IV–TR*, a disorder characterized by the repeated voluntary regurgitation of ingested food involving ejection or reswallowing, but without nausea. Individuals may develop potentially fatal weight loss and malnutrition. It lasts for a period of at least 1 month and generally occurs during infancy (age 3 to 12 months), following a period of normal feeding; however, it may also be observed in individuals with severe mental retardation.

rural health clinic (**RHC**) a clinic, physician practice, or country health department that, in compliance with the Rural Clinic Services Act, is located in a medically underserved area and uses a physician, PHYSICIAN ASSISTANT, NURSE PRACTITIONER, or some combination of these to deliver primary outpatient health care. See also NATIONAL ASSOCIATION OF RURAL HEALTH CLINICS.

rush *n.* the effect reported when someone receives an intravenous injection of amphetamine, cocaine, or methamphetamine. The sensation is sometimes described as a dramatic awakening accompanied by a high and sudden degree of euphoria.

RVS abbreviation for ROKEACH VALUE SURVEY.

RxP abbreviation for PRESCRIPTIVE AUTHORITY.

Ss

s symbol for SPECIFIC FACTOR.

SA abbreviation for SOCIAL AGE.

sacrificial paraphilia sexual interest and arousal involving staged or actual death, with ritualistic sacrifice features. This may involve, as the sacrificial objects, animals or people. See also PARAPHILIA.

SAD abbreviation for SEASONAL AFFECTIVE DISORDER.

S-adenosylmethionine (SAM) *n.* a nonprotein chemical compound that mediates numerous metabolic reactions, including those involving certain proteins, phospholipids, neurotransmitters, and nucleic acids. It is commonly used as a dietary supplement in the treatment of depression because it may increase levels of serotonin in the brain. It also has been implicated in Alzheimer's disease: Low S-adenosylmethionine levels often are observed in those with the disorder, which may be a sign of alteration of SAM metabolism.

sadism *n.* the derivation of pleasure through cruelty and inflicting pain, humiliation, and other forms of suffering on individuals. The term generally denotes SEXUAL SADISM. In psychoanalytic theory, sadism is attributed to the working of the DEATH INSTINCT and is manifested in innate aggressive tendencies expressed from the earliest stages of development. For example, during the ORAL-BITING PHASE the infant expresses sadism by taking pleasure in biting. See also ANAL SADISM; ORAL SADISM. [Donatien Alphonse François, Comte (Marquis) de **Sade** (1740–1814), French soldier and writer] **—sadist** *n.* **—sadistic** *adj.*

sadistic personality disorder in *DSM–III–R* (but not in *DSM–IV–TR*), a personality disorder characterized by an abusive and intimidating manner, inclined to gain satisfaction in coercing and humiliating others. Such people are often reckless and undaunted by danger or punishment.

sadness *n.* an emotional state of unhappiness, ranging in intensity from mild to extreme and usually aroused by the loss of something that is highly valued, for example, by the rupture or loss of a relationship. Persistent sadness is one of the two defining symptoms of a MAJOR DEPRESSIVE EPISODE, the other being ANHEDONIA. **—sad** *adj.*

sadomasochism *n.* **1.** sexual activity between consenting partners in which one partner enjoys inflicting pain (see SEXUAL SADISM) and the other enjoys experiencing pain (see SEXUAL MASOCHISM). **2.** a PARAPHILIA in which a person is both sadistic and masochistic, deriving sexual arousal from both giving and receiving pain. **—sadomasochist** *n.* **—sadomasochistic** *adj.*

sadomasochistic personality formerly, in psychoanalysis, the characterization of people who enjoy both exhibiting and receiving aggressive behavior.

SADS abbreviation for SCHEDULE FOR AFFECTIVE DISORDERS AND SCHIZOPHRENIA.

Saethre–Chotzen syndrome see CHOTZEN'S SYNDROME.

safe sex sexual activity in which the exchange of bodily fluids is inhibited as much as possible to help reduce the risk of unwanted pregnancy or contracting sexually transmitted diseases. Precautions may include avoidance of high-risk behaviors, careful selection of one's partners, and the use of preventive barriers (e.g., condoms, dental dams).

safety and health education instruction regarding health-related matters, including the causes and prevention of malnutrition, alcoholism, drug addiction, and sexually transmitted disease, as well as safety on the roads, in the workshop, at home, and on the playing field. See also ACCIDENT PREVENTION.

safety behavior a behavior performed by an anxious individual in an attempt to minimize or prevent a feared catastrophe. For example, a person with PANIC DISORDER might only go out when accompanied, and a person with SOCIAL PHOBIA might wear sunglasses indoors to avoid eye contact. Safety behaviors may also include internal mental processes: A person with social phobia might memorize what he or she plans to say at a social gathering. Safety behavior contributes to the maintenance of anxiety disorders when people believe that the behavior, rather than the lack of actual danger, is what prevents the feared catastrophe. Also called **safety cues**; **safety-seeking behavior**; **safety signals**. [first defined in 1991 by British psychologist Paul M. Salkovskis]

safety device in the therapeutic approach of German-born U.S. psychoanalyst Karen D. Horney (1885–1952), any psychic means used by an individual to protect himself or herself from threats, particularly the hostile elements of the environment. As such, the concept is similar to the classical psychoanalytic concept of the DEFENSE MECHANISM. See also BASIC ANXIETY.

safety need a desire for freedom from illness or danger and for a secure, familiar, predictable environment. Safety needs comprise the second level of MASLOW'S MOTIVATIONAL HIERARCHY, after basic PHYSIOLOGICAL NEEDS.

St. John's wort a perennial flowering plant, *Hypericum perforatum*, that has an extensive history of folk use, particularly as a sedative, a treatment for nerve pain and malaria, and a balm for wounds, burns, and insect bites. It is currently a highly popular product used in the treatment of mild to moderate depression, anxiety, and insomnia. There is some research supporting its effectiveness for these purposes, but studies have not demonstrated the superiority of St. John's wort over placebo in the management of major depression. There is also some research suggesting the herb possesses anti-inflammatory and antioxidant properties as well. The active agents are presumed to be HYPERICIN and related compounds. Hypericin is known to exert some effects common to other ANTIDEPRESSANTS, such as inhibition of the reuptake of norepinephrine, dopamine, and serotonin. It may also exert some effects by modulating the neurotransmitters GAMMA-AMINOBUTYRIC ACID (GABA) and GLUTAMATE. The agent should be used with caution, as it may interact adversely with or limit the effectiveness of a number of other drugs, particularly those used to treat HIV/AIDS and cancer and to prevent transplant rejection. Although rare, side effects may include dry mouth, dizziness, diarrhea, nausea, increased sensitivity to sunlight, and fatigue.

salicylates *pl. n.* a group of drugs that are based on **salicin**, a compound obtained from the bark of willow trees (*Salix*), and includes salicylic acid and its derivatives. The latter are used as analgesics, antipyretics, and anti-inflammatory agents. They act on both the peripheral and central nervous systems, particularly the thalamus, but also mimic some aspects of the adrenal hormones. The best known member is ASPIRIN (acetylsalicylic acid), introduced in 1899. Other salicylates include **salicylamide** and compounds used in topical formulations for the relief of muscle and joint pain.

salicylism *n.* poisoning with salicylates, the most common form of which is due to overdosage of ASPIRIN. Symptoms of mild salicylism include tinnitus, mental confusion, headache, nausea, and vomiting. More severe forms of salicylism are characterized by severe acidosis, hemorrhage, and changes in mental status that may lead to convulsions, coma, and death.

saliromania *n.* sexual interest and arousal associated with objects that are filthy, disgusting, or deformed.

SAM abbreviation for S-ADENOSYLMETHIONINE.

same-sex marriage a long-term, intimate, stable, and in some jurisdictions legally recognized relationship between two people of the same sex. It is less frequently called **homosexual marriage**. See DOMESTIC PARTNERSHIP.

SAMHSA abbreviation for SUBSTANCE ABUSE AND MENTAL HEALTH SERVICES ADMINISTRATION.

sample *n.* a subset of a POPULATION of interest that is selected for study. It is important to ensure that a sample is representative of the population as a whole.

sampling *n.* the process of selecting a limited number of subjects or cases for participation in experiments, surveys, or other research. There are a number of different types (e.g., STRATIFIED SAMPLING, OPPORTUNISTIC SAMPLING), each having a different potential of obtaining a sample appropriately representative of the POPULATION under study.

sampling bias any flaw in SAMPLING processes that makes the resulting sample unrepresentative of the population, hence possibly distorting research results.

sampling distribution the distribution of a statistic, such as the mean, over infinite repeated samples drawn from a population; that is, the theoretical distribution of a statistic.

sampling error the predictable margin of error that occurs in studies employing sampling, as reflected in the variation in the estimate of a parameter from its true value in the population. Sampling error is exacerbated by the use of samples that are not representative of the population from which they were drawn.

sampling frame a complete listing of all of the elements in a POPULATION from which a sample is to be drawn.

sampling population the POPULATION from which a SAMPLE is selected in experimental studies.

sampling with replacement a SAMPLING technique in which a selected unit is returned to the pool and may subsequently be redrawn in another sample. In **sampling without replacement** the sampling unit is not returned to the pool.

Sandimmune *n.* a trade name for CYCLOSPORINE.

S and M abbreviation for sadism and masochism. See SADOMASOCHISM.

sane society see Erich FROMM.

Sanfilippo's syndrome a disorder causing severe mental retardation associated with bone and joint defects and a tendency toward dwarfism. Affected children may also show signs of corneal opacities. The disease is transmitted as an autosomal recessive trait that causes a systemic form of MUCOPOLYSACCHARIDOSIS. After normal early mental development, the child shows mental regression. The ability to speak deteriorates and eventually is lost, as is motor control. Lifespan may be 10 to 20 years. Also called **heparitinuria**; **mucopolysaccharidosis Type III**; **polydystrophic oligophrenia**; **Sanfilippo (A, B, C, D)**. [described in 1963 by Sylvester **Sanfilippo**, U.S. pediatrician]

sangue dormido a CULTURE-BOUND SYNDROME found among inhabitants (indigenous and immigrant) of Cape Verde. Symptoms include pain, numbness, tremor, paralysis, convulsions, stroke, blindness, heart attack, infection, and miscarriage. [Portuguese, literally: "sleeping blood"]

sanity *n.* **1.** in law, the state of being not legally insane (see INSANITY), and therefore not suffering from a mental disease or defect that impairs one's ability to understand or appreciate one's acts or to conform to the requirements of the law. **2.** more generally, soundness of mind or judgment. **—sane** *adj.*

Sansert *n.* a trade name for METHYSERGIDE.

sapphism *n.* an older name for LESBIANISM.

Sarafem *n.* a trade name for FLUOXETINE.

sarcoma *n.* see CANCER.

SAR workshop abbreviation for SEXUAL ATTITUDE REASSESSMENT WORKSHOP.

satellite clinic a freestanding outpatient facility that is physically separate from but administratively attached to a parent medical facility. Staff interaction and sharing of services occur between the clinic and parent facility.

satiation *n.* **1.** the satisfaction of a desire or need, such as hunger or thirst; another name for satiety. **2.** the temporary loss of effectiveness of a REINFORCER due to its repeated presentation. **—satiate** *vb.*

satisfaction of instincts in psychoanalytic theory, the gratification of basic needs, such as hunger, thirst, sex, and aggression, which discharges tension, eliminates UNPLEASURE, and restores the organism to a balanced state. Satisfaction may occur on a conscious, preconscious, or unconscious level. Also called **gratification of instincts**. See also LIBIDO.

satyriasis *n.* excessive or insatiable desire in a male for sexual gratification. Sexual activity with one person is found not to be enough, and many other sexual partners are sought. See also DON JUAN; EROTOMANIA.

S

savant *n.* a person with mental retardation or an AUTISTIC SPECTRUM DISORDER (**autistic savant**) who demonstrates exceptional, usually isolated, cognitive abilities, such as rapid calculation, identifying the day of the week for any given date, or musical talent. The term **idiot savant** initially was used to denote such a person but has been discarded because of its colloquial, pejorative connotation.

sawtooth waves bursts of small, sharp waves recorded on an electroencephalogram during REM SLEEP.

SBS abbreviation for SHAKEN BABY SYNDROME.

sc abbreviation for *s*ub*c*utaneous.

scalability *n.* the characteristic of an item (e.g., in a test) that allows it to fit into a progression of scores or values.

scale *n.* a system for arranging items in a progressive series, for example, according to their magnitude or value.

scale development the process of constructing, standardizing, and validating a measuring instrument.

Scale of Prodromal Symptoms (**SOPS**) a psychological assessment instrument designed to identify and assess the PRODROMAL SYNDROME of schizophrenia and other psychotic disorders. It includes behaviorally defined diagnosis criteria and provides a six-point scale to quantitatively rate the severity of five ATTENUATED POSITIVE SYMPTOMS, four disorganization symptoms, and four general symptoms. [originally developed in 2001 by U.S. psychiatrist Thomas H. McGlashan (1941–) and colleagues]

scaling *n.* the process of constructing a SCALE to measure or assess some quantity or characteristic (e.g., height, weight, happiness, empathy).

scanning *n.* in medicine, the process of using radiological, magnetic, or other means (e.g., a BRAIN SCAN) to visualize and examine the body or a portion of it to diagnose a disease or disorder.

scanning hypothesis the hypothesis that RAPID EYE MOVEMENTS observed during dreaming sleep correspond to subjective gaze shifts of the dreamer looking around in the dream with fixations in specific locations.

scapegoating *n.* blaming: the process of directing one's anger, frustration, and aggression onto other, usually less powerful, groups or individuals and targeting them as the source of one's problems and misfortunes. **—scapegoat** *n., vb.*

scapegoat theory **1.** an analysis of violence and aggression that assumes that individuals undergoing negative experiences (such as failure or abuse by others) may blame an innocent individual or group for causing the experience. Subsequent mistreatment of this scapegoat then serves as an outlet for individuals' frustrations and hostilities (see DISPLACED AGGRESSION). It has also been suggested that when scapegoats have been targets for aggression over the years they may thus acquire the quality of a stimulus for aggression. **2.** an analysis of PREJUDICE that assumes that intergroup conflict is caused, in part, by the tendency of individuals to blame their negative experiences on other groups. The theory is supported by studies suggesting that racial prejudice increases during periods of economic downturn and high unemployment. See also FRUSTRATION–AGGRESSION HYPOTHESIS.

scatologia *n.* preoccupation with obscenities, lewdness, and filth, mainly of an excremental nature. The term is derived from the Greek word for dung. In psychoanalytic theory, scatalogia is usually associated with ANAL EROTICISM. Also called **scatology**. **—scatological** *adj.*

scatophilia *n.* sexual interest and arousal derived from talking about sexual or excremental matters and using obscene language.

scattering *n.* a type of thinking characterized by tangential or irrelevant associations that may be expressed in incomprehensible speech. It is observed in individuals with schizophrenia.

Schachenmann's syndrome see CAT'S-EYE SYNDROME.

Schachter–Singer theory the theory that experiencing and identifying emotional states are functions of both physiological AROUSAL and cognitive interpretations of the physical state. Also called **attribution of emotion**; **cognitive arousal theory of emotion**; **Schachter theory**; **two-factor theory of emotion**. [Stanley **Schachter** (1922–1997) and Jerome E. **Singer** (1924–2010), U.S. psychologists]

schadenfreude *n.* the gaining of pleasure or satisfaction from the misfortune of others. [from German *Schaden*, "harm," and *Freude*, "joy"]

scheduled awakening a form of behavior therapy for elimination of persistent nightmares (see NIGHTMARE DISORDER; SLEEP TERROR DISORDER). The procedure includes the regular wakening of the sleeper at intervals related to REM SLEEP.

scheduled drug any of various drugs whose prescription or use has been restricted by the U.S. Drug Enforcement Administration. Schedule I drugs are those for which all nonresearch use is illegal (e.g., LSD, heroin). Schedule II drugs include most opiates, stimulants (e.g., cocaine, amphetamines, and methylphenidate), barbiturates, and prescribed forms of tetrahydrocannabinol (dronabinol). For Schedule II drugs, no refills or telephone prescriptions are permitted. Schedule III drugs include some opioids, barbiturates, and stimulants subject to abuse; prescriptions must be rewritten after 6 months, with a maximum of five refills. Schedule IV drugs include certain opioids, some stimulants, and most of the benzodiazepines. Refills are limited to five, and prescriptions must be rewritten after 6 months. Schedule V drugs include several opiates with low abuse potential (low doses of codeine and others). The Schedule of Controlled Substances, originally designed to restrict the prescription of commonly abused drugs, is periodically updated as the popularity of new agents—generally drugs of abuse—reaches the attention of authorities.

Schedule for Affective Disorders and Schizophrenia (SADS) a STRUCTURED INTERVIEW to identify and describe in detail a range of psychopathological symptoms, used to make standardized and reliable diagnoses in adults. The SADS includes a progression of questions and criteria and provides for the rating of symptom severity, both for lifetime occurrence and most recent or current occurrence, using a 0–4, 0–6, or 0–7 scale. A version of the SADS for use with children and adolescents, the **Kiddie Schedule for Affective Disorders and Schizophrenia (KSADS)**, is also available. [originally developed in 1978 by U.S. psychiatrist Robert L. Spitzer and U.S. clinical psychologist Jean Endicott (1936–)]

schema *n.* (*pl.* **schemata**) **1.** a collection of basic knowledge about a concept or entity that serves as a guide to perception, interpretation, imagination, or problem solving. For example, the schema "dorm room" suggests that a bed and a desk are probably part of the scene, that a microwave oven might or might not be, and that expensive Persian rugs probably will not be. Also called **cognitive schema**. See also FRAME OF REFERENCE; PERCEPTUAL SCHEMA. **2.** an outlook or assumption that an individual has of the self, others, or the world that endures despite objective reality. For example, "I am a damaged person" and "Anyone I trust will eventually hurt me" are negative schemas that may result from negative experiences in early childhood. A goal of treatment, particularly stressed in COGNITIVE THERAPY, is to help the client to develop more realistic, present-oriented schemas to replace those developed during childhood or through traumatic experiences. See also SELF-IMAGE. **3.** in social psychology, a cognitive structure representing a person's knowledge about some entity or situation, including its qualities and the relationships between these. Schemas are usually ABSTRACTIONS and therefore simplify a person's world. In 1932 British psychologist Frederic C. Bartlett (1886–1969) showed that past experiences are stored in memory as schemas; impressions of other people are also thought to be organized in this way. **—schematic** *adj.*

schema change therapeutic techniques to alter cognitive, emotional, and physical patterns of meaning that individuals have derived about the self, other individuals, social groups, and situations from early experiences and that now interfere with adaptive living.

schizoaffective disorder in *DSM–IV–TR*, an uninterrupted illness featuring at some time a MAJOR DEPRESSIVE EPISODE, MANIC EPISODE, or MIXED EPISODE concurrently with characteristic symptoms of SCHIZOPHRENIA (e.g., delusions, hallucinations, disorganized speech, catatonic behavior) and, in the same period, delusions or hallucinations for at least 2 weeks in the absence of prominent mood symptoms. Also called **schizoaffective psychosis**; **schizoaffective schizophrenia**.

schizoid *adj.* denoting characteristics resembling SCHIZOPHRENIA but in a milder form: characterized by lack of affect, social passivity, and minimal introspection.

schizoid disorder of childhood or adolescence in *DSM–III*, a disorder characterized by absence of close friends other than relatives or isolated children, no apparent interest in making friends, no pleasure from peer interactions, general avoidance of social contacts, lack of interest in team sports and other activities that in-

S

volve other children, and a duration of at least three months. In DSM–IV–TR, this diagnostic category has been subsumed under PERVASIVE DEVELOPMENTAL DISORDERS.

schizoid–manic state a psychotic state combining features of both manic and schizophrenic excitement. Also called **schizomania**. [identified by Swiss-born U.S. psychiatrist Adolf Meyer (1866–1950), Austrian-born U.S. psychiatrist Abraham Brill (1874–1948), and Swiss psychiatrist Eugen Bleuler (1857–1939)]

schizoid personality disorder in *DSM–IV–TR*, a personality disorder characterized by long-term emotional coldness, absence of tender feelings for others, indifference to praise or criticism and to the feelings of others, and inability to form close friendships with more than two people. The eccentricities of speech, behavior, or thought that are characteristic of SCHIZOTYPAL PERSONALITY DISORDER are absent in those with schizoid personality disorder.

schizomania *n.* see SCHIZOID–MANIC STATE.

schizophrenia *n.* a psychotic disorder characterized by disturbances in thinking (cognition), emotional responsiveness, and behavior. Schizophrenia was first formally described in the late 19th century by German psychiatrist Emil Kraepelin (1856–1926), who named it DEMENTIA PRAECOX; in 1911 Swiss psychiatrist Eugen Bleuler (1857–1939) renamed the disorder "schizophrenia" and described what he regarded as its FUNDAMENTAL SYMPTOMS. According to *DSM–IV–TR*, which provides the criteria for diagnosis that are now most widely used, the characteristic disturbances must last for at least 6 months and include at least 1 month of active-phase symptoms comprising two or more of the following: delusions, hallucinations, disorganized speech, grossly disorganized or catatonic behavior, or NEGATIVE SYMPTOMS (e.g., lack of emotional responsiveness, extreme apathy). These signs and symptoms are associated with marked social or occupational dysfunction. Disorganized thinking (see FORMAL THOUGHT DISORDER; LOOSENING OF ASSOCIATIONS; SCHIZOPHRENIC THINKING) has been argued by some (beginning with Bleuler) to be the single most important feature of schizophrenia. But, lacking an objective definition of THOUGHT DISORDER and limited to evaluation of an individual's speech, *DSM–IV–TR* and its predecessors have not emphasized this feature. The age of onset is typically between the late teens and mid-30s, occasionally later. Five distinct subtypes of schizophrenia are described in *DSM–IV–TR* (see CATATONIC SCHIZOPHRENIA; DISORGANIZED SCHIZOPHRENIA; PARANOID SCHIZOPHRENIA; RESIDUAL SCHIZOPHRENIA; UNDIFFERENTIATED SCHIZOPHRENIA). In *DSM–III*, schizophrenia was viewed as comprising a group of SCHIZOPHRENIC DISORDERS. **—schizophrenic** *adj.*

schizophrenia in remission a diagnosis for cases in which individuals have experienced at least one schizophrenic episode and are currently free of schizophrenic symptoms.

Schizophrenia Patient Outcomes Research Team (**PORT**) a team of researchers established in 1992 by the Agency for Health Care Policy and Research and the National Institute of Mental Health. The team conducted a 5-year study to assess the treatment and management of schizophrenia (including pharmacotherapies, psychological and family interventions, vocational rehabilitation, and assertive community treatment) and subsequently developed 15 recommendations for improving patient outcomes. The researchers reviewed the literature on schizophrenia treatment outcomes and also surveyed a random sample of 719 individuals diagnosed with schizophrenia in two U.S. states to determine how the scientific evidence compared with actual clinical practice in outpatient and inpatient settings in both urban and rural areas. It was found that the overall rates at which patients' treatment conformed to the study recommendations were generally below 50%, indicating the need for greater efforts to ensure that treatment research results are translated into practice, and that the key to improving patient outcomes is adoption of a comprehensive and individualized strategy that includes not only proper doses of appropriate medications but also patient and family education and support.

schizophrenic disorders in *DSM–III*, a group of disorders that in *DSM–IV–TR* are regarded as subtypes of SCHIZOPHRENIA, namely: **catatonic type** (see CATATONIC SCHIZOPHRENIA), **disorganized type** (see DISORGANIZED SCHIZOPHRENIA), **paranoid type** (see PARANOID SCHIZOPHRENIA), **residual type** (see RESIDUAL SCHIZOPHRENIA), and **undifferentiated type** (see UNDIFFERENTIATED SCHIZOPHRENIA).

schizophrenic episode a period during which an individual exhibits promiment symptoms of schizophrenia, such as hallucinations, delusions, disordered thinking, and disturbances in emotional responsiveness and behavior. See also ACUTE SCHIZOPHRENIC EPISODE.

schizophrenic reaction a former diagnosis for the symptoms of schizophrenia that has its origin in the theories of Swiss-born U.S. psychiatrist Adolf Meyer (1866–1950). See also REACTION TYPE.

schizophrenic thinking pervasive, marked impairment of thinking in terms of LOOSENING OF ASSOCIATIONS and slowness of associations, representing POSITIVE SYMPTOMS and NEGATIVE SYMPTOMS, respectively, of schizophrenia. Because thinking must be inferred rather than merely observed, and because no single definition or test or technique of inference has been universally accepted, evaluation is usually limited to examining samples of speech or writing that the individual is inclined to express. On certain psychological tests (e.g., Rorschach, MMPI), schizophrenic thinking is identified in terms of

deviant verbalizations, which are unusual, exaggerated, or otherwise abnormal responses to items presented during the test, for example, inventing a word (see NEOLOGISM) to describe a Rorschach inkblot. On the Whitaker Index of Schizophrenic Thinking (WIST; 1980), which actively tests for both positive and negative schizophrenic thinking, schizophrenic impairment of thinking is defined as simultaneously illogical, impaired, and without apparent awareness, all to a marked degree.

schizophreniform disorder in *DSM–IV–TR*, a disorder whose essential features are identical to those of SCHIZOPHRENIA except that the total duration is between 1 and 6 months (i.e., intermediate between BRIEF PSYCHOTIC DISORDER and schizophrenia) and social or occupational functioning need not be impaired. The diagnosis applies without qualification to an episode of between 1 and 6 months' duration from which the individual has already recovered. The diagnosis is provisional when there is no certainty of recovery within the 6-month period. If the disturbance persists beyond 6 months, the diagnosis would be changed to schizophrenia.

schizophreniform psychosis a type of nonschizophrenic psychosis in which symptoms typical of NUCLEAR SCHIZOPHRENIA are present but there is good PREMORBID ADJUSTMENT, sudden onset in response to a clear precipitating event, and a good prognosis and high probability of return to normal levels of functioning. Characteristics of schizophreniform psychosis can be seen in the *DSM–IV–TR* diagnostic category of SCHIZOPHRENIFORM DISORDER. Also called **schizophreniform state**. [proposed in the late 1930s by Norwegian psychiatrist Gabriel Langfeldt (1895–1983)]

schizophrenogenic *adj.* denoting a factor or influence viewed as causing or contributing to the onset or development of schizophrenia.

schizophrenogenic mother the stereotypic mother of an individual with schizophrenia. She is held to be emotionally disturbed, cold, rejecting, dominating, perfectionistic, and insensitive. At the same time, however, she is overprotective, fosters dependence, and is both seductive and rigidly moralistic. Historically, this type of mother was considered to play a causal role in the development of schizophrenia, but this view is now no longer widely held. See also SCHIZOPHRENOGENIC PARENTS. [first defined in 1948 by German-born U.S. psychiatrist Frieda Fromm-Reichmann (1889–1957)]

schizophrenogenic parents parents whose harmful influences are presumed to cause schizophrenia in their offspring. This concept—the subject of much debate in the 1940s especially—is now considered an oversimplification. See also SCHIZOPHRENOGENIC MOTHER.

schizotaxia *n.* a genetic predisposition to schizophrenia, held to be necessary for the disorder to become manifest and to be activated by severe environmental stresses. [presented as a concept in 1962 by Paul Everett MEEHL]

schizotypal personality disorder in *DSM–IV–TR*, a personality disorder characterized by various oddities of thought, perception, speech, and behavior that are not severe enough to warrant a diagnosis of schizophrenia. Symptoms may include perceptual distortions, MAGICAL THINKING, social isolation, vague speech without incoherence, and inadequate rapport with others due to aloofness or lack of feeling.

schizotypy *n.* in research contexts, a type of personality organization defined by milder forms of POSITIVE SYMPTOMS of schizophrenia, such as COGNITIVE SLIPPAGE, and NEGATIVE SYMPTOMS, such as inability to experience pleasure (see ANHEDONIA). Schizotypy is studied in individuals and family members as a predictor of or liability for the later occurrence of schizophrenia.

Schmid-Fraccaro syndrome see CAT'S-EYE SYNDROME.

school avoidance see SCHOOL REFUSAL.

school counseling guidance, offered at or outside the school to students, parents, and other caregivers, that focuses on students' academic, personal, social, and career adjustment, development, and achievement. Counseling is offered by certified and licensed professionals at all educational levels, from elementary through college and professional school.

school phobia see SCHOOL REFUSAL.

school refusal persistent reluctance to go to school, which usually occurs during the primary school years and is often a symptom of an educational, social, or emotional problem. School refusal may be a feature of SEPARATION ANXIETY DISORDER. It may be triggered by a stressor (e.g., loss of a pet or loved one, a change of school, loss of a friend due to a move) or it may occur after a summer vacation when the child has spent more time with the primary caregiver. School refusal is often associated with physical symptoms (e.g., upset stomach, nausea, dizziness, headache) and anxiety at the start of the day along with complaints that the child is too sick to go to school. Also called **school avoidance**; **school phobia**.

school truancy see TRUANCY.

Schwann cell a type of nonneuronal peripheral nervous system cell (GLIA) that forms the MYELIN SHEATH around axons. Extensions of a single Schwann cell wind tightly and many times around several neighboring axons, so that the myelin sheath consists of multiple layers of the Schwann-cell plasma membrane. [Theodor **Schwann** (1810–1882), German histologist]

schwannoma *n.* a type of tumor that develops from SCHWANN CELLS. Although typically benign, schwannomas tend to displace and compress surrounding neurons as they grow. A schwannoma is very similar to a NEUROFIBROMA but is distinguished by its capsule.

SCID-I acronym for STRUCTURED CLINICAL INTERVIEW FOR DSM–IV AXIS I DISORDERS.

SCID-II acronym for STRUCTURED CLINICAL INTERVIEW FOR DSM–IV AXIS II PERSONALITY DISORDERS.

scientist-practitioner model a concept for the university training of doctoral clinical (or other applied) psychologists in the United States that is intended to prepare individuals both to provide services and to conduct research on mental health problems, essentially integrating these two functions in their professional work by making a laboratory of their applied settings and studying their phenomena and the results of their administrations scientifically. The purpose of the model is to ensure that practitioners contribute to the scientific development of their field. The training emphasizes research techniques applicable to applied (therapeutic) settings. The model emerged from a conference held in Boulder, Colorado, in 1949, which was sponsored by the U.S. Veterans Administration and the National Institute of Mental Health. Also called **Boulder model**.

SCL-90-R abbreviation for SYMPTOM CHECKLIST-90-REVISED.

scopolamine *n.* an ANTICHOLINERGIC DRUG found as an alkaloid in HENBANE and related plants. Its most common therapeutic use is for the prevention of motion sickness; in the past it was sometimes used in labor to produce twilight sleep (a conscious but drowsy state with lack of sensitivity to pain) and amnesia for the event. Small doses can have a sedative effect, but large doses may cause restlessness, agitation, or delirium. Also called **hyoscine**. U.S. trade names: Scopace; Transderm-Scop.

scopophilia *n.* sexual pleasure derived from watching others in a state of nudity, undressing, or engaging in sexual activity. If scopophilia is persistent, the condition is essentially VOYEURISM. Also called **scoptophilia**; **scotophilia**. See also ACTIVE SCOPOPHILIA; PASSIVE SCOPOPHILIA.

scotomization *n.* in psychoanalytic theory, the tendency to ignore or be blind to impulses or memories that would threaten the individual's EGO. Scotomization is a defensive process and may also be a form of RESISTANCE. Also called **scotomatization**. See also BLIND SPOT.

scotophilia *n.* see SCOPOPHILIA.

screen defense in psychoanalytic theory, a defense in which a memory, fantasy, or dream image is unconsciously employed to conceal the real but disturbing object of one's feelings.

screening *n.* **1.** a procedure or program to detect early signs of a disease in an individual or population. Individuals at increased hereditary risk of developing a disease are advised to follow regular screening plans. See also SCREENING TEST. **2.** the initial evaluation of a patient to determine his or her suitability for medical or psychological treatment generally, a specific treatment approach, or referral to a treatment facility. This evaluation is made on the basis of medical or psychological history, MENTAL STATUS EXAMINATION, diagnostic formulation, or some combination of these. **3.** the process of selecting items for a psychological test.

screening test any testing procedure designed to separate people or objects according to a fixed characteristic or property. Screening tests are typically used to distinguish people who have a disease, disorder, or predisease condition from those who do not; they may be used, for example, in primary health care settings to identify people who are depressed. Screening tests are designed to be broadly sensitive, and subsequent highly specific or focused testing is often required to confirm the results.

screening tests for young children checklists or assessment protocols that have been developed to detect DEVELOPMENTAL DELAYS, criterion behaviors, or other risk factors associated with certain conditions or disorders during infancy and early childhood through the primary school years. Such tests do not provide diagnostic information, but instead are used with large numbers of children in order to identify those who may require assessment for emotional disturbance, mental retardation, neurological conditions, or other disorders.

screen memory in psychoanalytic theory, a memory of a childhood experience, usually trivial in nature, that unconsciously serves the purpose of concealing or screening out an associated experience of a more significant and perhaps traumatic nature. Also called **cover memory**; **replacement memory**.

script *n.* a cognitive schematic structure—a mental road map—containing the basic actions (and their temporal and causal relations) that comprise a complex action. Also called **script schema**.

script analysis in TRANSACTIONAL ANALYSIS, the analysis of the client's unconscious life plan, or SCRIPT. The script is based on fantasies, attitudes, and games or ploys derived from the individual's early experiences. [developed by Canadian-born U.S. psychiatrist Eric Berne (1910–1970)]

script theory **1.** in TRANSACTIONAL ANALYSIS, the theory that an individual's approach to social situations follows a sequence that was learned and established early in life. **2.** the proposition that discrete affects, such as joy and fear, are prime motivators of behavior and that personality structure and function can be understood in terms of self-defining affective scenes and scripts. [proposed by U.S. personality psychologist Silvan S. Tomkins (1911–1991)]

SCU abbreviation for SPECIAL CARE UNIT.

sculpting *n.* see FAMILY SCULPTING.

SD abbreviation for STANDARD DEVIATION.

SDAT abbreviation for SENILE DEMENTIA OF THE ALZHEIMER'S TYPE.

S data see Q DATA.

SDS abbreviation for ZUNG SELF-RATING DEPRESSION SCALE.

Seashore Rhythm Test a neuropsychological test in which the participant listens to a recording of pairs of rhythmic patterns and indicates whether they are the same or different. The test is used by neuropsychologists to measure generalized cerebral function. [Carl **Seashore**, Swedish-born U.S. Psychologist (1866–1949)]

seasonal affective disorder (**SAD**) a MOOD DISORDER in which there is a predictable occurrence of MAJOR DEPRESSIVE EPISODES, MANIC EPISODES, or both at particular times of the year. The typical pattern is the occurrence of major depressive episodes during the fall or winter months. Also called **seasonal mood disorder**.

seasonality effect the proposal that individuals with schizophrenia are most likely to have been born during the period January to April. The hypothesized significance of the season of birth is uncertain. See also VIRAL HYPOTHESIS OF SCHIZOPHRENIA. [advanced by U.S. psychiatrist E. Fuller Torrey (1938–)]

seasonal mood disorder see SEASONAL AFFECTIVE DISORDER.

Seckel's bird-headed dwarfism a familial disorder, now linked to a defect on chromosome 3 (locus 3q22.1–24), marked by MICROCEPHALY, a beaklike nose, prominent eyes, narrow face, and short stature. Typically, affected individuals show intellectual skills consistent with mild to profound mental retardation. Also called **Seckel nanism**; **Virchow–Seckel syndrome**. [reported in 1960 by Helmut P. G. **Seckel** (1900–1960), German physician; the term "bird-headed dwarf" was introduced by Rudolf **Virchow** (1821–1902), German pathologist]

seclusiveness *n.* the tendency to isolate oneself from social contacts or human relationships. See also PRIVACY. **—seclusive** *adj.*

secondary aging changes due to biological aging, but accelerated by disabilities resulting from disease or produced by extrinsic factors, such as stress, trauma, lifestyle, and environment. Secondary aging is often distinguished from PRIMARY AGING, which is governed by inborn and age-related processes, but the distinction is not a precise one.

secondary amenorrhea see AMENORRHEA.

secondary appraisal in the COGNITIVE APPRAISAL THEORY of emotion, assessment of one's ability to cope with the consequences of an interaction with the environment, which follows a PRIMARY APPRAISAL. See also COPING POTENTIAL; CORE RELATIONAL THEMES. [proposed by U.S. psychologist Richard S. Lazarus (1922–2002)]

secondary autoeroticism a type of AUTOEROTICISM not involving direct masturbation but produced instead by indirect association with the erogenous zones (e.g., sexual arousal from contact with urine).

secondary care health care services provided by medical specialists (e.g., cardiologists, urologists, dermatologists), to whom, typically, patients are referred by the PRIMARY CARE PROVIDER. Compare PRIMARY CARE; TERTIARY CARE.

secondary cause a contributing factor to the onset of symptoms of a disorder that in itself would not be sufficient to cause the disorder.

secondary control behavior that, while not directly controlling, is aimed at producing a sense of control by altering oneself (e.g., one's values, priorities, behavior) so as to bring oneself in line with the environment. Compare PRIMARY CONTROL. See LOCUS OF CONTROL.

secondary coping a stress-management strategy in which a person seeks to adjust his or her hopes, expectations, attributions, and other aspects of the self to achieve a better fit with current events and prevailing conditions. This adaptation of oneself to the environment represents a more internally focused COPING STRATEGY that generally is applied when stressors cannot easily be counteracted directly. It includes such behaviors as distraction, positive thinking, COGNITIVE RESTRUCTURING, and rethinking about the stressor or problem in such a way as to facilitate acceptance. Also called **secondary control coping**. Compare PRIMARY COPING. [identified in 1982 by Fred M. Rothbaum (1949–2011) and John R. Weisz (1945–), U.S. clinical and developmental psychologists, and Samuel S. Snyder, U.S. developmental psychologist]

secondary defense symptoms a set of defensive measures employed by obsessive individuals when their primary defenses against repressed memories no longer offer protection. The secondary defenses usually include obsessional thinking, DOUBTING MANIA, and speculations, which may be expressed as phobias, ceremonials, superstitions, or pedantry.

secondary deviance see PRIMARY DEVIANCE.

secondary drive a learned drive; that is, a drive that is developed through association with or generalization from a PRIMARY DRIVE. For example, in an AVOIDANCE CONDITIONING experiment in which a rat must go from one compartment into another to escape from an electric shock, the secondary drive is fear of the shock and the primary drive with which it is associated is avoidance of pain. Also called **acquired drive**.

secondary elaboration in psychoanalysis, the process of altering the memory and description of a dream to make it more coherent and less fragmentary or distorted. See also DREAMWORK.

secondary emotion an emotion that is not

S

recognized or manifested universally across cultures or that requires social experience for its construction. For some theorists, PRIDE represents a secondary emotion, stemming from the conjunction of a PRIMARY EMOTION (JOY) and a favorable public reaction. Other secondary emotions include ENVY, LOVE, and JEALOUSY.

secondary environment an environment that is incidental or marginally important in a person's life and in which interactions with others are comparatively brief and impersonal. An example is a bank or a shop. Compare PRIMARY ENVIRONMENT.

secondary erectile dysfunction **1.** a condition in which a man is no longer capable of producing or maintaining a penile erection sufficient for sexual intercourse, although he was previously capable of performing intercourse successfully. **2.** a condition in which a man can have an erection in some situations (e.g., during masturbation) or with some partners, but not during sexual activity with his current primary partner. See also ERECTILE DYSFUNCTION; IMPOTENCE; MALE ERECTILE DISORDER. Compare PRIMARY ERECTILE DYSFUNCTION.

secondary gain in psychoanalytic theory, advantages derived from a NEUROSIS in addition to the PRIMARY GAINS of relief from anxiety or internal conflict. Examples are extra attention, sympathy, avoidance of work, and domination of others. Such gains are secondary in that they are derived from others' reactions to the illness instead of causal factors. They often prolong the neurosis and create resistance to therapy. Also called **advantage by illness**.

secondary group one of the larger, less intimate, more goal-focused groups typical of more complex societies. These social groups influence members' attitudes, beliefs, and actions, but as a supplement to the influence of small, more interpersonally intensive PRIMARY GROUPS. Whereas primary groups, such as families and children's play groups, are the initial socializing agents, adolescents and adults are increasingly influenced by such secondary groups as work groups, clubs, congregations, associations, and so on.

S

secondary identification in psychoanalytic theory, identification with admired figures other than the parents.

secondary memory (**SM**) memory that retains a large number of items relatively permanently, in contrast to PRIMARY MEMORY. The term was used in the DUAL-STORE MODEL OF MEMORY before being replaced by LONG-TERM MEMORY. [introduced by William JAMES]

secondary mental deficiency below average intelligence due to disease or brain injury rather than congenital factors.

secondary mood disorder a MOOD DISORDER that occurs in the context of another disorder and whose symptoms may be caused by the other disorder.

secondary motivation motivation that is created by personal or social incentives (e.g., the urge to learn classical music or become a movie star) rather than by primary, physiological needs (e.g., for food).

secondary personality a second discrete identity that repeatedly controls behavior in individuals with DISSOCIATIVE IDENTITY DISORDER. This personality state is in sharp contrast to the original, PRIMARY PERSONALITY and generally has a different name as well as dramatically different attitudes, behavior, manner of speaking, and style of dress.

secondary prevention intervention for individuals or groups that demonstrate early psychological or physical symptoms, difficulties, or conditions (i.e., subclinical-level problems), which is intended to prevent the development of more serious dysfunction or illness. Compare PRIMARY PREVENTION; TERTIARY PREVENTION.

secondary process in psychoanalytic theory, conscious, rational mental activities under the control of the EGO and the REALITY PRINCIPLE. These thought processes, which include problem-solving, judgment, and systematic thinking, enable individuals to meet both the external demands of the environment and the internal demands of their instincts in rational, effective ways. Also called **secondary process thinking**. Compare PRIMARY PROCESS.

secondary reinforcement **1.** in OPERANT CONDITIONING, the process in which a neutral stimulus acquires the ability to influence the future probability of a particular response by virtue of being paired with another stimulus that naturally enhances such probability. That is, the initially neutral stimulus or circumstance functions as effective REINFORCEMENT only after special experience or training. For example, a person teaching a dog to understand the command "sit" might provide a treat and a simultaneous popping noise from a clicker tool each time the dog successfully performs the behavior. Eventually, the clicker noise itself can be used alone to maintain the desired behavior, with no treat reward being necessary. **2.** the contingent occurrence of such a stimulus or circumstance after a response. Also called **conditioned reinforcement**. Compare PRIMARY REINFORCEMENT.

secondary repression see REPRESSION PROPER.

secondary sexual dysfunction any disturbance in sexual functioning (see SEXUAL DYSFUNCTION) that is not lifelong or that occurs only with some partners or in some situations. Compare PRIMARY SEXUAL DYSFUNCTION.

secondary stuttering dysfluency in speech characterized by uncomfortable awareness and attempts to modify the dysfluency. Effort, fear, and anxiety are typically conveyed through abnormal or unusual movements of the face, head, or body (e.g., tics, blinking, lip tremor, head jerks, fist clenching). Compare PRIMARY STUTTERING.

secondary symptoms **1.** according to Swiss psychiatrist Eugen Bleuler (1857–1939), those symptoms of SCHIZOPHRENIA, such as delusions and hallucinations, that are shared with other disorders and therefore not specifically diagnostic of schizophrenia. Bleuler theorized that these symptoms do not stem directly from the disease but rather begin to operate when the person reacts to some internal or external process. Also called **accessory symptoms**. Compare FUNDAMENTAL SYMPTOMS. **2.** symptoms that are not a direct result of a disorder but are associated with or incidental to those that are (e.g., social avoidance accompanying obsessive-compulsive disorder). **3.** symptoms that appear in the second stage of a disorder or that are derived from an earlier traumatic event, disease process, or disordered condition.

second-generation antipsychotic see ATYPICAL ANTIPSYCHOTIC.

second messenger an ion or molecule inside a cell whose concentration increases or decreases in response to stimulation of a cell RECEPTOR by an agonist (e.g., a neurotransmitter, hormone, or drug). The second messenger acts to relay and amplify the signal from the agonist (the "first messenger") by triggering a range of cellular activities. For example, receptors for catecholamine neurotransmitters (epinephrine and norepinephrine) are coupled to G PROTEINS, whose activation in postsynaptic neurons affects levels of second messengers that act to open or close certain ION CHANNELS. Second messengers include CYCLIC AMP, IP_3 (see INOSITOL PHOSPHATES), and calcium ions.

second-order factor a factor that results from the factoring of correlated factors by correlating the derived factors among themselves. Compare FIRST-ORDER FACTOR.

second-person perspective the point of view of one person addressing another and aware of the other's consciousness, characterized by "I–you" communication. Compare FIRST-PERSON PERSPECTIVE; THIRD-PERSON PERSPECTIVE.

SECs abbreviation for STIMULUS EVALUATION CHECKS.

sector therapy a therapeutic procedure in which patterns of association that have produced emotional problems in the client are replaced by more realistic and constructive patterns. Unlike DEPTH THERAPY, this process, described as **goal-limited adjustment therapy**, focuses on specific areas (sectors) revealed by the client's own autobiographical account. The procedure enables the client to understand his or her faulty associations and gradually establish new ones with the aid of the therapist. [developed by Felix Deutsch (1884–1964)]

secure attachment **1.** in the STRANGE SITUATION, the positive parent–child relationship, in which the child displays confidence when the parent is present, shows mild distress when the parent leaves, and quickly reestablishes contact when the parent returns. **2.** an adult attachment style that combines a positive INTERNAL WORKING MODEL OF ATTACHMENT of oneself, characterized by a view of oneself as worthy of love, and a positive internal working model of attachment of others, characterized by the view that others are generally accepting and responsive. Compare DISMISSIVE ATTACHMENT; FEARFUL ATTACHMENT; PREOCCUPIED ATTACHMENT.

secure treatment setting a locked residential setting providing safety and treatment services for adolescent or adult offenders, usually felons, with mental retardation or developmental disabilities.

security *n.* a sense of safety, confidence, and freedom from apprehension. In psychology, security is believed to be engendered by such factors as warm, accepting parents and friends; development of age-appropriate skills and abilities; and experiences that build EGO STRENGTH. The development of security in the psychotherapeutic context (most often referred to as **trust**) is seen as a mediating goal that encourages open exploration of emotional and behavioral issues and is viewed to be part of a strong and healthy THERAPIST–PATIENT RELATIONSHIP.

security blanket see TRANSITIONAL OBJECT.

security operations in the approach of U.S. psychoanalyst Harry Stack Sullivan (1892–1949), a variety of interpersonal defensive measures, such as arrogance, boredom, or anger, that are used as a protection against anxiety or loss of self-esteem.

sedative **1.** *n.* a drug that has a calming effect and therefore relieves anxiety, agitation, or behavioral excitement by depressing the central nervous system. The degree of sedation depends on the agent, the size of the dose, the method of administration, and the condition of the patient. A drug that sedates in small doses may induce sleep in larger doses and may be used as a HYPNOTIC; such drugs are commonly known as **sedative–hypnotics**. BENZODIAZEPINES are commonly used as sedatives. **2.** *adj.* producing sedation.

sedative amnestic disorder see SEDATIVE-, HYPNOTIC-, OR ANXIOLYTIC-INDUCED PERSISTING AMNESTIC DISORDER.

sedative, hypnotic, and anxiolytic drugs CNS DEPRESSANTS that have been developed for therapeutic use because of their calming effect (i.e., sedatives) and ability to induce sleep (i.e., hypnotics) and reduce anxiety (i.e., anxiolytics). They include the BARBITURATES, MEPROBAMATE, and the BENZODIAZEPINES. At low doses these drugs are prescribed for daytime use to reduce anxiety; at higher doses many of the same drugs are prescribed as sleeping pills. Although efficacious when used sparingly, over the long term all induce marked tolerance, and cessation of use can precipitate potentially life-threatening withdrawal phenomena. Acute abuse can yield dangerous intoxication effects, and chronic abuse can cause a range of other serious, irreversible conditions.

sedative, hypnotic, or anxiolytic abuse in *DSM–IV–TR*, a pattern of use of sedative, hypnotic, or anxiolytic drugs manifested by recurrent significant adverse consequences related to the repeated ingestion of these substances. This diagnosis is preempted by the diagnosis of SEDATIVE, HYPNOTIC, OR ANXIOLYTIC DEPENDENCE: If the criteria for sedative, hypnotic, or anxiolytic abuse and sedative, hypnotic, or anxiolytic dependence are both met, only the latter diagnosis is given.

sedative, hypnotic, or anxiolytic dependence in *DSM–IV–TR*, a cluster of cognitive, behavioral, and physiological symptoms indicating continued use of sedative, hypnotic, or anxiolytic drugs despite significant problems related to these substances. There is a pattern of repeated ingestion resulting in tolerance, characteristic withdrawal symptoms on cessation of use (see SEDATIVE, HYPNOTIC, OR ANXIOLYTIC WITHDRAWAL), and an uncontrollable drive to continue use. See also SEDATIVE, HYPNOTIC, OR ANXIOLYTIC ABUSE.

sedative-, hypnotic-, or anxiolytic-induced persisting amnestic disorder a disturbance in memory due to the persisting effects of sedative, hypnotic, or anxiolytic drugs. The ability to learn new information or to recall previously learned information is impaired severely enough to interfere markedly with social or occupational functioning and to represent a significant decline from a previous level of functioning. Unlike those diagnosed with ALCOHOL-INDUCED PERSISTING AMNESTIC DISORDER, people diagnosed with this disorder can recover memory functioning.

sedative, hypnotic, or anxiolytic intoxication a reversible syndrome specific to the recent ingestion of sedative, hypnotic, or anxiolytic drugs. It includes clinically significant behavioral or psychological changes (e.g., inappropriate sexual or aggressive behavior, mood lability, impaired judgment, and impaired social or occupational functioning), as well as one or more signs of physiological involvement (e.g., slurred speech, an unsteady gait, involuntary eye movements, memory or attentional problems, incoordination, and stupor or coma).

sedative, hypnotic, or anxiolytic withdrawal in *DSM–IV–TR*, a characteristic withdrawal syndrome, potentially life-threatening, that develops after cessation of (or reduction in) prolonged, heavy consumption of sedative, hypnotic, or anxiolytic drugs. Symptoms may include autonomic hyperactivity; increased hand tremor; insomnia; nausea or vomiting; transient visual, tactile, or auditory hallucinations or illusions; psychomotor agitation; anxiety; either a transient worsening (rebound) of the anxiety condition that prompted treatment or a recurrence of that condition; and tonic–clonic seizures. Risks of physiological dependence and withdrawal are present with long-term use of all benzodiazepines and similarly acting anxiolytics. Short-acting benzodiazepines pose particular withdrawal risks, and patients taking high doses of short-acting agents must be carefully withdrawn over an extended period to avoid adverse outcomes. See also SUBSTANCE WITHDRAWAL.

sedative, hypnotic, or anxiolytic withdrawal delirium a reversible syndrome that develops over a short period of time (usually hours to days) following cessation of prolonged, heavy consumption of sedative, hypnotic, or anxiolytic drugs. It involves disturbance of consciousness (e.g., reduced ability to focus, sustain, or shift attention), accompanied by changes in cognition (e.g., memory deficit, disorientation, or language disturbance) in excess of those usually associated with withdrawal from these substances. See also SEDATIVE, HYPNOTIC, OR ANXIOLYTIC WITHDRAWAL.

sedative–hypnotics *pl. n.* see SEDATIVE.

seduction *n.* **1.** the inducement of a person to participate in sexual intercourse, without the use of force. Local laws vary in their interpretation of seduction, and common law does not recognize it as a crime. However, some laws define seduction as a crime if it involves a promise by a man to marry a woman in the near future if she will submit to intercourse now. **2.** more generally, the act or process of attracting or alluring. **—seduce** *vb.*

segmentation *n.* a technique of BEHAVIOR MODIFICATION in which a complex sequence of behaviors is divided into parts so that the client can more easily learn and master one or two at a time.

segregated model in evaluation research, an administrative relationship, used in FORMATIVE EVALUATION, between the program director, the production unit, and the evaluation unit as three distinct entities. In this model the production unit and the evaluation unit share equal importance and improved access to the program director. Compare INTEGRATED MODEL.

seizure *n.* a discrete episode of uncontrolled, excessive electrical discharge of neurons in the brain. The resulting clinical symptoms vary based on the type and location of the seizure. See EPILEPSY.

selection *n.* the process of choosing an item (e.g., an individual or object) for a purpose, such as study, testing, classifying, or working (employee selection).

selective amnesia the forgetting of particular issues, people, or events that is too extensive to be explained by normal forgetfulness and that is posited to be organized according to emotional, rather than temporal, parameters. The selectivity appears to be of benefit to or convenient for

S

the person who cannot remember. See also DISSOCIATIVE AMNESIA.

selective attention concentration on certain stimuli in the environment and not others, enabling important stimuli to be distinguished from peripheral or incidental ones. Selective attention is typically measured by instructing participants to attend to some sources of information while ignoring others and then determining their effectiveness in doing this. Also called **controlled attention**; **directed attention**.

selective estrogen receptor modulators (**SERMs**) see ANTIESTROGEN.

selective inattention 1. unmindful absence or failure of attention to particular physical or emotional stimuli. **2.** a perceptual defense in which anxiety-provoking or threatening experiences are ignored or forgotten. [defined by U.S. psychiatrist Harry Stack Sullivan (1892–1949)]

selective mutism in *DSM–IV–TR*, a rare disorder, most commonly but not exclusively found in young children, characterized by a persistent failure to speak in certain social situations (e.g., at school) despite the ability to speak and to understand spoken language. Age of onset is usually before 5 years, and the failure to speak lasts at least 1 month (not counting the first month at school, when many children are shy about talking). Generally, these individuals function normally in other ways, although some may have additional disabilities. Most learn age-appropriate skills and academic subjects. Currently, selective mutism is thought to be related to severe anxiety and SOCIAL PHOBIA, but the exact cause is unknown. It was formerly (in *DSM–III* and earlier editions) called **elective mutism**.

selective optimization with compensation a process used in SUCCESSFUL AGING to adapt to biological and psychological deficits associated with aging. The process involves emphasizing and enhancing those capacities affected only minimally by aging (optimization) and developing new means of maintaining functioning in those areas that are significantly affected (compensation). [described by German psychologists Paul Baltes (1939–2006) and Margret Baltes (1939–1999)]

selective reminding test any memory test in which the participant is given the answer when it cannot be remembered so that he or she is more likely to answer correctly on subsequent trials. For instance, if the word "pencil" is presented on a list-learning task and the participant is unable to recall it, the word would then be presented along with other words not recalled.

selective response a response that has been differentiated from a group of possible alternative responses.

selective retention variation between individuals in the capacity to remember with respect to the vividness, accuracy, quantity, and specific contents of memory. This selectivity is usually determined by such factors as interest, experience, motivation, and emotional arousal.

selective serotonin reuptake inhibitor see SSRI.

selective silence in psychotherapy, a prolonged silence imposed by the therapist to generate tension that may encourage the client to speak, thus beginning or resuming communication in a session.

selegiline *n.* a drug used as an adjunct in the treatment of Parkinson's disease. At low doses it selectively inhibits the enzyme MONOAMINE OXIDASE B (MAO-B)—which degrades the neurotransmitter dopamine—and thereby increases levels of dopamine in the brain. Because selegiline is an irreversible MONOAMINE OXIDASE INHIBITOR (MAOI), and at higher doses it inhibits both MAO-A and MAO-B, great care must be taken not to exceed the therapeutic dosage in order to avoid the severe adverse effects of nonselective, irreversible MAOIs. Adverse drug interactions have been observed with commonly prescribed antidepressants, and concurrent administration of selegiline and these should be avoided. Also called **deprenyl**. U.S. trade name: **Eldepryl**.

self *n.* the totality of the individual, consisting of all characteristic attributes, conscious and unconscious, mental and physical. Apart from its basic reference to personal identity, being, and experience, the term's use in psychology is extremely wide-ranging and lacks uniformity. According to William JAMES, self can refer either to the person as the target of appraisal (i.e., one introspectively evaluates how one is doing) or to the person as the source of AGENCY (i.e., one attributes the source of regulation of perception, thought, and behavior to one's body or mind). Carl JUNG maintained that the self gradually develops by a process of INDIVIDUATION, which is not complete until late maturity is reached. Alfred ADLER identified the self with the individual's LIFESTYLE, the manner in which he or she seeks fulfillment. German-born U.S. psychoanalyst Karen D. Horney (1885–1952) held that one's REAL SELF, as opposed to one's idealized self-image, consists of one's unique capacities for growth and development. Gordon ALLPORT substituted the word PROPRIUM for self, and conceived of it as the essence of the individual, consisting of a gradually developing body sense, IDENTITY, self-estimate, and set of personal values, attitudes, and intentions. See also FALSE SELF; PHENOMENAL SELF; SENSE OF SELF; TRUE SELF.

self-abasement *n.* **1.** the act of degrading or demeaning oneself. **2.** extreme submission to the will of another person. Also called **self-debasement**.

self-abuse *n.* a euphemism for MASTURBATION. The term apparently evolved from an attempt by certain 18th-century religious and medical writers to identify masturbation as "the sin of Onan"

S

(see ONANISM) and to substantiate unscientific claims that a number of disorders (e.g., blindness and mental retardation) were produced by masturbation.

self-acceptance *n.* a relatively objective sense or recognition of one's abilities and achievements, together with acknowledgment and acceptance of one's limitations. Self-acceptance is often viewed as a major component of mental health.

self-accusation *n.* the act of blaming oneself unjustifiably for negative occurrences. It is often associated with a MAJOR DEPRESSIVE EPISODE.

self-activity *n.* the performance of actions that have been decided upon by oneself, without dependence on outside activators.

self-actualization *n.* the complete realization of that of which one is capable, involving maximum development of abilities and full involvement in and appreciation for life, particularly as manifest in PEAK EXPERIENCES. The term is associated particularly with Abraham MASLOW, who viewed the process of striving toward full potential as fundamental yet obtainable only after the basic needs of physical survival, safety, love and belongingness, and esteem are fulfilled. Also called **self-realization**.

self-advocacy *n.* the process by which people make their own choices and exercise their rights in a self-determined manner. For people with developmental and other disabilities, for example, self-advocacy might entail promoting increased control of resources related to services and making informed decisions about what services to accept, reject, or insist be altered. See also CONSUMER EMPOWERMENT.

self-affirmation *n.* **1.** any behavior by which a person expresses a positive attitude toward his or her self, often by a positive assertion of his or her values, attributes, or group memberships. SELF-AFFIRMATION THEORY assumes that the desire for self-affirmation is basic and pervasive and that many different behaviors reflect this motive. **2.** in psychotherapy, a positive statement or set of such statements about the self that a person is required to repeat on a regular basis, often as part of a treatment for depression, negative thinking, or low self-esteem. **3.** see COMPENSATORY SELF-ENHANCEMENT. **4.** in performance or competitive situations, any thought about oneself that is believable and vivid and that reinforces positive characteristics, abilities, or skills.

self-affirmation theory a theory postulating that people are motivated to maintain views of themselves as well adapted, moral, competent, stable, and able to control important outcomes. When some aspect of this self-view is challenged, people experience psychological discomfort. They may attempt to reduce this discomfort by directly resolving the inconsistency between the new information and the self, by affirming some other aspect of the self, or both. Self-affirmation theory has been used to provide an alternative explanation to COGNITIVE DISSONANCE THEORY for some phenomena. See also DISSONANCE REDUCTION; SELF-CONSISTENCY PERSPECTIVE OF COGNITIVE DISSONANCE THEORY. [originally proposed by U.S. psychologist Claude M. Steele (1946–)]

self-alienation *n.* a state in which the individual feels a stranger to himself or herself, typically accompanied by significant emotional distancing. The self-alienated individual is frequently unaware of or largely unable to describe his or her own intrapsychic processes.

self-alien syndrome any of various conditions in which an aspect of oneself is perceived as outside one's normal experience and control. This perception is common in neurological and psychological disorders but also occurs in such everyday situations as failures of impulse control.

self-analysis *n.* **1.** generally, the investigation or exploration of the SELF for the purpose of better understanding of personal thoughts, emotions, and behavior. Self-analysis occurs consciously and unconsciously in many contexts of daily life. To some degree or other, and with the assistance and sometimes interpretation of the therapist, it is a particularly crucial process within most forms of psychotherapy. **2.** an attempt to apply the principles of PSYCHOANALYSIS to a study of one's own drives, feelings, and behavior. It was proposed by Sigmund FREUD early in his career as part of the preparation of an analyst but later dropped in favor of a TRAINING ANALYSIS. Much of Freud's early theory of psychoanalysis was based on his own self-analysis as described in *The Interpretation of Dreams* (1900). **—self-analytic** *adj.*

self-appraisal *n.* see SELF-CONCEPT.

self as agent the aspect of the self that has goals, plans, and some degree of control over actions. It contrasts with the self as object and is synonymous with the "I" of William JAMES.

self as known the aspect of the self that is known through reflection. It is sometimes contrasted with the self as knower.

self-assertion *n.* the act of putting forward one's own opinions or taking actions that express one's needs, rights, or wishes. Self-assertion is often seen as a goal of treatment and in some cases is specifically targeted by structured group treatments. **—self-assertive** *adj.*

self-assessment *n.* see SELF-CONCEPT.

self-as-target effect the tendency to assume wrongly that, or to overestimate the degree to which, external events refer to the self. For example, a person may think quite wrongly that other people's conversations and actions, or even music lyrics, are directed at him or her. In its milder forms the self-as-target effect is common and normal, but extreme forms are associated with PARANOIA.

self-awareness *n.* self-focused attention or knowledge. There has been a continuing contro-

S

versy over whether nonhuman animals have self-awareness. Evidence of this in animals most often is determined by whether an individual can use a mirror to groom an otherwise unseen spot on its own forehead. A few chimpanzees, gorillas, and orangutans have passed this test.

self-awareness theory any hypothetical construct that attempts to describe how self-focused attention occurs and what purpose it serves. Distinctions are sometimes made between subjective self-awareness, arising directly from the observation and experience of oneself as the source of perception and behavior, and objective self-awareness, arising from comparison between the self and (a) the behaviors, attitudes, and traits of others or (b) some perceived standard for social correctness in any one of these areas.

self-blaming depression a MAJOR DEPRESSIVE EPISODE in which unreasonable guilt is a prominent feature.

self-care *n.* activities required for personal care, such as eating, dressing, or grooming, that can be managed by an individual without the assistance of others.

self-censure *n.* an individual's conscious self-blame, condemnation, or guilt in judging his or her own behavior to be inconsistent with personal values or standards of moral conduct.

self-completion theory the theory that many behaviors are performed to claim desired identities, so that by behaving in a certain way one is symbolically "proving" oneself to be a certain kind of person. Insecurity about being the sort of person one wants to be is often the reason for engaging in such self-completing acts. For example, a person who takes pride in being very fit and active may respond to the first signs of illness or exhaustion by increasing, rather than reducing, his or her activities.

self-complexity *n.* the degree to which different aspects of the SELF-CONCEPT are disconnected from one another. Low self-complexity entails considerable integration; high self-complexity results from COMPARTMENTALIZATION, so that what affects one part of the self may not affect other parts.

self-concept *n.* one's description and evaluation of oneself, including psychological and physical characteristics, qualities, and skills. Self-concepts contribute to the individual's sense of identity over time. The conscious representation of self-concept is dependent in part on unconscious schematization of the self (see SCHEMA). Although self-concepts are usually available to some degree to the consciousness, they may be inhibited from representation yet still influence judgment, mood, and behavioral patterns. Also called **self-appraisal**; **self-assessment**; **self-evaluation**; **self-rating**. See SELF-IMAGE; SELF-PERCEPTION.

self-concept test a type of personality assessment designed to determine how participants view their own attitudes, values, goals, body concept, personal worth, and abilities. The TENNESSEE SELF-CONCEPT SCALE is an example.

self-confidence *n.* self-assurance, or trust in one's own abilities, capacities, and judgment. Because it is most typically viewed as a positive personality trait, the encouragement or bolstering of self-confidence is often a mediate or end goal in psychotherapeutic treatment. —**self-confident** *adj.*

self-confrontation *n.* examining one's own attitudes, behaviors, and shortcomings to provide an impetus to change and to gain insight into how one is perceived by others.

self-conscious emotion an emotion that celebrates or condemns the self and its actions, generated when the self is known to be the object of another person's evaluation. Self-conscious emotions include SHAME, PRIDE, GUILT, and EMBARRASSMENT. Recently, the term **other-conscious emotions** has been suggested as a better name for these emotions, to emphasize the importance of the appraisal of other human beings in generating them.

self-consciousness *n.* **1.** a personality trait associated with the tendency to reflect on or think about oneself. Psychological use of the term refers only to individual differences in self-reflection, not to embarrassment or awkwardness. Some researchers have distinguished between two varieties of self-consciousness: (a) **private self-consciousness**, or the degree to which people think about private, internal aspects of themselves (e.g., their own thoughts, motives, and feelings) that are not directly open to observation by others; and (b) **public self-consciousness**, or the degree to which people think about public, external aspects of themselves (e.g., their physical appearance, mannerisms, and overt behavior) that can be observed by others. **2.** extreme sensitivity about one's own behavior, appearance, or other attributes and excessive concern about the impression one makes on others, which leads to embarrassment or awkwardness in the presence of others. —**self-conscious** *adj.*

self-consistency *n.* behavior or personality that has a high degree of internal harmony and stability.

self-consistency perspective of cognitive dissonance theory a variation of COGNITIVE DISSONANCE THEORY postulating that COGNITIVE DISSONANCE is particularly likely to occur when an inconsistency involves some aspect of the self. This perspective differs from SELF-AFFIRMATION THEORY in that it assumes that dissonance can only be reduced by resolving the specific inconsistency that gave rise to the discomfort; it does not allow for the possibility that dissonance can be reduced by affirming some other aspect of the self. [originally proposed by U.S. psychologist Elliot Aronson (1932–)]

self-construal *n.* any specific belief about the

SELF. The term is used particularly in connection with the distinction between INDEPENDENT SELF-CONSTRUALS and INTERDEPENDENT SELF-CONSTRUALS. A self-construal is much more specific than a SELF-CONCEPT.

self-control *n.* the ability to be in command of one's behavior (overt, covert, emotional, or physical) and to restrain or inhibit one's impulses. In circumstances in which short-term gain is pitted against long-term loss or long-term greater gain, it is the ability to opt for the long-term outcome. Choice of the short-term outcome is called **impulsiveness** (see IMPULSIVE). See also SELF-DISCIPLINE; SELF-REGULATION. **—self-controlled** *adj.*

self-control technique a technique in BEHAVIOR THERAPY in which clients are trained to evaluate their own behavior and reinforce desired behavior with appropriate material or social rewards.

self-control therapy a form of BEHAVIOR THERAPY that involves self-monitoring (e.g., diaries of behavior), self-evaluation, goal setting, BEHAVIORAL CONTRACTS, teaching, self-reinforcement, and relapse prevention. Also called **self-management therapy**. [developed by Austrian-born U.S. clinical psychologist Frederick H. Kanfer (1925–2002)]

self-correction *n.* any situation in which an individual makes an error but fixes it spontaneously, with no external instructions or cues.

self-criticism *n.* the examination and evaluation of one's behavior, with recognition of one's weaknesses, errors, and shortcomings. Self-criticism can have both positive and negative effects; for example, a tendency toward harsh self-criticism is thought by some to be a risk factor for depression. **—self-critical** *adj.*

self-debasement *n.* see SELF-ABASEMENT.

self-deception *n.* the process or result of convincing oneself of the truth of something that is false or invalid, particularly the overestimation of one's abilities and concurrent failure to recognize one's own limitations.

self-defeating behavior actions by an individual that invite failure or misfortune and thus prevent him or her from attaining goals or fulfilling desires. An example is a college student procrastinating about studying and subsequently getting a poor grade on an important exam.

self-defeating personality disorder in *DSM–III–R* (but not *DSM–IV–TR*), a personality disorder characterized by a reluctance to seek pleasurable activities, encouraging others to exploit or take advantage of oneself, focusing on one's very worst personal features, and a tendency to sabotage one's good fortunes. See also MASOCHISTIC PERSONALITY DISORDER.

self-degradation *n.* NEGATIVE IMAGERY or negative self-talk that causes one to think less of oneself and one's ability.

self-denial *n.* the act of suppressing desires and forgoing satisfactions.

self-derogation *n.* the tendency to disparage oneself, often unrealistically. It is often associated with a MAJOR DEPRESSIVE EPISODE.

self-desensitization *n.* a procedure used in BEHAVIOR THERAPY in which the individual, when confronted with objects or situations that arouse fear or anxiety, engages in coping strategies designed to reduce anxiety, for example, repeating positive self-statements, mentally rehearsing a potential confrontation, or employing muscle relaxation. See also DESENSITIZATION; SYSTEMATIC DESENSITIZATION.

self-destructiveness *n.* actions by an individual that are damaging and not in his or her best interests. The behavior may be repetitive and resistant to treatment, sometimes leading to suicide attempts. The individual may not be aware of the damaging influence of the actions or may on some level wish for the resulting damage. See also DEATH INSTINCT. **—self-destructive** *adj.*

self-determination *n.* the process or result of engaging in behaviors without interference or undue influence from other people or external demands. Self-determination refers particularly to behaviors that improve one's circumstances, including choice making, problem solving, self-management, self-instruction, and self-advocacy.

self-determination theory a theory that emphasizes the importance of AUTONOMY and INTRINSIC MOTIVATION for producing healthy adjustment. According to this theory, negative outcomes ensue when people are driven mainly by external forces and extrinsic rewards.

self-direction *n.* see SELF-DETERMINATION.

self-discipline *n.* the control of one's own impulses and desires, forgoing immediate satisfaction in favor of long-term goals or of improvement generally. See also SELF-CONTROL; SELF-REGULATION. **—self-disciplined** *adj.*

self-disclosure *n.* the act of revealing information about one's self, especially one's PRIVATE SELF, to other people. In psychotherapy, the revelation and expression by the client of personal, innermost feelings, fantasies, experiences, and aspirations is believed by many to be a requisite for therapeutic change and personal growth. In addition, pertinent revelation by the therapist of his or her personal details to the client can—if used with discretion—be a valuable tool to increase rapport and earn the trust of the client.

self-discovery *n.* the process of searching for and finding one's unique SELF or IDENTITY.

self-discrepancy *n.* an incongruence between different aspects of one's self-concept, particularly between one's ACTUAL SELF and either the IDEAL SELF or the OUGHT SELF. [derived from the theory of U.S. psychologist E. Tory Higgins (1946–)]

self-dynamism *n.* the pattern of motivations or

drives that comprise one's SELF-SYSTEM, including especially the pursuit of biological satisfaction, security, and freedom from anxiety. [proposed by U.S. psychiatrist Harry Stack Sullivan (1892–1949)]

self-effacement *n.* **1.** acting in such a way as not to draw attention to oneself or make oneself noticeable. **2.** in the approach of German-born U.S. psychoanalyst Karen D. Horney (1885–1952), a neurotic idealization of compliancy, dependency, and selfless love as a reaction to identification with the hated self. See also COMPLIANT CHARACTER; NEUROTIC TREND. **—self-effacing** *adj.*

self-efficacy *n.* an individual's capacity to act effectively to bring about desired results, especially as perceived by the individual (see PERCEIVED SELF-EFFICACY).

self-enhancement motive the desire to think well of oneself and to be well regarded by others. This motive causes people to prefer favorable, flattering feedback rather than accurate but possibly unfavorable information. Compare APPRAISAL MOTIVE; CONSISTENCY MOTIVE.

self-enucleation *n.* see AUTOENUCLEATION.

self-esteem *n.* the degree to which the qualities and characteristics contained in one's SELF-CONCEPT are perceived to be positive. It reflects a person's physical self-image, view of his or her accomplishments and capabilities, and values and perceived success in living up to them, as well as the ways in which others view and respond to that person. The more positive the cumulative perception of these qualities and characteristics, the higher one's self-esteem. A high or reasonable degree of self-esteem is considered an important ingredient of mental health, whereas low self-esteem and feelings of worthlessness are common depressive symptoms.

self-evaluation *n.* see SELF-CONCEPT.

self-expression *n.* free expression of one's feelings, thoughts, talents, attitudes, or impulses through such means as verbal communication; the visual, decorative, literary, and performing arts; and other commonplace activities (e.g., gardening and sports).

self-extension *n.* according to Gordon ALLPORT, an early stage in the development of the PROPRIUM or self, beginning roughly at age 4 and marked by the child's emerging ability to incorporate people, objects, and abstractions into the self-concept. Self-extension is the investment of ego in those objects outside the self with which the individual feels affinity or identification.

self-extinction *n.* in psychoanalytic theory, a form of neurotic behavior in which the patient lacks experience of himself or herself as an entity and identifies vicariously with the experiences and lives of others. [introduced by German-born U.S. psychoanalyst Karen D. Horney (1885–1952)]

self-focus *n.* **1.** the ability of human beings to direct conscious attention on themselves and their own thoughts, needs, desires, and emotions. **Trait self-focus** refers to a chronic habit or pattern of self-attention, whereas **state self-focus** refers to any temporary occurrence of the state. **2.** the capacity of an individual to analyze and evaluate his or her mental and emotive states. **3.** excessive concern for the self and its needs: selfishness. **—self-focused** *adj.*

self-fulfilling prophecy a belief or expectation that helps to bring about its own fulfillment, as, for example, when a person expects nervousness to impair his or her performance in a job interview or when a teacher's preconceptions about a student's ability influence the child's achievement for better or worse. See also DEMAND CHARACTERISTICS.

self-gratification *n.* the satisfaction of the needs of the self.

self-guide *n.* a specific image or goal of the SELF that can be used to direct SELF-REGULATION. In particular, self-guides include mental representations of valued or preferred attributes, that is, ideals and notions of how one ought to be; these may be chosen by the self or may come from others.

self-handicapping *n.* a strategy of creating obstacles to one's performance, so that future anticipated failure can be blamed on the obstacle rather than on one's own lack of ability. If one succeeds despite the handicap, it brings extra credit or glory to the self. The theory originally was proposed to explain alcohol and drug abuse among seemingly successful individuals. **—self-handicap** *vb.*

self-hate *n.* extreme SELF-DEROGATION.

self-help *n.* a focus on self-guided, in contrast to professionally guided, efforts to cope with life problems. This can involve self-reliance, drawing upon publicly available information and materials, or joining together with others similar to oneself, as is the case in SELF-HELP GROUPS.

self-help clearinghouse an organization that serves as an information and referral source about self-help groups in a given locality or region, providing up-to-date directories of all groups in that jurisdiction, as well as national self-help group resources. It serves as an important resource for citizens, groups, and professionals. Some clearinghouses also provide consultation to groups and group leaders and attempt to educate the public and professionals about the nature, value, and availability of groups. *The Self-Help Sourcebook* of a well-known clearinghouse in the United States, the American Self-Help Clearinghouse, provides an international listing of self-help clearinghouses.

self-help group a group composed of individuals who meet on a regular basis to help one another cope with a common life problem. Unlike therapy groups, self-help groups are not led by professionals, do not charge a fee for service, and do not place a limit on the number of members. They provide many benefits that professionals cannot provide, including friendship, emotional support, experiential knowledge, identity, meaningful roles, and a sense of belonging (see also SELF-HELP GROUP PROCESSES). Psychologists have become increasingly active in researching and supporting the development of self-help groups. Examples of self-help groups are ALCOHOLICS ANONYMOUS, COMPASSIONATE FRIENDS, and RECOVERY, INC. See also MUTUAL SUPPORT GROUP; SUPPORT GROUP.

self-help group ideology the set of beliefs about the cause and best means to address the problem that brings members of SELF-HELP GROUPS together. Each self-help group develops an ideology that is distinctive and that serves as an aid or "antidote" to its particular type of problem. For instance, in the case of ALCOHOLICS ANONYMOUS the group ideology includes the belief that alcoholism is a life-long problem and that the first step in addressing the problem is for group members to admit that they do not have control over it.

self-help group processes the means or mechanisms by which SELF-HELP GROUPS are thought to exert influence on their members. These include providing a sense of belonging, adaptive beliefs, emotional support, role models, specific coping approaches, practical information, and opportunities to contribute meaningfully to others and to expand or rebuild personal social networks.

self-help group typology classification of self-help groups according to type. Many typologies include addiction/compulsion groups (e.g., ALCOHOLICS ANONYMOUS), life stress/transition groups (e.g., COMPASSIONATE FRIENDS), mental illness/mental health problem groups (e.g., GROW, INC.), and physical illness/health/disability groups (e.g., the National Multiple Sclerosis Society).

self-hypnorelaxation *n.* a form of SELF-HYPNOSIS in which clients are trained to respond to their own relaxation suggestions.

self-hypnosis *n.* the process of putting oneself into a trance or trancelike state, sometimes spontaneously but typically through AUTOSUGGESTION. Also called **autohypnosis**.

self-ideal Q sort a technique designed to measure the discrepancy between an individual's existing and ideal SELF-CONCEPTS. The technique requires participants to sort descriptions of characteristics twice, once with regard to how they see themselves and then in terms of how they would like to be.

self-identity *n.* see IDENTITY.

self-image *n.* one's own view or concept of oneself. Self-image is a crucial aspect of an individual's personality that can determine the success of relationships and a sense of general well-being. A negative self-image is often a cause of dysfunctions and of self-abusive, self-defeating, or destructive behavior. See also SCHEMA.

self-inflicted wound a physical injury that results from self-injurious behavior or ATTEMPTED SUICIDE.

self-injurious behavior apparently intentional actions that inflict damage upon one's own body.

self-insight *n.* understanding oneself in some depth (see INSIGHT). It is a mediate goal or the desired outcome of many types of psychotherapy. See also DERIVATIVE INSIGHT.

self-instructional training a form of COGNITIVE BEHAVIOR THERAPY that aims to modify maladaptive beliefs and cognitions and develop new skills in an individual. In therapy, the therapist identifies the client's maladaptive thoughts (e.g., "Everybody hates me") and models appropriate behavior while giving spoken constructive **self-instructions** (or **self-statements**). The client then copies the behavior while repeating these instructions aloud. See also SELF-STATEMENT TRAINING. [developed by U.S. psychologist Donald Meichenbaum (1940–)]

self-inventory *n.* a questionnaire or series of statements on which participants check characteristics or traits that they perceive to apply to themselves.

selfishness *n.* the tendency to act excessively or solely in a manner that benefits oneself, even if others are disadvantaged. **—selfish** *adj.*

self-love *n.* **1.** regard for and interest in one's own being or contentment. **2.** excessive self-regard, or a narcissistic attitude toward one's own body, abilities, or personality. See EGOTISM; NARCISSISM.

self-managed reinforcement see SELF-REINFORCEMENT.

self-management *n.* **1.** an individual's control of his or her own behavior, particularly regarding the pursuit of a specific objective (e.g., weight loss). Self-management is usually considered a desirable aspect for the individual personally and within the social setting, but some forms of self-management may be detrimental to mental and physical health (see also COPING MECHANISM). Psychotherapy and counseling often seek to provide methods of identifying the latter and modifying them into the former. **2.** a BEHAVIOR-THERAPY program in which clients are trained to apply techniques that will help them modify an undesirable behavior, such as smoking, excessive eating, or aggressive outbursts. Clients learn to pinpoint the problem, set realistic goals for changing it, use various CONTINGENCIES to establish and maintain the desired behavior, and monitor progress.

self-management therapy see SELF-CONTROL THERAPY.

self-medication *n.* see MEDICATION.

self-monitoring *n.* **1.** a method used in behavioral management in which individuals keep a

S

record of their behavior (e.g., time spent, place of occurrence, form of the behavior, feelings during performance), especially in connection with efforts to change or regulate the self (see SELF-REGULATION). **2.** a personality trait reflecting an ability to modify one's behavior in response to situational pressures, opportunities, and norms. High self-monitors are typically more in tune with the demands of the situation, whereas low self-monitors tend to be more in tune with their internal feelings. **3.** a therapeutic technique in which the therapist assigns homework to encourage the client to record behavior, because behavior sometimes changes when it is closely self-monitored. **4.** a motivational technique used in exercise programs.

self-mutilation *n.* the act of disfiguring oneself. The most common type of self-mutilation is cutting.

self-objectification *n.* the achievement of objective knowledge about the self or self-understanding. It is one of Gordon ALLPORT's set of seven adaptive characteristics for psychological maturity.

self-perception *n.* a person's view of his or her self or of any of the mental or physical attributes that constitute the self. Such a view may involve genuine self-knowledge or varying degrees of distortion. Also called **self-percept**. See also PERCEIVED SELF; SELF-CONCEPT.

self-perception theory a theory postulating that people often have only limited access to their attitudes, beliefs, traits, or psychological states. In such cases, people must attempt to infer the nature of these internal cues in a manner similar to the inference processes they use when making judgments about other people. For example, a person may infer what his or her attitude is by considering past behaviors related to the ATTITUDE OBJECT: Approach behaviors imply a positive attitude; avoidance behaviors imply a negative attitude. Self-perception theory has been offered as an alternative explanation for some phenomena traditionally interpreted in terms of COGNITIVE DISSONANCE THEORY. [originally proposed by U.S. psychologist Daryl J. Bem (1938–)]

self-presentation *n.* any behaviors designed to convey a particular image of, or particular information about, the self to other people. Self-presentational motives explain why an individual's behavior often changes as soon as anyone else is thought to be present or watching. Some common strategies of self-presentation include self-promotion and SUPPLICATION. See also IMPRESSION MANAGEMENT. **—self-presentational** *adj.*

self-preservation instinct the fundamental tendency of humans and nonhuman animals to behave so as to avoid injury and maximize chances of survival (e.g., by fleeing from dangerous situations or predators). In his early formulations of classic psychoanalytic theory, Sigmund FREUD proposed that the instinct of self-preservation was one of two instincts that motivated human behavior, the other being the SEXUAL INSTINCT. In his later formulations he combined both instincts into the concept of EROS, or the LIFE INSTINCT, and opposed them to THANATOS, the DEATH INSTINCT. Also called **self-preservative instinct**; **survival instinct**.

self-protection *n.* any strategic behavior that is designed to avoid losing esteem, either SELF-ESTEEM or the esteem of others. Self-protection fosters a risk-avoidant orientation.

self psychology 1. any system of psychology focused on the SELF. **2.** a school of psychoanalytical theory that stresses the importance of an individual's relationships with others to healthy self-development and locates the source of many psychological problems in caregivers' lack of responsiveness to the child's emotional needs. In self-psychological therapy the therapist attempts to build an empathetic relationship with the client, rather than keeping an emotional distance as in classic psychoanalytical practice. [pioneered by Austrian-born U.S. psychoanalyst Heinz Kohut (1913–1981)]

self-punishment *n.* the act of inflicting physical or psychological harm on oneself for one's perceived misdeeds. Self-punishment ranges from SELF-ACCUSATION to SELF-MUTILATION or ATTEMPTED SUICIDE and commonly occurs in severe cases of MAJOR DEPRESSIVE DISORDER.

self-rating *n.* **1.** see SELF-CONCEPT. **2.** in psychological measurement, the act of reporting on or describing characteristics of oneself.

self-realization *n.* see SELF-ACTUALIZATION.

self-reference *n.* a persistent tendency to direct a discussion or the attention of others back to oneself, that is, to one's personal concerns and perceptions. **—self-refer** *vb.* **—self-referential** *adj.*

self-referral *n.* the act of consulting a clinical service provider or health care practitioner without being directed to by a medically qualified professional or similar person or without being forced to seek such help by an employer, a spouse, or the courts. Self-referred individuals are often viewed as more motivated for treatment and more likely to admit to problems.

self-reflection *n.* examination, contemplation, and analysis of one's thoughts and actions. The condition of or capacity for this is called **self-reflexivity**.

self-regulation *n.* the control of one's own behavior through the use of self-monitoring (keeping a record of behavior), self-evaluation (assessing the information obtained during self-monitoring), and self-reinforcement (rewarding oneself for appropriate behavior or for attaining a goal). Self-regulatory processes are stressed in BEHAVIOR THERAPY. See also SELF-CONTROL; SELF-MANAGEMENT.

S

self-regulatory resources theory a model stating that SELF-REGULATION depends on a global, but finite, pool of resources that can be temporarily depleted by situational demands. See EGO DEPLETION.

self-reinforcement *n.* the rewarding of oneself for appropriate behavior or the achievement of a desired goal. The self-reward may be, for example, buying a treat after studying for an exam. Also called **self-managed reinforcement**.

self-report *n.* a statement or series of answers to questions provided by an individual as to his or her state, feelings, beliefs, and so forth. Self-report methods rely on the honesty and self-awareness of the participant (see SELF-REPORT BIAS) and are used especially to measure behaviors or traits that cannot easily be directly observed.

self-report bias a methodological problem that arises when researchers rely on asking people to describe their thoughts, feelings, or behaviors rather than measuring these directly and objectively. People may not give answers that are fully correct, either because they do not know the full answer or because they seek to make a good impression (see SOCIAL DESIRABILITY). The self-report bias is often cited as a reason to use direct observation rather than SELF-REPORTS whenever practicable.

self-report inventory a type of questionnaire on which participants indicate the degree to which the descriptors listed apply to them.

self-repudiation *n.* denial of one's own pleasure or rights, usually out of a sense of guilt or low self-esteem.

self-respect *n.* a feeling of self-worth and SELF-ESTEEM, especially a proper regard for one's values, character, and dignity.

self-schema *n.* a cognitive framework comprising organized information and beliefs about the self that guides a person's perception of the world, influencing what information draws the individual's attention as well as how that information is evaluated and retained.

S

self-serving bias the tendency to interpret events in a way that assigns credit to the self for any success but denies the self's responsibility for any failure, which is blamed on external factors. The self-serving bias is regarded as a form of self-deception designed to maintain high SELF-ESTEEM.

self-statement *n.* see SELF-INSTRUCTIONAL TRAINING; SELF-STATEMENT TRAINING.

self-statement modification a technique designed to change maladaptive ideas about the self that are uncovered in COGNITIVE BEHAVIOR THERAPY. See also SELF-INSTRUCTIONAL TRAINING.

self-statement training (**SST**) a type of COGNITIVE REHEARSAL that involves periodically thinking or saying something positive, such as "I am a capable individual who is worthy of respect." It is used in SELF-INSTRUCTIONAL TRAINING. See also INNER DIALOGUE.

self-stimulation *n.* **1.** the act or process of inducing or increasing the level of arousal in oneself. It can be observed in various situations; for example, infants who are understimulated may explore their surroundings or babble to themselves. **2.** see PLEASURE CENTER. See also MASTURBATION; SELF-REINFORCEMENT.

self-suggestion *n.* see AUTOSUGGESTION.

self-system *n.* the relatively fixed personality of the individual resulting from relationships with his or her parents and other significant adults, in which approved attitudes and behavior patterns tend to be retained and disapproved actions and attitudes tend to be blocked out. [first described by U.S. psychiatrist Harry Stack Sullivan (1892–1949)]

self-talk *n.* an internal dialogue in which an individual utters phrases or sentences to him- or herself. The self-talk often confirms and reinforces negative beliefs and attitudes, such as fears and false aspirations, which have a correspondingly negative effect on the individual's feelings and reactions. In certain types of psychotherapy, one of the tasks of the therapist is to encourage the client to replace self-defeating, negative self-talk with more constructive, positive self-talk. In sport, athletes are trained to use positive self-talk to cue the body to act in particular ways, to cue attentional focus, to motivate, to reinforce SELF-EFFICACY, and to change mood. See also INTERNALIZED SPEECH; RATIONAL EMOTIVE BEHAVIOR THERAPY. [described by U.S. psychotherapist Albert Ellis (1913–2007)]

self-test *n.* a test that can be administered without the help of a trained professional.

self-transcendence *n.* the state in which an individual is able to look beyond him- or herself and adopt a larger perspective that includes concern for others. Some psychologists maintain that self-transcendence is a central feature of the healthy individual, promoting personal growth and development. [first described by Austrian psychiatrist Viktor Emil Frankl (1905–1998)]

self-understanding *n.* the attainment of knowledge about and insight into one's characteristics, including attitudes, motives, behavioral tendencies, strengths, and weaknesses. The achievement of self-understanding is one of the major goals of certain forms of psychotherapy.

self-verbalization *n.* **1.** self-directed private speech or thinking aloud. Self-verbalization can be a cognitive strategy that fosters internal self-regulation by verbally controlling behavior. Often used as a learning tool, it can be used to teach new skills, enhance problem-solving abilities, or alter previously held beliefs. Varying perspectives on this type of speech include the work of Lev VYGOTSKY, Jean PIAGET, and Alexander LURIA. **2.** see SELF-TALK.

self-verification hypothesis the hypothesis

that people seek information about themselves that confirms their existing SELF-CONCEPT, regardless of whether this is good or bad. According to this theory, the CONSISTENCY MOTIVE, which seeks self-verification, is often stronger than the SELF-ENHANCEMENT MOTIVE, which seeks favorable information about the self, or than the APPRAISAL MOTIVE, which seeks accurate information about the self (DIAGNOSTICITY). People seek self-verification (a) by engaging in situations that confirm their self-concept, (b) by seeking out and choosing to believe self-verifying feedback, and (c) by trying to persuade others of the validity of their own views of themselves.

self-worth *n.* an individual's evaluation of himself or herself as a valuable, capable human being deserving of respect and consideration. Positive feelings of self-worth tend to be associated with a high degree of SELF-ACCEPTANCE and SELF-ESTEEM.

SEM abbreviation for STRUCTURAL EQUATION MODELING.

semantic counseling a type of COUNSELING in which emphasis is placed on interpretations of meanings, particularly those related to adjustment and maladjustment.

semantic dementia a selective, progressive impairment in SEMANTIC MEMORY, leading to difficulties in naming, comprehension of words and their appropriate use in conversation, and appreciation and use of objects. Nonsemantic aspects of language, as well as perceptual and spatial skills, are preserved. The syndrome results from focal degeneration of the polar and inferolateral regions of the temporal lobes.

semantic differential a technique used to explore the connotative meaning that certain words or concepts have for the individuals being questioned. Participants are asked to rate the word or concept on a seven-point scale with reference to pairs of opposites, such as *good–bad, beautiful–ugly, hot–cold, big–small,* and so on. Responses are then averaged or summed to arrive at a final index of attitudes. This procedure is one of the most widely used methods of assessing attitudes and may be used in psychometric testing or (in advertising, politics, etc.) to gauge public reactions to a product, issue, or personality. See also ATTITUDE OBJECT. [developed in the 1950s by U.S. psychologists Charles E. OSGOOD, George J. Suci, and Percy H. Tannenbaum (1927–2009)]

semantic dissociation a distortion between words and their culturally accepted meanings that is characteristic of the THOUGHT DISORDER of individuals with schizophrenia. It includes **semantic dissolution**, marked by a complete loss of meaning and communication; **semantic dispersion**, in which meaning and syntax are lost or reduced; **semantic distortion**, in which meaning may be transferred to neologisms; or **semantic halo**, marked by coherent but vague and ambiguous language.

semantic encoding cognitive ENCODING of new information that focuses on the meaningful aspects of the material as opposed to its perceptual characteristics. This will usually involve some form of ELABORATION. See also DEEP PROCESSING; TOP-DOWN PROCESSING.

semantic memory memory for general factual knowledge and concepts, of the kind that endows information with meaning and ultimately allows people to engage in such complex cognitive processes as recognizing objects and using language. Examples of such **semantic** (or **generic**) **knowledge** include the location of the Eiffel Tower, the characteristics of a Labrador Retriever, or the elements associated with beauty. Impairments of semantic memory may be seen following brain injury as well as in certain neurological disorders, particularly DEMENTIA. For instance, people with ALZHEIMER'S DISEASE often find it increasingly difficult to categorize and name items (i.e., to refer to an apple as an apple) as their memory deficits worsen. Semantic memory is considered by many theorists to be one of the two forms of DECLARATIVE MEMORY, the other being EPISODIC MEMORY. [defined in 1972 by Endel Tulving (1927–), Estonian-born Canadian psychologist]

semantic psychosis the tendency of antisocial individuals to distort the meaning of words. They might say, for example, *I shouldn't have done that* when they merely mean *I'll say that because that's what he wants to hear, and then he'll let me go.* [defined by U.S. psychiatrist H. M. Cleckley (1905–1984)]

semantic therapy a form of psychotherapy in which the clients are trained to examine undesired word habits and distorted ideas so that they can think more clearly and critically about their aims, values, and relationships. This approach is based on an active search for the meaning of the key words the client uses and on practicing the formation of clear abstractions, as well as on uncovering hidden assumptions and increased awareness of the emotional tone behind the words the client has been using. Polish-born U.S. scientist Alfred Korzybski (1879–1950) and U.S. psychologist Wendell A. L. Johnson (1906–1965) were major early exponents of this approach.

semantogenic disorder a mental disorder originating in a misinterpretation of the meanings of emotion-colored words.

semiconscious *adj.* describing states of partial wakefulness, or alertness, such as drowsiness, stupor, or intermittent coma.

senile *adj.* **1.** relating to DEMENTIA associated with advanced age, used particularly with refernce to dementia or any other cognative or behavioral deterioration relating to old age. **2.** a lay term used to describe an older adult with dementia.

senile dementia see DEMENTIA.

S

senile dementia of the Alzheimer's type (**SDAT**) an older name for dementia of the Alzheimer's type with onset after age 65. See ALZHEIMER'S DISEASE.

senile plaque a clump of BETA-AMYLOID protein surrounded by degenerated dendrites that is particularly associated with symptoms of Alzheimer's disease. Increased concentration of senile plaques in the cerebral cortex of the brain is correlated with the severity of dementia. Also called **amyloid plaque**; **neuritic plaque**.

senilism *n.* an obsolete name for the appearance of symptoms of SENILITY in old age or before.

senility *n.* an obsolete term for DEMENTIA associated with advanced age. See also PSEUDOSENILITY.

sensate focus an approach to problems of sexual dysfunction in which people are trained to focus attention on their own natural biological sensual cues and gradually achieve the freedom to enjoy sensory stimuli. Therapy is conducted by teams of male and female professionals in joint interviews with the partners. The procedures involve prescribed body-massage exercises designed to give and receive pleasure, first not involving breasts and genitals, and then moving to these areas. This eliminates performance anxiety about arousal and allows the clients to relax and enjoy the sensual experience of body caressing without the need to achieve erection or orgasm. Sensate focus therapy is one component of the program developed by U.S. gynecologist William H. Masters (1915–2001) and U.S. psychologist Virginia E. Johnson (1925–).

sensation *n.* **1.** the process or experience of perceiving through the senses. **2.** an irreducible unit of experience produced by stimulation of a sensory RECEPTOR and the resultant activation of a specific brain center, producing basic awareness of a sound, odor, color, shape, or taste or of temperature, pressure, pain, muscular tension, position of the body, or change in the internal organs associated with such processes as hunger, thirst, nausea, and sexual excitement. Also called **sense datum**; **sense impression**; **sensum**. **3.** in the STRUCTURALISM of E. B. TITCHENER, one of the three structural elements of mental experience, the other two being images and feelings. **4.** in general usage, a thrilling or exciting experience. See SENSATION SEEKING. **—sensational** *adj.*

sensation seeking the tendency to search out and engage in thrilling activities as a method of increasing stimulation and arousal. Limited to human populations, it typically takes the form of engaging in highly stimulating activities accompanied by a perception of danger, such as skydiving or race-car driving.

sensation type in the ANALYTIC PSYCHOLOGY of Carl JUNG, a FUNCTIONAL TYPE dominated by sense perception, as opposed to thinking, feeling, or intuition. This type of individual lives a life of sense experience and enjoyment. The sensation type is one of Jung's two IRRATIONAL TYPES, the other being the INTUITIVE TYPE. See also FEELING TYPE; THINKING TYPE.

sense 1. *n.* any of the media through which one gathers information about the external environment or about the state of one's body in relation to this. They include the five primary senses—vision, hearing, taste, touch, and smell—as well as the senses of pressure, pain, temperature, kinesthesis, and equilibrium. Each sense has its own receptors, responds to characteristic stimuli, and has its own pathways to a specific part of the brain. Also called **sense modality**; **sensory modality**. **2.** *n.* a particular awareness of a physical dimension or property (e.g., time, space) or of an abstract quality, usually one that is desirable (e.g., humor, justice). **3.** *n.* good judgment or intelligence manifested by, or absent from, a person. **4.** *vb.* to perceive something using the senses. **5.** *vb.* to make an emotional or cognitive judgment about something, such as another person's mood.

sense of coherence 1. a perception of having clarity or intelligibility, that is, of being capable of thinking and expressing oneself in a clear and consistent manner. **2.** the ability to present a narrative of oneself in a way that is understandable and easy to follow.

sense of identity see IDENTITY.

sense of presence 1. the sense of being in a particular place or time. **2.** an awareness and understanding of one's current existence. **3.** in parapsychology, an awareness or consciousness of unusual phenomena, such as the existence or appearance of spirits.

sense of self an individual's feeling of IDENTITY, uniqueness, and self-direction. See also SELF-CONCEPT; SELF-IMAGE.

sensibility *n.* **1.** a capacity to respond to an emotional situation with refined or intense feeling. **2.** the capacity to receive sensory input.

sensible *adj.* **1.** showing reason and sound judgment. **2.** capable of receiving sensory input (e.g., feeling pain). **3.** receptive to external influences. **4.** felt or perceived as real or material.

sensitive 1. *adj.* having well-developed or intense mental and affective SENSIBILITY. **2.** *n.* in spiritualism and parapsychology, a person who is supposedly capable of receiving knowledge by paranormal means, as in clairvoyance and telepathy, or of perceiving AURAS and similar alleged phenomena beyond the range of normal perception. See also PSYCHIC.

sensitive period a stage in development when an organism can most advantageously acquire necessary skills or characteristics. For example, in humans the 1st year of life is considered significant for the development of a secure attachment bond. It is important to note, however, that lack of appropriate growth-dependent experiences during a sensitive period does not permanently and irreversibly affect development, as it

S

would during a CRITICAL PERIOD, but rather makes the acquisition process outside the period more difficult.

sensitivity *n.* **1.** the capacity to detect and discriminate. In SIGNAL DETECTION THEORY, sensitivity is measured by D PRIME (d′). **2.** the probability that a test gives a positive diagnosis given that the individual actually has the condition for which he or she is being tested. Compare SPECIFICITY. **3.** in physiology, the ability of a cell, tissue, or organism to respond to changes in its external or internal environment: a fundamental property of all living organisms. **4.** awareness of and responsiveness to the feelings of others.

sensitivity training a group process focused on the development of self-awareness, productive interpersonal relations, and sensitivity to the feelings, attitudes, and needs of others. The primary method used in sensitivity training is free, unstructured discussion with a leader functioning as an observer and facilitator, although other techniques, such as ROLE PLAY, may be used. Sensitivity training is employed in HUMAN RELATIONS TRAINING in industry and general life, with various types of groups (e.g., workers, executives, married couples) meeting, for example, once a week or over a weekend. See also PERSONAL-GROWTH LABORATORY; T-GROUP. [originated by Kurt LEWIN and Carl ROGERS]

sensitization *n.* **1.** a form of nonassociative learning in which an organism becomes more responsive to most stimuli after being exposed to unusually strong or painful stimulation. **2.** the increased effectiveness of an eliciting stimulus as a function of its repeated presentation. Water torture, in which water is dripped incessantly onto a person's forehead, is a good example. **3.** see REVERSE TOLERANCE.

sensorimotor *adj.* **1.** describing activity, behavior, or brain processes that combine sensory (afferent) and motor (efferent) function. **2.** describing a mixed nerve that contains both afferent and efferent fibers.

sensorimotor memory 1. a memory, commonly of a traumatic experience, that is encoded in SENSORIMOTOR, rather than verbal, forms. Frequently these are memories of events that occurred during the period of CHILDHOOD AMNESIA, which commonly lasts up to the age of 3 years. See also BODY MEMORY. **2.** see PROCEDURAL MEMORY.

sensorium *n.* the human sensory apparatus and related mental faculties considered as a whole. The state of the sensorium is tested through the traditional MENTAL STATUS EXAMINATION; the sensorium may be **clear** (i.e., functioning normally) or **clouded** (lacking ability to concentrate and think clearly).

sensory *adj.* relating to the SENSES, to SENSATION, or to a part or all of the neural apparatus and its supporting structures that are involved in any of these.

sensory aprosodia an inability to understand the emotional inflections of language, that is, the rhythm, pitch, and "melody" of speech.

sensory ataxia lack of muscular coordination (see ATAXIA) due to the loss of the sense of limb movements (see PROPRIOCEPTION).

sensory awareness training 1. the methods used in SENSATE FOCUS therapy and similar therapies to help an individual become more acutely aware of his or her own feelings and sensations and to accept new ways of experiencing them. **2.** in sport, training an athlete to become aware of the kinesthetic sensations experienced while performing and of the sensations related to AROUSAL level.

sensory consciousness consciousness of sensory stimuli, having visual, tactile, olfactory, auditory, and taste qualities. Compare HIGHER ORDER CONSCIOUSNESS.

sensory conversion symptoms one of two types of symptoms of CONVERSION DISORDER, the other being MOTOR CONVERSION SYMPTOMS. Examples of sensory conversion symptoms include loss of touch or pain sensation, double vision, blindness, deafness, tinnitus, and hallucinations.

sensory deficit a loss, absence, or marked impairment of a normal sensory function, such as vision, hearing, taste, touch, or smell.

sensory deprivation the reduction of sensory stimulation to a minimum in the absence of normal contact with the environment. Sensory deprivation may be experimentally induced (e.g., via the use of a **sensory deprivation chamber**) for research purposes or it may occur in a real-life situation (e.g., in deep-sea diving). Although short periods of sensory deprivation can be beneficial, extended sensory deprivation has detrimental effects, causing (among other things), hallucinations, delusions, hypersuggestibility, or panic.

sensory disorder any disturbance in the optimum transmission of information from a sense organ to its appropriate reception point in the brain or spinal cord, particularly when related to an anatomical or physiological abnormality. An auditory disorder, for example, may be due to damage from injury or disease to the cochlear structures.

sensory integration the neural processes involved in perceiving, organizing, and evaluating sensory information across modalities, such as vision and hearing, and producing an adaptive response via impulses transmitted through the motor nerves. Development or enhancement of **sensory-integrative functioning** is an important goal of OCCUPATIONAL THERAPY.

sensory integration dysfunction a condition characterized by difficulties in organizing, processing, and analyzing sensory input (touch, movement, body awareness, sight, sound, smell, and taste).

sensory intensity the perceived intensity of a

physical stimulus, predictably related to its actual intensity by psychophysical laws.

sensory memory brief storage of information from each of the senses in a relatively unprocessed form beyond the duration of a stimulus, for recoding into another memory (such as SHORT-TERM MEMORY) or for comprehension. For instance, sensory memory for visual stimuli, called iconic memory, holds a visual image for less than a second, whereas that for auditory stimuli, called ECHOIC MEMORY, retains sounds for a little longer. Also called **sensory-information store (SIS)**; **sensory register**.

sensory modulation dysfunction a condition characterized by difficulties in responding appropriately to sensory input (touch, movement, body awareness, sight, sound, smell, and taste). A person may be overresponsive or underresponsive to sensations or alternate rapidly between both response patterns.

sensory neglect inability to attend to sensory information, usually from one side of the body, as a result of brain injury.

sensory neuron a neuron that receives information from the environment, via specialized RECEPTOR cells, and transmits this—in the form of nerve impulses—through SYNAPSES with other neurons to the central nervous system.

sensory overload a state in which the senses are overwhelmed with stimuli, to the point that the person is unable to process or respond to all of them. See also INFORMATION OVERLOAD; STIMULUS OVERLOAD.

sensual *adj.* **1.** referring to the senses, particularly gratification of or appeal to the senses. **2.** referring to physical or erotic sensation.

sentence-completion test a language ability test in which the participant must complete an unfinished sentence by filling in the specific missing word or phrase. However, the test is used more often to evaluate personality, in which case the participant is presented with an introductory phrase to which he or she may respond in any way. An example might be "Today I am in a __ mood." As a projective test, the sentence-completion test is an extension of the WORD-ASSOCIATION TEST in that responses are free and believed to contain psychologically meaningful material. Also called **incomplete-sentence test**.

sentience *n.* **1.** the simplest or most primitive form of cognition, consisting of a conscious awareness of stimuli without association or interpretation. **2.** the state of being SENTIENT.

sentience need in the PERSONOLOGY of U.S. psychologist Henry Alexander Murray (1893–1988), a need to enjoy sights, sounds, and other sensuous experiences.

sentient *adj.* capable of sensing and recognizing stimuli.

sentimentality *n.* the quality or condition of being excessively or affectedly swayed by emotional situations, especially those of a romantic or maudlin nature. See also EMOTIONALITY. **—sentimental** *adj.*

sentinel event in health administration, an unexpected occurrence or variation to service delivery involving death or serious physical or psychological injury. The event is called "sentinel" because it sends a signal or sounds a warning that requires immediate attention.

separation anxiety the normal apprehension experienced by a young child when away (or facing the prospect of being away) from the person or people to whom he or she is attached (particularly parents). Separation anxiety is most active between 6 and 10 months. Separation from loved ones in later years may elicit similar anxiety.

separation anxiety disorder in *DSM–IV–TR*, an anxiety disorder occurring in childhood or adolescence that is characterized by developmentally inappropriate, persistent, and excessive anxiety about separation from the home or from major attachment figures. Other features may include marked ANTICIPATORY ANXIETY over upcoming separation and persistent and excessive worry about harm coming to attachment figures or about major events that might lead to separation from them (e.g., getting lost). There may also be SCHOOL REFUSAL, fear of being alone or going to sleep without major attachment figures present, separation-related nightmares, and repeated complaints of physical symptoms (e.g., vomiting, nausea, headaches, stomachaches) associated with anticipated separation. These symptoms cause clinically significant distress or impairment in functioning.

separation distress discomfort and anxiety felt by an individual upon losing contact with an attachment figure, for example, by a child upon losing contact with a caregiver or by an adult in reaction to the traumatic loss of a spouse or partner. See SEPARATION ANXIETY.

separation–individuation *n.* the developmental phase in which the infant gradually differentiates himself or herself from the mother, develops awareness of his or her separate identity, and attains relatively autonomous status. [defined by Austrian child psychoanalyst Margaret Mahler (1897–1985)]

sepsis *n.* the condition of tissues contaminated by the presence of pus-forming bacteria or other microorganisms or the toxic substances produced by such microorganisms. When spread throughout the bloodstream, the condition is called septicemia (see BLOOD POISONING). **—septic** *adj.*

septal area a region of the forebrain that contains the **septal nuclei** and the septum pellucidum, which separates the lateral ventricles. The septal nuclei, which include the nucleus accumbens, form an integral part of the LIMBIC SYSTEM; they contribute fibers to the medial forebrain bundle and have interconnections with the amygdala, hippocampus, and regions of the hypothalamus. Functionality of this area includes pleasure and anger suppression.

septicemia *n.* see BLOOD POISONING.

sequela *n.* (*pl.* **sequelae**) a residual effect of an illness or injury, or of an unhealthy or unstable mental condition, often (but not necessarily) in the form of persistent or permanent impairment. Examples include paralysis, which may be the sequela of poliomyelitis, and flashbacks, which may be the sequelae of traumatic stress.

sequence completion see NUMBER-COMPLETION TEST.

sequence effect in WITHIN-SUBJECTS DESIGNS, the effect of the treatments being administered in a particular sequence (e.g., the sequence ABC versus ACB, versus BCA, and so forth). This is often confused with the ORDER EFFECT.

sequential marriage see SERIAL POLYGAMY.

Serax *n.* a trade name for OXAZEPAM.

Serentil *n.* a trade name for MESORIDAZINE.

serial interpretation a psychoanalytic technique in which the analyst studies a series of consecutive DREAMS that, when taken as a group, provide clues that would be overlooked in interpretation of a single, isolated dream. See also RECURRENT DREAM.

serial killer an individual who repeatedly commits homicide, typically with a distinct pattern in terms of the selection of victims, location, and method.

serial monogamy see MONOGAMY.

serial polygamy a pattern of repeated marriage and divorce. Also called **sequential marriage**.

serial processing INFORMATION PROCESSING in which only one sequence of processing operations is carried on at a time. Those who hold that the human information-processing system operates in this way argue that the mind's apparent ability to carry on different cognitive functions simultaneously is explained by rapid shifts between different information sources. Also called **intermittent processing**; **sequential processing**. Compare PARALLEL PROCESSING. See also SINGLE-CHANNEL MODEL.

seriation *n.* the process of arranging a collection of items into a specific order (series) on the basis of a particular dimension (e.g., size). According to Jean PIAGET, this ability is necessary for understanding the concepts of number, time, and measurement and is acquired typically by children during the ages of 7 to 11 years.

SERMs abbreviation for selective estrogen receptor modulators. See ANTIESTROGEN.

Sernyl *n.* trade name for a brand of phencyclidine hydrochloride, an animal anesthetic with hallucinogenic properties sometimes taken as a drug of abuse (see PCP).

Seroquel *n.* a trade name for QUETIAPINE.

serotonin *n.* a common monoamine neurotransmitter in the brain and other parts of the central nervous system, also found in the gastrointestinal tract, in smooth muscles of the cardiovascular and bronchial systems, and in blood platelets. It is synthesized from the dietary amino acid L-tryptophan (see TRYPTOPHAN HYDROXYLASE), and in the pineal gland it is converted to MELATONIN. Significant amounts of serotonin are found in the upper brainstem. Serotonin is primarily degraded by MONOAMINE OXIDASE, which yields its principal metabolic product, 5-HYDROXYINDOLEACETIC ACID (5-HIAA). Serotonin has roles in numerous bioregulatory processes, including emotional processing, mood, appetite, and sleep as well as pain processing, hallucinations, and reflex regulation. For example, levels of serotonin correlate negatively with aggression, and release of serotonin may promote sleep. It is implicated in many psychological conditions, including depressive disorders, anxiety disorders, sleep disorders, aggression, and psychosis; many common psychotropic drugs affect NEUROTRANSMISSION mediated by serotonin. Also called **5-hydroxytryptamine** (**5-HT**).

serotonin and norepinephrine reuptake inhibitor see SNRI.

serotonin antagonists agents that oppose the action of SEROTONIN. They include CYPROHEPTADINE and METHYSERGIDE, which are used for the prevention of migraine attacks, and the antiemetic ONDANSETRON.

serotonin receptor any of various receptors that bind and respond to SEROTONIN (5-hydroxytryptamine; 5-HT). They occur in the brain and in peripheral areas and have different sensitivities that can be measured by susceptibility to ligands or blockers. At least 15 classes of serotonin receptors, affecting a variety of physiological and psychological processes, have been identified. They are designated by subscript numbers and letters (e.g., 5-HT_{1A}, 5-HT_{1B}, 5-HT_{1D}, 5-HT_{2A}, etc.).

serotonin-receptor agonists agents that increase the affinity for, or availability of, SEROTONIN at various SEROTONIN RECEPTORS in the brain or peripheral tissues. Commonly used INDIRECT AGONISTS are the SSRIS (e.g., fluoxetine, citalopram), which work by blocking the presynaptic reuptake of serotonin, thereby increasing the availability of serotonin at postsynaptic receptor sites. Other serotonin agonists exert their effects directly at the receptor site; for example, the TRIPTANS are direct agonists at receptor subtypes 5-HT_{1B} and 5-HT_{1D}. The anxiolytic agent BUSPIRONE is a PARTIAL AGONIST at the postsynaptic 5-HT_{1A} receptor, whereas the serotonin-like HALLUCINOGENS (e.g., LSD) act as partial agonists at 5-HT_{2A} receptors.

serotonin reuptake inhibitor (**SRI**) see SSRI.

serotonin syndrome a collection of symptoms, including agitation, confusion, delirium, and increased heart rate, due to excess activity of

S

the neurotransmitter serotonin. It may result from drug interactions that increase amounts of available serotonin to toxic levels.

sertraline *n.* an SSRI that is used for the treatment of depressive and anxiety disorders, including major depression, panic disorder, posttraumatic stress disorder, and obsessive-compulsive disorder. It has also been indicated for the treatment of premenstrual dysphoric disorder. U.S. trade name: **Zoloft**.

service delivery system see HUMAN SERVICE DELIVERY SYSTEM.

set *n.* a temporary readiness to respond in a certain way to a specific situation or stimulus. For example, a sprinter gets set to run when the starting gun fires (a motor set); a parent is set to hear his or her baby cry from the next room (a perceptual set); a poker player is set to use a tactic that has been successful in other games (a mental set).

seven plus or minus two the number of items that can be held in short-term memory at any given time and therefore accurately perceived and recalled after a brief exposure (see CHUNKING). The phrase originated in the title of an article (1956) by U.S. cognitive psychologist George Armitage Miller (1920–), "The magical number seven, plus or minus two: Some limitations on our capacity for processing information."

severe mental retardation a diagnostic category applying to those with IQs of 20 to 34, comprising about 7% of people with MENTAL RETARDATION. While able to manage basic self-care activities such as dressing and eating, these individuals typically do not acquire much more than rudimentary communication, social, educational, and vocational skills and generally require significant assistance and supervision. Additionally, sensory and motor deficits are common.

sex *n.* **1.** the traits that distinguish between males and females. Sex refers especially to physical and biological traits, whereas GENDER refers especially to social or cultural traits, although the distinction between the two terms is not regularly observed. **2.** the physiological and psychological processes related to procreation and erotic pleasure.

S

sex change see SEX REASSIGNMENT.

sex characteristic any of the traits associated with sex identity. **Primary sex characteristics** (e.g., testes in males, ovaries in females) are directly involved in reproduction of the species. **Secondary sex characteristics** are features not directly concerned with reproduction, such as voice quality, facial hair, and breast size. Also called **sexual characteristic**.

sex-chromosomal aberration any disorder of structure, function, or both that is associated with the complete or partial absence of a sex chromosome or with the presence of extra sex chromosomes. Examples of such disorders are KLINEFELTER'S SYNDROME, XYY SYNDROME, and TURNER'S SYNDROME.

sex chromosome a chromosome that determines the sex of an individual. Humans and other mammals have two sex chromosomes: the X CHROMOSOME, which carries genes for certain sexual traits and occurs in both females and males; and the smaller Y CHROMOSOME, which is normally found only in males. An individual usually is considered to be a female if the body cells contain the XX combination of chromosomes and male if the cells contain the XY combination, regardless of physical traits or signs of hermaphroditism. Disease genes that are carried only on a sex chromosome (usually the X chromosome) are responsible for SEX-LINKED inherited conditions.

sex counseling guidance provided by therapists to sex partners in such matters as birth control, infertility, and general feelings of inadequate sexual performance. Working on specific SEXUAL DYSFUNCTION problems is usually considered to be SEX THERAPY rather than sex counseling.

sex determination the genetic mechanism that determines the sex of the offspring. In humans a fertilized egg with two X CHROMOSOMES becomes a female, and a fertilized egg with one X and one Y CHROMOSOME becomes a male. See SEX DIFFERENTIATION.

sex differences 1. the differences in physical features between males and females. These include differences in brain structures as well as differences in primary and secondary SEX CHARACTERISTICS. **2.** the differences between males and females in the way they behave and think. Sex differences are often viewed as driven by actual biological gender disparity (nature), rather than by differing environmental factors (nurture), and affect both cognition and behavior. Compare SEX ROLE.

sex differentiation the process of acquiring distinctive sexual features during the course of development. Human sexual differentiation is determined genetically at the time of fertilization, primarily by the presence or absence of a Y CHROMOSOME. Fertilized eggs containing a Y chromosome develop as male embryos, whereas ones lacking a Y chromosome develop as females. This is due to the presence on the Y chromosome of a particular gene, called *SRY* (*sex reversal on Y*). It encodes a testis-determining factor that, via a cascade of signals, triggers the development of testes and other male reproductive organs. In the absence of this gene, the embryo develops along the default, female pathway, with ovaries and other female organs.

sex drive an arousal state precipitating the desire for sexual gratification and, ultimately, for sexual reproduction. Although it is not necessary for an individual's survival, it is considered a PRIMARY DRIVE as it is essential for species survival. In many animals, sexual activity is cyclical (e.g., seasonal or dependent on cyclical hormone release), although a variety of factors (e.g., external stimulation) may arouse the drive. Also called **sexual drive**. See LIBIDO.

sex feeling the pleasurable feeling associated with coitus or other sexual contact. Also called **sexual feeling**.

sex hormone any of the hormones that stimulate various reproductive functions. Primary sources of sex hormones are the male and female gonads (i.e., testis and ovary), which are stimulated to produce sex hormones by pituitary hormones. The principal male sex hormones (ANDROGENS) include testosterone; female sex hormones include the ESTROGENS, PROGESTERONE, and PROLACTIN.

sex hygiene the health-maintenance procedures related to sexual activity, for example, the prevention or control of sexually transmitted infections. Also called **sexual hygiene**.

sex identification see SEXUAL IDENTIFICATION.

sex identity 1. the purely biologically determined sexual condition or status of an individual. **2.** a person's sense of him- or herself as male or female, regardless of physical or biological considerations.

sex instinct see SEXUAL INSTINCT.

sex interest a readiness to engage or participate in discussions, viewing, or other activities related to or leading to sexual contact. Also called **sexual interest**.

sex-linked *adj.* describing a gene that is located on one of the SEX CHROMOSOMES, usually the X CHROMOSOME (**X-linked**), or a trait determined by such a gene. Sex-linked diseases, such as hemophilia, generally affect only males, because the defective gene is usually a RECESSIVE ALLELE. In females, who have two X chromosomes, it would be masked by the normal, dominant allele on the other X chromosome. In males, with just a single X chromosome, any sex-linked defective allele is expressed.

sex-negativity *n.* a negative attitude or stance toward any sexual behavior other than procreative marital coitus. Compare SEX-POSITIVITY.

sex object see SEXUAL OBJECT.

sex offense a sex act that is prohibited by law. An individual who has committed such an offense is called a **sex offender**. Some crimes are acts of violence involving sex, and others are violations of social taboos; there is much variation, by culture and jurisdiction, concerning which behaviors are considered crimes and how they may be punished. Some jurisdictions consider certain consensual sex acts to be illegal. Examples of sex offenses include forcible and statutory rape, incest, prostitution and pimping, bestiality, sodomy, sex murder, and forcible sexual assault without coitus. Also called **sexual offense**. See also MOLESTATION.

sexological examination the study of an individual's sexual behavior in terms of physiological, psychological, sociological, and specific genetic and environmental influences.

sexology *n.* the study of sexuality, particularly among human beings, including the anatomy, physiology, and psychology of sexual activity and reproduction. **—sexological** *adj.* **—sexologist** *n.*

sex perversion see SEXUAL PERVERSION.

sex-positivity *n.* a positive attitude or stance toward sexual activity between consenting individuals where this is seen as promoting healthy relationships and forms of self-expression. Sex is seen as neither good nor bad, per se, and the purpose of sexual relations is not deemed to be confined exclusively to procreation through marital coitus. Compare SEX-NEGATIVITY.

sex reassignment a process, involving hormone treatment and surgery, in which a person's sex characteristics are changed to conform to that person's sense of his or her own GENDER IDENTITY, particularly in cases of TRANSSEXUALISM. Also called **gender reassignment**; **sex change**. See also GENDER IDENTITY DISORDER.

sex role the behavior and attitudinal patterns characteristically associated with being male or female as defined in a given society. Sex roles thus reflect the interaction between biological heritage and the pressures of socialization, and individuals differ greatly in the extent to which they manifest typical sex-role behavior.

sex-role inversion a former name for TRANSSEXUALISM.

sex sensations the effects of stimulation of the genitalia and other erogenous zones. Also called **sexual sensations**.

sex service see PROSTITUTION.

sex therapy a multimodal therapeutic approach designed to improve sexual functioning, based on the assumption that sexual performance problems are caused by a combination of lack of knowledge, misinformation, and faulty learning. Several different techniques commonly are used in sex therapy (e.g., SENSATE FOCUS, COGNITIVE RESTRUCTURING, COUPLES THERAPY), but they share the goals of providing education, reducing performance anxiety, improving communication, and teaching skills to improve sexual pleasuring for both partners. Sex therapy incorporates homework assignments, ideally rehearsed with the participation of a partner.

sex typing the process by which particular activities are identified within particular cultures as appropriate expressions of maleness and femaleness.

sexual abuse violation or exploitation by sexual means. Although the term typically is used with reference to any sexual contact between adults and children, sexual abuse can also occur in other relationships of trust.

sexual addiction a problematic sexual behavior, such as a PARAPHILIA or HYPERSEXUALITY, regarded as a form of addiction similar to drug addiction. The defining features of a sexual addiction include sexual behavior that has become out of control, has severely negative consequences, and that the addict is unable to stop, despite a wish to do so. Other features include persistence in high-risk, self-destructive behavior; spending large amounts of time in sexual activity or fantasy; neglect of social, occupational, or other activities; and mood changes associated with sexual activity.

sexual adjustment the process of establishing a satisfactory relationship with one or more sexual partners. Sexual adjustment may depend on psychological as well as physical factors.

sexual and gender identity disorders in *DSM–IV–TR,* a category of disorders involving sexual or gender identity problems not attributable to another mental disorder. It includes SEXUAL DYSFUNCTIONS, PARAPHILIAS, and GENDER IDENTITY DISORDERS.

sexual anesthesia an absence of normal sensation during sexual activity, including coitus. Sexual anesthesia is usually psychogenic. However, although some patients report they obtain sexual pleasure in masturbation but not in sexual activity with a partner, many derive no pleasure from any form of sexual behavior. See also ERECTILE DYSFUNCTION; FEMALE SEXUAL AROUSAL DISORDER.

sexual anomaly a congenital or developmental abnormality of the reproductive system, for example, the presence of both male and female gonads in an infant.

sexual apathy lack of interest in sexual activity. See HYPOACTIVE SEXUAL DESIRE DISORDER.

sexual arousal a state of physiological arousal elicited by sexual contact or by other erotic stimulation (e.g., fantasies, dreams, odors, or objects), resulting in impulses being transmitted through the central nervous system to the sacral region of the spinal cord. The impulses also trigger the release of sex hormones, dilation of the arteries supplying the genital areas, and inhibition of vasoconstrictor centers of the lumbar nerves. The effects of sexual arousal are mediated through the hypothalamus. See SEXUAL-RESPONSE CYCLE.

sexual arousal disorder a class of sexual disorders characterized by the inability to attain or maintain an adequate physiological response in the excitement (arousal) phase of the SEXUAL-RESPONSE CYCLE. See FEMALE SEXUAL AROUSAL DISORDER; MALE ERECTILE DISORDER.

sexual assault violent sexual penetration of an individual. It includes forced vaginal, oral, and anal penetration. See also RAPE.

sexual attitude reassessment workshop (**SAR workshop**) a group educational experience in which participants view films on such issues as same-sex sexual orientation, sex in aging, sexual values, and education about sex. The workshop also involves group discussion and personal reflection on these issues.

sexual attitudes values and beliefs about sexuality. Manifested in a person's individual sexual behavior, these attitudes are based on family and cultural views about sexuality, sex education (both formal and informal), and prior sexual experiences.

sexual aversion disorder in *DSM–IV–TR,* negative emotional reactions (e.g., anxiety, fear, or disgust) to sexual activity, leading to active avoidance of it and causing distress in the individual or his or her partner. This can be lifelong or acquired, and although it usually applies to all sexual activity (**generalized type**), it may be specific to only some activities or some partners (**situational type**). This aversion is not caused by a medical condition, a medication, or a drug side effect.

sexual burnout loss of sexual function or interest due to a period of excessively frequent or demanding sexual activity. Sexual burnout also sometimes refers to the effects of advancing age on sexual activity, although age itself does not lead to loss of sexual interest or functioning.

sexual characteristic see SEX CHARACTERISTIC.

sexual contact any person-to-person contact that involves touching or connection of genital or erogenous skin or membrane surfaces, as in fondling, kissing, biting, or coitus.

sexual curiosity curiosity and interest in learning about sex and sexuality. In some cases this alone may be sufficient to produce sexual gratification or orgasm.

sexual desire disorder a class of sexual disorders, including HYPOACTIVE SEXUAL DESIRE DISORDER and SEXUAL AVERSION DISORDER, characterized by a chronic lack of interest in sexual activity that causes marked distress or interpersonal difficulty.

sexual deviance any sexual behavior that is regarded as significantly different from the standards established by a culture or subculture. The corresponding term in *DSM–IV–TR* is PARAPHILIA. Deviant forms of sexual behavior may include voyeurism, fetishism, bestiality, necrophilia, transvestism, sadism, and exhibitionism. Same-sex sexual behavior is considered deviant in some cultures, but not in all and not by most mental health professionals. Also called **sexual deviation**. See also SEXUAL PERVERSION.

sexual dimorphism the existence within a species of males and females that differ distinctly from each other in form. See SEX CHARACTERISTIC; SEX DIFFERENCES.

sexual disorder any impairment of sexual function or behavior. Sexual disorders include SEXUAL DYSFUNCTION and PARAPHILIAS. See also SEXUAL AND GENDER IDENTITY DISORDERS.

sexual disorder not otherwise specified

in *DSM–IV–TR*, a sexual problem that does not meet diagnostic criteria for SEXUAL DYSFUNCTION or PARAPHILIA. Examples include feelings of inadequacy about sexual performance, persistent and marked distress about sexual orientation (see EGO-DYSTONIC HOMOSEXUALITY), and distress about a pattern of repeated unsatisfactory or exploitative sexual relationships.

sexual drive see SEX DRIVE.

sexual dysfunction in *DSM–IV–TR*, a category of sexual disorders characterized by problems in one or more phases of the SEXUAL-RESPONSE CYCLE. Sexual dysfunctions include HYPOACTIVE SEXUAL DESIRE DISORDER, SEXUAL AVERSION DISORDER, FEMALE SEXUAL AROUSAL DISORDER, PRIMARY ERECTILE DYSFUNCTION, SECONDARY ERECTILE DYSFUNCTION, PREMATURE EJACULATION, MALE ORGASMIC DISORDER, FEMALE ORGASMIC DISORDER, DYSPAREUNIA, and VAGINISMUS.

sexual dysfunction not otherwise specified in *DSM–IV–TR*, a category that includes sexual dysfunctions outside the standard specific categories, such as absence of erotic sensations despite physiologically normal sexual excitement and orgasm or a dysfunction that may be due to a medical condition or substance abuse.

sexual erethism abnormal irritability or unpleasant sensitivity to stimulation of the sexual organs. It may be seen in individuals with SEXUAL AVERSION DISORDER.

sexual fantasy pleasant mental images or stories of sexual activity, not constrained by such real-world issues as partner availability or setting and situation.

sexual feeling see SEX FEELING.

sexual functioning the performance of sexual intercourse or the capability of performing sexual intercourse.

sexual harassment conduct of a sexual nature that is unwelcome or considered offensive, particularly in the workplace. In the United States, under Title VII of the 1964 Civil Rights Act, an employee is entitled to sue employers for sexual harassment. According to the U.S. Equal Employment Opportunity Commission (EEOC), there are two forms of sexual harassment: *quid pro quo* and behavior that makes for a HOSTILE WORK ENVIRONMENT. See also MERITOR SAVINGS BANK V. VINSON.

sexual hygiene see SEX HYGIENE.

sexual identification the gradual adoption of the attitudes and behavior patterns associated with being male or female. A clear concept of sexual identity gradually develops out of a perception of physical sex differences, starting during the first 3 or 4 years of life, and, somewhat later, awareness of psychological differences determined by the particular culture and particular family. Also called **sex identification**. See SEX ROLE.

sexual identity **1.** the individual's internal identification with heterosexual, homosexual, or bisexual preference, that is, with his or her SEXUAL ORIENTATION. **2.** an occasional synonym for SEX IDENTITY or GENDER IDENTITY.

sexual infantilism the tendency of a mature person to engage in sexual behavior characteristic of a small child. Sexual infantilism may be manifested in certain sexual disorders, such as VOYEURISM, FETISHISM, or in lovemaking that is limited to acts of foreplay (e.g., kissing, biting, or stroking the skin).

sexual inhibition suppression of the sexual impulse or the inability to feel sexual desire, to perform sexually, or to experience sexual gratification. See HYPOACTIVE SEXUAL DESIRE DISORDER; FEMALE ORGASMIC DISORDER; MALE ORGASMIC DISORDER.

sexual instinct **1.** the basic drive or urge to preserve the species through mating and the activities that precede it, or, by extension, simply to express the self and the self's physiological and psychological needs through sexual activity. **2.** in psychoanalytic theory, the instinct comprising all the erotic drives and sublimations of such drives. It includes not only genital sex, but also anal and oral manifestations and the channeling of erotic energy into artistic, scientific, and other pursuits. In his later formulations, Sigmund FREUD saw the sexual instinct as part of a wider LIFE INSTINCT that also included the self-preservative impulses of hunger, thirst, and elimination. Also called **sex instinct**. See also EROS; LIBIDO; SELF-PRESERVATION INSTINCT.

sexual intercourse see COITUS.

sexual interest see SEX INTEREST.

sexual inversion see INVERSION.

sexual involution sexual behavior that features deviant, unusual, involved, complicated, or ritualistic elements. PARAPHILIAS are considered to be an example of sexual involution.

sexuality *n.* **1.** the capacity to derive pleasure from all forms of sexual activity and behavior, particularly from sexual intercourse. **2.** all aspects of sexual behavior, including gender identity, orientation, attitudes, and activity. **3.** in psychoanalytic theory, the "organ pleasure" derived from all EROGENOUS ZONES and processes of the body, including the mouth, anus, urethra, breasts, skin, muscles, and genital organs, as well as such functions as sucking, biting, eating, defecating, urinating, masturbation, and intercourse.

Sexuality Information and Education Council of the United States (**SIECUS**) a nonprofit organization founded in 1964 that develops, collects, and disseminates information about sexuality, promotes sex education, and advocates the right of individuals to make sexual choices.

sexualization *n.* see EROTIZATION.

sexual latency in psychoanalytic theory, the

period from about 6 years of age until puberty, when the child has little, if any, interest in sex.

sexual lifestyle an individual pattern of sexual behavior in terms of orientation, number of partners, and types of sexual activity engaged in. Sexual lifestyle reflects such influences as early childhood observations of the family of origin, experiences with male and female contacts in childhood and adolescence, and cultural or religious values.

sexually dimorphic nucleus a nucleus of the central nervous system that differs in size between males and females. In humans, for example, a nucleus in the medial preoptic area of the hypothalamus that synthesizes GONADOTROPIN-RELEASING HORMONE tends to be larger and more active in males than in females because gonadotropin release is continuous (it is cyclical in females).

sexually transmitted disease (STD) an infection transmitted by sexual activity. More than 20 STDs have been identified, including those caused by viruses (e.g., hepatitis B, herpes, and HIV) and those caused by bacteria (e.g., chlamydia, gonorrhea, and syphilis). STDs are also known as **venereal diseases**, the term used traditionally for syphilis and gonorrhea.

sexual masochism in *DSM–IV–TR*, a PARAPHILIA in which sexual interest and arousal is repeatedly or exclusively achieved through being humiliated, bound, beaten, or otherwise made to suffer physical harm or threat to life. For the diagnosis, these activities must occur in real life, not fantasy, and must actually cause pain, not merely simulate painful experiences.

sexual metamorphosis a rare delusion in which the individual believes that his or her biological sex has been changed into the opposite sex.

sexual object 1. in general language, a person regarded only in terms of his or her sexual attractiveness. **2.** in psychoanalytic theory, a person, animal, or inanimate object external to the individual's own body or psyche toward whom or which the sexual energy of an individual is directed. Also called **sex object**.

sexual orientation one's enduring sexual attraction to male partners, female partners, or both. Sexual orientation may be heterosexual, same-sex (gay or lesbian), or bisexual. Also called **gender orientation**; **object choice**.

sexual orientation grid a method of classifying SEXUAL ORIENTATION on the basis of seven factors: sexual fantasy, sexual attraction, sexual behavior, emotional attraction, social attraction, social behavior, and self-identity. Each of these factors is evaluated in three time periods: past, present, and ideal future. Thus, a person's sexual orientation is described in terms of positions in a 3 × 7 grid. [developed by U.S. psychiatrist Fritz Klein (1932–2006), who considered Alfred KINSEY's single scale of sexual orientation to be too simplistic]

sexual pain disorder a class of sexual disorders, including DYSPAREUNIA and VAGINISMUS, characterized by persistent or recurring pain during sexual activity.

sexual perversion any sexual practice that is regarded by a community or culture as an abnormal means of achieving orgasm or sexual arousal. Sexual perversion is an older term that is little used nowadays, largely having been replaced by SEXUAL DEVIANCE or, in a psychiatric context, PARAPHILIA.

sexual preference 1. loosely, SEXUAL ORIENTATION. **2.** any particular sexual interest and arousal pattern, which may range from the relatively common (e.g., particular patterns of foreplay, particular positions) to those associated with a PARAPHILIA.

sexual reassignment see GENDER REASSIGNMENT.

sexual reflex 1. penile erection produced by stimulation of the male genitalia. **2.** vaginal secretion and lubrication and swelling of the clitoris produced by stimulation of the female genitalia. **3.** the reflex activity involved in ORGASM. **4.** components of sexual behavior that are not under direct control of the higher brain levels and may be stimulated through spinal or bulbar neural connections.

sexual response a reaction to sexual stimulation. The most noticeable sexual response in the male is erection of the penis. See SEXUAL AROUSAL.

sexual-response cycle a four-stage cycle of sexual response that is exhibited by both men and women, differing only in aspects determined by male or female anatomy. The stages include the **arousal** (or **excitement**) **phase**, which lasts several minutes to hours (see SEXUAL AROUSAL); the **plateau phase**, lasting 30 s to 3 min, marked by penile erection in men and vaginal lubrication in women; the **orgasmic phase**, lasting 15 s and marked by EJACULATION in men and ORGASM in women; and the **resolution phase**, lasting 15 min to 1 day (see REFRACTORY PHASE).

sexual revolution either of two periods in U.S. (and, to some extent, European) history marked by a significant change in sexual values and behavior. The first sexual revolution occurred in the early part of the 20th century, after the end of the Victorian era, and involved efforts to increase sexual knowledge, legitimize women's enjoyment of sex, and eliminate prostitution. The second sexual revolution, during the 1960s, was stimulated by such events as the development of oral contraception and the publication of the KINSEY reports on the sexual behavior of men and women. This led to more openness of sexual expression in literature and the media, an increase in sexual activity, more tolerance of what were previously considered "deviant" activities, and more acceptance of female sexuality.

sexual role see SEX ROLE.

sexual sadism a PARAPHILIA in which sexual excitement is achieved by intentional infliction of physical or psychological suffering on another person. The harm may be inflicted on a consenting partner, typically involving mildly injurious bodily suffering combined with humiliation. When practiced with nonconsenting partners, sexual sadism may involve inflicting extensive, permanent, or possibly fatal bodily injury. This activity is likely to be repeated, with the severity of the sadistic acts increasing over time. See also SADISM; SADOMASOCHISM.

sexual sensations see SEX SENSATIONS.

sexual stimulation see GENITAL STIMULATION.

sexual synergism sexual arousal that results from a combination of stimuli experienced at the same time. The stimuli may appear to be somewhat contradictory, such as love and hate, fear, pain, or fright.

sexual tension a condition of anxiety and restlessness associated with the sex drive and a normal desire for release of sexual energy. Sexual tension may be complicated by fear of inadequate performance, fear of an unwanted pregnancy, fear of discovery, or other concerns.

sexual trauma any disturbing experience associated with sexual activity, such as rape, incest, and other sexual offenses. It is one of the most common causes of POSTTRAUMATIC DISORDERS and DISSOCIATIVE DISORDERS.

sexual-value system **1.** the system of sexual stimulation and response that an individual feels is necessary for a satisfactory sexual relationship. **2.** a person's beliefs about what is normal, moral, and acceptable sexual behavior and activity.

shadow *n.* in the ANALYTIC PSYCHOLOGY of Carl JUNG, an ARCHETYPE that represents the "darker side" of the human psyche, mainly the sexual and aggressive instincts that tend to be unacceptable to the conscious ego and that are more comfortably projected onto others.

shadowing *n.* in cognitive testing, a task in which a participant repeats aloud a message word for word at the same time that the message is being presented, often with other stimuli being presented in the background. It is mainly used in studies of ATTENTION.

shaken baby syndrome (**SBS**) the neurological consequences of a form of child abuse in which a small child or infant is repeatedly shaken. The shaking causes diffuse, widespread damage to the brain; in severe cases it may cause death.

shallow affect significant reduction in appropriate emotional responses to situations and events. See also FLAT AFFECT.

shallow processing cognitive processing of a stimulus that focuses on its superficial, perceptual characteristics rather than its meaning. It is considered that processing at this shallow level produces weaker, shorter-lasting memories than DEEP PROCESSING. [proposed in 1972 by Canadian psychologists Fergus I. M. Craik (1935–) and Robert S. Lockhart]

shaman *n.* in various indigenous cultures, especially those that include nature and ancestor worship, a spiritual leader, male or female, who uses allegedly supernatural or magical powers for divination (particularly diagnosis) and to heal mental or physical illness. The status of shamans is not conferred by recognized organizations but is held to arise from a significant personal physical or mental crisis or to be hereditary. **Shamanism** includes a wide spectrum of traditional beliefs and practices, many of which involve communication with the spirit and animal worlds in pursuit of physical or mental healing. **—shamanic** *adj.* **—shamanistic** *adj.*

shamanic trance an ALTERED STATE OF CONSCIOUSNESS induced by hallucinogens, rhythmic actions and music, suggestion, experiences of possession, or by similar means. See SHAMAN.

sham disorder a colloquial name for FACTITIOUS DISORDER.

shame *n.* a highly unpleasant SELF-CONSCIOUS EMOTION arising from the sense of there being something dishonorable, ridiculous, immodest, or indecorous in one's conduct or circumstances. It is typically characterized by withdrawal from social intercourse, for example by hiding or distracting the attention of another from one's shameful action, which can have a profound effect on psychological adjustment and interpersonal relationships. Shame may motivate not only avoidant behavior, but also defensive, retaliative anger. Psychological research consistently reports a relationship between proneness to shame and a whole host of psychological symptoms, including depression, anxiety, eating disorders, subclinical sociopathy, and low self-esteem. Shame is also theorized to play a more positive adaptive function by regulating experiences of excessive and inappropriate interest and excitement and by diffusing potentially threatening social behavior. **—shameful** *adj.*

shamelessness *n.* behavior marked by an apparent absence of feelings of shame. This may arise as the result of psychological problems or reflect a loss of judgment after brain injury. **—shameless** *adj.*

sham rage sudden aggressive behavior and motor activity occurring disproportionally in response to a weak or relatively innocuous stimulus. Sham rage initially was observed by researchers in the 1920s: following surgical removal of the outer layer of the cortex, cats responded to the touch of a hand by growling, spitting, lashing the tail, arching the back, protracting the claws, erecting the hairs, jerking the limbs, rapidly moving the head from side to side, and attempting to bite. It subsequently has been demonstrated to occur with direct electrical stimulation of the LIMBIC SYSTEM as well. Additionally, sham rage has been seen in some pathological human conditions involving similar damage to the cerebral cortex that removes its inhibitory influence over the activities of the HYPOTHALAMUS and other deeper, more primitive structures.

shaping *n.* the production of new forms of OPERANT BEHAVIOR by reinforcement of successive approximations to the behavior. Also called **approximation conditioning**; **behavior shaping**.

shared environment in behavior genetic analyses, those aspects of an environment that individuals living together (e.g., biologically related individuals in a family household) share and that therefore cause them to become more similar to each other than would be expected on the basis of genetic influences alone. Examples of shared environmental factors include parental child-rearing style, divorce, or family income and related variables. Compare NONSHARED ENVIRONMENT.

shared paranoid disorder in *DSM–III*, a disorder characterized by a persecutory DELUSIONAL SYSTEM that develops as a result of a close relationship with another person or (rarely) persons who already have such delusional beliefs. This disorder has been subsumed under the *DSM–IV–TR* category of SHARED PSYCHOTIC DISORDER.

shared psychotic disorder in *DSM–IV–TR*, a disorder in which the essential feature is an identical or similar delusion that develops in an individual who is involved with another individual (sometimes called the **inducer** or the **primary case**) who already has a psychotic disorder with prominent delusions. Shared psychotic disorder can involve many people (e.g., an entire family), but is most commonly seen in relationships of only two, in which case it is known as FOLIE À DEUX. In *DSM–III–R*, shared psychotic disorder was referred to as **induced psychotic disorder**.

Sheldon's constitutional theory of personality the theory that every person possesses some degree of three primary temperamental components that relate to three basic body builds (SOMATOTYPES), measured on a seven-point scale. The three body types ECTOMORPH, ENDOMORPH, and MESOMORPH are correlated with the three components of temperament CEREBROTONIA, VISCEROTONIA, and SOMATOTONIA. Constitution provides a substructure, but nutrition and early experiences also influence the physique and temperament, respectively. [William H. **Sheldon** (1899–1970), U.S. psychologist]

S

shell shock the name used during World War I for COMBAT STRESS REACTIONS. At the time the disorder was attributed solely to minor brain hemorrhages or brain concussion due to exploding shells and bombs, without involving psychological factors.

shelter care the provision of a facility without physical restrictions for the temporary care of children who have been taken into custody pending investigation and placement. Shelter care is a form of FOSTER CARE.

sheltered workshop a work-oriented rehabilitation facility for individuals with disabilities that provides a controlled, noncompetitive, supportive working environment and individually designed work settings, using work experience and related services to assist individuals with disabilities to achieve specific vocational goals. Sheltered workshops differ from SUPPORTED EMPLOYMENT in that the latter occurs in a competitive, noncontrolled working environment.

shenjing shuairuo see SHINKEISHITSU.

shen-k'uei (**shenkui**) *n.* a CULTURE-BOUND SYNDROME occurring in males of Chinese or Taiwanese cultures and characterized by symptoms of anxiety, panic, and SOMATIZATION, such as sexual dysfunction, insomnia, and dizziness. Symptoms cannot be linked to a physical cause and are typically ascribed to excessive loss of semen due to unrestrained sexual activity. See also DHAT; JIRYAN; SUKRA PRAMEHA.

shin-byung *n.* a CULTURE-BOUND SYNDROME found in Korea, characterized by anxiety and such physical complaints as general weakness, dizziness, loss of appetite, insomnia, and gastrointestinal problems, followed by dissociation and alleged possession by ancestral spirits (see DISSOCIATIVE TRANCE DISORDER). It is considered by those affected to be a "divine illness," in which the individual experiences hallucinations of becoming a shaman, and a cure occurs when this conversion takes place.

shinkeishitsu *n.* a CULTURE-BOUND SYNDROME prevalent in Japan, with symptoms that include obsessions, perfectionism, ambivalence, social withdrawal, physical and mental fatigue, hypersensitivity, and hypochondriasis. Japanese psychiatrist Shoma Morita (1874–1938), a pioneer in the study of shinkeishitsu, postulated that there is a shinkeishitsu-prone innate temperament, which he called "hypochondriacal temperament." According to Morita, people who are born with this temperament are overly sensitive, self-reflective, and notice even minimal changes in their mental and physical states. This disorder is also prevalent in China, where it is known as **shenjing shuairuo**. See also MORITA THERAPY.

Shipley Institute of Living Scale (**SILS**) a short assessment of general cognitive functioning consisting of two subtests: vocabulary, in which participants must choose which of a group of words is most similar in meaning to a target word; and abstraction, in which participants must provide the final element in a sequence of numbers, letters, or words. The scale was originally developed in 1940 for use in psychiatric settings to identify and evaluate the intellectual decline associated with certain mental disorders. Also called **Shipley–Hartford Institute of Living Scale**. [Walter C. **Shipley** (1903–1966), U.S. psychologist]

shock *n.* **1.** the application of electric current. See ELECTROCONVULSIVE THERAPY. **2.** a condition of lowered excitability of neural centers following cutting of their connections with other neural centers. For example, spinal shock occurs when connections between the spinal cord and the brain are severed. **3.** acute reduction of blood flow in the body due to failure of circulatory control or loss of blood or other bodily fluids, marked by hypotension, coldness of skin, usually tachycardia, and sometimes anxiety. **4.** a sudden disturbance of equilibrium.

shock therapy the treatment of severe mental disorders by administering drugs or an electric current to produce shock to the central nervous system in order to induce loss of consciousness or convulsions. Also called **shock treatment**. See COMA THERAPY; ELECTROCONVULSIVE THERAPY.

shoe anesthesia see STOCKING ANESTHESIA.

shoe fetishism see RETIFISM.

shook yong see KORO.

Short Portable Mental Status Questionnaire (**SPMSQ**) a brief questionnaire that is typically used to screen older adults for DEMENTIA and other neurologically based cognitive deficits and to determine the severity of impairment. It consists of 10 simple questions relating to orientation (e.g., "What is the date today?", "What is the name of this place?"), knowledge of current events, short- and long-term memory, and calculation. [developed in 1975 by U.S. geriatric psychiatrist Eric A. Pfeiffer]

short-term memory (**STM**) the reproduction, recognition, or recall of a limited amount of material after a period of about 10–30 s. STM is often theorized to be separate from LONG-TERM MEMORY, and the two are the components of the DUAL-STORE MODEL OF MEMORY. STM is frequently tested in intelligence or neuropsychological examinations. See also IMMEDIATE MEMORY; PRIMARY MEMORY.

short-term psychodynamic psychotherapy see BRIEF PSYCHODYNAMIC PSYCHOTHERAPY.

short-term psychotherapy see BRIEF PSYCHOTHERAPY.

shrink *n.* slang for a psychologist, psychiatrist, or other mental health professional who conducts psychotherapy. It is short for **headshrinker**, an allusion to the practice of HEADSHRINKING.

shuk yang see KORO.

shunt *n.* a congenitally occurring or surgically created passage diverting the flow of bodily fluids such as blood or cerebrospinal fluid from one part of an organ or body to another. For example, a **ventriculoatrial shunt** is an artificially formed passage for draining cerebrospinal fluid from the brain to the external jugular vein to relieve symptoms of HYDROCEPHALUS.

shyness *n.* anxiety and inhibition in social situations, typically involving three components: (a) global feelings of emotional arousal and specific physiological experiences (e.g., upset stomach, pounding heart, sweating, and blushing); (b) acute public self-consciousness, self-deprecation, and worries about being evaluated negatively by others; and (c) observable behavior such as cautiousness, quietness, gaze aversion, and social withdrawal. Extremely shy individuals are at an increased risk of developing anxiety disorders such as SOCIAL PHOBIA. Also called **timidity**. See also SOCIAL ANXIETY. **—shy** *adj.*

shyness disorder see AVOIDANT DISORDER OF CHILDHOOD OR ADOLESCENCE.

sibling rivalry competition among siblings for the attention, approval, or affection of one or both parents or for other recognition or rewards, for example, in sports or school grades.

sib-pair method a technique used in genetics, particularly in attempting to discover the extent of inherited psychiatric factors, in which the incidence of a disorder among blood relatives is compared with the distribution of the disorder in the general population. Sib-pair method studies have found a higher incidence of schizophrenia in twins and close family members than in the general population.

sibutramine *n.* an APPETITE SUPPRESSANT used for the management of obesity. Sibutramine acts on the central nervous system to inhibit the reuptake of the neurotransmitter epinephrine and, to a lesser extent, serotonin and dopamine. Sibutramine may cause raised blood pressure and, because of its ability to release monoamines, it should not be used in conjunction with MONOAMINE OXIDASE INHIBITORS. Like other appetite suppressants, it is effective only in conjunction with dietary restriction. Due to concerns about serious adverse effects, it has been removed from the market in many countries, including the United States. U.S. trade name: **Meridia**.

sick role the behavior expected of a person who is physically ill, mentally ill, or injured. Such expectations can be the individual's own or those of the family, the community, or society in general. They influence both how the person behaves and how others will react to him or her. In his pioneering discussion of the subject, U.S. sociologist Talcott Parsons (1902–1979) noted in 1951 that people with a sick role were expected to cooperate with caregivers and to want to get well, but were also provided with an exemption from normal obligations. See also FACTITIOUS DISORDER.

side effect any reaction secondary to the intended therapeutic effect that may occur following administration of a drug or other treatment. Often these are undesirable but tolerable (e.g., headache or fatigue), although more serious effects (e.g., liver failure, seizures) may also occur. Occasionally, harmful side effects are unexpected, in which case they more properly are termed ADVERSE DRUG REACTIONS.

SIDS acronym for SUDDEN INFANT DEATH SYNDROME.

SIECUS abbreviation for SEXUALITY INFORMATION AND EDUCATION COUNCIL OF THE UNITED STATES.

sign 1. *n.* an objective, observable indication of a disorder or disease. See also SOFT SIGN. **2.** *vb.* to communicate using sign language.

signal *n.* **1.** an intelligible sign communicated from one individual or electromagnetic device to another. **2.** a presentation of information, usually one that evokes some action or response. **3.** as used in SIGNAL DETECTION THEORY, a stimulus.

signal anxiety in psychoanalytic theory, anxiety that arises in response to internal conflict or an emerging impulse, and functions as a sign to the EGO of impending threat, resulting in the use of a DEFENSE MECHANISM. Compare PRIMARY ANXIETY.

signal detection theory (**SDT**) a body of concepts and techniques from communication theory, electrical engineering, and decision theory that were applied during World War II to the detection of radar signals in noise. These concepts were applied to auditory and visual psychophysics in the late 1950s and are now widely used in many areas of psychology. An important methodological contribution of SDT has been the refinement of psychophysical techniques to permit the separation of sensitivity from criterial, decision-making factors. SDT has also provided a valuable theoretical framework for describing perceptual and other aspects of cognition and for quantitatively relating psychophysical phenomena to findings from sensory physiology. A key notion of SDT is that human performance in many tasks is limited by variability in the internal representation of stimuli due to internal or external NOISE. Many of the theoretical notions of SDT were anticipated by Louis THURSTONE. Also called **detection theory**. See D PRIME; RECEIVER-OPERATING CHARACTERISTIC CURVE.

significance level in null hypothesis SIGNIFICANCE TESTING, the probability of rejecting the null hypothesis when it is in fact true (i.e., of making a Type I error). It is set at some criterion, α, usually .01 or .05, and the actual value for a particular test is denoted p. Thus when the p value is less than α, the null hypothesis is rejected. Also called **alpha level**.

significance testing a set of procedures that is used to differentiate between two models. In the most common form of significance testing, one model (the NULL HYPOTHESIS) specifies a condition in which the treatment being studied has no effect and the other model (the ALTERNATIVE HYPOTHESIS) specifies that the treatment has some effect. Significance testing may also be used to differentiate beween two models (as in MULTIPLE REGRESSION analysis) where the two models differ in terms of the number of parameters specified in them.

significant difference the situation in which a SIGNIFICANCE TESTING procedure indicates that the two models being compared are legitimately different and do not reflect chance variation.

significant other any individual who has a profound influence on a person, particularly his or her self-image and SOCIALIZATION. Although the term most often denotes a spouse or other person with whom one has a committed sexual relationship, it is also used to refer to parents, peers, and others.

signifier *n.* in the theory of French psychoanalyst Jacques Lacan (1901–1981), a symbol, such as a word or symptom, that stands for some aspect of the patient's unconscious. Lacan's use of the term reflects his central belief that the unconscious is structured as a language.

sign system an epithet for PSYCHOTHERAPY, which highlights the discipline's dependence on language as the major tool for exploring and understanding the hidden causes of cognitive, affective, and behavioral problems and disorders. [introduced by Austrian-born U.S. psychologist Paul Schilder (1886–1940)]

silok *n.* a CULTURE-BOUND SYNDROME found in the Philippines, with symptoms similar to those of LATAH.

SILS abbreviation for SHIPLEY INSTITUTE OF LIVING SCALE.

Silver–Russell syndrome a congenital disorder characterized by short stature, hypertrophy of one side of the body, and elevated urinary gonadotropin hormones without precocious sexual maturity. Motor development is often delayed because of muscle weakness. Physical features include **pseudohydrocephalus**, a condition of normal head circumference but a small face, giving the appearance of an enlarged head. Various studies have found a higher than average incidence of mental retardation among the patients. Also called **Silver's syndrome**. [Henry K. **Silver** (1918–1991), U.S. pediatrician; Alexander **Russell** (1914–), British pathologist]

Simenon's syndrome a delusional condition characterized by the false perception or belief that one is loved by or has had a sexual affair with a public figure or other individual. See EROTIC DELUSION; EROTIC PARANOIA. See also CLÉRAMBAULT'S SYNDROME. [named for Georges Joseph Christian **Simenon** (1903–1989), Belgian-born French novelist, possibly because the condition featured in one of his stories]

Simmonds' disease a disorder of the pituitary gland caused by necrosis and failure of the anterior lobe (adenohypophysis) of the gland, which may be partial or complete. This results in secondary failure of the gonads, adrenal cortex, and thyroid gland, which depend upon the hor-

S

monal stimulation of the pituitary. Anorexia, atrophy of sexual features, absence of libido, hypotension, bradycardia, and hypoglycemia are symptoms of the disorder. [Morris **Simmonds** (1855–1925), German physician]

simple depression a less common name for MILD DEPRESSION.

simple deteriorative disorder in *DSM–IV–TR,* a disorder in which the essential feature is the development over the course of at least 1 year of prominent NEGATIVE SYMPTOMS, which represent a clear change from a preestablished baseline and are severe enough to result in a significant deterioration in occupational or academic functioning. The individual gradually loses emotional responsivity, ambition, and interest in self-care and becomes socially withdrawn or isolated. POSITIVE SYMPTOMS, if they appear, are not prominent. Historically, and in other classifications, this disorder is known as SIMPLE SCHIZOPHRENIA.

simple effect in an experimental design involving multiple independent variables, the consistent total effect on a dependent variable of a particular level (quantity, magnitude, or category) of one independent variable at a particular level of another independent variable.

simple factorial design an experimental design in which the two or more levels of each INDEPENDENT VARIABLE or factor are observed in combination with the two or more levels of every other factor. See also FACTORIAL DESIGN.

simple phobia see SPECIFIC PHOBIA.

simple schizophrenia one of the four major types of schizophrenia described by German psychiatrist Emil Kraepelin (1856–1926) and Swiss psychiatrist Eugen Bleuler (1857–1939), characterized primarily by gradual withdrawal from social contact, lack of initiative, and emotional apathy. The current psychiatric diagnosis is SIMPLE DETERIORATIVE DISORDER.

simple stepfamily a STEPFAMILY in which only one of the parents brings a child or children from a previous union to the new family unit.

simulated family a technique used in training and therapy in which hypothetical family situations are enacted. In training, the enactment is by clinicians or other professionals. In FAMILY THERAPY, one or more members of the family may participate with others, who play the roles of other family members. See also ROLE PLAY.

simulation *n.* **1.** an experimental method used to investigate the behavior and psychological processes and functioning of individuals in social and other environments, often those to which investigators cannot easily gain access, by reproducing those environments in a realistic way. **2.** the artificial creation of experiment-like data through the use of a mathematical or computer model of behavior or data. **3.** resemblance or imitation, particularly the mimicking of symptoms of one disorder by another or the faking of an illness.

Sinemet *n.* a U.S. trade name for a drug combination of LEVODOPA and **carbidopa**, used in the treatment of Parkinson's disease, the symptoms of which are due to lack of striatal dopamine. Carbidopa inhibits the action of the enzyme DOPA DECARBOXYLASE in peripheral tissues, thereby enabling levodopa to be administered in lower doses to achieve an effective concentration in the brain, where it is converted by striatal enzymes into dopamine.

Sinequan *n.* a trade name for DOXEPIN.

single blind see BLIND.

single-case experimental design an experimental design involving only a single participant or other sampling unit. The individual serves as his or her own CONTROL, and typically a number of observations are obtained at different times over the course of treatment. Also called **intrasubject replication design**; **N-of-1 experimental design**; **n=1 research**; **single-subject design**.

single-case methods and evaluation a type of PSYCHOTHERAPY RESEARCH based on systematic study of one client before, during, and after intervention.

single-episode depression a MAJOR DEPRESSIVE EPISODE in an individual who does not have a history of major depressive episodes. It is thought that the effects of treatment in people having single episodes may be different from those in individuals who have a history of depression.

single-gene disorder a disease or condition that is due to the presence of a single mutated gene. Single-gene disorders are relatively rare; many diseases exhibit MULTIFACTORIAL INHERITANCE and are also influenced by environmental factors. Huntington's disease and sickle-cell disease are examples of single-gene disorders. Generally, the single mutation causes a failure to synthesize a normally functioning enzyme that is required for a specific step in building body tissue or for a vital stage in the metabolism of a food component.

single-nucleotide polymorphism (**SNP**) a common, tiny variation in human DNA, occurring roughly every 1000 bases along the molecule and affecting single nucleotides. Such variations can be used as GENETIC MARKERS to track the inheritance of particular defective genes in families.

single parent a person who rears a child without the assistance of a partner.

single photon emission computed tomography (**SPECT**) a functional imaging technique that uses gamma radiation from a radioactive dye to create a picture of blood flow in the body. In the brain it can be used to measure cerebral blood flow, which is a direct measure of cerebral metabolism and activity.

single-session therapy (**SST**) therapy that ends after one session, usually by choice of the client but also as indicated by the type of treatment (e.g., ERICKSONIAN PSYCHOTHERAPY, SOLUTION-FOCUSED BRIEF THERAPY). Some clients claim enough success with one hour of therapy to stop treatment, although some therapists believe that this claim represents a FLIGHT INTO HEALTH or temporary relief from symptoms. Preparation for the session (e.g., by telephone) increases the likelihood of the single-therapy session being successful.

single-subject design see SINGLE-CASE EXPERIMENTAL DESIGN.

sinistration *n.* leftward direction. MIRROR WRITING, for example, shows sinistration.

sissy behavior slang for effeminate behavior in boys, which is often a source of ridicule by others. See ROLE CONFUSION; TOMBOYISM.

SIT 1. abbreviation for SMELL IDENTIFICATION TEST. **2.** abbreviation for STRESS-INOCULATION TRAINING.

situational attribution the ascription of one's own or another's behavior, an event, or an outcome to causes outside the person concerned, such as luck, pressure from other people, or external circumstances. Also called **environmental attribution**; **external attribution**. Compare DISPOSITIONAL ATTRIBUTION.

situational determinant an environmental condition that exists before and after an organism's response and influences the elicitation of this behavior: one of the four variables considered in behavioral analysis. See SORC.

situational homosexuality same-sex sexual behavior that develops in a situation or environment in which the opportunity for heterosexual activity is missing and where close contact with individuals of the same sex occurs, such as a prison, school, or military setting where individuals are living together, segregated according to their sex. Once away from this setting, the person typically returns to heterosexual activity. See also OCCASIONAL INVERSION.

situationally predisposed panic attack a PANIC ATTACK that occurs in response to a specific situational trigger but is not invariably induced by it. Compare CUED PANIC ATTACK; UNCUED PANIC ATTACK.

situational orgasmic dysfunction the inability of a woman to experience orgasm with a particular sex partner or in a particular situation. See FEMALE ORGASMIC DISORDER.

situational psychosis a severe but temporary reaction to a traumatic event or situation (such as imprisonment) involving such symptoms as delusions and hallucinations. Also called **reactive psychosis**; **traumatic psychosis**.

situational restraint the use of environmental arrangements (e.g., screens on windows, immovable furniture), as opposed to physical restraint of the individual, to minimize the risk of dangerous or destructive acts by patients with mental or emotional problems.

situational-stress test a SITUATION TEST with stress as an integral component.

situational test see SITUATION TEST.

situational therapy see ENVIRONMENTAL THERAPY.

situation awareness conscious knowledge of the immediate environment and the events that are occurring in it. Situation awareness involves perception of the elements in the environment, comprehension of what they mean and how they relate to one another, and projection of their future states. In ergonomics, for example, it refers to the operator's awareness of the current status and the projected future status of a system. Situation awareness is influenced by a number of factors, including stress.

situation test a test that places an individual in a natural setting, or in an experimental setting that approximates a natural one, to assess either the individual's ability to solve a problem that requires adaptive behavior under stressful conditions or the individual's reactions to what is believed to be a stressful experience. For example, a course of DESENSITIZATION therapy aimed at reducing phobic reactions might begin with a situation test in which the individual encounters the phobic object. The individual's reactions are then assessed and considered in relation to individual needs or a specific therapy program. Also called **situational test**. See also SITUATIONAL-STRESS TEST.

Sixteen Personality Factor Questionnaire (**16PF**) the fifth edition (1993) of a comprehensive self-report PERSONALITY INVENTORY. The instrument assesses personality on 16 key scales: warmth, vigilance, reasoning, abstractedness, emotional stability, privateness, dominance, apprehension, liveliness, openness to change, rule-consciousness, self-reliance, social boldness, perfectionism, sensitivity, and tension. The 16 factors (called SOURCE TRAITS) are grouped into 5 "global factors": extraversion, independence, tough-mindedness, anxiety, and self-control. [developed by British psychologist Raymond B. Cattell (1905–1998) and his associates]

Sjögren–Larsson syndrome an autosomal recessive condition characterized by scaly skin, spasticity, and mental retardation, caused by several different genetic factors. Sweat glands are sparse or deficient. The scaliness varies in specific cases among populations from different regions of the world. [reported in 1957 by Torsten **Sjögren** (1896–1974), Swedish physician, and Tage Konrad Leopold **Larsson** (1905–1998), Swedish scientist]

sketchpad see WORKING MEMORY.

skewness *n.* a measure of the degree or extent to which a batch of scores lack symmetry in their distribution around their measure of CENTRAL TENDENCY.

skilled nursing facility (**SNF**) a licensed or approved facility, whether freestanding or affiliated with a hospital, that provides continuous rehabilitation and medical care of a lesser intensity than that provided in an acute-care hospital setting. See also CONTINUING CARE UNIT; CONVALESCENT CENTER.

skill learning learning to perform a task with proficiency, as defined by ease, speed, and accuracy of performance, acquired through a high degree of practice. Skills may be motor, perceptual, cognitive, or a combination of these (as in reading and playing music).

Skinner, Burrhus Frederic (1904–1990) U.S. psychologist. Skinner earned his doctorate from Harvard University in 1931 and subsequently taught at the University of Minnesota and Indiana University before returning to Harvard in 1948. He spent the rest of his career there. Arguably the most famous experimental psychologist of the 20th century, Skinner was best known as the originator of OPERANT CONDITIONING, a distinctive form of BEHAVIORISM that he called RADICAL BEHAVIORISM. Operant conditioning, which he contrasted with PAVLOVIAN CONDITIONING, was based on the view that an organism's environment shapes its behavior; actions that are reinforced by the environment will increase in frequency, while those that are punished will decrease in frequency. Skinner invented a laboratory method utilizing the Skinner box (operant conditioning chamber) to make detailed studies of the SCHEDULES OF REINFORCEMENT that shape behavior in rats and pigeons. Not content to confine himself to laboratory research, Skinner initiated the field of APPLIED BEHAVIOR ANALYSIS by applying his ideas to educational methods (programmed instruction), child rearing, language acquisition, psychotherapy, and cultural analysis. His most famous writings include his *Behavior of Organisms* (1938) and *Verbal Behavior* (1957) as well as more popular works, such as *Walden Two* (1948), *Beyond Freedom and Dignity* (1971), and *About Behaviorism* (1974). Among Skinner's many honors were his election to the National Academy of Sciences and the Society of Experimental Psychologists and his receipt of both the Distinguished Scientific Contribution Award and the Lifetime Scientific Contribution Award from the American Psychological Association. See also DESCRIPTIVE BEHAVIORISM.

skin popping slang for the injection of a substance containing an opioid—usually HEROIN—under the skin, as opposed to mainlining (i.e., injecting into a vein).

sl abbreviation for *sub*/*ingual*.

SLD abbreviation for SPECIFIC LEARNING DISABILITY.

SLE abbreviation for systemic lupus erythematosus (see LUPUS ERYTHEMATOSUS).

sleep *n.* a state of the brain characterized by partial or total suspension of consciousness, muscular relaxation and inactivity, reduced metabolism, and relative insensitivity to stimulation. Other mental and physical characteristics that distinguish sleep from wakefulness include amnesia for events occurring during the loss of consciousness and unique sleep-related electroencephalogram and brain-imaging patterns (see SLEEP STAGES). These characteristics also help distinguish normal sleep from a loss of consciousness due to injury, disease, or drugs. See also DREAM STATE; NREM SLEEP; REM SLEEP.

sleep apnea the temporary cessation of breathing while asleep, which occurs when the upper airway briefly becomes blocked (**obstructive sleep apnea**) or when the respiratory centers in the brain fail to stimulate respiration (**central sleep apnea**). It can cause severe daytime sleepiness, and evidence is building that untreated severe sleep apnea may be associated with high blood pressure and risk for stroke and heart attack.

sleep cycle a recurring pattern of SLEEP STAGES in which a period of SLOW-WAVE SLEEP is followed by a period of REM SLEEP. In humans, a sleep cycle lasts approximately 90 min.

sleep deprivation deliberate prevention of sleep, particularly for experimental purposes. Studies show that the loss of one night's sleep has a substantial effect on physical or mental functioning; participants score significantly lower on tests of judgment and simple reaction time and show impairments in daytime alertness and memory. Sleep loss also may be detrimental to the immune and endocrine systems.

sleep disorder a persistent disturbance of typical sleep patterns, including the amount, quality, and timing of sleep, or the chronic occurrence of abnormal events or behavior during sleep. In *DSM–IV–TR* sleep disorders are broadly classified according to apparent cause, which may be endogenous or conditioning factors (**primary sleep disorders**), another mental disorder, a medical condition, or substance use. Primary sleep disorders are subdivided into DYSSOMNIAS and PARASOMNIAS. A classification system introduced in 1979 by the Association of Sleep Disorders Centers groups sleep disorders according to individuals' presenting symptoms: DISORDERS OF INITIATING AND MAINTAINING SLEEP; DISORDERS OF EXCESSIVE SOMNOLENCE; DISORDERS OF THE SLEEP–WAKE CYCLE SCHEDULE; and DYSFUNCTIONS ASSOCIATED WITH SLEEP, SLEEP STAGES, OR PARTIAL AROUSALS.

sleep efficiency the ratio of total time asleep to total time in bed. Sleep efficiency can be reduced in various psychological conditions (e.g., depression, anxiety) as well as by the use of some pharmacological agents (e.g., certain antidepressants).

sleep enuresis see BED-WETTING.

sleep hygiene techniques for the behavioral

treatment of insomnia that involve instruction given to the client to follow certain routines aimed at improving sleep patterns. Typical recommendations to the client include using the bed only for sleeping and sex (e.g., the client is instructed not to read in bed), not napping during the day, decreasing caffeine intake or eliminating it after a certain point in the day, going to bed regularly at a set time, and keeping a sleep diary.

sleeping sickness an infection, found only in tropical Africa, caused by parasitic protozoans of the genus *Trypanosoma* (*T. gambiense* and *T. rhodesiense*), which are transmitted by the bite of infected tsetse flies. Initial symptoms include fever, headaches, sweating, and swollen lymph nodes, progressing—upon inflammation of the brain and its protective membranes —to lethargy, excessive sleepiness (see HYPERSOMNIA), and confusion. If untreated, sleeping sickness can result in coma and eventually death. In *DSM–IV–TR*, the condition is categorized as SLEEP DISORDER due to a general medical condition: hypersomnia type. Also called **African trypanosomiasis**.

sleep inversion a tendency to sleep or be somnolent by day and to remain awake at night.

sleep laboratory a research facility designed to monitor patterns of activity during sleep, such as eye movement, breathing abnormalities, heartbeat, brain waves, and muscle tone. Sleep laboratories are typically found in neurology departments in hospitals and universities or in sleep disorder clinics.

sleep latency the amount of time it takes for an individual to fall asleep once the attempt to do so is made. Sleep latency is measured in the diagnosis of SLEEP DISORDERS. Sleeping pills (e.g., benzodiazepines) are designed to decrease sleep latency so that the individual can fall asleep more quickly.

sleeplessness *n.* see INSOMNIA.

sleep-onset insomnia a DYSSOMNIA characterized by persistent difficulty initiating sleep. Also called **onset insomnia**. See also INSOMNIA; PRIMARY INSOMNIA.

sleep paralysis brief inability to move or speak just before falling asleep or on awakening often accompanied by terrifying hallucinations. It may occur in any individual but is seen especially in individuals with NARCOLEPSY and may be due to a temporary dysfunction of the RETICULAR ACTIVATING SYSTEM.

sleep pattern a habitual, individual pattern of sleep, such as two 4-hour periods, daytime napping, various forms of insomnia (e.g., initial or intermittent insomnia), or excessive sleep. See also SLEEP–WAKE CYCLE.

Sleep Questionnaire and Assessment of Wakefulness (**SQAW**) an extensive questionnaire developed in 1979 by U.S. physician Laughton E. Miles at the Stanford University Sleep Disorders Clinic and Research Center to assess sleep behaviors and sleep disorders.

sleep spindles characteristic spindle-shaped patterns recorded on an electroencephalogram (EEG) during STAGE 2 SLEEP. They are short bursts of waves with a frequency of about 15 Hz that progressively increase then decrease in amplitude and they indicate a state of light sleep. Sleep spindles are often accompanied by K COMPLEXES.

sleep stages the four-cycle progression in electrical activity of the brain during a normal night's sleep, as recorded on an electroencephalogram (EEG). The regular pattern of ALPHA WAVES characteristic of the relaxed state of the individual just before sleep becomes intermittent and attenuated in STAGE 1 SLEEP, which is marked by drowsiness with rolling eyeball movements. This progresses to STAGE 2 SLEEP (light sleep), which is characterized by SLEEP SPINDLES and K COMPLEXES. In STAGE 3 SLEEP and STAGE 4 SLEEP (deep sleep), DELTA WAVES predominate (see SLOW-WAVE SLEEP). These stages comprise NREM SLEEP and are interspersed with periods of dreaming associated with REM SLEEP. After a period of deep sleep, the sleeper may return to either light sleep or REM sleep or to both, and the cycles can recur multiple times over the course of the sleep period.

sleep terror disorder a SLEEP DISORDER characterized by repeated episodes of abrupt awakening from NREM SLEEP accompanied by signs of disorientation, extreme panic, and intense anxiety. More intense than NIGHTMARES and occurring during the first few hours of sleep, these episodes typically last between 1 and 10 min and involve screaming and symptoms of autonomic arousal, such as profuse perspiration, dilated pupils, rapid breathing, and a rapidly beating heart. The individual is difficult to wake or comfort and does not have detailed recall of the dream upon waking; complete loss of memory for the episode is common. The disorder occurs most often in children and generally resolves itself during adolescence. In adults, it is often associated with psychopathology and a more chronic course. See also PARASOMNIA.

sleep–wake cycle the natural, brain-controlled bodily rhythm that results in alternate periods of sleep and wakefulness. The sleep–wake cycle may be disrupted by a number of factors, such as flight across time zones, shift work, drug use, or stress (see CIRCADIAN RHYTHM SLEEP DISORDER; DISORDERS OF THE SLEEP–WAKE CYCLE SCHEDULE). Also called **sleep rhythm**; **sleep–wakefulness cycle**. See also MONOPHASIC SLEEP; POLYPHASIC SLEEP.

sleep–wake schedule disorder see CIRCADIAN RHYTHM SLEEP DISORDER.

sleepwalking disorder a SLEEP DISORDER characterized by persistent incidents of complex motor activity during slow-wave NREM SLEEP. These episodes typically occur during the first hours of sleep and involve getting out of bed and walking, although the individual may also perform more complicated tasks, such as eating, talking, or operating machinery. While in this state, the individual stares blankly, is essentially unresponsive, and can be awakened only with great difficulty; he or she does not remember the episode upon waking. Also called **noctambulation**; **somnambulism**. See also PARASOMNIA.

slip *n.* an error, such as a SLIP OF THE TONGUE, that is committed unintentionally, even while knowing that it is an error. It implies a momentary loss of conscious control.

slip of the pen see FREUDIAN SLIP; PARAPRAXIS.

slip of the tongue a minor error in speech that is episodic and not related to a speech disorder or a stage of second-language acquisition. Psychoanalysts have long been interested in the significance of such slips, referring to them as FREUDIAN SLIPS and believing them to reveal unconscious associations, motivations, or wishes. Also called **lapsus linguae**; **speech error**. See also FREUDIAN SLIP; PARAPRAXIS; VERBAL LEAKAGE.

slippage *n.* see COGNITIVE SLIPPAGE.

slope *n.* the steepness or slant of a line on a graph, measured as the change of value on the *y*-axis associated with a change of one unit of value on the *x*-axis. In a REGRESSION EQUATION, slope is represented by the variable *b*, with +*b* indicating an upward slope to the line and –*b* indicating a downward slope.

slow learner a child of lower-than-average intelligence. Such children are so designated despite the fact that a somewhat lower-than-average IQ does not necessarily imply slow learning. Slow learners are estimated at 15–17% of the average school population. They do not show marked variations from physical, social, and emotional norms and are usually placed in regular classes. The term "slow learner" is often imprecisely applied to children with MILD MENTAL RETARDATION as well as to children of normal capacity whose intellectual progress is slow.

slow-release preparation a drug preparation that is formulated in such a way that the active ingredient is released over an extended period. For example, drugs may be administered in the form of transdermal patches, which are applied to skin, through which they slowly release their contents; or as extended-release capsules, which contain quantities of the active drug surrounded by separate coatings that dissolve at different rates in stomach and intestines. Injectable slow-release forms (depot preparations) are often oil based; these are taken up into fat stores in the body and released over extended periods of days to weeks. Also called **extended-release preparation**; **sustained-release preparation**.

slow-wave sleep deep sleep that is characterized by DELTA WAVES on the electroencephalogram, corresponding to stages 3 and 4 of sleep. It is controlled by SEROTONIN-rich cells in the brainstem: Increased levels of serotonin stimulate slow-wave sleep, whereas abnormally low levels of serotonin result in insomnia. Slow-wave sleep has a restorative function that helps eliminate feelings of fatigue. See also SLEEP STAGES.

Smell Identification Test (**SIT**) a 40-item test of odor-identification ability for individuals aged 5 years and older. It is used to assess olfactory sensitivity and diagnose or evaluate olfactory impairment, which has been recognized as an important clinical indicator of neurological and psychiatric disorders (e.g., Alzheimer's disease, Parkinson's disease). Test participants scratch and sniff a scent-impregnated patch and then identify the odor from a list of four answer choices, repeating the procedure for all 40 test stimuli. A brief version of the test (**B–SIT**) using 12 odorant stimuli determines gross dysfunction of olfactory sensitivity. The SIT, initially developed in 1981, is now in its third edition. Also called **University of Pennsylvania Smell Identification Test** (**UPSIT**). [developed by U.S. psychologist Richard L. Doty (1944–)]

smile *n.* a bilateral upturning of the lips, typically taking place when greeting another or sharing certain states of pleasure with another. See also DUCHENNE SMILE; ENDOGENOUS SMILE.

Smith–Lemli–Opitz syndrome an autosomal recessive disorder marked by MICROCEPHALY, a broad, short nose, syndactyly (fused digits) or polydactyly (extra digits), and mental retardation. Nearly all affected males have urethral or other genital anomalies, whereas females have no obvious abnormalities of the external genitalia, a factor that led early investigators to believe erroneously that the syndrome affected only males. This disorder may be caused by mutations in the sterol delta-7-reductase gene (*DHCR7*), on chromosome 11 (locus 11q12–13). Also called **RSH syndrome** (from the names of the three affected families originally reported); **Smith syndrome**. [reported in 1964 by David W. **Smith** (1926–1981), U.S. pediatrician; Luc **Lemli** (1935–), Belgian pediatrician; and John M. **Opitz** (1935–), U.S. geneticist]

S

smoking *n.* the act of drawing the smoke of burning TOBACCO or other substances, such as marijuana, into the mouth or lungs. See CANNABIS; NICOTINE; TOBACCO.

smoking cessation treatment interventions to help people quit smoking that typically involve behavioral techniques (e.g., reinforcement), social support, environmental change, and healthy activity substitution (e.g., exercise), which may be used in conjunction with nicotine replacement therapy or other drugs. Group treatment is often offered in community settings.

smoothing *n.* a collection of techniques used to reduce the irregularities (random variation) in a batch of data or in a plot (curve) of that data, particularly in TIME SERIES analyses, so as to more clearly see the underlying trends.

snake phobia a persistent and irrational fear of snakes, formerly called **ophidiophobia**. This type of fear is classified as a SPECIFIC PHOBIA, animal type. See also ANIMAL PHOBIA.

SNF abbreviation for SKILLED NURSING FACILITY.

snow *n.* slang for COCAINE or, sometimes, HEROIN or AMPHETAMINE.

SNP abbreviation for SINGLE-NUCLEOTIDE POLYMORPHISM.

SNRI serotonin and norepinephrine reuptake inhibitors: any of a class of antidepressants that exert their therapeutic effects by interfering with the reabsorption of both serotonin and norepinephrine by the neurons that released them. They include VENLAFAXINE and duloxetine.

sociability *n.* the tendency to seek out companionship, engage in interpersonal relations, and participate in social activities. **—sociable** *adj.*

sociability rating an evaluation of an individual's degree of sociability based on the amount of time devoted to social activities.

social age (SA) a numerical scale unit expressing how mature a person is in terms of his or her interpersonal skills and ability to fulfill the norms and expectations associated with particular social roles, as compared to others of the same CHRONOLOGICAL AGE. SA is similar to MENTAL AGE and is derived from ratings gathered from the individual or, in the case of young children, from parents or caregivers using instruments such as the Vineland Adaptive Behavior Scales.

social agency a private or governmental organization that supervises or provides personal services, especially in the fields of health, welfare, and rehabilitation. The general objective of a social agency is to improve the quality of life of its clients.

social animal the concept that some animals are inherently social creatures with interpersonal needs and wants. When referring to humans, the term **social man** is sometimes used. Also called **social being**; **zoon politikon**. See also SOCIAL INSTINCT.

social anxiety fear of social situations (e.g., making conversation, meeting strangers, or dating) in which embarrassment may occur or there is a risk of being negatively evaluated by others (e.g., seen as stupid, weak, or anxious). Social anxiety involves apprehensiveness about one's social status, role, and behavior. When the anxiety causes an individual significant distress or impairment in functioning, a diagnosis of SOCIAL PHOBIA may be warranted.

social anxiety disorder see SOCIAL PHOBIA.

social bond an affective relation between individuals, such as the connection between two friends or the emotional link between family members.

social breakdown syndrome a symptom pattern observed primarily in institutionalized individuals with chronic mental illness but also in such populations as long-term prisoners and older people. Symptoms include withdrawal, apathy, submissiveness, and progressive social and vocational incompetence. Previously considered to be symptomatic of mental illness, this decline is now attributed to internalized negative stereotypes, such as identification with the SICK ROLE and the impact of labeling (see LABELING THEORY), the absence of social support, and such institutional factors as a lack of stimulation, overcrowding, unchanging routine, and disinterest on the part of the staff. Also called **chronicity**; **institutionalism**; **institutional neurosis**; **social disability syndrome**.

social casework see CASEWORK.

social cognition cognition in which people perceive, think about, interpret, categorize, and judge their own social behaviors and those of others. The study of social cognition involves aspects of both cognitive psychology and social psychology. Major areas of interest include ATTRIBUTION THEORY, SOCIAL INFLUENCE, and the cognitive processes involved in moral judgments.

social-cognitive theory a theoretical framework in which the functioning of personality is explained in terms of cognitive contents and processes acquired through interaction with the sociocultural environment. [advanced by Albert BANDURA and U.S. personality psychologist Walter Mischel (1930–)]

social cohesion see COHESION.

social comparison theory the proposition that people evaluate their abilities and attitudes in relation to those of others (i.e., through a process of comparison) when objective standards for the assessment of these abilities and attitudes are lacking. The way people compare themselves with others (their **comparison group** or reference group) was most fully described by Leon FESTINGER in 1954. He also held that those chosen as the comparison group are generally those whose abilities or attitudes are relatively similar to the person's own abilities or views.

social competence effectiveness or skill in interpersonal relations and social situations, increasingly considered an important component of mental health. Social competence involves the ability to evaluate social situations and determine what is expected or required; to recognize the feelings and intentions of others; and to select social behaviors that are most appropriate for that given context. It is important to note, however, that what is required and appropriate for effective social functioning is likely to vary across settings.

social constructivism the school of thought that recognizes knowledge as embedded in social context and sees human thoughts, feelings, language, and behavior as the result of interchanges with the external world. Social constructivism argues that there is no separation between subjectivity and objectivity and that the dichotomy between the person and the situation is false: the person is intimately and intricately bound within social, cultural, and historical forces and cannot be understood fully without consideration of these social forces. According to social constructivism, not only knowledge but reality itself is created in an interactive process and thus people are solely what their society shapes them to be.

social deficit inability, unwillingness, or poor judgment in the performance of social activities commensurate with chronological age, intelligence, or physical condition. Such a deficit is presumed to reduce a person's ability to obtain social support and is therefore a target of treatment, especially in behavior therapy and with severely disturbed individuals.

social deprivation **1.** limited access to society's resources due to poverty, discrimination, or other disadvantage. See CULTURAL DEPRIVATION. **2.** lack of adequate opportunity for social experience.

social desirability **1.** the extent to which someone or something (a trait, attribute, or the like) is admired or considered valuable within a social group. **2.** the bias or tendency of individuals to present themselves in a manner that will be viewed favorably by others. In an experiment, for example, it manifests as the **social desirability response set**, which is the tendency of participants to give answers that are in accordance with social norms or the perceived desires of the researcher rather than genuinely representative of their views. This is a CONFOUND to be controlled for in certain research, as it often reduces the validity of interviews, questionnaires, and other self-reports. See IMPRESSION MANAGEMENT.

social determinism the theory or doctrine that individual behaviors are determined by societal events and other interpersonal experiences. See also CULTURAL DETERMINISM; DETERMINISM.

social disability syndrome see SOCIAL BREAKDOWN SYNDROME.

social drift see DRIFT HYPOTHESIS.

social drinker an imprecise categorization generally agreed to signify an individual who tends to drink alcohol only in a social setting and usually in moderation.

Social–Emotional scale see BAYLEY SCALES OF INFANT AND TODDLER DEVELOPMENT.

social exchange theory a theory envisioning social interactions as an exchange in which the participants seek to maximize their benefits within the limits of what is regarded as fair or just. Intrinsic to this hypothesis is the RECIPROCITY NORM: People are expected to reciprocate for the benefits they have received. Social exchange theory is similar to **equity theory**, which also maintains that people seek fairness in social relationships and that fairness exists when each party in the relationship has the same ratio of outcomes (benefits) to inputs (resources brought to the relationship). [proposed by Austrian sociologists George C. Homans (1910–1989) and Peter Blau (1918–2002)]

social facilitation the improvement in an individual's performance of a task that often occurs when others are present. This effect tends to occur with tasks that are uncomplicated or have been previously mastered through practice. There is some disagreement as to whether the improvement is due to a heightened state of arousal, a greater self-awareness, or a reduced attention to unimportant and distracting peripheral stimuli. By contrast, the presence of other people is frequently an impediment to effective performance when the task is complicated, particularly if it is not well learned. See also AUDIENCE EFFECT.

social factors factors (e.g., attitudes) that affect thought or behavior in social contexts or that affect SELF-CONCEPT vis-à-vis other individuals or groups.

social growth the development of the individual's knowledge and ability with regard to dealings with other individuals and groups. Social growth is not limited to conformity; much social growth can lie outside the range of cultural expectations.

social hunger a desire to be accepted by others.

social identity **1.** the personal qualities that one claims and displays to others so consistently that they are considered to be part of one's essential, stable self. This public persona may be an accurate indicator of the private, personal self, but it may also be a deliberately contrived image. **2.** see COLLECTIVE SELF.

social imperception disorder a condition characterized by a lack of awareness of common social interaction and interpersonal behaviors, difficulty in recognizing and understanding other people's feelings and emotions, and a very limited awareness of typical social interpersonal issues.

social influence **1.** any change in an individual's thoughts, feelings, or behaviors caused by other people, who may be actually present, imagined, expected, or only implied. **2.** those interpersonal processes that can cause individuals to change their thoughts, feelings, or behaviors.

social instinct **1.** the desire for social contact and a feeling of belonging, as manifested by the tendency to congregate, affiliate, and engage in group behaviors. **2.** in the INDIVIDUAL PSYCHOLOGY of Alfred ADLER, an innate drive for cooperation that leads normal individuals to incorporate social interest and the common good into their efforts to achieve self-realization.

social intelligence the ability to understand people and effectively relate to them. It is often contrasted with ABSTRACT INTELLIGENCE and CONCRETE INTELLIGENCE.

social interest in the INDIVIDUAL PSYCHOLOGY of Alfred ADLER, communal feeling based on a recognition that people live in a social context; are an integral part of their family, community, humanity, and the cosmos itself; and have a natural aptitude for acquiring the skills and understanding necessary to solve social problems and to take socially affirmative action. Adler believed, however, that social interest is only partially inherent in adaptive development and needs to be actively cultivated in any individual.

social intervention social action programs designed to increase some type of social goods or services.

social introversion a behavioral trait manifested by shy, inhibited, and withdrawn attitudes.

social isolation voluntary or involuntary absence of contact with others. See also ISOLATE; LONELINESS.

sociality *n.* the tendency to live as part of a group with clear organization of social interactions and the ability to cooperate with and adapt to the demands of the group.

sociality corollary a concept proposing that an individual's ability to communicate or otherwise interact with another individual is based on an understanding of the other's PERSONAL CONSTRUCT. [proposed by U.S. psychologist George A. Kelly (1905–1967)]

socialization *n.* **1.** the process by which individuals acquire social skills, beliefs, values, and behaviors necessary to function effectively in society or in a particular group. **2.** the process by which employees adjust to the organizational culture and learn the knowledge, skills, attitudes, and values expected of them by superiors, peers, subordinates, customers, and others. **3.** the process whereby individuals become aware of alternative lifestyles and behaviors. It enables individuals to learn the social or group value-system behavior pattern and what is considered normal or desirable for the social environment in which they will be members. —**socialize** *vb.*

socialized delinquency violations of the law by individuals under age 18 that result from their adherence to the attitudes and values of a subculture, such as a gang, that glorifies criminal or antisocial conduct. Also called **subcultural delinquency**.

socialized drive any PRIMARY DRIVE that has been modified through social learning so that drive satisfaction is achieved through socially acceptable behaviors, for example, sexual gratification achieved through mutually consensual adult sex.

social learning theory the general view that learning is largely or wholly due to imitation, modeling, and other social interactions. Behavior is assumed to be developed and regulated (a) by external stimulus events, such as the influence of other individuals; (b) by external reinforcement, such as praise, blame, and reward; and (c) by the effects of cognitive processes, such as thinking and judgment, on the individual's behavior and on the environment that influences him or her. [developed by Albert BANDURA]

social maladjustment **1.** inability to develop relationships that satisfy affiliative needs. **2.** lack of social finesse or tact. **3.** a breakdown in the process of maintaining constructive social relationships.

social maturity scale an instrument that assesses the degree to which an individual performs age-appropriate behaviors. These behaviors are primarily concerned with functioning in the family and community and are sometimes considered in conjunction with measures of intellectual impairment to establish the presence of retardation.

social need see LOVE NEED.

social-network therapy a form of psychotherapy in which various people who maintain significant relationships with the patient or client in different aspects of life (e.g., relatives, friends, coworkers) are assembled with the client present in small or larger group sessions. See also NETWORK THERAPY.

social norm any of the socially determined consensual standards that indicate (a) what behaviors are considered typical in a given context (descriptive norms) and (b) what behaviors are considered proper in the context (injunctive norms). Whether implicitly or explicitly, these norms not only prescribe the socially appropriate way to respond in the situation (the "normal" course of action) but also proscribe actions that should be avoided if at all possible. Unlike statistical norms, social norms of both types include an evaluative quality such that those who do not comply and cannot provide an acceptable explanation for their violation are evaluated negatively. Social norms apply across groups and social settings, whereas **group norms** are specific to a particular group.

social ossification ingrained social behavior that is difficult to change, for example, when a person moves to a new environment with different social rules and standards.

social phobia an anxiety disorder that is characterized by extreme and persistent SOCIAL ANXIETY or PERFORMANCE ANXIETY that causes significant distress or prevents participation in everyday activities. The feared situation is most often avoided altogether or else it is endured with marked discomfort. Also called **social anxiety disorder**.

social psychology the study of how an individual's thoughts, feelings, and actions are affected by the actual, imagined, or symbolically represented presence of other people. **Psychological social psychology** differs from **sociological social psychology** in that the former tends to give greater emphasis to internal psychological processes, whereas the latter focuses on factors that affect social life, such as status, role, and class.

social quotient the ratio between SOCIAL AGE and CHRONOLOGICAL AGE. A social quotient is a parallel concept to an IQ, where a score of 100 indicates average performance for age and scores less than 100 indicate below average functioning.

social recovery restoration of an adaptive, highly functional mental state through SOCIAL THERAPY and improvement in social skills. [first described by U.S. psychiatrist Harry Stack Sullivan (1892–1949)]

social rehabilitation 1. the achievement of a higher level of social functioning in individuals with mental disorders or disabilities through group activities and participation in clubs and other community organizations. **2.** the achievement of a higher level of independent functioning in individuals with physical impairments or disabilities through provision of assistance with ACTIVITIES OF DAILY LIVING as well as other more social aspects of living, such as employment and the need for transportation and appropriate housing, that often present barriers to participation for those with disabilities. **3.** services and assistance provided to help criminal offenders establish new, noncriminal ways of life and become productive members of the community.

social reinforcement a positive interpersonal stimulus, such as verbal praise, a smile, touch, or other sign of approval, that increases the frequency of the behavior that immediately precedes it. See REINFORCEMENT.

social representation a system, model, or code for unambiguously naming and organizing values, ideas, and conduct, which enables communication and social exchange (i.e., at the levels of language and behavior) among members of a particular group or community.

social role valorization a principle, developed in succession to the NORMALIZATION PRINCIPLE, that stresses the importance of creating or supporting socially valued roles for people with disabilities. According to this principle, fulfillment of valued social roles increases the likelihood that a person will be socially accepted by others and will more readily achieve a satisfactory quality of life. [formulated in 1983 by German-born Canadian sociologist and special educator Wolf Wolfensberger (1934–2011)]

social schema a cognitive structure of organized information, or representations, about social norms and collective patterns of behavior within society. Whereas a SELF-SCHEMA involves a person's conception of herself or himself as an individual and in terms of a particular personal role (or roles) in life, social schemata often underlie behavior of the person acting within group—particularly larger-group or societal—contexts.

Social Security a comprehensive social program providing basic retirement income and insurance, as well as disability, survivor, and MEDICARE benefits. Established in 1935, the program is operated by the U.S. Social Security Administration.

social self 1. the aspects of the SELF that are important to or influenced by social relations. See also COLLECTIVE SELF; PUBLIC SELF; SOCIAL IDENTITY. **2.** a person's characteristic behavior in social situations. **3.** the facade that an individual may exhibit when in contact with other people, as contrasted with his or her real self.

social services 1. services provided by government and nongovernment agencies and organizations to improve social welfare for those in need, including people with low income, illness or disability, older adults, and children. Services might include health care, insurance, subsidized housing, food subsidies, and the like. **2.** government services to improve standards of living for all citizens, including such services as roads and public transportation, clean water, electricity, telecommunications, and public health institutions.

social skills training (**SST**) a form of individual or group therapy for those who need to overcome social inhibition or ineffectiveness. It uses many techniques for teaching effective social interaction in specific situations (e.g., job interviews, dating), including ASSERTIVENESS TRAINING and behavioral and cognitive REHEARSAL.

social support the provision of assistance or comfort to others, typically in order to help them cope with a variety of biological, psychological, and social stressors. Support may arise from any interpersonal relationship in an individual's social network, involving family members, friends, neighbors, religious institutions, colleagues, caregivers, or support groups. It may take the form of practical help with chores or money; informational assistance (e.g., advice or guidance); and, at the most basic level, emotional support that allows the individual to feel valued, accepted, and understood. Social support has generally been shown to have positive physical and psychological effects, particularly in protecting against the deleterious effects of stress. See also COPING.

social therapy therapeutic and rehabilitative approaches that use social structures and experiences to improve the interpersonal functioning of individuals, for example, MILIEU THERAPY and the THERAPEUTIC COMMUNITY.

social withdrawal retreat from society and interpersonal relationships, usually accompanied by an attitude of indifference, detachment, and aloofness. Social withdrawal is often associated with such disorders as schizophrenia, autism, and depression. See also WITHDRAWAL REACTION.

social work a profession devoted to helping individuals, families, and other groups deal with personal and practical problems within the larger community context of which they are a part. Social workers address a variety of problems, including those related to mental or physical disorder, poverty, living arrangements, child care, occupational stress, and unemployment, especially through involvement in the provision of SOCIAL SERVICES.

societal-reaction theory see LABELING THEORY.

Society for Psychotherapy Research an international, interdisciplinary organization dedicated to the scientific study of psychotherapy in all of its various forms. It publishes the journal *Psychotherapy Research.*

sociobiology *n.* the systematic study of the biological basis for social behavior. **Sociobiologists** believe that populations tend to maintain an optimal level of density (neither overpopulation nor underpopulation) by such controls as aggression, stress, fertility, emigration, predation, and disease. Such controls are held to operate through the Darwinian principle of natural selection. [pioneered by U.S. biologist Edward Osborne Wilson (1929–)] **—sociobiological** *adj.*

sociocentrism *n.* **1.** the tendency to put the needs, concerns, and perspective of the social unit or group before one's individual, egocentric concerns. See also ALLOCENTRIC. **2.** the practice of perceiving and interpreting situations from the point of view of the social group rather than from one's own personal perspective. **3.** the tendency to judge one's own group as superior to other groups across a variety of domains. Whereas ethnocentrism refers to the selective favoring of one's ethnic, religious, racial, or national groups, sociocentrism usually means the favoring of smaller groups characterized by face-to-face interaction among members. Compare EGOCENTRISM. **—sociocentric** *adj.*

sociocognitive bias a subtle bias in judgment to which evaluators may be susceptible. Unlike values, sociocognitive biases are inaccurate judgments that result from shortcomings in cognitive processing; they appear to be universals that intrude regardless of values or ethics.

S

sociocultural deprivation see PSYCHOSOCIAL DEPRIVATION.

sociocultural factors environmental conditions that play a part in healthy and adaptive behavior and well-being or in maladaptive behavior and the etiology of mental disorder and social pathology. Examples of sociocultural factors of a positive nature are a strong sense of family and community support and mentorship, good education and health care, availability of recreational facilities, and exposure to the arts. Examples of a negative nature are slum conditions, poverty, extreme or restrictive occupational pressures, lack of good medical care, and inadequate educational opportunities.

sociocultural mental retardation see CULTURAL-FAMILIAL MENTAL RETARDATION.

sociodrama *n.* a technique for enhancing human relations and social skills that uses dramatization and ROLE PLAY. See also PSYCHODRAMA.

sociogenic *adj.* resulting from social factors. For example, a **sociogenic hypothesis** of schizophrenia posits that social conditions, such as living in impoverished circumstances, are major contributors to and causal agents of the disorder.

sociogram *n.* a graphic representation of the relations among members of a social unit or group. In most cases each member of the group is depicted by a symbol, such as a lettered circle or square, and the types of relations among members (e.g., communication links, friendship pairings) are depicted by arrows. SOCIOMETRY, as originally developed by Romanian-born U.S. psychiatrist and philosopher Jacob L. Moreno (1889–1974), uses objective data collected by observers or the self-reports provided by members of the group to generate sociograms. Moreno himself used four types of sociograms to represent any given situation: (a) an intuitive sociogram, based on relationships noted by the therapist in the first session; (b) an observer's sociogram, consisting of the cotherapist's impressions; (c) an objective sociogram, based on a sociometric test; and (d) a perceptual sociogram, in which each member indicates which other members appear to accept or reject him or her. In practice, sociograms are used mainly to emphasize the patterns of liking and disliking (ATTRACTION RELATIONS) in a group.

sociological measure 1. a formal measure of aspects of society that may affect the development or maintenance of normal behaviors or mental health problems. Sociological measures may assess the interrelationships between people or the structural components of a society, for example, and include both quantitative and qualitative methods. See also SOCIOMETRY. **2.** see PRIMARY PREVENTION.

sociometry *n.* a field of research in which various techniques are used to analyze the patterns of intermember relations within groups and to summarize these findings in mathematical and graphic form. In most cases researchers ask the group members one or more questions about their fellow members, such as "Whom do you most like in this group?", "Whom in the group would you like to work with the most?", or "Whom do you like the least?". These choices can then be summarized in a SOCIOGRAM, in which each member is represented by a numbered or lettered symbol and the various choices are identified by lines between them with arrows indicating the direction of relationships. In most cases the diagram is organized into a meaningful pattern by placing those individuals who are most frequently chosen (stars) in the center of the diagram and the ISOLATES about the periphery. The method also yields various indices of group structure and group cohesion, including choice status (the number of times a person is chosen by the other group members), rejection status (the number of times a person is rejected by others), the relative number of mutual pairs in a group, and so on. [developed by Romanian-born U.S. psychiatrist and philosopher Jacob L. Moreno (1889–1974)] **—sociometric** *adj.*

sociopath *n.* a former name for an individual with an ANTISOCIAL PERSONALITY DISORDER.

sociopathic behavior see DYSSOCIAL BEHAVIOR.

sociopathic disorder see ANTISOCIAL PERSONALITY DISORDER.

sociopathic personality see ANTISOCIAL PERSONALITY DISORDER.

sociopathy *n.* see ANTISOCIAL PERSONALITY DISORDER.

sociosexual assessment an assessment of an individual to identify or measure his or her awareness of cultural standards regarding social relationships and sexual activity, knowledge of facts about sexuality and the nature and consequences of sexual interaction, and engagement (type and nature) in sexual activities. It may also include an assessment of risks that the individual may engage in culturally sanctioned sexual activities.

sociotherapy *n.* a supportive therapeutic approach based on modification of an individual's environment with the aim of improving the individual's interpersonal adjustment. The approach may be used in a variety of contexts, including working with parents and prospective foster parents, family counseling, vocational retraining, and assistance in readjusting to community life following hospitalization for severe mental illness.

sociotropy *n.* the tendency to place an inordinate value on relationships over personal independence, thought to leave one vulnerable to depression in response to the loss of relationships or to conflict.

Socratic dialogue a process of structured inquiry and discussion between two or more people to explore the concepts and values that underlie their everyday activities and judgments. In some psychotherapies, it is a technique in which the therapist poses strategic questions designed to clarify the client's core beliefs and feelings and, in the case of COGNITIVE THERAPY, to enable the client to discover the distortions in his or her habitual interpretation of a given situation. In psychotherapy, it is also known as the **Socratic-therapeutic method**.

Socratic-therapeutic method see SOCRATIC DIALOGUE.

sodium Amytal interview see AMOBARBITAL.

sodium channel see ION CHANNEL.

sodomy *n.* **1.** ANAL INTERCOURSE between human beings or sexual intercourse of any kind between a human being and an animal (see ZOOERASTY). This word is derived from the name of the corrupt town of Sodom described in Genesis 18–19. **2.** in legal contexts, any sexual assault that does not involve penile–vaginal penetration.

soft sign a clinical, behavioral, or neurological sign that may reflect the presence of neurological impairment. Soft signs are subtle, nonspecific, and ambiguous (because they are also seen in individuals without neurological impairment). Examples include slight abnormalities of speech, gait, posture, or behavior; sleep disturbances; slow physical maturation; sensory or perceptual deficits; and short attention span. Also called **equivocal sign**; **soft neurological sign**.

Sohval–Soffer syndrome a rare, presumably hereditary, disease characterized by mental retardation and testicular deficiency, as well as skeletal anomalies and diabetes mellitus. A small number of affected individuals studied had psychotic disorder and low intelligence. The penis and testes are small, and facial and pubic hair is sparse. [reported in 1953 by Arthur R. **Sohval** (1904–1985) and Louis J. **Soffer** (1904–), U.S. physicians]

solution-focused brief therapy BRIEF PSYCHOTHERAPY that focuses on problems in the HERE AND NOW, with specific goals that the client views as important to achieve in a limited time.

solvent abuse see INHALANT ABUSE.

soma *n.* **1.** the physical body (Greek, "body"), as distinguished from the mind or spirit. See MIND–BODY PROBLEM. **2.** in neuroscience, the CELL BODY of a neuron. **3.** a plant regarded as sacred (and personified as the plant god Soma) by ancient Aryan peoples, which some experts have hypothesized to be FLY AGARIC (*Amanita muscaria*).

Soma *n.* a trade name for CARISOPRODOL.

somatic concern worries about one's bodily health, including concern over physical symptoms (e.g., chest pain, nausea, diarrhea, headaches, pain, shortness of breath) and distressing beliefs about bodily illness or dysfunction. See HYPOCHONDRIASIS.

somatic delusion a false belief related to one or more bodily organs, such as that they are functioning improperly or are diseased, injured, or otherwise altered. Although standard tests do not confirm this belief, the individual nonetheless continues to maintain this conviction. Also called **somatopsychic delusion**.

somatic depression a MAJOR DEPRESSIVE EPISODE in which physical symptoms are prominent.

somatic disorder an organic physical disorder, as distinguished from a FUNCTIONAL DISORDER or a PSYCHOGENIC DISORDER.

somatic hallucination the false perception of a physical occurrence within the body, such as feeling electric currents.

somatic nervous system the part of the nervous system comprising the sensory and motor neurons that innervate the sense organs and the skeletal muscles, as opposed to the AUTONOMIC NERVOUS SYSTEM.

somatic obsession preoccupation with one's body or any part of it. This concern may be associated with compulsive checking of the body part (e.g., in a mirror or by touch), comparison with others, and seeking reassurance. Somatic obsession is the central feature of BODY DYSMORPHIC DISORDER but may also be a feature of OBSESSIVE-COMPULSIVE DISORDER if other obsessive-compulsive symptoms are present.

somatic therapy the treatment of mental disorders by physical methods that directly influence the body, such as the administration of drugs (PHARMACOTHERAPY) or the application of a controlled, low-dose electric current (ELECTROCONVULSIVE THERAPY). Also called **somatotherapy**.

somatic weakness the hypothesized vulnerability, due to congenital susceptibility, of an organ or organ system to the effects of psychological stress. The organ is thus predisposed to becoming the focus of a PSYCHOSOMATIC DISORDER.

somatist *n.* a person who considers mental disorders to be manifestations of organic disease.

somatization *n.* the expression of psychological disturbance in physical (bodily) symptoms. The first use of the word has controversially been attributed to Austrian psychoanalyst Wilhelm Stekel (1868–1940) to describe what is now called CONVERSION. Some investigators use the word in reference not only to the physical symptoms that occur in almost every type of anxiety disorder but also to the expression of symptoms in such PSYCHOSOMATIC DISORDERS as psychogenic asthma and peptic ulcers.

somatization disorder in *DSM–IV–TR,* a SOMATOFORM DISORDER involving a history of multiple physical symptoms (at least eight, one of which must be a PSEUDONEUROLOGICAL symptom) of several years' duration, for which medical attention has been sought but which are apparently not due to any physical disorder or injury. The complaints are often described in vague yet colorful or exaggerated terms by the patient, who often appears anxious or depressed. Among the complaints are feelings of sickliness, difficulty in swallowing or walking, blurred vision, abdominal pain, nausea, diarrhea, painful or irregular menstruation, sexual indifference, painful intercourse, pain in the back or joints, shortness of breath, palpitations, and chest pain.

somatoform disorder in *DSM–IV–TR,* any of a group of disorders marked by physical symptoms suggesting a specific medical condition for which there is no demonstrable organic evidence and for which there is positive evidence or a strong probability that they are linked to psychological factors. The symptoms must cause marked distress or significantly impair normal social or occupational functioning. See SOMATIZATION DISORDER; UNDIFFERENTIATED SOMATOFORM DISORDER; CONVERSION DISORDER; PAIN DISORDER; HYPOCHONDRIASIS; BODY DYSMORPHIC DISORDER.

somatoform disorder not otherwise specified in *DSM–IV–TR,* a diagnostic category reserved for disorders with unexplained physical symptoms that do not meet the criteria for a more specific SOMATOFORM DISORDER. It should not be confused with UNDIFFERENTIATED SOMATOFORM DISORDER.

somatoform pain disorder see PAIN DISORDER.

somatogenesis *n.* **1.** the process by which germ-cell material develops into body cells. **2.** the development of behavioral or personality traits or disorders as a result of anatomical, physiological, or biochemical changes in the body. Also called **organogenesis**. **—somatogenic** or **somatogenetic** *adj.*

somatognosia *n.* awareness of one's own body or body parts. Denial of one's body parts is called asomatognosia and is commonly seen in individuals with NEGLECT.

somatophrenia *n.* a tendency to imagine or exaggerate bodily ills. See also HYPOCHONDRIASIS.

somatopsychic delusion see SOMATIC DELUSION.

somatopsychology *n.* the study of the psychological impact of physiological disease or disability: The term is little used, and the subject matter of the study is now largely included under the rubric of HEALTH PSYCHOLOGY.

somatopsychosis *n.* **1.** a psychosis marked by delusions that involve the person's body or body parts. **2.** a psychosis that is due to a bodily (physical) disease. [defined by U.S. psychiatrist Elmer Ernest Southard (1876–1920)]

somatosensory area either of two main areas of the CEREBRAL CORTEX that can be mapped with EVOKED POTENTIALS to reveal points that respond to stimulation of the various senses related to touch (somatosense). Also called **somatic sensory area**; **somatic area**; **somatosensory cortex**.

somatosensory system the parts of the nervous system that serve perception of touch, vibration, pain, temperature, and position. Also called **somatic sensory system**.

somatotherapy *n.* **1.** treatment of bodily or physical disorders. **2.** see SOMATIC THERAPY.

somatotonia *n.* the personality type that, according to SHELDON'S CONSTITUTIONAL THEORY OF PERSONALITY, is associated with a mesomorphic physique (see MESOMORPH). Somatotonia is characterized by a tendency toward energetic activity, physical courage, and love of power. **—somatotonic** *adj.*

somatotype *n.* the body build or physique of a person, particularly as it relates to his or her temperament or behavioral characteristics (see CON-

STITUTIONAL TYPE). Numerous categories of somatotypes have been proposed by various investigators since ancient times. The classification of individuals in this way is called **somatotypology**.

somesthetic disorder any dysfunction involving the senses involving touch (somatosenses), such as difficulty in maintaining postural or positional awareness or lack of sensitivity to pain, touch, or temperature. Somesthetic disorders are usually related to PARIETAL LOBE damage.

somnambulism *n.* see SLEEPWALKING DISORDER.

somnambulistic state a state of mind in which walking, talking, or other complex acts occur during sleep (see SLEEPWALKING DISORDER). Historically, it refers to a hypnotic phase in which the individual in a deep TRANCE may appear to be awake and in control of his or her actions but is actually under the influence of the hypnotist.

somnolence *n.* excessive sleepiness or drowsiness, which is sometimes pathological. The condition may be due, for example, to medication, a sleep disorder, or a medical condition (e.g., HYPOTHYROIDISM). **—somnolent** *adj.*

somnolentia *n.* unnatural drowsiness.

somnophilia *n.* an obsolete term for sexual interest and arousal derived from intruding on a sleeping person. It may involve fondling the person or masturbating while watching the person sleep.

Sonata *n.* a trade name for ZALEPLON.

soporifics *pl. n.* agents that are capable of producing sleep, particularly a deep sleep. Also called **sopoforics**.

SOPS abbreviation for SCALE OF PRODROMAL SYMPTOMS.

SORC *n.* an acronym for the four variables employed in behavioral analysis: stimuli (see SITUATIONAL DETERMINANT), ORGANISMIC VARIABLES, responses, and consequences (reinforcement contingencies). A functional analysis of behavior may seek to determine how the presentation of certain stimuli leads to specific responses (perhaps influenced by individual, or organismic, variables), which are followed by consequences that may then reinforce the elicited responses.

sorcery drugs a group of plant alkaloids that includes belladonna, the opium alkaloids, mandrake, aconite, and hemlock. The substances have been chewed, smoked, or brewed into potions since ancient times for purposes of healing or intoxication. Medicinal herbs were usually grown and administered by shamans or native healers; some, such as the opiates and anticholinergics, are used in modern medical pharmacology.

Sotos syndrome an inherited condition characterized by MACROCEPHALY, distinctive facial features (including wide-set eyes), nonprogressive cerebral disorder, mental retardation, increased birth weight, and excessive growth during early childhood. Mild dilation of the cerebral ventricles, nonspecific EEG (electroencephalogram) changes, and seizures have been observed in affected individuals. Handicaps may be fewer than previously believed and tend to improve with age. Also called **cerebral gigantism; Nevo syndrome**. [reported in 1964 by J. F. **Sotos** (1927–), U.S. pediatrician]

soul image in the ANALYTIC PSYCHOLOGY of Carl JUNG, the deeply unconscious portion of the psyche that is composed of the ANIMUS (or male archetype) and ANIMA (or female archetype).

source amnesia impaired memory for how, when, or where information was learned despite good memory for the information itself. Source amnesia is often linked to frontal lobe pathology.

source confusion misattribution of the origins of a memory. This may distort eyewitness accounts of the events surrounding a crime. For example, an eyewitness hearing from a police officer that the perpetrator carried a gun may later believe that he or she saw the gun at the crime scene.

source memory remembering the origin of a memory or of knowledge, that is, memory of where or how one came to know what one now remembers.

source trait in CATTELL'S PERSONALITY TRAIT THEORY, any of 16 personality traits, determined by FACTOR ANALYSIS, that underlie and determine SURFACE TRAITS. Examples are social boldness, dominance, and openness to change. See also ABILITY TRAIT; DYNAMIC TRAIT; TEMPERAMENT TRAIT.

SOV abbreviation for ALLPORT–VERNON–LINDZEY STUDY OF VALUES.

spasm *n.* a sudden, involuntary muscle contraction. It may be continuous or sustained (tonic) or it may alternate between contraction and relaxation (clonic). A spasm may be restricted to a particular body part; for example, a **vasospasm** involves a blood vessel, and a **bronchial spasm** involves the bronchi. **—spasmodic** *adj.*

spasmodic dysphonia a rare VOICE DISORDER whose symptoms include momentary periods of uncontrolled vocal spasms, stuttering, tightness in the throat, and recurrent hoarseness. The cause is unknown, but the condition may be attributed to a neurological or physiological disturbance or to psychological factors. Spasmodic dysphonia (formerly known as **spastic dysphonia**) particularly affects public speakers.

spastic colitis see IRRITABLE BOWEL SYNDROME.

spastic dysphonia see SPASMODIC DYSPHONIA.

spatial neglect a disorder in which individuals are unaware of a portion of their surrounding physical, personal, or extrapersonal space, usually on the left side. For example, if approached on the left side, an individual with spatial neglect may not notice the approaching person but would respond normally when approached on the right side.

spatial-temporal reasoning the ability to conceptualize the three-dimensional relationships of objects in space and to mentally manipulate them as a succession of transformations over a period of time. Spatial-temporal reasoning is a cognitive ability that plays an important role in such fields as architecture, engineering, and mathematics, among others, and in such basic tasks as everyday movement of the body through space.

speaking in tongues see GLOSSOLALIA.

Spearman rank correlation coefficient (symbol: ρ) see RANK CORRELATION COEFFICIENT. [Charles Edward **Spearman** (1863–1945), British psychologist and psychometrician)]

special care unit (**SCU**) a unit in a health care institution designed to provide specialized care for people with severe problems, such as dementia, head injuries, or spinal cord injuries.

special child a child with SPECIAL NEEDS who requires SPECIAL EDUCATION and training. Such children may have learning disabilities, mental retardation, physical disabilities, or emotional difficulties. See also EXCEPTIONAL CHILD.

special education specially designed programs, services, and instruction provided to children with learning, behavioral, or physical disabilities (e.g., visual impairment, hearing loss, or neurological disorders) to assist them in becoming independent, productive, and valued members of their communities.

special needs the requirements of individuals with physical, mental, or emotional disabilities or financial, community-related, or resource disadvantages. Special needs may include SPECIAL EDUCATION, training, or therapy.

S

special psychiatric rapid intervention team (**SPRINT**) a multidisciplinary U.S. Navy team, consisting of psychologists, psychiatrists, social workers, and chaplains, that provides short-term mental health and emotional support immediately after a crisis. The team may also provide educational and consultative services to local supporting agencies.

specific ability an ability used only for a particular intellectual task or a single test in a battery of tests. It does not correlate with other abilities, as opposed to GENERAL ABILITY, which correlates at least moderately with other abilities. Also called **special aptitude**. See also SPECIFIC FACTOR.

specific-attitudes theory the viewpoint that certain psychosomatic disorders are associated with particular attitudes. An example is an association between the feeling of being mistreated and the occurrence of hives. See also SPECIFIC-REACTION THEORY.

specific developmental disorders in *DSM–III*, disorders in which some distinctive and circumscribed ability or area of functioning fails to develop properly from an early age, but difficulties are not attributable to mental retardation, autism, or any other condition. In *DSM–IV–TR*, such disorders are categorized as LEARNING DISORDERS or COMMUNICATION DISORDERS.

specific factor (symbol: *s*) a specialized ability that is postulated to come into play in particular kinds of cognitive tasks. Specific factors, such as mathematical ability, are contrasted with the GENERAL FACTOR (*g*), which underlies every cognitive performance. Also called **special factor**. [proposed in 1904 by British psychologist and psychometrician Charles Edward Spearman (1863–1945)]

specificity *n.* **1.** the quality of being unique, of a particular kind, or limited to a single phenomenon. For example, a stimulus that elicits a particular response or a symptom localized in a particular organ (e.g., the stomach) is said to have specificity. **2.** the probability that a test yields a negative diagnosis given that the individual does not have the condition for which he or she is being tested. Compare SENSITIVITY.

specificity doctrine of traits the proposition that personality traits are expressed with respect to specific classes of social contexts rather than being expressed globally in all situations.

specificity of behavior 1. the fact that certain behavior is elicited only by particular stimuli and therefore does not generalize beyond specific situations. **2.** a fixed pattern of expected behavior in a situation.

specificity theory a theory holding that the mechanism of pain is—like vision and hearing—a specific modality with its own central and peripheral apparatus. According to this theory, pain is produced by nerve impulses that are generated by an injury and are transmitted directly to a pain center in the brain. Compare GATE-CONTROL THEORY.

specific language disability see LANGUAGE DISABILITY.

specific learning disability (**SLD**) a substantial deficit in scholastic or academic skills that does not pervade all areas of learning but rather is limited to a particular aspect, for example, reading or arithmetic difficulty. In U.S. federal legislation, this term is used interchangeably with LEARNING DISABILITY.

specific phobia an ANXIETY DISORDER, formerly called **simple phobia**, characterized by a marked and persistent fear of a specific object, activity, or situation (e.g., dogs, blood, flying, heights). The fear is excessive or unreasonable and is invariably triggered by the presence or anticipation of the feared object or situation; consequently, this is either avoided or endured with marked anxiety or distress. In *DSM–IV–TR*, specific phobias are classified into five subtypes: (a) **animal type**, which includes fears of animals or insects (e.g., cats, dogs, birds, mice, insects, or snakes); (b) **natural environment type**, which includes fears of objects in the natural surroundings (e.g., heights, storms, water, or lightning); (c) **blood-injection-injury type**, which includes fears of seeing blood or an injury and of receiving an injection or other invasive medical procedure; (d) **situational type**, which includes fear of public transportation, elevators, bridges, driving, flying, enclosed places (see CLAUSTROPHOBIA), and so forth; and (e) **other type**, which includes fears that cannot be classified under any of the other subtypes (e.g., fears of choking, vomiting, or contracting an illness and children's fears of clowns or loud noises).

specific-reaction theory a concept that an innate tendency of the autonomic nervous system to react in a particular way to a stressful situation accounts for psychosomatic symptoms. See also SPECIFIC-ATTITUDES THEORY.

spectator effect the effect on performance when a task is carried out in the presence of others. When an individual is confident of being able to perform the task, that is, has high task confidence, spectators improve performance; when task confidence is low, they worsen it.

spectator role a behavior pattern in which one's natural sexual responses are blocked by performance anxiety. It involves observing oneself closely and worrying about how well or poorly one is performing sexually, rather than participating fully in the sexual activity; this prevents sexual arousal from occurring. [first described by U.S. gynecologist William H. Masters (1915–2001) and U.S. psychologist Virginia E. Johnson (1925–)]

spectator therapy the beneficial effect upon members of a therapy group of observing the therapy of fellow members with similar or related problems.

spectrum of consciousness 1. in TRANSPERSONAL PSYCHOLOGY, the full range of human psychological and spiritual experiences concomitant with states of being. **2.** in neuroscience, the full range of awareness. See CONSCIOUSNESS.

speech, language, and hearing center a professionally staffed clinic or center that provides diagnostic and treatment services to people with communication impairments. Staff typically consists of experts in audiology, speech and language pathology, and speech and hearing sciences. Also called **community speech and hearing center**.

speech and language disorder any disorder that affects verbal or written communication. A **speech disorder** is one that affects the production of speech, potentially including such problems as poor audibility or intelligibility; unpleasant tonal quality; unusual, distorted, or abnormally effortful sound production; lack of conventional rhythm and stress; and inappropriateness in terms of age or physical or mental development. A **language disorder** is one that affects the expression or reception (comprehension) of ideas and feelings, potentially including such problems as reduced vocabulary, omissions of articles and modifiers, understanding of nouns but not verbs, difficulties following oral instructions, and syntactical errors. Although speech disorders and language disorders are two distinct entities, they often occur together and thus generally are referred to together.

speech and language pathology 1. inadequate or maladaptive communication behavior and disorders of speech, language, and hearing. **2.** the clinical field that studies, evaluates, and treats speech, voice, and language disorders.

speech and language therapy the application of remedies, treatment, and counseling for the improvement of verbal or written communication.

speech anxiety see PUBLIC-SPEAKING ANXIETY.

speech derailment see DERAILMENT.

speech impairment any problem that affects the production of speech: an occasional synonym for speech disorder (see SPEECH AND LANGUAGE DISORDER).

speech rehabilitation training to restore a lost or impaired speech function. Also called **speech reeducation**.

speech therapy the application of remedies, treatment, and counseling for the improvement of speech and language.

speed *n.* slang for an amphetamine, especially METHAMPHETAMINE.

speedball *n.* a colloquial name for a mixture of HEROIN and a powerful stimulant (e.g., COCAINE or an AMPHETAMINE).

spell *n.* **1.** a hypnotic influence or suggestion. **2.** a lay term for an episode of a physical or mental disorder.

spelling dyslexia see WORD-FORM DYSLEXIA.

Spence, Kenneth Wartinbee (1907–1967) U.S. psychologist. Spence received his PhD in 1933 from Yale University, where he studied with Robert M. Yerkes (1876–1956). He spent the bulk of his career at the University of Iowa, heading its psychology department for 22 years. Spence was an experimental psychologist whose research involved a skillfully designed series of experiments on DISCRIMINATION LEARNING in animals and Pavlovian eyeblink conditioning in humans. Together with Clark L. HULL, he developed a version of NEOBEHAVIORISM that was very influential in the 1940s and 1950s. The Hull–Spence model offered a theoretical system that explained animal learning and motivation based on principles of PAVLOVIAN CONDITIONING, in contrast to Skinnerian (OPERANT CONDITIONING) principles. Spence was awarded many honors, including election to the National Academy of Sciences and the Society of Experimental Psychologists and receipt of the Distinguished Scientific Contribution Award from the American Psychological Association in 1956. See also

S

ASSOCIATIONISM; CONTIGUITY LEARNING THEORY; MAZE LEARNING.

Sperry, Roger Wolcott (1913–1994) U.S. psychologist. Sperry earned his MA in psychology from Oberlin College in 1937 and his PhD in zoology from the University of Chicago in 1941, studying under the neuroembryologist Paul Weiss (1898–1989). He spent four postdoctoral years working with Karl LASHLEY at the Yerkes Laboratories of Primate Biology in Florida and then several years on the faculty of the University of Chicago. In 1954 he accepted a newly created chair of psychobiology at the California Institute of Technology, where he spent the remainder of his career. Sperry is best known for his nerve-regeneration theory and his research into the functions of the two hemispheres of the brain using the split-brain technique (see COMMISSUROTOMY). Throughout his career, Sperry sought answers to fundamental questions regarding the nature of consciousness and its interaction with the body. Representative works include "Neurology and the Mind–Brain Problem" (*American Scientist,* 1952), "Hemispheric Disconnection and Unity in Conscious Awareness" (*American Psychologist,* 1968), and his book *Science and Moral Priority* (1983). Sperry's many honors included membership in the American Academy of Arts and Sciences and receipt of the American Psychological Association's Lifetime Achievement Award. In 1981 he received the Nobel Prize for Physiology or Medicine.

sphincter control the ability to control the muscles that open and close the openings of the body, especially the anal and urinary sphincters. This ability is an important stage in physical development.

sphincter morality in psychoanalytic theory, personality characteristics and behaviors such as obstinacy, extreme orderliness, and parsimony, which are associated with an anal-retentive personality. See also ANAL PERSONALITY; ANAL STAGE.

sphingomyelin lipidosis see NIEMANN–PICK DISEASE.

S

spider phobia a persistent and irrational fear of spiders. In *DSM–IV–TR,* spider phobia is classified as a SPECIFIC PHOBIA, animal type. Also called **arachneophobia**; **arachnophobia**. See also ANIMAL PHOBIA.

spike-and-wave discharges a pattern of BRAIN WAVES on an electroencephalogram (see ELECTROENCEPHALOGRAPHY) that is characteristic of ABSENCE SEIZURES. It consists of a sharp spike followed by a low-amplitude DELTA WAVE and occurs at a frequency of three per second.

spinal cord the part of the CENTRAL NERVOUS SYSTEM that extends from the lower end of the MEDULLA OBLONGATA, at the base of the brain, through a canal in the center of the spine as far as the lumbar region. In transverse section, the cord consists of an H-shaped core of gray matter (see PERIAQUEDUCTAL GRAY) surrounded by white matter consisting of tracts of long ascending and descending nerve fibers on either side of the cord. The spinal cord is enveloped by protective membraneous layers (meninges) and is the origin of the 31 pairs of SPINAL NERVES.

spinal cord injury any damage to the spinal cord caused by sudden or progressive external forces. Spinal cord injuries include contusion (bruising), hemorrhage, laceration, transection, spinal shock, and compression.

spinal nerve any of the 31 pairs of nerves that originate in the gray matter of the SPINAL CORD and emerge through openings between the vertebrae of the spine to extend into the body's dermatomes (skin areas) and skeletal muscles. The spinal nerves comprise 8 cervical nerves, 12 thoracic nerves, 5 lumbar nerves, 5 sacral nerves, and 1 coccygeal nerve. Each attaches to the spinal cord via two short branches, a dorsal root and a ventral root.

spirit *n.* **1.** the nonphysical part of a person: the mental, moral, and emotional characteristics that make up the core of someone's identity (e.g., *a noble spirit; it broke her spirit*). **2.** a vital force seen as animating the bodies of living creatures, sometimes identified with the soul and seen as surviving death. **3.** an immaterial being, possessed of some permanence, to which are ascribed many or most of the activities of a living person. **4.** a supernatural being, such as a ghost or a deity. **5.** in idealist philosophies, a universal mind or idea seen as a fundamental reality and a moving force of events in the world. **6.** the mood, temper, or disposition that temporarily or permanently characterizes a person. **7.** loyalty or morale.

spiritual healing see FAITH HEALING.

spirituality *n.* **1.** a concern for or sensitivity to the things of the spirit or soul, especially as opposed to material things. **2.** more specifically, a concern for God and a sensitivity to religious experience, which may include the practice of a particular religion but may also exist without such practice.

split brain a brain in which the cerebral hemispheres have been separated by severence of the corpus callosum (see COMMISSUROTOMY). Surgical transection of the corpus callosum is used to create split-brain animals for experimental purposes and is also occasionally performed on humans to alleviate some forms of severe epilepsy. Split brain can also occur without surgical intervention as a result of injury or disease of the corpus callosum. Study of individuals or animals with split brain helps to define the roles of the two hemispheres. Also called **divided brain**.

split-half reliability a measure of the ability of a test to measure an attribute consistently, obtained by correlating scores on one half of the test with scores on the other half. Also called **split-half correlation**.

split personality a lay term for an individual with DISSOCIATIVE IDENTITY DISORDER. It is sometimes confused with SCHIZOPHRENIA, which means literally "splitting of the mind" but does not involve the formation of a second personality.

splitting *n.* **1.** in KLEINIAN analysis, the most primitive of all DEFENSE MECHANISMS, in which OBJECTS that evoke ambivalence and therefore anxiety are dealt with by compartmentalizing positive and negative emotions (see PART-OBJECT), leading to images of the self and others that are not integrated. In general, it results in polarized viewpoints that are projected onto different people. This mechanism is found not only in infants and young children, who are as yet incapable of combining these polarized viewpoints, but also in adults with dysfunctional patterns of dealing with ambivalence; it is often associated with BORDERLINE PERSONALITY DISORDER and plays a central role in FAIRBAIRNIAN THEORY. Also called **splitting of the object**. **2.** in COTHERAPY, an appeal by a client to one of the therapists when he or she feels that that therapist would be more sympathetic than the other. Also called **splitting situation**.

SPMSQ abbreviation for SHORT PORTABLE MENTAL STATUS QUESTIONNAIRE.

spontaneity test a type of sociometric test in which an individual in a therapy group is encouraged to improvise freely in reenactments of typical life situations with other members of the group who have been judged to be emotionally related, positively or negatively, to that individual. The object is to gain insight into interpersonal relationships not revealed by the standard sociometric test, which deals only with attraction and repulsion. [devised by Romanian-born U.S. psychiatrist Jacob Levi Moreno (1889–1974)]

spontaneity training a personality-training program in which a client learns to act naturally and spontaneously in real-life situations by practicing such behavior in graduated sessions. Also called **spontaneity therapy**. [introduced by Romanian-born U.S. psychiatrist Jacob Levi Moreno (1889–1974)]

spontaneous alternation the instinctive, successive alternation of responses between alternatives in a situation involving discrete choices or exploration. For example, in a learning and memory experiment, a rat in a T-shaped maze tends to choose the left arm on one trial, the right arm on the next, the left arm again, and so on.

spontaneous movement movement that results from impulse, occurring without premeditation or planning. Spontaneous movement decreases in some disorders, such as Parkinson's disease.

spontaneous regression a phenomenon in which a person suddenly relives an event from an earlier age (e.g., childhood) and may exhibit appropriate behavior for that age.

spontaneous remission a reduction or disappearance of symptoms without any therapeutic intervention, which may be temporary or permanent. It most commonly refers to medical, rather than psychological, conditions. See also WAITING-LIST PHENOMENON.

spontaneous speech speech that is not in response to a specific question or direction.

spontaneous trait inference a judgment about an individual's personality traits that is made automatically, based on observed behavior. More specifically, it is the phenomenon by which people who hear others describe negative or positive behaviors in individuals attribute the qualities implied by those behaviors to the speaker.

sports hypnosis hypnosis used to assist participants in sport to eliminate mind-sets that interfere with athletic performance or to develop those that enhance it.

spreading activation **1.** in neuroscience, a hypothetical process in which the activation of one neuron is presumed to spread to connected neurons, making it more likely that they will fire. **2.** in cognitive psychology, an analogous model for the association of ideas, memories, and the like, based on the notion that activation of one item stored in memory travels through associated links to activate another item. As each item is activated, further activation may spread through the network, making it more likely that associated items will be recalled. Spreading activation is a feature of some models of SEMANTIC MEMORY.

spreading depression a propagating wave of silence in neuronal activity accompanied by a relatively large negative electric potential. Spreading depression occurs in regions of gray matter, including the cerebral cortex and hippocampus. It may occur spontaneously or be evoked by intense local electrical, chemical, or mechanical stimuli. Cortical spreading depression is related to migraine headaches.

SPRINT acronym for SPECIAL PSYCHIATRIC RAPID INTERVENTION TEAM.

SQAW acronym for SLEEP QUESTIONNAIRE AND ASSESSMENT OF WAKEFULNESS.

squeeze technique a technique for overcoming PREMATURE EJACULATION. The penis is stimulated until the man is well aroused, then the partner squeezes the penis briefly where the head of the penis joins the shaft. When the squeeze is released, a pause in stimulation is taken for 30 s to 1 min. The squeeze and pause lowers arousal, and stimulation is then resumed. After several stimulate–squeeze–pause–stimulate cycles, the man is stimulated to ejaculation. This procedure conditions the man to maintain an erection longer before ejaculation. [devised by U.S. gynecologist William H. Masters (1915–2001) and U.S. psychologist Virginia E. Johnson (1925–)]

SQUID acronym for SUPERCONDUCTING QUANTUM INTERFERENCE DEVICE.

SRI abbreviation for serotonin reuptake inhibitor. See SSRI.

S sleep abbreviation for SLOW-WAVE SLEEP or SYNCHRONIZED SLEEP, that is, NREM SLEEP. Compare D SLEEP.

SSRI selective serotonin reuptake inhibitor: any of a class of antidepressants that are thought to act by blocking the reuptake of serotonin into serotonin-containing presynaptic neurons in the central nervous system (see also SEROTONIN-RECEPTOR AGONISTS). The SSRIs have demonstrated efficacy in the treatment of not only depression but also panic disorder and obsessive-compulsive disorder as well as eating disorders and premenstrual dysphoric disorder. However, the relationship of the reuptake mechanism to the therapeutic qualities of these agents has not been clearly elucidated. SSRIs also block the activity of certain subtypes of serotonin AUTORECEPTORS, and this may also be associated with their therapeutic effects. SSRIs have less adverse side effects than the TRICYCLIC ANTIDEPRESSANTS and the MONOAMINE OXIDASE INHIBITORS; common side effects include nausea, headache, anxiety, and tremor, and some patients may experience sexual dysfunction. SSRIs include FLUOXETINE, PAROXETINE, SERTRALINE, CITALOPRAM, and FLUVOXAMINE. Also called **SRIs** (serotonin reuptake inhibitors).

SST 1. abbreviation for SELF-STATEMENT TRAINING. **2.** abbreviation for SINGLE-SESSION THERAPY. **3.** abbreviation for SOCIAL SKILLS TRAINING.

S-state *n.* the *s*leeping (or *s*leep) state, as opposed to the D-state (see DREAM STATE) and the W-state (waking state).

stability *n.* **1.** the absence of variation or motion, as applied, for example, to genetics (invariance in characteristics), personality (few emotional or mood changes), or body position (absence of body sway). **2.** in developmental psychology, the degree to which a person maintains over time the same rank order with respect to a particular characteristic (e.g., intelligence test performance) in comparison with peers. **3.** the property of a system, either open or closed, that regulates its internal environment and tends to maintain a stable, constant condition.

S

stability–instability bipolar dimensions of the single trait of EMOTIONAL STABILITY.

Stablon *n.* a trade name for TIANEPTINE.

Stadol *n.* a trade name for BUTORPHANOL.

stage fright an anxiety reaction associated with speaking or performing in public. The individual becomes tense and apprehensive and may stutter, forget lines, or escape the situation. The apprehension may develop into panic symptoms or even a PANIC ATTACK. See also PERFORMANCE ANXIETY.

stage 1 sleep the initial stage of sleep, which is characterized by low-amplitude BRAIN WAVES (4–6 Hz) of irregular frequency, slow heart rate, and reduced muscle tension. See SLEEP STAGES.

stage 2 sleep a stage of sleep that is defined by regular bursts of 14–18 Hz waves (called SLEEP SPINDLES) that progressively increase and then decrease in amplitude. See SLEEP STAGES.

stage 3 sleep a stage of SLOW-WAVE SLEEP that is defined by the SLEEP SPINDLES seen in STAGE 2 SLEEP interspersed with larger amplitude DELTA WAVES (slow waves of 1–4 Hz). See SLEEP STAGES.

stage 4 sleep a stage of SLOW-WAVE SLEEP that is defined by the presence of high-amplitude DELTA WAVES (slow waves of 1–4 Hz). See SLEEP STAGES.

stages of change the five steps involved in changing health behavior proposed in the TRANSTHEORETICAL MODEL: (a) precontemplation (not thinking about changing behavior), (b) contemplation (considering changing behavior), (c) preparation (occasionally changing behavior), (d) action (participating in the healthful behavior on a regular basis, resulting in major benefits), and (e) maintenance (continuing the behavior after 6 months of regular use). [developed by U.S. clinical psychologist James O. Prochaska (1942–)]

stages of grief a hypothetical model, originally described in 1969 by Swiss-born U.S. psychiatrist Elisabeth Kübler-Ross (1926–2004), depicting psychological states, moods, or coping strategies that occur during the DYING PROCESS or during periods of BEREAVEMENT, great loss, or TRAUMA. These begin with the denial stage, followed by the anger stage, bargaining stage, depression stage, and acceptance stage. The model is nonlinear in that the stages do not necessarily occur in the given sequence or for a set period of time; moreover, they can recur and overlap before some degree of psychological and emotional resolution occurs. Also called **grief cycle model**.

stagnation *n.* see GENERATIVITY VERSUS STAGNATION.

STAI abbreviation for STATE–TRAIT ANXIETY INVENTORY.

stalking *n.* a repeated pattern of following or observing a person in an obsessional, intrusive, or harassing manner. Often associated with a failed relationship with the one pursued, stalking may involve direct threats, the intent to cause distress or bodily harm, and interpersonal violence. It may alternatively follow from an instance of EROTIC DELUSION. See also DOMESTIC VIOLENCE.

standard *n.* **1.** a criterion for evaluating the goodness or worth of a person, action, or event. **2.** any positive idea about how things might be, such as an ideal, norm, value, expectation, or previous performance, that is used to measure and judge the way things are. Evaluation of the self is often based on comparing the current reality (or perceptions of the current reality) against one or more standards.

standard deviation (symbol: *SD*) a measure of the variability of a set of scores or values within a group, indicating how narrowly or broadly they deviate from the MEAN. A small standard deviation indicates data points that cluster around the mean, whereas a large standard deviation indicates data points that are dispersed across many different values. The standard deviation is expressed in the same units as the original values in the sample or population, so that the standard deviation of a series of measurements of weight would be in e.g. pounds. The standard deviation is equal to the square root of the VARIANCE. If a population of n values has a mean μ, then the standard deviation is $\sqrt{[\Sigma(X_i - \mu)^2/n]}$. For a sample of the population, with a mean value $\bar{X}$, the **sample standard deviation** is taken to be

$$\sqrt{[\Sigma(X_i - \bar{X})^2/(n-1)]},$$

that is, the divisor is $(n - 1)$ rather than n.

standard error (symbol: *SE*) in statistical analysis, a quantification of the inherent inaccuracy of a calculated POPULATION value that is attributable to random fluctuations within the SAMPLE data upon which it is based. Some degree of imprecision is present whenever a value for a large group (the population) is estimated by studying a subset of that group (the sample), and the standard error provides a numerical description of that variability. It is expressed as the STANDARD DEVIATION of the SAMPLING DISTRIBUTION. For example, the sample mean is the usual estimator of a population mean yet different samples drawn from that same population nonetheless will yield different values for the mean. Thus, to determine how much sample variability exists the STANDARD ERROR OF THE MEAN may be obtained by taking the standard deviation of all of the means over all of the samples taken. Standard error is expressed in units, given in the same scale of measurement that was used for the sample data (e.g., for a set of means that are given in weight the standard error unit is also a weight). The more samples involved in determining the standard error, the smaller its value; the smaller the standard error, the more reliable the calculated population value.

standard error of estimate (symbol: *SEE*) for a relationship between two variables (X and Y) given by a regression line or REGRESSION EQUATION, an index of how closely the predicted value of Y for a specific value of X matches its actual value. If y' is an estimated value from a regression line and y is the actual value, then the standard error of estimate is $\sqrt{[\Sigma(y - y')^2/n]}$, where n is the number of points. The smaller the standard error of estimate, the better the degree of relationship (CORRELATION) between X and Y and the more confident one can be in the accuracy of the estimated (predicted) Y value. Also called **standard error of prediction**. See also STANDARD ERROR.

standard error of measurement (symbol: *SEM*) an index of the RELIABILITY of an assessment instrument, representing the variation of an individual's scores across multiple administrations of the same test. A perfectly reliable instrument will have a standard error of measurement of 0.00, which means that an individual will have the same score upon repeated testings with the instrument. Otherwise, the standard error of measurement will be between 0.00 and 1.00 and the individual will have different scores on different occasions; the larger the error the greater the variation across administrations. In essence, the standard error of measurement provides an indication of how confident one may be that an individual's obtained score on any given measurement opportunity represents his or her TRUE SCORE. See also STANDARD ERROR.

standard error of the mean (symbol: σ_M) a statistic that indicates how much the average value (MEAN) for a particular SAMPLE is likely to differ from the average value for the larger POPULATION from which it is drawn. It is the STANDARD DEVIATION of the SAMPLING DISTRIBUTION of the mean, equal to $\sigma/\sqrt{n}$, where σ is the standard deviation of the original distribution and n is the sample size. Less commonly called **standard error of the population mean**.

standardization *n.* **1.** the process of establishing NORMS for a test. **2.** the use of uniform procedures in test administration to ensure that all participants take the same test under the same conditions and are scored by the same criteria, which in turn ensures that results can be compared to each other. **3.** the transformation of data into a distribution of STANDARDIZED SCORES having a mean of 0 and a STANDARD DEVIATION of 1, which produces derived measures of relative standing and allows comparison of raw scores from different distributions.

standardization group a sample used to establish reliable norms for the population that it represents. This is done by analysing the results of the test administered to the sample and ascertaining the average performance level and the relative frequency of each deviation from the mean. The NORMAL DISTRIBUTION thus created is then used for comparison with any specific future test score. It is important to note, however, that the standardization group must be representative of the intended population of test takers in order to yield valid information. Also called **standardization sample**.

standardized test 1. an assessment instrument whose VALIDITY and RELIABILITY have been established by thorough empirical investigation and analysis. It has clearly defined norms, such that a person's score is an indication of how well he or she did in comparison to a large group of individuals representative of the population for which the test is intended. Also called **standardized measure**. **2.** an assessment instrument administered in a predetermined manner, such that the questions, conditions of administration, scoring, and interpretation of responses are consistent from one occassion to another.

standardized score a value derived from a raw score by subtracting the mean value of all scores

S

in the set and dividing by the STANDARD DEVIATION of the set. The advantage of standardized scores is that they are not reflective of the units of the measuring device from which they were obtained and thus can be compared to one another regardless of the device's scale values. Several types of standardized score exist, such as T SCORES. Also called **standard score**. See also STANDARDIZATION.

standards of practice a set of guidelines that delineate the expected techniques and procedures, and the order in which to use them, for interventions with individuals experiencing a range of psychological, medical, or educational conditions. Standards of practice have been developed by the American Psychological Association and other professional associations to ensure that practitioners use the most researched and validated treatment plans.

Stanford–Binet Intelligence Scale (**SB**) a standardized assessment of intelligence and cognitive abilities for individuals aged 2 to 89 years. It currently includes five verbal subtests and five nonverbal subtests that yield Verbal, Nonverbal, and Full Scale IQs (with a mean of 100 and a standard deviation of 15) as well as Fluid Reasoning, Knowledge, Quantitative Reasoning, Visual-Spatial Processing, and Working Memory index scores. The Stanford–Binet test was so named because it was brought to the United States by Lewis M. TERMAN, a professor at Stanford University, in 1916, as a revision and extension of the original **Binet–Simon Scale** (the first modern intelligence test) developed in 1905 by Alfred BINET and French physician Théodore Simon (1873–1961) to assess the intellectual ability of French children. The present Stanford–Binet Intelligence Scale (**SB5**), developed by U.S. psychologist Gale H. Roid (1943–) and published in 2003, is the fourth revision of the test; the first and second revisions were made in 1937 and 1960, respectively, by Terman and U.S. psychologist Maud Merrill (1888–1978), and the third in 1986 by U.S. psychologists Robert L. Thorndike (1910–1990), Elizabeth P. Hagen (1915–2008), and Jerome M. Sattler (1931–).

S

Stanford Hypnotic Susceptibility Scale a standardized 12-item scale used to measure HYPNOTIC SUSCEPTIBILITY by means of the participant's response to such suggestions as falling forward, closing the eyes, or lowering an outstretched arm for mild hypnosis and hallucinating a fly or posthypnotic amnesia for deeper hypnosis. [developed at Stanford University by Ernest R. HILGARD]

stanolone *n.* a semisynthetic analog of dihydrotestosterone used in the treatment of some breast cancers because of its tumor-suppressing capabilities.

startle response an unlearned, rapid, reflexlike response to sudden, unexpected, intense stimuli (loud noises, flashing lights, etc.). This response includes behaviors that serve a protective function, such as closing the eyes, frowning by drawing the eyebrows together, compressing the lips, lowering the head, hunching the shoulders, and bending the trunk and knee. The reaction can be neutralized by context, inhibition, and habituation. Also called **startle reaction**.

starvation reactions physical and psychological effects of chronic undernourishment, which is experienced by perhaps well over one quarter of the world's population. Common physical effects include general weakness or asthenia, hunger pangs, sluggishness, and susceptibility to disease. Psychological effects include slowing down of thought processes, difficulty in concentration, apathy, irritability, reduced sexual desire, and loss of care in appearance. Psychotic reactions seldom occur except when starvation is accompanied by infection or extreme stress.

stasis *n.* a condition of stability, equilibrium, or inactivity, as opposed to a state of flux or change. Compare LABILE. **—static** *adj.*

state *n.* the condition or status of an entity or system at a particular time that is characterized by relative stability of its basic components or elements. Although the components or elements are essentially qualitatively stable, it is possible for them also to be dynamic, as in a hyperactive state or a state of flux.

state anxiety anxiety in response to a specific situation that is perceived as threatening or dangerous. State anxiety varies in intensity and fluctuates over time. Compare TRAIT ANXIETY. [defined in 1972 and 1983 by U.S. psychologist Charles D. Spielberger (1927–)]

state-dependent behavior actions that are affected by one's emotional state, for example, saying something hurtful to another while in a state of anger.

state-dependent learning learning that occurs in a particular biological or psychological state and is better recalled when the individual is subsequently in the same state. Recall may be diminished when the individual is in a different state. For example, an animal trained to run a maze while under the influence of a psychoactive drug (e.g., pentobarbital) may not run it successfully without the drug. Also called **dissociated learning**. See also CONTEXT-SPECIFIC LEARNING.

state-dependent memory a condition in which memory for a past event is improved when the person is in the same biological or psychological state as when the memory was initially formed. Thus, alcohol may improve recall of events experienced when previously under the influence of alcohol (although this level of recall is lower than recall under conditions where both ENCODING and RETRIEVAL occur in sober states). A distinctive state may arise from a drug, a mood, or a particular place. See CONTEXT-SPECIFIC LEARNING; MOOD-DEPENDENT MEMORY; STATE-DEPENDENT LEARNING.

statement validity analysis a collection of

techniques used to assess the truth of statements given during investigations, such as the truth of allegations made by children during interviews concerning sexual abuse. The focus is on the words themselves, independent of case facts. Such analysis is based on the assumption that the current and quality of truthful statements is different from fabricated ones and involves examining such things as the use of nouns, pronouns, and verbs; the inclusion of extraneous information; the use of phrases like "I think," which indicate lack of connection; and the balance between descriptions of activities before, during and after the event in question. These provide various criteria enabling interviewers to distinguish between plausible and implausible accounts. See also CRITERION-BASED CONTENT ANALYSIS.

state of consciousness see CONSCIOUSNESS; ALTERED STATE OF CONSCIOUSNESS.

State–Trait Anxiety Inventory (**STAI**) a self-report assessment device that includes separate measures of STATE ANXIETY and TRAIT ANXIETY. The state anxiety items measure the intensity of anxiety experienced by participants in specific situations; the trait anxiety items assess the frequency with which respondents experience anxiety in the face of perceived threats in the environment. [devised in 1970 by U.S. psychologist Charles D. Spielberger (1927–) and colleagues]

static marriage see CLOSED MARRIAGE.

statistical association see ASSOCIATION.

statistical control the use of statistical methods to reduce the effect of factors that could not be eliminated or controlled during an experiment.

statistical error any error of sampling, measurement, or analysis that interferes with drawing a valid conclusion from the data so obtained, for example, in the context of experimental results.

statistical significance the degree to which a result cannot reasonably be attributed to the operation of chance or random factors alone.

status comparison the comparison of one's own abilities and status with those of others.

STD abbreviation for SEXUALLY TRANSMITTED DISEASE.

steady state a condition of stability or equilibrium. For example, in behavioral studies it is a state in which behavior is practically the same over repeated observations in a particular context. In pharmacology, it refers to a state in the body in which the amount of drug administered is equal to that excreted.

steatopygia *n.* the presence of large quantities of fat in the buttocks. In some cultures steatopygia is considered an element of female beauty.

Stelazine *n.* a trade name for TRIFLUOPERAZINE.

stenosis *n.* the abnormal narrowing of a body conduit or passage. **Carotid stenosis** is narrowing of a carotid artery, for example by atherosclerosis, which limits blood flow to the brain; **aortic stenosis** is narrowing of the aortic valve leading from the left ventricle, thereby restricting blood flow from the heart to the general circulation; **pyloric stenosis** restricts the flow of stomach contents into the small intestine; **spinal stenosis** is a narrowing of the opening in the spinal column, thereby restricting the space needed for the spinal cord and resulting in numbness and pain in the lower back and legs. **—stenotic** *adj.*

stepfamily *n.* a family unit formed by the union of parents one or both of whom brings a child or children from a previous union (or unions) into the new household. Also called **blended family**; **reconstituted family**.

stepwise regression a group of regression techniques that enter predictor (independent) variables into (or delete them from) the REGRESSION EQUATION one variable (or block of variables) at a time according to some predefined criterion. It is contrasted with ordinary **least squares regression**, which enters all variables simultaneously.

stereotaxy *n.* determination of the exact location of a specific area within the body (e.g., the exact location of a nerve center in the brain) by means of three-dimensional measurements. Stereotaxy is used for positioning microelectrodes or other devices in the brain for diagnostic, experimental, or therapeutic purposes and for locating an area of the brain prior to surgery. It involves the coordinated use of a **stereotactic atlas**, a map of the brain featuring a coordinate system and consisting of images and schematic representations of nerve fibers and other structures and serial sections of the brain, and a **stereotactic instrument**, a device that prohibits damage to neighboring tissues by holding the individual's head absolutely still in the appropriate position. Also called **stereotactic localization**; **stereotactic technique**. **—stereotactic** or **stereotaxic** *adj.*

stereotype *n.* a set of cognitive generalizations (e.g., beliefs, expectations) about the qualities and characteristics of the members of a particular group or social category. Stereotypes, like SCHEMAS, simplify and expedite perceptions and judgments, but they are often exaggerated, negative rather than positive, and resistant to revision even when perceivers encounter individuals with qualities that are not congruent with the stereotype (see PREJUDICE). Unlike individually held expectations about others based on their category memberships, stereotypes are widely shared by group members. See NEGATIVE STEREOTYPE; POSITIVE STEREOTYPE. See also GENDER STEREOTYPE; INSTANCE THEORY; KERNEL-OF-TRUTH HYPOTHESIS. **—stereotypic** *adj.*

stereotyped behavior **1.** inflexible behavior that follows a particular pattern and does not alter with changing conditions. **2.** see STEREOTYPY.

stereotyped movement a repeated movement or gesture, such as a tic, rocking, or head banging.

stereotypic movement disorder in *DSM–IV–TR,* a disorder characterized by repetitive, nonfunctional, and often self-injurious behaviors, such as head banging, biting or hitting parts of the body, rocking, or hand waving. It may be associated with mental retardation and can arise at any age. Stereotypic movement disorder is distinguished from other disorders marked by stereotyped movements, such as TIC DISORDERS and PERVASIVE DEVELOPMENTAL DISORDERS.

stereotypy *n.* persistent repetition of the same words, movements, or other behavior, particularly as a symptom of disorder (e.g., autism, obsessive-compulsive disorder, schizophrenia). Stereotypy is also seen in nonhuman animals under conditions of social isolation, early social deprivation, or neglect. See STEREOTYPIC MOVEMENT DISORDER.

sterility *n.* **1.** the condition of being incapable of producing offspring, either because of INFERTILITY or surgical or medical intervention. **2.** the condition of being incapable of supporting microbial life because of treatment with chemicals, radiation, or heat. **—sterile** *adj.*

Stevens–Johnson syndrome a condition marked by eruptions of fluid-filled blisters on the skin, mucous membranes, eyes, and genitals. It has a fatality rate of 1–5% and may be associated with an adverse reaction to ANTICONVULSANT and antibiotic agents. Also called **erythema multiforme bullosum**; **erythema multiforme exudativum**; **erythema multiforme major**. [Albert M. **Stevens** (1884–1945) and Frank C. **Johnson** (1894–1934), U.S. pediatricians]

stigma *n.* the negative social attitude attached to a characteristic of an individual that may be regarded as a mental, physical, or social deficiency. A stigma implies social disapproval and can lead unfairly to discrimination against and exclusion of the individual.

stigmatophilia *n.* sexual interest in and arousal by a partner who is tattooed or has scars, or by having oneself tattooed, particularly in the genital area.

stilted speech formal, affected, or pompous speech. It may be characteristic of a particular individual, but is also observed as a speech disturbance in some individuals with particular disorders, such as schizophrenia or certain forms of APHASIA.

stimulant *n.* any of various agents that excite functional activity in an organism or in a part of an organism. Stimulants are usually classified according to the body system or function excited (e.g., cardiac stimulants, respiratory stimulants). In psychology, the term usually refers to the CNS STIMULANTS (or psychostimulants).

stimulus *n.* (*pl.* **stimuli**) **1.** any agent, event, or situation—internal or external—that elicits a response from an organism. See CONDITIONED STIMULUS; UNCONDITIONED STIMULUS. **2.** any change in physical energy that activates a sensory RECEPTOR.

stimulus-bound *adj.* **1.** relating to a perception that is largely dependent on the qualities of the stimulation and thus involves little or no interpretation. **2.** describing behavior that occurs in response to the presence of a specific stimulus (e.g., hungering for and eating a specific food after seeing it). **3.** characterizing an individual whose behavior tends to be inflexible and determined primarily by the nature of the stimulus. **4.** describing a person, usually a child, who has a poor attention span, is distracted by irrelevant stimuli, and therefore performs below his or her intellectual capacity.

stimulus evaluation checks (**SECs**) assessments made on several dimensions when an individual evaluates the impact of an event and hence its emotional intensity and quality. Examples of SECs include checks for novelty, goal relevance, and congruity–incongruity of actions or events with social expectations. [proposed by Swiss psychologist Klaus Scherer (1943–) in his theory of appraisal]

stimulus overload the condition in which the environment presents too many stimuli to be comfortably processed, resulting in stress and behavior designed to restore equilibrium.

stimulus sampling a procedure for increasing the generalizability of research results by using multiple stimuli within a category as representative of an experimental condition, as opposed to selecting a single stimulus whose unique characteristics may distort results. For example, a study investigating the effects of gender on monetary generosity would demonstrate stimulus sampling if it employed a variety of different males and females to elicit donations from participants, instead of using a single male and a single female.

stimulus situation all the components of an occurrence or experience that, taken as a whole, comprise a stimulus to which an organism responds. The term is used to highlight the complexity of behavior-arousing events that are unitary patterns comprising many elements (e.g., a concert, an athletic competition). This approach differs from that of traditional behavior analysts, who tend to break down stimuli into smaller, separate elements.

stimulus word a word presented to a participant with the object of eliciting a response.

STM abbreviation for SHORT-TERM MEMORY.

stochastic variable see RANDOM VARIABLE.

Stockholm syndrome a mental and emotional response in which a captive (e.g., a hostage) displays seeming loyalty to—even affection for—the captor. The captive may come to see law enforcement or rescuers as the enemy because they endanger the captor. The name derives from the case of a woman who in 1973 was held hostage at a bank in Stockholm, Sweden, and became so emotionally attached to one of the robbers that she broke her engagement to another man and remained faithful to her former captor during his prison term. [term coined by Swedish psychiatrist and criminologist Nils Bejerot (1921–1988)]

stocking anesthesia a SENSORY CONVERSION SYMPTOM in which there is a loss of sensitivity in the foot and in part of the calf (i.e., areas that would be covered by a stocking) that cannot be explained by a general medical condition or organic dysfunction. Also called **foot anesthesia**; **shoe anesthesia**. See also GLOVE ANESTHESIA.

storm-and-stress period a period of emotional turmoil. The phrase was used by G. Stanley HALL to characterize adolescence, which he believed to correspond to the turbulent transition from savagery to civilization. It is a translation of the German *Sturm und Drang*, which was the title of a 1776 drama by Friedrich Maximilian von Klinger and was subsequently applied to a German literary movement. Also called **Sturm und Drang period**.

storytelling *n.* **1.** the recounting by a client of the events, concerns, and problems that led him or her to seek treatment. Therapists can learn much about the motives and origins of conflicts by attending carefully (see ACTIVE LISTENING) to the stories that clients bring to the session. **2.** the use of symbolic talk and allegorical stories by the therapist to aid the client's understanding of issues. Also called **therapeutic storytelling**.

STP see DOM.

straight 1. *adj.* a colloquial term for heterosexual. **2.** *n.* slang for a heterosexual person.

straitjacket *n.* an article of clothing that was formerly used to restrain patients in mental hospitals from injuring themselves or others and, in some cases, for punishment. It consisted of a canvas shirt with long sleeves that could be fastened behind the patient's back after folding his or her arms in front of the body. If a means of physical restraint for a mental patient is needed now, a system of belts that limit the patient's range of motion is used. Also called **camisole**.

stranger anxiety the distress and apprehension experienced by young children when they are around individuals who are unfamiliar to them. Stranger anxiety is a normal part of cognitive development: Babies differentiate caregivers from other people and display a strong preference for familiar faces. Stranger anxiety usually begins around 8 or 9 months of age and typically lasts into the second year. Also called **fear of strangers**; **stranger fear**. See also SEPARATION ANXIETY; XENOPHOBIA.

Strange Situation an experimental technique used to assess quality of ATTACHMENT in infants and young children (up to the age of 2). The procedure subjects the child to increasing amounts of stress induced by a strange setting, the entrance of an unfamiliar person, and two brief separations from the parent. The reaction of the child to each of these situations is used to evaluate the security or insecurity of his or her attachment to the parent. See AMBIVALENT ATTACHMENT; AVOIDANT ATTACHMENT; DISORGANIZED ATTACHMENT; INSECURE ATTACHMENT; SECURE ATTACHMENT. [devised in 1978 by Canadian-born U.S. psychologist Mary D. Salter Ainsworth (1913–1999)]

strangulated affect in psychoanalytic theory, an inhibition or retention of the normal discharge of emotion, leading to a substitute discharge in the form of physical symptoms. This theory was advanced in Sigmund FREUD's early formulations to explain the dynamics of CONVERSION HYSTERIA; it was later supplanted by the concept of REPRESSION. See also AFFECT.

strategic family therapy a group of approaches to FAMILY THERAPY in which the focus is on identifying and applying novel interventions to produce behavioral change rather than on helping the family gain insight into the sources of their problems. Also called **strategic intervention therapy**.

strategic intervention therapy see STRATEGIC FAMILY THERAPY.

stratified sampling a technique in which a population is divided into subdivisions (strata) and individuals or cases are selected for study from each strata. The sample obtained (called a **stratified sample**) thus includes a number of individuals representing each stratum (e.g., young and old or men and women), the goal being to reproduce as accurately as possible their proportional representation in the population of interest. Typically, RANDOM SAMPLING is used to select the cases from each stratum, in which case the technique is referred to as **stratified random sampling**.

stream of consciousness the concept of consciousness as a continuous, dynamic flow of ideas and images rather than a static series of discrete components. It emphasizes the subjective quality of conscious experience as a never-ending and never-repeating stream. Also called **stream of thought**. [introduced in 1890 by William JAMES]

street hustlers see MALE HOMOSEXUAL PROSTITUTION.

strephosymbolia *n.* **1.** a perceptual disorder characterized by the mirrorlike reversal of objects. **2.** a reading difficulty characterized by a tendency to transpose or reverse letters while reading or writing (e.g., *tap* for *pat* or *p* for *q*). Also called **twisted symbols**. [defined in 1937 by U.S. psychiatrist Samuel Torrey Orton (1879–1948)]

stress *n.* a state of physiological or psychological

S

response to internal or external stressors. Stress involves changes affecting nearly every system of the body, influencing how people feel and behave. For example, it may be manifested by palpitations, sweating, dry mouth, shortness of breath, fidgeting, faster speech, augmentation of negative emotions (if already being experienced), and longer duration of stress fatigue. Severe stress is manifested by the GENERAL ADAPTATION SYNDROME. By causing these mind–body changes, stress contributes directly to psychological and physiological disorder and disease and affects mental and physical health, reducing the quality of life. [first described in the context of psychology around 1940 by Canadian physician Hans Selye (1907–1982)]

stress casualty a member of the armed forces who is unable to perform his or her duties because of exposure to operational stresses or risk factors. Such stress may result in somatic and behavioral symptoms. The primary cause is an imminent external threat to life, leading to inability to cope with the threat and a consequent overwhelming feeling of helplessness.

stress-decompensation model a concept of the development of abnormal behavior as a result of high levels of stress that lead to the gradual but progressive deterioration of normal behavior to a level that is highly disorganized and dysfunctional.

stress immunity 1. a highly developed capacity to tolerate emotional strain. **2.** failure to react to stressful situations or events.

stress immunization the concept that mild stress early in life makes an individual better able to handle stress later in life.

stress incontinence 1. a type of URINARY INCONTINENCE that occurs during exertion or other physical activities, such as laughing or coughing, that apply increased pressure to the abdomen and bladder. **2.** any form of INCONTINENCE whose origin is a high level of stress.

stress-induced analgesia a reduced sensitivity to pain that an organism may experience when exposed to extreme physical trauma. For example, soldiers in combat may ignore injuries and instead respond to other threats to their lives, and injured animals fleeing predators may ignore their injuries in order to avoid capture. The precise mechanism is uncertain but may be related to the production of large quantities of ENDORPHINS.

stress-inoculation training (**SIT**) a four-phase training program for stress-management often used in COGNITIVE BEHAVIOR THERAPY. Phase 1 entails the identification of reactions to stress and their effects on functioning and psychological well-being; phase 2 involves learning relaxation and self-regulation techniques; phase 3 consists of learning coping self-statements (see SELF-STATEMENT TRAINING); phase 4 involves assisted progression through a series of increasingly stressful situations using imagery, video, role playing, and real-life situations until the individual is able to cope with the original stress-inducing situation or event. [developed by U.S. psychologist Donald Meichenbaum (1940–)]

stress management the use of specific techniques, strategies, or programs—such as relaxation training, anticipation of stress reactions, and breathing techniques—for dealing with stress-inducing situations and the state of being stressed. See also PREVENTIVE STRESS MANAGEMENT.

stressor *n.* any event, force, or condition that results in physical or emotional stress. Stressors may be internal or external forces that require adjustment or COPING STRATEGIES on the part of the affected individual.

stress reaction maladaptive or pathological behavior resulting from conditions of pressure or strain. Examples are extreme feelings of tension or panic, disorganized speech patterns, and accidents caused by the effects of alcohol, drugs, or emotional stress.

stress test 1. an examination or evaluation designed to ascertain an individual's capacity to perform a relatively complex task under purposefully stressful conditions. **2.** a medical evaluation designed to assess the effects of stress, typically induced by physical exercise, on cardiac function. The most common of such procedures is a test in which the patient walks or runs on a treadmill while cardiac, respiratory, or other physiological processes are monitored.

stress tolerance the capacity to withstand pressures and strains and the consequent ability to function effectively and with minimal anxiety under conditions of stress. See also STRESS IMMUNITY.

stress training activities designed to help individuals understand the causes of stress and learn strategies for managing and preventing it. Realistic training and simulation (e.g., water survival, escape training, firefighting) are seen as necessary instructional strategies to prepare personnel in certain types of work to operate in stressful environments.

stress–vulnerability model in schizophrenia and mood disorders, the theory that a genetic or biological predisposition to these illnesses exists and that psychological and social factors can increase the likelihood of symptomatic episodes. See also DIATHESIS–STRESS MODEL.

stridor dentium see BRUXISM.

striving for superiority in the INDIVIDUAL PSYCHOLOGY of Alfred ADLER, the idea that human beings are motivated by an innate, sovereign drive for realizing their full potential. This drive is defined as the urge for completion and perfection rather than for superiority in the sense of social status or domination over others.

stroke *n.* disruption of blood flow to the brain, which deprives the tissue of oxygen and nutrients, causing tissue damage and loss of normal function and, potentially, tissue death. A stroke may result from a hemorrhage of a blood vessel in the brain (see HEMORRHAGIC STROKE) or an embolism or thrombus blocking an artery in the brain (see EMBOLIC STROKE; THROMBOTIC STROKE). This term is often used interchangeably with CEREBROVASCULAR ACCIDENT. See also CEREBRAL INFARCTION; CEREBROVASCULAR DISEASE; TRANSIENT ISCHEMIC ATTACK.

Stroop Color–Word Interference Test a three-part test in which (a) color names are read as fast as possible; (b) the colors of bars or other shapes are rapidly named; and, most importantly, (c) color hues are named quickly when used to print the names of other colors (such as the word *green* printed in the color red). The degree to which the participants are subject to interference by the printed words is a measure of their cognitive flexibility and selective attention. Also called **Stroop test**. [John Ridley **Stroop** (1897–1973), U.S. psychologist]

Stroop effect the finding that the time it takes a participant to name the color of ink in which a word is printed is longer for words that denote incongruent color names than for neutral words or for words that denote a congruent color. For example, if the word *blue* is written in red ink (incongruent), participants take longer to say "red" than if the word *glue* is written in red ink (neutral) or if the word *red* is written in red ink (congruent). See STROOP COLOR–WORD INTERFERENCE TEST. [John **Stroop**]

structural analysis 1. in psychology, any theory of the organization of mind or personality that attempts to differentiate between component parts and to define the relationship of part to part and part to whole. Such an analysis can be contrasted with one based on function, dynamics, or behavior. See PERSONALITY STRUCTURE; STRUCTURAL MODEL. **2.** any analysis based on the ideas or methods of STRUCTURALISM.

structural approach see STRUCTURAL MODEL.

structural equation modeling (**SEM**) a statistical modeling technique that includes LATENT VARIABLES as causal elements. SEM is an advanced statistical method for testing causal models involving constructs that cannot be directly measured but are, rather, approximated through several measures presumed to assess part of the given construct.

structural family therapy a type of FAMILY THERAPY that assesses the subsystems, boundaries, hierarchies, and coalitions within a family (its structure) and focuses upon direct interactions between the family members (enactment) as the primary method of inducing positive change. Structural family therapy assumes the competence and uniqueness of families with problems, stressing that when appropriately induced to do so families will discover their own alternatives to their ineffective patterns of relating to one another and that this process of discovery cannot proceed in a specific predetermined form but instead can only be directed toward a fairly well-defined area of functioning. For example, a structural family therapist working with a family whose daughter is anorexic would examine such family issues as the framework of authority, the rules that govern the assumption of roles, the various functions members perform, and the coalitions created by the bonding of certain family members, and then encourage the mother, daughter, and father to use this information to develop more productive patterns of functioning. Also called **structural therapy**.

structural group a therapeutic group made up of individuals selected for those characteristics that would make them most likely to be successful in achieving the goals sought in the therapy. People of different types, temperaments, personalities, and educational levels are combined in a group, based on the concept that their interaction will maximize each other's benefits in the therapeutic process. Also called **structured group**. [devised by Romanian-born U.S. psychiatrist Jacob Levi Moreno (1889–1972)]

structural hypothesis see STRUCTURAL MODEL.

structural integration see ROLFING.

structuralism 1. a movement considered to be the first school of psychology as a science, independent of philosophy. Usually attributed to Wilhelm WUNDT, but probably more strongly and directly influenced by Edward Bradford TITCHENER, structuralism defined psychology as the study of mental experience and sought to investigate the structure of such experience through a systematic program of experiments based on trained INTROSPECTION. Also called **structural psychology**. **2.** a movement in various disciplines that study human behavior and culture that enjoyed particular currency in the 1960s and 1970s.

structuralist 1. *n.* a therapist who believes that changing the organizational structure of a group or system, such as a family, will change and improve its patterns of interaction. **2.** *n.* an adherent of structuralism. **3.** *adj.* of or relating to structuralism.

structural matrix see STRUCTURED INTERACTIONAL GROUP PSYCHOTHERAPY.

structural model in psychoanalytic theory, the view that the total personality comprises three divisions or functions: (a) the ID, which represents instinctual drives; (b) the EGO, which controls id drives and mediates between them and external reality; and (c) the SUPEREGO, which comprises moral precepts and ideals. Sigmund FREUD proposed this model in 1923 to replace his earlier TOPOGRAPHIC MODEL, in which the mind was divided into three regions: the UNCONSCIOUS, PRECONSCIOUS, and CONSCIOUS. Also called **structural approach**; **structural hypothesis**; **structural theory**. See also DYNAMIC MODEL; ECONOMIC MODEL.

S

structural therapy 1. see STRUCTURAL FAMILY THERAPY. **2.** a system of treatment for children with AUTISTIC DISORDER, which provides a structured environment emphasizing physical and verbal stimulation in a gamelike setting. The purpose is to increase the amount and variety of stimuli received by the children, thereby helping them to relate to their environment in a more realistic manner.

structured autobiography see AUTOBIOGRAPHY.

Structured Clinical Interview for DSM–IV Axis I Disorders (**SCID-I**) an instrument used by clinicians to make standardized and reliable diagnoses of the 37 most frequently seen *DSM–IV* Axis I clinical disorders and avoid the common problem of premature focus on one diagnostic possibility. Assessment involves a standard set of questions asked in an interview with the patient.

Structured Clinical Interview for DSM–IV Axis II Personality Disorders (**SCID-II**) an instrument used by researchers and clinicians to make standardized and reliable diagnoses of the 10 *DSM–IV* personality (Axis II) disorders, as well as DEPRESSIVE PERSONALITY DISORDER, PASSIVE-AGGRESSIVE PERSONALITY DISORDER, and personality disorder not otherwise specified. Assessment involves a set of questions asked in an interview with the patient.

structured group see STRUCTURAL GROUP.

structured interactional group psychotherapy a form of GROUP THERAPY in which the therapist provides a **structural matrix** for the group's interactions. This is usually achieved by selecting a different member of the group to be the focus of the interaction—the TARGET PATIENT—in each session. [developed by U.S. psychiatrists Harold I. Kaplan (1928–1998) and Benjamin J. Sadock (1933–)]

structured interview an interview consisting of a predetermined set of questions or topics. Structured interviews are popular in marketing research because they produce data that can be easily tabulated; they may also be used in personnel selection and other fields. Compare PATTERNED INTERVIEW; UNSTRUCTURED INTERVIEW. See also STANDARDIZED INTERVIEW SCHEDULE.

structured item a response item with fixed options.

structured learning a complex system of psychotherapy based on the idea of psychological skills training, that is, teaching individuals the skills and behaviors associated with leading healthy and satisfying lives and then helping them gain the ability to consistently and reliably apply these skills outside of the therapeutic setting. This approach involves four essential components: MODELING, ROLE PLAY, performance feedback, and the influence of prior learning on new learning (transfer of training). The individual is provided with examples of specific behavior to be imitated, is allowed to practice that behavior, is given feedback regarding the performance of the behavior, and completes HOMEWORK assignments that encourage the use of the behavior in real-world situations. [developed in the mid-1970s by U.S. psychologists Arnold P. Goldstein (1933–), Robert P. Sprafkin (1940–), and N. Jane Gershaw (1945–)]

structured stimulus a well-defined, well-organized stimulus.

structuring *n.* **1.** the explanation by a counselor or therapist, usually during the first session of a course of treatment, of the specific procedures and conditions of the process. This includes the intended results of treatment, time restrictions, fees, and the function and responsibilities of both client and counselor or therapist. See also CONTRACT. **2.** in education, the use of behavioral instructions to a student to decrease disruptions in the classroom.

strychnine *n.* an alkaloid derived from NUX VOMICA. It is a stimulant of the central nervous system (see CNS STIMULANT)—through its ability to antagonize the inhibitory neurotransmitter glycine—and a powerful convulsant, with death usually resulting from paralysis of muscles of respiration. Strychnine has long been used as a rodenticide, and this use continues to the present; there are, however, no clinical applications for strychnine. No marked tolerance develops for strychnine, and increased susceptibility to poisoning is likely from repeated exposure.

student counseling see EDUCATIONAL COUNSELING.

student's disease the condition of individuals who believe they have the symptoms of a disease or mental disorder that they have been studying or that they have read or heard about.

Student's t distribution see T DISTRIBUTION. [**Student**, pseudonym of William S. Gosset (1876–1937), British statistician]

Study of Values see ALLPORT–VERNON–LINDZEY STUDY OF VALUES.

stupor *n.* **1.** a state of lethargy and impaired consciousness, in which an individual is unresponsive and immobile and experiences DISORIENTATION. **2.** inability to speak (see MUTISM).

Sturge–Weber syndrome a congenital disorder marked by malformation of meningeal blood vessels (hemi- or leptomeningeal angioma), a facial port-wine stain, glaucoma, and focal-motor seizures. Skin pigmentation may occur on one or both sides of the face or extend into the scalp area. About half of affected individuals have mental retardation, and others may have specific cognitive difficulties or disabilities detected by neuropsychological testing. Other characteristics may include contralateral hemiplegia, intracranial calcification, and emotional or behavioral disorders. Also called **encephalofacial angiomatosis**; **Kalischer syndrome**; **Parkes–Weber syndrome**; **Sturge–Weber–Dimitri syndrome**. [William A.

Sturge (1850–1919) and Frederick Parkes **Weber** (1863–1962), British physicians; Vicente **Dimitri** (1885–1955), Austrian physician; S. **Kalischer**, German physician]

Sturm und Drang period see STORM-AND-STRESS PERIOD.

stuttering *n.* in *DSM–IV–TR*, a disturbance in the normal fluency and time patterning of speech. It is characterized by frequent repetition or prolongation of sounds, syllables, or words, with hesitations and pauses that disrupt speech. The disorder occurs in about 1% of all children. Mild cases usually recover spontaneously by the age of 16; chronic stuttering is exacerbated in situations where communication is important or stressful. Also called **stammering**. See also PRIMARY STUTTERING; SECONDARY STUTTERING. **—stutter** *vb., n.*

stuttering gait a gait characterized by hesitancy in taking steps: a walking pattern observed in certain patients with schizophrenia or conversion disorder. In some cases it is neurological in origin, as with PARKINSON'S DISEASE.

style *n.* a typically stable characteristic mode or manner of expressing oneself or acting. Various psychological researchers have examined particular areas of human activity to identify and classify modal differences, as for example in COGNITIVE STYLE and leadership style.

subception *n.* a reaction to an emotion-provoking stimulus that is not clearly enough perceived to be reportable, although its effects may be observed indirectly by the electrodermal response or by a longer than expected reaction time.

subconscious 1. *adj.* denoting mental processes that occur outside consciousness but can easily be brought into awareness. **2.** *n.* in Sigmund FREUD's structural model, the concept of the mind beneath the level of consciousness, comprising the PRECONSCIOUS.

subcortical center any region of the brain at a level below the CEREBRAL CORTEX that has a particular function or functions. Subcortical centers include the THALAMUS, HYPOTHALAMUS, and BASAL GANGLIA. Within each subcortical structure may be several special centers, such as nuclei of the hypothalamus that regulate sleep, water balance, protein metabolism, and sexual activity.

subcortical dementia dementia caused by damage to or dysfunction of the subcortical (deeper) structures of the brain that may be due, for example, to Parkinson's disease. It is marked by cognitive slowing, memory impairment, visuospatial abnormalities, and mood and affect disturbances. Compare CORTICAL DEMENTIA.

subcutaneous injection injection of a drug beneath the skin, often in the upper arm or thigh, where there is an adequate layer of subcutaneous tissue. Although the subcutaneous route is used mainly to inject fluids, medications may also be administered subcutaneously in the form of slowly absorbed pellets. Also called **hypodermic injection**. See also ADMINISTRATION.

subdelirious state the precursor of full DELIRIUM, marked by restlessness, headache, irritability, hypersensitivity to sound and visual stimuli, and emotional instability. Also called **subdelirium**.

subgoal *n.* a goal that serves as an intermediary step to attaining an ultimate goal (i.e., the GOAL OBJECT). For example, completing an outline of an essay may be a subgoal of completing the essay itself—the ultimate goal.

subject *n.* the individual human or nonhuman animal that takes part in an experiment or research study and whose responses or performance are reported or evaluated. PARTICIPANT is now often the preferred term for human subjects, because the word "subject" is depersonalizing and implies passivity and submissiveness on the part of the experimentee.

subjective *adj.* **1.** taking place or existing only within the mind. **2.** particular to a specific person and thus intrinsically inaccessible to the experience or observation of others. **3.** based on or influenced by personal feelings, interpretations, or prejudices. Compare OBJECTIVE.

subjective well-being a judgment that people make about the overall quality of their lives by summing emotional ups and downs to determine how well their actual life circumstances match their wishes or expectations concerning how they should or might feel.

subject of consciousness the observing ego, the "I," or an individual's subjectivity. See also SELF AS AGENT. Compare OBJECT OF CONSCIOUSNESS.

sublimation *n.* in psychoanalytic theory, a DEFENSE MECHANISM in which unacceptable sexual or aggressive drives are unconsciously channeled into socially acceptable modes of expression. Thus, the unacceptable drives and energies are redirected into new, learned behaviors, which indirectly provide some satisfaction for the original instincts. For example, an exhibitionistic impulse may gain a new outlet in choreography; a voyeuristic urge may lead to scientific research; and a dangerously aggressive drive may be expressed with impunity on the football field. As well as allowing for substitute satisfactions, such outlets are posited to protect individuals from the anxiety induced by the original drive. **—sublimate** *vb.*

Sublimaze *n.* a trade name for FENTANYL.

subliminal consciousness a level of consciousness in which a stimulus may affect behavior even though the person is not aware of it. See SUBLIMINAL PERCEPTION.

subliminal learning information, habits, or attitudes acquired from exposure to stimuli that were presented below the threshold for conscious awareness (i.e., subliminally).

subliminal perception the registration of stimuli below the level of awareness, particularly stimuli that are too weak (or too rapid) to affect the individual on a conscious level. It is questionable whether responses to subliminal stimuli actually occur and whether it is possible for subliminal commands or advertising messages to influence behavior. Evidence indicates that subliminal commands do not directly affect behavior but may influence responses via SUBLIMINAL PRIMING.

subliminal priming unconscious (below the threshold of awareness) stimulation that increases the probability of the later occurrence of related cognitive tasks. See PRIMING.

subliminal stimulation stimulation that is below the threshold intensity required to elicit a response (see SUBLIMINAL PERCEPTION). Also called **subliminal stimulus**.

submission *n.* compliance with or surrender to the requests, demands, or will of others. Compare DOMINANCE; ASSERTIVENESS.

submissiveness *n.* a tendency to comply with the wishes or obey the orders of others. **—submissive** *adj.*

subscale *n.* a SCALE that taps some specific constituent or otherwise differentiated category of information as part of a larger, overall scheme. For example, the current version of the WECHSLER ADULT INTELLIGENCE SCALE consists of several subscales (or subtests) assessing such cognitive abilities as verbal comprehension, processing speed, and working memory.

substance *n.* in psychopathology, a drug of abuse (e.g., alcohol, cannabis, cocaine, an inhalant), a medication (e.g., a sedative or anxiolytic), or a toxin that is capable of producing harmful effects when ingested or otherwise taken into the body. See SUBSTANCE-RELATED DISORDER.

substance abuse a pattern of compulsive substance use manifested by recurrent significant social, occupational, legal, or interpersonal adverse consequences, such as repeated absences from work or school, arrests, and marital difficulties. DSM–IV–TR identifies nine drug classes associated with abuse: alcohol, amphetamines, cannabis, cocaine, hallucinogens, inhalants, opioids, phencyclidines, and sedatives, hypnotics, or anxiolytics. This diagnosis is preempted by the diagnosis of SUBSTANCE DEPENDENCE: If the criteria for substance abuse and substance dependence are both met, only the latter diagnosis is given.

Substance Abuse and Mental Health Services Administration (**SAMHSA**) an agency of the U.S. Department of Health and Human Services (HHS), established in 1992, charged with improving the quality and availability of prevention, treatment, and rehabilitative services in order to reduce illness, death, disability, and cost to society resulting from substance abuse and mental illness. SAMHSA has three program divisions: the Center for Mental Health Services, the Center for Substance Abuse Prevention, and the Center for Substance Abuse Treatment. See also ALCOHOL, DRUG ABUSE AND MENTAL HEALTH ADMINISTRATION.

substance abuse treatment inpatient and outpatient programs for individuals diagnosed with substance dependence (i.e., dependence on alcohol or any other drug) to achieve abstinence. These include but are not limited to short- and long-term residential programs (colloquially known as "rehab"), clinic- and hospital-based outpatient programs, METHADONE MAINTENANCE THERAPY, and TWELVE-STEP PROGRAMS. Also called **drug abuse treatment**. See also ALCOHOLISM TREATMENT.

substance dependence a cluster of cognitive, behavioral, and physiological symptoms indicating continued use of a substance despite significant substance-related problems. There is a pattern of repeated substance ingestion resulting in tolerance, withdrawal symptoms if use is suspended, and an uncontrollable drive to continue use. DSM–IV–TR identifies 10 drug classes associated with dependence: alcohol, amphetamines, cannabis, cocaine, hallucinogens, inhalants, nicotine, opioids, phencyclidines, and sedatives, hypnotics, or anxiolytics. This term currently is preferred over the equivalent ADDICTION. See also SUBSTANCE ABUSE.

substance-induced anxiety disorder clinically significant anxiety (e.g., generalized anxiety, panic attacks, phobic symptoms, or obsessive-compulsive symptoms) caused by the direct physiological effects of exposure to a drug, toxin, or other substance. The anxiety symptoms may be associated with substance intoxication (e.g., alcohol, amphetamines, caffeine), substance withdrawal (e.g., alcohol, cocaine, sedatives), medication use (e.g., anesthetics, anticholinergics, thyroid medication), or exposure to heavy metals and toxins (e.g., gasoline, paint, carbon dioxide).

substance-induced mood disorder in *DSM–IV–TR*, significant and persistent mood disturbance (with depressive symptoms, manic symptoms, or both) believed to be caused directly by the physiological effects of a substance, which may be a drug of abuse, a medicinal drug, or a heavy metal or toxin (e.g., gasoline, paint, an organophosphate insecticide). When caused by a drug of abuse, the mood disturbance must occur during or within a month of intoxication or withdrawal and must be more severe than that normally experienced as part of a SUBSTANCE INTOXICATION or SUBSTANCE WITHDRAWAL syndrome. Medications that can cause mood disturbance include antihypertensives, steroids, psychotropic drugs, and many others.

substance-induced persisting amnestic disorder a disturbance in memory due to the persisting effects of a substance (see AMNESTIC DISORDER). The ability to learn new information or to recall previously learned information is impaired severely enough to interfere markedly with social or occupational functioning and torepresent a significant decline from a previous level of functioning. See ALCOHOL-INDUCED PERSISTING AMNESTIC DISORDER; SEDATIVE-, HYPNOTIC-, OR ANXIOLYTIC-INDUCED PERSISTING AMNESTIC DISORDER.

substance-induced persisting dementia multiple COGNITIVE DEFICITS due to the persisting effects of substance abuse. The most notable feature is impaired memory, but there may also be aphasia (impaired expression or understanding of language), apraxia (inability to perform skilled or complex movements), agnosia (impaired ability to interpret sensations correctly), and EXECUTIVE DYSFUNCTION. See also ALCOHOL-INDUCED PERSISTING DEMENTIA.

substance-induced psychotic disorder prominent hallucinations or delusions due to the direct physiological effects of a substance. Also called **hallucinosis**. See ALCOHOL-INDUCED PSYCHOTIC DISORDER; AMPHETAMINE-INDUCED PSYCHOTIC DISORDER; CANNABIS-INDUCED PSYCHOTIC DISORDER; HALLUCINOGEN-INDUCED PSYCHOTIC DISORDER.

substance intoxication a reversible syndrome due to the recent ingestion of a specific substance, including clinically significant behavioral or psychological changes, as well as one or more signs of physiological involvement. Although symptoms vary by substance there are some common manifestations, for example, perceptual disturbances; mood changes; impairments of judgment, attention and memory; alterations of heartbeat and vision; and speech and coordination difficulties. DSM–IV–TR identifies 10 drug classes associated with intoxication: alcohol, amphetamines, caffeine, cannabis, cocaine, hallucinogens, inhalants, opioids, phencyclidines, and sedatives, hypnotics, or anxiolytics.

substance intoxication delirium a reversible substance-specific syndrome that develops over a short period of time (usually hours to days) following heavy consumption of the substance. It includes disturbance of consciousness (e.g., reduced ability to focus, sustain, or shift attention), accompanied by changes in cognition (e.g., memory deficit, disorientation, or language disturbance) in excess of those usually associated with intoxication with that substance. See ALCOHOL INTOXICATION DELIRIUM; AMPHETAMINE INTOXICATION DELIRIUM; COCAINE INTOXICATION DELIRIUM; PCP INTOXICATION DELIRIUM.

substance P a NEUROPEPTIDE that functions as a neurotransmitter in both peripheral and central nervous systems. It belongs to the neurokinin family of transmitters. High concentrations of neurons containing substance P are localized in the dorsal horn of the spinal cord, where they play a role in the modulation of pain. In peripheral tissues, substance P acts as a vasodilator. It also has a role in sexual behavior and has been implicated in the regulation of mood.

substance-related disorder any of various disorders caused by the effects of a drug or a toxin. This DSM–IV–TR category encompasses the substance use disorders (substance abuse and substance dependence) and the substance-induced disorders (e.g., intoxication).

substance withdrawal a syndrome that develops after cessation of prolonged, heavy consumption of a substance. Symptoms vary by substance but generally include physiological, behavioral, and cognitive manifestations, such as nausea and vomiting, insomnia, mood alterations, and anxiety. DSM–IV–TR identifies six drug classes associated with withdrawal: alcohol, amphetamines, cocaine, nicotine, opioids, and sedatives, hypnotics, or anxiolytics.

substantia nigra a region of gray matter in the midbrain, named for its dark pigmentation, that sends DOPAMINERGIC neurons to the BASAL GANGLIA. Depletion of dopaminergic neurons in this region is implicated in PARKINSON'S DISEASE.

substitute formation see SYMPTOM FORMATION.

substituting *n.* in GROUP THERAPY, providing social support by such behavior as a smile, a pat, or a hug, rather than by words.

substitution *n.* the replacement of one thing with another. More specifically, particularly in psychoanalytic theory, it denotes the replacement of unacceptable emotions or unattainable goals with alternative satisfactions or feelings. Substitution may be viewed as a positive adaptation or solution (e.g., adoption when one cannot have a child of one's own) or as a negative, maladaptive response (e.g., emotional eating after a frustrating day at the office). See also DEFENSE MECHANISM.

substrate *n.* **1.** a basis or foundation, such as the physical medium on which an animal or plant lives or grows. **2.** a chemical compound that is acted on by an enzyme. The substrate binds specifically to the enzyme's active site, thereby lowering the energy required for the reaction, which therefore can proceed much faster. When the process is over, the enzyme is unchanged but the substrate has been changed into different molecules called reaction products. The released enzyme then repeats the process with another substrate of the same composition.

subthalamic nucleus a part of the subthalamus that receives fibers from the GLOBUS PALLIDUS as a part of the descending pathway from the BASAL GANGLIA. It forms part of the EXTRAPYRAMIDAL TRACT.

subthalamus *n.* a part of the DIENCEPHALON of the brain, wedged between the THALAMUS and the HYPOTHALAMUS. It contains the subthalamic nucleus and functions in the regulation of movements controlled by skeletal muscles, together with the BASAL GANGLIA and the SUBSTANTIA NIGRA. **—subthalamic** *adj.*

subtherapeutic dose a dose of a drug that does not achieve a particular therapeutic effect. Although this is generally not desired, drugs intended for one purpose may be administered in subtherapeutic doses to achieve a different effect. For example, the TRICYCLIC ANTIDEPRESSANTS are rarely used in current practice in doses sufficient to alleviate depression; however, they are often used in low (subtherapeutic) doses to promote sleep or alleviate pain.

successful aging avoidance of disease and disability, maintenance of cognitive capacity, continued active engagement in life, and adaptation to the aging process through such strategies as SELECTIVE OPTIMIZATION WITH COMPENSATION.

succinimide *n.* any of a group of chemically related drugs that are effective in the treatment of absence seizures. Discovered in a search for an antidote for drug-induced convulsions, they produce a sedative effect and may cause behavioral changes. **Ethosuximide** is an example of a succinimide and is sold in the United States under the trade name **Zarontin**.

succinylcholine *n.* a drug that relaxes skeletal muscles, used intravenously in anesthesia and before electroconvulsive treatment. It is a neuromuscular blocking agent that does not relieve pain or produce sedation. U.S. trade name (among others): **Anectine**.

succorance need in the PERSONOLOGY of U.S. psychologist Henry Alexander Murray (1893–1988), the need for protection, aid, and support.

sucking reflex a basic reflex in which the young of many mammals (including human infants) grasp the nipple with their lips and draw milk into their mouths by suction.

sudden infant death syndrome (**SIDS**) the sudden and unexpected death of a seemingly healthy infant during sleep for no apparent reason. The risk of SIDS is greatest between 2 and 6 months of age and is a common cause of death in infants less than 1 year old. Also called **cot death**; **crib death**.

S

sudden insight sudden knowledge or understanding of the truth or essential nature of something, for example, a problem, an issue, or a complex situation. See AHA EXPERIENCE; DISCONTINUITY HYPOTHESIS; EUREKA TASK; INSPIRATION.

sufentanil *n.* a short-acting OPIOID that binds to OPIOID RECEPTORS and is used as an analgesic supplement in the maintenance of balanced general anesthesia. See also FENTANYL. U.S. trade name: **Sufenta**.

suffering *n.* the experience of pain or acute distress, either psychological or physical, in response to a significant event, particularly one that is threatening or involves loss (e.g., the death of a loved one) or a physical trauma.

suggestibility *n.* **1.** a state in which the ideas, beliefs, attitudes, or actions of others are readily and uncritically adopted. **2.** an occasional synonym for HYPNOTIC SUSCEPTIBILITY.

suggestion *n.* **1.** the process of inducing acceptance of an idea or course of action in an individual through indirect means. Suggestion is usually expressed in words but may also be pictorial, as in advertisements, or subliminal. **2.** an idea or potential course of action presented to another for consideration. See also AUTOSUGGESTION; PRESTIGE SUGGESTION.

suggestion therapy a type of psychotherapy in which distressing symptoms are alleviated by direct suggestion and reassurance. The technique is sometimes used in HYPNOTHERAPY. A suggestion may be accompanied by an explanation of the meaning and the purpose of the symptoms, but no attempt is made to modify the client's basic personality.

suicidal crisis a situation in which suicide is threatened or attempted.

suicidal gesture an ATTEMPTED SUICIDE or similar self-destructive behavior, especially one where the risk of death is quite low.

suicidal ideation suicidal thoughts or a preoccupation with suicide, often as a symptom of a MAJOR DEPRESSIVE EPISODE. Most instances of suicidal ideation do not progress to ATTEMPTED SUICIDE.

suicidality *n.* the risk of suicide, usually indicated by suicidal ideation or intent.

suicide *n.* the act of killing oneself. Frequently, suicide occurs in the context of a MAJOR DEPRESSIVE EPISODE, but it may also occur as a result of a substance-use or other disorder. It sometimes occurs in the absence of any psychiatric disorder, especially in untenable situations, such as bereavement or declining health. See also ATTEMPTED SUICIDE; PASSIVE SUICIDE. **—suicidal** *adj.*

suicide attempt see ATTEMPTED SUICIDE.

suicide-prevention center a CRISIS-INTERVENTION facility dealing primarily with individuals who have suicidal thoughts or who have threatened or attempted suicide. Suicide-prevention centers are usually staffed by social workers or paraprofessionals with mental health preparation who are trained to deal with such emergencies in person or over a telephone hotline. Suicide-prevention centers additionally provide community education and outreach, and staff may provide bereavement support for the relatives and loved ones of an individual who has killed himself or herself.

suicidology *n.* a multiprofessional discipline devoted to the study of suicidal phenomena and their prevention. Major groups involved are (a) scientists (epidemiologists, sociologists, statisticians, demographers, and social psychologists), (b) clinicians (clinical psychologists, psychiatrists, social workers, trained volunteers, and members of the clergy), and (c) educators (public health educators and school and college personnel).

sukra prameha a CULTURE-BOUND SYNDROME found in Sri Lanka, with symptoms similar to those of SHEN-K'UEI.

suk-yeong *n.* see KORO.

Sullivan's interpersonal theory a theory that emphasizes social influences on development, focusing on key relationships and how they develop and change over time. It proposes that an individual's concept of selfhood is a reflection of others' attitudes toward that person (i.e., arising out of interpersonal relationships and situations) and posits that, although personal self-concept develops slowly, the need for personal security is present from the beginning of existence. Sullivan hypothesized that threats to self-respect are experienced as anxiety and that assaults on self-esteem emanate from sources outside the person, particularly those most intimately related to the individual across early and adolescent development. The theory proposes three phases of relationship development: (a) during preadolescence, intimacy with a same-sex friend; (b) in early adolescence, changes from same-sex cliques to mixed-sex cliques; (c) in late adolescence, full participation in intimate reciprocal relationships with a romantic partner. [Harry Stack **Sullivan** (1892–1949), U.S. psychiatrist]

sumatriptan *n.* see TRIPTANS.

summa libido see ACME.

summative evaluation **1.** in educational evaluation research, the appraisal of a student's achievement at the conclusion of an educational program. Also called **terminal assessment**. **2.** in evaluation research, an attempt to assess the overall effectiveness of a program after it is in operation (in contrast to FORMATIVE EVALUATION, which is used to help in the development of the program). Also called **ex post facto evaluation**. See also OUTCOME EVALUATION.

summer depression an atypical variant of SEASONAL AFFECTIVE DISORDER in which MAJOR DEPRESSIVE EPISODES tend to occur in the summer months.

sum of squares the total obtained by adding together the squares of each deviation score in a sample (i.e., each score minus the sample mean squared, and then added together). Thus, for a set of variables X_i, $\Sigma(X_i - \bar{X})^2$, where $\bar{X}$ is the mean value of X_i.

sundown syndrome the tendency, particularly among older adults with dementia or individuals in institutional care, to experience reduced levels of psychological functioning late in the day. Also called **sundowning**.

suo yang see KORO.

superconducting quantum interference device (SQUID) a device used in MAGNETOENCEPHALOGRAPHY for detecting magnetic waves in the brain. These highly sensitive devices must be used in rooms that are screened from all outside magnetic sources. They are useful in the study of in vivo human brain processes.

superconscious *n.* **1.** a New Age term for transpersonal awareness. **2.** in certain Eastern traditions, with variation (Buddhism; Hinduism; Taoism), a state in which the individual attains highest knowledge, freedom from pain, and perfect spiritual insight because the mind is free from passion and desire. At their most profound level, the practices of MEDITATION and YOGA (among others) may be directed toward the ultimate achievement of the superconscious state.

superego *n.* in psychoanalytic theory, the moral component of the personality that represents society's standards and determines personal standards of right and wrong, or conscience, as well as aims and aspirations (see EGO-IDEAL). In the classic Freudian tripartite structure of the psyche, the EGO, which controls personal impulses and directs actions, operates by the rules and principles of the superego, which basically stem from parental demands and prohibitions. The formation of the superego occurs on an unconscious level, beginning in the first 5 years of life and continuing throughout childhood and adolescence and into adulthood, largely through identification with the parents and later with admired models of behavior. See also HETERONOMOUS SUPEREGO; PRIMITIVE SUPEREGO.

superego anxiety in psychoanalytic theory, anxiety caused by unconscious superego activity that produces feelings of guilt and demands for atonement. Compare EGO ANXIETY; ID ANXIETY.

superego resistance in psychoanalytic theory, a type of RESISTANCE to the psychoanalytic process created by the superego. It generates a sense of guilt and gives rise to the need for punishment in the form of persistent symptoms. Compare REPRESSION-RESISTANCE; ID RESISTANCE.

superego sadism in psychoanalytic theory, the aggressive, rigid, and punitive aspect of the superego, or conscience. Its energy is derived from the destructive forces of the ID, and its intensity and strength are dependent upon the violent and sadistic fantasies of the child's primordial strivings. See SADISM.

superior function in the ANALYTIC PSYCHOLOGY of Carl JUNG, the dominating function among the four basic functions—seeing, thinking, intuiting, and feeling—that rules the conscious ego and dominates the other three, which become INFERIOR FUNCTIONS in the unconscious. The superior function determines the FUNCTIONAL TYPE of the individual.

superiority complex in the INDIVIDUAL PSYCHOLOGY of Alfred ADLER, an exaggerated opinion of one's abilities and accomplishments that derives from an overcompensation for feelings of inferiority. See COMPENSATION. Compare INFERIORITY COMPLEX.

superstitious control the illusion that one

can influence outcomes through various practices designed to protect oneself, alter the environment, or affect a situation. Such practices include following specific behavior patterns and rituals. Some people maintain that superstitious control serves a positive psychological function in averting the development of LEARNED HELPLESSNESS. See FAITH HEALING; MAGICAL THINKING.

supervalent thought an extreme preoccupation with a single topic. See OBSESSION; RUMINATION.

supervised analysis see CONTROL ANALYSIS.

supervision *n.* oversight: critical evaluation and guidance provided by a qualified and experienced person—the supervisor—to another individual—the trainee—during the learning of a task or process. In psychotherapy and counseling, supervision by a senior therapist or counselor is required while the trainee learns therapeutic techniques. A prescribed number of hours of supervision is required by state licensing boards as part of the requirements for obtaining a license in a mental health field.

supervisory analysis see CONTROL ANALYSIS.

supervisory attentional system (**SAS**) a theoretical higher level cognitive mechanism active in nonroutine or novel situations, responsible for troubleshooting and decision making when habitual responses or automatic processes are ineffective or otherwise unsatisfactory. Thought to be involved in carrying out a variety of other EXECUTIVE FUNCTIONS as well, it is considered a network for the coordination and control of cognitive activity and intentional behavior.

supplementary motor area an area of the MOTOR CORTEX with somatotopic organization involved in planning and learning new movements that have coordinated sequences. In contrast to the PREMOTOR AREA, neuronal input to the supplementary motor area is triggered more by internal representations than by external events.

supplication *n.* in SELF-PRESENTATION theory, a strategy that involves depicting oneself as weak, needy, or dependent, so as to motivate others to provide assistance or care. —**supplicate** *vb.*

supported employment a VOCATIONAL REHABILITATION program that places individuals with disabilities directly into the paid competitive working environment as quickly as possible. With an emphasis on matching an individual with an appropriate employer and work environment rather than adapting the person to the environment, it involves individualized, rapid placement and ongoing support, training, and assessment that integrates both vocational and personal needs. Supported employment differs from a SHELTERED WORKSHOP in that the latter occurs in a controlled, noncompetitive working environment. See also TRANSITIONAL EMPLOYMENT.

supported living a situation in which people with mental retardation live singly or in small groups in apartments or houses (usually rented but sometimes leased or purchased) where drop-in assistance in performing activities of daily living and learning independent living skills is available. Varying degrees of assistance are provided by staff, depending on the skills of the particular residents.

supported retirement a daily or regular program or schedule of activity for an aging or aged person with mental retardation that emphasizes socialization and recreational engagement, rather than the habilitation activities and vocational involvement typical of adult mental retardation day services.

support group a group similar in some ways to a SELF-HELP GROUP, in that members who share a problem come together to provide help, comfort, and guidance. A primary distinguishing feature of support groups is in their leadership: a professional or agency-based facilitator who often does not share the problem of members. In addition, support groups often last for only a limited predetermined number of sessions, and a fee for attendance is sometimes charged.

supportive ego a member of an ACTIVITY-THERAPY group who helps a fellow member work out difficulties within his or her psyche, mind, or personality. [first described by Russian-born U.S. psychotherapist Samuel Richard Slavson (1890–1981)]

supportive-expressive psychotherapy a form of brief PSYCHODYNAMIC PSYCHOTHERAPY that focuses on the therapist–client relationship and on relationships outside of therapy to define a central relationship pattern that is the focus of treatment. [developed by U.S. clinical psychologists Lester Luborsky (1920–2009) and Paul Crits-Christoph]

supportiveness *n.* in psychotherapy and counseling, an attitude or response of acceptance, encouragement, or reassurance displayed by the therapist or counselor.

supportive psychotherapy a form of therapy that aims to relieve emotional distress and symptoms without probing into the sources of conflicts or attempting to alter basic personality structure. Specific methods used include reassurance, reeducation, advice, persuasion, environmental changes, pastoral counseling, bereavement therapy, bibliotherapy, remotivation, and encouragement of desirable behavior. Such measures are frequently applied to individuals with relatively minor or limited problems, as well as to fragile or hospitalized patients, as a means of maintaining morale and preventing deterioration.

supportive services **1.** programs ancillary to the treatment or rehabilitation of people with illnesses or disabilities. **2.** social service programs (e.g., child care or transportation) that are necessary to enable an individual to participate in the workforce or function more independently.

suppository *n.* a bullet-shaped medicinal preparation for rectal administration. It dissolves in the rectum to release its active component, which is absorbed through the rectal mucosa. Vaginal suppositories are available for treating gynecological conditions.

suppression *n.* a conscious effort to put disturbing thoughts and experiences out of mind, or to control and inhibit the expression of unacceptable impulses and feelings. It is distinct from the unconscious DEFENSE MECHANISM of REPRESSION in psychoanalytic theory. **—suppress** *vb.*

suppressive therapy a form of psychotherapy directed toward the reinforcement of the client's defense mechanisms and the suppression (rather than expression) of distressing experiences and feelings. Compare EXPRESSIVE THERAPY.

surface dyslexia a form of acquired dyslexia (see ALEXIA) in which a person is overly reliant on spelling-to-sound correspondence and therefore has difficulty reading irregularly spelled words. Surface dyslexia manifested as a form of DEVELOPMENTAL DYSLEXIA has also been described. See also DEEP DYSLEXIA. [first described in 1973 by British neuropsychologists John C. Marshall and Freda Newcombe (1925–2001)]

surface therapy psychotherapy directed toward relieving the client's symptoms and emotional stress through such measures as reassurance, suggestion, and direct attempts to modify attitudes and behavior patterns, rather than through exploration and analysis of unconscious motivation and underlying dynamics. Compare DEPTH THERAPY.

surface trait in CATTELL'S PERSONALITY TRAIT THEORY, a characteristic manifested as a group of interrelated observable behaviors. For example, arriving early for appointments and leaving the office only after one's work is complete are visible verifications of the characteristic of conscientiousness. Surface traits appear consistently and are thought to cluster and form SOURCE TRAITS, which are regarded as the underlying building blocks of personality.

surgency *n.* in trait psychology, a personality trait marked by cheerfulness, responsiveness, spontaneity, and sociability, but at a level below that of EXTRAVERSION or MANIA. [defined by British psychologist Raymond Cattell (1905–1998)] **—surgent** *adj.*

surprise *n.* an emotion typically resulting from the violation of an expectation or the detection of novelty in the environment. According to various theories, it is considered to be one of the emotions that have a universal pattern of facial expression. The physiological response includes raising or arching the eyebrows, opening the eyes wide, opening the mouth wide in an oval shape, and gasping.

surrogate decision making a provision in law or a regulation permitting the appointment of a surrogate for a person, frequently a person with mental retardation, dementia, or a mental disorder, who is not competent to make specific decisions regarding consent to medical, surgical, or other health care procedures. The surrogate makes these determinations on behalf of the person.

surrogate father see FATHER SURROGATE.

surrogate mother see MOTHER SURROGATE.

survival instinct see SELF-PRESERVATION INSTINCT.

survivor guilt remorse or guilt for having survived a catastrophic situation when others did not or for not suffering the ills that others had to endure. It is a common reaction stemming in part from a feeling of having failed to do enough to prevent the tragedy or to save those who did not survive. Survivor guilt is also experienced by family members who are found not to carry deleterious genetic mutations that have led to disease and, often, death in other family members or simply by family or friends who feel that they did not do enough to succor their loved ones prior to death.

survivorship *n.* **1.** the state of having a typical life and life span after overcoming severe diseases (e.g., cancer), traumatic life events (e.g., child abuse), or environmental disaster (e.g., earthquake). **2.** the state of living into very old age.

susceptibility *n.* vulnerability: readily affected by or at increased risk of acquiring a particular condition, such as an infection, injury, or disorder.

suspiciousness *n.* an attitude of mistrust toward the motives or sincerity of others. Although a degree of suspiciousness in certain situations can be natural and likely serves the purposes of self-preservation or survival, extreme, pervasive suspiciousness is a common characteristic of individuals with PARANOID PERSONALITY DISORDER.

sustained operations (**SUSOPS**) an extended work schedule under demanding conditions. A sustained workload can combine with fatigue and reduced or fragmented sleep to degrade performance, productivity, safety, and the effectiveness of an operation.

sustained-release preparation see SLOW-RELEASE PREPARATION.

susto *n.* a CULTURE-BOUND SYNDROME occurring among Latinos in the United States and populations in Mexico, Central America, and South America. After experiencing a frightening event, individuals fear that their soul has left their body. Symptoms include weight loss, fatigue, muscle pains, headache, diarrhea, unhappiness, troubled sleep, lack of motivation, and low self-esteem. Also called **chibih**; **espanto**; **pasmo**; **perdida del alma**; **tripa ida**.

swinging *n.* slang for uninhibited sexual expres-

S

sion, for example, partner swapping, one-night stands, group sex, and experimentation with sexual activities.

switching *n.* **1.** in psychotherapy, changing the course of the discussion during a session. This may be done by the client, either purposefully or unconsciously, when the discussion is too close to sensitive issues. Switching may also be done by the therapist to change the discussion to more relevant therapeutic issues. **2.** in multiple personality disorders, the often rapid movement between one personality and another.

switch process the process by which a person with a BIPOLAR DISORDER experiences the transition from a MAJOR DEPRESSIVE EPISODE to a MANIC EPISODE or vice versa. These processes usually include brief periods of relatively unimpaired functioning.

symbiosis *n.* **1.** in developmental psychology, the stage in infantile development when the infant's dependence is total and he or she is neither biologically nor psychologically separated from the mother. See also SEPARATION–INDIVIDUATION. [proposed by Hungarian-born U.S. psychoanalyst Margaret S. Mahler (1897–1985)] **2.** a mutually reinforcing relationship in which one individual is overdependent on another to satisfy needs. Such a relationship hampers the development or independence of both individuals and usually results in dysfunction when the dominant individual is unwilling to provide for the dependent individual. Also called **symbiotic relationship**. **—symbiotic** *adj.*

symbiotic infantile psychosis see SYMBIOTIC PSYCHOSIS.

symbiotic marriage a marriage or partnership of two individuals who are dependent upon each other for the gratification of certain psychological needs. Both partners may have neurotic or otherwise unusual needs that could not be satisfied easily outside of their relationship. Compare SYNERGIC MARRIAGE.

symbiotic psychosis an obsolete name for a condition, occurring in children between the ages of 2 and 5, that is characterized by complete emotional dependence on the mother, inability to tolerate separation from her, reactions of anger and panic if any separation is threatened, and developmental lag. Some of these features are characteristic of SEPARATION ANXIETY DISORDER. Also called **symbiotic infantile psychosis**; **symbiotic infantile psychotic syndrome**. [first described by Hungarian-born U.S. psychoanalyst Margaret Mahler (1897–1985)]

symbiotic relationship see SYMBIOSIS.

symbol *n.* **1.** any object, figure, or image that represents something else, such as a flag, a logo, a pictogram, or a religious symbol (e.g., a cross). In literature and art, symbols are generally suggestive rather than explicit in their meaning: For example, a rose may suggest ideas of beauty, love, femininity, and transience without being limited to any of these meanings in particular. Carl JUNG maintained that the symbols of religion, mythology, and art throw special light on the racial unconscious. See also SIGN. **2.** in psychoanalytic theory, a disguised representation of a repressed idea, impulse, or wish. See also SYMBOLISM. **—symbolic** *adj.*

Symbolic *n.* the realm of symbols or SIGNIFIERS: one of three aspects of the psychoanalytic field defined by French psychoanalyst Jacques Lacan (1901–1981). The achievement of symbolization marks the beginning of ego differentiation and is associated with the infant's entrance into the world of language, culture, law, and morality. The other two realms are the IMAGINARY and the REAL. See also MIRROR PHASE; NAME-OF-THE-FATHER.

symbolic action see SYMPTOMATIC ACT.

symbolic consciousness awareness of events whose meaning goes beyond their sensory contents.

symbolic displacement the process of transferring a response, usually emotional, from its original stimulus to one that represents it. For example, a man who harbors homicidal impulses might develop a morbid fear of knives or guns.

symbolic interactionism a sociological theory that assumes that self-concept is created through interpretation of symbolic gestures, words, actions, and appearances exhibited by others during social interaction. In contrast to Freudian and other approaches that postulate extensive inner dispositions and regard social interaction as resulting from them, symbolic interactionists believe that inner structures result from social interactions. U.S. social thinkers George Herbert Mead (1863–1931) and Charles Horton Cooley (1864–1929) are recognized exponents of this view. See REFLECTED APPRAISALS.

symbolic play a form of play in which the child uses objects as representations of other things. For example, a child may put a leash on a stuffed animal, take it for a walk, and make it eat from a bowl. Symbolic play may or may not be social. See also IMAGINARY COMPANION.

symbolic process **1.** in cognitive psychology, any cognitive activity in which ideas, images, or other MENTAL REPRESENTATIONS serve as mediators of thought. The term is often used to distinguish the HIGHER MENTAL PROCESSES from either (a) lower cognitive functions, such as perception, or (b) those neurophysiological processes that underlie processing at the symbolic level. See also SYMBOLIC THINKING; THINKING. **2.** in psychoanalysis, any operation in which a SYMBOL is substituted for a repressed thought or impulse. See also SYMBOLIZATION.

symbolic realization the fulfillment of a blocked desire or goal through a substitute that represents it. For example, a person who has not been able to rebel against an authoritarian father may rebel against all symbols of authority, such as the laws or customs of the society in which he or she lives.

symbolic representation the process of representing experiences in the mind symbolically, for example, through words and sounds: one of three modes of representing knowledge. [proposed by U.S. developmental psychologist Jerome Seymour Bruner (1915–)]

symbolic reward something that has no intrinsic value but is nevertheless prized because it represents something of value. For example, being listed in a city's social register may be regarded as a symbolic reward for attainment of high social standing.

symbolic thinking the ability to think about objects and events that are not within the immediate environment. It involves the use of signs, symbols, concepts, and abstract relations, as evidenced by language, numeracy, and artistic or ritual expression. Archaeological finds suggest that symbolic thinking may have evolved in humans much earlier than previously thought, possibly toward the end of the Lower Paleolithic (i.e., over 70,000 years ago). See also SYMBOLIC PROCESS.

symbolism *n.* **1.** in psychoanalytic theory, the substitution of a SYMBOL for a repressed impulse or threatening object in order to avoid censorship by the superego (e.g., dreaming of a steeple or other PHALLIC SYMBOL instead of a penis). Also called **symbolization**. **2.** the use of symbols in literature and the visual arts or in human culture generally. A specific, early modernist movement, referred to as **Symbolism**, developed in France in the mid- to late 19th century. The writing, primarily poetry and drama, was highly evocative and made extensive use of indirect symbolic language to represent character, situation, and action.

symbolization *n.* **1.** see SYMBOLISM. **2.** in Albert BANDURA'S SOCIAL-COGNITIVE THEORY, the ability to think about one's social behavior in terms of words and images. **—symbolize** *vb.*

Symmetrel *n.* a trade name for AMANTADINE.

symmetry compulsion a compulsion to arrange objects in a certain way (e.g., in a room) or in a particular order (e.g., on a desk). Symmetry compulsion is associated with obsessions about neatness or perfection. It can be a symptom of OBSESSIVE-COMPULSIVE DISORDER or, sometimes, of OBSESSIVE-COMPULSIVE PERSONALITY DISORDER.

sympathectomy *n.* a surgical procedure in which portions of the SYMPATHETIC NERVOUS SYSTEM are excised, severed, or otherwise disrupted. In **chemical sympathectomy**, this is accomplished by the administration of specific drugs.

sympathetic induction the process in which one person's expressed emotion elicits a similar emotion in another person. See EMPATHY; SYMPATHY.

sympathetic nervous system one of the two divisions of the AUTONOMIC NERVOUS SYSTEM (ANS, which controls smooth muscle and gland functions), the other being the PARASYMPATHETIC NERVOUS SYSTEM. Anatomically it consists of preganglionic autonomic neurons whose fibers run from the thoracic and lumbar regions of the spinal cord to the chains of sympathetic ganglia. From these arise the fibers of postganglionic autonomic neurons, which innervate organs ranging from the eye to the reproductive organs. It is defined functionally in terms of its ability to act as an integrated whole in affecting a large number of smooth muscle systems simultaneously, usually in the service of enhancing "fight or flight" (see FIGHT-OR-FLIGHT RESPONSE). Typical sympathetic changes include dilation of the pupils to facilitate vision, constriction of the peripheral arteries to supply more blood to the muscles and the brain, secretion of epinephrine to raise the blood-sugar level and increase metabolism, and reduction of stomach and intestinal activities so that energy can be directed elsewhere. Thus, the sympathetic nervous system tends to antagonize the effects of the parasympathetic nervous system. Also called **sympathetic division**.

sympathetic vibration a state in which the thoughts and feelings of two or more people are in harmony.

sympathism *n.* see SYMPATHY SEEKING.

sympathomimetic drug any pharmacological agent that stimulates activity in the sympathetic nervous system because it potentiates the activity of norepinephrine or epinephrine or has effects similar to these neurotransmitters (hence they are also known as **adrenergic drugs**). Sympathomimetic drugs include the amphetamines and ephedrine.

sympathy *n.* **1.** feelings of concern or compassion resulting from an awareness of the suffering or sorrow of another. **2.** more generally, a capacity to share in and respond to the concerns or feelings of others. See also EMPATHY. **3.** an affinity between individuals on the basis of similar feelings, inclinations, or temperament. **—sympathetic** *adj.* **—sympathize** *vb.*

sympathy seeking the tendency to seek emotional support or elicit the assistance of others by arousing sympathy. Also called **sympathism**.

symphorophilia *n.* sexual interest and arousal derived from stage-managing the occurrence of a disaster and then watching it. The person may masturbate either while the disaster occurs or afterward, with memories or pictures of the event. **—symphorophile** *n.*

symptom *n.* any deviation from normal functioning that is considered indicative of physical or mental disorder. A recognized pattern of symptoms is usually necessary in order for an individual to be judged as having a SYNDROME or psychological disorder. **—symptomatic** *adj.*

symptomatic act an action that appears to be

S

intended for one purpose (or to have no particular purpose) but that betrays a hidden intention or meaning. In psychoanalytic theory, such acts are thought to represent repressed impulses. See also FREUDIAN SLIP; PARAPRAXIS; SYMPTOM FORMATION.

symptomatic treatment treatment directed toward the relief of distressing symptoms, as opposed to treatment focused on underlying causes and conditions. Symptomatic treatment of chronic migraines, for example, would involve the use of analgesics to relieve pain without attempting to discover why they are occurring.

symptomatology *n.* **1.** the combined signs, markers, or indications of a disease or disorder. **2.** the scientific study of the markers and indications of a disease or disorder.

symptom bearer see IDENTIFIED PATIENT.

Symptom Checklist-90-Revised (**SCL-90-R**) a 90-item self-report inventory that measures the psychological symptoms and distress of community, medical, and psychiatric respondents along nine primary symptom dimensions and three global indices. The SCL-90-R adds four dimensions to the five assessed in the HOPKINS SYMPTOM CHECKLIST, of which it is a direct outgrowth: hostility, phobic anxiety, paranoid ideation, and psychoticism.

symptom cluster a group of related symptoms that usually occur together, as in a SYNDROME.

symptom complex see SYNDROME.

symptom-context method a system of gathering data as symptoms arise in vivo in the psychotherapy session as an aid to psychotherapy research, case formulation, and treatment. It is similar to the CORE CONFLICTUAL RELATIONSHIP THEME method. [developed by U.S. clinical psychologist Lester Luborsky (1920–2009)]

symptom formation **1.** in psychoanalytic theory, the development of a somatic or behavioral manifestation of an unconscious impulse or conflict that provokes anxiety. Also called **substitute formation**. **2.** the process by which the indications of physical or psychological illness or disease develop.

symptom removal in psychotherapy, elimination of symptoms through direct treatment without addressing underlying issues and unconscious motivation. See also SURFACE THERAPY.

symptom specificity a hypothesis stating that people with PSYCHOSOMATIC DISORDERS display abnormal responses to stress in particular physiological systems. According to this hypothesis, a person's complaints will center around a particular organ (e.g., the heart) and set of related symptoms (e.g., cardiovascular symptoms) rather than involving a variety of complaints about different organs or systems.

symptom substitution in the classic psychoanalytic theory of Sigmund FREUD, the development of a symptom to replace one that has cleared up as a result of treatment. It is said to occur if the unconscious impulses and conflicts responsible for the original symptom are not dealt with. Symptom substitution is often used as an argument against therapies aimed at symptom removal alone, as in behavior therapy, suggestion, and some forms of hypnotherapy; however, this hypothesis has not been validated.

Synanon *n.* a residential drug treatment program that utilized confrontation and peer pressure to encourage its members to deal with their addiction. Founded in California in 1958 by Charles Dederich (1914–1997), himself a recovering alcoholic, Synanon was the first major drug treatment program in the United States, and its TOUGH LOVE approach to overcoming addiction was widely publicized as innovative and effective. It evolved into an experimental commune that Dederich proclaimed as a religion in the mid-1970s. Thereafter, amid accusations of authoritarian practices within the community and Dederich's no-contest plea to charges of attempted murder, Synanon declined in prominence and was eventually disbanded in 1991.

synapse *n.* the specialized junction through which neural signals are transmitted from one neuron (the presynaptic neuron) to another (the postsynaptic neuron). In most synapses the knoblike ending (terminal button) of the axon of a presynaptic neuron faces the dendrite or cell body of the postsynaptic neuron across a narrow gap, the synaptic cleft. The arrival of a neural signal triggers the release of NEUROTRANSMITTER from synaptic vesicles in the terminal button into the synaptic cleft. Here the molecules of neurotransmitter activate receptors in the postsynaptic membrane and cause the opening of ION CHANNELS in the postsynaptic cell. This may lead to excitation or inhibition of the postsynaptic cell, depending on which ion channels are affected. Also called **synaptic junction**. **—synaptic** *adj.*

synaptic bouton see AXON.

synaptic cleft the gap within a synapse between the knoblike ending of the axon of one neuron and the dendrite or cell body of a neighboring neuron. The synaptic cleft is typically 20–30 nm wide. Also called **synaptic gap**.

synaptic pruning a neurodevelopmental process, ocurring both before birth and up to the second decade of life, in which the weakest synapses between neurons are eliminated. In schizophrenia research, it is hypothesized that premature or excessive pruning may account for some forms of the disease.

synaptic transmission see NEUROTRANSMISSION.

synchronicity *n.* in the ANALYTIC PSYCHOLOGY of Carl JUNG, the simultaneous occurrence of events that appear to have a meaningful connection when there is no explicable causal relationship between these events, as in extraordinary coincidences or purported examples of telepa-

S

thy. Jung suggested that some simultaneous occurrences possess significance through their very coincidence in time.

synchronized sleep DELTA-WAVE sleep, when electroencephalogram recordings show slow, synchronous waves. See also SLEEP STAGES.

syncope *n.* fainting: a transient loss of consciousness resulting from sudden reduction in the blood supply to the brain. **—syncopal** *adj.*

syndrome *n.* a set of symptoms and signs that are usually due to a single cause (or set of related causes) and together indicate a particular physical or mental disease or disorder. Also called **symptom complex**.

synergic marriage a marriage or partnership that is enhanced by the contributions the partners can make in satisfying each other's psychological needs in a positive manner. Compare SYMBIOTIC MARRIAGE.

synergism *n.* the joint action of different elements such that their combined effect is greater than the sum of their individual effects, as, for example, in DRUG SYNERGISM or SEXUAL SYNERGISM. **—synergistic** *adj.*

synergy *n.* the coordination of forces or efforts to achieve a goal, as when a group of muscles work together in order to move a limb. Also called **coordinative structure**. **—synergic** *adj.*

synesthesia *n.* a condition in which stimulation of one sensory system arouses sensations in another. For example, sounds (and sometimes tastes and odors) may be experienced as colors while they are being heard, and specific sounds (e.g., different musical notes) may yield specific colors. Research suggests that about one in 2,000 people regularly experience synesthesia, and some experts suspect that as many as one in 300 people have some variation of the condition. Also called **concomitant sensation**; **secondary sensation**.

syntaxic mode the highest stage in experiencing the world, characterized by CONSENSUAL VALIDATION, the development of syntaxic thinking, and the expression of ideas in a commonly accepted language. [defined by U.S. psychiatrist Harry Stack Sullivan (1892–1949)]

syntaxic thinking the highest level of cognition, which includes logical, goal-directed, reality-oriented thinking. [defined by U.S. psychiatrist Harry Stack Sullivan (1892–1949)]

syntaxis *n.* a way of thinking and communicating that is logical and based on reality. See SYNTAXIC MODE; SYNTAXIC THINKING. **—syntaxic** *adj.*

synthesis *n.* the bringing together of disparate parts or elements—whether they be physical or conceptual—into a whole. For example, BIOSYNTHESIS is the process by which chemical or biochemical compounds are formed from their constituents and mental synthesis involves combining ideas and images into meaningful objects of thought. **—synthetic** *adj.*

synthetic opioids see OPIOID.

syntonia *n.* a high degree of emotional responsiveness to the environment. **—syntonic** *adj.*

syphilis *n.* a contagious disease caused by infection with the spirochete bacterium *Treponema pallidum*. Syphilis is usually a SEXUALLY TRANSMITTED DISEASE, but it can be transmitted through a break or cut in the skin or mucous membrane; it can also be transmitted by an infected pregnant woman to an unborn child. Untreated, syphilis progressively destroys body tissues, particularly those of the heart and nervous system. See also CEREBRAL SYPHILIS; GENERAL PARESIS.

system *n.* **1.** any collective entity consisting of a set of interrelated or interacting elements that have been organized together to perform a function. **2.** an orderly method of classification or procedure (e.g., the Library of Congress system). **3.** a structured set of facts, concepts, and hypotheses that provide a framework of thought or belief, as in a philosophical system. See CONCEPTUAL SYSTEM. **4.** a living organism or one of its major bodily structures (e.g., the respiratory system). **—systematic** *adj.*

systematic approach see TOPOGRAPHIC MODEL.

systematic desensitization a form of BEHAVIOR THERAPY in which COUNTERCONDITIONING is used to reduce anxiety associated with a particular stimulus. It involves the following stages: (a) The client is trained in deep-muscle relaxation; (b) various anxiety-provoking situations related to a particular problem, such as fear of death or a specific phobia, are listed in order from weakest to strongest; and (c) each of these situations is presented in imagination or in reality, beginning with the weakest, while the client practices muscle relaxation. Since the muscle relaxation is incompatible with the anxiety, the client gradually responds less to the anxiety-provoking situations. See also COVERT DESENSITIZATION; IN VIVO DESENSITIZATION; RECIPROCAL INHIBITION. [introduced by South African-born U.S. psychologist Joseph Wolpe (1915–1997)]

systematic error an error in data or in a conclusion drawn from the data that is regular and repeatable as a result of improper collection methods or statistical treatment of the data.

systematic rational restructuring a system of psychotherapy in which the client is encouraged to imagine anxiety-provoking situations while talking about them in a realistic manner that reduces his or her anxieties. See also IMPLOSIVE THERAPY.

systematized delusion a false, irrational belief that is highly developed and organized, with multiple elaborations that are coherent, consistent, and logically related. Compare FRAGMENTARY DELUSION.

systemic 1. *adj.* concerning or having impact on an entire system. For example, a systemic disorder affects an entire organ system or the body as a whole. **2.** *n.* the interplay of reciprocal processes between interactional partners, as in a family.

systemic lupus erythematosus (**SLE**) see LUPUS ERYTHEMATOSUS.

systemic mucopolysaccharidosis see MAROTEAUX–LAMY SYNDROME.

systems of support a framework for identifying the nature and profile of services and supports required by a person with mental retardation. This is based on considerations of intellectual functioning and adaptive skills, psychological and emotional factors, physical health and etiological factors, and environmental or situational factors.

systems theory see GENERAL SYSTEMS THEORY.

S

Tt

T_3 abbreviation for TRIIODOTHYRONINE.

T_4 abbreviation for THYROXINE.

TA abbreviation for TRANSACTIONAL ANALYSIS.

tabanka (**tabanca**) *n.* a CULTURE-BOUND SYNDROME found in Trinidad, with symptoms that include depression associated with a high rate of suicide. It is seen in men who have been abandoned by their wives.

taboo (**tabu**) **1.** *n.* a religious, moral, or social convention prohibiting a particular behavior, object, or person. The word derives from *tabu,* the Polynesian term for "sacred," which was used specifically in reference to objects, rites, and individuals consecrated to sacred use or service and, therefore, seen as forbidden, unclean, or untouchable in secular contexts. **2.** *adj.* prohibited or strongly disapproved.

tachycardia *n.* see ARRHYTHMIA.

tachyphemia *n.* a kind of speech that is characterized by persistent volubility and rapidity. See LOGORRHEA. See also PRESSURED SPEECH.

tachyphylaxis *n.* a rapidly decreasing response to repeated administration of a drug. For example, the blood pressure of a patient might continue to rise despite repeated injections of a drug that normally would lower the blood pressure. —**tachyphylactic** *adj.*

tacit knowledge knowledge that is informally acquired rather than explicitly taught (e.g., knowledge of social rules) and allows a person to succeed in certain environments and pursuits. It is stored without self-reflective awareness and therefore not easily articulated. PRACTICAL INTELLIGENCE requires a facility for acquiring tacit knowledge. Also called **implicit knowledge**; **unconscious knowledge**. See TRIARCHIC THEORY OF INTELLIGENCE. [proposed by U.S. psychologist Robert J. Sternberg (1949–)]

tacrine *n.* an ACETYLCHOLINESTERASE INHIBITOR used for the treatment of mild to moderate dementia associated with Alzheimer's disease (see NOOTROPIC). A common adverse reaction to tacrine is liver dysfunction, which limits its use. U.S. trade name: **Cognex**.

tactile agnosia loss or impairment of the ability to recognize and understand the nature of objects through touch. Several distinct subtypes have been identified, including **amorphagnosia**, impaired recognition of the size and shape of objects; **ahylognosia**, impaired recognition of such object qualities as weight and texture; and **finger agnosia**, impaired recognition of one's own or another person's fingers.

Tactile Form Perception a test in which participants use one hand to feel a geometric figure made of sandpaper, which is hidden from view, and then identify it from among a set of 12 drawings. There is a total of 20 geometric figures; 10 are presented to one hand and 10 to the other. The test assesses nonverbal tactile information-processing ability and is scored for the number of correct identifications. [developed in 1983 by U.S. neuropsychologist Arthur Lester Benton (1909–2006) and colleagues]

tactile hallucination a false perception involving the sense of touch. These sensations occur in the absence of any external stimulus and may include itching, feeling electric shocks, and feeling insects biting or crawling under the skin. Also called **haptic hallucination**; **tactual hallucination**.

tactual hallucination see TACTILE HALLUCINATION.

Tactual Performance Test (**TPT**) a NEUROPSYCHOLOGICAL TEST—part of the HALSTEAD–REITAN NEUROPSYCHOLOGICAL BATTERY—that requires a blindfolded individual to place wooden shapes (e.g., stars) into a formboard placed at a 45° angle to the vertical. Performances for the dominant, nondominant, and both hands simultaneously are obtained, and then the blindfold is removed and the individual is asked to draw the shapes and their relative positions on the formboard. The test measures motor skills, tactile perception, nonverbal memory, problem solving, and other executive functions.

taijin kyofusho a phobia, similar to SOCIAL PHOBIA and unique to Japan, that is characterized by an intense fear that one's body parts, bodily functions, or facial expressions are embarrassing or offensive to others (e.g., in appearance, odor, or movement).

talion *n.* retaliation, especially retaliation in kind, as in the biblical injunction "an eye for an eye, a tooth for a tooth." The **talion principle** or **law** plays an important part in psychoanalytic theory, because it includes the general idea of retribution for defying the SUPEREGO and the specific fear (**talion dread**) that all transgressions, accidental or intentional, will be punished in kind. For example, a person wishing consciously or unconsciously for the death of another person might suffer extreme anxiety caused by the fear that he himself or she herself is dying.

talking cure a colloquial expression used for psychotherapy. The term is apt in that the very essence of certain psychotherapeutic approaches is for the client to "talk out" his or her problems with the therapist. First used in the context of psychoanalysis, the term was coined by the landmark patient ANNA O.

talk therapy see PSYCHOTHERAPY.

taming of the instinct see NEUTRALIZATION.

tandem therapy in marriage therapy (see COUPLES THERAPY), a practice in which the therapist meets individually with each partner.

tangentiality *n.* a thought disturbance that is marked by oblique speech in which the person constantly digresses to irrelevant topics and fails to arrive at the main point. In extreme form it is a manifestation of LOOSENING OF ASSOCIATIONS, a symptom most frequently found in schizophrenia. Compare CIRCUMSTANTIALITY.

tangential speech verbal communication that repeatedly diverges from the original subject. Often resulting from disorganized thought processes or a diminished ability to focus attention, these digressions may continue until the original subject is no longer the focus of the conversation. This type of conceptual disorganization is often associated with schizophrenia and delirium.

tantric sex an approach to sex based on the Chinese philosophical and religious system of Taoism. The approach highly values sex, with the belief that long life and even immortality can be reached by sexual activity. Sexual techniques are aimed at mutual and equal sexual pleasure for each partner. Prolonged love-making sessions, with much general body stroking, and techniques to prolong intercourse are stressed in the tantric approach.

tapering *n.* in pharmacology, a gradual reduction in the dose of a drug in order to avoid undesirable effects that may occur with rapid cessation. Such effects may be extreme (e.g., convulsions) or relatively mild (e.g., head pain, mild gastrointestinal distress). Drugs that produce physiological dependence (e.g., opiates, benzodiazepines) must be tapered to prevent a withdrawal syndrome; seizures can result from sudden cessation of benzodiazepines (see SEDATIVE, HYPNOTIC, OR ANXIOLYTIC WITHDRAWAL).

taphophilia *n.* a morbid attraction to cemeteries.

Taractan *n.* a trade name for CHLORPROTHIXENE.

Tarasoff decision the 1976 California Supreme Court decision in *Tarasoff v. Regents of the University of California*, which placed limits on a client's right to confidentiality by ruling that mental health practitioners who know or reasonably believe that a client poses a threat to another person are obligated to protect the potential victim from danger. Depending on the circumstances, that protection may involve such actions as warning the potential victim, notifying the police of the potential threat posed by the client, or both. The decision was based on a case in which an individual confided to his therapist that he intended to kill a friend and later did so. See also DUTY TO PROTECT; DUTY TO WARN.

tardive *adj.* denoting delayed or late-arriving symptoms or disease characteristics, as in TARDIVE DYSKINESIA.

tardive dyskinesia a movement disorder associated with the use of ANTIPSYCHOTICS, particularly conventional antipsychotics that act primarily as DOPAMINE-RECEPTOR ANTAGONISTS. It is more common with prolonged use (months or years), and older patients, females, and patients with mood disorders are thought to be more susceptible. Symptoms include tremor and spasticity of muscle groups, particularly orofacial muscles and muscles in the extremities. Onset is insidious and may be masked by continued use of the antipsychotic, only appearing when the drug is discontinued or the dose lowered. Its incidence is estimated at up to 40% of long-term users of conventional antipsychotics; the incidence is lower with atypical antipsychotics. No effective treatment is known.

tardive dysmentia a behavioral disorder associated with long-term use of antipsychotic drugs and characterized by changes in affect, social behavior, and level of activity. Symptoms may include an inappropriately loud voice and loquaciousness, euphoria, intrusive behavior (including invasion of others' privacy), and thought disorder. In addition, the individual may exhibit episodes of social withdrawal interspersed with episodes of hyperactivity, as well as excessive emotional reactivity and explosive hostility. The condition is considered the behavioral equivalent of TARDIVE DYSKINESIA. Also called **iatrogenic schizophrenia**; **tardive psychosis**.

target *n.* **1.** an area or object that is the focus of a process, inquiry, or activity. **2.** the goal object in a task. For example, the target in a visual search might be to find a letter *S* in a randomly arranged array of letters. Where a search has more than one item as its goal, these are known as the **target set**. **3.** a tissue, organ, or type of cell that is selectively affected by a particular hormone, neurochemical, drug, or microorganism. **4.** a NEURON that attracts the growth of the DENDRITES or AXONS of other neurons toward it.

target behavior the specific behavior or behavioral pattern selected for modification in BEHAVIOR THERAPY.

target patient in STRUCTURED INTERACTIONAL GROUP PSYCHOTHERAPY, the group member who becomes the focus of attention and discussion.

target population the population that a study is intended to research and to which generalizations from samples are to be made.

target stimulus a specific stimulus to which participants in a test or experimental procedure must attend or respond. For example, in tests of hearing the target stimulus may be a specific tone that must be identified.

TAS abbreviation for TELLEGEN ABSORPTION SCALE.

task *n.* any goal-oriented activity undertaken by an individual or a group. When such an activity is the subject of observation in an experimental setting (e.g., in problem-solving and decision-making studies or in studies of perception and cognition), the researcher may set particular objectives and control and manipulate those objectives, stimuli, or possible responses, thus changing task parameters to observe behavioral adjustments.

TAT abbreviation for THEMATIC APPERCEPTION TEST.

Tavistock Clinic a major British provider of clinical mental health services, set up in Tavistock Square, London, England, in 1919. It became a part of the National Health Service in 1947, when the separate **Tavistock Institute of Human Relations** was founded to relate the psychological and social sciences to the needs of society. In 1994 the Tavistock Clinic and the PORTMAN CLINIC became a trust of the National Health Service and its leading organization for providing postgraduate training in mental health.

Taylor Manifest Anxiety Scale a 65-item self-report scale, derived from the MINNESOTA MULTIPHASIC PERSONALITY INVENTORY, that was first developed in 1951 and modified and shortened to 50 items in 1953. The scale, consisting of statements (e.g., "I cannot keep my mind on one thing") to which participants respond "true" or "false," formerly enjoyed frequent use in research as a general measure of anxiety symptoms. It correlates with other anxiety measures and with physiological indicators of anxiety. Also called **Manifest Anxiety Scale**. See ANXIETY SCALE. [devised by U.S. psychologist Janet **Taylor** Spence (1923–)]

TBI abbreviation for TRAUMATIC BRAIN INJURY.

TCA abbreviation for TRICYCLIC ANTIDEPRESSANT.

T data *t*est data: information about an individual gathered from formal scientific measurement and objective testing. See also L DATA; O DATA; Q DATA.

t distribution a theoretical PROBABILITY DISTRIBUTION that plays a central role in testing hypotheses about population means among other parameters. It is the sampling distribution of the statistic $(M - \mu_0)/s$, where μ_0 is the population mean of the population from which the sample is drawn, M is the data estimate of the mean of the population, and s is the standard deviation of the batch of scores. Also called **Student's t distribution**.

tease *vb.* to bother, provoke, or torment another person through various types of irritating behavior, such as name-calling, insults, or repetitive annoyances. Teasing can be playful and affectionate or malicious and bullying.

technical eclecticism in INTEGRATIVE PSYCHOTHERAPY, the use of techniques from various theoretical frameworks to deal with the complex issues of a client. Technical eclecticism uses a systematic and carefully thought out approach that balances theoretical perspectives and treatment processes. [developed by South African-born U.S. psychologist Arnold Allan Lazarus (1932–)]

teeth grinding see BRUXISM.

teething *n.* the process in which the teeth erupt through the gums, typically occurring between 4 and 9 months of age. During this process, the infant may exhibit several accompanying symptoms, such as an increase in irritability, sleep disturbance, temporary rejection of breast or bottle feeding, gum inflammation, and excessive drooling.

Tegretol *n.* a trade name for CARBAMAZEPINE.

telecanthus-hypospadias syndrome a hereditary disorder marked by widely spaced eyes, a high nose bridge, and a urethral opening on the ventral side of the penis. Some affected individuals also show mental retardation, with IQs in the 40s and 50s. Recent research suggests that the condition is genetically heterogeneous, with both X-linked and autosomal forms. Also called **BBBG** (or **GBBB**) **syndrome** (from the names of the affected families originally reported); **Opitz–Frias syndrome**.

telehealth *n.* the use of telecommunications and information technology to provide access to health assessment, diagnosis, intervention, and information across a distance, rather than face to face. Also called **telemedicine**.

telemedicine *n.* see TELEHEALTH.

teleologic regression see PROGRESSIVE TELEOLOGIC REGRESSION.

telephone counseling 1. a method of treating and dealing with the problems of clients by telephone. The skills for telephone counseling include (a) careful selection of problems that lend themselves to the medium, (b) ACTIVE LISTENING for cues to issues and ramifications of the problems, (c) good verbal skills that guide the client appropriately, and (d) ability to respond quickly to avoid gaps and awkward silences. **2.** free HOTLINE telephone services that provide listening and referral services rather than formal counseling. Hotline volunteers are trained to provide emotional support in serious situations, especially those involving suicidal thoughts, but not to give formal advice. See also DISTANCE THERAPY.

telephone scatologia a PARAPHILIA in which an individual obtains sexual pleasure by making obscene telephone calls. See SCATOPHILIA.

telepsychotherapy *n.* see DISTANCE THERAPY.

telic *adj.* purposeful or goal-directed in nature, as in **telic behavior**.

Tellegen Absorption Scale (**TAS**) a measure of a person's ability to become deeply involved in a task or other aspect of the environment. Consisting of 34 statements (e.g., "I like to watch cloud shapes change in the sky") to which participants respond "true" or "false," it is considered to be a reliable indication of the ease with which an individual can be hypnotized. See ABSORPTION. [devised in 1974 by U.S. psychologist Auke **Tellegen** (1930–)]

temazepam *n.* an intermediate-acting BENZODIAZEPINE used for the short-term treatment of insomnia. Temazepam is readily processed in the liver to form an inactive metabolic product; it therefore has a relatively predictable HALF-LIFE and does not accumulate in the body with repeated doses. However, as with other benzodiazepine HYPNOTICS, TOLERANCE can occur with repeated use. U.S. trade name: **Restoril**.

temper *n.* **1.** a display of irritation or anger, or a tendency to be quick to anger. **2.** a personality characteristic, disposition, or mood.

temperament *n.* the basic foundation of personality, usually assumed to be biologically determined and present early in life, including such characteristics as energy level, emotional responsiveness, demeanor, mood, response tempo, and willingness to explore. In animal behavior, temperament is defined as an individual's constitutional pattern of reactions, with a similar range of characteristics.

temperament theory the belief that behavioral tendencies are biologically based and present from birth, forming the DISPOSITION of the individual.

temperament trait 1. a biologically based, inherited personality characteristic. **2.** a personality trait that involves emotional qualities and affective styles of behavior. It is one of three classes of SOURCE TRAITS in CATTELL'S PERSONALITY TRAIT THEORY, the other two being ABILITY TRAITS and DYNAMIC TRAITS.

T

temperance *n.* any form of auspicious self-restraint, manifested as self-regulation in monitoring and managing one's emotions, motivation, and behavior and as self-control in the attainment of adaptive goals.

temporal gradient a pattern of retrograde AMNESIA characterized by greater loss of memory for events from the recent past (i.e., close to the onset of the amnesia) than for events from the remote past. See also RIBOT'S LAW.

temporal lobe one of the four main lobes of each CEREBRAL HEMISPHERE in the brain, lying immediately below the lateral sulcus on the lower lateral surface of each hemisphere. It contains the auditory projection and auditory association areas and also areas for higher order visual processing. The MEDIAL TEMPORAL LOBE contains regions important for memory formation.

temporal lobe amnesia a memory disorder, secondary to injury of the temporal lobe (particularly medial structures, such as the hippocampus), that prevents the formation of new memories.

temporal lobectomy the surgical excision of a temporal lobe or a portion of the lobe. It may be performed in the treatment of temporal lobe epilepsy, the location and size of the lesion determining which tissues and related functions may be affected.

temporal lobe illusions distorted perceptions that may be associated with COMPLEX PARTIAL SEIZURES arising from abnormal discharge of neurons in the temporal lobe. They often include distortions of the sizes or shapes of objects, recurring dreamlike thoughts, or sensations of déjà vu. Hallucinations, such as the sound of threatening voices, may also be experienced. Also called **temporal hallucinations**; **temporal lobe hallucinations**.

temporal lobe syndrome a group of personality and behavioral disturbances associated with temporal lobe epilepsy in some individuals. These may include a profound sense of righteousness, preoccupation with details, compulsive writing or drawing, religiosity, and changes in sexual attitudes.

temporary commitment emergency INVOLUNTARY HOSPITALIZATION of a patient with a mental disorder for a limited period of observation or treatment.

tend-and-befriend response a proposed physiological and behavioral stress regulatory system in females, in which tending involves nurturant activities designed to protect the self and offspring, to promote a sense of safety, and to reduce distress, and befriending is expressed in the creation and maintenance of social networks that aid in this process. This model has been characterized as a human stress response in females that is secondary to the classic FIGHT-OR-FLIGHT RESPONSE. Neuroendocrinal evidence from animal and human research suggests an underlying physiological mechanism mediated by OXYTOCIN and moderated by female sex hormones and opioid peptide mechanisms.

tendentious apperception the tendency to perceive what one wishes to perceive in an event or situation. See APPERCEPTION. See also PERCEPTUAL SET.

tender-mindedness *n.* a personality trait characterized by intellectualism, idealism, optimism, dogmatism, religiousness, and monism. Compare TOUGH-MINDEDNESS. [first described by William JAMES] **—tender-minded** *adj.*

Tenex *n.* a trade name for GUANFACINE.

Tennessee Self-Concept Scale (**TSCS**) a self-report assessment currently consisting of descriptive statements to which participants respond using a 5-point scale, ranging from "always false" to "always true." It is available in two forms—Adult, containing 82 items for use with individuals aged 13 years and older, and Child, containing 76 items for use with individuals aged 7 to 14 years—and yields measurements on six substantive dimensions of SELF-CONCEPT (Physical, Moral, Personal, Family, Social, Academic/Work) within three domains (Identity, Satisfaction, Behavior). The TSCS was originally published in 1964; the most recent version is the **TSCS–2**, published in 1996. [originally developed by U.S. psychologist William H. Fitts (1918–)]

tense 1. *adj.* in a state of nervous activity. **2.** *adj.* stretched tight or strained.

tension *n.* **1.** a feeling of physical and psychological strain accompanied by discomfort, uneasiness, and pressure to seek relief through talk or action. **2.** the force resulting from contraction or stretching of a muscle or tendon.

tension headache a persistent headache produced by acute or prolonged emotional tension and usually accompanied by insomnia, irritability, and painful contraction of the neck muscles.

tension reduction alleviation of feelings of tension. A variety of techniques may be used for this purpose, for example, RELAXATION THERAPY, tranquilizing drugs, muscle relaxants, hypnotic suggestion, periods of MEDITATION, verbal CATHARSIS, or MOVEMENT THERAPY.

tenting *n.* lengthening and expansion of the vagina and elevation of the uterus during the excitement and plateau phases of the female SEXUAL-RESPONSE CYCLE. These changes facilitate entry of the penis and make intercourse more pleasurable.

ten–twenty system a standardized system of imaginary lines on the head that allows for placement of electrodes during ELECTROENCEPHALOGRAPHY.

Tenuate *n.* a trade name for DIETHYLPROPION.

teratogen *n.* an agent that induces developmental abnormalities in a fetus. The process that results in such abnormal developments is called **teratogenesis**; a **teratomorph** is a fetus or offspring with developmental abnormalities.

teratology *n.* the study of developmental abnormalities and their causes. **—teratological** *adj.*

Terman, Lewis Madison (1877–1956) U.S. psychologist. Terman earned his doctorate at Clark University in 1905, worked for 4 years at the Los Angeles Normal School, and then went to Stanford University, where he spent the remainder of his career. Terman's career was primarily devoted to the development and application of psychological tests. He was responsible for validation and revision of the Binet scales for use in the United States, resulting in the STANFORD–BINET INTELLIGENCE SCALE; construction of the Army tests administered during World War I; development of the Stanford Achievement Test; and creation of questionnaires designed to reveal *Psychological Factors in Marital Happiness* (1938). He is also noted for developing a series of studies of gifted children and eminent adults (see GENIUS; TERMAN'S GIFTEDNESS STUDY).

terminal behavior 1. relatively unvaried behavior that is predominant in the period shortly before reinforcement occurs during operant or instrumental conditioning. **2.** a response that either falls outside an organism's current behavioral repertoire or is not occurring at a desired rate, strength, or magnitude. Increasing terminal behavior is the aim of specific behavioral interventions.

terminal button see AXON.

terminal care services for people with terminal illness, now usually provided by HOSPICES, which may be either freestanding units or associated with a hospital, nursing home, or extended care facility. The emphasis is on PALLIATIVE CARE, pain control, supportive psychological services, and involvement in family and social activities, with the goal of enabling patients to live out their lives in comfort, peace, and dignity.

terminal drop a rapid decline in cognitive abilities immediately before death. The cognitive abilities that appear to be most prone to terminal drop are those least affected by normal aging (see HOLD FUNCTIONS). Also called **terminal drop-decline**.

terminal insomnia a form of INSOMNIA in which the individual habitually awakens very early, feels unrefreshed, and cannot go back to sleep. It is a common symptom of a MAJOR DEPRESSIVE EPISODE. Compare INITIAL INSOMNIA; MIDDLE INSOMNIA.

termination *n.* in therapy, the conclusion of treatment. Termination may be suggested by the client or therapist or may be by mutual agreement. Termination can be immediate or prolonged; in the latter case, a date for the final session is established and sessions are sometimes scheduled less frequently over a period. In **premature termination**, treatment is ended before either the therapist or client considers the therapy complete. This may result, for example, from difficulties in the relationship between the therapist and client, misunderstanding of the required length of treatment, a change in the client's financial circumstances, or departure of the client to another location.

terror *n.* intense and overwhelming fear.

terror management theory a theory proposing that control of death-related anxiety is the primary function of society and the main motivation in human behavior. Individual SELF-ESTEEM and a sense of being integrated into a powerful human culture are regarded as the most effective ways for human beings to defend themselves against the frightening recognition of their own mortality (see DEATH ANXIETY). [based on the work of U.S. cultural anthropolo-

T

gist Ernest Becker (1925–1974) and developed by U.S. psychologists Jeff Greenberg (1954–), Sheldon Solomon (1953–), and Tom Pyszczynski (1954–)]

tertiary care highly specialized care given to patients who are in danger of disability or death. Tertiary care often requires sophisticated technologies provided by highly specialized practitioners and facilities, for example, neurologists, neurosurgeons, thoracic surgeons, and intensive care units. Compare PRIMARY CARE; SECONDARY CARE.

tertiary prevention intervention and treatment for individuals or groups with already established psychological or physical conditions, disorders, or diseases. Tertiary interventions include attempts to minimize negative effects, prevent further disease or disorder related to complications, prevent relapse, and restore the highest physical or psychological functioning possible. Compare PRIMARY PREVENTION; SECONDARY PREVENTION.

test anxiety tension and apprehensiveness associated with taking a test (see PERFORMANCE ANXIETY).

test bias the tendency of a test to systematically over- or underestimate the true scores of individuals to whom that test is administered, for example because they are members of particular groups (e.g., ethnic minorities, sexes, etc.). See also CULTURAL TEST BIAS.

testing the limits **1.** a method used to study adult age differences in cognition in which research participants are required to perform a task to the best of their ability and are then tested after extensive practice on the task. [developed by German psychologist Paul Baltes (1939–2006) and his associates] **2.** in psychological testing, allowing a participant to proceed beyond time limits (or waiving other standardized requirements) to see if he or she can complete an item or do better under alternate conditions. **3.** in general psychology, attempts by an individual to see how far he or she can test rules before the rules are enforced. An example would be seeing how much talking one can get away with in a class before being reprimanded by the teacher.

T

test item a constituent part, or the smallest scoreable unit, of a test.

testosterone *n.* a male sex hormone and the most potent of the ANDROGENS produced by the testes. It stimulates the development of male reproductive organs, including the prostate gland, and secondary SEX CHARACTERISTICS, such as beard, bone, and muscle growth. Women normally secrete small amounts of testosterone from the adrenal cortex and ovary.

test–retest correlation a CORRELATION that represents the stability of a variable over time.

test selection the process of choosing the most useful or appropriate test or set of assessment instruments in order to provide accurate diagnostic or other psychological information. Test selection is made on the basis of psychological history (often in conjunction with medical history), interviews, other pretest knowledge of the individual or group to be tested, or some combination of these.

tetrabenazine *n.* a drug used in the treatment of HUNTINGTON'S DISEASE and other hyperkinetic movement disorders. It acts by depleting brain stores of the monoamine neurotransmitters dopamine, norepinephrine, and serotonin and produces such side effects as PARKINSONISM, sedation, and depression. U.S. trade name: **Xenazine**. Canadian trade name: **Nitoman**.

tetrahydrocannabinol (**THC**) *n.* one of a number of CANNABINOIDS occurring in the CANNABIS plant that is the agent principally responsible for the psychoactive properties of cannabis. THC is available in a synthetic pharmaceutical preparation known as **dronabinol** (U.S. trade name: **Marinol**) for use in the treatment of chemotherapy-induced nausea and vomiting and as an appetite stimulant for the treatment of HIV-related anorexia. Research suggests it may also be effective in reducing intraocular pressure and as an analgesic.

TGA abbreviation for TRANSIENT GLOBAL AMNESIA.

T-group *n.* *t*raining group: a type of experiential group, usually of up to a dozen or so people, concerned with fostering the development of "basic skills," such as effective leadership and communication, and attitude change. **T-group training** was developed by the National Training Laboratory in Group Development in the late 1940s and grew out of Kurt LEWIN'S work in the area of small-group dynamics. Although sometimes used synonymously with ENCOUNTER GROUP, the emphasis is less on personal growth and more on SENSITIVITY TRAINING and practical interpersonal skills, for example, as stressed in management training. One of the goals of T-groups is to foster greater understanding of group dynamics and of the individual members' roles within the group or organization.

thalamic lesion a loss of structure or function of a part of the THALAMUS resulting in such effects as avoidance-learning deficits. Animals that have experienced a thalamic lesion take much longer to learn to avoid an electric shock, although they learn eventually. Effects vary somewhat with the part of the thalamus affected.

thalamus *n.* (*pl.* **thalami**) a mass of gray matter, forming part of the DIENCEPHALON of the brain, whose two lobes form the walls of the third VENTRICLE. It consists of a collection of sensory, motor, autonomic, and associational nuclei, serving as a relay for nerve impulses traveling between the spinal cord and brainstem and the cerebral cortex. Specific areas of the body surface and cerebral cortex are related to specific parts of the thalamus. See also SUBTHALAMUS. **—thalamic** *adj.*

thalidomide *n.* a drug reintroduced into the United States in 1998 as an immunosuppressant for treatment of cutaneous manifestations of erythema nodosum leprosum (a severe, acute form of leprosy). A derivative of the sedative GLUTETHIMIDE, it was originally (in the late 1950s and early 1960s) used to treat anxiety and morning sickness in pregnancy until its association with severe, life-threatening birth defects became apparent. Numerous fetal abnormalities, including abnormal limb development and gastrointestinal, cardiac, and neurological deficits were common, and the drug was withdrawn. Prescription requires special training by prescribers and pharmacists, and thalidomide must not be taken by women who are pregnant; both women and men who are taking thalidomide must comply with various mandatory conditions and contraceptive measures. Its mechanism of action is unclear. U.S. trade name: **Thalomid**.

thanatology *n.* the study of death and death-related behaviors, thoughts, feelings, and phenomena. Death was mostly the province of theology until the 1960s, when existential thinkers and a broad spectrum of care providers, educators, and social and behavioral scientists became interested in death-related issues. **—thanatologist** *n.*

thanatomania *n.* see VOODOO DEATH.

thanatophobia *n.* a persistent and irrational fear of death or dying. This fear may focus on the death of oneself or others and is often associated with HYPOCHONDRIASIS. **—thanatophobic** *adj.*

Thanatos *n.* the personification of death and the brother of Hypnos (sleep) in Greek mythology, whose name was chosen by Sigmund FREUD to designate a theoretical set of strivings oriented toward the reduction of tension and life activity (see DEATH INSTINCT). In Freud's DUAL INSTINCT THEORY, Thanatos is seen as involved in a dialectic process with EROS (love), the striving toward sexuality, continued development, and heightened experience (see LIFE INSTINCT). See also DESTRUDO; NIRVANA PRINCIPLE; PRINCIPLE OF INERTIA.

THC abbreviation for TETRAHYDROCANNABINOL.

Theater of Spontaneity an experimental theater established in Vienna in 1921 by Romanian-born U.S. psychiatrist Jacob Levi Moreno (1889–1974). The process of playing unrehearsed, improvised parts in the theater proved to be not only effective training for actors but frequently had a beneficial effect on their interpersonal relationships. This technique evolved into PSYCHODRAMA, which Moreno brought to the United States in 1925.

thebaine *n.* an OPIUM ALKALOID that is chemically similar to morphine but has stimulatory effects. It comprises about 0.2% of natural opium. Although thebaine lacks the analgesic effect of morphine, it can be converted to several important opioid agonists and antagonists (e.g., buprenorphine, naloxone).

thema *n.* in the PERSONOLOGY of U.S. psychologist Henry Alexander Murray (1893–1988), a unifying "theme," or unit of interplay, between an individual and the environment in which a need and a PRESS interact to yield satisfaction.

Thematic Apperception Test (**TAT**) a projective test, developed by U.S. psychologist Henry Alexander Murray (1893–1988) and his associates, in which participants are held to reveal their attitudes, feelings, conflicts, and personality characteristics in the oral or written stories they make up about a series of relatively ambiguous black-and-white pictures. Prior to administering the test, the examiner assures the participant that there are no right or wrong answers and indicates that the narratives should have a beginning, middle, and ending. At the end, the stories are discussed for diagnostic purposes. Systematic coding schemes, with demonstrated reliability and validity, have been developed to assess different aspects of personality functioning derived from TAT stories, including motivation for achievement, power, affiliation, and intimacy; gender identity; DEFENSE MECHANISMS; and mental processes influencing interpersonal relations. The TAT is one of the most frequently used and researched tests in psychology, particularly in clinical settings for diagnosis, personality description, and assessment of strengths and weakness in personality functioning.

thematic paralogia a speech characteristic marked by the incessant, distorted dwelling of the mind on a single theme or subject.

thematic paraphasia incoherent speech that wanders from the theme or subject.

thematic test any examination in which a participant is required to tell a story from which interpretations are made about the individual's psychological functioning, especially his or her unconscious wishes and needs.

theobromine *n.* a METHYLXANTHINE alkaloid that occurs naturally in the seeds of *Theobroma cacao*, the COCOA plant. Theobromine is structurally similar to caffeine in coffee and theophylline in tea but has less pharmacological potency than these methylxanthines.

theomania *n.* a delusion in which the person believes himself or herself to be inspired by or possessed of divinity.

theophylline *n.* see METHYLXANTHINES.

theoretical integration the integration of theoretical concepts from different approaches to produce meaningful frames of reference that may help explain the dynamics or causes of problems or the functioning of an individual when any single traditional theoretical approach individually fails to explain the behavior adequately.

theory *n.* **1.** a principle or body of interrelated principles that purports to explain or predict a number of interrelated phenomena. See CONSTRUCT; MODEL. **2.** in the philosophy of science, a set of logically related explanatory hypotheses that are consistent with a body of empirical facts and that may suggest more empirical relationships. **—theoretical** *adj.*

theory of mental self-government a model of COGNITIVE STYLES that proposes several dimensions to describe the preferred ways in which individuals think or express their cognitive abilities. The dimensions include (a) governmental—preferences in the legislative, executive, and judicial functions of cognition (i.e., in planning, implementing, and evaluating); (b) problem solving—styles labeled monarchic (a tendency to pursue one goal at a time), hierarchic (multiple goals with different priorities), oligarchic (multiple, equally important goals), and anarchic (unstructured, random problem solving); (c) global versus local thinking—preferring to think about large, abstract issues on the one hand or concrete details on the other; (d) internal versus external thinking—related to introversion–extraversion, social skills, and cooperativeness; and (e) conservative or progressive—rule-based leanings versus those that are creative and change-oriented. [proposed in 1988 by U.S. psychologist Robert J. Sternberg (1949–)]

theory of mind the ability to imagine or make deductions about the mental states of other individuals: What does the other individual know? What actions is that individual likely to take? Theory of mind is an essential component of attributing beliefs, intentions, and desires to others, specifically in order to predict their behavior. It begins to appear around 4 years of age in human beings; there has been considerable controversy about whether nonhuman animals have this ability. See also BELIEF–DESIRE REASONING; MINDBLINDNESS.

theory verification the process of developing and citing empirical evidence to increase or decrease the tenability of theories.

therapeutic 1. *adj.* pertaining to **therapeutics**, the branch of medical science concerned with the treatment of diseases and disorders and the discovery and application of remedial agents or methods. **2.** *adj.* having beneficial or curative effects. **3.** *n.* a compound that is used to treat specific diseases or medical conditions.

therapeutic agent any means of advancing the treatment process, such as a drug, occupational therapy, a therapist, or a THERAPEUTIC COMMUNITY. The therapeutic agent is presumed to be the causative agent in patient change.

therapeutic alliance a cooperative working relationship between client and therapist, considered by many to be an essential aspect of successful therapy. Derived from the concept of the psychoanalytic working alliance, the therapeutic alliance comprises bonds, goals, and tasks. Bonds are constituted by the core conditions of therapy, the client's attitude toward the therapist, and the therapist's style of relating to the client; goals are the mutually negotiated, understood, agreed upon, and regularly reviewed aims of the therapy; and tasks are the activities carried out by both client and therapist. See THERAPIST–PATIENT RELATIONSHIP. [concept developed by U.S. psychologist Edward S. Bordin (1913–1992)]

therapeutic atmosphere an environment of acceptance, empathic understanding, and UNCONDITIONAL POSITIVE REGARD in which clients feel most free to verbalize and consider their thoughts, behaviors, and emotions and make constructive changes in their attitudes and reactions.

therapeutic camp a camp that may provide part-time care, therapeutic treatment, rehabilitation, or a combination of these for individuals, often children and adolescents, with a variety of conditions, disorders, and illnesses. Examples include camps for children with learning disabilities, for children and adolescents living with HIV/AIDS, for SCHOOL REFUSAL adolescents, and for individuals with head injury.

therapeutic communication any comment or observation by the therapist that increases the client's awareness or self-understanding.

therapeutic community a setting for individuals requiring therapy for a range of psychosocial problems and disorders that is based on an interpersonal, socially interactive approach to treatment, both among residents and among residents and staff (i.e., "community as method or therapy"). The term covers a variety of short- and long-term residential programs as well as day treatment and ambulatory programs. The staff is typically multidisciplinary and may consist of human services professionals and clinicians providing mental health, medical, vocational, educational, fiscal, and legal services, among others. Originating as an alternative to conventional medical and psychiatric approaches, therapeutic communities have become a significant form of psychosocial treatment. See MILIEU THERAPY. [developed by 20th-century British psychiatrist Maxwell Shaw Jones]

therapeutic crisis a turning point in the treatment process, usually due to sudden insight or a significant revelation on the part of the client or patient. The crisis may have positive or negative implications and may lead to a change for the better or the worse, depending on how it is handled.

therapeutic factors curative factors that operate across models and techniques in GROUP THERAPY. Factors identified include altruism, catharsis, cohesion, family reenactment, feedback, hope, identification, interpersonal learning, reality testing, role flexibility, universality, and vicarious learning. Therapeutic factors are often confused with COMMON FACTORS because both delineate effective change factors across theoretical models and techniques of therapy; however, common factors refer to individual psychotherapy, whereas therapeutic factors refer to group psychotherapy.

therapeutic group a group of individuals who meet under the leadership of a therapist for the express purpose of working together toward improvement in the mental and emotional health of the members.

therapeutic group analysis see GROUP-ANALYTIC PSYCHOTHERAPY.

therapeutic index any of several indices relating the clinical effectiveness of a drug to its safety factor, the most common being the THERAPEUTIC RATIO. Other therapeutic indices include the ratio of the minimum toxic dose to the minimum EFFECTIVE DOSE and the difference between the minimum effective dose and the minimum toxic dose.

therapeutic matrix in COUPLES THERAPY, the specific combination of therapist and clients that is used in the sessions, for example, a different therapist for each partner in COLLABORATIVE THERAPY or seeing the couple together in CONJOINT THERAPY.

therapeutic process see PSYCHOTHERAPEUTIC PROCESS.

therapeutic ratio an index relating the clinical effectiveness of a drug to its safety factor, calculated by dividing the median LETHAL DOSE (LD_{50}) by the median EFFECTIVE DOSE (ED_{50}). A drug is often considered safe only if its therapeutic ratio is at least 10. [introduced by German bacteriologist and immunologist Paul Ehrlich (1854–1915)]

therapeutic recreation see RECREATIONAL THERAPY.

therapeutic relaxation see RELAXATION THERAPY.

therapeutic role the functions of the therapist or other THERAPEUTIC AGENT in treating psychological disorders, alleviating painful responses or symptoms resulting from a distressing condition, or altering maladaptive thinking or behavior.

therapeutic soliloquy a procedure in which clients speak about themselves to a group without interruption. [developed by Romanian-born U.S. psychiatrist Jacob Levi Moreno (1889–1974)]

therapeutic storytelling see STORYTELLING.

therapeutic touch see TOUCH THERAPY.

therapeutic window the range of plasma levels of a drug within which optimal therapeutic effects occur. Suboptimal effects may occur both below and above the therapeutic window. Evidence for true therapeutic windows was never well established; possibly the best evidence existed for the tricyclic antidepressant NORTRIPTYLINE. Few modern psychotropic drugs require therapeutic monitoring, although LITHIUM is a notable exception; it has a very narrow therapeutic range below which it has no therapeutic effect and above which adverse effects and toxicity dominate. Therapeutic windows are increasingly becoming less significant in modern clinical psychopharmacology.

therapeutist *n.* a former name for a THERAPIST.

therapist *n.* an individual who has been trained in and practices one or more types of therapy to treat mental or physical disorders or diseases: often used synonymously with psychotherapist (see PSYCHOTHERAPY).

therapist–patient relationship the relationship formed in therapy between a psychotherapist and the patient (client) receiving therapy. There has been much theory and research concerning this interaction: how it varies and changes over time and the significant implications that the dynamic has for the way in which treatment is offered and its outcomes. The relationship has ethical dimensions that are often specified in PRACTICE GUIDELINES. See also THERAPEUTIC ALLIANCE.

therapy *n.* **1.** remediation of physical, mental, or behavioral disorders or disease. **2.** see PSYCHOTHERAPY.

therapy group climate see GROUP CLIMATE.

therapy puppet a puppet used for ROLE PLAY in therapy with children. The use of a therapy puppet is sometimes more conducive to the child's revelation of thoughts and feelings than direct communication by the child with the therapist.

therapy supervision see SUPERVISION.

there-and-then approach an historical approach to therapy, focusing on the roots of the client's difficulties in past experience, as opposed to the here-and-now approach (see HERE AND NOW).

theta wave in electroencephalography, a type of BRAIN WAVE with a frequency of 4–7 Hz. Theta waves are observed in the REM SLEEP of animals, STAGE 2 SLEEP in humans, and in the drowsiness state of newborn infants, adolescents, and young adults. Theta waves are also recorded in TRANCES, HYPNOSIS, and deep DAYDREAMS. Neurologically, the hippocampus is one well-known source of theta activity. Also called **theta rhythm**.

thiazide diuretics a group of synthetic chemicals developed in the 1950s and widely used as DIURETICS in the treatment of hypertension. Thiazides cause the excretion of approximately equal amounts of sodium and chloride with an accompanying volume of water, thereby lowering blood pressure. Also called **benzothiadiazides**.

thienobenzodiazepine *n.* any member of a class of chemically related compounds that include OLANZAPINE, an ATYPICAL ANTIPSYCHOTIC introduced into the U.S. market in 1996.

thinking *n.* cognitive behavior in which ideas, images, MENTAL REPRESENTATIONS, or other hypothetical elements of thought are experienced or manipulated. In this sense thinking includes imagining, remembering, problem solving, daydreaming, FREE ASSOCIATION, concept formation, and many other processes. Thinking may be said to have two defining characteristics: (a) It is covert, that is, it is not directly observable but must be inferred from behavior or self-reports; and (b) it is symbolic, that is, it seems to involve operations on mental symbols or representations, the nature of which remains obscure and controversial (see SYMBOLIC PROCESS).

thinking style see COGNITIVE STYLE.

thinking through a typically multistage, multilayered thought process in which the individual attempts to understand and achieve insight into his or her own reactions, thought processes, or behavior, for example through consideration and analysis of cause and effect.

thinking type in the ANALYTIC PSYCHOLOGY of Carl JUNG, a FUNCTIONAL TYPE exemplified by the individual who evaluates information or ideas rationally and logically. The thinking type is one of Jung's two RATIONAL TYPES, the other being the FEELING TYPE. See also INTUITIVE TYPE; SENSATION TYPE.

thiopental *n.* an ultrashort-acting BARBITURATE used primarily as an anesthetic that can be administered intravenously to produce almost immediate loss of consciousness. It may also be used as an antidote to overdosage of stimulants or convulsants. Formerly it was occasionally used in psychotherapy to induce a state of relaxation and suggestibility. In nonmedical circles, it gained notoriety as a TRUTH SERUM. U.S. trade name: **Pentothal**.

thioridazine *n.* a low-potency antipsychotic of the piperidine PHENOTHIAZINE class that, like others of its class, causes sedation and significant anticholinergic effects. Adverse effects unique to thioridazine include the potential to cause retinal changes possibly leading to blindness (retinitis pigmentosum) at doses exceeding 800 mg/day. It can also cause severe disturbances in heart rhythm: Its ability to prolong the Q-T interval may cause fatal arrhythmias (see ELECTROCARDIOGRAPHIC EFFECT). It should not be taken by patients who have cardiac arrhythmias or who are taking other drugs that may prolong the Q-T interval. U.S. trade name: **Mellaril**.

thioxanthenes *pl. n.* a group of ANTIPSYCHOTIC drugs, generally of intermediate potency, that resemble the PHENOTHIAZINES in pharmacological activity and molecular structure. Thioxanthenes are used mainly in the treatment of psychotic disorders. Like the phenothiazines, they are associated with cardiovascular and anticholinergic side effects, as well as EXTRAPYRAMIDAL SYMPTOMS common to all dopamine-blocking agents. Their use has largely been supplanted by newer antipsychotics. Thioxanthenes include **thiothixene** (U.S. trade name: Navane), flupenthixol, and ZUCLOPENTHIXOL. Only thiothixene is currently available in the United States.

third-party administrator (**TPA**) in health insurance, a fiscal intermediary organization that provides administrative services, including claims processing and underwriting, for other parties (e.g., insurance companies or employers) but does not carry any insurance risk.

third-party payer an organization, usually an insurance company, prepayment plan, or government agency, that pays for the health expenses incurred by the insured. The third party (to the agreement) is distinguished from the first party, the individual receiving the services, and the second party, the individual or institution providing the services.

third-person perspective a public, external, objective point of view on human behavior and experience. Compare FIRST-PERSON PERSPECTIVE; SECOND-PERSON PERSPECTIVE.

Thomas S. class action a class action lawsuit in North Carolina that established a special class of people with mental retardation who lived in state psychiatric hospitals. Many class members had both mental retardation and severe and persistent or recurring mental illness (MR/MI). The court order specified required services and supports. Although the class was dissolved in 1998, the case resulted in the establishment of a division that administers MR/MI services within the state-led agency for mental retardation services.

Thorazine *n.* a trade name for CHLORPROMAZINE.

thought *n.* **1.** the process of THINKING. **2.** an idea, image, opinion, or other product of thinking. **3.** attention or consideration given to something or someone.

thought avoidance the ability to evade or not consider unpleasant or dissonant mental events. It is a kind of psychological DEFENSE MECHANISM as well as a means of therapeutic change.

thought broadcasting the delusion that one's thoughts are being disseminated throughout the environment for all to hear.

thought deprivation see BLOCKING.

thought derailment disorganized, disconnected thought processes, as manifested by a tendency to shift from one topic to another that is indirectly related or completely unrelated to the first. Thought derailment is a symptom of schizophrenia; the term is essentially equivalent to COGNITIVE DERAILMENT. See DERAILMENT.

thought disorder a disturbance in the cognitive processes that affects communication, language, or thought content, including POVERTY OF IDEAS, NEOLOGISMS, PARALOGIA, WORD SALAD, and DELUSIONS. A thought disorder is considered by some to be the most important mark of schizophrenia (see also SCHIZOPHRENIC THINK-

ING), but thought disorders are also associated with mood disorders, dementia, mania, and neurological diseases (among others). Also called **thought disturbance**. See CONTENT-THOUGHT DISORDER; FORMAL THOUGHT DISORDER.

thought echoing see ÉCHO DES PENSÉES.

thought experiment the process of imagining a theoretical research setup and what the result might be of conducting the imagined experiment, in the hope that this process will lead to a better designed real experiment. In cases in which the experiment cannot actually be performed, the intent is to arrive at a well-reasoned conclusion. In physics, such experiments—also called **Gedanken experiments**—are sometimes held in high regard.

thought insertion a delusion in which the individual believes that thoughts are irresistibly forced into his or her mind and ascribes these thoughts to outside sources.

thought intrusion interruption of the stream of consciousness by unwanted mental contents. See INTRUSIVE THOUGHTS.

thought obstruction see BLOCKING.

thought pressure see PRESSURE OF IDEAS.

thought process any of the COGNITIVE PROCESSES involved in mental activities that are beyond perception, such as reasoning, remembering, imagining, problem solving, and making judgments. See THINKING. See also HIGHER MENTAL PROCESS; SYMBOLIC PROCESS.

thought-process disorder see FORMAL THOUGHT DISORDER.

thought stopping the skill of using a physical or cognitive cue to stop negative thoughts and redirect them to a neutral or positive orientation. This skill is taught in some behavior therapies, when the therapist shouts "Stop!" to interrupt a trend toward undesirable thoughts and trains clients to apply this technique to themselves.

thought suppression the attempt to control the content of one's mental processes and specifically to rid oneself of undesired thoughts or images.

thought withdrawal the delusion that one's thoughts are being removed from one's mind by other people or forces outside oneself.

threat *n.* **1.** a condition that is appraised as a danger to one's self or well-being or to a group. **2.** an indication of unpleasant consequences for failure to comply with a given request or demand, used as a means of coercion. **3.** any event, information, or feedback that is perceived as conveying negative information about the self. **—threaten** *vb.* **—threatening** *adj.*

threat appraisal the cognitive and emotional processes involved in assessing the potentiality and level of threat.

threat to self-esteem model a theory stating that help from another is sometimes perceived as a threat to the self, because it implies that the recipient is incapable or inferior. In these circumstances the recipient may respond negatively.

threshold *n.* **1.** in psychophysics, the magnitude of a stimulus that will lead to its detection 50% of the time. **2.** the minimum intensity of a stimulus that is necessary to evoke a response. For example, an auditory threshold is the slightest perceptible sound; an excitatory threshold is the minimum stimulus that triggers an ACTION POTENTIAL in a neuron; a renal threshold is the concentration of a substance in the blood required before the excess is excreted. Also called **limen**; **response threshold**.

threshold theory a hypothesis in GROUP DYNAMICS positing that conflict is beneficial and useful provided it does not exceed the tolerance threshold of the group members for too long. [developed by U.S. communication theorist Ernest G. Bormann (1925–2008)]

thrombosis *n.* the presence or formation of a blood clot (THROMBUS) in a blood vessel, including blood vessels in the heart (**coronary thrombosis**). Formation of a blood clot in a vein is called **venous thrombosis**. Thrombosis is likely to develop where blood flow is impeded by disease, injury, or a foreign substance. A thrombosis in the brain (**cerebral thrombosis**) can cause a THROMBOTIC STROKE or CEREBROVASCULAR ACCIDENT. **—thrombotic** *adj.*

thrombotic stroke the most common type of STROKE, occurring when blood flow to the brain is blocked by a cerebral THROMBOSIS. A thrombotic stroke typically results from narrowing or occlusion of a large blood vessel in the brain, especially the carotid or middle cerebral artery, by ATHEROSCLEROSIS. Onset of symptoms can be gradual and is frequently preceded by TRANSIENT ISCHEMIC ATTACKS.

thrombus *n.* a blood clot that forms in a blood vessel (see THROMBOSIS). A thrombus that becomes detached from its point of origin and is carried in the blood to obstruct another site is called an embolus (see EMBOLISM).

thumb sucking a common though not universal habit among infants and young children, formerly classified as a habit disturbance when persisting beyond 3 or 4 years. It is commonly explained as a basic sucking impulse from which the child derives pleasure as well as comfort and relaxation.

Thurstone, Louis Leon (1887–1955) U.S. psychologist. After receiving a master's degree in engineering from Cornell University in 1912, Thurstone began studying psychology at the University of Chicago under James Rowland ANGELL and at the Carnegie Institute of Technology under Walter Van Dyke Bingham (1880–1952). He was awarded his doctorate in 1917 from the University of Chicago. Thurstone is best known as a pioneer in PSYCHOMETRICS, the field of psychological tests and measurements.

T

He and his wife, Thelma Gwinn Thurstone (1897–1993), developed and maintained for more than 20 years the American Council of Education's Examination for High School Graduates and College Freshmen, which was the forerunner of the Scholastic Assessment Test (SAT). His contributions to methodology include his development of the statistical technique of factor analysis to tease out PRIMARY ABILITIES. Thurstone founded the Psychometric Society in 1936 and launched the Society's journal *Psychometrika*. Among his many honors were his election to the National Academy of Sciences and the American Academy of Arts and Sciences.

thymus *n.* an organ, located in the lower neck region, that is part of the IMMUNE SYSTEM. The thymus reaches maximum size at puberty, then shrinks. During infancy it is the site of formation of T lymphocytes.

thyroid gland an endocrine gland forming a shieldlike structure on the front and sides of the throat, just below the thyroid cartilage. It produces the iodine-containing THYROID HORMONES (thyroxine and triiodothyronine) in response to thyroid-stimulating hormone from the anterior pituitary gland. C cells (parafollicular cells) in the thyroid produce the hormone calcitonin, which controls levels of calcium and phosphate in the blood.

thyroid hormones any of the hormones synthesized and released by the THYROID GLAND. The primary thyroid hormone, THYROXINE (T_4), is metabolized to TRIIODOTHYRONINE (T_3) within target tissues. Plasma levels of T_4 are much higher than those of T_3, but T_3 has the more potent physiological activity. Both hormones play a central role in regulating basic metabolic processes and the early development and differentiation of the brain. Extremes in secretion of these hormones have major effects on metabolism and cognitive function (see CONGENITAL HYPOTHYROIDISM; MYXEDEMA; THYROTOXICOSIS). Calcitonin, a hormone released by parafollicular cells of the thyroid gland, plays a crucial role in calcium and phosphate metabolism.

T

thyrotoxicosis *n.* a condition caused by an excess of THYROID HORMONES, which may be produced by an overactive thyroid gland or administered therapeutically. **Endogenous thyrotoxicosis** may be familial and can involve an autoimmune reaction in which the patient's antibodies stimulate rather than destroy the cells producing thyroid hormone. Thyrotoxicosis is characterized by nervousness, tremor, palpitation, weakness, heat sensitivity with sweating, and increased appetite with weight loss. Thyrotoxicosis is frequently associated with HYPERPLASIA (enlargement) of the thyroid gland, as in GRAVES' DISEASE, or the development of thyroid nodules (**Plummer's disease**), which occurs in older people. See also HYPERTHYROIDISM.

thyroxine (**T_4**) *n.* an iodine-containing hormone produced by the thyroid gland: the principal THYROID HORMONE. It helps regulate metabolism by controlling oxidation rate in cells. See also TRIIODOTHYRONINE.

TIA abbreviation for TRANSIENT ISCHEMIC ATTACK.

tianeptine *n.* a novel antidepressant compound with a modified tricyclic structure that enhances, rather than blocks, the presynaptic reuptake of serotonin (see SSRI) and thus decreases serotonin neurotransmission, unlike the majority of anti depressants. Its efficacy compares favorably to currently used antidepressants, and it is being investigated for clinical use in the United States. French trade name: **Stablon**.

tic *n.* a sudden, involuntary contraction of a small group of muscles (motor tic) or vocalization (vocal tic) that is recurrent, nonrhythmic, and stereotyped. Tics may be simple (e.g., eye blinking, shoulder shrugging, grimacing, throat clearing, grunting, yelping) or complex (e.g., hand gestures, touching, jumping, ECHOLALIA, COPROLALIA). Tics may be psychogenic in origin; alternatively, they may occur as an adverse effect of a medication or other substance or result from a head injury, neurological disorder, or general medical condition.

tic disorder in *DSM–IV–TR*, any one of a group of disorders characterized by the occurrence many times a day of motor tics, vocal tics, or both that is not due to a general medical condition or the effects of a medication. The group includes TOURETTE'S DISORDER, CHRONIC MOTOR OR VOCAL TIC DISORDER, TRANSIENT TIC DISORDER, and TIC DISORDER NOT OTHERWISE SPECIFIED.

tic disorder not otherwise specified in *DSM–IV–TR*, a disorder characterized by the presence of tics that does not meet the diagnostic criteria for a specific TIC DISORDER. Examples are bouts of tics lasting less than 4 weeks and tics that appear after the age of 18.

time and rhythm disorders speech and language problems related to the timing of sounds and syllables, including repetitions, prolongations, and stuttering. The disorders are often functional and may be complicated by feelings of guilt. The condition may be treated with a combination of psychotherapy and speech therapy, using such techniques as cancellation (interrupted stuttering), voluntary stuttering, or rewarding or reinforcing fluent speech.

time disorientation loss of the ability to keep track of time or the passage of time. Inability to accurately state the correct year, month, day, or hour is a common symptom of mental disorder. See DISORIENTATION.

time distortion a type of perceptual distortion, sometimes experienced in altered states of consciousness, in which time appears to pass either with great rapidity or with extreme slowness.

Perception of past and future may also be transformed.

time-extended therapy a form of GROUP THERAPY in which prolonged sessions replace or alternate with sessions of normal length. The experience is usually highly emotional and revealing since, due to fatigue and other reasons, the participants have insufficient energy for defensive games. See also ACCELERATED INTERACTION; MARATHON GROUP.

time-lag design a type of QUASI-EXPERIMENTAL RESEARCH in which participants of the same age are compared at different time periods. For example, a time-lag study of intelligence might compare a group of people who were 20 years old in 2005 with groups who were 20 years old in 2006, 2007, and 2008. Used in examining human developmental processes, time-lag designs have the benefit of controlling for time of testing effects but the drawbacks of low INTERNAL VALIDITY and the difficulty in separating cohort effects from age effects.

time-lagged correlation the correlation of a measure at one point in time with the value of that same measure at a different point in time; for example, the correlation of IQ scores of individuals at 5 years of age with their IQ scores when they are 10 years of age.

timeless moment **1.** an infinitely small dimension of the present instant as conceptualized by traditional linear time. See PSYCHOLOGICAL MOMENT; SPECIOUS PRESENT. **2.** an experience in which one's normal awareness of time dissolves and one feels a sense of holistic involvement with another person or thing or with the universe as a whole. Such PEAK EXPERIENCES are of particular interest in HUMANISTIC PSYCHOLOGY. See BEING COGNITION.

time-limited day treatment an outpatient all-day therapeutic community approach used with clients diagnosed with personality disorders that capitalizes on the positive attributes of the clients as a group. [developed by Canadian psychologist William E. Piper (1945–)]

time-limited psychotherapy (**TLP**) therapy that is limited to a predetermined and agreed-upon number of sessions over a specified period of time. Also called **limited-term psychotherapy**. See also BRIEF PSYCHOTHERAPY.

time out (**TO**) **1.** a technique, originating in BEHAVIOR THERAPY, in which undesirable behavior is weakened and its occurrence decreased, typically by moving the individual away from the area that is reinforcing the behavior. For example, a child may be temporarily removed from an area when misbehaving. The technique is used in schools and by parents to decrease the undesirable behavior by isolating the misbehaver for a period. Also called **time out from reinforcement**. **2.** in OPERANT CONDITIONING, a time interval during which a behavior does not occur. A time-out procedure may be used to eliminate stimulus effects of earlier behaviors or as a marker in a series of events.

time sampling a strategy commonly used in direct observation that involves noting and recording the occurrence of a target behavior whenever it is seen during a stated time interval. The process may involve fixed time periods (e.g., every 5 min) or random time intervals. For example, a researcher may observe a group of children for 10 s every 5 min for a specific 30 min period each day, noting the occurrence or nonoccurrence of particular behaviors. Observations taken during these periods are known as **time samples**.

time series a set of measures on a single attribute measured repeatedly over time.

time-series design an experimental design that involves the observation of units (e.g., people or countries) over a defined time period.

timidity *n.* **1.** the tendency to take great caution in approaching a perceived risk or to avoid the risk altogether. **2.** see SHYNESS. **—timid** *adj.*

tinnitus *n.* noises in one or both ears, including ringing, buzzing, or clicking sounds due to acute ear problems, such as Ménière's disease, disturbances in the receptor mechanism, side effects of drugs (especially tricyclic antidepressants), or epileptic aura. Occasionally tinnitus is due to psychogenic factors (see SENSORY CONVERSION SYMPTOMS).

tip-of-the-tongue phenomenon (**TOT phenomenon**) the experience of attempting to retrieve from memory a specific name or word but not being able to do so: The fact is ordinarily accessible and seems to hover tantalizingly on the rim of consciousness. See also RETRIEVAL BLOCK.

Titchener, Edward Bradford (1867–1927) British-born U.S. psychologist. A member of the founding generation of American psychologists, Titchener studied under Wilhelm WUNDT, earning his doctorate from the University of Leipzig in 1892. After a brief period at Oxford University, in 1895 Titchener became a professor of psychology at Cornell University, where he spent the remainder of his career. Determined to make psychology a rigorously experimental science, Titchener became the chief exponent of STRUCTURALISM in America, emphasizing the use of systematic introspection in a laboratory setting to uncover the elements of experience (sensations, images, and feelings). He also developed experimental techniques, which were more fully accepted than his atomistic approach. To promote further his vision of psychology as an experimental science, Titchener founded a club called The Experimentalists, which eventually became the Society of Experimental Psychologists. His club was controversial among psychologists because of its exclusivity (membership was by invitation only and did not include experimentalist women). Titchener's multivolume textbook, *Experimental Psychology: A Manual of Labo-*

T

ratory Practice (1901–1905), was widely influential. See also IMAGELESS THOUGHT.

titration *n.* a technique used in determining the optimum dose of a drug needed to produce a desired effect in a particular individual. The dosage may be either gradually increased until a noticeable improvement is observed in the patient or adjusted downward from a level that is obviously excessive because of unwanted adverse effects or toxicity. To avoid unpleasant side effects when starting pharmacotherapy, some drugs must be slowly titrated upward to a therapeutic dose. Likewise, many drugs should be slowly titrated downward upon cessation of therapy both to avoid discontinuation side effects as well as to monitor for the recurrence of symptoms. See TAPERING.

TLP abbreviation for TIME-LIMITED PSYCHOTHERAPY.

TM abbreviation for TRANSCENDENTAL MEDITATION.

TMA abbreviation for TRIMETHOXYAMPHETAMINE.

TMJ syndrome a disorder of muscles operating the lower jaw at the temporomandibular joint (TMJ) just in front of the ear. The condition, which may be due to tension or stress, arthritis, dislocation or other injury, or a tumor, is often marked by facial pain, limited jaw movement, and clicking of the jaw during movement.

TMS abbreviation for TRANSCRANIAL MAGNETIC STIMULATION.

TO abbreviation for TIME OUT.

tobacco *n.* the dried leaves of the plant *Nicotiana tabacum* and other *Nicotiana* species (native to tropical America but now cultivated worldwide), which are smoked, chewed, or sniffed for their stimulant effects. The main active ingredient is NICOTINE. The leaves also contain volatile oils, which give tobacco its characteristic odor and flavor. Tobacco has no therapeutic value but is of great commercial and medical importance because of its widespread use and associated detrimental cardiovascular, pulmonary, and carcinogenic effects. Indeed, smoking tobacco cigarettes was first identified by the U.S. Surgeon General in the 1960s as the major preventable cause of death and disability.

T

tobacco dependence see NICOTINE DEPENDENCE.

Tofranil *n.* a trade name for IMIPRAMINE.

token economy in BEHAVIOR THERAPY, a program, sometimes conducted in an institutional setting (e.g., a hospital or classroom), in which desired behavior is reinforced by offering tokens that can be exchanged for special foods, television time, passes, or other rewards. See also BACKUP REINFORCER; BEHAVIOR MODIFICATION; OPERANT CONDITIONING THERAPY.

Token Test a test of auditory-language processing in which participants are asked to manipulate tokens of different shapes, sizes, and colors in response to increasingly complex instructions. The Token Test is used to identify and evaluate receptive language dysfunction associated with APHASIA. [originally developed in 1962 by Italian neuropsychologists Ennio De Renzi and Luigi A. Vignolo]

tolerance *n.* **1.** a condition, resulting from persistent use of a drug, characterized by a markedly diminished effect with regular use of the same dose of the drug or by a need to increase the dose markedly over time to achieve the same desired effect. Tolerance is one of the two prime indications of physical dependence on a drug, the other being a characteristic withdrawal syndrome. Development of drug tolerance involves several mechanisms, including pharmacological ones (i.e., metabolic tolerance and PHARMACODYNAMIC TOLERANCE) and a behavioral one (i.e., a behavioral conditioning process). Also called **drug tolerance**. See SUBSTANCE DEPENDENCE. **2.** acceptance of others whose actions, beliefs, physical capabilities, religion, customs, ethnicity, nationality, and so on differ from one's own. **3.** a fair and objective attitude toward points of view different from one's own. **4.** permissible or allowable deviation from a specified value or standard. **—tolerant** *adj.*

Tolman, Edward Chace (1886–1959) U.S. psychologist. Tolman earned his doctorate from Harvard University in 1915, studying under Hugo Münsterberg (1863–1916) After teaching for 3 years at Northwestern University, he joined the faculty of the University of California, Berkeley, where he remained for the rest of his career. Tolman, along with Clark Leonard HULL and B. F. SKINNER, is known as a founder of NEOBEHAVIORISM who followed in the path set by John B. WATSON and his theory of behaviorism. Tolman differed from Hull, Skinner, and Watson, however, in the importance that he gave such mentalist concepts as purpose and COGNITIVE MAPS. In his theory of purposive behaviorism, Tolman held that behavior, far from being randomly initiated, was persistently directed toward a goal until the goal was attained. Drawing on the FIELD THEORY of psychologist Kurt LEWIN, Tolman also argued that behavior can be described in terms of goal-directed vectors and valences within a field. His selected papers are collected in two important books, *Purposive Behavior in Animals and Men* (1932) and *Behavior and Psychological Man* (1951). Among Tolman's many honors were election to the National Academy of Sciences (1937) and to the presidency of the American Psychological Association (1937). He also received the American Psychological Association's Distinguished Scientific Contribution Award (1957).

toloache *n.* a plant, *Datura innoxia*, belonging to the nightshade family and closely related to JIMSONWEED, that contains numerous alkaloids with powerful ANTICHOLINERGIC EFFECTS. The plant has been used by indigenous peoples of

North and Central America in religious ceremonies and adolescent rituals.

toluene *n.* a volatile solvent that, when chronically inhaled, can cause kidney failure and death. See INHALANT.

Tolvon *n.* a trade name for MIANSERIN.

tomato effect the rejection of an effective treatment because it does not fit an established medical model or because it does not make sense in light of currently accepted medical theories. It has been applied to BIOFEEDBACK TRAINING. The tomato effect is so named because in America the tomato—known to be a member of the nightshade family—was originally thought to be poisonous; for this reason, tomatoes were not consumed in America until 1820, even though Europeans had been eating them for generations without harm.

tomboyism *n.* the tendency of girls to adopt behavior traditionally associated with boys. See also ROLE CONFUSION; SISSY BEHAVIOR.

tomomania *n.* a compulsive urge to undergo surgery. See also MUNCHAUSEN SYNDROME.

tonic–clonic seizure a seizure characterized by both tonic and clonic motor movements (it was formerly known as a **grand mal seizure**). In the tonic phase the muscles go into spasm and the individual falls to the ground unconscious; breathing may be suspended. This is followed by the clonic phase, marked by rapidly alternating contraction and relaxation of the muscles, resulting in jaw movements (the tongue may be bitten) and urinary incontinence. Also called **generalized tonic–clonic seizure**.

topalgia *n.* pain that is localized in one spot or small area without any lesion or trauma to account for it. Topalgia often is a symptom of a SOMATOFORM DISORDER, particularly in cases in which the pain seems to occur in unlikely segments of nerve or circulatory patterns.

Topamax *n.* a trade name for TOPIRAMATE.

topdog *n.* a set of internal moral standards or rules of conduct that produce anxiety and conflict in the individual when they are not fulfilled or carried out. The topdog is an ego state of superiority over the UNDERDOG. [defined by German-born U.S. psychiatrist Frederick (Fritz) R. Perls (1893–1970)]

top-down analysis a deductive approach to problem solving that begins with a hypothesis or general principle and proceeds from this to an examination of empirical data or specific instances. Compare BOTTOM-UP ANALYSIS. Also called **above-down analysis**.

topectomy *n.* a former psychosurgical procedure in which selected areas of the frontal cortex were excised in cases of refractory mental illness (e.g., schizophrenia) that had not responded to electroconvulsive therapy or other types of treatment.

topical application the administration of a drug by applying it to the surface of the skin or other tissue surface, such as a mucous membrane. The drug is absorbed through the surface and produces its effects on underlying tissues. Some therapeutic drugs that are poorly absorbed through the skin are formulated with inert substances with better penetrating powers, which act as carriers.

topiramate *n.* an ANTICONVULSANT drug that is also used as a MOOD STABILIZER in the treatment of bipolar disorders. Topiramate works by slowing neurotransmission through blockade of sodium channels (see ION CHANNEL); it also apparently facilitates the activity of the neurotransmitter GAMMA-AMINOBUTYRIC ACID (GABA) and limits activity at GLUTAMATE RECEPTORS. Psychomotor slowing and somnolence are commonly reported adverse effects. U.S. trade name: **Topamax**.

topographical amnesia impairment in topographical memory, that is, memory for places and spatial layouts.

topographical psychology the process of mapping the mind, or locating the various mental processes in different regions or systems of the mind. Carl JUNG, for example, divided the mind into the conscious ego, the PERSONAL UNCONSCIOUS, and the COLLECTIVE UNCONSCIOUS; Sigmund FREUD divided the mind into three levels: **conscious**, **preconscious**, and **unconscious**. Also called **mental topography**.

topographic model the original division of the psyche into three regions or systems as proposed by Sigmund FREUD in 1913. The divisions are: (a) the system UNCONSCIOUS (Ucs), made up of unconscious impulses clustering around specific drives or instincts, such as hunger, thirst, and sex, as well as repressed childhood memories associated with them; (b) the system CONSCIOUS (Cs), which enables the individual to adapt to society, distinguish between inner and outer reality, delay gratification, and anticipate the future; and (c) the system PRECONSCIOUS (Pcs), which stands between the conscious and unconscious systems and is made up of logical, realistic ideas intermingled with irrational images and fantasies. Also called **descriptive approach**; **systematic approach**; **topographic hypothesis**. Compare DYNAMIC MODEL; ECONOMIC MODEL. See also STRUCTURAL MODEL.

torpor *n.* a condition of total inactivity or lethargy. Only a very strong stimulus can elicit a response from an individual in such a condition.

Torrance Tests of Creative Thinking (TTCT) two batteries of pencil-and-paper test items—a verbal test (thinking creatively with words) and a figural test (thinking creatively with pictures)—that can be used at all stages from kindergarten to graduate school. Typical "activities," as they are called, involve listing possible consequences of the action in an intriguing picture, citing ways of improving a toy, and incorporating a curved line in drawing an unusual picture. The object is to test for four characteristics of creative thinking: fluency, flexibility, originality, and elaboration. See CREATIVITY TEST. [originally devised in 1966 by Ellis Paul **Torrance** (1915–2003), U.S. psychologist]

torsades de pointes see ELECTROCARDIOGRAPHIC EFFECT.

torticollis *n.* a continuous or spasmodic contraction of the neck muscles, resulting in rotation of the chin and twisting of the head to one side. This form of dystonia may be neurological or congenital and may respond to drug treatment or BIOFEEDBACK TRAINING. However, it may also be psychogenic. Torticollis is sometimes classed as a complex (dystonic) TIC. **—torticollar** *adj.*

torture *n.* the subjection of individuals to severe, painful physical abuse and violence, which often includes treatment that simulates death or near-death experiences. Torture may also involve mental or psychological abuse.

total institution 1. a highly organized and restrictive social INSTITUTION that maintains a high degree of control over the activities of those individuals who are members of, or confined to, it. Prisons, mental health facilities, and military bases are (in many cases) examples, because nearly all the activities of prisoners, patients, and personnel are regulated by the staff or officers. **2.** a traditional social institution that becomes so rigid that it takes on many of the qualities of a restrictive social institution. Marriage, for example, has been characterized as a total institution because it often creates a high degree of uniformity in the lifestyles and choices of adults.

total recall 1. the ability to remember an event completely and accurately. **2.** in a recall task, the total number of items recalled across conditions or tests.

totem *n.* **1.** a revered animal, plant, natural force, or inanimate object that is conceived as the ancestor, symbol, protector, or tutelary spirit of a people, clan, or community. It is usually made the focus of certain ritual activities and TABOOS, typically against killing or eating it. **2.** as interpreted by Sigmund FREUD in *Totem and Taboo* (1912–1913), any symbol or representation of the primal father. **—totemic** *adj.* **—totemism** *n.*

toucherism *n.* sexual interest and arousal obtained from touching a stranger on a erotic part of the body, particularly the breasts, buttocks, or genitals. This is often done as an apparent accident, in doorways or hallways. See also FROTTEURISM.

touch therapy treatment that involves touching or manipulating parts of an individual's body to ease physical pain or to promote relaxation and a general sense of well-being. Touch therapy has been shown to have numerous benefits for children (among others), improving, for example, the physical and psychological development of preterm infants and bringing about a greater tolerance of touch by children with autism, which has resulted in improved bonding and communication with their parents. Also called **therapeutic touch**. See also COMPLEMENTARY AND ALTERNATIVE MEDICINE; MASSAGE.

tough love the fostering of individuals' well-being by requiring them to act responsibly and to seek professional assistance when they find it difficult to act in their own best interests. Often, strict oversight and restrictions of personal freedom and privileges must be willingly accepted by the target individual. Tough love is sometimes seen as a stance taken by a therapist or counselor or in interventions by family and friends of individuals with problem behaviors (e.g. substance abuse, violent behavior).

ToughLove International a voluntary organization for parents, children, or communities who seek help in dealing with the out-of-control behavior of a family member. Parent SUPPORT GROUPS aim to help parents take a firm stand in helping their children take responsibility for their behavior.

tough-mindedness *n.* **1.** a personality trait reflecting the extent to which people demonstrate low levels of compassion and high levels of aggression in social interactions. [proposed by Hans J. EYSENCK] **2.** a personality trait characterized by empiricism, materialism, skepticism, and fatalism. Compare TENDER-MINDEDNESS. [first described by William JAMES] **—tough-minded** *adj.*

Tourette's disorder a TIC DISORDER characterized by many motor tics and one or more vocal tics, such as grunts, yelps, barks, sniffs, and in a few cases an irresistible urge to utter obscenities (see COPROLALIA). The tics occur many times a day for more than a year, during which time any period free of tics is never longer than 3 months. The age of onset for the disorder is before 18 years; in most cases it starts during childhood or early adolescence. Also called **Gilles de la Tourette's syndrome**. [first described in 1885 by Georges Gilles de la **Tourette** (1857–1904), French physician]

toxic delirium DELIRIUM resulting from the action of a poison.

toxicity *n.* the capacity of a substance to produce toxic (poisonous) effects in an organism. The toxicity of a substance—whether a drug, an industrial or household chemical, or other agent—generally is related to the size of the dose per body weight of the individual, expressed in terms of milligrams of chemical per kilogram of body weight. Toxicity also may be expressed in terms of the median LETHAL DOSE (LD_{50}). See also BEHAVIORAL TOXICITY.

toxicomania *n.* **1.** a morbid desire to consume poisons. **2.** a severe dependency on drugs.

toxic psychosis any PSYCHOSIS resulting from

ingestion of poisons or drugs or caused by toxins produced within the body.

toy test any of a variety of projective tests for children that make use of dolls, puppets, or other toys. See PROJECTIVE TECHNIQUE.

TPA abbreviation for THIRD-PARTY ADMINISTRATOR.

TPD abbreviation for trance and possession disorder (see DISSOCIATIVE TRANCE DISORDER).

TPT abbreviation for TACTUAL PERFORMANCE TEST.

trace *n.* see MEMORY TRACE.

tract *n.* **1.** a bundle or group of nerve fibers within the central nervous system. The name of a tract typically indicates its site of origin followed by its site of termination; for example, the reticulospinal tract runs from the reticular formation of the brainstem to the spinal cord. Compare NERVE. **2.** a series of organs that as a whole accomplishes a specific function (e.g., the digestive tract). **3.** a region, passage, or pathway.

tractotomy *n.* the surgical interruption of a nerve tract in the brainstem or spinal cord. One form of tractotomy is of benefit in bipolar disorder that is resistant to other forms of treatment.

trademark *n.* any word, phrase, name, symbol, device, or combination thereof used by manufacturers or merchants to identify their products. While a trademark identifies products, a **trade name** identifies the company that makes or sells them. In the area of pharmacology, the two terms are often used interchangeably to refer to PROPRIETARY DRUGS.

traditional marriage 1. a marriage according to the traditional norms of a given society, usually for the primary purpose of establishing a family. Although prenuptial customs vary in different cultures, a traditional marriage generally follows a period of courtship, public announcement of wedding plans, and a wedding ceremony. Compare NONTRADITIONAL MARRIAGE. **2.** a marriage of husband and wife, wherein the former is the primary or sole breadwinner and the latter holds primary or sole responsibility for maintaining the home and managing child care.

tradition-directed *adj.* describing or relating to individuals whose values, goals, and behavior are largely determined by their traditional cultural heritage, that is, by the social norms transmitted by their parents. Compare INNER-DIRECTED; OTHER-DIRECTED. [introduced by U.S. sociologist David Riesman (1909–2002)]

Trail Making Test (**TMT**) a connect-the-dot task that forms part of the HALSTEAD–REITAN NEUROPSYCHOLOGICAL BATTERY. **Trails A** requires the connection in sequence of 25 dots labeled by numbers. **Trails B** requires the connection in sequence of 25 dots labeled by alternating numbers and letters (1–A–2–B–3–C). The test, one of the most widely used for cognitive impairment, is purported to measure several functions, particularly cognitive flexibility, attention, sequencing, visual search, and motor speed. The TMT, originally developed in 1938 by U.S. psychologists John E. Partington and Russell G. Leiter, was initially known as the **Divided Attention Test** and subsequently as **Partington's Pathways Test**.

train 1. *vb.* to teach or condition an individual to perform certain responses, behaviors, tasks, or activities, particularly in a learning experiment. **2.** *n.* a succession of mild electrical impulses, such as is given in brain stimulation.

trainable mentally retarded formerly, describing people, usually children or young adults, with moderate mental retardation (IQ 35 to 49) who did not appear to profit from academic education in special classes but were able to achieve a degree of self-care, social adjustment at home, and vocational usefulness in such settings as sheltered workshops.

trainer *n.* **1.** in mental health, a professional leader or facilitator of a sensitivity-training group (see T-GROUP). **2.** a teacher or supervisor of individuals learning to practice psychotherapy.

training analysis PSYCHOANALYSIS of a trainee analyst. Its purpose is not only to provide training in the concepts and techniques of psychoanalysis, but also to increase insight into personal sensitivities or other emotional reactions that might interfere with the process of analyzing patients in the form of a COUNTERTRANSFERENCE. Also called **didactic analysis**.

training group see T-GROUP.

training school formerly, a rehabilitation facility for children or adults with mental retardation, utilizing interdisciplinary teams of therapists and allied health care practitioners to provide residential, health, training, vocational, and leisure services. Although such facilities attempted to provide homelike settings, this was seldom achieved in practice. Their use, once common, greatly diminished in the late 20th century. See also PUBLIC RESIDENTIAL FACILITY.

trait *n.* **1.** an enduring personality characteristic that describes or determines an individual's behavior across a range of situations. **2.** in genetics, an attribute resulting from a hereditary predisposition (e.g., hair color or facial features).

trait anxiety proneness to experience anxiety. People with high trait anxiety tend to view the world as more dangerous or threatening than those with low trait anxiety and to respond with STATE ANXIETY to situations that would not elicit this response in people with low trait anxiety. [defined in 1972 and 1983 by U.S. psychologist Charles D. Spielberger (1927–)]

trait organization the way in which an individual's personal traits are related and comprise a unique, integrated whole.

trait profile a graphic display of test scores in which each score represents an individual trait.

These scores or ratings are often arranged on a common scale to enable them to be interpreted quickly. Also called **psychogram**.

trait theory approaches that explain personality in terms of TRAITS, that is, internal characteristics that are presumed to determine behavior. Some examples are ALLPORT'S PERSONALITY TRAIT THEORY, CATTELL'S PERSONALITY TRAIT THEORY, and the FIVE-FACTOR PERSONALITY MODEL.

trance *n.* **1.** a state characterized by markedly narrowed consciousness and responsiveness to stimuli. **2.** a state induced by HYPNOSIS or AUTOSUGGESTION and characterized by openness, or availability, to suggestion (see HYPNOTIC SUSCEPTIBILITY). The hypnotized person may experience a **light trance**, accepting such suggestions as inability to open the eyes or rigidity or lack of sensation in a limb, or a **medium trance**, in which there might be partial amnesia, POSTHYPNOTIC AMNESIA, and POSTHYPNOTIC SUGGESTION. A DEEP TRANCE might be characterized by such effects as an inability to open the eyes without affecting the trance, complete somnambulism, positive and negative posthypnotic hallucinations, and hyperesthesia (excessive sensibility). Also called **hypnotic trance**.

trance and possession disorder (**TPD**) see DISSOCIATIVE TRANCE DISORDER.

trance disorder see DISSOCIATIVE TRANCE DISORDER.

trance logic the presumed tendency of hypnotized individuals to engage simultaneously in logically contradictory or paradoxical trains of thought. It has been suggested that trance logic represents evidence of PARALLEL PROCESSING in that there appears to be simultaneous registration of information at different levels of awareness. See DIVIDED CONSCIOUSNESS; NEODISSOCIATIVE THEORY.

tranquilizer *n.* a drug that is used to reduce physiological and subjective symptoms of anxiety. In the past, distinctions were made between so-called major tranquilizers (ANTIPSYCHOTICS) and minor tranquilizers (ANXIOLYTICS, e.g., benzodiazepines).

tranquilizer chair a heavy wooden chair used in early psychiatry in which patients were strapped at the chest, abdomen, ankles, and knees, with their head inserted in a wooden box. This method of restraint was preferred to the STRAITJACKET because it reduced the flow of blood to the head and did not interfere with bloodletting, one of the standard treatments of the time. [devised by U.S. physician and psychiatrist Benjamin Rush (1745–1813)]

transaction *n.* **1.** any interaction between the individual and the social or physical environment, especially during encounters between two or more people. **2.** in some psychotherapies, the interplay between the therapist and the patient and ultimately between the patient and other individuals in his or her environment.

transactional analysis (**TA**) a theory of personality and a form of dynamic group or individual psychotherapy focusing on characteristic interactions that reveal internal EGO STATES and the games people play in social situations. Specifically, the approach involves: (a) a study of three primary ego states (parent, child, adult) and determination of which one is dominant in the transaction in question; (b) identification of the tricks and expedients, or games, habitually used in the client's transactions; and (c) analysis of the total script (see SCRIPT ANALYSIS), or unconscious plan, of the client's life, in order to uncover the sources of his or her emotional problems. [developed in the 1950s by Canadian-born U.S. psychologist Eric Berne (1910–1970)]

transactional psychotherapy psychotherapy that emphasizes the daily interactions between the client and others in his or her life. TRANSACTIONAL ANALYSIS is a specific type of therapy that is based on types of transactions that are considered dysfunctional.

transcendence *n.* in metaphysics and in the study of CONSCIOUSNESS, a state of existence or perception that exceeds—and is not definable in terms of—normal understanding or experience. The term implies states that go beyond the physical world and the nature of material existence. **—transcendent** *adj.*

transcendence need in the psychoanalysis of Erich FROMM, the human need to create so as to rise above passivity and attain a sense of meaning and purpose in an impermanent and seemingly random or accidental universe. Both creativity and destructiveness are considered by Fromm to be manifestations of the transcendence need.

transcendence therapy a form of therapy that is spiritually oriented and intended to help people achieve an inner sense of peace by first understanding their role in the larger picture of life and then using that understanding to overcome disappointments, difficulties, and other hardships. It is based on the concept of **formative spirituality**, which postulates that humans are not passive givers or receivers of information or experience but, rather, active interpreters of reality, engaging in an inner dialogue to recognize, relate to, and modify individual construals of existence. [developed by Dutch-born U.S. psychologist Adrian van Kaam (1920–2007)]

transcendental meditation (**TM**) a technique of CONCENTRATIVE MEDITATION for achieving a TRANSCENDENTAL STATE of consciousness. Based on the *Bhagavadgita* and other ancient Hindu writings, it was introduced in the United States in 1959 by Indian-born guru Maharishi Mahesh Yogi. The modern version of the original discipline consists of six steps that culminate in sitting with one's eyes closed, while repeating a MANTRA, for two 20-minute periods a day. Repetition of the mantra serves to block distracting thoughts and to induce a state of relaxation in which images and ideas can arise from deeper levels of the mind and from the cosmic source of all thought and being. The result is said to be not only a greater sense of well-being but also more harmonious interpersonal relations and the achievement of a state of ultimate self-awareness and restful alertness. See also MYSTIC UNION.

transcendental state a level of consciousness believed to reach beyond waking, sleeping, and hypnotic states. It is characterized physically by lowered metabolism and reduced adrenergic functions and psychologically by alleviation of tension, anxiety, and frustration and a high level of tranquillity. See also TRANSCENDENTAL MEDITATION.

transcendent counseling a form of counseling that is based on the notion that behavior is a product of an individual's lifestyle and that behavior change can only be achieved through lifestyle change. Various directive and action-oriented techniques and activities are employed, such as interpersonal counseling, the use of relaxation and meditation, and adoption of exercise and nutrition programs. [developed by U.S. psychologist Frederick D. Harper (1943–)]

transcranial magnetic stimulation (TMS) localized electrical stimulation of the brain through the skull caused by changes in the magnetic field in coils of wire placed around the head. Depending on the parameters, TMS may elicit a response or disrupt functioning in the region for a brief time. The technique was originally devised and is primarily used as an investigatory tool to assess the effects of electrical stimulation of the motor cortex. It is also being investigated as a possible therapy for some types of movement disorders and psychological conditions, such as depression, obsessive-compulsive disorder, and Tourette's disorder. **Repetitive transcranial magnetic stimulation** (**rTMS**) consists of a series of TMS pulses.

transcription *n.* in genetics, the process whereby the genetic information contained in DNA is transferred to a molecule of MESSENGER RNA (mRNA), which subsequently directs protein synthesis. The base sequence of the mRNA is complementary to that of the coding DNA strand and faithfully represents the instructions for assembling the component amino acids of the protein encoded by the gene (see GENETIC CODE).

transcultural psychotherapy any form of PSYCHODYNAMIC PSYCHOTHERAPY that emphasizes cultural sensitivity and awareness, including culturally defined concepts of emotion, psychodynamics, and behavior. In the psychiatric community the term is used somewhat more often in a sense similar to MULTICULTURAL THERAPY in clinical psychology.

transdermal patch an adhesive application that is designed to release a drug at a steady rate through absorption through the skin into the bloodstream. Transdermal patches are used, for example, to administer nicotine in progressively smaller doses to people who are trying to give up smoking.

Transderm-Scop *n.* a trade name for SCOPOLAMINE.

transfer 1. *vb.* to shift or change from one location to another, one form to another, or one situation or condition to another. **2.** *n.* the shift or change thus produced. **3.** *n.* in GESTALT PSYCHOLOGY, the use of the solution to one problem in solving a second problem that has elements in common with the first.

transference *n.* in psychoanalysis, the DISPLACEMENT or PROJECTION onto the analyst of unconscious feelings and wishes originally directed toward important individuals, such as parents, in the patient's childhood. This process, which is at the core of the psychoanalytic method, brings repressed material to the surface where it can be reexperienced, studied, and worked through. In the course of this process, it is posited that the sources of neurotic difficulties are frequently discovered and their harmful effects alleviated. Although quite specific to psychoanalysis, the term's meaning has had an impact far beyond its narrow confines, and transference—as unconscious repetition of earlier behaviors and projection onto new subjects—is acknowledged as ubiquitous in human interactions. The role of transference in counseling and short-term dynamic psychotherapy is well recognized, and ongoing attempts to study its role in a range of therapeutic encounters promise to expand and elucidate its meanings. See also ANALYSIS OF THE TRANSFERENCE; COUNTERTRANSFERENCE; NEGATIVE TRANSFERENCE; POSITIVE TRANSFERENCE; TRANSFERENCE RESISTANCE.

transference analysis see ANALYSIS OF THE TRANSFERENCE.

transference cure see FLIGHT INTO HEALTH.

transference neurosis in psychoanalysis, neurotic reactions released by the TRANSFERENCE process that result from the revival and reliving of the patient's early conflicts and traumas. These reactions are posited to replace the original neurosis and help the patient become aware that his or her attitudes and behavior are actually repetitions of infantile drives. It is believed that the transference neurosis must be resolved if the patient is to free himself or herself from the harmful effects of past experiences and adopt more appropriate attitudes and responses.

transference remission see FLIGHT INTO HEALTH.

transference resistance in psychoanalysis, a form of RESISTANCE to the disclosure of unconscious material, in which the patient maintains silence or attempts to act out feelings of love or hate transferred from past relationships to the analyst. See also ANALYSIS OF THE TRANSFERENCE.

transformation *n.* **1.** any change in appearance, form, function, or structure. See also METAMORPHOSIS. **2.** the conversion of data to a different form through a rule-based, usually mathematical process. **3.** in psychoanalytic theory, the process by which unconscious wishes or impulses are disguised in order that they can gain admittance to CONSCIOUSNESS. **—transform** *vb.* **—transformational** *adj.*

transgender *adj.* having or relating to gender identities that differ from culturally determined gender roles and biological sex. Transgender states include transsexualism, some forms of transvestism, and intersexuality. These states should not be confused with same-sex orientation. Also called **transgendered**. See also GENDER IDENTITY DISORDER. **—transgenderism** *n.*

transgenerational patterns patterns of behavior or personality characteristics that appear in successive generations, often referring to negative or maladaptive behaviors (e.g., drug abuse, adolescent pregnancy, child abuse).

transience *n.* impermanence that implies ending and may invoke anticipation of loss. In classical psychoanalytic theory, the idea that everything is transient may interfere with enjoyment and preclude the establishment of deep or lasting relationships. **—transient** *adj.*

transient global amnesia (**TGA**) a sudden GLOBAL AMNESIA—a form of transient AMNESTIC DISORDER—that typically resolves within 24 hours and occurs in the absence of any other neurological abnormalities. Individuals with TGA appear confused and disoriented and ask frequent repetitive questions to try and make sense of their experience. They are unable to acquire new memories (anterograde amnesia); they also exhibit amnesiafor recently experienced events (retrograde amnesia). As the episode of TGA clears, new learning gradually returns to normal and retrograde amnesia shrinks; individuals are left with a dense memory gap for the period of TGA. TGA may be triggered by precipitating events, such as physical exertion. The mechanism responsible for its occurrence is poorly understood.

transient ischemic attack (**TIA**) an episode during which an area of the brain is suddenly deprived of oxygen because its blood supply is temporarily interrupted, for example by thrombosis, embolism, or vascular spasm. Symptoms are the same as those of STROKE but disappear completely, typically within 24 hours.

transient situational disturbance a *DSM–II* category for disturbances that in *DSM–IV–TR* are classified as ADJUSTMENT DISORDERS. See also ADJUSTMENT REACTION.

transient situational personality disorder a *DSM–I* designation for POSTTRAUMATIC STRESS DISORDER, replacing the older term **traumatic neurosis**. This category also included what are classified in *DSM–IV–TR* as ADJUSTMENT DISORDERS. See also ADJUSTMENT REACTION.

transient tic disorder a TIC DISORDER involving the presence of single or multiple tics occurring many times a day for a period of between 4 weeks and 1 year. The tics may be simple (e.g., eye blinking, facial grimacing, throat clearing, or sniffing) or more complex (e.g., hand gestures, stomping, ECHOLALIA, or meaningless change in vocal pitch or volume).

transitional employment a VOCATIONAL REHABILITATION program that places individuals with disabilities or those who are economically, socially, or otherwise disadvantaged (e.g., those who are homeless or dependent on long-term welfare) in paid entry-level positions in a competitive working environment to gain the skills and experience needed to eventually obtain a permanent job in the community workforce. Positions are often provided by participating companies, and each placement typically lasts 6–9 months. Program participants may hold several transitional employment positions before obtaining permanent employment. See also SUPPORTED EMPLOYMENT.

transitional living a supervised living situation that allows psychiatric or neurological patients to make the transition from the dependence of a hospital setting to greater independence before returning to fully independent living.

transitional object 1. a thing (e.g., a doll or a blanket) used by a child to ease the anxiety of separation from his or her first external OBJECT, the mother, until the child has established a secure internal object, or mental representation of her, that provides a sense of security and comfort. [first described by British psychoanalyst Donald W. Winnicott (1896–1971)] **2.** by extension, any person or thing that provides comfort, security, and emotional well-being.

transitional phenomenon an internal representation of the relationship between an individual's inner subjective representation of the world and the objective reality of that world. See also TRANSITIONAL OBJECT. [first described by British psychoanalyst Donald W. Winnicott (1896–1971)]

transitivism *n.* the illusory assumption of one's symptoms or other characteristics by other people. For example, individuals with schizophrenia might believe that others are also experiencing their hallucinations (e.g., hearing voices) or delusions (e.g., of being persecuted).

transitory problem 1. a passing or short-lived symptom, sequela, or other sign of an illness or disorder. **2.** a problem or cause of concern that is short-lived and of brief duration.

translation and back-translation as used primarily in cross-cultural research, a method of ensuring that the translation of an assessment instrument into another language is adequate. A bilingual person translates items from the source language to the target language, and a different bilingual person then independently translates the items back into the source language. The researcher can then compare the original with the back-translated version to see if anything important was changed in the translation.

transorbital lobotomy see LOBOTOMY.

transparency *n.* **1.** genuineness in relating to other people, with minimal attempts to make a good impression. **2.** the state of being "invisible," that is, trying not to be noticed in certain social situations (e.g., when volunteers are sought for a task), for example, by avoiding eye contact, remaining still, or hiding behind another person.

transpersonal psychology an area in HUMANISTIC PSYCHOLOGY concerned with the exploration of the nature, varieties, causes, and effects of "higher" states of consciousness and transcendental experiences. "Transpersonal" refers to the concern with ends that transcend personal identity and individual, immediate desires. See also BEING COGNITION; PEAK EXPERIENCE.

transplantation *n.* **1.** the surgical implantation of a tissue or organ from one part of the body to another or from one person (the donor) to another (the recipient). Such procedures often induce pre- and postoperative anxieties, resistance, and other behavioral manifestations that may have ramifications for psychological health and intervention. **2.** the removal of a person from a permanent home to a temporary residence or nursing home, which may result in anxiety, depression, and other disturbances.

transporter *n.* a protein complex that spans a cell membrane and conveys neurotransmitters, ions, or other substances between the exterior and interior of the cell. For example, at SYNAPSES between neurons, transporters in the presynaptic membrane recognize and bind to neurotransmitter molecules and return them to the presynaptic neuron for reuse (see REUPTAKE). Transporters may use passive transport, in which a substance is transported into or out of a cell according to its concentration gradient across the cell membrane; or active transport, which is an energy-dependent process often relying on the hydrolysis of ATP to provide energy to facilitate movement of a substance from one side of the cell membrane to the other.

transposition of affect the transfer of the affective component associated with a particular idea or object to an unrelated idea or object, as frequently occurs in OBSESSIVE-COMPULSIVE DISORDER. Also called **displacement**; **displacement of affect**.

transsexualism *n.* a GENDER IDENTITY DISORDER consisting of a persistent sense of discomfort and inappropriateness relating to one's anatomical sex, with a persistent wish to be rid of one's genitals and to live as a member of the other sex. In *DSM–IV–TR*, the diagnosis is applicable only if the condition is not due to another mental disorder, such as schizophrenia, and is not associated with INTERSEXUALITY or genetic abnormality. Many transsexuals feel that they belong to the opposite sex and are somehow trapped in the wrong body. They therefore seek to change their sex through surgical and hormonal means (see SEX REASSIGNMENT). **—transsexual** *adj., n.*

transtheoretical model (**TTM**) a five-stage theory to explain changes in people's health behavior (see STAGES OF CHANGE). It suggests that change takes time, that different interventions are effective at different stages, and that there are multiple outcomes occurring across the stages (e.g., belief structure, self-efficacy). [developed in the 1970s by U.S. clinical psychologist James O. Prochaska (1942–)]

transvestic fetishism in *DSM–IV–TR*, a PARAPHILIA consisting of the persistent wearing by a heterosexual male of female clothes with the purpose of achieving sexual excitement and arousal. It typically begins in childhood or adolescence and should not be confused with transvestism, the nonpathological CROSS-DRESSING by men or women of any sexual preference.

transvestism *n.* the process or habit of wearing the clothes of the opposite sex. Transvestism, or CROSS-DRESSING, is distinct from TRANSVESTIC FETISHISM. Also called **transvestitism**. **—transvestic** *adj.* **—transvestite** *n.*

Tranxene *n.* a trade name for CLORAZEPATE.

tranylcypromine *n.* see MONOAMINE OXIDASE INHIBITOR.

trauma *n.* **1.** any disturbing experience that results in significant fear, helplessness, DISSOCIATION, confusion, or other disruptive feelings intense enough to have a long-lasting negative impact on a person's attitudes, behavior, and other aspects of functioning. Traumatic events include those caused by human behavior (e.g., rape, toxic accidents) as well as by nature (e.g., earthquakes) and often challenge an individual's view of the world as a just, safe, and predictable place. **2.** any serious physical injury, such as a widespread burn or a blow to the head. **—traumatic** *adj.*

T

trauma management therapy a treatment program intended to alleviate the anxiety and fear, manage the anger, and enhance the interpersonal functioning of combat veterans with posttraumatic stress disorder. It is a sequential approach that combines (a) education, in which the client is informed about the symptom chronicity, skill deficits, and extreme social maladjustment associated with posttraumatic stress disorder; (b) EXPOSURE THERAPY, in which the client reexperiences—in imagination or through virtual reality—his or her specific traumatic events during individually administered weekly sessions; (c) programmed practice, in which the client performs exposure-related homework assigned by the therapist; and (d) socioemotional rehabilitation, in which the client participates in structured, group-administered social and emotional skills training sessions. [developed in 1996 by clinical psychologists B. Christopher Frueh (1963–), Samuel M. Turner (1944–2005), Deborah C. Beidel, and Robert F. Mirabella and health administrator and political scientist Walter J. Jones]

traumatic brain injury (**TBI**) damage to brain tissue caused by external mechanical forces, as evidenced by objective neurological findings, posttraumatic amnesia, skull fracture, or loss of consciousness because of brain trauma.

traumatic disorder any disorder that results from physical or psychological trauma.

traumatic grief a severe form of separation distress that usually occurs following the sudden and unexpected death of a loved one. Numbness and shock are frequently accompanied by a sense of futility and purposelessness. A defining characteristic of traumatic grief is a sense of the meaninglessness of life, although the total syndrome includes many other painful and dysfunctional responses.

traumatic neurosis see TRANSIENT SITUATIONAL PERSONALITY DISORDER.

traumatic psychosis see SITUATIONAL PSYCHOSIS.

trazodone *n.* a chemically unique antidepressant that was introduced as a safer alternative to the tricyclic agents. However, it was of limited use as an antidepressant due to its pronounced sedative effects and its association with prolonged, painful, and unwanted erections (priapism) in a very small number of men who took the drug. Its mechanism of antidepressant action is unclear; it is not a potent inhibitor of either serotonin or norepinephrine reuptake and it is an antagonist at the 5-HT_2 serotonin receptor. Although of little use as an antidepressant, trazodone is commonly used in low doses for bedtime sedation or in controlling agitation and hostility in geriatric patients. A related agent, NEFAZODONE, which is less sedating and less associated with priapism, is now available. U.S. trade name: **Desyrel**.

T

Treacher Collins syndrome a principally autosomal dominant hereditary disorder characterized by facial anomalies, including a small retracted chin, small eyes with defects of the iris, and deformed external ears. It is caused by several genetic variations, including one that is autosomal recessive. Many affected individuals have conductive hearing loss; some have mental retardation. Also called **Berry syndrome**; **Franceschetti–Zwahlen–Klein syndrome**; **mandibulofacial dysostosis**. [Edward **Treacher Collins** (1862–1919), British ophthalmologist]

treatment *n.* **1.** the administration of appropriate measures (e.g., drugs, surgery, therapy) that are designed to relieve a pathological condition. **2.** the level of an INDEPENDENT VARIABLE in an experiment, or the independent variable itself. See TREATMENT LEVEL.

treatment audit a procedure that measures quality assurance in health care. Audit activities include assessment of the structure, process, and outcome of the services provided. Audits occur in a cyclical process, thus enabling the results of the assessment to be fed back to improve or maintain the services assessed.

treatment bias 1. a tendency for the type of treatment given to a patient to be determined or influenced by the social class or cultural background of that patient. **2.** a practitioner's or researcher's unrealistically positive or negative bias toward a particular type of intervention stategy.

treatment effect the magnitude of the effect of a treatment (i.e., the INDEPENDENT VARIABLE) upon the response variable (i.e., the DEPENDENT VARIABLE) in a study. It is usually measured as the difference between the level of response under a control condition and the level of response under the treatment condition in standardized units.

treatment integrity see PROGRAM INTEGRITY.

treatment level a specific condition to which a group or participant is exposed in a study or experiment. For example, in a design employing four groups, each of which is exposed to a different dosage of a particular drug, each dosage amount represents a level of the treatment factor.

treatment plan the recommended steps for intervening that the therapist or counselor devises after an assessment of the client has been completed. Many MANAGED CARE plans require submission of formal, written treatment plans prior to approving mental health treatment. Compare TREATMENT PROTOCOL.

treatment protocol the formal procedures used in a system of psychotherapy. In some systems, such as EXPERIENTIAL PSYCHOTHERAPY, few explicit "rules" apply, whereas in others, such as BEHAVIOR THERAPY, strict adherence to a treatment protocol is often used to guide the therapist's work. Compare TREATMENT PLAN.

treatment resistance 1. refusal or reluctance on the part of an individual to accept psychological or medical treatment or unwillingness to comply with the therapist's or physician's instructions or prescribed regimens. In psychotherapy it is the lack of a positive response by a client to the techniques being used or to what the client feels is a rupture in the THERAPEUTIC ALLIANCE, which requires the use of other strategies or efforts to repair the alliance by the therapist. Examples of treatment resistance are noncompliance with assignments, extended silences, talking about tangential issues, and seemingly pointless debates about the therapist's approach, suggestions, and interpretations. See also NONADHERENCE. **2.** failure of a disease or disorder to respond positively or significantly to a particular treatment method.

treatment-seeking behavior the active pursuit of treatment by a person who is mentally or physically ill, uneasy, or disturbed. See HELP-SEEKING BEHAVIOR.

treatment validity see PROGRAM INTEGRITY.

treatment withholding discontinuing medical treatment that has no benefit to the patient in terms of an eventual cure or short-term alleviation of symptoms.

tremor *n.* any involuntary trembling of the body or a part of the body (e.g., the hands) due to neurological or psychological causes. **Psychological** (or **psychogenic**) **tremor** may be mild, due to tension, or violent and uncontrolled in severe disturbances. Toxic effects of drugs or heavy metals may produce a **transient tremor**. A **coarse tremor** involves a large muscle group in slow movements, whereas a **fine tremor** is caused by a small bundle of muscle fibers that move rapidly. Some tremors occur only during voluntary movements (**action tremor**); others occur in the absence of any voluntary movements (**resting tremor**). A **senile tremor** is one that is associated with aging.

triad *n.* a set of three people involved in a dynamic relationship, for example, a therapist and a couple receiving marital therapy. The three people are presumed to form a triangle that has peculiar group characteristics and internal alliances.

triad training model an approach to training therapists and counselors that fosters an understanding of clients of other cultures and develops multicultural counseling competencies. The didactic simulation matches a trainee therapist or counselor from a particular culture with a three-person team: (a) a "procounselor," representing the trainee therapist's or counselor's own culture; (b) a coached "client," who is hostile or resistant to the trainee, the therapy, or the trainee's culture; and (c) a catalyst "anticounselor," who represents the client's ethnic group, religion, or other affiliation. The catalyst serves as a bridge of communication and support for the client, and the dynamic among all parties reveals issues, content, and effective approaches to the trainee. See also MULTICULTURAL THERAPY. [developed by U.S. psychologist Paul Bodholdt Pedersen (1936–)]

triage *n.* **1.** a method of enhancing the effects of treatment that involves the selection and sorting of patients in an orderly and systematic fashion. The patients are then routed to the most appropriate treatment services available. **2.** in evaluation research, a method of allocating scarce resources among social programs in which only programs that need and are most likely to benefit from the resources are considered.

trial *n.* **1.** in testing, conditioning, or other experimentation, one performance of a given task (e.g., one run through a maze) or one presentation of a stimulus (e.g., an ordered list of three-letter words). **2.** see CLINICAL TRIAL.

trial consultant a social scientist who assists attorneys with various aspects of a trial in which his or her expertise is relevant. **Trial consultation** typically includes helping to prepare individuals for testimony, developing surveys to help in jury selection and trial strategy development, and conducting change of venue surveys. Also called **jury consultant**.

trial design an outline or plan of the conditions of a CLINICAL TRIAL that must be satisfied in order to optimally evaluate the efficacy of a new treatment.

trial marriage an arrangement by which a couple attempts to determine their compatibility and suitability for formal marriage by living together for a period of time.

trial therapy a planned process of temporary treatment, either in the early sessions of therapy or as a set of sessions prior to the initiation of long-term therapy, to test whether the client is suitable or ready for a commitment to the therapeutic process. Trial therapy is also used to assess whether the therapist believes that his or her treatment approach is compatible with the client and is able to resolve the problem.

triangular theory of love the proposition that the various kinds of love can be characterized in terms of the degree to which they possess the three basic components of love relationships: passion, intimacy, and commitment. See COMPANIONATE LOVE; EROTIC LOVE; PASSIONATE LOVE; ROMANTIC LOVE. [advanced in 1988 by U.S. psychologist Robert J. Sternberg (1949–)]

triangulation *n.* **1.** the process of confirming a hypothesis by collecting evidence from multiple source or experiments or using multiple procedures. The data from each source, experiment, or procedure support the hypothesis from a somewhat different perspective. **2.** in FAMILY THERAPY, a situation in which two members of a family in conflict each attempt to draw another member onto their side. Triangulation can occur, for example, when two parents are in conflict and their child is caught in the middle. **—triangulate** *vb.*

triarchic theory of intelligence a theory of intelligence proposing three key abilities—analytical, creative, and practical—which are viewed as largely although not entirely distinct. According to the theory, intelligence comprises information-processing components, which are applied to experience (especially novel experiences) in order to adapt to, shape, and select environments. The theory is triarchic because it contains three subtheories: one specifying the components of intelligence (componential subtheory), another specifying the kinds of experience to which the components are applied (experiential subtheory), and a third specifying how the components are applied to experience to be used in various kinds of environmental contexts (contextual subtheory). [proposed in

1985 by Robert J. Sternberg (1949–), U.S. psychologist]

Triavil *n.* a trade name for a combination of the tricyclic antidepressant AMITRIPTYLINE and the antipsychotic PERPHENAZINE, used for the treatment of concurrent anxiety and depression.

triazolam *n.* a short-acting BENZODIAZEPINE used primarily as a HYPNOTIC and also to manage anxiety associated with dental procedures. Following reports of severe psychological disturbances associated with its use, including behavioral disinhibition, aggression, agitation, and short-term memory impairment (anterograde amnesia), its sale was prohibited in the United Kingdom in 1991. U.S. trade name: **Halcion**.

tribade *n.* a woman who achieves sexual pleasure by rubbing her genitals against those of another woman. This activity is known as **tribadism**, which is also occasionally used as a synonym for lesbianism. **—tribadic** *adj.*

trichomegaly-retinal degeneration syndrome a rare disorder marked by abnormally short stature, long eyebrows and eyelashes, and poor vision due to retinal pigment degeneration. Some affected individuals exhibit slow psychomotor development and may have IQs of less than 70; in others, average-range intelligence has been reported.

trichophagy *n.* the act of persistently biting and eating one's hair.

trichorrhexis nodosa with mental retardation a congenital disorder marked by stubby, brittle hair, thin tooth enamel, defective nails, and severe mental retardation. Affected individuals who have been studied have shown MICROCEPHALY; X-rays have revealed a small cranial vault. Also called **Pollitt syndrome**.

trichotillomania *n.* an impulse-control disorder characterized by persistent hair pulling at any part of one's body on which hair grows, often with conspicuous hair loss. Feelings of increasing tension before the act and feelings of release or satisfaction on completion are common. In *DSM–IV–TR* trichotillomania is included in the category IMPULSE-CONTROL DISORDERS NOT ELSEWHERE CLASSIFIED.

tricyclic antidepressant (**TCA**) any of a group of drugs, developed in the 1950s, that were the original FIRST-LINE MEDICATIONS for treatment of depression. They are presumed to act by blocking the reuptake of monoamine neurotransmitters (serotonin, dopamine, and norepinephrine) into the presynaptic neuron, thereby increasing the amount of neurotransmitter available for binding to postsynaptic receptors. Tricyclic antidepressants have a characteristic three-ring molecular core. They may be tertiary amines (e.g., IMIPRAMINE, AMITRIPTYLINE) or their metabolites, which are secondary amines (e.g., DESIPRAMINE, NORTRIPTYLINE). Other members of the group include CLOMIPRAMINE, **protriptyline** (U.S. trade name: **Vivactil**), DOXEPIN, and **trimipramine** (U.S. trade name: **Surmontil**). Side effects of TCAs include significant anticholinergic effects (e.g., dry mouth, blurred vision, constipation, urinary retention), drowsiness or insomnia, confusion, anxiety, nausea, weight gain, and impotence. They can also cause cardiovascular complications (particularly disturbances in heart rhythm). The tricyclics represented the mainstay of antidepressant treatment from the introduction of imipramine in 1957 until fluoxetine (Prozac)—the first SSRI—was introduced in 1987. Although they are effective as antidepressants, their adverse side effects and—more significantly—their lethality in overdose have led to a profound decline in their use. They remain, however, the standard against which other antidepressants are compared; no other class of antidepressants has demonstrated more clinical efficacy.

tridimensional theory of feeling the theory that feelings can vary along three dimensions: pleasantness–unpleasantness (hedoric quality), excitement–calmness, and arousal–relaxation. The tridimensional theory is used to define different combinations and successions of feelings and describe the course of change of the feelings along each of the three dimensions. [introduced by Wilhelm WUNDT]

trifluoperazine *n.* a HIGH-POTENCY ANTIPSYCHOTIC of the piperazine PHENOTHIAZINE class. Like other agents of this class, it acts primarily by blocking postsynaptic dopamine D2 receptors. Trifluoperazine is appropriate for the treatment of schizophrenia in both adults and children and severe, nonpsychotic anxiety in adults only. It may also be used to control behavioral symptoms associated with dementia. Because of its potentially severe side effects (e.g., TARDIVE DYSKINESIA, NEUROLEPTIC MALIGNANT SYNDROME)—and the availability of other, relatively nontoxic anxiolytics (e.g., the benzodiazepines)—it is not recommended for routine use in anxiety. U.S. trade name: **Stelazine**.

trigger 1. *n.* a stimulus that elicits a reaction. For example, an event could be a trigger for a memory of a past experience and an accompanying state of emotional arousal. **2.** *vb.* to act as a trigger.

triggering cause a stimulus or phenomenon that initiates the immediate onset of a behavior problem. See also PRECIPITATING CAUSE. Compare PREDISPOSING CAUSE.

trihexyphenidyl *n.* an ANTICHOLINERGIC DRUG used in the treatment of drug-induced parkinsonian symptoms, such as those produced with use of conventional antipsychotics, and as an adjunctive treatment for PARKINSON'S DISEASE. It acts by exerting a direct inhibitory effect on the parasympathetic nervous system and a relaxing effect on smooth musculature. U.S. trade name: **Artane**.

triiodothyronine (**T_3**) *n.* an iodine-containing hormone that, together with THYROXINE, regulates metabolic activity. See THYROID HORMONES.

Trilafon *n.* a trade name for PERPHENAZINE.

trimethoxyamphetamine (TMA) *n.* a synthetic AMPHETAMINE derivative that is a CNS STIMULANT with purported hallucinogenic properties similar to LSD and the naturally occurring hallucinogen MESCALINE. Side effects and toxicity of TMA and other "designer psychedelics" are similar to those of MDMA.

tripa ida see SUSTO.

triple-X condition see XXX SYNDROME.

triptans *pl. n.* a class of VASOCONSTRICTOR drugs used in the treatment of migraine headache, the prototype of which is **sumatriptan**. Triptans exert their therapeutic effect by acting as SEROTONIN-RECEPTOR AGONISTS at 5-HT_{1B} and 5-HT_{1D} receptors, causing the constriction of cerebral blood vessels. Triptans should not be administered concurrently with MONOAMINE OXIDASE INHIBITORS and should be used cautiously with SSRIS to avoid the risk of precipitating a SEROTONIN SYNDROME.

21 trisomy see TRISOMY 21.

trisomy *n.* see AUTOSOME. **—trisomic** *adj.*

trisomy 13–15 see CHROMOSOME-13 TRISOMY.

trisomy 17–18 a congenital disorder characterized by low birth weight with various facial anomalies, a prominent occiput, overlapping of the index finger over the third finger, and visual abnormalities. Severe mental retardation accompanies the defect, which is due to NONDISJUNCTION of one of the chromosomes in the 17–18 group. Also called **Edwards syndrome**; **E trisomy**.

trisomy 21 a condition associated with 85% of instances of DOWN SYNDROME, characterized by the presence of three number 21 chromosomes in the body cells rather than the normal pair. The extra chromosome may be contributed by either the father or the mother. Also called **21 trisomy**.

troilism *n.* sexual activity involving three people. A **troilist** is a person who, in such a relationship, enjoys engaging in heterosexual activities with a partner as well as observing the partner in sexual activities with a third person. The third person may be of the same sex as the partner or the troilist. If the third person is of the same sex as the troilist, only observation occurs. If the third person is of the same sex as the troilist's partner, the troilist may engage in sexual activity with both of them.

truancy *n.* absence from school without permission. Persistent truancy before the age of 13 is an example of a serious violation of major rules, one of the symptoms of CONDUCT DISORDER. Also called **school truancy**. **—truant** *adj.*

true schizophrenia see NUCLEAR SCHIZOPHRENIA.

true score in CLASSICAL TEST THEORY, that part of a measurement or score that reflects the actual amount of the attribute possessed by the individual being measured.

true self in psychoanalytic theory, the total of an individual's potentialities that could be developed under ideal social and cultural conditions. The term is used in the context of Erich FROMM's approach to neurosis as a reaction to cultural pressures and repressed potentialities. The concept is also used in the CLIENT-CENTERED THERAPY of Carl ROGERS. The realization of the true self is a major goal of therapy.

true variance naturally occurring variability within or among research participants. This variance is inherent in the nature of the participant and is not due to measurement error, imprecision of the model used to describe the variable of interest in the research (e.g., a particular behavior), or other extrinsic factors.

trust 1. *n.* reliance on or confidence in the worth, truth, or value of someone or something. Trust is considered by most psychological researchers to be a primary component in mature relationships with others, whether intimate, social, or therapeutic. See BASIC TRUST VERSUS MISTRUST; INTERPERSONAL TRUST; SECURITY. **2.** *vb.* to have trust in someone or something.

trust exercise a common procedure in GROUP THERAPY and GROWTH GROUPS intended to help members of the group learn to trust other people. The trust exercise may involve putting a member in a vulnerable position so that he or she depends on the other group members for support. See also BLIND WALK.

trust versus mistrust see BASIC TRUST VERSUS MISTRUST.

truth serum a colloquial name for drugs, especially the barbiturates AMOBARBITAL, PENTOBARBITAL, or THIOPENTAL, that are injected intravenously in mild doses to help elicit information by inducing a relaxed, semihypnotic state in which an individual is less inhibited and more communicative. The term is derived from the reported use of such drugs by police to extract confessions from suspects.

tryptamine derivatives a group of drugs that are chemically related to SEROTONIN (5-hydroxytryptamine). They include a number of agents with hallucinogenic effects similar to those of LSD, including DMT (dimethyltryptamine), DET (diethyltryptamine), BUFOTENIN, and PSILOCIN. Tryptamine derivatives may also be classified as substituted indolealkylamines.

tryptophan *n.* one of the essential amino acids of the human diet. It is a precursor of the neurotransmitter SEROTONIN and plays a role in general physiological processes. In plants and many animals it is also a precursor of the B vitamin nicotinic acid. Tryptophan depletion—loss of tryptophan in the brain—may be induced for research purposes.

tryptophan hydroxylase an enzyme that

catalyzes the first step in the biosynthesis of SEROTONIN. It uses tetrahydrobiopterin as a coenzyme to transform the dietary amino acid L-tryptophan to 5-HYDROXYTRYPTOPHAN (5-HTP). This reaction is the rate-limiting step in serotonin synthesis, limited by levels of tryptophan in the brain as well as by levels of activity of neurons that use serotonin as a neurotransmitter.

T score any of a set of scores scaled so that they have a MEAN equal to 50 and STANDARD DEVIATION equal to 10.

TSCS abbreviation for TENNESSEE SELF-CONCEPT SCALE.

t test any of a class of statistical tests based on the fact that the test statistic follows the T DISTRIBUTION when the null hypothesis is true. Most *t* tests deal with hypotheses about the mean of a population or about differences between means of different populations.

tuberoinfundibular tract one of three major neural pathways in the brain that use dopamine as their principal neurotransmitter (see DOPAMINERGIC). The cell bodies of this tract, which is a local circuit in the hypothalamus, project short axons to the pituitary gland. The tuberoinfundibular tract is associated with regulation of hypothalamic function and specific hormones (e.g., prolactin). Alterations in hormone function involving this tract are often seen in patients taking phenothiazine ANTIPSYCHOTICS.

tumor *n.* **1.** see NEOPLASM. **2.** swelling, one of the cardinal signs of inflammation.

Turner's syndrome a chromosomal disorder, specific to women, marked by the absence of all or a part of one of the two X (female) chromosomes. The effects include underdevelopment or absence of primary and secondary SEX CHARACTERISTICS, infertility, and various physical abnormalities (e.g., short stature, lack of menstruation). See also NOONAN'S SYNDROME. [reported in 1938 by Henry H. **Turner** (1892–1970), U.S. endocrinologist]

twelve-step program a distinctive approach to overcoming addictive, compulsive, or behavioral problems that was developed initially in ALCOHOLICS ANONYMOUS (AA) to guide recovery from alcoholism and is now used, often in an adapted form, by a number of other SELF-HELP GROUPS. In the context of alcoholism, for instance, the twelve-step program in AA asks each member to (a) admit that he or she cannot control his or her drinking; (b) recognize a supreme spiritual power, which can give the member strength; (c) examine past errors, a process that is carried out with another member who serves as sponsor; (d) make amends for these errors; (e) develop a new code and style of life; and (f) help other alcoholics who are in need of support. Variations of this model also exist for drug abuse and addiction, gambling addiction, and other problems.

twenty-four-hour therapy a procedure in psychotherapy in which a patient is supervised 24 hours a day by the therapist, who has legal, medical, and financial control over the patient, or by the therapist's assistants, who maintain control over the patient under the direction of the therapist. Sometimes mobile telephones or other communication devices are used by the assistants to receive and obtain direction and information from the therapist. Often a parent or partner of the patient initiates this process when the situation is so desperate that no other method seems possible. [developed by U.S. psychologist Eugene E. Landy (1934–2006)]

twilight state a state of clouded consciousness in which the individual is temporarily unaware of his or her surroundings, experiences fleeting auditory or visual hallucinations, and responds to them by performing irrational acts, such as undressing in public, running away, or committing violence. The disturbance occurs primarily in temporal lobe epilepsy, dissociative reactions, and alcoholic intoxication. On regaining normal consciousness, individuals usually report that they felt they were dreaming and have little or no recollection of their behavior. See also DREAM STATE.

twin control in a TWIN STUDY, a method in which the target twin—that is, the one who has had certain experiences or training or has been exposed to the experimental conditions—is compared against the twin who has not had the experiences, training, or treatment and therefore serves as a CONTROL. Also called **cotwin control**.

twins *pl. n.* see DIZYGOTIC TWINS; MONOZYGOTIC TWINS.

twin study research using twins. The purpose of such research is usually to assess the relative contributions of heredity and environment to some attribute. Specifically, twin studies often involve comparing the characteristics of identical and fraternal twins and comparing twins of both types who have been reared together or reared apart. For example, two types of study have been used to investigate intelligence in twins: (1) Identical twins reared apart. Here the genotypes (genetic makeups) are identical but as there is no shared environment disparity in intelligence must result from the different environments. (2) Comparisons between identical twins reared together and fraternal twins reared together. Here one can assume that each pair of twins shares the same environment, but while the identical twins have 100% of their genes in common, the fraternal twins share only 50% of their genes. The assumptions made in these studies are, however, never completely fulfilled. For example, the identical twins reared apart have had some common environment, if only their intrauterine experiences. Moreover, identical twins reared together usually have more similar environments than fraternal twins raised together. These differences can make the estimations of heritability of intelligence open to some doubts.

twisted symbols see STREPHOSYMBOLIA.

twitching *n.* a series of small muscular contractions.

two-by-two factorial design an experimental design in which there are two INDEPENDENT VARIABLES each having two levels. When this design is depicted as a matrix, two rows represent one of the independent variables and two columns represent the other independent variable. See FACTORIAL DESIGN.

two-chair technique see EMPTY-CHAIR TECHNIQUE.

two-factor design a FACTORIAL DESIGN in which two INDEPENDENT VARIABLES are manipulated. Also called **two-way factorial design**.

two-factor theory of emotion see SCHACHTER–SINGER THEORY.

two-spirit *n.* in some Native American cultures, a person, typically male, who takes on the gender identity of the opposite sex with the approval of the society. The culture often views such individuals as having a special spiritual or guidance role in the community. In the Navajo culture such a person is termed a **nadle**, in the Lakota culture the term **winkte** is used, and in other cultures a literal translation of "man-woman" might be used. The traditional scholarly term **berdache** is now used less frequently because of its negative implications of male prostitution or of a "kept" status.

two-tailed test a statistical test of an experimental hypothesis that does not specify the expected direction of an effect or a relationship. Also called **nondirectional test**. Compare ONE-TAILED TEST.

two-way analysis of variance a statistical test analyzing the joint and separate influences of two INDEPENDENT VARIABLES on a DEPENDENT VARIABLE.

two-way factorial design see TWO-FACTOR DESIGN.

Tylenol *n.* a trade name for ACETAMINOPHEN.

Type A behavior a behavior pattern that may be associated with increased risk of coronary heart disease. It is marked by competitiveness, achievement motivation, aggression and hostility, impatience and a distorted sense of time urgency, and **polyphasic activity** (e.g., shaving or eating while reading a newspaper). Compare TYPE B BEHAVIOR.

Type A personality a personality pattern characterized by chronic competitiveness, high levels of ACHIEVEMENT MOTIVATION, and hostility. The lifestyles of Type A individuals are said to predispose them to coronary heart disease. Compare TYPE B PERSONALITY. [outlined in the 1970s by U.S. physicians Meyer Friedman (1910–2001) and Ray H. Rosenman]

Type B behavior a behavior pattern that is free of aggression and hostility, marked by an absence of time urgency and lack of a need to display or discuss one's accomplishments and achievements. Compare TYPE A BEHAVIOR.

Type B personality a personality pattern characterized by low levels of competitiveness and frustration and a relaxed, easy-going approach. Type B individuals typically do not feel the need to prove their superiority or abilities. Compare TYPE A PERSONALITY. [outlined in the 1970s by U.S. physicians Meyer Friedman (1910–2001) and Ray H. Rosenman]

Type III error an error in direction (positive/negative, higher/lower) when two groups are shown empirically to be different. Researchers frequently investigate the direction rather than the size of a relationship (e.g., investigating "Which is more?" or "Which is better?"), and they make a Type III error when they use a nondirectional TWO-TAILED TEST to make a directional decision: After conducting the test and finding STATISTICAL SIGNIFICANCE, the researcher inspects data visually to decide (incorrectly) upon the direction of the observed relationship.

Type D personality a "distressed" personality pattern, characterized by a high degree of negative affectivity (i.e., a tendency to experience negative emotions) in combination with a conscious tendency to suppress self-expression in social interaction. Accumulating evidence suggests that Type D individuals are at increased risk of developing CORONARY HEART DISEASE and other chronic medical conditions.

Type I error the error of rejecting the NULL HYPOTHESIS when it is in fact true. Investigators make this error when they believe they have detected an effect or a relationship that does not actually exist. Also called **alpha error**.

Type II error the error of failing to reject the NULL HYPOTHESIS when it is in fact not true. Investigators make this error if they conclude that a particular effect or relationship does not exist when in fact it does. Also called **beta error**.

type theory any hypothetical proposition or principle for the grouping of people by kind of personality or by personality characteristics. An example of such a theoretical system of personality classification is that of Swiss psychoanalyst Carl Jung (1875–1961), who divided individuals into types according to (a) attitudes of INTROVERSION and EXTRAVERSION and (b) the dominant functions of the psyche.

typhomania *n.* DELIRIUM occurring in individuals with typhoid fever and typhus.

typical antipsychotic see ANTIPSYCHOTIC.

typical schizophrenia see NUCLEAR SCHIZOPHRENIA.

typology *n.* any analysis of a particular category of phenomena (e.g., individuals, things) into classes based on common characteristics, for example, a typology of personality. —**typological** *adj*.

tyramine *n*. a BIOGENIC AMINE found in high concentrations in a variety of sources, including ripe cheese, broad beans, ergot, mistletoe, some wines, and many foodstuffs that are produced via enzymatic action. Tyramine is derived from the amino acid tyrosine and is sympathomimetic, causing an increase in blood pressure and heart action. Foods containing tyramine react with MONOAMINE OXIDASE INHIBITORS, preventing normal metabolism of the tyramine and resulting in a greatly aggravated effect on blood pressure. As a consequence, the patient may suffer a hypertensive crisis.

tyrosine hydroxylase an enzyme that catalyzes the first, and rate-limiting, step in the biosynthesis of the catecholamine neurotransmitters DOPAMINE, norepinephrine, and epinephrine. It transforms dietary tyrosine, using the coenzyme tetrahydrobiopterin and molecular oxygen, to L-DOPA.

Uu

UCR fees abbreviation for usual, customary, and reasonable fees (see CUSTOMARY, PREVAILING, AND REASONABLE FEES).

Ucs abbreviation for UNCONSCIOUS.

ulcer *n.* an erosion of a tissue surface, such as the mucosal lining of the digestive tract. **Peptic ulcers**, which affect the stomach and duodenum, are associated with increased secretion of hydrochloric acid and pepsin, a digestive enzyme, or increased susceptibility of the lining of the stomach and duodenum to the effects of these substances. See also DYSPEPSIA.

Ullrich–Noonan syndrome see NOONAN'S SYNDROME. [Otto **Ullrich** (1894–1957), German pediatrician; Jacqueline **Noonan** (1921–), U.S. pediatrician]

ultimate opinion testimony opinion testimony by an expert witness that directly informs the court about the issue in dispute. For example, an expert witness who testifies that the defendant is insane is giving ultimate opinion testimony.

Ultiva *n.* a trade name for remifentanil. See FENTANYL.

ultrasonic irradiation a form of psychosurgery in which sound waves of a frequency of 1000 kHz are directed through trephine openings in the skull for up to 14 min. It is an alternative to prefrontal lobotomy (see LOBOTOMY) and is rarely used now.

ultrasound *n.* sound whose frequency exceeds the human audibility range, often used in order to measure and record structures and structural change within the body in the imaging technique called **ultrasonography** (or **sonography**). Echoes from ultrasound waves reflected from tissue surfaces are recorded to form structural images for diagnostic purposes, for example, to examine a growing fetus during pregnancy or to examine internal organs, such as the heart, liver, kidneys, and gallbladder, for signs of health or disease.

ululation *n.* **1.** a shrill lament or wailing associated with emotional expression and ritual behavior in various cultures. **2.** a rare name for the incoherent wailing of some individuals with psychosis.

unbiased *adj.* impartial or without net error. In unbiased procedures, studies, and the like any errors that do occur are RANDOM ERROR and therefore self-cancelling in the long run.

unbiased sampling a survey design in which the values produced by the samples coincide in the long run with the true values in the population.

uncertainty avoidance 1. a COGNITIVE STYLE characterized by a tendency to adhere to what is already known, thought, or believed. It contrasts with **uncertainty orientation**, which is the tendency to seek out new information and ideas and to enjoy exploring and mastering uncertainty. **2.** an intolerance of ambiguity or uncertainty and a psychological need for formal rules. See also NEED FOR CLOSURE. [defined by Dutch cultural psychologist Geert Hofstede (1928–)]

uncertainty orientation see UNCERTAINTY AVOIDANCE.

unconditional love see UNCONDITIONAL POSITIVE REGARD.

unconditional positive regard an attitude of caring, acceptance, and prizing expressed by others irrespective of an individual's behavior and without regard to the other's personal standards, which is considered conducive to self-awareness, self-worth, and personality growth. Posited by Carl ROGERS to be a universal human need essential to healthy development, unconditional positive regard is the centerpiece of his CLIENT-CENTERED THERAPY and is also emphasized in many other therapeutic approaches. Compare CONDITIONAL POSITIVE REGARD.

unconditioned reinforcement see PRIMARY REINFORCEMENT.

unconditioned response (**UCR**; **UR**) the unlearned response to a stimulus: any original response that occurs naturally and in the absence of conditioning (e.g., salivation in response to the presentation of food). The unconditioned response is a REFLEX that serves as the basis for establishment of the CONDITIONED RESPONSE in PAVLOVIAN CONDITIONING.

unconditioned stimulus (**UCS**; **US**) a stimulus that elicits an UNCONDITIONED RESPONSE, as in withdrawal from a hot radiator, contraction of the pupil on exposure to light, or salivation when food is in the mouth. Also called **unconditional stimulus**. Compare CONDITIONED STIMULUS.

unconscious 1. (**Ucs**) *n.* in psychoanalytic theory, the region of the psyche that contains memories, emotional conflicts, wishes, and repressed impulses that are not directly accessible to awareness but that have dynamic effects on thought and behavior. Sigmund FREUD sometimes used the term **dynamic unconscious** to distinguish this concept from that which is merely descriptively unconscious but "static" and with little psychological significance. Compare CONSCIOUS; PRECONSCIOUS. See also COGNITIVE UNCONSCIOUS; COLLECTIVE UNCONSCIOUS; PERSONAL UNCONSCIOUS. **2.** *adj.* relating to or marked by absence of awareness or lack of consciousness.

unconscious cognition cognitive processes, such as thinking, memory processing, and linguistic processing, that occur in the absence of awareness. See COGNITIVE UNCONSCIOUS.

unconscious homosexuality see LATENT HOMOSEXUALITY.

unconscious inference theory the hypothesis that perception is indirectly influenced by inferences about current sensory input that make use of the perceiver's knowledge of the world and prior experience with similar input. For example, consider two trees of the same height but different distances from the perceiver. The images of the trees that appear on the retina are of different sizes, but the knowledge that one tree is farther away than the other leads the perceiver to infer, without conscious effort, that in actuality the two trees are the same size. [proposed by German physiologist Hermann von Helmholtz (1821–1894)]

unconscious motivation in psychoanalytic theory, wishes, impulses, aims, and drives of which the self is not aware. Examples of behavior produced by unconscious motivation are purposive accidents, slips of the tongue, and dreams that express unfulfilled wishes. See also PARAPRAXIS.

unconscious perception a phenomenon, the existence of which is controversial, in which a stimulus that is not consciously perceived nonetheless influences behavior. See PREATTENTIVE PROCESSING.

unconscious process 1. in psychoanalytic theory, a psychical process that takes place in the UNCONSCIOUS, for example, REPRESSION. **2.** in cognitive psychology, a mental process that occurs without a person's awareness and subserves cognitive activity. Also called **preattentive process**; **subliminal process**. Compare CONSCIOUS PROCESS.

unconscious resistance in psychoanalytic theory, RESISTANCE proper, as opposed to CONSCIOUS RESISTANCE.

U

uncontrolled *adj.* not regulated or measured, particularly by an investigator in the course of research.

uncontrolled variable a characteristic factor that is not regulated or measured by the investigator during an experiment or study, such that it is not the same for all participants in the research. For example, if the investigator collects data on participants having varying levels of education, then education is an uncontrolled variable. If the investigator, however, were to collect data only on participants with college degrees then education would be a controlled variable.

unconventional therapy treatment that may be unique, controversial, or both, in that it is not traditionally accepted by the health care professions. See COMPLEMENTARY AND ALTERNATIVE MEDICINE.

uncovering *n.* in psychotherapy, the process of peeling away an individual's defenses and passing beyond a focus on symptoms to get to the underlying roots of a problem. **Uncovering techniques** may include psychoanalysis and other psychodynamic or depth therapies, deep exploration of issues, and the use of trust to encourage truthfulness on the part of the client.

uncriticalness *n.* a nonjudgmental attitude on the part of the therapist, which is considered essential in Carl ROGERS's nondirective approach (see CLIENT-CENTERED THERAPY) as well as in other forms of psychotherapy. Criticism is held to inhibit clients' efforts to recognize and revise their self-defeating patterns of thought and behavior.

uncued panic attack a PANIC ATTACK that occurs unexpectedly rather than being brought on by a specific situation or trigger. It is therefore perceived to have occurred spontaneously. Also called **unexpected panic attack**. Compare CUED PANIC ATTACK; SITUATIONALLY PREDISPOSED PANIC ATTACK.

underdog *n.* the rationalizations and self-justifications employed by an individual to allay the sense of guilt or shame arising from an inability to meet the demands of internal moral standards or other rules of conduct (the TOPDOG). [first described by German-born U.S. psychiatrist Frederick (Fritz) R. Perls (1893–1970)]

understanding *n.* **1.** the process of gaining insight about oneself or others or of comprehending the meaning or significance of something, such as a word, concept, argument, or event. See also APPREHENSION; COMPREHENSION. **2.** in counseling and psychotherapy, the process of discerning the network of relationships between a client's behavior and his or her environment, history, aptitudes, motivation, ideas, feelings, relationships, and modes of expression. **—understand** *vb.*

undifferentiated schizophrenia in *DSM–IV–TR*, a subtype of SCHIZOPHRENIA in which the individual exhibits prominent psychotic features, such as delusions, hallucinations, disorganized thinking, or grossly disorganized behavior, but does not meet the criteria for any of the other subtypes of the disorder. The *DSM–III* designation was **undifferentiated type schizophrenic disorder**.

undifferentiated somatoform disorder in *DSM–IV–TR*, a SOMATOFORM DISORDER in which one or more physical complaints persist for 6 months or longer and cannot be explained by a known medical condition. Unlike FACTITIOUS DISORDER or MALINGERING, these symptoms are not intentionally feigned or produced.

It should not be confused with SOMATOFORM DISORDER NOT OTHERWISE SPECIFIED.

unfinished business in therapy and counseling, the personal experiences that have been blocked or tasks that have been avoided because of feared emotional or interpersonal effects. Many therapists believe that people have an urge to complete unfinished business in order to achieve satisfaction and peace. Those working with the dying and their families believe that dealing with unfinished business is an important aspect of the dying and grieving processes.

unfinished story PROJECTIVE TECHNIQUE in which participants are required to complete a story by role play, discussion, or writing. It is intended to reveal information about the participants' concerns.

unfitness *n.* **1.** the state or condition of lacking fitness or health. **2.** in biology, the inability of an organism to produce viable offspring in a given environment. Compare FITNESS.

unfreezing *n.* a therapeutic goal to rid an individual of rigid beliefs and stereotypes of self, others, and the world.

unidimensional *adj.* having a single dimension or composed of a single or a pure factor. Compare MULTIDIMENSIONAL.

unidimensional concept see BIPOLAR CONCEPT.

Unified Tri-Service Cognitive Performance Assessment Battery (UTCPAB) a battery of tests compiled in 1984 by a group of experimental research psychologists. It presents computerized, clinically relevant psychomotor and neuropsychological tests for the rapid assessment of the integrity of the nervous system.

unilateral couple counseling the counseling of one partner on his or her relationship to the other. Even when only one partner participates in counseling, the focus is on the partners' relationship. See also COUPLES COUNSELING.

unilateral neglect a disorder resulting from damage to the PARIETAL LOBE of the brain and characterized by a loss of conscious perception of objects in the half of the visual field (usually the left half) that is opposite the location of the lesion, ALIEN LIMB SYNDROME, and other striking neuropsychological features. Also called **hemineglect**.

unimodal distribution a set of scores with a single peak, or MODE, around which values tend to fluctuate, such that the frequencies at first increase and then decrease. Compare BIMODAL DISTRIBUTION; MULTIMODAL DISTRIBUTIONS.

unipolar depression any DEPRESSIVE DISORDER, that is, any mood disorder marked by one or more MAJOR DEPRESSIVE EPISODES or a prolonged period of depressive symptoms with no history of manic or hypomanic symptoms or MIXED EPISODES.

unipolar disorder persistent or pervasive DEPRESSION that does not involve a MANIC EPISODE, a HYPOMANIC EPISODE, or a MIXED EPISODE. As such, it contrasts with BIPOLAR DISORDER. The term is sometimes used synonymously with MAJOR DEPRESSIVE DISORDER.

unipolar mania a BIPOLAR DISORDER in which only MANIC EPISODES have occurred. Except in rare cases, manic episodes tend eventually to be followed by one or more MAJOR DEPRESSIVE EPISODES.

unipolar rating scale a type of survey that prompts a respondent to evaluate the degree to which a single quality or attribute is present. For example, consider a five-point scale with the following anchors: (1) not at all satisfied, (2) slightly satisfied, (3) moderately satisfied, (4) very satisfied, and (5) completely satisfied. Since there is no anchor that represents the opposing quality of dissatisfaction, the scale has one pole. Also called **unipolar scale**. Compare BIPOLAR RATING SCALE.

unique trait see IDIOGRAPHIC TRAIT.

United Nations Declaration on the Rights of Mentally Retarded Persons a 1971 declaration by the United Nations affirming the human rights of people with mental retardation. These issues were largely subsumed under the 1993 Standard Rules on the Equalization of Opportunities for Persons with Disabilities. See RIGHTS OF PEOPLE WITH MENTAL RETARDATION.

unity of consciousness the concept that the contents of awareness are coherent, internally consistent, or shaped by a common goal. From this it follows that mutually inconsistent events cannot simultaneously appear in awareness.

univariate *adj.* characterized by a single variable. Compare MULTIVARIATE. See also BIVARIATE.

universal design a quality of a product or built environment so conceived as to make it optimally usable and comfortable for people of all ages and abilities. Universal design as a concept goes beyond mere accessibility and removal of barriers, in accordance with the mandates of such laws as the Americans With Disabilities Act (ADA), by emphasizing the inclusiveness of design to accommodate a wide range of physical and cognitive abilities. Also called **transgenerational design**. See also BARRIER-FREE ENVIRONMENT.

universality *n.* **1.** the tendency to assume that one's personal qualities and characteristics, including attitudes and values, are common in the general social group or culture. **2.** in mob and crowd settings, the tendency for individuals to assume that atypical, unusual behaviors are allowable because many others in the situation are performing such actions ("everybody's doing it"). See CONTAGION. **3.** in self-help and psychotherapy groups, a curative factor fostered by members' recognition that their problems and difficulties are not unique to them, but instead are experienced by many of the group members.

Also called **impression of universality**. See also CURATIVE FACTORS MODEL.

universality of emotions the finding that certain emotional expressions, appraisals, and manifestations are the same or highly similar across cultures and societies. Compare CULTURAL SPECIFICITY OF EMOTIONS. See also PRIMARY EMOTION.

unlearning *n.* see DECONDITIONING.

unobtrusive measure a measure obtained without disturbing the participant or alerting him or her that a measurement is being made. The behavior or responses of such participants are thus assumed to be unaffected by the investigative process or the surrounding environment. Compare OBTRUSIVE MEASURE.

unpleasantness *n.* an emotional state that is experienced when an event is incongruent with one's goals or is associated with pain. See also DIMENSIONAL THEORY OF EMOTION. **—unpleasant** *adj.*

unpleasure *n.* in psychoanalytic theory, the psychic pain, tension, and EGO suffering that is consciously felt when instinctual needs and wishes, such as hunger and sex, are blocked by the ego and denied gratification. [translation of German *Unlust*, "reluctance" or "listlessness"]

unresolved *adj.* **1.** in psychotherapy, denoting emotional or psychic conflicts not yet sufficiently dealt with and assimilated or understood. See also UNFINISHED BUSINESS. **2.** describing any stimulus whose characteristics cannot be determined by the perceiver.

unshared environment see NONSHARED ENVIRONMENT.

unsociable *adj.* lacking SOCIABILITY because of a disinclination to interact and form relationships with others.

unspecified mental retardation the diagnosis made when an individual is presumed to have mental retardation but is too severely impaired or uncooperative to be evaluated through the use of standard intelligence tests and adaptive behavior measures. The *DSM–IV–TR* designation is **mental retardation, severity unspecified**.

unstable personality disorder see BORDERLINE PERSONALITY DISORDER.

unstructured autobiography see AUTOBIOGRAPHY.

unstructured interview an interview that imposes minimal structure by asking open-ended (rather than set) questions and allowing the interviewee to steer the discussion into areas of his or her choosing. Unstructured interviews are used in a variety of contexts but are particularly popular in personnel selection, the idea is that such an approach will reveal more of the applicant's traits, interests, priorities, and interpersonal and verbal skills than a STRUCTURED INTERVIEW. The appropriateness of the technique will depend on the nature of the occupation or position; it will also require an experienced and confident interviewer.

uppers *pl. n.* slang for various drugs that stimulate the central nervous system, such as amphet amine and methamphetamine. See CNS STIMULANT.

UR 1. abbreviation for UNCONDITIONED RESPONSE. **2.** abbreviation for UTILIZATION REVIEW.

Urecholine *n.* a trade name for BETHANECHOL.

urethral eroticism in psychoanalytic theory, sexual pleasure derived from urination. Also called **urethral erotism**. See UROLAGNIA.

urethritis *n.* inflammation of the urethra, with symptoms of painful urination (dysuria) and urethral discharge. The infection may be transmitted by sexual contact, as in the case of GONORRHEA.

urinary incontinence loss of conscious control of urination due to an organic condition, such as a neurological disorder or age-related changes in the bladder or kidneys. Compare ENURESIS.

urolagnia *n.* sexual interest focused on urine and urination. This may involve watching others urinate, being urinated on during sexual activity, urinating on the partner during sexual activity, or drinking one's own urine. See also URETHRAL EROTICISM.

urophilia *n.* a PARAPHILIA involving urine and urination as a major source of arousal during sexual activity.

U.S. Department of Veterans Affairs (VA) an agency of the U.S. government established in 1930 to administer the laws providing benefits and other services to veterans, their dependents, and their beneficiaries. Its mission is to serve U.S. veterans and their families with compassion; to be their principal advocate in ensuring that they receive medical care, benefits, social support, and lasting memorials; and to promote the health, welfare, and dignity of all veterans in recognition of their service to the nation.

Usher syndrome a genetic disorder, inherited as an autosomal recessive trait (see RECESSIVE ALLELE), causing sensorineural deafness, deterioration of vision due to retinitis pigmentosa, and, in some cases, loss of balance. [Charles Howard **Usher** (1865–1942), British ophthalmologist]

usual, customary and reasonable fees (UCR fees) see CUSTOMARY, PREVAILING, AND REASONABLE FEES.

UTCPAB abbreviation for UNIFIED TRI-SERVICE COGNITIVE PERFORMANCE ASSESSMENT BATTERY.

uterine orgasm see VULVAL ORGASM.

utility standards the information requirements of those for whom an evaluation research study is carried out. These standards include identifying all stakeholders, selecting evaluation objectives appropriate to the intended recipients of the findings, providing clear and timely reporting of information, and following procedures that maximize the study's utilization. See also ACCURACY STANDARDS; FEASIBILITY STANDARDS; PROPRIETY STANDARDS.

utilization review (**UR**) a formal review of the necessity and quality of services provided in a hospital or clinic or by an individual provider. Conducted by a specially appointed committee, a utilization review often addresses whether the level of service provided is the most appropriate to the severity of the presenting problem. See also CONTINUED-STAY REVIEW; EXTENDED-STAY REVIEW.

uxoricide *n.* the murder of a wife by her husband.

Vv

VA abbreviation for U.S. DEPARTMENT OF VETERANS AFFAIRS.

VABS abbreviation for VINELAND ADAPTIVE BEHAVIOR SCALES.

vagabond neurosis see DROMOMANIA.

vagina dentata in psychoanalytic theory, the unconscious fantasy that the vagina is a mouth with teeth that can castrate the male partner. In women, the fantasy is believed to stem from intense PENIS ENVY and a desire to castrate the partner as an act of revenge; in men, it is believed to stem from CASTRATION ANXIETY.

vaginal administration see ADMINISTRATION.

vaginal envy a psychological characteristic of men who desire the ability to become pregnant and bear children. See also FEMININITY COMPLEX; WOMB ENVY.

vaginal orgasm 1. female orgasm achieved through vaginal stimulation. **2.** in early psychoanalytic theory, the "mature, feminine" orgasm, as opposed to "immature, masculine" orgasms produced from clitoral stimulation. This view has long since been refuted. Indeed, researchers have demonstrated that the clitoris is the focus of female sexual response and that vaginal orgasms are primarily related to indirect stimulation of the clitoris and labia during intercourse. See COITAL ANORGASMIA.

vaginal sex sexual intercourse by means of vaginal penetration. See COITUS.

vaginismus *n.* a sexual dysfunction in which spasmic contractions of the muscles around the vagina occur during or immediately preceding sexual intercourse, causing the latter to be painful or impossible. Vaginismus is not diagnosed if the dysfunction is due solely to the effects of a medical condition, although medical conditions may be involved as a factor in the problem. See also FUNCTIONAL VAGINISMUS.

vagotomy *n.* surgical cutting or interruption of the VAGUS NERVE, which has motor, sensory, and physiological functions.

vagus nerve the tenth CRANIAL NERVE, a mixed nerve with both sensory and motor fibers that serves many functions. The sensory fibers innervate the external ear, vocal organs, and thoracic and abdominal viscera. The motor nerves innervate the tongue, vocal organs, and—through many ganglia of the PARASYMPATHETIC NERVOUS SYSTEM—the thoracic and abdominal viscera. Also called **cranial nerve X**; **pneumogastric nerve**.

valence *n.* **1.** in the FIELD THEORY of Kurt LEWIN, the subjective value of an event, object, person, or other entity in the LIFE SPACE of the individual. An entity that attracts the individual has **positive valence**, while one that repels has **negative valence**. **2.** in certain theories of motivation, the anticipated satisfaction of attaining a particular goal or outcome.

validating marriage a long-lasting marriage in which the partners express mutual respect even when they disagree.

validation *n.* the process of establishing the truth or logical cogency of something, for example determining the accuracy of a research instrument in measuring what it is designed to measure. In some forms of psychotherapy, validation may take the form of MIRRORING of the client's judgment or experience by the therapist. **—validate** *vb.*

validity *n.* **1.** the characteristic of being founded on truth, accuracy, fact, or law. **2.** the degree to which a test or measurement accurately measures or reflects what it purports to measure. There are various types of validity, for example CONCURRENT VALIDITY and CONSTRUCT VALIDITY. **—valid** *adj.*

validity criterion an external CRITERION that is used to define the attribute that an instrument is purported to measure and that is used to estimate the VALIDITY of the measurement instrument.

Valium *n.* a trade name for DIAZEPAM.

valor *n.* see COURAGE.

valproic acid a carboxylic acid (also formulated as **valproate sodium**; U.S. trade name: **Depacon**) used as an ANTICONVULSANT and MOOD STABILIZER. Although exact mechanisms of action remain unclear, valproic acid may exert its effects by reducing membrane sodium-channel activity (see ION CHANNEL), thereby slowing neuronal activity. It may also stimulate the synthesis of the inhibitory neurotransmitter gamma-aminobutyric acid (GABA). Valproic acid and valproate sodium are officially approved by the U.S. Food and Drug Administration for the management of seizures and of manic episodes associated with bipolar disorders. Although in general less toxic than lithium, these drugs have been associated with fatalities due to liver failure, particularly in children under 2 years of age, as well as pancreatitis; serum monitoring of drug levels and liver function is therefore required, particularly on starting treatment. Valproic acid and valproate sodium should not be taken during pregnancy due to risks of NEURAL TUBE DEFECTS in the fetus. U.S. trade name: **Depakene**.

value-drive care a federally backed movement to improve quality and reduce costs in U.S. health care by increasing system transparency and encouraging consumer choice. Such an emphasis on quality contrasts with the current volume-driven model of care in which consumers are passive recipients of treatments and providers are reimbursed for the number of cases they handle, regardless of patient outcome or the standard of services rendered. The central premise underlying value-driven care is that informed consumers are active and discriminating decision makers who will examine their available service options and choose those that will be the most beneficial and cost effective, which in turn will foster competition among providers to provide better services at reduced costs (e.g., by eliminating waste, improving cooperation and coordination among providers, preventing foreseeable patient complications, etc.). For example, if a person needing an operation could review readily available statistics on outcome, price, and so forth, he or she likely will avoid choosing hospitals, procedures, or medical professionals having poor success rates or costing too much. According to the U.S. government, however, the success of value-driven care requires not only the consistent measurement and public reporting of provider quality and cost information, but also the nationwide adoption of standardized, interoperable health information technology and the use of incentives that motivate all parties within the system—payors, patients, providers, and health care facilities—to achieve better care for less money.

values clarification any process intended to promote an individual's awareness and understanding of his or her moral principles and ethical priorities and their relationships to behavior and place in daily life. Individuals may be asked to carry out a series of exercises to this effect in some forms of psychotherapy.

vampirism *n.* a belief in the existence of vampires. In the portrayal of vampirism in literature, sexual pleasure is often associated with sucking blood from another person, a representation of the "love bite." Vampirism is variously interpreted by some psychoanalytic thinkers as oral sadism, oedipal strivings, fear of castration, or aggressive hostile feelings.

vandalism *n.* willful defacement or destruction of property. A persistent pattern of vandalism is one symptom of CONDUCT DISORDER.

vanishing cues methodology a computer-assisted training technique designed to teach new, complex knowledge to individuals with memory impairment. The technique takes advantage of the patient's preserved ability to respond to partial cues. Initially, as much information is provided as is needed for the patient to make a correct response. Across learning trials, information is gradually withdrawn until the patient can respond correctly in the absence of any cues.

variability *n.* **1.** the quality of being subject to change or variation in behavior or emotion. **2.** in statistics and experimental design, the degree to which members of a group or population differ from each other.

variable *n.* a quantity in an experiment or test that varies, that is, takes on different values (such as test scores, ratings assigned by judges, and other personal, social, or physiological indicators) that can be quantified (measured). Also called **variate**.

variance (symbol: σ^2) *n.* a measure of the spread, or DISPERSION, of scores within a sample, whereby a small variance indicates highly similar scores, all close to the sample mean, and a large variance indicates more scores at a greater distance from the mean and possibly spread over a larger range. Also called **index of variability**.

variate *n.* a specific value of a particular VARIABLE.

vascular dementia severe loss of cognitive functioning as a result of cerebrovascular disease. It is often due to repeated strokes. Also called **multi-infarct dementia**.

vascular depression a MAJOR DEPRESSIVE EPISODE that occurs shortly after the onset or treatment of cardiovascular disease or that is assumed to be caused by cardiovascular disease. Often, this episode is characterized by ANHEDONIA rather than depressed mood.

vascular insufficiency failure of the cardiovascular system to deliver an adequate supply of blood to the body tissues. This may involve large regions of the body or a particular organ or area of an organ. ATHEROSCLEROSIS, for example, can reduce the blood supply to the leg muscles, causing cramplike pains and limping; the heart, resulting in angina pectoris; or the brain, causing symptoms of stroke.

vasoconstrictor *n.* any drug or other agent (e.g., the hormone vasopressin) that causes constriction of blood vessels so that the diameter of the vessels is reduced. The vasomotor nerves of the SYMPATHETIC NERVOUS SYSTEM also serve as vasoconstrictors. Vasoconstrictor drugs are used to increase blood pressure that has fallen to dangerously low levels. Also called **vasopressor**.

V

vasodilator *n.* any drug or other agent that serves to increase the diameter of blood vessels, generally by relaxing smooth muscle in arterial walls. Vasodilators are commonly used in the treatment of hypertension and angina pectoris.

vasopressin *n.* a PEPTIDE hormone produced in the paraventricular nucleus and supraoptic nucleus of the hypothalamus and released by the posterior PITUITARY GLAND into the blood as controlled by osmoreceptors. It has two forms that differ by a single amino acid—**lysine vaso-**

pressin (**LVP**) in pigs and **arginine vasopressin** (**AVP**) in humans and all other mammals—and that bind to one of three distinct receptors, called V1a, V1b, and V2. Both forms increase fluid retention in the body by signaling the kidneys to reabsorb water instead of excreting it in urine, and also raise blood pressure by signaling specific smooth muscle cells to contract and narrow small blood vessels. In addition to these and various other physiological functions, vasopressin modulates complex cognitive functions—such as attention, learning, and the formation and recall of memories—and may also modulate emotion. Additionally, vasopressin and the chemically related peptide hormone OXYTOCIN have been implicated in a range of mammalian social behaviors including aggression, territoriality, maternal and paternal care, PAIR-BOND formation and mating, social recognition, attachment, affiliation, vocalization, and spacing behavior, as well as components of human social behaviors and the etiology of AUTISM. AVP secretion also appears to play a critical role in the stress response through activation of the HYPOTHALAMIC–PITUITARY–ADRENOCORTICAL SYSTEM (HPA system): In times of stress the HPA axis secretes CORTICOTROPIN-RELEASING FACTOR and AVP to synergistically stimulate the release of CORTICOTROPIN from the anterior pituitary gland, culminating in a rise in circulating GLUCOCORTICOIDS. Vasopression may also be involved in the modulation of anxiety and in the pathophysiology of anxiety disorders, including POSTTRAUMATIC STRESS DISORDER, and has been implicated in the pathophysiology of depression as well. The hormone is produced synthetically (U.S. trade names **DDAVP**, **Minirin**, or **Stimate**) as well for such therapeutic purposes as helping the body conserve fluids (e.g., in the treatment of DIABETES INSIPIDUS), restoring blood pressure (e.g., in the treatment of HYPOTENSION), and facilitating blood clotting (e.g., in the treatment of hemophilia). Also called **antidiuretic hormone** (**ADH**).

VD abbreviation for venereal disease. See SEXUALLY TRANSMITTED DISEASE.

vegetative *adj.* **1.** pertaining to basic physiological functions, such as those involved in growth, respiration, sleep, digestion, excretion, and homeostasis, which are governed primarily by the AUTONOMIC NERVOUS SYSTEM. **2.** living without apparent cognitive neurological function or responsiveness, as in PERSISTENT VEGETATIVE STATE.

vegetative state a condition in which an individual is immobile and noncommunicative, unaware of self or the environment, and unresponsive to stimuli. The condition occurs primarily in individuals with serious brain injury and is characterized by a nonfunctioning cerebral cortex. See PERSISTENT VEGETATIVE STATE.

vegetotherapy *n.* see ORGONE THERAPY.

venereal disease see SEXUALLY TRANSMITTED DISEASE.

venlafaxine *n.* an antidepressant that works by inhibiting the reuptake of both serotonin and norepinephrine; it belongs to a class called the SNRIs (serotonin and norepinephrine reuptake inhibitors). Its mechanism of action therefore differs from that of the SSRIS, which—some believe—makes it a more effective treatment for depression than SSRIs. It is also appropriate for treatment of generalized anxiety disorder and social anxiety disorder. Like other antidepressants, it should not be administered concurrently with MONOAMINE OXIDASE INHIBITORS. U.S. trade name: **Effexor**.

ventilation *n.* in psychotherapy and counseling, a client's full and free expression of feelings or emotions, especially in session.

ventral stream a series of specialized visual regions in the cerebral cortex of the brain that originate in the striate cortex (primary visual cortex) of the occipital lobe and project forward and downward into the lower temporal lobe. It is known informally as the "what" pathway of perception. Compare DORSAL STREAM.

ventricle *n.* **1.** an anatomical cavity in the body, such as any of the ventricles of the heart. **2.** any of the four interconnected cavities inside the brain, which serve as reservoirs of cerebrospinal fluid. Each of the two lateral ventricles communicates with the third ventricle via the intervventricular foramen; the third and fourth ventricles communicate with each other, via the cerebral aqueduct, and with the central canal of the spinal cord and the subarachnoid space. Also called **cerebral ventricle**. **—ventricular** *adj.*

ventricular puncture a surgical procedure in which an opening from the outside is made to the lateral ventricle areas of the brain. The procedure may be performed in order to reduce INTRACRANIAL PRESSURE, to inject medications (e.g., antibiotics) directly into the brain, or to obtain cerebrospinal fluid. See also VENTRICULOATRIAL SHUNT.

ventriculoatrial shunt a surgically created passage for draining cerebrospinal fluid from the ventricles of the brain to the external jugular vein, as in the treatment of HYDROCEPHALUS. The shunt carries the fluid through a catheter to the venous system that empties into the right atrium of the heart.

verapamil *n.* see CALCIUM-CHANNEL BLOCKER.

veratrine *n.* see HELLEBORE.

verbal automatism see AUTOMATISM.

verbal behavior therapy a form of BEHAVIOR THERAPY, developed in the 1960s, that is based upon the principles of OBSERVATIONAL LEARNING and CONDITIONING and incorporates the notion of RECIPROCAL DETERMINISM. The process involves a thorough inventory of symptoms and behavioral problems, the identification of those problems that will be the focus of the therapy, a careful FUNCTIONAL ANALYSIS of these target problems, development of specific reasonable goals for behavior change for each target problem, and the selection of appropriate therapeutic techniques to achieve the specific goal for each target problem. [developed by Albert BANDURA]

Verbal Comprehension Index on the WECHSLER ADULT INTELLIGENCE SCALE and other Wechsler tests, a subset of verbal tests thought to measure verbal knowledge and comprehension more purely than the other tests included in the VERBAL IQ.

verbal fluency test any of a group of tests in which participants are required, within a limited period, to generate words that fit a specific category or have specific characteristics (e.g., they may all start with the same letter). Compare DESIGN FLUENCY TEST.

verbal intelligence the ability to use words and combinations of words effectively in communication and problem solving.

verbal IQ a broad measure of verbal ability as obtained on standardized intelligence tests and affected by native verbal skills, experience, education, test tasking skills, and test motivation. See IQ.

verbalization *n.* **1.** the expression of thoughts, feelings, and fantasies in words. Verbalization is a common feature of most forms of psychotherapy, which has led to the use of the terms SIGN SYSTEM and TALKING CURE to refer to the discipline and practice. Apart from the general communication that occurs between therapist and client as part of the PSYCHOTHERAPEUTIC PROCESS, a particularly striking form of verbalization occurs in the use of FREE ASSOCIATION. **2.** in psychiatry, a symptom involving excessive or uncontrolled speech, as in CIRCUMSTANTIALITY or PRESSURED SPEECH. **—verbalize** *vb.*

verbal leakage SLIPS OF THE TONGUE, verbal ambiguities, or other aspects of speech thought to reveal information about an individual's motives and behavior that he or she has attempted to conceal. Body language that is similarly revealing is described by some psychologists as **nonverbal leakage**. See also FREUDIAN SLIP; PARAPRAXIS; SYMPTOMATIC ACT.

verbal masochism a sexual disorder in which an individual enjoys hearing words that are humiliating and insulting and derives sexual excitement from the abuse. According to Austrian-born U.S. psychologist Theodore Reik (1888–1969), the sexual excitement may depend on the choice and emphasis of words or sentences used.

verbigeration *n.* apparently meaningless repetition of specific words or phrases. Also called **catalogia**; **cataphasia**.

verbomania *n.* see LOGORRHEA.

verification *n.* the process of establishing the truth or accuracy of something, especially the use of objective, empirical data to test or support the truth of a statement, conclusion, or hypothesis.

Versed *n.* a trade name for MIDAZOLAM.

vertigo *n.* an unpleasant, illusory sensation of movement or spinning of oneself or one's surroundings due to neurological disorders, psychological stress (e.g., anxiety), or activities that disturb the labyrinth (which contains the organs of balance) in the inner ear (as in a roller-coaster ride).

vestibular system a system in the body that is responsible for maintaining balance, posture, and the body's orientation in space and plays an important role in regulating locomotion and other movements. It consists of the vestibular apparatus in the inner ear, the vestibular nerve, and the various cortical regions associated with the processing of vestibular (balance) information.

vestigial body image the subjective or internal image of one's appearance that is not necessarily modified by changes to one's external features. For example, individuals who have lost large amounts of weight may continue to have a vestigial body image of an overweight individual.

vestured genital apposition sexual activity in which clothed participants place their genital regions together and thrust or rub against each other, simulating COITUS. The activity may or may not be carried to the point of orgasm for one or both partners.

vibrator *n.* an appliance containing a small electric motor that produces a vibrating action, used to stimulate the genitals and other sensitive areas during masturbation or sexual activity with a partner. The device may be powered by batteries or by household electric current. Some vibrators strap on the hand, making the fingers vibrate during sexual stimulation. Another type has a vibrating mechanism on which a number of attachments of different size, shape, and texture can be placed, and these stimulate the body directly. Other vibrators are cylinders that can be used externally or inserted into the vagina or anus.

Vicodin *n.* a trade name for a combination of HYDROCODONE and ACETAMINOPHEN.

vicarious *adj.* **1.** substitutive or second-hand: applied, for example, to the satisfaction obtained by viewing the experiences of others in television programs. It is widely believed that human conditioning of fear responses can occur through vicarious means, and that gratification of needs can be partially accomplished through watching the actions of others. **2.** occurring when one organ performs part of the functions normally performed by another.

vicarious function a theory to explain the ability to recover from the effects of brain damage. It is based on evidence that many functions are not strictly localized in the brain, and that many brain areas can assume a function previously performed by a brain area that has been damaged.

vicarious learning see OBSERVATIONAL LEARNING.

vicarious traumatization (**VT**) the impact on a therapist of repeated emotionally intimate contact with trauma survivors. More than COUNTERTRANSFERENCE, VT affects the therapist across clients and situations. It results in a change in the therapist's own worldview and sense of the justness and safety of the world. Therapist isolation and overinvolvement in trauma work can increase the risk of vicarious traumatization.

vicious circle a situation or behavioral pattern in which an individual's or group's problems become increasingly difficult because of a tendency to "address" or ignore them repetitively through unhealthy defensive reactions that, in fact, compound them.

victim *n.* **1.** an individual who is the target of another person's violent, discriminatory, harassing, or assaultive behaviors. **2.** an individual who has experienced an accident or natural disaster. **—victimization** *n.*

victim blaming see BLAMING THE VICTIM.

videotape methods in clinical psychology and psychiatry, the use of videotape recordings of therapy sessions for therapeutic, research, or teaching purposes. Videotaped sessions are typically reviewed as a part of clinical supervision and are useful in providing trainees with feedback. Occasionally patients are invited to view the videotape with the therapist and recall their thoughts and emotions.

Vienna Psychoanalytic Society see WEDNESDAY EVENING SOCIETY.

Viennese School a group of early 20th-century practitioners of psychoanalysis, based in Vienna, who followed the theories of Sigmund FREUD. Also called **Vienna School**; **Wiener Schule**. See also WEDNESDAY EVENING SOCIETY.

vigilance *n.* a state of extreme awareness and watchfulness directed by one or more members of a group toward the environment, often toward potential threats (e.g., predators, intruders, enemy forces in combat). In animal behavior, vigilance increases in females after the birth of their young and in response to alarm calls. In large groups there can be a division of labor, with individuals taking turns in vigilance. In a millitary context, vigilance tasks (e.g., sentry duty, ship and air traffic control, antiaircraft and missile defense tracking) demand maximum physiological and psychological attention and readiness to react, characterized by an ability to attend and respond to stimulus changes for uninterrupted periods of time. This level of vigilance can produce significant cognitive stress and occasional physiological stress reactions. **—vigilant** *adj.*

vigor *n.* physical and mental robustness and energy. **—vigorous** *adj.*

Vineland Adaptive Behavior Scales (**VABS**) an assessment of an individual's personal and social functioning in four domains: communication, daily living skills, socialization, and motor skills. The VABS, which is a modification and replacement of the 1935 **Vineland Social Maturity Scale**, currently contains items covering the age range from birth to 90 years. Data are gathered through a rating form or semistructured interview with the person's parents or caregivers. The scales are used not only to diagnose and evaluate individuals with various disabilities—dementia, brain injuries, mental retardation, autism, or other developmental problems—but also to formulate educational and treatment (habilitative or rehabilitative) programs. The VABS was originally published in 1984; the most recent version is the **VABS–II**, published in 2005. [originally developed by psychologists Sara S. Sparrow (1933–2010), David A. Balla, and Domenic V. Cicchetti (1937–)]

violence *n.* **1.** the expression of hostility and rage with the intent to injure or damage people or property through physical force. See also DOMESTIC VIOLENCE. **2.** passion or intensity of emotions or declarations. **—violent** *adj.*

viral hypothesis of schizophrenia the theory, first suggested in the early 20th century, that psychoses resembling schizophrenia are associated with influenza epidemics. It was later observed that several types of viral encephalitis may include schizophrenia-like symptoms, and many studies have investigated the effect of exposure to viral agents, especially in utero, on subsequent development of schizophrenia. In particular, U.S. psychiatrist E. Fuller Torrey (1938–) has noted that the viral hypothesis accounts for the greater number of people with schizophrenia who are born from January to April (see SEASONALITY EFFECT), a period during which there is a high incidence of viral infections. More recently, however, it has been suggested that virus exposure is a risk factor for—rather than a key causative event in—the development of schizophrenia.

Virchow–Seckel syndrome see SECKEL'S BIRD-HEADED DWARFISM.

virginity *n.* the state of a person who has not participated in sexual intercourse. Traditionally, a woman was assumed to be a virgin if her hymen was not ruptured, but a ruptured hymen is no longer regarded as prima facie evidence of loss of virginity, as other events can cause this.

virility *n.* the state of possessing the qualities of an adult male, especially capacity for coitus. See also MALENESS; MASCULINITY. **—virile** *adj.*

virtual reality therapy a form of IN VIVO EXPOSURE therapy in which clients are active participants immersed in a three-dimensional computer-generated interactive environment that allows them a sense of actual presence in scenarios related to their presenting problems. This treatment is currently used primarily for anxiety-related disorders, such as fear of flying.

visceral brain the area of the brain that is involved in the neurophysiological control of emotional behavior and experience (including motivated behavior). Its major structures are the AMYGDALA, HIPPOCAMPAL FORMATION, and SEPTAL AREA. These structures are considered to regulate responses organized, in principle, by the hypothalamus and basal ganglia and to provide them with much of the necessary information. It integrates cognitive aspects with commands for action.

visceral drive a drive that is derived from a physiological need. Also called **viscerogenic drive**.

viscerogenic need in the PERSONOLOGY of U.S. psychologist Henry Alexander Murray (1893–1988), one of the primary, physiological needs that arise from organic processes and lead to physical gratification. They include the needs for air, water, food, sex, urination, and defecation. Compare PSYCHOGENIC NEED.

viscerotonia *n.* the personality type that, according to SHELDON'S CONSTITUTIONAL THEORY OF PERSONALITY, is associated with an endomorphic physique (see ENDOMORPH) and is characterized by a tendency toward love of comfort, love of food, relaxation, and sociability. **—viscerotonic** *adj.*

vision *n.* **1.** the sense of sight, in which the eye is the receptor and the stimulus is radiant energy in the visible spectrum. **2.** a visual hallucination often involving a religious or mystical experience. **3.** a mental image of something or someone, produced by the imagination. **—visual** *adj.*

vision rehabilitation the REHABILITATION of individuals with visual impairment ranging from blindness to low vision. Services provided include functional assessments of a person's visual abilities, if any; orientation and mobility training; rehabilitation teaching (e.g., adaptive skills training in managing one's ACTIVITIES OF DAILY LIVING); instruction in the use of optical devices and ASSISTIVE TECHNOLOGY; career services and training; and psychological counseling.

visiting nurse a REGISTERED NURSE who provides nursing services to patients in their homes. Visiting nurses are usually employed by a local visiting nurse association.

Vistaril *n.* a trade name for HYDROXYZINE.

visual agnosia loss or impairment of the ability to recognize and understand the nature of visual stimuli. Classically, a distinction between **apperceptive** and **associative** forms of visual agnosia has been made. Individuals with the former are said to have deficits in the early stages of perceptual processing, whereas those with the latter either do not display such problems or do so to a degree not sufficient to impair substantially the ability to perform perceptual operations. Subtypes of each form exist, based on the type of visual stimulus the person has difficulty recognizing, such as objects (**visual object agnosia** or **visual form agnosia**), multiple objects or pictures (**simultanagnosia**), faces (**prosopagnosia**), or colors (**color agnosia**).

visual apperception test a PROJECTIVE TECHNIQUE in which participants (most often children and adolescents) are presented with a visually oriented task, for example, to draw a person, object, or situation; to finish an incomplete drawing; or to create a narrative from a single or multiple visual stimuli.

visual attention disorder any disturbance of a person's ability to detect and attend to visual stimuli. Examples include BÁLINT'S SYNDROME and VISUAL NEGLECT.

visual dyslexia a form of acquired dyslexia (see ALEXIA) characterized by multiple reading errors involving the substitution or transposition of letters within words (see PARALEXIA). The resulting misread words are often very similar to the actual words (e.g., reading *wife* as *life*, or *bug* as *dug*). [proposed in 1973 by British neuropsychologists John C. Marshall and Freda Newcombe (1925–2001)]

visual hallucination visual perception in the absence of any external stimulus. Visual hallucinations may be unformed (e.g., shapes, colors) or complex (e.g., figures, faces, scenes). In hallucination associated with psychoses (e.g., paranoid schizophrenia, alcohol- or hallucinogen-induced psychotic disorder), the individual is unaware of the unreality of the perception, whereas insight is retained in other conditions (e.g., pathological states of the visual system). Visual hallucinations may arise in association with lesions of the peripheral or central visual pathway or visual cortical areas; they are often present in temporal-lobe epilepsy and may appear during prolonged isolation. See also PEDUNCULAR HALLUCINOSIS.

visual illusion a misperception of external visual stimuli that occurs as a result of a misinterpretation of the stimuli, such as a geometric illusion. Visual illusions are among the most common type of illusion.

visual imagery mental imagery that involves the sense of having "pictures" in the mind. Such images may be memories of earlier visual experiences or syntheses produced by the imagination (as, for example, in visualizing a pink kangaroo). Visual imagery can be used for such purposes as dealing with traumatic events, establishing DESENSITIZATION hierarchies, or improving physical performance. See VISUALIZATION.

visual impairment partial or total inability to see, or to see normally, due to partial or complete loss or absence of vision or to visual dysfunction. Visual impairment encompasses the continuum from BLINDNESS to LOW VISION. It can result from disease or degenerative disorder (e.g., cataract, glaucoma, diabetic retinopathy, or macular degeneration), injury, or congenital defects (e.g., refractive errors, astigmatism). The degree of visual impairment is assessed in terms of disability in everyday life. Also called **vision impairment**.

visualization *n.* **1.** the process of creating a visual image in one's mind (see VISUAL IMAGERY) or mentally rehearsing a planned movement in order to learn skills or enhance performance. **2.** in psychotherapy, the intentional formation by a client of mental visual images of a scene or historical incident that may be inhibited or the source of anxiety. The purpose is to bring the visualized scene into the present therapeutic situation where it can be discussed and worked out to reduce its negative implications. See also GUIDED AFFECTIVE IMAGERY. **3.** a hypnotic method used to induce or increase relaxation in which the individual is asked to imagine, for example, sitting comfortably at home and then to use all senses in perceiving the scene (e.g., the curtains blowing in the windows, the texture of the armchair). The more fully the individual concentrates on these features, the more deeply relaxed he or she becomes. **—visualize** *vb.*

visual neglect a form of SENSORY NEGLECT in which the individual is unaware of half the visual field. This occurs most often in the left visual field following right parietal damage or dysfunction. See NEGLECT.

visuoconstructive test any of a wide range of tests that require a combination of visual and motor skills in the construction of an end product as an evaluation of these nonverbal skills. The most common examples of these tests are drawing tests, block-design tests, and jigsaw-puzzle tests. Also called **visual-construction test**.

vitality *n.* physical or intellectual vigor or energy: the state of being full of zest and enthusiastic about ongoing activities. See also FITNESS.

vitamin *n.* an organic substance that in minute quantities is essential for normal growth and health. Many vitamins function as coenzymes, aiding in the metabolism of carbohydrates, fats, and proteins. A few vitamins can be synthesized in the human body, but most must be supplied in the diet. The most important are vitamin A, the vitamin B complex (including thiamine, riboflavin, pyridoxine, cyanocobalamin [B_{12}], folic acid, nicotinic acid, and pantothenic acid), vitamin C (ascorbic acid), vitamin E, and vitamin K. Vitamins were so named in 1913 by Polish-born U.S. biochemist Casimir Funk (1884–1967), based on his belief that all vitamins were amines.

vitamin and mineral therapy the treatment of mental or physical conditions through a daily intake of diagnostic-specific vitamins or mineral supplements (or both) in specific dosages. These are typically prescribed in conjunction with some psychopharmacological agent, and effectiveness is still a matter of debate and research. See also MEGAVITAMIN THERAPY.

vitamin A toxicity a condition caused by excessive intake of vitamin A (retinol). A large overdose of vitamin A—500,000 IU or more—can cause headache, vomiting, bone pain, weakness, blurred vision, irritability, and flaking of the skin. Long-term intake of 100,000 IU or more per day can also lead to toxicity. Symptoms include hair loss, headache, bone thickening, an enlarged liver and spleen, anemia, menstrual problems, stiffness, joint pain, weakness, and dry skin. On the other hand, high doses of beta-carotene (which can be converted to vitamin A in the body) have no toxic effects.

vitamin deficiency lack of a vitamin needed for normal bodily functions. For example, deficiency of thiamine (vitamin B_1) is often associated with severe and chronic alcoholism (see WERNICKE'S ENCEPHALOPATHY; WERNICKE–KORSAKOFF SYNDROME).

vitamin D toxicity a condition caused by excessive intake of vitamin D. Long-term overdose of vitamin D can cause irreversible damage to the kidneys and cardiovascular system and can retard growth in children. Excessive amounts of the vitamin may lead to high blood pressure and premature hardening of the arteries. Nausea, abdominal pain, loss of appetite, weight loss, seizures, and an irregular heartbeat may be signs of overdose.

vitex agnus castus see AGNUS CASTUS.

VMI abbreviation for DEVELOPMENTAL TEST OF VISUAL–MOTOR INTEGRATION.

vocational counseling 1. a counseling service provided to employees who seek guidance on such matters as adjusting to new jobs or roles, developing their careers within organizations, or any personal or other problems affecting job satisfaction or job performance. See also OUTPLACEMENT COUNSELING. **2.** see VOCATIONAL GUIDANCE.

vocational guidance the process of helping an individual to choose an appropriate vocation through such means as (a) in-depth interviews; (b) administration of aptitude, interest, and personality tests; and (c) discussion of the nature and requirements of specific types of work in which the individual expresses an interest. Also called **vocational counseling**.

vocational rehabilitation the REHABILITATION of individuals with mental or physical disabilities or those who have been injured or ill in order to develop or restore productivity. A vocational rehabilitation program includes assessment, VOCATIONAL GUIDANCE, and training and involves helping the individual to develop skills that have been lost or neglected and to find or return to employment in the competitive job market or another setting (see SHELTERED WORKSHOP; TRANSITIONAL EMPLOYMENT). Also called **occupational rehabilitation**. See also WORK REHABILITATION CENTER.

vocational services VOCATIONAL GUIDANCE, testing, and training, together with practical assistance in finding employment, as provided by a school, college, hospital, clinic, or rehabilitation center.

voice disorder any disorder that affects the pitch, loudness, tone, or resonance of the voice. See also COMMUNICATION DISORDER NOT OTHERWISE SPECIFIED.

voice-stress analyzer an instrument that detects minute alterations in the voice, undetectable to the human ear, that presumably occur when a person is under stress. It is sometimes used as a lie detector, although its reliability and validity are controversial, and the results are not accepted as evidence in many U.S. courts of law.

voice therapy the diagnosis and remediation of voice disorders by a specialist in the physiology and pathology of voice production. See also SPEECH AND LANGUAGE THERAPY.

volatile marriage a long-lasting marriage marked by both passionate arguments and expressions of affection, but with more positive than negative interactions.

volubility *n.* excessive, uncontrollable talkativeness: a common symptom of a MANIC EPISODE.

volume of distribution (symbol: V_d) the amount of a drug in the body in relation to its concentration in various body fluids (e.g., blood, plasma, extracellular fluid). It is expressed by the equation V_d = dose (amount of drug in body)/concentration in body fluid.

voluntary admission admission of a patient to a mental hospital or other inpatient unit at his or her own request, without coercion. Such hospitalization can end whenever the patient sees fit, unlike INVOLUNTARY HOSPITALIZATION, the length of which is determined by a court or the hospital. Also called **voluntary commitment**; **voluntary hospitalization**.

voluntary behavior behavior that is intentional in nature (e.g., walking, tapping at a key to receive food), as opposed to REFLEXIVE BEHAVIOR. See also OPERANT BEHAVIOR.

voluntary commitment see VOLUNTARY ADMISSION.

voluntary hospitalization see VOLUNTARY ADMISSION.

volunteerism *n.* the act or practice of donating (i.e., without pay) one's time and energy to activities that contribute to the common good.

vomiting *n.* ejecting the contents of the stomach through the mouth. Normally occurring as an autonomic physiological reaction to the ingestion of toxic substances, vomiting may also be self-induced, as in BULIMIA NERVOSA, as an inappropriate means of managing body weight (see PURGING).

von Domarus principle an explanation of SCHIZOPHRENIC THINKING based on the concept that the individual perceives two things as identical merely because they have identical predicates or properties. [developed by Eilhard **von Domarus**, German psychiatrist]

von Recklinghausen's disease an autosomal dominant hereditary disorder in which the common anomalies are pigmented (pale brown) patches on the skin and tumors of the peripheral nervous system (NEUROFIBROMAS); the latter may be firm subcutaneous nodules or soft cutaneous lumps that invaginate (form a pocket) when pressed. Visual, hearing, and other neurological anomalies may occur, and about a quarter of affected individuals show mental retardation. It is popularly called **Elephant Man's disease** (so named after a 19th-century patient, John Merrick, who was known as "the Elephant Man"). Also called **neurofibromatosis**. [described in 1882 by Friedrich D. **von Recklinghausen** (1833–1910), German pathologist]

voodoo death a CULTURE-BOUND SYNDROME observed in Haiti, Africa, Australia, and islands of the Pacific and the Caribbean. An individual who has disobeyed a ritual or taboo is hexed or cursed by a medicine man or sorcerer (often by pointing a bone at the culprit) and dies within a few days. U.S. physiologist Walter B. Cannon (1871–1945), one of the first researchers of voodoo death, suggested that the individual's strong belief in the curse caused physiological reactions in the body resulting in death. Also called **bone pointing**; **thanatomania**. See also PSYCHIC SUICIDE.

voyeurism *n.* a PARAPHILIA in which preferred or exclusive sexual interest and arousal is focused on observing unsuspecting people who are naked or in the act of undressing or engaging in sexual activity. Although the **voyeur** seeks no sexual activity with the person observed, orgasm is usually produced through masturbation during the act of "peeping" or later, while visualizing and remembering the event. Also called **inspectionalism**. **—voyeuristic** *adj.*

VT abbreviation for VICARIOUS TRAUMATIZATION.

vulnerability *n.* susceptibility to developing a condition, disorder, or disease when exposed to specific agents or conditions. **—vulnerable** *adj.*

vulnerability factor a variable that, if experienced or triggered, affects the probability that an individual will develop a condition, disorder, or disease.

vulval orgasm orgasm produced from stimulation of the vulva (including the clitoris and labia). Some researchers have proposed that there are two types of orgasm, vulval and uterine, the latter involving deep vaginal penetration that results in contractions of the uterus during orgasm. Uterine contractions are said not to occur with vulval orgasms. This theory suggests that a more complete or satisfying orgasm results from intercourse than from stimulation of the vulva alone. However, many women have reported that whether or not uterine contractions accompany orgasm does not depend on

V

the type of stimulation or sexual activity but rather on how intense the orgasm is, and that the most intense orgasms occur in such activities as cunnilingus or during vibrator stimulation of the clitoris. See also VAGINAL ORGASM.

Vygotsky, Lev Semenovich (or **Vigotsky**; 1896–1934) Russian psychologist. Vygotsky earned his doctorate in 1925 from the Psychological Institute in Moscow, where he remained on the research staff for the remainder of his career, although he also lectured and supervised research in Leningrad and Kharkov. Vygotsky is best known for his sociocultural theory of cognitive development, stressing the interaction of the child's natural capabilities with the symbolic mediators (e.g., written and oral language) available in his or her culture. In contrast to Jean PIAGET, who held that cognitive stages unfold naturally and inevitably and that education should follow these stages, Vygotsky held that the stages are in part driven by education and that therefore education should take place within a "zone of proximal development," aiming to stretch the child's capabilities beyond the current stage. Vygotsky's views were banned in the Soviet Union for political reasons from the 1930s to mid-1950s; they reached the West only after considerable delay, but are now quite influential. Among his most important writings are *Thought and Language* (1934) and the posthumously published *Mind in Society* (1978).

Ww

WAB abbreviation for WESTERN APHASIA BATTERY.

Wada test a presurgical and diagnostic technique for determining hemispheric functions, typically memory and language, by injecting a small dose of a barbiturate into an internal carotid artery. While each hemisphere is separately anesthetized, various cognitive tasks are administered; impairments on these tasks suggest that these functions are represented in the anesthetized hemisphere. The Wada test is typically used prior to TEMPORAL LOBECTOMY in severe epilepsy. Also called **intracarotid amobarbital procedure**; **intracarotid sodium amytal test (ISA)**; **Wada dominance test**; **Wada technique**. [Juhn Atsushi **Wada** (1924–), Japanese-born Canadian neurosurgeon]

WAIS abbreviation for WECHSLER ADULT INTELLIGENCE SCALE.

waiting-list control group a group of research participants that will receive the same intervention given to the EXPERIMENTAL GROUPS but at a later time, thus functioning as a CONTROL GROUP in the interim.

waiting-list phenomenon in psychotherapy and counseling, the unusual occurrence of a "cure" in a person who is on a waiting list for treatment. Such occurrences suggest that the anticipation of treatment, in and of itself, has profound psychological effects, which are similar to the PLACEBO EFFECT.

wakefulness *n.* a condition of awareness of one's surroundings, generally coupled with an ability to communicate with others or to signal understanding of what is being communicated by others. It is characterized by low-amplitude, random, fast-wave electrical activity in the brain, as recorded on an electroencephalogram.

waking dream 1. a metaphor for a vision. **2.** a dream process in the psychoanalytic theory of British psychiatrist Wilfred Ruprecht Bion (1897–1979).

waking hypnosis a technique—or the state produced by such a technique—in which hypnotic effects (see HYPNOTIC SUSCEPTIBILITY) are achieved in a participant's normal state of consciousness without reference to sleep or a relaxed state. It is induced through an apparently natural, but carefully considered, choice of simple words, gestures, and directives upon which to focus. There are almost as many definitional variations as there are practitioners, but the criteria of participants being in a normal state of awareness and there being no reference to sleep or trance are common to most.

walk-in clinic a clinic in which diagnostic or therapeutic service is available without an appointment. See also DROP-IN CENTER.

wandering behavior a disturbance of motor activity that involves directionless, disoriented movement. This behavior typically occurs in individuals with neurological impairment, dementia, alcohol dependence, or extreme stress.

wanderlust *n.* (German: desire for wandering) a tendency or compulsion to travel or roam. See also DROMOMANIA.

warehousing *n.* the practice of confining patients with mental disorders to large institutions for long-term, often lifetime, custodial care. This colloquial term implies lack of treatment beyond housing and feeding.

Watson, John Broadus (1878–1958) U.S. psychologist. Watson earned his PhD in 1903 from the University of Chicago, where he studied biology and neurophysiology with Jacques Loeb (1859–1924) and Henry H. Donaldson (1857–1938), as well as philosophy and psychology with James Rowland ANGELL and John DEWEY. He then became an instructor and head of the university's psychological laboratory. From 1908 to 1920 he headed the program in experimental psychology at Johns Hopkins University but was forced to resign because of a divorce scandal. Thereafter, he worked for the J. Walter Thompson advertising company in New York City while continuing to write popular psychological works. Watson, an important figure in the early history of comparative psychology, is best known as the founder of BEHAVIORISM, which eschewed the then-current emphasis on the study of consciousness through the method of INTROSPECTION and favored instead an objective study of observable, measurable behavior, molded on the methods of natural science. In applying this approach, major emphasis was placed on learned behavior, stimulus–response connections, and PAVLOVIAN CONDITIONING, which Watson introduced to American psychology. Watson served as president of the American Psychological Association in 1915. Among his most influential works were his 1913 *Psychological Review* article, "Psychology as the Behaviorist Views It," and *Psychology From the Standpoint of a Behaviorist* (1919).

Watson–Glaser critical thinking appraisal a measure of CRITICAL THINKING in which participants are asked to read and evaluate various statements, such as arguments, theses, problems, and interpretations. [Goodwin B. **Watson** (1899–1976) and Edward Maynard **Glaser** (1911–1993), U.S. psychologists]

waxy flexibility see CATALEPSY.

Ways of Coping Questionnaire (**WAYS**) a 66-item questionnaire administered to identify thoughts and behaviors that adults use to cope with stressful encounters in everyday life. It consists of statements (e.g., "I talked to someone to find out more") to which participants must respond using a 4-point LIKERT SCALE, ranging from "does not apply and/or not used" to "used a great deal." The WAYS measures coping processes, not coping styles. [developed by U.S. psychologists Susan Folkman (1938–) and Richard S. Lazarus (1922–2002)]

WCST abbreviation for WISCONSIN CARD SORTING TEST.

weak ego see EGO WEAKNESS.

Wechsler, David (1896–1981) German-born U.S. psychologist. Wechsler earned his doctorate at Columbia University in 1925 under Robert S. Woodworth (1869–1962). During World War I he worked under Edwin G. Boring (1886–1968), scoring the Army's Alpha tests of intelligence and administering and scoring the Beta tests. After the war Wechsler studied with Charles Spearman (1863–1945) and Karl Pearson (1857–1936) in London, then went into private practice until becoming chief psychologist at Bellevue Psychiatric Hospital in New York City in 1932. It was there that Wechsler first developed the Wechsler–Bellevue Intelligence Scale, which provided subtest scores for different components of intelligence, such as verbal and quantitative ability, in contrast to the single-score tests of the STANFORD–BINET INTELLIGENCE SCALE. Wechsler's test was ultimately standardized as the WECHSLER ADULT INTELLIGENCE SCALE (WAIS). It and the WECHSLER INTELLIGENCE SCALE FOR CHILDREN (WISC) are still the dominant tests worldwide for measuring cognitive abilities. See also WECHSLER PRESCHOOL AND PRIMARY SCALE OF INTELLIGENCE.

Wechsler Adult Intelligence Scale (**WAIS**) an intelligence test, for individuals aged 16 years to 90 years. The WAIS was originally published in 1955 (revised in 1981) as a modification and replacement of the Wechsler–Bellevue Intelligence Scale (1939) , which consisted of subtests that yielded separate verbal and performance IQs as well as an overall IQ. The third edition (WAIS-III, 1997) included seven verbal subtests (Information, Comprehension, Arithmetic, Similarities, Digit Span, Vocabulary, Letter–Number Sequencing) and seven performance subtests (Digit Symbol, Picture Completion, Block Design, Picture Arrangement, Object Assembly, Matrix Reasoning, Symbol Search). Depending on the specific combination of subtests administered, the test yielded a Verbal Comprehension, a Perceptual Organization, a Processing Speed, and a Working Memory index score; a Verbal IQ, a Performance IQ, and a Full Scale IQ with a mean of 100 and a standard deviation of 15; or both index scores and IQs. The current version, **WAIS-IV** (2008), retains most of the subtests of WAIS-III but has modified some of them and added three new ones (Visual Puzzles, Figure Weights, and Cancellation). The core battery of 10 subtests yields a Full Scale IQ and index scores on the same four domains of cognitive ability (verbal comprehension, perceptual organization, processing speed, and working memory). [David WECHSLER]

Wechsler Intelligence Scale for Children (**WISC**) an intelligence test developed initially in 1949 and standardized for children aged from 6 years to 16 years 11 months. It currently includes 10 core subtests (Similarities, Vocabulary, Comprehension, Block Design, Picture Concepts, Matrix Reasoning, Digit Span, Letter–Number Sequencing, Coding, Symbol Search) and 5 supplemental subtests (Word Reasoning, Information, Picture Completion, Arithmetic, Cancellation) that measure verbal comprehension, perceptual reasoning, processing speed, and working memory capabilities, yielding index scores for each as well as a Full Scale IQ with a mean of 100 and a standard deviation of 15. The most recent version of the test is the **WISC–IV**, published in 2003. [David WECHSLER]

Wechsler Memory Scale (**WMS**) a collection of tests that assesses different memory functions in individuals aged 16 to 90 years old. It has undergone several revisions since its original publication in 1945, including in the **Wechsler Memory Scale–Revised** (**WMS–R**, 1987), the **WMS-III** (1997), and the most current version, the **WMS-IV** (2009). The latter's standard battery measures an individual's memory performance on seven subtests and yields scores in five indexes: Immediate Memory, Delayed Memory, Visual Memory, Visual Working Memory, and Auditory Memory. [David WECHSLER]

Wechsler Preschool and Primary Scale of Intelligence (**WPPSI**) an intelligence test for children aged 2 years 6 months to 7 years 3 months that currently includes seven verbal subtests (Information, Vocabulary, Receptive Vocabulary, Word Reasoning, Similarities, Comprehension, Picture Naming) and seven performance subtests (Picture Completion, Picture Concepts, Block Design, Object Assembly, Matrix Reasoning, Symbol Search, Coding). These subtests yield Verbal, Performance, and Full Scale IQs with a mean of 100 and a standard deviation of 15 as well as General Language and Processing Speed index scores. The WPPSI was originally published in 1967; the most recent version is the **WPPSI–III**, published in 2002. A new edition, **WPPSI-IV**, is expected in 2012. [David WECHSLER]

Wednesday Evening Society an informal group of Sigmund FREUD's disciples who met with him for instruction in psychoanalysis, beginning in 1902. The Society evolved into the larger **Vienna Psychoanalytic Society** in 1910. See also VIENNESE SCHOOL.

weekend hospitalization a form of PARTIAL HOSPITALIZATION in which psychiatric patients function in the community during the week but spend the weekend in the hospital.

weight *n.* **1.** heaviness: the extent of downward gravitational force exerted on an object or body. **2.** a coefficient or multiplier used in an equation or statistical investigation and applied to a particular variable to reflect the contribution to the data.

weighted item an item on a test or scale that is multiplied by a WEIGHT other than 1.0 before scores on items are combined.

weighted test a test in a test battery that has been multiplied by a WEIGHT other than 1.0 before scores on tests are combined.

Weight Watchers a widely available weight loss and control program that includes aspects of both SUPPORT GROUPS and SELF-HELP GROUPS.

well-being *n.* a state of happiness, contentment, low levels of distress, overall good physical and mental health and outlook, or good quality of life.

Wellbutrin *n.* a trade name for BUPROPION.

well-defined problem a problem with clear initial conditions and goals and standard methods for proceeding from the former to the latter.

well-integrated personality see INTEGRATED PERSONALITY.

wellness *n.* a dynamic state of physical, mental, and social WELL-BEING. Some researchers and clinicians have viewed wellness as the result of four key factors over which an individual has some control: biology (i.e., body condition and fitness), environment, lifestyle, and health care management. The **wellness concept** is the notion that individual health care and health care programs should actively involve the promotion of good mental and physical health rather than merely being concerned with the prevention and treatment of illness and disease.

wellness program a health care program emphasizing the WELLNESS concept.

Welsh Figure Preference Test (WFPT) a nonverbal personality assessment in which participants indicate "like" or "dislike" for each of 400 black-and-white figures varying in complexity from simple line drawings of geometric figures to detailed, multiline abstractions. Initially designed to diagnose psychiatric disorders, the WFPT currently includes several scales intended to measure a variety of constructs, both pathological (e.g., anxiety, repression) and nonpathological (e.g., creativity, originality). [originally developed in 1949 by George S. **Welsh** (1918–1990), U.S. psychologist]

Werner's disease a rare hereditary disorder affecting both sexes and characterized by signs of premature aging that may appear before the age of 20. The patients are usually of short stature. The symptoms include graying and loss of hair, skin atrophy, underactivity of the endocrine glands, accumulation of calcium deposits in the tissues, and a form of arthritis. Also called **progeria adultorum**; **Werner's syndrome**. [Carl Otto **Werner** (1879–1936), German physician]

Wernicke–Korsakoff syndrome a syndrome resulting from chronic alcoholism or nutritional insufficiency, associated with deficiency of vitamin B_1 (thiamine). The syndrome is characterized by an acute confusional stage, ATAXIA, and oculomotor problems (see WERNICKE'S ENCEPHALOPATHY), followed by chronic changes in mental status and memory (see KORSAKOFF'S SYNDROME). Lesions are centered in the midbrain, cerebellum, and diencephalon. [Karl **Wernicke** (1848–1904), German neurologist; Sergei S. **Korsakoff** (1854–1900), Russian psychiatrist]

Wernicke's aphasia a loss of the ability to comprehend sounds or speech (auditory amnesia), and in particular to understand or repeat spoken language (see APHASIA) and to name objects or qualities (see ANOMIA). The condition is a result of brain damage and may be associated with other disorders of communication, including ALEXIA, ACALCULIA, or AGRAPHIA. Also called **auditory aphasia**; **cortical sensory aphasia**. [Karl **Wernicke**]

Wernicke's encephalopathy a neurological disorder caused by a deficiency of vitamin B_1 (thiamine). The principal symptoms are confusion, oculomotor abnormalities (gaze palsy and NYSTAGMUS), and ataxia. The disorder is most frequently associated with chronic alcoholism but is also found in cases of pernicious anemia, gastric cancer, and malnutrition. These symptoms are likely to resolve with thiamine treatment, although most individuals then develop severe retrograde and anterograde amnesia as well as impairment in other areas of cognitive functioning, including executive functions (see KORSAKOFF'S SYNDROME). Also called **cerebral beriberi**; **Wernicke's disease**. [first described in 1881 by Karl **Wernicke**]

Wertheimer, Max (1880–1943) German-born U.S. psychologist. Wertheimer earned his doctorate at the University of Würzburg in 1904, studying with Karl Marbe (1869–1953) and Oswald Külpe (1862–1915). After a number of years lecturing at the University of Frankfurt, he moved to the University of Berlin, where he was appointed professor in 1922. He returned to Frankfurt as chair in 1929, but with the Nazi rise to power he emigrated to the United States in 1933 and taught at the New School for Social Research in New York City. Wertheimer is widely regarded as the founder of GESTALT PSYCHOLOGY, along with Wolfgang KÖHLER and Kurt KOFFKA. His most important contributions included his early experiments on the phi phe-

W

nomenon, which is the perception of apparent movement when two separate stationary lines are presented in rapid succession. Unable to account for this phenomenon on the basis of existing theories of perception, Wertheimer suggested in a 1912 paper that certain perceptions, such as the phi phenomenon, were based not on the isolated elements contained in the thing perceived but in the PERCEPT taken as a whole (gestalt). Wertheimer is also famous for his work on the GESTALT PRINCIPLES OF ORGANIZATION and PRODUCTIVE THINKING. The latter research was published posthumously as the book *Productive Thinking* (1945), which has been influential in the field of cognitive psychology.

Westermarck effect the proposal that people who grow up in close proximity in the same household do not find one another sexually attractive later in life. It is based on the observation that people who had extensive contact with one another as children rarely ever married, despite being available as mates. [Edward **Westermarck** (1862–1939), Finnish anthropologist]

Western Aphasia Battery (**WAB**) a test battery that evaluates numerous aspects of language—spontaneous speech, comprehension, repetition, naming, etc.—and is used to determine the severity and type of a language disturbance as well as to assess such skills as writing, reading, and calculation. The current version, **Western Aphasia Battery–Revised** (**WAB-R**), was published in 2006. [developed by Canadian psychologist Andrew Kertesz (1935–)]

wet dream see NOCTURNAL EMISSION.

wet pack see HYDROTHERAPY.

WFPT abbreviation for WELSH FIGURE PREFERENCE TEST.

whipping *n.* striking a person with a rod, lash, or similar instrument. See FLAGELLATION.

white matter parts of the nervous system composed of nerve fibers that are enclosed in a MYELIN SHEATH, which gives a white coloration to otherwise grayish neural structures. The sheaths cover only the fibers, so regions containing mainly CELL BODIES are gray. Compare GRAY MATTER.

whiteout syndrome a psychosis occurring in individuals (e.g., arctic explorers and mountaineers) who are exposed to the same white, impoverished environment for long periods of time.

whitiko *n.* see WINDIGO.

WHO abbreviation for WORLD HEALTH ORGANIZATION.

W

WHO (10) Well-Being Index a 10-item questionnaire, commissioned by the World Health Organization, that includes negative and positive aspects of well-being in a single unidimensional scale. The index has been used to examine well-being in patients experiencing chronic diseases.

Wiener Schule see VIENNESE SCHOOL.

wife beating see BATTERED WOMEN.

wife swapping a form of GROUP SEX in which two or more married couples exchange spouses by mutual agreement for the purpose of sexual intercourse. The practice of wife swapping may also include watching the husband or wife participate in sexual intercourse with another person's spouse. Also called **mate swapping**; **partner swapping**. See also SWINGING.

wihtigo (**wihtiko**) *n.* see WINDIGO.

Wildervanck's syndrome a hereditary disorder associated with KLIPPEL–FEIL SYNDROME and characterized by deafness and paralysis of the abducens nerve. Cranial asymmetry and mental retardation may also occur. [reported in 1952 by L. S. **Wildervanck**, Dutch geneticist]

will disturbance a deficiency or lack of willpower identified by Swiss psychiatrist Eugen Bleuler (1857–1939) as a basic symptom of schizophrenia. The person may appear apathetic and lacking in objectives and motivation. Another form of will disturbance is characterized by a high degree of activity that is trivial, inappropriate, or purposeless.

Wille zur Macht see WILL TO POWER.

Williams syndrome (**Williams–Barratt syndrome**; **Williams–Beuren syndrome**) a rare disorder caused by deletion of a segment of chromosome 7. In addition to mental retardation, it is characterized by FAILURE TO THRIVE, high concentrations of calcium in the blood, narrowing of blood vessels (particularly the aorta, which restricts blood flow from the heart), and unusual facial features (e.g., short nose with a broad tip, wide mouth, small chin). Additionally, individuals with Williams syndrome are highly sociable and have superior verbal (compared to nonverbal) skills. [described in the 1960s by J. C. P. **Williams**, 20th-century New Zealand cardiologist; Brian Gerald **Barratt-Boyes** (1924–2006), New Zealand cardiologist; and Alois J. **Beuren** (1919–1984), German cardiologist]

Willie M. class action a class action lawsuit in North Carolina, settled out of court in 1979, that established a special class of children aged 18 years and younger. Class members have emotional, mental, or neurological disabilities, are violent or assaultive, have been placed in residential programs, and have not received appropriate treatment or educational services. Related service entitlements are specified in the agreement between the defendants and plaintiffs. The class persists to the present day.

Willowbrook Consent Judgment a landmark agreement in 1975 between agencies, parents, and friends of the court (the plaintiffs) and New York State (the defendant), detailing the rights of people with mental retardation who lived at the Willowbrook State School in Staten Island, NY, for several years. It set out standards for the residents' living environment, evaluation of services, personnel, education, recreation, food and nutrition services, dental services, psychological services, physical therapy services, speech and audiology services, medical and nursing services, safety procedures, treatment and medication, building maintenance, emergencies, records, and movement to community settings. Willowbrook State School was later renamed Staten Island Developmental Center; it closed during the 1980s. Also called **Willowbrook Consent Decree**.

willpower *n.* the ability to carry out one's intentions. See SELF-CONTROL.

will psychology see ACTION THEORY.

will therapy a form of psychotherapy based on the theory that neuroses can be avoided or overcome by asserting the will (or "counterwill") and by achieving independence. According to this theory, will is central to personality formation and life is a long struggle to separate oneself from the mother psychologically, just as one is physically separated from the mother during birth. Also called **Rankian therapy**. See also BIRTH TRAUMA. [developed by Austrian psychoanalyst Otto Rank (1884–1939)]

will to meaning the need to find a suitable meaning and purpose for one's life. Will to meaning is the basis and fundamental motivation of LOGOTHERAPY, a technique for addressing problems related to the experience of MEANINGLESSNESS.

will to power 1. in the individual psychology of Alfred ADLER, the determination to strive for superiority and domination, which he believed to be particularly strong in men who feel a need to escape the feelings of insecurity and inferiority that they associate with femininity. **2.** in the thought of German philosopher Friedrich Nietzsche (1844–1900), the determination to affirm oneself through courage, strength, and pride, which necessitates casting off the "slave morality" of Christianity, democracy, and false compassion. Also called **Wille zur Macht**.

windigo *n.* a severe CULTURE-BOUND SYNDROME occurring among northern Algonquin Indians living in Canada and the northeastern United States. The syndrome is characterized by delusions of becoming possessed by a flesh-eating monster (the windigo) and is manifested in symptoms including depression, violence, a compulsive desire for human flesh, and sometimes actual cannibalism. Also called **whitiko**; **wihtigo**; **wihtiko**; **witigo**; **witiko**; **wittigo**.

WISC abbreviation for WECHSLER INTELLIGENCE SCALE FOR CHILDREN.

Wisconsin Card Sorting Test (**WCST**) a test that requires participants to deduce from feedback (right vs. wrong) how to sort a series of cards depicting different geometric shapes in various colors and quantities. Once the participant has identified the underlying sorting principle (e.g., by color) and correctly sorts 10 consecutive cards, the principle is changed without notification. Although the task involves many aspects of brain function, it is primarily considered a test of EXECUTIVE FUNCTIONS. [originally developed in 1948 by U.S. psychologists David A. Grant (1916–) and Esta A. Berg]

wish *n.* **1.** in psychoanalytic theory, the psychological manifestation of a biological INSTINCT that operates on a CONSCIOUS or UNCONSCIOUS level. **2.** in general language, any desire or longing.

wish-fulfillment *n.* in psychoanalytic theory, the gratification, in fantasy or in a dream, of a WISH associated with a biological INSTINCT.

wishful thinking a thought process in which one interprets a fact or reality according to what one wishes or desires it to be.

withdrawal *n.* see SUBSTANCE WITHDRAWAL.

withdrawal-destructiveness *n.* in the psychoanalysis of Erich FROMM, a style of relating based on withdrawal and isolation from others, destructive behavior directed toward others, or a combination of the two. Fromm held that this style of relating was motivated by a need to establish emotional distance arising from a fear of dependency.

withdrawal reaction 1. an extreme form of SOCIAL WITHDRAWAL that sometimes occurs in severe cases of MAJOR DEPRESSIVE EPISODE. **2.** a reemergence or exacerbation of symptoms as a result of cessation of treatment with medication, such as anxiolytics.

withdrawal reflex a reflex that may be elicited by any painful stimulus or unexpected threat to the well-being of the individual. It is characterized by sudden movement away from the potentially damaging stimulus, which requires rapid coordination of neuromuscular units.

withdrawing response in behavioral psychology, any behavior designed to sever contact with a noxious stimulus. See also ESCAPE BEHAVIOR.

within-cell variance see POOLED VARIANCE.

within-group variance variation in experimental scores among identically treated individuals within the same group who experienced the same experimental conditions. It is determined through an ANALYSIS OF VARIANCE and compared with BETWEEN-GROUPS VARIANCE to obtain an F RATIO.

within-subjects design an experimental design in which the effects of treatments are seen through the comparison of scores of the same participant observed under all the treatment conditions. Also called **repeated measures design**; **within-group design**. Compare BETWEEN-SUBJECTS DESIGN.

witigo (**witiko**) *n.* see WINDIGO.

wittigo *n.* see WINDIGO.

Wittmaack–Ekbom syndrome see EKBOM'S SYNDROME. [Theodor **Wittmaack**, German phy-

W

sician; Karl-Axel **Ekbom** (1907–1977), Swedish physician]

Witzelsucht *n.* a type of joking mania (from German, literally, "compulsive wisecracking"), characterized by a morbid desire to tell poor jokes and meaningless stories, that can be a symptom of damage to the FRONTAL LOBE of the brain. See also MORIA.

WMS abbreviation for WECHSLER MEMORY SCALE.

Wolf Man in the annals of psychoanalysis, a landmark case reported by Sigmund FREUD in 1918. It involved a conversion symptom (constipation), a phobia (for wolves and other animals), a religious obsession (piety alternating with blasphemous thoughts), and an appetite disturbance (anorexia), all of which proved to be reactions to early experiences. Freud saw this case as confirmation for his theory of infantile sexuality.

woman-centered psychology an approach to psychology that emphasizes the physical, psychological, and social experiences that are particularly characteristic of women. See ENGENDERING PSYCHOLOGY; FEMINIST PSYCHOLOGY.

womb envy 1. in psychoanalytic theory, the envy felt by some men for the reproductive capacity of women, regarded as an unconscious motive that leads them to denigrate women. See also VAGINAL ENVY. [proposed by German-born U.S. psychoanalyst Karen D. Horney (1885–1952)] **2.** the desire of a transsexual, or of a transvestite male whose gender identity is female, to wear female clothing or have sex-change surgery.

womb fantasy in psychoanalytic theory, the FANTASY of returning to the womb or existing in the womb, usually expressed in symbolic form, for example, living under water or being alone in a cavern.

word approximation a speech disturbance in which conventional words are used in unconventional or inappropriate ways (as in METONYMY), or new but understandable words are constructed out of ordinary words (e.g., *easify* for *simplify*).

word-association test a projective test in which the participant responds to a stimulus word with the first word that comes to mind. The technique was invented by British scientist Sir Francis Galton (1822–1911) in 1879 for use in exploring individual differences, and German psychiatrist Emil Kraepelin (1856–1926) was the first to apply it to the study of abnormality.

word-form dyslexia a type of acquired DYSLEXIA characterized by the inability to recognize and read whole words, which can be read only by spelling them out letter by letter. Also called **spelling dyslexia**.

word-frequency study a study in which the frequency of to-be-remembered words is manipulated to investigate the effect of this variable on later memory. Typically, in studies of FREE RECALL, higher frequency words are better remembered, but in studies of recognition memory, lower frequency words are better remembered.

word-recognition threshold in tests involving word recognition, the minimum amount of time that a word must be exposed for a person to identify it correctly.

word salad severely disorganized and virtually incomprehensible speech or writing, marked by severe LOOSENING OF ASSOCIATIONS strongly suggestive of schizophrenia. The person's associations appear to have little or no logical connection. Also called **jargon aphasia**; **paraphrasia**; **word hash**. See also NEOLOGISTIC JARGON; SCHIZOPHRENIC THINKING.

workaholic *n.* a colloquial name for an individual who has a compulsive need to work, works to an excessive degree, and has trouble refraining from work. This type of driven overinvolvement in work is often a source of significant stress, interpersonal difficulties, and health problems. See also ERGOMANIA.

work-for-pay unit an inpatient or aftercare work facility constituting a component of a comprehensive rehabilitation program for patients with mental disorders. Such units offer prevocational screening and evaluation, vocational training, ego-strength assessment, and simple to complex work-related tasks, performed under supervision, for which patients receive payment. See SHELTERED WORKSHOP.

working hypothesis a provisional HYPOTHESIS readily subject to revision upon further experimentation.

working memory as originally described in 1960 by U.S. cognitive psychologist George Armitage Miller (1920–), U.S. experimental psychologist Eugene Galanter (1924–), and Austrian-born U.S. neuropsychologist Karl H. Pribram (1919–), any of various hypothetical systems involved in the brief retention of information in a highly accessible state. The term has evolved, however, to refer primarily to the 1974 model of British cognitive psychologists Alan D. Baddeley (1934–) and Graham J. Hitch for the short-term maintenance and manipulation of information necessary for performing complex cognitive tasks such as learning, reasoning, and comprehension. According to their multicomponent conceptualization, working memory comprises a **phonological loop** for temporarily manipulating and storing speech-based information and a **visuospatial sketchpad** that performs a similar function for visual and spatial information. Both are supervised by a limited capacity **central executive**, a control system responsible for the distribution of attention and general coordination of ongoing processes. A fourth component, the **episodic buffer**, was added to the model in 2000; it binds together information about the same stimulus or event from the different subsidiary systems to form an integrated representation that is essential to LONG-TERM MEMORY storage. The Baddeley and Hitch working memory model, which introduced an element of assessment and planning into the memory mechanism, has replaced the idea of a unitary SHORT-TERM MEMORY system and become one of the most influential and well-known concepts within memory psychology, continuing to stimulate research and debate more than 35 years after its introduction. Indeed, the model has proved valuable in accounting for experimental data from a wide range of participants under a rich array of task conditions. Current interest focuses most strongly on the link between working memory and long-term memory and on the processes allowing the integration of information from the component subsystems.

Working Memory Index an index used in the WECHSLER MEMORY SCALE as well as the Wechsler intelligence tests that evaluates the ability to manipulate and process visual and auditory stimuli in short-term or working memory.

working self-concept see PHENOMENAL SELF.

working through 1. in psychotherapy, the process by which clients identify, explore, and deal with psychological issues, on both an intellectual and emotional level, through the presentation of such material to, and in discussion with, the therapist. **2.** in psychoanalysis, the process by which patients gradually overcome their RESISTANCE to the disclosure of unconscious material and are repeatedly brought face to face with the repressed feelings, threatening impulses, and internal conflicts at the root of their difficulties.

work rehabilitation center a facility in which employees who have been injured recuperate and prepare for returning to employment. Rehabilitation efforts focus on an individual's specific therapeutic needs, include participation in simulated work activities, and incorporate workplace education designed to prevent future injury. See also VOCATIONAL REHABILITATION.

work therapy the use of compensated or uncompensated work activities as a therapeutic agent for individuals with mental or physical disorders. For example, self-esteem or interpersonal or cognitive skills may be enhanced when these individuals function in a safe, controlled environment, where they may either acquire fundamental training for new skills or receive retraining in skills that have been lost or diminished.

work-up *n.* in health care, a total patient evaluation, which may include laboratory assessments, radiologic series, medical history, and diagnostic procedures.

World Federation for Mental Health an international, nongovernmental association of organizations and individuals formed in 1948 to advance the prevention of mental and emotional disorders, the proper treatment and care of those with such disorders, and the promotion of mental health worldwide. The federation organizes World Mental Health Day.

World Health Organization (WHO) a specialized agency of the United Nations that promotes technical medical cooperation among nations, carries out programs to control and eradicate disease, and strives to improve the quality of human life. Founded in 1948, the WHO has four main functions: (a) to give worldwide guidance in the field of health; (b) to set global standards for health; (c) to cooperate with governments in strengthening national health programs; and (d) to develop and transfer appropriate health technology, information, and standards. The WHO defines health as "a state of complete physical, mental and social well-being and not merely the absence of disease or infirmity." Its headquarters are in Geneva, Switzerland.

worry *n.* a state of mental distress or agitation due to concern about an impending or anticipated event, threat, or danger.

WPPSI abbreviation for WECHSLER PRESCHOOL AND PRIMARY SCALE OF INTELLIGENCE.

wraparound services a philosophy of care and related services that includes a planning process involving a focal person, concerned family members, and providers of services. It results in a highly individualized set of closely coordinated community services and natural supports for the person and his or her family, which achieves a variety of intervention outcomes. Wraparound services have been developed in several service sectors, including mental health, child welfare, and developmental disabilities, and have been proven effective as an alternative to residential services for multiproblem individuals and their families.

writer's block inhibited ability to start or continue working on a piece of writing. Such difficulty is attributed primarily to psychological factors (e.g., fear of failure) but may also result from fatigue or BURNOUT. Suggested remedies often include writing spontaneously about an unrelated topic, doing more reading, and changing something about the physical environment.

writer's cramp a painful spasm of the muscles involved in writing or typing, which may be a form of OCCUPATIONAL CRAMP or a FUNCTIONAL DISORDER. See also REPETITIVE STRAIN INJURY.

W-state *n.* the *w*aking state (see WAKEFULNESS), as opposed to the D-state (see DREAM STATE) and the S-state (sleeping state).

Wundt, Wilhelm Max (1832–1920) German psychologist and physiologist. Wundt received his medical degree in 1855 and his second doctorate in 1857, studying under Johannes Müller (1801–1858). He then served as an assistant to Hermann Von Helmholtz (1821–1894), who had a great influence on him. Wundt became the founder of EXPERIMENTAL PSYCHOLOGY when he established the first official psychological laboratory in Leipzig in 1879. There he and his students applied introspective and psychophysical methods to a wide range of subjects, including reaction time, word associations, attention, judgment, and emotions. A man of encyclopedic knowledge, Wundt published monumental works not only on the history and foundations of psychology, but also on logic, ethics, and the psychological interpretation of history and anthropology. Because his research laboratory became the premier locus of study for the new science of psychology in the late 19th century, Wundt's influence extended around the globe, with his students founding laboratories and university departments when they returned to their countries of origin. His most important works include his *Grundzüge der physiologischen Psychologie* (1873–1874); *Völkerpsychologie: Eine Untersuchung der Entwicklungsgesetze von Sprache, Mythus, und Sitte* (1900–1920); and his many papers published in the journal he founded in 1881, *Philosophische Studien*. See also FOLK PSYCHOLOGY; STRUCTURALISM.

Wyatt v. Stickney decision a 1972 Alabama District Court decision stipulating that the state could not hold people involuntarily in hospital facilities without proper standards. These standards include a humane environment, adequate staff, and appropriate treatment.

W

Xx

Xanax *n.* a trade name for ALPRAZOLAM.

xanthines *pl. n.* see METHYLXANTHINES.

X chromosome the SEX CHROMOSOME that is responsible for determining femaleness in humans and other mammals. The body cells of normal females possess two X chromosomes (XX), whereas males have one X chromosome and one Y CHROMOSOME (XY). In humans, various authorities estimate that the X chromosome carries between 1,000 and about 2,000 genes, including many responsible for hereditary diseases (see SEX-LINKED). Abnormal numbers of X chromosomes lead to genetic imbalance and a range of disorders and syndromes. See also FRAGILE X SYNDROME.

Xenazine *n.* a U.S. trade name for TETRABENAZINE.

xenoglossophilia *n.* a tendency to use strange or foreign words, particularly in a pretentious manner.

xenophobia *n.* **1.** a strong and irrational, sometimes pathological, fear of strangers. **2.** hostile attitudes or aggressive behavior toward people of other nationalities, ethnic groups, or even different regions or neighborhoods. **—xenophobic** *adj.*

xenorexia *n.* the pathological ingestion of inedible objects.

xeroderma pigmentosum a syndrome acquired as an autosomal recessive trait (see RECESSIVE ALLELE) and marked by extreme photosensitivity. It is caused by a defect in the ability of the body to repair damage to DNA resulting from exposure to ultraviolet light, which leads to cancerous changes in skin cells and increased mortality. MICROCEPHALY, mental retardation, and dwarfism may also be present.

X-linked *adj.* see SEX-LINKED.

XO syndrome see TURNER'S SYNDROME.

XXX syndrome a rare chromosomal disorder characterized by the presence of three X (female) chromosomes. The majority of affected females are physically and mentally normal. Delays in mental development, when present, are usually mild. This disorder is sometimes associated with PRADER–WILLI SYNDROME. Also called **triple-X condition**.

XXXX syndrome a chromosomal disorder in which a female has four X chromosomes instead of the normal pair. Affected females are likely to have minor physical anomalies and mental retardation; IQs of affected individuals have ranged from 30 to 80 in studies.

XXXXX syndrome a rare chromosomal disorder in which a female has five X chromosomes instead of the normal pair. All affected individuals studied had mental retardation, and some had ocular or other anomalies, such as patent ductus arteriosus (a heart defect), MICROCEPHALY, or limb abnormalities.

XXXXY syndrome a rare chromosomal disorder in which a male inherits three extra X chromosomes resulting in a variety of anomalies, including abnormally small genitalia, a short, broad neck, and hypotonia (flaccid muscles). Most affected individuals have mental retardation, with IQs of less than 60.

XXXY syndrome a relatively rare chromosomal disorder in which a child inherits the full complement of both male and female sex chromosomes. Affected individuals have a normal penis but small testes and prostate, and about half develop enlarged breasts. IQs of those tested have ranged from 20 to 76. Most cases have been found by screening projects in mental institutions and may not represent the spectrum of cases in the general population.

XXY syndrome see KLINEFELTER'S SYNDROME.

XXYY syndrome a chromosomal disorder in which a male is born with a double complement of the normal XY chromosome pair. Skeletal deformities, genital anomalies, and mental retardation are common effects. More than half the affected individuals tested had IQs below 70, and some exhibited bizarre behavior. Enlarged breasts and eunuchoid abdominal and hip fat are among the physical traits.

xylene *n.* a volatile solvent that, when chronically inhaled, can cause kidney failure and death. See INHALANT.

Xyrem *n.* a trade name for GHB.

XYY syndrome a chromosomal anomaly discovered in 1961 and associated with males who were aggressive or violent in institutions for criminals. It was originally assumed that the extra Y chromosome predisposes males to such behavior, but the theory was modified when XYY anomalies were later found among normal males. Also called **double-Y condition**.

Yy

yagé *n.* see AYAHUASCA.

yakee *n.* see EPENA.

yantra *n.* a visual pattern on which attention is focused during CONCENTRATIVE MEDITATION. Compare MANTRA.

yaupon *n.* see CASSINA.

yawning *n.* the act of drawing in through the mouth a volume of air that is much larger than that inhaled in normal respiration, serving to improve oxygen supplies to the brain. Some research indicates that yawning is mediated by the same NEUROTRANSMITTERS in the brain that affect emotions, mood, appetite, and so forth (i.e., serotonin, dopamine, glutamic acid, and nitric oxide). The more of these compounds that are activated in the brain, the greater the frequency of yawns. Yawns can be a form of NONVERBAL COMMUNICATION in that they are contagious and can indicate boredom or disagreement as well as sleepiness.

Y chromosome the SEX CHROMOSOME that is responsible for determining maleness in humans and other mammals. The body cells of normal males possess one Y chromosome and one X CHROMOSOME (XY). The Y chromosome is much smaller than the X chromosome and is thought to carry just a handful of functioning genes. Hence, males are far more susceptible to SEX-LINKED diseases than females, because the Y chromosome cannot counteract any defective genes carried on the X chromosome.

yea-saying *n.* answering questions positively regardless of their content, which can distort the results of surveys, questionnaires, and similar instruments. Also called **response acquiescence**. Compare NAY-SAYING.

Yerkes–Dodson law see INVERTED-U HYPOTHESIS. [Robert M. **Yerkes** (1876–1956), U.S. psychobiologist, and John Dillingham **Dodson** (1879–1955), U.S. psychologist]

yoga *n.* a school or tradition of Hindu philosophy and practical teaching that ultimately seeks to achieve MYSTIC UNION of the self with the Supreme Being, or of the human spirit with the universal spirit, through a prescribed mental discipline and physical exercises. Yoga exercises, including regulation of breathing and the adaptation of bodily postures (see ASANA), are used as a means of releasing tension and redirecting energy (i.e., prana; see CHI) and achieving a state of self-control, physical and mental relaxation, and finally deep contemplation. [Sanskrit, "union" or "yoke"]

yohimbine *n.* a stimulant alkaloid derived from the bark of the African tree *Pausinystalia yohimbe* and from *Rauwolfia serpentina* root. It acts as an antagonist at α_2-adrenoreceptors (see ALPHA-ADRENERGIC RECEPTOR); at high doses, it is a MONOAMINE OXIDASE INHIBITOR and can cause serious adverse effects when taken together with antidepressants, tyramine-containing foods (e.g., liver, cheeses), or over-the-counter products containing phenylpropanolamine, such as nasal decongestants and diet aids. Yohimbine has achieved a reputation as a sexual enhancer in men, but there is little clinical evidence suggesting its efficacy is greater than placebo. It has also been studied as a potential treatment for erectile dysfunction, with contradictory results regarding its effectiveness. Chemically related to reserpine (see RAUWOLFIA DERIVATIVES), yohimbine is a SYMPATHOMIMETIC DRUG and may increase anxiety or produce panic attacks in susceptible individuals. Side effects may include nervousness, irritability, dizziness, skin flushing, or headache. More serious effects, including renal failure, seizures, and death, have also been reported, calling into question the safety of yohimbine-containing products. Yohimbine should not be taken by people with hypotension (low blood pressure), diabetes, or heart, liver, or kidney disease. It is available as an herbal remedy and also in prescription form (U.S. trade name: **Yocon**).

Youngberg v. Romeo the initial lawsuit that culminated in the PENNHURST CONSENT DECREE. In this action, the U.S. Supreme Court held that people with mental retardation who were involuntarily committed to state mental retardation institutions have a constitutional right to reasonably safe conditions, freedom from unreasonable restraints, and the services reasonably required to protect their liberty and interests.

youpon *n.* see CASSINA.

you statement see I STATEMENT.

youth counseling consultation that provides advice, information, and support to young people, usually in adolescence or slightly younger. Youth counseling may focus on any issue that raises concerns or conflicts related to studying, family involvement, sexuality and gender identity, or peer relationships. It may be used to counter low self-image and feelings of inadequacy often experienced by young people.

Zz

zaar *n.* see ZAR.

zaleplon *n.* a nonbenzodiazepine HYPNOTIC used for short-term treatment of insomnia. It has a rapid onset but short duration of action. Side effects are less frequent compared with other classes of hypnotics but commonly include headache, dizziness, abdominal pain, nausea, and amnesia. Although chemically unrelated to the benzodiazepines, zaleplon acts at the same $GABA_A$ RECEPTOR and carries a similar potential for abuse. U.S. trade name: **Sonata**.

zar (**zaar**) *n.* a CULTURE-BOUND SYNDROME, occurring in North African and Middle Eastern cultures, that is attributed to spirit possession. Occurring most frequently in women, zar often involves dissociative, somatic, and affective symptoms, such as shouting, laughing, apathy, and refusal to perform daily tasks.

Zarontin *n.* a trade name for ethosuximide. See SUCCINIMIDE.

Zelmid *n.* a trade name for ZIMELDINE.

zelotypia *n.* extreme overzealousness in advocating a cause.

Zen therapy psychotherapy that is informed by and incorporates the philosophy and practices of Zen Buddhism and that, like EXISTENTIALISM, is concerned with the unique meaning of the client's life within the universal context, rather than with simple adjustment to or removal of symptoms. Contemplation, through meditation and intuition, of human nature and human existence are believed to lead to a therapeutic alignment of the client with a sense of the oneness of the universe and to spiritual (and, thus, cognitive, affective, and behavioral) transformation. See also MYSTIC UNION.

zest *n.* see VITALITY.

zimeldine *n.* an antidepressant with SSRI properties that was removed from the worldwide market in 1983 due to its severe neurological side effects. Former European trade name: **Zelmid**.

ZIOF abbreviation for zone of individual optimal functioning (see ZONE OF OPTIMAL FUNCTIONING).

ziprasidone *n.* an ATYPICAL ANTIPSYCHOTIC that is used for the treatment of schizophrenia and of acute manic or mixed episodes associated with bipolar disorders. It may prolong the Q-T interval of the cardiac cycle (see ELECTROCARDIOGRAPHIC EFFECT) and should therefore not be taken by patients with abnormal heart rhythms or by those who have had a recent heart attack or are taking antiarrhythmic drugs. Common side effects include ORTHOSTATIC HYPOTENSION and sedation. U.S. trade name: **Geodon**.

ZOF abbreviation for ZONE OF OPTIMAL FUNCTIONING.

Zofran *n.* a trade name for ONDANSETRON.

Zoloft *n.* a trade name for SERTRALINE.

zolpidem *n.* a nonbenzodiazepine HYPNOTIC for short-term management of insomnia. Although structurally different from the benzodiazepines, it acts similarly by binding to a specific site on the $GABA_A$ RECEPTOR. Though infrequent compared with other agents, side effects typically include dizziness, headache, nausea and vomiting, and amnesia. U.S. trade name: **Ambien**.

zone of optimal functioning (**ZOF**) the range of physiological AROUSAL within which an individual can perform at the peak of physical, mental, and skillful ability. Also called **zone of individual optimal functioning** (**ZIOF**).

zooerasty *n.* sexual excitement or gratification obtained through anal or genital intercourse or other sexual contact with an animal. In *DSM–IV–TR* the corresponding term is ZOOPHILIA. Also called **zooerastia**; **bestiality**. See also SODOMY.

zoolagnia *n.* sexual attraction to animals. See ZOOERASTY; ZOOPHILIA.

zoomania *n.* an extremely intense or active form of ZOOERASTY or ZOOPHILIA.

zoophilia *n.* a PARAPHILIA in which animals are repeatedly preferred or exclusively used to achieve sexual excitement and gratification. The animal, which is usually a household pet or farm animal, is either used as the object of intercourse or is trained to lick or rub the human partner, referred to as a **zoophile**. The most commonly used animals are pigs and sheep, in rural settings. Also called **zoophilism**. See also ZOOERASTY.

zoosadism *n.* a PARAPHILIA in which sexual arousal and satisfaction are obtained from torturing an animal. This may occur during direct sexual contact with the animal, or the person may masturbate later, using memories of the event as masturbatory fantasies.

Z transformation see FISHER'S R TO Z TRANSFORMATION.

zuclopenthixol *n.* a conventional (typical or first-generation) ANTIPSYCHOTIC of the THIOXANTHENE class. Side effects include sedation, neuromuscular rigidity, and dystonia, and—like similar agents—it is associated with long-term risk of TARDIVE DYSKINESIA. Zuclopenthixol is not available in the United States. Canadian trade name: **Clopixol**.

Zung Self-Rating Depression Scale (**SDS**) a widely used adult self-report depression-screening instrument designed to measure the intensity of depressive or mood-related symptoms. It is also a tool for tracking a client's response to depression treatment over time. The SDS consists of 20 statements to which participants must respond using a 4-point LIKERT SCALE, ranging from "none or little of the time" to "most or all of the time." Half of the questions are worded positively (e.g., "I have trouble sleeping") and half are worded negatively (e.g., "I do not feel hopeful"). [originally developed in 1965 by William W. K. **Zung**, U.S. psychiatrist]

Zurich School a group of psychoanalysts who were early followers of Carl JUNG in Zurich, as opposed to the VIENNESE SCHOOL of Sigmund FREUD's followers.

Zyban *n.* a trade name for BUPROPION.

Zydis *n.* a trade name for OLANZAPINE.

zygote *n.* a fertilized egg, or ovum, with a DIPLOID set of chromosomes, half contributed by the mother and half by the father. The zygote divides to become an embryo, which continues to divide as it develops and differentiates—in humans eventually forming a FETUS. **—zygotic** *adj.*

Zyprexa *n.* a trade name for OLANZAPINE.

Appendixes

Biographical Entries

Adler, Alfred (1870–1937), Austrian psychiatrist
Allport, Gordon Willard (1897–1967), U.S. psychologist
Angell, James Rowland (1869–1949), U.S. psychologist
Asch, Solomon E. (1907–1996), Polish-born U.S. psychologist
Bandura, Albert (1925–), Canadian-born U.S. psychologist
Binet, Alfred (1857–1911), French psychologist
Bowlby, Edward John Mostyn (1907–1990), British psychiatrist
Brown, Roger (1925–1997), U.S. psychologist
Cronbach, Lee J. (1916–2001), U.S. psychologist
Dewey, John (1859–1952), U.S. philosopher, educator, and psychologist
Erikson, Erik H. (1902–1994), German-born U.S. psychologist
Eysenck, Hans Jurgen (1916–1997), German-born British psychologist
Festinger, Leon (1919–1989), U.S. psychologist
Freud, Anna (1895–1982), Austrian-born British psychoanalyst
Freud, Sigmund (1856–1939), Austrian neurologist and psychiatrist
Fromm, Erich (1900–1980), German-born U.S. psychoanalyst
Guilford, Joy Paul (1897–1987), U.S. psychologist
Hall, Granville Stanley (1844–1924), U.S. psychologist
Hilgard, Ernest R. (1904–2001), U.S. psychologist
Hull, Clark Leonard (1884–1952), U.S. psychologist
James, William (1842–1910), U.S. psychologist and philosopher
Jung, Carl Gustav (1875–1961), Swiss psychiatrist and psychoanalyst
Kinsey, Alfred (1894–1956), U.S. zoologist and sex researcher
Klein, Melanie (1882–1960), Austrian-born British psychoanalyst
Koffka, Kurt (1886–1941), German experimental psychologist
Köhler, Wolfgang (1887–1967), German experimental psychologist
Lashley, Karl Spencer (1890–1958), U.S. psychologist
Lewin, Kurt (1890–1947), German-born U.S. psychologist
Luria, Alexander R. (1902–1977), Russian neuropsychologist
Maslow, Abraham Harold (1908–1970), U.S. psychologist
May, Rollo (1909–1994), U.S. psychologist, psychoanalyst, and existentialist
McClelland, David (1917–1998), U.S. psychologist
Meehl, Paul Everett (1920–2003), U.S. psychologist
Miller, Neal Elgar (1909–2002), U.S. psychologist
Osgood, Charles Egerton (1916–1991), U.S. psychologist
Pavlov, Ivan Petrovich (1849–1936), Russian physiologist
Piaget, Jean (1896–1980), Swiss child psychologist and epistemologist
Rogers, Carl (1902–1987), U.S. psychologist
Rorschach, Hermann (1884–1922), Swiss psychiatrist
Skinner, Burrhus Frederic (1904–1990), U.S. psychologist
Spence, Kenneth Wartinbee (1907–1967), U.S. psychologist
Sperry, Roger Wolcott (1913–1994), U.S. psychologist
Terman, Lewis Madison (1877–1956), U.S. psychologist
Thurstone, Louis Leon (1887–1955), U.S. psychologist
Titchener, Edward Bradford (1867–1927), British-born U.S. psychologist
Tolman, Edward Chace (1886–1959), U.S. psychologist
Vygotsky, Lev Semenovich (or Vigotsky; 1896–1934), Russian psychologist
Watson, John Broadus (1878–1958), U.S. psychologist
Wechsler, David (1896–1981), Romanian-born U.S. psychologist
Wertheimer, Max (1880–1943), German-born U.S. psychologist
Wundt, Wilhelm Max (1832–1920), German psychologist and physiologist

Psychotherapy and Psychotherapeutic Approach Entries

acceptance and commitment therapy
action-oriented therapy
active analytic psychotherapy
active therapy
activity-group therapy
activity-interview group psychotherapy
adaptational approach
adjunctive therapy
adjuvant therapy
affirmative therapy
ahistoric therapy
analytical psychotherapy
analytic group psychotherapy
anamnestic analysis
anger control therapy
animal-assisted therapy
art therapy
assignment therapy
atropine-coma therapy (ACT)
attitude therapy
attribution therapy
aversion therapy
Beck therapy
behavioral couples therapy
behavioral family therapy
behavioral group therapy
behavioral relaxation training
behavioral sex therapy
behavioral weight control therapies
behavior modification
behavior therapy
bereavement therapy
bibliotherapy
biological therapy
brain-wave therapy
brief group therapy
brief intensive group cognitive behavior therapy
brief psychodynamic psychotherapy
brief stimulus therapy (BST)
carbon dioxide therapy
cerebral electrotherapy (CET)
child analysis
child psychotherapy
chronotherapy
client-centered therapy
cognitive-analytic therapy
cognitive behavioral couples therapy
cognitive behavioral group therapy
cognitive behavior therapy (CBT)
cognitive processing therapy (CPT)
cognitive therapy (CT)
collaborative therapy
coma therapy
combination therapy
combined therapy
computerized therapy
concurrent therapy
configurational analysis
conjoint therapy
constructivist psychotherapy
contact desensitization
convulsive therapy
coping-skills training
core conflictual relationship theme
correspondence training
cortical undercutting
cotherapy
couples therapy
covert desensitization
covert sensitization
creative arts therapy
dance therapy
Dauerschlaf
depth-oriented brief therapy
depth therapy
developmental therapy
dialectical behavior therapy
didactic group therapy
directive group psychotherapy
directive play therapy
directive therapy
distance therapy
drama therapy
dynamic psychotherapy
eclectic psychotherapy
ecosystemic approach
educational therapy
ego analysis
electroconvulsive therapy (ECT)
electronarcosis
electrosleep therapy
electrotherapy
emergency psychotherapy
emetic therapy
emotional reeducation
emotion-focused couples therapy
emotion-focused therapy
environmental therapy
Ericksonian psychotherapy
e-therapy
ethnotherapy
evocative therapy
exercise therapy
existential analysis

existential–humanistic therapy
existential psychotherapy
experiential psychotherapy
exposure therapy
expressive therapy
extended-family therapy
eye-movement desensitization and reprocessing (EMDR)
family group psychotherapy
family therapy
feminist family therapy
feminist therapy
focal psychotherapy
frontal lobotomy
functional family therapy
geriatric psychotherapy
gestalt therapy
group-analytic psychotherapy
group psychotherapy
half-show
holistic education
horticultural therapy
humanistic therapy
hydrotherapy
hypnotherapy
imaginal exposure
imago therapy
implosive therapy
indirect method of therapy
individual therapy
insight therapy
instigation therapy
integrative behavioral couples therapy
integrative psychotherapy
integrityy group psychotherapy
intensive psychotherapy
interpersonal group psychotherapy
interpersonal psychotherapy (IPT)
interpersonal reconstructive psychotherapy
interpretive therapy
in vivo exposure therapy
Kleinian analysis
leaderless group therapy
leukotomy
light therapy
lobectomy
lobotomy
logotherapy
long-term therapy
LSD psychotherapy
maintenance therapy
manual arts therapy
manualized therapy
marital therapy
medical family therapy
medical psychotherapy
megadose pharmacotherapy
megavitamin therapy
metaphor therapy
methadone maintenance therapy
Metrazol shock treatment
milieu therapy
Milligan annihilation method
monotherapy
moral therapy
Morita therapy
motivational enhancement therapy
movement therapy
multicultural therapy
multimodal therapy (MMT)
multiple family therapy
multiple-impact therapy
multiple marital therapy
multiple monitored electroconvulsive treatment (MMECT)
music therapy
naikan
narcotherapy
narrative psychotherapy
network therapy
nondirective play therapy
nondirective therapy
objective psychotherapy
operant conditioning therapy
organic therapies
panic control treatment
paraverbal therapy
parent effectiveness training (PET)
parent management training
pastoral counseling
personal construct therapy
persuasion therapy
phenomenological therapy
phototherapy
play-group psychotherapy
play therapy
poetry therapy
polypharmacy
process experiential psychotherapy
projective play
projective psychotherapy
psychedelic therapy
psychoanalysis
psychoanalytic group psychotherapy
psychoanalytic play technique
psychoanalytic psychotherapy
psychodynamic group psychotherapy
psychodynamic psychotherapy
psychopharmacotherapy
psychosocial therapy
psychosurgery
psychotherapy by reciprocal inhibition
puppetry therapy
quadrangular therapy
radical therapy
rational emotive behavior therapy (REBT)
reality therapy
reconditioning therapy
reconstructive psychotherapy
recreational therapy
reeducation
regressive electroshock therapy
reinforcement therapy
relationship therapy

release therapy
reminiscence therapy
reparative therapy
response prevention
restoration therapy
role-divided psychotherapy
role therapy
scheduled awakening
sector therapy
self-control therapy
self-instructional training
self-management
semantic therapy
sensate focus
sex therapy
shock therapy
short-term psychodynamic psychotherapy
single-session therapy (SST)
social-network therapy
social skills training (SST)
social therapy
sociotherapy
solution-focused brief therapy
somatic therapy
spontaneity training
strategic family therapy
stress-inoculation training (SIT)
structural family therapy
structural therapy
structured interactional group psychotherapy
structured learning
suggestion therapy
supportive-expressive psychotherapy
supportive psychotherapy
suppressive therapy
surface therapy
systematic desensitization
systematic rational restructuring
tandem therapy
time-extended therapy
time-limited day treatment
time-limited psychotherapy (TLP)
topectomy
tractotomy
transactional psychotherapy
transcendence therapy
transcultural psychotherapy
transorbital lobotomy
trial therapy
ultrasonic irradiation
verbal behavior therapy
virtual reality therapy
vitamin and mineral therapy
will therapy
work therapy
Zen therapy

For Reference

Not to be taken from this room